W9-BMW-995

2ND EDITION

Business Statistics

ROBERT A. DONNELLY, JR.

PEARSON

Boston Columbus Indianapolis New York San Francisco Upper Saddle River
Amsterdam Cape Town Dubai London Madrid Milan Munich Paris Montréal Toronto
Delhi Mexico City São Paulo Sydney Hong Kong Seoul Singapore Taipei Tokyo

Editor in Chief: Deirdre Lynch
Acquisitions Editor: Marianne Stepanian
Development Editor: Dana Bettez
Assistant Editor: Sonia Ashraf
Senior Managing Editor: Karen Wernholm
Associate Managing Editor: Tamela Ambush
Senior Production Project Manager: Peggy McMahon
Associate Director of Design, USHE EMSS/HSC/EDU: Andrea Nix
Art Director/Cover Designer: Beth Paquin
Interior Design: Nancy Goulet, Studio Wink
Marketing Manager: Erin Lane
Marketing Assistant: Kathleen DeChavez
Senior Author Support/Technology Specialist: Joe Vetere
Project Supervisor, MyStatLab: Robert Carroll
QA Manager, Assessment Content: Marty Wright
Media Producer: Jean Choe
Image Manager: Rachel Youdelman
Image Research: Integra
Procurement Manager: Vincent Scelta
Procurement Specialist: Debbie Rossi
Production Coordination, Technical Illustrations, and Composition: PreMediaGlobal
Printer/Binder: Courier/Kendallville
Cover Printer: Lehigh-Phoenix Color/Hagerstown

Credits and acknowledgments borrowed from other sources and reproduced, with permission, in this textbook appear on page 935 in the back of this book.

Library of Congress Cataloging-in-Publication Data
Donnelly, Robert A.
Business statistics / Robert A. Donnelly, Jr.—2nd ed.
p. cm.
ISBN 978-0-321-92512-1
1. Commercial statistics. 2. Industrial management—Statistical methods. I. Title.
HF1017.S74 2013
519.5024'65—dc23

2012005942

10 9 8 7 6 5 4 3 2 1—V011—16 15 14 13

ISBN 10: 0-321-92512-2
ISBN 13: 978-0-321-92512-1

To my wife, Debbie,
who supported and
encouraged me every
step of the way.
I could not have done this
without you, Babe.

ABOUT THE Author

ROBERT A. DONNELLY, JR.

Robert (Bob) A. Donnelly, Jr. is a professor at Goldey-Beacom College in Wilmington, Delaware, with more than 25 years of teaching experience. He teaches classes in statistics, operations management, spreadsheet modeling and project management at both the undergraduate and graduate level. Bob earned an undergraduate degree in chemical engineering from the University of Delaware, after which he worked for several years as an engineer with the Diamond Shamrock Corporation in a chlorine plant. Despite success in this field, Bob felt drawn to pursue a career in education. It was his desire to teach that took him back to school to earn his MBA and Ph.D. in Operations Research, also from the University of Delaware. Bob also teaches in the MBA program at the International School of Management in Paris, France. He thoroughly enjoys discussing research methods and business statistics with both his French and American students.

Bob's working experience gathered prior to his teaching career has provided him with many opportunities to incorporate real-life examples into classroom learning. His students appreciate his knowledge of the business world as well as his mastery of the course subject matter. Many former students seek Bob's assistance in work-related issues that deal with his expertise. Typical student comments focus on his genuine concern for their welfare and his desire to help them succeed in reaching their goals.

BRIEF Contents

TABLE OF Contents

Preface

BUSINESS STATISTICS, ***second edition***, is a one- or two-semester textbook written in a conversational tone designed to reduce the level of anxiety that many business students experience when taking a statistics course.

Many of today's business students are intimidated by their statistics textbook. These students often view their textbook as an obstacle to overcome rather than a tool to help them succeed. To address this issue, I have written *Business Statistics* in a straightforward, conversational tone that helps to reduce the anxiety many students experience with this course. My experience as both a writer and a teacher has taught me that students learn more effectively when they feel a personal connection with their instructor. Many traditional textbooks tend to "talk down" to students in a manner that many find difficult to understand. I prefer a textbook that "talks to" the students as I do in the classroom providing them a sense that I'm on their side, encouraging them every step of the way.

I strongly believe that students learn most effectively when they solve statistics problems as they learn new concepts rather than later (often right before the next exam). To facilitate this philosophy, I provide the student with a parallel problem that I have labeled "Your Turn," which allows them to work alongside the example that I am demonstrating in the chapter. I attempt to motivate them to do these exercises with a little levity but it's not beneath me to downright beg them to give it a try. I show the entire solution at the end of the chapter, so they can quickly check if their answer is correct. I call this my "learn it, do it, check it" cycle, where students learn by reading an example, doing a similar problem on their own, and finally checking their answer to confirm they understand. In effect, the textbook also plays the role of a workbook for the student, keeping them actively engaged in the learning process. Too often, students skim through an example that is completely solved for them in the text and convince themselves they understand the concept—that is, until they are trying to solve a similar problem in an exam for the first time. My approach encourages students to work through examples and confirm they grasp the concept before moving on to the next topic.

I have inserted many author's comments in the margins throughout each chapter, that provide useful insights along the way. This feature is analogous to the side comments you would make to your students during a lecture to help them better understand the material. I have found this to be an effective technique to help keep students focused on material that they may find confusing or overwhelming.

To help students be successful in your course, *Business Statistics,* second edition, has the following attributes:

- **Is written in a straightforward, conversational tone**—to help reduce the anxiety that many business students experience with the topic of statistics.
- **Utilizes a "learn it, do it, check it" cycle**—by providing parallel Your Turn problems throughout each chapter, the textbook essentially serves as a workbook allowing students to convince themselves they really understand a concept before moving on to the next topic.
- **Incorporates author's comments in the margins**—which are analogous to the side comments that an instructor would make during a lecture to help students better understand the material.

NEW TO THIS EDITION

I am very excited to offer several new features to the second edition of *Business Statistics*. I have

- Added two new online chapters: Chapter 17, Decision Analysis, and Chapter 18, Nonparametric Statistics. Chapter 17, Decision Analysis, provides a detailed discussion of decision making under uncertainty and decision making under risk along with a step-by-step description on the construction and analysis of decision trees. Chapter 18, Nonparametric Statistics, provides a detailed description of the following procedures: Sign Test, Wilcoxon Rank-Sum Test, Wilcoxon Signed-Rank Test, Kruskal-Wallis One-Way ANOVA, and Spearman Rank-Order Correlation Coefficient. These chapters can be found on the textbook's Web site www.pearsonhighered.com/donnelly.

- Updated technology coverage to Microsoft Excel 2013, with instructions for Excel 2011 for Mac and Excel 2010 for Windows provided online as needed. Through my experience in the classroom, I have been aware of the increasing number of Mac users who have been frustrated with software compatibility issues. The version of the Excel Add-in PHStat that is utilized in this edition is compatible with Excel 2011 for Mac. These instructions can be found on the textbook's Web site www.pearsonhighered.com/donnelly.
- Increased the number of problems by 25%, totaling over 1,110 business-related problems. Additionally, 35% of the problems in the text are new or updated.
- Doubled the number of data sets included in problems, examples, and Your Turns, totaling over 340 data sets.
- Introduced topics of covariance and the correlation coefficient at the end of Chapter 3, Calculating Descriptive Statistics. The correlation coefficient is also covered in Chapter 14, Correlation and Simple Linear Regression.
- Used Excel functions to determine *p*-values and critical scores for hypothesis tests that use the normal, student's *t*, *F*, and chi-square distributions. This feature provides students with more options for this type of analysis.
- Removed critical sample mean and critical sample proportion as optional steps to hypothesis testing in Chapters 9 and 10 to streamline these procedures. These two topics are now included in the section describing Type II Errors at the end of Chapter 9.
- Added learning objectives to each chapter opener, which describe the skills that the student is expected to acquire after studying this material.
- Added an Index of Applications that allows faculty and students to conveniently locate specific types of problems and examples.

TEXTBOOK FEATURES

- **Current business examples that keep the students' interest**—Statistical procedures are applied to products and services that students can relate to such as the following:
  - Approximating the probability of an accident similar to the BP oil spill in the Gulf of Mexico occurring again in the near future
  - Liberty Mutual Insurance Company comparing the proportion of auto accident claims for clients with and without good student discounts
  - Comparing satisfaction scores for various smartphone brands
  - The shortage of Internet protocol (IP) addresses using the original IPv4 format

YOUR TURN #7

My college requires instructors to have an average approval rating of 9.0 on a scale of 1–10 from student evaluations as a condition for employment. This current semester, I have 120 students, of whom 30 completed the evaluation. My average score on the evaluation was 8.8. Historical data have indicated that the standard deviation for student evaluations in the college is 3.2. My dean has scheduled a meeting with me today to discuss my future employment with the college. Can you help me save my job?

Answer can be found on ▶ **page 331**

- **Your Turn problems after every major section**—These problems are strategically placed throughout the chapter and are designed to reinforce key concepts. Complete solutions to these problems can be found at the end of the chapter. I feel that students learn more effectively when they actively solve problems rather than skim through examples that are completely solved for them.
- **Step-by-step approach to complicated statistical procedures**—Many students tend to get "lost in the forest" when facing complicated procedures such as hypothesis testing, analysis of variance (ANOVA), and regression. My approach is to break these procedures down into bite-size, repeatable steps that can be applied to solve a variety of problems. As a result, the student has a consistent road map to follow when deciding how to proceed with a specific technique.

In other words, if customers are arriving every 4 minutes, 15 customers arrive in 1 hour (there are 15 four-minute intervals in an hour). It's simply a matter of explaining the same information two different ways. However, the terms μ and λ must be based on the same units. If μ is expressed in minutes per customer, then λ must be expressed in customers per minute.

We're now ready to use the EXPON.DIST function to calculate $P(x \leq 2)$ with $\lambda = 0.25$.

$$=\text{EXPON.DIST}(2, 0.25, \text{TRUE}) = 0.3935$$

As you can see, our result, $P(x \leq 2) = 0.3935$ matches what we obtained using Equation 6.4.

- **Highlighted text**—Throughout the textbook, I have highlighted text to draw the student's attention to a key point in the chapter. This will help to reinforce important concepts that could otherwise be overlooked by the student.

In quality control settings, businesses prefer a smaller standard deviation, which is an indication of more consistency in the process.

- **Author's comments**—In the margins, you will find comments that help clarify specific topics. These comments often point to an appropriate location in the chapter and are analogous to the comments you as an instructor might make in class to provide your students with some additional insight to the material.
- **Statistics in Practice**—Throughout the textbook, examples of how statistics is used in today's business environment are described in specially marked sections within the chapter. Examples include the following:
  - Government reports of unemployment figures using confidence intervals and the interpretation of these results
  - Comparison of customer feedback for different snack food products from Herr's Food Company
  - A statistical technique that health care insurance companies can rely on to investigate unusual billing practices from doctors' offices
  - Comparison of performances of Olympic athletes across different sporting events

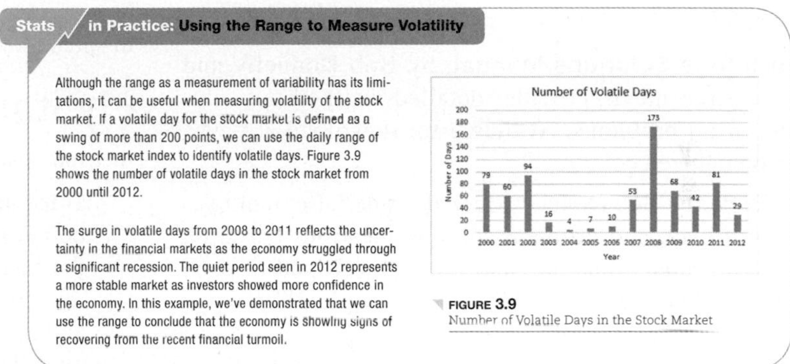

Stats in Practice: Using the Range to Measure Volatility

Although the range as a measurement of variability has its limitations, it can be useful when measuring volatility of the stock market. If a volatile day for the stock market is defined as a swing of more than 200 points, we can use the daily range of the stock market index to identify volatile days. Figure 3.9 shows the number of volatile days in the stock market from 2000 until 2012.

The surge in volatile days from 2008 to 2011 reflects the uncertainty in the financial markets as the economy struggled through a significant recession. The quiet period seen in 2012 represents a more stable market as investors showed more confidence in the economy. In this example, we've demonstrated that we can use the range to conclude that the economy is showing signs of recovering from the recent financial turmoil.

FIGURE 3.9
Number of Volatile Days in the Stock Market

- **The integration of Microsoft Excel® 2013**—I utilize Excel to demonstrate the use of technology in business statistics, but not at the expense of understanding the underlying concepts. I have spoken to students who tell me that they know how to perform a procedure such as ANOVA on the computer, but do not feel comfortable interpreting the results. By letting Excel do all the work they miss the opportunity to understand the underlying concepts of the technique. The philosophy employed in this textbook avoids this unfortunate situation.

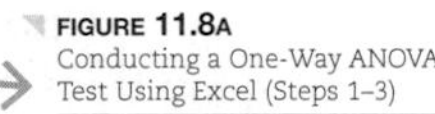

FIGURE 11.8A
Conducting a One-Way ANOVA Test Using Excel (Steps 1–3)

Supplements

STUDENT RESOURCES

Student Solutions Manual, by Bob Donnelly and Roman Erenshteyn, provides detailed, worked-out solutions to all even-numbered problems (ISBN-10: 0-321-93070-3; ISBN-13: 978-0-321-93070-5).

Study Cards for Business Statistics Software. This series of study cards, available for Excel® with XLSTAT™, Excel® 2013, Minitab®, JMP®, SPSS®, R®, StatCrunch™, and TI-83/84 graphing calculators, provides students with easy, step-by-step guides to the most common business statistics software. Available at www.myPearsonStore.com.

INSTRUCTOR RESOURCES

- **Instructor's Solutions Manual**, by Bob Donnelly and Roman Erenshteyn, provides detailed, worked-out solutions for all problems. Available for download at www.pearsonhighered.com/irc.
- **Test Bank**, by Bob Donnelly, includes true/false, multiple-choice, fill-in, and problem-solving questions based on the definitions, concepts, and ideas developed in each chapter of the text. Available for download at www.pearsonhighered.com/irc.
- **TestGen®** (www.pearsonhighered.com/testgen) enables instructors to build, edit, print, and administer tests, using a computerized bank of questions developed to cover all the objectives in the text. TestGen is algorithmically based, allowing instructors to create multiple but equivalent versions of the same question or test with the click of a button. Instructors can also modify test bank questions or add new questions. Tests can be printed or administered online. The software and test bank are available for download from Pearson Education's online catalog (www.pearsonhighered.com/irc).

TECHNOLOGY RESOURCES

Online Resources can be downloaded from www.pearsonhighered.com/donnelly and include the following:

- Chapters 17, Decision Analysis, and Chapter 18, Nonparametric Statistics.
- **Data sets** in Excel format for chapter problems, examples, and Your Turns.
- **Excel for Mac 2011/Excel 2010 for Windows instructions** for students to refer to when Excel instructions shown in the textbook are not compatible with the Excel for Mac 2011 or Excel 2010 for Windows versions of Excel.
- **Online case files and answers**, by Bob Donnelly, can be used in conjunction with the chapters to further class discussions or to use as class projects or homework assignments.

PHStat, the latest version of PHStat, the Pearson statistical add-in for Windows-based Excel 2003, 2007, and 2010. This version is also compatible with Excel 2011 for Mac. PHStat can be downloaded from www.pearsonhighered.com/phstat.

MyStatLab™ Online Course (access code required) MyStatLab is a course management systems that delivers proven results in helping individual students succeed. MyStatLab can be successfully implemented in any environment—lab-based, hybrid, fully online, traditional—and demonstrates the quantifiable difference that integrated usage has on student retention, subsequent success, and overall achievement. MyStatLab's comprehensive online gradebook automatically tracks students' results on tests, quizzes, homework, and in the study plan. Instructors can use the gradebook to provide positive feedback or intervene if students have trouble. Gradebook data can be easily exported to a variety of spreadsheet programs, such as Microsoft Excel.

MyStatLab™ **MyStatLab** provides engaging experiences that personalize, stimulate, and measure learning for each student.

- **Tutorial Exercises with Multimedia Learning Aids:** The homework and practice exercises in MyStatLab align with the exercises in the textbook, and they regenerate algorithmically to give students unlimited opportunity for practice and mastery. Exercises offer immediate helpful feedback, guided solutions, sample problems, animations, videos, and eText clips for extra help at point-of-use.
- **Adaptive Study Plan:** Pearson now offers an optional focus on adaptive learning in the study plan to allow students to work on just what they need to learn when it makes the most sense to learn it.
- **Additional Statistics Question Libraries:** In addition to questions that are aligned with your textbook, MyStatLab courses come with two additional question libraries. **Four hundred and fifty Getting Ready for Statistics** questions offer the developmental math topics students need for the course. **One thousand Conceptual Question Library** require students to apply their statistical understanding.
- **StatCrunch™:** MyStatLab includes a Web-based statistical software, StatCrunch, within the online assessment platform so that students can easily analyze data sets from exercises and the text. In addition, MyStatLab includes access to **www.StatCrunch.com**, a Web site where users can access shared data sets, conduct online surveys, perform complex analyses, and generate compelling reports.
- **Integration of Statistical Software:** Knowing that students often use external statistical software, we make it easy to copy our data sets, both from the ebook and the MyStatLab questions, into software programs. Students also have access to a variety of support tools—Technology Instruction Videos, Technology Study Cards, and Manuals for select titles.
- **Business Insight Videos:** Ten engaging videos show managers at top companies using statistics in their everyday work. Assignable questions available.

- **StatTalk Videos:** Fun-loving statistician Andrew Vickers takes to the streets of Brooklyn, New York, to demonstrate important statistical concepts through interesting stories and real-life events. A series of 24 videos with accompanying assessment questions and instructor's guide available.
- **Expert Tutoring:** Although many students describe the whole of MyStatLab as "like having your own personal tutor," students also have access to live tutoring with qualified statistics instructors via MyStatLab.

And, MyStatLab comes from a **trusted partner** with educational expertise and an eye on the future.

- Knowing that you are using a Pearson product means knowing that you are using quality content. That means that our eTexts are accurate, that our assessment tools work, and that our questions are error free. And whether you are just getting started with MyStatLab, or have a question along the way, we're here to help you learn about our technologies and how to incorporate them into your course.

To learn more about how MyStatLab combines proven learning applications with powerful assessment, visit **www.mystatlab.com** or contact your Pearson representative.

MyStatLab™ Ready to Go Course (access code required): These new Ready to Go courses provide students with all the same great MyStatLab features that you're used to, but make it easier for instructors to get started. Each course includes pre-assigned homework and quizzes to make creating your course even simpler. Ask your Pearson representative about the details for this particular course or to see a copy of this course.

MathXL® for Statistics Online Course (access code required): MathXL® is the homework and assessment engine that runs MyStatLab. (MyStatLab is MathXL plus a learning management system.)

With MathXL for Statistics, instructors can

- Create, edit, and assign online homework and tests using algorithmically generated exercises correlated at the objective level to the textbook.
- Create and assign their own online exercises and import TestGen tests for added flexibility.
- Maintain records of all student work, tracked in MathXL's online gradebook.

With MathXL for Statistics, students can

- Take chapter tests in MathXL and receive personalized study plans and/or personalized homework assignments based on their test results.
- Use the study plan and/or the homework to link directly to tutorial exercises for the objectives they need to study.
- Knowing that students often use external statistical software, we make it easy to copy our data sets, both from the ebook and the MyStatLab questions, into software like StatCrunch™, Minitab, Excel, and more.

MathXL for Statistics is available to qualified adopters. For more information, visit our Web site at www.mathxl.com or contact your Pearson representative.

StatCrunch™ StatCrunch is powerful Web-based statistical software that allows users to perform complex analyses, share data sets, and generate compelling reports of their data.

- **Collect.** Users can upload their own data to StatCrunch or search a large library of publicly shared data sets, spanning almost any topic of interest. An online survey tool allows users to quickly collect data via Web-based surveys.
- **Crunch.** A full range of numerical and graphical methods allow users to analyze and gain insights from any data set. Interactive graphics help users understand statistical concepts, and are available for export to enrich reports with visual representations of data.
- **Communicate.** Reporting options help users create a wide variety of visually appealing representations of their data.

Full access to StatCrunch is available with a MyStatLab kit, and StatCrunch is available by itself to qualified adopters. For more information, visit our Web site at www.StatCrunch.com or contact your Pearson representative.

PowerPoint® Lecture Slides. These presentations are available for each chapter. The PowerPoint slides provide an instructor with individual lecture outlines to accompany the text. The slides include many of the figures and tables from the text. Instructors can use these lecture notes as is or can easily modify the notes to reflect specific presentation needs.

The Student Edition of Minitab® is a condensed edition of the professional release of Minitab statistical software. It offers the full range of statistical methods and graphical capabilities, along with worksheets that can include up to 10,000 data points. Individual copies of the software can be bundled with the text (ISBN-10: 0-13-143661-9; ISBN-13: 978-0-13-143661-9).

JMP Student Edition is an easy-to-use, streamlined version of JMP desktop statistical discovery software from AS Institute, Inc., and is available for bundling with this text (ISBN-10: 0-321-89164-3; ISBN-13: 978-0-321-89164-8).

SPECIAL THANKS

I would like especially to thank Deirdre Lynch and Marianne Stepanian for their support and guidance with this second edition, Dana Bettez for keeping the entire project on schedule, Erin Lane for promoting this edition with her marketing skills, Joe Vetere for producing professional quality figures and screenshots in the textbook, Peggy McMahon for coordinating the production process with PreMediaGlobal, Sonia Ashraf for coordinating the reviewers, Amy Ray for improving my writing with her editorial skills, Cathy Zucco-Teveloff and Dirk Tempelaar for their accuracy checking to ensure an error-free textbook, and David Stephan for the development of the Excel Add-in, PHStat.

And most importantly, I would like to thank my wife, Debbie, for her constant love and support throughout the entire project.

Acknowledgments

This textbook was shaped and contributed to by dozens of class testers, consultants, focus group participants, and reviewers who gave generously of their time, expertise, and creativity.

REVIEWERS FOR THE SECOND EDITION

Henry Ander, *Arizona State University*
Kristian Braekkan, *Gustavus Adolphus College*
Chen-Huei Chou, *College of Charleston*
Mark Dahlke, *Colorado State University*
Joan Donohue, *University of South Carolina*
Levent Kaan, *University of Texas Dallas*
Andrew Koch, *James Madison University*
Latika Lagalo, *Emory University*
Rutilio Martinez, *University of Northern Colorado*
Lee McClain, *Western Washington University*
Angela Mitchell, *Wilmington College*
Alex Olbrecht, *Ramapo College of New Jersey*
Robert Patterson, *Penn State-Erie*
Leonard Presby, *William Patterson University*
Carol Puttman, *Penn State-Erie*
Mike Racer, *University of Memphis*
Jena Shafai, *Bellvue University*
Ruben Veliz, *Marymount College*
Candace Sorenson, *Marylhurst University*
Ronald Young, *Stark State College*

Class Testers/Consultant Board/Focus Group Participants/Reviewers for the First Edition

ALABAMA

Scott Bailey, *Troy University*

ARIZONA

Jason Bronowitz, *Arizona State University*
Linda Chattin, *Arizona State University*
Ashley Jacobson, *Chandler Gilbert Community College*
Nicolas Rouse, *Phoenix College*
Susan Sandblom, *Scottsdale Community College*
Yvonne M. Sandoval, *Pima Community College*

ARKANSAS

Tony Hunnicutt, *Ouachita Technical College*

CALIFORNIA

Asatar Bair, *City College of San Francisco*
Michael Brady, *California State University, Dominguez Hills*
Min Li, *California State University, Sacramento*
Khosrow Moshirvaziri, *California State University, Long Beach*
Christopher O'Byrne, *San Diego State University*
Ozgur Ozluk, *San Francisco State University*
Hamid Pourmohammadi, *California State University–Dominquez Hills*
Hindupur Ramakrishna, *University of Redlands*
Sunil Sapra, *California State University, Los Angeles*
Mark Tendall, *Stanford University*

COLORADO

Dale DeBoer, *University of Colorado, Colorado Springs*
Eric Huggins, *Fort Lewis College*
Alexandre Probst, *Colorado Christian University*
Richard Turley, *Colorado State University*

CONNETICUT

Matt Rafferty, *Quinnipiac University*

DELAWARE

Roman Erenshteyn, *Goldey-Beacom College*
James Ford, *University of Delaware*
Angela Mitchell, *Wilmington College*

FLORIDA

Dipankar Basu, *Miami University*
James Mirabella, *Jacksonville University*
Gary Smith, *Florida State University*

GEORGIA

Kim Gilbert, *University of Georgia*
Katherine McClain, *University of Georgia*
Komanduri Murty, *Fort Valley State University*
Hilde Patron-Boenheim, *University of West Georgia*

ILLINOIS

Harold Beck, *Southern Illinois University Edwardsville*
Yanli Cui, *University of Illinois at Chicago*
Jian Li, *Northeastern Illinois University*

INDIANA

Jason Davidson, *Butler University*
Ellen Gundlach, *Purdue University*
Keith Starcher, *Indiana Wesleyan University*

IOWA

Rick Jerz, *St. Ambrose University*
Blake Whitten, *University of Iowa*

KENTUCKY

Bob Gillette, *University of Kentucky*
Kusum Singh, *University of Kentucky*
Meenu Singh, *Murray State University*

LOUSIANA

Brandi Guidry, *University of Lousiana Lafayette*
Begona Perez-Mira, *Northwestern State University of Louisiana*
Zhiwei Zhu, *University of Louisiana at Lafayette*

MARYLAND

John Beyers, *University of Maryland–University College*
Michael Kulansky, *University of Maryland—University College*
Elkanah Faux, *Bowie State University*
Steve South, *Montgomery College, Germantown*

MASSACHUSETTS

Richard McGowan, *Boston College*
Bharatendra Rai, *UMASS–Dartmouth*

MICHIGAN

Fred Gruhl, *Washtenaw Community College*

MISSISSIPPI

Daniel Cameron Montgomery, *Delta State University*
Stephen Trouard, *Mississippi College*

MISSOURI

Eli Snir, *Washington University in St. Louis*

NEBRASKA

Karl Petersen, *Bellevue University*
Jena Shafai, *Bellevue University*

NEW HAMPSHIRE

Irwin Bramson, *New Hampshire College*

NEW JERSEY

Emma Bojinova, *Canisius College*
Ellen Benowitz, *Mercer County Community College*
Raed Dandan, *William Paterson University*
Martin Gritsch, *William Paterson University*
David Letcher, *The College of New Jersey*
Lan Nygren, *Rider University*
Penina Orenstein, *Seton Hall University*
Leonard Presby, *William Paterson University*
Harold Schneider, *Rider University*

NEW MEXICO

Sue Stockly, *Eastern New Mexico University*

NEW YORK

Chen-Huei Chou, *College of Charleston*
Kevin Caskey, *SUNY–New Paltz*
Ann Brandwein, *Baruch College*
Chun-Pin Hsu, *York College, City University of New York*
Jan Pitera, *Broome Community College*
Sean Simpson, *Westchester Community College*

NORTH CAROLINA

Alexander Deshkovski, *North Carolina Central University*
Casey DiRienzo, *Elon University*
Mahour Parast, *University of North Carolina–Penbroke*

OHIO

Pam Boger, *The Ohio State University*
Susan Emens, *Kent State University at Trumbull*
Eugene Jones, *The Ohio State University*
Joe Nowakowski, *Muskingum University*
Eddy Patuwo, *Kent State University*
Roxana Postolache, *Capital University*
Deborah Rumsey-Johnson, *The Ohio State University*
Anthony Sterns, *Kent State University, University of Maryland—University College*
Robert Stoll, *Cleveland State University*
Michael Welker, *Franciscan University of Steubenville*

OKLAHOMA

Ramona Piearcy, *Connors State College*
Allen White, *Bacone College*
Diana Wolfe, *Oklahoma State University at Oklahoma City*

PENNSLYVANIA

Mohamed Albohali, *Indiana University of Pennsylvania*
Ozgun Caliskan Demirag, *Pennsylvania State-Behrend*
Deborah Gougeon, *University of Scranton*
Ian Langella, *Shippensburg University of Pennsylvania*
Edward Mathis, *Villanova University*
Jerrold H. May, *KGSB/University of Pittsburg*h
Robert O. Neidigh, *Shippensburg University*
Rick Tannery, *Slippery Rock University*
Ray Venkataraman, *Pennsylvania State–Behrend*
Charles Wilf, *Duquesne University*

SOUTH CAROLINA

Joan Donohue, *University of South Carolina*
Lisa Bosman, *Clemson University*
Chen-Huei Chou, *College of Charleston*
Kent Foster, *Winthrop University*
Renu Singh, *South Carolina State University*

TENNESSEE

Mohammad Ahmadi, *The University of Tennessee at Chattanooga*
Michael Racer, *University of Memphis*
Carolyn Rochelle, *East Tennessee State University*
Jeffrey Schultz, *Christian Brothers University*

TEXAS

Jacob Dell, *University of Texas at San Antonio*
Levon R. Hayrapetyan, *Houston Baptist University*
Mark Leung, *University of Texas at San Antonio*
Carolyn Monroe, *Baylor University*
Ranga Ramasesh, *Texas Christian University*
Joseph C. Rhodes Jr., *Lone Star College*
Jesus Tanguma, *The University of Texas–Pan American*
Grace Vaughn, *El Paso Community College*

UTAH

Camille Fairbourn, *Utah State University Brigham City Regional Campus*
Don Gren, *Salt Lake Community College*

VIRGINIA

Kelly Alvey, *Old Dominion University*
Niels-Hugov Blunch, *Washington and Lee University*
Stephen Custer, *Virginia Commonwealth University*
Drew Koch, *James Madison University*
Quinton Nottingham, *Virginia Polytechnic Institute and State University*
Harvey Singer, *George Mason University*
Faye Teer, *James Madison University*

WAHINGTON

Sung Ahn, *Washington State University*

Stergio Fotopoulos, *Washington State University*

WASHINGTON D.C.

Rick Gibson, *American University*

Darius Singpurwalla, *George Washington University*

Ernest Zampelli, *Catholic University of America*

WISCONSIN

Patricia A. Mullins, *University of Wisconsin–Madison*

Cathy Poliak, *University of Wisconsin–Milwaukee*

Lee J. Van Scyoc, *University of Wisconsin–Oshkosh*

Student Reviewers/Focus Group Participants for the First Edition

This textbook was shaped and contributed to by hundreds of students who gave generously of their time, expertise, and creative unique perspective as students. This is who this textbook is for and we appreciate your input. Of particular note, are the following students:

Jay Bhatt, *Goldey-Beacom College*
Rafie K. Boghozian, *East Tennessee State University*
Lisa Bosman, *College of Menominee Nation*
Anne Drougas, *Dominican University*
Ashraf El-Houbi, *Lamar University*
Douglas Evans, *The Ohio State University*
Kevin Foster, *City College of New York*
Fred Howington, *Washtenaw Community College*
Molly Jensen, *University of Arkansas*
Constance McLaren, *Indiana State University*
Lan Ma Nygren, *Rider University*
Eric Ozsen, *San Francisco State Universtiy*
Gopi Parimi, *Goldey Beacom College*
Robert Patterson, *Penn State–Erie, The Behrend College*
Nora Perrone, *Newmann University*
Phillip Pfaff, *Canisius College*
Hamid Pourmohammadi, *California State University–Dominquez Hills*
Alex Riker, *Boston College*
Sanjani Shah, *Goldey-Beacom College*
Tim Sullivan, *Southern Illinois University Edwardsville*
Minghe Sun, *The University of Texas at San Antonio*
Cori Thompson, *Madison Area Technical College*
Linda Williams, *Tidewater Community College*

DEAR STUDENTS

Information overload is a recognized mark of our time, and the daily data tsunami isn't going to recede any time soon. There's no doubt you will be exposed to an unprecedented volume of data and information throughout your career. While many around you are crying "I'm overwhelmed!" or even "man overboard!" you can take a different, much better approach. Developing the skills needed to organize and interpret important information is a key to success, especially in business.

The business statistics course you are beginning will give you invaluable tools that enable you to use data to make good business decisions. For example, if you were a manager for AT&T or Verizon, could you conclude that the dropped-call rates for the two companies are significantly different based on a sample of customers from each company? Would that data alone be enough to affect how you manage your business? Or, would you want to break it down further and analyze it by some additional other factor, the locations of dropped calls perhaps? After you have completed Chapter 10, you'll be able to analyze data such as this and answer these questions with a high degree of reliability.

Throughout your business career you will find people at every level making decisions that have real consequences affecting business profitability and the jobs of real people. A skilled data analysis can give you an amazing window on aspects of a business that are simply not apparent without it.

I have written this textbook with you, the student, as my focus and the overall goal of helping you succeed both in this course and later in your career. I developed my approach over many years of teaching, and on the basis of that experience, I offer the following advice to help you achieve your own goals:

- Make it to class regularly. If you don't, you'll miss the details that help you master the subject. No textbook, no matter how well written, can take the place of your instructor and the classroom interaction. Seriously, go to class!
- Take advantage of the "Your Turn" problems placed throughout the chapters. Solving them will reinforce key concepts and let you know if you fully understand the material. The solutions to the problems at the end of each chapter give you immediate feedback, so I encourage you not to peek at the answers before you solve the problems or you won't really know how you are doing!
- Solve as many of the chapter problems as you can before exams. Business statistics is not a subject that rewards cramming or winging it. The saying "practice makes perfect" holds true in this field, and working through a variety of problems will build your confidence during the semester. I have provided solutions to all the even-numbered problems in Appendix B at the end of the book.

I hope that you come to share my enthusiasm for the value of business statistics this semester and that what you learn in this course contributes to your future success in the business world.

BOB DONNELLY

INDEX OF Applications

An Introduction to Business Statistics

IN THIS CHAPTER, YOU WILL LEARN:

- How statistics is used in the business world
- About the sources and data and the methods for collecting it.
- How to classify data by the level of measurement.
- To distinguish between time series and cross-sectional data.
- To distinguish between descriptive and inferential statistics.
- About the ethical implications of misusing statistics.

CHAPTER 1 MAP

Welcome to the world of statistics! Although some of you might be excited about learning statistics, others of you are probably less than thrilled about it. Perhaps you have to take "sadistics" because your major requires it. However, before you write off the value of this learning opportunity, let's discuss the role that statistics can play in your life. In today's world, everyone is a consumer of statistics. By this, I mean that you are continually surrounded by data and statements about those data in an effort to influence you to purchase something, vote for someone, or change your opinion about an issue. Consider the following examples:

- When CBS Sports announces that 109 million viewers tuned in to the 2013 Super Bowl, do you understand the method used to determine this number? (How does CBS know that I, you, or anyone else watched the game?)
- When we hear on TV that President Barack Obama's approval rating is 56% and in small print see ±4%, do you understand the significance of this percentage?
- When you read an advertisement claiming that a new product is recommended by four out of five doctors, do you question the validity of the claim? (For instance, were the doctors paid for their endorsements?)
- When an online survey reports that Canon digital cameras are preferred to Nikon, does it concern you that the majority of the respondents could be Canon loyalists who repeatedly voted, skewing the results, or that the survey was conducted on a Canon user's forum?

Never before in the history of humankind have people had more data and information at their fingertips than you do at this moment. Statistics can have a powerful effect on our feelings, our opinions, and the decisions that we make in our personal and professional lives. As a result, it's very important that the statistics we report are both accurate and unbiased to ensure that they are properly utilized.

1.1 Business Statistics and Their Uses

Statistics is the mathematical science that deals with the collection, analysis, and presentation of data, which can then be used as a basis for inference and induction.

Statistics is the mathematical science that deals with the collection, analysis, and presentation of data—data that can then be used as a basis for inference and induction. **Business statistics** are statistics applied to the business world in an effort to improve people's decision making in fields such as marketing, operations, finance, and human resources, to name a few. Let's look at a few examples of how business statistics can help an organization's decision makers.

Marketing Research

Organizations rely heavily on business statistics when they conduct marketing research to determine what consumers want. For example, Kellogg's could perform a taste test to determine if consumers prefer the company's Cheez-It crackers to Nabisco's Cheese Nips. (Being a life-long Cheez-It addict, I know where my vote will go.) Kellogg's could also gather information about each consumer participating in the test in an effort to determine if the people who prefer one brand to the other share similar characteristics. This would be useful information for Kellogg's future marketing efforts.

In the 1980s, Marriott conducted an extensive survey to see how potential customers felt about the company's current hotel offerings. Based on the results, Marriott designed a new hotel chain known as Courtyard by Marriott, which has been a huge success.

Advertising

Television networks set their advertising rates for commercials based on the sizes of viewing audiences. The networks receive the information from Nielsen Media Research, which collects data from approximately 25,000 U.S. households. The sample of households surveyed has been carefully selected so that the results can be used to infer the viewing habits of the entire country. Statistics are used to ensure the sample is properly chosen and to process the data into meaningful information for the networks. Based on this information, CBS was able to charge a record $3.8 million for a 30-second Super Bowl ad in 2013.

Business statistics are statistics applied to the business world to help improve decision making.

Operations

Statistics can also be used to help businesses operate better. Quality control, for example, is a vital concern for all successful organizations. The combination of business statistics and quality control is a marriage made in heaven. If properly implemented, statistics can help manufacturing and service organizations monitor their processes and determine when quality problems begin to occur. For instance, Kellogg's can use statistics to determine if my Cheez-Its are overbaked or too salty. (Based on the box I'm sampling from at this moment, I'd say the company is doing an excellent job with its statistical quality control.)

Finance

When I began writing this textbook, the U.S. economy was in the middle of a deep recession. Part of the economic downturn was due to the poor lending practices of banks, particularly in the mortgage industry. If used properly, business statistics is an excellent tool to help banks identify consumers who are good credit risks and those who are not based on characteristics such as income, education, and home-ownership. For example, Fair Isaac Corporation (FICO) developed the credit scoring system (FICO score) currently used by the industry and which is based on a variety of statistical techniques.

Stats in Practice: Careers in Statistics

It's a great time to be in the job market if you have an interest and aptitude for statistics. This is due to an increase in demand for the skills of individuals who have developed a level of statistical literacy. The biggest driver for this demand is a global society that is both data-rich and data-dependent as technology advances at an explosive rate. In recognition of this development more than 150 professional organizations, including the American Statistical Association, have designated 2013 as the International Year of Statistics.

There are abundant employment opportunities in today's business world that require expertise in statistics. The following jobs are just a small sampling of the type of jobs available to people who have mastered this skill set.

- Transportation statistician—Our daily lives are surrounded by transportation systems that require ongoing attention by people with statistical talents. Examples include:
  - Delivery companies such as FedEx and UPS, which are always seeking opportunities to improve the efficiency of their delivery systems by analyzing data.
  - Airlines such as American Airlines rely on statistics for their yield management system which determines airfares on a continuous basis. You can thank these systems when you experience unexpected swings in airfare as you book your next vacation!
- Financial analyst—Using a variety of statistical tools, financial analysts provide investment advice to businesses and individuals. Banks and investment firms are examples of organizations seeking this type of position.
- Actuary—In order to maintain profitability, insurance companies need actuaries to analyze risk factors for their customers in order to establish appropriate premiums for their service. Statistical techniques play a major role in this analysis. Hospitals, banks, and government agencies are other examples of organizations that rely on these skills.
- Sports statistician—Many professional baseball, basketball, and football teams have hired statisticians in an effort to gain a competitive advantage. Examples include:
  - Assistant General Manager Peter Brand, who was dramatized in the 2011 film *Moneyball*, used statistical analysis to help the Oakland Athletics assemble a competitive Major League Baseball team during the 2002 season. The Boston Red Sox won the World Series in 2004 (their first since 1918!) relying on some of the same statistical modeling used by the Oakland Athletics.
  - The Memphis Grizzlies, an NBA team, recently hired a vice president of basketball operations because of his statistical expertise.
- Political analyst—A great deal of attention has been paid to predicting political outcomes, such as elections, using statistical tools.
  - Nate Silver is an American statistician who has developed an impressive reputation for his accurate predictions in the political arena. I recommend visiting his Web site, fivethirtyeight.blogs.nytimes.com, to gain some insight into the benefits of statistics in this field.

And of course I'd be remiss not mentioning one last type of employment in the field of statistics—education. I can personally testify that teaching statistics to students and writing books to help them learn has been a very rewarding experience.

1.2 Data

Data are values assigned to observations or measurements and are the building blocks of statistical analysis.

Data are the foundation of the field of statistics and can be defined as the values assigned to specific observations or measurements. If I'm collecting data on my wife's snoring behavior, I can do so in different ways. I can measure how many times Deb snores over a 10-minute period. I can measure the length of each snore in seconds. I could also measure how loud each snore is using a descriptive phrase like "That one sounded like a bear just waking up from hibernation" or "Wow! That one sounded like a sea lion calling for its young." (How a sound like that can come from a person who can fit into a pair of size 2 jeans is beyond me.)

In each instance, I would be recording data on the same event but in a different form. In the first instance, I would be measuring a frequency, or number of occurrences. In the second instance, I would be measuring duration, or length of time. And in the final instance, I would be measuring the event by describing its volume using words rather than numbers.

Information is data that are transformed into useful facts that can be used for a specific purpose, such as making a decision.

However, data all by themselves are not particularly useful. By definition, data are just the raw facts and figures that pertain to a measurement of interest. **Information**, on the other hand, is derived from the facts for the purpose of making decisions. One of the major reasons to use statistics is to transform data into information. For example, Table 1.1 shows my golf scores over a two-month period. (For those of you who are non-golfers, lower scores are better.)

TABLE 1.1 | GOLF-SCORE DATA

DATE	SCORE
June 13	94
June 20	96
June 27	93
July 10	89
July 16	86
July 24	89

Each individual golf score would be considered a data point. By themselves, the data points have limited value, other than to suggest that I should not quit my day job. (To quit my day job and become a professional golfer, I would need a score in the 65–70 range.) To these data, let's add the fact that in my desperate efforts to buy a better golf game, I quietly purchased a brand new driver on July 1, thinking my wife would not notice a new club in my golf bag (she did). We may be able to conclude, with the help of statistics, that the purchase helped improve my game (imagine a doubtful look on Deb's face). In order to answer this question, we will need to employ a statistical analysis that will be covered later in this text. Stay tuned as I use statistics hopefully to convince my wife that I really needed this new club!

The Sources of Data

The Internet has become a rich source of data for statistics published by various industries. I once found a Japanese study on the effect of fluoride on toad embryos. Before this discovery, I had no idea toads even had teeth, much less a cavity problem!

We classify the sources of data into two broad categories: primary data and secondary data. **Secondary data** are data somebody else has collected and made available for others to use. The U.S. government collects and publishes a variety of data that are readily available online. The U.S. Department of Labor collects mountains of data on topics such as consumer prices, inflation, unemployment, and productivity. The home page for the department's Web site is shown in Figure 1.1.

Every 10 years the U.S. Department of Commerce conducts a nationwide census to gather a wide variety of data related to the country's population. The data are used by Congress to make decisions about the funding for community services throughout the United States. The data are used to adjust the number of representatives each state is allowed to elect to Congress. You can find census data on the Department of Commerce's Web site.

Secondary data are data collected by someone else that you are "borrowing."

FIGURE 1.1
The Home Page of the Bureau of Labor Statistics

The U.S. Geological Survey (USGS) provides an impressive assortment of scientific information that is used to manage water, energy, biological, and mineral resources across the Earth. For instance, did you know there are 250 species of squirrels in the world? If you don't believe me, you can look the information up at the USGS's Web site and become the local squirrel "expert" in your area.

The main drawback of using secondary data is that you have no control over how the data were collected. People tend to believe anything that's in print, even if it's not true. (You believe me, don't you?) Some of it is wrong, and, as you will learn later in the chapter, some of it is deliberately biased. The advantage to secondary data is that they are cheap (sometimes free) and that they are immediately available. For someone looking for data quickly, secondary data provide instant gratification (assuming the data are accurate, of course).

Primary data are data that you have collected for your own use.

Primary data, on the other hand, are data collected by the person or organization that eventually uses the data. This type of data can be expensive to acquire, but the main advantage is that primary data are your data, and you have nobody else to blame but yourself if you make a mess of it. You can obtain primary data in many ways, such as by direct observation, via experiments, and through surveys.

Direct observation is a method of gathering data while the subjects of interest are in their natural environment, often unaware they are being watched.

Direct observation is a method of gathering data while the subjects of interest are in their natural environment, often unaware they are being watched. Observing wild animals stalking their prey in the forest or teenagers at the mall on Friday night are two examples. (Or are they the same example?) The advantage of this method is that the subjects will unlikely be influenced by the data collection process.

A **focus group** is a direct observational technique whereby individuals are often paid to discuss their attitudes toward products or services in a group setting controlled by a moderator.

A **focus group** is a direct observational technique whereby individuals are often paid to discuss their attitudes toward products or services in a group setting controlled by a moderator. For example, Fisher Price heavily relies on focus groups of both adults and children to obtain valuable feedback on new toy ideas. The participants are aware they are being observed.

In an **experiment**, subjects are exposed to certain treatments and the data of interest are recorded.

In an **experiment**, subjects are exposed to certain treatments and the data of interest are recorded. An experiment that tests the use of a new medical drug is an example. Two different groups would be established: The first group would receive the new drug; the second group would be the control group. People in the control group would be told they are getting the new drug but would in fact get a placebo with no medication. The reactions from each group would be measured and compared to determine whether the new drug is effective.

The benefit of experiments is that they allow statisticians to control factors that could influence the results, such as the gender, age, and education of a participant. One major concern about collecting data through experiments is that the response of the subjects might be influenced by the fact they are participating in a study.

A **survey** involves directly asking people a series of questions and can be administered by e-mail, via the Web, through snail mail, face to face, or over the telephone.

A **survey** involves directly asking people a series of questions. Surveys can be administered by e-mail, via the Web, through snail mail, face to face, or over the telephone. (It's the telephone survey I'm most fond of, especially when I get the call just as I'm sitting down to dinner, getting into the shower, or finally making some progress on the chapter I'm writing.) The questionnaire needs to be carefully designed to avoid any bias that could affect

Research has shown that a question posed in a positive tone will tend to evoke a more positive response. A question posed in a negative tone will tend to evoke a more negative response. A good strategy is to pre-test your questionnaire before releasing it to the actual participants.

participants' responses or confuse them. Bias can occur when a question is stated in a way that encourages or leads a respondent to a particular answer. For example, "Wouldn't you agree that all drivers should wear a seat belt?" is a biased question. The influence the survey itself has on the responses of participants can also affect the quality of the data collected. Some participants will respond in a way they feel the survey would like them to. Figure 1.2 shows a portion of a survey I developed for users of the Claymont Community Center in Delaware. To encourage respondents to participate, an effective survey will state its purpose in the beginning, ask questions in a clear and concise manner, and place the more personal demographic questions last—when the respondents feel more comfortable with the process.

FIGURE 1.2
An Example of a Survey

Claymont Community Center
Health Clinic
Customer Service Survey

Dear Customer,

Our goal is to provide you with the best service possible. You can help us by taking a few minutes to answer the following questions about the Claymont Community Center (CCC). This valuable information will be used to help us to improve our services in the near future. The information gathered with this survey will be kept strictly confidential. Thank you for helping us.

(Please place this form in the Customer Survey Box in the Health Clinic. If you need more time, you may return the form on your next visit or ask for a stamped envelope to return it by mail.)

1. How long have you been using the Health Clinic? (Check one)
____ Less than one month
____ 1 to 6 months
____ 6 months to a year
____ 1 to 3 years

2. How satisfied are you with the quality of service being provided by the medical staff at the Health Clinic?
____ Very Satisfied
____ Satisfied
____ Dissatisfied
____ Very Dissatisfied
Comment________________________________
____

3. Please provide the following personal information. Again, all information will remain confidential.

Zip code of your residence:______________

Gender: _____ Male _____ Female Age: _____

Marital Status: _____ Married _____ Single
_____ Separated _____ Divorced _____ Widowed

Are you the head of your household?
_____ Yes _____ No

What is your annual gross income?
_____ Less than $10,000 _____ $30–40
_____ $10–20 _____ $40+
_____ $20–30

We relied on SurveyMonkey to develop this textbook. Faculty and students tested the book before publication and provided valuable feedback through this Web site. I'm a satisfied customer!

Online surveys are a convenient way to acquire data. Companies such as SurveyMonkey provide people with a low-cost way to design surveys, collect responses, and analyze the data. The SurveyMonkey Web site claims that 80% of the Fortune 100 companies are users of the service. However, there are challenges to Internet surveys, which will be discussed later in this chapter.

To test your understanding of data sources, I encourage you to spend a few minutes answering the questions in the following Your Turn section.

YOUR TURN #1

Identify if the data required for each example are primary or secondary. For primary data, determine the best way in which the data should be collected. In other words, should the data be collected via observation, experiment, or survey?

1. Apple would like to measure the satisfaction levels of customers who purchased its new iPad product.
2. Pepsi would like to determine if consumers prefer the taste of Diet Pepsi to Diet Coke.
3. Cleveland State University needs to determine the current inflation rate to determine the annual salary increases for its staff for the upcoming year.
4. McDonald's would like to determine the average wait time for customers who use its drive-through windows during the lunch hour.

Answers can be found on ▶ **page 19**

The Two Main Types of Data

Another way to classify data is by whether they are quantitative or qualitative:

Quantitative data use numerical values while **qualitative data** relies on descriptive terms to describe something of interest.

- **Quantitative data** use numerical values to describe something of interest either by measuring it (such as its weight, height, or distance) or by counting it (such as the number of customers or repeat customers a business receives).
- **Qualitative data** use descriptive terms to measure or classify something of interest. One example of qualitative data is the name of a respondent in a survey and his or her level of education. Mathematical operations such as addition, subtraction, multiplication, and division cannot be performed on this type of data.

Classifying Data by Their Level of Measurement

Another important way to classify data is by the *way* the data are measured. This distinction is critical because it affects which statistical techniques we can use in our analysis of the data. The four levels of measurement are nominal, ordinal, interval, and ratio.

Nominal data are data that are described as a category or a label. Examples are gender (male or female), marital status (married, single, divorced, widowed), or yes/no responses.

A **nominal level of measurement** deals strictly with qualitative data assigned to predetermined categories. One example is the gender of a survey respondent, with the categories being male and female. This type of data is referred to as nominal data, or categorical data. It does not allow us to perform any mathematical operations on it, such as adding or multiplying. We can only give the data names and categorize them. (The word *nominal* actually means "pertaining to names.") We also cannot rank-order the data in any way from highest to lowest. An example is the state in which the survey respondent resides, such as Delaware or New Jersey (although I would try to rank my home state of Delaware on top.)

Other examples of nominal data are zip codes and telephone numbers, which can't be added, subtracted, or placed in a meaningful order of greater than or less than. Even though the data consist of numbers, they are handled just like qualitative data. Nominal data are considered the lowest level of data, and, as a result, the statistical techniques used to analyze them are the most restrictive.

Ordinal data have all the properties of nominal data, with the added feature that we can rank-order the values from highest to lowest.

An **ordinal level of measurement** can be conducted on data that are on the next level up on the food chain. Ordinal data has all the properties of nominal data, with the added feature that we can rank-order the values from highest to lowest. The following example explains ordinal measurement: Recently, I felt my manhood challenged by two neighbors who claimed their lawnmowers were faster than mine. Naturally, this had to be settled by a lawnmower race down our street, Gaebel Lane. Sadly, I present Figure 1.3, which shows that I lost the race. My neighbor Tom came in first (1), my neighbor Scott came in second (2), and I came in third (3).

FIGURE 1.3
An Example of Ordinal Measurement: Tom, Me, and Scott (from left to right) on Our Mowers

We still can't perform mathematical operations on this type of data, but we can say that Tom's lawnmower was faster than mine and Scott's. However, we cannot say how *much* faster because we didn't record the times of the lawnmowers. We just noted who came in first, second, and third. Ordinal data that have been collected do not allow us to make measurements between the categories or to say, for instance, that Scott's lawnmower is twice as fast as Bob's. For that, we need a different type of data. (In case you were wondering, I have been unsuccessful at convincing Deb that I need more horsepower to restore our family honor at the Second Annual Gaebel Lane Lawnmower Race.)

Education level is another example of ordinal data. A master's degree is ranked higher than a bachelor's degree, which in turn is ranked higher than a high school diploma. However, we are unable to measure the difference between these degrees in a meaningful, mathematical way. For instance, it would not be accurate to claim the difference between a master's and a bachelor's degree is more than the difference between a bachelor's and a high school degree. A property of ordinal data is that the differences between categories are not meaningful and, therefore, cannot be measured.

Ordinal data can also be numerical. One example of numerical ordinal data is when we rate movies with one, two, three, or four stars. Although we can order the movies by their ratings, we can't, for example, claim that a four-star movie is four times as good as a one-star movie.

Interval data, which are strictly quantitative, allow us to measure the differences between the categories with actual numbers in a meaningful way.

The **interval measurement level** is yet a higher level of measurement. It measures interval data, which are strictly quantitative. Temperature measurements in degrees Fahrenheit are an example of interval data. With this level, we can measure the differences between the categories with actual numbers in a meaningful way. For instance, 70°F is 5 degrees warmer than 65°F. However, multiplication and division can't be performed on this level of data. Why not? Simply because we cannot argue that 100°F is twice as warm as 50°F. The logic of this claim becomes more obvious when we convert the temperatures to the Celsius scale. The same two temperatures convert to 38°C and 10°C, respectively, so the twice-as-warm argument does not hold true. To help explain this, try baking a cake at twice the recommended temperature in half the recommended time. Yuck!

Another characteristic of interval data is that they do not have a true zero point. The term *true zero point* means that a zero data value indicates the absence of the object being measured. For instance, 0°F and 0°C do not represent the absence of temperature, even though it may feel like it.

Your grade point average (GPA) is another example of interval data. We can measure the difference between a 4.0 and a 2.0 GPA by simply subtracting the two values. However, it would not be an accurate statement to claim that a 4.0 student is twice as smart as a 2.0 student. Also, GPA has no true zero point because a 0.0 GPA does not indicate the absence of a grade point average.

Ratio data have all the features of interval data, with the added benefit of having a true zero point.

The most versatile of data types is the **ratio level of measurement**. Ratio data are as good as it gets as far as data are concerned. Examples of this type of data are ages, weights, prices, and salaries. Ratio data have all the features of interval data, with the added benefit of a true zero point. For instance, a zero salary indicates the absence of any salary. With a true zero point, we can say that a person who is six feet in height is twice as tall as a three-foot person or that a 20-year-old person is half the age of a 40-year-old.

For example, dollars are considered to be ratio data because $20 is twice as much as $10.

The distinction between interval and ratio data is a fine line. To help identify the proper scale, use the "twice as much" rule. If the phrase "twice as much" accurately describes the relationship between two values that differ by a multiple of two, then the data can be considered to be ratio level.

Table 1.2 summarizes the properties of the four levels of data measurement, and Figure 1.4 shows the relationship between the levels of data measurement and the two main types of data,

FIGURE 1.4
The Two Main Types of Data and Their Corresponding Levels

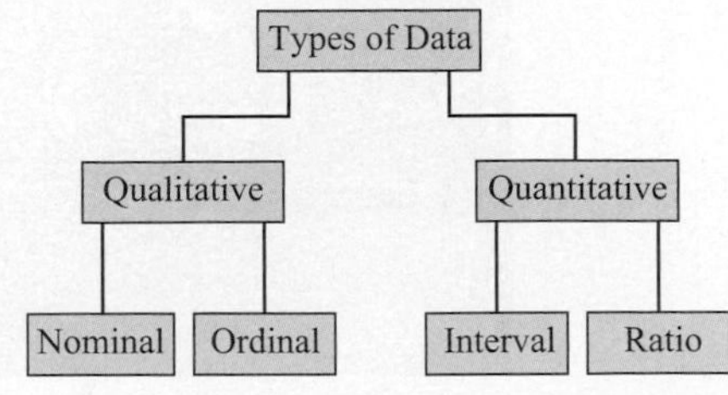

TABLE 1.2 | THE FOUR LEVELS OF DATA MEASUREMENT: A SUMMARY

LEVEL	DESCRIPTION	EXAMPLE
Nominal	Arbitrary labels for data No ranking allowed	Zip Codes (19808, 76137)
Ordinal	Ranking allowed No measurable meaning to the number differences	Education level (master's degree, doctorate degree)
Interval	Meaningful differences No true zero point	Calendar year (2014, 2015)
Ratio	Meaningful differences True zero point	Income ($48,000, $0)

which creates data measurement scales. As we explore different statistical techniques later in this book, we will revisit these different measurement scales. You will discover that specific techniques require certain types of data.

We can summarize classifying data by the level of measurement with the following baseball analogy:

- **Nominal data**. The numbers on the players' uniforms would be nominal data because these values are simply a label and are not used for any type of measurement. A player with the number 30 is not necessarily better than the player wearing number 15.
- **Ordinal data**. The batting order of the players would be considered ordinal data because we can rank-order the players going to the plate to hit. However, there is no useful or meaningful way to measure the differences between a player hitting 5th and a player hitting 6th.
- **Interval data**. The birth years of the players would be considered interval data. We can say that a player born in 1984 is three years older than a player born in 1987, but the "twice-as-much rule" does not hold true for calendar years. A person born in the year 1000 is not twice as old as a person born in the year 2000. This is because there is no true zero point with calendar years. The year 0 does not indicate the absence of age or time; it is merely an arbitrary reference point.
- **Ratio data**. The number of home runs hit by the best hitter on the team is an example of ratio data. A player with 20 home runs has twice as many as a player with 10 home runs. There is a true zero point for these data because zero home runs represent the absence of home-run hits.

Because this is such an important concept, which will be used later in the course, take a few minutes to answer the questions in the following Your Turn section before moving on in the chapter.

YOUR TURN #2

Identify the type of data (qualitative/quantitative) and the level of measurement for each of the following data sources:

a. Your IQ score
b. The price for one gallon of gasoline
c. The letter grade earned in your statistics course
d. The number of boxes of Frosted Flakes on the shelf of a grocery store
e. The types of cars driven by students in your class

Answers can be found on ▶ **page 19**

Time Series vs. Cross-Sectional Data

Time series data are values that correspond to specific measurements taken over a *range* of time periods.

Data can also be classified as time series or cross-sectional. Table 1.3 shows the average unemployment rates for the Unites States, California, Delaware, Michigan, and Texas during the month of January for indicated years. **Time series data** are values that correspond to specific measurements taken over a *range* of time periods. Each of the last five columns in Table 1.3 represents a time series of unemployment rates. Figure 1.5 shows a line graph of one of the columns, U.S. unemployment rates from 2008 until 2012. The upward trend in unemployment in 2008 and 2009 reflects the economic recession that occurred during that time period.

TABLE 1.3 | Unemployment Rate Data, 2008–2012

YEAR	UNITED STATES %	CA %	DE %	MI %	TX %
2008	4.9	5.9	3.8	7.1	4.3
2009	7.6	10.1	6.7	11.6	6.4
2010	9.7	12.3	8.8	13.7	8.2
2011	9.0	12.4	8.5	10.7	8.3
2012	8.3	10.9	7.0	9.0	7.3

Based on: http://www.bls.gov.

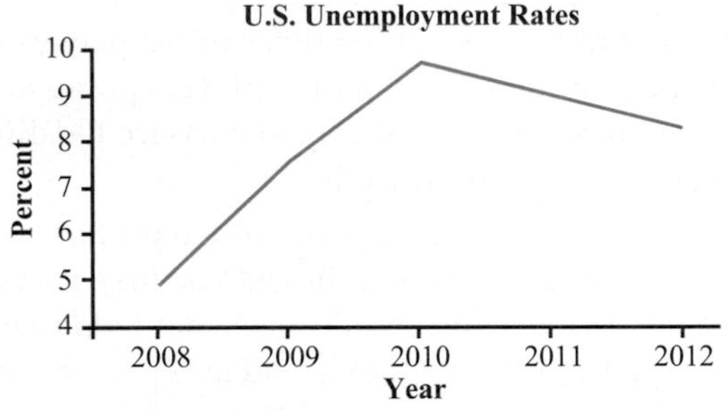

FIGURE 1.5
A Time Series Graph of U.S. Unemployment Rates, 2008–2012

Cross-sectional data are values collected from a number of subjects (firms, individual, states, regions, and so forth) during a single time period.

Unlike time series data, which measure values over a range of time, **cross-sectional data** are values collected from a number of subjects (firms, individual, states, regions, and so forth) during a single time period. Each of the five rows labeled 2008–2012 in Table 1.3 represents a cross-section of unemployment rates for the entire country and the various states during a single year. Figure 1.6 shows a column graph of the 2012 U.S. unemployment rates for the country and the states in the table. Michigan's high unemployment rate reflects the impact that the recession had on the automotive industry. Both time series and cross-sectional data told their own stories from the same data set—the data shown in Table 1.3.

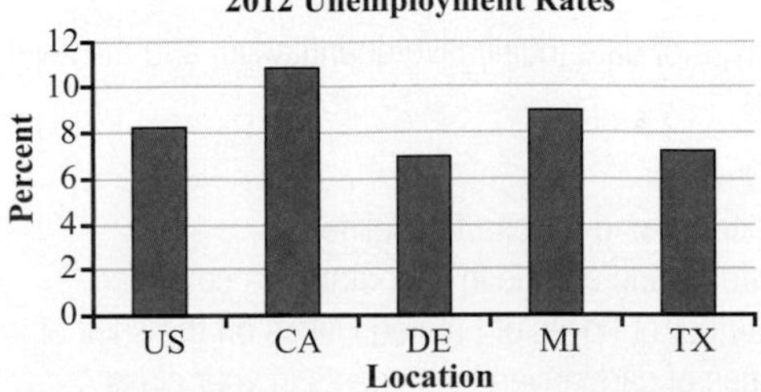

FIGURE 1.6
A Cross-Sectional Graph of 2012 Unemployment Rates

Try the next Your Turn problems to test your understanding of time series and cross-sectional data.

YOUR TURN #3

Identify the following data as either time series data or cross-sectional data.

1. The following table shows the final win/loss records of the National League Central Division for Major League Baseball at the end of the 2012 season.

Team	Wins	Losses
Cincinnati Reds	91	65
St. Louis Cardinals	88	74
Milwaukee Brewers	83	79
Pittsburgh Pirates	79	83
Chicago Cubs	61	107
Houston Astros	55	107

2. The following table shows the final win/loss records of my favorite Major League Baseball team that I love to hate, the Pittsburgh Pirates, for the 2005–2012 seasons. (This is so painful to list.)

Year	Wins	Losses
2005	67	95
2006	67	95
2007	68	94
2008	67	95
2009	62	99
2010	57	105
2011	72	90
2012	79	83

Answers can be found on ▶ **page 19**

1.3 Descriptive and Inferential Statistics

The purpose of **descriptive statistics** is simply to summarize, or display, data so we can quickly get an overview of the information.

The two main branches of statistics are descriptive and inferential. The main focus of **descriptive statistics** is to summarize and display data. Descriptive statistics plays an important role today because of the vast amount of data readily available at our fingertips. With a basic computer and an Internet connection, we can access volumes of data in no time at all. Being able to summarize all of these data accurately in order to get a look at the "big picture," either graphically or numerically, is the job of descriptive statistics.

The majority of statistics that you encounter in your day-to-day life are descriptive. Figures 1.5 and 1.6 are examples of descriptive statistics for unemployment rates. An average is another popular descriptive statistic, such as the average exam score in your statistics class. The statistic provides your instructor with an overview of how well your class performed on the test.

Descriptive statistics are useful, but have limitations. By summarizing large quantities of data, you lose information. For instance, your current GPA is a descriptive statistic summarizing your academic performance. However, this value alone does not provide information about the level of difficulty of the courses you have taken or how your GPA compares to your classmates'.

Inferential statistics allows us to make claims or conclusions about the data based on a sample of them.

A **population** represents all possible subjects of interest. A **sample** is a subset of a population.

As important as descriptive statistics are to us number crunchers, we really get excited about **inferential statistics**. This category covers a large variety of techniques that allow us to make actual claims about a population based on a sample of data. We use the term **population** in statistics to represent all possible subjects that are of interest to us in a particular study. The term **sample** refers to a portion of the population that is representative of the population from which it was selected. Figure 1.7 illustrates this important concept.

FIGURE 1.7
The Relationship Between a Population and a Sample

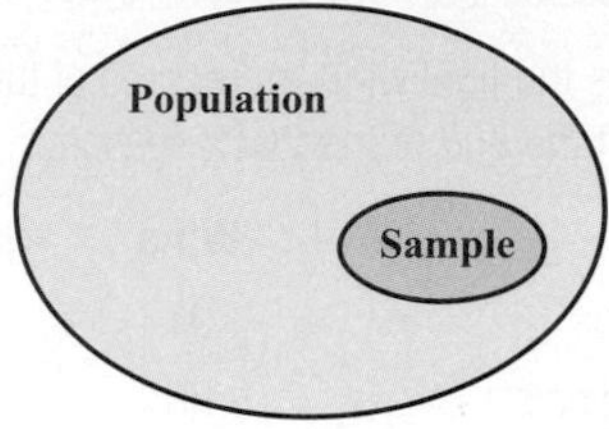

Because much of Alaska is a rainforest, mosquitoes grow large—so large that Alaskans refer to them as the state's unofficial bird!

Many populations are too large or inaccessible to measure completely, so looking at a sample of the population of interest is the only feasible way to estimate it. For instance, it would not be practical to measure the average life span of the mosquito population in Alaska. We would need to measure the life span of a random sample of mosquitoes and use these data to estimate the average life span of the entire population.

Suppose I would like to estimate the average weight per box of my favorite cereal, Kellogg's Frosted Flakes, in the population. (No, I don't own stock in Kellogg's, but I really like Frosted Flakes, so I want the company to stay in business.) For Kellogg's sake, I hope the population average is very close to the target weight of 18 ounces per box. Filling boxes with less than 18 ounces could result in dissatisfied customers (me included), whereas overfilling boxes is giving away free cereal and will reduce profits. To accomplish this task, I would randomly select a sample of cereal boxes and measure their average weight. Let's say the average weight is 18.2 ounces. With inferential statistics, I could determine the likelihood that the average weight of the population of boxes is actually 18 ounces if my sample average were 18.2 ounces. Even if the likelihood were very low, say less than 1%, I would still have to conclude that the average weight of the population of boxes is more than 18 ounces. I would then proceed to check Kellogg's filling process to see why the company is giving away free Frosted Flakes. This example demonstrates the usefulness of statistics in quality control programs. Figure 1.8 summarizes the process of inferential statistics.

FIGURE 1.8
Using Inferential Statistics for Quality Control Purposes: An Example

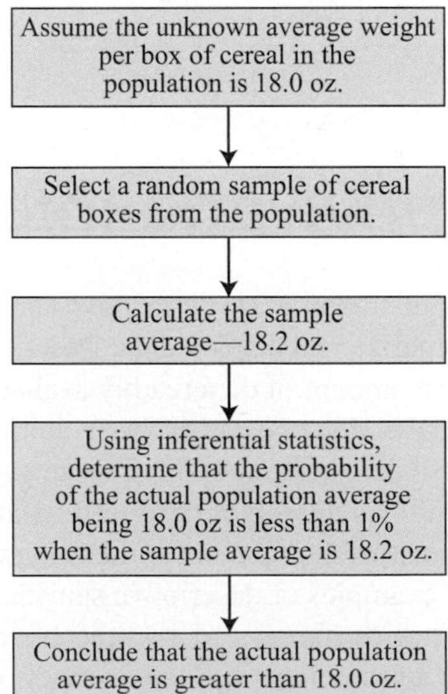

Descriptive statistics describe a sample while **inferential statistics** draw a conclusion about a population.

The following are other examples of inferential statistics:

- Based on a recent sample, I am 95% certain that the average age of my customers is between 32 and 35 years.
- Based on a random survey, the average salary for male employees in a particular job category across the country is higher than for comparable female employees.

In summary, descriptive statistics reports only on the observations at hand and nothing more. Inferential statistics makes a statement about a population based solely on results from a sample taken from that population.

Data that describe a characteristic about a population are known as **parameters**.

Data that describe a characteristic about a sample are known as **statistics**.

Two more terms need to be mentioned here regarding populations and samples. Data used to describe something of interest about a population are known as **parameters**. An example of a parameter is the average weight of the population of Frosted Flake boxes (assumed to be 18 ounces). Data that describe a sample from that population are known as **statistics**. In our previous example, the sample average of 18.2 ounces would be considered a statistic.

Let's check your understanding of this important concept with the following questions.

YOUR TURN #4

Identify each of the following as either descriptive or inferential statistics.

1. Households with children under the age of 18 are more likely to have access to the Internet (77%) than family households with no children (68%).
2. Julie, who cuts and styles hair in her home salon, had 23 customers last week.
3. The average exam score for my statistics exam was an 88.
4. A recent poll showed that 57% of Americans had a favorable opinion of the president of the United States.

Answers can be found on ▶ **page 19**

Stats in Practice: Using Smartphone Data to Monitor Health

With today's technology, our smartphones have become a rich data source of our day-to-day activities. Researchers at the Massachusetts Institute of Technology used this data from student volunteers and found they could reliably conclude when they were ill. Sick students moved around much less than normal and depressed students had fewer calls and text messages. As a result of this research, a company called Ginger.io was formed whose mission is to provide tools to monitor the health of individuals using their smartphone data. When there is a disruption in someone's normal daily pattern, Ginger.io can send a message similar to a car's "check engine light" to that person's friends or doctors. In order to accomplish this task, Ginger.io must analyze massive amounts of smartphone data and link it to health patterns. Sounds like this company can really use the talent of a few good statisticians! Anybody out there interested?

1.4 Ethics and Statistics—It's a Dangerous World of Data Out There

People often use statistics when attempting to persuade you to accept their point of view. Perhaps they are motivated to convince you to purchase something or to support a cause they are advocating. This motivation can lead to the misuse of statistics in several ways. One of the most common misuses is choosing a sample that ensures results consistent with the desired outcome rather than choosing a sample representative of the population of interest. This is known as having a **biased sample**.

A **biased sample** is a sample that does not represent the intended population and that can lead to distorted findings. Biased sampling can occur either intentionally or unintentionally.

Suppose I'm a lobbyist for the golf industry, and my task is to convince Congress to establish a national golf holiday. During this honored day, all government and business offices would be closed so that we all could run out to chase a little white ball into a hole that's way too small with sticks purposely designed by the evil golf club companies to make the task impossible. Sounds like fun to me! Somehow, I need to demonstrate to Congress that the average level-headed American is in favor of this. Here is where the genius part of my plan lies: Rather than survey the general American public, I pass out my survey form only at golf courses. But wait—it only gets better. I design the survey to read as follows:

> We would like to propose a national golf holiday. Everybody gets the day off from work and can play golf *all day*. (You would not need permission from your spouse to play.) Are you in favor of this proposal?
>
> **A.** Yes, most definitely.
>
> **B.** Sure, why not?
>
> **C.** No, I would rather spend the entire day at work.
>
> P.S. If you choose C, your golfing privileges will be permanently revoked everywhere in the country for the rest of your life. We are dead serious.

Granted, this is an extreme example, but my point is that survey results can easily be manipulated by how we ask questions and who is responding to them. And often, major decisions rest on these results.

Another way to misuse statistics is to make differences seem greater or lesser depending on the way the data are graphed. Earlier in the chapter, I presented Figure 1.5, which showed a rather dramatic increase in the U.S. unemployment rate in 2008 and 2009. Figure 1.9 graphs the same data, but the increase in unemployment appears much less dramatic. The trick I employed (no pun intended) was to flatten the graph by simply changing the scale of the *y*-axis, which shows the unemployment rate. In Figure 1.5, the scale ranges from 4% to 10%, whereas in Figure 1.9, the scale has been expanded to 0%–40%. By simply expanding the scale, I made the increase in unemployment rates seem less pronounced.

FIGURE 1.9
Misusing Statistics: A Graphical Example, U.S. Unemployment Rates, 2008–2012

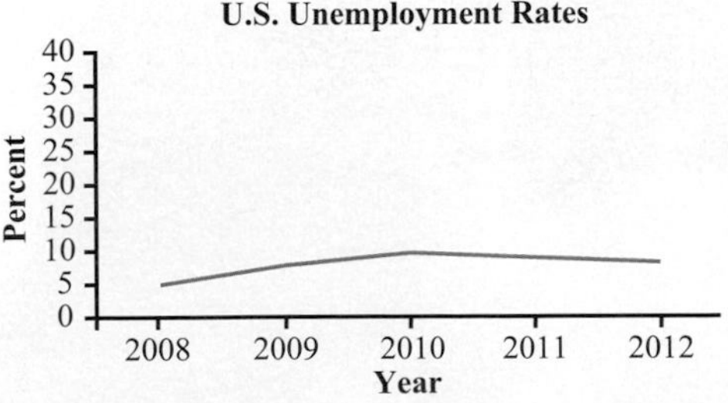

Many of the polls we see on the Internet represent another potential misuse of statistics. I'm sure you have visited Web sites that encourage you to vote on a question of the day. The results of these informal polls are unreliable simply because those collecting the data have no control over who responds to the polls or how many times they respond. As stated earlier, a valid statistical study depends on selecting a sample representative of the population of interest. This is not possible when any person surfing the Internet can participate in the poll. Even though most of these polls state that the results are not scientific, it's still a natural human tendency to be influenced by the results we see.

Many times statistical mishaps occur simply due to poor decision making. One of the most famous snafus took place during the 1936 presidential race. The *Literary Digest*, an influential magazine at the time, conducted a presidential election poll, based on questionnaires mailed to readers and potential readers, and published the results before the election. Unfortunately, the magazine predicted that Alf Landon would win the election over Franklin D. Roosevelt. Even if history is not your best subject, you should realize that somebody at the *Digest* had some serious explaining to do after that election day. The problem was that the *Digest* drew its sample from phone books and automobile registrations. People with phones and cars in 1936 tended to be wealthier Republicans (who voted for Landon) and were not representative of the entire voting population.

A more recent example of poor decision making that was based on statistical analysis occurred in the 1980s when Coca-Cola was feeling the pressure because Pepsi's market share was rising. To halt the trend, Coca-Cola decided to reformulate its nearly 100-year-old recipe for Coke. The new formula was sweeter than both the old formula and Pepsi's product. After scoring well in the taste tests, Coke decided to replace its original product with the new formula. However, the test failed to consider two important factors. First, people might prefer a sweeter taste when they are drinking small quantities of a beverage as they were at time of the test. However, they don't like to drink larger quantities of it. Second, and more importantly, Coke failed to measure the psychological impact making such a major change to a well-established product would have on consumers. Many Coke drinkers were outraged that the product they loved to drink suddenly no longer existed. After a huge public outcry, Coca-Cola admitted its mistake and brought the original formula back to market as Coke Classic and relabeled the new formulation New Coke. What a mess! The lesson here is that even large, successful corporations can misuse statistics, which can result in poor business decisions.

CHAPTER 1 Summary

- Statistics is the process of collection, analysis and presentation of data, which can then be used for inference.
  - Business statistics helps improve people's decision making in fields such as marketing, operations, finance, and human resources.
- Data are the foundation for the field of statistics.
- Data is defined as the values assigned to specific observations or measurements.
- Information is derived from data for the purpose of making decisions.
- Data sources are either primary or secondary.
  - Secondary data are data collected by someone else that you are "borrowing."
  - Primary data are data that you have collected for your own use through direct observation, experiments, or surveys.
    - Direct observation focuses on gathering data while the subjects of interest are in their natural environment.
    - In an experiment, subjects are exposed to certain treatments and data of interest are recorded.
    - A survey involves directly asking subjects a series of questions.
- Data can be classified in different ways.
  - Quantitative—characterized by numerical values.
  - Qualitative—characterized by terms describing the data.
  - By the way they are measured.
    - A nominal level of measurement deals strictly with qualitative data.
    - Ordinal level data have all the properties of data measured at the nominal level, but we can rank-order the values from highest to lowest.
    - At the interval level of measurement, the differences between the data can be measured with actual numbers giving measurable meaning to the differences.
    - Ratio data have all the properties of interval data, along with a true zero point.
      - A zero data value indicates the absence of the object being measured.
    - As time series or cross-sectional data.
      - Times series data are values that correspond to a specific measurement over a range of time periods.
      - Cross-sectional data are values that correspond to a specific time period.
- Two main branches of statistics are as follows.
  - Descriptive statistics summarize and display sample data.
  - Inferential statistics makes a statement about a population based on sample data from that population.
- Statistics can be misused by the following.
  - Employing a biased sample that is not representative of the population of interest.
  - Manipulating a graph by adjusting the scale of the data.
  - Relying on Internet surveys with no control over who responds or how many times they respond to the survey.

CHAPTER 1 Key Terms

Business statistics. Statistics applied to the business world to help improve people's decision making in fields such as marketing, operations, finance, and human resources.

Biased sample. A sample that does not represent the intended population and that can lead to distorted findings.

Cross-sectional data. Data values that correspond to a specific time period.

Data. The values assigned to specific observations or measurements.

Descriptive statistics. The branch of statistics that focuses on summarizing, or displaying, data.

Direct observation. A method of gathering primary data by observing subjects of interest in their natural environment.

Experiment. A method of gathering primary data by exposing subjects to certain treatments and recording the data of interest.

Focus group. A direct observational technique whereby individuals are often paid to discuss their attitudes toward products or services in a group setting controlled by a moderator.

Inferential statistics. The field of statistics that allows us to make claims or conclusions about a population based on a sample of data from that population.

Information. Data that are transformed into useful facts that can be used for a specific purpose, such as making a decision.

Interval level of measurement. Quantitative data that can measure the difference between categories with actual numbers, giving measurable meaning to the differences.

Nominal level of measurement. Qualitative data observations that are assigned to predetermined categories.

Ordinal level of measurement. Data that have all the properties of nominal data but that also permit the rank-ordering of values from highest to lowest.

Parameter. Data that describe characteristics of a population.

Population. A population represents all possible outcomes or measurements of interest.

Primary data. Data collected by the person or organization that eventually uses the data.

Qualitative data. Data that use descriptive terms to measure or classify something of interest.

Quantitative data. Data that use numerical values to describe something of interest.

Ratio level of measurement. Data that have all the features of interval data, with the added benefit of a true zero point. The term *true zero point* means that a zero data value indicates the absence of the object being measured.

Sample. A subset of a population.

Secondary data. Data that somebody else has collected and made available for others to use.

Statistic. Data that describe characteristics about a sample.

Statistics. The mathematical science that deals with the collection, analysis, and presentation of data, which can then be used as a basis for inference and induction.

Survey. A method of collecting primary data by asking subjects a series of questions.

Time series data. Data values that correspond to a specific measurement over a range of time periods.

CHAPTER 1 Problems

Identify the type of data (qualitative/quantitative) and the level of measurement for Problems 1.1 through 1.18. Explain your choice.

1.1 The average monthly temperature in degrees Fahrenheit for the city of Wilmington, Delaware, throughout the year

1.2 The average monthly rainfall in inches for the city of Wilmington throughout the year

1.3 The education level of survey respondents

Level	Number of Respondents
High school	168
Bachelor's degree	784
Master's degree	212

1.4 The marital status of survey respondents

Status	Number of Respondents
Single	28
Married	189
Divorced	62

1.5 The ages of the respondents in a survey

1.6 The genders of the respondents in a survey

1.7 The years in which the respondents to a survey were born

1.8 The voting intentions of the respondents in a survey classified as Republican, Democrat, or Undecided

1.9 The race of the respondents in a survey classified as White, African American, Asian, or Other

1.10 The performance rating of employees classified as Above Expectations, Meets Expectations, or Below Expectations

1.11 The uniform number of each member on a sports team

1.12 A list of the graduating high school seniors by class rank

1.13 Final exam scores for your statistics class on a scale of 0 to 100

1.14 The state in which the respondents in a survey reside

1.15 SAT scores for graduating high school students

1.16 Movie ratings: G, PG, PG-13, R

1.17 In order to promote the development of electric cars, the government has proposed rating passenger vehicles on a letter scale of A–D based on fuel efficiency and emissions. The following five vehicles were given these ratings:

Vehicle	Rating
Nissan Leaf	A+
Toyota Prius	A−
Ford Focus	B
Jeep Grand Cherokee	C+
Ferrari 612 Scaglietti	D

1.18 S&P provides ratings for the creditworthiness of countries around the world on a letter scale from AAA (highest) to D (lowest). The following table shows the S&P rating for various countries in January 2013.

Country	Rating
Germany	AAA
United States	AA+
France	AA+
Italy	BBB+
Spain	BBB−
Portugal	BB

Identify the data shown in Problems 1.19 and 1.20 as either time series or cross-sectional.

1.19 The following table shows the closing price of the three major stock markets on February 4, 2013:

Stock Market	Closing Price
Dow Jones Industrial	13,880
NASDAQ	3,131
S&P 500	1,496

1.20 The following table shows the closing price of the Dow Jones Industrial stock market during 2012:

Date	Closing Price
September 28, 2012	13,437
October 31, 2012	13,096
November 30, 2012	13,026
December 31, 2012	13,104

Problems 1.21 and 1.22 refer to the following data, which show the median weekly earnings of full-time workers by gender over a five-year period:

Year	Men	Women
2008	$798	$638
2009	$819	$657
2010	$824	$669
2011	$854	$691
2012	$832	$684

1.21 Identify the time series data in the table.

1.22 Identify the cross-sectional data in the table.

Problems 1.23 and 1.24 refer to the following data, which shows the number of photographs sold at Island Art, a retail store in Stone Harbor, New Jersey, by print-size of a four-year period:

Year	Print-Size		
	8 × 10	11 × 14	13 × 19
2010	117	102	160
2011	92	125	146
2012	105	111	133
2013	112	89	138

1.23 Identify the cross-sectional data in the table.

1.24 Identify the time series data in the table.

Identify each of the following as either descriptive or inferential statistics.

1.25 The average salary of a random sample of 50 high school teachers in 2013 was $52,400.

1.26 Based on a random sample of hotels in Chicago and a random sample of hotels in Atlanta, it was concluded that the average cost of a hotel room in Chicago was greater than one in Atlanta.

1.27 A study has concluded that the average credit card debt of college graduates has increased from 2012 to 2013.

1.28 The average Amazon.com rating of the book *The Complete Idiot's Guide to Statistics* by 26 reviewers is 4.6 on a scale of 1 to 5.

1.29 The average American viewer watches 151 hours of TV per month.

1.30 Seventy-eight percent of customers at the Holiday Inn hotel in Dover, Delaware, arrived before 6 PM last week.

CHAPTER 1 Solutions to Your Turn

YOUR TURN #1

1. Primary data through a survey
2. Primary data through an experiment
3. Secondary data
4. Primary data through direct observation

YOUR TURN #2

a) Quantitative/Interval. The differences between IQ scores are meaningful, but there is no true zero point because an IQ of 0 does not indicate the absence of intelligence.

b) Quantitative/Ratio. The differences between prices are meaningful, and there is a true zero point because gasoline that is $0 per gallon is free!

c) Qualitative/Ordinal. You can rank letter grades, but the differences between the grades cannot be consistently measured.

d) Quantitative/Ratio. The differences between inventory levels are meaningful, and there is a true zero point because zero boxes on the shelf indicates an absence of the product.

e) Qualitative/Nominal. The types of cars are merely labels with no ranking or meaningful differences.

YOUR TURN #3

1. Cross-sectional
2. Time series

YOUR TURN #4

1. Inferential statistics, because it would not be feasible to survey every household in the country. These results would be based on a sample of the population and used to make an inference on the entire population.
2. Descriptive statistics, because this data describes a sample, the number of customers last week.
3. Descriptive statistics, because the average exam score describes a sample, which is students in my class.
4. Inferential statistics, because it would not be feasible to survey every American in the country. These results would be based on a sample of the population and used to make an inference about the entire population.

CHAPTER 2

Displaying Descriptive Statistics

IN THIS CHAPTER, YOU WILL LEARN TO:

- Use Excel to display data with charts and graphs.
- Construct a frequency distribution and histogram.
- Construct and interpret polygons.
- Display qualitative data using bar charts and pie charts.
- Display quality control issues with a Pareto chart.
- Organize data in a contingency table.
- Present the frequency of data using a stem and leaf display.
- Show the relationship between two variables using scatter plots.

CHAPTER 2 MAP

In Chapter 1, we learned that the purpose of descriptive statistics is to summarize or display data so that we can quickly obtain an overview of the information of interest. In this chapter, we will explore the methods by which data can be displayed in tables and graphs to facilitate better understanding. I find that some students (not you, of course) often underestimate the importance of presenting graphical data and information in a clear and convincing manner to lend support to their ideas. There's no better way to make your point than with a creative chart your audience can quickly absorb.

By contrast, presenting lots of data in a table format is a surefire way to lose your audience. Our brains do not process information very effectively when faced with reading a list of numbers. We do much better at comprehending data when we are presented with a picture such as a graph or chart. For instance, Table 2.1 shows the selling price, in thousands of dollars, of 60 two-bedroom condominiums in Myrtle Beach, South Carolina, during a recent time period. Most people, including me, do not have the attention span to read every single number in this table.

TABLE 2.1 | DATA PRESENTED AS A TABLE: CONDOMINIUM PRICES IN MYRTLE BEACH

$281.0	$262.1	$291.2	$277.1	$294.5	$298.2
$247.8	$344.9	$322.5	$258.0	$226.3	$320.0
$306.0	$287.5	$228.2	$209.6	$220.0	$218.4
$247.2	$395.0	$291.4	$329.4	$335.5	$325.9
$446.3	$302.3	$257.7	$278.8	$296.8	$343.8
$254.1	$193.0	$174.4	$380.9	$198.6	$270.7
$199.0	$298.8	$268.3	$193.3	$383.6	$348.3
$295.5	$254.1	$301.2	$375.0	$359.9	$260.4
$227.8	$360.3	$299.0	$274.1	$195.9	$337.8
$246.4	$292.6	$237.0	$339.0	$300.2	$271.9

A much better approach would be to construct a chart that provides an effective snapshot of these 60 data points. You don't need to work as hard to understand the data in the chart, which is always a good thing, in my book.

By examining the chart in Figure 2.1, we can see the range that contains the highest number of condominiums is $250,000 to under $300,000. This information is not readily observable by merely looking at the data in the table.

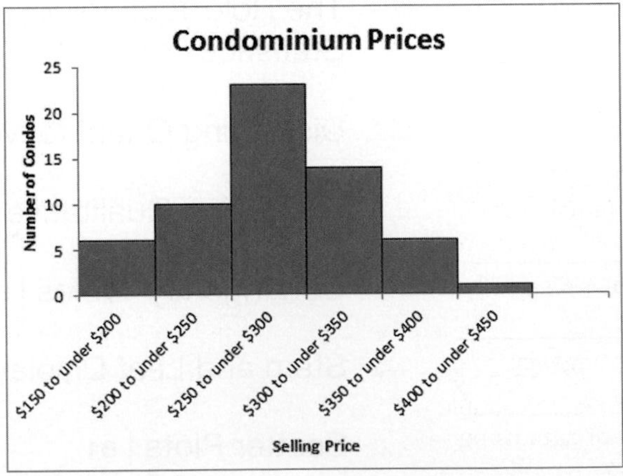

FIGURE 2.1 Data Presented Graphically: Condominium Prices in Myrtle Beach

This chapter will provide you with a solid foundation to display descriptive statistics in a way that is sure to impress your future boss and colleagues. Using Microsoft Excel 2013, you will be cranking out fancy graphs like the one shown in Figure 2.1 in no time.

In addition to creating graphs, as a reader and a consumer of information you will also find yourself interpreting data that have been presented to you in a graphical format.

Publications such as the *Wall Street Journal* and *USA Today* present data graphically to capture the attention of their readers and to summarize complex issues efficiently. Being well versed in the art of interpreting graphical data will make you a better decision maker.

2.1 The Role Technology Plays in Statistics

Technology plays a major role in the field of statistics. Throughout this book, we will be using Excel 2013 for Windows to assist you in your efforts to construct various charts and graphs as well as to perform many of the calculations required in statistics.

When I was a youthful engineering undergraduate student in the 1970s, the words *personal computer* had no meaning. Windows were something you looked through, and no self-respecting consumer electronics company would dream of naming itself after a fruit. I performed calculations on a clever gadget fondly known as a slide rule. For those of you who weren't even alive during this time period, I've included a picture of a slide rule in Figure 2.2.

FIGURE 2.2
A Slide Rule Circa 1975.

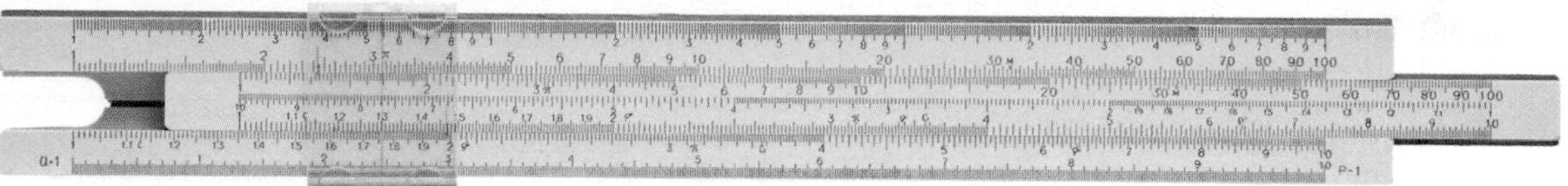

As you can see, this device looks like a ruler on steroids. It can perform all sorts of mathematical calculations, but is far from being user friendly. During my freshman year in college, I purchased my first handheld calculator, a Texas Instrument model that could perform only the basic math functions. It was the approximate size of a cash register. I proudly wore this device like a badge of honor on my belt, which I suspect contributed to my current back problems. Oh well, the things we do to look cool!

Fortunately, we have advanced from the Dark Ages and now have awesome, user-friendly computing power at our fingertips. Powerful programs such as SAS, SPSS, Minitab, and Excel are readily accessible to those of us who don't know a thing about computer programming. Yet the programs allow us to perform some of the most sophisticated statistical analysis known to humankind. The next section describes how we can prepare Excel 2013 to assist us with various ways to display data and perform calculations required in statistics.

Statistical Analysis Using Excel 2013

In addition to the basic statistical functions found in Excel 2013 for Windows, we will be relying on two Excel Add-ins:

- Data Analysis ToolPak—available as a standard feature in Excel (Windows version).
- PHStat—developed by Pearson Education. This program provides statistical tools not available in Excel's Data Analysis ToolPak and can be downloaded at www.pearsonhighered.com/phstat. Installation instructions can also be found in this download site.

If you are a Mac user (like myself), there are some compatibility issues that we have to address for which there is good news and bad news. First the bad news—Excel for Mac (2011 or older) is not compatible with Data Analysis ToolPak. Now the good news—the version of PHStat mentioned in the previous paragraph is compatible with Excel 2011 for Mac. Also (more good news), the basic Excel statistical functions used in this book are compatible with Windows and Mac versions. Whenever Excel instructions shown in this textbook are not compatible with the Mac version, I will make a note to direct you to the textbook's Web site mentioned earlier to download Excel for Mac instructions (for versions 2011 and older) for that particular task. Often, you will be able to rely on PHStat for these situations.

I also need to address those using Excel 2010 for Windows with this textbook. For the most part, the instructions used in this textbook can be easily applied to your software. Whenever there is a discrepancy between the two versions, I will make a note to direct you to the book's Web site to download Excel 2010 instructions.

We are now ready to activate Excel's Data Analysis ToolPak (Windows version only) by using the following steps:

1. With Excel 2013 open, click on the **File** tab found in the upper left corner of your computer screen.
2. Click **Options** shown in the left margin in Figure 2.3. This will open the **Excel Options** dialog box shown in Figure 2.4.
3. Select **Add-Ins** in the left margin as shown in Figure 2.4.
4. Click on **Go** at the bottom of the screen.

FIGURE 2.3
Excel's File Drop-Down Menu

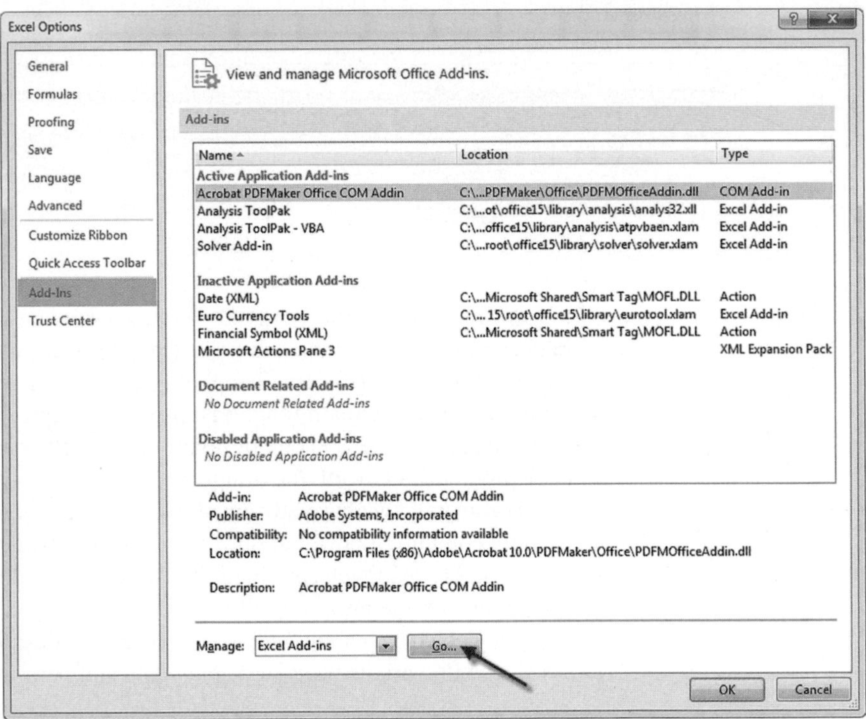

FIGURE 2.4
Excel's Options

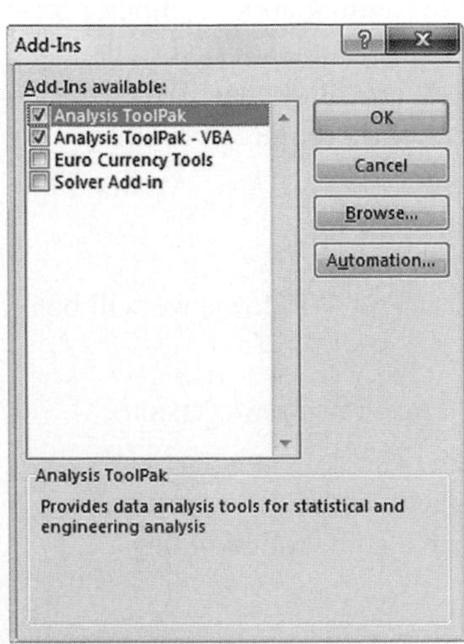

FIGURE 2.5
Excel's Add-Ins Pop-Up Menu

5. Select the check boxes for **Analysis ToolPak** and **Analysis ToolPak - VBA** in the pop-up menu and click **OK** as shown in Figure 2.5.
6. Select the Data tab. Click on **Data Analysis** on the right as shown in Figure 2.6. The Data Analysis pop-up menu should appear in the spreadsheet.

Your Excel software is now ready to perform all sorts of statistical magic as we explore various techniques throughout this textbook. At this point, you can click Cancel and close out Excel. Each time you open Excel in the future, the Data Analysis option will be available under the Data tab.

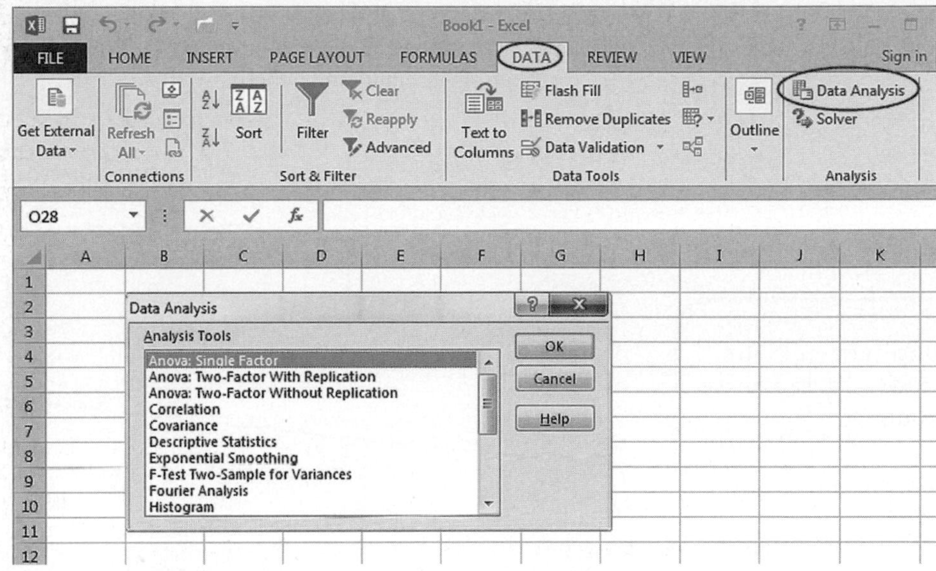

FIGURE 2.6 Excel's Data Analysis Pop-Up Menu

2.2 Displaying Quantitative Data

In Chapter 1, we made a distinction between quantitative data, which consist of numerical values, and qualitative data, which use descriptive categories. In this section, we will discuss the various methods used to display quantitative data. In a later section, we will cover the qualitative data.

Constructing a Frequency Distribution

A **frequency distribution** is a table that shows the number of data observations that fall into specific intervals.

One of the simplest ways to describe data is through a **frequency distribution**, which shows the number of data observations that fall into specific intervals. I'll use the following example to demonstrate the construction of a frequency distribution using quantitative data. The 50 values in Table 2.2 represent the number of iPads sold at an Apple store in each of the past 50 days.

TABLE 2.2 | The Number of iPads Sold in Each of 50 Days

4	2	3	2	5
5	1	3	3	2
3	2	2	3	2
2	2	3	0	1
3	1	1	5	4
1	2	4	3	5
2	0	0	3	2
3	3	3	2	2
0	4	2	4	3
1	1	4	0	1

Three iPads were sold on this Particular day.

Table 2.3 on the next page shows these same data as a frequency distribution. The first column in the table lists all the possible daily values that occurred over the 50 days: 0, 1, 2, 3, 4, or 5 iPads sold. The second column counts the number of observations for each of these values during the past 50 days. Notice that the total number of frequencies (50) shown in Table 2.3

matches the total number of observations in Table 2.2. Because the number of iPads sold per day is a numerical value rather than a descriptive value, this is an example of a frequency distribution summarizing quantitative data.

TABLE 2.3 | FREQUENCY DISTRIBUTION FOR THE NUMBER OF IPADS SOLD IN THE PAST 50 DAYS

NUMBER SOLD PER DAY	FREQUENCY
0	5
1	8
2	14
3	13
4	6
5	4
Total	**50**

Two iPads were sold in 14 of the 50 days that the data were collected.

A **class** is a category in a frequency distribution.

We call each row in a frequency distribution table a **class**. In our iPad example, the first class represents the number of days that no iPads were sold, the second class shows the number of days one iPad was sold, and so on.

Discrete data are values based on observations that can be counted and are typically represented by whole numbers.

Before we move on, I have one more data type to throw your way. The data in Table 2.2 are known as **discrete data**, which means the values represent something that has been counted. Discrete data typically take on whole numbers such as 0, 1, 2, 3, and so on. Because selling partial iPads is not a good business decision let alone possible, values such as 2.8 or 4.3 would not be considered discrete data in this example.

Continuous data are values that can take on any real numbers, including numbers that contain decimal points.

Data that can take on any real numbers, including numbers that contain decimal points, are known as **continuous data**. Continuous data are usually measured rather than counted. Examples of continuous data are weight, time, and distance. I'll show you an example using continuous data later in this chapter.

Here's a helpful way to distinguish between continuous and discrete data. Continuous data are often the result of measuring observations, whereas discrete data often involve counting them.

The acid test for determining which type of data we are dealing with is to ask ourselves, "How many data values can be found in a specific interval of numbers?" Because discrete data can be counted, they have a finite number of values within an interval, whereas continuous data have an infinite number of values available. Let's take the interval 0–3 as an example. Remembering that iPad sales were discrete data, only four possible values of iPad sales can occur within this interval (0, 1, 2, or 3). If we were measuring time, which is continuous, there are an infinite number of possible values within this interval (2.0 minutes, 2.04 minutes, 2.046 minutes, and so on). The only limitation in the number of continuous data values is the level of precision of our measuring instrument.

Discrete vs. continuous data is an important concept throughout this textbook, so let's take a minute to test your understanding in the following Your Turn box.

YOUR TURN #1

Identify the following as either discrete or continuous data:

1. The number of students absent from your statistics class today
2. The number of hours a light bulb burned before going out
3. The number of light bulbs that burned for more than 1,000 hours in a quality control program
4. The number of minutes an airline flight was late
5. The number of red cars a dealer has on its sales lot
6. The number of inches in a person's height
7. The number of runs scored by the Pittsburgh Pirates tonight

Answers can be found on ▶ **page 73**

Relative Frequency Distributions

Relative frequency distributions display the proportion of observations of each class relative to the total number of observations.

Another way to display frequency data is by using a **relative frequency distribution**. Rather than displaying the *number* of observations in each class, this method calculates the *proportion* of observations in each class by dividing each frequency by the total number of observations. A relative frequency distribution tells us what proportion, or fraction, a class's observations are relative to the total observations made. Table 2.4 shows the relative frequency distribution for our iPad example.

TABLE 2.4 | Relative Frequency Distribution for the Number of iPads Sold in the Past 50 Days

NUMBER SOLD PER DAY	FREQUENCY	RELATIVE FREQUENCY
0	5	$5/50 = 0.10$
1	8	$8/50 = 0.16$
2	14	$14/50 = 0.28$
3	13	$13/50 = 0.26$
4	6	$6/50 = 0.12$
5	4	$4/50 = 0.08$
Total	**50**	**1.00**

Notice that the fractions in the relative frequency distribution add up to 1.00. Because of rounding, the total relative frequency will sometimes not add up to exactly 1.00, but it should be very close.

According to Table 2.4, two iPads were sold on 28% of the days.

Cumulative Relative Frequency Distributions

A **cumulative relative frequency distribution** totals the proportion of observations that are less than or equal to the class at which you are looking.

A cousin of the relative frequency distribution (a pun I couldn't resist) simply totals the proportions of each class as you move down the column. It is called the **cumulative relative frequency distribution**. A cumulative relative frequency distribution provides you with the proportion of observations that are less than or equal to the class you are looking at—the accumulated proportion, in other words. This technique would be useful if the manager of the Apple store wanted to determine the percentage of days that three or fewer iPads were sold. The cumulative relative frequency distribution for our iPad example is shown in Table 2.5.

TABLE 2.5 | Cumulative Relative Frequency Distribution for the Number of iPads Sold in the Past 50 Days

NUMBER SOLD PER DAY	FREQUENCY	RELATIVE FREQUENCY	CUMULATIVE RELATIVE FREQUENCY
0	5	0.10	0.10
1	8	0.16	$0.10 + 0.16 = 0.26$
2	14	0.28	$0.26 + 0.28 = 0.54$
3	13	0.26	$0.54 + 0.26 = 0.80$
4	6	0.12	$0.80 + 0.12 = 0.92$
5	4	0.08	$0.92 + 0.08 = 1.00$
Total	**50**	**1.00**	

Note that the last cumulative relative frequency should equal 1.00 (or very close to 1.00 due to rounding).

Looking at Table 2.5, we can now conclude that three iPads or less were sold on 80% of the business days.

Excel's FREQUENCY Function

A **histogram** is a graph showing the number of observations in each class of a frequency distribution.

Now that I've tortured you with constructing frequency distributions by hand, I'll demonstrate how to use Excel's FREQUENCY function to construct a distribution and generate a graph known as a histogram. A **histogram** is simply a graph showing the number of observations in each class of a frequency distribution. Figure 2.1, the chart in which we graphed condominium prices, is an example of a histogram.

Figure 2.7A shows the iPad data from Table 2.2 along with a column labeled "Bins," which is Excel's strange term for the classes in our distribution. Use the following steps to construct the frequency distribution.

1. Open the Excel file **iPad sales.xlsx** or type in the data in Column A and Column C as shown in Figure 2.7A (except Column D).
2. Place your cursor in Cell D2 and highlight cells D2:D7. This is where our frequency distribution will be placed.
3. With cells D2:D7 highlighted, type=**FREQUENCY(A2:A51,C2:C7).** Do not hit the Enter key just yet!
4. Hit the **Control + Shift + Enter** keys together.
5. Voila! (pronounced "vwa-la") The frequency distribution appears before your very eyes in the highlighted cells in Column D, as shown in Figure 2.7A (circled in red).

FIGURE 2.7A
Constructing a Frequency Distribution with Excel

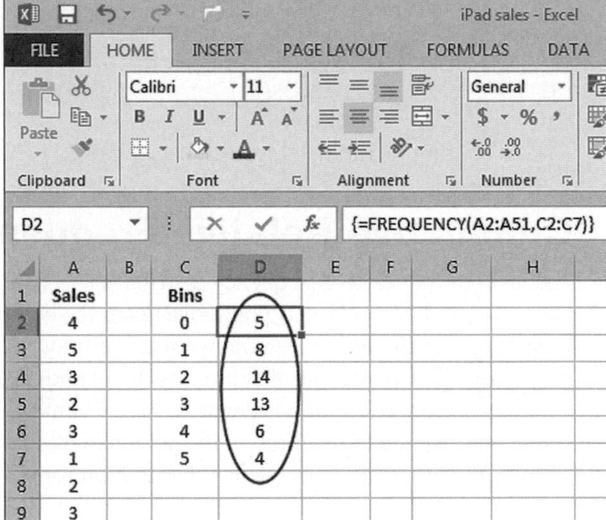

Using a Histogram to Graph a Frequency Distribution

www.pearsonhighered.com/donnelly

The following steps will guide you through the process of constructing a histogram in Excel for Windows. See the textbook's Web site for Excel for Mac instructions. We'll start with Figure 2.7B, which shows the iPad data and the bins column.

1. Select the **Data** tab, and click on **Data Analysis** in the upper right corner. The Data Analysis pop-up menu will appear as shown in Figure 2.7B.
2. In the pop-up menu, select **Histogram** and click **OK**.
3. Figure 2.7C shows the **Histogram** dialog box. In the **Input Range** text box, highlight the data in cells A1:A51.
4. In the **Bin Range** text box, highlight the bin values in cells C1:C7 and check the **Labels** box.
5. For **Output options**, select **New Worksheet Ply** and **Chart Output**.
6. Click **OK**.

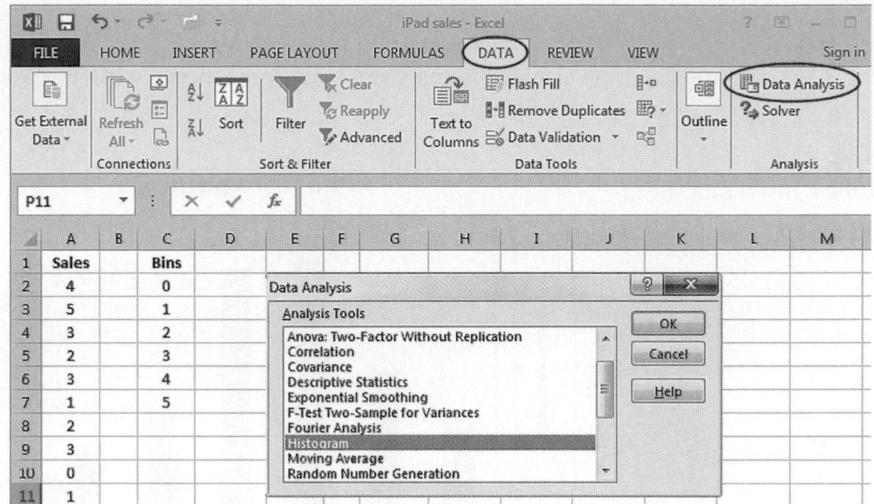

FIGURE 2.7B
Constructing a Histogram with Excel (Steps 1 and 2)

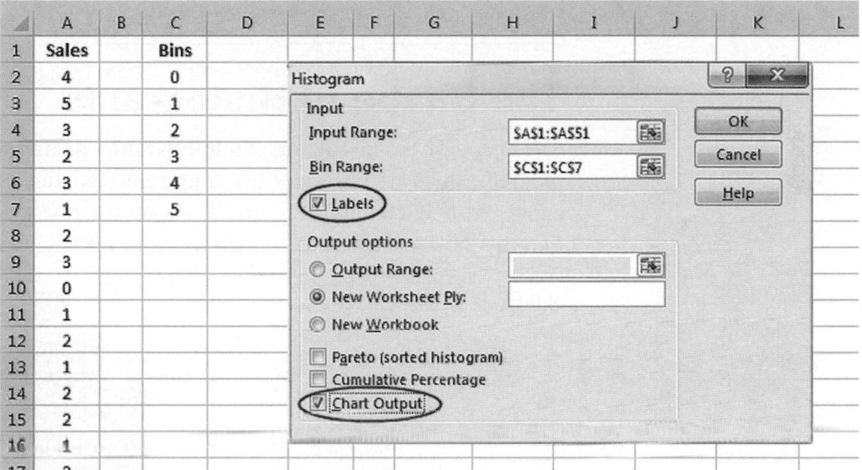

FIGURE 2.7C
Constructing a Histogram with Excel (Steps 3 and 4)

7. Figure 2.7D shows the fruits of your labor, but a few extra steps can make it look prettier.
8. Excel tends to produce a histogram that looks like an elephant sat on it. If you click on the histogram, a border will appear around the histogram that will allow you to grab a corner with your cursor and stretch out your chart.
9. By default, Excel adds a "More" bin that doesn't serve much purpose here. Delete cells A8 and B8 in the frequency distribution to remove this class from your histogram.
10. The labels on the histogram can be modified by highlighting the label and typing over them.
11. The "Frequency" legend to the right of the histogram can be removed by clicking on it and hitting **Delete**.

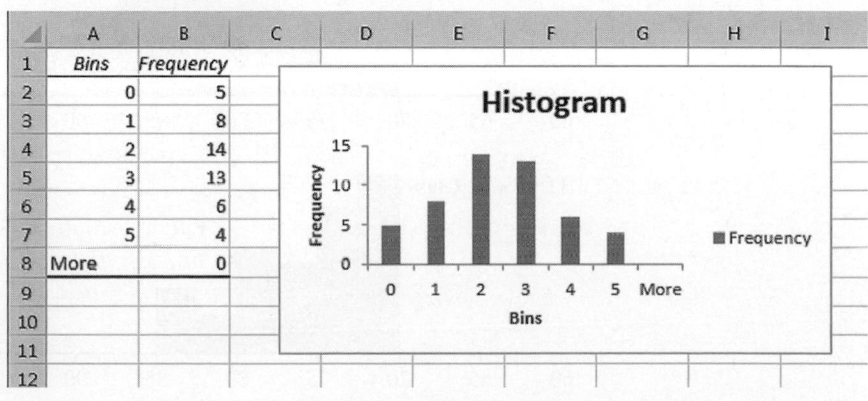

FIGURE 2.7D
Constructing a Histogram with Excel (Steps 5–7)

Figure 2.7E shows our finished histogram, which I think looks much better than Figure 2.7D. By default, Excel inserts gaps between the bars in the histogram, which is the appropriate way to display discrete data. In a later section, I will show you how to display continuous data in a histogram.

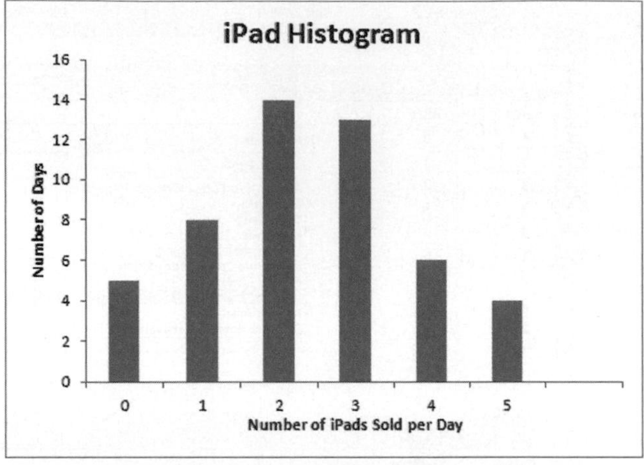

FIGURE 2.7E Constructing a Histogram with Excel (Final Result)

The Shape of Histograms

The shape of the histogram can tell us some useful information about our data. For example, let's say I am currently teaching four statistics classes and that I just finished grading exams from each class. Figure 2.8 shows the histogram for each class. You can clearly see that my 8:00 A.M. class performed the best, with many students scoring in the low 90s.

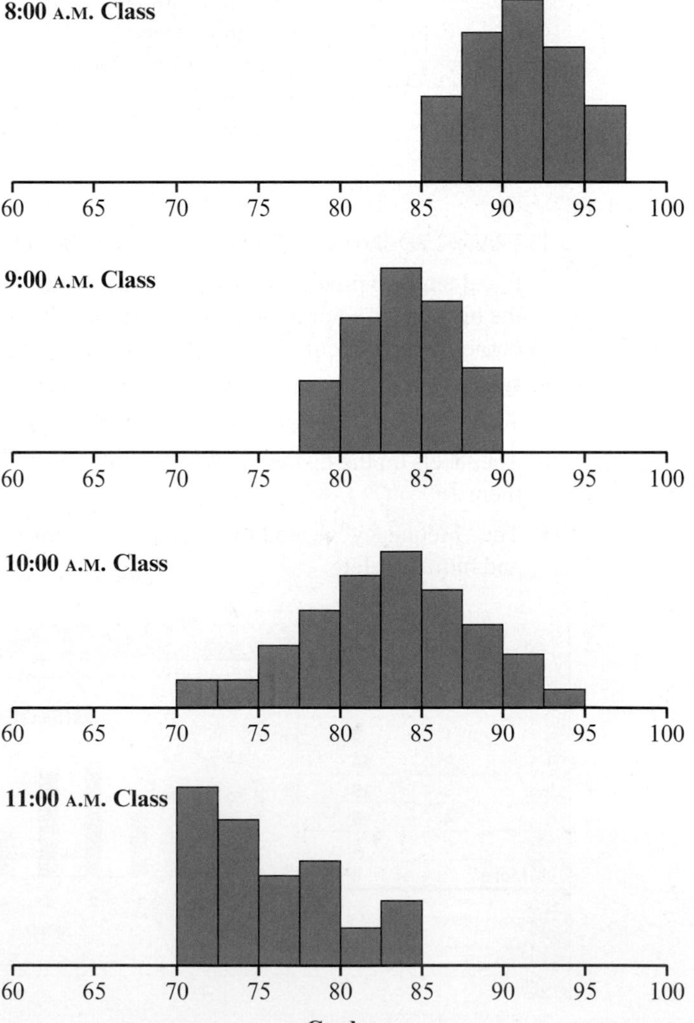

FIGURE 2.8 Histograms of My Four Statistics Classes

A **symmetrical distribution** is one in which the right side of the distribution is the mirror image of the left side of the distribution.

The grade distribution appears symmetrical, with most of the scores in the middle of the range. A **symmetrical distribution** is one in which the right side of the distribution is the mirror image of the left side of the distribution. The shape of the histogram for the 9:00 A.M. class is similar to the one for the 8:00 A.M. class. However, the 9:00 A.M. class did not do as well—many of the students' scores were in the mid-80s. The histogram for the 10:00 A.M. class also appears symmetrical and is centered in the mid-80s. However, the scores in this class are more spread out than those of the 9:00 A.M. class. They range from 70 to 95, whereas the 9:00 A.M. class scores range from the upper 70s to 90. Finally, my poor 11:00 A.M. class appears to have really struggled with the exam. Notice that this distribution is more concentrated on the left side, in the low 70s, so it is not symmetrical. Each histogram provides me with a quick overview of how each class performed. We will revisit the shapes of distributions in Chapter 3 when we cover calculating descriptive statistics.

While these concepts are still fresh in your brain, take a crack at a problem in the following Your Turn box before moving on to the next topic.

YOUR TURN #2

The following table shows the number of stars that 25 reviewers gave Amazon's Kindle, a device for reading electronic books.

4	4	5	5	5	4	3	5	3	5
5	5	4	5	2	4	5	1	5	4
3	5	5	4	1					

Construct the following:

1. A frequency distribution
2. A relative frequency distribution
3. A cumulative relative frequency distribution
4. A histogram

Answers can be found on ▶ **page 74**

Constructing a Frequency Distribution Using Grouped Quantitative Data

Each class in the iPad frequency distribution from the last section consisted of a single value. Some data sets, particularly those with continuous data, require several values to be grouped together in a single class. This grouping prevents having too many classes in the frequency distribution, which can make it difficult to detect patterns. Ideally, the number of classes in a frequency distribution should be between 4 and 20.

To demonstrate grouped data in a frequency distribution, I'll use the following example: In an effort to improve customer service, Dell monitors the time customers wait on hold when calling in for support. Table 2.6 lists the wait times in minutes for the last 50 callers.

TABLE 2.6 | DELL'S CUSTOMER-SUPPORT HOLD TIMES

0.6	3.9	5.4	8.3	10.2
1.2	4.4	5.5	8.7	10.5
1.3	4.4	5.8	9.0	10.9
2.5	4.6	6.1	9.3	12.2
2.8	4.6	6.4	9.3	12.5
3.2	4.6	6.9	9.5	13.1
3.2	4.8	7.0	9.5	13.3
3.5	4.9	8.0	9.7	13.6
3.8	5.1	8.1	9.8	14.4
3.9	5.2	8.1	9.9	17.4

The times are sorted from shortest to longest. These data can also be found in the Excel file **Dell hold times.xlsx**.

Number of Classes

For grouped data, we need to determine the number of classes in our frequency distribution. One method is to use the $2^k \geq n$ rule, where

$$k = \text{Number of classes}$$
$$n = \text{Number of data points}$$

The trick is to find the lowest value of k that satisfies the rule. For our Dell example, $n = 50$.

$$2^5 = 32 \leq 50 \; (k = 5 \text{ is too small})$$
$$2^6 = 64 \geq 50 \; (k = 6 \text{ is a good choice})$$

Class Width

Once we decide to set $k = 6$, we need to determine the width of each class. The width is the breadth, or range, of numbers we plan to put into each class. We can use the following equation to find a good class width:

$$\text{Estimated class width} = \frac{\text{Maximum data value} - \text{Minimum data value}}{k}$$

$$\text{Estimated class width} = \frac{17.4 - 0.6}{6} = 2.8$$

This is one of the few areas in statistics where there is more than one correct answer, so enjoy it!

The previous equation provides a rough estimate for the class width. Round this estimate to a useful whole number that makes the frequency distribution more readable. For convenience, it would be best to round this class width up to three, but other values such as four could also be considered. There is no one correct answer for the class width. The goal of constructing a frequency distribution is to identify a useful pattern in the data, and often there is more than one acceptable way to accomplish this.

Class Boundaries

The class boundaries represent the minimum and maximum values for each class. Choosing the lowest boundary in the first class is an important step. If we choose the minimum time in Table 2.6, which is 0.6 minutes, the first class would be 0.6 to less than 3.6 minutes. This is not a very convenient choice. A more useful class boundary that is easier to read would start at 0 minutes and end at less than 3 minutes. The following list shows the boundaries for the Dell example:

0 to less than 3 minutes
3 to less than 6 minutes
6 to less than 9 minutes
9 to less than 12 minutes
12 to less than 15 minutes
15 to less than 18 minutes

Because the Dell example involves continuous data (minutes), there are no gaps in the boundaries between classes. By establishing the upper boundary of the first class as "less than 3 minutes" and the lower boundary of the next class as "3 minutes," we eliminate any gap between these classes. In this example, we were able to set up six classes, which matches the value for k that we determined earlier using the $2^k > n$ rule. However, it doesn't always work out this way, which is fine. If we had chosen a class width equal to 4 minutes, we would have ended up with five classes rather than six:

0 to less than 4 minutes
4 to less than 8 minutes

Occasionally you will end up with $k + 1$ or $k - 1$ classes to cover the entire range of data. No worries!

8 to less than 12 minutes

12 to less than 16 minutes

16 to less than 20 minutes

Either case would be acceptable. We will continue the Dell example with a class width of three minutes and six classes.

Class Frequencies

Figuring out the frequency is the easy part. Simply count up the number of observations in each class and record the total to obtain the frequency. This job is much easier when the data are sorted, as is the case with the Dell data in Table 2.6. Table 2.7 shows our finished frequency distribution along with the relative frequency and cumulative relative frequency.

Sorting the raw data from lowest to highest value makes it easier to count the number of observations contained in each class of a frequency distribution.

TABLE 2.7 | Frequency Distribution for Dell's Customer-Support Hold Times

NUMBER OF MINUTES	FREQUENCY	RELATIVE FREQUENCY	CUMULATIVE RELATIVE FREQUENCY
0 to less than 3	5	0.10	0.10
3 to less than 6	18	0.36	0.46
6 to less than 9	9	0.18	0.64
9 to less than 12	11	0.22	0.86
12 to less than 15	6	0.12	0.98
15 to less than 18	1	0.02	1.00
Total	**50**	**1.00**	

Based on this summary, we can conclude that the largest group of customers (18 of them) waited between 3 and 6 minutes and that nearly half the customers (46%) waited less than 6 minutes on the phone for customer support.

When constructing classes for grouped data, be sure to follow these rules:

1. **Equal-size classes.** All classes in the frequency distribution must be of equal width. Without equal sizes, patterns in the distribution could be misleading.
2. **Mutually exclusive classes.** This is a fancy term that simply means the class boundaries cannot overlap. For example, the following two classes overlap:

   0 to less than 3 minutes

   2.5 to less than 5.5 minutes

   If a person waited 2.7 minutes for customer support, this observation would appear in both classes and violate the rule. (Violating rules in statistics is a really bad idea!)
3. **Include all data values.** This rule is pretty self-explanatory. If your data set has 50 observations, make sure that all 50 are accounted for in the total row of the frequency distribution.
4. **Avoid empty classes.** If our class widths are too narrow, some classes might not have any observations. However, most populations do *not* have empty intervals; there are at least a few observations within each. Because the observations we collect should be representative of the population, it is undesirable for our histogram to display a class so narrow that there are no observations in it.
5. **Avoid open-ended classes (if possible).** An example of an open-ended class would be to add **18-over** as the last class in the distribution to include any callers who waited more than 18 minutes for service. Open-ended classes violate the first rule of equal class sizes, but sometimes they cannot be avoided.

Constructing a Histogram with Grouped Quantitative Data

We will now call on the Histogram tool in the Data Analysis ToolPak in Excel to construct the histogram for the Dell example. For grouped data, the bins in Excel are the upper boundary for each class. Table 2.8 shows the bins that can be used for the Dell data. For example, I need to choose a value to represent "less than 3" which in this case is 2.9. I could have also chosen 2.99.

TABLE 2.8 | Bins for Dell Data

CLASS	BINS
0 to less than 3 minutes	2.9
3 to less than 6 minutes	5.9
6 to less than 9 minutes	8.9
9 to less than 12 minutes	11.9
12 to less than 15 minutes	14.9
15 to less than 18 minutes	17.9

Histograms displaying continuous data do not have gaps between their bars. By contrast, histograms displaying discrete data do have gaps between their bars.

We can create a histogram by following the steps laid out for the iPad sales example earlier in the chapter. Figure 2.9 shows the "raw" histogram that Excel has generated for us, but it needs some work. Because our grouped data are continuous, we need to remove the gaps between the bars in the histogram by taking the following steps:

1. A right-click on any bar in the histogram will cause a pop-up menu to appear.
2. Left-click on **Format Data Series**.
3. In the dialog box, move the **Gap Width** slide all the way to the left.
4. Close the **Format Data Series** dialog box.

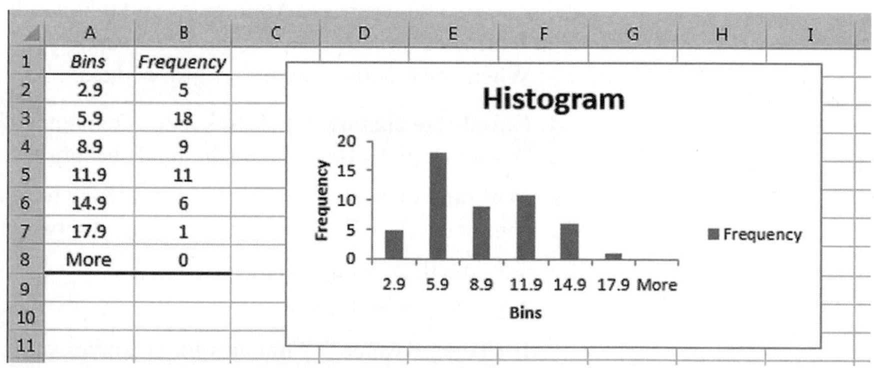

FIGURE 2.9
Raw Histogram for Grouped Data

Our final touch is to re-label the bins along the horizontal axis to reflect the entire range of each class. We can do this simply by changing the values in cells A2 to A7 as shown in Figure 2.10. Excel 2010 users should go to the book's Web site for these instructions. We can also angle the labels along the horizontal axis, as shown in this figure, by doing the following:

1. Right-click the labels for the horizontal axis to open the drop-down menu.
2. Left-click on **Format Axis**.
3. In the **Format Axis** dialog box, left-click on the **Size & Properties** icon, which looks like this:
4. Change the **Custom angle** to **−45** in the text box.
5. Close the **Format Axis** dialog box.

Now that's what I call a great-looking histogram for grouped data!

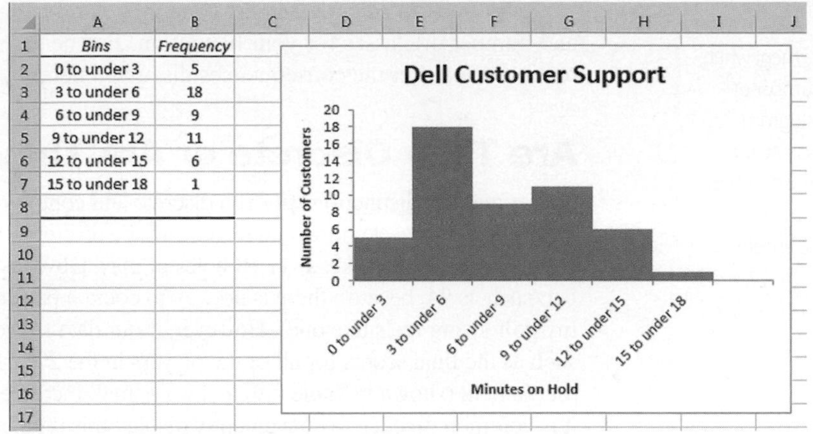

Bins	Frequency
0 to under 3	5
3 to under 6	18
6 to under 9	9
9 to under 12	11
12 to under 15	6
15 to under 18	1

FIGURE 2.10
Finished Histogram for Grouped Data

The Consequences of Too Few or Too Many Classes

The purpose of a histogram is to provide some insight into the natural shape of the distribution of interest. Using very wide classes results in a small number of classes, which may obscure important patterns. For example, Figure 2.11 shows a histogram for our Dell data with a class width of 9 minutes. A 9-minute width results in only two classes. This looks more like a picture of two toy blocks and tells us little about the distribution of customers waiting on hold for support.

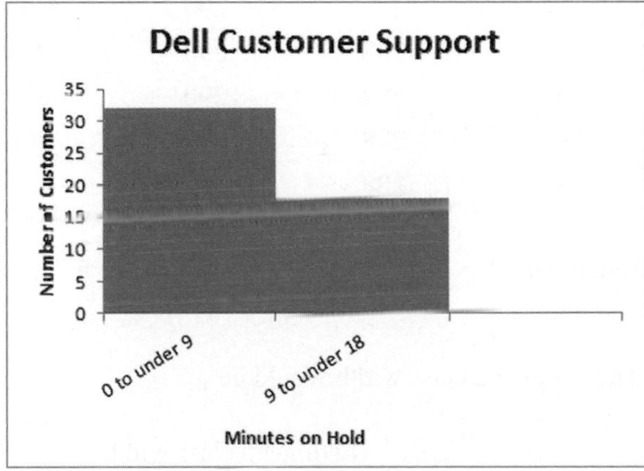

FIGURE 2.11
Too Few Histogram Classes

Creating too many classes in our histogram also has consequences. Figure 2.12 shows the Dell data with a class width of 1 minute, which results in 18 classes. This results in a histogram with a very jagged shape and three empty classes. I'm sure there are Dell customers in the population who have waited between 11 and 11.9 minutes on hold, but according to our histogram, they do not exist.

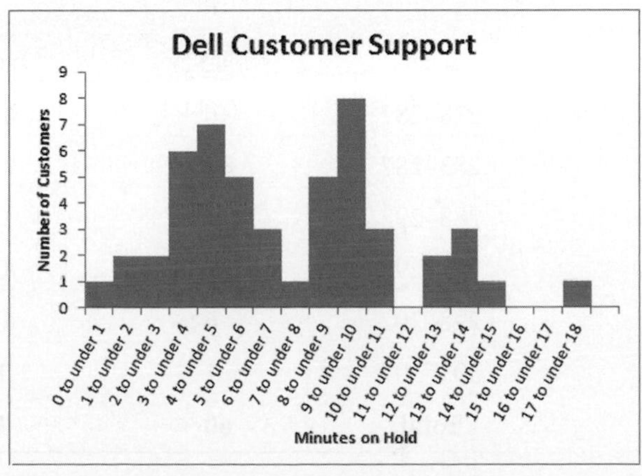

FIGURE 2.12
Too Many Histogram Classes

Exercise good judgment when deciding on the number of classes in your histogram. Too few classes can obscure the natural shape of the distribution. Too many classes can result in some classes being empty.

As I mentioned earlier in the chapter, you do have some flexibility in deciding the width and number of classes for your histogram. Just be careful not to wander too far in either direction and suffer the consequences discussed here.

Are They Discrete or Are They Continuous Data?

Sometimes the distinction between discrete and continuous data is not obvious. For instance, my golf score next weekend would technically be discrete data because this value is arrived at by counting my total strokes over 18 holes of play. Obviously, this value needs to be a whole number, such as 94, because there is no way to count a partial stroke (even though there are times my golf swing feels like one). However, if our data set contains a wide range of golf scores, such as the final scores for all of the players in the 2012 Masters, a major professional golf tournament (shown in Table 2.9) and very small increments between scores (that is, one stroke), it is common practice to conveniently display this type of information in a grouped-continuous format. These data can also be found in the Excel file titled **2012 Masters Scores.xlsx.**

TABLE 2.9 | FINAL GOLF SCORES OF THE 2012 MASTERS

278	286	288	291	293	296
278	286	289	291	294	297
280	286	289	291	294	297
280	286	289	291	294	298
280	286	290	292	295	299
280	287	290	292	295	299
283	287	290	292	295	299
284	288	290	293	296	301
284	288	290	293	296	302
284	288	291	293	296	306
285	288				

Using the $2^k > n$ rule with $n = 62$, I'll set $k = 6$ because

$$2^6 = 64 \geq 62$$

The estimated class width would be

$$\text{Estimated class width} = \frac{306 - 278}{6} = 4.67$$

Setting the actual class width to either four or five would be reasonable, so I'll go with five, starting with 278, as shown in Table 2.10. Also in this table I'm showing the frequency, relative frequency, and cumulative relative frequency for each class.

TABLE 2.10 | FREQUENCY DISTRIBUTION FOR THE FINAL GOLF SCORES OF THE 2012 MASTERS

SCORE	FREQUENCY	RELATIVE FREQUENCY	CUMULATIVE RELATIVE FREQUENCY
278–282	6	0.097	0.097
283–287	12	0.194	0.291
288–292	21	0.339	0.630
293–297	16	0.258	0.888
298–302	6	0.097	0.985
303–307	1	1.016	1.001
Total	**60**	**1.001**	

Recall that bins in Excel represent the higher end of each class (something that I sometimes can't remember).

Using bins of 282, 287, 292, 297, 302, and 307 in Excel, I display the histogram of golf scores in a grouped-continuous format in Figure 2.13.

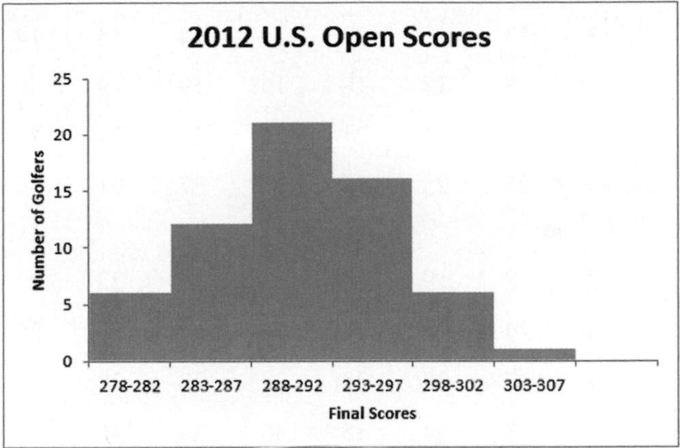

FIGURE 2.13 Finished Histogram for the Final Golf Scores of the 2012 Masters

According to this histogram, the class with the largest percentage of golfers was the one with final scores between 288 and 292.

Income and age are also examples of data that are technically discrete (we count our money and our years, not measure them), but they are normally displayed in a continuous format. To test your skills on frequency distributions with grouped data, take on the following Your Turn before moving on to the next section.

YOUR TURN #3

A survey was performed in the Philadelphia area that recorded the annual salaries of marketing managers. The following table shows the responses from 30 managers. The numbers are in thousands of dollars.

$40.0	$58.7	$63.4	$68.6	$74.8
$46.6	$60.0	$65.7	$68.7	$77.1
$49.0	$60.7	$65.9	$69.2	$78.2
$52.9	$61.2	$66.4	$71.7	$79.2
$54.7	$62.5	$66.8	$72.3	$83.1
$55.5	$63.0	$67.7	$72.6	$87.7

Construct the following:

1. A frequency distribution
2. A relative frequency distribution
3. A cumulative relative frequency distribution
4. A histogram

Answers can be found on ▶ **page 74**

The Polygon

The **percentage polygon** graphs the midpoint of each class as a line rather than a column. The height of each midpoint represents the relative frequency of the corresponding class.

When you want to compare the shape of two or more distributions on one graph, histograms are not your best choice because the overlapping columns of the two histograms will make the comparison difficult to interpret. A better choice is the **percentage polygon**, which graphs the midpoints of each class as a line rather than columns. The midpoint is the center position between the upper and lower boundaries. The height of each midpoint represents the relative frequency of the corresponding class. To demonstrate the percentage polygon, consider the data in Table 2.11 on the next page, which lists the number of minutes that call centers in Denver and Phoenix spent with 50 customers. The numbers are shown in ascending order and can be found in the Excel file **call center times.xlsx**.

TABLE 2.11 | Number of Minutes Spent with 50 Customers at Each of Two Call Centers

DENVER												
13	13	13	13	14	14	14	14	14	16	16	17	17
18	18	18	18	19	19	19	20	20	20	20	20	21
21	21	21	21	21	21	21	23	23	23	24	24	24
24	25	25	26	26	27	31	32	33	34	36		
PHOENIX												
12	18	19	20	21	21	22	22	22	22	23	23	23
24	24	24	24	24	24	24	25	25	25	25	26	26
27	27	28	28	28	28	28	29	29	29	30	30	31
32	33	34	35	36	36	36	37	38	39	39		

PHStat will be used to generate the percentage polygon. First, however, we need to set up the class boundaries for the data. Using the $2^k \geq n$ rule with $n = 50$, I'll set $k = 6$ because

$$2^6 = 64 \geq 50$$

I'll use the data from Phoenix to estimate the class widths for both distributions as follows. (Using the Denver data would produce similar results.)

$$\text{Estimated class width} = \frac{39 - 12}{6} = 4.5$$

Rounding the class widths up to 5 minutes will result in the class boundaries shown in Table 2.12. I have also indicated the bin and midpoint for each class in the table. I'll need these values for PHStat.

TABLE 2.12 | Classes and Midpoints for the Call Centers

CLASS	BIN	MIDPOINT
10 to less than 15 minutes	14.9	12.5
15 to less than 20 minutes	19.9	17.5
20 to less than 25 minutes	24.9	22.5
25 to less than 30 minutes	29.9	27.5
30 to less than 35 minutes	34.9	32.5
35 to less than 40 minutes	39.9	37.5

	A	B	C	D
1	Denver	Phoenix	Bins	Midpoints
2	13	12	9.9	12.5
3	13	18	14.9	17.5
4	13	19	19.9	22.5
5	13	20	24.9	27.5
6	14	21	29.9	32.5
7	14	21	34.9	37.5
8	14	22	39.9	
9	14	22		
10	14	22		

FIGURE 2.14A Constructing a Polygon with PHStat (Data)

I have set up these data in Excel as shown in Figure 2.14A. Only the first nine values from Table 2.12 are shown in Columns A and B. Your actual Excel sheet would contain all 50 values. PHStat requires the first bin of a distribution to be open-ended toward negative infinity. Consequently, I added a class of "less than 10," which has a bin equal to 9.9 in the spreadsheet. Because this class is open-ended (the lowest value could be any number less than 10), it does not have a midpoint. The first midpoint in Column D (12.5) corresponds to the second bin in Column C (14.9).

Take the following steps to use PHStat to construct the polygon for these data (Windows and Mac):

1. Go to **Add-Ins > PHStat > Descriptive Statistics > Histogram & Polygons**, as shown in Figure 2.14B.
2. Fill in the **Histogram & Polygons** dialog box as shown in Figure 2.14C. Click **OK**.

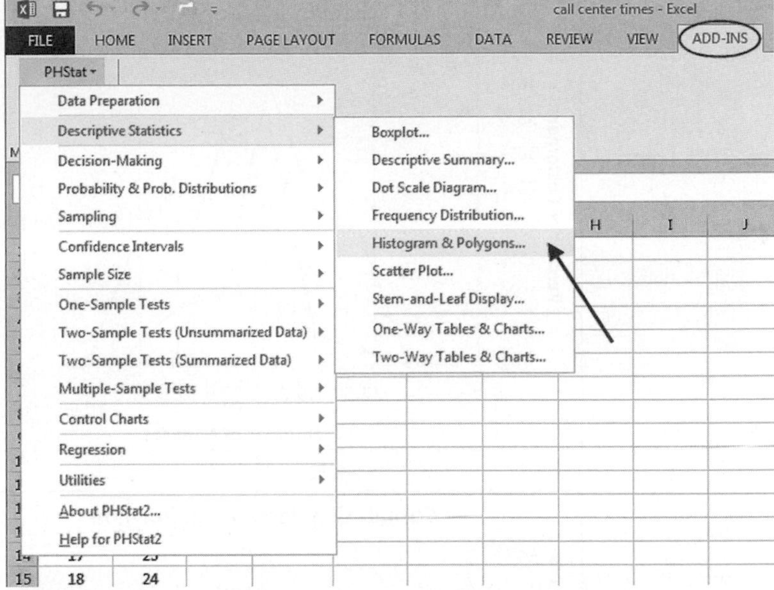

FIGURE 2.14B
Constructing a Polygon with PHStat (Step 1)

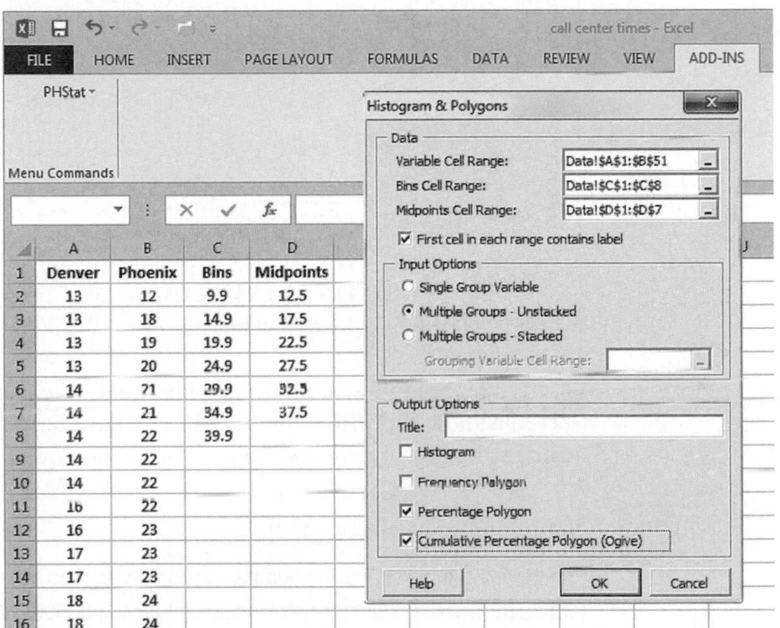

FIGURE 2.14C
Constructing a Polygon with PHStat (Step 2)

Figure 2.14D on the next page shows our percentage polygon for the two call centers. We can conclude from the distributions that the call times for Denver tend to be shorter than the call times for Phoenix. At the lower end of the distribution (shorter times) the Denver percentages are higher than the Phoenix percentages. For instance, nearly 20% of Denver's call times fall into the 12.5-minute interval compared with less than 5% of the calls to Phoenix. On the higher end of the distribution, roughly 15% of Phoenix's calls are in the 37.5-minute interval, whereas less than 5% of Denver's are.

The **cumulative percentage polygon**, or **ogive**, is a line graph that plots the cumulative relative frequency distribution.

As Figure 2.14E shows on the next page, using PHStat you can also create a **cumulative percentage polygon**, also known as an **ogive**. A cumulative percentage polygon is a line graph that plots the cumulative relative frequency distribution. For example, in Figure 2.14E, 20% of the calls in Denver fall in the ≤14.9-minute interval, 40% fall in the ≤19.9-minute interval, 80% fall in the ≤24.9-minute interval, and so forth. A full 100% of the calls fall in the ≤39.9-minute interval. There are no calls that last 40 minutes or longer. Now let's look at the calls for Phoenix: Roughly 40% of them fall into the ≤24.9-minute interval, compared with 80% of the Denver times. Notice that the Phoenix line is to the right of the Denver line. In other words, the Phoenix line is falling at the higher end of the distribution, where the times are longer. This is consistent with our findings in Figure 2.14D.

FIGURE 2.14D
The Percentage Polygon

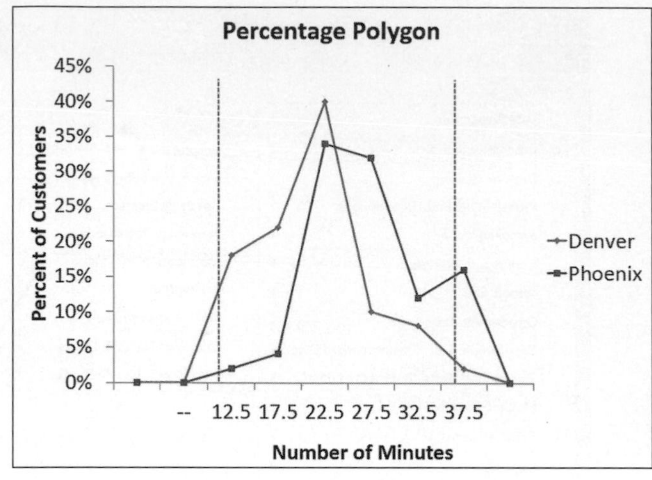

FIGURE 2.14E
The Cumulative Percentage Polygon (Ogive)

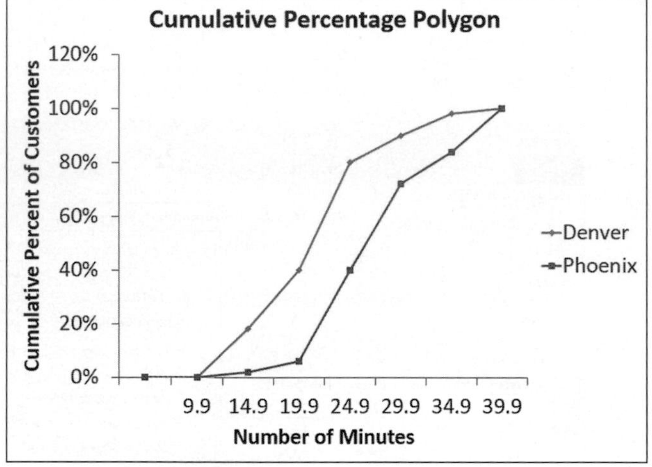

While these steps are fresh in your mind, take some time to construct polygons to observe just how badly my Pittsburgh Pirates have been performing lately compared with a team that has a winning tradition, the New York Yankees.

YOUR TURN #4

The following table shows the number of wins per season for the New York Yankees and Pittsburgh Pirates from 1974 until 2012, not including the strike-shortened seasons of 1981, 1994, and 1995. These data can also be found in the Excel file **Pirates Yankees wins.xlsx.**

NEW YORK YANKEES

95	97	95	103	89	94	97	95	101	101	103	95
87	98	114	96	92	88	76	71	67	74	85	89
90	97	87	91	79	103	89	100	100	97	83	89

PITTSBURGH PIRATES

79	72	57	62	67	68	67	67	72	75	72	62
69	78	69	79	73	75	96	98	95	74	85	80
64	57	75	84	84	83	98	88	96	92	92	88

Use seven classes, each with a class width of 10. Start with 51–60, 61–70, and so on, and then construct a percentage and cumulative percentage polygon using PHStat. What conclusions can you draw when you compare the distributions of the two teams?

Answers can be found on ▶ **page 74**

2.2 Section Problems

Basic Skills

2.1 Using the $2^k \geq n$ rule, determine the number of classes needed for the following data set sizes.

a. $n = 100$
b. $n = 300$
c. $n = 1{,}000$
d. $n = 2{,}000$

2.2 A data set that consists of 50 numbers has a minimum value of 16 and a maximum value of 74. Determine the class boundaries using the $2^k \geq n$ rule if the data are

a. discrete
b. continuous

2.3 Consider the following discrete data:

2 4 3 3 1 1 5 2 2 1 1 3
5 2 1 4 3 4 2 2 1 3 4 5

a. Construct a frequency distribution.
b. Construct a relative frequency distribution.
c. Construct a cumulative relative frequency distribution.

2.4 Consider the following continuous data.

17.5 19.8 29.9 28.1 15.7 21.7
33.6 21.1 19.8 32.7 15.1 13.9
31.8 39.8 33.1 19.6 23.5 42.8
21.7 36.8 35.6 14.5 24.2 14.7
19.2 21.8 20.7 26.9 26.7 35.2

a. Construct a frequency distribution using the $2^k \geq n$ rule.
b. Construct a relative frequency distribution.
c. Construct a cumulative relative frequency distribution.

Applications

2.5 The results of a survey that collected the current credit card balances for 36 undergraduate college students are shown in the following table. These data can also be found in the Excel file **college credit card.xlsx**.

$2,467 $3,373 $434 $1,426 $4,628 $167
$5,927 $4,064 $4,503 $2,600 $3,673 $4,231
$1,788 $5,805 $5,395 $733 $4,890 $1,455
$5,817 $1,145 $846 $739 $4,370 $986
$5,729 $1,159 $1,021 $1,563 $967 $499
$353 $2,297 $289 $375 $162 $1,740

a. Using the $2^k \geq n$ rule, construct a frequency distribution for these data.
b. Using the results from part a, calculate the relative frequencies for each class.
c. Using the results from part a, calculate the cumulative relative frequencies for each class.
d. Construct a histogram for these data.

2.6 The following table shows the number of students in the 25 classes being taught this semester at Goldey-Beacom College.

32 42 42 24 33 25 37 23 35 18 46 37 34
25 45 38 28 42 32 43 43 36 28 27 40

a. Using the $2^k \geq n$ rule, construct a frequency distribution for these data.
b. Using the results from part a, calculate the relative frequencies for each class.
c. Using the results from part a, calculate the cumulative relative frequencies for each class.
d. Construct a histogram for these data.

2.7 A major U.S. airline records the number of no-shows on a flight that operates each day from Philadelphia to Paris. A no-show is a passenger who purchases a ticket but fails to arrive at the gate at time of departure. The following table indicates the number of no-shows during the last 70 flights. These data can also be found in the Excel file **no-shows.xlsx**.

1 2 1 2 3 2 1 2 2 2
1 3 3 3 3 4 2 4 3 3
1 2 4 2 4 2 4 1 0 1
1 3 2 1 2 3 1 1 3 1
2 3 1 1 2 2 0 0 3 2
4 2 1 2 1 2 3 1 4 2
3 1 2 1 1 2 1 3 4 2

a. Construct a frequency distribution for these data.
b. Using the results from part a, calculate the relative frequencies for each class.
c. Using the results from part a, calculate the cumulative relative frequencies for each class.
d. Construct a histogram for these data.

2.8 A major electronics retailer was recently sued by 40 employees who were laid off by the company. The employees claimed they were victims of age discrimination, which is illegal in the United States. The first of the two following tables shows the ages of the 40 employees who were laid off. The second of the following tables shows the age of a random sample of 40 employees currently working for the company. These data can be found in the Excel file **employee ages.xlsx**.

Ages of Laid-Off Employees

38 35 39 44 54 59 39 43 60 61
56 57 56 53 51 56 53 43 19 42
42 56 75 64 38 62 39 61 43 74
65 44 40 51 46 51 44 45 67 51

Ages of a Sample of Current Employees

34	46	41	33	39	38	35	44	34	19
39	36	37	36	35	28	37	28	35	30
76	31	29	32	42	39	32	30	47	21
39	26	27	42	27	30	33	32	60	38

a. Construct a percentage polygon for these data.
b. Construct a cumulative percentage polygon for these data.
c. Does it appear that the employees suing this company have a case?

2.9 The Excel file labeled **Lowes.xlsx** lists the receipt total for 350 randomly selected customers for Lowes, a home improvement store.

a. Using Excel and the $2^k \geq n$ rule, construct a frequency distribution for these data.
b. Using the results from part a, calculate the relative frequencies for each class.
c. Using the results from part a, calculate the cumulative relative frequencies for each class.
d. Construct a histogram for these data.

2.10 The Hawaii Island Chamber of Commerce collects ocean temperature data to help promote tourism for local businesses. The Excel file titled **Hawaii ocean temps.xlsx** lists daily ocean temperatures for the past 125 days.

a. Using Excel, construct a frequency distribution for these data.
b. Using the results from part a, calculate the relative frequencies for each class.
c. Using the results from part a, calculate the cumulative relative frequencies for each class.
d. Construct a histogram for these data.
e. For what percentage of days was the ocean temperature less than 77 degrees Fahrenheit?

2.3 Displaying Qualitative Data

Qualitative data are values that are categorical (nominal or ordinal measurement levels) and that describe a characteristic, such as gender or level of education. This type of data is handled differently when displayed.

Constructing a Frequency Distribution Using Qualitative Data

Frequency distributions help display qualitative data by indicating the number of occurrences of various categories. To demonstrate this procedure, we'll use Table 2.13, which shows the final letter grade of 30 students from my statistics class. These data can also be found in the Excel file **final grades.xlsx**. I would like to determine the percentage of students who passed the course with a grade of C or better.

TABLE 2.13 | FINAL GRADES IN A STATISTICS CLASS

B	C	A	A	B	F	B	C	B	D
B	C	A	B	B	C	F	A	C	B
B	B	C	B	A	A	A	B	B	B

In an earlier section, we used Excel's FREQUENCY function to summarize quantitative data. However, this function does not work with qualitative data, so I will use Excel's COUNTIF function as shown in Figure 2.15A. This neat function will count the number of A's, B's, C's, D's, and F's in our data set using the following characteristics:

=COUNTIF(range, criteria)

where

range = the range of cells from which you are counting

criteria = the value that you are counting

FIGURE 2.15A
Excel's COUNTIF Function

	A	B	C	D	E	F
1	Grade		Bins	Frequency	Relative Frequency	Cumulative Relative Frequency
2	B		A	=COUNTIF($A$2:$A$31,C2)	=D2/$D$7	=E2
3	C		B	=COUNTIF($A$2:$A$31,C3)	=D3/$D$7	=F2+E3
4	A		C	=COUNTIF($A$2:$A$31,C4)	=D4/$D$7	=F3+E4
5	A		D	=COUNTIF($A$2:$A$31,C5)	=D5/$D$7	=F4+E5
6	B		F	=COUNTIF($A$2:$A$31,C6)	=D6/$D$7	=F5+E6
7	F		Total	=SUM(D2:D6)		
30	B					
31	B					
32						
33	Rows 8-29 are hidden					
34						

1. Open the Excel file **final grades.xlsx** or enter the grade data in Column A and the Bins in Column C as seen in Figure 2.15B.
2. To count the number of A's in the class, type **=COUNTIF($A$2:$A$31,C2)** in Cell D2.
3. Copy and paste this formula in Cells D3 to D6 to count the number of B's, C's, D's, and F's.
4. The formulas for the relative and cumulative frequencies are also shown in Columns E and F. These are the same calculations we did manually in the previous sections.

Figure 2.15B shows the frequency distribution for our final grades example.

FIGURE 2.15B
The Frequency Distribution for the Final Grades Example

	A	B	C	D	E	F
1	Grade		Bins	Frequency	Relative Frequency	Cumulative Relative Frequency
2	B		A	7	0.233	0.233
3	C		B	14	0.467	0.700
4	A		C	6	0.200	0.900
5	A		D	1	0.033	0.933
6	B		F	2	0.067	1.000
7	F		Total	30		
30	B					
31	B					
32						
33	Rows 8-29 are hidden					
34						

Based on the value calculated in Cell F4 in Figure 2.15B, 90% of the students passed the course with a grade of C or better. I'm sure you're itching to try your hand at generating frequency distributions with Excel, so take a shot at the following Your Turn.

YOUR TURN #5

In 2013, the companies that dominated the U.S. cell phone carrier market were AT&T, Sprint, Verizon, and T-Mobile. The following table shows the results of a survey that asked 20 people to name the company that provides their current cell phone service. These data can be found in the Excel file **cell phone carriers.xlsx.**

Sprint	AT&T	Sprint	AT&T
Sprint	Sprint	Verizon	AT&T
AT&T	Sprint	Verizon	Verizon
AT&T	Sprint	AT&T	Verizon
T-Mobile	AT&T	Sprint	AT&T

Construct the following:

1. Frequency distribution
2. Relative frequency distribution

Answers can be found on ▶ **page 75**

Bar Charts

Bar charts are a good tool for displaying qualitative data that have been organized in categories and can be arranged in a vertical or horizontal orientation.

Bar charts are a good tool for displaying qualitative data that have been organized in categories. The bars in a bar chart can be arranged either horizontally or vertically. We'll start with a vertical bar chart and use Excel 2013 for Windows to construct the chart. See the textbook's Web site for Excel 2011 for Mac or Excel 2010 for Windows instructions. Let's explore the world of bar charts with the data in Figure 2.16A, which shows the grade distribution from my statistics class.

FIGURE 2.16A
Constructing a Vertical Bar Chart with Excel (Steps 1–3)

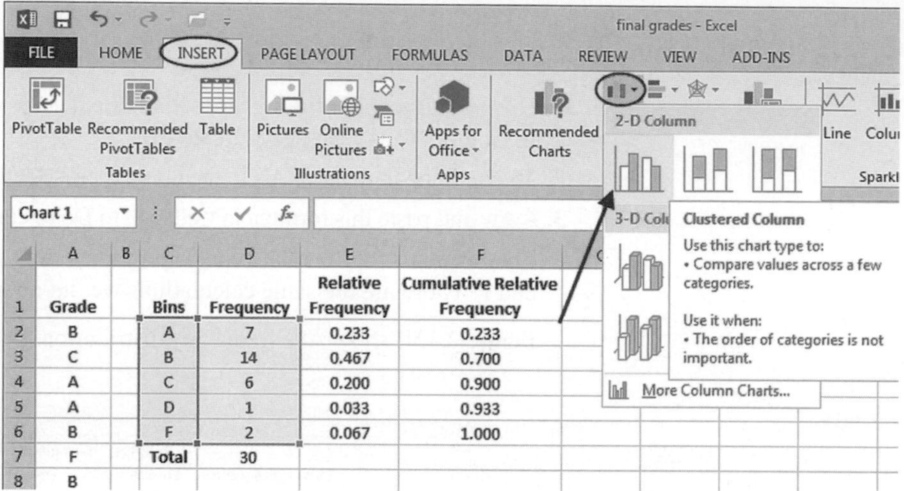

1. Using the frequency distribution from Figure 2.15, highlight Cells C2:D6 as shown in Figure 2.16A.
2. Select the **Insert** tab and the Insert Column Chart icon which are both circled in red in Figure 2.16A.
3. Click on the first **2-D Column** icon in the pop-down menu.
4. To add labels to your bar chart, click on the bar chart Excel created to activate the **Chart Tools** and choose the **Design** tab as shown in Figure 2.16B.

FIGURE 2.16B
Constructing a Vertical Bar Chart with Excel (Steps 4–7)

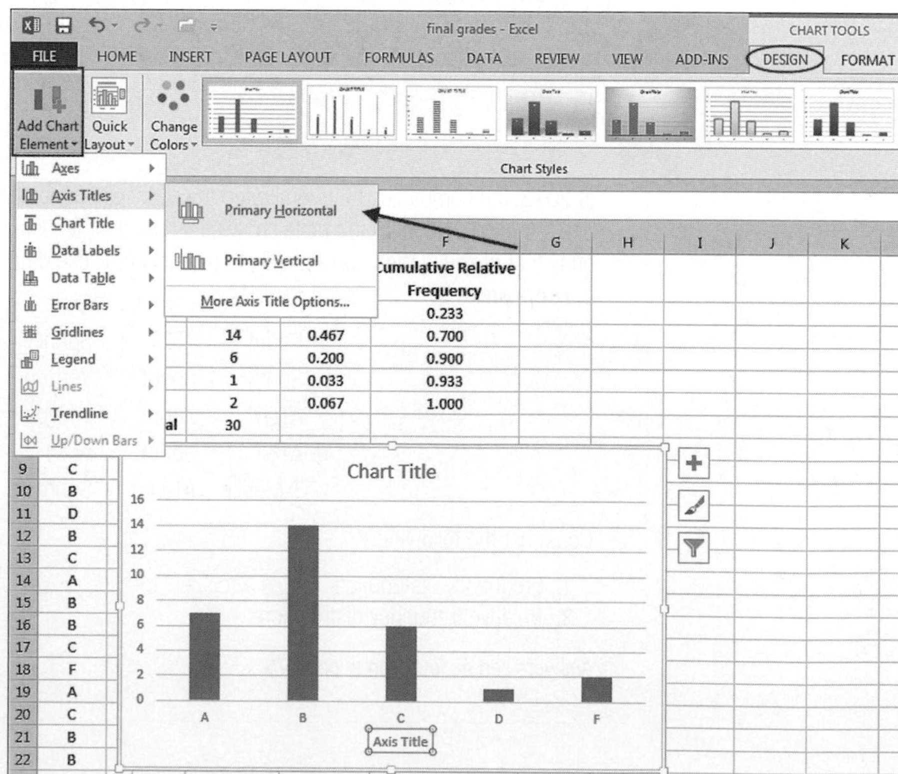

5. Select **Add Chart Element > Axis Titles > Primary Horizontal** as shown in Figure 2.16B to insert a title along the horizontal axis.
6. Select **Add Chart Element > Axis Titles > Primary Vertical** to insert a title along the vertical axis.
7. Select **Add Chart Element > Chart Title > Above Chart** to insert a title at the top of the histogram.

Figure 2.16C shows our finished vertical bar chart displaying the qualitative grade data.

FIGURE 2.16C
Constructing a Vertical Bar Chart with Excel (Final Result)

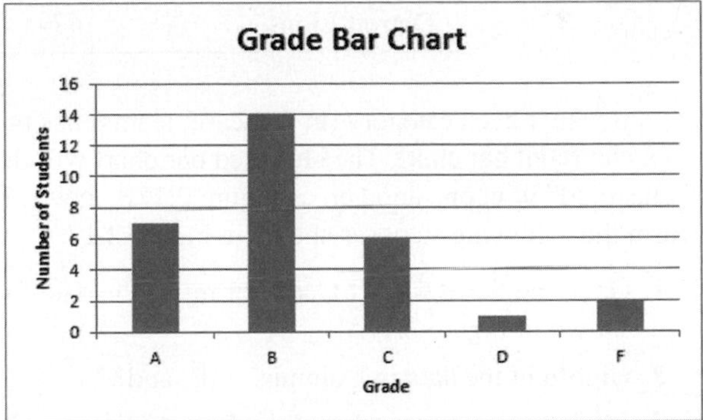

If you've just realized Figure 2.16C looks very much like the histograms that we've already discussed, you are right. However, there is a subtle difference. Histograms display quantitative data using vertical bars that are separated for discrete data and joined together for continuous data. Bar charts, on the other hand, display qualitative (categorical) data. The bars can be vertical or horizontal.

Horizontal bar charts display the bars in a horizontal direction.

Bar charts can also be displayed in the horizontal direction and are called—you guessed it—**horizontal bar charts**. The following steps show how these charts are constructed in Excel.

1. Highlight the Grade data from Figure 2.16A in Cells C2:D6.
2. Click on the **Insert** tab and select the **Insert Bar Chart** icon which is to the right of the **Insert Column Chart** icon that was just used.
3. Click on the first **2-D Bar** icon.
4. Add titles as we did with the vertical bar chart (note the axes are reversed here).

The resulting horizontal bar chart is shown in Figure 2.16D.

FIGURE 2.16D
Horizontal Bar Chart with Excel

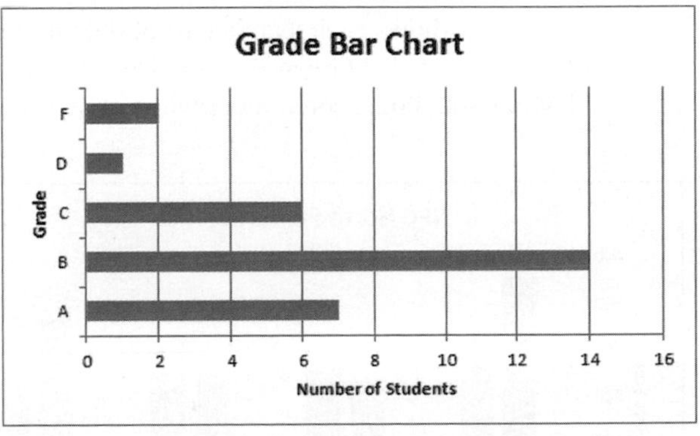

Now that you have mastered basic bar charts, let's take it up a notch with the next example, shown in Table 2.14 on the next page, which provides the total points scored by the football teams in the NFC (National Football Conference) North Division in 2011 and 2012. These data can be found in the Excel file **NFC.xlsx**.

TABLE 2.14 | POINTS SCORED BY THE FOOTBALL TEAMS IN THE NFC NORTH DIVISION, 2011 AND 2012

TEAM	POINTS SCORED	
	2011	2012
Green Bay Packers	560	433
Minnesota Vikings	340	379
Chicago Bears	353	375
Detroit Lions	474	372

Clustered bar charts group several values side by side within the same category in a vertical direction.

Because each category (in this case, teams) has two data points, we can display the data in a **clustered bar chart**. The clustered bar chart will display the two data points together, or "clustered" with one another, as Figure 2.17B shows. To get the data to look like this, perform the following steps, as shown in Figure 2.17A.

1. Open the Excel file **NFC.xlsx** or insert the data from Table 2.14 into an Excel file, as shown in Figure 2.17A.
2. Highlight the data in Columns A, B, and C.
3. Click on the **Insert** tab and the **Insert Column Chart** icon which are both circled in red in Figure 2.17A.
4. Click on the **Clustered Column** icon, which is the first **2-D Column** icon in the row.

FIGURE 2.17A
Constructing a Clustered Bar Chart in Excel

Do not insert a title in cell A1 in Figure 2.17A. Doing so will interfere with the proper construction of the clustered bar chart in Excel. If you don't believe me, go on and try it!

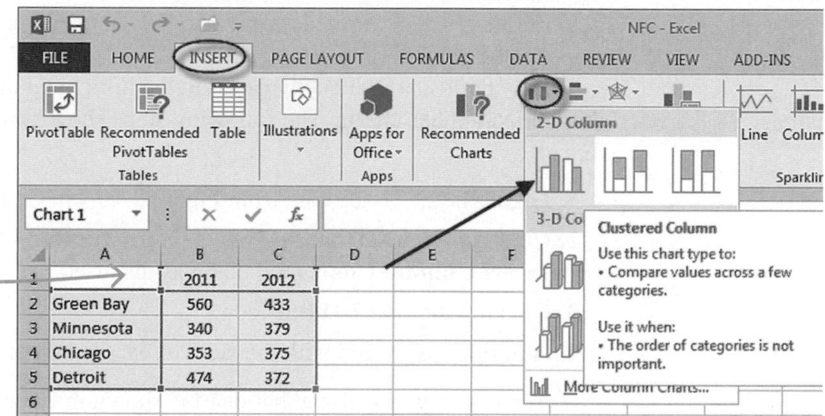

Figure 2.17B shows each team's pair of data points in a bar graph format. According to this chart, we can see that Green Bay and Detroit scored fewer points in 2012, whereas Chicago and Minnesota both scored more when compared with the 2011 season.

FIGURE 2.17B
Finished Clustered Bar Chart

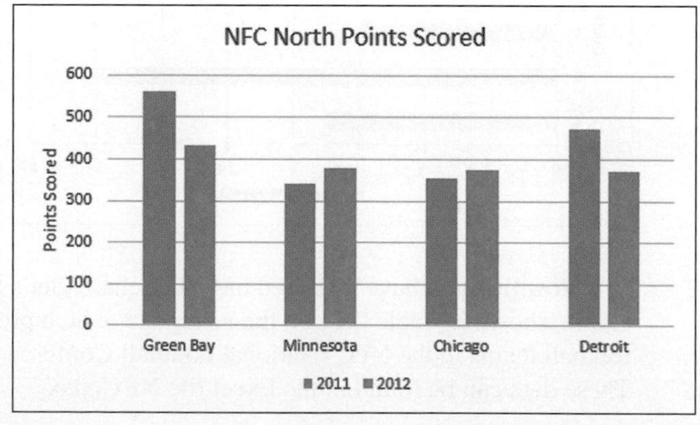

Stacked bar charts group several values in a single column within the same category in a vertical direction.

We can also arrange our data in a **stacked bar chart**, as shown in Figure 2.17C. To construct this chart in Excel, follow the steps in the clustered bar chart example but choose the second 2-D Column icon rather than the first.

FIGURE 2.17C
Stacked Bar Chart

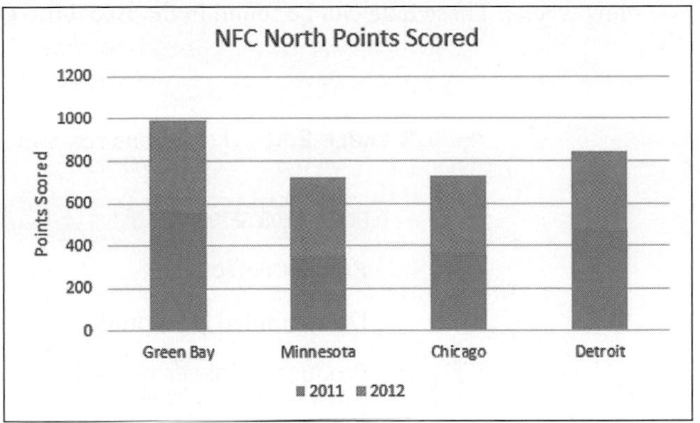

Clustered charts work well when you are comparing data within categories, whereas stacked bar charts are more effective at displaying totals in each category.

Looking at Figure 2.17C, we can easily see that Green Bay scored the most points over the two-year span, with Detroit scoring the second-most points.

Choosing between clustered and stacked bar graphs depends on the purpose of the chart. Clustered charts work well when you are comparing data within categories, such as which team scored more points in 2011 when compared with 2012. Stacked bar charts are more effective at displaying totals in each category, such as which team scored the most points over the two-year period (which, in case you forgot, was my favorite team since 1967, the Green Bay Packers).

Take a stab at bar charts with some Facebook data in the next Your Turn problem.

YOUR TURN #6

The data in the following table show the unemployment rate (as a percentage of the workforce) for five states at the end of 2011 and 2012. These data can be found in the Excel file **unemployment.xlsx**.

State	2011 (%)	2012 (%)
Arizona	9.0	7.9
Florida	9.9	8.0
Nebraska	3.7	4.2
North Carolina	10.4	9.2
Virginia	6.1	5.5

Construct the most appropriate bar chart (stacked or clustered) if the goal is to display changes in unemployment rate from 2011 to 2012 for each state.

Answers can be found on ▶ **page 75**

Pareto Charts

Pareto charts are essentially bar charts that show the frequency of the categories that cause quality control problems. The charts show the categories in a decreasing order.

Pareto charts are a specific type of bar chart used in quality control programs by businesses to display the causes of problems graphically. The charts are essentially histograms that show, in decreasing order, the frequency of the categories that cause problems. In other words, the most problematic categories are listed first. Pareto charts are named after Vilfredo Pareto (1848–1923), an Italian industrialist who helped develop the field of microeconomics (which has tortured more students than the field of statistics, your author included). Pareto observed that 80% of the land in Italy was owned by 20% of the population. In the 1940s, the quality control consultant Joseph Juran came across Pareto's work and began calling it Pareto's 80/20 rule. Pareto's rule states that 20% of defects cause 80% of quality control problems.

I'll use the following example to demonstrate the use of Pareto charts. QVC, a major home shopping retailer (and my wife's very favorite company in the world) maintains records of the reasons customers return products they purchased. The data in Table 2.15 show the reasons for the returns and the number of incidences for each category during the past few weeks. These data can be found in the Excel file **QVC.xlsx**.

TABLE 2.15 | Reasons for and Number of Returns to QVC

REASON FOR RETURN	FREQUENCY
Product defective	46
Disappointed with product	22
Product no longer wanted	14
Late delivery of product	5
Other	3

Pareto charts also plot the cumulative relative frequency as a line on the chart. This line is known as an ogive, which was discussed earlier in the chapter. To construct a Pareto chart in Excel, we first need to calculate the relative and cumulative relative frequencies for our data, as shown in Figure 2.18A. See Figure 2.15 if you need a refresher on how to calculate the values in Columns C and D.

FIGURE 2.18A
Spreadsheet for Constructing a Pareto Chart

	A	B	C	D
1	Reason	Frequency	Relative Frequency	Cumulative Relative Frequency
2	Defective	46	0.511	0.511
3	Disappointed	22	0.244	0.756
4	No longer wante	14	0.156	0.911
5	Late delivery	5	0.056	0.967
6	Other	3	0.033	1.000
7				

Use the following steps to construct our Pareto chart with Excel 2013. See the textbook's Web site for Excel 2011 for Mac or Excel 2010 for Windows instructions.

1. Highlight Cells A1:A6.
2. Holding down the CTRL key, highlight Cells C1:C6.
3. Holding down the CTRL key, highlight Cells D1:D6.
4. Click on the **Insert** tab and select **Column**.
5. Click on **Clustered Column**, the first **2-D Column** icon shown in the list.

Your chart will look like the one in Figure 2.18B. But we still have a little work to do here.

1. Right-click on one of the Cumulative Relative Frequency bars (the red ones).
2. In the drop-down menu, select **Change Series Chart Type**.

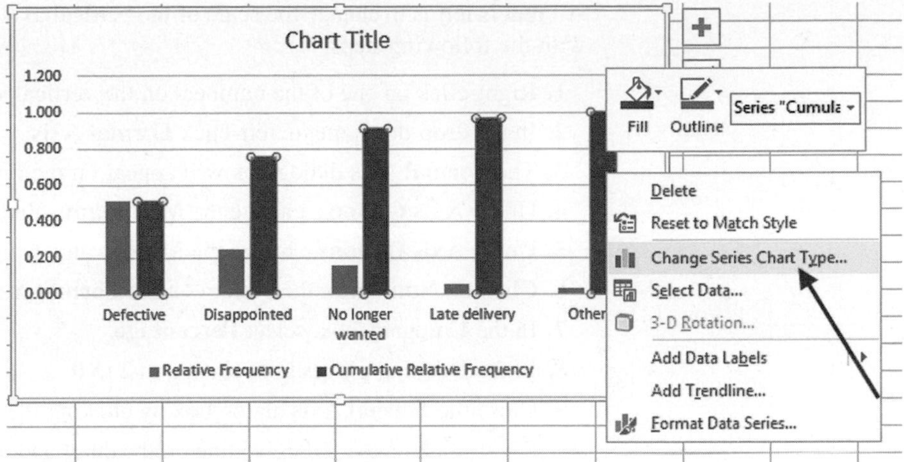

FIGURE 2.18B
Preliminary Pareto Chart

The **Change Chart Type** dialog box will appear as seen in Figure 2.18C.

1. Click on the drop-down box to the right of **Cumulative Relative Frequency** in the **Series Name** box which is circled in Figure 2.18C.
2. Select the first **Line** graph in the drop-down menu as seen in Figure 2.18C.
3. Click **OK**.

FIGURE 2.18C
Excel's Change Chart Type Dialog Box

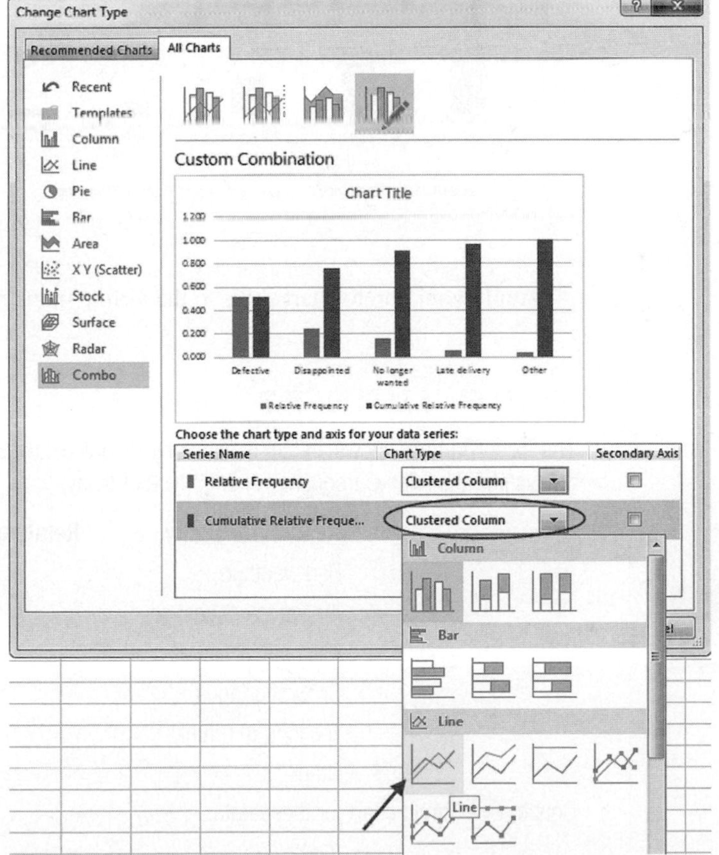

All that is left is to change the scale of the vertical axis and add data points to the line graph with the following steps.

1. Right-click on one of the numbers on the vertical axis.
2. In the drop-down menu, left-click **Format Axis**.
3. The **Format Axis** dialog box will appear on the right side of your spreadsheet.
4. Under **Axis Options**, change the **Maximum** value from 1.2 to **1.0**.
5. Under **Axis Options**, change the **Major** value from 0.1 to **0.2**.
6. Click on **Number** at the bottom on the **Format Axis** menu to expand the options.
7. In the **Category** box, select **Percentage.**
8. In the **Decimal places** box, change to 2 to **0**.
9. Close the **Format Axis** dialog box by clicking the **X** in the right-hand corner.
10. Right-click on the red ogive line on the chart and left-click on **Add Data Labels**.

Figure 2.18D shows our completed Pareto chart for QVC. As you can see, Pareto charts are an efficient way to summarize quality control issues. From this example, you can see by looking at the ogive, or cumulative relative frequency line, that 75.6% of the returns are due to the first two categories—defective merchandise and customers being disappointed with the merchandise.

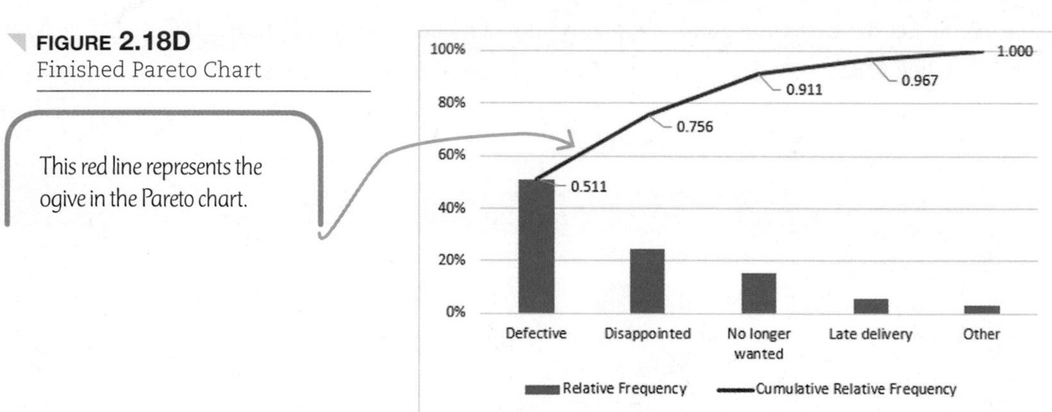

FIGURE 2.18D Finished Pareto Chart

Apply your Pareto chart skills to the airline industry in this next Your Turn section.

YOUR TURN #7

The following table shows an airline company's flight-delay data. The table shows the reasons for the delays and the relative frequency of each type of delay.

Reason for Delay	Relative Frequency (%)
Bad weather	33
Air traffic congestion	22
Mechanical issues	18
Crew shortages	13
Too long to refuel	9
Other	5

Construct a Pareto chart for these data.

Answer can be found on ▶ **page 75**

Pie Charts

Pie charts are another excellent tool for comparing proportions for categorical data. Each category occupies a segment of the pie that represents the relative frequency of that category.

Pie charts are another excellent tool for comparing proportions for qualitative (categorical) data. To demonstrate, we'll use Table 2.16, which shows the number of computers shipped by leading computer manufacturers during the third quarter of 2012 in the United States. These data can be found in the Excel file **computer shipments.xlsx**.

TABLE 2.16 | ESTIMATED U.S. COMPUTER SHIPMENTS, THIRD QUARTER, 2012

COMPANY	UNITS SHIPPED (000S)
HP	4,142
Dell	3,271
Apple	2,079
Lenovo	1,358
Acer	990
Others	2,548

Based on: http://www.gartner.com.

Perform the following steps, as shown in Figure 2.19A, to construct a pie chart with Excel 2013. See the textbook's Web site for Excel 2011 for Mac or Excel 2010 for Windows instructions.

1. Highlight Cells A1:B7.
2. Click on the **Insert** tab and select the **Insert Pie** icon circled in Figure 2.19A.
3. Click on the first **2-D Pie** icon.

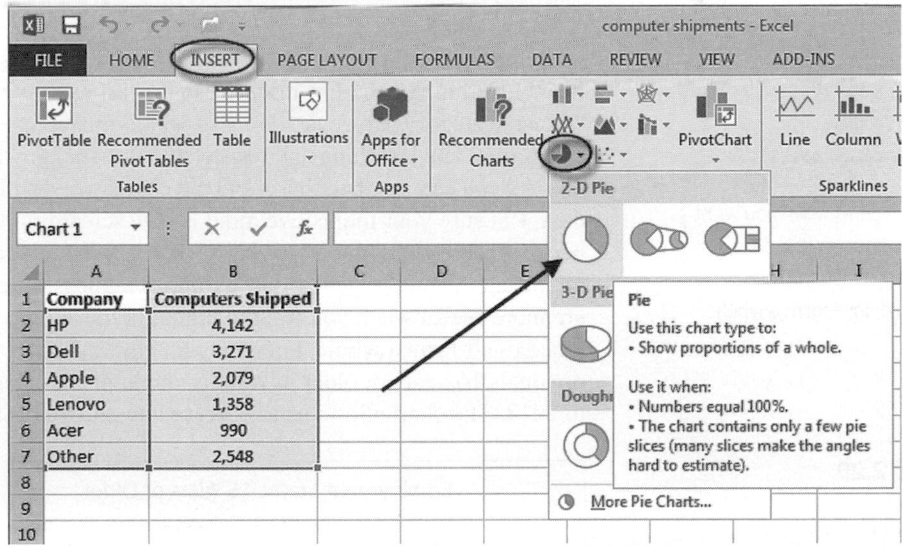

FIGURE 2.19A Constructing a Pie Chart in Excel (Steps 1–3)

The pie chart will appear in your spreadsheet on the next page. Click on the chart and take the following steps to populate your pie chart with percentages:

4. Select the **Design** tab as seen in Figure 2.19B.
5. Select the **Chart Style** circled in Figure 2.19B.

FIGURE 2.19B
Constructing a Pie Chart in Excel (Steps 4–5)

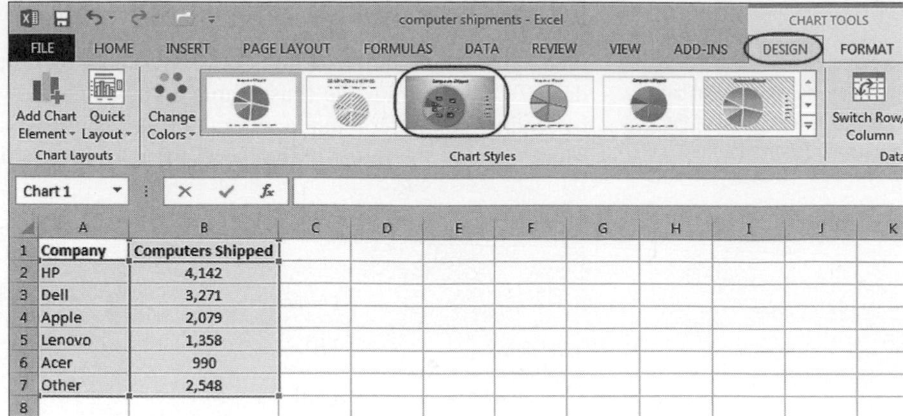

Figure 2.19C shows our finished pie chart, complete with U.S. market share percentages for the computer industry during the third quarter of 2012. Looking at this chart, it is easy to conclude that HP and Dell together controlled over half the U.S. market share in computers shipped during this time period.

FIGURE 2.19C
Constructing a Pie Chart in Excel (Final Result)

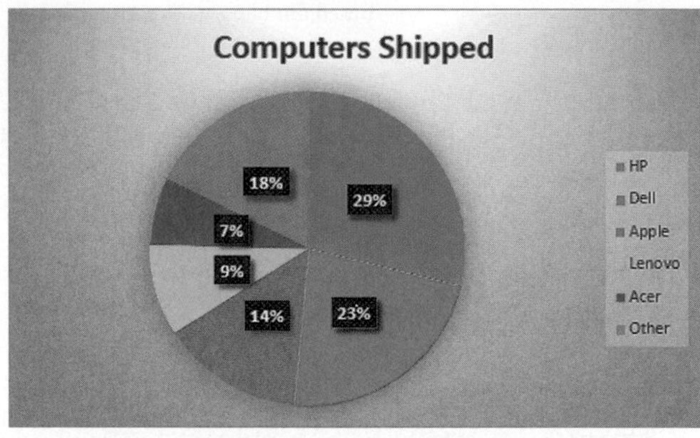

Use a pie chart if you want to compare the relative sizes of the classes to one another and together they comprise all possible categories.

One word of warning about constructing pie charts: All categories in the data set must be included in the pie. For instance, in the last example, it may be tempting to omit the "Other" category. However, doing so would misrepresent the market share for the remaining categories. The last thing any respectable statistician wants to do is misrepresent anything.

Use a bar chart when you want to highlight the actual data values and when the classes combined don't form a whole.

As you can see, bar charts and pie charts work with the same type of data—qualitative data. I'm sure your inquisitive mind is now screaming with the question, "How do I choose between a pie chart and a bar chart?" If you want to compare the relative sizes of the classes to one another and together they comprise all possible categories, use a pie chart. Bar charts are more useful when you want to highlight the actual data values and when the classes combined don't form a whole. For example, Figure 2.20 is a bar chart showing the number of individuals 16 years or older in various employment categories in the United States from 2004 to 2013. The chart allows us to observe how the trends in the categories have changed over

FIGURE 2.20
Employment Status for Individuals 16 Years or Older, 2004–2013

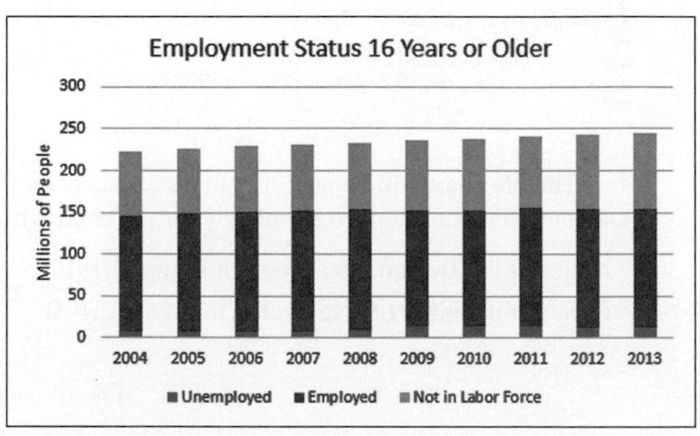

time. One pie chart would not be able to display all this information. It could not display the trends in these categories over the 10-year span. The best we could do with a pie chart is to show the three categories for a specific year.

Before we move on, try your hand at making some Excel pie charts.

YOUR TURN #8

A recent Gallup Poll surveyed 1,145 people who had visited emergency rooms within the past year. The people surveyed were asked to rate the quality of care they received. The results are shown in the following table.

Rating	Frequency
Very good	527
Good	492
Poor	80
Very poor	46

Based on: USA Today/Gallup Poll.

Construct a pie chart summarizing these data.

Answer can be found on ▶ **page 75**

2.3 Section Problems

Applications

2.11 The following table shows the results of a survey that asked users of the Internet to identify their favorite search engine. These data can be found in the Excel file **search engine.xlsx**. (For your information, Baidu is a Chinese-language search engine.)

Google	Google	Yahoo	Google	Google	Bing
Google	Yahoo	Google	Google	Baidu	Google
Google	Other	Yahoo	Google	Google	Google
Yahoo	Bing	Baidu	Google	Google	Google
Google	Google	Google	Yahoo	Google	Google

a. Using Excel, construct a frequency distribution for these data.

b. Using the results from part a, calculate the relative frequencies for each search engine.

c. Construct a vertical bar chart for these data.

2.12 A restaurant manager surveys her customers after their dining experience. Customers rate their experience as Excellent (E), Good (G), Fair (F), or Poor (P). The following table records the experience of 60 customers and can be found in the Excel file **dining experience.xlsx**.

G	G	E	G	F	G	G	E	G	E	F	G
P	G	E	E	G	F	G	G	E	E	F	E
G	E	P	G	G	F	E	G	E	G	G	G
G	F	E	G	E	E	G	P	G	G	E	G
P	F	E	F	G	G	P	G	G	G	G	G

a. Construct a frequency distribution for these data.

b. Using the results from part a, calculate the relative frequencies for each class.

c. Using the results from part a, calculate the cumulative relative frequencies for each class.

d. Construct a horizontal bar chart for these data.

e. What percentage of customers rated their dining experience as either Excellent or Good?

2.13 Recently, a salary survey was conducted to measure the impact of having an MBA degree in various industries with four years of work experience. The following table summarizes these results:

Four Years' Experience

Occupation	No MBA	MBA
Consulting	$66,271	$101,137
Energy	$66,461	$84,701
Finance	$80,236	$89,169
Manufacturing	$71,013	$90,435
Media	$63,745	$97,295
Telecom	$74,378	$106,142

Based on: http://www.topmba.com.

Construct a clustered bar chart that summarizes these data.

2.14 A recent business trend is for companies to purchase online software applications (applications that can be run on the Internet) rather than to own and install the applications on their own computer systems. A recent survey asked 210 small business owners if they would pay a monthly subscription fee to use the various online software applications shown in the following table. The percentages of owners who answered *yes* were determined for January and May and are shown in the following table:

Use of Software	January (%)	May (%)
Business applications	22	44
Support for information technology	14	42
Computer security	15	49
Electronic storage	15	37

Based on: AMI Partners data.

Construct a clustered bar chart that summarizes these data.

2.15 The following table shows the number of graduating students in 2012 and 2013 with various majors at Sussex College.

Major	2012	2013
Management	38	30
Marketing	24	39
Finance	31	40
Economics	13	16
Accounting	25	20

With the goal of comparing the number of graduating students from 2012 and 2013 for each major, construct a stacked bar chart that summarizes these data.

2.16 The following table lists the reasons customers provided when they rated their dining experience unsatisfactory at a particular restaurant:

Reason	Relative Frequency (%)
Service too slow	37
Long wait for table	16
Mistake with order	14
Poor food quality	13
Poor atmosphere	11
Other	9

Construct a Pareto chart for these data.

2.17 A manager at a local restaurant records the number of customers who ordered each of four types of entrées. The following table summarizes the results:

Entrée Type	Frequency
Beef	25
Fish	17
Chicken	11
Vegetarian	7

Construct a pie chart summarizing these data as percentages.

2.18 The following table shows the breakdown of gasoline prices in terms of its components.

Component	Percentage
Crude oil	60.9
Taxes	15.1
Refining	13.7
Distribution and marketing	10.3

Based on: Energy Information Administration data.

Construct a pie chart summarizing these data.

2.19 Opinion Research Corporation asked adults to describe the category that best describes their health care costs. The following table shows the number of adults in each category:

Category	Number of Adults
Fairly priced	426
Expensive	274
Low cost	256
Don't know	47

Construct a display that best describes these data.

2.20 The following table shows the economic output, or gross domestic product (GDP), for various countries in 2002 and 2012:

	GDP ($ trillion)	
Country	2002	2012
United States	$10.5	$15.7
Japan	$4.0	$6.0
China	$1.3	$8.3
Germany	$2.0	$3.4
France	$1.4	$2.6
United Kingdom	$1.6	$2.4
Italy	$1.2	$2.0

Construct a display that best describes these data.

2.4 Contingency Tables

Contingency tables provide a format to display the frequencies of two qualitative variables.

All of the examples so far in this chapter have consisted of observations with a single value. For instance, each student had one grade and each manager had one salary. **Contingency tables** provide a format to display the frequencies of two qualitative variables. The following example will be used to demonstrate this procedure.

The manager of a 7-Eleven convenience store recorded the genders of the last 20 customers and their types of payment (credit, debit, or cash), which are shown in Table 2.17. These data can also be found in the Excel file **payment types.xlsx**.

TABLE 2.17 | GENDERS AND PAYMENT TYPES FOR 7-ELEVEN'S CUSTOMERS

CUSTOMER	GENDER	PAYMENT	CUSTOMER	GENDER	PAYMENT
1	Female	Cash	11	Male	Cash
2	Female	Credit	12	Male	Credit
3	Female	Credit	13	Female	Cash
4	Male	Cash	14	Male	Credit
5	Male	Debit	15	Male	Cash
6	Female	Credit	16	Female	Debit
7	Male	Cash	17	Female	Credit
8	Female	Credit	18	Female	Debit
9	Female	Debit	19	Male	Cash
10	Female	Credit	20	Female	Credit

The raw data in Table 2.17 are summarized more efficiently as the contingency table shown in Table 2.18.

TABLE 2.18 | CONTINGENCY TABLE FOR 7-ELEVEN'S CUSTOMERS

	GENDER		
PAYMENT	FEMALE	MALE	TOTAL
Cash	2	5	**7**
Credit	7	2	**9**
Debit	3	1	**4**
Total	**12**	**8**	**20**

Five customers from Table 2.17 were male and paid in cash.

The "Female" column in Table 2.18 shows the number of female customers who paid with cash (2), credit cards (7), and debit cards (3), which accounts for all 12 female customers in Table 2.17. The "Male" column shows the number of male customers who paid with cash (5), credit cards (2), and debit cards (1), which accounts for all eight male customers in Table 2.17. The last column in Table 2.18 shows the total number of customers, both male and female, who paid with cash (7), credit cards (9), and debit cards (4). This column accounts for all 20 customers.

We can also convert the frequencies in Table 2.18 to relative frequencies, as we did with the frequency distributions earlier in the chapter, by dividing all the values in Table 2.18 by 20, the total number of observations. These results are shown in Table 2.19 on the next page.

TABLE 2.19 | Relative Contingency Table for 7-Eleven's Customers

	GENDER		
PAYMENT	FEMALE	MALE	TOTAL
Cash	0.10	0.25	0.35
Credit	0.35	0.10	0.45
Debit	0.15	0.05	0.20
Total	**0.60**	**0.40**	**1.00**

Five males out of 20 paid with cash, so $5/20 = 0.25$

Contingency tables help us identify relationships between two or more variables. Based on the 20 customers from Table 2.18, we can conclude that over half the female customers paid with credit (7 out of 12) and over half the male customers paid with cash (5 out of 8). From Table 2.19 we can conclude that 10% of the customers were both female and paid with cash. These conclusions certainly were not obvious looking at the raw data shown in Table 2.17 (at least not to me).

Constructing a Contingency Table in Excel (Windows)

Excel for Mac users can find instructions for pivot tables on the textbook's Web site.

Contingency tables can be rather tedious to construct by hand (especially when there are lots of data), so I'm going to show you a cool feature in Excel known as a pivot table, which is really just a contingency table in disguise. First, arrange the data from Table 2.17 as shown in Figure 2.21A. Because we are counting the number of customers who are female or male and have paid by cash, credit, or debit, we need to include a Customer column in our spreadsheet. This new column allows Excel to count the number of rows (customers) associated with each category.

1. Click on any cell within your data.
2. Choose the **Insert** tab.
3. Click on the **Pivot Table** icon as shown in Figure 2.21A.
4. A **Create Pivot Table** dialog box will appear. Simply click **OK**.

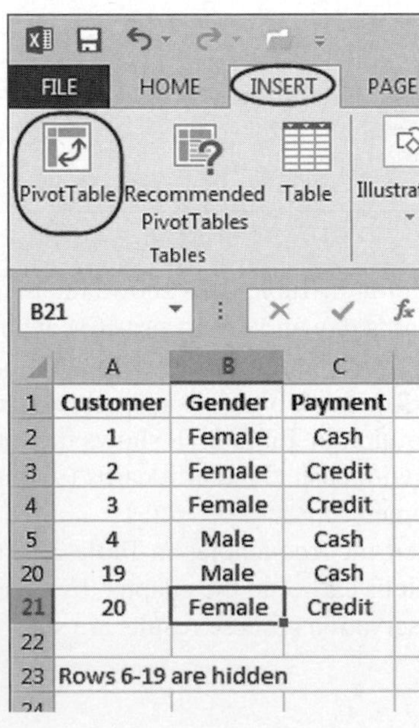

FIGURE 2.21A
Creating a Pivot Table in Excel (Steps 1–4)

5. A new worksheet will be created for your pivot table. From the **Pivot Table Fields** found to the right of this worksheet,
   a. Drag the **Gender** field down into the **Column Labels** box below, as shown in Figure 2.21B.
   b. Drag the **Payment** field down into the **Row Labels** box below.
   c. Drag the **Customer** field down into the **Values** box below.
6. Your spreadsheet should look like Figure 2.21B.

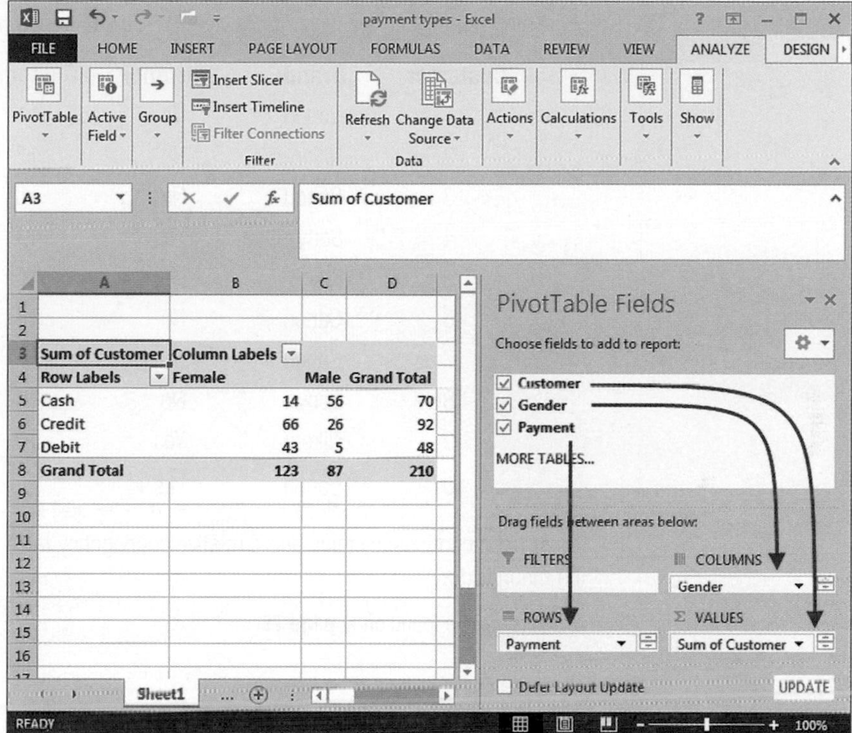

FIGURE 2.21B
Creating a Pivot Table in Excel (Steps 5–6)

Don't panic when you see that the values in our pivot table are not correct. By default, Excel sums up all the values in the Customer column in our pivot table, which doesn't help us since these values are arbitrary customer numbers from 1 to 20. We want Excel to count the number of customers in each category. To do this,

7. Left-click anywhere within the pivot table.
8. Right-click on the cell you selected.
9. In the drop-down menu, select **Summarize Data By > Count**.

You can now let out a big sigh of relief as our pivot table converts the observations to a frequency distribution and counts the number of them in each category, as shown in Figure 2.21C.

FIGURE 2.21C
Creating a Pivot Table in Excel (Final Result)

	A	B	C	D
1				
2				
3	Count of Customer	Column Labels		
4	Row Labels	Female	Male	Grand Total
5	Cash	2	5	7
6	Credit	7	2	9
7	Debit	3	1	4
8	Grand Total	12	8	20
9				

After a little practice with this, you will find pivot tables very useful tools for organizing complex data sets. Pivot tables work with both quantitative and qualitative data, as well as grouped data. These tables can also work with more than two variables in a data set.

Test your newly discovered pivot table skills with this next Your Turn problem.

YOUR TURN #9

The digital camera manager at Best Buy was investigating the relationship between the camera brand a customer purchased and whether the person also purchased an extended warranty. The following table shows the purchasing behavior of the last 20 customers who bought a digital camera.

Customer	Brand	Warranty	Customer	Brand	Warranty
1	Canon	No	11	Nikon	No
2	Nikon	No	12	Sony	Yes
3	Canon	No	13	Canon	No
4	Sony	Yes	14	Sony	Yes
5	Nikon	No	15	Sony	No
6	Canon	No	16	Canon	No
7	Canon	No	17	Canon	No
8	Sony	No	18	Nikon	No
9	Nikon	Yes	19	Canon	No
10	Canon	Yes	20	Nikon	No

Construct a contingency table and a relative contingency table for these data. What conclusions might the manger draw?

Answers can be found on ▶ **page 75**

2.4 Section Problems

Applications

2.21 The following table shows the final grades and genders of 24 students in a statistics class. These data can be found in the Excel file **grade distribution.xlsx**.

Grade	Gender	Grade	Gender
B	Male	C	Female
A	Female	A	Male
B	Female	A	Female
C	Male	B	Male
B	Male	B	Female
B	Female	B	Male
A	Female	C	Male
C	Female	A	Female
B	Male	B	Male
C	Male	A	Male
A	Female	B	Female
B	Male	B	Female

Develop a contingency table for these data. What conclusions can be drawn about the grade distribution?

2.22 A regional manager at Sears compares customer satisfaction ratings (1, 2, 3, or 4 stars) at the company's Media, Pennsylvania, store (M); Exton, Pennsylvania, store (E); and Darby, Pennsylvania, store (D). The following table shows these data from 50 customers, which can also be found in the Excel file **Sears ratings.xlsx**.

Store	Rating	Store	Rating	Store	Rating
M	3	M	2	E	1
D	4	M	3	E	2
E	3	D	3	M	3
M	2	E	3	D	3
E	3	E	2	M	2
M	1	D	3	M	4
D	4	D	2	E	3
E	2	D	4	E	3
D	3	E	3	E	1

Store	Rating	Store	Rating	Store	Rating
M	4	M	1	E	3
E	4	M	2	D	2
M	2	M	3	M	1
E	4	M	3	D	4
D	3	D	4	M	2
M	2	D	3	E	4

Store	Rating	Store	Rating	Store	Rating
D	4	M	2	M	3
M	3	D	4		

Develop a contingency table for these data. What conclusions can be drawn about the store location and customer satisfaction?

2.5 Stem and Leaf Display

The **stem and leaf display** splits the data values into stems (the larger place values) and leaves (the smaller place value). By listing all of the leaves to the right of each stem, we can graphically describe how the data are distributed.

The **stem and leaf display** is another graphical technique you can use to display quantitative data. A statistician named John Tukey originated the concept during the 1970s. The major benefit of this approach is that all the original data points are visible on the display and that they are very easy to construct by hand.

To demonstrate the method, I will use test scores from a recent statistics exam, which are shown in Table 2.20.

TABLE 2.20 | EXAM SCORES

81	86	78	80	81	82	92	90
79	83	84	95	85	88	80	78
84	79	80	83	79	87	84	80

The first step in constructing a stem and leaf display is to sort the data from lowest to highest, as shown in Table 2.21.

TABLE 2.21 | SORTED EXAM SCORES

78	78	79	79	79	80	80	80
80	81	81	82	83	83	84	84
84	85	86	87	88	90	92	95

Figure 2.22 shows the stem and leaf display for the scores.

FIGURE 2.22
A Stem and Leaf Display for the Exam Scores

```
7 | 8 8 9 9 9
8 | 0 0 0 0 1 1 2 3 3 4 4 4 5 6 7 8
9 | 0 2 5
```

The "stem" in this display is the first column of numbers, which represents the first digit of the exam scores. The "leaf" in the display is the second digit of the exam scores, with one digit for each score. The values 0, 2, and 5 on the 9 stem represent the exam scores 90, 92, and 95.

If we choose to, we can break this display down further by adding more stems. Figure 2.23 on the next page shows this approach of splitting the stems in half. Here, the stem labeled 7 (5) stores all the scores between 75 and 79. The stem 8 (0) stores all the scores between 80 and 84. After examining this display, I can see a pattern that's not as obvious when looking at Figure 2.22: The majority of the exam scores are in the low 80s.

FIGURE 2.23
Splitting the Stems in Half

7(5)	8	8	9	9	9								
8(0)	0	0	0	0	1	1	2	3	3	4	4	4	
8(5)	5	6	7	8									
9(0)	0	2											
9(5)	5												

Sorting the data from lowest to highest makes constructing the stem and leaf display much easier and less prone to mistakes.

A common mistake that my students make is to omit stems that have no leaves. Figure 2.24 shows a stem and leaf display for the following data, which represent the weekly demand for milk at a local Costco warehouse store.

105 111 111 113 116 119 132 138 140 143 143 147

FIGURE 2.24
A Stem and Leaf Display with an Empty Stem

10	5				
11	1	1	3	6	9
12					
13	2	8			
14	0	3	3	7	

Be sure to include all the stems in the distribution, even the ones with no leaves, as shown in Figure 2.24.

Because each data point has three digits, we'll use the first two digits for the stems and the third digit for the leaves. Even though the 12 stem has no leaves, including this stem in the display provides a more accurate picture of this distribution. The lesson here is "don't cut your leafless stems."

The beauty of the stem and leaf display is its simplicity. It does not require computer software to construct, shows each of the data values, and provides a histogram-like picture of the distribution. Before moving on to the next section, use the following Your Turn example to test your stem and leaf skills on this next data set.

The space between the numbers in the leaves for a stem and leaf display should be equal so that the shape of the frequency distribution is properly displayed. In other words, a string of six numbers should appear twice as long as a string of three numbers.

YOUR TURN #10

The following table shows the ages of employees who work in an AT&T Wireless retail facility. Construct a stem and leaf display for these data by splitting the stems in half.

48	40	38	37	37	37	36	34	33	33
33	33	32	32	29	29	29	28	28	27
27	27	26	26	25	25	25	25	25	25

Answer can be found on ▶ **page 75**

2.5 Section Problems

Basic Skills

2.23 Construct a stem and leaf display for the following data, which also can be found in the Excel file **Prob 2-23 data .xlsx**.

72 120 83 79 137 99 75 86 71 122 87 125 130
111 134 118 110 97 116 139 112 115 80 100 94 73
86 90 78 78 107 101 87 90 126 134 120 107 111

2.24 Construct a stem and leaf display for the following data, which also can be found in the Excel file **Prob 2-24 data .xlsx**.

130 123 122 121 113 114 112 100 125 150 113 127 139
132 111 110 105 121 123 102 140 126 137 136 137 140
108 127 145 129 146 115 121 108 137 142 109 114 132

Applications

2.25 The following table shows the number of cars that arrived at a local Burger King drive-through during lunch hour (12:00–1:00 P.M.) over the past 39 days. These data can also be found in the Excel file **Burger King.xlsx**.

50	27	52	22	29	54	44	37	35	40	55	40	24
51	42	49	48	44	38	67	23	43	45	59	41	50
21	43	37	37	13	45	52	64	51	58	16	48	47

a. Construct a stem and leaf display for these data.
b. Construct a stem and leaf display, splitting the stems from part a.

2.26 The following table shows the ages of the top 25 golfers on the 2012 PGA money list which represents the top earners that year. These data can also be found in the Excel file **PGA money list.xlsx**.

23	37	32	35	34	36	32	42	30	26	34	42	35
35	30	43	27	45	28	35	24	31	37	39	32	

Based on: http://www.espn.com

a. Construct a stem and leaf display for these data.
b. Construct a stem and leaf display, splitting the stems from part a.

2.6 Scatter Plots

Scatter plots provide a picture of the relationship between two quantitative variables that are paired together.

Up to this point, most of the data we have summarized involved only a single value, such as the number of computers shipped by HP or the number of defective returns to QVC. **Scatter plots** provide a picture of the relationship between two quantitative variables that are paired together. To demonstrate scatter plots, we'll use the data in Table 2.22, which shows the selling price of various sizes of Samsung LCD televisions that were listed recently on Best Buy's Web site. These data can also be found in the Excel file **Samsung TV.xlsx**.

TABLE 2.22 | SIZE AND PRICE DATA FOR SAMSUNG LCD TELEVISIONS

SIZE (IN.)	PRICE ($)	SIZE (IN.)	PRICE ($)
43	500	60	1,100
55	900	46	1,600
51	900	19	200
32	400	55	2,200
51	1,200	60	1,700
37	500	55	2,000
60	2,800	22	300
60	1,100	40	600
46	1,600	40	900

Based on: http://www.bestbuy.com.

There are a total of 18 observations (televisions) in Table 2.22, each consisting of a size and the corresponding price of a television. There is an important relationship between the size and price of a television. Common sense tells us that as the size of the television increases, the price will also increase. In this example, we call the television price the **dependent variable** because we believe that the price will depend on the television's size. The television size is known as the **independent variable**.

The **dependent variable**, which is placed on the vertical axis, of the scatter plot is influenced by changes in the **independent variable**, which is placed on the horizontal axis.

When constructing a scatter plot, the independent variable is placed on the horizontal axis, or x-axis. The dependent variable is placed on the vertical axis, or y-axis. Perform the following steps, as shown in Figure 2.25A on the next page, to construct the scatter plot in Excel 2013. See the textbook's Web site for Excel 2011 for Mac or Excel 2010 for Windows instructions.

1. Open the Excel file **Samsung TV.xlsx** or type in the data as seen on Figure 2.25A. If you type in the data, be sure to place the independent variable (size) in the first column and the dependent variable (price) in the second column.
2. Highlight Cells A1:B17.
3. Select the **Insert** tab and select the **Insert Scatter Chart** icon circled in Figure 2.25A.
4. Click on the first **Scatter** icon.

FIGURE 2.25A Constructing a Scatter Plot in Excel (Steps 1–4)

	A	B
1	Size (in.)	Price ($)
2	43	500
3	55	900
4	51	900
5	32	400
6	51	1200
7	37	500
8	60	2800
9	60	1100
10	46	1600
11	19	200
12	55	2200
13	60	1700
14	55	2000
15	22	300
16	40	600
17	40	900
18		

We now have a preliminary scatter plot that could use a little work. Perform the following steps to construct the scatter plot shown in Figure 2.25B:

5. Add axis titles by clicking on the scatter plot and selecting the **Design** tab under **Chart Tools**.
6. Insert the chart title and axis titles by clicking on **Add Chart Element** (like we did in Figure 2.16B).
7. Format the television prices on the vertical axis to currency by right-clicking on one of the prices and use the **Format Axis** menu (like we did in Figure 2.18D).

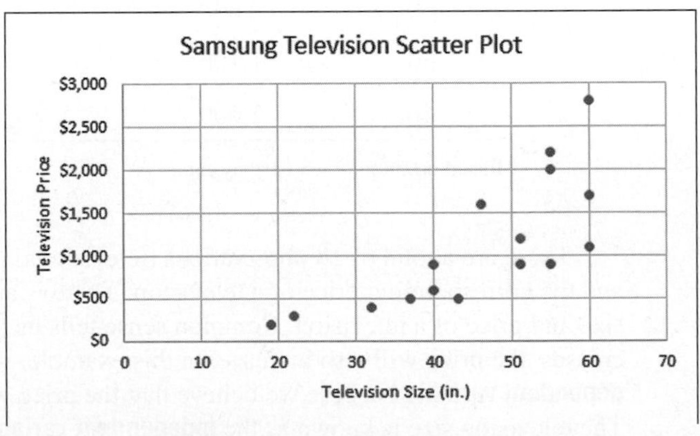

FIGURE 2.25B Constructing a Scatter Plot in Excel (Final Result)

There are 16 data points on the scatter plot in Figure 2.25B. Each point represents one television from Table 2.22. For instance, the far-left data point corresponds to the 19-in.

television that sells for $200. Our scatter plot shows an upward trend in price as the size of the television increases. This makes sense, as we would expect larger televisions to cost more.

Use caution when deciding which variable in your scatter plot is independent and which is dependent. The relationship between independent and dependent variables exists only in one direction, as shown in the following equation:

$$\text{Independent variable } (x) \rightarrow \text{Dependent variable } (y)$$

$$\text{Size } (x) \rightarrow \text{Price } (y)$$

The relationship does not make sense in the opposite direction. For instance, if Best Buy reduces the price of a television, doing so does not reduce the size of the television.

Line Charts

A **line chart** is a special type of scatter plot in which the data points in the scatter plot are connected with a line.

A **line chart** is a special type of scatter plot in which the data points in the scatter plot are connected with a line. To demonstrate this type of chart, I'll use the data in Table 2.23, which shows the annual revenues for The Walt Disney Company from 1993 to 2012. These data can also be found in the Excel file **Disney revenue.xlsx**.

TABLE 2.23 | ANNUAL REVENUE FOR THE WALT DISNEY COMPANY

YEAR	REVENUE ($ BILLIONS)	YEAR	REVENUE ($ BILLIONS)
1993	8.5	2003	27.1
1994	10.4	2004	30.8
1995	12.5	2005	31.9
1996	18.7	2006	33.7
1997	22.5	2007	35.5
1998	23.0	2008	37.8
1999	23.4	2009	36.1
2000	25.4	2010	38.1
2001	25.8	2011	40.9
2002	25.4	2012	42.3

Based on: Disney Annual Reports.

A data set is known as a **time series** when each data point is associated with a specific point in time.

The data set shown in Table 2.23 is known as a **time series** because each data point is associated with a specific point in time. (We first discussed time series data and charts in Chapter 1, if you recall.) We can construct a line chart using these data by performing the following steps:

1. List the data in Columns A and B as shown in Figure 2.26A on the next page. Because Year is the independent variable, place it in Column A.
2. Highlight Cells A1:B19.
3. Select the **Insert** tab and select the **Insert Scatter Chart** icon circled in Figure 2.26A.
4. Click on the second **Scatter** icon.

FIGURE 2.26A Constructing a Line Chart in Excel

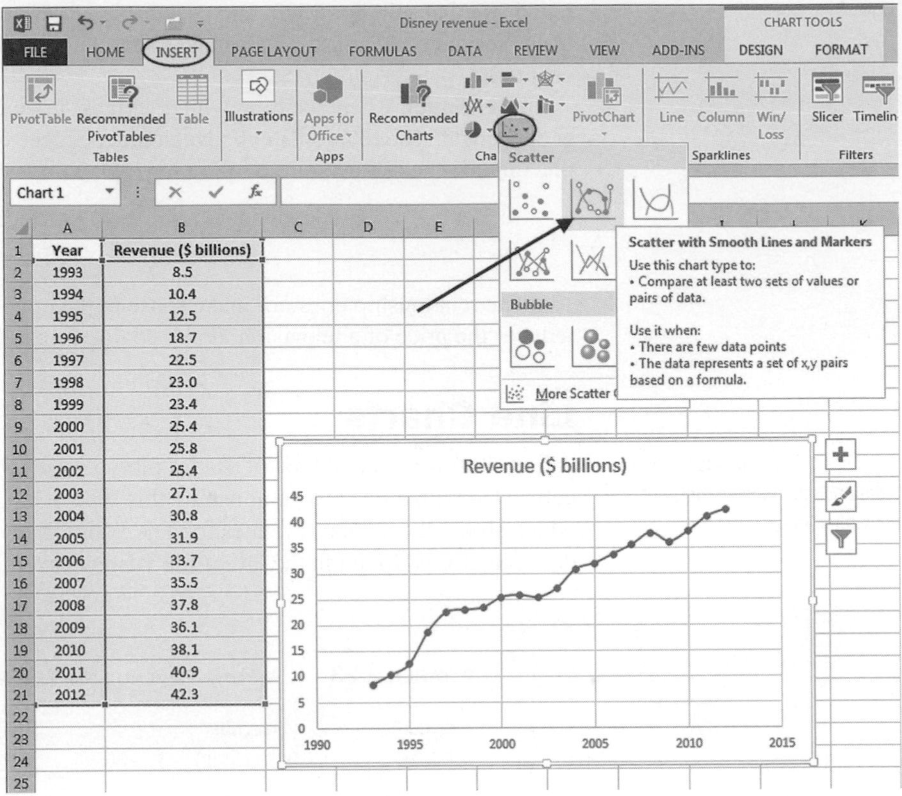

A **line chart** is a special type of scatter plot in which the data points in the scatter plot are connected with a line.

Figure 2.26B shows our **line chart** with titles added. This chart provides much better information than Table 2.23. We can see that Disney experienced the most significant revenue growth in the mid-1990s, followed by a few years of flat revenues and then significant increases from 2004 to 2008. Connecting the data points with a line helps readers of the chart visualize the movement in the data over time. Now, who wants to go see Mickey?

FIGURE 2.26B Line Chart Showing Disney's Revenues, 1993–2012

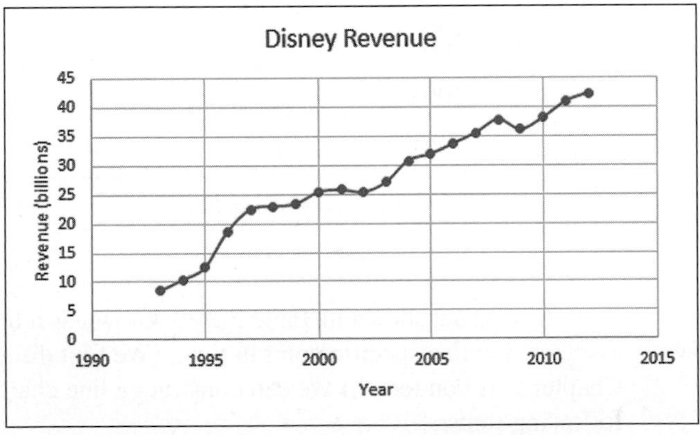

When graphing a time series such as the Disney example, the convention is to place the time data on the horizontal axis of the graph. This is accomplished by placing the time data in Column A in the Excel spreadsheet and the other data in Column B, as shown in Figure 2.26A.

Let's wrap this chapter up with one final Your Turn to test your scatter plot skills by engaging in one of my favorite activities—car shopping.

YOUR TURN #11

A few years ago, I had the opportunity to "bond" with my son Brian as we shopped for his first car when he turned 16. Brian had visions of Mercedes and BMWs dancing in his head, whereas I was thinking more along the line of Chevys and Toyotas. After many "discussions" on the matter, we compromised by looking for 1999 Volkswagen Jettas. However, Brian had two requirements:

- The car had to be black.
- It had to be the "new body" style.

Apparently, somebody at Volkswagen had the brilliant idea back in 1999 to subtly change the design of the Jetta halfway through the production year. Personally, I would never have noticed the difference. Brian, on the other hand, wouldn't be caught dead driving in the original body style, which essentially eliminated half the used 1999 Volkswagen Jettas on the market. Undeterred, I searched the world over, asking each seller, "Is it the new body style?" The things we do for our children. What follows is a table showing the mileage of eight Jettas with the new body style and the asking price of each:

Mileage	Price ($)	Mileage	Price ($)
21,900	16,000	65,900	10,300
34,300	11,400	72,200	12,400
41,000	13,500	76,700	8,000
53,500	14,700	84,800	9,600

Construct a scatter plot for these data. Describe the relationship between the mileage and the price of Jettas with these data.

Answers can be found on ▶ page 75

2.6 Section Problems

2.27 Netflix is a company that provides online video streaming and a DVD-by-mail service for members since 1997. The following table shows the number of U.S. subscribers, in millions, each quarter from 2007 to 2012. These data can also be found in the Excel file **Netflix subscribers.xlsx**.

Quarter	2007	2008	2009	2010	2011	2012
1	6.8	8.2	10.3	14.0	22.8	23.4
2	6.7	8.4	10.6	15.0	24.6	23.9
3	7.0	8.7	11.1	16.8	23.8	25.1
4	7.5	9.4	12.3	19.5	24.4	27.1

Construct a line chart using these data. Describe the relationship between time and number of subscribers.

2.28 Suppose the Internet retailer Buy.com would like to investigate the relationship between the amount of time in minutes a purchaser spends on its Web site and the amount of money he or she spends on an order. The following table shows the data from a random sample of 12 customers. These data can also be found in the Excel file titled **Buy.com.xlsx**.

Time	Order Size ($)	Time	Order Size ($)
18	69	5	58
13	26	37	365
26	94	6	127
23	199	36	160
2	49	24	75
14	38	9	250

Construct a scatter plot using these data. Describe the relationship between the amount of time in minutes a purchaser spends on its Web site and the amount of money he or she spends on an order.

2.29 Take-Two Interactive Software, Inc., produces video games such as Grand Auto Theft and NBA 2K9. The following table lists the company's quarterly profits and losses from 2007 to 2012. These data can also be found in the Excel file **Take Two.xlsx**.

Q	2007 ($)	2008 ($)	2009 ($)	2010 ($)	2011 ($)	2012 ($)
1	−21.5	−38.0	−53.8	−33.8	−22.0	−66.8
2	−51.2	98.2	−10.1	16.9	6.4	−93.8
3	−58.5	51.8	−55.5	12.4	−47.4	−12.5
4	−7.1	−15.0	−22.0	40.9	14.1	71.3

http:/ir.take2games.com

Construct a line chart using these data.

CHAPTER 2 Summary

- Technology, such as Excel, provides an excellent tool to display descriptive data in a graphical format.
- A frequency distribution shows the number of data observations that fall into specific intervals.
    - Relative frequency distributions display the percentage of observations of each class relative to the total number of observations.
    - Cumulative relative frequency distributions indicate the percentage of observations that are less than or equal to the current class.
    - A histogram graphically displays the frequency distribution as a bar graph showing the number of observations in each class as the height of each bar.
    - Ideally, the number of classes in a frequency distribution should be between 4 and 20.
    - Some data sets require several values to be grouped together in a single class using the following rules:
        - Create equal class sizes.
        - Use mutually exclusive classes.
        - Include all data values.
        - Avoid open-ended classes.
    - Histograms displaying
        - discrete data have gaps between the bars indicating the frequency of each class.
        - continuous data do not have gaps between the bars.
    - A percentage polygon graphs the midpoints of each class as a line rather than columns.
        - The height of each midpoint represents the relative frequency of the corresponding class.
        - The cumulative percentage polygon, or ogive, is a line graph that plots the cumulative frequency distribution.
- Contingency tables provide a format to display the frequencies of two qualitative variables.
    - Contingency tables are constructed with Excel as pivot tables.
- The stem and leaf display is a graphical technique used to present quantitative data by splitting the data values into stems (the first digits in the value) and leaves (the remaining digit in the value).
- Bar charts are used to display data that has been organized in categories and can be arranged in a vertical or horizontal orientation.
- Pareto charts show in a decreasing order the frequency of the classes that cause quality-control problems.
    - A Pareto chart also plots the cumulative relative frequency as a line on the chart known as an ogive.
- Pie charts are a tool for comparing proportions for categorical data.
    - Each category occupies a segment of the pie that represents the relative frequency of that category.
- Scatter plots display the relationship between two quantitative variables that are paired together on an *x*-*y* graph.
    - A line chart is a type of scatter plot in which the data points in the scatter plot are connected with a line.

CHAPTER 2 Key Terms

Bar chart. A chart that displays qualitative data that have been organized in categories and can be arranged vertically or horizontally.

Class. A category in a frequency distribution.

Clustered bar chart. A bar chart that groups several values side by side within the same category in a vertical direction.

Contingency table. A table that provides a format to display the frequencies of two qualitative variables.

Continuous data. Values that can take on any value within a given range; continuous data are often the result of measuring observations rather than counting them.

Cumulative percentage polygon (ogive). A line graph that plots the cumulative relative frequency distribution.

Cumulative relative frequency distribution. A frequency distribution that totals the proportion of observations that are less than or equal to the class at which you are looking.

Dependent variable. The dependent variable is the variable in the scatter plot that is influenced by changes in the other variable, the independent variable; the dependent variable is placed on the vertical axis.

Discrete data. Values based on observations that can be counted; they are restricted to integer values (whole numbers).

Frequency distribution. A table that shows the number of data observations that fall into specific intervals.

Histogram. A bar graph showing the number of observations in each class as the height of each bar.

Horizontal bar chart. A bar chart that displays the bars in a horizontal direction.

Independent variable. The independent variable is the variable in the scatter plot that is not affected by changes in the other variable; the independent variable is placed on the horizontal axis.

Line chart. A special type of scatter plot in which the data points in the scatter plot are connected with a line.

Pareto chart. A bar chart that shows in a decreasing order the frequency of the categories that cause quality control problems.

Percentage polygon. Graphs the midpoint of each class as a line rather than a column. The height of each midpoint represents the relative frequency of the corresponding class.

Pie chart. A chart that displays categories in the shape of a pie; each segment of the pie represents the relative frequency of that category.

Relative frequency distribution. A frequency distribution that displays the proportion of observations of each class relative to the total number of observations.

Scatter plot. A chart that provides a picture of the relationship between two quantitative variables that are paired together on a graph with a horizontal and vertical axis.

Stacked bar chart. A bar chart that groups several values in a single column within the same category in a vertical direction.

Stem and leaf display. A chart that splits data values into stems (the larger place values) and leaves (the smaller place values).

Symmetrical distribution. The shape of a distribution when its two halves mirror one another.

Time series. A data set where each data point is associated with a specific point in time.

CHAPTER 2 Problems

2.30 The following table shows the number of complaints received each day by a customer service department over the past 40 days. These data can also be found in the Excel file **complaints.xlsx**.

8	10	8	2	4	13	23	10	6	3
18	16	11	3	3	17	12	8	10	6
3	19	9	10	21	11	8	10	0	7
20	13	18	3	5	19	2	8	10	9

a. Using the $2^k \geq n$ rule, construct a frequency distribution for these data.

b. Using the results from part a, calculate the relative frequencies for each class.

c. Using the results from part a, calculate the cumulative relative frequencies for each class.

d. Construct a histogram for these data.

2.31 The Arizona Diamondbacks and the city of Phoenix are considering building a new baseball stadium for the Major League Baseball team. A decision needs to be made whether to enclose the new facility with a roof. To help make this decision, data were gathered on the number of days per month it rained during the baseball season, which are shown in the following table. These data can also be found in the Excel file **Diamondbacks.xlsx**.

0	3	5	0	3	0	1	0	5	0
2	1	0	4	1	1	0	2	3	2
0	1	1	3	3	3	3	4	0	3
2	4	0	4	0	1	3	0	2	0
1	0	0	4	2	2	1	0	3	3

a. Construct a frequency distribution for these data.
b. Using the results from part a, calculate the relative frequencies for each class.
c. Using the results from part a, calculate the cumulative relative frequencies for each class.
d. Construct a histogram for these data.
e. What is the likelihood that a month during the baseball season will experience one day or less of rain?

2.32 The following table shows the number of minutes that 48 Verizon Wireless customers used on their cell phone accounts last month. These data can also be found in the excel file **wireless.xlsx**.

235	406	339	544	78	327
922	58	76	860	549	179
492	63	1,187	188	288	90
235	353	964	577	524	43
731	45	343	170	178	338
169	136	728	678	74	483
522	279	863	373	255	692
87	486	238	218	550	402

a. Using the $2^k \geq n$ rule, construct a frequency distribution for these data.
b. Using the results from part a, calculate the relative frequencies for each class.
c. Using the results from part a, calculate the cumulative relative frequencies for each class.
d. Construct a histogram for these data.

2.33 The following table lists the math SAT scores for 72 students. These data can also be found in the excel file **math SAT scores.xlsx**.

586	621	613	493	552	449	559	672	428	409	571	449
498	457	578	369	511	726	566	412	795	382	607	701
739	359	354	517	384	196	496	515	439	493	508	535
507	509	428	612	530	556	660	576	626	522	515	374
190	601	499	593	538	509	450	690	571	252	599	362
505	555	323	519	524	281	580	412	553	394	555	541

a. Using the $2^k \geq n$ rule, construct a frequency distribution for these data.
b. Using the results from part a, calculate the relative frequencies for each class.
c. Using the results from part a, calculate the cumulative relative frequencies for each class.
d. Construct a histogram for these data.

2.34 The following data show the exam grades for two different sections of a statistics class that I teach. The first group of data is from a day section of traditional students. The second group of data is from my evening section, which is comprised mostly of older students who work full-time during the day. These data can also be found in the Excel file **statistics grades.xlsx**. Note: Consider these data as discrete data because fractional grades will not occur.

Day

71	69	68	90	87	76	90	66	90	71
66	75	78	80	75	90	76	77	80	100
75	75	66	86	85	86	77	75	66	77

Evening

96	98	88	94	88	86	100	99	95	89
96	98	92	85	93	83	90	88	91	89
87	82	83	87	88	88	81	93	77	90

a. Construct a percentage polygon for these data.
b. Construct a cumulative percentage polygon for these data.
c. What conclusions can be drawn about the grade distribution of these two sections?

2.35 On-time arrival is a critical measurement in the airline industry. The Excel file titled **airline arrivals.xlsx** lists the number of minutes that a particular flight either arrived early (negative value) or late (positive value) over the past 300 days of operation.

a. Using Excel and the $2^k \geq n$ rule, construct a frequency distribution for these data.
b. Using the results from part a, calculate the relative frequencies for each class.
c. Using the results from part a, calculate the cumulative relative frequencies for each class.
d. Construct a histogram for these data.
e. What approximate percentage of flights did not arrive late during this time period?

2.36 The following data show the average monthly revenue a store earned per customer by selling six different types of cell phones:

Phone	Average Revenue Per Customer ($)
iPhone	95
Blackberry	85
LG	60
Samsung	55
Motorola	55
Prepaid	20

a. Construct a vertical bar chart for these data.
b. Construct a horizontal bar chart for these data.

2.37 The recent downturn in the housing market can be measured by the number of days homes are on the market before they are sold. To compare the health of the housing market between the communities of Wayne, Pennsylvania, and Dover, Delaware, these data were collected for 100 homes from each city and can be found in the Excel file **days on the market.xlsx**.

a. Construct a percentage polygon for these data.
b. Construct a cumulative percentage polygon for these data.
c. What conclusions can be drawn about the housing market in these two communities?

2.38 Charles Schwab conducted a survey that asked 1,252 young adults between the ages of 22 and 28 the following question: "What most surprised you as you began life on your own?" The following table summarizes the responses:

Response	Percentage
High cost of living	26
Difficulty saving money	22
Number of financial decisions	13
Difficulty paying all the bills	12
Challenges finding a job	10

Based on: Charles Schwab.

a. Construct a vertical bar chart for these data.
b. Construct a horizontal bar chart for these data.

2.39 The following table shows the number of wins for baseball teams in the National League Central Division for the 2011 and 2012 seasons:

Team	2011	2012
St. Louis Cardinals	90	88
Chicago Cubs	71	61
Milwaukee Brewers	96	83
Cincinnati Reds	79	97
Houston Astros	56	55
Pittsburgh Pirates	72	79

Based on: http://www.espn.com.

Construct a horizontal stacked bar chart that summarizes these data.

2.40 The following table lists the reasons customers provided over the phone when they rated their customer service experience with a particular cable company unsatisfactory.

Reason	Frequency
Too long on hold	47
Not knowledgeable	22
Not courteous	18
Hard to understand	15
Too many transfers	10
Other	8

Construct a Pareto chart for these data.

2.41 AutoBeef is a Web site to which customers post complaints about their cars. The following table lists the number of complaints and the type of complaints posted about used Ford Explorers:

Complaint	Frequency
Transmission	721
Body	437
Wheels	164
Drivetrain	139
Windows	89
Engine	55
Interior	45
Electrical	44
Steering	42
Suspension	41
Air conditioner/heater	26
Brakes	22
Other	47

Based on: http://www.carcomplaints.com/Ford/Explorer/2002.

Construct a Pareto chart for these data.

2.42 A survey conducted by NetApplications in January 2013 on the use of Internet browsers reported the following market shares:

Browser	Market Share (%)
Internet Explorer	55.2
Firefox	20.0
Chrome	17.5
Safari	5.2
Opera	1.8
Other	0.3

Construct a pie chart to display these data.

2.43 SnagAJob.com surveyed 551 hiring managers to ask them what recruiters looked for when hiring seasonal employees. The following table shows the results:

Response	Percentage
Positive attitude	36
Ability to work the daily schedule	27
Previous experience in the industry	23
Commitment to work for the entire summer	14

Construct a pie chart to display these data.

2.44 The following table shows the sources of our electricity, according to the U.S. Department of Energy:

Source	Percentage
Coal	48
Natural gas	21
Nuclear	20
Hydro	6
Other	4
Oil	1

Construct a pie chart to display these data.

2.45 Data were collected about the time per day children 8 to 18 years old spent with various types of media. The following table reports the average time the children spent with each media category:

Media	Time
Television content	4 hours 29 minutes
Music/audio	2 hours 31 minutes
Computer	1 hour 29 minutes
Video games	1 hour 13 minutes
Print	38 minutes
Movies	25 minutes

Construct a display that best describes these data.

2.46 The following table shows the average number of viewers aged 18–49 who watch the ABC, CBS, FOX, or NBC networks at 10:00 P.M. The data were collected by Nielsen during the last week of January 2012 and 2013.

Network	Average Number of Viewers (Thousands)	
	2012	**2013**
CBS	4,071	3,542
NBC	3,163	3,669
ABC	3,174	2,910
FOX	4,162	3,155

Construct a display that best describes these data.

2.47 The following table indicates the market share for LCD televisions in the fourth quarter of 2011.

Brand	Market Share %
Samsung	23.6
Vizio	15.4
LG	12.4
Sony	8.0
Toshiba	7.8

Construct a display that best describes these data.

2.48 A Scottrade survey asked adults how much money they have saved for retirement. The data are as follows:

How Much	Percentage
Less than $25,000	39
$25,001 to $100,000	14
$100,001 to $250,000	9
$250,001 to $500,000	7
More than $500,000	7
Not sure	24

Construct a display that best describes these data.

2.49 The number of television coverage hours for six Winter Olympics is shown in the following table:

Winter Olympics	Television Coverage Hours
Albertville (1990)	116
Lillehammer (1994)	120
Nagano (1998)	124
Salt Lake City (2002)	376
Torino (2006)	398
Vancouver (2010)	835

Construct a display that best describes these data.

2.50 The following table shows the average 401(k) balances, in thousands of dollars, by age group according to the AARP.

Age Group	Balance ($)
50–54	224
55–59	250
60–64	234
65–69	228
70 and older	230

Construct a display that best describes these data.

2.51 The following table displays the average mathematics scores from the Trends in International Mathematics and Science Study (TIMSS) for fourth graders in 1995 and 2011 for various countries.

	Average Math Score	
Country	**1995**	**2011**
Singapore	590	606
Japan	567	585
Great Britain	484	542
United States	518	541
Australia	531	508

Construct a display that best presents these data with the goal of comparing scores between 1995 and 2012 for each country.

2.52 A survey conducted to determine how students pay for college reported the following results.

Source	Percentage
Grants/scholarships	29
Parent income and savings	28
Student borrowing	18
Student income and savings	12
Parent borrowing	9
Friends/relatives	4

Construct a display that best presents these data.

2.53 The following table provides the new housing starts, in thousands, in different regions in the United States over a three-year period.

Region	2010	2011	2012
Northeast	71.6	67.7	77.8
Midwest	97.9	100.9	128.8
South	297.5	307.8	398.7
West	119.9	132.5	174.7

Based on: U.S. Department of Commerce.

Construct a display that best presents these data with the goal of comparing total housing starts over this three-year period for each region in the country.

2.54 The following data shows the ages of 55 current BMW owners. These data can also be found in the Excel file **BMW owners.xlsx**.

28	50	37	51	42	27	40	38	46	48	56
29	44	40	42	46	50	30	60	30	43	66
32	36	35	48	47	43	39	26	44	32	35
47	42	47	34	39	34	60	43	26	50	43
61	42	32	45	46	49	54	51	39	26	49

a. Using the $2^k \geq n$ rule, construct a frequency distribution for these data.
b. Using the results from part a, calculate the relative frequency distributions for each class.
c. Using the results from part a, calculate the cumulative relative frequency distributions for each class.
d. Construct a histogram for these data.

2.55 A survey asked 614 small-business owners if they found their company's Facebook presence valuable. The results are shown in the following table.

Response	Percentage
Yes	42
No	30
Don't have a presence	23
No longer have a presence	5

Construct a display that best presents these data.

2.56 The following data represent the number of student absences for a large, two-semester statistic class. These data can also be found in the Excel file **absence.xlsx**.

3	5	2	5	5	3	2	6	2	2	0	2
4	4	0	5	5	2	4	2	3	5	2	3
6	5	4	3	2	7	3	7	3	4	5	3
3	5	6	4	4	3	2	3	3	3	2	6
2	4	4	5	2	1	3	4	7	3	4	3

a. Construct a frequency distribution for these data.
b. Using the results from part a, calculate the relative frequency distributions for each class.
c. Using the results from part a, calculate the cumulative relative frequency distributions for each class.
d. Construct a histogram for these data.
e. What is the likelihood that more than four students will be absent from this statistics class?

2.57 The following data represent the number of cars per day that used the drive-through lane for a fast food restaurant.

117	104	102	98	97	96	95	91	90	90	89	88
87	87	86	85	83	82	81	78	77	77	76	75
74	71	71	71	70	70	70	69	69	67	67	64

a. Construct a stem and leaf display for these data.
b. Construct a stem and leaf display for these data, splitting the stems from part a.

2.58 A marketing research firm would like to display the relationship between a family's weekly food costs and the number of family members living in the household. The following table shows the monthly food costs and the number of family members for 16 families. These data can also be found in Excel file **food costs.xlsx**.

People	Costs ($)	People	Costs ($)
4	926	6	1,263
5	1,155	3	1,023
3	962	8	1,265
4	909	3	1,114
4	1,084	7	1,322
2	755	2	937
4	949	5	962
4	1,000	3	829

Construct a scatter plot using these data. Describe the relationship between the number of household members and the family's monthly food costs.

2.59 The following table represents the average new-home size, in square feet, in the United States over various years.

Year	Average Size
1985	1,785
1990	2,080
1995	2,100
2000	2,266
2005	2,434
2010	2,392

Construct a display that best describes these data.

2.60 The term *never events* in the health care industry refers to mistakes that should never happen in the operating room. Researchers identified the following "never events" and their relative frequency of occurring.

Event	Relative Frequency (%)
Foreign objects left behind	49.8
Wrong procedure	25.1
Wrong site	24.8
Wrong patient	0.3

Construct a Pareto chart for these data.

2.61 As a long-time lover of Cheez-It crackers, I find myself offended when somebody claims that Cheese Nips, which is a competing product, is just as good. To put an end to this silly argument, I performed a taste test with 24 unbiased individuals, asking them to state their preference and listed the results in the following table. Those with no preference were recorded as "No Prefer." These data can also be found in the Excel file titled **Cheezits.xlsx**.

Cheez-Its	Cheez-Its	Cheese Nips	Cheez-Its	Cheez-Its	Cheese Nips
Cheez-Its	Cheez-Its	No Prefer	Cheez-Its	Cheese Nips	Cheez-Its
Cheez-Its	Cheez-Its	Cheez-Its	No Prefer	Cheese Nips	Cheez-Its
Cheez-Its	No Prefer	Cheez-Its	Cheese Nips	Cheese-Its	Cheez-Its

a. Construct a frequency distribution for these data.
b. Construct a relative frequency distribution for these data.

2.62 The following data represents the total annual snowfall (in inches) for 30 cities.

12	13	15	18	21	21	23	26	26	27
27	28	30	33	33	35	36	36	39	40
40	42	42	44	46	47	49	50	51	57

Construct a stem and leaf display using these data.

2.63 The following table shows the percentage of children at various age groups who use smartphones and laptop computers according to a survey conducted by the NPD Group.

Age	Smartphones (%)	Laptops (%)
4–5	37	22
6–8	35	28
9–11	38	37
12–14	47	43

Construct a display that best presents these data with the goal of comparing percentages between devices for each age group.

2.64 A grocery store manager records the purchases of soda by the brands Coke (C), Pepsi (P), and Mt. Dew (M). The type of soda is also noted (regular or diet). The following table shows the brand and type of soda for the last 33 customers. These data can also be found in the Excel file **soda.xlsx**.

Brand	Type	Brand	Type	Brand	Type
P	Reg	C	Diet	M	Reg
C	Diet	M	Reg	P	Diet
P	Diet	P	Diet	C	Reg
M	Reg	C	Diet	P	Reg
C	Reg	P	Reg	M	Reg
P	Reg	C	Reg	P	Reg
C	Diet	M	Reg	C	Reg
C	Diet	M	Diet	M	Reg
M	Diet	C	Reg	P	Reg
C	Reg	M	Reg	C	Diet
P	Diet	P	Reg	M	Reg

Develop a contingency table for these data. What conclusions can be drawn about the brands and types of soda sales?

2.65 Golf Galaxy, a major golf equipment retailer, would like to investigate the relationship between the brand of golf clubs (Taylor Made, Nike, and Callaway) and the age of the golfer who purchased them. The Excel file titled **golf clubs.xlsx** lists the golf club brand purchased by the last 100 customers along with the customers' ages. Using Excel, construct a pivot table for these data. What conclusions can be drawn about the golf club brand and age of the customer? Hint: Group the ages of the customers with a class width of 10 years using the following steps:

a. After the initial pivot table is constructed, right-click on one of the ages.
b. In the drop-down menu, left-click on **Group**.
c. In the **Group** dialog box, input the following values:
   1. Starting at = 20
   2. Ending at = 59
   3. By = 10
d. Click **OK**.

2.66 The class sizes for 40 courses currently being taught at Neumann University this semester are shown in the following table. These data can also be found in the Excel file **class size.xlsx**.

28	26	35	28	20	43	31	22	25	18
35	39	19	29	23	31	45	35	22	28
28	20	41	36	32	32	39	33	25	30
19	43	23	31	31	51	46	20	36	25

a. Construct a stem and leaf display for these data.
b. Construct a stem and leaf display, splitting the stems from part a.

2.67 The following table shows the number of customers who have visited a T-Mobile retail store during the past 40 days. These data can also be found in the Excel file **T-Mobile.xlsx**.

72	99	99	100	119	91	101	74	102	130
81	76	70	97	77	70	130	85	82	131
94	125	97	112	118	72	93	93	75	95
93	104	92	105	77	138	88	77	90	92

a. Construct a stem and leaf display for these data.
b. Construct a stem and leaf display, splitting the stems from part a.

2.68 The Excel file **MLB payroll.xlsx** provides the payroll and number of wins for all the Major League Baseball teams during the 2012 season. Construct a scatter plot using these data. Describe the relationship between payroll and number of wins.

2.69 The Excel file titled **gasoline prices.xlsx** lists the average monthly price per gallon of regular gasoline in the United States from August 1990 to January 2013 from the U.S. Energy Information Administration. Construct a line chart using these data and describe the trend.

2.70 The Excel file titled **airline performance.xlsx** lists the status of 100 flights as either "on time" or "late" along with the airline for that flight.

a. Construct a contingency table for these data.
b. Construct a relative contingency table for these data.
c. What conclusions could be drawn from these data?

2.71 The amount of time required to navigate through airport security can vary from city to city. The Excel file titled **TSA times.xlxs** shows the number of minutes that 60 passengers spent going through security at Chicago's O'Hare International Airport and Seattle International Airport. Construct a display that will allow a direct comparison of the security times for both airports.

2.72 The Excel file titled **US Housing Starts.xlsx** lists the number of housing starts in the United States each year from 1970 to 2012 provided by the U.S. Department of Commerce. Construct a display that best describes these data.

CHAPTER 2 Solutions to Your Turn

YOUR TURN #1

1. Discrete
2. Continuous
3. Discrete
4. Continuous
5. Discrete
6. Continuous
7. Discrete

YOUR TURN #2

Number of Stars	Frequency	Relative Frequency	Cumulative Relative Frequency
1	2	0.08	0.08
2	1	0.04	0.12
3	3	0.12	0.24
4	7	0.28	0.52
5	12	0.48	1.00
Total	**25**	**1.00**	

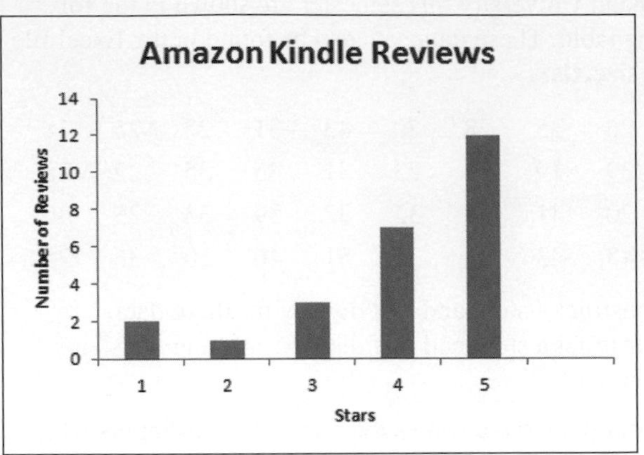

YOUR TURN #3

$2^5 = 32 \geq 30$, therefore use five classes.

$$\text{Estimated class width} = \frac{\$87.7 - \$40.0}{5} = \$9.54 \approx \$10$$

Salary	Frequency	Relative Frequency	Cumulative Relative Frequency
40–49.9	3	0.100	0.100
50–59.9	4	0.133	0.233
60–69.9	14	0.467	0.700
70–79.9	7	0.233	0.933
80–89.9	2	0.067	1.000
Total	**30**	**1.000**	

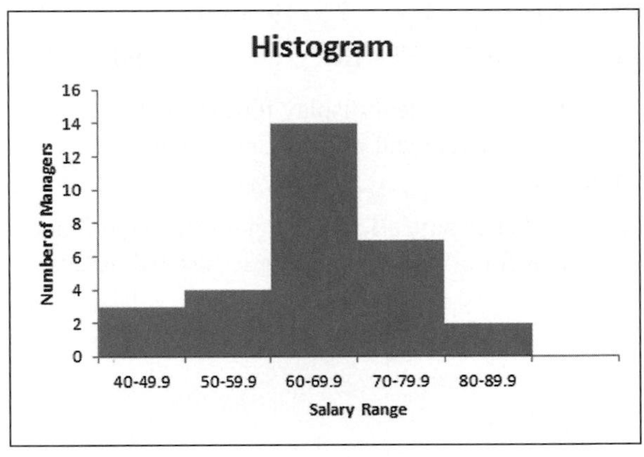

YOUR TURN #4

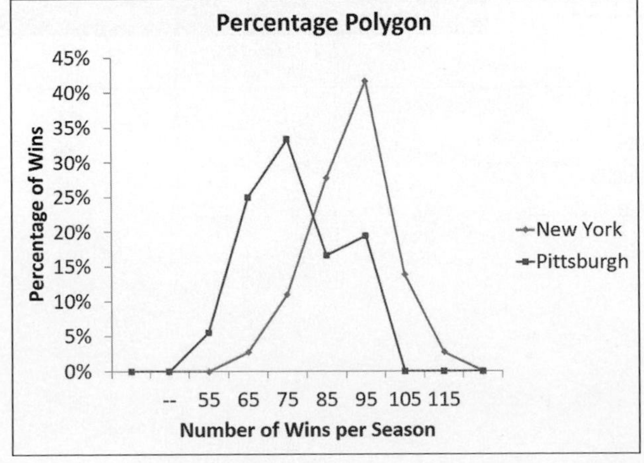

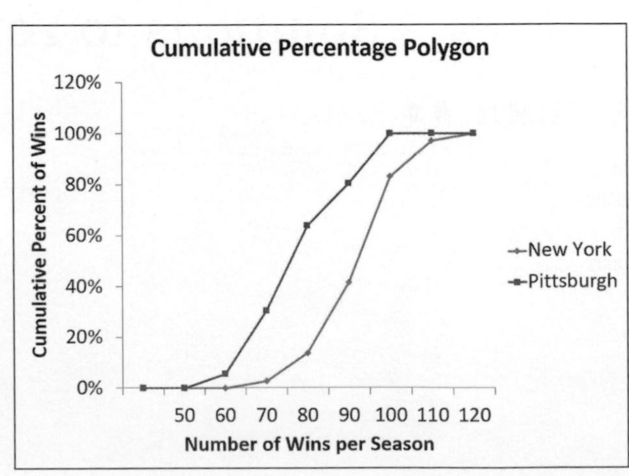

YOUR TURN #5

	A	B	C	D	E
1	Company		Bins	Frequency	Relative Frequency
2	Sprint		AT&T	8	0.40
3	Sprint		Sprint	7	0.35
4	AT&T		Verizon	4	0.20
5	AT&T		T-Mobile	1	0.05
6	T-Mobile		Total	20	1.00
7	AT&T				

YOUR TURN #6

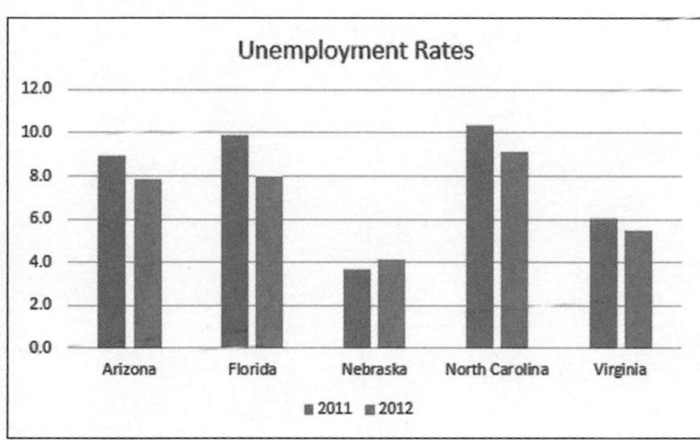

A clustered bar chart would be more appropriate because it provides a convenient way to compare unemployment rates for all five states between 2011 and 2012.

YOUR TURN #7

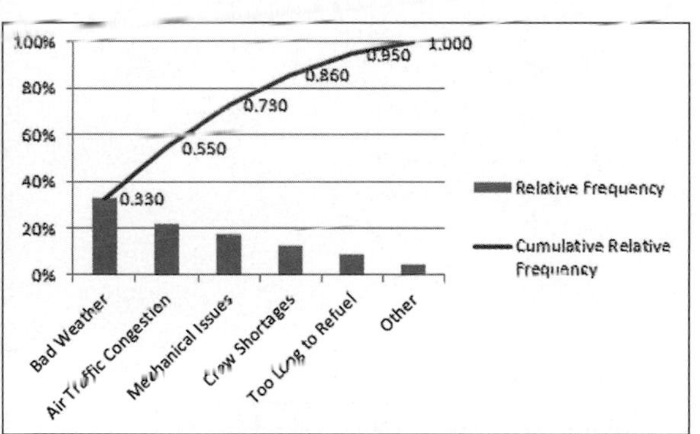

YOUR TURN #8

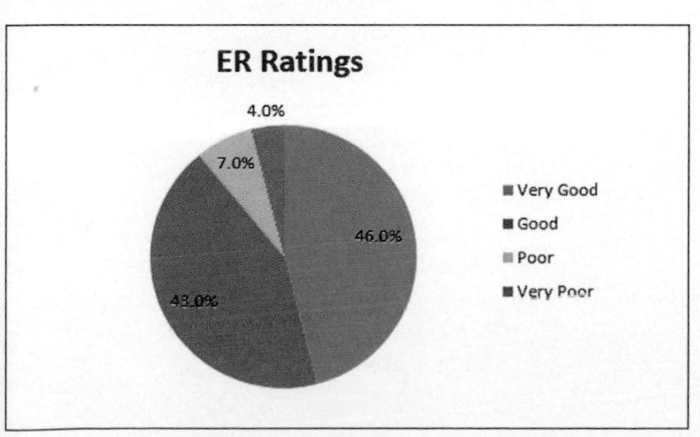

YOUR TURN #9

	Warranty		
Brand	**Yes**	**No**	**Total**
Canon	1	8	**9**
Nikon	1	5	**6**
Sony	3	2	**5**
Total	**5**	**15**	**20**

	Warranty		
Brand	**Yes**	**No**	**Total**
Canon	0.05	0.40	**0.45**
Nikon	0.05	0.25	**0.30**
Sony	0.15	0.10	**0.25**
Total	**0.25**	**0.75**	**1.00**

Based on these data, it appears that Sony customers are more likely to purchase an extended warranty when compared with Canon and Nikon customers.

YOUR TURN #10

2(5) | 5 5 5 5 5 5 6 6 7 7 7 8 8 9 9 9

3(0) | 2 2 3 3 3 3 4

3(5) | 6 7 7 7 8

4(0) | 0

4(5) | 8

YOUR TURN #11

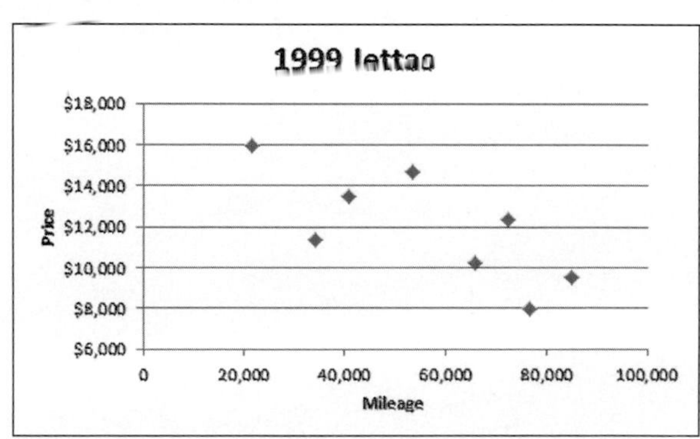

As expected, as mileage increases, the selling price decreases.

Calculating Descriptive Statistics

IN THIS CHAPTER, YOU WILL LEARN TO:

- Calculate the mean, weighted mean, median, and mode.
- Identify the most appropriate measure of central tendency to describe data.
- Calculate and interpret the range, variance, and standard deviation.
- Understand the coefficient of variation, z-score, the empirical rule, and Chebyshev's Theorem.
- Calculate the mean and standard deviation of grouped data.
- Calculate percentiles, percentile rank, and quartiles for a data set.
- Construct and interpret box-and-whisker plots.
- Calculate and interpret the covariance and the correlation coefficient for two data sets.

CHAPTER 3 MAP

Stats in Practice: Using the Median to Compare Salaries

The Bureau of Labor Statistics (BLS) is an agency of the federal government that collects and reports labor data for the economy. Their Web site, www.bls.gov, provides a wealth of information on earnings and employment status for various characteristics such as age, gender, and education. According to BLS, women's wages have increased at a higher rate than men's since the start of the recent economic recession. Between 2007 and 2012, women's wages have risen 12.5% compared to an 11.5% increase for men.

The median weekly wage for men in 2012 was $854, compared with a median wage of $691 per week for women. However, men had a higher unemployment rate during 2012 when compared to women: 8.2% vs. 7.9%.

According to BLS, education also played a role in wages. An individual without a high school diploma earned a median of $451 a week in 2011, compared to $1,150 for an individual with at least a bachelor's degree.

Based on: http://www.bls.gov.

The emphasis in Chapter 2 was on demonstrating ways to display our data graphically so that our brain cells could quickly absorb the big picture. With that task behind us, we can proceed to the next step—summarizing our data numerically. Chapter 3 focuses on how to calculate descriptive statistics manually and, if you so choose, how to verify these results with our good friend Excel. The *Stats in Practice* at the start of this chapter relied on the median to present income data over a five-year period. We will explore this measurement, along with many others, throughout Chapter 3. Also, I hope the **opening example** sends you another message loud and clear: Stay in school and get your degree!

3.1 Measures of Central Tendency

Central tendency is a single value used to describe the center point of a data set.

Most data sets have a tendency to concentrate around a specific value. For example, the histogram in Figure 3.1 shows that U.S. adult males from a sample have a tendency to cluster around a height of 70 in. This value is known as the **central tendency** for our data set. As we learned in Chapter 2, a histogram is a great tool for providing a picture to show where the central tendency can be found. In this chapter, we will explore how to precisely calculate the

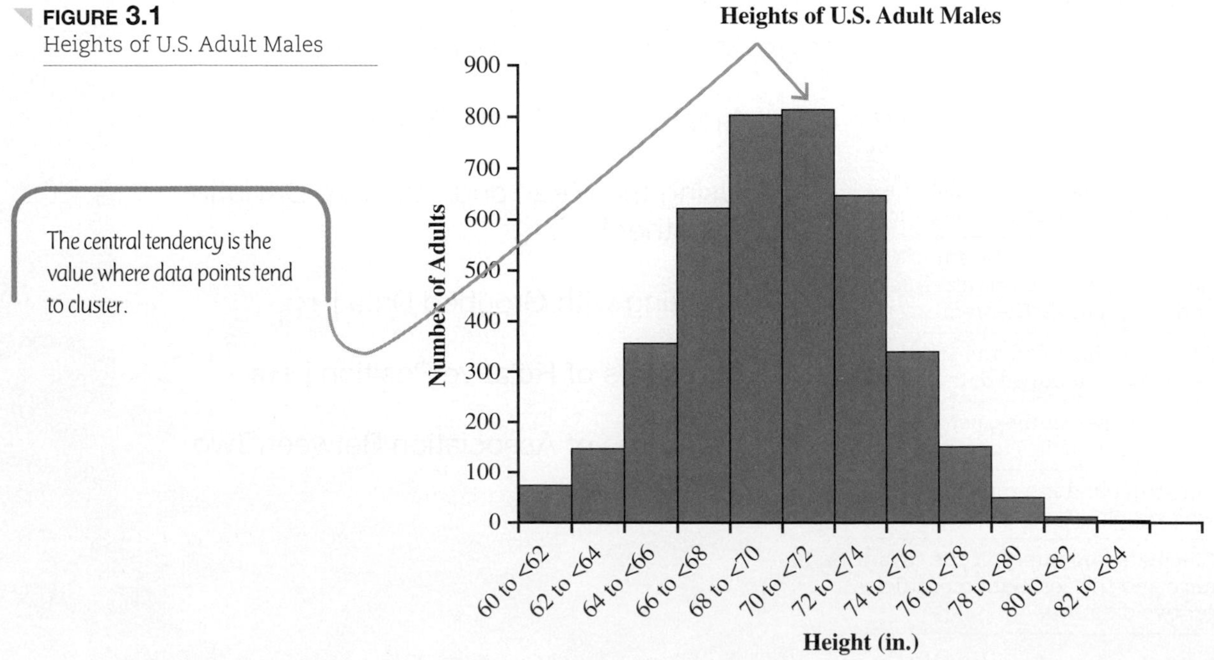

FIGURE 3.1 Heights of U.S. Adult Males

value that represents the central tendency of our data. As we will see in the following sections, our choices of central tendency measures are the mean, median, and mode.

The Mean

The **mean**, or **average**, which is the most common measure of central tendency, is calculated by adding all the values in a data set and then dividing the result by the number of observations.

The most common measure of central tendency is the **mean**, or **average**. We calculate the mean by adding all the values in our data set and then dividing the result by the number of observations. The mathematical formula for the mean differs slightly depending on whether you're referring to the mean of the sample or the mean of the population. The formula for the sample mean is shown in Equation 3.1.

Don't panic when you see the symbol $\sum_{i=1}^{n} x_i$. If our data sample contains the values 5, 8, and 2, then $n = 3, x_1 = 5, x_2 = 8$, and $x_3 = 2$, resulting in the following expression:

$$\sum_{i=1}^{3} x_i = x_1 + x_2 + x_3$$
$$= 5 + 8 + 2 = 15$$

Formula 3.1 for the Sample Mean

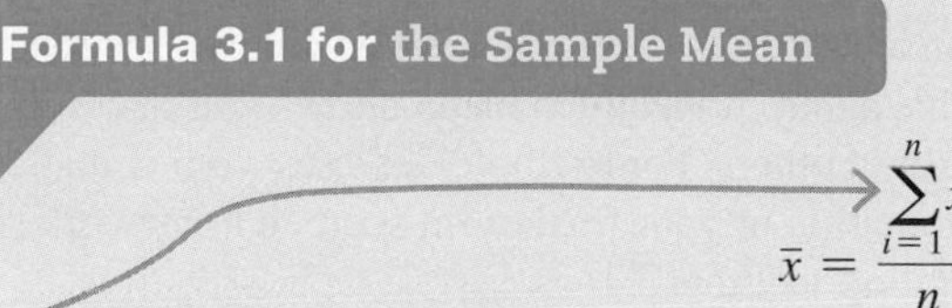

$$\bar{x} = \frac{\sum_{i=1}^{n} x_i}{n}$$

where

$\bar{x} =$ The sample mean
$x_i =$ The values in the sample ($x_1 =$ the first data value, $x_2 =$ the second data value, and so on)
$\sum_{i=1}^{n} x_i =$ The sum of all the data values in the sample
$n =$ The number of data values in the sample

To see how the sample mean is calculated, look at the following data set, which shows the annual household incomes (in thousands of dollars) of five randomly selected families in Delaware.

$87.2 $118.9 $76.2 $107.7 $61.5

These data values are a sample because they represent a subset of all of the households in Delaware.

The sample mean is found as follows:

$$\bar{x} = \frac{\sum_{i=1}^{n} x_i}{n} = \frac{87.2 + 118.9 + 76.2 + 107.7 + 61.5}{5} = \frac{451.5}{5} = \$90.3$$

The average income from our sample of five Delaware households is $90,300.

The population mean is calculated in the same way as the sample mean; the only difference is in the notation. The formula for determining the population mean is shown in Equation 3.2.

Formula 3.2 for the Population Mean

$$\mu = \frac{\sum_{i=1}^{N} x_i}{N}$$

where

$\mu =$ The population mean
$N =$ The number of data values in the population

Let's say you have just completed a statistics course that had four exams, and your scores are as follows:

89 95 87 97

This data set is a population because all of your exam scores for the course are included.

The population mean is shown as follows:

$$\mu = \frac{\sum_{i=1}^{N} x_i}{N} = \frac{89 + 95 + 87 + 97}{4} = \frac{368}{4} = 92$$

Your exam average was a 92. Very impressive!

The Weighted Mean

A **weighted mean** allows you to assign more weight to certain values and less weight to others.

When we calculated the average exam score in the previous example, we gave each data value the same weight in the calculation. A *weighted mean* refers to a mean that needs to go on a diet. Just kidding; I was checking to see whether you were paying attention. Let's try this again. A **weighted mean** allows you to assign more weight to certain values and less weight to others. For example, let's say your statistics grade this semester will be based on a combination of your final exam score, a homework score, and a final project, each weighted according to Table 3.1.

TABLE 3.1 | SCORES FROM A STATISTICS CLASS

TYPE	SCORE	WEIGHT (%)
Exam	94	50
Project	92	35
Homework	100	15

We can calculate your final grade using the following formula for a weighted average (Equation 3.3).

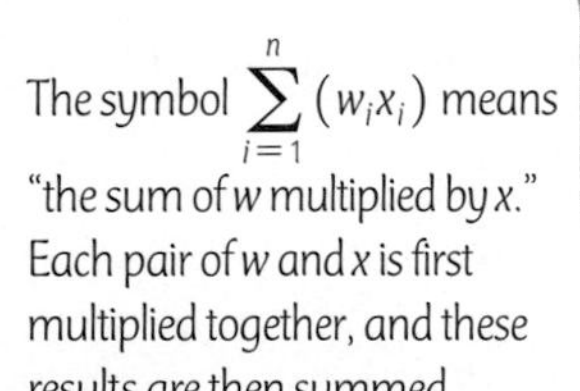

Formula 3.3 for the Weighted Mean

$$\bar{x} = \frac{\sum_{i=1}^{n} (w_i x_i)}{\sum_{i=1}^{n} w_i}$$

Note that in this equation, we are dividing by the sum of the weights rather than by the number of data values.

where

$w_i =$ The weight for each data value x_i

$\sum_{i=1}^{n} w_i =$ The sum of the weights

Table 3.2 sets up how to use Equation 3.3 for our statistics class example.

TABLE 3.2 | DATA USED TO CALCULATE A WEIGHTED MEAN

TYPE		SCORE	WEIGHT	WEIGHT × SCORE
	i	x_i	w_i	$(w_i x_i)$
Exam	1	94	0.50	47.0
Project	2	92	0.35	32.2
Homework	3	100	0.15	15.0

$$\sum_{i=1}^{3} w_i = 0.50 + 0.35 + 0.15 = 1.0$$

$$\sum_{i=1}^{3} (w_i x_i) = 47.0 + 32.2 + 15.0 = 94.2$$

We can obtain the same result by plugging the numbers directly into Equation 3.3, the formula for a weighted average:

$$\bar{x} = \frac{(0.50)(94) + (0.35)(92) + (0.15)(100)}{0.50 + 0.35 + 0.15} = \frac{47.0 + 32.2 + 15.0}{1.0} = 94.2$$

Congratulations—you earned an A!

The weights in a weighted average do not need to add up to 1.0 like they do in our example. For instance, the mean of a frequency distribution is simply a weighted mean calculation, as shown in the next example.

An airline company recorded the number of no-shows (people who fail to arrive at the gate on time to board a plane) for the past 120 flights. The frequencies are shown in Table 3.3. For 37 of the 120 flights, all of the passengers made it on board in time. There were zero no-shows, in other words. Thirty-one flights each had one passenger missing, 20 flights each had two passengers missing, and so on down the table. We would like to calculate the average number of no-shows per flight.

TABLE 3.3 | Frequency of No-Shows for Airline Flights

NUMBER OF NO-SHOWS	NUMBER OF FLIGHTS
0	37
1	31
2	20
3	16
4	12
5	4

To calculate the average number of no-shows per flight, use Equation 3.3. The weights would be the number of flights for each number of no-shows.

$$\bar{x} = \frac{\sum w_i x_i}{\sum w_i} = \frac{(37)(0) + (31)(1) + (20)(2) + (16)(3) + (12)(4) + (4)(5)}{37 + 31 + 20 + 16 + 12 + 4}$$

$$\bar{x} = \frac{187}{120} = 1.56 \text{ passengers}$$

The average number of no-shows per flight is 1.56 passengers.

Even though we can't have 1.56 passengers not show up for a particular flight, the average number of no-shows can be a fraction.

The Advantages and Disadvantages of Using the Mean to Summarize Data

The mean is a convenient measurement for summarizing a data set with a single value. Most students will agree with me when I say it's a pretty easy calculation to perform and understand. However, you need to beware of the mean's potential pitfalls.

I'll use the following example to demonstrate the first drawback of the mean. Suppose you have just been hired as a quality control manager for Kellogg's, and you are responsible for ensuring that each box of Frosted Flakes is properly filled with 18 ounces of cereal.

On Friday afternoon, your staff informs you that a sample of filled cereal boxes has an average weight of 18.1 ounces. Satisfied that the process is working well, you head home for a relaxing weekend, only to return Monday to customer complaints that their Frosted Flakes boxes were missing some Frosted Flakes! How can this be? When you ask to see the data from Friday's sample, you are shocked. The weights of the boxes sampled ranged widely. As the following equation shows, one box contained only 13.1 ounces of Frosted Flakes, whereas another contained a whopping 22.7 ounces!

When you rely on the mean to summarize many data values, you lose important information about the original data.

$$\bar{x} = \frac{\sum_{i=1}^{n} x_i}{n} = \frac{14.2 + 19.6 + 22.7 + 13.1 + 20.9}{5} = \frac{90.5}{5} = 18.1 \text{ ounces}$$

Obviously, the process was over-filling and under-filling boxes, resulting in a sample mean that led you to believe all was well. This example highlights one drawback of using the mean: When you summarize data with a single value, you lose information about the original data, which in this case was critical. On Tuesday, you find yourself updating your resume and searching the Internet for a new job.

Outliers are values that are much higher or lower than most of the data. The mean can be heavily influenced by outliers.

Another concern about relying on the mean involves how it is affected by outliers in the data. **Outliers** are extreme values above or below the mean that require special consideration. They could be caused by data entry errors or measurement errors. In this case, you should consider deleting these values from the data set to avoid distorting the analysis. However, the outlier could be a legitimate value that just happens to be very large or small and should remain in the analysis. Consequently, you will have to judge carefully whether to include the outlier. For example, the following data represent the appraised value of five homes in a particular cul-de-sac:

$300,000 $320,000 $270,000 $210,000 $8,000,000

The average value of the homes, in thousands of dollars, is

This outlier is causing the mean of this data set to be much higher than most of the remaining values, which can be misleading.

$$\mu = \frac{\sum_{i=1}^{N} x_i}{N} = \frac{300 + 320 + 270 + 210 + 8{,}000}{5} = \frac{9{,}100}{5} = \$1{,}820$$

As you can see, the average home value of $1,820,000 is much higher than most of the houses in the cul-de-sac. The one extreme home value of $8,000,000 distorts the population mean, making the rest of the homes in the cul-de-sac seem much more expensive than they actually are. We will discuss more about outliers and how to deal with them later in the chapter.

I don't mean to be mean, but I'm going to have you test your mean skills on this Your Turn.

YOUR TURN #1

1. The following data indicate the number of minutes eight randomly selected airline flights were either early (negative values) or late (positive values) arriving at their destinations. Calculate the sample mean.

   14 −17 31 −10 0 11 5 18

2. A company has four locations at which customers were surveyed about their satisfaction levels. The following table shows the average customer rating for each of the four locations along with the number of customers at each location who responded. Calculate the average customer rating for the entire company.

Location	Average Rating	Number of Customers
1	7.2	116
2	8.8	80
3	6.0	67
4	7.5	91

Answers can be found on ▶ **page 141**

The Median

The **median** is the value in the data set for which half the observations are higher and half the observations are lower.

The next measure of central tendency that we will explore is the median. The **median** is the value in the data set for which half the observations are higher and half the observations are lower. To demonstrate the technique for finding the median, consider the following data set, which represents nine quiz scores for a particular statistics student:

86 95 74 83 92 70 88 81 91

We find the median by first arranging the data values in ascending order:

70 74 81 83 86 88 91 92 95

The **index point** is used to determine the position of the median in the data set.

To determine the position of the median in our data set, we calculate the index point. The **index point**, *i*, marks the middle of the data values. We can calculate it using Equation 3.4.

Formula 3.4 for the Index Point for the Median

$$i = 0.5(n)$$

where n equals the number of data points, which in this case is nine.

$$i = 0.5(n) = 0.5(9) = 4.5$$

Whenever the index point is not a whole number, we round the value up to the next highest whole number, which, in this case, is five. The median exam score is therefore in the fifth position of our sorted data set and is shown in red:

When there are an odd number of data values, the median is always the middle value in the data set.

70 74 81 83 **86** 88 91 92 95

The median of our quiz scores is 86. Notice that our index point using Equation 3.4 found the middle value, which is the definition of the median. There are four quiz scores below and four quiz scores above the median.

In the last section, we discussed the fact that outliers in our data set can heavily affect the mean. This is not so with the median, as I will now demonstrate. Let's replace the quiz score of 70 with an abysmal score of 20, as shown as follows. (Aren't you glad it wasn't you that scored the 20?)

The outlier in this data set does not influence the median, which remains at 86.

20 74 81 83 **86** 88 91 92 95

Notice that the change has no impact on the median calculation. With nine data points, the median will always be in the fifth position, regardless of the values above and below it. One of the nice features of the median is that it is not influenced by outliers as the mean was in the previous section. Unfortunately, most instructors don't calculate grades based on the median but on the mean. The mean quiz score from this last example is 78.9 with the outlier data point, much lower than the median score of 86!

When we have an even number of data values, the procedure for finding the median differs slightly. Table 3.4 shows the closing stock prices for Dick's Sporting Goods at the end of each month between July and December 2012.

TABLE 3.4 | Closing Stock Prices for Dick's Sporting Goods

DATE	STOCK PRICE ($)
July 31	49.12
August 31	49.76
September 28	51.85
October 31	50.00
November 30	52.51
December 31	45.49

First, sort the stock prices from low to high:

$45.49 $49.12 $49.76 $50.00 $51.85 $52.51

Next, calculate the index point using Equation 3.4:

$$i = 0.5(n) = 0.5(6) = 3$$

When you have an even number of data points, and the index point is a whole number, the median lies halfway between the index point and next highest data point.

Here is where the difference lies when there is an even number of data points: When the index point is an even whole number, the position of the median is halfway between the index point (i) and the next highest data point (the $i + 1$ position). Because $i = 3$, the median is the midpoint between the 3rd value ($49.76) and 4th value ($50.00).

Median ↓

$45.49 $49.12 **$49.76** **$50.00** $51.85 $52.51

In other words, the median is halfway between the two middle values whenever we have an even number of data points. The following equation shows you how to find it:

$$\text{Median} = \frac{\$49.76 + \$50.00}{2} = \$49.88$$

YOUR TURN #2

A concept that some of my students struggle with is correctly assigning the median to the index point rather than the point between the middle two values in the data set. You can practice right now with this Your Turn section.

1. The following data represent the ages of 10 employees in a marketing department at a specific company. Identify the median age.

   26 45 39 28 57 31 43 45 50 62

2. The following data are the math SAT scores of nine students from St. Mark's High School. Identify the median SAT score.

   560 610 490 670 700 460 510 590 650

Answers can be found on ▶ **page 141**

The Mode

The **mode** is the value that appears most often in a data set.

The last measure of central tendency we'll discuss in this chapter is the mode, which gets the least amount of attention when compared with the mean and median. Nonetheless, the mode has some useful characteristics. The **mode** is simply the value that appears most often in a data set, as seen in the following example.

Table 3.5 shows last week's sales for a particular style of a woman's dress at my wife's favorite clothing store. The sales are shown by dress size.

TABLE 3.5 | DRESS SALES BY SIZE

SIZE	NUMBER SOLD
4	7
6	7
8	14
10	15
12	5
14	9

A word of warning: Some of my students mistakenly think that the mode equals 15, which is the number of dresses sold. Other students make the mistake of telling me the mode in this problem is 7 because it is the frequency that appears most often.

The mode for this data set is Size 10 because this is the dress size that had the most sales last week (15).

For this example, the mean or median would not be very useful. For instance, to report that the average dress size sold last week was 9.1 isn't very helpful to the manager of this department because there is no such dress size in the store.

The mode is a particularly useful way to describe categorical data such as the dress sizes in Table 3.5. Table 3.6 shows another distribution of categorical data—television sales categorized by brand. Suppose the data in Table 3.6 show the number of televisions by brand sold by a particular Walmart store last month.

TABLE 3.6 | TELEVISIONS SOLD BY WALMART

BRAND	NUMBER SOLD
Sony	21
Panasonic	9
Samsung	18
Sharp	11
Toshiba	15
Vizio	11

Categorical data are data that are described as a category or a label. Examples are gender (male or female), marital status (married, single, widowed), or yes/no responses.

I'm hoping that you recognize the data in Table 3.6 as **categorical data** from what you learned in Chapters 1 and 2. The mode is the only choice for describing this type of data because it is qualitative rather than quantitative. The Sony television brand would be the mode here because it had the highest frequency (21). When dealing with categorical data, the mode is the category with the highest frequency, rather than the actual frequency for that category.

Note that the mode is not 21. Nor is the mode equal to 11, the frequency that appears most often.

If no data value or category repeats more than once, then we say that the mode does not exist. Consider the following data, which represent the number of years of service for the faculty members in my department:

16 10 3 7 9 2 6

Because no value in this data set repeats itself, there is no mode.

Be careful not to claim that the mode is zero in this example. That is an incorrect statement because the value zero does not occur most frequently.

Also, more than one mode can exist, as the following data set shows. The data set indicates the number of students absent from my last 10 statistics classes.

2 0 1 3 1 4 2 0 1 2

We can sort the data to make identifying the mode easier.

0 0 **1 1 1 2 2 2** 3 4

The modes for the data, which are shown in red, are one student and two students because both values appear three times. Because the distribution has two modes, it is called a bimodal distribution.

Even if you're not in the "mode," I encourage you to take a minute to be sure you understand how to find the mode in this Your Turn section.

YOUR TURN #3

1. The following data represent the average hourly earnings in the United States for each month during 2012 according to www.data360.org. Determine the mode for these data.

Month	Earnings ($)	Month	Earnings ($)
January 2012	16.90	July 2012	16.85
February 2012	16.85	August 2012	16.75
March 2012	16.75	September 2012	16.71
April 2012	16.74	October 2012	16.73
May 2012	16.74	November 2012	16.86
June 2012	16.81	December 2012	16.94

2. The following data show the number of touchdown passes thrown by the NFL's top quarterbacks during the 2012 football season. Determine the mode for these data.

43	39	37	34	32	28	27	27	26	26	26	26
24	23	22	22	22	21	20	20	19	19	18	14

3. The following data represent the number of customers per day at a hardware store during the past 14 days. Determine the mode for these data.

67 62 57 31 69 32 83 49 80 53 38 36 46 41

4. The demand for various flavors of Rita's Water Ice yesterday is shown in the following table. Identify the mode.

Flavor	Number Sold
Lemon	37
Grape	46
Cherry	60
Orange	46
Lime	19

Answers can be found on ▶ **page 141**

The Shapes of Frequency Distributions

The positions of the mean and median will influence the shape of the frequency distribution for the data. Figure 3.2 shows a case in which the mean and median are approximately equal. This results in a symmetrical frequency distribution. Recall from Chapter 2 that a symmetrical distribution is one in which the right side of the distribution looks like the mirror image of the left side of the distribution.

In a symmetrical frequency distribution, the mean and median are roughly equal to each other.

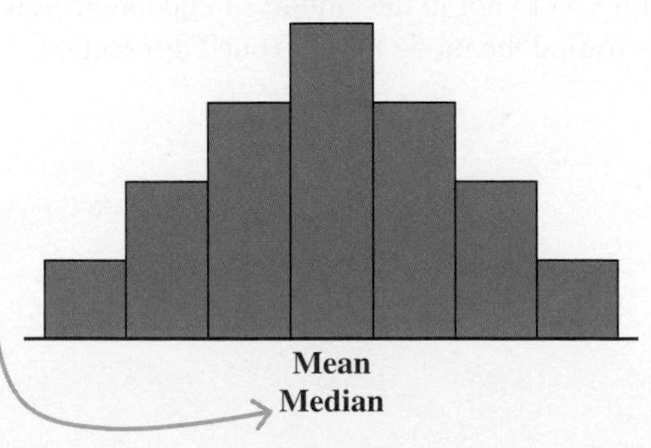

FIGURE 3.2
A Symmetrical Frequency Distribution

In a **left-skewed** distribution, the median is larger than the mean.

Figure 3.3 shows a distribution that's not symmetrical. Such a distribution is said to be skewed. Notice that higher data values dominate the data set. As you can see in this figure, the median is larger than the mean. As a result, the shape of the distribution is **left-skewed**, even though the data are concentrated on the right side. An easy way to remember this distribution is left-skewed is to observe that if you were skiing down the long slope of the graph, you would be moving in the left direction. For example, if grade inflation exists at your institution, which occurs when the grade point average (GPA) of the student body steadily increases over time, then a histogram of student GPAs will resemble a left-skewed distribution, as shown in Figure 3.3.

FIGURE 3.3
A Left-Skewed Frequency Distribution

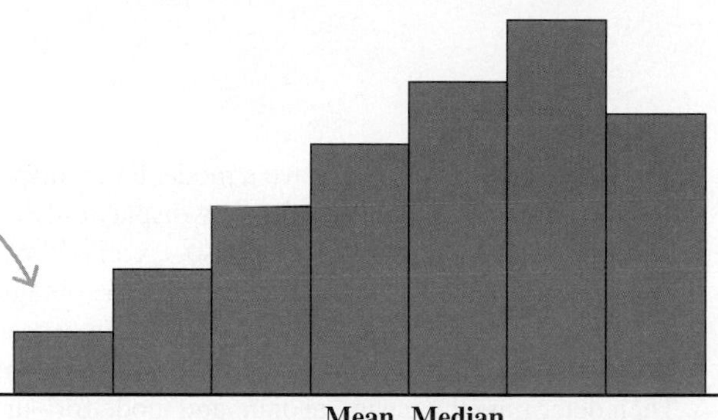

This distribution is left-skewed because if we were skiing down this slope, we would be moving toward the left.

In a **right-skewed** distribution, the median is less than the mean.

Figure 3.4 shows the opposite scenario, one in which the data are concentrated on the lower end of the distribution. Here the median is less than the mean. The shape of the distribution is **right-skewed** because we ski toward the right as we move down the slope. For example, annual income data tend to be right-skewed because most of us hardworking individuals tend to be in either the middle or somewhat to the left side of the income scale, whereas a few ultra-rich Warren Buffet–types of people are spread far to the right side of the distribution.

FIGURE 3.4
A Right-Skewed Frequency Distribution

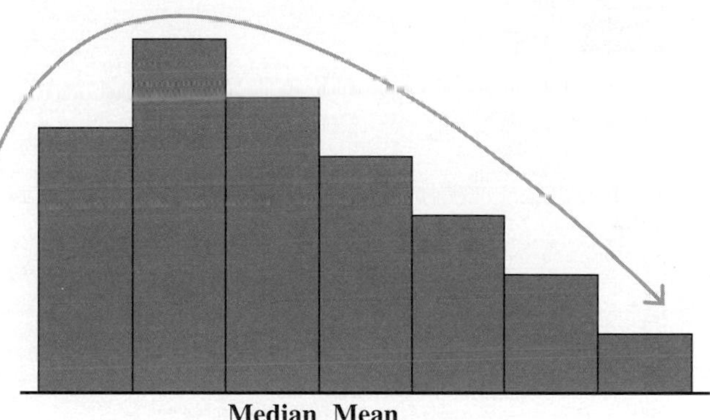

This distribution is right-skewed because if we were skiing down this slope, we would be moving toward the right.

Using Excel to Calculate the Mean, Median, and Mode

Excel provides a convenient method for determining the mean, median, and mode for your data set. We will demonstrate this with the following example. The following data represent the number of magazine subscriptions from 12 households:

4 1 0 8 2 5 4 6 1 5 2 1

Figure 3.5 shows the Excel equations used to calculate the mean, median, and mode for this data set. The Excel functions for these calculations are as follows:

=AVERAGE(*data values*)
=MEDIAN(*data values*)
=MODE.SNGL(*data values*)

As you can see from Figure 3.5, the mean = 3.25, the median = 3, and the mode = 1.

FIGURE 3.5
Excel Equations Used to Calculate the Mean, Median, and Mode

	A	B	C	D	E
1	4				
2	1		Mean	3.25	=AVERAGE(A1:A12)
3	0		Median	3	=MEDIAN(A1:A12)
4	8		Mode	1	=MODE.SNGL(A1:A12)
5	2				
6	5				
7	4				
8	6				
9	1				
10	5				
11	2				
12	1				
13					

Be sure you're aware of some of Excel's deficiencies when handling the mode.

If the data set does not have a mode, Excel displays "#N/A" in the cell. If there is more than one mode, Excel will incorrectly display only one mode from the data set, so use caution when relying on this feature. Also, Excel will not identify the mode for categorical data.

The mean, median, and mode can also be obtained using the Data Analysis tool in Excel for Windows. See the textbook's Web site (www.pearsonhighered.com/donnelly) for Excel for Mac instructions. If you haven't activated the tool yet, refer to Chapter 2 for instructions. Then determine the mean, median, and mode for our data by taking the following steps:

1. Place the data in Cells A1 through A12 as shown in Figure 3.6.
2. Select **Data > Data Analysis.**
3. In the **Data Analysis** dialog box, select **Descriptive Statistics** and click **OK.**

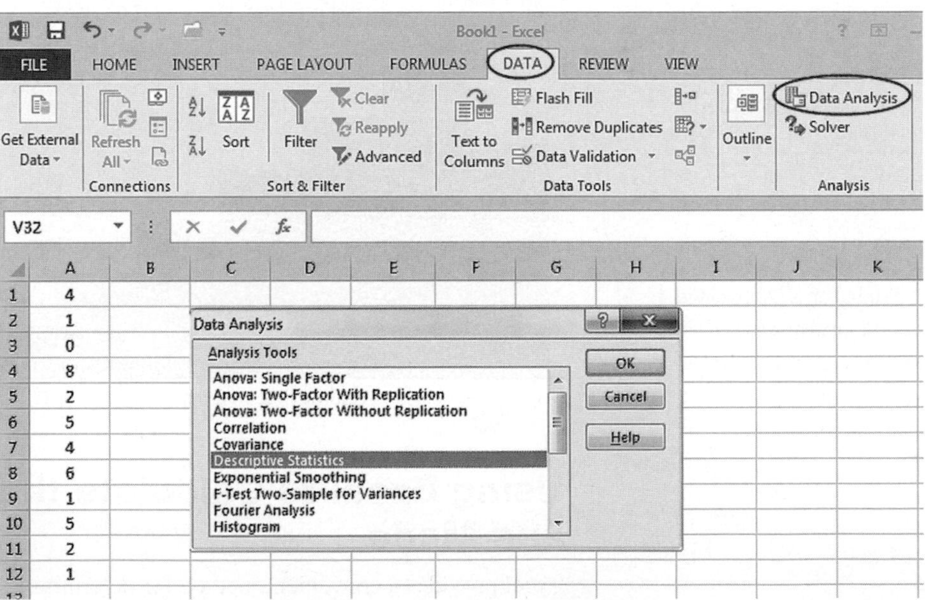

FIGURE 3.6
Using Excel's Data Analysis Tool to Calculate the Mean, Median, and Mode (Steps 1–3)

4. In the **Descriptive Statistics** dialog box, click on the textbox for **Input Range:** and select Cells A1:A12 as shown in Figure 3.7.
5. Click on the textbox for **Output Range:** and select Cell C1.
6. Check **Summary statistics**, and click **OK.**

The results are shown highlighted in red in Figure 3.8, which shows the mean = 3.25, the median = 3, and the mode = 1. We will discuss other values in this figure later on in the chapter.

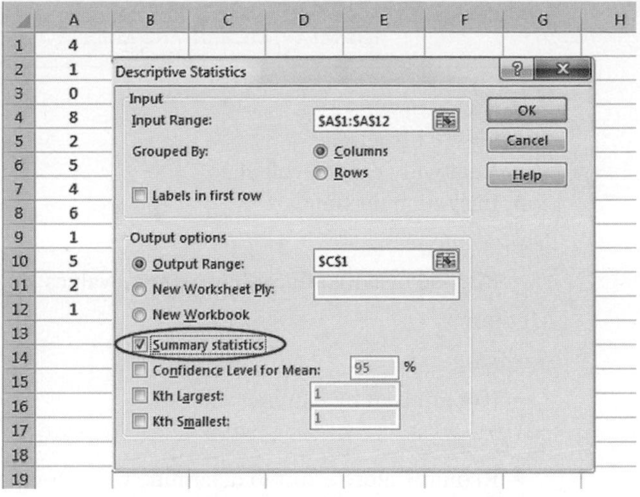

FIGURE 3.7
Using Excel's Data Analysis Tool to Calculate the Mean, Median, and Mode (Steps 4–6)

FIGURE 3.8
Using Excel's Data Analysis Tool to Calculate the Mean, Median, and Mode (Final Result)

	A	B	C	D
1	4		*Column1*	
2	1			
3	0		Mean	3.25
4	8		Standard Error	0.708445
5	2		Median	3
6	5		Mode	1
7	4		Standard Deviation	2.454125
8	6		Sample Variance	6.022727
9	1		Kurtosis	-0.64932
10	5		Skewness	0.495431
11	2		Range	8
12	1		Minimum	0
13			Maximum	8
14			Sum	39
15			Count	12
16				

Which Measure of Central Tendency Should You Use: The Mean, Median, or Mode?

Each of these measures of central tendency has its advantages and disadvantages. The mean is relatively easy to determine and most widely understood by people with little statistical training. As a result, it is by far the most popular choice for measuring the central tendency. However, as you learned, the mean can be heavily affected by outliers, which at times can be misleading.

When outliers are present in the data, the median is often the best choice because it is unaffected by them. However, the median requires a little more effort to determine if you are not using computer software such as Excel, especially when several data points are involved. The data need to be sorted from low to high values, and the index point needs to be calculated. In the many statistics exams I have given over the years (please don't ask how many), I have found that students struggle more with calculating the median when compared with calculating the mean. So give the median some extra practice when preparing for your next exam.

When describing the central tendency for categorical data, the mode is your only choice. However, there are two main drawbacks to using the mode. First, in many data sets, a mode does not exist. Second, there may be more than one mode in the data set, a situation that Excel does not properly identify. Table 3.7 summarizes our discussion of central tendency.

TABLE 3.7 | A Summary of the Advantages and Disadvantages of Using the Mean, Median, and Mode

Mean

Advantages

- Relatively easy to calculate
- Easy to understand

Disadvantages

- May be heavily affected by extreme values

Median

Advantages

- Not affected by extreme values

Disadvantages

- Requires more effort to determine when compared with the mean

Mode

Advantages

- Can be used with categorical data

Disadvantages

- Might not exist in some data sets
- Might not be unique (more than one mode may exist)

3.1 Section Problems

Basic Skills

3.1 Consider the following data values:

18 12 7 10 15 12 6 12 14

a. Calculate the mean.
b. Calculate the median.
c. Determine the mode.
d. Describe the shape of this distribution.

3.2 Consider the following data values:

6 14 17 1 16 17 6 19

a. Calculate the mean.
b. Calculate the median.
c. Determine the mode.
d. Describe the shape of this distribution.

3.3 Consider the following data values:

14 62 0 20 26 38 8

a. Calculate the mean.
b. Calculate the median.
c. Determine the mode.
d. Describe the shape of this distribution.

3.4 Consider the following data values:

25 18 −7 10 34 −12

a. Calculate the mean.
b. Calculate the median.
c. Determine the mode.
d. Describe the shape of this distribution.

Applications

3.5 The following table shows the monthly unemployment rate in the United States from January 2011 until January 2013. These data can also be found in the Excel file titled **US unemployment.xlsx.**

9.1 9.0 8.9 9.0 9.0 9.1 9.0 9.0 9.0 8.9 8.6 8.5 8.3

8.3 8.2 8.1 8.2 8.2 8.2 8.1 7.8 7.9 7.8 7.8 7.9

Based on: http://www.bls.gov.

a. Calculate the mean.
b. Calculate the median.
c. Determine the mode.
d. Describe the shape of this distribution.

3.6 Bank of America stock prices at the end of each month from February 2012 until January 2013 are shown as below. These data can also be found in the Excel file titled **Bank of America.xlsx.**

$7.97 $9.57 $8.11 $7.35 $8.18 $7.34

$7.99 $8.83 $9.32 $9.86 $11.61 $11.32

Based on: http://www.bigcharts.com

a. Calculate the mean.
b. Calculate the median.
c. Determine the mode.
d. Describe the shape of this distribution.

3.7 The following frequency distribution shows the various levels of demand for a particular laptop computer sold by Costco during the last 50 business days. Determine the average number of laptops sold per day.

Number of Laptops	Frequency
0	14
1	8
2	8
3	12
4	5
5	3

3.8 The following table shows the 2009 carbon emissions, in tons per capita, for various countries around the world. These data can also be found in the Excel file titled **emissions.xlsx.**

Country	Emissions	Country	Emissions
United States	17.7	Canada	16.2
Mexico	4.0	France	6.3
Italy	7.0	Russia	11.2
China	5.8	United Kingdom	8.4
Australia	19.6	Qatar	79.8
Brazil	2.1	Peru	1.3
India	1.4	Japan	8.6

Based on: International Energy Agency Data.

a. Calculate the mean.
b. Calculate the median.
c. Determine the mode.
d. Which of these three measurements would best describe the central tendency of the data?
e. Describe the shape of this distribution.

3.9 The following data represent the exchange rates for the euro in terms of U.S. dollars from March 2011 until February 2013. These data can also be found in the Excel file titled **Euro.xlsx**.

1.40	1.44	1.43	1.44	1.43	1.43
1.38	1.37	1.36	1.32	1.29	1.32
1.32	1.32	1.28	1.25	1.23	1.24
1.29	1.30	1.28	1.31	1.33	1.35

Based on: http://www.oanda.com.

a. Calculate the mean.
b. Calculate the median.
c. Determine the mode.
d. Which of these three measurements would best describe the central tendency of the data?
e. Describe the shape of this distribution.

3.10 Mark McGwire, a former Major League Baseball player who broke Roger Maris's single-season record for home runs in 1998, recently admitted to using performance-enhancing steroids, primarily during the second half of his 16-year career. McGwire claimed he used the steroids strictly for rehabilitation purposes and that they did not give him more power to hit home runs. The following data show the number of home runs McGwire hit during his first eight years of his career followed by the number hit during his last eight years.

1986–1993

3 49 32 33 39 22 42 9

1994–2001

9 39 52 58 70 65 32 29

For both data sets,

a. Calculate the mean.
b. Calculate the median.
c. Determine the mode.
d. Describe the shape of this distribution.
e. What conclusions can be drawn concerning Mark McGwire's claim?

3.2 Measures of Variability

Measures of variability show how much spread is present in the data.

Another way to describe a data set is through **measures of variability**, which determine how much spread is present in the data. For example, a student who gets A's in half of his classes and F's in the other half has the same GPA as a student who gets straight C's. However, the first student—the one with more variability in his grades—has to retake many courses. The second student—the one with less variability—does not have to retake any courses and can graduate on schedule. In business, less variability is an indication of more consistency, which is usually more desirable, especially in the area of quality control. Recall my example earlier in the chapter regarding the filling process for Frosted Flakes and how troublesome high variability was.

The most common measures of variability are the range, variance, and standard deviation. Although these measures are not as widely used by the typical person as the mean and median, they are extremely important to those in the field of statistics.

The Range

The **range**, which is one measure of variability, can found by subtracting the lowest value from the highest value in the data set.

The **range** is the difference between the highest value and the lowest value in a data set. The range, which is the simplest measure of a distribution's variability, can be found using Equation 3.5.

Formula 3.5 for the Range

$$\text{Range} = \text{Highest value} - \text{Lowest value}$$

The following data set shows five online donations recently received by the American Red Cross:

$35 $10 $50 $20 $60

The range for these data is shown as follows:

The range is the easiest measure of variability to calculate, but it has the most limitations, one being that it is highly affected by outliers.

$$\text{Range} = \$60 - \$10 = \$50$$

The benefit of the range is that it is easy to calculate and understand. However, this measure of variability has the following two drawbacks: (1) It is based only on two numbers in the data set, and (2) it is highly affected by outliers. For instance, if the last donation were changed from $60 to $1,000, the range would be $1,000 − $10 = $990, instead of $50. The $990 range does not accurately reflect the overall variability of our donations because most of the values lie between $10 and $50.

Stats in Practice: Using the Range to Measure Volatility

Although the range as a measurement of variability has its limitations, it can be useful when measuring volatility of the stock market. If a volatile day for the stock market is defined as a swing of more than 200 points, we can use the daily range of the stock market index to identify volatile days. Figure 3.9 shows the number of volatile days in the stock market from 2000 until 2012.

The surge in volatile days from 2008 to 2011 reflects the uncertainty in the financial markets as the economy struggled through a significant recession. The quiet period seen in 2012 represents a more stable market as investors showed more confidence in the economy. In this example, we've demonstrated that we can use the range to conclude that the economy is showing signs of recovering from the recent financial turmoil.

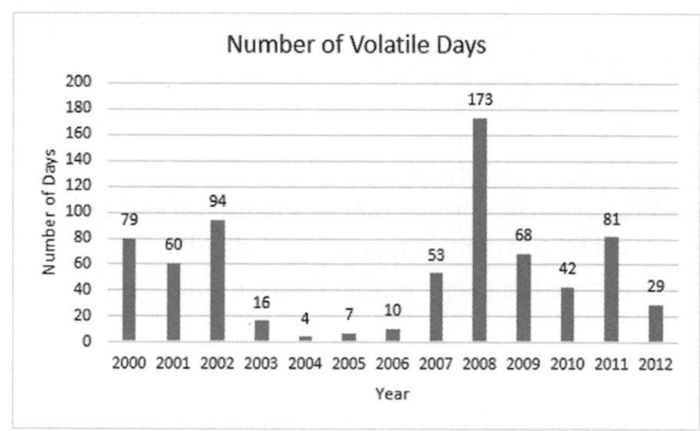

FIGURE 3.9
Number of Volatile Days in the Stock Market

The Variance and Standard Deviation

The **variance** measures the variability, or spread, of the data points in a set around the set's mean.

A much more useful measure of variability is the **variance**, which is determined by using all of the data values rather than only the highest and lowest. The variance measures the variability, or spread, of the data points in a set around the set's mean. The formula for calculating a variance will depend on whether your data set is a sample or a population. Next, we look at each scenario.

The Variance and Standard Deviation for a Sample

If our data set is a sample from a larger population, the sample variance, s^2, is found using Equation 3.6.

Formula 3.6 for the Sample Variance

$$s^2 = \frac{\sum_{i=1}^{n}(x_i - \bar{x})^2}{n-1}$$

where

$s^2 =$ The sample variance
$\bar{x} =$ The sample mean
$n =$ The sample size (number of data values)
$(x_i - \bar{x}) =$ The difference between each data value and the sample mean

Using our Red Cross donation data, we start the sample variance calculation by determining the sample mean:

$$\bar{x} = \frac{35 + 10 + 50 + 20 + 60}{5} = \frac{175}{5} = 35$$

Table 3.8 summarizes the following steps used to calculate the variance:

Step 1. Calculate the mean of the data set.

Step 2. Subtract the mean $(\bar{x})$ from each donation (x_i) in order to find the distance, or difference, between the mean and each donation. The differences are shown in the third column of Table 3.8.

Step 3. Square the differences that we calculated in Step 2. The squared differences are shown in the fourth column of Table 3.8.

Step 4. Add up the squared differences in the fourth column in Table 3.8, which in our Red Cross example equals 1,700.

TABLE 3.8 | SAMPLE VARIANCE CALCULATIONS FOR THE RED CROSS DONATIONS

x_i	$\bar{x}$	$(x_i - \bar{x})$	$(x_i - \bar{x})^2$
35	35	0	0
10	35	−25	625
50	35	15	225
20	35	−15	225
60	35	25	625
			Total $= \sum_{i=1}^{5}(x_i - \bar{x})^2 = 1{,}700$

We are now ready to calculate the sample variance by plugging our values into Equation 3.6:

$$s^2 = \frac{\sum_{i=1}^{n}(x_i - \bar{x})^2}{n-1} = \frac{1{,}700}{5-1} = 425$$

Your curious mind may be asking why we square the differences in Table 3.8. Well, I commend your curiosity. If we simply sum the differences between the mean and each data value (the third column in Table 3.8), we get the following:

$$\sum_{i=1}^{5}(x_i - \bar{x}) = 0 + (-25) + 15 + (-15) + 25 = 0$$

This result will happen with any data set—the sum of these differences will always be zero. The negative differences cancel out the positive differences. By squaring the differences, we remove the negative signs and get a true measure of the variation in our data set. This total squared difference is known as the sum of squares, which you will see more of in future chapters.

Now, I have a question for you: What is the unit of measure for the variance? Because the original data set is in dollars, and the variance calculation has squared the difference between each donation and the average donation, the unit of measure is dollars^2 (dollars squared). I know this unit of measure sounds strange, which leads me to the next measure of variability, the standard deviation.

The **standard deviation** is the square root of the variance. The unit of measure for the standard deviation is the same as the unit for the original data.

The **standard deviation** also measures the average distance between all of a set's data points and the mean. However, a nice feature of the standard deviation is that unlike the variance, the unit is not squared. Consequently, it matches those of the original data.

Next, let's look at how the standard deviation is calculated for a sample and then for a population.

The standard deviation is the most common and most important measure of variability throughout this textbook. Keep this section in mind for future reference!

The sample standard deviation, s, is the square root of the sample variance. Equation 3.7 shows the formula for finding the sample standard deviation.

Formula 3.7 for the Sample Standard Deviation

$$s = \sqrt{s^2} = \sqrt{\frac{\sum_{i=1}^{n}(x_i - \bar{x})^2}{n - 1}}$$

In our Red Cross donation example, the sample standard deviation is determined as follows:

$$s = \sqrt{s^2} = \sqrt{425} = 20.62$$

Therefore, the standard deviation from our donation sample is \$20.62. Feel better?

As you can see from the variance and standard deviation equations, we are simply measuring how far on average each data value is from the mean of the sample. The farther each value is from the mean, the larger a distribution's variance and standard deviation are. To help you grasp this important concept, Table 3.9 calculates the standard deviation for a sample in which all five donations are \$35. Because all five donations are \$35, the mean (average) donation is also \$35.

TABLE 3.9 | Sample Variance Calculations for the Red Cross Donations

x_i	$\bar{x}$	$(x_i - \bar{x})$	$(x_i - \bar{x})^2$
35	35	0	0
35	35	0	0
35	35	0	0
35	35	0	0
35	35	0	0
			$\sum_{i=1}^{5}(x_i - \bar{x})^2 = 0$

When all the data values in the sample are the same, the sample standard deviation equals zero.

$$s = \sqrt{\frac{\sum_{i=1}^{n}(x_i - \bar{x})^2}{n - 1}} = \sqrt{\frac{0}{5 - 1}} = \$0$$

Because there is no variability in the sample (all numbers are the same), the standard deviation equals \$0. Note that the variance and the standard deviation should *never* be negative values. If you obtain a negative result in your calculations, stop and go back to find your mistake.

Short-Cut Formulas for the Sample Variance and Standard Deviation

Now that I've tortured you with the nasty standard deviation equation, I'm going to show you a short-cut equation that gives you the same results with a little less work. I recommend using this method when you are calculating the variance and standard deviation manually.

Formula 3.8 for the Sample Variance (Short-Cut)

$$s^2 = \frac{\sum_{i=1}^{n} x_i^2 - \frac{\left(\sum_{i=1}^{n} x_i\right)^2}{n}}{n - 1}$$

where

$\sum_{i=1}^{n} x_i^2 =$ The sum of each data value after it has been squared

$\left(\sum_{i=1}^{n} x_i\right)^2 =$ The square of the sum of all data values

$n =$ The sample size

Formula 3.9 for the Sample Standard Deviation (Short-Cut)

$$s = \sqrt{\frac{\sum_{i=1}^{n} x_i^2 - \frac{\left(\sum_{i=1}^{n} x_i\right)^2}{n}}{n - 1}}$$

I recommend using this short-cut equation when calculating the standard deviation by hand, especially when the sample size is relatively large.

where

$\sum_{i=1}^{n} x_i^2 =$ The sum of each data value after it has been squared

$\left(\sum_{i=1}^{n} x_i\right)^2 =$ The square of the sum of all data values

$n =$ The sample size

I can imagine the look on your face right now. It's the same expression that I get from my students when I show them this so-called short-cut method. I admit that these equations appear nastier than the first ones we used, but before you call me crazy, let me demonstrate why they really aren't, using our Red Cross data.

The following steps, summarized in Table 3.10 for our Red Cross data, are used to calculate the variance using the short-cut formula:

Step 1. Sum up the total of the data values (x_i), shown in the first column of Table 3.10. For our Red Cross example, the sum of the donations is $\sum_{i=1}^{5} x_i = 175$.

Step 2. Square the result of Step 1. For our Red Cross example, the squared sum of the donations is $\left(\sum_{i=1}^{n} x_i\right)^2 = (175)^2 = 30{,}625$.

Step 3. Square each value from the first column (x_i^2). The squared values are shown in the second column of Table 3.10.

Step 4. Sum up the values in the second column of Table 3.10. For our Red Cross example, the sum of the squared donations is $\sum_{i=1}^{5} x_i^2 = 7{,}825$.

To calculate $\sum_{i=1}^{n} x_i^2$ (the sum of the squared values), square each data value and then add up the squared terms. To calculate $\left(\sum_{i=1}^{n} x_i\right)^2$ (the square of the sum), add up all the data values first and then square that sum.

TABLE 3.10 | Sample Variance Calculations for the Red Cross Donations (Short-Cut Method)

DATA VALUE (x_i)	DATA VALUE SQUARED (x_i^2)
35	1,225
10	100
50	2,500
20	400
60	3,600

Sum of the data values: $\sum_{i=1}^{5} x_i = 175$ **Sum of the squared data values:** $\sum_{i=1}^{5} x_i^2 = 7{,}825$

Squared sum of the data values: $\left(\sum_{i=1}^{n} x_i\right)^2 = (175)^2 = 30{,}625$

Now carefully plug in the values from Table 3.10 into Equation 3.8. Note that $n = 5$ because we have five donations in our sample.

The variance and the standard deviation should never be negative values. If you obtain a negative result in your calculations, stop and go back to find your mistake.

$$s^2 = \frac{\sum_{i=1}^{n} x_i^2 - \frac{\left(\sum_{i=1}^{n} x_i\right)^2}{n}}{n-1} = \frac{7{,}825 - \frac{30{,}625}{5}}{5-1} = \frac{7{,}825 - 6{,}125}{4} = 425$$

This result matches the sample variance we found earlier with less work. The short-cut method for calculating the variance by hand is less work than using Equation 3.6 because you don't have to (1) calculate the sample mean and (2) subtract the sample mean from each and every observation. These benefits become more substantial as the number of data points in the sample increases.

The Variance and Standard Deviation for a Population

If our data set represents an entire population rather than a sample from a population, the variance is determined using Equation 3.10.

Formula 3.10 for the Population Variance

$$\sigma^2 = \frac{\sum_{i=1}^{N} (x_i - \mu)^2}{N}$$

where

$\sigma^2 =$ The population variance
$\mu =$ The population mean
$N =$ The population size
$(x_i - \mu) =$ The difference between each data value and the population mean

The population standard deviation would simply be the square root of Equation 3.10.

Formula 3.11 for the Population Standard Deviation

$$\sigma = \sqrt{\frac{\sum_{i=1}^{N} (x_i - \mu)^2}{N}}$$

Rather than use these equations to calculate the population variance and standard deviation, I present the population short-cut versions to make your life easier.

Formula 3.12 for the Population Variance (Short-Cut)

$$\sigma^2 = \frac{\sum_{i=1}^{N} x_i^2 - \frac{\left(\sum_{i=1}^{N} x_i\right)^2}{N}}{N}$$

Formula 3.13 for the Population Standard Deviation (Short-Cut)

$$\sigma = \sqrt{\frac{\sum_{i=1}^{N} x_i^2 - \frac{\left(\sum_{i=1}^{N} x_i\right)^2}{N}}{N}}$$

where

$\sum_{i=1}^{N} x_i^2$ = The sum of each data value after it has been squared

$\left(\sum_{i=1}^{N} x_i\right)^2$ = The square of the sum of all data values

For example, suppose that at your school there are six statistics classes with the following student sizes:

34 25 41 32 25 29

These data would be considered a population because all current classes are included. Table 3.11 summarizes the population variance calculations.

TABLE 3.11 | POPULATION VARIANCE CALCULATIONS FOR THE CLASS SIZE

DATA VALUE (x_i)	DATA VALUE SQUARED (x_i^2)
34	1,156
25	625
41	1,681
32	1,024
25	625
29	841

Sum of the data values: $\sum_{i=1}^{6} x_i = 186$ **Sum of the squared data values:** $\sum_{i=1}^{6} x_i^2 = 5{,}952$

Squared sum of the data values: $\left(\sum_{i=1}^{6} x_i\right)^2 = (186)^2 = 34{,}596$

As with our previous example, we plug the results from Table 3.11 into Equation 3.12 to obtain the population variance for our class sizes.

$$\sigma^2 = \frac{\sum_{i=1}^{N} x_i^2 - \frac{\left(\sum_{i=1}^{N} x_i\right)^2}{N}}{N} = \frac{5{,}952 - \frac{34{,}596}{6}}{6} = \frac{5{,}952 - 5{,}766}{6} = 31$$

The population standard deviation is simply the square root of the population variance.

$$\sigma = \sqrt{\sigma^2} = \sqrt{31} = 5.57 \text{ students}$$

Using Excel to Calculate the Variance and Standard Deviation

We can also rely on Excel to calculate the sample variance and standard deviation from our Red Cross example, as shown in Figure 3.10. The Excel functions for the sample variance and standard deviation are shown here. Notice the letter S in VAR.S and STDEV.S, which indicates "sample."

=VAR.S(*data values*)

=STDEV.S(*data values*)

FIGURE 3.10
Calculating the Sample Variance and Standard Deviation Using Excel Formulas

	A	B	C	D	E
1	35				
2	10		Variance	425	=VAR.S(A1:A5)
3	50		Standard Deviation	20.62	=STDEV.S(A1.A5)
4	20				
5	60				

Measures of sample variability can also be determined using the Data Analysis Add-In. The following steps describe this procedure using our Red Cross donation data:

1. Place the Red Cross donation data in Cells A1 through A5.
2. Select **Data > Data Analysis**.
3. In the **Data Analysis** dialog box, select **Descriptive Statistics** and click **OK**.
4. In the **Descriptive Statistics** dialog box, click on the text box for **Input Range:** and select Cells A1:A5.
5. Click on the text box for **Output Range:** and select Cell C1.
6. Check **Summary statistics**, and click **OK**.

Figure 3.11 shows the Data Analysis output for our Red Cross example. The spreadsheet shows the sample standard deviation, variance, and range values in red that we calculated earlier in this section.

FIGURE 3.11
Calculating the Sample Variance and Standard Deviation Using Excel Data Analysis

	A	B	C	D
1	35		*Column1*	
2	10			
3	50		Mean	35
4	20		Standard Error	9.219544
5	60		Median	35
6			Mode	#N/A
7			Standard Deviation	20.61553
8			Sample Variance	425
9			Kurtosis	-1.89273
10			Skewness	0
11			Range	50
12			Minimum	10
13			Maximum	60
14			Sum	175
15			Count	5
16				

Excel also provides the following functions to calculate the population variance and standard deviation, for our class size example as shown in Figure 3.12. Notice the letter *P* in VAR.P and STDEV.P, which indicates "population."

=VAR.P(*data values*)

=STDEV.P(*data values*)

FIGURE 3.12
Calculating the Population Variance and Standard Deviation Using Excel Formulas

	A	B	C	D	E
1	34				
2	25		Variance	31	=VAR.P(A1:A6)
3	41		Standard Deviation	5.57	=STDEV.P(A1:A6)
4	32				
5	25				
6	29				
7					

Before you go any further in this chapter, try your hand at calculating the variances and standard deviations in the next Your Turn box.

YOUR TURN #4

The following data represent the number of books that seven adults have read during the past 12 months. Determine the variance and standard deviation of these data.

10 10 4 8 13 6 11

A local PNC Bank branch employs eight employees whose ages are shown here. Determine the variance and standard deviation of these data.

32 40 27 29 34 38 46 24

Answers can be found on ▶ **page 141**

Why Divide by $n - 1$ for the Sample Variance?

A common question that my students often ask is why the denominator in the population variance equation is N and the denominator for the sample variance equation is $n - 1$? As you will see in later chapters, we use the sample variance to provide a good estimate for the population variance. This is because we rarely know the population variance but we always have enough information to calculate the sample variance. As it turns out, using $n - 1$ in the denominator for the sample variance in Equation 3.6 is a much better estimate of the true population variance when compared to dividing by n. There are two ways to convince you of this phenomenon. The first way is to use a mathematical proof which will cause your eyes to glaze over and send your mind off to some faraway place. Or I can use a numerical example that might possibly result in an "ahha moment." I choose the latter.

Suppose I play the following game with my two-year old grandson, Caleb. I have three plastic cups turned upside down on the table in which I have hidden one, three, and five M&Ms, respectively. After moving the cups around on the table like a shell game, Caleb gets to pick one cup and eat the contents of his choice. (I'm assuming his mother will not be reading this. After all, that's what grandparents are for!) What I have described is a population with values 1, 3, and 5 $(N = 3)$ with the following mean and variance:

$$\mu = \frac{\sum_{i=1}^{N} x_i}{N} = \frac{1 + 3 + 5}{3} = 3$$

$$\sigma^2 = \frac{\sum_{i=1}^{N} (x_i - \mu)^2}{N} = \frac{(1 - 3)^2 + (3 - 3)^2 + (5 - 3)^2}{3} = \frac{8}{3} = 2.67$$

After replacing the M&M's that Caleb has eaten from his first choice, I move the cups around and we repeat the game one more time. At this point, I have drawn a sample size of two from this population $(n = 2)$ by allowing Caleb to pick a cup twice. The real challenge is to now convince Caleb that the game is over. Table 3.12 shows the following information:

Column 1: All of the possible combinations of M&M's that Caleb will eat after twice choosing a cup.

Column 2: The sample mean for each of the combinations in Column 1 using Equation 3.2.

Column 3: The sample variance for each of the combinations in Column 1 using Equation 3.6.

Column 4: The result of replacing $n - 1$ with n in the denominator of Equation 3.6.

The variance calculations for the first two samples in this table are shown for you.

TABLE 3.12 | POSSIBLE COMBINATIONS OF CHOOSING A SAMPLE OF SIZE TWO FROM A POPULATION OF SIZE THREE

(1) Possible Combinations	(2) Sample Mean	(3) Sample Variance	(4)
	$\bar{x} = \frac{\sum_{i=1}^{n} x_i}{n}$	$s^2 = \frac{\sum_{i=1}^{n} (x_i - \bar{x})^2}{n - 1}$	$\frac{\sum_{i=1}^{n} (x_i - \bar{x})^2}{n}$
(1,1)	1	$\frac{(1-1)^2 + (1-1)^2}{2-1} = 0$	$\frac{(1-1)^2 + (1-1)^2}{2} = 0$
(1,3)	2	$\frac{(1-2)^2 + (3-2)^2}{2-1} = 2$	$\frac{(1-2)^2 + (3-2)^2}{2} = 1$
(1,5)	3	8	4
(3,1)	2	2	1
(3,3)	3	0	0
(3,5)	4	2	1
(5,1)	3	8	4
(5,3)	4	2	1
(5,5)	5	0	0

Caleb might not understand statistics (yet) but he sure loves finding five M&Ms!

If the sample variance is a good estimate of the true population variance, then I would expect that the *average* sample variance from all nine samples (Column 3) in Table 3.12 would be equal to the population variance. Let's check it out:

$$\text{Average Sample Variance} = \frac{0 + 2 + 8 + 2 + 0 + 2 + 8 + 2 + 0}{9} = \frac{24}{9} = 2.67$$

Even though none of the sample variances in Column 3 of Table 3.12 equals the population variance (2.67), their average does equal 2.67. Because if this phenomenon, we call the sample variances found in Column 3 **unbiased estimators** of the population variance.

The sample variance is an **unbiased estimator** of the population variance because we would expect the average of many sample variances taken from a population would be equal to the true population variance.

The same can't be said for the average of Column 4 where we used n rather than $n - 1$ in the denominator:

$$\text{Average of Column 4} = \frac{0 + 1 + 4 + 1 + 0 + 1 + 4 + 1 + 0}{9} = \frac{12}{9} = 1.33$$

I hope this little demonstration convinced you that using $n - 1$ in the denominator of the sample variance calculation provides a better estimate of the true population variance in comparison to using n. (Special thanks to Caleb Nelson for his invaluable participation in this highly important experiment.)

3.2 Section Problems

Basic Skills

3.11 Consider the following sample data values:

18 12 7 10 15 12 6 12 14

a. Calculate the range.
b. Calculate the variance.
c. Calculate the standard deviation.

3.12 Consider the following sample data values:

5 11 17 23 14 16 11 17

a. Calculate the range.
b. Calculate the variance.
c. Calculate the standard deviation.

3.13 Consider the following population data values:

14 41 0 20 26 38 8

a. Calculate the range.
b. Calculate the variance.
c. Calculate the standard deviation.

3.14 Consider the following population data values:

25 18 −7 10 34 −12

a. Calculate the range.
b. Calculate the variance.
c. Calculate the standard deviation.

Applications

3.15 A local Holiday Inn asked customers to rate their stays on a scale of 1–10. The following list shows the ratings given by the last 10 customers:

8 8 7 10 6 9 5 7 6 8

a. Calculate the range.
b. Calculate the variance.
c. Calculate the standard deviation.

3.16 The following list represents the number of absent students from my last nine statistics classes:

2 4 0 1 6 1 3 2 3

a. Calculate the range.
b. Calculate the variance.
c. Calculate the standard deviation.

3.17 Every 10 years, the U.S. Census Bureau asks people about the number of people living within their households. The following list shows how eight households responded to the question.

5 1 2 6 4 4 3 5

a. Calculate the range.
b. Calculate the variance.
c. Calculate the standard deviation.

3.18 The following values represent the number of iPhones sold per day at a local AT&T retail store during the last 10 business days:

14 5 6 11 18 10 10 12 3 15

a. Calculate the range.
b. Calculate the variance.
c. Calculate the standard deviation.

3.19 The following list shows the starting salaries, in thousands of dollars, for 11 recent college graduates with business degrees:

36 32 40 35 32 41 35 44 38 37 40

a. Calculate the range.
b. Calculate the variance.
c. Calculate the standard deviation.

3.3 Using the Mean and Standard Deviation Together

The standard deviation is a common measure of consistency in business applications, particularly in the area of quality control. Let's go back to our Frosted Flakes example from earlier in the chapter, where we sampled five 18-ounce boxes and weighed the contents. Sample 1 in Table 3.13 represents the sample that caused customers to complain about missing Frosted Flakes. The mean of the sample appears to be satisfactory at 18.1 ounces. Consequently, you figured the population of boxes was OK, which cost you your job. The problem lies with too much variability in the sample, which is reflected by a standard deviation of 4.23 ounces. Sample 2 in Table 3.13 is a more acceptable sample from a quality control perspective. The sample mean is still 18.1 ounces, but the variability is much lower: The standard deviation is only 0.12 ounces. The standard deviation calculations are also shown in Table 3.13. This example demonstrates the fact that the sample mean alone does not provide sufficient information in a quality control setting. The sample standard deviation must also be investigated to confirm the filling process is working properly.

TABLE 3.13 | Frosted Flakes Samples: The Mean vs. the Standard Deviation

	Sample 1 (oz)	Sample 2 (oz)
Box 1	14.2	18.2
Box 2	19.6	17.9
Box 3	22.7	18.1
Box 4	13.1	18.1
Box 5	20.9	18.2
Mean	18.1	18.1
Standard deviation	**4.23**	**0.12**

	Sample 1		Sample 2	
	x (oz)	x^2 (oz^2)	x (oz)	x^2 (oz^2)
	14.2	201.64	18.2	331.24
	19.6	384.16	17.9	320.41
	22.7	515.29	18.1	327.61
	13.1	171.61	18.1	327.61
	20.9	436.81	18.2	331.24
Total	**90.5**	**1,709.51**	**90.5**	**1,638.11**

Sample 1

$$s_1 = \sqrt{\frac{\sum_{i=1}^{n} x_i^2 - \frac{\left(\sum_{i=1}^{n} x_i\right)^2}{n}}{n-1}}$$

$$s_1 = \sqrt{\frac{1{,}709.51 - \frac{(90.5)^2}{5}}{5-1}}$$

$$s_1 = 4.23 \text{ oz}$$

Sample 2

$$s_2 = \sqrt{\frac{\sum_{i=1}^{n} x_i^2 - \frac{\left(\sum_{i=1}^{n} x_i\right)^2}{n}}{n-1}}$$

$$s_1 = \sqrt{\frac{1{,}638.11 - \frac{(90.5)^2}{5}}{5-1}}$$

$$s_2 = 0.12 \text{ oz}$$

In quality control settings, businesses prefer a smaller standard deviation, which is an indication of more consistency in the process.

In this example, we were able to compare two different standard deviations because the means from both samples were identical. When sample means are very different, comparing standard deviations can be misleading. This is because the size of the standard deviation is affected by the scale of the data. Larger data values will tend to generate larger standard deviations. This scenario is covered in the following section.

The Coefficient of Variation

The **coefficient of variation,** *CV*, measures the standard deviation in terms of its percentage of the mean.

The **coefficient of variation**, *CV*, measures a distribution's standard deviation in terms of its percentage of the mean. A high *CV* is an indication of high variability, or less consistency, in the data. In other words, the data points vary widely among themselves.

Comparing the consistency between two data sets when their means are very different is best done with the coefficient of variation. It is a useful measure because two different data sets are likely to have different means. The coefficient of variation gives us a common measure—a percentage—we can use to compare the two sets. That way, instead of comparing apples to oranges, we can compare apples to apples (or oranges to oranges, depending on the fruit you prefer).

Equation 3.14 shows the formula for the coefficient of variation for a sample. Equation 3.15 shows the formula for the coefficient of variation for a population.

Formula 3.14 for the Sample Coefficient of Variation

$$CV = \frac{s}{\bar{x}}(100)$$

where

$s =$ The sample standard deviation
$\bar{x} =$ The sample mean

Formula 3.15 for the Population Coefficient of Variation

$$CV = \frac{\sigma}{\mu}(100)$$

where

$\sigma =$ The population standard deviation
$\mu =$ The population mean

As you can see, the coefficient of variation measures the standard deviation in terms of its percentage of the mean. When comparing two samples, the smaller CV indicates more consistency (or less variability) within the sample or population.

A smaller coefficient of variation indicates more consistency within a set of data values.

To demonstrate this approach, let's compare the stock price of Nike to that of Google during the same six-month period to determine which company's stock price was more consistent. Table 3.14 shows the stock prices along with the mean and standard deviation for each of the two stocks.

TABLE 3.14 | STOCK PRICES FOR NIKE AND GOOGLE

DATE	NIKE ($)	GOOGLE ($)
September 14, 2012	48.32	709.68
October 15, 2012	47.81	740.98
November 15, 2012	45.42	647.26
December 14, 2012	48.46	701.96
January 15, 2013	53.64	724.93
February 15, 2013	54.95	792.89
Mean	49.77	719.62
Standard deviation	3.70	47.96

Based on: http://www.bigcharts.com.

The coefficient of variation for each sample is computed as follows:

$$\text{Nike:} \quad CV = \frac{s}{\bar{x}}(100) = \frac{\$3.70}{\$49.77}(100) = 7.4\%$$

$$\text{Google:} \quad CV = \frac{s}{\bar{x}}(100) = \frac{\$47.96}{\$719.62}(100) = 6.7\%$$

Even though Google's stock price has a higher standard deviation than Nike's does, it is more consistent because its coefficient of variation is lower. Take this opportunity to check out the following Your Turn box. Here you will have the chance to compare the home-run consistency of two Major League Baseball players. Sounds like fun to me!

YOUR TURN #5

The following table shows the number of home runs hit by Jimmy Rollins and Albert Pujols over eight consecutive Major League Baseball seasons. These data can also be found in the Excel file titled **homerun cv.xlsx**. Who was the more consistent home-run hitter?

Year	Rollins	Pujols
2005	12	41
2006	25	49
2007	30	32
2008	11	37
2009	21	47
2010	8	42
2011	16	37
2012	23	30

Based on: http://www.espn.com.

Answer can be found on ▶ **page 142**

Stats in Practice: Variability Is Not Always a Bad Thing

Earlier in this section, we discussed the problems that a high variability causes in a quality control setting. However, there are situations in the business world in which variability is viewed positively. For instance, Herr Foods, a producer of a variety of salty snacks (including my favorite potato chips), performs taste tests to compare how consumers react to its products. A product such as horseradish cheddar chips is considered a polarizing product because it has a very strong taste. Consumers tend to rate the product very high or very low, which results in highly variable taste-test ratings for the product. A more standard product, such as regular tortilla chips, typically receives more consistent ratings. Suppose the following table shows how seven customers rated each product on a scale of 1–10. The mean and standard deviation for each sample are also shown in the table.

	Horseradish Cheddar Chips	Tortilla Chips
	4	8
	10	8
	10	7
	3	8
	10	8
	9	10
	10	7
Mean	**8.0**	**8.0**
Standard deviation	**3.1**	**1.0**

(continued)

Even though both products have the same average (mean) rating, the horseradish cheddar results are viewed more positively from a marketing perspective because of the higher standard deviation. Herr Foods does not consider high variability in the testing scores a problem if the product has a strong flavor.[1]

[1] Special thanks to Don Kirkley from Herr Foods for providing this material.

The z-Score

The ***z*-score** identifies the number of standard deviations a particular value is from the mean of its distribution.

One of the most common measurements in statistics is the ***z*-score**, which identifies the number of standard deviations a particular value is from the mean of its population or sample. Equation 3.16 shows how the z-score for a population is computed.

I assure you that this equation will be used over and over again throughout this textbook, so be sure to become familiar with it.

Formula 3.16 for the Population z-score

$$z = \frac{x - \mu}{\sigma}$$

where

$x =$ The data value of interest
$\mu =$ The population mean
$\sigma =$ The population standard deviation

If our data are from a sample, we would use Equation 3.17 to compute the z-score.

Formula 3.17 for the Sample z-score

$$z = \frac{x - \bar{x}}{s}$$

where

$x =$ The data value of interest
$\bar{x} =$ The sample mean
$s =$ The sample standard deviation

To illustrate z-scores, we'll use Table 3.15, which shows the number of calories contained in a sample of fast-food hamburgers. Also shown are the mean and standard deviation for the sample, which you can verify using Excel. (Try not to drool lest you get your textbook wet.)

TABLE 3.15 | CALORIES FOR VARIOUS FAST-FOOD HAMBURGERS

HAMBURGER TYPE	RESTAURANT	CALORIES
Cheeseburger	McDonald's	300
Single with everything	Wendy's	430
Big Mac	McDonald's	540
Whopper	Burger King	670
Bacon cheeseburger	Sonic	780
Baconator	Wendy's	840
Triple whopper with cheese	Burger King	1,230
⅔ lb. Monster thickburger	Hardee's	1,420
	Sample Mean	**776.3**
	Sample Standard Deviation	**385.1**

Let's calculate the z-score for the Triple Whopper with Cheese using Equation 3.17:

$$z = \frac{x - \bar{x}}{s} = \frac{1{,}230 - 776.3}{385.1} = \frac{453.7}{385.1} = 1.18$$

What does the number 1.18 tell us? Well, our Triple Whopper w/Cheese is 453.7 calories above the sample mean. If one standard deviation is 385.1 calories, then our burger is slightly more than one standard deviation (1.18) above the sample mean.

The z-score for the Big Mac demonstrates this concept for values below the mean:

$$z = \frac{x - \bar{x}}{s} = \frac{540 - 776.3}{385.1} = \frac{-236.3}{385.1} = -0.61$$

The Big Mac is 236.3 calories below our sample mean, which translates to -0.61 standard deviations. Our z-score is negative, indicating our data value is lower than the sample mean.

Had one of our hamburgers in our sample been exactly 776.3 calories, the z-score for this selection would be as follows:

$$z = \frac{x - \bar{x}}{s} = \frac{776.3 - 776.3}{385.1} = \frac{0}{385.1} = 0.0$$

In general, z-scores will always have the following attributes:

- Positive for values above the mean
- Negative for values below the mean
- Zero for values equal to the mean

Think of the z-score calculation as simply converting the value of x to a different set of units, like converting feet to inches.

The z-score is analogous to expressing the original data in other units, such as converting 2 feet to 24 in. In our example, the 540 calories for the Big Mac is being converted to a z-score of -0.61. However, the z-score itself has no units, even though the original values will normally be expressed in units such as dollars, years, pounds, and calories.

The following *Stats in Practice* box highlights another use of the z-score.

Stats in Practice: Comparing Olympic Performances

How does one compare great performances of athletes competing in different sports? Take, for example, the 2010 Winter Olympic Games in Vancouver. How does the performance of Switzerland's Simon Ammann, who won the Large Hill Ski Jumping event by a margin of 14.2 points, compare to the United State's Shani Davis, who won the 1,000-m Speedskating event by 0.18 seconds? Which performance was more dominant?

This question was answered in the *Wall Street Journal* article titled "The Best Olympic Performances So Far" by Matthew Futterman. In order to compare performances across sporting events, we need to convert the winning scores to a common measurement scale. The z-scores that we have been discussing in this chapter provide the perfect solution.

Mr. Futterman calculated the z-scores for the winning time or score for Olympic events. These values represent the number of standard deviations the winning performance was from the average performance in that particular event. Congratulations to France's Jay Vincent, who is credited with the most dominant performance of the 2010 Winter Olympics. His 12.2-second margin of victory in the 10K Sprint Biathlon event is 2.13 standard deviations below the average time in this event.

Now, back to our first question of whose performance was more dominant: Simon Ammann's Large Hill Ski Jumping Event or Shani Davis' 1,000-m Speedskating event. Ammann's 14.2-point margin was 2.01 standard deviations above the average score whereas Shani Davis' 0.18-second margin was less—1.81 standard deviations below the average time.

Based on: Matthew Futterman, "The Best Olympic Performances So Far," *Wall Street Journal*, February 24, 2010, http://online.wsj.com.

Outliers are extreme values in the data set that require special consideration.

Finally, we can use z-scores to identify outliers in the data set. Data values that have z-scores above $+3$ or below -3 are categorized as **outliers**. Table 3.16 shows the z-scores for the calories in each of our fast-food hamburgers.

TABLE 3.16 | z-SCORES FOR FAST-FOOD HAMBURGERS

HAMBURGER TYPE	CALORIES		
	x_i	$(x_i - \bar{x})$	z
Cheeseburger	300	−476.3	−1.24
Single with everything	430	−346.3	−0.90
Big Mac	540	−236.3	−0.61
Whopper	670	−106.3	−0.28
Bacon cheeseburger	780	3.7	0.01
Baconator	840	63.7	0.17
Triple whopper with cheese	1,230	453.7	1.18
⅔ lb. Monster thickburger	1,420	643.7	1.67

None of the hamburgers listed in Table 3.16 would be classified as an outlier because all of the z-scores are within ± 3 standard deviations from the sample mean. Even the gut-busting, stroke-inducing Monster Thickburger didn't qualify as an outlier because its z-score was only 1.67 standard deviations above the mean. (Please don't use this as an endorsement to consume one!)

The STANDARDIZE function in Excel will calculate z-scores for us using Equation 3.17 and is executed as follows:

$$= \text{STANDARDIZE}(x, \text{mean}, \text{standard deviation})$$

Using our Big Mac example, we have the following:

$$= \text{STANDARDIZE}(540, 776.3, 385.1) = -0.61$$

In Chapter 8 we will use z-scores to explore how statistics can be used to make inferences about a population based on a sample taken from that population. As I mentioned earlier, z-scores will be used extensively in this textbook. So file this information somewhere safe in your brain for easy access later.

The Empirical Rule

According to the **empirical rule,** if a distribution follows a bell-shaped, symmetrical curve centered around the mean, we would expect approximately 68%, 95%, and 99.7% of the values to fall within one, two, and three standard deviations above and below the mean, respectively.

The values of many large data sets sometimes cluster around the mean or median so that the data distribution in the histogram resembles a bell-shape, symmetrical curve. When this is the case, according to the **empirical rule** (sounds like a decree from the emperor) approximately 68%, 95%, and 99.7% of the values will fall within $\pm$ one, two, and three standard deviations of the mean, respectively. In other words, almost all of the values—99.7%—will fall within $\pm$ three standard deviations of the mean. (The empirical rule is also sometimes called the 68-95-99.7 rule.)

For example, suppose that the average exam score for my large statistics class is 80 points, the standard deviation is 5.0 points, and the distribution of grades is bell-shaped around the mean, as shown in the shaded region in Figure 3.13. Because one standard deviation above the mean would be 85 $(80 + 5)$ and one standard deviation below the mean would be 75 $(80 - 5)$, the empirical rule tells us that approximately 68% of the exam scores will fall between 75 and 85 points.

We can also calculate these exam scores by rearranging Equation 3.16 in terms of x (the population) rather than z (the z-score), as shown in Equation 3.18 on the next page.

If the data are bell-shaped and somewhat symmetrical, we expect practically all the data values to lie with three standard deviations from the center of the data.

Formula 3.18 for Expressing the z-Score in Terms of x

$$x = \mu + z\sigma$$

We can find the exam scores that are one standard deviation above and below the mean by setting $z = 1$ and $z = -1$.

$$x = \mu + z\sigma$$
$$x = 80 + (1)(5) = 85$$
$$x = 80 + (-1)(5) = 75$$

FIGURE 3.13 Percentage of Exam Scores That Are One Standard Deviation Around the Mean

The empirical rule applies only to bell-shaped curves that are relatively symmetrical.

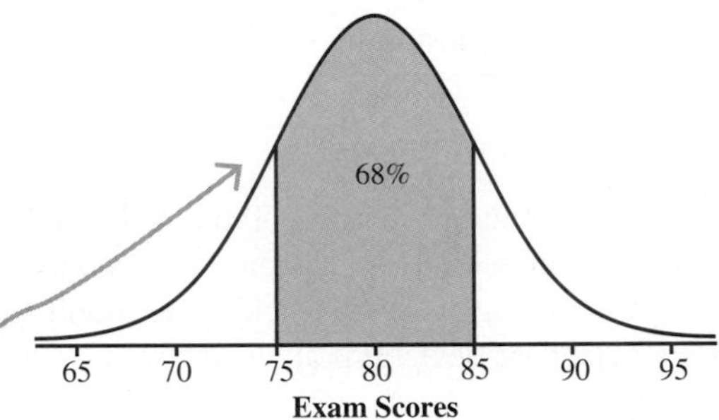

The empirical rule also states that approximately 95% of the data values will fall within two standard deviations above and below the mean. In our example, the exam scores that are two standard deviations from the mean are as follows:

$$x = 80 + (2)(5) = 90$$
$$x = 80 + (-2)(5) = 70$$

According to Figure 3.14, approximately 95% of the exam scores will be between 70 and 90 points.

FIGURE 3.14 Percentage of Exam Scores That Are Two Standard Deviations Around the Mean

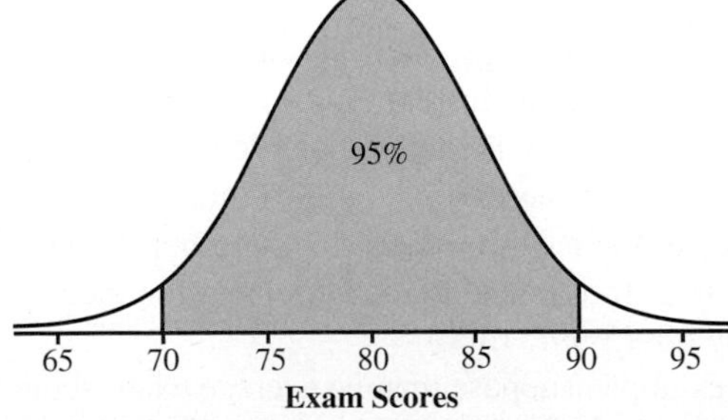

Taking this one final step, the empirical rule states that, under these conditions, approximately 99.7% of the data values will fall within three standard deviations above and below the mean. In our example, the exam scores that are three standard deviations from the mean are as follows:

$$x = 80 + (3)(5) = 95$$
$$x = 80 + (-3)(5) = 65$$

According to Figure 3.15, I would expect nearly all the exam scores to be between 65 and 95.

FIGURE 3.15
Percentage of Exam Scores That Are Three Standard Deviations Around the Mean

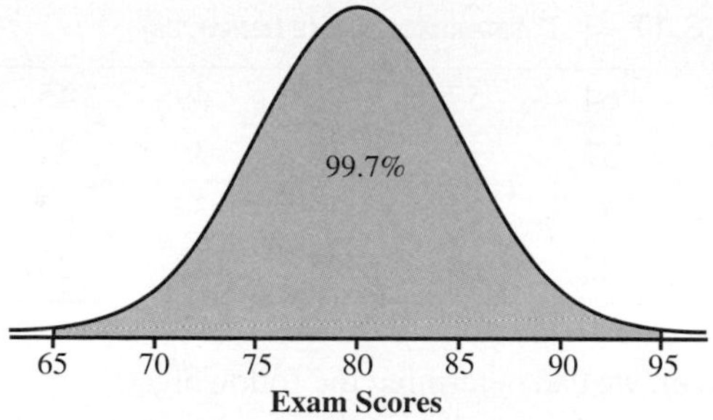

This is further evidence that values outside three standard deviations around the mean are rare and are considered outliers.

Chebyshev's Theorem can be applied to any distribution regardless of its shape.

Chebyshev's Theorem

Chebyshev's Theorem is a mathematical rule similar to the empirical rule except that it applies to any distribution rather than just bell-shaped, symmetrical distributions. The theorem states that for any z score greater than 1, the percent of the values that fall within z standard deviations above and below the mean will be *at least* the result obtained using Equation 3.19.

Chebyshev's Theorem states that for any number z greater than 1, the percent of the values that fall within z standard deviations from the mean will be at least $\left(1 - \frac{1}{z^2}\right) \times 100$.

Formula 3.19 for Chebyshev's Theorem

$$\left(1 - \frac{1}{z^2}\right) \times 100$$

So, according to the theorem, using Equation 3.19 we can state the following:

- When $z = 2$, *at least* $\left(1 - \frac{1}{2^2}\right) \times 100\% = 75\%$ of the data values will fall within two standard deviations above and below the mean.
- When $z = 3$, *at least* $\left(1 - \frac{1}{3^2}\right) \times 100\% = 89\%$ of the data values will fall within three standard deviations above and below the mean.
- When $z = 4$, *at least* $\left(1 - \frac{1}{4^2}\right) \times 100\% = 94\%$ of the data values will fall within four standard deviations above and below the mean.

In other words, regardless of whether a distribution is bell-shaped, *at least* 94% of the data values will fall within four standard deviations of the mean; *at least* 89% of the data values will fall within three standard deviations of the mean; and *at least* 75% of the data values will fall within two standard deviations of the mean. Chebyshev's Theorem can be applied to any distribution of data but can only be stated for z scores that are *greater* than 1.

Let's check out Chebyshev's Theorem to see whether it really works. Airlines define turnaround time as the number of minutes required to prepare a plane for its next flight. Reducing this time is a key factor in the airline's efforts to improve profitability in a very competitive market. Table 3.17 shows the turnaround times, in minutes, for a sample of 30 domestic flights.

Pafnuty Chebyshev (also known as Tchebysheff) was a Russian mathematician who lived from 1821–1894.

TABLE 3.17 | TURNAROUND TIME (MINUTES)

73	64	57	49	49	45	41	39	38	38
37	37	37	36	36	34	34	34	34	34
33	31	31	30	30	29	27	27	27	25
25	25	25	25	25	23	23	22	22	21

Using Excel, we can determine the following:

$$\bar{x} = 34.3 \text{ (sample mean)}$$
$$s = 11.4 \text{ (sample standard deviation)}$$

To verify that at least 75% of the observations fall within two standard deviations from the mean, we'll rearrange Equation 3.17 in terms of x rather than z, as seen in Equation 3.20. We are using $\bar{x}$ and s here because our data represent a sample rather than a population.

Formula 3.20 for Expressing the z-Score (z) in Terms of x (Sample)

$$x = \bar{x} + zs$$

We can find the turnaround times that are two standard deviations above and below the mean by setting $z = 2$ and $z = -2$.

$$x = \bar{x} + zs$$
$$x = 34.3 + (2)(11.4) = 57.1$$
$$x = 34.3 + (-2)(11.4) = 11.5$$

All but the top two turnaround times fall within this interval. Therefore, the percent of observations that falls within two standard deviations of the mean is as follows:

$$\frac{38}{40}(100) = 95\%$$

It's important to remember that Chebyshev's Theorem states that at least 75% of the data will be two standard deviations from the mean. Therefore, 95% satisfies the theorem.

Because 95% is greater than 75%, Chebyshev's Theorem holds true.

Table 3.18 verifies that Chebyshev's Theorem also holds true for three and four standard deviations from the mean of our sample.

TABLE 3.18 | VERIFYING CHEBYSHEV'S THEOREM

z	$\bar{x}$	s	$\bar{x} + zs$	$\bar{x} - zs$	CHEBYSHEV'S PERCENT	ACTUAL PERCENT
2	34.3	11.4	57.1	11.5	75	95
3	34.3	11.4	68.5	0.1	89	97.5
4	34.3	11.4	79.9	−11.3	94	100

As you can see in each case, the actual percent of values for 2, 3, and 4 standard deviations above and below the mean exceeds Chebyshev's percent, which confirms the theorem works. One downside of using Chebyshev's Theorem is that when it is applied to a bell-shaped, symmetrical distribution, it will tend to understate the percentage of observations that will fall within an interval. Now, to see if you have been paying attention, let's see if you can handle the following Your Turn section before moving on in the chapter.

YOUR TURN #6

1. Assume that the average tuition for a four-year, in-state public college is $7,000 per year with a standard deviation of $850 per year. Calculate the *z*-score for the following tuitions:
   a. $6,000
   b. $8,400
2. Assume that the average weekly rental charge for a compact car from Avis is $322 with a standard deviation of $25 per week and that the distribution for these data is bell-shaped. Find the interval of weekly charges that includes the following:
   a. 68% of the car rentals around the mean
   b. 95% of the car rentals around the mean
   c. 99.7% of the car rentals around the mean
3. Assume that the average annual premium for health care insurance for an employee is $1,920 per year with a standard deviation of $160 per year and that the distribution of these data is not bell-shaped. Find the interval of annual premiums that will include at least the following:
   a. 75% of the employees around the mean
   b. 85% of the employees around the mean (Hint: You'll need to calculate *z* using Chebyshev's Theorem.)
   c. 94% of the employees around the mean

Answers can be found on ▶ **pages 142–143**

3.3 Section Problems

Basic Skills

3.20 Consider the following two sample data sets.

Set 1:

4 7 6 9 5

Set 2:

2 11 14 4 3

a. Calculate the coefficient of variation for each data set.
b. Which data set has more variability?

3.21 Consider the following two sample data sets.

Set 1:

11 21 15 24 20

Set 2:

3 8 0 5 6

a. Calculate the coefficient of variation for each data set.
b. Which data set has more variability?

3.22 Consider a sample with a mean equal to 40 and a standard deviation equal to 12. Calculate the *z*-scores for the following values:

a. 50 **b.** 65
c. 35 **d.** 10

3.23 Consider the following sample data:

9 7 15 10 4 12

Calculate the *z*-scores for the following values:

a. 13 **b.** 16
c. 8 **d.** 4

Applications

3.24 Assume the average price of a laptop computer is $800 with a standard deviation of $75. The following data represent the prices of a sample of laptops at Best Buy. Calculate the *z*-score for each of the following prices:

a. $699 **b.** $949
c. $625 **d.** $849
e. $999

3.25 The following data represent the number of minutes customers at Wendy's had to wait in the drive-through line before their order was taken.

1 4 6 0 4 3 10 0 4

Calculate the *z*-scores for the following times:

a. 1 minute **b.** 3 minutes
c. 7 minutes **d.** 12 minutes

3.26 Assume the average selling price for houses in a certain county is $325,000 with a standard deviation of $40,000.

a. Determine the coefficient of variation.
b. Calculate the *z*-score for a house that sells for $310,000.
c. Using the empirical rule, determine the range of prices that includes 95% of the homes around the mean.
d. Using Chebyshev's Theorem, determine the range of prices that includes at least 94% of the homes around the mean.

3.27 The following data represent the number of touchdown passes per season thrown by the Benedict Arnold of the National Football League, Brett Favre (can you tell I'm a diehard Green Bay Packer fan?), during his first 18 seasons.

0	18	19	33	38	39	35	31	22
20	32	27	32	30	20	18	28	22

Verify that Chebyshev's Theorem holds true by determining the percent of observations that fall within ± two and three standard deviations from the mean.

3.28 Assume the average age of an MBA student is 31.6 years old with a standard deviation of 2.8 years.

a. Determine the coefficient of variation.

b. Calculate the z-score for an MBA student who is 28 years old.

c. Using the empirical rule, determine the range of ages that will include 99.7% of the students around the mean.

d. Using Chebyshev's Theorem, determine the range of ages that will include at least 94% of the students around the mean.

e. Using Chebyshev's Theorem, determine the range of ages that will include at least 80% of the students around the mean.

3.4 Working with Grouped Data

Back in Chapter 2, you learned about frequency distributions that were organized as grouped data instead of individual data points. We can calculate the mean, the variance, and the standard deviation for this type of data using the following example.

A survey that collected demographic data from respondents asked for their ages as grouped data. This is often done to increase the likelihood of getting people to respond to surveys. People tend to feel more comfortable selecting an age category rather than owning up to their actual ages. The number of respondents in each age group is shown in Table 3.19.

TABLE 3.19 | Number of Respondents and Their Age Groups

AGE GROUP	NUMBER OF RESPONDENTS (f_i)
20 to under 30	20
30 to under 40	41
40 to under 50	19
50 to under 60	9
60 to under 70	11
Total	**100**

The following sections will demonstrate the procedures for computing the mean, variance, and standard deviation for the age of the respondents.

The Mean of Grouped Data

The **midpoint** is the halfway point in each group and can be found by taking the average of the endpoints for each class.

To calculate the average age in our frequency distribution, we first need to find the midpoint for each range of ages. The **midpoint** is the halfway point in each age group. You can find it by taking the average of the endpoints for each class, or group. For example, the midpoint for the first group is found as follows:

$$\frac{20 + 30}{2} = 25$$

Table 3.20 shows the midpoints for each class in our example.

TABLE 3.20 | THE MIDPOINTS FOR THE RESPONDENTS' AGE GROUPS

AGE GROUP	MIDPOINT (m_i)
20 to under 30	25
30 to under 40	35
40 to under 50	45
50 to under 60	55
60 to under 70	65

Equation 3.21 can be used to calculate the average age of this sample of grouped data.

Formula 3.21 for the Sample Mean: Grouped Data

$$\bar{x} \approx \frac{\sum_{i=1}^{k} (f_i m_i)}{n}$$

where

f_i = The frequency for class i
m_i = The midpoint for class i

$n = \sum_{i=1}^{k} f_i$ (the total number of observations)

k = number of classes

Did you notice the "squiggly" equal sign in Equation 3.21? This symbol indicates that this equation is only an approximation of the average age of the respondents. By grouping the ages, we are losing information about individual respondents. Because the midpoint approximates only the ages within each class, our final result is merely an approximation of the average age of all the respondents.

The approximate sample mean for our respondents' ages is calculated as follows:

Because the midpoint estimates only the ages in each class, the weighted average is only an approximate value.

$$\bar{x} \approx \frac{\sum_{i=1}^{k} (f_i m_i)}{n} = \frac{(20)(25)+(41)(35)+(19)(45)+(9)(55)+(11)(65)}{20 + 41 + 19 + 9 + 11}$$

$$\bar{x} \approx \frac{500 + 1{,}435 + 855 + 495 + 715}{100} = \frac{4{,}000}{100} = 40 \text{ years}$$

The average age of the respondents is about 40 years.

If our grouped data are a population, the population mean is found using Equation 3.22.

Formula 3.22 for the Population Mean: Grouped Data

$$\mu \approx \frac{\sum_{i=1}^{k} (f_i m_i)}{N}$$

Equation 3.22 is identical to Equation 3.21, except μ replaces $\bar{x}$ and N replaces n.

The Variance and Standard Deviation of Grouped Data

We can also determine the variability of grouped data. The sample variance for grouped data is computed using Equation 3.23.

Formula 3.23 for the Sample Variance: Grouped Data

$$s^2 \approx \frac{\sum_{i=1}^{k}(m_i - \bar{x})^2 f_i}{n - 1}$$

where

$\bar{x}$ = The approximate sample mean
f_i = The frequency for class i
m_i = The midpoint for class i
$n = \sum_{i=1}^{n} f_i$ (the total number of observations)
k = number of classes

Table 3.21 summarizes the sample variance calculations for our respondents' age example. Notice that we are using $\bar{x} = 40$ from the previous section.

TABLE 3.21 | Variance Calculations for the Respondents' Ages

AGE	m_i	f_i	$(\bar{x})$	$(m_i - \bar{x})$	$(m_i - \bar{x})^2$	$(m_i - \bar{x})^2 f_i$
20–30	25	20	40	−15	225	4,500
30–40	35	41	40	−5	25	1,025
40–50	45	19	40	5	25	475
50–60	55	9	40	15	225	2,025
60–70	65	11	40	25	625	6,875
$n = \sum f_i = 100$						$\sum (m_i - \bar{x})^2 f_i = 14{,}900$

$$s^2 \approx \frac{\sum_{i=1}^{n}(m_i - \bar{x})^2 f_i}{n - 1} = \frac{14{,}900}{100 - 1} = 150.5$$

The standard deviation of grouped data is also just an estimate, for the same reasons the mean is.

The sample standard deviation for the respondents' ages is

$$s = \sqrt{s^2} \approx \sqrt{150.5} = 12.3 \text{ years}$$

If our data represent a population, the variance equation is calculated using Equation 3.24.

Formula 3.24 for the Population Variance: Grouped Data

$$\sigma^2 \approx \frac{\sum_{i=1}^{k}(m_i - \mu)^2 f_i}{N}$$

Equation 3.24 is identical to Equation 3.23, except that μ replaces $\bar{x}$ and N replaces $n - 1$.

Now work the following Your Turn problem to see if you understand the procedure for calculating the mean and standard deviation of grouped data.

YOUR TURN #7

The following table summarizes the GPAs of a sample of MBA students graduating from Goldey-Beacom College this year. Calculate the mean GPA of the class, along with the variance and standard deviation.

GPA	Frequency
3.0 to under 3.2	6
3.2 to under 3.4	8
3.4 to under 3.6	6
3.6 to under 3.8	14
3.8 to 4.0	6

Answer can be found on ▶ **page 143**

3.4 Section Problems

Basic Skills

3.29 Consider the following grouped sample data:

Values	Frequency
0 to under 2	4
2 to under 4	2
4 to under 6	9
6 to under 8	7

a. Calculate the approximate mean of these sample data.
b. Calculate the approximate standard deviation of these sample data.

3.30 Consider the following grouped sample data:

Values	Frequency
5 to under 10	15
10 to under 15	9
15 to under 20	21
20 to under 25	24
25 to under 30	6

a. Calculate the approximate mean of these sample data.
b. Calculate the approximate standard deviation of these sample data.

3.31 Consider the following grouped sample data:

Values	Frequency
10 to under 30	26
30 to under 50	35
50 to under 70	51
70 to under 90	33

a. Calculate the approximate mean of these sample data.
b. Calculate the approximate standard deviation of these sample data.

Applications

3.32 A survey that collected demographic data from respondents asked them to categorize their annual incomes (in thousands of dollars) into the groups in the following table. The number of respondents for each income group is also shown in the table.

Income	Number of Respondents
\$20 to under \$30	67
\$30 to under \$40	111
\$40 to under \$50	125
\$50 to under \$60	21
\$60 to under \$70	38

a. Calculate the approximate average income of the respondents.
b. Calculate the approximate variance and standard deviation of the incomes of the respondents.

3.33 A walk-in clinic for emergency room services maintains records of the number of patients it treats per day. The following table shows the frequency of the patient arrivals over the course of a 150-day period:

Number of Patients per Day	Frequency
20 to under 40	10
40 to under 60	16
60 to under 80	25
80 to under 100	65
100 to under 120	34

a. Calculate the approximate average number of patients per day.
b. Calculate the approximate variance and standard deviation of the number of patients per day.

3.34 The Olive Garden Italian Restaurant records the amount of time customers wait for a table on Saturday evenings.

The following table lists the frequency of wait times for the last 100 customers.

Number of Minutes per Customer	Frequency
0 to under 10	6
10 to under 20	22
20 to under 30	10
30 to under 40	18
40 to under 50	28
50 to under 60	16

a. Calculate the approximate average wait time per customer.

b. Calculate the approximate variance and standard deviation of the wait time per customer.

3.35 The following data represent the number of home runs Hank Aaron hit each year during his 23-year baseball career.

13	27	26	44	30	39	40	34	45	44	24	32
44	39	29	44	38	47	34	40	20	12	10	

a. Calculate the mean and standard deviation of these data.

b. Group these data into four classes with class boundaries of 10 to under 20, 20 to under 30, 30 to under 40, and 40 to under 50.

c. Calculate the approximate mean and standard deviation of these grouped data.

d. Explain the difference in the results of part c from those of part a.

3.5 Measures of Relative Position

Measures of relative position compare the position of one value in relation to other values in the data set.

In addition to central tendency, data can also be described in terms of **relative position**, which compares the position of one value in relation to other values in the data set. Percentiles and quartiles are the most common measures of relative position.

Percentiles

Percentiles measure the approximate percentage of values in the data set that are below the value of interest.

The ***p*th percentile** of a data set (where *p* is any number between 1 and 100) is the value that *at least p* percent of the observations will fall below.

Percentiles and percentages are not the same thing. Be sure you understand the difference.

Percentiles measure the approximate percentage of values in the data set that are below the value of interest. Standardized test scores are often reported in terms of percentiles. For example, when my daughter Christin informed me that she scored a 36 on the MCAT, which is the admission test for medical schools, I wasn't sure how to respond. However, when she explained to me that this score was in the 97th percentile, I then realized it was time to celebrate because she did better than at least 97% of the students who took the test. (It looks like there's going to be another Dr. Donnelly in the family!)

The formal definition of the ***p*th percentile** of a data set (where *p* is any number between 1 and 100) is the value that *at least p* percent of the observations will fall below.

Some of my students confuse percentiles with percentages, so be careful not to make this mistake. In the MCAT example, the maximum score is a 45. Christin's percentage score is therefore $36/45 = 80\%$, which is not the same as the 97th percentile.

There's more than one way to determine percentiles manually, and the results from the various approaches differ slightly. I'll present the same method used to determine the median, which uses the index point.

The median, discussed earlier in this chapter, is the 50th percentile.

To demonstrate the manual technique for determining percentiles, we'll use the following data. The numbers are the total seconds 15 customers of PNC Bank took to complete their ATM transactions. Let's determine the value that represents the 70th percentile.

124	137	88	156	66	142	96	122
69	107	104	87	111	93	99	

We first need to sort our data from lowest to highest, as shown in Table 3.22, and indicate their position.

TABLE 3.22 | Sorted ATM Times (in Seconds)

TIME	POSITION	TIME	POSITION
66	1	107	9
69	2	111	10
87	3	122	11
88	4	124	12
93	5	137	13
96	6	142	14
99	7	156	15
104	8		

Next, we need to identify the index point, i, by using the Equation 3.25.

Formula 3.25 for the Index Point for the *pth* Percentile

$$i = \frac{P}{100}(n)$$

where

$P =$ The percentile of interest
$n =$ The number of data values

Because we have 15 ATM observations and we are looking for the 70th percentile,

$$i - \frac{P}{100}(n) - \frac{70}{100}(15) - 10.5$$

Pay close attention to these two rules for finding the position of the percentile of interest.

However, 10.5 is not a whole number. So what do we do? We follow the same rule that we used to determine the median:

- If i is not a whole number, round i to the next whole number. The ith position represents our value of interest.
- If i is a whole number, the midpoint between the ith and $i + 1$ position is our value of interest.

Because $i = 10.5$, the 70th percentile is the data value in the 11th position, which is 122 seconds. In other words, 122 seconds constitutes the 70th percentile. Thus, 70% of the data values in the set are below 122 seconds.

Another red flag here—some students will mistakenly claim that the 70th percentile is 11. Remember, the index point, i, is not the *value* of interest. It is merely the *position* of the value of interest in our sorted data.

Be sure not to confuse the value of i for the percentile. The value of i represents the position of the percentile, not the value of the percentile.

Excel will calculate percentiles for us with the PERCENTILE.EXC function:

=PERCENTILE.EXC(*array*, *k*)

where

array = The data range of interest
$k =$ The percentile of interest between 0 and 1 inclusive

Figure 3.16 illustrates how this function is used to find the 70th percentile for our ATM example, with the result shown in Cell D1.

To demonstrate the use of our second index rule, we'll find the 40th percentile from our ATM example using the following equation:

$$i = \frac{P}{100}(n) = \frac{40}{100}(15) = 6$$

FIGURE 3.16
Excel's PERCENTILE.EXC Function

	A	B	C	D	E	F	G
1	124	69		122.4			
2	137	107					
3	88	104					
4	156	87					
5	66	111					
6	142	93					
7	96	99					
8	122						
9							

D1 =PERCENTILE.EXC(A1:B8,0.7)

Excel's value for the 70th percentile (122.4) is slightly different from the value for the 70th percentile we obtained by hand (122) because Excel uses a different method to calculate percentiles.

Because $i = 6$, the 40th percentile is the data value midway between the sixth (96) and seventh (99) positions in Table 3.22, as the following calculation shows:

$$40\text{th percentile} = \frac{96 + 99}{2} = 97.5 \text{ seconds}$$

Notice that the percentile does not need to be an actual value in the data set.

Now, let's throw this procedure in reverse. In the previous example, we determined the value in the data set that corresponds to a certain percentile. Now, I'll show you how to determine the **percentile rank**, which identifies the percentile of a particular value within a set of data (sounds pretty exciting to me).

The **percentile rank** identifies the percentile of a particular value within a set of data.

Table 3.23 shows the credit scores for 16 individuals. These data can also be found in the Excel file titled **percentile rank.xlsx**.

TABLE 3.23 | Credit Scores

NAME	SCORE	NAME	SCORE
Lori	726	Marc	690
Chris	643	Kendra	747
John	777	Peter	618
Sam	695	Jordan	701
Katie	796	Teresa	660
Carole	743	David	716
Irina	642	Gia	742
Lisa	819	Ryan	682

Let's determine the percentile rank for John, who has a credit score of 777. First, we need to sort the data from lowest to highest, as follows. The point total for John is highlighted in red.

618 642 643 660 682 690 695 701
716 726 742 743 747 777 796 819

Next, we count the number of people who have a lower credit score than John which is 13. To find the approximate percentile rank for John, we use the Equation 3.26.

Formula 3.26 for the Percentile Rank

$$\text{Percentile Rank} = \frac{(\text{Number of values below } x) + 0.5}{\text{Total number of values}}(100)$$

The percentile rank must be between 0 and 100.

In our example, the x in the equation stands for John's credit score of 777. Because we know there are 13 people with credit scores less than 777, we can calculate John's percentile rank as follows:

$$\text{Percentile Rank} = \frac{(13) + 0.5}{16}(100) = \frac{13.5}{16}(100) = 84th$$

John's credit score of 777 puts him in the 84th percentile, which places him above at least 84% of this group of 16 people.

Excel will also calculate the percentile rank with the PERCENTRANK.EXC function:

=PERCENTRANK.EXC(*array*, *x*, *significance*)

where

array = The data range of interest
x = The value for which you want the percentile rank
significance = the number of decimal places displayed for the percentile rank

Figure 3.17 shows how this function is used to find the percentile rank of John. The result is shown in Cell D1.

FIGURE 3.17
Excel's PERCENTRANK.EXC Function

D1 =PERCENTRANK.EXC(B2:B17, 777, 3)

	A	B	C	D	E	F	G
1	Name	Score		0.823			
2	Lori	726					
3	Chris	643					
4	John	777					
16	Gia	742					
17	Ryan	682					
18							
19	Rows 5-15 are hidden						
20							

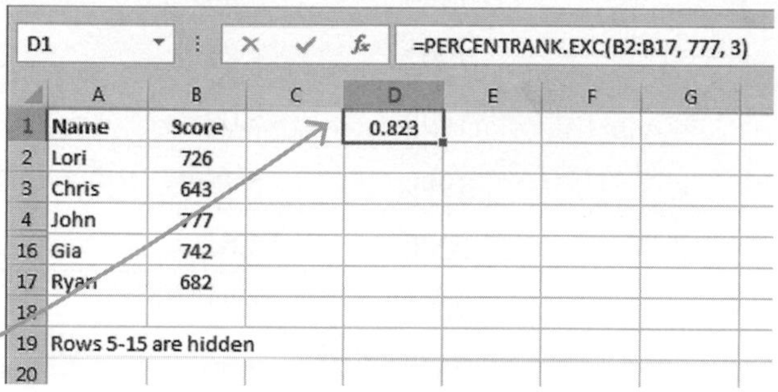

Excel's value for the 86th percentile is different from the value for the 84th percentile we obtained by hand because Excel uses a different method to calculate percentile ranks.

We can use percentile ranks to compare two different values from two different data sets. Table 3.24 lists the exam scores from a math class and a physics class. A particular student scored an 88 on her math test and a 76 on her physics test. Which of her two exam scores is higher relative to those of her classmates? To answer this question, we need to find the percentile ranks.

Percentile ranks are very useful when comparing values from two different data sets.

TABLE 3.24 | EXAM SCORES

MATH EXAM SCORES

59	62	66	69	72	72	75	75	78	81	83	84	85
86	88	89	90	91	92	93	94	94	95	97	98	

PHYSICS EXAM SCORES

47	48	53	56	57	58	60	61	61	62	63	64	71
72	74	75	**76**	82	89	95						

There are a total of 25 math scores, of which 14 are below an 88. Therefore, the approximate math percentile rank is as follows:

$$\text{Percentile Rank} = \frac{(14) + 0.5}{25}(100) = \frac{14.5}{25}(100) = 58\text{th}$$

There are a total of 20 physics scores, of which 16 are below a 76. Therefore, the approximate physics percentile rank is as follows:

$$\text{Percentile Rank} = \frac{(16) + 0.5}{20}(100) = \frac{16.5}{20}(100) = 83\text{th}$$

Even though the student's math score (88) was higher than her physics score (76), the student performed better on the physics test relative to her classmates because of the higher percentile rank.

Quartiles

The first, second, and third **quartiles** in a data set are the values for the 25th, 50th (median), and 75th percentiles, respectively.

Quartiles are simply specific percentiles of interest. The first quartile is the value that constitutes the 25th percentile, the second quartile is the value that constitutes the 50th percentile, and the third quartile is the value that constitutes the 75th percentile. The three quartiles are designated Q_1, Q_2, and Q_3, respectively. The second quartile, Q_2, is also the median, which was discussed earlier in the chapter.

Table 3.25 lists the number of mishandled baggage reports per 1,000 passengers from 1995 to 2012 during the month of July for the largest U.S. air carriers. These data can also be found in the Excel file titled **mishandled bags.xlsx**. Notice the upward trend from 2005 to 2007! This was a good time to drive to your vacation spot. Let's find the three quartiles in these data.

TABLE 3.25 | MISHANDLED BAGGAGE REPORTS PER 1,000 PASSENGERS

YEAR	REPORTS	YEAR	REPORTS
1995	5.18	2004	4.99
1996	5.30	2005	7.71
1997	4.82	2006	6.51
1998	5.09	2007	7.93
1999	5.75	2008	4.87
2000	5.64	2009	3.98
2001	4.48	2010	3.69
2002	3.99	2011	3.72
2003	4.37	2012	3.52

Based on: U.S. Department of Transportation data.

We'll start by sorting our 18 values from lowest to highest:

3.52 3.69 3.72 3.98 3.99 4.37
4.48 4.82 4.87 4.99 5.09 5.18
5.30 5.64 5.75 6.51 7.71 7.93

We now can identify the index point for the first quartile. Using Equation 3.25 to determine the index point, we set $P = 25$ because the first quartile is the 25th percentile.

$$\text{Index point for } Q_1\text{: } i = \frac{P}{100}(n) = \frac{25}{100}(18) = 4.5$$

Because 4.5 is a fraction, we round up like we did when we were trying to find the median in a data set. Doing so puts Q_1 in the fifth position of our sorted data, which corresponds to 3.99.

Because the second quartile is the median, set $P = 50$ to find the index point for Q_2.

$$\text{Index point for } Q_2\text{: } i = \frac{P}{100}(n) = \frac{50}{100}(18) = 9$$

Q_2 is the midpoint between the 9th (4.87) and 10th (4.99) position; therefore,

$$Q_2 = \frac{4.87 + 4.99}{2} = 4.93$$

The index point for the third quartile, which is the 75th percentile, is shown as follows:

$$\text{Index point for } Q_3\text{: } i = \frac{P}{100}(n) = \frac{75}{100}(18) = 13.5$$

Q_3 is in the 14th position of our sorted data; therefore, $Q_3 = 5.64$. Thus, the three quartiles were found to be as follows:

$$Q_1 = 3.99 \quad Q_2 = 4.93 \quad Q_3 = 5.64$$

Excel will calculate quartiles with the QUARTILE.EXC function

$$=\text{QUARTILE.EXC}(array, quart)$$

where

$array =$ The data range of interest
$quart =$ 1, 2, or 3 for the first, second, or third quartile, respectively

Figure 3.18 shows how this function is used to find the quartiles for our mishandled baggage example. The results are shown in Cells E2 through E4.

FIGURE 3.18
Excel's QUARTILE.EXC Function

	A	B	C	D	E	F
1	Year	Mishandled Bags				
2	1995	5.18		Q1	3.99	=QUARTILE.EXC(B2:B19,1)
3	1996	5.30		Q2	4.93	=QUARTILE.EXC(B2:B19,2)
4	1997	4.82		Q3	5.67	=QUARTILE.EXC(B2:B19,3)
18	2011	3.72				
19	2012	3.52				
20						
21	Rows 5-17 are hidden					
22						

Once again, the value shown in Cell E4 is slightly different from the results that we calculated manually because Excel uses a different technique to determine quartiles.

The **interquartile range**, ***IQR***, describes the middle 50% of a range.

The **interquartile range, *IQR***, describes the middle 50% of a range. We can find it by discarding the values in the upper and lower quartile ranges of the distribution so that only the middle values remain. To find the interquartile range, subtract the first quartile from the third quartile, as Equation 3.27 shows.

Formula 3.27 for the Interquartile Range

$$IQR = Q_3 - Q_1$$

The interquartile range for our mishandled baggage data is calculated as follows:

$$IQR = 5.64 - 3.99 = 1.65$$

What remains—1.65—represents the span of the *IQR*, or the range in which 50% of the values fall.

This is a good time to see if you "get it" by testing your percentile skills on this next Your Turn section.

YOUR TURN #8

The following table lists the U.S. and Canadian box-office revenues for the highest grossing films of all time (in millions of dollars). These data can also be found in the Excel file titled **boxoffice revenues.xlsx**.

Film	Adjusted Revenue* ($000,000)
Gone with the Wind (1939)	$1,538
Star Wars: A New Hope (1977)	$1,355
The Sound of Music (1965)	$1,084
E.T. the Extra-Terrestrial (1982)	$1,080
The Ten Commandments (1956)	$998
Titanic (1997)	$977
Jaws (1975)	$975
Doctor Zhivago (1965)	$945
The Exorcist (1973)	$841
Snow White and the Seven Dwarfs (1937)	$829
One Hundred and One Dalmatians (1961)	$760

Film	Adjusted Revenue* ($000,000)
Star Wars: The Empire Strikes Back (1980)	$747
Ben-Hur (1959)	$746
Avatar (2009)	$742
Star Wars: Return of the Jedi (1983)	$716
The Sting (1973)	$678
Raiders of the Lost Ark (1981)	$671
Jurassic Park (1993)	$656
The Graduate (1967)	$651
Star Wars: The Phantom Menace (1999)	$646
Fantasia (1941)	$632
The Godfather (1972)	$601

Based on: http://www.boxofficemojo.com.

*In U.S. dollars adjusted to the estimated 2010 average ticket price of $7.61.

Using these data, determine the following:

1. The three quartiles and the *IQR*
2. The 65th percentile
3. The percentile rank for the film *The Sting* (one of my favorites)

Answers can be found on ▶ **page 143**

Box-and-Whisker Plots

A **box-and-whisker plot** is a graphical display showing the relative position of the three quartiles as a box on a number line along with the minimum and maximum values in the data set and any outliers.

A **box-and-whisker plot** is a graphical display showing the relative position of the three quartiles as a box on a number line. The display also shows the minimum and maximum values in the data set along with any extreme values, or outliers.

To illustrate the box-and-whisker plot, I'll use the data in Table 3.26, which lists the number of visitors, in millions, for 15 U.S. National Parks during 2012. These data can also be found in the Excel file titled **national parks.xlsx**.

My wife, Deb, at a spot known as the Jump Off in the Great Smoky Mountain National Park.

TABLE 3.26 | NATIONAL PARK VISITORS, 2012

PARK	NUMBER OF VISITORS (IN MILLIONS)
Great Smoky Mountains (TN, NC)	9.69
Grand Canyon (AZ)	4.42
Yosemite (CA)	3.85
Yellowstone (WY)	3.45
Rocky Mountain (CO)	3.23
Zion (UT)	2.97
Olympic (WA)	2.82
Grand Teton (WY)	2.71
Acadia (ME)	2.43
Cuyahoga Valley (OH)	2.30
Glacier (MT)	2.16
Bryce Canyon (UT)	1.39
Shenandoah (VA)	1.21
Everglades (FL)	1.14
Denali (AK)	0.39

Based on: http://www.nature.nps.gov/stats.

Box-and-whisker plots are constructed by taking the following steps:

Step 1. Determine the three quartiles.

$$\text{Index point for } Q_1\text{: } i = \frac{P}{100}(n) = \frac{25}{100}(15) = 3.75$$

Q_1 is in the fourth position of our sorted data; therefore, $Q_1 = 1.39$ million visitors.

$$\text{Index point for } Q_2\text{: } i = \frac{P}{100}(n) = \frac{50}{100}(15) = 7.5$$

Q_2 is in the eighth position of our sorted data; therefore, $Q_2 = 2.71$ million visitors.

$$\text{Index point for } Q_3\text{: } i = \frac{P}{100}(n) = \frac{75}{100}(15) = 11.25$$

Q_3 is in the 12th position of our sorted data; therefore, $Q_3 = 3.45$ million visitors. Thus, the three quartiles were found to be as follows:

$$Q_1 = 1.39 \quad Q_2 = 2.71 \quad Q_3 = 3.45$$

Step 2. Draw a horizontal number line that spans the length of the data values, as shown in Figure 3.19.

Step 3. Draw a box over the number line that has vertical lines at Q_1, Q_2, and Q_3, as shown in Figure 3.19.

FIGURE 3.19
The Box in a Box-and-Whisker Plot

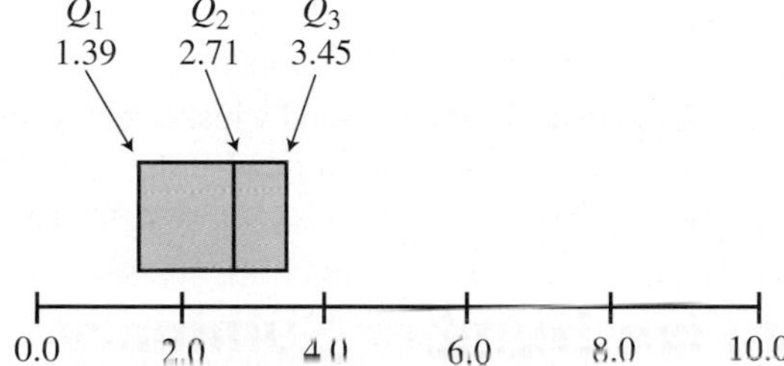

Step 4. Determine if any outliers exist in the data. Recall that outliers are extreme values in the data set that require special consideration.

Earlier in this chapter, we identified outliers as having z-scores greater than ± 3 standard deviations from the mean. John Tukey (1915–2000), who was a famous American statistician, proposed defining outliers as values that are above the upper limit found in Equation 3.28 or below the lower limit determined by Equation 3.29.

Formulas 3.28 and 3.29 for the Upper and Lower Limits of Outliers

$$\text{Upper Limit} = Q_3 + 1.5(IQR)$$
$$\text{Lower Limit} = Q_1 - 1.5(IQR)$$

Paul Velleman, who was a student of John Tukey, tells a well-traveled story about the origin of these equations. When asked why the factor 1.5 is used to define outliers, Tukey responded, "Because 1 is too small and 2 is too large." When John Tukey spoke, people listened!

For a data set that is normally distributed, these equations will define approximately 1 out of 100 values as outliers.

For our National Park data, the IQR is calculated as follows:

$$IQR = Q_3 - Q_1$$
$$IQR = 3.45 - 1.39 = 2.06$$

This results in the following upper and lower limits:

$$\text{Upper Limit} = 3.45 + 1.5(2.06) = 6.54$$
$$\text{Lower Limit} = 1.39 - 1.5(2.06) = -1.70$$

Any data value below −1.70 or above 6.54 would be considered an outlier in this example. Because the number of visitors at Great Smoky Mountain is above 6.54, 9.69 would be labeled as an outlier.

Step 5. Draw the whiskers on each end of the box as shown in Figure 3.20. The whiskers are the horizontal dotted lines that extend from each side of the box. The right whisker extends out to the *highest* data value in our National Park example that is not an outlier, which is 4.42 (million visitors) and which corresponds to Grand Canyon National Park. The left whisker extends to the *lowest* data value that is not an outlier, which is 0.39 (million visitors). It corresponds to Denali National Park.

Step 6. Identify outliers if present. If outliers exist in the data set, they are plotted with an asterisk on the number line, as shown in Figure 3.20.

FIGURE 3.20 The Whiskers in a Box-and-Whisker Plot

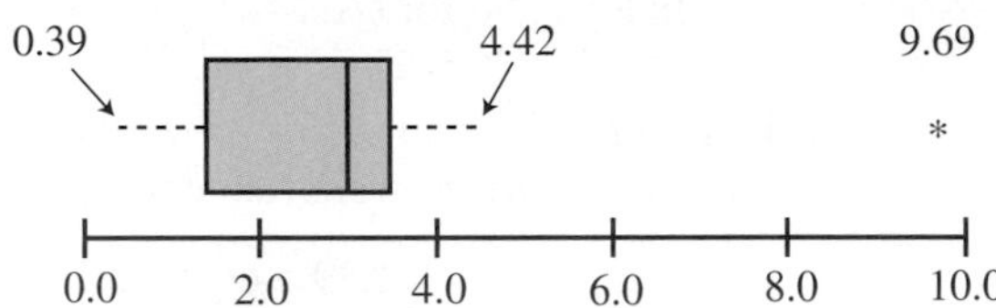

The finished box-and whisker plot for our National Park example is shown in Figure 3.21.

FIGURE 3.21 Finished Box-and-Whisker Plot

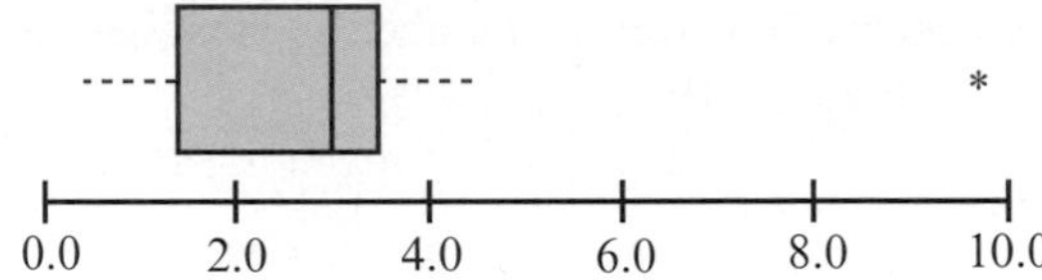

As you can see, the box-and whisker plot provides an easy-to-understand picture of where the data are concentrated along a number line, as well as information about outliers. Now, let's take a look at one other way to describe our data set.

The Five-Number Summary

The **five-number summary** consists of a distribution's minimum value; the values for the first, second, and third quartiles; and the maximum value.

We can also summarize data using a **five-number summary**, which consists of—you guessed it—the following five numbers for a distribution:

- The minimum value
- The first quartile
- The second quartile
- The third quartile
- The maximum value

Using the National Park data, our five-number summary would be as follows:

- 0.39
- 1.39
- 2.71
- 3.45
- 9.69

Notice that outliers are included in a five-number summary. Therefore, we include 9.69 in our summary, even though it was identified as an outlier in our box-and-whisker plot.

The following Your Turn will test your box-and-whisker skills, so I encourage you to give it a shot while all those steps are still fresh in your mind.

YOUR TURN #9

Use the following credit card balances for 16 Citibank customers to construct a box-and-whisker plot and a five-number summary.

$3,414	$10,827	$8,128	$12,437
$7,960	$378	$9,970	$9,038
$19,400	$11,499	$5,030	$11,113
$8,048	$15,783	$11,349	$10,162

Answer can be found on ▶ page 144

3.5 Section Problems

Basic Skills

3.36 Consider the following data set:

38 55 76 20 30 66 17 54

a. Determine the 20th percentile.
b. Determine the 40th percentile.
c. Determine the 60th percentile.

3.37 Consider the following data set:

22 5 18 20 13 33 30 8 39

a. Determine the 15th percentile.
b. Determine the 35th percentile.
c. Determine the 85th percentile.

3.38 Consider the following data set:

71 40 45 67 5 15 43 37 13 10

Determine the percentile rank for the following values:

a. 50
b. 30
c. 15

3.39 Consider the following data set:

106 83 63 104 118 124 117 136 82 97 65 141

Determine the percentile rank for the following values:

a. 100
b. 75
c. 120

3.40 Consider the following data set:

14 24 20 18 23 20 12 16 22 18 14 26 15

a. Determine the quartiles for these data.
b. Calculate the interquartile range for these data.

3.41 Identify the five-number summary for the following data set:

35 24 54 2 36 23 16 43 59 55 28 81

Applications

3.42 The following table shows the estimated populations of the 12 largest U.S. cities from the 2010 Census. These data can also be found in the Excel file titled **city populations.xlsx.**

City	Population (in millions)
New York, NY	8.18
Los Angeles, CA	3.79
Chicago, IL	2.70
Houston, TX	2.10
Philadelphia, PA	1.53
Phoenix, AZ	1.45
San Antonio, TX	1.33
San Diego, CA	1.31
Dallas, TX	1.20
San Jose, CA	0.95
Jacksonville, FL	0.82
Indianapolis, IN	0.82

a. Calculate the 60th percentile for the data.
b. Calculate the 20th percentile for the data.
c. Calculate the 85th percentile for the data.

3.43 The following table shows the total runs scored by the 16 National League teams in Major League Baseball during the 2012 season. These data can also be found in the Excel file titled **MLB runs.xlsx.**

Team	Runs	Team	Runs
Brewers	776	Reds	669
Cardinals	765	Pirates	651
Rockies	758	Padres	651
Diamondbacks	734	Mets	650

Team	Runs	Team	Runs
Nationals	731	Dodgers	637
Giants	718	Cubs	613
Braves	700	Marlins	609
Phillies	684	Astros	583

a. Find the percentile rank for the runs scored by the Mets.
b. Find the percentile rank for the runs scored by the Braves.
c. Find the percentile rank for the runs scored by the Phillies.

3.44 The following data set refers to the number of customers per day at a jewelry kiosk in Christiana Mall during a 20-day period:

8	10	18	58	58	59	63	64	69	71
75	78	80	82	84	84	86	87	87	88

a. Identify the first, second, and third quartiles.
b. Determine the interquartile range.

3.45 The following table shows the number of graduating students with business majors at Neumann University over the past 30 years in descending order:

269	261	242	238	225	223	217	212	208	204
199	198	197	195	195	193	193	191	189	185
181	179	177	174	174	172	171	171	170	170

a. Construct a box-and-whisker plot for these data.
b. Identify the five-number summary.

3.6 Measures of Association Between Two Variables

The statistics that have been discussed in this chapter to this point have all dealt with describing one variable at a time, such as Nike's stock price or the number of televisions sold at Walmart. In this last section, you will learn about measurements that will describe the relationship between two variables. For example, suppose we are interested in the relationship between the number of hours that a student studies for an exam and the resulting exam score. Table 3.27 shows values for these two variables from a small sample of students.

TABLE 3.27 | EXAM GRADES

STUDENT	HOURS OF STUDY	EXAM GRADE
1	3	86
2	7	98
3	5	92
4	4	83
5	3	78
6	2	79

Figure 3.22 shows the scatter plot for the sample data in Table 3.27.

FIGURE 3.22
Scatter Plot of Hours and Exam Scores

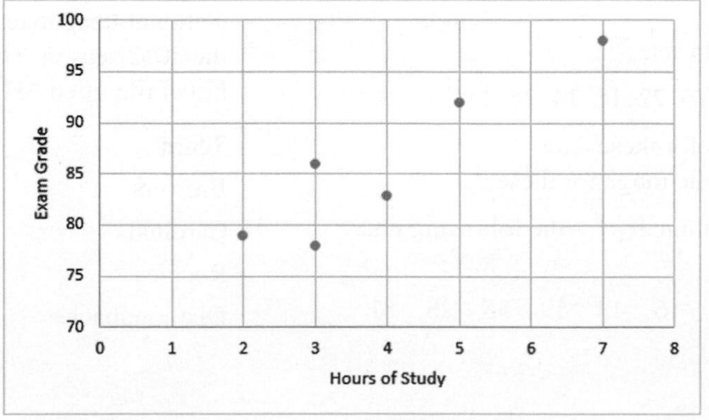

Notice that the data points in Figure 3.22 tend to move in a relatively straight-line pattern across the scatter plot. As a result, we can describe this relationship between hours and exam scores as linear. In the following pages, we will examine two descriptive statistics that will measure the linear relationship between variables such as those seen in Table 3.27—the sample covariance and the sample correlation coefficient.

Sample Covariance

The **sample covariance**, s_{xy}, measures the direction of the linear relationship between two variables.

The **sample covariance**, s_{xy}, measures the direction of the linear relationship between two variables by using Equation 3.30.

Formula 3.30 for the Sample Covariance

$$s_{xy} = \frac{\sum_{i=1}^{n}(x_i - \bar{x})(y_i - \bar{y})}{n - 1}$$

where

s_{xy} = The sample covariance between variables x and y
$\bar{x}$ = The sample mean of the x variable
$\bar{y}$ = The sample mean of the y variable
$(x_i - \bar{x})$ = The difference between each data value and the sample mean for the x variable
$(y_i - \bar{y})$ = The difference between each data value and the sample mean for the y variable
n = The sample size

For this example, I am making the following arbitrary assignment of variables:

I could have also chosen to reverse these assignments of x and y—the choice is completely arbitrary.

x = the hours of study
y = the exam score

We need to calculate the sample average for each variable. Notice that $n = 6$ because our sample consists of six students. Using Equation 3.1, we have:

$$\text{Hours of Study: } \bar{x} = \frac{\sum_{i=1}^{n} x_i}{n} = \frac{3 + 7 + 5 + 4 + 3 + 2}{6} = 4.0$$

$$\text{Exam Score: } \bar{y} = \frac{\sum_{i=1}^{n} y_i}{n} = \frac{86 + 98 + 92 + 83 + 78 + 79}{6} = 86.0$$

Table 3.28 shows the calculations needed for the numerator of the covariance Equation 3.30 for our exam score example.

TABLE 3.28 | COVARIANCE CALCULATIONS

x_i	$\bar{x}$	$(x_i - \bar{x})$	y_i	$\bar{y}$	$(y_i - \bar{y})$	$(x_i - \bar{x})(y_i - \bar{y})$
3	4	−1	86	86	0	0
7	4	3	98	86	12	36
5	4	1	92	86	6	6
4	4	0	83	86	−3	0
3	4	−1	78	86	−8	8
2	4	−2	79	86	−7	14
						$\sum(x_i - \bar{x})(y_i - \bar{y}) = 64$

We are now ready to plug our results into Equation 3.30:

$$s_{xy} = \frac{\sum_{i=1}^{n}(x_i - \bar{x})(y_i - \bar{y})}{n - 1} = \frac{64}{6 - 1} = 12.8$$

Because our covariance is a positive value (12.8), we describe the relationship between hours of study and exam scores as a positive linear one. In general, a positive linear relationship means that as one variable increases, the second variable also tends to increase. This type of relationship fits our example well—students who study more tend to earn higher grades!

A negative covariance indicates a negative linear relationship. In this scenario, as one variable increases in value, the second variable tends to decrease. An example of this type of relationship would be price and demand for a product. As the price of the product increases, demand for that product tends to decrease.

Finally, a covariance close to zero indicates no relationship between the two variables. As the value of one variable increases, the value of second variable will have no consistent pattern.

Students may be tempted to conclude that the larger the covariance, the stronger the relationship between the two variables. Unfortunately, this statement is not true. The size of the covariance is influenced by the scale of the data. Very large data values tend to generate a large covariance. The covariance is useful in describing the *direction* of the relationship but not the strength of the relationship. The next descriptive statistic that we are examining, the correlation coefficient, describes both for us.

Sample Correlation Coefficient

The **sample correlation coefficient**, r_{xy}, measures both the strength and direction of the linear relationship between two variables.

The **sample correlation coefficient**, r_{xy}, measures both the strength and direction of the linear relationship between two variables and can be calculated using Equation 3.31.

Formula 3.31 for the Sample Correlation Coefficient

$$r_{xy} = \frac{s_{xy}}{s_x s_y}$$

where

r_{xy} = The sample correlation coefficient
s_{xy} = The sample covariance between variables x and y
s_x = The sample standard deviation for the x variable
s_y = The sample standard deviation for the y variable

As you can see, Equation 3.31 relies on the covariance calculation that we just computed in the last section. We also need to calculate the sample standard deviations from each variable which I show here using Equation 3.6.

Hours of Study:

$$s_x = \sqrt{\frac{\sum_{i=1}^{n}(x_i - \bar{x})^2}{n - 1}}$$

$$s_x = \sqrt{\frac{(3-4)^2 + (7-4)^2 + (5-4)^2 + (4-4)^2 + (3-4)^2 + (2-4)^2}{6 - 1}}$$

$$s_x = \sqrt{\frac{16}{5}} = \sqrt{3.2} = 1.79$$

Exam Grade:

$$s_y = \sqrt{\frac{\sum_{i=1}^{n}(y_i - \bar{y})^2}{n-1}}$$

$$s_y = \sqrt{\frac{(86-86)^2 + (98-86)^2 + (92-86)^2 + (83-86)^2 + (78-86)^2 + (79-86)^2}{6-1}}$$

$$s_y = \sqrt{\frac{302}{5}} = \sqrt{60.4} = 7.77$$

We are now ready to calculate our sample correlation coefficient using Equation 3.31.

$$r_{xy} = \frac{s_{xy}}{s_x s_y} = \frac{12.8}{(1.79)(7.77)} = 0.920$$

The values of r_{xy} range from between -1.0 and $+1.0$. When r_{xy} is positive, the linear relationship between x and y is positive, which means that as the value of x increases, the value of y tends to increase. By contrast, when r_{xy} is negative, the linear relationship between x and y is negative. So, as the value of x increases, the value of y tends to decrease. When $r_{xy} = 0$, there is no relationship between the x and y variables.

The strength of the linear relationship between x and y is measured by how close the correlation coefficient is to $+1.0$ or -1.0. Figure 3.23 illustrates the strengths of various correlation coefficients.

FIGURE 3.23
The Strength and Direction of Various Linear Relationships, Along with Their Correlation Coefficients

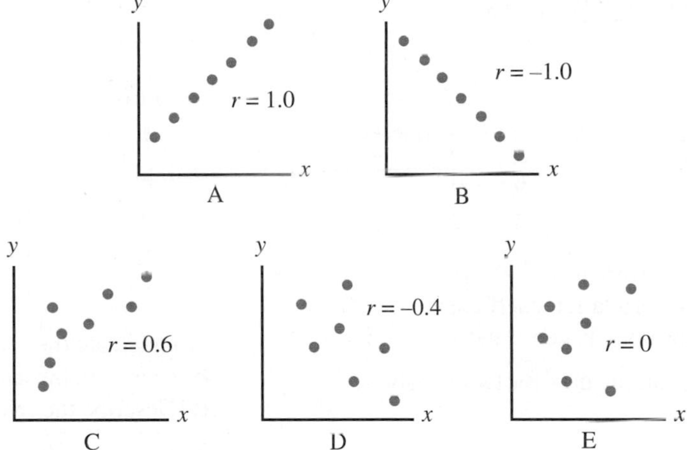

With $r_{xy} = 0.920$, we can conclude that there is a strong positive relationship between the number of hours that students study and their exam score—good news for us teachers!

I do have one important word of warning here. Just because the sample correlation coefficient tells us there is a strong relationship between the variables does not prove that one variable *caused* the change in the other variable. To prove causation, you need to have evidence that one variable is causing the other to move, which the correlation coefficient alone does not provide. For example, if our two variables were the left and right shoe sizes of people, we would expect a very high correlation. This is not the result of one foot causing the other foot to be a certain size. These two variables just tend to move together naturally.

The following Your Turn exercise will give you the chance to calculate the covariance of correlation coefficient for a negative relationship to test your skills on this topic.

YOUR TURN #10

Suppose Best Buy would like to examine the relationship between the price and weekly demand for a popular Epson printer. The following data represent the weekly demand for various price levels that were used for this printer.

Price and Demand Data for an Epson Printer

Price ($)	Demand
70	18
75	23
80	10
85	16
90	17
95	15
100	6

a. Calculate the sample covariance for these variables.
b. Calculate the sample correlation coefficient for these variables.
c. Describe the relation between price and demand for this printer.

Answers can be found on ▶ **pages 144–145**

3.6 Section Problems

Basic Skills

3.46 Consider the following sample data for two variables.

x	4	7	2	6	6
y	4	9	5	5	7

a. Calculate the sample covariance.
b. Calculate the sample correlation coefficient.
c. Describe the relationship between x and y.

3.47 Consider the following sample data for two variables.

x	7	6	2	3
y	6	8	11	5

a. Calculate the sample covariance.
b. Calculate the sample correlation coefficient.
c. Describe the relationship between x and y.

Business Applications

3.48 Comcast's customer service department asks its customers to rate their over-the-phone service on a scale of 1–20 immediately after their service has been completed. The company then matches each customer's rating with the number of minutes the person waited on hold. The following table shows the ratings and number of minutes on hold for 10 randomly selected customers and can also be found in the Excel file **hold.xlsx**.

Minutes	Rating	Minutes	Rating
4	15	2	16
8	13	10	14
0	18	3	20
5	10	8	14
6	14	4	13

a. Calculate the sample covariance.
b. Calculate the sample correlation coefficient.
c. Describe the relationship between x and y.

3.49 Suppose the EPA would like to investigate the relationship between the engine size of sedans and the miles per gallon (MPG) they get. The following table shows the engine size in cubic liters and rated miles per gallon for a selection of 2011 sedans and can also be found in the Excel file **engine size.xlsx**.

Car	Engine Size	MPG
1	2.0	26
2	2.2	30
3	2.4	25
4	3.3	21
5	3.0	23
6	2.0	28
7	2.4	24
8	2.0	29
9	3.2	19

a. Calculate the sample covariance.
b. Calculate the sample correlation coefficient.
c. Describe the relationship between x and y.

3.50 A regional manager at Acme Markets would like to develop a model to predict weekly sales of pet food based on the shelf space. The following table shows the results of data collected from nine randomly selected stores and can also be found in the Excel file **Acme.xlsx**.

Shelf Space (Feet)	Sales ($100)	Shelf Space (Feet)	Sales ($100)
2	3	2	4
3	3	4	5
4	6	5	7
6	5	5	12
5	18		

a. Calculate the sample covariance.
b. Calculate the sample correlation coefficient.
c. Describe the relationship between x and y.

3.51 The American Board of Family Medicine would like to investigate the theory that a mother's shoe size can be used to predict an infant's birth weight. The following table records a random sample of the shoe sizes of 10 mothers and the birth weights of their infants and can also be found in the Excel file **ABFM.xlsx**.

Shoe Size	Weight	Shoe Size	Weight
7.5	7.6	8.0	6.9
8.0	7.8	8.5	9.2
9.0	8.0	7.5	6.5
8.5	9.4	8.0	9.1
8.5	7.7	9.5	9.8

a. Calculate the sample covariance.
b. Calculate the sample correlation coefficient.
c. Describe the relationship between x and y.

CHAPTER 3 Summary

- Measures of central tendency describe the center point of our data set with a single value by using the mean, median, or mode.
- The simple mean or average is the most common measure of central tendency and is calculated by adding all the values in our data set and then dividing the result by the number of observations.
  - One drawback of the mean is that it can be heavily influenced by outliers.
- The weighted mean allows you to assign more weight to certain values and less weight to others.
- The median is the value in the data set for which half the observations are higher and half the observations are lower.
  - The median is more difficult than the mean to calculate manually, but it is not influenced by outliers.
- The mode is simply the value that appears most often in a data set.
  - The mode is particularly useful when it comes to describing categorical data.
  - The mode might not be unique in a data set or even exist in certain data sets.
- The mean, median, and mode are roughly equal to each other in symmetrical frequency distributions.
  - In left-skewed distributions, the median is greater than the mean.
  - In right-skewed distributions, the median is less than the mean.
- Measures of variability determine how much spread is in your data by using the range, variance, and standard deviation.
- The range is a measure of variability that is found by subtracting the lowest value from the highest value in the data set.
  - The benefit of the range is that it is easy to calculate and understand but is has its drawbacks.
    - It is based only on two numbers in the data set.
    - It is highly affected by outliers.
- The variance measures the squared difference between each data point and the mean.
- The standard deviation is the square root of the variance and is in the same units as the original data.
- The coefficient of variation, *CV*, measures the standard deviation in terms of its percentage to the mean rather than units to the mean.
  - When comparing two samples, the smaller *CV* indicates more consistency (less variability).
- The *z*-score identifies the number of standard deviations that a particular value is from the mean of its distribution and is positive for values above the mean and negative for values below the mean.
- The empirical rule states that if a distribution follows a bell-shape, symmetrical curve centered around the mean, approximately 68%, 95%, and 99.7% of the values will fall above and below one, two, and three standard deviations around the mean, respectively.
- Chebyshev's theorem states that regardless of whether a distribution is bell-shaped or not, *at least* 94% of data values will fall within four standard deviations of the mean; *at least* 89% of data values will fall within three standard deviations of the mean; and *at least* 75% of data values will fall within two standard deviations of the mean.
- The mean and standard deviation can be calculated for grouped data by using the midpoint of each class to approximate all the data within that class.
  - Because the midpoint approximates only the data within each class, our final result is merely an approximation of the average and standard deviation.

- Measures of relative position compare the position of one value in relation to other values in the data set.
- Percentiles measure the approximate percentage of values in the data set that are below the value of interest.
- Quartiles are simply specific percentiles of interest.
  - The first quartile is the 25th percentile, the second quartile is the 50th percentile, and the third quartile is the 75th percentile.
- The interquartile range, *IQR*, is the difference between the first and third quartile.
- A box-and-whisker plot is a graphical display showing the relative position of the three quartiles as a box on a number line along with the minimum and maximum values in the data set.
- The five-number summary consists of a distribution's minimum value, values for the first, second, and third quartiles, and maximum value.
- Measures of association describe the relationship between two variables.
- The sample covariance measures the direction of the linear relationship between two variables.
  - A positive covariance indicates a positive linear relationship, which means as one variable increases, the second variable also tends to increase.
  - A negative covariance indicates a negative linear relationship, which means as one variable increases, the second variable tends to decrease.
- The sample correlation coefficient measures both the strength and the direction of the linear relationship between two variables.
  - The correlation coefficient ranges between -1.0 and $+1.0$.
  - When the correlation coefficient is positive, the linear relationship between x and y is positive.
  - When the correlation coefficient is negative, the linear relationship between x and y is negative.
  - The strength of the linear relationship between x and y is measured by how close the correlation coefficient is to $+1.0$ or -1.0.

CHAPTER 3 Key Terms

Box-and-whisker plot. A graphical display showing the relative position of a distribution's three quartiles as a box on a number line, along with the minimum and maximum values.

Categorical Data. Data that are described as a category or label.

Chebyshev's Theorem. A theorem that states that regardless of whether a distribution is bell-shaped, *at least* 94% of data values will fall within ± four standard deviations of the mean, *at least* 89% of data values will fall within ± three standard deviations of the mean, and *at least* 75% of data values will fall within ± two standard deviations of the mean.

Coefficient of variation. A measure of the standard deviation in terms of its percentage of the mean.

Empirical rule. A rule which states that if a distribution follows a bell-shaped, symmetrical curve centered around the mean, approximately 68%, 95%, and 99.7% of the values fall within one, two, and three standard deviations around the mean, respectively.

Five-number summary. A list that consists of a distribution's minimum value; first, second, and third quartiles; and maximum value.

Index point. The index point, *i*, marks the middle of the data values and is used to determine the position of the median in the data set.

Interquartile range, *IQR*. The difference between the first and third quartiles. It corresponds to the data in the middle 50% of the range.

Left-skewed distribution. The shape of the distribution when the median is higher than the mean.

Mean. A measure of central tendency that is calculated by adding up all of the values in a data set and then dividing the result by the number of observations.

Measures of central tendency. Measures that use a single value to describe the center point of a data set.

Measures of relative position. Measures that compare the position of one value in relation to other values in a data set.

Measures of variability. Measures that determine how much of a spread there is within a data set.

Median. The value in a data set for which half the observations are higher and half the observations are lower.

Midpoint. The halfway point in a set of data. It can be found by taking the average of the endpoints for each class.

Mode. The value that appears most often in a data set.

Outliers. Outliers are values that are much higher or lower than most of the data.

Percentiles. Measure the approximate percentage of values in the data set that are below the value of interest.

Percentile rank. Identifies the percentile of a particular value within a set of data.

***P*th percentile.** The approximate percentage of values in the data set that are below the value of interest (where p is any number between 1 and 100).

Quartiles. The first, second, and third quartiles are the 25th, 50th (median), and 75th percentiles, respectively.

Range. A measure of variability that is found by subtracting the lowest value from the highest value in a data set.

Right-skewed distribution. The shape of a distribution when its mean is higher than its median.

Sample Correlation Coefficient, r_{xy}. Measures both the strength and direction of the linear relationship between two variables.

Sample Covariance, s_{xy}. Measures the direction of the linear relationship between two variables.

Standard deviation. The square root of a distribution's variance.

Variance. A measure of variation that describes the relative distance between the data points in a set around the mean of the data set.

Weighted mean. A weighted mean allows you to assign more weight to certain values and less weight to others when calculating the mean.

***z*-score.** A measure that identifies the number of standard deviations a particular value is from the mean of its distribution.

CHAPTER 3 Equations

3.1 Central Tendency (pp 78–91)

Formula 3.1 for the Sample Mean

$$\bar{x} = \frac{\sum_{i=1}^{n} x_i}{n}$$

Formula 3.2 for the Population Mean

$$\mu = \frac{\sum_{i=1}^{N} x_i}{N}$$

Formula 3.3 for the Weighted Mean

$$\bar{x} = \frac{\sum_{i=1}^{n} (w_i x_i)}{\sum_{i=1}^{n} w_i}$$

Formula 3.4 for the Index Point for the Median

$$i = 0.5(n)$$

3.2 Measures of Variability (pp 91–101)

Formula 3.5 for the Range

$$\text{Range} = \text{Highest value} - \text{Lowest value}$$

Formula 3.6 for the Sample Variance

$$s^2 = \frac{\sum_{i=1}^{n} (x_i - \bar{x})^2}{n - 1}$$

Formula 3.7 for the Sample Standard Deviation

$$s = \sqrt{s^2} = \sqrt{\frac{\sum_{i=1}^{n} (x_i - \bar{x})^2}{n - 1}}$$

Formula 3.8 for the Sample Variance (Short-Cut)

$$s^2 = \frac{\sum_{i=1}^{n} x_i^2 - \frac{\left(\sum_{i=1}^{n} x_i\right)^2}{n}}{n - 1}$$

Formula 3.9 for the Sample Standard Deviation (Short-Cut)

$$s = \sqrt{\frac{\sum_{i=1}^{n} x_i^2 - \frac{\left(\sum_{i=1}^{n} x_i\right)^2}{n}}{n - 1}}$$

Formula 3.10 for the Population Variance

$$\sigma^2 = \frac{\sum_{i=1}^{N} (x_i - \mu)^2}{N}$$

Formula 3.11 for the Population Standard Deviation

$$\sigma = \sqrt{\frac{\sum_{i=1}^{N} (x_i - \mu)^2}{N}}$$

Formula 3.12 for the Population Variance (Short-Cut)

$$\sigma^2 = \frac{\sum_{i=1}^{N} x_i^2 - \frac{\left(\sum_{i=1}^{N} x_i\right)^2}{N}}{N}$$

Formula 3.13 for the Population Standard Deviation (Short-Cut)

$$\sigma = \sqrt{\frac{\sum_{i=1}^{N} x_i^2 - \frac{\left(\sum_{i=1}^{N} x_i\right)^2}{N}}{N}}$$

3.3 Using the Mean and Standard Deviation Together (pp 101–112)

Formula 3.14 for the Sample Coefficient of Variation

$$CV = \frac{s}{\overline{x}}(100)$$

Formula 3.15 for the Population Coefficient of Variation

$$CV = \frac{\sigma}{\mu}(100)$$

Formula 3.16 for the Population z-score

$$z = \frac{x - \mu}{\sigma}$$

Formula 3.17 for the Sample z-score

$$z = \frac{x - \overline{x}}{s}$$

Formula 3.18 for Expressing the z-Score in Terms of x

$$x = \mu + z\sigma$$

Formula 3.19 for Chebyshev's Theorem

Chebyshev's Theorem states that for any number z greater than 1, the percent of the values that fall within z standard deviations from the mean will be *at least plus or minus*

$$\left(1 - \frac{1}{z^2}\right) \times 100$$

Formula 3.20 for Expressing the z-Score (z) in Terms of the Sample (x)

$$x = \overline{x} + zs$$

3.4 Working with Grouped Data (pp 112–116)

Formula 3.21 for the Sample Mean: Grouped Data

$$\overline{x} \approx \frac{\sum_{i=1}^{k} (f_i m_i)}{n}$$

Formula 3.22 for the Population Mean: Grouped Data

$$\mu \approx \frac{\sum_{i=1}^{k} (f_i m_i)}{N}$$

Formula 3.23 for the Sample Variance: Grouped Data

$$s^2 \approx \frac{\sum_{i=1}^{k} (m_i - \overline{x})^2 f_i}{n - 1}$$

Formula 3.24 for the Population Variance: Grouped Data

$$\sigma^2 \approx \frac{\sum_{i=1}^{k} (m_i - \mu)^2 f_i}{N}$$

3.5 Measures of Relative Position (pp 116–126)

Formula 3.25 for the Index Point for the *p*th Percentile

$$i = \frac{P}{100}(n)$$

Formula 3.26 for the Percentile Rank

$$\text{Percentile Rank} = \frac{(\text{Number of values below } x) + 0.5}{\text{Total number of values}}(100)$$

Formula 3.27 for the Interquartile Range

$$IQR = Q_3 - Q_1$$

Formulas 3.28, 3.29 for the Upper and Lower Limits for Outliers

$$\text{Upper Limit} = Q_3 + 1.5(IQR)$$
$$\text{Lower Limit} = Q_1 - 1.5(IQR)$$

3.6 Measures of Association Between Two Variables (pp 126–131)

Formula 3.30 for the Sample Covariance

$$s_{xy} = \frac{\sum_{i=1}^{n}(x_i - \bar{x})(y_i - \bar{y})}{n - 1}$$

Formula 3.31 for the Sample Correlation Coefficient

$$r_{xy} = \frac{s_{xy}}{s_x s_y}$$

CHAPTER 3 Problems

3.52 You are car shopping (lucky you!) and are considering a Ford, a Chevy, and a Honda. You are basing your decision on the criteria in the following table. You have also ranked each of the criterions based on its importance to you, with a rank of 5 being the most important: price (5), reliability (4), looks (3), gas mileage (3), and resale value (2). You have scored each car for each criterion on a scale of 1–10 (10 = highest), as shown in the following table. Calculate the average score for each car.

Criteria	Ford	Chevy	Honda
Price	7	8	3
Reliability	7	6	9
Looks	5	7	5
Gas mileage	4	6	8
Resale value	7	4	8

3.53 The following data represent the number of days homes were on the market before being sold in New Castle County, Delaware, in 2014:

80 74 62 79 55 56 64 44 13
74 98 87 45 142 88 47 79

a. Calculate the mean.
b. Calculate the median.
c. Determine the mode.
d. Which of these three measurements would best describe the central tendency of the data?
e. Describe the shape of this distribution.

3.54 The average number of hours that people of Brazil spend per month on social networking sites is nearly double the worldwide average, drawing the attention of companies such as Facebook. The following data represent the number of hours that a sample of people from Brazil spent on a social networking site last month.

1.5 1.0 2.3 12.1 8.8 13.2 40.2 1.5 12.4

a. Calculate the mean.
b. Calculate the median.
c. Determine the mode.
d. Which of these three measurements would best describe the central tendency of the data?
e. Describe the shape of the distribution.

3.55 Internet service providers compete on services such as download speeds that are measured in megabits per second (Mbps). The following data represent the download speeds that 16 Comcast customers experienced recently.

6	18	7	8	8	6	10	16
11	5	14	6	12	12	16	13

a. Calculate the mean.
b. Calculate the median.
c. Determine the mode.
d. Describe the shape of the distribution.

3.56 The Fan Cost Index measures the average cost for a typical family to attend a Major League Baseball game. The index comprises the prices of two adult average-price tickets, two child average-price tickets, two small draft beers, four small soft drinks, four regular-size hot dogs, parking for one car, two game programs, and two adult-size adjustable caps (the least expensive). The Excel file **Fan Cost Index** lists the index for each MLB team for the 2012 season. Using Excel,

a. Calculate the mean.
b. Calculate the median.
c. Determine the mode.
d. Which of these three measurements would best describe the central tendency of the data?
e. Describe the shape of this distribution.

3.57 A country's fertility rate can have a major long-term impact on its economic health. Low fertility rates eventually cause the average age of the population to skew higher, making it more difficult to fund programs such as social security. The following data represent a sample showing the number of children from 10 families.

1 5 3 1 2 2 1 4 0 1

a. Calculate the range.
b. Calculate the variance.
c. Calculate the standard deviation.

3.58 The following table lists the average monthly unemployment rate from July to September 2012 for various European countries.

Country	Rate	Country	Rate
Belgium	7.4	Denmark	8.1
France	10.7	Germany	5.4
Spain	25.5	Ireland	15.0
United Kingdom	7.9	The Netherlands	5.3
Austria	4.5	Sweden	7.7

a. Calculate the range.
b. Calculate the variance.
c. Calculate the standard deviation.

3.59 Delta is one of the largest airlines in the world and also has one of the oldest fleets of planes. The following data represent the age, in years, of a sample of eight planes from Delta's fleet.

17 22 8 19 20 21 7 14

a. Calculate the range for this sample.
b. Calculate the variance for this sample.
c. Calculate the standard deviation for this sample.

3.60 The following data represent the number of pounds lost by 10 individuals who participated in a weight loss program. A negative number represents a weight loss, whereas a positive number represents a weight gain.

−12 −8 −15 −10 4 −6 −9 5 −8 −10

a. Calculate the range.
b. Calculate the variance.
c. Calculate the standard deviation.

3.61 Text messages have been a major source of revenue for cell phone carriers and for the first time in history the average number of text messages per month decreased from the second to the third quarter of 2012. The Excel file **text messages.xlsx** lists the number of text messages sent last month from a sample of 70 cell phone customers. Using Excel, determine the range, variance, and standard deviation for this sample.

3.62 A company operates two retail outlets at different locations. The following table lists the customer satisfaction ratings on a scale of 1–10 for each location:

Store 1	Store 2
7	8
4	7
6	10
3	8
9	8

Which location provides a more consistent level of customer satisfaction?

3.63 The following table shows the number of wins per season for the New England Patriots and Detroit Lions NFL teams from 2004 through 2012. This data can also be found in the Excel file **NFL wins.xlsx.**

Year	New England	Detroit
2004	14	6
2005	10	5
2006	12	3
2007	16	7
2008	11	0
2009	10	2
2010	14	6
2011	13	10
2012	12	4

Which team experienced more variability with games won per season?

3.64 The following table lists the 20 largest companies in the world in 2013 ranked by their market capitalizations (in billions of dollars). A company's market capitalization is defined as the number of its shares multiplied by the price per share. This data can also be found in the Excel file **market cap.xlsx.**

Company	Market Cap ($)	Company	Market Cap ($)
Apple	423	Procter & Gamble	210
Exxon	407	AT&T	203
Google	264	Pfizer	202
Berkshire Hathaway	252	Wells Fargo	189
General Electric	245	JPMorgan Chase	186
Wal-Mart	236	Coca-Cola	172
Microsoft	233	Oracle	165
IBM	227	Phillip Morris	156
Chevron	227	Merck	131
Johnson & Johnson	211	Verizon	130

a. Determine the coefficient of variation.
b. Calculate the z-score for a company with a market capitalization of $200 billion.
c. Test to determine if the empirical rule holds true by determining the percentage of observations that fall within ± one standard deviation from the mean.
d. Verify that Chebyshev's Theorem holds true by determining the percentage of observations that fall within ± two standard deviations from the mean.

3.65 Suppose I recorded the attendance of my students in a recent statistics class because I wanted to investigate the relationship between the number of classes they missed and their final grades. The following table shows this data for a random sample of nine students. This data can also be found in the Excel file **missed classes.xlsx.**

Missed Classes	Final Grade	Missed Classes	Final Grade
4	81	2	84
7	79	0	90
2	93	5	86
5	70	2	95
0	96		

a. Calculate the sample covariance.
b. Calculate the sample correlation coefficient.
c. Describe the relationship between x and y.

3.66 As a measure of productivity, Verizon Wireless records the number of customers each of its retail employees activates weekly. An activation is defined as either a new customer signing a cell phone contract or an existing customer renewing a contract. The following table shows the number of weekly activations for eight randomly selected employees along with their job-satisfaction levels rated on a scale of $1-10$ $(10 = \text{most satisfied})$. This data can also be found in the Excel file **Verizon satisfaction.xlsx.**

Activations	Satisfaction	Activations	Satisfaction
36	8.0	19	6.1
25	7.9	28	7.0
40	8.5	33	8.2
38	9.0	25	7.7

a. Calculate the sample covariance.
b. Calculate the sample correlation coefficient.
c. Describe the relationship between x and y.

3.67 The Excel file labeled **Customer service champs.xlsx** lists the top 25 companies, with the best customer service scores ranked by *Business Week* in 2012.

a. Determine the coefficient of variation.
b. Calculate the z-score for a company with a score of 900.
c. Test if the empirical rule holds true by determining the percentage of observations that fall within ± two standard deviations from the mean.
d. Verify that Chebyshev's Theorem holds true by determining the percentage of observations that fall within ± three standard deviations from the mean.

3.68 The following table shows the frequency distribution for the golf scores recorded during the 2012 Masters tournament:

Score	Frequency
278–282	6
283–287	12
288–292	21
293–297	16
298–302	6
303–307	1

a. Calculate the approximate average golf score for the tournament.
b. Calculate the approximate variance and standard deviation for the tournament.

3.69 The following table shows the frequency distribution for the mileage on a sample of Avis rental cars:

Mileage	Frequency
5,000 to under 6,000	16
6,000 to under 7,000	11
7,000 to under 8,000	24
8,000 to under 9,000	10
9,000 to under 10,000	15
10,000 to under 11,000	9

a. Calculate the approximate average mileage per car for the sample.
b. Calculate the approximate variance and standard deviation for the sample.

3.70 The following data represent the tips left by 21 customers for the waitstaff at a local restaurant:

$18.40	$10.35	$12.15	$ 7.75	$14.00	$ 9.50	$11.45
$16.00	$15.50	$12.75	$10.50	$12.40	$13.75	$10.75
$ 8.40	$17.85	$16.50	$17.60	$14.10	$10.00	$11.00

a. Calculate the 30th percentile for the data.
b. Calculate the 45th percentile for the data.
c. Calculate the 65th percentile for the data.

3.71 The following data represent the number of students enrolled in 20 business classes this semester at Wilmington University:

29 33 45 26 30 19 21 42 42 24
34 30 28 24 20 25 13 46 40 32

a. Calculate the 20th percentile for the data.
b. Calculate the 70th percentile for the data.
c. Calculate the 90th percentile for the data.

3.72 The following table lists the SAT scores for 27 college students:

845	1,040	815	1,345	1,554	668	1,165	919	1,175
629	490	1,074	387	894	1,419	941	454	673
696	974	564	1,245	1,535	665	1,471	1,188	680

a. Identify the first, second, and third quartiles.
b. Determine the interquartile range.

3.73 The following data represent the number of customers per day that entered an AT&T wireless retail center in Orlando over a 30-day period.

114 106 124 84 86 104 161 183 146 123
189 138 157 166 121 153 222 103 168 147
202 115 156 183 201 202 178 122 94 227

a. Identify the first, second, and third quartiles.
b. Determine the interquartile range.

3.74 The following tables record the times of swimmers in the 50-m freestyle and 100-m backstroke events at a recent meet. A particular swimmer swam the freestyle event in 33 seconds and the backstroke in 72 seconds. In which event did the swimmer perform better relative to the competition?

50-m Freestyle Times
26 29 31 32 32 33 34 35

100-m Backstroke Times
68 71 72 75 76 78 78 78 79 80

3.75 The following table shows the final exam scores for the students from my last statistics class:

78 100 88 84 73 78 70 99 92 96 87 89 81
79 80 84 86 85 79 80 72 69 89 66 76

Determine the percentile ranks for the following scores:

a. 70
b. 75
c. 82
d. 90

3.76 The following data indicate the battery life, in minutes, on a single charge, for 25 iPads:

215 219 229 230 236 239 240 244 247 255
262 264 271 279 280 282 285 285 290 296
301 310 326 327 330

a. Construct a box-and-whisker plot for these data.
b. Identify the five-number summary.

3.77 The following data set represents the odometer mileage, in thousands of miles, of 30 used cars currently in inventory at Mojo Motors:

109.6	107.2	104.4	103.2	100.5	99.9
98.6	97.6	96.2	93.2	93.1	92.9
88.9	86.8	86.4	83.6	83.5	82.8
81.5	80.9	76.8	75.2	75.1	70.7
69.9	69.7	67.2	63.0	61.0	59.8

a. Construct a box-and-whisker plot for these data.
b. Identify the five-number summary.

3.78 Fair Isaac, the company that developed the current credit score model used by most lenders today, would like to examine the relationship between the age and credit score of an individual. The following table shows the credit scores and ages of 10 randomly selected people. This data can also be found in the Excel file **Fair Isaac.xlsx**.

Age	Credit Score	Age	Credit Score
36	675	47	790
24	655	35	720
54	760	59	760
28	615	40	685
31	660	46	610

a. Calculate the sample covariance.
b. Calculate the sample correlation coefficient.
c. Describe the relationship between x and y.

3.79 Suppose *Consumer Reports* would like to investigate the relationship between the battery life, in hours, and the screen size, in diagonal inches, of a laptop computer. The following table shows a random sample of eight laptops and the battery life, in hours, and corresponding screen size, in inches, of each. This data can also be found in the Excel file **laptop battery.xlsx**.

Battery Life	Screen Size	Battery Life	Screen Size
3.6	15.6	3.1	14.5
4.5	17.3	3.4	13.3
4.2	14.5	4.8	11.6
4.5	11.6	3.9	13.6

a. Calculate the sample covariance.
b. Calculate the sample correlation coefficient.
c. Describe the relationship between x and y.

CHAPTER 3 Solutions to Your Turn

YOUR TURN #1

1. $\bar{x} = \dfrac{\sum x}{n} = \dfrac{14 + (-17) + 31 + (-10) + 0 + 11 + 5 + 18}{8} = \dfrac{52}{8} = 6.5 \text{ minutes}$

2. $\bar{x} = \dfrac{\sum w_i x_i}{\sum w_i} = \dfrac{(116)(7.2) + (80)(8.8) + (67)(6.0) + (91)(7.5)}{116 + 80 + 67 + 91} = \dfrac{2{,}623.7}{354} = 7.41$

YOUR TURN #2

1. The sorted ages are as follows:

26 28 31 39 43 45 45 50 57 62

$i = 0.5(n) = 0.5(10) = 5$

The median is the midpoint between the fifth (43) and sixth (45) values.

$$\text{Median} = \frac{43 + 45}{2} = 44$$

2. The sorted SAT scores are as follows:

460 490 510 560 590 610 650 670 700

$i = 0.5(n) = 0.5(9) = 4.5$

The median is the fifth value, which is 590.

YOUR TURN #3

1. Mode = \$16.74, \$16.75, and \$16.85. All three values appear twice.
2. Mode = 26. This value appears four times.
3. No mode exists because no value repeats in the data set.
4. Mode = Cherry. This flavor has the highest number of sales. This is not a coincidence, as it happens to be my favorite!

YOUR TURN #4

1. These data are considered a sample because only a subset of adults in the general population is included in the problem.

x_i	x_i^2
10	100
10	100
4	16
8	64
13	169
6	36
11	121

$$\sum_{i=1}^{7} x_i = 62 \quad \sum_{i=1}^{7} x_i^2 = 606$$

$$\left(\sum_{i=1}^{n} x_i\right)^2 = (62)^2 = 3{,}844$$

$$s^2 = \frac{\sum_{i=1}^{n} x_i^2 - \frac{\left(\sum_{i=1}^{n} x_i\right)^2}{n}}{n-1} = \frac{606 - \frac{3{,}844}{7}}{7-1}$$

$$= \frac{606 - 549.14}{6} = 9.48$$

$$s = \sqrt{s^2} = \sqrt{9.48} = 3.08$$

2. These data are considered a population because the ages of all eight employees in the bank branch are included in the problem.

x_i	x_i^2
32	1,024
40	1,600
27	729
29	841
34	1,156
38	1,444
46	2,116
24	576

$$\sum_{i=1}^{8} x_i = 270 \quad \sum_{i=1}^{8} x_i^2 = 9{,}486$$

$$\left(\sum_{i=1}^{N} x_i\right)^2 = (270)^2 = 72{,}900$$

$$\sigma^2 = \frac{\sum_{i=1}^{N} x_i^2 - \frac{\left(\sum_{i=1}^{N} x_i\right)^2}{N}}{N} = \frac{9{,}486 - \frac{72{,}900}{8}}{8}$$

$$= \frac{9{,}486 - 9{,}112.5}{8} = 46.7$$

$$\sigma = \sqrt{\sigma^2} = \sqrt{46.7} = 6.8$$

YOUR TURN #5

	Rollins		Pujols	
	x	x^2	x	x^2
	12	144	41	1,681
	25	625	49	2,401
	30	900	32	1,024
	11	121	37	1,369
	21	441	47	2,209
	8	64	42	1,764
	16	256	37	1,369
	23	529	30	900
Total	146	3,080	315	12,717

Rollins

$$s_R = \sqrt{\frac{\sum_{i=1}^{n} x_i^2 - \frac{\left(\sum_{i=1}^{n} x_i\right)^2}{n}}{n-1}}$$

$$s_R = \sqrt{\frac{3{,}080 - \frac{(146)^2}{8}}{8-1}}$$

$$s_R = \sqrt{\frac{3{,}080 - 2{,}664.50}{7}}$$

$$s_R = \sqrt{59.36}$$

$$s_R = 7.70$$

$$\bar{x}_R = \frac{\left(\sum_{i=1}^{n} x_i\right)}{n} = \frac{146}{8} = 18.25$$

$$CV_R = \frac{s_R}{\bar{x}_R}(100)$$

$$CV_R = \frac{7.70}{18.25}(100) = 42.2\%$$

Pujols

$$s_P = \sqrt{\frac{\sum_{i=1}^{n} x_i^2 - \frac{\left(\sum_{i=1}^{n} x_i\right)^2}{n}}{n-1}}$$

$$s_P = \sqrt{\frac{12{,}717 - \frac{(315)^2}{8}}{8-1}}$$

$$s_P = \sqrt{\frac{12{,}717 - 12{,}403.13}{7}}$$

$$s_P = \sqrt{44.84}$$

$$s_P = 6.70$$

$$\bar{x}_P = \frac{\left(\sum_{i=1}^{n} x_i\right)}{n} = \frac{315}{8} = 39.38$$

$$CV_P = \frac{s_P}{\bar{x}_P}(100)$$

$$CV_P = \frac{6.70}{39.38}(100) = 17.0\%$$

Albert Pujols is a more consistent home-run hitter because he has a lower CV.

YOUR TURN #6

1. a) $z = \frac{x - \bar{x}}{s} = \frac{\$6{,}000 - \$7{,}000}{\$850} = -1.18$

b) $z = \frac{x - \bar{x}}{s} = \frac{\$8{,}400 - \$7{,}000}{\$850} = 1.65$

2. a) $x = \bar{x} + zs$

$x = \$322 + (1)(\$25) = \$347$

$x = \$322 + (-1)(\$25) = \$297$

b) $x = \$322 + (2)(\$25) = \$372$

$x = \$322 + (-2)(\$25) = \$272$

c) $x = \$322 + (3)(\$25) = \$397$

$x = \$322 + (-3)(\$25) = \$247$

3. a) $x = \bar{x} + zs$

$x = \$1{,}920 + (2)(\$160) = \$2{,}240$

$x = \$1{,}920 + (-2)(\$160) = \$1{,}600$

b) $\left(1 - \frac{1}{z^2}\right) = 0.85$

$\frac{1}{z^2} = 0.15$

$z^2 = \frac{1}{0.15} = 6.67$

$z = \sqrt{6.67} = 2.58$

$x = \bar{x} + zs$

$x = \$1{,}920 + (2.58)(\$160) = \$2{,}332.80$

$x = \$1{,}920 + (-2.58)(\$160) = \$1{,}507.20$

c) $x = \$1{,}920 + (4)(\$160) = \$2{,}560$

$x = \$1{,}920 + (-4)(\$160) = \$1{,}280$

YOUR TURN #7

GPA	Midpoint
3.0 to under 3.2	3.1
3.2 to under 3.4	3.3
3.4 to under 3.6	3.5
3.6 to under 3.8	3.7
3.8 to 4.0	3.9

$$\bar{x} \approx \frac{\sum_{i=1}^{k}(f_i m_i)}{n}$$

$$\bar{x} \approx \frac{(6)(3.1) + (8)(3.3) + (6)(3.5) + (14)(3.7) + (6)(3.9)}{6 + 8 + 6 + 14 + 6}$$

$$= \frac{141.2}{40} = 3.53$$

GPA	m_i	f_i	$\bar{x}$	$(m_i - \bar{x})$	$(m_i - \bar{x})^2$	$(m_i - \bar{x})^2 f_i$
3.0–3.2	3.1	6	3.53	−0.43	0.1849	1.1094
3.2–3.4	3.3	8	3.53	−0.23	0.0529	0.4232
3.4–3.6	3.5	6	3.53	−0.03	0.0009	0.0054
3.6–3.8	3.7	14	3.53	0.17	0.0289	0.4046
3.8–4.0	3.9	6	3.53	0.37	0.1369	0.8214

$n = \Sigma f_i = 40 \quad \Sigma(m_i - \bar{x})^2 f_i = 2.764$

$$s^2 \approx \frac{\sum_{i=1}^{k}(m_i - \bar{x})^2 f_i}{n - 1} = \frac{2.764}{40 - 1} = 0.0709.$$

$$s \approx \sqrt{0.0709} = 0.267$$

YOUR TURN #8

1. $n = 22$

$$Q_1: i = \frac{P}{100}(n) = \frac{25}{100}(22) = 5.5$$

Q_1 is in the 6th position of our data sorted from lowest to highest; therefore, $Q_1 = \$671$.

$$Q_2: i = \frac{P}{100}(n) = \frac{50}{100}(22) = 11$$

Q_2 is the midpoint between the 11th ($747) and 12th ($760) positions; therefore,

$$Q_2 = \frac{\$747 + \$760}{2} = \$753.5$$

The calculation for the third quartile index point is shown as follows:

$$Q_3: i = \frac{P}{100}(n) = \frac{75}{100}(22) = 16.5$$

Q_3 is in the 17th position of our sorted data; therefore, $Q_3 = 977$. Thus, the three quartiles were found to be as follows:

$$Q_1 = \$671 \quad Q_2 = \$753.5 \quad Q_3 = \$977$$

$$IQR = \$977 - \$671 = \$306$$

2. $i = \frac{P}{100}(n) = \frac{65}{100}(22) = 14.3$

The 65th percentile is the data value in the 15th position and is equal to $945.

3. There are a total of 22 films, of which 6 are below *The Sting.*Therefore, the approximate percentile for *The Sting* is as follows:

$$\text{Percentile} = \frac{(6) + 0.5}{22}(100) = \frac{6.5}{22}(100) = 30\text{th}$$

YOUR TURN #9

Sort the data from lowest to highest:

$$Q_1 : i = \frac{P}{100}(n) = \frac{25}{100}(16) = 4$$

\$378	\$8,048	\$10,162	\$11,499
\$3,414	\$8,128	\$10,827	\$12,437
\$5,030	\$9,038	\$11,113	\$15,783
\$7,960	\$9,970	\$11,349	\$19,400

Q_1 is midway between the fourth (7,960) and the fifth (8,048) positions of our sorted data.

$$Q_1 = \frac{7{,}960 + 8{,}048}{2} = 8{,}004$$

$$Q_2 : i = \frac{P}{100}(n) = \frac{50}{100}(16) = 8$$

Q_2 is midway between the eighth (9,970) and the ninth (10,162) positions of our sorted data.

$$Q_2 = \frac{9{,}970 + 10{,}162}{2} = 10{,}066$$

$$Q_3 : i = \frac{P}{100}(n) = \frac{75}{100}(16) = 12$$

Q_3 is midway between the 12th (11,349) and the 13th (11,499) positions of our sorted data.

$$Q_3 = \frac{11{,}349 + 11{,}499}{2} = 11{,}424$$

$$IQR = Q_3 - Q_1$$
$$IQR = 11{,}424 - 8{,}004 = 3{,}420$$
$$\text{Upper Limit} = Q_3 + 1.5(IQR)$$
$$\text{Upper Limit} = 11{,}424 + 1.5(3{,}420) = 16{,}554$$
$$\text{Lower Limit} = Q_1 - 1.5(IQR)$$
$$\text{Lower Limit} = 8{,}004 - 1.5(3{,}420) = 2{,}874$$

There are two outliers in the data set: \$378 and \$19,400.

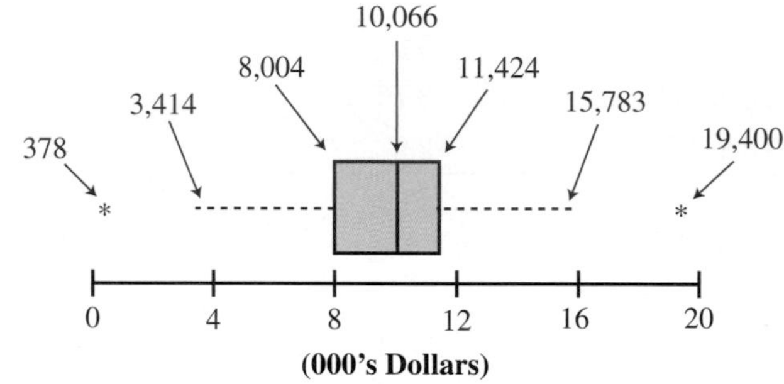

Five-number summary: 378, 8,004, 10,066, 11,424, 19,400

YOUR TURN #10

a) Price: $\bar{x} = \frac{\sum_{i=1}^{n} x_i}{n} = \frac{70 + 75 + 80 + 85 + 90 + 95 + 100}{7} = 85.0$

Demand: $\bar{y} = \frac{\sum_{i=1}^{n} y_i}{n} = \frac{18 + 23 + 10 + 16 + 17 + 15 + 6}{7} = 15.0$

x_i	$\bar{x}$	$(x_i - \bar{x})$	y_i	$\bar{y}$	$(y_i - \bar{y})$	$(x_i - \bar{x})(y_i - \bar{y})$
70	85	−15	18	15	3	−45
75	85	−10	23	15	8	−80
80	85	−5	10	15	−5	25
85	85	0	16	15	1	0
90	85	5	17	15	2	10
95	85	10	15	15	0	0
100	85	15	6	15	−9	−135
						$\sum(x_i - \bar{x})(y_i - \bar{y}) = -225$

b) $$s_{xy} = \frac{\sum_{i=1}^{n}(x_i - \bar{x})(y_i - \bar{y})}{n - 1} = \frac{-225}{7 - 1} = -37.5$$

$$s_x = \sqrt{\frac{\sum_{i=1}^{n}(x_i - \bar{x})^2}{n - 1}}$$

$$s_x = \sqrt{\frac{(70 - 85)^2 + (75 - 85)^2 + (80 - 85)^2 + (85 - 85)^2 + (90 - 85)^2 + (95 - 85)^2 + (100 - 85)^2}{7 - 1}}$$

$$s_x = \sqrt{\frac{700}{6}} = \sqrt{116.67} = 10.80$$

$$s_y = \sqrt{\frac{\sum_{i=1}^{n}(y_i - \bar{y})^2}{n - 1}}$$

$$s_y = \sqrt{\frac{(18 - 15)^2 + (23 - 15)^2 + (10 - 15)^2 + (16 - 15)^2 + (17 - 15)^2 + (15 - 15)^2 + (6 - 15)^2}{7 - 1}}$$

$$s_y = \sqrt{\frac{184}{6}} = \sqrt{30.67} = 5.54$$

$$r_{xy} = \frac{s_{xy}}{s_x s_y} = \frac{-37.5}{(10.80)(5.54)} = -0.627$$

c) We have discovered a negative relationship between price and demand for this printer. As the price increases, weekly demand tends to decrease, which would be expected.

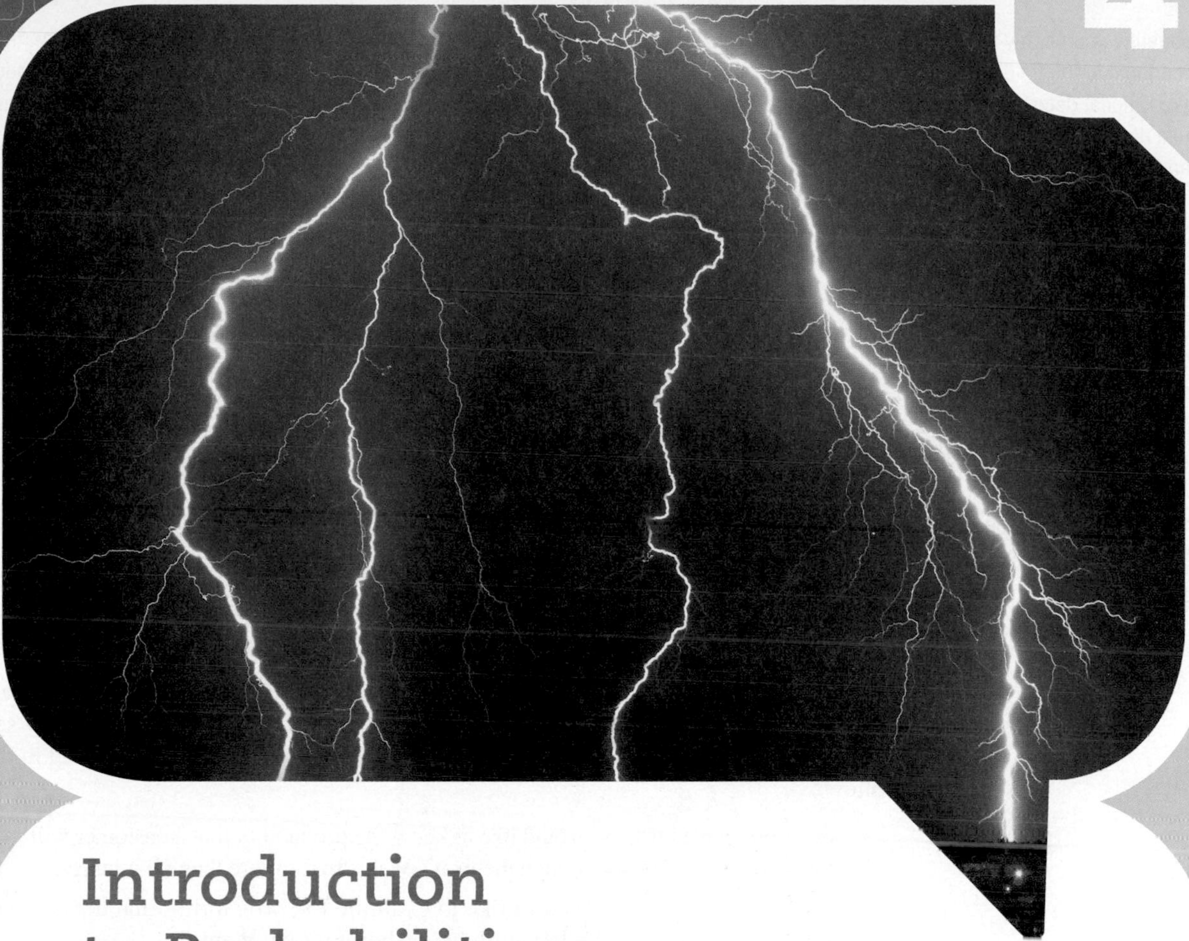

Introduction to Probabilities

IN THIS CHAPTER, YOU WILL LEARN TO:

- Distinguish between classical, empirical, and subjective probability.
- Identify the basic properties of probability.
- Calculate and interpret the intersection and union of events.
- Use the addition rule and multiplication rule for probability.
- Interpret the meaning of conditional probability.
- Use Bayes' Theorem to calculate revised probabilities from prior probabilities.
- Count the total number of possible outcomes using the fundamental counting principle.
- Distinguish between permutations and combinations.

CHAPTER 4 MAP

Stats in Practice: Statistics Author Sent Out by Wife to Purchase Lottery Tickets During Thunderstorm: What's Wrong with This Picture?

Probability is probably (no pun intended) the most misunderstood topic in the field of statistics. People often struggle to make rational decisions when dealing with probabilities because it's difficult to judge the likelihood of complex events. For example, most people (including my wife) are much more optimistic about winning the state lottery than the actual numbers merit. A common type of lottery is called 6/49. The goal of it is to correctly choose 6 out of 49 numbers. As you will see later in the chapter, the chance of winning this lottery is an infinitesimal 0.00000007, or nearly 1 out of 14 million. The probability is so low that it is difficult to fathom. If you purchase one lottery ticket every day of the year, you can expect to win once every 38,286 years. To give this some perspective, 38,000 years ago humans were living in caves during the Stone Age.

Let's compare your probability of winning the 6/49 lottery to the likelihood that you will be struck by lightning. According to the National Oceanic and Atmospheric Administration (NOAA), the federal agency that monitors atmospheric conditions, the odds of being struck by lightning in the United States on any given day are approximately 1 out of 400,000. According to these statistics, you are 35 times more likely to be struck by lightning today than win the lottery.

In spite of presenting this useful information to my wife in what I considered to be a very convincing manner, she still insisted that I go out and buy lottery tickets during a severe thunderstorm when the jackpot was unusually large. The good news is that I returned home safely without getting lit up like a Christmas tree. The bad news is that we didn't win the lottery (big surprise), as evidenced by the fact that I haven't quit my day job.

Organizations in today's business world face a great deal of uncertainty when they are making decisions. Probability provides a valuable tool to quantify this uncertainty so that managers can make better decisions. Some examples of how probability is used in business follow:

- An e-commerce business would like to know the probability that a customer will make a purchase after browsing through the firm's Web site for more than 10 minutes.
- A credit card executive would like to examine the probability that a customer with a poor credit score will be late with his or her next payment.
- A media consultant is asked to determine the probability that the viewing audience for next year's Super Bowl will exceed 130 million people.
- A company's sales department would like to establish the probability that a male customer will purchase an extended warranty after buying a laptop computer.

In this chapter, we will explore the topic of probability and discover its usefulness in a variety of business settings.

4.1 An Introduction to Probabilities

A **probability** is a numerical value ranging from 0 to 1. It indicates the chance, or likelihood, of a specific event occurring. If there is no chance of the event occurring, the probability is 0. If the event is absolutely going to occur, the probability of it occurring is 1.

A **probability** is a numerical value that indicates the chance, or likelihood, of a specific event occurring. Weather forecasters commonly use probabilities when referring to the chance of rain the following day. A probability is expressed by statisticians as a number ranging from 0 to 1. The number is translated into a percentage. For example, if an event cannot occur, then it is assigned a probability of 0, which is stated as 0%. By contrast, if the event will absolutely occur, the probability of it occurring is 1, or 100%.

But before we go any further, we need to tackle some new statistics jargon. The following terms are widely used when talking about probability:

An outcome is just a fancy word for a result of an experiment. For example, if I roll a single die and get a six, the outcome of the experiment is a six.

- **Experiment.** The process of measuring or observing an activity for the purpose of collecting data. An example is rolling a single six-sided die.
- **Sample space.** All the possible outcomes, or results, of an experiment. The sample space for our single-die experiment is the numbers {1, 2, 3, 4, 5, 6}. Statisticians put the numbers in braces to signal that they represent the sample space.

- **Event.** One or more outcomes of an experiment. The outcome, or outcomes, is a subset of the sample space. An example of an event is rolling a pair with two dice.
- **Simple event.** An event with a single outcome in its most basic form that cannot be simplified. An example of a simple event is rolling a five with a single die.

Table 4.1 shows some other examples of experiments and their corresponding sample spaces.

The event "rolling a pair with two dice" is not a simple event because it contains two outcomes—the numbers from each die.

TABLE 4.1 | EXAMPLES OF EXPERIMENTS AND THEIR SAMPLE SPACES

EXPERIMENT	SAMPLE SPACE
Flip a coin	{heads, tails}
Answer a multiple-choice question	{a, b, c, d, e}
Inspect a product	{defective, not defective}
Draw a card from a standard deck	{52 cards in the deck}

There are three methods of assigning probability that we will discuss in this chapter: classical, empirical, and subjective.

Classical Probability

Classical probability is used when we know the number of possible outcomes of the event of interest and can calculate the probability of that event using Equation 4.1.

Classical probability is used when we know the number of possible outcomes of the event of interest and can calculate the probability of that event using Equation 4.1.

Formula 4.1 for Classical Probability

$$P(A) = \frac{\text{Number of possible outcomes that constitute Event } A}{\text{Total number of possible outcomes in the sample space}}$$

where

$P(A) =$ The probability that Event A will occur

For our single-die experiment, our sample space has six possible outcomes, as shown in Figure 4.1.

FIGURE 4.1
The Sample Space for a Single Die

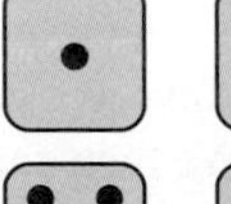

If the simple Event A is defined as rolling a five, which has only one possible way of occurring, then the probability of Event A occurring is calculated as follows:

$$P(A) = \frac{1}{6} = 0.167$$

Classical probability requires that you know the number of outcomes that pertain to a particular event. You also need to know the total number of possible outcomes in the sample space.

In other words, there is a 16.7% probability of rolling a five. This is an example of **simple probability** because we are considering the likelihood of a single (simple) event occurring by itself. Later in this chapter, we will expand this concept to consider two or more events occurring.

Simple probability represents the likelihood of a single (simple) event occurring by itself.

Classical probability assumes that each event in the sample space has the same likelihood of occurring. That is, the chance of rolling a one is the same as rolling a two, and so forth. You also need to know the total number of possible outcomes in the sample space.

The sample space {male, female} would be an example of collectively exhaustive events because a person's gender must be one or the other.

A sample space is described as **collectively exhaustive** if it includes every possible simple event that can occur.

If the sample space includes every possible simple event that can occur, then we say that set of events is **collectively exhaustive** (sounds like how I feel when I'm trying to make my publisher's writing deadlines). For example, the events 1, 2, 3, 4, 5, and 6 are collectively exhaustive when we roll a single die. When we roll the die, one of these outcomes must occur.

We can expand our classical probability example to rolling two dice together. This changes the sample space to the following one, which has 36 possible outcomes. Each pair of numbers represents the outcome of the two dice. Let's define Event A as obtaining a sum of five. There are four ways in which a sum of five could be rolled; they are highlighted in yellow in the following sample space.

Sample Space When Rolling Two Dice to Obtain a Sum of Five

{(1,1) (1,2) (1,3) (1,4) (1,5) (1,6)
(2,1) (2,2) (2,3) (2,4) (2,5) (2,6)
(3,1) (3,2) (3,3) (3,4) (3,5) (3,6)
(4,1) (4,2) (4,3) (4,4) (4,5) (4,6)
(5,1) (5,2) (5,3) (5,4) (5,5) (5,6)
(6,1) (6,2) (6,3) (6,4) (6,5) (6,6)}

We can now calculate the probability of rolling a sum of five with our two dice. Because there are four ways to obtain a sum of five out of the 36 possible outcomes,

$$P(A) = \frac{4}{36} = 0.111$$

In other words, there is an 11.1% chance of two dice summing to the number five.

Try your luck on this card example to test your understanding of classical probability.

YOUR TURN #1

1. What is the probability of randomly selecting a spade from a standard 52-card deck?
2. What is the probability of obtaining a sum of eight when rolling two dice?

Answers can be found on ▶ **page 189**

Empirical Probability

Empirical probability involves conducting an experiment to observe the frequency with which an event occurs.

With classical probability, we understand the underlying process of what we are working with, such as "There are 4 aces in a deck of 52 cards, so the probability of drawing an ace is 4/52." When we don't have the information needed to determine the number of outcomes associated with an event (there is no "known" sample space, in other words), we rely on **empirical probability**. Empirical probability involves conducting an experiment to observe the frequency with which an event occurs. We then calculate the ratio of the number of times the event occurred relative to the total number of times we observed that it both did and did not occur (Equation 4.2),

Empirical probability requires that you count the frequency that an event occurs through an experiment and calculate the probability from the experiment's relative frequency distribution.

Formula 4.2 for Empirical Probability

$$P(A) = \frac{\text{Frequency in which Event } A \text{ occurs}}{\text{Total number of observations}}$$

Say for example, I am a store owner and would like to know the probability that a person who walks in my store will make a purchase. Classical probability is no help to me here because I don't have any information about why someone makes a purchase. I need to use empirical probability by counting how many customers come to my store over a period of time and how many of those customers made a purchase. If 100 customers walked into my store today and 15 made a purchase, then my empirical probability for this event would be $15/100 = 0.15$.

On a recent trip to the Nautica Factory Outlet store in Hilton Head, South Carolina, I was presented a scratch card from the salesperson that entitled me to a discount between 5% and 50% on my purchase. My discount card turned out to be 15%. Hoping to do better, I quietly told my wife to pretend she didn't know me (which she was happy to do) and to get her own card. I'm sad to report Deb came back with a whopping 5% discount. For the sake of this example, let's suppose that when Deb approached her, the salesperson had 20 cards with the discounts shown in Table 4.2.

TABLE 4.2 | NAUTICA FACTORY OUTLET DISCOUNT CARDS

DISCOUNT (%)	NUMBER OF CARDS
5	9
10	4
15	2
20	3
30	0
40	1
50	1
Total	**20**

For instance, the 5% discount has a frequency of nine because there were nine of these cards in the salesperson's hand. We can determine the probability of Deb receiving each of the discounts using the relative frequency distribution procedure discussed in Chapter 3. This gives us the empirical probabilities of Deb receiving the discounts shown in Table 4.3.

TABLE 4.3 | CALCULATING EMPIRICAL PROBABILITIES

DISCOUNT (%)	NUMBER OF CARDS	PROBABILITY
5	9	$9/20 = 0.45$
10	4	$4/20 = 0.20$
15	2	$2/20 = 0.10$
20	3	$3/20 = 0.15$
30	0	$0/20 = 0.00$
40	1	$1/20 = 0.05$
50	1	$1/20 = 0.05$
Total	**20**	$\mathbf{20/20 = 1.00}$

Empirical probability is also known as the relative frequency approach because it relies on relative frequencies that were discussed in Chapter 2.

As Table 4.3 shows, the probability of Deb getting a 5% discount is 45%. What was the probability that her discount would exceed my 15%? Because there were 5 cards out of the 20 that were greater than 15%, the probability of Deb's discount exceeding 15%, which I'll define as Event A, was as follows:

There are three cards with 20%, one card with 40%, and one card with 50%.

$$P(A) = \frac{5}{20} = 0.25$$

Oh well, it was worth a try!

There is an important connection between classical and empirical probabilities that can be explained with the following example. Suppose I flip a fair coin (one with an equal chance of observing a heads or tails) three times and observe three tails. The empirical probability for this experiment is shown in Table 4.4.

TABLE 4.4 | THE EMPIRICAL PROBABILITIES OF A COIN FLIP

OUTCOME	FREQUENCY	PROBABILITY
Heads	0	0/3 = 0.00
Tails	3	3/3 = 1.00
Total	**3**	**3/3 = 1.00**

Even though the empirical probability of a tails in this example is 100%, we all know the classical probability is 50%. If we flipped the coin, say, 500 times, the empirical probability would be very close to 50%. What we have discovered here is the **law of large numbers**, which states that when an experiment is conducted a large number of times, the empirical probabilities of the process will converge to the classical probabilities.

The **law of large numbers** states that when an experiment is conducted a large number of times, the empirical probabilities of the process will converge to the classical probabilities.

The following Your Turn problem will give you an opportunity to test your newly learned empirical probability skills.

YOUR TURN #2

In a recent survey of 1,025 adults conducted by the poll-taking company Gallup asked how much money they planned to spend on Christmas gifts. The results are shown in the following table:

Amount	Frequency
$1,000 or more	297
$500–$999	246
$250–$499	144
$100–$249	164
Less than $100	41
No opinion	133
Total	**1,025**

a) What is the probability that a randomly selected person is planning to spend between $250 and $499 for Christmas?

b) What is the probability that a randomly selected person is planning to spend $250 or more for Christmas?

Answers can be found on ▶ **page 189**

Subjective Probability

We use **subjective probability** when classical and empirical probabilities are not available. These are instances in which data or experiments are not available to calculate probabilities. Instead, we rely on our experience and judgment to estimate the probabilities.

We use **subjective probability** when classical and empirical probabilities are not available and instead we rely on experience and intuition to estimate the probabilities.

The following examples demonstrate how subjective probability is used in the business world:

- A director of marketing estimates that there is a 20% probability that her company's biggest competitor will reduce its prices in the next month.
- A human resource manager reports that there is a 75% chance that his company will institute a hiring freeze for the upcoming year.
- A market analyst believes that there is a 50% probability that Apple will announce a new version of the iPhone next month.

In each case, it would be very difficult to determine these probabilities using classical or empirical methods. Rather, these subjective probabilities would most likely be based on the expertise and judgment of the individuals. We often engage in this type of assessment in our day-to-day lives, albeit more informally. Have you, perhaps, at some point in your college career mulled over the possibility of passing tomorrow's exam after staying out late with your friends the night before? If you have, you have put subjective probability to work!

Let's see if you can distinguish between the three different types of probabilities in the next Your Turn problem.

YOUR TURN #3

Indicate whether classical, empirical, or subjective probability should be used to determine each of the following:

a. The probability that the baseball player Josh Hamilton will hit a home run during his next at bat
b. The probability of drawing a jack from a deck of cards
c. The probability that I will shoot lower than a 90 during my next round of golf
d. The probability of winning your state's lottery
e. The probability that the price of gasoline will exceed $4.00 per gallon next summer
f. The probability that I will finish writing my next textbook before my deadline

Answers can be found on ▶ **page 190**

Basic Properties of a Probability

Our next step is to review the "rules and regulations" that govern probability theory. The basic ones are as follows:

Probability Rule 1

If $P(A) = 1$, then with certainty, Event A must occur. An example is Event A = Rolling a single six-sided die and observing a 1, 2, 3, 4, 5, or 6.

Probability Rule 2

If $P(A) = 0$, then with certainty, Event A will not occur. An example is Event A = Drawing five cards from a 52-card deck without replacing any of them and observing five aces in your hand. (A 52-card deck only has four aces. The only way this event can occur is if somebody is cheating and has another ace up his or her sleeve!)

Probability Rule 3

The probability of any event must range from 0 to 1. Probabilities can never be negative or greater than 1. For example, the probability of my wife buying a pair of shoes next month could be 0 (0%), 1 (100%), or some number in between. However, the probability could never be -1 (-100%) or 2 (200%). (My experience tells me my subjective probability of this event occurring will be closer to 100% than 0%, but I should keep that assessment to myself.)

Probability Rule 4

The sum of all the probabilities for the simple events in the sample space must be equal to 1. For example, Table 4.5 shows the way in which patients arrived at the University of Virginia Medical Center's emergency room during a recent 24-hour period.

Note that the sum of the probabilities in the third column adds to 1.00 because every simple event in the sample space is included in the table. In other words, the only recorded methods of arrival are those listed in Table 4.5.

TABLE 4.5 | EMERGENCY ROOM ARRIVAL METHODS

METHOD OF ARRIVAL	FREQUENCY	PROBABILITY
Walk-in	132	$132/197 = 0.67$
Ambulance	61	$61/197 = 0.31$
Helicopter	2	$2/197 = 0.01$
Prison guard	2	$2/197 = 0.01$
Total	**197**	$\mathbf{197/197 = 1.00}$

Probability Rule 5

The **complement** to Event *A* is defined as all the outcomes in the sample space that are not part of Event *A* and is denoted as A'.

The **complement** to Event *A* is defined as all of the outcomes in the sample space that are not part of Event *A*. The complement is denoted as A'. Using this definition, we can state the following:

Formula 4.3 for The Complement Rule

$$P(A) + P(A') = 1 \text{ or}$$
$$P(A) = 1 - P(A')$$

In other words, the probability of the complement of an event occurring is 100% minus the probability of the event itself occurring. We can see this graphically in Figure 4.2, which shows a Venn diagram. The box represents the entire sample space, and the shaded circle represents Event *A*. The area outside the circle within the box represents the complement of Event *A*.

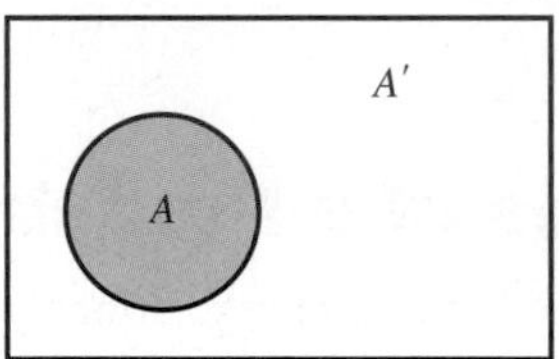

FIGURE 4.2 Venn Diagram Illustrating the Complement Rule

Table 4.6 demonstrates the complement rule by showing the results of a survey conducted by Impulse Research for the Downtown Cookie Company. In the survey, 1,033 adults were asked to identify their favorite cookie.

TABLE 4.6 | FAVORITE COOKIE SURVEY

FAVORITE COOKIE	FREQUENCY	PROBABILITY
Chocolate chip	548	0.53
Peanut butter	165	0.16
Oatmeal	155	0.15
Sugar/shortbread	114	0.11
Other	51	0.05
Total	**1,033**	**1.00**

We'll define Event *A* as selecting a person whose favorite cookie was chocolate chip. This means that Event A' represents the probability of selecting a person whose favorite cookie was *not* chocolate chip. From Table 4.6, we can determine $P(A')$ as follows:

$$P(A) = 0.53$$
$$P(A') = 1 - P(A) = 1 - 0.53 = 0.47$$

The probability of selecting someone whose favorite cookie is not chocolate chip is 47%. Notice that the complement rule saved us some work because it is easier to calculate than adding up all the following probabilities:

$$P(A') = 0.16 + 0.15 + 0.11 + 0.05 = 0.47$$

Test your newfound skills in the following Your Turn box before moving on to the next section.

YOUR TURN #4

1. Identify which of the following values are valid and not valid numbers for a probability:

a. 0.19	**f.** 124%
b. −0.6	**g.** $\frac{2}{3}$
c. 0	**h.** 1
d. 51%	**i.** $-\frac{1}{6}$
e. 1.08	

2. The following table shows the average change in salaries for full-time permanent employees over a recent one-year period as determined by a survey of 2,795 human resource professionals by Harris Interactive:

Change in Salary	Frequency	Probability
11% or more	58	0.02
4%–10%	351	0.13
1%–3%	720	0.26
No change	1,491	0.53
Decrease	175	0.06
Total	**2,795**	**1.00**

Use the complement rule to determine the probability that an employee did not take a pay cut.

Answers can be found on ▶ **page 190**

4.1 Section Problems

Basic Skills

4.1 Identify which of the following values are valid and not valid numbers for a probability:

a. $\frac{5}{4}$	**f.** 14%
b. 0.04	**g.** $-\frac{3}{3}$
c. 200%	**h.** 0%
d. 0.5	**i.** 1.2
e. $\frac{1}{8}$	

4.2 What is the probability of randomly selecting a diamond from a standard 52-card deck?

4.3 Consider the experiment of rolling two dice.

a. What is the probability of obtaining a sum of seven?

b. What is the probability of obtaining a sum of three or less?

c. What is the probability of obtaining a sum of ten or more?

4.4 Indicate whether classical, empirical, or subjective probability should be used to determine each of the following:

a. The probability that the Green Bay Packers will make the playoffs this year.

b. The probability that no students will be absent from my next statistics class.

c. The probability that I will draw three of a kind in a five-card hand.

d. The probability that the local bakery will sell more than five loaves of rye bread tomorrow.

e. The probability that I will randomly select a red M&M from a bowl that contains five red, eight yellow, and seven green M&Ms.

Applications

4.5 A customer survey asked respondents to indicate their highest levels of education. The only three choices in the survey were high school, college, and other. If 29% indicated high school and 53% indicated college, determine the percentage of respondents who chose the "other" category.

4.6 A survey was conducted in which 125 families were asked how many cats lived in their households. The results are as follows:

Number of Cats	Number of Households
0	76
1	32
2	12
3	3
4	2
Total	**125**

a. What is the probability that a randomly selected family has one cat?
b. What is the probability that a randomly selected family has more than one cat?
c. What is the probability that a randomly selected family has cats?
d. Is this an example of classical, empirical, or subjective probability?

4.7 A total of 200 adults responded to a survey asking them to name their favorite national park. The relative frequencies are as follows:

Park	Relative Frequency (%)
Yellowstone	33
Great Smoky Mountains	19
Yosemite	19
Acadia	7
Other	?
Total	**100**

a. What percentage of respondents chose the "Other" category?
b. How many respondents selected Yellowstone?
c. How many respondents selected either Yosemite or Acadia?
d. Is this an example of classical, empirical, or subjective probability?

4.8 The following table shows the frequencies of executives' salary ranges at a particular organization:

Salary Range	Frequency
Under \$60,000	2
\$60,000 to under \$70,000	5
\$70,000 to under \$80,000	7
\$80,000 to under \$90,000	4
\$90,000 to under \$100,000	6
\$100,000 or more	?
Total	**26**

a. How many executives at this organization earned \$100,000 or more per year?
b. What is the probability that a randomly selected executive earned \$100,000 or more per year?
c. What is the probability that a randomly selected executive earned \$60,000 or more per year?
d. What is the probability that a randomly selected executive earned between \$70,000 and \$90,000 per year?

4.9 Braun Research recently surveyed U.S. adults about the number of cups of coffee they drink per day and per week. The percentages are as follows:

Number of Cups	Percentage
Two or more cups a day	33
One cup a day	19
Two cups a week	11
One cup a week	9
Don't drink coffee	28

a. What percentage of adults drink coffee?
b. What percentage of adults drink two cups or more of coffee a week?
c. What percentage of adults drink one or two cups per week?

4.2 Probability Rules for More Than One Event

Up until now, we have focused on basic probability concepts that primarily deal with a single event. However, in the business world, situations are rarely this simple. Oftentimes, they involve two or more events that intersect with one another. For example, a banking manager might want to know the probability that a customer who has a poor credit score will default on her mortgage. In this case there are two events to consider:

Event A = Customer defaults on mortgage

Event B = Customer has a low credit score

To address this type of probability, we need to explore the concepts presented in this section.

The Intersection of Events

To demonstrate working with probabilities of multiple events, I will use the following example. Now that my children are older and living away from home, I cherish those moments when the phone rings and I see one of their names appear on my caller ID. Experience has taught me that I can categorize these calls as either "crisis"—involving such things as a computer, a car, an ATM card, or a cell phone—or "noncrisis"—when the kids call just to see if I'm alive and well so that I'll be available for their next crisis.

A **contingency table** indicates the number of occurrences of events that are classified according to two categorical variables.

Table 4.7, which is called a **contingency table**, categorizes the last 50 phone calls by child and type of call.

TABLE 4.7 | A Contingency Table for Phone Calls

CHILD	CRISIS	NONCRISIS	TOTAL
Christin	12	7	19
Brian	10	4	14
John	6	11	17
Total	28	22	50

I received a total of 14 phone calls from Brian, of which 10 were crisis and 4 were noncrisis.

Contingency tables show the actual or relative frequency of two categorical variables at the same time. In this case, the categorical variables are the child and type of call. I'll assume that this past pattern of calls will hold true in the near future. We'll define Events A and B as follows:

Event A = The next phone call will come from Christin

Event B = The next phone call will involve a crisis

We can use the contingency table to calculate the simple probability that the next phone call will come from Christin:

There were a total of 19 calls from Christin (12 crisis and 7 noncrisis) in Table 4.7.

$$P(A) = \frac{19}{50} = 0.38$$

The probability that the next phone call will involve a crisis would be as follows:

There were a total of 28 crisis calls between all three kids in Table 4.7.

$$P(B) = \frac{28}{50} = 0.56$$

Marginal probability is another term used for simple probability.

The **intersection** of Events A and B represents the number of instances in which Events A and B occur at the same time (that is, the same phone call is both from Christin and a crisis).

These simple probabilities are also known as **marginal probabilities** in some settings.

What about the probability that the next phone call will come from Christin *and* will involve a crisis? This event is known as the **intersection** of Events A and B and is described as $A \cap B$. Figure 4.3 shows a Venn diagram describing the intersection of Events A and B. It is the shaded region shared by both events.

FIGURE 4.3
Venn Diagram Illustrating the Intersection of A and B

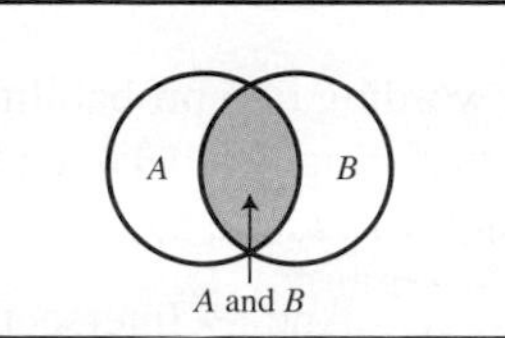

The number of phone calls from our contingency table that meet both criteria is found at the intersection of the Crisis column and the Christin row in Table 4.7, which is 12; therefore,

$$P(A \text{ and } B) = P(A \cap B) = \frac{12}{50} = 0.24$$

The probability of the intersection of two events is known as a **joint probability**.

This explains why I hold my breath as I pick up the phone! The probability of the intersection of two events is known as a **joint probability**.

The Union of Events

The **union** of Events *A* and *B* represents the number of instances where either Event *A* or *B* occur or both events occur together.

The **union** of Events *A* and *B* represents the number of instances in which either Event *A* or Event *B* or both occur together. The union is denoted as $A \cap B$. Figure 4.4 shows a Venn diagram describing the union of Events A and *B*. It consists of all three shaded regions.

FIGURE 4.4
Venn Diagram Illustrating the Union of Events A and B

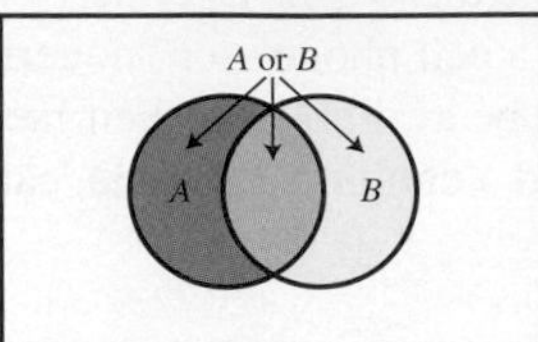

Using our previous example, the highlighted numbers in Table 4.8 show the instances that include either

- A call—crisis or noncrisis—from Christin (Event *A*)

or

- A crisis phone call from any of the three kids (Event *B*)

Note that there were a total of 35 such calls $(12 + 7 + 10 + 6 = 35)$.

TABLE 4.8 | A Contingency Table Showing the Union of Two Events: Phone Calls

CHILD	CRISIS	NONCRISIS	TOTAL
Christin	12	7	19
Brian	10	4	14
John	6	11	17
Total	28	22	50

CHILD	TYPE OF CALL	NUMBER OF CALLS
Christin	Crisis	12
Christin	Noncrisis	7
Brian	Crisis	10
John	Crisis	6
		Total = 35

Therefore, the probability that the next phone call is either from Christin (Event *A*) or a crisis (Event *B*) is as follows:

$$P(A \text{ or } B) = P(A \cup B) = \frac{35}{50} = 0.70$$

Many of us college professors have been accused of tricking our poor defenseless students with the use of and and or in exams. Convince yourself that you understand the difference.

Pay close attention to the wording of a probability question. Does it include the word *and* or the word *or*? One way to distinguish between the use of *and* and *or* is to remember the following relationships that always hold true:

And → Intersection

Or → Union

The probability of the intersection of two events occurring can never be more than the probability of the union of two events occurring.

Our previous example shows that there is a big difference between the probability of the intersection of two events occurring and the probability of the union of two events occurring:

$$\text{Intersection: } P(A \text{ and } B) = P(A \cap B) = \frac{12}{50} = 0.24$$

$$\text{Union: } P(A \text{ or } B) = P(A \cup B) = \frac{35}{50} = 0.70$$

Notice that the probability of the union occurring is 70%, whereas the probability of the intersection occurring is just 24%. Why is this so? Because the union of Events *A* and *B* include the intersection of Events *A* and *B* (the orange region in Figure 4.4) as well as the red and yellow regions in Figure 4.4. You will never encounter a situation in which the probability of the intersection of two events is greater than the union.

Understanding the difference between the intersection and the union of events and how to calculate them is very important. For example, suppose Comcast Cable is tracking customer complaints and would like to know the probability that an unsatisfied customer is male and has a premium channel package. This question requires the use of the intersection of events (AND). If the union of events (OR) is erroneously used, the resulting probability will be higher than the true value. Take a few minutes to test your understanding in the following Your Turn problem before moving on.

YOUR TURN #5

The following table indicates the number of customers at Walmart who purchased a digital camera with and without extended warranties. The contingency table also identifies the age group of the customers.

Age Group	Warranty	No Warranty	Total
Less than 40	5	34	39
40 or Older	6	15	21
Total	11	49	60

What is the probability that a randomly selected customer

a. chose to purchase the warranty?
b. was less than 40 years old?
c. was 40 years or older and chose not to purchase a warranty?
d. was less than 40 or chose not to purchase a warranty?

Answers can be found on ▶ page 100

The Addition Rule

The **addition rule** for probabilities is used to calculate the probability of the union of events, that is, the probability that Event *A*, or Event *B*, or both events will occur.

Two events are considered to be **mutually exclusive** if they cannot occur at the same time during the experiment.

In the previous sections, we defined the intersection and union of events in general terms. Now it is time to use the **addition rule** for probabilities to calculate the probability of the union of events, that is, the probability that Event *A*, or Event *B*, or both events will occur. However, the addition rule requires us to first learn on a new concept: mutually exclusive events.

Two events are considered to be **mutually exclusive** if they cannot occur at the same time during the experiment. To demonstrate this, refer to Table 4.9, which shows the grade distribution of one of my statistics classes along with the genders of the students.

TABLE 4.9 | Grade Distribution of My Statistics Class (by Gender)

GRADE	FEMALE	MALE	TOTAL
A	6	3	9
B	4	8	12
C	0	4	4
Total	10	15	25

Consider the following two events:

Event A = Student earned an A grade

Event B = Student earned a B grade

The addition rule depends on whether or not the two events are mutually exclusive. Events A and B would be considered mutually exclusive because a student cannot receive both an A and a B grade at the same time. This concept is shown graphically in the Venn diagram in Figure 4.5. As you can see, mutually exclusive events have no overlap in the sample space.

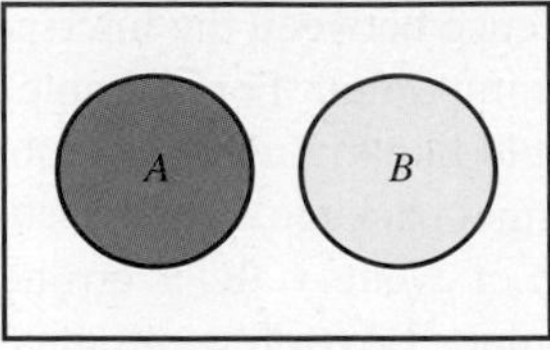

FIGURE 4.5 Venn Diagram Illustrating Mutually Exclusive Events

For mutually exclusive events, the addition rule states that the probability of two events occurring is simply the sum of their individual probabilities. Equation 4.4 shows how the addition rule is written.

An example of two events that are not mutually exclusive: Event A = a randomly selected student gets an A grade on the exam and Event B = a randomly selected student is female. Both of these events can occur together.

Formula 4.4 for The Addition Rule for Mutually Exclusive Events

$$P(A \text{ or } B) = P(A) + P(B)$$

For our grade-distribution example, the probability that a randomly selected student earned either an A or a B grade is calculated as follows:

$$P(A) = \frac{9}{25} = 0.36 \quad P(B) = \frac{12}{25} = 0.48$$

$$P(A \text{ or } B) = P(A) + P(B)$$

$$P(A \text{ or } B) = 0.36 + 0.48 = 0.84$$

Next, let's consider the following two events from the grade example:

Event A = Student earned an A grade

Event B = Student is female

Now, Events A and B are not mutually exclusive. This is because a student can receive an A grade and be female at the same time. This concept is shown graphically in the Venn diagram in Figure 4.6.

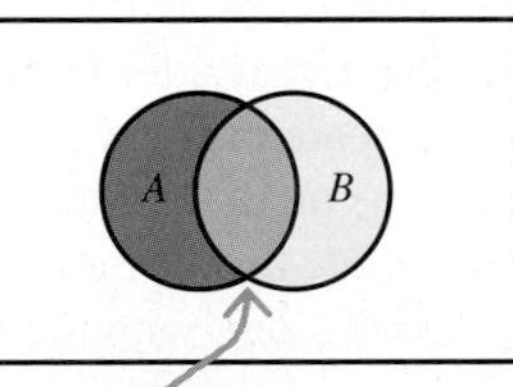

FIGURE 4.6 Venn Diagram Illustrating Events That Are Not Mutually Exclusive

$P(A \text{ and } B)$ is shown in the orange-shaded region.

You can see in Figure 4.6 that there is overlap between Events A and B (orange-shaded region). For events that are not mutually exclusive, the addition rule states that the probability of the two events occurring is the sum of their individual probabilities occurring minus the probability of the intersection of two events, as shown in Equation 4.5.

Formula 4.5 for The Addition Rule for Events That Are Not Mutually Exclusive

$$P(A \text{ or } B) = P(A) + P(B) - P(A \text{ and } B)$$

This term represents the orange-shaded region in Figure 4.6. We subtract it out of Equation 4.5 to avoid double counting this orange region.

For our grade-distribution example, the probability that a randomly selected student either earned an A (Event A) or is female (Event B) is determined as follows.

Nine of the 25 students in the class received A's (Event *A*). Ten of the 25 students in the class are female (Event *B*). Therefore,

$$P(A) = \frac{9}{25} = 0.36 \quad P(B) = \frac{10}{25} = 0.40$$

P(*A* and *B*) is the intersection of the two events: both receiving an A and being female. Our data from Table 4.8 show that six women received A's. Thus,

$$P(A \text{ and } B) = \frac{6}{25} = 0.24$$

Now we are ready to calculate the probability that a randomly selected student either earned an A (Event *A*) or is female (Event *B*) using Equation 4.5.

$$P(A \text{ or } B) = P(A) + P(B) - P(A \text{ and } B)$$
$$P(A \text{ or } B) = 0.36 + 0.40 - 0.24 = 0.52$$

Why do we need to subtract the intersection of Events *A* and *B* in the addition rule in Equation 4.5 when they are not mutually exclusive? Figure 4.7 shows what happens when the probabilities of the two events are added together. A total of nine students earned an A grade, of which six were female. There were a total of 10 female students, of which 6 earned an A. Adding the probabilities of Events *A* and *B* results in counting the six female students who earned an A grade twice. The overlap for these six students is evident in Figure 4.7. To avoid counting these students twice, we subtract this intersection of Events *A* and *B* in Equation 4.5.

FIGURE 4.7 The Addition Rule for Events That Are Not Mutually Exclusive: The Grade Distribution

Grade	Female	Male	Total
A	6	3	9
B	4	8	12
C	0	4	4
Total	10	15	25

Before moving on, this would be a good time to convince yourself that you understand the addition rule with the following Your Turn problem.

YOUR TURN #6

The following table shows the number of Bank of America customers who have overdue accounts. The data are broken down by the credit card type and number of days overdue.

	Card Type		
Days Overdue	**Standard**	**Gold**	**Total**
30 days or less	165	90	255
31–60 days	96	121	217
61–90 days	42	49	91
More than 90 days	22	15	37
Total	325	275	600

Determine the probability that a randomly selected customer

a. has a Standard card and is 31–60 days overdue
b. has a Standard card or is 30 days or less overdue
c. has a Gold card and is 61–90 days overdue
d. is 31–60 days or is 30 days or less overdue
e. is 31–60 days and is 61–90 days overdue

Answers can be found on ▶ **page 190**

Conditional Probability

Conditional probability is the probability of Event *A* occurring, given the condition that Event *B* has occurred.

Conditional probability is the probability of Event *A* occurring, knowing, or given the *condition*, that Event *B* has already occurred. In other words, the likelihood of Event *A* occurring can be affected by the fact that Event *B* has already occurred.

Consider the following example of a conditional probability: The SAT is a nationally administered test that many colleges use to evaluate student admissions. The math portion of the exam is scored on a scale of 0–800. Some students will enroll in a preparation course in the hopes of increasing their chances of a higher score. Table 4.10 shows the number of students in different categories of math scores and identifies the number of students who participated in a preparation class.

TABLE 4.10 | MATH SAT SCORES WITH AND WITHOUT A PREP CLASS

SCORE RANGE	PREP CLASS	NO PREP CLASS	TOTAL
201–400	8	53	61
401–600	40	107	147
601–800	22	20	42
Total	70	180	250

40 students who took the prep class scored in the 401–600 range

Consider the following two events:

Event A = Student scored in the 601–800 range in math

Event B = Student participated in a prep class

We would like to investigate whether the prep class increased the chance of scoring in the 601–800 range. Conditional probability can help us answer this question.

Because the sample space for Event *A* is 250 students and the number of students who scored in the 601–800 range is 42, the simple probability, $P(A)$, is calculated as follows:

$$P(A) = \frac{42}{250} = 0.168$$

There is a 16.8% chance that a randomly selected student scored in the 601–800 range. This simple probability is also known as a **prior probability** because it is determined without any additional information.

Prior probability is the probability of Event *A* occurring as determined without any additional information that could influence the event.

However, what if we had some additional information regarding the randomly selected student? Suppose we know the student participated in a prep class. We are now seeking the probability that the student scored in the 601–800 range, given he or she participated in a prep class. The notation for the probability of Event *A*, given the condition that Event *B* occurred, is shown as follows:

$$P(A|B)$$

For this conditional probability, the sample space of interest is reduced to those students who took the prep class, which is 70. Out of those 70 students, 22 scored in the 601–800 range. Therefore, the probability of a student scoring in the 601–800 range, given he or she participated in a prep class, is as follows:

$$P(A|B) = \frac{22}{70} = 0.314$$

Based on this evidence, it appears that the prep class has influenced the probability of scoring in the 601–800 range because

$$P(A) = 0.168$$
$$P(A|B) = 0.314$$

Students who take the prep class have nearly twice the probability of scoring in the 601–800 range than a randomly selected student from the sample space.

What we have learned is that students who take the prep class have a higher probability of scoring in the 601–800 range.

Equations 4.6 and 4.7 show how a conditional probability is calculated.

Formulas 4.6 and 4.7 for Calculating a Conditional Probability

$$P(A|B) = \frac{P(A \text{ and } B)}{P(B)}$$

or

$$P(B|A) = \frac{P(A \text{ and } B)}{P(A)}$$

Equation 4.6 requires that $P(B) > 0$, whereas Equation 4.7 requires that $P(A) > 0$.

We can apply this equation to our example, as follows, to verify our SAT result:

$$P(A \text{ and } B) = \frac{22}{250} = 0.088$$

$$P(B) = \frac{70}{250} = 0.280$$

$$P(A|B) = \frac{P(A \text{ and } B)}{P(B)} = \frac{0.088}{0.280} = 0.314$$

This result matches the probability that we found earlier using Table 4.10.

A conditional probability is also known as a **posterior probability**, which is a revision of the prior probability using additional information.

Whichever way you calculate it, a conditional probability is also known as a **posterior probability** (I'll resist using a "behind" joke here), which is a revision of the prior probability using additional information. In this case, the additional information is the fact that the student participated in the prep class.

Conditional probabilities have many applications in the business environment, such as the following:

- A bank would be very interested to know how probable it is that a customer with a credit-card balance of less than $3,000 will pay his entire balance in any given month.
- A car manufacturer would like to know the probability that a 40-year-old female customer will choose to purchase an extended warranty from the factory.

The following Your Turn problem will use the 2008 Summer Olympics to test your understanding of conditional probability.

YOUR TURN #7

The following table lists the number of medals won by particular countries during the 2012 Summer Olympics in London.

	Gold	Silver	Bronze	Total
United States	46	29	29	104
China	38	27	23	88
Russia	24	26	32	82
Other	194	222	272	688
Total	302	304	356	962

a. What is the probability that a randomly selected medal is gold?
b. What is the probability that a randomly selected medal was won by Russia?
c. What is the probability that a randomly selected medal was silver and won by the United States?
d. What is the probability that a randomly selected medal was bronze or won by China?
e. Given that a medal is gold, what is the probability that it was won by the United States?
f. Given that a medal was won by Russia, what is the probability that it was Bronze?

Answers can be found on ▶ **page 190**

Independent and Dependent Events

Two events are considered **independent** of one another if the occurrence of one event has no impact on the occurrence of the other event.

Two events are considered **independent** of each other if the occurrence of one event has no impact on the occurrence of the other event. Consider the following two independent events:

Event A: Today, I join the multitudes and decide to purchase the current version of Apple's iPhone.

Event B: Later that same day, Apple announces the development of the newest version of the iPhone with several cool features that the current version does not have.

Even though the timing of these two events may feel like the cruel work of fate, obviously they are independent of one another. I would have a difficult time convincing any rational person that Apple's management was waiting for my purchase before making this announcement.

If the occurrence of one event affects the occurrence of another event, the events are considered **dependent**.

If the occurrence of one event affected the probability of another event, we would call these events **dependent**. Consider the following two dependent events:

Event A: You earn an A grade on your statistics exam.

Event B: You study many hours preparing for your statistics exam.

As a teacher, I am confident that the occurrence of Event B will have an impact on the probability of Event A, making these two events dependent.

To apply this concept, I'll use the following example. My wife, Deb, is an avid tennis player, and we enjoy playing matches against each other. We do, however, have one difference of opinion on the court. Deb likes to have a nice long warm-up session at the start, where we hit the ball back and forth and back and forth for what seems like an eternity to me. All during this time, a little voice in my head is saying, "Who's winning?" and "What's the score?" My ideal warm-up is to bend at the waist to tie my sneakers. Deb tells me that when we rush through the warm-up, she doesn't play as well. "Hogwash!" I say, and I'll use conditional probability to show her who's right. Table 4.11 shows the outcomes of our last 25 matches, along with the type of warm-up before we started keeping score.

TABLE 4.11 | A Contingency Table for Tennis Matches

WARM-UP TIME	DEB WINS	BOB WINS	TOTAL
Short	4	11	15
Long	7	3	10
Total	**11**	**14**	**25**

We'll define the following events of interest:

Event A = Deb wins the tennis match

Event B = The warm-up time is long

First, using the totals columns in Table 4.11, we'll calculate the marginal probability of Deb winning the match, $P(A)$. The calculation is as follows:

$$P(A) = \frac{11}{25} = 0.44$$

Next, we'll calculate the conditional probability of Deb winning the match, given that the warm-up period was long, $P(A|B)$, using Equation 4.6:

$$P(A \text{ and } B) = \frac{7}{25} = 0.28$$

$$P(B) = \frac{10}{25} = 0.40$$

$$P(A|B) = \frac{P(A \text{ and } B)}{P(B)} = \frac{0.28}{0.40} = 0.70$$

Because this probability is not equal to 70%, Events *A* and *B* are not independent. It seems that Deb's chance of winning is affected by the length of the warm-up.

If the warm-up period has no impact on Deb's chances of winning (the events are independent events), then I would expect the conditional probability that she will win because of a long warm-up to be equal to the marginal probability that she will win regardless of the length of the warm-up. In other words, $P(A|B)$ would equal $P(A)$.

Unfortunately for me, once again Deb seems to be right. The probability of her winning regardless of the length of the warm-up is just 44%. The probability of her winning given the condition of a long warm-up is 70%. These two events are dependent on one another. Excuse me while I go apologize to my wife.

In general, the definition of two events that are independent is shown in Equation 4.8.

Formula 4.8 for Determining if Events A and B Are Independent

$$P(A|B) = P(A)$$

Otherwise, Events *A* and *B* are dependent.

Spend a few minutes on the next Your Turn problem to be sure you understand the concept of independent and dependent events.

YOUR TURN #8

The following table shows the number of adults (in thousands) in the United States who were employed and unemployed in 2012 along with their marital statuses.

Status	Employed	Unemployed	Total
Married	95,886	6,480	102,366
Never Married	39,348	6,025	45,373
Total	135,234	12,505	147,739

Event A = Person is unemployed
Event B = Person is married

Determine whether Events *A* and *B* are independent or dependent.

Answer can be found on ▶ **page 191**

The Multiplication Rule

The **multiplication rule** is used to determine the probability of the intersection (joint probability) of two events occurring, or *P* (*A* and *B*).

Earlier, I introduced the addition rule for probability to calculate the *union* of Events *A* and *B*. In this section, I will use the **multiplication rule** to determine the probability of the *intersection* of two events occurring, or *P*(*A* and *B*). Recall that this situation is known as the joint probability. We can derive the multiplication rule, shown in Equation 4.9, by rearranging the conditional probability equation, Equation 4.6, and using algebra to solve for *P*(*A* and *B*). Likewise, the multiplication rule shown in Equation 4.10 can be derived from Equation 4.7. These equations assume that Events *A* and *B* are dependent.

Formulas 4.9 and 4.10 for The Multiplication Rule for Dependent Events

$$P(A|B) = \frac{P(A \text{ and } B)}{P(B)}$$

$$P(A \text{ and } B) = P(B)P(A|B)$$

or

$$P(B|A) = \frac{P(A \text{ and } B)}{P(A)}$$

$$P(A \text{ and } B) = P(A)P(B|A)$$

To demonstrate the multiplication rule for dependent events, consider a grocery store that unknowingly received a potato chip order containing an unusually high percentage of bags with salt content below quality control standards. The day you walk in the store to purchase two bags, there are 32 bags on the shelf, 9 of which have low salt content. What is the probability that both bags you select will have low salt content?

To answer this question, we first define the following events:

Event A = The first bag has low salt content

Event B = The second bag has low salt content

The two events are dependent because if the first bag selected is removed from the shelf, the sample space for selecting the second is reduced from 32 to 31 bags, which affects the probabilities. We can use the multiplication rule shown in Equation 4.10 to determine the probability that both bags will be low on salt, or $P(A \text{ and } B)$. First, recognize that the probability of Event A occurring is determined as follows:

$$P(A) = \frac{9}{32} = 0.281$$

The conditional probability $P(B|A)$ refers to the probability that the second bag is low on salt given that the first bag selected was also low on salt. Because the first bag selected was not replaced on the shelf, there is one less low-salt bag among the remaining 31 bags. This means that

Only 8 of the remaining 31 bags have low salt because the first bag selected was also low salt.

$$P(B|A) = \frac{8}{31} = 0.258$$

Therefore, using the multiplication rule, we can tell that the joint probability that both bags selected will be low salt is as follows:

$$P(A \text{ and } B) = P(A)P(B|A)$$
$$P(A \text{ and } B) = (0.281)(0.258) = 0.072$$

There is slightly more than a 7% chance that you will leave the grocery store with two bags low on salt content.

As we have explained, Events A and B are independent if $P(B|A) = P(B)$. When two events are independent, the probability of them both occurring is simply the product of their individual probabilities of occurring. In this case, the multiplication rule can be simplified as shown in Equation 4.11.

Formula 4.11 for The Multiplication Rule for Two Independent Events

$$P(A \text{ and } B) = P(A)P(B)$$

Independence means that the probability of the second person ordering the Chef's Special is the same regardless of whether the first person ordered the Chef's Special.

For example, the Club Bistro restaurant in Wilmington, Delaware, has observed that a customer will order the Chef's Special for the evening 18% of the time. Assuming that customer orders are independent of one another, we can use Equation 4.11 to calculate the joint probability of the following two events occurring:

Event A = The first customer orders the Chef's Special

Event B = The second customer orders the Chef's Special

$$P(A \text{ and } B) = P(A)P(B)$$
$$P(A \text{ and } B) = (0.18)(0.18) = 0.032$$

In case you were wondering, the multiplication rule for independent events is not limited to only two events. It can be used to calculate any number of independent events, as Equation 4.12 shows:

Formula 4.12 for The Multiplication Rule for *n* Independent Events

$$P(A_1 \text{ and } A_2 \text{ and} \ldots \text{and } A_n) = P(A_1)P(A_2)\ldots P(A_n)$$

To demonstrate this rule, suppose you walk into class and your teacher surprises you with a five-question true/false pop quiz. If you randomly guess at all five answers, what is the probability you will answer all of them correctly? I'll define the following events:

$$A_1 = \text{Answering question 1 correctly}$$
$$A_2, A_3, A_4, \text{and } A_5 = \text{Answering questions 2, 3, 4, and 5 correctly}$$

Because you are randomly guessing (shame on you!), you have a 50% chance of Event A_1 occurring. You have the same chance (50%) of answering each of the other four questions right. Therefore,

$$P(\text{of 5 correct answers}) = P(A_1)P(A_2)P(A_3)P(A_4)P(A_5)$$
$$P(\text{of 5 correct answers}) = (0.5)(0.5)(0.5)(0.5)(0.5) = 0.031$$

You have a 3% chance of correctly guessing at all five true/false answers. As you can see, this is not a great test-taking strategy!

The multiplication rule is very helpful in a business setting because people's intuition often leads them astray when they are assessing probabilities. To illustrate, consider the following two statements:

> **Statement 1:** You will complete all of the goals that were assigned to you by your boss this year.
>
> **Statement 2:** You will complete all of the goals that were assigned to you by your boss this past year, and you will receive an above-average salary increase based on your performance.

Which statement has the higher probability of occurring? One research study found that most people selected choices similar to Statement 2 as being more likely. Including the above-average salary increase apparently gives Statement 2 more credibility. But now that you are well versed in the multiplication rule, I hope you see that this is not possible. To prove my point, let's define the following events:

Statement 1 = Event *A* occurring, while Statement 2 = Event (*A* and *B*) occurring.

> **Event *A*:** You will complete all of the goals that were assigned to you by your boss this year.
>
> **Event *B*:** You will receive an above-average salary increase based on your performance.

Statement 2 corresponds to *P*(*A* and *B*), which, according to the multiplication rule, equals $P(A)P(B|A)$. Mathematically, it is impossible for *P*(*A* and *B*) > *P*(*A*), which means Statement 2 could never be more likely than Statement 1, no matter how convincing your intuition happens to be. Be sure to give the next Your Turn problem a try to make sure the multiplication rule makes sense to you.

YOUR TURN #9

1. Draw two cards from a standard 52-card deck *without* replacing the first card. What is the probability that the first card will be a red queen and the second card will be a red card?
2. Draw two cards from a standard 52-card deck, replacing the first card after you draw it. What is the probability that the first card will be a red queen and the second card will be a red card?

Answers can be found on ▶ **page 191**

Contingency Tables with Probabilities

So far in the chapter, we have used contingency tables to show the frequency of events. We will now convert those frequencies into probabilities. We do so by dividing each number in the table by the total number of observations. Let's say Club Bistro has two types of entrée, meat and fish. Customers are individually asked after their meals if they were satisfied with them. Table 4.12 shows the contingency table for the past 200 customers.

TABLE 4.12 | Frequency of Customer Satisfaction by Entrée Type

RESPONSE	MEAT	FISH	TOTAL
Satisfied	70	100	170
Not Satisfied	10	20	30
Total	80	120	200

Table 4.13 converts each frequency into a probability by dividing each number in Table 4.12 by 200, the total number of customers.

TABLE 4.13 | Probability of Customer Satisfaction by Entrée Type

RESPONSE	MEAT	FISH	TOTAL
Satisfied	$70/200 = 0.35$	$100/200 = 0.50$	$170/200 = 0.85$
Not Satisfied	$10/200 = 0.05$	$20/200 = 0.10$	$30/200 = 0.15$
Total	$80/200 = 0.40$	$120/200 = 0.60$	$200/200 = 1.00$

What can we conclude about Table 4.13? Figure 4.8 summarizes the various types of probabilities discussed in this chapter using the following events:

Event A = Customer is satisfied with the meal
Event B = Customer is not satisfied with the meal
Event C = Customer orders a meat entrée
Event D = Customer orders a fish entrée

FIGURE 4.8 A Summary of Customer Satisfaction Probabilities by Entrée Type

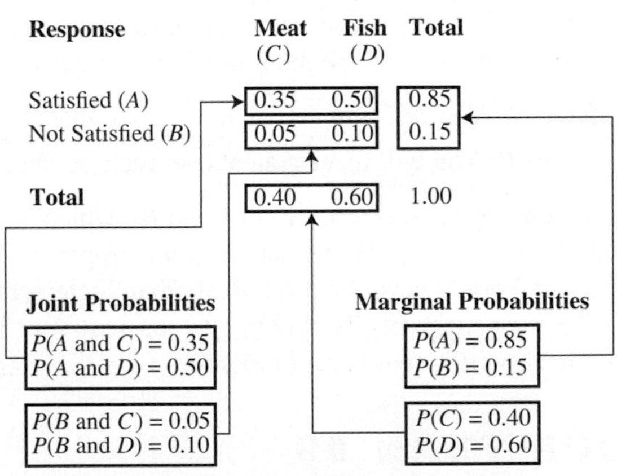

Conditional Probabilities

$$P(A|C) = \frac{P(A \text{ and } C)}{P(C)} = \frac{0.35}{0.40} = 0.875$$

$$P(A|D) = \frac{P(A \text{ and } D)}{P(C)} = \frac{0.50}{0.60} = 0.833$$

$$P(B|C) = \frac{P(B \text{ and } C)}{P(C)} = \frac{0.05}{0.40} = 0.125$$

$$P(B|D) = \frac{P(B \text{ and } D)}{P(D)} = \frac{0.10}{0.60} = 0.167$$

From Figure 4.8, we can conclude that the probability of a customer being satisfied with his or her meal is $P(A) = 0.85$. The probability that a customer is satisfied with his or her meal *and* had a meat entrée is $P(A \text{ and } C) = 0.35$. (This is one of the joint probabilities shown in Figure 4.8.) Finally, the probability that a customer is satisfied with his or her meal, given he or she had a meat entrée, is $P(A|C) = 0.875$. (This is one of the conditional probabilities shown in Figure 4.8.) We can also display the joint probabilities from Figure 4.8 using the **decision tree** shown in Figure 4.9.

Decision trees are used to display marginal and joint probabilities from a contingency table.

FIGURE 4.9
Decision Tree for Club Bistro

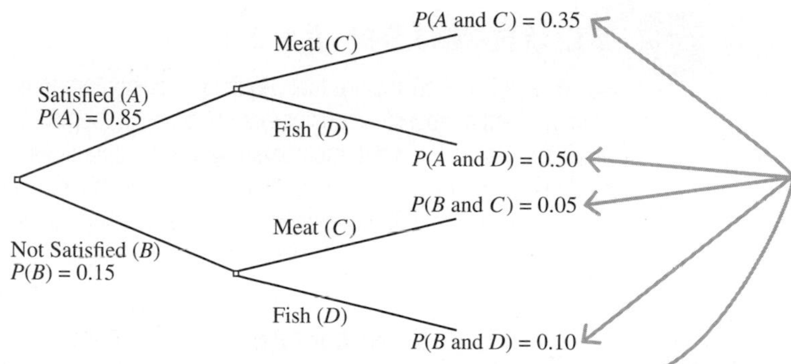

These four probabilities add up to 1.0 because they represent the entire sample space $(0.35 + 0.50 + 0.05 + 0.10 = 1.0)$.

The first two branches on the left side of the tree represent the events that a customer is satisfied with his or her meal (A) or is not satisfied with his or her meal (B). The four branches on the right side of the tree represent the joint probabilities for all the combinations of satisfaction and lack of satisfaction by entrée. Summing these four probabilities $(0.35 + 0.50 + 0.05 + 0.10)$ results in 1.0, which represents the entire sample space. Note that decision trees can also be used to display marginal probabilities.

In Figure 4.9, I chose to start the tree branches on the left side with the Satisfied/Not Satisfied events. I could have just as easily chosen the Meat/Fish events on the left side of the decision tree. Either tree structure would be acceptable.

Mutually Exclusive and Independent Events

Earlier in the chapter we discussed mutually exclusive events being events that could not occur at the same time. Using our Club Bistro example, Events A and B would be mutually exclusive because a customer could not be satisfied and not satisfied at once. Also, Events C and D are mutually exclusive because we are assuming that an entrée must be either a meat or a fish dish. Therefore, we can state the following:

$$P(A \text{ and } B) = 0$$
$$P(C \text{ and } D) = 0$$

I have one final word on mutually exclusive and independent events. Two events cannot be both independent and mutually exclusive. Think about it: Independent events can occur at the same time. One the other hand, by definition, mutually exclusive events can't occur at the same time. Let's look at an example:

Consider Event A (the customer is satisfied) and Event B (the customer is not satisfied.) These two events are mutually exclusive because the customer cannot be satisfied and not satisfied at the same time. As a result, these events cannot be independent and are therefore dependent on one another based on the following logic.

We know from Figure 4.3 that $P(A) = 0.85$. If Events A and B are independent, then $P(A|B)$ should also equal 0.85. But if we are told that Event B has occurred (the customer is not satisfied), then the probability of Event A occurring (the customer is satisfied) cannot be 0.85. Instead, it must equal 0 because there is no chance the customer can also be satisfied. Therefore, these mutually exclusive events must be dependent because

Remember, Events A and B are independent if $P(A|B) = P(A)$.

$$P(A|B) \neq P(A)$$

This argument holds true for any two mutually exclusive events. I do have one word of caution here. It is not accurate to describe the terms *mutually exclusive* and *independent* as opposites of one another. In other words, you *cannot* conclude that because events are not independent they will be mutually exclusive.

In this next Your Turn section, you'll get the chance to use a contingency table and decision tree to help one of Deb's favorite stores, Costco, evaluate the spending patterns of its members.

YOUR TURN #10

Costco is a warehouse store that requires its customers to have a membership to purchase items. Costco offers nonbusiness customers two types of membership. Gold Star members pay an annual fee of \$50, whereas Executive members pay a \$100 annual fee but also earn a 2% reward on most Costco purchases. The following contingency table shows the number of customers who had check-out totals above and below \$200 along with their corresponding membership type.

	Membership	
Check-Out Total	**Gold**	**Executive**
\$200 or less	66	21
More than \$200	15	48

Set up a contingency table similar to that in Figure 4.8 showing the following:

a. Marginal probabilities
b. Joint probabilities
c. Conditional probabilities
d. Display these probabilities in a decision tree using check-out total as the starting branches.
e. What conclusions can be made concerning the spending patterns of each membership type?

Answers can be found on ▶ **page 191**

Bayes' Theorem

Thomas Bayes (1701–1761) developed a mathematical rule that calculates $P(A|B)$ from information about $P(B|A)$. In other words, if we know something about the probability of Event B occurring, given that Event A occurred, we can calculate the reverse—that is, we can calculate the probability of Event A occurring, given that Event B occurs. Bayes' Theorem has many practical applications, such as determining the probability of discovering a terrorist with airport security measures in place and evaluating the effectiveness of drug testing athletes.

Before we go any further, it's very important to convince yourself that the two conditional probabilities we just discussed are not identical. I'll use the following example to explain this difference and to demonstrate Bayes' Theorem.

I want to play golf tomorrow, but the local weather forecast calls for rain. Let's define the following events:

Event A_1 = It rains tomorrow
Event A_2 = It does not rain tomorrow
Event B = Rain is predicted in tomorrow's weather forecast

Events A_1 and A_2 are mutually exclusive because if one event occurs, the other cannot. They are also collectively exhaustive because one of them *must* occur tomorrow. I am interested in discovering the probability that it will rain tomorrow, given the forecast calls for rain. This is represented as the conditional probability $P(A_1|B)$.

To answer this question, I gathered the following information. The average number of days per year that rain is recorded in my hometown is 91. Therefore, the simple probability that rain will occur on any given day is as follows:

$$P(A_1) = \frac{91}{365} = 0.25$$

The probabilities $P(A_1)$ and $P(A_2)$ are known as **prior probabilities** because they are determined without any other information, such as a weather forecast.

Because Events A_1 and A_2 are mutually exclusive and collectively exhaustive, the probability that it will not rain on any given day is calculated as follows:

$$P(A_2) = 1 - 0.25 = 0.75$$

So far, though, we only know the probability of Events A_1 and A_2 occurring. What we need to know is the probability of rain being predicted for tomorrow (Event B). Otherwise, we won't be able to determine $P(A_1|B)$, which is the probability of it raining, given that rain is in the forecast.

To determine the probability of Event B—the probability of rain being predicted— I counted the number of days that it *actually* rained in the past year and checked the historical forecast for those days. I discovered that on 85% of the days that it actually rained, rain had been predicted. Based on this fact, I set the following conditional probability:

$$P(B|A_1) = 0.85$$

$P(B|A_1)$ is the probability that rain will be in tomorrow's forecast, given that it actually *does* rain tomorrow.

Notice the important distinction between the following two conditional probabilities:

This probability is what we ultimately want to determine.

$P(A_1|B)$ = The probability that it will rain tomorrow, given rain is in the forecast.

We just determined that this probability is 0.85.

$P(B|A_1)$ = The probability that rain will be in tomorrow's forecast, given that it actually does rain tomorrow.

Even though these two statements sound similar, their meanings are very different.

Pay careful attention to the distinction between $P(A_1|B)$ and $P(B|A_1)$. Some of my students really struggle with this distinction.

Finally, I identified the number of days that it did not rain in the past year and checked the historical forecast for those days. I discovered that, on 20% of the days that it did not rain, rain had been in the forecast. Based on this fact, I set the following conditional probability:

$$P(B|A_2) = 0.20$$

Bayes' Theorem is used to update prior probabilities with new information.

$P(B|A_2)$ is the probability that rain will be in tomorrow's forecast, given that it *doesn't* rain tomorrow. Now I'm ready to call on **Bayes' Theorem**, shown in Equation 4.13, to answer my question: What is the probability that it will rain tomorrow, given the forecast calls for rain?

Formula 4.13 for the Bayes' Theorem

$$P(A_i|B) = \frac{P(A_i)P(B|A_i)}{P(A_1)P(B|A_1) + P(A_2)P(B|A_2) + \cdots + P(A_n)P(B|A_n)}$$

where

A_i = The ith event of interest from a choice of n events
B = An event that has *already* occurred

It must either rain or not rain tomorrow.

In our weather example, $i = 1$ because we are interested in determining $P(A_1|B)$, and $n = 2$ because the events A_1 and A_2 are collectively exhaustive. Carefully plug in the probabilities that we have acquired into Equation 4.13:

$$P(A_1|B) = \frac{P(A_1)P(B|A_1)}{P(A_1)P(B|A_1) + P(A_2)P(B|A_2)}$$

$$P(A_1|B) = \frac{(0.25)(0.85)}{(0.25)(0.85) + (0.75)(0.20)}$$

$$P(A_1|B) = \frac{0.2125}{0.2125 + 0.15} = \frac{0.2125}{0.3625} = 0.586$$

Given that tomorrow's forecast calls for rain, there is a 58.6% chance that it will actually rain tomorrow. This probability is known as a revised, or posterior, probability. Without any weather forecast, the prior probability of rain was 25%. Now that we have a weather forecast calling for rain, we have revised this probability to 58.6%. Oh well, I better prepare myself for a soggy day on the course.

If using Equation 4.13 makes you squeamish, the revised probabilities that Bayes' Theorem provides can also be derived in a table, as Table 4.14 shows. Columns 2 and 3 represent the prior and conditional probabilities with which we started. These two columns are multiplied together to calculate the joint probabilities shown in Column 4.

When Column 4 is summed, we have the probability that Event B has occurred, which in this example is the probability that rain is in tomorrow's forecast (36.25%).

Column 5 shows our final result, the revised probabilities. Note that this calculation is the same as Equation 4.6, which determined conditional probability earlier in the chapter.

$$P(A|B) = \frac{P(A \text{ and } B)}{P(B)}$$

This table summarizes the calculations for Equation 4.13.

TABLE 4.14 | AN EXAMPLE OF BAYES' THEOREM IN TABLE FORM

(1) EVENT	(2) PRIOR PROB	(3) CONDITIONAL PROB	(4) JOINT PROB	(5) REVISED PROB
A_i	$P(A_i)$	$P(B\|A_i)$	$P(A_i \text{ and } B)$	$P(A_i\|B)$
A_1	0.25	0.85	0.2125	$0.2125/0.3625 = 0.586$
A_2	0.75	0.20	0.1500	$0.1500/0.3625 = 0.414$
			$P(B) = 0.3625$	Total $= 1.000$

Let's look at the following example to see what happens to Bayes' Theorem when we have more than two collectively exhaustive events. PNC Bank classifies its credit card customers into three categories by their credit scores. Table 4.15 shows the percentage of customers who fall into each group.

TABLE 4.15 | CREDIT SCORES OF PNC BANK CUSTOMERS

EVENT	CREDIT SCORE	PERCENTAGE	$P(A_i)$
A_1	Less than 600	25	0.25
A_2	600 to 700	45	0.45
A_3	More than 700	30	0.30

We'll define Event B as follows:

Event B = Customer is late on his or her current credit card payment

We also know the following historical information:

- Customers with credit scores of less than 600 are late with their payments 40% of the time, or $P(B|A_1) = 0.40$.
- Customers with credit scores between 600 and 700 are late with their payments 10% of the time, or $P(B|A_2) = 0.10$. Customers with credit scores of more than 700 are late with their payments 5% of the time, or $P(B|A_3) = 0.05$.

Suppose PNC Bank wants to use Bayes' Theorem to determine the probability that a customer has a credit score of less than 600 given that he or she is late on his or her current credit card payment, or $P(A_1|B)$.

$$P(A_1|B) = \frac{P(A_1)P(B|A_1)}{P(A_1)P(B|A_1) + P(A_2)P(B|A_2) + P(A_3)P(B|A_3)}$$

$$P(A_1|B) = \frac{(0.25)(0.40)}{(0.25)(0.40) + (0.45)(0.10) + (0.30)(0.05)}$$

$$P(A_1|B) = \frac{0.10}{0.10 + 0.045 + 0.015} = \frac{0.10}{0.16} = 0.625$$

There is a 62.5% chance that a late payment is from a customer with a credit score of less than 600. All the revised probabilities for this example are shown in Table 4.16.

TABLE 4.16 | BAYES' THEOREM IN TABLE FORM

(1) EVENT	(2) PRIOR PROB	(3) CONDITIONAL PROB	(4) JOINT PROB	(5) REVISED PROB
A_i	$P(A_i)$	$P(B\|A_i)$	$P(A_i \text{ and } B)$	$P(A_i\|B)$
A_1	0.25	0.40	0.100	$0.100/0.16 = 0.625$
A_2	0.45	0.10	0.045	$0.045/0.16 = 0.281$
A_3	0.30	0.05	0.015	$0.015/0.16 = 0.094$
			$P(B) = 0.160$	Total $= 1.000$

The answer to PNC Bank's question can also be found here in the table.

Now that you're a Bayes' Theorem expert, show off your newfound skills by completing the following Your Turn problem.

YOUR TURN #11

Suppose that there is a 90% chance that a test for performance-enhancing drugs will provide a positive test for an athlete who actually took them. In addition, there is a 15% chance that the same test will provide a positive test for an athlete who did not take them. (This is known as a false positive.) Assume that 8% of the athlete population is currently taking performance-enhancing drugs. Using Bayes' Theorem, determine the probability that a randomly selected athlete who tests positive is actually a user of performance-enhancing drugs.

Answer can be found on ▶ **page 192**

4.2 Section Problems

Basic Skills

Use the following contingency table to answer questions from Problems 4.10 to 4.14.

	Event *A*	Event *B*
Event *C*	9	6
Event *D*	4	21
Event *E*	7	3

4.10 Determine the following probabilities:

a. $P(A)$
b. $P(B)$
c. $P(C)$
d. $P(D)$
e. $P(E)$

4.11 Determine the following probabilities:

a. $P(A \text{ and } C)$
b. $P(A \text{ and } D)$
c. $P(B \text{ and } E)$
d. $P(A \text{ and } B)$

4.12 Determine the following probabilities:

a. $P(B \text{ or } C)$
b. $P(B \text{ or } D)$
c. $P(A \text{ or } E)$
d. $P(A \text{ or } B)$

4.13 Determine the following probabilities:

a. $P(A|C)$
b. $P(C|A)$
c. $P(B|E)$
d. $P(E|B)$

4.14 Use Bayes' Theorem to determine $P(B|D)$.

Applications

4.15 Consider the following experiment that involves rolling a pair of dice:

Event A = Rolling a nine

Event B = Rolling a pair (both dice the same)

a. Are these two events mutually exclusive? Why or why not?
b. Are these two events independent? Why or why not?

4.16 Consider the following experiment that involves flipping a single coin and rolling one six-sided die:

Event A = Coin comes up tails

Event B = Rolling a four with the die

a. Are these two events mutually exclusive? Why or why not?
b. Are these two events independent? Why or why not?

4.17 Consider an experiment with a standard 52-card deck from which one card is randomly selected and not replaced. Then a second card is randomly selected. Define the following events:

Event A = The first card is a heart

Event B = The second card is a heart

a. Are these two events mutually exclusive? Why or why not?
b. Are these two events independent? Why or why not?

4.18 A recent survey found that 75% of households had Internet access and 80% of households had cable television. Also, it was reported that 70% of the households in the survey had both Internet and cable television. Determine the probability that a randomly selected household in the survey had either Internet access or cable.

4.19 A local car dealership currently has 36 used GM, Ford, and Toyota vehicles on the lot that can be classified as either cars or trucks. The following data are available:

- Twenty-six vehicles are cars.
- Eleven vehicles are GMs.
- Fifteen vehicles are Fords.
- Three vehicles are both Toyotas and trucks.
- Fourteen vehicles are both Fords and cars.

a. What is the probability that a randomly selected vehicle is a Toyota?
b. What is the probability that a randomly selected vehicle is a truck?
c. What is the probability that a randomly selected vehicle is a either a Ford or a car?
d. What is the probability that a randomly selected vehicle is a GM truck?
e. What is the probability that a randomly selected vehicle is a Toyota, given it is a car?
f. What is the probability that a randomly selected vehicle is a truck, given it is a Ford?
g. Construct a decision tree for these events.

4.20 The following table shows the frequencies that the Green Bay Packers of the NFL called a running play or a passing play for various down and distance situations for the first five games of a recent season. (Yes, I actually counted these frequencies myself.)

Down and Distance	**Run**	**Pass**
First down and 10 or more yards to go	55	81
Second down and 6 or more yards to go	27	52
Second down and 5 or less yards to go	18	10
Third down and 2 or more yards to go	3	60
Third down and 1 yard to go	1	2

What is the probability that the Packers will do the following:

a. Pass the ball on any given down
b. Run the ball on second down
c. Pass the ball, given that it is third down and they have 1 yard to go
d. Run the ball on first down
e. Run the ball, given that it is second down and they have 6 or more yards to go
f. Construct a decision tree for these events.

4.21 At a local restaurant, 22% of the customers order takeout. If 8% of the customers order takeout and choose a hamburger, determine the probability that a customer who orders takeout will order a hamburger.

4.22 A recent *Wall Street Journal* poll found that 70% of Americans felt the U.S. government was not working well. If seven people were randomly selected, what is the probability that all seven felt the government is not working well?

4.23 The following table shows the number of people, in thousands, in the United States with and without health insurance in 2011, according to the U.S. Census Bureau:

Age Group	Insured	Uninsured
Under 18 years	66,835	6,902
18 to 24 years	22,491	7,649
25 to 34 years	29,690	11,529
35 to 44 years	31,588	8,399
45 to 64 years	68,544	13,382
65 years and older	40,817	690

a. What percentage of the U.S. population in 2011 did not have health insurance and was between the ages of 18 to 24 years?
b. What percentage of the U.S. population in 2011 did not have health insurance or was between the ages of 25 to 34 years?
c. What percentage of the U.S. population in 2011 did have health insurance, given they were 65 years or older?
d. Do age group and health insurance appear to be independent or dependent events? Define Event A as a person 45 to 64 years old and Event B as the person insured. What conclusions can be drawn with this information?

Based on: U.S. Census Bureau data.

4.24 Thirty-five percent of customers who purchased products from an e-commerce site had orders exceeding \$100. If 20% of the customers have orders exceeding \$100 and also pay with the e-commerce site's sponsored credit card, determine the probability that a customer whose order exceeds \$100 will pay with the sponsored credit card.

4.25 A single card is drawn from a standard 52-card deck. What is the probability that the card is either

a. A king, or a four, or a five
b. A diamond, or a heart, or club
c. A two, or a three, or a club
d. A six, or a seven, or a spade, or a diamond

4.26 In 2012, 37% of taxpayers who filed their tax return electronically self-prepared their taxes. If the IRS randomly selected three tax returns submitted electronically, what is the probability that all three were self-prepared?

4.27 The following table shows the number of men and women, in thousands, enrolled in degree-granting institutions in the United States in 2010. The men and women are categorized by their age groups.

Age Group	Men	Women
14 to 17 years old	92	19
18 and 19 years old	1,842	2,276
20 and 21 years old	1,931	2,120
22 to 24 years old	1,666	2,008
25 to 29 years old	1,414	1,783
30 to 34 years old	745	1,078
35 years old and over	1,354	2,587

Based on: National Center for Education Statistics

Determine the probability that a randomly selected student

a. Was a female
b. Was 22 to 24 years old
c. Was a woman who was 35 years old or older
d. Was either a women or 25 to 29 years old
e. Was a man, given that the student was 22 to 24 years old
f. Was 30 to 34 years old, given that the student was a man

4.28 A hotel asked its customers to rate their stays as Excellent, Good, Fair, or Poor. The following table shows the frequency of each rating as well as the gender of the customer.

Rating	Men	Women
Excellent	3	9
Good	20	12
Fair	16	7
Poor	6	2

Determine the probability that a randomly selected customer

a. Rated his or her stay as Excellent
b. Rated his or her stay as either Good or Fair
c. Rated his or her stay as other than Poor
d. Was a man who rated his stay as Good
e. Either was a woman or rated his or her stay as Fair
f. Rated her stay as Good, given the customer was a woman
g. Was a woman, given the person rated the stay as Poor
h. Construct a decision tree for these events.

4.29 Super D is a major video distributor that purchases blank DVDs from two sources: Disk Makers, which provides 62% of the DVDs, and Media Supply, which provides the remaining 38%. Historically, 3% of the DVDs Super D has purchased from Disk Makers have been defective, whereas 2% of the DVDs purchased from Media Supply have been defective. A randomly selected DVD is found to be defective. Use Bayes' Theorem to determine the probability that the DVD came from Disk Makers.

4.30 A sporting goods company operates retail stores in the New York and Atlanta areas. Customers were asked to rate their shopping experiences, the results of which are summarized in the following table:

Shopping Experience	Percentage
Poor	15
Average	45
Good	40

Consider the following information:

- 67% of the customers who rated their store Poor came from the Philadelphia area.
- 36% of the customers who rated their store Average came from the Philadelphia area.
- 30% of the customers who rated their store Good came from the Philadelphia area.

Use Bayes' Theorem to determine the probability that a customer who shopped in the Philadelphia area rated his or her experience as Good.

4.3 Counting Principles

To use classical probability, which we introduced at the beginning of this chapter, we need to be able to count the number of events of interest along with the total number of events that are possible in the sample space. For simple events, like rolling a single die, the number of possible outcomes (six) is obvious. But for more complex events, like a state lottery drawing, we need to rely on techniques known as counting principles to arrive at the correct answer. Let's look at these techniques.

The Fundamental Counting Principle

After a tough round of golf on a hot afternoon, Brian, John, and I decide to revive our spirits at the ice cream store on the way home. I'm desperately trying to decide from among four flavors and three toppings in which to indulge. Let's have

k_1 = The number of ice cream flavors I'm trying to decide from among

and

k_2 = The number of topping flavors I'm trying to decide from among

How many different combinations of ice cream and toppings am I faced with, assuming I can choose only one flavor and one topping? (After all, I am watching my weight.) Fortunately, I can use the **fundamental counting principle**, which tells me that if one event (my ice cream choice) can occur in k_1 ways and a second event (my topping choice) can occur in k_2 ways, the total number of ways both events can occur together is $(k_1)(k_2) = (4)(3) = 12$ ways.

The **fundamental counting principle** states that if there are k_1 choices for the first event, k_2 choices for the second event ... and k_n choices for the *nth* event, then the total number of possible outcomes is $(k_1)(k_2)(k_3) \cdots (k_n)$.

Now I can extend this principle to more than two events. In addition to flavors and toppings, I have another tempting choice: A choice between a small and large serving. That leaves me with a mind-boggling number of combinations to choose from: $(k_1)(k_2)(k_3) = (4)(3)(2) = 24$. The combinations are summarized in Table 4.17.

TABLE 4.17 | Ice Cream Combinations

ICE CREAM FLAVORS	TOPPINGS	SIZE
CH = Chocolate	HF = Hot Fudge	LG = Large
VA = Vanilla	BS = Butterscotch	SM = Small
ST = Strawberry	SP = Sprinkles	
CF = Coffee		

LIST OF COMBINATIONS (BY FLAVOR, TOPPING, AND SIZE)			
CH-HF-LG	VA-HF-LG	ST-HF-LG	CF-HF-LG
CH-HF-SM	VA-HF-SM	ST-HF-SM	CF-HF-SM
CH-BS-LG	VA-BS-LG	ST-BS-LG	CF-BS-LG
CH-BS-SM	VA-BS-SM	ST-BS-SM	CF-BS-SM
CH-SP-LG	VA-SP-LG	ST-SP-LG	CF-SP-LG
CH-SP-SM	VA-SP-SM	ST-SP-SM	CF-SP-SM

In general, the fundamental counting principle tells me that if there are k_1 choices for the first event, k_2 choices for the second event, and k_n choices for the nth event, then the total number of possible outcomes is as shown in Equation 4.14.

Formula 4.14 for the Fundamental Counting Rule

$$(k_1)(k_2)(k_3)\cdots(k_n)$$

where

k_i = The number of choices for the ith event
n = The number of events

Another demonstration of the fundamental counting principle is to calculate the number of unique combinations for a state's automobile license plates. Suppose the state plates have three letters followed by four numbers. The state doesn't allow the number zero and the letter O to be used because their resemblance to one another can cause confusion. Because we have 25 possible letters (all of the numbers of the alphabet except O) and 9 possible numbers (1–9), the total number of unique combinations is as follows:

This number represents $k_1 = 25$ because there are 25 possible choices for the first letter in the license plate.

FIRST LETTER	SECOND LETTER	THIRD LETTER	FIRST NUMBER	SECOND NUMBER	THIRD NUMBER	FOURTH NUMBER
25	25	25	9	9	9	9

$$25 \times 25 \times 25 \times 9 \times 9 \times 9 \times 9 = 102{,}515{,}625$$

That's 102,515,625 possible license plates.

Stats in Practice: Running Out of Internet Addresses

Every device that communicates on the Internet, whether it be a desktop computer or a smartphone, needs a unique IP address so that it can be identified. Think of the IP address as basically a postal address for your Internet device.

Those who designed the Internet back in the 1970s used the Internet Protocol Addressing Scheme version 4 (IPv4). Because computers speak a binary language, they only recognize zeros and ones. The IPv4 address format that the Internet was established on consists of a string of 32 zero/one digits. An example of an IPv4 address is as follows:

00001101.10110000.11110011.00110001

Because each digit must be a zero or one, we can use the Fundamental Counting Principle to find that there are 2^{32} combinations or a total of

$$2^{32} = 4{,}294{,}967{,}296$$

unique IP addresses available. Years ago, the founders of the Internet figured this would be an ample number of addresses. Today we know differently.

With the huge growth in devices that depend on an Internet connection over the past few years such as Apple's iPhone and iPad, it was projected that we would run out of IP addresses with the IPv4 format in 2012. Another contributing factor to the shortage of IP addresses is the rapid increase in the demand for technology in developing countries like China and India. Lack of IP address have many consequences; Internet connections will slow down and computers will have difficulty communicating with each other.

To address this shortage on IP addresses (pun intended), a new protocol system, known as IPv6, has been developed. This new format allows for a combination of 128 zero/one digits, as seen in the following example:

00001101.10110000.11110011.00110001.
00110000.10000001.00011000.11100011.
10100101.01101010.11001010.00001001.
10111001.11101101.01111001.01010111

Using the IPv6 format, there are a total of 2^{128} combinations, which provides

$$2^{128} = 340{,}282{,}366{,}920{,}938{,}000{,}000{,}000{,}000{,}000{,}000{,}000$$

unique IP addresses. To facilitate the transition from IPv4 to IPv6, the Internet community organized World IPv6 Launch Day on June 6, 2012. The goal of this event was to obtain a commitment from the Internet industry, such as equipment manufacturers and ISPs, to hasten the conversion to IPv6.

When I told my daughter about IPv6, her first reaction was, "They'll never run out of all of those addresses."

"Yeah, that's what they said in the 1970s," I replied.

Permutations are the number of different ways in which objects can be arranged in order. The number of permutations of n objects selected x at a time can be found by $_nP_x = \frac{n!}{(n-x)!}$.

Permutations

Permutations are the number of different ways in which different objects can be arranged in order. In a permutation, there can be only one of each arrangement of the objects. As an example, there are six permutations for the numbers 1, 2, and 3. The permutations are as follows:

123 132 213 231 312 321

But what if we had many numbers instead of just three? How many permutations would there be? Finding all of the permutations by manually writing them down as we just did would be time consuming. Instead, we can use Equation 4.15. By definition, the number of permutations of n distinct objects is $n!$

Formula 4.15 for the Permutations of n Distinct Objects

$$n! = n(n-1)(n-2)(n-3)\cdots(2)(1)$$

By definition, $0! = 1$.

Let's use our previous example to work out Equation 4.15. The number of permutations of the three distinct objects in our example is 3! Now you can plug 3! into Equation 4.15 to find the number of permutations more easily.

Using the $n!$ permutation rule, we find the following:

$$3! = (3)(2)(1) = 6$$

There are six permutations for the numbers 1, 2, and 3. This is the same result we got by arranging the numbers manually.

Now suppose we have six numbers instead of three. Using Equation 4.15, we find that the number of permutations associated with six numbers is as follows:

$$6! = (6)(5)(4)(3)(2)(1) = 720$$

Let's work another problem. Before the beginning of a professional basketball game, the starting five players are announced one at a time. How many different ways can we arrange the order in which the players are announced? The number of permutations is calculated as follows:

$$5! = (5)(4)(3)(2)(1) = 120$$

Suppose we want to select only some of the objects in the group. If there are 12 players on the team, how many different ways can any five players on the team be announced at the start of the game?

We can find the number of permutations for this problem using Equation 4.16.

Formula 4.16 for the Permutations of n Objects Selected x at a Time

$$_nP_x = \frac{n!}{(n-x)!}$$

where

n = The total number of objects
x = The number of objects to be selected

Using our basketball example again, if there are 12 players on the team, how many different ways can any 5 players on the team be announced to start the game? In this case, because $n = 12$ and $x = 5$, the number of permutations is as follows:

$$_{12}P_5 = \frac{12!}{(12-5)!} = \frac{(12)(11)(10)(9)(8)(7)(6)(5)(4)(3)(2)(1)}{(7)(6)(5)(4)(3)(2)(1)}$$

$$_{12}P_5 = (12)(11)(10)(9)(8) = 95{,}040$$

I'm sure glad it's not my job to decide the order of the announcements.

It's easier to calculate the number of permutations using Equation 4.17, which is algebraically the same as Equation 4.16.

I recommend using this equation to calculate permutations. It requires less effort than Equation 4.16.

Formula 4.17 for the Permutations of n Objects Selected x at a Time

$$_nP_x = \frac{n!}{(n-x)!} = n(n-1)(n-2)\cdots(n-x+1)$$

This works because every value in the denominator (the bottom of the fraction) will cancel out with many values in the numerator (the top of the fraction). I will show you why with the following demonstration. Suppose we have 10 objects ($n = 10$), and we are removing 2 at a time ($x = 2$). How many permutations will we have?

Recall that Equation 4.16 is as follows:

$$_nP_x = \frac{n!}{(n-x)!}$$

Plugging our numbers into 4.16 we get the following:

$$_{10}P_2 = \frac{10!}{(10-2)!} = \frac{(10)(9)(8)(7)(6)(5)(4)(3)(2)(1)}{(8)(7)(6)(5)(4)(3)(2)(1)} = (10)(9) = 90$$

Equation 4.17 is as follows:

$$_nP_x = \frac{n!}{(n-x)!} = n(n-1)(n-2)\cdots(n-x+1)$$

Equation 4.17 is easier to use than Equation 4.16 because it cancels out the numbers 1 through 8 in the numerator and denominator that are present when using Equation 4.16. We are left with x number of factors, which in this case is two (10 and 9)

Plugging our numbers into Equation 4.17, we get the following:

$$(n-x+1) = 10 - 2 + 1 = 9$$

$$_{10}P_2 = \frac{n!}{(n-x)!} = (10)(9) = 90$$

As you can see, Equation 4.17 has fewer calculations.

Sometimes the order of events is not of consequence. We'll discuss those cases in the next section.

Combinations

Combinations are the number of different ways in which objects can be arranged without regard to order. The number of combinations of n objects selected x at a time can be found by $_nC_x = \frac{n!}{(n-x)!x!}$.

Combinations are similar to permutations, except that the order of the objects is not important. The number of combinations of n objects selected x at a time can be found using Equation 4.18.

Formula 4.18 for the Combinations of n Objects Selected x at a Time

$$_nC_x = \frac{n!}{(n-x)!x!}$$

where

$n =$ The total number of objects
$x =$ The number of objects to be selected

As with permutations, it's easier to calculate the number of combinations using Equation 4.19, which is algebraically the same as Equation 4.18.

Formula 4.19 for the Combinations of n Objects Selected x at a Time

$$_nC_x = \frac{n!}{(n-x)!x!} = \frac{n(n-1)(n-2)\cdots(n-x+1)}{x!}$$

For example, in poker, 5 cards are selected randomly from a deck of 52 cards. How many five-card combinations exist?

$$_{52}C_5 = \frac{52!}{(52-5)!5!} = \frac{(52)(51)(50)(49)(48)}{(5)(4)(3)(2)(1)} = 2{,}598{,}960$$

How many five-card permutations exist?

$$_{52}P_5 = \frac{52!}{(52-5)!} = (52)(51)(50)(49)(48) = 311{,}875{,}200$$

There are more five-card permutations than combinations. For example, the 2 five-card groups (or hands) hands shown below have the same combination of cards but are considered two different permutations. Recall that the order matters with permutations. By contrast, with combinations the order doesn't matter. Consequently, the two hands would be counted as only one hand, or combination, because they consist of the same cards, only in a different order:

When the order of objects is important, use permutations. When the order of objects does not matter, like a poker hand, use combinations.

HAND 1	HAND 2
Ace of spades	Ace of spades
Queen of hearts	Ten of spades
Ten of spades	Queen of hearts
Ten of diamonds	Ten of diamonds
Three of clubs	Three of clubs

Now that we know the total number of five-card combinations from a 52-card deck, we can calculate the probability of a flush, which is any five cards that are all the same suit (spades, clubs, hearts, or diamonds). For you poker veterans, I am including a royal flush and a straight flush in this calculation.

First, we need to count the number of five-card flushes of one suit, let's say diamonds. Because there are 13 diamonds in the deck, the number of combinations of these 13 diamonds, selected 5 at a time, is as follows:

$$_{13}C_5 = \frac{13!}{(13-5)!5!} = \frac{(13)(12)(11)(10)(9)}{(5)(4)(3)(2)(1)} = 1{,}287$$

Because there are four suits in the deck, the total number of five-card flushes from any suit is $(1{,}287)(4) = 5{,}148$. Therefore, the probability of being dealt a flush, including royal and straight, in a five-card hand is calculated as follows:

$$P(\text{Flush}) = \frac{5{,}148}{2{,}598{,}960} = 0.00198$$

roughly twice in 1,000 hands of poker. Ready to deal?

Combinations are also useful for calculating the probability of winning a state lottery drawing. At the start of this chapter, I referred to a typical lottery game that requires you to pick 6 numbers out of a possible 49. The number of 6-number combinations from a pool of 49 numbers is as follows:

Because the order of the numbers in a lottery does not matter, we use the combination rather than the permutation formula.

$$_{49}C_6 = \frac{49!}{(49-6)!6!} = \frac{(49)(48)(47)(46)(45)(44)}{(6)(5)(4)(3)(2)(1)} = 13{,}983{,}816$$

Because there are nearly 14 million different six-number combinations, the probability that your combination is the winner is as follows:

$$P(\text{Winning a } 6/49 \text{ Lottery}) = \frac{1}{13{,}983{,}816} = 0.00000007$$

With those chances of winning the lottery, you better not quit your day job just yet.

This is one of the biggest misconceptions in probability, especially in gambling. No matter how many consecutive heads are observed when tossing a coin, the probability of the next toss being a heads is always 50%. The coin has no memory of previous tosses.

Probability does not have a memory. The same six numbers selected in last week's lottery drawing have the exact same probability of being chosen again in this week's lottery. That's because the two drawings are independent events and have absolutely no influence on each other. Therefore, choosing a lottery number because it has not been selected recently does not increase your odds of winning. Sorry if I ruined your favorite strategy!

Here's something you will like: Rather than deal with all those nasty factorial calculations, we can let Excel figure out the number of permutations or combinations for us. The functions are as follows:

$$= \text{PERMUT}(n,x)$$
$$= \text{COMBIN}(n,x)$$

For example, if we type =PERMUT(52,5) from our five-card poker example into Excel, the result will be 311,875,200. If we type =COMBIN(52,5), the result will be 2,598,960.

Combinations are useful in business when a product or service is available with different options. For example, suppose a car model has five different option packages available. The manufacturer will probably be interested in knowing, for production reasons, how many variations of the model exist when customers choose two options.

To be sure you understand the counting rules we have discussed, work out the problems in the following Your Turn section.

YOUR TURN #12

1. A restaurant has a menu with four appetizers, seven entrées, four desserts, and three drinks. If a meal consists of an appetizer, an entrée, a desert, and a drink, how many different meals can you order?
2. The NBA teams with the 13 worst records at the end of the season participate in a lottery to determine the order in which they will draft new players for the next season. How many different arrangements exist for the drafting order for these 13 teams?
3. A combination lock has a total of 40 numbers and will unlock with the proper three-number sequence. How many possible combinations exist?
4. I would like to select 3 paperback books from a list of 11 books to take on vacation. How many different sets of three books can I choose?

Answers can be found on ▶ **page 192**

4.3 Section Problems

Basic Skills

4.31 If the order of objects is of importance, how many ways can I select eight objects three at a time?

4.32 If the order of objects is of importance, how many ways can I select nine objects two at a time?

4.33 If the order of objects is not of importance, how many ways can I select eight objects three at a time? Why is this result different from Problem 4.31?

4.34 If the order of objects is not of importance, how many ways can I select nine objects two at a time? Why is this result different from Problem 4.32?

Applications

4.35 I would like to customize a desktop computer online. I have to choose among the following categories:

- processor (five choices)
- hard drive (four choices)
- memory (three choices)
- monitor (four choices)
- keyboard (two choices)

How many unique computers can I configure with these choices?

4.36 In a race with eight swimmers, how many ways can the swimmers finish first, second, and third?

4.37 A panel of 12 jurors needs to be selected from a group of 50 people. How many different juries can be selected?

4.38 What is the probability of being dealt a full house (three-of-a-kind and a pair) in five-card poker?

4.39 What is the probability of winning a 4/20 lottery game where 4 numbers are picked from a range of 20?

4.40 There are four teams in the NFL's NFC North Division. How many different ways can the four teams finish at the end of the season in the standings?

4.41 An event planner needs to decide a seating arrangement for eight people at a table. Calculate the total number of possible arrangements available from which to choose.

4.42 A research study needs to select three people to participate from a group of nine. Calculate the total number of unique groups that can be formed.

4.43 An executive needs to select 4 stores from a total of 10 to participate in a customer service program. Determine the number of possible groups of four stores.

4.44 Determine the number of ways in which a jury of 6 men and 6 women can be selected from a group of 13 men and 15 women.

CHAPTER 4 Summary

- A probability is a numerical value ranging from zero to one that represents the likelihood of an event occurring.
    - Classical probability refers to a situation in which we know the number of possible outcomes of the event of interest.
    - Empirical probability observes the number of occurrences of an event through an experiment and calculates their probability from a relative frequency distribution.
    - Subjective probability relies on people's experience and intuition to estimate the probabilities.
- If the sample space includes every possible event that can occur, then we say that the events are collectively exhaustive.
- Simple probability represents the likelihood of a single event occurring.
- The law of large numbers states that when an experiment is conducted a large number of times, the empirical probabilities of the process will converge to the classical probabilities.
- A contingency table indicates the number of occurrences of events classified according to two variables.
    - Marginal probabilities are simple probabilities found by using the total occurrences in the margins of a contingency table.
- The intersection of Events *A* and *B* represents the number of instances in which Events *A* and *B* occur at the same time.
    - The probability of the intersection of two events is known as a joint probability.
- The union of Events *A* and *B* represents the number of instances in which either Event *A* or *B* occurs or both events occur together.
- Two events are considered to be mutually exclusive if they cannot occur at the same time during an experiment.
- Prior probability is the probability of Event *A* occurring without your knowing any additional information that could affect the event.
- Conditional probability is the probability of Event *A* occurring when you know Event *B* has already occurred.
    - Conditional probability is also known as a posterior probability.
    - Two events are considered independent of one another if the occurrence of one event has no impact on the probability of the other event.
    - If the occurrence of one event affected the probability of another event, the events are dependent events.
- The multiplication rule is used to determine the probability of the intersection of two events, or *P*(*A* and *B*), otherwise known as the joint probability.
- Thomas Bayes (1701–1761) developed a mathematical rule, known as Bayes' Theorem, for calculating $P(A|B)$ from information about $P(B|A)$.
- The fundamental counting principle states that if there are k_1 choices for the first event, k_2 choices for the second event, and k_n choices for the *n*th event, then the total number of possible outcomes is $(k_1)(k_2)(k_3)\cdots(k_n)$.
- Permutations are the number of different ways in which objects can be arranged in order.
- Combinations are similar to permutations, except that the order of the objects is not important.

CHAPTER 4 Key Terms

Addition rule. A mathematical rule used to calculate the probability of the union of events.

Bayes' Theorem. A theorem used to calculate $P(A|B)$ from information about $P(B|A)$.

Classical probability. A probability that is determined by dividing the number of possible outcomes of an event by the total number of possible outcomes in the sample space.

Collectively exhaustive. Describes a set of events where at least one of the events must occur during an experiment.

Combinations. The number of different ways in which objects can be arranged without regard to order.

Complement. All of the outcomes in the sample space that are not part of the event of interest.

Conditional probability (of *A* given *B*). The probability of Event *A* occurring given the condition that Event *B* has already occurred.

Contingency table. A table that shows the number of occurrences of events of an experiment classified by two variables.

Decision trees. Display marginal and joint probabilities from a contingency table.

Dependent events. Events wherein the occurrence of one event affects the occurrence of another event.

Empirical probability. A probability determined by counting the frequency of an event during an experiment.

Event. One or more outcomes of an experiment that are a subset of the sample space.

Experiment. The process of measuring or observing an activity for the purpose of collecting data.

Fundamental counting principle. A principle that states that if there are k_1 choices for the first event, k_2 choices for the second event, ... and k_n choices for the *n*th event, then the total number of possible outcomes is $(k_1)(k_2)(k_3)\cdots(k_n)$.

Independent events. Events that have no impact on the probability of each other occurring.

Intersection (of Events *A* and *B*). The number of instances in which Events *A* and *B* occur at the same time.

Joint probability. The probability of the intersection of two events.

Law of large numbers. A law that states that when an experiment is conducted a large number of times, the empirical probabilities of the process will converge to the classical probabilities.

Marginal probabilities. Simple probabilities found in the margins, or row and column totals, of a contingency table.

Multiplication rule. A rule used to determine the probability of the intersection of two events.

Mutually exclusive events. Events that cannot occur at the same time.

Permutations. The number of different ways in which objects can be arranged in order.

Posterior probability. A probability that is a revision of a prior probability using additional information.

Prior probability. The probability of an event occurring as determined without any additional information that could affect the event.

Probability. A numerical value ranging from zero to one that represents the likelihood of a specific event occurring.

Sample space. A set of all possible outcomes of an experiment.

Simple event. An event with a single outcome in its most basic form that cannot be simplified.

Simple probability. The likelihood of a single event occurring.

Subjective probability. A probability that is calculated based on the experience and intuition of a person (or people). A subjective probability is made when classical and empirical probabilities cannot be calculated.

Union (of Events *A* and *B*). All of the instances in which Event *A* or Event *B* or both occur.

CHAPTER 4 Equations

4.1 An Introduction to Probabilities (pp 148–156)

Formula 4.1 for the Classical Probability

$$P(A) = \frac{\text{Number of possible outcomes that constitute Event } A}{\text{Total number of possible outcomes in the sample space}}$$

Formula 4.2 for the Empirical Probability

$$P(A) = \frac{\text{Frequency in which Event } A \text{ occurs}}{\text{Total number of observations}}$$

Formula 4.3 for The Complement Rule

$$P(A) + P(A') = 1 \text{ or}$$
$$P(A) = 1 - P(A')$$

4.2 Probability Rules for More Than One Event (pp 156–175)

Formula 4.4 for The Addition Rule for the Mutually Exclusive Events

$$P(A \text{ or } B) = P(A) + P(B)$$

Formula 4.5 for The Addition Rule for the Events That Are Not Mutually Exclusive

$$P(A \text{ or } B) = P(A) + P(B) - P(A \text{ and } B)$$

Formulas 4.6 and 4.7 for Calculating a Conditional Probability

$$P(A|B) = \frac{P(A \text{ and } B)}{P(B)}$$

or

$$P(B|A) = \frac{P(A \text{ and } B)}{(A)}$$

Formula 4.8 for Determining If Events A and B Are Independent

$$P(A|B) = P(A)$$

Formulas 4.9 and 4.10 for The Multiplication Rule for Dependent Events

$$P(A|B) = \frac{P(A \text{ and } B)}{P(B)}$$

$$P(A \text{ and } B) = P(B)P(A|B)$$

or

$$P(B|A) = \frac{P(A \text{ and } B)}{P(A)}$$

$$P(A \text{ and } B) = P(A)P(B|A)$$

Formula 4.11 for The Multiplication Rule for Two Independent Events

$$P(A \text{ and } B) = P(A)P(B)$$

Formula 4.12 for The Multiplication Rule for *n* Independent Events

$$P(A_1 \text{ and } A_2 \text{ and } \cdots \text{ and } A_n) = P(A_1)P(A_2)\cdots P(A_n)$$

Formula 4.13 for the Bayes' Theorem

$$P(A_i|B) = \frac{P(A_i)P(B|A_i)}{P(A_1)P(B|A_1) + P(A_2)P(B|A_2) + \cdots + P(A_n)P(B|A_n)}$$

4.3 Counting Principles (pp 176–182)

Formula 4.14 for the Fundamental Counting Rule

$$(k_1)(k_2)(k_3)\cdots(k_n)$$

Formula 4.15 for the Permutations of *n* Distinct Objects

$$n! = n(n-1)(n-2)(n-3)\cdots(2)(1)$$

Formulas 4.16 and 4.17 for the Permutations of *n* Objects Selected *x* at a Time

$$_nP_x = \frac{n!}{(n-x)!}$$

or

$$_nP_x = \frac{n!}{(n-x!)} = n(n-1)(n-2)\cdots(n-x+1)$$

Formulas 4.18 and 4.19 for the Combinations of *n* Objects Selected *x* at a Time

$$_nC_x = \frac{n!}{(n-x)!x!}$$

or

$$_nC_x = \frac{n!}{(n-x)!x!} = \frac{n(n-1)(n-2)\cdots(n-x+1)}{x!}$$

CHAPTER 4 Problems

4.45 Identify which of the following values are valid and not valid numbers for a probability:

a. 2.1
b. $\frac{4}{4}$
c. 76%
d. 0.8
e. $\frac{9}{8}$
f. 110%
g. $-\frac{1}{3}$
h. 1
i. 0.007

4.46 What is the probability of randomly selecting a heart from a standard 52-card deck?

4.47 Consider the experiment of rolling two dice.

a. What is the probability of obtaining a sum of eight?
b. What is the probability of obtaining a sum of eight or less?
c. What is the probability of obtaining a sum of four or more?

4.48 Indicate whether classical, empirical, or subjective probability should be used to determine each of the following:

a. The probability that it will rain tomorrow
b. The probability that you will roll doubles when throwing two dice
c. The probability that I will pass tomorrow's statistics exam
d. The probability that I will select a Milky Way candy bar out of a bowl of Halloween candy

4.49 A survey was conducted in which 150 households were asked how many working televisions they owned. The results are as follows:

Number of Televisions	Number of Households
0	5
1	34
2	50
3	29
4	12
5	12
6	8
Total	**150**

a. What is the probability that a randomly selected household has one television?
b. What is the probability that a randomly selected household has more than two televisions?
c. What is the probability that a randomly selected household has fewer than four televisions?
d. Is this an example of classical, empirical, or subjective probability?

4.50 A recent survey administered by ZoneDiet.com asked 1,000 adults, "How far are you from your ideal weight?" The results are shown in the following table:

Response	Frequency
1–5 lbs	150
6–10 lbs	140
11–15 lbs	90
16 or more	380
I'm content	?
Total	**1,000**

a. How many adults responded that they are content with their current weight?
b. What is the probability that a randomly selected adult is content with his or her weight?
c. What is the probability that a randomly selected adult is 1–5 lbs from his or her ideal weight?
d. What is the probability that a randomly selected adult is 6 lbs or more from his or her ideal weight?

4.51 The following table indicates the frequency of laptops sold per day at a local Best Buy store during a particular time period. During the period, there were never any days in which more than seven laptops were sold.

Daily Demand	Frequency
0	7
1	11
2	26
3	13
4	15
5	5
6	8
7	5

a. What is the probability that three laptops will be sold tomorrow?
b. What is the probability that four or more laptops will be sold tomorrow?
c. What is the probability that either one or two laptops will be sold tomorrow?
d. What is the probability that less than two laptops will be sold tomorrow?
e. Is this an example of classical, empirical, or subjective probability?

4.52 Consider an experiment with the following two events:

A = A statistics test is scheduled for 8:00 A.M.
B = Every student arrives to class on time for the test

a. Are these two events mutually exclusive?
b. Are these two events independent?

4.53 Consider the following experiment—a card is chosen randomly from a 52-card deck, observed, and then replaced. After shuffling the deck, a second card is drawn and observed. Consider the following events:

A = The first card is the jack of diamonds
B = The second card is the jack of diamonds

a. Are these two events mutually exclusive?
b. Are these two events independent?

4.54 Consider the following experiment—a card is chosen randomly from a 52-card deck, observed, and *not* replaced. A second card is drawn and observed. Consider the following events:

A = The first card is the jack of diamonds
B = The second card is the jack of diamonds

a. Are these two events mutually exclusive?
b. Are these two events independent?

4.55 A local university has a student population that is 57% male. Sixty-four percent of the students are undergraduates; 40% are both male and undergraduates.

a. What is the probability that a randomly selected student is both female and an undergraduate?
b. What is the probability that a randomly selected student is either male or an undergraduate?

4.56 The airline industry defines an on-time flight as one that arrives within 15 minutes of its scheduled time. The following table shows the number of on-time and late flights leaving Philadelphia and arriving in Orlando during a recent time period by airline:

Airline	On-Time	Late
Southwest	239	68
US Airways	288	130
Air Tran	180	63

a. What is the probability that a randomly selected flight was from Southwest and was on time?
b. What is the probability that a randomly selected flight was from Air Tran or was on time?
c. Given that the flight was late, what is the probability that it was from US Airways?
d. Given that the flight was from Southwest, what is the probability that it was late?
e. Construct a decision tree for these probabilities.

4.57 A test has multiple-choice questions, with four choices of answers from which to choose. After reading the first four questions, you realize you have no idea what any of the correct answers are. Assume you randomly guess at the answers for all four questions.

a. What is the probability that you answered the first question correctly?
b. What is the probability that you answered the first two questions correctly?
c. What is the probability that you answered the first three questions correctly?
d. What is the probability that you answered all four questions correctly?
e. What assumption are you making with these calculations?

4.58 The following table shows the number of students who earned an A, B, C, and D grade in a business statistics class along with their year in their program.

Grade	Sophomore	Junior
A	14	30
B	31	38
C	20	16
D	11	5

a. What percentage of students in this class are juniors?
b. What percentage of students in this class earned a B grade?
c. What percentage of students in this class were sophomores and earned a B grade?
d. What percentage of students in this class were juniors or earned an A grade?
e. What percentage of students in this class earned a C grade, given they were sophomores?
f. What percentage of students in this class were sophomores, given they earned a C grade?
g. Do course grade and year in the program appear to be independent or dependent? Define Event *A* as earning an A grade and Event *B* as a student in his or her sophomore year.

4.59 In college basketball, a turnover is defined as losing possession of the basketball to the opposing team without scoring a basket. In theory, reducing the number of turnovers increases the likelihood of winning a game. The following table categorizes the number of wins and losses by the number of turnovers made by the Villanova Wildcats during two recent seasons.

Turnovers Per Game	Win	Lose
5–8	6	0
9–12	17	5
13–16	22	10
17–20	7	4
21–24	0	2

Assume that a randomly selected game was chosen during one of the two seasons. What is the probability that the game

a. was won by Villanova?
b. had 9–12 turnovers made by Villanova?
c. was lost by Villanova, and Villanova made 13–16 turnovers?
d. was won by Villanova or Villanova made 5–8 turnovers?
e. was won by Villanova, given that Villanova made 9–12 turnovers?
f. had 21–24 turnovers made by Villanova, given that Villanova lost the game?
g. Construct a decision tree for these probabilities.
h. Do winning and turnovers appear to be independent or dependent events for Villanova? Define Event *A* as a game with 13–16 turnovers and Event *B* as a win. What conclusions can be drawn about these events?

4.60 A snack-food company produces potato chips on three different production lines. Line 1 produces 20% of the total output, Line 2 produces 30%, and Line 3 produces the balance. Each line is sampled to ensure the salt content is within the proper range. Historically, 4% of Line 1's output does not meet the salt standards, 3% of Line 2's fails to meet the standards, and 2% of Line 3's does not meet the salt standards. A random bag of potato chips was selected and did not meet the salt standards. What is the probability that the chips were produced in Line 3?

4.61 A computer program consists of 1,000 lines of code. For the program to work properly, all 1,000 lines must be correct. Assume that the probability of any line of code being correct is 0.9999.

a. What is the probability that the program will work properly?
b. What assumptions do you need to make to determine this probability?

4.62 According to Internet World Stats, 79% of North American adults used the Internet in 2012. If five people are randomly chosen, what is the probability that all five use the Internet?

4.63 A call center for customer support records the time each customer requires for service and whether the call occurred during the week (Monday through Friday) or during the weekend (Saturday and Sunday). The results are shown in the following table:

Time (Minutes)	Week	Weekend
Less than 5	15	3
5 to less than 10	26	4
10 to less than 15	11	9
15 to less than 20	22	6
More than 20	10	14

Determine the probability that a randomly selected call

a. was during the week
b. was less than 20 minutes
c. was 10 to less than 20 minutes
d. was more than 20 minutes during the weekend
e. was 15 to less than 20 minutes or occurred during the weekend
f. was 5 to less than 10 minutes, given it occurred during the week
g. occurred during the week, given it was 5 to less than 10 minutes
h. Construct a decision tree for these events.

4.64 Ann is the owner of Pizzas R Us, a small company that delivers pizza from two different locations. The Mayfair site handles 40% of the total orders while the Claymont location delivers the remaining orders. In its promotional materials, Pizzas R Us strives to deliver all orders within 45 minutes. Historically, the Claymont location has experienced 5% of its orders taking longer than 45 minutes to deliver. The Mayfair store has been late on 15% of its orders. Ann has just spoken to a customer whose order was delivered 1 hour after it was placed but did not remember which location the order originated. What is the probability that the late order came from the Mayfair store?

4.65 I would like to order a car from the factory and I have to choose among the following categories:

- exterior color (four choices)
- interior color (four choices)
- engine size (three choices)
- transmission (two choices)
- option packages (four choices)

How many unique cars can I choose from with these choices?

4.66 What is the probability of winning a 5/30 lottery game where 5 numbers are picked from a range of 30?

4.67 A multiple-choice test has 10 questions, with each question having four choices.

a. How many different ways can a student answer the 10 questions?
b. What is the probability that a student who randomly answers each question will answer all of them correctly?

4.68 How many different ways can 10 new movies be ranked first, second, and third by a movie critic?

4.69 My bank requires me to establish a four-digit pin number for my debit card.

a. How many possible pin numbers can I choose from?
b. What is the probability that someone can correctly guess my pin number?

4.70 A director for a play has to choose an actor to play a lead male role and an actress to play a lead female role. The director has to choose from among five males and seven females. Determine how many possible male–female combinations the director has to choose from for the two lead roles.

4.71 If a salesperson is responsible for eight stores in her territory, determine how many different ways she can schedule a visit with five of them today.

4.72 A graduate class has 12 students with A grades and 16 students with B grades. Calculate the number of ways in which 4 A students and 5 B students can be uniquely selected.

4.73 The NFL has 32 teams that are evenly divided into two conferences, the NFC and the AFC. One team from each conference will play in the Super Bowl to determine the NFL champion.

a. How many unique pairs of teams exist that can play in the Super Bowl?
b. Do you have enough information from this problem to calculate the probability that the two Super Bowl teams will be the Green Bay Packers and the Pittsburgh Steelers? Why or why not?

CHAPTER 4 Solutions to Your Turn

YOUR TURN #1

1. $P(\text{Spade}) = \dfrac{13}{52} = 0.25$

2. $P(8) = \dfrac{5}{36} = 0.139$

YOUR TURN #2

1. $P(250 - 499) = \dfrac{144}{1025} = 0.140$

2. $P(>250) = \dfrac{144 + 246 + 297}{1025} = \dfrac{687}{1025} = 0.670$

YOUR TURN #3

a. empirical, because we have historical data for the number of home runs Josh Hamilton normally hits
b. classical, because we know the number of cards and the number of jacks in the deck
c. If I have data from my last several rounds of golf, this would be empirical; otherwise, subjective.
d. classical, because we can calculate the probability based on the lottery rules
e. subjective, because I would not be collecting data for this experiment
f. subjective, because I would not be collecting data for this experiment

YOUR TURN #4

1. a. valid probability
   b. not a valid probability because probability cannot be less than zero
   c. valid probability
   d. valid probability
   e. not a valid probability because probability cannot be more than one
   f. not a valid probability because probability cannot be more than one
   g. valid probability
   h. valid probability
   i. not a valid probability because probability cannot be less than zero
2. $P(\text{No pay cut}) = 1 - (0.02 + 0.13 + 0.26 + 0.53) = 1 - 0.94 = 0.06$

YOUR TURN #5

a. $P(\text{warranty}) = \frac{11}{60} = 0.183$

b. $P(<40) = \frac{39}{60} = 0.65$

c. $P(\geq 40 \text{ and no waranty}) = \frac{15}{60} = 0.25$

d. $P(<40 \text{ or no waranty}) = \frac{5}{60} + \frac{34}{60} + \frac{15}{60} = \frac{54}{60} = 0.90$

YOUR TURN #6

a. $P(\text{Standard and } 31\text{–}60) = \frac{96}{600} = 0.16$

b. $P(\text{Standard or} < 30) = \frac{325}{600} + \frac{255}{600} - \frac{165}{600} = \frac{415}{600} = 0.692$

c. $P(\text{Gold and } 61\text{–}90) = \frac{49}{600} = 0.082$

d. $P(31\text{–}60 \text{ or } <30) = \frac{217}{600} + \frac{255}{600} = \frac{472}{600} = 0.787$

e. $P(31\text{–}60 \text{ and } 61\text{–}90) = \frac{0}{600} = 0.0$

YOUR TURN #7

a. $P(\text{Gold}) = \frac{302}{962} = 0.314$

b. $P(\text{Russia}) = \frac{82}{962} = 0.085$

c. $P(\text{Silver and United States}) = \frac{29}{962} = 0.030$

d. $P(\text{Bronze or China}) = \frac{356}{962} + \frac{88}{962} - \frac{23}{962} = \frac{421}{962} = 0.438$

e. $P(\text{United States} \mid \text{Gold}) = \frac{P(\text{United States and Gold})}{P(\text{Gold})}$

$P(\text{United States and Gold}) = \frac{46}{962} = 0.048$

$P(\text{Gold}) = \frac{302}{962} = 0.314$

$P(\text{United States} \mid \text{Gold}) = \frac{0.048}{0.314} = 0.153$

f. $P(\text{Bronze} \mid \text{Russia}) = \frac{P(\text{Bronze and Russia})}{P(\text{Russia})}$

$P(\text{Bronze and Russia}) = \frac{32}{962} = 0.033$

$P(\text{Russia}) = \frac{82}{962} = 0.085$

$P(\text{Bronze} \mid \text{Russia}) = \frac{0.033}{0.085} = 0.388$

YOUR TURN #8

$$P(A) = \frac{12{,}505}{147{,}739} = 0.085$$

$$P(A|B) = \frac{P(A \text{ and } B)}{P(B)}$$

$$P(A \text{ and } B) = \frac{6{,}480}{147{,}739} = 0.044 \qquad P(B) = \frac{102{,}366}{147{,}739} = 0.693$$

$$P(A|B) = \frac{0.044}{0.693} = 0.063$$

$$P(A|B) \neq P(A)$$

Events A and B are dependent.

YOUR TURN #9

1. Define A = First card is a red queen
Define B = Second card is red

$$P(A) = \frac{2}{52} = 0.038$$

$$P(B|A) = \frac{25}{51} = 0.490$$

$$P(A \text{ and } B) = P(A)P(B|A) = (0.038)(0.490) = 0.0186$$

2. Define A = First card is a red queen
Define B = Second card is red

$$P(A) = \frac{2}{52} = 0.038$$

$$P(B) = \frac{26}{52} = 0.50$$

$$P(A \text{ and } B) = P(A)P(B) = (0.038)(0.50) = 0.019$$

YOUR TURN #10

a., b., c.

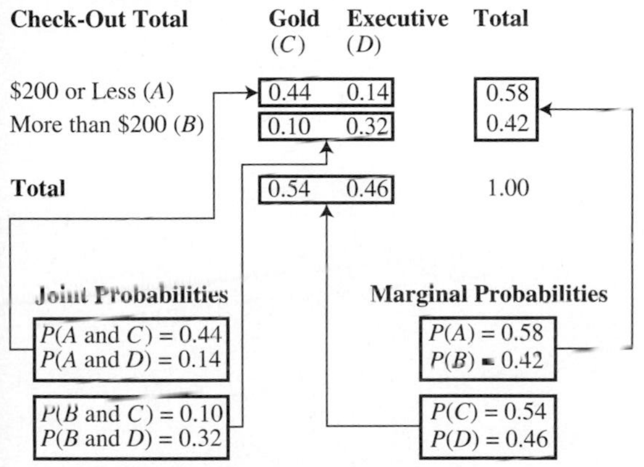

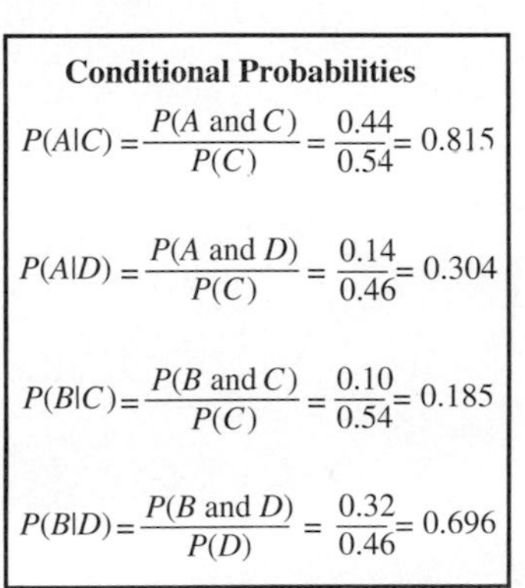

d.

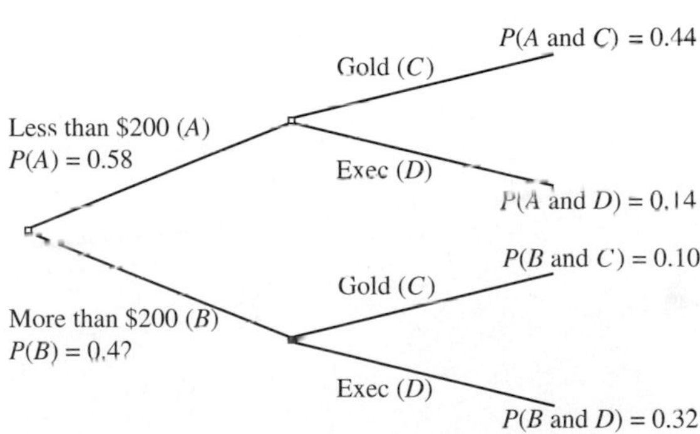

e. Because the conditional probabilities are $P(A|C) = 0.815$, we can conclude that Gold Star members are more likely to spend less than \$200. And because $P(B|D) = 0.696$, we can conclude that executive members are more likely to spend more than \$200.

YOUR TURN #11

Define A_1 = Player used drug, A_2 = Player did not use drug, and B = Player tested positive for the drug.

$$P(A_1) = 0.08$$
$$P(A_2) = 1 - 0.08 = 0.92$$
$$P(B|A_1) = 0.90$$
$$P(B|A_2) = 0.15$$

$$P(A_1|B) = \frac{P(A_1)P(B|A_1)}{P(A_1)P(B|A_1) + P(A_2)P(B|A_2)}$$
$$P(A_1|B) = \frac{(0.08)(0.90)}{(0.08)(0.90) + (0.92)(0.15)}$$
$$P(A_1|B) = \frac{0.072}{0.072 + 0.138} = \frac{0.072}{0.21} = 0.343$$

YOUR TURN #12

1. $4 \times 7 \times 4 \times 3 = 336$ different meals

2. $13! = 6{,}227{,}020{,}800$ different ordered arrangements

3. ${}_{40}P_3 = \frac{40!}{(40-3)!} = (40)(39)(38) = 59{,}280$

4. ${}_{11}C_3 = \frac{11!}{(11-3)!3!} = \frac{(11)(10)(9)}{(3)(2)(1)} = 165$

CHAPTER

5

Discrete Probability Distributions

IN THIS CHAPTER, YOU WILL LEARN TO:

- Identify the rules of a discrete probability distribution.
- Calculate and interpret the mean and standard deviation of a discrete distribution.
- Understand the characteristics of a binomial experiment.
- Calculate binomial probabilities.
- Calculate and interpret the mean and standard deviation of a binomial distribution.
- Understand the characteristics of a Poisson process.
- Calculate Poisson probabilities.
- Approximate binomial probabilities using the Poisson distribution.
- Calculate hypergeometric probabilities.

CHAPTER 5 MAP

We discussed the difference between discrete and continuous data back in Chapter 2. If you are counting the number of customers visiting your store on a given day, you are working with discrete data. In this case, the values are typically whole numbers (or integers) such as 10 or 16. In most applications, discrete data cannot take on fractional values like 30.5 because having 30.5 customers visit your store in one day is not physically possible. By contrast, continuous data, which are the focus of Chapter 6, can take on any real number, including fractional values. Unlike discrete data, which are counted, continuous data are typically measured. Examples are the height and weight of people, which can take on an infinite number of possible values. For example, a hypothetical statistics author's weight could be 186.1 lbs or 186.1456 lbs. The number of possibilities is limited only by the precision of the measurement.

This chapter will show you how to determine discrete probabilities. Discrete probabilities are probabilities that describe the likelihood that certain discrete data will occur. For example, consider Tony's Pizza, which offers on its menu three pizza sizes that sell for $5, $10, and $15. Table 5.1 shows the historic probabilities of customers ordering each size.

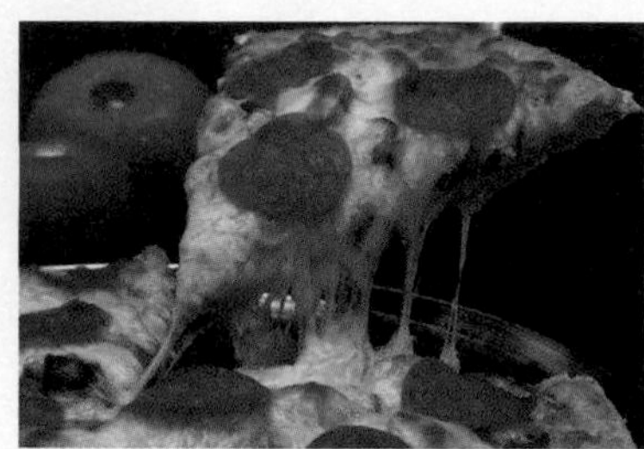

TABLE 5.1 | Discrete Probabilities for Tony's Pizza

PRICE ($)	PROBABILITY (%)
5	30
10	25
15	45

The price of the pizza would be considered discrete data because the values are limited to these three prices. Table 5.1 describes the discrete probability distribution for these sizes. We can see from these data that the $15 pizza is the most popular size, whereas the $10 is the least popular. Probabilities, in general, are often difficult to assess when we rely on our intuition or judgment. For example, you might be surprised by how low the probability is of your passing a multiple-choice test you are completely unprepared for and must guess the answers to. (Not that you would ever try such a crazy thing!) Table 5.2 summarizes the probabilities for such a scenario based on the number of test questions. (Assume that 70% is a passing grade.)

TABLE 5.2 | Probabilities of Passing an Exam when Guessing at the Answers

NUMBER OF TEST QUESTIONS	PROBABILITY OF PASSING
10	0.0035
20	0.0000295
40	0.0000000028

For example, the probability of correctly guessing at least 7 (70%) of the 10 multiple-choice questions each with four choices is only 0.0035 (less than 1%). For a 40-question test, the probability drops to an infinitesimal 0.0000000028. This translates to passing the exam once in every 357,142,857 attempts. I'm not sure your professor is going to let you try the exam that many times to pass. In this chapter, you will learn how to calculate the probabilities displayed in Table 5.2.

Our test-taking example brings to mind a recurring nightmare I have experienced for as long as I can remember: In the dream, I am back in college. Suddenly, I realize I'm enrolled in a math course I have never attended. I finally work up the nerve to walk into the classroom and find myself face to face with . . . *an exam*. At this point, I wake up in a cold sweat, thankful that I had only been dreaming. After calculating the probability of passing an exam in this situation, you surely have come to the same conclusion that I did many years ago: It doesn't pay to take a multiple-choice exam unprepared and by guessing at the answers. Table 5.2 provides proof.

Businesses often rely on discrete probabilities to help them make important decisions, including the following:

- Forecasting customer demand to plan for staffing and inventory needs
- Quantifying the risk of producing defective items to provide better control of a manufacturing process
- Gauging different customer satisfaction scores to improve customer service

These and other types of discrete probabilities will be considered throughout this chapter.

5.1 Introduction to Discrete Probability Distributions

In Chapter 4, we discussed conducting experiments to acquire data. A simple experiment would be to roll a fair six-sided die (one with an equal chance of observing each number). Examples of more complex experiments businesses might conduct to calculate probabilities would be the following:

- To record the number of customers who enter a Best Buy store each hour during the business day
- To randomly select six customers who walked into an AT&T Wireless store and count the number who signed new cell phone contracts
- To request that each customer checking out of a Marriott Hotel rate his or her satisfaction with the stay as a 1, 2, 3, 4, or 5

Each of these experiments would generate discrete data, such as the following:

- Twenty-six customers entered the Best Buy store between 10:00 and 11:00 A.M.
- One of the six customers at the AT&T store signed a cell phone contract.
- Four is the satisfaction rating, on a scale of 1–5, provided by the last customer to check out of the Marriott Hotel.

Discrete Random Variables

Discrete random variables have outcomes that typically take on whole numbers as a result of conducting an experiment.

Discrete random variables have outcomes that typically take on whole numbers as a result of conducting an experiment. The values 26, 1, and 4 are examples of values that a discrete random variable often takes on. The term *random* is used because the value of the variable cannot be known with certainty before the experiment. For example, it would be unreasonable to expect me (or anyone else) to accurately predict that 26 customers will arrive during the first hour of business at the Best Buy store. The value of the random variable becomes known with certainty *after* the experiment is conducted. By convention, the value of the random variable is often denoted by x.

Continuous random variables have outcomes that take on any numerical value as a result of conducting an experiment.

Some experiments will generate continuous data and are known as **continuous random variables**. Continuous random variables have outcomes that take on any numerical value as a result of conducting an experiment. Examples of continuous random variables include the following:

- The length of time a customer waits in a checkout line at a Whole Foods grocery store
- The ounces of soda consumed by an adult in one month
- The weight of a tractor-trailer at a weigh station on Interstate 95

The acid test for determining whether we are dealing with discrete or continuous random variables is to ask ourselves, "How many data values can be found in a specific interval of numbers?" Discrete random variables have outcomes that are limited to a finite number of values within an interval, whereas continuous random variables have an infinite number of outcomes within an interval. In the Marriot Hotel (discrete) example, there are only five possible outcomes within the interval 1–5 for a customer to choose from when rating his or her satisfaction. In the Whole Foods (continuous) example, there are an infinite number of wait times within the interval 0–5 minutes. Possible wait times could be 3 minutes, 3.2 minutes, or 3.27 minutes. Because we are measuring time on a continuous scale, the only limitation in the number of values within this 0- to 5-minute interval is our measuring instrument's level of precision.

As mentioned in Chapter 2, there are some exceptions to these guidelines, especially when the outcome of the random variable covers a wide range of values. Income values, for instance, are technically discrete data (we count our money, not measure it). But because of the very large number of possible income values, it is more practical to consider these data as continuous.

We will discuss continuous random variables in more detail in Chapter 6.

Rules for Discrete Probability Distributions

A listing of all the possible outcomes of an experiment for a discrete random variable along with the relative frequency of each outcome is called a **discrete probability distribution**.

A listing of all the possible outcomes of an experiment for a discrete random variable along with the relative frequency of each outcome is called a **discrete probability distribution**. To demonstrate this concept, let's consider the Olive Garden restaurant, which records the frequencies of group sizes that arrive for dinner. The Olive Garden wants to know this information so that it can arrange its available seating in the most efficient manner.

Table 5.3 shows these frequencies. The "Group Size" column shows the discrete random variables in our experiment. Notice how the group sizes are all whole numbers (the Olive Garden won't see a party of 2.6 people). The "Frequency" column displays the number of times each random variable occurred during the experiment. The "Relative Frequency" column shows the relative frequencies for each group size for the last 50 tables. Relative frequencies are a proportion of the total, so they can consist of fractions. (Recall that relative frequency distributions were discussed at length in Chapter 2.)

Group size represents discrete data because there are only a finite number (five) of possible values for the outcome of this random variable within the interval 2–6.

TABLE 5.3 | Olive Garden's Probability Distribution for Group Sizes

GROUP SIZE	FREQUENCY	RELATIVE FREQUENCY
2	17	$17/50 = 0.34$
3	6	$6/50 = 0.12$
4	16	$16/50 = 0.32$
5	4	$4/50 = 0.08$
6	7	$7/50 = 0.14$
Total	50	1.00

The relative frequencies in Table 5.3 represent the probabilities for each outcome of the discrete random variable (group size). If the 50 tables are representative of a typical evening, we can conclude the probability is greatest (34%) that the next group arriving for dinner will consist of two people.

Figure 5.1 shows the probability distribution in graphical form. See Chapter 2 for a refresher on how to construct this chart in Excel.

FIGURE 5.1
Graph Showing Olive Garden's Probability Distribution for Group Sizes

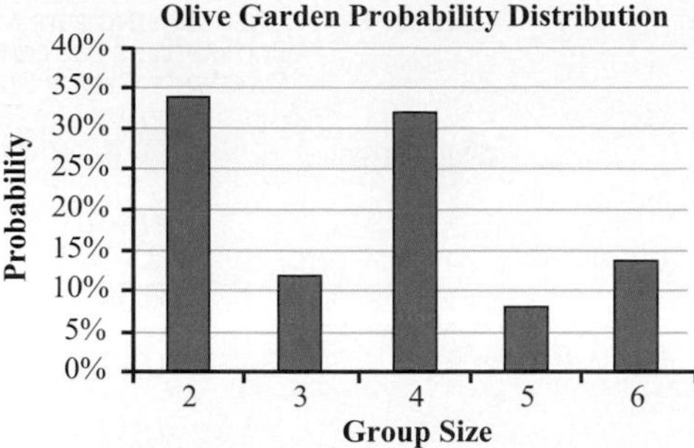

A discrete probability distribution meets the following conditions:

- Each outcome in the distribution needs to be mutually exclusive with other outcomes in the distribution—that is, the value of the random variable cannot fall into more than one of the frequency distribution classes. For example, it is not possible for the same group to consist of both two and three people.
- The probability of each outcome, $P(x)$, must be between 0 and 1 (inclusive); that is, $0 \leq P(x) \leq 1$ for all values of x. In the previous example, $P(x = 4) = 0.32$, which falls between 0 and 1.
- The sum of the probabilities for all the outcomes in the distribution needs to add up to 1—that is, $\sum_{i=1}^{n} P(x_i) = 1$, where n equals the total number of possible outcomes.

In Table 5.3, notice that the "Relative Frequency" (probability) column adds to 1.00. Occasionally, rounding errors occur when probabilities are added, causing the total to be slightly more or less than 1, such as 0.999 or 1.001. We normally assume that values such as these are close enough to 1 for our purposes.

The Mean of a Discrete Probability Distribution

The mean of a discrete probability distribution is simply the weighted average of the outcomes of the random variable that comprise it. We can calculate it using Equation 5.1.

Formula 5.1 for the Mean of a Discrete Probability Distribution

$$\mu = \sum_{i=1}^{n} x_i P(x_i)$$

where

μ = The mean of the discrete probability distribution
x_i = The value of the random variable for the ith outcome
$P(x_i)$ = The probability that the ith outcome will occur
n = The number of outcomes in the distribution

Table 5.4 shows the calculations that determined the mean of our discrete probability distribution for our Olive Garden example. The third column in the table is the product of the first two columns.

TABLE 5.4 | Calculating the Mean of a Discrete Probability Distribution (for Olive Garden's Group Sizes)

GROUP SIZE	PROBABILITY	
x_i	$P(x_i)$	$x_iP(x_i)$
2	0.34	0.68
3	0.12	0.36
4	0.32	1.28
5	0.08	0.40
6	0.14	0.84
Total	**1.00**	**3.56**

The table shows us that the mean group size at the Olive Garden is 3.56 people. Obviously, 3.56 will never be the actual size of any one particular group arriving for dinner. Rather, it represents the average group size over the last 50 tables. The mean of a discrete probability distribution does not have to equal one of the values of the outcome for the random variables (2, 3, 4, 5, or 6 in this case).

The mean of a discrete probability distribution is the weighted average of the outcomes of the random variable in the distribution.

We could have also directly calculated the mean by using Equation 5.1:

$$\mu = \sum_{i=1}^{n} x_iP(x_i)$$

$$\mu = (2)(0.34) + (3)(0.12) + (4)(0.32) + (5)(0.08) + (6)(0.14)$$

$$\mu = 0.68 + 0.36 + 1.28 + 0.40 + 0.84$$

$$\mu = 3.56 \text{ people}$$

Expected value is another term for the mean of a probability distribution.

Another term for describing the mean of a discrete probability distribution is the **expected value**, $E(x)$. We can calculate the expected value using Equation 5.2.

Formula 5.2 for the Expected Value of a Discrete Probability Distribution

$$E(x) = \mu = \sum_{i=1}^{n} x_iP(x_i)$$

where

$E(x)$ = The expected value of the discrete probability distribution
μ = The mean of the discrete probability distribution
x_i = The value of the random variable for the ith outcome
$P(x_i)$ = The probability that the ith outcome will occur
n = The number of outcomes in the distribution

The Variance and Standard Deviation of a Discrete Probability Distribution

Just when you thought it was safe to get back into the water, along comes another variance and standard deviation! Fear not. If you've seen one variance and standard deviation calculation, you've seen them all. Remember, we learned in Chapter 3 that the variance measures the spread of the individual values around the mean of a data set and that the standard deviation is the square root of the variance. We can calculate the variance for a discrete probability distribution using Equation 5.3.

Formula 5.3 for the Variance of a Discrete Probability Distribution

$$\sigma^2 = \sum_{i=1}^{n} (x_i - \mu)^2 P(x_i)$$

where

σ^2 = The variance of the discrete probability distribution
x_i = The value of the random variable for the ith outcome
$P(x_i)$ = The probability that the ith outcome will occur
n = The number of outcomes in the distribution

To demonstrate the use of these equations, we'll use the Olive Garden distribution shown in Table 5.4. The calculations for the variance are summarized in Table 5.5. Columns 1, 2, and 3 are the results from Table 5.4. The remaining columns are found as follows:

Column 4 = Column 1 minus Column 3 $\rightarrow x_i - \mu$
Column 5 = Column 4 squared $\rightarrow (x_i - \mu)^2$
Column 6 = Column 5 multiplied by Column 2 $\rightarrow (x_i - \mu)^2 P(x_i)$

The sum of Column 6 (1.93) equals the variance of the discrete probability distribution.

TABLE 5.5 | CALCULATING THE VARIANCE OF A DISCRETE PROBABILITY DISTRIBUTION (FOR OLIVE GARDEN'S GROUP SIZES)

(1)	(2)	(3)	(4)	(5)	(6)
x_i	$P(x_i)$	μ	$x_i - \mu$	$(x_i - \mu)^2$	$(x_i - \mu)^2 P(x_i)$
2	0.34	3.56	−1.56	2.43	0.83
3	0.12	3.56	−0.56	0.31	0.04
4	0.32	3.56	0.44	0.19	0.06
5	0.08	3.56	1.44	2.07	0.17
6	0.14	3.56	2.44	5.95	0.83
					Total = 1.93

The units of the variance are the squared units of the original data.

$$\sigma^2 = \sum_{i=1}^{n} (x_i - \mu)^2 P(x_i) = 1.93 \text{ people squared}$$

Recall that the standard deviation (σ) is the square root of the variance:

$$\sigma = \sqrt{\sigma^2}$$

The standard deviation of our example distribution is as follows:

$$\sigma = \sqrt{\sigma^2} = \sqrt{1.93} = 1.39 \text{ people}$$

A more efficient way to calculate the variance of a discrete probability distribution is to use Equation 5.4.

Formula 5.4 for Calculating the Variance of a Discrete Probability Distribution (Shortcut)

$$\sigma^2 = \left(\sum_{i=1}^{n} x_i^2 P(x_i)\right) - \mu^2$$

where

σ^2 = The variance of the discrete probability distribution
x_i = The value of the random variable for the ith outcome
$P(x_i)$ = The probability that the ith outcome will occur
μ = The mean of the discrete probability distribution
n = The number of outcomes in the distribution

Table 5.6 summarizes the calculations needed to solve Equation 5.4. The second column is the square of the first column. The fourth column is the product of the second and third columns.

TABLE 5.6 | CALCULATING THE VARIANCE OF A DISCRETE PROBABILITY DISTRIBUTION (FOR OLIVE GARDEN'S GROUP SIZES)

x_i	x_i^2	$P(x_i)$	$x_i^2P(x_i)$
2	4	0.34	1.36
3	9	0.12	1.08
4	16	0.32	5.12
5	25	0.08	2.00
6	36	0.14	5.04
			Total = 14.60

$$\sum_{i=1}^{n} x_i^2P(x_i) = 14.60$$

$$\sigma^2 = \left(\sum_{i=1}^{n} x_i^2P(x_i)\right) - \mu^2$$

$$\sigma^2 = 14.60 - (3.56)^2 = 14.60 - 12.67 = 1.93$$

A large standard deviation indicates that the size of the party from one group to the next varies quite a bit. A small standard deviation tells us that most of the group sizes are close to the average group size (3.56).

Again, the variance equals 1.93, so the standard deviation for our example is again 1.39 people. However, Equation 5.4 requires a lot less effort to calculate.

As explained in Chapter 3, the standard deviation measures the dispersion of the outcome of the discrete random variables in relation to the distribution's mean. The closer each group size is to 3.56, the lower the standard deviation is. If the individual group sizes tend to be far from 3.56, the standard deviation will be larger. If the Olive Garden discovers that on certain nights the standard deviation of the group size tends to be higher, it may want to set up tables differently on those nights than on nights when the group sizes tend to be more consistent (where the standard deviation tends to be smaller).

I can sense that look of doubt on your face, so let me convince you by changing the Olive Garden example as follows. Let's assume all 50 groups that arrived consisted of four people. In this case, $P(x = 4) = 1.0$ and all of the other discrete probabilities are equal to zero, as shown in Table 5.7.

TABLE 5.7 | CALCULATING THE VARIANCE OF A DISCRETE PROBABILITY DISTRIBUTION (FOR OLIVE GARDEN'S GROUP SIZES)

x_i	x_i^2	$P(x_i)$	$x_i^2P(x_i)$
2	4	0.0	0.0
3	9	0.0	0.0
4	16	1.0	16.0
5	25	0.0	0.0
6	36	0.0	0.0
			Total = 16.0

Because all 50 tables consisted of four people, the mean of this distribution is 4.0, or $\mu = 4.0$. The variance for this new distribution is calculated as follows:

$$\sum_{i=1}^{n} x_i^2 P(x_i) = 16.0$$

$$\sigma^2 = \left(\sum_{i=1}^{n} x_i^2 P(x_i)\right) - \mu^2$$

$$\sigma^2 = 16.0 - (4.0)^2 = 16.0 - 16.0 = 0.0$$

This result demonstrates that the variance of the distribution measures the degree of dispersion of the random variable from the mean of the distribution. Because all outcomes of the discrete random variable equal four and the mean is four, the variance is zero. Have I convinced you yet?

The mean and standard deviation for discrete probability distributions are useful when comparing two different distributions. For example, the two best-selling statistics reference books on the market at the time of this writing are *Statistics for Dummies* and *The Complete Idiot's Guide to Statistics*. Both books are sold on the Amazon Web site, which provides the distribution for the number of stars reviewers gave each book. (The rating scale is from one to five stars.) Table 5.8 provides these data.

TABLE 5.8 | RATINGS FOR TWO STATISTICS BOOKS ON AMAZON

	NUMBER OF REVIEWERS	
NUMBER OF STARS	*DUMMIES*	*IDIOT'S GUIDE*
5	16	19
4	8	7
3	4	3
2	6	0
1	2	0
Total	**36**	**29**

First, we need to convert these frequencies to probabilities, as shown in Table 5.9.

TABLE 5.9 | PROBABILITY DISTRIBUTION FOR TWO STATISTICS BOOKS ON AMAZON

	DUMMIES		*IDIOT'S GUIDE*	
STARS	FREQUENCY	PROBABILITY	FREQUENCY	PROBABILITY
5	16	$16/36 = 0.444$	19	$19/29 = 0.655$
4	8	$8/36 = 0.222$	7	$7/29 = 0.241$
3	4	$4/36 = 0.111$	3	$3/29 = 0.103$
2	6	$6/36 = 0.167$	0	$0/29 = 0.000$
1	2	$2/36 = 0.056$	0	$0/29 = 0.000$
Total	**36**	**1.000**	**29**	**0.999**

Occasionally, summing all of the probabilities for a discrete distribution will not add up to exactly 1.0 because of rounding.

Using Equation 5.1, we calculate the mean number of stars for each book:

Dummies:

$$\mu = \sum_{i=1}^{n} x_i P(x_i)$$

$$\mu = (5)(0.444) + (4)(0.222) + (3)(0.111) + (2)(0.167) + (1)(0.056)$$

$$\mu = 2.220 + 0.888 + 0.333 + 0.334 + 0.056$$

$$\mu = 3.831$$

Idiot's Guide:

$$\mu = \sum_{i=1}^{n} x_i P(x_i)$$

$$\mu = (5)(0.655) + (4)(0.241) + (3)(0.103) + (2)(0.0) + (1)(0.0)$$

$$\mu = 3.275 + 0.964 + 0.309 + 0.0 + 0.0$$

$$\mu = 4.548$$

According to these calculations, the *Idiot's Guide* book has a higher average rating from reviewers than the *Dummies* book.

Let's next examine the variances and standard deviations. Table 5.10 shows the variance calculations for both books.

This column was calculated in Table 5.9

TABLE 5.10 | VARIANCE CALCULATIONS FOR TWO STATISTICS BOOKS ON AMAZON

		DUMMIES		IDIOT'S GUIDE	
x_i	x_i^2	$P(x_i)$	$x_i^2P(x_i)$	$P(x_i)$	$x_i^2P(x_i)$
5	25	0.444	11.100	0.655	16.375
4	16	0.222	3.552	0.241	3.856
3	9	0.111	0.999	0.103	0.927
2	4	0.167	0.668	0.000	0.000
1	1	0.056	0.056	0.000	0.000
Total			**16.375**		**21.158**

We calculate the standard deviations for the reviews of each book as follows:

Dummies:

$$\sum_{i=1}^{n} x_i^2 P(x_i) = 16.375$$

$$\sigma^2 = \left(\sum_{i=1}^{n} x_i^2 P(x_i)\right) - \mu^2$$

$$\sigma^2 = 16.375 - (3.831)^2 = 16.375 - 14.677 = 1.698$$

$$\sigma = \sqrt{\sigma^2} = \sqrt{1.698} = 1.303$$

Idiot's Guide:

$$\sum_{i=1}^{n} x_i^2 P(x_i) = 21.158$$

$$\sigma^2 = \left(\sum_{i=1}^{n} x_i^2 P(x_i)\right) - \mu^2$$

$$\sigma^2 = 21.158 - (4.548)^2 = 21.158 - 20.684 = 0.474$$

$$\sigma = \sqrt{\sigma^2} = \sqrt{0.474} = 0.688$$

Because the *Idiot's Guide* book has a lower standard deviation, the customer reviews for this book are more consistent than those of the *Dummies book.* By observing the original data in Table 5.8, you can see that the number of stars ranges from three to five for the *Idiot's Guide* book, whereas the number of stars for the *Dummies* book varies from one to five. This is shown graphically in Figure 5.2, which compares the two distributions.

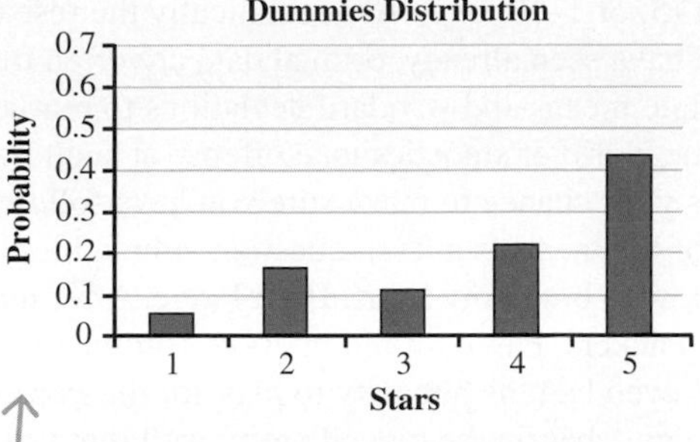

FIGURE 5.2A Ratings Distribution for the *Statistics for Dummies* Book

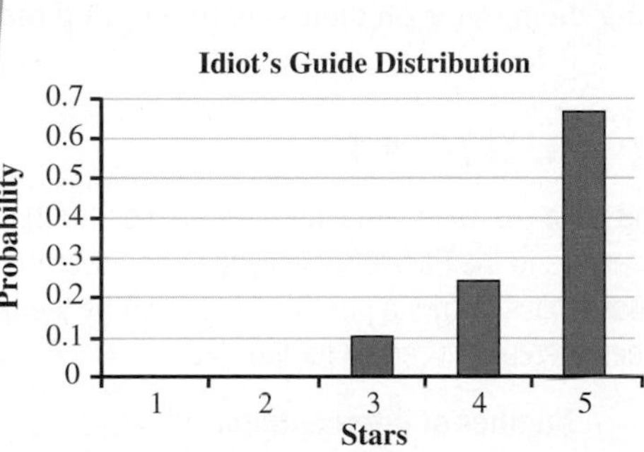

FIGURE 5.2B Ratings Distribution for *The Complete Idiot's Guide to Statistics* Book

The Dummies distribution is more spread out than the Idiot's Guide distribution, which provides visual evidence that the Dummies standard deviation is higher.

I have one word of warning concerning this last example. Technically, the book reviewer data are ordinal data. I'm sure you remember that back in Chapter 1, we defined ordinal data as measurements that are rank-ordered with no assurance that the differences between the ranks are uniform. In our book example, we have no certainty that the difference between a two-star and three-star rating is identical to the difference between a three-star and four-star rating. By contrast, the intervals between the Olive Garden data are consistent, making the Olive Garden data interval data. Everyone agrees that the difference between a party of two and a party of three is the same as the difference between a party of four and a party of five.

Because of the ambiguity of the intervals, technically it's not proper to calculate the mean and standard deviation of ordinal data. Nonetheless, it's common practice when it comes to data such as book ratings. For example, Amazon graphically shows the mean number of stars for books on its Web site.

Another example of this statistical "controversy" is the use of the Likert Scale, which is often used in survey questions, such as the one shown in Table 5.11.

TABLE 5.11 | LIKERT SCALE EXAMPLE

PLEASE CIRCLE THE NUMBER INDICATING YOUR AGREEMENT OR DISAGREEMENT TO THE FOLLOWING STATEMENT:	
I LOVE STATISTICS.	
Strongly Agree	5
Agree	4
Neither Agree nor Disagree	3
Disagree	2
Strongly Disagree	1

Again, we are dealing with ordinal data here because we can't say with certainty that the difference between "strongly disagree" and "disagree" is the same as the difference between "strongly agree" and "agree." However, it is often assumed that the differences between the categories are close enough to consider Likert scales to be interval data.

There are plenty of other examples of this issue in the world of statistics. Anytime a researcher gathers data by asking respondents to rate something such as their satisfaction on a scale of 1–5, or 1–10, or 1–100, technically the researcher is collecting ordinal data. However, as we have seen already, ordinal data are often treated as interval data, which allows us to calculate means and standard deviations to our heart's delight. Just be aware that some people in the world of statistics take offense at such liberties.

Now is your chance to make sure you have followed this discussion so far. I'm particularly fond of this next Your Turn question, which highlights the performance of the NFL quarterback who broke my heart, Brett Favre. After many years of playing for my beloved Green Bay Packers, Favre retired in 2008. But then in 2009, he came out of retirement (again) and even had the audacity to play for the Packer's division rival, the Minnesota Vikings. To my chagrin, he played pretty well that year, beating Green Bay *twice* in the process. Revenge is sweet, however. In 2010, the Packers put Favre and the Vikings in their place, beating them twice on their way to winning the Super Bowl.

YOUR TURN #1

The following table shows the frequency distribution for the number of interceptions thrown per game by Brett Favre relative to the Packer's wins and losses over the course of his career. (An interception occurs when the quarterback throws a pass that is caught by the opposing team.) Favre currently holds the all-time career interception record for the NFL.

Number of Interceptions per Game	Games Won	Games Lost
0	91	12
1	59	37
2	23	29
3	9	21
4	0	5
5	0	1

a. Develop a discrete probability distribution of interceptions thrown by Brett Favre for the games won. Next, develop a discrete probability distribution of interceptions thrown by Brett Favre for the games lost.

b. What was the average number of interceptions thrown by Brett Favre per game that was won?

c. What was the average number of interceptions thrown by Brett Favre per game that was lost?

d. Calculate the variance and standard deviation for both distributions.

e. What conclusions can you draw about Brett Favre's interceptions during his career (other than he threw too many)?

Answers can be found on ▶ **page 242**

The Expected Monetary Value

The **expected monetary value (EMV)** is the mean of a discrete probability distribution when the discrete random variable is expressed in terms of dollars.

When the discrete random variable is expressed in terms of dollars, the mean of the distribution is known as the **expected monetary value (EMV)**. The EMV is commonly used to evaluate the profit potential of projects or the financial return of investment portfolios. We can use Equation 5.2 to calculate the EMV. The following example will demonstrate this concept.

The RAD Construction Company has been awarded a contract with the state of California to replace a bridge on Pike Creek Road. If the project is completed on time, which is defined as during the month of September, RAD expects to earn \$100,000 in profit. If the project is completed before September, the state contract calls for a \$20,000 bonus to be paid to RAD. If the project is completed after September, there is a \$10,000 penalty. RAD estimates the probability of completing the project early, on time, and late to be 25%, 60%, and 15%, respectively. What is the EMV of the project for RAD? Table 5.12 summarizes the information that has been provided so far.

TABLE 5.12 | RAD Construction Example

COMPLETION	NET PROFIT ($)	PROBABILITY
Before September	120,000	0.25
September	100,000	0.60
After September	90,000	0.15

We can use Equation 5.2 to calculate the EMV for this project:

$$EMV = \mu = \sum_{i=1}^{n} x_i P(x_i)$$

$$EMV = (\$120{,}000)(0.25) + (\$100{,}000)(0.60) + (\$90{,}000)(0.15)$$

$$EMV = \$103{,}500$$

The EMV represents the long-term average profit for this project, as if this project occurred over and over again.

Once the project is complete, RAD will earn $90,000, $100,000, or $120,000, depending on the completion time. What does the $103,500 represent in the context of this example? (Don't worry—when I ask this question of my students, I often get a blank look.) The EMV is the long-term average profit for this project. Even though the actual project will occur only once, to determine the EMV we need to consider the hypothetical case that the project occurs over and over again. There will be times the profit will be $90,000, other times it will be $100,000, and other times it will be $120,000, with the frequencies reflected in the probabilities shown in Table 5.12. The long-term average of all these profits, weighted with their respective probabilities, is expected to be $103,500.

See how the EMV can help you win a bet playing basketball in the following Your Turn problem.

YOUR TURN #2

Your best friend proposes a bet on the basketball court. You get to attempt one free throw. If you make the free throw, your friend will pay you $20. If you miss the free throw, you will pay your friend $25. Based on your past performance on the court, you estimate the probability that you will make the free throw to be 65%. Should you take the bet? Why or why not?

Answer can be found on ▶ **page 243**

5.1 Section Problems

Basic Skills

5.1 Consider the following discrete probability distribution:

Outcome	Probability
0	0.06
1	0.11
2	0.24
3	0.27
4	0.20
5	?

Determine the missing probability for the random variable that equals 5.

5.2 Consider the following discrete probability distribution:

Outcome	Probability
1	0.18
2	0.25
3	0.35
4	0.22

a. Calculate the mean of this distribution.
b. Calculate the standard deviation of this distribution.

5.3 Consider the following discrete probability distribution:

Outcome	Probability
10	0.10
15	0.30
20	0.20
25	0.30
30	0.10

a. Calculate the mean of this distribution.
b. Calculate the standard deviation of this distribution.

5.4 The following table provides five different distributions for the daily demand for loaves of sourdough bread at a local bakery. Identify which distributions are valid discrete probability distributions and which ones are not. Explain your answers.

Daily	Probability Distributions				
Demand	A	B	C	D	E
0	0.1	0.0	0.1	0.1	0.1
1	0.1	0.1	0.1	0.1	0.1
2	0.2	0.2	0.2	0.2	0.2
3	0.4	0.3	0.3	0.4	0.2
4	0.3	0.3	0.2	1.3	0.2
5	0.1	0.1	0.1	0.1	0.1

Applications

5.5 A survey recorded the number of children 18 years old or younger who lived in 200 households. The following table shows the results:

Number of Children	Number of Families
0	88
1	40
2	42
3	20
4	7
5	3

a. Determine the mean number of children per household.
b. Determine the standard deviation for the number of children per household.

5.6 Steve Blass owns two fast-food restaurants in Delaware: one located in Stanton and another located in Newark. Steve has recorded customer satisfaction ratings for both locations on a scale of 1 to 5 (5 = Most satisfied). The following table summarizes the data:

	Number of Customers	
Rating	Stanton	Newark
1	4	12
2	12	12
3	8	18
4	36	15
5	20	18

a. Calculate the mean satisfaction rating at each location.
b. Calculate the standard deviation of each distribution.
c. What conclusions can be drawn from these results?

5.7 The following table shows the discrete probability distribution for the number of bedrooms per house in a certain community:

Number of Bedrooms	Probability
3	0.23
4	0.57
5	0.14
6	0.06

a. Determine the mean number of bedrooms per house.
b. Determine the standard deviation for the number of bedrooms per house.

5.8 Kohls Candy Company developed a new consumer product that is expected to earn $4,000 in profit each year if consumer demand is low, $20,000 per year if consumer demand is moderate, and $36,000 per year if consumer demand is high. The probability of low, moderate, and high demand is 30%, 45%, and 25%, respectively. Determine the EMV for the new product.

5.9 Avalon Bakery would like you to recommend how many loaves of its famous marble rye bread to bake at the beginning of the day. Each loaf costs the bakery $3.00 and can be sold for $6.00. Leftover loaves at the end of each day are donated to charity. Research has shown that the probabilities for demands of 25, 50, and 75 loaves are 35%, 25%, and 40%, respectively. Make a recommendation for Avalon to bake 25, 50, or 75 loaves each morning.

5.2 Binomial Distributions

We are now ready to address a specific type of discrete probability distribution known as the binomial distribution. In the previous section, we defined an experiment as the process of measuring or observing an activity for the purpose of collecting data. Let's say our experiment involves counting the customers who sign cell phone contracts at an AT&T Wireless store. Each customer would be considered a trial for the experiment. For this particular experiment, we have only two possible outcomes for each trial: either the customer signs a contract (a success) or the customer doesn't sign a contract (a failure). Because we can have only two possible outcomes for each trial, this is known as a **binomial experiment**.

A **binomial experiment** has the following characteristics: (1) The experiment consists of a fixed number of trials, denoted by n; (2) each trial has only two possible outcomes, a success or a failure; (3) the probability of a success and the probability of a failure are constant throughout the experiment; (4) each trial is independent of the other trials in the experiment.

The Characteristics of a Binomial Experiment

Let's say that, historically, 10% of the customers who walk into an AT&T store sign cell phone contracts. Therefore, the probability of a success, p, for any given customer is 0.10. Because there are only two outcomes possible, the probability of a failure for any given customer, q, is 0.90. For a binomial experiment, the probability of a success, p, and the probability of a failure, q, must be the same for every trial in the experiment. Because only two outcomes are allowed in a binomial experiment, $p = 1 - q$ always holds true.

The word *success* does not have to be assigned to the positive outcome, and the word *failure* need not apply to the negative one. These are merely labels that can be assigned to either outcome. Just be sure to keep the two straight:

Assigning the terms success and failure to outcomes is completely arbitrary. I could have easily assigned success to a customer not signing a contract and failure to a customer signing a contract.

$$p = \text{The probability of a success}$$
$$q = \text{The probability of a failure}$$

Another characteristic of a binomial experiment is that each trial is independent of any other trials. In other words, the probability of the second customer signing a contract is not affected by whether the first customer signed or did not sign a contract.

Finally, a binomial experiment consists of a fixed number of trials, denoted by n. We count the number of successes in those trials, which we label as the value of x. For example, if our experiment consists of six randomly selected customers, and one of them signs a contract, we have the following parameters:

$$n = 6$$
$$x = 1$$

Recall that we already established that the probability of a success, p, and the probability of a failure, q, are as follows:

$$p = 0.10$$
$$q = 0.90$$

Given this information, we can calculate the probability that one customer of the six will sign a contract.

Other examples of binomial experiments include the following:

- Testing whether a part is defective or not defective after it has been manufactured
- Observing whether a customer purchases or does not purchase an extended warranty for a new laptop
- Recording whether a household watched or did not watch the series finale of ABC's *Lost*

Using Binomial Distributions

A binomial probability distribution allows us to calculate the probability of a specific number of successes for a certain number of trials. Therefore, the random variable for this distribution would be the number of successes that were observed. To demonstrate a binomial distribution, let's use the following example.

Orange Lake Golf Resort in Orlando, Florida, provides a free 1-hour golf clinic every Monday for its guests. Historically, 20% of the guests who attend the clinic register for paid golf lessons during the remainder of the week. I have long suspected this is why they provide the "free" clinics. If we randomly select three attendees—call them Bob, Kate, and Roger—what is the probability that one of the attendees will pay for golf lessons this week? This is a job for the binomial probability distribution.

Let's define Event A as follows:

$$\text{Event } A = \text{Bob pays for lessons, whereas Kate and Roger do not}$$

We can calculate the probability of Event A by identifying the following simple probabilities:

$$P(\text{Bob} = \text{Yes}) = 0.20 \quad P(\text{Kate} = \text{No}) = 0.80 \quad P(\text{Roger} = \text{No}) = 0.80$$

If we define a success as a person paying for lessons and a failure as a person not paying for lessons, then $p = 0.20$ and $q = 0.80$. We have three trials in this example $(n = 3)$ because each of the three people can either pay or not pay for golf lessons. The probability that all three of these simple events will occur together (Event A) can be found using the multiplication rule for independent events, shown as Equation 4.12 in Chapter 4.

These three simple events are independent because we are assuming that, for example, if Bob decides to pay for lessons, the probability of Kate or Roger paying for lessons is still 20%. The decision of one person does not influence the decision of another.

$$P(A) = pqq = pq^2 = (0.2)(0.8)^2 = 0.128$$

However, this probability represents the likelihood that only Bob pays for lessons, not the likelihood that any one of the three people will pay for lessons. If Kate pays for lessons, whereas Bob and Roger decline (let's call this Event B), we have the following sequence and probability:

$$P(\text{Bob} = \text{No}) = 0.80 \quad P(\text{Kate} = \text{Yes}) = 0.20 \quad P(\text{Roger} = \text{No}) = 0.80$$
$$P(B) = qpq = pq^2 = (0.2)(0.8)^2 = 0.128$$

Lastly, if Roger is the only person from the group paying for the lessons (Event C), we have the following sequence and probability:

$$P(\text{Bob} = \text{No}) = 0.80 \quad P(\text{Kate} = \text{No}) = 0.80 \quad P(\text{Roger} = \text{Yes}) = 0.20$$
$$P(C) = qqp = pq^2 = (0.2)(0.8)^2 = 0.128$$

We have a total of three ways in which one person from the group will pay for lessons, with each scenario having a 12.8% chance of occurring. Therefore, the probability that exactly one person from this group of three will pay for golf lessons is the probability that Event A or Event B or Event C will occur. We can find this probability by using the addition rule for mutually exclusive events, shown as Equation 4.4 in Chapter 4.

Events A, B, and C are mutually exclusive because if one of these events occurs, the other two events cannot.

$$\begin{aligned} P(A \text{ or } B \text{ or } C) &= P(A) + P(B) + P(C) \\ &= 0.128 + 0.128 + 0.128 = (3)(0.128) = 0.384 \end{aligned}$$

The value "3" in this analysis represents the number of ways in which three people can be selected one at a time. We explored this concept with combinations in Chapter 4. In general, the number of ways in which n objects can be selected x at a time is shown in Equation 5.5.

Formula 5.5 for Combinations of n Objects Selected x at a Time

$${}_nC_x = \frac{n!}{(n-x)!x!}$$

where

$$n! = n(n-1)(n-2)(n-3)\ldots(4)(3)(2)(1)$$

For our Orange Lake example, $n = 3$ and $x = 1$.

$${}_nC_x = \frac{n!}{(n-x)!x!} = \frac{3!}{(3-1)!1!} = \frac{(3)(2)(1)}{(2)(1)(1)} = 3$$

So far, we have calculated a binomial probability the hard way by breaking it down step by step. Let me show you a much easier way to calculate these probabilities using the general equation for a binomial distribution, which is shown in Equation 5.6. This equation determines the probability of exactly x successes from n trials.

Formula 5.6 for the Binomial Probability Distribution

$$P(x, n) = \frac{n!}{(n-x)!x!} p^x q^{n-x}$$

where

$P(x, n)$ = The probability of observing x successes in n trials
n = Number of trials
x = Number of successes
p = Probability of a success
q = Probability of a failure

We can calculate the probability that one of our three resort guests will pay for golf lessons this week in one step using Equation 5.6:

$$P(x, n) = \frac{n!}{(n-x)!x!} p^x q^{n-x}$$

$$P(1, 3) = \frac{3!}{(3-1)!1!}(0.20)^1(0.80)^{3-1}$$

$$P(1, 3) = \frac{(3)(2)(1)}{(2)(1)(1)}(0.20)(0.80)^2$$

$$P(1, 3) = (3)(0.20)(0.64) = 0.384$$

The number of successes, x, can never exceed the number of trials, n, in a binomial experiment.

What other values can the random variable x take on in this example other than 1? Because this example includes only Bob, Kate, and Roger, the number of successes is limited to the values 0, 1, 2, and 3. In general, the number of successes in a binomial experiment must range from zero to n. The number of successes can never exceed the number of trials. Let's first look at the probability that none of the three resort guests pay for golf lessons.

$$P(x, n) = \frac{n!}{(n-x)!x!} p^x q^{n-x}$$

$$P(0, 3) = \frac{3!}{(3-0)!0!}(0.20)^0(0.80)^{3-0}$$

$$P(0, 3) = \frac{(3)(2)(1)}{(3)(2)(1)(1)}(0.20)^0(0.80)^3$$

$$P(0, 3) = (1)(1)(0.512) = 0.512$$

Remember that $0! = 1$ and $x^0 = 1$ for any value of x.

What is the probability that two of the three resort guests pay for golf lessons?

$$P(2, 3) = \frac{3!}{(3-2)!2!}(0.20)^2(0.80)^{3-2}$$

$$P(2, 3) = \frac{(3)(2)(1)}{(1)(2)(1)}(0.20)^2(0.80)^1$$

$$P(2, 3) = (3)(0.04)(0.80) = 0.096$$

Finally, the probability that all three of the resort guests pay for golf lessons is as follows:

$$P(3, 3) = \frac{3!}{(3-3)!3!}(0.20)^3(0.80)^{3-3}$$

$$P(3, 3) = \frac{(3)(2)(1)}{(1)(3)(2)(1)}(0.20)^3(0.80)^0$$

$$P(3, 3) = (1)(0.008)(1) = 0.008$$

Notice that the probability of 0 or 1 or 2 or 3 successes sums to 1.0, as shown in the following equation, because we have three trials in our experiment.

$$P(x = 0 \text{ or } 1 \text{ or } 2 \text{ or } 3) = 0.512 + 0.384 + 0.096 + 0.008 = 1.0$$

When we conduct our experiment, the value of our random variable, x, must be equal to 0, 1, 2, or 3. This is consistent with the discrete probability distribution rule that states that the sum of the probabilities for all the random variables in the distribution must sum to 1. Figure 5.3 shows this binomial distribution graphically.

FIGURE 5.3 The Golf Lesson Binomial Distribution

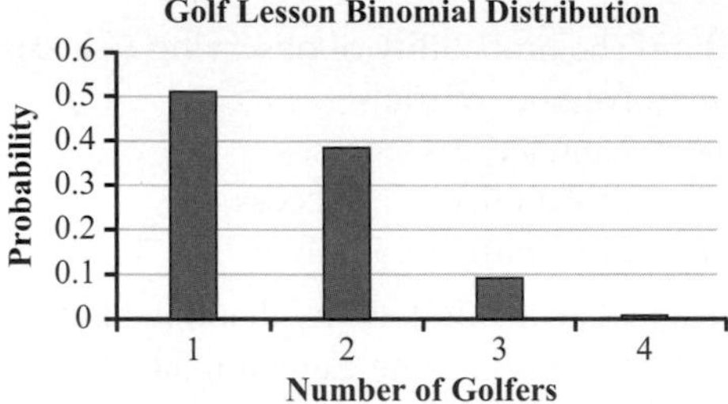

Let's revisit our AT&T Wireless store example and calculate the probability that exactly one customer of the six randomly selected will sign a cell phone contract. Remember, 10% of the customers who walk in the store sign a contract. For this example, our variables are as follows:

$$n = 6 \quad x = 1 \quad p = 0.10 \quad q = 0.90$$

Using Equation 5.6, we have the following:

$$P(x, n) = \frac{n!}{(n - x)!x!} p^x q^{n-x}$$

$$P(1, 6) = \frac{6!}{(6 - 1)!1!}(0.10)^1(0.90)^{6-1}$$

$$P(1, 6) = \frac{(6)(5)(4)(3)(2)(1)}{(5)(4)(3)(2)(1)(1)}(0.10)(0.90)^5$$

$$P(1, 6) = (6)(0.10)(0.5905) = 0.3543$$

There is a 35.4% chance that exactly one customer from a group of six will sign a cell phone contract. What about the probability that none of the six customers will sign a contract?

$$P(0, 6) = \frac{6!}{(6 - 0)!0!}(0.10)^0(0.90)^{6-0}$$

$$P(0, 6) = \frac{(6)(5)(4)(3)(2)(1)}{(6)(5)(4)(3)(2)(1)(1)}(0.10)^0(0.90)^6$$

$$P(0, 6) = (1)(1)(0.5314) = 0.5314$$

Here's a tricky question that causes some of my students to struggle. What is the probability that more than one of the six selected customers will sign a contract? This event includes two, three, four, five, or six customers signing a contract. Using the notation that $P(x) =$ The probability of x successes, I'm looking for the following:

$$P(2) + P(3) + P(4) + P(5) + P(6)$$

Equation 4.3 stated that $P(A) = 1 - P(A')$. That is, the probability of Event A equals one minus the probability that Event A does not occur (its complement).

In order to calculate this probability directly, I would have to employ Equation 5.6 five separate times and add all of the results. A much smarter approach (and a lot less work) is to call on the complement rule of probability that we learned in Chapter 4. From our previous discussions about discrete probability distributions, we know the following to be true:

$$P(0) + P(1) + P(2) + P(3) + P(4) + P(5) + P(6) = 1.0$$

By simply rearranging the above equation with a little bit of algebra, I can answer my question with fewer calculations.

$$P(2) + P(3) + P(4) + P(5) + P(6) = 1.0 - P(0) - P(1)$$
$$P(2) + P(3) + P(4) + P(5) + P(6) = 1.0 - 0.5314 - 0.3543 = 0.1143$$

There is an 11.4% probability that more than one of our six customers will sign a cell phone contract.

The Mean and Standard Deviation of a Binomial Distribution

Earlier in the chapter, we calculated the mean and standard deviation of a discrete probability distribution. The mean for a binomial probability distribution can be calculated using Equation 5.7.

Formula 5.7 for Calculating the Mean of a Binomial Distribution

$$\mu = np$$

where

μ = The mean of the binomial distribution
n = The number of trials
p = The probability of a success

For our AT&T example, the mean of the distribution is as follows:

$$\mu = np = (6)(0.1) = 0.6 \text{ customer}$$

In other words, out of six randomly selected customers, we expect an average of 0.6 (10% of them) to sign a new contract. The mean of the binomial distribution represents the long-term average number of successes to expect based on the number of trials conducted.

To demonstrate the mean of this binomial distribution, let's consider five different groups that consist of six customers. Suppose that zero customers signed a contract from the first group of six. The second group of six had one customer sign, whereas the third and fourth groups also had zero customers sign a contract. From the last (fifth) group of six customers, two signed a contract. The mean number of customers who signed a contract from each group is calculated as follows:

$$\frac{0 + 1 + 0 + 0 + 2}{5} = 0.6 \text{ customer}$$

The standard deviation for a binomial probability distribution can be calculated using Equation 5.8.

Formula 5.8 for Calculating the Standard Deviation of a Binomial Distribution

$$\sigma = \sqrt{npq}$$

where

σ = The standard deviation of the binomial distribution
n = The number of trials
p = The probability of a success
q = The probability of a failure

The standard deviation of a binomial distribution represents the variation that we would see in the number of successes over n trials, assuming the chance of a success is p.

For our AT&T example, the standard deviation of the distribution is calculated as follows:

$$\sigma = \sqrt{npq} = \sqrt{(6)(0.1)(0.9)}$$
$$\sigma = \sqrt{0.54} = 0.735 \text{ customer}$$

This value represents the variation that we would see in the number of successes over six trials, assuming the chance of a success is 10%. The larger the standard deviation is, the more variation we would expect in the number of successes.

Take a few minutes to see if you can correctly determine some binomial probabilities in the next Your Turn problem.

YOUR TURN #3

Suppose a recent survey conducted by Cafe Napoli found that 84% of their customers were satisfied with their most recent meal.

a. Calculate the probability that exactly four of the next five customers will be satisfied.
b. Calculate the probability that less than four of the next five customers will be satisfied.
c. Calculate the mean for this distribution.
d. Calculate the standard deviation for this distribution.
e. What assumptions need to be made to validate your results?

Answers can be found on ▶ **page 243**

Binomial Probability Tables

As the number of trials increases in a binomial experiment, calculating probabilities using Equation 5.6 will really drain the batteries in your calculator and possibly even your brain. An easier way to arrive at these probabilities is to use a binomial probability table, which is provided in Table 1 in Appendix A in the back of this textbook. Table 5.13 is an excerpt from this appendix.

The probability table is organized by values of n, the total number of trials. The number of successes, x, makes up the rows of each section, and the probability of success, p, makes up the columns. Notice that the sum of each block of probabilities for a particular value of p adds to 1.0.

Let's go back to our Orange Lake Golf Resort example, where three resort guests attended the free golf clinic on Monday. Recall that 20% of the attendees pay for golf lessons later in the week. The probabilities that we calculated earlier for each value of x are highlighted in yellow in Table 5.13.

TABLE 5.13 | BINOMIAL PROBABILITIES FROM TABLE 1 IN APPENDIX A

		p								
n	***x***	**0.10**	**0.15**	**0.20**	**0.25**	**0.30**	**0.35**	**0.40**	**0.45**	**0.50**
2	**0**	0.8100	0.7225	0.6400	0.5625	0.4900	0.4225	0.3600	0.3025	0.2500
	1	0.1800	0.2550	0.3200	0.3750	0.4200	0.4550	0.4800	0.4950	0.5000
	2	0.0100	0.0225	0.0400	0.0625	0.0900	0.1225	0.1600	0.2025	0.2500
3	**0**	0.7290	0.6141	0.5120	0.4219	0.3430	0.2746	0.2160	0.1664	0.1250
	1	0.2430	0.3251	0.3840	0.4219	0.4410	0.4436	0.4320	0.4084	0.3750
	2	0.0270	0.0574	0.0960	0.1406	0.1890	0.2389	0.2880	0.3341	0.3750
	3	0.0010	0.0034	0.0080	0.0156	0.0270	0.0429	0.0640	0.0911	0.1250

The highlighted values represent the probabilities that 0, 1, 2, or 3 people from 3 randomly selected people will pay for golf lessons at Orange Lake.

It's now time to revisit the question I posed at the start of the chapter: What is the probability that a student will pass a 10-question, multiple-choice test by randomly guessing at each answer? We assumed each question had four choices, so if a student were guessing, the success of correctly answering a question would be 25%. Therefore, $p = 0.25$, which would mean $q = 0.75$. Each question represents a trial, so the number of trials, n, equals 10. We also assumed that 70% was a passing grade, which would mean the student would need to answer 7, 8, 9, or 10 questions correctly to pass.

Table 5.14 shows the section of Appendix A that we need to answer this question. The probability of earning a score of 70% or better is the sum of the four probabilities under the $p = 0.25$ column that are highlighted in yellow.

TABLE 5.14 | BINOMIAL PROBABILITY TABLES FROM APPENDIX A

		P								
n	*x*	**0.10**	**0.15**	**0.20**	**0.25**	**0.30**	**0.35**	**0.40**	**0.45**	**0.50**
10	**0**	0.3487	0.1969	0.1074	0.0563	0.0282	0.0135	0.0060	0.0025	0.0010
	1	0.3874	0.3474	0.2684	0.1877	0.1211	0.0725	0.0403	0.0207	0.0098
	2	0.1937	0.2759	0.3020	0.2816	0.2335	0.1757	0.1209	0.0763	0.0439
	3	0.0574	0.1298	0.2013	0.2503	0.2668	0.2522	0.2150	0.1665	0.1172
	4	0.0112	0.0401	0.0881	0.1460	0.2001	0.2377	0.2508	0.2384	0.2051
	5	0.0015	0.0085	0.0264	0.0584	0.1029	0.1536	0.2007	0.2340	0.2461
	6	0.0001	0.0012	0.0055	0.0162	0.0368	0.0689	0.1115	0.1596	0.2051
	7	0.0000	0.0001	0.0008	0.0031	0.0090	0.0212	0.0425	0.0746	0.1172
	8	0.0000	0.0000	0.0001	0.0004	0.0014	0.0043	0.0106	0.0229	0.0439
	9	0.0000	0.0000	0.0000	0.0000	0.0001	0.0005	0.0016	0.0042	0.0098
	10	0.0000	0.0000	0.0000	0.0000	0.0000	0.0000	0.0001	0.0003	0.0010

Notice that the probability of answering exactly nine correctly is 0.0000 according to Table 5.14. If we use Equation 5.6, the actual probability for this event is 0.000029. However, because we have space for only four decimal places in the table, the probability was rounded to 0.0000. The same situation holds true in this table for the probability of answering exactly 10 questions correctly.

Using the yellow highlighted numbers in Table 5.14, we can determine the probability of passing the multiple-choice (MC) test by guessing as follows:

$$P(\text{Passing MC Test}) = 0.0031 + 0.0004 = 0.0035$$

Notice that this is the probability I reported in Table 5.2.

Table 5.14 also has highlighted (in green) the probabilities needed to determine the chance of passing a 10-question true/false (TF) test, under the $p = 0.50$ column.

$$P(\text{Passing TF Test}) = 0.1172 + 0.0439 + 0.0098 + 0.0010$$
$$P(\text{Passing TF Test}) = 0.1719$$

This probability is much higher than those for the multiple-choice test because the probability of success is higher $(p = 0.50)$ when there are only two choices for each question. In other words, the student has a 50% chance of answering one of the true/false questions right but only a 25% chance of answering one of the multiple-choice questions right when guessing.

We saved ourselves a lot of work in this last example by using Table 1 in Appendix A rather Equation 5.6. However, the tables are limited to specific combinations of values for n, x, and p. As a result, some binomial probabilities cannot be determined using the tables.

The next Your Turn problem will give you the chance to test your understanding of the binomial probability tables.

YOUR TURN #4

It is estimated that 40% of drivers passing through a particular tollbooth use E-ZPass, an electronic toll collection system. Use the binomial tables in Appendix A to determine the probability of the following:

a. Exactly three of the next seven cars will use the E-ZPass system
b. At least five of the next seven cars will use the E-ZPass system

Answers can be found on ▶ **page 243**

Using Excel and PHStat to Calculate Binomial Probabilities

Another convenient way to calculate binomial probabilities is to rely on Excel's BINOM.DIST function which has the following characteristics:

$$=\text{BINOM.DIST}(x, n, p, \text{cumulative})$$

where

x = Number of successes
n = Number of trials
p = Probability of a success
cumulative = FALSE, if you want to determine the probability of exactly x successes occurring
cumulative = TRUE, if you want to determine the probability of x or fewer successes occurring

Consider the following example. According to First American CoreLogic, 45% of the mortgages in Florida were underwater in 2012. The term *underwater* refers to a situation in which borrowers owe more on their mortgages than their properties are worth. If we randomly select three Florida mortgages, what is the probability that exactly two of them are underwater?

We can use Table 5.13 to see that this probability equals 0.3341.We can also use Excel's BINOM.DIST function to give us the same result.

$$=\text{BINOM.DIST}(2, 3, 0.45, \text{FALSE}) = 0.3341$$

We specify FALSE because we want to determine the probability of *exactly* two mortgages from our sample being underwater. Excel will also calculate the probability that two or fewer mortgages from our sample will be underwater.

$$=\text{BINOM.DIST}(2, 3, 0.45, \text{TRUE}) = 0.9089$$

We specify TRUE because we want to determine the probability of two *or fewer* mortgages from our sample being underwater. The probability of this event is 0.9089, which can be confirmed using Table 5.13 and the following equation:

$$P(x \leq 2) = P(0) + P(1) + P(2)$$
$$P(x \leq 2) = 0.1664 + 0.4084 + 0.3341 = 0.9089$$

In other words, there is nearly a 91% chance that zero, one, or two mortgages from our Florida sample of three will be underwater. This is also known as the cumulative probability because it sums up all the individual probabilities of two or less.

Finally, we can calculate binomial probabilities using the Excel Add-In PHStat for Windows. See the textbook's Web site (www.pearsonhighered.com/donnelly) for Excel for Mac instructions. The following steps demonstrate this technique for our Florida mortgage example:

1. Go to **Add-Ins > PHStat > Probability & Prob. Distributions > Binomial**, as shown in Figure 5.4.

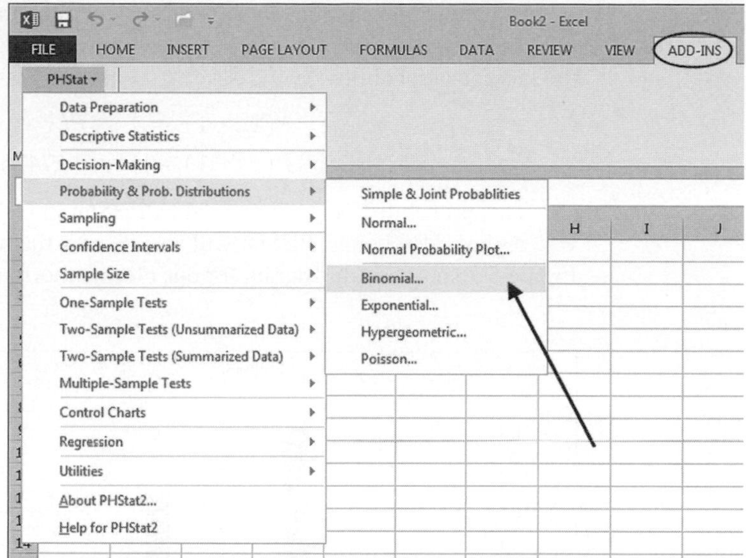

FIGURE 5.4 PHStat's Function for Calculating Binomial Distributions (Step 1)

2. Fill in the **Binomial Probability Distribution** dialog box as shown in Figure 5.5. Click **OK**.

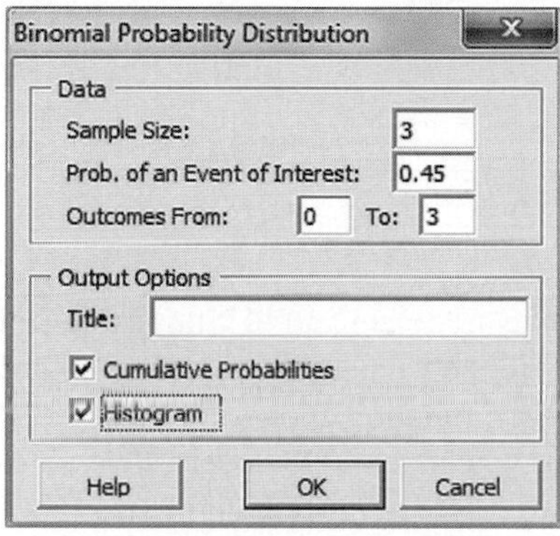

FIGURE 5.5 PHStat's Function for Calculating Binomial Distributions (Step 2)

Figure 5.6 shows the binomial probabilities that we found in Table 5.13 as well as the mean and standard deviation for this distribution. Notice that cumulative probabilities are also displayed in the output. For example, the probability that one or fewer mortgages from our sample of three are underwater is calculated as follows:

$$P(x \le 1) = P(0) + P(1) = 0.57475$$

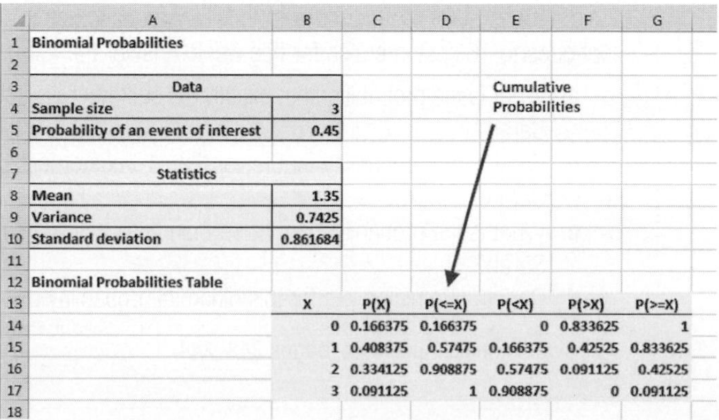

	A	B	C	D	E	F	G
1	Binomial Probabilities						
2							
3	Data				Cumulative Probabilities		
4	Sample size	3					
5	Probability of an event of interest	0.45					
6							
7	Statistics						
8	Mean	1.35					
9	Variance	0.7425					
10	Standard deviation	0.861684					
11							
12	Binomial Probabilities Table						
13		X	P(X)	P(<=X)	P(<X)	P(>X)	P(>=X)
14		0	0.166375	0.166375	0	0.833625	1
15		1	0.408375	0.57475	0.166375	0.42525	0.833625
16		2	0.334125	0.908875	0.57475	0.091125	0.42525
17		3	0.091125	1	0.908875	0	0.091125
18							

FIGURE 5.6 Final Binomial Probabilities Calculated Using PHStat

From this information, we can easily determine the probability that more than one mortgage from our sample of three are underwater by recognizing that this is the complement of the previous probability:

$$P(x > 1) = 1 - P(x \leq 1)$$
$$P(x > 1) = 1 - 0.57475 = 0.42525$$

This probability is also provided by PHStat in Cell F15 in Figure 5.6.

As an added bonus, PHStat will also display the histogram for a binomial distribution. Figure 5.7 shows the histogram for our Florida mortgage example.

FIGURE 5.7 Final Binomial Probabilities Calculated Using PHStat: A Histogram

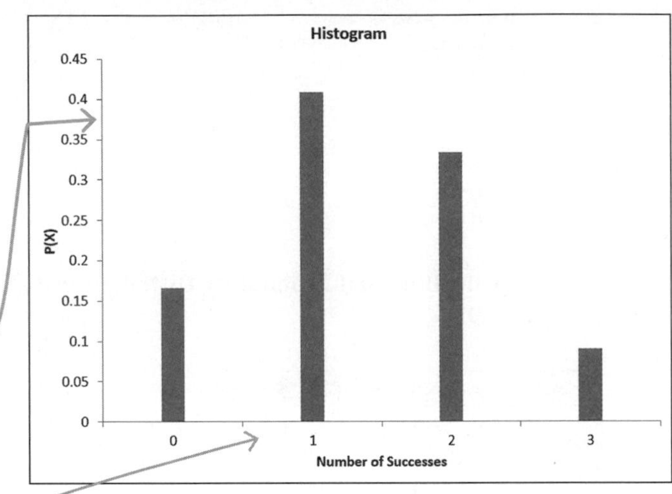

The *x*-axis shows the number of mortgages that are underwater (successes) while the *y*-axis denotes the probability for observing the exact number of successes in the sample.

One benefit of using Excel and PHStat to determine binomial probabilities is that you are not limited to the values of n, x, and p shown in the binomial table in Appendix A. Excel's BINOM.DIST function allows you to use any value between zero and one for p and any value for n that you choose. Obviously, the value of x—the number of successes—will always be limited to whole numbers ranging from zero to n.

Use the next Your Turn example to determine the probability that customers will purchase insurance for their cell phones.

YOUR TURN #5

Cell phone retailers offer insurance plans for customers that provide protection if the phone is lost or accidently damaged. Sarah is a sales representative for Verizon Wireless, and historically has sold insurance plans to 53% of her customers who purchase new cell phones. Suppose that Sarah has sold cell phones to 16 customers so far this week. Answer the following questions using Excel and PHStat.

a. What is the probability that exactly 10 customers purchased insurance plans this week from Sarah?

b. What is the probability that fewer than 10 customers purchased insurance plans this week from Sarah?

c. What is the probability that more than five customers purchased insurance plans this week from Sarah?

d. Construct a histogram for this binomial probability distribution.

Answers can be found on ▶ **pages 243–244**

5.2 Section Problems

Basic Skills

5.10 Consider a binomial probability distribution with $p = 0.60$ and $n = 7$. Determine the following probabilities:

a. $P(x = 2)$
b. $P(x \leq 1)$
c. $P(x > 5)$

5.11 Consider a binomial probability distribution with $p = 0.35$ and $n = 8$. Determine the following probabilities:

a. exactly three successes
b. less than three successes
c. six or more successes

5.12 Consider a binomial probability distribution with $p = 0.25$. Determine the probability of exactly four successes for the following conditions:

a. $n = 5$
b. $n = 7$
c. $n = 10$

5.13 Consider a binomial probability distribution with $p = 0.65$ and $n = 15$. Determine the mean and standard deviation of this distribution.

Applications

5.14 If a student estimated that the probability of correctly answering each question in a multiple-choice question is 80%, use the binomial tables to determine the probability of earning at least a 70% grade on a 20-question exam.

5.15 A recent survey taken by Adecco of 1,047 employees found that 28% of them would lay off their bosses if they could. Answer the following questions based on a random sample of 10 employees:

a. What is the probability that exactly three employees would lay off their bosses?
b. What is the probability that three or fewer employees would lay off their bosses?
c. What is the probability that five or more employees would lay off their bosses?
d. What are the mean and standard deviation for this distribution?
e. Construct a histogram for this distribution.

5.16 A hotel claims that 90% of its customers are very satisfied with its service. Answer the following questions based on a random sample of eight customers:

a. What is the probability that exactly seven customers are very satisfied?
b. What is the probability that more than seven customers are very satisfied?
c. What is the probability that less than six customers are very satisfied?
d. Suppose that of the eight customers selected, four responded that they are very satisfied. What conclusions can be drawn about the hotel's claim?

5.17 The budgeting Web site HelloWallet reported that 25% of U.S. households have withdrawn money from a 401(k) or other retirement account for needs other than retirement in 2013. A random sample of 11 U.S. households was selected.

a. What is the probability that exactly two households withdrew funds from a retirement account for needs other than retirement?
b. What is the probability that less than three households withdrew funds from a retirement account for needs other than retirement?
c. What is the probability that more than five households withdrew funds from a retirement account for needs other than retirement?
d. What are the mean and standard deviation for this distribution?
e. Construct a histogram for this distribution.

5.18 According to a survey by Apartments.com, 35% of apartment renters in 2013 had owned a home at one point. Consider a random sample of nine apartment renters.

a. What is the probability that exactly three renters from this sample previously owned a home?
b. What is the probability that less than four renters from this sample previously owned a home?
c. What is the probability that exactly six or seven renters from this sample previously owned a home?
d. What are the mean and standard deviation for this distribution?
e. Construct a histogram for this distribution.

5.19 According to Catalyst, based on a survey of Fortune 500 companies, 14% of Executive Officer positions in 2012 were female. Answer the following questions based on a random sample of 12 corporate officers:

a. What is the probability that one corporate officer was female?
b. What is the probability that less than four corporate officers were female?
c. What is the probability that more than two corporate officers were female?
d. What are the mean and standard deviation for this distribution?
e. Construct a histogram for this distribution.

5.20 An e-commerce Web site claims that 6% of people who visit the site make a purchase. Answer the following questions based on a random sample of 15 people who visited the Web site.

a. What is the probability that none of the people will make a purchase?
b. What is the probability that less than three people will make a purchase?

c. What is the probability that more than one person will make a purchase?
d. Construct a histogram for this distribution.
e. Suppose that out of the 15 customers, 4 made a purchase. What conclusions can be drawn about the e-commerce site's claim?

5.21 According to IDC, 70% of smartphones in the world use Google's Android operating system in the fourth quarter of 2012. Answer the following questions based on a random sample of 14 smartphone users.

a. What is the probability that exactly nine people from this sample have a smartphone using the Android operating system?
b. What is the probability that all 14 people from this sample have a smartphone using the Android operating system?
c. What is the probability that 11 or fewer people from this sample have a smartphone using the Android operating system?
d. What are the mean and standard deviation for this distribution?
e. Construct a histogram for this distribution.

5.3 Poisson Distributions

This probability distribution is named after Simeon Poisson, a French mathematician who developed the distribution during the early 1800s.

Now that we have mastered the binomial probability distribution, we are ready to move on to the next discrete distribution, the Poisson.

A Poisson distribution is useful for calculating the probability that a certain number of events will occur over a specific interval of time or space. For example, we could use the distribution to determine the likelihood that 10 customers will walk into a store during the next hour or that two car accidents will occur at a busy intersection this month. So, let's grab some crepes and croissants and learn about some math cooked up by the French.

The Characteristics of a Poisson Process

A **Poisson process** has the following characteristics: (1) The experiment consists of counting the number of occurrences of an event over a period of time, area, distance, or any other type of measurement; (2) the mean of the Poisson distribution has to be the same for each equal interval of measurement; (3) the number of occurrences during one interval has to be independent of the number of occurrences in any other interval; (4) the intervals that are defined in the Poisson process cannot overlap.

A Poisson process does not count successes and failures like the binomial. Rather, it counts the number of occurrences of a particular event over a specific interval such as time or distance.

In our last section, we defined a binomial experiment as one in which the number of successes are counted over a specific number of trials. The result of each trial is either a success or a failure. A **Poisson process** counts the number of occurrences of an event over a period of time, area, distance, or any other type of measurement.

In a binomial experiment, the value of the random variable (number of successes) was limited to the number of trials. By contrast, the Poisson process can have any number of outcomes. For instance, the number of customers who walk into our local convenience store during the next hour could be zero, one, two, three, or so on. The outcome for the random variable for the Poisson distribution would be the actual number of occurrences—in this case, the number of customers arriving during the next hour.

The mean for a Poisson distribution is the average number of occurrences that would be expected over the unit of measurement. For a Poisson process, the mean has to be the same for each equal interval of measurement. For instance, if the average number of customers walking into the store each hour is 11, this average needs to apply to every 1-hour increment.

Another characteristic of a Poisson process is that the number of occurrences during one interval is independent of the number of occurrences in other intervals. In other words, if six customers walk into the store during the first hour of business, this would have no effect on the number of customers arriving during the second hour.

Finally, the intervals that are defined in the Poisson process cannot overlap. Using our previous example, if we are interested in counting the number of customers arriving during 1-hour periods, the time segments cannot overlap one another. For example, using the 1-hour intervals 1:00–2:00 P.M. and 1:30–2:30 P.M would violate this requirement.

Examples of the random variables that could be used in a Poisson probability distribution include the following:

- The number of cars that arrive at a tollbooth over a specific period of time
- The number of typographical errors found in a manuscript
- The number of customers who call to complain about a service problem this month
- The total number of home runs hit in Major League Baseball games today

Now that you understand the basics of a Poisson process, let's calculate some probability distributions.

Using Poisson Probability Distributions

If a random variable follows a pattern consistent with a Poisson probability distribution, we can calculate the probability of a certain number of occurrences over a given interval. To make this calculation, we need to know the average number of occurrences for the event over the interval. To demonstrate the use of the Poisson probability distribution, I'll use this example.

The following story is true, and the names have not been changed because nobody in this story is innocent. For many years, when my sons Brian and John were teenagers they would accompany me on a golf pilgrimage to Myrtle Beach, South Carolina. On our last night one particular year, we were browsing through Martin's Golf Superstore. Brian somehow convinced me to purchase a used, fancy, brand-name golf club that he swore he absolutely had to have in order to reach his full potential as a golfer. Even used, the club cost more than any club I had ever purchased new.

Early the following morning, we packed our bags, checked out of the hotel, and drove to our final round of golf, which I had cleverly planned to be along our route back home. On the first tee, Brian pulled out his new, used prize possession and proceeded to hit a "duck hook," which is a golfer's term for a ball that goes very short and very left, often into a bunch of trees, rarely to be seen again. I smiled nervously at Brian and tried to convince myself that he'd be fine on the next hole. After hitting duck hooks on holes two, three, and four, I found myself physically restraining Brian from throwing his new, used, prized possession into the lake.

After our round was over, I patiently drove *back* to Myrtle Beach to return the club, adding an hour to what would have been a 10-hour car ride. At Martin's, the woman cheerfully said she would take the club back as long as I had *the receipt* (cue scary music). I vaguely remembered putting the receipt someplace "special" just in case I would need it, but after packing, checking out, and playing golf, I would have had a better chance of discovering a cure for cancer than remembering where I had put that piece of paper.

Not being one to give up easily, I marched back to the car and started unpacking everything. After a short while, during which time I had spread out our dirty underwear and socks all over the parking lot, the same woman walked out to tell me the store would gladly refund my money *without the receipt* if I would just pack up my things and put them back in the car. Apparently, I was scaring some customers away. (I recommend you consider this strategy when you're trying to return something without the darned receipt.)

Anyway, let's assume that during Brian's brief career as a golfer, the mean number of golf balls he will lose during a round is 4.2. Because this value is an average, it does not have to be a whole number. We will also assume that the actual number of Brian's lost golf balls during one round follows the Poisson distribution.

To test this assumption that the number of golf balls that Brian loses during one round follows the Poisson distribution, we'll need to perform a goodness-of-fit test, a procedure that will be discussed in Chapter 12.

We can use the Poisson probability distribution to calculate the probability that Brian will lose x number of golf balls during his next round with Equation 5.9.

Formula 5.9 for the Poisson Probability Distribution

$$P(x) = \frac{\lambda^x e^{-\lambda}}{x!}$$

where

x = The number of occurrences of interest over the interval
λ = The mean number of occurrences over the interval
$e \approx 2.71828$
$P(x)$ = The probability of exactly x occurrences over the interval

I recommend carrying out the intermediate Poisson calculations out to six decimal places to avoid rounding errors in the final results. Check with your instructor about rounding your final results.

We can now calculate the probability that Brian will lose exactly two golf balls during his next round. With $\lambda = 4.2$ and $x = 2$, Equation 5.9 becomes as follows:

$$P(2) = \frac{\lambda^x e^{-\lambda}}{x!} = \frac{(4.2^2)(2.71828^{-4.2})}{2!}$$

$$P(2) = \frac{(17.64)(0.014996)}{2} = 0.1323$$

In other words, Brian has a 13.2% chance of losing exactly two golf balls during his next round. We can also calculate the cumulative probability that Brian will lose no more than two golf balls using the following equations:

$$P(x \leq 2) = P(0) + P(1) + P(2)$$

$$P(0) = \frac{(4.2^0)(2.71828^{-4.2})}{0!} = \frac{(1)(0.014996)}{1} = 0.0150$$

$$P(1) = \frac{(4.2^1)(2.71828^{-4.2})}{1!} = \frac{(4.2)(0.014996)}{1} = 0.0630$$

$$P(x \leq 2) = 0.0150 + 0.0630 + 0.1323 = 0.2103$$

There is a 21% chance that Brian will lose no more than two golf balls during his next round.

There is no upper limit to the number of occurrences for the Poisson distribution. Mathematically, there are an infinite number of terms in this equation.

I have one final question: What is the probability that Brian will lose four or more golf balls during his next round? You can express this probability as follows:

$$P(x \geq 4) = P(4) + P(5) + \cdots$$

Notice from this equation that the probability of x being greater than or equal to four includes an infinite number of events. Mathematically, with a Poisson distribution, there is no upper limit to the number of occurrences during an interval. If Brian is having a particularly bad round of golf, he could lose a lot of balls with no limit other than his patience. (Unfortunately, I have personally observed this on occasion.) Because we cannot add all the probabilities for an infinite number of occurrences, we need to take another approach. From our rules of discrete probability distributions, we know the following:

$$P(0) + P(1) + P(2) + P(3) + P(4) + P(5) + \cdots = 1.0$$

With a little algebra, we can rearrange the previous equation as follows:

$$P(4) + P(5) + \cdots = 1.0 - P(0) - P(1) - P(2) - P(3)$$

Therefore, the probability that Brian will lose four or more golf balls can be expressed in the following manner:

$$P(x \geq 4) = 1.0 - P(0) - P(1) - P(2) - P(3)$$

We have previously used the complement rule of probability discussed in Chapter 4 to solve the problem of summing an infinite number of occurrences. Note that we already calculated the probabilities on the right side of the equation except for $P(3)$. Like we did before, we can use the Poisson distribution equation to find $P(3)$:

$$P(3) = \frac{(4.2^3)(2.71828^{-4.2})}{3!} = \frac{(74.088)(0.014996)}{(3)(2)(1)} = 0.1852$$

Now we can plug in the values of all of the probabilities and calculate the answer:

$$P(x \geq 4) = 1.0 - P(0) - P(1) - P(2) - P(3)$$

$$P(x \geq 4) = 1.0 - 0.0150 - 0.0630 - 0.1323 - 0.1852 = 0.6045$$

There is a 60.45% chance that Brian will lose four or more golf balls during his next round. I see we will be visiting the golf store very soon to buy more golf balls! Not Martin's Golf Superstore, however. Apparently, the Donnelly family has been given a lifetime ban after the suitcase "incident."

There's one more cool feature of the Poisson distribution: As Equation 5.10 shows, the variance of the distribution is the same as the mean.

Formula 5.10 for the Variance of a Poisson Distribution

$$\sigma^2 = \lambda$$

The variance of the Poisson distribution is equal to the mean.

So, for this distribution there are no nasty variance calculations such as those we dealt with in previous chapters. For our golf ball example, the variance is as follows:

$$\sigma^2 = \lambda = 4.2$$

The standard deviation then is calculated as follows:

$$\sigma = \sqrt{\lambda} = \sqrt{4.2} = 2.05$$

Using a Poisson Distribution to Calculate the Probability of Arrivals

One of the more common uses of the Poisson distribution is to determine the probability of customer arrivals. For example, a local PNC Bank branch has a drive-through window. On average, 12 customers per hour arrive at the window, and we'll assume these arrivals follow the Poisson distribution. What is the probability that exactly four customers will arrive during the next 30 minutes?

To answer this question, we need to adjust the average number of arrivals per hour to a 30-minute interval. If the bank averages 12 customers arriving per hour, it would average 6 customers every 30 minutes, so $\lambda = 6.0$. To find the probability that 4 customers will arrive during the next 30 minutes, we use Equation 5.9 with $x = 4$:

$$P(x) = \frac{\lambda^x e^{-\lambda}}{x!}$$

$$P(4) = \frac{(6^4)(2.71828^{-6})}{4!} = \frac{(1{,}296)(0.002479)}{(4)(3)(2)(1)} = 0.1339$$

How about the probability that two customers will arrive during the next 15 minutes? Some students will tell me that this probability is the same as our last example, which was four customers over 30 minutes (0.1339). I'll show you that this is not the case. First, we need to convert the arrival average to a 15-minute interval. If we average six customers arriving every 30 minutes, then we average three customers every 15 minutes, which makes $\lambda = 3.0$. To find the probability that two (half of the four for the 30-minute interval) customers will arrive during the next 15 minutes, we have the following:

$$P(2) = \frac{(3^2)(2.71828^{-3})}{2!} = \frac{(9)(0.049787)}{(2)(1)} = 0.2240$$

You can see this probability is not the same as our previous example. I'm sure you're itching to see if you understand how to calculate a Poisson probability distribution—the next Your Turn problem will give you a chance.

YOUR TURN #6

Suppose the average number of complaints received by Christiana Hospital from patients is 7.4 every four weeks. Assuming the number of complaints per month follows the Poisson distribution, determine the following probabilities:

a. Exactly three complaints during the next four weeks
b. Three or fewer complaints during the next four weeks
c. Five or more complaints during the next four weeks
d. Exactly three complaints during the next two weeks

Answers can be found on ▶ **page 244**

Poisson Probability Tables

Just like binomial distributions, for certain mean values, Poisson probability distributions can be looked up in a table. You can find the Poisson distribution table in Table 2 in Appendix A of this book. Table 5.15 is an excerpt from this appendix for the probabilities from our golf ball example.

TABLE 5.15 | POISSON PROBABILITY TABLES FROM APPENDIX A

	λ									
x	**4.10**	**4.20**	**4.30**	**4.40**	**4.50**	**4.60**	**4.70**	**4.80**	**4.90**	**5.00**
0	0.0166	0.0150	0.0136	0.0123	0.0111	0.0101	0.0091	0.0082	0.0074	0.0067
1	0.0679	0.0630	0.0583	0.0540	0.0500	0.0462	0.0427	0.0395	0.0365	0.0337
2	0.1393	0.1323	0.1254	0.1188	0.1125	0.1063	0.1005	0.0948	0.0894	0.0842
3	0.1904	0.1852	0.1798	0.1743	0.1687	0.1631	0.1574	0.1517	0.1460	0.1404
4	0.1951	0.1944	0.1933	0.1917	0.1898	0.1875	0.1849	0.1820	0.1789	0.1755
5	0.1600	0.1633	0.1662	0.1687	0.1708	0.1725	0.1738	0.1747	0.1753	0.1755
6	0.1093	0.1143	0.1191	0.1237	0.1281	0.1323	0.1362	0.1398	0.1432	0.1462
7	0.0640	0.0686	0.0732	0.0778	0.0824	0.0869	0.0914	0.0959	0.1002	0.1044
8	0.0328	0.0360	0.0393	0.0428	0.0463	0.0500	0.0537	0.0575	0.0614	0.0653
9	0.0150	0.0168	0.0188	0.0209	0.0232	0.0255	0.0281	0.0307	0.0334	0.0363
10	0.0061	0.0071	0.0081	0.0092	0.0104	0.0118	0.0132	0.0147	0.0164	0.0181
11	0.0023	0.0027	0.0032	0.0037	0.0043	0.0049	0.0056	0.0064	0.0073	0.0082
12	0.0008	0.0009	0.0011	0.0013	0.0016	0.0019	0.0022	0.0026	0.0030	0.0034
13	0.0002	0.0003	0.0004	0.0005	0.0006	0.0007	0.0008	0.0009	0.0011	0.0013
14	0.0001	0.0001	0.0001	0.0001	0.0002	0.0002	0.0003	0.0003	0.0004	0.0005
15	0.0000	0.0000	0.0000	0.0000	0.0001	0.0001	0.0001	0.0001	0.0001	0.0002

The probability table is organized by values of λ, the average number of occurrences. The probability that Brian will lose two golf balls during his next round when he averages losing 4.2 balls is highlighted in yellow (0.1323). This value was calculated earlier using the Poisson distribution equation. If you add up the probabilities in a column for a particular value of λ, they will sum to 1. As with the binomial tables, one limitation of using the Poisson tables is that you are restricted to using only the values of λ that are shown in the table.

The next Your Turn problem will give you the chance to test your understanding of the Poisson probability tables.

YOUR TURN #7

While working on research for my Ph.D. dissertation back in the Stone Age, I spent time at a DuPont facility in Buffalo, New York, that produced Tedlar. Tedlar is a thin film used to protect a variety of surfaces. It is produced in sheets that resemble plastic wrap. To inspect the Tedlar for defects, three-foot squares of it are placed on light panels and examined. Assume the number of defects in a three-foot square follows the Poisson distribution. The average number of defects per square is 0.05. Use the Poisson probabilities in Appendix A to answer the following:

a. What is the probability that there is exactly one defect in the square?
b. What is the probability that there is a defect in the square?

Answers can be found on ▶ **page 244**

Stats in Practice: Using the Poisson Distribution to Estimate the Probability of an Oil Spill

Is this something that could happen once in a million times? Is it something that could happen once in a thousand times, or once every 5,000 times? What exactly are the risks involved?

—President Barack Obama, following the BP oil spill in the Gulf of Mexico

President Obama's question was on the minds of many people following BP's disastrous oil spill in the Gulf of Mexico beginning in the spring of 2010. Increasing oil prices in the last decade have made it economically feasible to drill in deep waters. During this time, the number of deepwater wells in the Gulf of Mexico increased from 17 to 130. But just how safe is deepwater drilling?

We can use the Poisson distribution to determine the probability of future oil spills, but to do so, we need to assign a value for λ, which represents the average number of major oil spills per year. Given the fact that we have experienced one major spill during the 10-year period when deepwater drilling became more prevalent, a rough estimate for λ could be set at 0.1 spills per year. Using this assumption, what is the probability that a major oil spill will occur during the next 20 years? First, we need to convert λ to a 20-year interval by multiplying 0.1 by 20. With $\lambda = 2.0$ spills per 20-year period and $x = 1$, we have the following:

$$P(1) = \frac{\lambda^x e^{-\lambda}}{x!} = \frac{(2.0^1)(2.71828^{-2.0})}{1!}$$

$$P(1) = \frac{(2.0)(0.135335)}{1} = 0.2707$$

Based on our assumptions, there is a 27% chance of another major deepwater oil spill occurring during the next 20 years. I have to admit that this conclusion is based on a very small amount of data; nevertheless, I imagine this is not a statistic that President Obama would be thrilled to hear.

Using Excel and PHStat to Calculate Poisson Probabilities

You can also conveniently calculate Poisson probabilities using Excel. The built in POISSON.DIST function has the following characteristics:

$$=\text{POISSON.DIST}(x, \lambda, \text{cumulative})$$

where

cumulative = FALSE, if you want to determine the probability of exactly x occurrences
cumulative = TRUE, if you want to determine the probability of x or fewer occurrences

We can use Excel's POISSON.DIST function to calculate the probability that Brian will lose exactly two golf balls during his next round of golf when he averages losing 4.2 balls.

$$=\text{POISSON.DIST}(2, 4.2, \text{FALSE}) = 0.1323$$

Excel will also calculate the cumulative probability that Brian will lose two balls or less during his next round.

$$=\text{POISSON.DIST}(2, 4.2, \text{TRUE}) = 0.2102$$

Earlier in the chapter, we calculated this probability as being 0.2103. This (very) slight difference is due to the fact that Excel uses more significant figures in the Poisson calculations than we used with our calculator.

We can also calculate Poisson probabilities using the Excel Add-In PHStat for Windows. See the textbook's Web site for Excel for Mac instructions. The following steps demonstrate this technique for our golf ball example.

1. Go to **Add-Ins > PHStat > Probability & Prob. Distributions > Poisson**, as shown in Figure 5.4.
2. Fill in the **Poisson Probability Distribution** dialog box as shown in Figure 5.8 on the next page. Click **OK**.

FIGURE 5.8
PHStat's Function for Calculating a Poisson Distribution

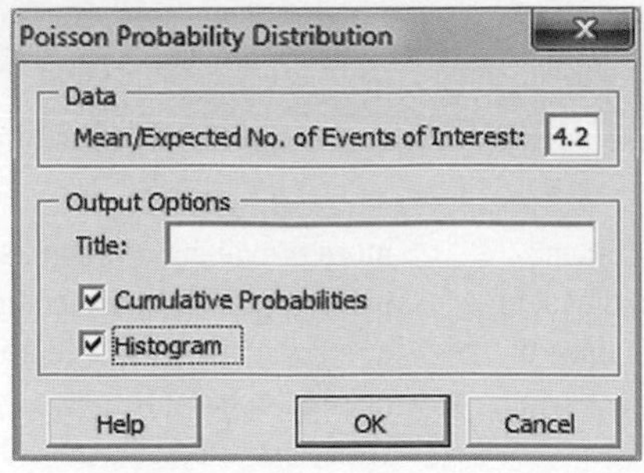

Figure 5.9 shows the Poisson probabilities that we saw in Table 5.15. Isn't technology wonderful?

FIGURE 5.9
Final Poisson Probabilities Calculated Using PHStat

	A	B	C	D	E	F	G	H
1	Poisson Probabilities							
2								
3	Data							
4	Mean/Expected number of events of interest:				4.2			
5								
6	Poisson Probabilities Table							
7		X	P(X)	P(<=X)	P(<X)	P(>X)	P(>=X)	
8		0	0.014996	0.014996	0.000000	0.985004	1.000000	
9		1	0.062981	0.077977	0.014996	0.922023	0.985004	
10		2	0.132261	0.210238	0.077977	0.789762	0.922023	
11		3	0.185165	0.395403	0.210238	0.604597	0.789762	
12		4	0.194424	0.589827	0.395403	0.410173	0.604597	
13		5	0.163316	0.753143	0.589827	0.246857	0.410173	
14		6	0.114321	0.867464	0.753143	0.132536	0.246857	
15		7	0.068593	0.936057	0.867464	0.063943	0.132536	
16		8	0.036011	0.972068	0.936057	0.027932	0.063943	
17		9	0.016805	0.988873	0.972068	0.011127	0.027932	
18		10	0.007058	0.995931	0.988873	0.004069	0.011127	
19		11	0.002695	0.998626	0.995931	0.001374	0.004069	
20		12	0.000943	0.999569	0.998626	0.000431	0.001374	
21		13	0.000305	0.999874	0.999569	0.000126	0.000431	
22		14	0.000091	0.999966	0.999874	0.000034	0.000126	
23		15	0.000026	0.999991	0.999966	0.000009	0.000034	
24		16	0.000007	0.999998	0.999991	0.000002	0.000009	
25		17	0.000002	1.000000	0.999998	0.000000	0.000002	
26		18	0.000000	1.000000	1.000000	0.000000	0.000000	
27		19	0.000000	1.000000	1.000000	0.000000	0.000000	
28		20	0.000000	1.000000	1.000000	0.000000	0.000000	
29								
30								
31	Cumulative Probabilities							

Notice that we also have the cumulative probabilities displayed in Column D in Figure 5.9. For example, we calculated earlier that the probability of Brian losing two or fewer balls in his next round was as follows:

$$P(x \leq 2) = P(0) + P(1) + P(2)$$
$$P(x \leq 2) = 0.0150 + 0.0630 + 0.1323 = 0.2103$$

This result is shown in Figure 5.9 in Cell D10. The slight difference in probabilities is due to rounding.

We also calculated the probability that Brian will lose four or more balls on his next round as being 0.6045. You can find this value in Figure 5.9 as well, in Cell G12.

As we discovered earlier, PHStat can also display the histogram for our Poisson distribution; Figure 5.10 shows the histogram for our golf ball example.

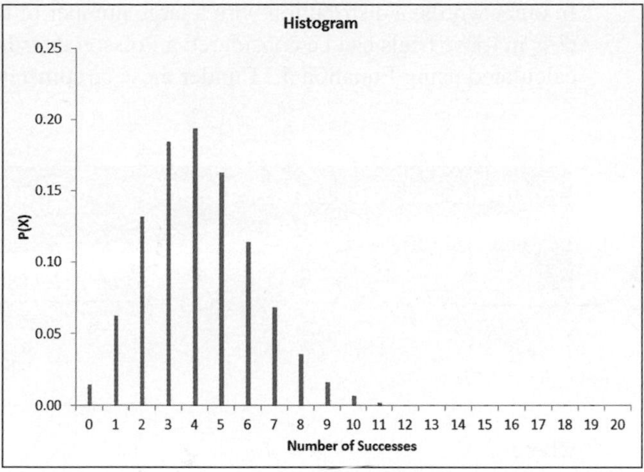

FIGURE 5.10 Final Poison Probabilities Displayed Using PHStat: A Histogram

One benefit of using Excel to determine Poisson probabilities is that you are not limited to the values of λ shown in the Poisson table in Appendix A. Excel's POISSON.DIST function allows you to use any value for λ.

Use the next Your Turn problem to see if you understand how to use Excel and PHStat to calculate Poisson probabilities.

YOUR TURN #8

As a young engineer, I spent several years working for Diamond Shamrock Corporation at its chlorine plant in Delaware City, Delaware. Each month, we would track the number of recordable injuries, which are defined by the Occupational Safety and Health Administration as injuries to employees that require medical treatment beyond routine first aid. Assume the number of recordable injuries each month follows a Poisson distribution with an average of 1.4 injuries per month. Use Excel to answer the following questions:

a. What is the probability that exactly one recordable injury will occur next month?

b. What is the probability that less than two recordable injuries will occur next month?

c. What is the probability that four or more recordable injuries will occur next month?

d. Construct a histogram of the probabilities for this Poisson distribution using PHStat.

Answers can be found on ▶ **page 245**

Using Poisson Distributions to Approximate Binomial Distributions

We can calculate binomial probabilities using the Poisson distribution when the following conditions are present:

- When the number of trials, n, is greater than or equal to 20

  and

- When the probability of a success, p, is less than or equal to 0.05

In other words, a distribution with a large number of trials and a small probability for success in those trials can be considered a Poisson distribution. Binomial probabilities can be calculated using Equation 5.11 under these circumstances.

If you need to calculate binomial probabilities with the number of trials, n, greater than or equal to 20 and the probability of a success, p, less than or equal to 0.05, you can use the equation for the Poisson distribution to approximate the binomial probabilities.

Formula 5.11 for Using the Poisson Equation to Calculate Binomial Probabilities

$$P(x) = \frac{(np)^x 2.71828^{-(np)}}{x!}$$

where

x = Number of successes
n = The number of trials
p = The probability of a success

You might be asking yourself at this moment just why you would want to do this. The answer is because the Poisson formula has fewer computations than the binomial formula and, under the stated conditions, the distributions are very close to one another. I'm all for taking the easy way when I have a choice.

I'll demonstrate this point with an example. Avon Products ships boxes to its representatives that contain the products that the representatives ordered. Historically, 2% of the boxes do not contain the correct products. Twenty boxes are randomly selected and inspected to ensure they have the proper contents. We want to determine the probability that exactly two of these boxes do not have the correct items. This is a binomial experiment with $n = 20$, $x = 2$, and $p = 0.02$. Using Equation 5.6, we can calculate the binomial probability as follows:

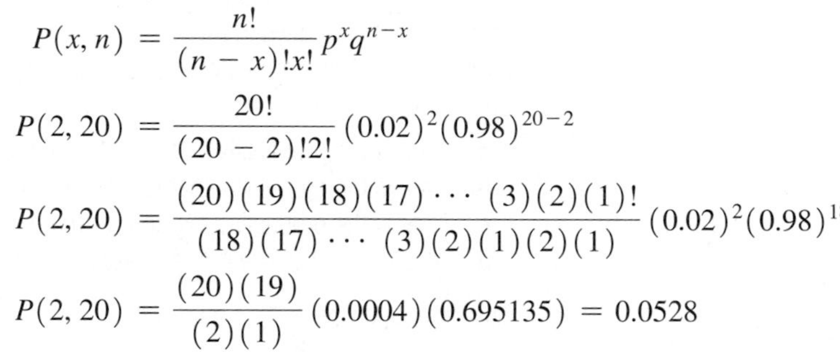

$$P(x, n) = \frac{n!}{(n - x)!x!} p^x q^{n-x}$$

$$P(2, 20) = \frac{20!}{(20 - 2)!2!} (0.02)^2 (0.98)^{20-2}$$

$$P(2, 20) = \frac{(20)(19)(18)(17) \cdots (3)(2)(1)!}{(18)(17) \cdots (3)(2)(1)(2)(1)} (0.02)^2 (0.98)^{18}$$

$$P(2, 20) = \frac{(20)(19)}{(2)(1)} (0.0004)(0.695135) = 0.0528$$

Now, I'll use Equation 5.11, the Poisson approximation to the binomial distribution, to prove my point:

$$np = (20)(0.02) = 0.4$$

$$P(x) = \frac{(np)^x 2.71828^{-(np)}}{x!}$$

$$P(2) = \frac{(0.4)^2 2.71828^{-(0.4)}}{2!} = \frac{(0.16)(0.670320)}{2} = 0.0536$$

In my opinion, these probabilities are close enough (5.3% versus 5.4%), and fewer calculations were needed using Equation 5.11. If you need further evidence, Figures 5.11 and 5.12 show the histograms for each distribution.

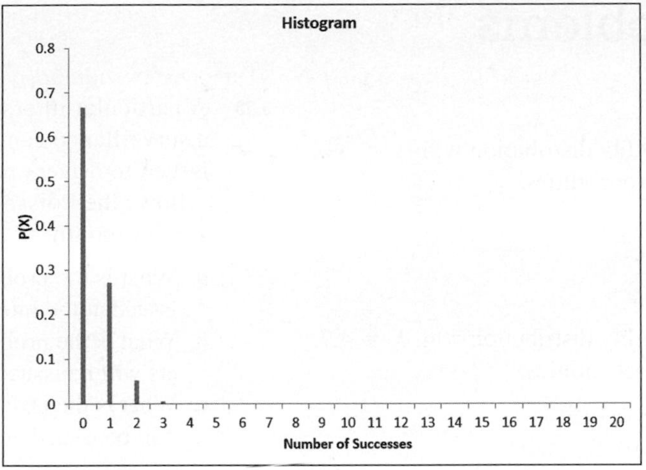

FIGURE 5.11 The Binomial Probability Distribution When $n = 20$ and $p = 0.02$

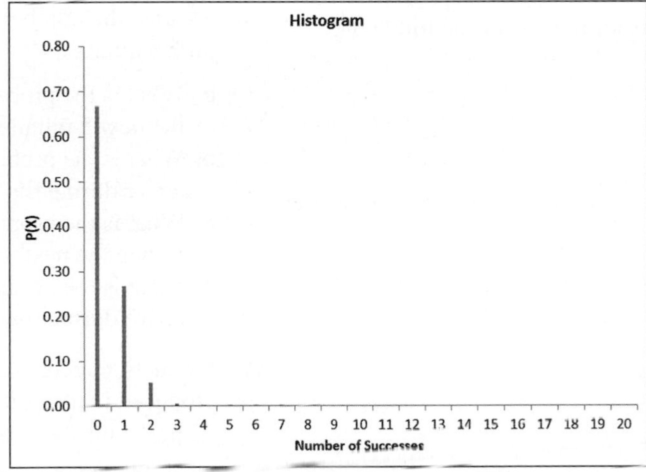

FIGURE 5.12 The Poisson Probability Distribution When the Mean = 0.4

Even to a skeptic, these two distributions look very much alike. So, my advice to you is to use the Poisson equation if you're faced with calculating binomial probabilities when $n \geq 20$ and $p \leq 0.05$.

The following Your Turn problem will give you the chance to use this approximation technique to predict the probability that your next fast-food order will not be correct.

YOUR TURN #9

A fast-food manager claims that only 3% of the orders that are filled are inaccurate. Use the first 20 orders of the day to answer the following:

a. Use Equation 5.6 to calculate the probability that exactly three orders from the first 20 are not correct.

b. Use Equation 5.11 to calculate the probability that exactly three orders from the first 20 are not correct.

c. How do the two probabilities compare?

d. Suppose that of the first 20 orders of the day, four were not correct. What conclusions can be drawn about the manager's claim?

Answers can be found on ▶ **page 245**

5.3 Section Problems

Basic Skills

5.22 Consider a Poisson probability distribution with $\lambda = 3.0$. Determine the following probabilities.

a. $P(x = 3)$
b. $P(x \leq 2)$
c. $P(x > 4)$

5.23 Consider a Poisson probability distribution with $\lambda = 4.7$. Determine the following probabilities.

a. exactly five occurrences
b. more than six occurrences
c. three or fewer occurrences

5.24 Consider a Poisson probability distribution. Determine the probability of exactly four occurrences for the following conditions:

a. $\lambda = 2.0$
b. $\lambda = 3.0$
c. $\lambda = 4.0$
d. What conclusions can be made about how these probabilities change with λ?

5.25 Consider a Poisson probability distribution with $\lambda = 8.5$. Determine the mean and standard deviation of this distribution.

Applications

5.26 Assume the number of births in a local hospital follows a Poisson distribution and averages 2.6 per day.

a. What is the probability that no births will occur today?
b. What is the probability that less than four births will occur today?
c. What is the probability that more than one birth will occur today?

5.27 Sara is a salesperson for Camera's Etc. which is a retailer for high-end digital cameras. Historically, Sara has averaged selling 2.1 extended warranties per day for cameras that she sells. Assume the number of camera warranties that Sara sells per day follows the Poisson distribution.

a. What is the probability that Sara will sell five extended warranties tomorrow?
b. What is the probability that Sara will not sell an extended warranty tomorrow?
c. What is the probability that Sara will sell more than two extended warranties tomorrow?
d. What is the standard deviation for this distribution?

5.28 A particular intersection in Delaware is equipped with a surveillance camera. The number of traffic tickets issued to drivers passing through the intersection follows the Poisson distribution and averages 4.5 per month.

a. What is the probability that seven traffic tickets will be issued at the intersection next month?
b. What is the probability that less than three traffic tickets will be issued at the intersection next month?
c. What is the probability that five or more traffic tickets will be issued at the intersection next month?

5.29 A customer support center for a computer manufacturer receives an average of 1.5 phone calls every 5 minutes. Assume the number of calls received follows the Poisson distribution.

a. What is the probability that no calls will arrive during the next 5 minutes?
b. What is the probability that three or more calls will arrive during the next 5 minutes?
c. What is the probability that three calls will arrive during the next 10 minutes?
d. What is the probability that no more than two calls will arrive during the next 10 minutes?

5.30 Production records indicate that 1.5% of the light bulbs produced in a facility are defective. A random sample of 22 light bulbs was selected.

a. Use the binomial distribution to determine the probability that two defective bulbs are found.
b. Use the Poisson approximation to the binomial distribution to determine the probability that two defective bulbs are found.
c. How do these two probabilities compare?

5.31 Research in Motion (RIM) developed the Blackberry cell phone that was widely adopted by businesses for their employees. However, with the increase in popularity of Apple's iOS and Google's Android operating systems for mobile devices, sales of Blackberry devices have declined recently. The market share for devices using RIM's operating system was estimated to be 1.6% in 2013. A random sample of 25 mobile devices was selected.

a. Use the binomial distribution to determine the probability that less than three devices from this ample use the RIM operating system.
b. Use the Poisson distribution to determine the probability that less than three devices from this ample use the RIM operating system.

5.4 The Hypergeometric Distribution

One of the key features of the binomial and Poisson distributions was that the events are independent of one another. The underlying assumption with these distributions is that you are sampling with replacement or from a very large population without replacement so that the probabilities of a success or number of occurrences remains constant. However, sometimes samples are randomly selected from a small population without being replaced. Under these conditions, the probabilities of success change repeatedly because the sample space becomes smaller after each selection. Have no fear, worried student, when you are faced with these odds. This is a job for the **hypergeometric distribution** (cue the superhero music)!

The **hypergeometric distribution** is used when samples are taken from a small population without being replaced.

Calculating Probabilities for a Hypergeometric Distribution

The best way to explain the "superpowers" of a hypergeometric distribution is to start with an example: A Pennsylvania retailer currently employs 22 sales associates, of which 8 are more than 55 years in age. (We'll refer to the people over 55 as the "older employees" in this problem to differentiate them from younger employees.) Due to a recent downturn in the economy, the retailer decided to reduce its sales force by seven employees. Of the seven people laid off, five were older employees. If the employees who were laid off were randomly selected, what is the probability that five of them would be from the older group? This information would be useful for a lawyer who is investigating a possible age discrimination case.

Remember, a success does not need to be defined as a positive outcome.

I'll define a success as an older employee being selected to be laid off. This example involves sampling without replacement because once an employee is selected to be laid off, he or she can't be selected again to be laid off. As a result, the probability of future employees being selected changes due to the reduction in the sample space. To demonstrate, let's define the following event:

$$\text{Event } A = \text{Randomly selected laid-off employee is older than 55}$$

Because 8 of the 22 employees are older than 55, the probability of a success is then as follows:

$$P(A) = \frac{8}{22} = 0.364$$

However, the probability isn't constant throughout the sampling process. Let's assume the first employee laid off was older than 55. What is the probability that the next laid-off employee is older than 55? Well, because we are sampling without replacement, the sample space has been reduced from 22 to 21. Because one of the older employees has been previously selected, the number of remaining older employees is down to seven. Therefore, the probability that an older employee will be selected to be laid off (a success) is now given as follows:

Because the first employee selected was older and we are sampling without replacement, only 7 of the remaining 21 employees are older.

$$P(A) = \frac{7}{21} = 0.333$$

It is important to realize that the probability of success in our example changes during the sampling process, which violates the requirements for a binomial probability distribution. Therefore, the binomial distribution is not appropriate here, and we need the hypergeometric distribution to step in and save the day (sort of like Underdog).

For events that have only two possible outcomes, such as success or failure, the hypergeometric probability is calculated using Equation 5.12.

Formula 5.12 for the Hypergeometric Distribution

$$P(x) = \frac{{}_{N-R}C_{n-x} \cdot {}_{R}C_{x}}{{}_{N}C_{n}}$$

where

$N =$ The population size
$R =$ The number of successes in the population
$n =$ The sample size
$x =$ The number of successes in the sample

We have seen the term ${}_nC_x$ in both this chapter and in Chapter 4. It represents the number of combinations of n objects selected x at a time. In this example, the objects are employees. In Chapter 4, I showed you the following short-cut method for calculating combinations (Equation 4.19):

$$ {}_nC_x = \frac{n!}{(n-x)!x!} = \frac{n(n-1)((n-2))\cdots(n-x+1)}{x!} $$

Based on our definition of a success, we have the following variables for our example:

$N =$ The total number of employees $= 22$
$R =$ The number of older employees $= 8$
$n =$ The number of employees laid off $= 7$
$x =$ The number of older employees laid off $= 5$

If we plug these data into Equation 5.12, we can find the probability that five of the seven laid-off employees will be older than 55 if they are chosen randomly:

$$ P(x) = \frac{{}_{N-R}C_{n-x} \cdot {}_RC_x}{{}_NC_n} $$

$$ P(5) = \frac{{}_{22-8}C_{7-5} \cdot {}_8C_5}{{}_{22}C_7} = \frac{{}_{14}C_2 \cdot {}_8C_5}{{}_{22}C_7} $$

We still need to calculate the value of each of the three combinations. Using Equation 4.19, we can start with the result of ${}_{14}C_2$:

$$ {}_nC_x = \frac{n!}{(n-x)!x!} = \frac{n(n-1)(n-2)\cdots(n-x+1)}{x!} $$

$$ {}_{14}C_2 = \frac{14!}{(14-2)!2!} $$

$$ (n-x+1) = (14-2+1) = 13 $$

$$ {}_{14}C_2 = \frac{(14)(13)}{(2)(1)} = \frac{182}{2} = 91 $$

This value represents the number of ways that younger employees can be selected to be laid off.

There are 91 ways in which we can choose two employees from a group of 14. In our example, there were 14 employees who were younger than 55, and two of them were laid off.

Next, we obtain the value of ${}_8C_5$ as follows:

$$ {}_8C_5 = \frac{8!}{(8-5)!5!} $$

$$ (n-x+1) = (8-5+1) = 4 $$

$$ {}_8C_5 = \frac{(8)(7)(6)(5)(4)}{(5)(4)(3)(2)(1)} = \frac{6{,}720}{120} = 56 $$

This value represents the number of ways that older employees can be selected to be laid off.

There are 56 ways in which we can choose five employees from a group of eight. In our example, there were eight employees older than 55, and five of them were laid off.

Finally, we obtain the value of ${}_{22}C_7$ as follows:

$$ {}_{22}C_7 = \frac{22!}{(22-7)!7!} $$

$$ (n-x+1) = (22-7+1) = 16 $$

$$ {}_{22}C_7 = \frac{(22)(21)(20)(19)(18)(17)(16)}{(7)(6)(5)(4)(3)(2)(1)} = \frac{859{,}541{,}760}{5{,}040} = 170{,}544 $$

This value represents the total number of ways all 22 employees can be selected 7 at a time. In other words, this is the entire sample space.

There are 170,544 ways in which we can choose seven employees randomly from a group of 22. In our example, there were 22 employees in the population, and seven of them were being laid off.

We are now ready for our final result (drum roll, please). The probability that five of the seven laid-off employees will be older than 55 if they are chosen randomly is calculated as follows:

$$P(5) = \frac{{}_{14}C_2 \cdot {}_{8}C_5}{{}_{22}C_7} = \frac{(91)(56)}{(170{,}544)} = 0.0299$$

What we have learned is that there is less than a 3% chance that five older employees will be in this group of seven who are laid off, if the laid-off employees were randomly selected. It sounds like the lawyers might have a field day with this retailer if they file an age-discrimination case. Results such as these are often used in courts to help substantiate the claims of plaintiffs.

Just like the distributions we discussed previously in this chapter, the hypergeometric distribution also has a mean and a standard deviation, shown with Equations 5.13 and 5.14, respectively.

Formula 5.13 for the Mean of the Hypergeometric Distribution

$$\mu = \frac{nR}{N}$$

Formula 5.14 for the Standard Deviation of the Hypergeometric Distribution

$$\sigma = \sqrt{\frac{nR(N-R)}{N^2}}\sqrt{\frac{N-n}{N-1}}$$

where

N = The population size
R = The number of successes in the population
n = The sample size

For our retailer example, the mean of the distribution represents the expected number of older employees to be laid off such that the proportion of laid-off employees who are older matches the proportion of older employees in the sales force as a whole. Using Equation 5.13, we have the following:

$$\mu = \frac{nR}{N} = \frac{(7)(8)}{22} = 2.55$$

The fact that five older employees were laid off, which is nearly twice as high as expected, confirms the low probability (3%) that laid-off employees were chosen randomly. I smell a lawsuit!

If seven employees are laid off randomly, we would expect 2.55 of them to be older based on the number of older employees in the sales force.

The standard deviation of this distribution is found using Equation 5.14:

$$\sigma = \sqrt{\frac{nR(N-R)}{N^2}}\sqrt{\frac{N-n}{N-1}} = \sqrt{\frac{(7)(8)(22-8)}{(22)^2}}\sqrt{\frac{22-7}{22-1}}$$

$$\sigma = \sqrt{\frac{784}{484}}\sqrt{\frac{15}{21}} = \sqrt{1.6198}\sqrt{0.7143} = (1.273)(0.845) = 1.076$$

If we randomly select seven employees to be laid off over and over again, $\sigma = 1.076$ represents the variation we expect to see in the number of older employees in the laid-off group.

Now that we have drained our calculator batteries with all these combination calculations, let me show you a simpler approach with Excel in the following section.

Using Excel and PHStat to Calculate Hypergeometric Probabilities

A much more convenient way to calculate hypergeometric probabilities is to rely on Excel's HYPGEOM.DIST function which has the following characteristics:

$$=\text{HYPGEOM.DIST}(x, n, R, N, \text{cumulative})$$

where

N = The population size
R = The number of successes in the population
n = The sample size
x = The number of successes in the sample
cumulative = FALSE, if you want to determine the probability of exactly x occurrences
cumulative = TRUE, if you want to determine the probability of x or fewer occurrences

We can use Excel's HYPGEOM.DIST function to calculate the probability that exactly five of the seven laid-off employees will be older than 55 years.

$$=\text{HYPGEOM.DIST}(5, 7, 8, 22, \text{FALSE}) = 0.0299$$

Excel will also calculate the cumulative probability that five or fewer of the seven laid-off employees will be older than 55 years.

$$=\text{HYPGEOM.DIST}(5, 7, 8, 22, \text{TRUE}) = 0.9977$$

As you can see, this function returns the result 0.0299, matching the probability from our manual calculations with a whole lot less work!

Finally, we can calculate hypergeometric probabilities using the Excel add-in PHStat for Windows. See the textbook's Web site for Excel for Mac instructions. The following steps demonstrate this technique for our retailer example:

1. Go to **Add-Ins > PHStat > Probability & Prob. Distributions > Hypergeometric**, as shown in Figure 5.4.
2. Fill in the **Hypergeometric Probability Distribution** dialog box as shown in Figure 5.13. Click **OK**.

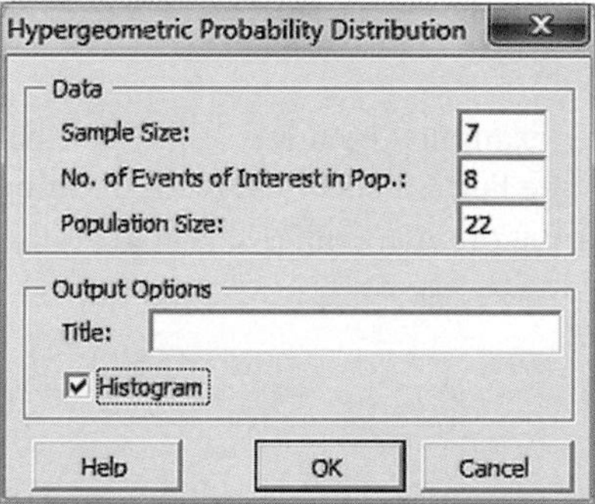

FIGURE 5.13
Using PHStat to Calculate Hypergeometric Probabilities

Figure 5.14 shows the hypergeometric probabilities for all the possible values of x (0 to n). Remember, x represents the number of successes from the sample, and n represents the size of the sample. As a result, the probabilities in Column C sum to 1.0. Note that the probability in Cell C15 represents the probability that our sample consisted of five older employees $(x = 5)$ and that this value matches what we manually calculated (0.0299).

FIGURE 5.14
Final Hypergeometric Probabilities Calculated Using PHStat

	A	B	C	D
1	**Hypergeometric Probabilities**			
2				
3	**Data**			
4	**Sample size**	7		
5	**No. of events of interest in population**	8		
6	**Population size**	22		
7				
8	**Hypergeometric Probabilities Table**			
9		X	P(X)	
10		0	0.020124	
11		1	0.140867	
12		2	0.328689	
13		3	0.328689	
14		4	0.149404	
15		5	0.029881	
16		6	0.002299	
17		7	4.69E-05	
18				

PHStat will also display the histogram for a hypergeometric probability. Figure 5.15 shows the histogram for our retailer example.

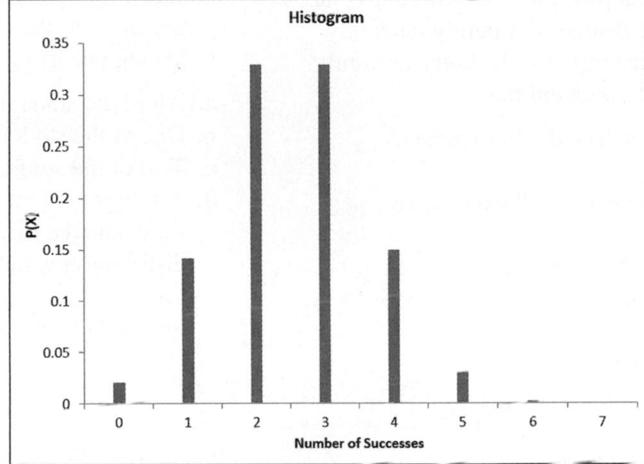

FIGURE 5.15
Final hypergeometric Probabilities Calculated Using PHStat: A Histogram

Now it's your turn to see what you have learned in this section. Give this next Your Turn problem your full attention to be sure you can handle a hypergeometric probability distribution on your own.

YOUR TURN #10

An assembly process has just produced 16 laptop computers. Three of them have a defect of which the manufacturer is unaware. A school just placed an order for 5 of the 16 computers.

a. Determine the probability that two of the laptops delivered to the school will have the defect.
b. Calculate the mean and standard deviation for this distribution.
c. Confirm your answer in part a with Excel and PHStat.

Answers can be found on ▶ **pages 245–246**

5.4 Section Problems

Basic Skills

5.32 Consider a hypergeometric probability distribution with $n = 5, R = 6$, and $N = 12$. Calculate the following probabilities:

a. $P(x = 3)$
b. $P(x = 2)$
c. $P(x \leq 1)$
d. Calculate the mean and standard deviation of this distribution.

5.33 Consider a hypergeometric probability distribution with $n = 3, R = 5$, and $N = 9$. Calculate the following probabilities:

a. $P(x = 0)$
b. $P(x > 1)$
c. $P(x < 3)$
d. Calculate the mean and standard deviation of this distribution.

5.34 An urn contains six blue balls and eight yellow balls. If four balls are selected randomly without being replaced, what is the probability that of the balls selected, three of them will be blue and one of them will be yellow?

Applications

5.35 I find a bowl of Christmas M&M's (only red and green) that Deb has hidden from me in the house one day. I quickly grab a handful before being caught. Before shoving them into my mouth to get rid of the evidence, I notice that I have selected six red M&M's and no green ones. Let's say there were 8 green and 10 red M&M's in the bowl before my discovery. What is the probability of this event occurring?

5.36 White boxers are dogs that have a genetic disposition for going deaf within the first year after they are born. Suppose a litter of nine white boxer puppies contained two dogs that would eventually experience deafness. A family randomly selected two puppies from this litter to take home as family pets. Determine the following probabilities:

a. None of the two puppies selected will experience deafness.
b. One of the two puppies selected will experience deafness.
c. Both puppies selected will experience deafness.
d. Calculate the mean and standard deviation of this distribution.
e. Verify these results with Excel.

5.37 A political committee consists of seven Democrats and five Republicans. A subcommittee of six people needs to be formed from this group. Determine the probability that this subcommittee will consist of the following:

a. Two Democrats and four Republicans if they were randomly selected
b. Four Democrats and two Republicans if they were randomly selected
c. Three Democrats and three Republicans if they were randomly selected
d. Calculate the mean and standard deviation for the distribution which defines selecting a Republican as a success.
e. Verify these results with Excel.

5.38 I have a statistics class of 20 students, of whom 12 are female. I randomly select three students to make a group presentation to the class. What is the probability of the following occurring?

a. All of the students in the group are male.
b. One of the students in the group is male.
c. Two of the students in the group are male.
d. All three students in the group are female.
e. Calculate the mean and standard deviation for the distribution which defines selecting a male as a success.
f. Verify these results with Excel.

CHAPTER 5 Summary

- Discrete random variables have outcomes that take on whole numbers when an experiment is conducted.
- A discrete probability distribution meets the following conditions:
  - Each outcome in the distribution needs to be mutually exclusive.
  - The probability of each outcome, $P(x)$, must be between 0 and 1 (inclusive).
  - The sum of the probabilities for all the outcomes in the distribution needs to add up to 1.
- The mean of a discrete probability distribution is a weighted average of the outcomes of the random variables in the distribution.
- The expected value is another term for the mean of a probability distribution.
- The expected monetary value (EMV) is the dollar outcome that can be expected based on a probability distribution.
- The standard deviation of a discrete probability distribution measures the dispersion of the outcomes of the discrete random variables in relation to the distribution mean.
- A binomial experiment has the following characteristics:
  - The experiment consists of a fixed number of trials denoted by n.
  - Each trial has only two possible outcomes, a success or a failure.
  - The probability of success and the probability of failure are constant throughout the experiment.
  - Each trial is independent of any other trial in the experiment.
- The number of successes in a binomial experiment must range from zero to n.
- The mean of the binomial distribution represents the long-term average number of successes to expect based on the number of trials.
- The standard deviation of the binomial distribution represents the variation we would see in the number of successes over n trials, assuming the chance of a success is p.
- A Poisson process has the following characteristics:
  - The experiment consists of counting the number of occurrences of an event over a period of time, area, distance, or any other type of measurement.
  - The mean of the Poisson distribution has to be the same for each interval of measurement.
  - The number of occurrences during one interval is independent of the number of occurrences in any other interval.
- Mathematically, with a Poisson distribution, there is no upper limit to the number of occurrences during the interval.
- The variance of the Poisson distribution is equal to the mean.
- You can use the equation for the Poisson distribution to approximate the binomial probabilities when the number of trials is greater than or equal to 20 and the probability of a success is less than or equal to 0.05.
- When samples are randomly selected from a finite population without being replaced, the hypergeometric distribution is the appropriate choice rather than calculating a binomial distribution.
  - Under these conditions, the probabilities of success change repeatedly because the sample space becomes smaller after each selection.
  - The mean of a hypergeometric distribution represents the expected number of successes such that the proportion of successes in the sample matches the proportion of successes in the population.

CHAPTER 5 Key Terms

Binomial experiment. An experiment with the following characteristics: (1) The experiment consists of a fixed number of trials denoted by n; (2) each trial has only two possible outcomes, a success or a failure; (3) the probability of success and the probability of failure are constant throughout the experiment; (4) each trial is independent of any other trial in the experiment.

Continuous random variables. Have outcomes that take on any numerical value, including fractions, as a result of conducting an experiment.

Discrete probability distribution. A listing of all the possible outcomes of an experiment for a discrete random variable along with the relative frequency, or probability, of each outcome.

Discrete random variables. Have outcomes that take on whole numbers as a result of conducting an experiment.

Expected monetary value (EMV). The dollar outcome that can be expected based on a probability distribution. Specifically, the EMV is the weighted dollar average for the distribution if the dollar values are associated with discrete probabilities.

Expected value. Another term for the mean of a discrete probability distribution.

Hypergeometric distribution. A probability distribution that occurs when samples are randomly selected from a finite population without being replaced. Under these conditions, the probabilities of success change repeatedly because the sample space becomes smaller after each selection.

Poisson process. An experiment with the following characteristics: (1) The experiment involves counting the number of occurrences of an event over a period of time, area, distance, or any other type of measurement; (2) the mean of the Poisson distribution has to be the same for each interval of measurement; (3) the number of occurrences during one interval is independent of the number of occurrences in any other interval.

CHAPTER 5 Equations

5.1 Introduction to Discrete Probability Distributions (pp 195–206)

Formula 5.1 for the Mean of a Discrete Probability Distribution

$$\mu = \sum_{i=1}^{n} x_i P(x_i)$$

Formula 5.2 for the Expected Value of a Discrete Probability Distribution

$$E(x) = \mu = \sum_{i=1}^{n} x_i P(x_i)$$

Formula 5.3 for the Variance of a Discrete Probability Distribution

$$\sigma^2 = \sum_{i=1}^{n} (x_i - \mu)^2 P(x_i)$$

Formula 5.4 for the Variance of a Discrete Probability Distribution (Shortcut)

$$\sigma^2 = \left(\sum_{i=1}^{n} x_i^2 P(x_i) \right) - \mu^2$$

5.2 Binomial Distributions (pp 207–218)

Formula 5.5 for Combinations of n Objects Selected x at a Time

$${}_nC_x = \frac{n!}{(n - x)!x!}$$

Formula 5.6 for the Binomial Probability Distribution

$$P(x, n) = \frac{n!}{(n - x)!x!} p^x q^{n-x}$$

Formula 5.7 for Calculating the Mean of a Binomial Distribution $\mu = np$

Formula 5.8 for Calculating the Standard Deviation of a Binomial Distribution $\sigma = \sqrt{npq}$

5.3 Poisson Distributions (pp 218–228)

Formula 5.9 for the Poisson Probability Distribution $P(x) = \frac{\lambda^x e^{-\lambda}}{x!}$

Formula 5.10 for the Variance of a Poisson Distribution $\sigma^2 = \lambda$

Formula 5.11 for Using the Poisson Equation to Calculate Binomial Probabilities $P(x) = \frac{(np)^x 2.71828^{-(np)}}{x!}$

5.4 The Hypergeometric Distribution (pp 229–234)

Formula 5.12 for the Hypergeometric Distribution $P(x) = \frac{{}_{N-R}C_{n-x} \cdot {}_{R}C_{x}}{{}_{N}C_{n}}$

Formula 5.13 for the Mean of the Hypergeometric Distribution $\mu = \frac{nR}{N}$

Formula 5.14 for the Standard Deviation of the Hypergeometric Distribution $\sigma = \sqrt{\frac{nR(N-R)}{N^2}}\sqrt{\frac{N-n}{N-1}}$

CHAPTER 5 Problems

5.39 AIG, an international insurance and financial services organization, recently announced that the performance of employees would be rated on a scale from 1 to 4. The top 10% of employees would receive a 1 rating, 20% of the employees would be rated with a 2, and 50% would be rated with a 3. The remaining employees would receive a 4 rating. The rating scheme is known as a forced-ranking system. It was begun after the government bailed out AIG and forced the company to link compensation to performance. Suppose the Wilmington, Delaware, facility of AIG has 450 employees. Determine the number of employees who can receive each rating.

5.40 The following distribution list displays the number of no-shows for a particular Delta Airlines flight and the historical probability that each number of no-shows will occur. A no-show is a person who has a reservation for a flight but fails to arrive prior to its departure.

No-Shows	Probability
0	0.23
1	0.32
2	0.22
3	0.15
4	0.08

a. Determine the mean number of no-shows for this flight.
b. Determine the standard deviation for the number of no-shows for this flight.

5.41 A survey was conducted to determine the number of cats living in individual households. The results are summarized in the following table:

Number of Cats	Probability
0	0.37
1	0.28
2	0.21
3	0.10
4	0.04

a. Determine the mean number of cats per household.
b. Determine the standard deviation for the number of cats per household.

5.42 I am currently teaching two statistics classes, one at 8:00 A.M. and the other at 10:00 A.M. The following table summarizes my attendance records by showing the probability of the number of absent students per class:

	Probability	
Number of Absent Students	8 A.M. Class	10 A.M. Class
0	0.06	0.16
1	0.19	0.32
2	0.25	0.25
3	0.20	0.16
4	0.21	0.06
5	0.09	0.05

a. Calculate the mean number of students absent for each class.
b. Calculate the standard deviation for the number of students absent for each class.
c. Are these results to be expected?

5.43 Travel insurance reimburses travelers for the cost of their trips if the trips are canceled for a variety of reasons. If a \$10,000 policy costs \$400 and you estimate that there is a 3% chance your trip will be canceled, should you purchase the insurance?

5.44 An investor has two portfolios to consider. Portfolio A is more heavily invested in bonds, whereas Portfolio B contains more stocks. The following table provides the annual returns for both portfolios under three different market conditions as well as the probability for each market condition in the upcoming year. Which portfolio should the investor choose to maximize her annual return?

	Market Conditions		
Portfolio	Weak	Normal	Strong
A (\$)	−1,500	2,500	4,000
B (\$)	−4,000	3,000	6,000
Probabilities (%)	25	60	15

5.45 Tees R Us, which manufactures and sells T-shirts for sporting events, is providing shirts for an upcoming tournament. Each shirt will cost \$10 to produce and will be sold for \$16. Any unsold shirts left over at the end of the tournament can be sold for \$5 apiece in the near future. Tees R Us assumes the demand for the shirts will be 1,000, 2,000, 3,000, or 4,000. The company also estimates that the probabilities of each of these sales level occurring will be 15%, 25%, 30%, and 30%, respectively. Determine the expected monetary value of the project if Tees R Us chooses to print 3,000 shirts for the tournament.

5.46 The following table shows Bob's Bookstore's estimated demand for a new calendar. The bookstore needs to decide whether to order 100, 200, or 300 calendars for the start of the year. Each calendar costs the store \$6 to purchase and can be sold for \$14. The store can sell any unsold calendars back to its supplier for \$2 each. Determine the number of calendars Bob's Bookstore should order to maximize its expected monetary value.

Demand	Probability
100	0.25
200	0.40
300	0.35

5.47 At the start of each Super Bowl, the NFL championship game between the winners of the NFC and AFC, a coin toss determines the team that will receive the opening kickoff. The NFC team won the coin toss 14 straight years from 1998 until 2011. Determine the probability of one team winning this coin toss 14 straight times.

5.48 A recent survey found that only 45% of Americans were satisfied with their current jobs. Answer the following questions based on a random sample of 15 American workers:

a. What is the probability that exactly six employees were satisfied with their current jobs?
b. What is the probability that exactly nine employees were satisfied with their current jobs?
c. What is the probability that either four or five employees were satisfied with their current jobs?
d. What are the mean and standard deviation for this distribution?
e. Construct a histogram for this distribution.

5.49 A foreclosure is a legal process that a lender uses to recover the balance of a mortgage owed by a homeowner who has stopped making payments. An unusually high volume of foreclosures occurred during the most recent recession, and as a result, errors were made in the foreclosure process to a significant number of borrowers. For example, auditors found that 24% of foreclosures processed by PNC Financial Services had errors that would have required compensation for the borrowers. A random sample of five foreclosures was selected from PNC Financial Services.

a. What is the probability that exactly three foreclosures from this sample will have an error that would have required compensation?
b. What is the probability that none of the foreclosures from this sample will have an error that would have required compensation?
c. What is the probability that two or fewer foreclosures from this sample will have an error that would have required compensation?
d. Construct a histogram for this distribution.

5.50 The Center for Disease Control and Prevention estimated that 37% of Americans received a flu shot during the winter of 2012–2013. A random sample of seven Americans was selected.

a. What is the probability that exactly four people from this sample received a flu shot that winter?
b. What is the probability that more than two people from this sample received a flu shot that winter?
c. What are the mean and standard deviation for this distribution?
d. Construct a histogram for this distribution.

5.51 A golfer claims that 80% of the time, he will score less than 90 on the golf course he normally plays. Consider his next 10 rounds of golf.

a. What is the probability that he will score lower than 90 on all 10 rounds?
b. What is the probability that he will score lower than 90 on eight or more rounds?
c. What is the probability that he will score lower than 90 on either six or seven rounds?
d. Construct a histogram for this distribution.
e. Suppose that out of the 10 rounds, he scores lower than 90 on five of them. What conclusions can be drawn about the golfer's claim?

5.52 In 2012, 79% of Southwest Airlines flights arrived at their destinations on time. Suppose a random sample of 12 Southwest Airlines flights was selected.

a. What is the probability that all 12 flights were on time?
b. What is the probability that more than nine flights were on time?
c. What is the probability that seven or fewer flights were on time?
d. What are the mean and standard deviation for this distribution?
e. Construct a histogram for this distribution.

5.53 According to the NPD Group, 70% of the basketball shoes purchased by American men are never worn on a basketball court. Answer the following questions based on a random sample of 13 men who purchased basketball shoes:

a. What is the probability that 12 men will not use their shoes on a basketball court?
b. What is the probability that more than 10 men will not use their shoes on a basketball court?
c. What is the probability that less than 12 men will not use their shoes on a basketball court?
d. Construct a histogram for this distribution.
e. Suppose that out of the 13 men, 5 will not use their shoes on a basketball court. What conclusions can be drawn about the claim by the NPD Group?

5.54 According to the University Business Officers, 86% of first-time, full-time freshman at private colleges were the recipients of some form of financial aid in 2011. A random sample of six freshmen in 2011 was selected.

a. What is the probability that all six freshmen from this sample received financial aid in 2011?
b. What is the probability that four or more freshmen from this sample received financial aid in 2011?
c. What is the probability that less than five freshmen from this sample received financial aid in 2011?
d. What are the mean and standard deviation for this distribution?
e. Construct a histogram for this distribution.

5.55 Regifting is defined as the act of taking a gift that has been given to you and presenting it as a gift to someone else. According to survey conducted by American Express regarding consumer spending, 79% of the respondents felt that it was socially acceptable to regift during the holiday season (big sigh of relief). Suppose a random sample of 10 holiday shoppers was selected.

a. What is the probability that nine shoppers from this sample felt that regifting was socially acceptable?
b. What is the probability that more than seven shoppers from this sample felt that regifting was socially acceptable?
c. What is the probability that less than 10 shoppers from this sample felt that regifting was socially acceptable?
d. What are the mean and standard deviation for this distribution?
e. Construct a histogram for this distribution.

5.56 When iPhone was first released in 2007, Google Maps was the default mapping software that was included in Apple's mobile operating system. In September 2012, Apple released an upgraded operating system for the iPhone which replaced Google Maps with its own newly developed Apple Maps. Unfortunately, Apple Maps was plagued with many mapping errors and did not contain all of the features found in Google Maps. In a December 2012 survey of iPhone users, 45% of the respondents said that they "hated Apple Maps." Using the binomial tables, answer the following questions based on a random sample of 20 iPhone users:

a. What is the probability that 12 iPhone users from this sample hated Apple Maps?
b. What is the probability that more than 12 iPhone users from this sample hated Apple Maps?
c. What is the probability that less than 10 iPhone users from this sample hated Apple Maps?

d. What are the mean and standard deviation for this distribution?
e. Construct a histogram for this distribution.

5.57 According to the Pew Research Center, 23% of American adults read an e-book during 2012. A random sample of nine adults was selected.

a. What is the probability that exactly two adults from this sample read an e-book last year?
b. What is the probability that less than four adults from this sample read an e-book last year?
c. What is the probability that five or more adults from this sample read an e-book last year?
d. What are the mean and standard deviation for this distribution?
e. Construct a histogram for this distribution.

5.58 According to the Graduate Management Admission Council, applications to two-year MBA programs have been on the decline during the past few years. A survey during 2012 reported that 62% of U.S. schools experienced fewer applications when compared to 2011. A random sample of eight U.S. schools with a two-year MBA program was selected.

a. What is the probability that exactly two schools from this sample experienced a decline in applications in 2012?
b. What is the probability that more than five schools from this sample experienced a decline in applications in 2012?
c. What is the probability that three or fewer schools from this sample experienced a decline in applications in 2012?
d. What are the mean and standard deviation for this distribution?
e. Construct a histogram for this distribution.

5.59 A first draft of a 400-page manuscript has 36 typos that are spread randomly across the pages. Assume the number of typos per page follows the Poisson distribution.

a. What is the probability that there is one typo in the first 10 pages?
b. What is the probability that there is one typo in the first 20 pages?
c. What is the probability that there are four typos in the first 50 pages?
d. What is the probability that there are 12 typos in the first 110 pages?

5.60 Methodist Hospital serves as a major trauma center for Indianapolis with one of the largest emergency departments in the country, averaging 11.0 ED patients per hour. Assume the number of ED patients arriving per hour follows the Poisson distribution.

a. What is the probability that six ED patients will arrive during the next hour?
b. What is the probability that three ED patients will arrive during the next 30 minutes?
c. What is the probability that seven or more ED patients will arrive during the next hour? (I suggest using Excel or the Poisson tables for this question.)
d. What is the probability that less than 10 ED patients will arrive during the next hour? (I suggest using Excel or the Poisson tables for this question.)

5.61 In college basketball, a turnover is defined as losing possession of the basketball to the opposing team. During a recent basketball season, the Villanova Wildcats averaged 13 turnovers per game. Assume the number of turnovers per game follows the Poisson distribution.

a. What is the probability that Villanova will have eight turnovers during a game?
b. What is the probability that Villanova will have less than 10 turnovers during a game? (I suggest using Excel for this problem.)
c. What is the probability that Villanova will have more than 15 turnovers during a game? (I suggest using Excel for this problem.)
d. What is the probability that Villanova will have four turnovers during the first half of a game?

5.62 Customers arrive at a local ice cream stand at an average rate of 16 per hour and follow a Poisson distribution.

a. What is the probability that two customers will arrive during the next 15 minutes?
b. What is the probability that four customers will arrive during the next 15 minutes?
c. What is the probability that six customers will arrive during the next 30 minutes?
d. What is the probability that six customers will arrive during the next 45 minutes?

5.63 According to the Department of Transportation, United Airlines lost an average of 3.87 bags per 1,000 passengers during 2012. Assume the number of lost bags follows the Poisson distribution.

a. What is the probability that, over the next 1,000 United passengers, nobody will lose their bag?
b. What is the probability that, over the next 1,000 United passengers, less than three will lose their bag?
c. What is the probability that, over the next 500 United passengers, nobody will lose their bag?
d. What is the probability that, over the next 500 United passengers, less than three will lose their bag?

5.64 According to the National Hurricane Center, the average number of hurricanes during the Atlantic season, which runs from June 1 to November 30, was 6.5 hurricanes per year from 1982 to 2012. Assume the number of hurricanes per year follows the Poisson distribution.

a. What is the probability that one hurricane will occur in the Atlantic next year?
b. What is the probability that less than three hurricanes will occur in the Atlantic next year?

c. What is the probability that more than four hurricanes will occur in the Atlantic next year?
d. What is the standard deviation for this distribution?

5.65 Harv& Marv's Outback Alaska provides personalized 4-hour or 8-hour whale watching tours in Juneau Alaska. (Count Deb and I as two very satisfied customers.) Suppose the number of whales spotted during a 4-hour tour follows the Poisson distribution and averages 5.3.

a. What is the probability that exactly three whales will be spotted during the next 4-hour tour?
b. What is the probability that less than four whales will be spotted during the next 4-hour tour?
c. What is the probability that more than five whales will be spotted during the next 4-hour tour?
d. What is the probability that exactly six whales will be spotted during the next 8-hour tour?

5.66 According to Experian, 2.5% of car-loan payments were 30 days past due in 2012, the lowest percentage since 2007. Lenders prefer auto loans to home mortgages because, when borrowers get into financial trouble, they tend to pay the auto loan first because cars are more easily seized by banks. A random sample of 24 car loans was randomly selected.

a. Use the binomial distribution to determine the probability that exactly one loan is 30 days past due from this sample.
b. Use the binomial distribution to determine the probability that exactly four loans are 30 days past due from this sample.
c. Use the Poisson distribution to determine the probability that exactly one loan is 30 days past due from this sample.
d. Use the Poisson distribution to determine the probability that exactly four loans are 30 days past due from this sample.

5.67 According to hybridcars.com, the market share of hybrid cars in the United States in February 2013 is 3.4%. Consider a random sample of 20 cars in the United States.

a. Use the binomial distribution to determine the probability that there are no hybrid cars from this sample.
b. Use the binomial distribution to determine the probability that there are less than two hybrid cars from this sample.
c. Use the Poisson distribution to determine the probability that there are no hybrid cars from this sample.
d. Use the Poisson distribution to determine the probability that there are less than two hybrid cars from this sample.

5.68 The U.S. Census reports that 3.5% of households have at least three generations living under one roof. Consider a random sample of 24 households.

a. Use the binomial equation to determine the probability that three households have at least three generations living in the same house.
b. Use the Poisson equation to determine the probability that three households have at least three generations living in the same house.
c. How do these two probabilities compare?

5.69 A grocery store has 18 two-liter bottles of diet cola on the shelf, four of which have exceeded their shelf-life date. You randomly select three bottles of diet cola without checking the expiration date. Determine the probability of the following:

a. None of the bottles have exceeded their expiration date.
b. At least two of the bottles have exceeded their expiration date.
c. Calculate the mean and standard deviation of this distribution.
d. Verify your results with Excel.

5.70 An IRS agent has 19 tax returns on her desk, of which 14 were filed using the short form (1040A). She randomly chooses eight returns to audit. Determine the probability of the following:

a. All eight were filed using the short form.
b. At least six were filed using the short form.
c. Explain why it is not possible for none of the tax returns to be filed using the short form.
d. Calculate the mean and standard deviation of this distribution.
e. Verify your results with Excel.

5.71 My department at school is comprised of 10 faculty and 6 administrators. I need to organize a committee of six people from the department. If I randomly select these committee members, determine the probability that the committee consists of the following:

a. Two faculty and four administers
b. Four faculty and two administers
c. All faculty and no administrators
d. Calculate the mean and standard deviation for the distribution which defines selecting a faculty as a success.
e. Verify your results with Excel.

5.72 Winner Automotive has a current inventory of 14 used cars and 8 used trucks. Management needs to select 10 used vehicles to participate in a special used vehicle sale at the local shopping mall. If the vehicles are selected randomly, determine the probability of the following occurring:

a. Four trucks have been selected.
b. Four cars have been selected.
c. Explain why these probabilities are so different.
d. Calculate the mean and standard deviation for the distribution which defines selecting a truck as a success.
e. Verify your results with Excel.

5.73 Packer Fan Tours is the official tour company for the Green Bay Packers of the NFL. One of the events in its package is to sponsor a reception the night before a game for fans that is attended by three of the players from the team. There are 53 players on the Green Bay Packers' roster, of which 22 are starters. Assume that the three players attending the reception this week are chosen randomly. Determine the probability of the following occurring:

a. None of the players at the reception are starters.
b. All of the players at the reception are starters.
c. Two of the players at the reception are starters.
d. Calculate the mean and standard deviation of this distribution.
e. Verify your results with Excel.

5.74 In a standard 52-deck of cards, there are 12 face cards consisting of four jacks, queens, and kings. You are randomly dealt a five-card hand from the deck. What is the probability that your hand will contain the following?

a. No face cards
b. One face card
c. Two face cards
d. Four face cards
e. Calculate the mean and standard deviation of this distribution.
f. Verify your results with Excel.

CHAPTER 5 Solutions to Your Turn

YOUR TURN #1

a.

Inter	Wins Freq	Wins Probability	Losses Freq	Losses Probability
0	91	91/182 = 0.500	12	12/105 = 0.114
1	59	59/182 = 0.324	37	37/105 = 0.352
2	23	23/182 = 0.126	29	29/105 = 0.276
3	9	9/182 = 0.049	21	21/105 = 0.200
4	0	0/182 = 0.000	5	5/105 = 0.048
5	0	0/182 = 0.000	1	1/105 = 0.010
Total	**182**	**0.999**	**105**	**1.000**

b. Wins:

$$\mu = \sum_{i=1}^{n} x_i P(x_i)$$

$$\mu = (0)(0.5) + (1)(0.324) + (2)(0.126) + (3)(0.049) + (4)(0.0) + (5)(0.0)$$

$$\mu = 0.0 + 0.324 + 0.252 + 0.147 + 0.0 + 0.0$$

$$\mu = 0.723$$

c. Losses:

$$\mu = \sum_{i=1}^{n} x_i P(x_i)$$

$$\mu = (0)(0.114) + (1)(0.352) + (2)(0.276) + (3)(0.2) + (4)(0.048) + (5)(0.010)$$

$$\mu = 0.0 + 0.352 + 0.552 + 0.6 + 0.192 + 0.05$$

$$\mu = 1.746$$

Brett Favre averaged 0.723 interceptions per game during games that his team won and 1.746 interceptions per game during games that his team lost.

d.

		Wins		Losses	
x_i	x_i^2	$P(x_i)$	$x_i^2P(x_i)$	$P(x_i)$	$x_i^2P(x_i)$
0	0	0.500	0.000	0.114	0.000
1	1	0.324	0.324	0.352	0.352
2	4	0.126	0.504	0.276	1.104
3	9	0.049	0.441	0.200	1.800
4	16	0	0.000	0.048	0.768
5	25	0	0.000	0.010	0.250
Total			**1.269**		**4.274**

Wins:

$$\sum_{i=1}^{n} x_i^2 P(x_i) = 1.269$$

$$\sigma^2 = \left(\sum_{i=1}^{n} x_i^2 P(x_i)\right) - \mu^2$$

$$\sigma^2 = 1.269 - (0.723)^2 = 1.269 - 0.523 = 0.746$$

$$\sigma = \sqrt{\sigma^2} = \sqrt{0.746} = 0.864$$

Losses:

$$\sum_{i=1}^{n} x_i^2 P(x_i) = 4.275$$

$$\sigma^2 = \left(\sum_{i=1}^{n} x_i^2 P(x_i)\right) - \mu^2$$

$$\sigma^2 = 4.274 - (1.746)^2 = 4.274 - 3.049 = 1.225$$

$$\sigma = \sqrt{\sigma^2} = \sqrt{1.225} = 1.107$$

e. Favre averaged one more interception per game during games that his team lost compared with those that his team won. His interceptions per game were more consistent during wins than they were during losses based on the standard deviations of the two distributions.

YOUR TURN #2

$$EMV = \mu = \sum_{i=1}^{n} x_i P(x_i)$$

$$EMV = (\$20)(0.65) + (-\$25)(0.35)$$

$$EMV = \$4.25$$

Because the EMV is positive, you should take the bet.

YOUR TURN #3

a. $P(x,n) = \dfrac{n!}{(n-x)!x!}p^x q^{n-x}$

$$P(4,5) = \frac{5!}{(5-4)!4!}(0.84)^4(0.16)^{5-4}$$

$$P(4,5) = \frac{(5)(4)(3)(2)(1)}{(1)(4)(3)(2)(1)}(0.84)^4(0.16)^1$$

$$P(4,5) = (5)(0.4979)(0.16) = 0.3983$$

There is a 39.8% chance that exactly four out of five customers will be satisfied.

b. $P(x,n) = \dfrac{n!}{(n-x)!x!}p^x q^{n-x}$

$$P(5,5) = \frac{5!}{(5-5)!5!}(0.84)^5(0.16)^{5-5}$$

$$P(5,5) = \frac{(5)(4)(3)(2)(1)}{(1)(5)(4)(3)(2)(1)}(0.84)^5(0.16)^0$$

$$P(5,5) = (1)(0.4182)(1) = 0.4182$$

$$P(0) + P(1) + P(2) + P(3) = 1.0 - P(4) - P(5)$$

$$P(0) + P(1) + P(2) + P(3) = 1.0 - 0.3983 - 0.4182 = 0.1835$$

There is an 18.35% chance that less than four out of five customers will be satisfied.

c. $\mu = np = (5)(0.84) = 4.2$

d. $\sigma = \sqrt{npq} = \sqrt{(5)(0.84)(0.16)} = 0.820$

e. The probability of each customer being satisfied is the same and the satisfaction of customers is independent of one another.

YOUR TURN #4

n	x	0.10	0.15	0.20	0.25	0.30	0.35	0.40	0.45	0.50
7	0	0.4783	0.3206	0.2097	0.1335	0.0824	0.0490	0.0280	0.0152	0.0078
	1	0.3720	0.3960	0.3670	0.3115	0.2471	0.1848	0.1306	0.0872	0.0547
	2	0.1240	0.2097	0.2753	0.3115	0.3177	0.2985	0.2613	0.2140	0.1641
	3	0.0230	0.0617	0.1147	0.1730	0.2269	0.2679	0.2903	0.2918	0.2734
	4	0.0026	0.0109	0.0287	0.0577	0.0972	0.1442	0.1935	0.2388	0.2734
	5	0.0002	0.0012	0.0043	0.0115	0.0250	0.0466	0.0774	0.1172	0.1641
	6	0.0000	0.0001	0.0004	0.0013	0.0036	0.0084	0.0172	0.0320	0.0547
	7	0.0000	0.0000	0.0000	0.0001	0.0002	0.0006	0.0016	0.0037	0.0078

a. There is a 29.03% chance that three of the next seven cars will use E-ZPass.

b. The probability that at least five cars will use E-ZPass is

$$0.0774 + 0.0172 + 0.0016 = 0.0962.$$

YOUR TURN #5

a. Use $=$ BINOM.DIST(10, 16, 0.53, FALSE) in Excel to find the probability $= 0.1510$.

b. Use $=$ BINOM.DIST(9, 16, 0.53, TRUE) in Excel to find the probability $= 0.6932$.

c. $P(x > 5) = 1 - P(x \leq 5) = 1 -$ BINOM.DIST(5, 16, 0.53, TRUE) $= 1 - 0.0674 = 0.9326$

d.

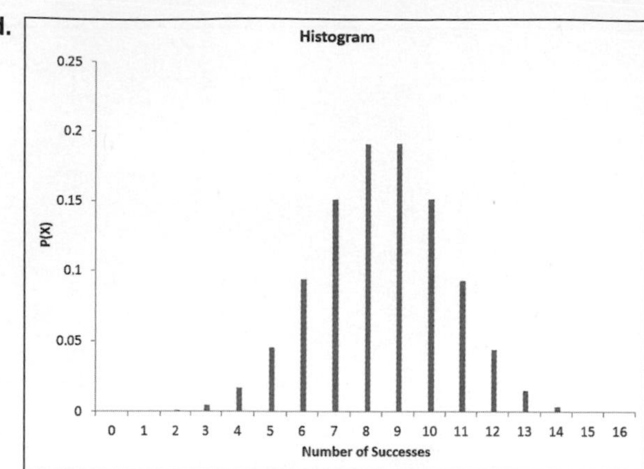

YOUR TURN #6

a. $\lambda = 7.4 \quad x = 3$

$$P(3) = \frac{\lambda^x e^{-\lambda}}{x!} = \frac{(7.4^3)(2.71828^{-7.4})}{3!}$$

$$P(3) = \frac{(405.224)(0.000611)}{(3)(2)(1)} = 0.0413$$

b. $P(x \leq 3) = P(0) + P(1) + P(2) + P(3)$

$$P(0) = \frac{(7.4^0)(2.71828^{-7.4})}{0!} = \frac{(1)(0.000611)}{1} = 0.0006$$

$$P(1) = \frac{(7.4^1)(2.71828^{-7.4})}{1!} = \frac{(7.4)(0.000611)}{1} = 0.0045$$

$$P(2) = \frac{(7.4^2)(2.71828^{-7.4})}{2!} = \frac{(54.76)(0.000611)}{2} = 0.0167$$

$$P(x \leq 3) = 0.0006 + 0.0045 + 0.0167 + 0.0413 = 0.0631$$

c. $P(x \geq 5) = 1.0 - P(0) - P(1) - P(2) - P(3) - P(4)$

$$P(4) = \frac{(7.4^4)(2.71828^{-7.4})}{4!} = \frac{(2{,}998.6576)(0.000611)}{(4)(3)(2)(1)} = 0.0763$$

$$P(x \geq 5) = 1.0 - 0.0006 - 0.0045 - 0.0167 - 0.0413 - 0.0763 = 0.8606$$

d. $\lambda = \frac{7.4}{2} = 3.7 \qquad x = 3$

$$P(3) = \frac{\lambda^x e^{-\lambda}}{x!} = \frac{(3.7)^3(2.71828^{-3.7})}{3!}$$

$$P(3) = \frac{(50.653)(0.024724)}{(3)(2)(1)} = 0.2087$$

YOUR TURN #7

x	0.005	0.01	0.02	0.03	0.04	0.05	0.06	0.07	0.08	0.09
0	0.9950	0.9900	0.9802	0.9704	0.9608	0.9512	0.9418	0.9324	0.9231	0.9139
1	0.0050	0.0099	0.0196	0.0291	0.0384	0.0476	0.0565	0.0653	0.0738	0.0823
2	0.0000	0.0000	0.0002	0.0004	0.0008	0.0012	0.0017	0.0023	0.0030	0.0037
3	0.0000	0.0000	0.0000	0.0000	0.0000	0.0000	0.0000	0.0001	0.0001	0.0001

a. $P(1) = 0.0476$

b. The probability that there is a defect is $P(x \geq 1) = 1.0 - P(0) = 1.0 - 0.9512 = 0.0488$.

YOUR TURN #8

a. =POISSON.DIST(1, 1.4, FALSE) = 0.3452

b. $P(x < 2) = P(x \le 1) =$ POISSON.DIST(1,1.4,TRUE) = 0.5918

c. $P(x \ge 4) = 1 - P(x \le 3) = 1 -$ POISSON.DIST(3,1.4,TRUE) = 0.0537

d.

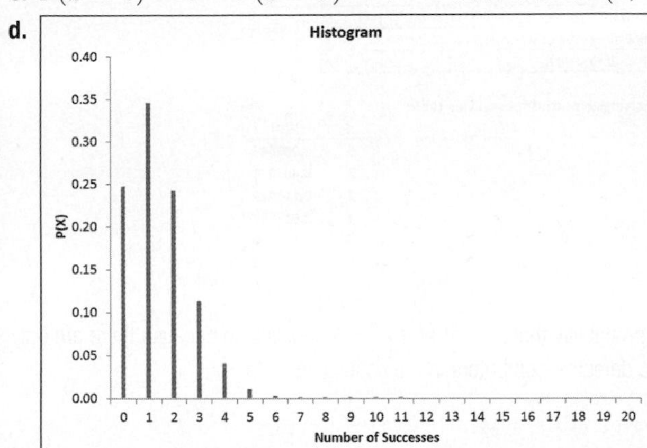

YOUR TURN #9

a. $$P(x,n) = \frac{n!}{(n-x)!x!}p^x q^{n-x}$$

$$P(3,20) = \frac{20!}{(20-3)!3!}(0.03)^3(0.97)^{20-3}$$

$$P(3,20) = \frac{(20)(19)(18)(17)\cdots(3)(2)(1)}{(17)\cdots(3)(2)(1)(3)(2)(1)}(0.03)^3(0.97)^{17}$$

$$P(3,20) = \frac{(20)(19)(18)}{(3)(2)(1)}(0.000027)(0.595826) = 0.0183$$

b. $np = (20)(0.03) = 0.6$

$$P(x) = \frac{(np)^x 2.71828^{-(np)}}{x!}$$

$$P(3) = \frac{(0.6)^3 2.71828^{-(0.6)}}{3!}$$

$$= \frac{(0.216)(0.548812)}{(3)(2)(1)} = 0.0198$$

c. 1.83% and 1.98% are very close to one another.

d. $$P(4) = \frac{(0.6)^4 2.71828^{-(0.6)}}{4!}$$

$$= \frac{(0.1296)(0.548812)}{(4)(3)(2)(1)} = 0.0030$$

If the true probability of not correctly filling an order is 3%, there is only a 0.3% chance that 4 orders from the first 20 are incorrect. Therefore, it is doubtful that the true probability of not correctly filling an order is 3%.

YOUR TURN #10

a. $N =$ The total number of computers $= 16$

$R =$ The number of defective computers $= 3$

$n =$ The number of computers ordered by the school $= 5$

$x =$ The number of defective computers delivered to the school $= 2$

$$P(x) = \frac{{}_{N-R}C_{n-x} \cdot {}_{R}C_x}{{}_{N}C_n}$$

$$P(2) = \frac{{}_{16-3}C_{5-2} \cdot {}_{3}C_2}{{}_{16}C_5} = \frac{{}_{13}C_3 \cdot {}_{3}C_2}{{}_{16}C_5}$$

$${}_{n}C_x = \frac{n!}{(n-x)!x!}$$

$$= \frac{n(n-1)(n-2)\cdots(n-x+1)}{x!}$$

$${}_{13}C_3 = \frac{13!}{(13-3)!3!}$$

$(n - x + 1) = (13 - 3 + 1) = 11$

$${}_{13}C_3 = \frac{(13)(12)(11)}{(3)(2)(1)} = \frac{1{,}716}{6} = 286$$

$${}_{3}C_2 = \frac{3!}{(3-2)!2!}$$

$(n - x + 1) = (3 - 2 + 1) = 2$

$$_3C_2 = \frac{(3)(2)(1)}{(2)(1)} = \frac{6}{2} = 3$$

$$_{16}C_5 = \frac{16!}{(16-5)!5!}$$

$$(n - x + 1) = (16 - 5 + 1) = 12$$

$$_{13}C_3 = \frac{(16)(15)(14)(13)(12)}{(5)(4)(3)(2)(1)} = \frac{524{,}160}{120} = 4{,}368$$

$$P(2) = \frac{_{13}C_3 \cdot {_3C_2}}{_{16}C_5} = \frac{(286)(3)}{4{,}368} = 0.1964$$

b. $\mu = \frac{nR}{N} = \frac{(5)(3)}{16} = 0.9375$

$$\sigma\sqrt{\frac{nR(N-R)}{N^2}}\sqrt{\frac{N-n}{N-1}}$$

$$= \sqrt{\frac{(5)(3)(16-3)}{(16)^2}}\sqrt{\frac{16-5}{16-1}}$$

$$\sigma\sqrt{\frac{195}{256}}\sqrt{\frac{11}{15}} = \sqrt{0.7617}\sqrt{0.7333}$$

$$= (0.873)(0.856) = 0.747$$

c. $=\text{HYPGEOM.DIST} = (2, 5, 3, 16) = 0.1964$

	A	B	C
1	Hypergeometric Probabilities		
2			
3	Data		
4	Sample size	5	
5	No. of events of interest in population	3	
6	Population size	16	
7			
8	Hypergeometric Probabilities Table		
9		X	P(X)
10		0	0.294643
11		1	0.491071
12		2	0.196429
13		3	0.017857
14		4	0
15		5	0
16			

The probability that $x = 4$ and $x = 5$ equals zero because there are only three defective computers in the population.

CHAPTER 6

Continuous Probability Distributions

IN THIS CHAPTER, YOU WILL LEARN TO:

- Understand the properties of continuous random variables.
- Identify the characteristics of the normal probability distribution.
- Calculate normal probabilities.
- Interpret z-scores for the normal probability distribution.
- Use the normal distribution to approximate the binomial distribution.
- Identify the characteristics of the exponential probability distribution.
- Calculate exponential probabilities.
- Identify the characteristics of the uniform probability distribution.
- Calculate uniform probabilities.

CHAPTER 6 MAP

Our focus in Chapter 5 was on discrete data. The values for discrete data are typically whole numbers such as 0, 1, or 2. They are found as a result of counting observations while conducting an experiment. By contrast, a continuous data value can take on any real number, including fractional values. These data are usually measured rather than counted. Examples of continuous data include time, distance, and weight. This chapter explores the probability of continuous data values occurring. Discrete probability distributions work well when you have small counts of observations; however, businesses are often faced with large quantities that they must measure—hence the need for continuous probability distributions.

The road behind your author's home after a major snowstorm.

Consider the following example: During the winter of 2009–2010, the Philadelphia area—the largest metropolitan area near my home in Delaware—experienced record-breaking snowfall amounts. Because we measure snowfall levels with values that can include decimal points, the data are considered continuous. Between 1884, the first year snowfall amounts were recorded, and 2012, Philadelphia averaged 22.3 in. of snow per winter. During the 2009–2010 winter season, Philadelphia received 78.7 in. of snow. Two major storms in February alone resulted in unprecedented snowfall levels, wreaking havoc with both governments and businesses in the Northeast.

The cost of removing the extraordinary amount of snow in the Philadelphia area that year led to budget shortfalls. Airlines estimated that the winter storms in the Northeast corridor cost $100 million due to flight delays and cancellations. General Motors announced that February 2010 car sales in the Northeast United States were down 22% because of these weather incidents. Apparently, selling cars that are buried under three feet of snow is difficult. Later in the chapter, you will learn how to calculate the probability of certain snowfall amounts based on historical data.

As I was examining the 128 years of Philadelphia snowfall data for this chapter, my attention was drawn to the one year in which there was no snowfall: the winter of 1972–1973. Coincidentally, in the fall of 1972, as an ambitious college student I decided to invest my entire savings into a used truck and snowplow. My dreams of rolling in money gradually faded away as week after snowless week went by that winter.

After Philadelphia's record-setting winter in 2010, I suggested to Deb, my wife, that we purchase a snow blower for next season. She just laughed and reminded me of how well my last snow-removal investment had worked out. (Although I explained to her how low the probability was of no snowfall occurring and cleverly reminded her that probability has no memory—a concept discussed in Chapter 4—there doesn't appear to be a snow blower in my near future.)

6.1 Continuous Random Variables

Continuous random variables are outcomes that take on any numerical value in an interval, as determined by conducting an experiment.

Experiments that involve continuous data generate **continuous random variables,** which are outcomes that take on any numerical value in an interval, including numbers with decimal points. Tracking the number of calories consumed daily by a middle-aged statistics author who is working late at night on a continuous probability chapter is an example of such an experiment. Some examples of experiments in the business environment that generate continuous random variables are as follows:

- Measuring the weight of a randomly selected box of Cheez-It crackers at a manufacturing plant
- Recording the flight time of a American Airlines flight bound from Philadelphia to Orlando
- Recording the amount of time a customer spends on the phone with a cable company's customer service representative

These experiments could generate continuous random variables, such as the following:

- 16.12 ounces of Cheez-It crackers in a selected box
- 2.4 hours of flight time for a American Airlines flight bound from Philadelphia and Orlando
- 6.49 minutes spent by a customer on the phone with a customer service representative

The number of ounces of Cheez-Its and hours of flight time are continuous "random" variables because they cannot be known with certainty before conducting the experiments. The values 16.12 and 2.4 are the values that these random variables have taken on during the experiment. The purpose of this chapter is to identify the probability that specific continuous random variables will occur using continuous probability distributions.

The value of a random variable is often denoted by x. When we discussed discrete random variables in Chapter 5, we calculated the probability that x would equal a specific value. For instance, if we flip a coin once, the probability of observing exactly one head is $P(x = 1) = 0.5$. However, continuous random variables can take on an infinite number of values. The flight time from Philadelphia to Orlando can be 2.4, 2.45, 2.451, or 2.4519 hours, for example.

Continuous variables can take on values between whole integers that contain decimal points.

The value of a continuous random variable depends on the level of precision in its measurement. Keep in mind that we aren't counting flights that are late or that arrive on time like we did with discrete probability distributions. We are measuring an interval. Because there are an infinite number of possible times, the probability of one specific flight time occurring is theoretically equal to zero or $P(x = 2.4) = 0$. Some of my students struggle with this concept, so let me try to explain further. Because there are an infinite number of possible flight times, the probability of any one specific flight time occurring is so small; it is essentially equal to zero. We can use Equation 4.2 from Chapter 4 to calculate this probability as follows:

$$P(x = 2.4) = \frac{\text{Frequency in which } x = 2.4 \text{ occurs in the interval}}{\text{Total number of possible values of } x \text{ in the interval}}$$

$$P(x = 2.4) = \frac{1}{\infty} \approx 0.000$$

This holds true for any specific flight time, not just $x = 2.4$ hours. However, we can calculate the probability that a continuous random variable will fall within a specific interval, such as $P(x \leq 2.4)$. Calculating this type of probability will be the focus of much of this chapter.

Also, because $P(x = 2.4) = 0$, we can also claim that

$$P(x \leq 2.4) = P(x = 2.4) + P(x < 2.4)$$
$$P(x \leq 2.4) = 0 + P(x < 2.4)$$
$$P(x \leq 2.4) = P(x < 2.4)$$

For continuous distributions, the probability that x is less than or equal to a value is the same as the probability that x is less than that value.

The probability of a continuous random variable being a specific value is always equal to zero.

Continuous probability distributions can have a variety of shapes, depending on their data values. Figure 6.1 shows the shapes of three common continuous distributions that will be discussed in this chapter.

FIGURE 6.1 Common Continuous Probability Distributions

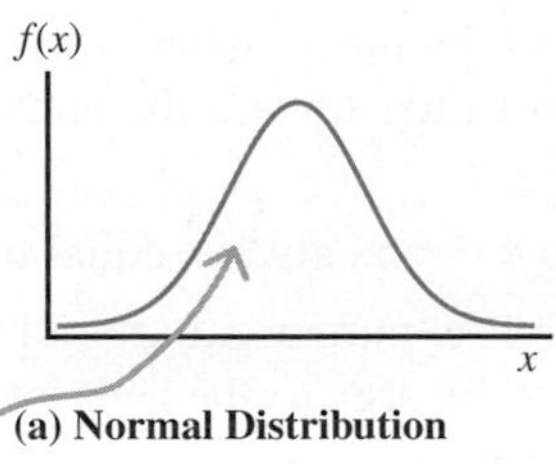

(a) Normal Distribution

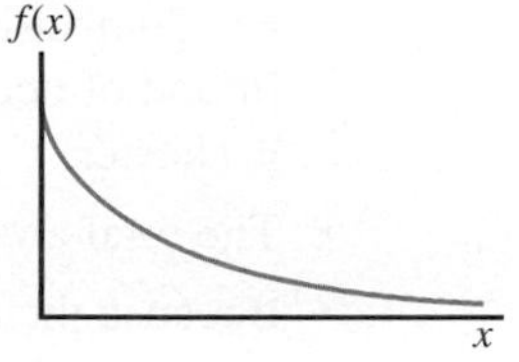

(b) Exponential Distribution

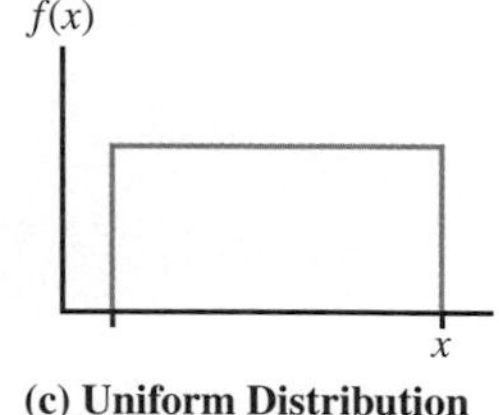

(c) Uniform Distribution

Because it is so common, the normal probability distribution is a statistician's workhorse. It will be used to calculate many types of inferential statistics throughout the rest of this textbook.

The normal probability distribution seen in Figure 6.1 is useful when the data tend to fall into the center of the distribution and when very high and very low values are fairly rare. You will see this type of distribution in a quality control setting, such as filling boxes of Frosted Flakes cereal.

The exponential distribution is used to describe data where lower values tend to dominate and higher values don't occur very often. The time between customer arrivals is a common application for the exponential distribution.

Finally, the uniform distribution describes data where all the values have the same chance of occurring. Download times on the Internet could be an application where the uniform distribution would be useful.

Keep in mind that this is not an exhaustive list of continuous distributions. There are many others that could be used in a business setting. The following section will introduce the most common type of continuous probability distribution, the normal distribution.

6.2 Normal Probability Distributions

As we saw in Figure 6.1, the normal probability distribution is useful when the majority of the data tend to be in the middle of the distribution. We will use this distribution repeatedly throughout this text, so it would be a good idea for you to become very familiar with it by studying the following sections.

Characteristics of the Normal Probability Distribution

A continuous random variable that follows the normal probability distribution has several distinctive features. Let's say the number of minutes a customer spends on the phone with customer service for a cable company follows the normal distribution with a mean of 12 minutes (μ) and a standard deviation of 2 minutes (σ). The probability distribution for such a random variable is shown in Figure 6.2.

FIGURE 6.2
A Normal Distribution with a Mean of 12 and a Standard Deviation of 2

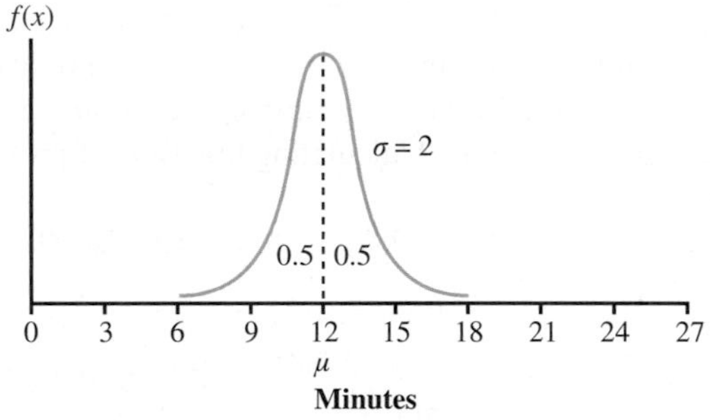

Normal probability distribution. A continuous distribution that is bell shaped and symmetrical around its mean.

We can make the following observations about the **normal probability distribution** like the one shown in Figure 6.2:

- The distribution is bell-shaped and symmetrical around the mean.
- Because the shape of the distribution is symmetrical, the mean and median are the same value, in this case 12 minutes (see Chapter 2).
- Random variables around the mean, where the curve is the tallest, have a higher likelihood of occurring than values toward the ends of the distribution, where the curve is shorter.
- The total area under the curve is always equal to 1.0.
- Because the distribution is symmetrical around the mean, the area to the left of the mean equals 0.5, as does the area to the right of the mean.
- The left and right ends of the normal probability distribution extend indefinitely, never quite touching the horizontal axis.

The standard deviation plays an important role in the shape of the curve. Looking at Figure 6.2, we can see that nearly all the phone calls would last between 6 and 18 minutes. Now look at Figure 6.3, which shows the effect of changing the standard deviation from 2 minutes (blue curve) to 3 minutes (red curve). The mean of both of these normal distributions is still 12 minutes.

FIGURE 6.3
The Effect of Changing a Normal Distribution's Standard Deviation from 2 to 3 (While Leaving the Mean at 12)

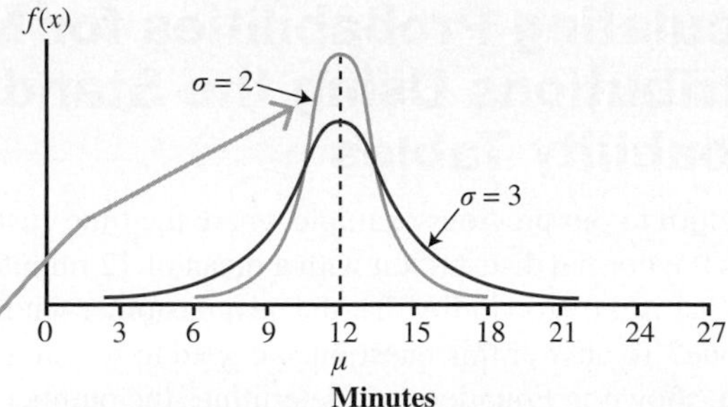

A smaller standard deviation results in a skinnier curve that is tighter and taller around the mean. By contrast, a larger σ (standard deviation) makes for a fatter curve that is more spread out and not as tall.

In this figure, you see a red curve, with a standard deviation of 3 ($\sigma = 3$). Notice that it is more spread out around the mean than the blue curve, which has a standard deviation of 2 ($\sigma = 2$). The red curve shows that almost all of the call times are between 3 and 21 minutes. What this shows us is that a smaller standard deviation results in a skinnier curve that is tighter and taller around the mean. By contrast, a larger σ (standard deviation) makes for a fatter curve that is more spread out and not as tall.

Figure 6.4 shows the impact of changing the mean of the distribution from 12 to 21 minutes, leaving the standard deviation at 2 minutes. Notice that the curve is simply shifted to the right.

FIGURE 6.4
Normal Distributions with Means of 12 and 21 and a Standard Deviation of 2

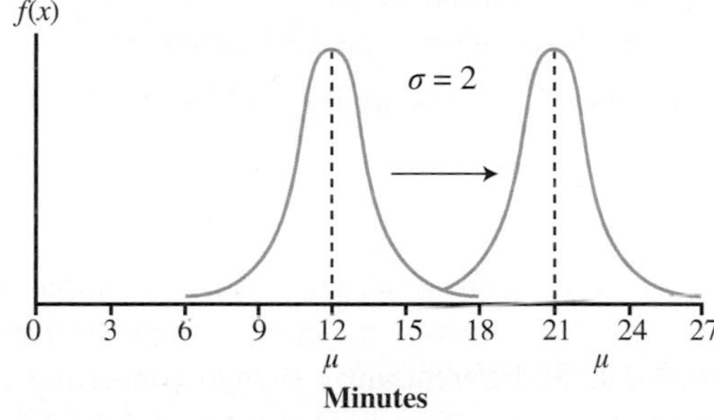

A distribution's mean (μ) and standard deviation (σ) completely describe its shape.

In each of the previous figures, the characteristics of the normal probability distribution hold true. In each case, the values of μ, the mean, and σ, the standard deviation, completely describe the shape of the distribution.

Normal probability density function. The mathematical expression that describes the shape of the normal probability distribution.

The mathematical expression that describes the shape of normal curves like those shown in the last three figures is known as the **normal probability density function**. It is shown in Equation 6.1.

Formula 6.1 for the Normal Probability Density Function

$$f(x) = \frac{1}{\sigma\sqrt{2\pi}} e^{-(1/2)[(x-\mu)/\sigma]^2}$$

where

$e = 2.71828$
$\pi = 3.14159$
$\mu =$ The mean of the distribution
$\sigma =$ The standard deviation of the distribution
$x =$ Any continuous number of interest

Fortunately for us, we will not have to use this intimidating equation to calculate probabilities. Instead, we can calculate the probability of normal distributions using tables and Microsoft Excel. Let's move on to the next section, and I will show you how this is done. Hint: It involves converting a normal distribution to the standard normal distribution, discussed next.

Calculating Probabilities for Normal Distributions Using the Standard Normal Probability Tables

Let's return to our previous example where the time customers spend on the phone for service follows the normal distribution with a mean of 12 minutes and a standard deviation of 3 minutes. What is the probability that the next customer who calls will spend 14 minutes or less on the phone? To answer this question, we need to revisit a concept introduced in Chapter 3. The ***z*-score**, shown in Equation 6.2, determines the number of standard deviations that a particular value, x, is from the mean of its distribution.

The ***z*-score** determines the number of standard deviations that a particular value, *x*, is from the mean of its distribution.

Formula 6.2 for the z-score

$$z = \frac{x - \mu}{\sigma}$$

where

$x =$ The continuous data value of interest
$\mu =$ The distribution's mean
$\sigma =$ The distribution's standard deviation

Using Equation 6.2, the z-score for $x = 14$ is

$$z_{14} = \frac{x - \mu}{\sigma} = \frac{14 - 12}{3} = 0.67$$

The z-score determines the number of standard deviations that a particular value, x, is from the mean of its distribution.

In other words, a customer who spends 14 minutes on the phone is 0.67 standard deviations from the distribution mean of 12 minutes. The z-score is analogous to expressing the original data in different units, such as converting two feet to 24 in. In our example, the 14-minute time is being converted to a z-score of 0.67. However, the z-score itself has no units even though the original values for x will normally be expressed in units such as minutes, dollars, years, and pounds. Table 6.1 shows the z-scores for this example for various call times.

Table 6.1 highlights the following features of z-scores:

- z-Scores are negative for values of x that are less than the distribution mean.
- z-Scores are positive for values of x that are more than the distribution mean.
- The z-score at the mean of the distribution equals zero.

TABLE 6.1 | z-SCORES FOR TIMES SPENT ON THE PHONE WITH CUSTOMER SERVICE

MINUTES				
x	μ	$x - \mu$	σ	$z = (x - \mu)/\sigma$
6	12	−6	3	−2.00
8	12	−4	3	−1.33
10	12	−2	3	−0.67
12	12	0	3	0.00
14	12	2	3	0.67
16	12	4	3	1.33
18	12	6	3	2.00

The z-score follows a normal distribution with $\mu = 0$ and $\sigma = 1$, which is known as the **standard normal distribution.**

When the original random variable, x, follows the normal distribution, z-scores also follow a normal distribution with $\mu = 0$ and $\sigma = 1$, which is shown in Figure 6.5. This is known as the **standard normal distribution**.

FIGURE 6.5
The Standard Normal Distribution (Mean = 0 and Standard Deviation = 1)

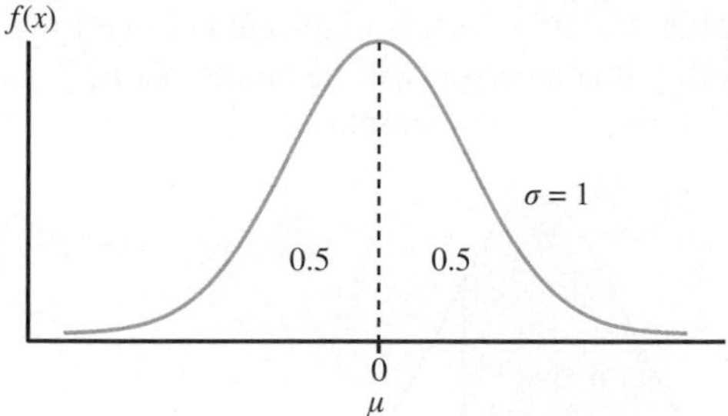

At this point, you might be wondering: So what does the standard normal distribution have to do with a random variable that follows the normal probability distribution? Essentially, we are converting the value of the random variable to a z-score that follows the standard normal distribution (like converting feet to inches). Once our normal random variable is converted to the z-score, its mean will equal zero, as Figure 6.5 shows, and the standard deviation will equal 1. We can then use the standard normal probability tables shown in Appendix A at the back of the book to calculate the probabilities for our normal distribution. (Looking up the probabilities in the tables will be much easier than using Equation 6.1, which requires an advanced math degree.) Keep in mind that this works for any normal distribution. Any normally distributed values can be standardized with z-scores.

Now, let us return to our original question. We can use the standard normal distribution tables to determine the probability that a person will spend 14 minutes or less on the phone with customer service. Table 6.2 shows a portion of Table 4 in Appendix A. This table

TABLE 6.2 | Cumulative Standardized Normal Table Excerpted from Appendix A for Positive Z-Scores

FIRST DIGIT OF Z	SECOND DIGIT OF Z									
z	0.00	0.01	0.02	0.03	0.04	0.05	0.06	0.07	0.08	0.09
0.0	0.5000	0.5040	0.5080	0.5120	0.5160	0.5199	0.5239	0.5279	0.5319	0.5359
0.1	0.5398	0.5438	0.5478	0.5517	0.5557	0.5596	0.5636	0.5675	0.5714	0.5753
0.2	0.5793	0.5832	0.5871	0.5910	0.5948	0.5987	0.6026	0.6064	0.6103	0.6141
0.3	0.6179	0.6217	0.6255	0.6293	0.6331	0.6368	0.6406	0.6443	0.6480	0.6517
0.4	0.6554	0.6591	0.6628	0.6664	0.6700	0.6736	0.6772	0.6808	0.6844	0.6879
0.5	0.6915	0.6950	0.6985	0.7019	0.7054	0.7088	0.7123	0.7157	0.7190	0.7224
0.6	0.7257	0.7291	0.7324	0.7357	0.7389	0.7422	0.7454	0.7486	0.7517	0.7549
0.7	0.7580	0.7611	0.7642	0.7673	0.7704	0.7734	0.7764	0.7794	0.7823	0.7852
0.8	0.7881	0.7910	0.7939	0.7967	0.7995	0.8023	0.8051	0.8078	0.8106	0.8133
0.9	0.8159	0.8186	0.8212	0.8238	0.8264	0.8289	0.8315	0.8340	0.8365	0.8389
1.0	0.8413	0.8438	0.8461	0.8485	0.8508	0.8531	0.8554	0.8577	0.8599	0.8621
1.1	0.8643	0.8665	0.8686	0.8708	0.8729	0.8749	0.8770	0.8790	0.8810	0.8830
1.2	0.8849	0.8869	0.8888	0.8907	0.8925	0.8944	0.8962	0.8980	0.8997	0.9015
1.3	0.9032	0.9049	0.9066	0.9082	0.9099	0.9115	0.9131	0.9147	0.9162	0.9177
1.4	0.9192	0.9207	0.9222	0.9236	0.9251	0.9265	0.9279	0.9292	0.9306	0.9319
1.5	0.9332	0.9345	0.9357	0.9370	0.9382	0.9394	0.9406	0.9418	0.9429	0.9441
1.6	0.9452	0.9463	0.9474	0.9484	0.9495	0.9505	0.9515	0.9525	0.9535	0.9545
1.7	0.9554	0.9564	0.9573	0.9582	0.9591	0.9599	0.9608	0.9616	0.9625	0.9633

provides the cumulative area under a standard normal distribution curve that lies to the left of the z-score. Because the z-score that corresponds to 14 minutes is 0.67, we use the 0.6 row, which corresponds to the first digit in our z-score, and the 0.07 column, which corresponds to the second digit in our z-score. At the intersection of the two columns, we find the value 0.7486, which is highlighted in yellow. The value 0.7486 (74.86%) represents the probability that a person will be on the phone 14 minutes or less. The shaded area in Figure 6.6 shows this value graphically.

FIGURE 6.6
The Area Under a Normal Curve When $x \leq 14$

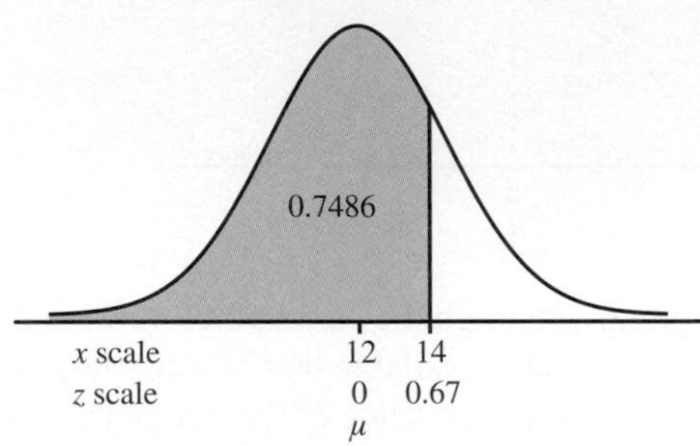

There is a 74.86% chance that the next person will be on the phone 14 minutes or less, which can be expressed as

$$P(x \leq 14) = 0.7486$$

Remember, this is the same probability as less than 14 minutes because $P(x = 14) = 0$.

What about the probability that the next customer will be on the phone for *more* than 14 minutes? Because we know the area under the normal curve equals 1.0,

$$P(x > 14) = P(z > 0.67) = 1.0 - 0.7486 = 0.2514$$

You only need to calculate the z-score out to two decimal places because this is the level of precision that Table 6.2 provides.

In other words, there is a 25.14% chance that the customer will be on the phone for more than 14 minutes. The shaded region in Figure 6.7 shows this probability.

FIGURE 6.7
The Area Under a Normal Curve When $x > 14$

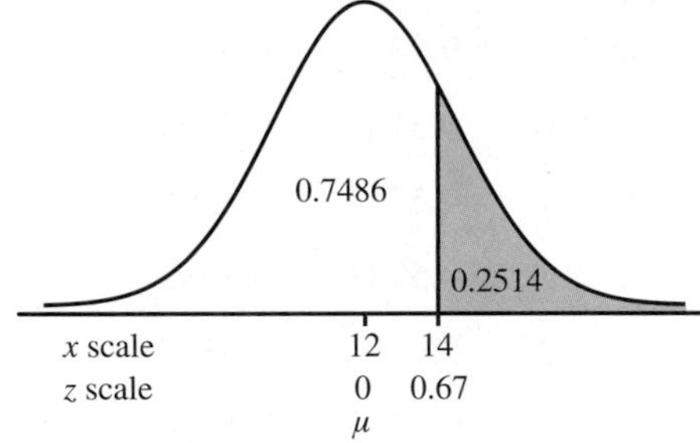

Suppose that management at a cable company has a goal that 95% of its customers will require less than 18 minutes per call on the phone with customer service. Is this goal being met with the current probability distribution, which has a mean of 12 and standard deviation of 3? To answer this question, we need to determine how many standard deviations to the right of the mean are needed to include 95% of the area under the curve. We do so by using Figure 6.8 and taking the following steps:

- First, we recognize that the area to the left of our point of interest includes 95% of the total area under the curve.

FIGURE 6.8
Finding the Value (x) That Corresponds to 95% of the Area Under a Normal Curve

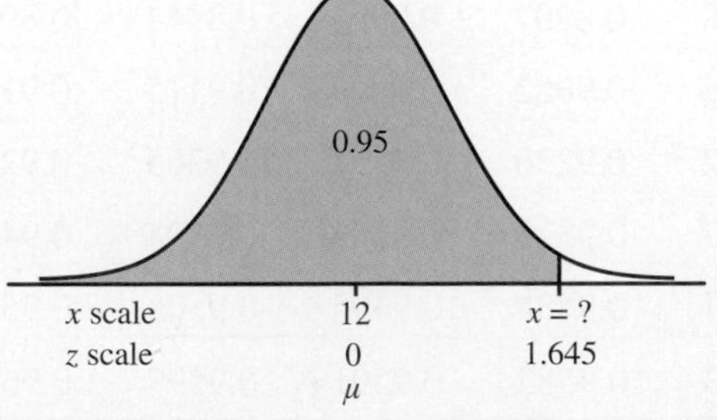

- Second, we search Table 6.2 to find the value in the body of the table closest to 0.95. This value is half-way between 0.9495 and 0.9505, which I have shown in the red box. These values are found in the 1.6 row and the 0.04 and 0.05 columns. This means our point of interest is halfway between these columns at 1.6 + 0.045, or 1.645 standard deviations to the right of the mean. In other words, $z = 1.645$.
- Third, we need to determine the value of x that corresponds to $z = 1.645$ by rearranging Equation 6.2 in terms of x, as follows:

$$z = \frac{x - \mu}{\sigma}$$

$$x = \mu + z\sigma$$

$$x = 12 + (1.645)(3) = 12 + 4.94 = 16.94 \text{ minutes}$$

- Finally, we can conclude that 95% of the people calling customer service will spend less than 16.94 minutes on the phone. Because this time is less than 18 minutes, management's goal appears to have been achieved. The value 16.94 can also be described as the 95th percentile, because 95% of the values in the distribution fall below it.

Now it's time to move over to the left side of the distribution's mean. Let's examine the probability that a customer will be on the phone for 8.5 minutes or less. First, we calculate the z-score for $x = 8.5$ using Equation 6.2:

$$z_{8.5} = \frac{x - \mu}{\sigma} = \frac{8.5 - 12}{3} = -1.17$$

Table 6.3 shows an excerpt from Table 3 in Appendix A. The values in this table are the cumulative normal probabilities for negative z-scores, which are always on the left side of the standard normal distribution (remember, the mean of this distribution is zero).

TABLE 6.3 | CUMULATIVE STANDARDIZED NORMAL TABLE EXCERPTED FROM APPENDIX A FOR NEGATIVE Z-SCORES

FIRST DIGIT OF Z	SECOND DIGIT OF Z									
z	0.00	0.01	0.02	0.03	0.04	0.05	0.06	0.07	0.08	0.09
−3.0	0.0013	0.0013	0.0013	0.0012	0.0012	0.0011	0.0011	0.0011	0.0010	0.0010
−2.9	0.0019	0.0018	0.0018	0.0017	0.0016	0.0016	0.0015	0.0015	0.0014	0.0014
−2.8	0.0026	0.0025	0.0024	0.0023	0.0023	0.0022	0.0021	0.0021	0.0020	0.0019
−2.7	0.0035	0.0034	0.0033	0.0032	0.0031	0.0030	0.0029	0.0028	0.0027	0.0026
−2.6	0.0047	0.0045	0.0044	0.0043	0.0041	0.0040	0.0039	0.0038	0.0037	0.0036
−2.5	0.0062	0.0060	0.0059	0.0057	0.0055	0.0054	0.0052	0.0051	0.0049	0.0048
−2.4	0.0082	0.0080	0.0078	0.0075	0.0073	0.0071	0.0069	0.0068	0.0066	0.0064
−2.3	0.0107	0.0104	0.0102	0.0099	0.0096	0.0094	0.0091	0.0089	0.0087	0.0084
−2.2	0.0139	0.0136	0.0132	0.0129	0.0125	0.0122	0.0119	0.0116	0.0113	0.0110
−2.1	0.0179	0.0174	0.0170	0.0166	0.0162	0.0158	0.0154	0.0150	0.0146	0.0143
−2.0	0.0228	0.0222	0.0217	0.0212	0.0207	0.0202	0.0197	0.0192	0.0188	0.0183
−1.9	0.0287	0.0281	0.0274	0.0268	0.0262	0.0256	0.0250	0.0244	0.0239	0.0233
−1.8	0.0359	0.0351	0.0344	0.0336	0.0329	0.0322	0.0314	0.0307	0.0301	0.0294
−1.7	0.0446	0.0436	0.0427	0.0418	0.0409	0.0401	0.0392	0.0384	0.0375	0.0367
−1.6	0.0548	0.0537	0.0526	0.0516	0.0505	0.0495	0.0485	0.0475	0.0465	0.0455
−1.5	0.0668	0.0655	0.0643	0.0630	0.0618	0.0606	0.0594	0.0582	0.0571	0.0559
−1.4	0.0808	0.0793	0.0778	0.0764	0.0749	0.0735	0.0721	0.0708	0.0694	0.0681
−1.3	0.0968	0.0951	0.0934	0.0918	0.0901	0.0885	0.0869	0.0853	0.0838	0.0823
−1.2	0.1151	0.1131	0.1112	0.1093	0.1075	0.1056	0.1038	0.1020	0.1003	0.0985
−1.1	0.1357	0.1335	0.1314	0.1292	0.1271	0.1251	0.1230	0.1210	0.1190	0.1170
−1.0	0.1587	0.1562	0.1539	0.1515	0.1492	0.1469	0.1446	0.1423	0.1401	0.1379

This table provides the cumulative area under a standard normal distribution curve that lies to the left of the negative z-score. Because the z-score that corresponds to 8.5 minutes is -1.17, we look at the -1.1 row, which corresponds to the first digit in our z-score. Then we look at the 0.07 column, which corresponds to the second digit in our z-score. At the intersection of the two columns, we find the value 0.1210, which is highlighted in yellow. The value 0.1210 (12.1%) represents the probability that a person will be on the phone 8.5 minutes or less. The shaded area in Figure 6.9 shows this value graphically.

FIGURE 6.9
The Area Under a Normal Curve When $x \leq 8.5$

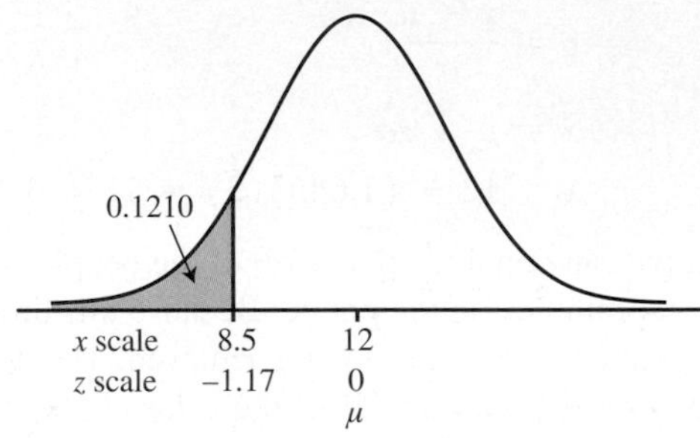

Let's wrap up this section with one last probability. What is the probability that a person will be on the phone for more than 8.5 minutes? The answer can be found in the shaded area in Figure 6.10.

FIGURE 6.10
The Area Under a Normal Curve When $x > 8.5$

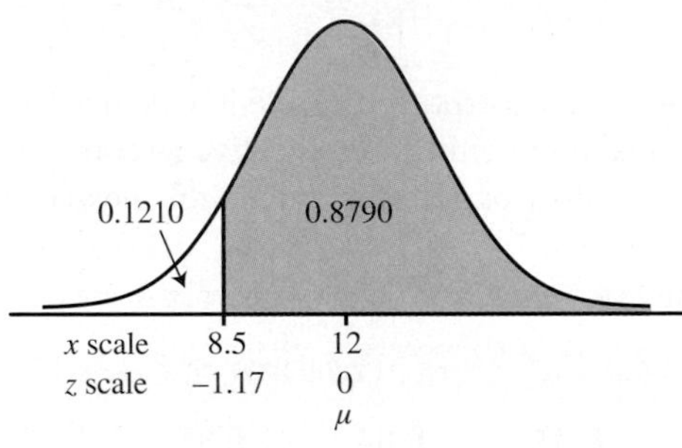

Remember, the total area under the normal curve equals 1.0.

Using Figure 6.10, we can see that this probability will be

$$P(x > 8.5) = P(z > -1.17) = 1.0 - 0.1210 = 0.8790$$

Thus, there is an 87.9% probability that the next person will be on the phone with customer service for more than 8.5 minutes.

YOUR TURN #1

A local gas station waits 4 days to receive a delivery of regular gasoline to replenish its inventory. The wait period to receive inventory is known as the lead time. The demand during the lead-time period for regular gasoline, as measured in gallons, follows the normal distribution with a mean of 930 gallons and standard deviation of 140 gallons.

a. What is the probability that, during the next lead time, the demand for regular gasoline will be less than 800 gallons?
b. What is the probability that, during the next lead time, the demand for regular gasoline will be less than 1,000 gallons?
c. What is the probability that, during the next lead time, the demand for regular gasoline will be equal to 900 gallons?
d. The station manager places the next order for regular gasoline when the inventory is 1,200 gallons (known as the reorder point). What is the probability that the station will not run out of gasoline before the order arrives?
e. Determine the reorder point that will ensure the station a 90% probability that it will have enough inventory of regular gasoline until the next order arrives.

Answers can be found on ▶ **page 286**

When solving these problems, I strongly encourage you to take the time to draw the distribution curves as I have shown you in this chapter. This will help you identify the proper area of interest.

Revisiting the Empirical Rule

According to the **empirical rule**, if a distribution follows a bell-shape, symmetrical curve centered around the mean, approximately 68%, 95%, and 99.7% of its values will fall within one, two, and three standard deviations above and below the mean, respectively.

Back in Chapter 3, we introduced the **empirical rule**, which states if a distribution is symmetrical and bell-shaped, approximately 68%, 95%, and 99.7% of its data values will fall within one, two, and three standard deviations above and below the mean, respectively. We now have the tools to verify these percentages using Tables 3 and 4 in Appendix A.

Figure 6.11 illustrates the empirical rule using our previous example. Recall that people spend an average of 12 minutes on the phone with customer service, with a standard deviation of 3 minutes. Each vertical line in Figure 6.11 represents an increment of one standard deviation from the mean. Because one standard deviation equals 3 minutes, the time interval between vertical lines represents 3 minutes on the phone.

FIGURE 6.11 The Empirical Rule for Customer Service Call Length

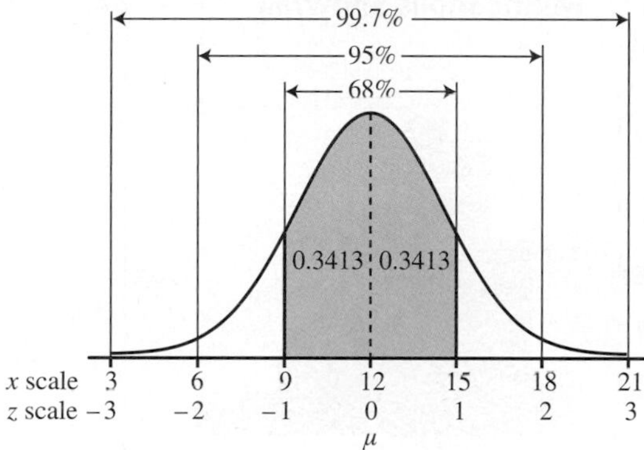

Let's examine the shaded region in Figure 6.11, which represents ± one standard deviation around the mean. According to Table 4 in Appendix A, the area to the left of $z = 1.0$ is 0.8413. Subtracting 0.5 (the area to the left of the mean) from this value gives us 0.3413 (the area of the shaded region to the right of the mean). Adding the two shaded areas together provides us with the 68% (approximately) stated in the empirical rule. We would expect that 68% of the callers spend between 9 and 15 minutes on the phone.

We'll use the same logic for ± two standard deviations around the mean. According to Table 4 in Appendix A, the area to the left of $z = 2.0$ is 0.9772. Subtracting 0.5 from this value gives us 0.4772 (the area to the right of the mean). Adding the two areas on either side of the mean together $(0.4772 + 0.4772)$ provides us with the 95% (approximately) stated in the empirical rule. We would expect that 95% of the callers spend between 6 and 18 minutes on the phone.

Finally, Table 4 in Appendix A shows that the area to the left of $z = 3.0$ is 0.9987. Subtracting 0.5 from this value gives us 0.4987. Adding the two areas on either side of the mean together $(0.4987 + 0.4987)$ provides us with the 99.7% (approximately) stated in the empirical rule. We would expect that practically all of the callers spend between 3 and 21 minutes on the phone with customer service.

The following Your Turn section will give you the chance to see if you've mastered the empirical rule.

YOUR TURN #2

Suppose the average fuel economy for the 2013 Ford C Max hybrid car is reported to be 39.2 miles per gallon (mpg) with a standard deviation of 3.7 mpg. Assume the fuel economy for each tankful of gas for this car follows the normal distribution. Determine the interval of miles per gallon around the mean that include the following:

a. Approximately 68% of the reported fuel economies for this car
b. Approximately 95% of the reported fuel economies for this car
c. Approximately 99.7% of the reported fuel economies for this car

Answers can be found on ▶ **page 286**

Other Normal Probability Intervals

We can examine other types of probability intervals using the normal distribution. Let's look at our snowfall example from the beginning of the chapter. I researched many cities in the United States and found that the annual snowfall amounts in Minneapolis, Minnesota, from 1884 until 2012 tended to follow a normal distribution with a mean of 46.3 in. and a standard deviation of 18.4 in. The histogram for these data are shown in Figure 6.12. As you can see, the data are slightly right-skewed, but they are close enough to a normal distribution for our purposes. (In Chapter 12, I will show you a procedure to test a distribution to see if its data values allow it to be categorized as a normal distribution.)

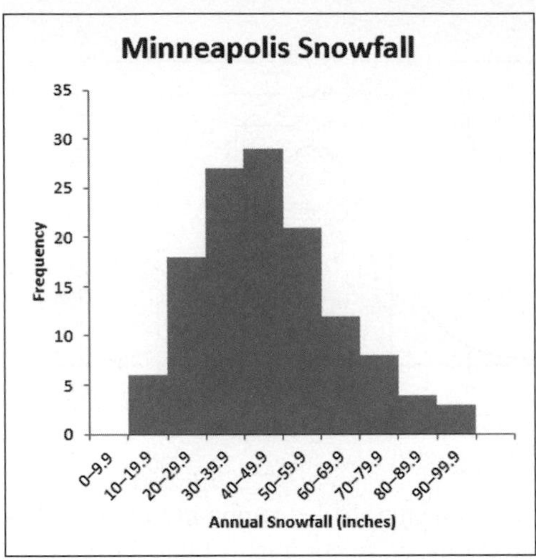

FIGURE 6.12 A Histogram Showing the Annual Snowfall in Minneapolis

If the historical data in the figure are a good indicator of future events, what is the probability that between 30 and 70 in. of snow will fall in Minneapolis next year? The area of interest straddles the distribution's mean of 46.3 inches. For this, we need to calculate the z-scores for $x = 30$ and $x = 70$ using Equation 6.2. (Remember, $\mu = 46.3$ and $\sigma = 18.4$.)

$$z_{30} = \frac{x - \mu}{\sigma} = \frac{30 - 46.3}{18.4} = -0.89$$

$$z_{70} = \frac{x - \mu}{\sigma} = \frac{70 - 46.3}{18.4} = 1.29$$

You can find this value in the 1.2 row and 0.09 column in Table 6.2.

According to Figure 6.13, the probability of less than 70 in. of snow falling in Minneapolis is

$$P(x \le 70) = P(z \le 1.29) = 0.9015$$

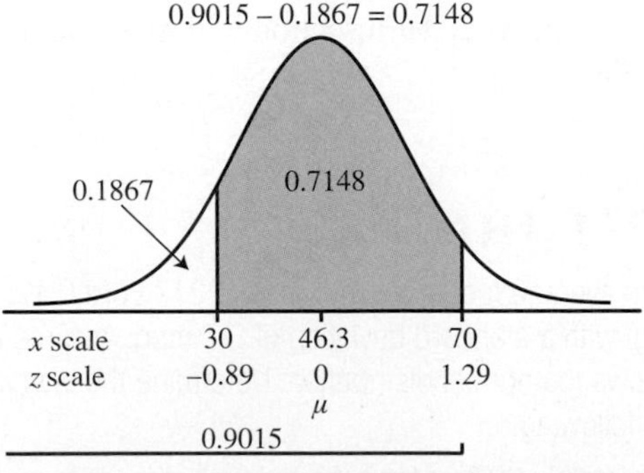

FIGURE 6.13 The Probability of Between 30 and 70 in. of Snow Falling in Minneapolis

You can find this value in the −0.8 row and 0.09 column in Table 3 in Appendix A.

However, this probability includes the event that less than 30 inches of snow will fall, so we need to subtract this out to get our final result, which is the shaded region in Figure 6.13.

$$P(x \le 30) = P(z \le -0.89) = 0.1867$$

$$P(30 \le x \le 70) = 0.9015 - 0.1867 = 0.7148$$

In other words, there is a greater than 71% chance that between 30 and 70 in. will fall. That's a lot of snow.

The next example has caused some of my students to accuse me of trickery when they see it on an exam. (OK, it's a little different from the examples we have looked at so far, but trickery? Decide for yourself.) What is the probability that between 60 and 75 in. of snow will fall in Minneapolis next year? When you examine Figure 6.14, you'll see the entire shaded area of interest falls to the right of the distribution's mean of 46.3 in. As with the last example, we need to calculate the z-scores for $x = 60$ and $x = 75$ using Equation 6.2.

$$z_{60} = \frac{x - \mu}{\sigma} = \frac{60 - 46.3}{18.4} = 0.74$$

$$z_{75} = \frac{x - \mu}{\sigma} = \frac{75 - 46.3}{18.4} = 1.56$$

According to Figure 6.14, the probability of less than 75 in. of snow falling in Minneapolis is

$$P(x \leq 75) = P(z \leq 1.56) = 0.9406$$

However, this probability includes the event that less than 60 in. of snow will fall, so we need to subtract this out to get our final result, which is the shaded region in Figure 6.14.

The probability of less than 75 in. falling includes the probability of less than 60 in. falling. Therefore, we need to remove this probability (0.7704) to obtain our final result.

$$P(x \leq 60) = P(z \leq 0.74) = 0.7704$$

$$P(60 \leq x \leq 75) = 0.9406 - 0.7704 = 0.1702$$

FIGURE 6.14
The Probability of Between 60 and 75 in. of Snow Falling in Minneapolis

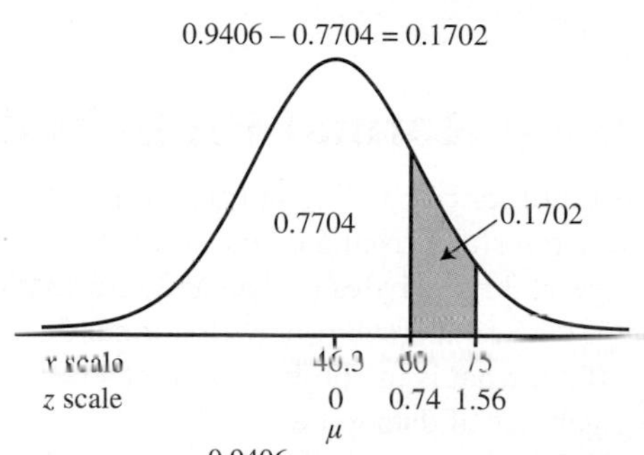

In other words, the probability of this much snow falling is considerable less—only a little over a 17% chance. Again, so that you don't get confused (or tricked), draw the distribution to show the area of probability more clearly.

Let's wrap up this section by calculating a shaded area to the left of the mean. (I don't want to discriminate against you left-handers). Figure 6.15 shows the probability that between 12 and 35 inches of snow will fall in Minneapolis next year. First, we show the z-scores for $x = 12$ and $x = 35$ using Equation 6.2:

$$z_{12} = \frac{x - \mu}{\sigma} = \frac{12 - 46.3}{18.4} = -1.86$$

$$z_{35} = \frac{x - \mu}{\sigma} = \frac{35 - 46.3}{18.4} = -0.61$$

FIGURE 6.15
The Probability of Between 12 and 35 in. of Snow Falling in Minneapolis

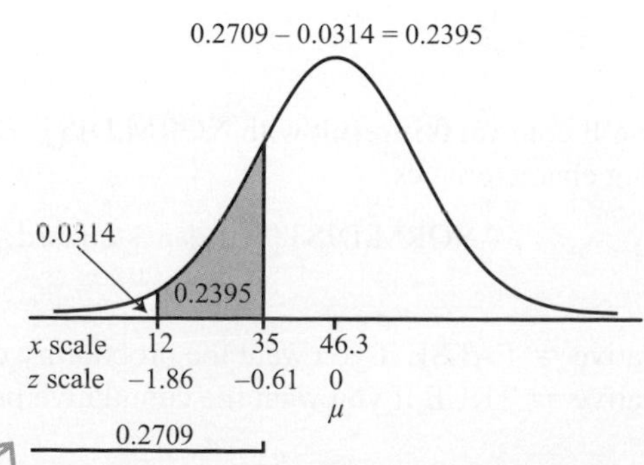

This is the probability that less than 35 in. of snow will fall next year.

Following the logic from the two previous examples and using Table 3 in Appendix A, we have

$$P(x \le 35) = P(z \le -0.61) = 0.2709$$
$$P(x \le 12) = P(z \le -1.86) = 0.0314$$
$$P(12 \le x \le 35) = 0.2709 - 0.0314 = 0.2395$$

At this point, I have tortured you with every possible type of interval under a normal distribution. Make me proud and nail this type of question in this next example by solving the following Your Turn problem.

YOUR TURN #3

The *Wall Street Journal* studied four National Football League games during a recent season to determine the number of minutes of actual playing time that occurred during a 3-hour game. Surprisingly (at least to me), the average playing time was only 10.7 minutes per game! Assume the actual playing time per game follows the normal distribution with a standard deviation of 0.8 minutes. Determine the probability that the actual playing time for the next game will be between

a. 9.8 and 11.9 minutes
b. 11.0 and 12.1 minutes
c. 9.7 and 10.3 minutes

Answers can be found on ▶ **page 286**

Calculating Normal Probabilities Using Excel

Excel is a great tool for calculating normal probabilities. To demonstrate its use, I'm going to rely on a research study from the University of California that reported Americans consume an average of 34 gigabytes of data and information per day. Let's assume that the daily consumption of data per person follows a normal distribution with a standard deviation of 10 gigabytes. If so, what is the probability that a randomly selected American will consume less than 46 gigabytes of data today?

First, we'll calculate this probability using Table 6.2 and Figure 6.16:

$$z_{46} = \frac{x - \mu}{\sigma} = \frac{46 - 34}{10} = 1.20$$
$$P(x \le 46) = P(z \le 1.20) = 0.8849$$

The probability is 88.49%.

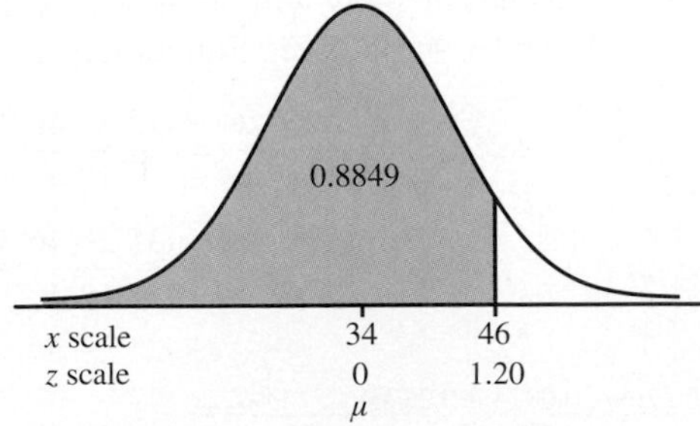

FIGURE 6.16 The Probability of an American Consuming Less Than 46 Gigabytes of Data a Day

Now we'll confirm this result with NORM.DIST, Excel's built-in function, which has the following characteristics:

=NORM.DIST(*x*, mean, standard_dev, cumulative)

where

cumulative = FALSE if you want the probability density function (we don't)
cumulative = TRUE if you want the cumulative probability (we do)

We'll choose the cumulative probability option (TRUE) because we want to include the probability of 46 gigabytes or less, which is shown in the shaded region in Figure 6.16.

=NORM.DIST(46, 34, 10, TRUE) = 0.8849

We can also use Excel's NORM.S.DIST function to determine the probability that a randomly selected American will consume 27 gigabytes or less today. We'll start by using Table 3 in Appendix A and Figure 6.17 to find this probability:

$$z_{27} = \frac{x - \mu}{\sigma} = \frac{27 - 34}{10} = -0.70$$

$$P(x \leq 27) = P(z \leq -0.70) = 0.2420$$

The probability is only 24.2%.

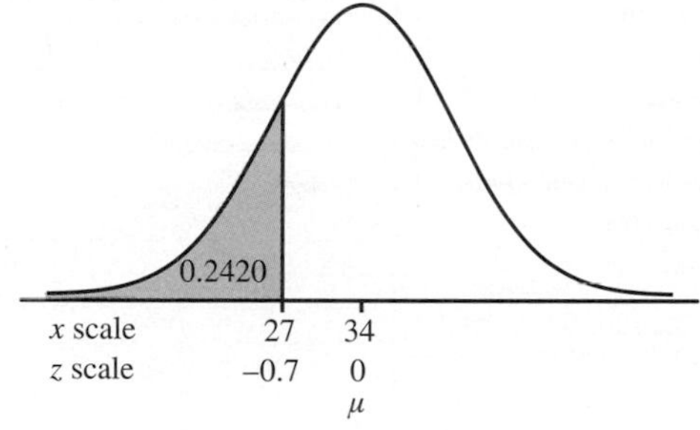

FIGURE 6.17 The Probability of an American Consuming Less Than 27 Gigabytes of Data a Day

We can confirm this result with Excel's NORM.S.DIST function which provides a probability for a specific z-score and has the following characteristics:

=NORM.S.DIST(z, cumulative)

We'll set cumulative = TRUE because we want to determine the probability of 27 gigabytes or less as shown here:

=NORM.S.DIST(−0.70, TRUE) = 0.2420

This result is consistent with the probability found using Table 3 in Appendix A. Occasionally, there will be a slight discrepancy between the probabilities determined from Tables 3 and 4 in Appendix A and those from Excel's NORM.DIST and NORM.S.DIST functions. This is because Tables 3 and 4 use only two decimal places for z-scores, whereas Excel uses many more. The rounding difference between the two methods is small enough to be ignored.

PHStat has the capability of providing not only the cumulative probabilities just illustrated but also the probabilities of intervals. For example, I'll use PHStat for Windows to determine the probability that a randomly selected American will consume *between* 27 and 46 gigabytes of data today. Using the probabilities shown in Figure 6.16 and Figure 6.17, we can construct the probability of interest, which is shown in Figure 6.18.

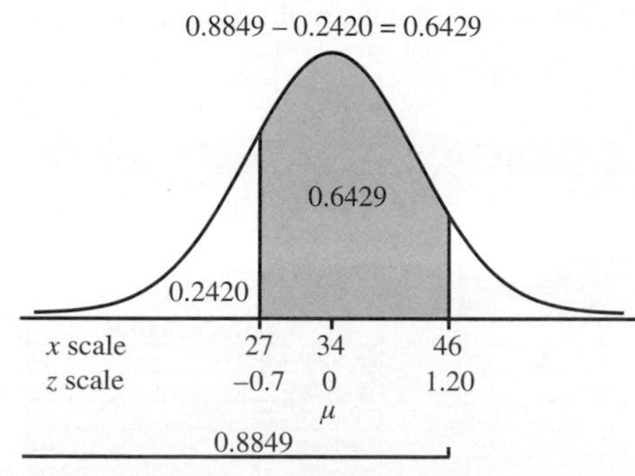

FIGURE 6.18 The Probability of an American Using Between 27 and 46 Gigabytes of Data a Day

According to Figure 6.18,

$$P(x \leq 46) = P(z \leq 1.20) = 0.8849$$
$$P(x \leq 27) = P(z \leq -0.70) = 0.2420$$
$$P(27 \leq x \leq 46) = 0.8849 - 0.2420 = 0.6429$$

We can use PHStat to calculate this probability directly by taking the following two steps:

1. Go to **Add-Ins > PHStat > Probability & Prob. Distributions > Normal**, as shown in Figure 6.19A.

FIGURE 6.19A
Calculating a Normal Probability Using PHStat (Step 1)

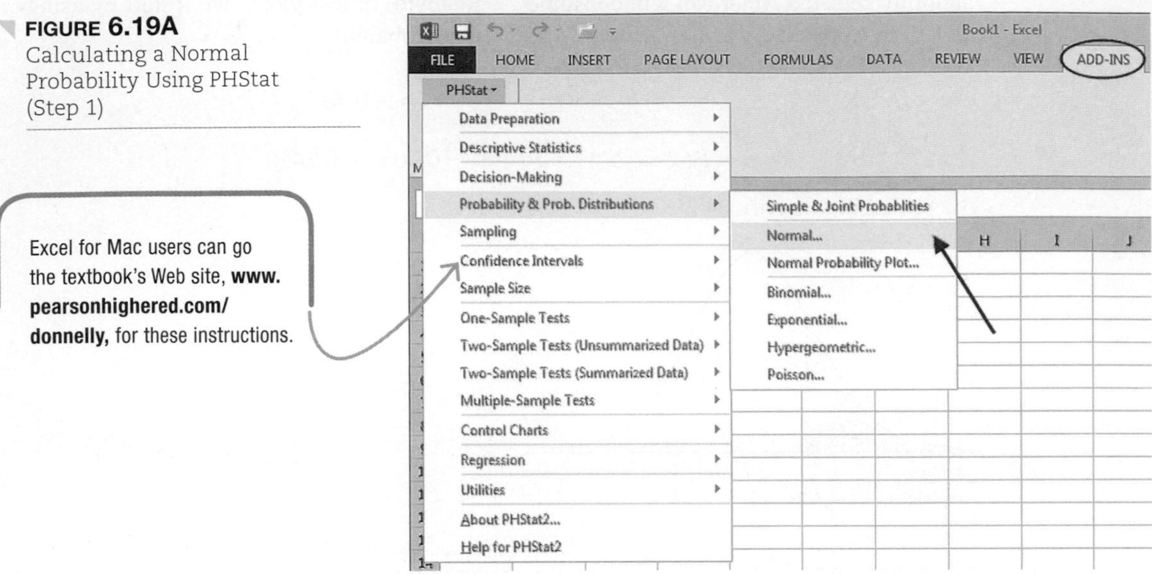

Excel for Mac users can go the textbook's Web site, **www.pearsonhighered.com/donnelly,** for these instructions.

2. Fill in the **Normal Probability Distribution** dialog box as shown in Figure 6.19B. Click **OK**.

FIGURE 6.19B
Calculating a Normal Probability Using PHStat (Step 2)

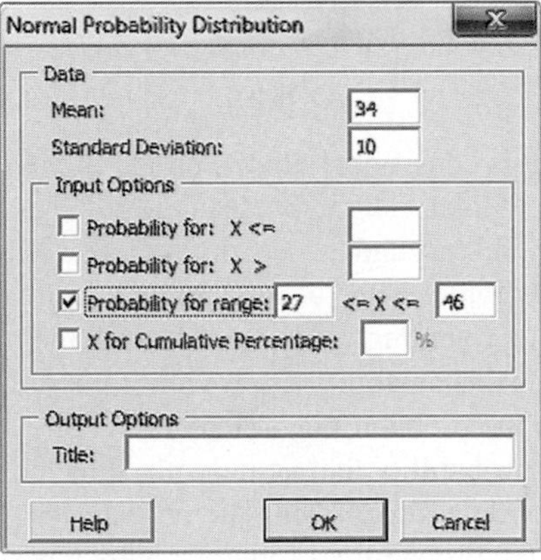

Figure 6.19C shows the normal probability we found in Figure 6.18. The slight discrepancy is due to rounding.

FIGURE 6.19C
Finished Normal Probabilities Calculated Using PHStat

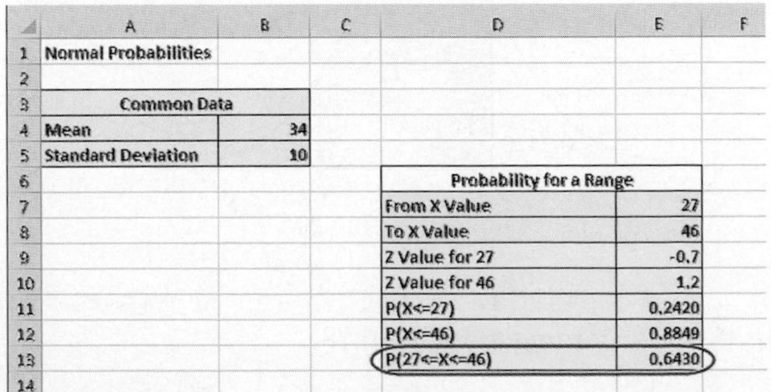

	A	B	C	D	E	F
1	Normal Probabilities					
2						
3	Common Data					
4	Mean	34				
5	Standard Deviation	10				
6				Probability for a Range		
7				From X Value	27	
8				To X Value	46	
9				Z Value for 27	-0.7	
10				Z Value for 46	1.2	
11				P(X<=27)	0.2420	
12				P(X<=46)	0.8849	
13				P(27<=X<=46)	0.6430	
14						

The following Your Turn section will help you hone your skills when it comes to calculating normal probabilities.

YOUR TURN #4

A weight-loss program claims that the average weight people lose during the first two weeks of the program is 5.0 lbs. Assuming the weight loss follows the normal distribution with a standard deviation of 3.0 lbs, use Excel and PHStat to answer the following questions.

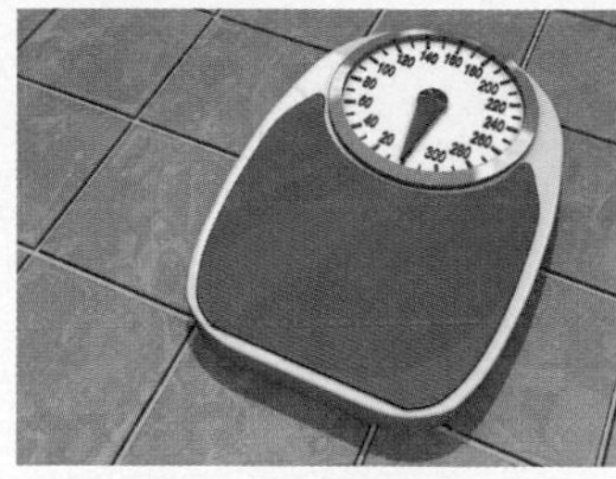

a. What is the probability that a person on the program will lose less than 7.0 lbs after two weeks?

b. What is the probability that a person on the program will gain weight after two weeks? (Hint: For example, losing 2 lbs means $x = 2$. Gaining 3 lbs results in $x = -3$. Continuous random variables can take on negative values.)

c. What is the probability that a person will lose between 1.0 and 4.0 lbs after two weeks?

Answers can be found on ▶ **page 286**

Using the Normal Distribution to Approximate the Binomial Distribution

Under the proper conditions, we can use the normal distribution to approximate the binomial probability distribution. Recall from Chapter 5 that a binomial probability distribution is a discrete probability distribution in which only two outcomes—either a success or a failure (hence the term "*bi*nomial"). Recall also that the binomial equation will calculate the probability of r successes in n trials, with $p =$ probability of a success for each trial and $q =$ probability of a failure.

The problem is that using the binomial formula from Chapter 5 to calculate probabilities gets very tedious if you have a large number of trials. This is where the normal distribution becomes a convenient tool to use to approximate the binomial distribution. If $np \geq 5$ and $nq \geq 5$, we can use the normal distribution to approximate the binomial probability, even though the normal distribution is a continuous distribution and the binomial distribution is not. In other words, if a decent-sized number of successes and number of failures are observed (such that $np \geq 5$ and $nq \geq 5$), the calculations for a normal distribution—with a few modifications—will work for the binomial distribution.

We can use the normal distribution to approximate the binomial distribution when $np \geq 5$ and $nq \geq 5$

Binominal approximations are often used in the business world in the area of quality control. For example, Carl's Jr., a fast-food chain with over 1,000 locations, recently experienced a 10% error rate in its drive-through orders. Carl's has defined a success as an order that was processed incorrectly, and a failure as an order that was processed correctly. Remember, the term *success* used with the binomial distribution is just a label for an outcome and is not necessarily associated with a positive result.

In the following year, the error rate fell to 6%. The reduction was attributed to the chain being able to hire employees with better language skills following a rise in unemployment rates during the period. Essentially, Carl's Jr. was able to choose applicants from a larger labor pool.

Assuming the chain has a 6% error rate, what is the probability that exactly 7 out of its next 120 drive-through customers will experience mistakes with their orders?

Recall from Chapter 5 that the BINOM.DIST function has the following characteristics:

$$=\text{BINOM.DIST}(x, n, p, \text{cumulative})$$

where

cumulative = FALSE, if you want to determine the probability of exactly x successes occurring

cumulative = TRUE, if you want to determine the probability of x or fewer successes occurring

Because we are counting individual customers, we are using discrete data rather than continuous data. We can use Excel to calculate this binomial probability as follows:

x represents the number of customers from the 120 whose order was not filled correctly.

$$x = 7 \quad n = 120 \quad p = 0.06$$

=BINOM.DIST(7, 120, 0.06, FALSE) = 0.1531

We use FALSE in the BINOM.DIST function because we are interested in the probability of exactly seven orders being incorrect.

Also from Chapter 5, the mean and standard deviation of this distribution are as follows:

$$\mu = np = (120)(0.06) = 7.2$$
$$\sigma = \sqrt{npq} = \sqrt{(120)(0.06)(1 - 0.06)} = \sqrt{6.768} = 2.60$$

The normal approximation can be used here to calculate binomial probabilities because the following conditions have been met:

$$np = (120)(0.06) = 7.2 \geq 5$$
$$nq = (120)(1 - 0.06) = 112.8 \geq 5$$

We can approximate the probability of exactly 7 orders from the next 120 customers being incorrect using the normal distribution. However, we know from earlier in this chapter that $P(x = 7) = 0$ because the normal distribution is a continuous distribution.

For the normal distribution, we can calculate only the probability for an interval, so we need to make a modification. We create an interval by subtracting 0.5 from 7.0 and adding 0.5 to 7.0, which is known as the **continuity correction factor**.

We then calculate the z-scores for $x = 6.5$ and $x = 7.5$.

The continuity correction factor allows us to approximate the binomial distribution with the normal distribution by adding and subtracting the value 0.5 to create the interval of interest.

$$z_{6.5} = \frac{x - \mu}{\sigma} = \frac{6.5 - 7.2}{2.6} = -0.27$$

$$z_{7.5} = \frac{x - \mu}{\sigma} = \frac{7.5 - 7.2}{2.6} = 0.12$$

Using Tables 3 and 4 in Appendix A, Figure 6.20, and the normal approximation, we can calculate the probability that exactly seven of the orders will be incorrect as follows:

$$P(x = 7) = P(6.5 \leq x \leq 7.5)$$
$$P(x \leq 7.5) = P(z \leq 0.12) = 0.5478$$
$$P(x \leq 6.5) = P(z \leq -0.27) = 0.3936$$
$$P(6.5 \leq x \leq 7.5) = 0.5478 - 0.3936 = 0.1542$$

FIGURE 6.20
The Probability of Exactly 7 Incorrect Orders Occurring Out of 120 Orders

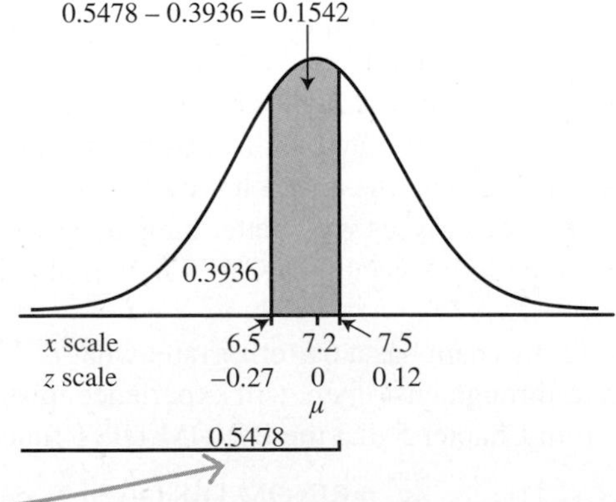

This is the probability that less than 7.5 of the 120 customers will have an incorrect order.

Notice that this is very close to the results of Excel's BINOM.DIST function, 0.1531. If we wanted to expand our example to calculate the probability of exactly 7, 8, or 9 incorrect orders, we would examine the area between 6.5 and 9.5 under the normal curve. I'll be sure to give you a chance to try this type of question in the next Your Turn section.

Let's explore the probability of 4 or fewer orders of the next 120 being incorrect. Using Excel, we can determine the binomial probability:

=BINOM.DIST(4, 120, 0.06, TRUE) = 0.1473

We use TRUE in the BINOM.DIST function because we are interested in not just the probability of four orders being correct, but the probability of 0, 1, 2, 3, or 4 orders being incorrect.

Using the continuity correction factor to calculate the normal approximation, we add 0.5 to 4, the right boundary of our interval. The left side of the normal distribution is $-\infty$ and therefore does not need a correction factor. We now calculate the z-score for $x = 4.5$:

$$z_{4.5} = \frac{x - \mu}{\sigma} = \frac{4.5 - 7.2}{2.6} = -1.04$$

Figure 6.21 shows the normal approximation to the probability that 4 or fewer of Carl's Jr. drive-through customers from the next 120 arrivals will experience a mistake with their order.

$$P(x \le 4.5) = P(z \le -1.04) = 0.1492$$

FIGURE 6.21
The Probability of 4 or Fewer Incorrect Orders Occurring Out of 120 Orders

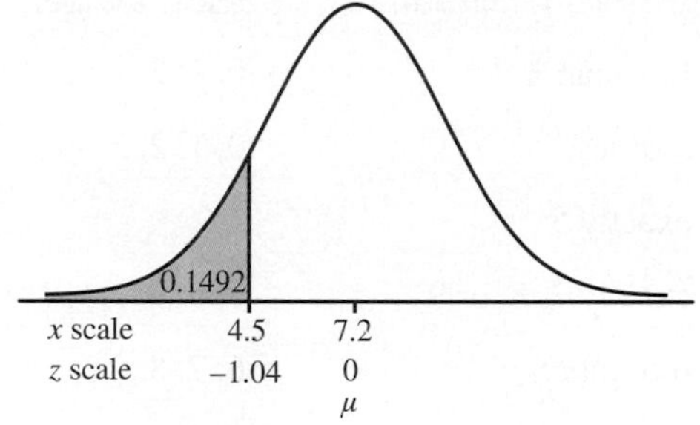

Notice that this is very close to the results of Excel's BINOM.DIST function, 0.1473.

Finally, let's examine the binomial probability that more than 8 of 120 drive-through customers will receive incorrect orders. Because this question includes the discrete values 9, 10, 11, and 12, on up to the value of 120, we determine this probability as follows using Excel:

$$P(x \ge 9) = 1 - P(x \le 8)$$
$$=\text{BINOM.DIST}(8, 120, 0.06, \text{TRUE}) = 0.7061$$
$$P(x > 8) = P(x \ge 9) = 1 - 0.7061 = 0.2939$$

Now we need to construct the interval for the normal approximation using the continuity correction factor. Because the value 9 is on the left side of the boundary, we subtract 0.5 from 9. The right side of the normal distribution is $+\infty$ and therefore does not need a correction factor. We now calculate the z-score for $x = 8.5$:

$$z_{8.5} = \frac{x - \mu}{\sigma} = \frac{8.5 - 7.2}{2.6} = 0.5$$

Figure 6.22 shows the normal approximation for the probability of more than 8 of 120 drive-through customers experiencing mistakes with their orders.

$$P(x > 8.5) = P(z > 0.5) = 1.0 - 0.6915 = 0.3085$$

FIGURE 6.22
The Probability of More Than 8 Incorrect Orders Occurring Out of 120 Orders

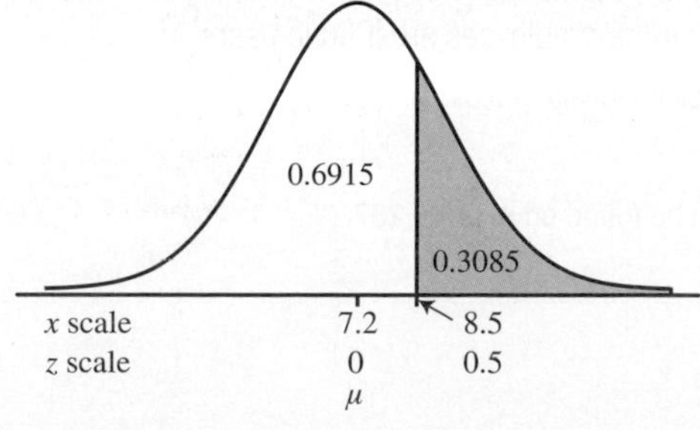

This probability is fairly close to the results of Excel's BINOM.DIST function, 0.2939.

Sometimes my students have difficulty deciding when to add and when to subtract the 0.5 continuity correction factor. In general, the rules are as follows:

- Subtract 0.5 from the left side of the boundary, which moves it slightly to the left.
- Add 0.5 to the right side of the boundary, which moves it slightly to the right.
- If the left boundary is $-\infty$ or the right boundary is $+\infty$, no correction factor is needed for that boundary.

Table 6.4 summarizes these rules and lists some examples to help clarify them.

Be careful of the wording of the probability statement so that you don't confuse phrases like "less than 3" with "3 or less"; they refer to different discrete values.

TABLE 6.4 | RULES FOR ADDING AND SUBTRACTING THE CONTINUITY CORRECTION FACTOR WHEN APPROXIMATING A BINOMINAL DISTRIBUTION

PROBABILITY STATEMENT	DISCRETE VALUES	NORMAL PROBABILITY
less than 3	0, 1, 2	$P(x \leq 2.5)$
3 or less	0, 1, 2, 3	$P(x \leq 3.5)$
exactly 5	5	$P(4.5 \leq x \leq 5.5)$
exactly 7, 8, or 9	7, 8, 9	$P(6.5 \leq x \leq 9.5)$
6 or more	6, 7, 8, . . ., n	$P(x \geq 5.5)$
more than 6	7, 8, . . ., n	$P(x \geq 6.5)$

As promised, the next Your Turn section will help you test your skills on this procedure.

YOUR TURN #5

A March 13, 2010, *Wall Street Journal* article reported that, to the chagrin of Microsoft management, approximately 10% of Microsoft employees were iPhone users. Of course, iPhones are a product of Apple, Inc., Microsoft's biggest competitor. The following is an excerpt from the article, titled "Forbidden Fruit: Microsoft Workers Hide Their iPhones" which highlighted the risk of being an iPhone user at a Microsoft function in September, 2009.

"At an all-company meeting in a Seattle sports stadium, one hapless employee used his iPhone to snap photos of Microsoft Chief Executive Steve Ballmer. Mr. Ballmer snatched the iPhone out of the employee's hands, placed it on the ground and pretended to stomp on it in front of thousands of Microsoft workers, according to people present."

Suppose 60 Microsoft employees are randomly selected. Use the normal approximation to the binomial distribution to determine the probability that

a. less than five employees are iPhone users.
b. exactly six, seven, eight, or nine employees are iPhone users.
c. nine or more employees are iPhone users.

Based on: Nick Wingfield, "Forbidden Fruit: Microsoft Workers Hide Their iPhones," *Wall Street Journal,* March 12, 2010.

Answers can be found on ▶ **page 287**

6.2 Section Problems

Basic Skills

6.1 For a standard normal distribution, determine the following:

a. $P(z \leq 1.50)$
b. $P(z \leq -1.22)$
c. $P(-0.86 \leq z \leq 1.76)$
d. $P(0.32 \leq z \leq 2.15)$

6.2 For a standard normal distribution, determine the following:

a. $P(z > 1.35)$
b. $P(z > -0.42)$
c. $P(-1.70 \leq z \leq -0.65)$
d. $P(-1.69 \leq z \leq 0.20)$

6.3 A random variable follows the normal probability distribution with a mean of 80 and a standard deviation of 20. What is the probability that a randomly selected value from this population

a. is less than 90?
b. is less than 65?
c. is more than 110?
d. is more than 40?

6.4 A random variable follows the normal probability distribution with a mean of 124 and a standard deviation of 27. What is the probability that a randomly selected value from this population

a. is between 100 and 140?
b. is between 130 and 170?
c. is between 65 and 90?
d. is between 120 and 180?

6.5 A binomial distribution has $p = 0.60$ and $n = 40$.

a. What are the mean and standard deviation for this distribution?
b. What is the probability of exactly 27 successes?
c. What is the probability of less than 30 successes?
d. What is the probability of more than 20 successes?

6.6 A binomial distribution has $p = 0.22$ and $n = 75$.

a. What are the mean and standard deviation for this distribution?
b. What is the probability of exactly 11 successes?
c. What is the probability of 10 to 18 successes?
d. What is the probability of 8 to 15 successes?

Applications

6.7 The average number of miles driven on a full tank of gas in a Hyundai Veracruz before its low-fuel light comes on is 320. Assume this mileage follows the normal distribution with a standard deviation of 30 miles. What is the probability that, before the low-fuel light comes on, the car will travel

a. less than 330 miles on the next tank of gas?
b. more than 308 miles on the next tank of gas?
c. between 305 and 325 miles on the next tank of gas?
d. exactly 340 miles on the next tank of gas?

6.8 According to a recent survey by Smith Travel Research, the average daily rate for a luxury hotel in the United States is \$237.22. Assume the daily rate follows a normal probability distribution with a standard deviation of \$21.45.

a. What is the probability that a randomly selected luxury hotel's daily rate will be
 1. less than \$250?
 2. more than \$260?
 3. between \$210 and \$240?
b. The managers of a local luxury hotel would like to set the hotel's average daily rate at the 80th percentile, which is the rate below which 80% of hotels' rates are set. What rate should they choose for their hotel?

6.9 Major League Baseball teams have become concerned about the length of games. During a recent season, games averaged 2 hours and 52 minutes (172 minutes) to complete. Assume the length of games follows the normal distribution with a standard deviation of 16 minutes.

a. What is the probability that a randomly selected game will be completed in
 1. 200 minutes or less?
 2. more than 200 minutes?
 3. 150 minutes or less?
 4. more than 150 minutes?
 5. exactly 150 minutes?
b. What is the completion time in which 90% of the games will be finished?

6.10 A study conducted by Hershey's discovered that Americans consumed an average of 11.4 pounds of chocolate per year (seems low to me). Let's assume that the annual chocolate consumption follows the normal distribution with a standard deviation of 3.6 pounds.

a. What is the probability that I will consume
 1. less than 7 lbs of chocolate next year?
 2. more than 9 lbs of chocolate next year?
 3. between 8 and 12 lbs of chocolate next year?
 4. exactly 10 lbs of chocolate next year?
b. What is the annual consumption of chocolate that represents the 60th percentile?

6.11 According to the Internal Revenue Service, the average income tax refund for the 2011 tax year was \$2,913. Assume the refund per person follows the normal probability distribution with a standard deviation of \$950.

a. What is the probability that a randomly selected tax return refund from the 2011 tax year will be
 1. more than \$2,000?
 2. between \$1,600 and \$2,500?
 3. between \$3,200 and \$4,000?

b. Confirm the answers to part a using Excel or PHStat.
c. What refund amount represents the 35th percentile of tax returns?

6.12 Assume the cost of an extended 100,000 mile warranty for a particular SUV follows the normal distribution with a mean of $1,600 and a standard deviation of $75.

a. Determine the interval of warranty costs from various companies that are
1. one standard deviation around the mean.
2. two standard deviations around the mean.
3. three standard deviations around the mean.
b. You see an ad for an extended warranty for this type of vehicle for $1,900. Based on the previous results, what conclusions can you make?

6.13 The average price of a 42-in. television on Best Buy's Web site is $790. Assume the price of these televisions follows the normal distribution with a standard deviation of $160.

a. What is the probability that a randomly selected television from the site sells for
1. less than $700?
2. between $400 and $500?
3. between $900 and $1,000
b. Confirm the answers to part a using Excel or PHStat.
c. The price intervals in parts a)2 and a)3 are equal ($100). Why are the probabilities so different?
d. Suppose I am shopping on Best Buy's Web site for a new 42-in. television and my wife (also known as she-who-has-veto-power-over-all-electronic-purchases) suggests we set a budget of $750 for the purchase. There are 15 42-inch televisions on the site. How many televisions are within my budget?

6.14 A credit score measures a person's creditworthiness. According to the credit-scoring company Experian, the average credit score for Americans in March 2013 was 736. Assume the scores are normally distributed with a standard deviation of 40. Determine the interval of credit scores that are

a. one standard deviation around the mean.
b. two standard deviations around the mean.
c. three standard deviations around the mean.

6.15 According to eMarketer, adults in the United States average 82 minutes per day on mobile devices in 2012. Assume that minutes per day on mobile devices follow the normal distribution and has a standard deviation of 27 minutes.

a. What is the probability that the amount of time spent today on mobile devices by a particular U.S. adult is
1. less than 70 minutes?
2. more than 65 minutes?
3. between 85 and 110 minutes?
b. Confirm the answers to part a using Excel or PHStat.
c. Which number of minutes per day represents the 75th percentile?

6.16 Curling is a Winter Olympic sport in which people slide a stone along a sheet of ice toward a target area. The game is similar to shuffleboard. Two sweepers with brooms lead the stone along the ice, attempting to influence its path toward the target. According to the *Journal of Sports Science and Medicine,* the average heart rate of a person who sweeps is 185 beats per minute, as compared with 80 beats per minute for an adult at rest. Assume the heart rate for a sweeper follows the normal distribution with a standard deviation of 5 beats per minute.

a. What is the probability that a sweeper's heart rate is
1. more than 187 beats per minute?
2. less than 181 beats per minute?
3. between 180 and 183 beats per minute?
4. between 188 and 193 beats per minute?
b. Confirm the answers to part a using Excel or PHStat.

6.17 Census data show that 67% of U.S. students went to college or a trade school within a year of graduating from high school. A random sample of 20 high school graduates is selected. Use the normal approximation to the binomial distribution to answer the following:

a. What are the mean and standard deviation for this distribution?
b. What is the probability that less than 16 of the 20 students will go to college?
c. What is the probability that exactly 16 of the 20 students will go to college?
d. What is the probability that more than 14 of the 20 students will go to college?
e. What is the probability that 10, 11, 12, 13, or 14 of the 20 students will go to college?

6.18 According to the Pew Research Center, 33% of U.S. adults owned a tablet in 2012. Use the normal approximation to the binomial distribution to calculate the probability that, from a sample of 24 U.S. adults,

a. less than 10 adults own a tablet.
b. 6, 7, 8, 9, or 10 adults own a tablet.
c. 11, 12, 13, or 14 adults own a tablet.
d. exactly seven adults own a tablet.

6.19 According to FlightStats.com, 82.8% of American Airline flights were on time during 2012. Assume this percentage still holds true for American Airlines. Using the normal approximation to the binomial distribution, determine the probability that, of the next 30 American Airlines flights,

a. less than 22 flights will arrive on time.
b. exactly 26 flights will arrive on time.
c. 21, 22, 23, or 24 will arrive on time.
d. 24, 25, 26, 27, or 28 flights will arrive on time.

6.20 According to Gartner, Inc., 39.2% of mobile phones worldwide use the Android operating system in 2013. A random sample of 30 mobile phone users was selected in 2013. Assuming this estimate is true, use the normal approximation to the binomial distribution to answer the following:

a. Calculate the mean and standard deviation for this distribution.

b. What is the probability that 13 or more of the 30 mobile phone users have an Android operating system?

c. What is the probability that exactly 14 of the 30 mobile phone users have an Android operating system?

d. What is the probability that 7, 8, or 9 of the 30 mobile phone users have an Android operating system?

e. What is the probability that 14, 15, or 16 of the 30 mobile phone users have an Android operating system?

6.3 Exponential Probability Distributions

The **exponential probability distribution** is a continuous distribution that is commonly used to measure the time between events of interest such as the time between customer arrivals or the time between failures in a business process.

Exponential probability density function the mathematical expression that describes the shape of the exponential probability distribution.

The **exponential probability distribution** is a continuous distribution that is commonly used to measure the time between events of interest, such as the time between customer arrivals or the time between failures in a business process. The mathematical expression that describes the shape of the curve of such a distribution is known as the **exponential probability density function.** The function for the curve is shown in Equation 6.3.

Formula 6.3 for the Exponential Probability Density Function

$$f(x) = \lambda e^{-\lambda x}$$

where

$e = 2.71828$
$\lambda =$ The mean number of occurrences over the interval
$x =$ Any continuous number of interest

You were first introduced to the symbol λ (lambda) back in Chapter 5 when the Poisson probability distribution was discussed. In the example used in Chapter 5, λ represented the average number of customers who arrived per hour at a drive-through window for a bank. If $\lambda = 12$ customers per hour, then the average number of minutes between customers, or μ, is

$$\mu = \frac{1}{\lambda} = \frac{1 \text{ hour}}{12 \text{ customers}} \times \frac{60 \text{ minutes}}{1 \text{ hour}} = 5 \text{ minutes per customer}$$

When the number of arrivals per hour follows the Poisson distribution, the average time between arrivals will follow the exponential distribution. In other words, a discrete random variable that follows the Poisson distribution with a mean equal to λ has a counterpart continuous random variable that follows the exponential distribution with a mean equal to $\mu = 1/\lambda$.

A discrete random variable that follows the Poisson distribution with a mean equal to λ has a counterpart continuous random variable that follows the exponential distribution with a mean equal to $\mu = 1/\lambda$.

The shapes of exponential distributions are shown in Figure 6.23 on the next page. As you can see, the shape of each curve is right-skewed and depends on its mean, μ. Recall from Chapter 3, a right-skewed distribution is one where the data are concentrated on the right end of the distribution and as we "ski down the slope" of the distribution, we are moving toward the right.

FIGURE 6.23
Three Exponential Probability Distributions When $\lambda = 3.0$, $\lambda = 2.0$, and $\lambda = 1.0$

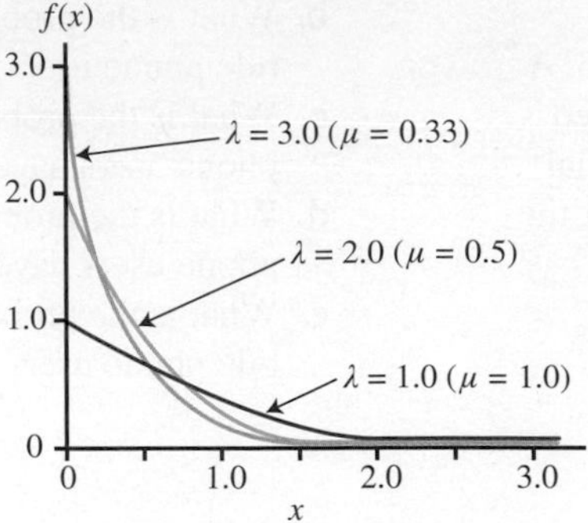

There are three major differences between exponential and normal distributions:

1. The exponential distribution is right-skewed, whereas the normal distribution is bell-shaped and symmetrical.
2. The shape of the exponential distribution is completely described by only one parameter, μ. On the other hand, the normal distribution requires two parameters, μ and σ, to describe its shape.
3. The values for an exponential random variable cannot be negative. For example, it doesn't make sense for the next customer to arrive −2 minutes after the previous customer. There is no such restriction for normal random variables.

As I mentioned earlier, the exponential distribution is particularly good at describing random variables, such as time between customer arrivals, where the majority of the data values tend to be on the left side, or lower end, of the distribution.

Calculating Exponential Probabilities

Let's put the exponential distribution to work with the following example. Suppose the average time between customer arrivals at the deli counter of a Piggly Wiggly grocery store (awesome name for a store) is 4 minutes. What is the probability that the next customer will arrive at the counter within the next 2 minutes? Figure 6.24 shows the exponential distribution for the deli counter. We are looking for the shaded area under the curve labeled $P(x \leq 2)$.

FIGURE 6.24
An Exponential Distribution for Customer Arrivals When $P(x \leq 2)$

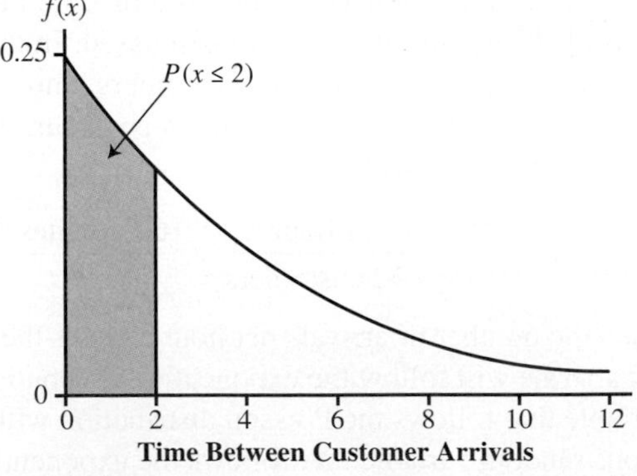

Exponential cumulative distribution function used to calculate the probability that a random variable that follows the exponential distribution is less than a specific value.

To find that area, we use Equation 6.4, which shows the formula for the **exponential cumulative distribution function**.

Formula 6.4 for the Exponential Cumulative Distribution Function

$$P(x \leq a) = 1 - e^{-a\lambda}$$

where

$e = 2.71828$
$\lambda =$ The mean number of occurrences over the interval
$a =$ Any number of interest

First, we need to decide on the value for λ, which, quite honestly, is a decision with which some of my students struggle. One way to help you remember is to realize that λ is always a countable rate, such as number of arriving customers per hour. In contrast, μ is always a measurable interval, such as the number of minutes between customer arrivals. In our example, we are told that $\mu = 4$ minutes per customer, so we need to find λ as follows:

$$\lambda = \frac{1}{\mu} = \frac{1 \text{ customer}}{4 \text{ minutes}} = 0.25 \text{ customers per minute}$$

The parameter λ is always a countable rate, such as number of arriving customers per hour. In contrast, μ is always a measurable interval, such as the number of minutes between customer arrivals.

It's important to remember that λ and μ are expressed in the same units (that is., minutes in this example). Applying Equation 6.4 to our example with $a = 2$ minutes, we have the following:

$$P(x \le a) = 1 - e^{-a\lambda}$$
$$P(x \le 2) = 1 - e^{-(2)(0.25)} = 1 - (2.71828)^{-0.5}$$
$$P(x \le 2) = 1 - 0.6065 = 0.3935$$

There is about a 39% chance that the next customer will arrive within the next 2 minutes.

What about the probability that the next customer will arrive between 4 and 8 minutes from now? We can still use Equation 6.4 by recognizing that

$$P(4 \le x \le 8) = P(x \le 8) - P(x \le 4)$$
$$P(x \le 8) = 1 - e^{-(8)(0.25)} \qquad P(x \le 4) = 1 - e^{-(4)(0.25)}$$
$$= 1 - 0.1353 \qquad = 1 - 0.3679$$
$$= 0.8647 \qquad = 0.6321$$
$$P(4 \le x \le 8) = 0.8647 - 0.6321 = 0.2326$$

Figure 6.25 also shows this shaded area, which is labeled $P(4 \le x \le 8)$.

FIGURE 6.25
An Exponential Distribution for Customer Arrivals When $P(4 \le x \le 8)$

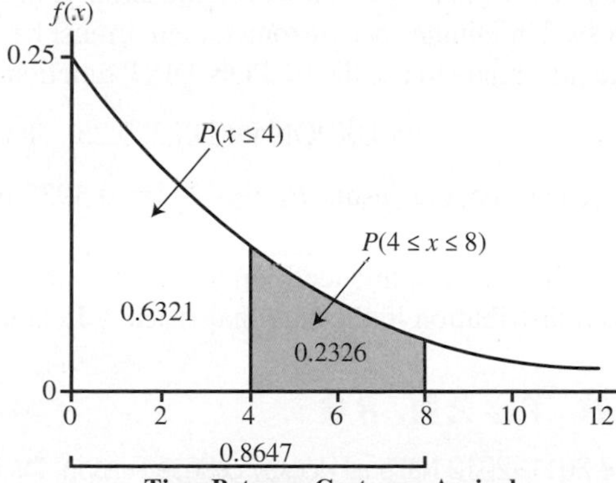

Therefore, there is a 23.26% chance that the next person will arrive at the Piggly Wiggly deli counter within the next 4 to 8 minutes.

The standard deviation of the exponential distribution is the same as the mean, as Equation 6.5 shows.

Formula 6.5 for the Standard Deviation of the Exponential Distribution

$$\sigma = \mu = \frac{1}{\lambda}$$

So, for exponential distributions, there are no nasty standard deviation calculations that we dealt with in previous chapters. For our Piggly Wiggly example, the standard deviation is simply as follows:

$$\sigma = \mu = 4 \text{ minutes}$$

As with our previous distributions, the standard deviation of the exponential distribution measures the average variability around the mean of the distribution.

Calculating Exponential Probabilities Using Excel

We can confirm the probability that the next customer at a Piggly Wiggly will arrive at the deli counter within the next two minutes using EXPON.DIST, Excel's built-in function, which has the following characteristics:

$$=\text{EXPON.DIST}(x, \lambda, \text{cumulative})$$

where

cumulative = FALSE if you want the probability density function
cumulative = TRUE if you want the cumulative probability

We choose the TRUE option for cumulative because we want the probability that the next customer will arrive in 2 minutes *or less.* The parameter λ refers to the average *rate* of arrivals over a specific interval. In our Piggly Wiggly example, customers arrive, on average, every four minutes (μ). We can convert this average value into a rate (λ) as follows:

$$\mu = 4 \text{ minutes per customer}$$

$$\lambda = \frac{1}{\mu} = \frac{1 \text{ customer}}{4 \text{ minutes}} = 0.25 \text{ customers per minute}$$

An average of 0.25 customers each minute is equivalent to

$$\left(\frac{0.25 \text{ customers}}{\text{minute}}\right)\left(\frac{60 \text{ minutes}}{\text{hour}}\right) = 15 \text{ customers per hour}$$

In other words, if customers are arriving every 4 minutes, 15 customers arrive in 1 hour (there are 15 four-minute intervals in an hour). It's simply a matter of explaining the same information two different ways. However, the terms μ and λ must be based on the same units. If μ is expressed in minutes per customer, then λ must be expressed in customers per minute.

We're now ready to use the EXPON.DIST function to calculate $P(x \leq 2)$ with $\lambda = 0.25$.

$$=\text{EXPON.DIST}(2, 0.25, \text{TRUE}) = 0.3935$$

As you can see, our result, $P(x \leq 2) = 0.3935$ matches what we obtained using Equation 6.4.

Take a shot (no pun intended) on the next Your Turn problem that involves using the exponential distribution in the National Hockey League.

YOUR TURN #6

During the 2011–2012 National Hockey League season, the Detroit Red Wings led the league in shots on goal, averaging 32.2 per 60-minute game. Assume that the number of minutes between shots on goal follows the exponential distribution.

a. Calculate the following probabilities using Equations 6.4 and 6.5 and verify them using Excel.

  1. The probability that the next shot on goal will occur during the next minute.

  2. The probability that the next shot on goal will occur between 2 and 3 minutes from now.

b. Verify your answers from part a using Excel.

c. What is the standard deviation for this distribution?

(Because I'm such a nice guy, I'll give you the following hint: You need to convert 32.2 shots per hour into minutes between shots.)

Answers can be found on ▶ **page 287**

6.3 Section Problems

Basic Skills

6.21 An exponential probability distribution has a mean equal to 10 minutes per customer. Calculate the following probabilities for the distribution:

a. $P(x \leq 12)$
b. $P(x \leq 2)$
c. $P(x \leq 10)$
d. $P(x \leq 5)$

6.22 An exponential probability distribution has a mean equal to 7 minutes per customer. Calculate the following probabilities for the distribution:

a. $P(x > 12)$
b. $P(x > 3)$
c. $P(7 \leq x \leq 10)$
d. $P(1 \leq x \leq 5)$

6.23 An exponential probability distribution has lambda equal to 24 customers per hour. What is the probability that the next customer will arrive

a. within the next minute?
b. within the next 30 seconds?
c. within the next 5 minutes?
d. within the next 10 minutes?

6.24 An exponential probability distribution has lambda equal to 18 customers per hour. What is the probability that the next customer will arrive

a. within the next 45 seconds?
b. within the next 1 to 3 minutes?
c. within the next 2 to 5 minutes?
d. within the next 4 to 10 minutes?

Applications

6.25 Suppose that the average time a fully charged 6-volt laptop battery will operate a computer is 3.2 hours and follows the exponential probability distribution.

a. Determine the probability that the next charge will last
  1. less than 2 hours.
  2. between 2.5 and 4.0 hours.
  3. more than 3.5 hours.
b. Confirm the answers to part a using Excel.

6.26 Assume the average time between students walking up to my desk during a statistics exam to ask a question in a desperate attempt to gain some insight into how to solve a problem is 8 minutes and follows the exponential probability distribution.

a. What is the probability that the next desperate student will approach my desk
  1. within the next 2 minutes?
  2. within the next 4 minutes?
  3. between the next 3 to 5 minutes?
  4. in more than 10 minutes?
b. Confirm the answers to part a using Excel.

6.27 Customers arrive at a local ATM at an average rate of 15 per hour. Assume the time between arrivals follows the exponential probability distribution.

a. What is the probability that the next customer will arrive
  1. within the next 3 minutes?
  2. in more than 7 minutes?
  3. between 4 and 8 minutes?
b. Confirm the answers to part a using Excel.

6.28 During lunch hour, customers arrive at a fast-food drive-through window, on average, every 2.5 minutes. Assume arrival time follows the exponential probability distribution.

a. What is the probability that the next customer will arrive
  1. within the next 2 minutes?
  2. in more than 5 minutes?
  3. between 1 and 4 minutes?
b. Confirm the answers to part a using Excel.

6.4 Uniform Probability Distributions

With the **continuous uniform probability distribution**, the probability of any interval in the distribution is equal to any other interval with the same width.

Our third and final continuous distribution is the **continuous uniform probability distribution**, where the probability of any interval in the distribution is equal to any other interval with the same width. To illustrate this distribution, I'll use the following example. I have always considered myself an incredibly lucky man because I have a wife who loves to play golf almost as much as I do. As a matter of fact, Deb's last birthday present was a golf club. (I'll take shopping for golf equipment over jewelry anytime!)

The pace of play is a very important statistic for golf course management. Courses that have a reputation for slow play risk losing golf clientele who do not wish to spend their entire round waiting for the group in front of them to finish. Suppose the time that it takes to play a round of golf at Deerfield Golf Club follows the uniform probability distribution with a minimum time of 4 hours (240 minutes) and a maximum time of 4 hours and 50 minutes (290 minutes). This means that any 1-minute interval within this range of time has the same probability of occurring. Let's explore how to determine the probability that our next round of golf at Deerfield will take less than 4 hours and 12 minutes (252 minutes).

For example, the probability of finishing a round between 240 and 250 minutes is the same as the probability of finishing between 260 and 270 minutes. Both intervals are 10 minutes long.

The mathematical expression that describes the shape of the uniform distribution is known as the **continuous uniform probability density function.** The formula for the function is shown in Equation 6.6.

Continuous uniform probability density function the mathematical expression that describes the shape of the continuous uniform probability distribution.

Formula 6.6 for the Continuous Uniform Probability Density Function

$$f(x) = \frac{1}{b - a} \quad \text{if } a \leq x \leq b$$

$$f(x) = 0 \quad \text{otherwise}$$

where

a = Smallest allowable continuous random variable
b = Largest allowable continuous random variable

For our Deerfield example,

$$a = 240 \text{ (4 hours)}$$

$$b = 290 \text{ (4 hours 50 minutes)}$$

$$f(x) = \frac{1}{b - a} = \frac{1}{290 - 240} = \frac{1}{50} = 0.02$$

The shape of the uniform probability distribution, which is shown in Figure 6.26, is rectangular. This particular uniform distribution has a height of $f(x) = 0.02$ between $a = 240$ and $b = 290$ minutes.

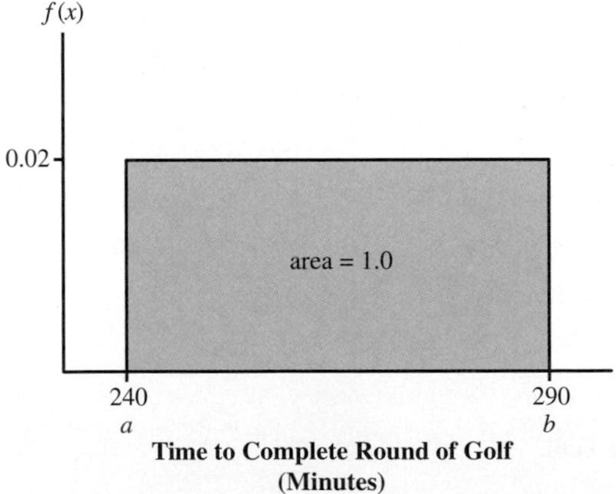

FIGURE 6.26 A Continuous Uniform Distribution

The value $f(x)$ in Figure 6.26 refers to the probability of a one-unit interval within the distribution occurring. For example, the probability that the next round of golf will be completed between the 240th and 241st minutes equals 2%. The probability that the next round of golf will be completed between the 241st and 242nd minute also equals 2%, and so on. Because there are 50 of these 1-minute intervals in this distribution, the total probability, or area, for our distribution equals

$$(0.02)(50) = 1.0$$

Uniform cumulative distribution function used to calculate the probability that a random variable that follows the uniform distribution is between two specific values.

To find the probability that a continuous uniform random variable will fall between two particular values, which we will refer to as x_1 and x_2, we use Equation 6.7, which shows the **uniform cumulative distribution function.**

Formula 6.7 for the Uniform Cumulative Distribution Function

$$P(x_1 \le x \le x_2) = \frac{x_2 - x_1}{b - a}$$

This equation essentially calculates the area of the distribution between the values x_1 and x_2. To determine the probability that the next round of golf at Deerfield will take less than 252 minutes, we use Equation 6.7, as follows:

$$x_1 = 240 \qquad x_2 = 252$$

$$P(x_1 \le x \le x_2) = \frac{x_2 - x_1}{b - a}$$

$$P(240 \le x \le 252) = \frac{252 - 240}{290 - 240} = \frac{12}{50} = 0.24$$

There is a 24% chance that the next round of golf at Deerfield will be completed in less than 4 hours and 12 minutes (252 minutes). The shaded area in Figure 6.27 illustrates this probability.

FIGURE 6.27
A Continuous Uniform Distribution When $P(240 \le x \le 252)$

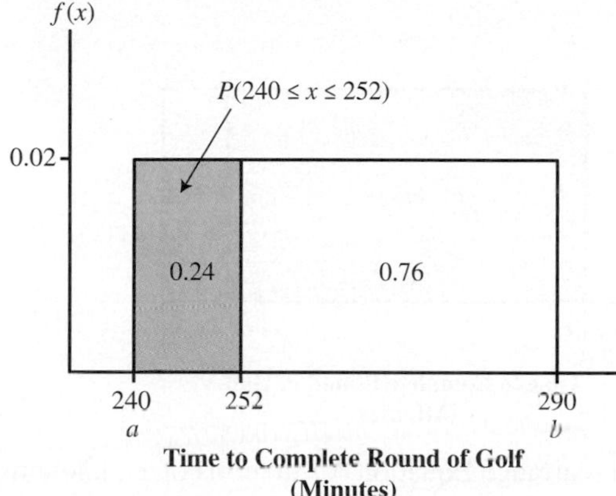

Next, we'll look at the probability that the next round of golf at Deerfield will be completed between 4 hours and 10 minutes (250 minutes) and four hours and 45 minutes (285 minutes) using Equation 6.7.

$$x_1 = 250 \qquad x_2 = 285$$

$$P(x_1 \le x \le x_2) = \frac{x_2 - x_1}{b - a}$$

$$P(250 \le x \le 285) = \frac{285 - 250}{290 - 240} = \frac{35}{50} = 0.70$$

There is a 70% chance that the next round of golf at Deerfield will be completed within this time interval. The shaded area in Figure 6.28 illustrates this probability.

FIGURE 6.28
A Continuous Uniform Distribution When $P(250 \le x \le 285)$

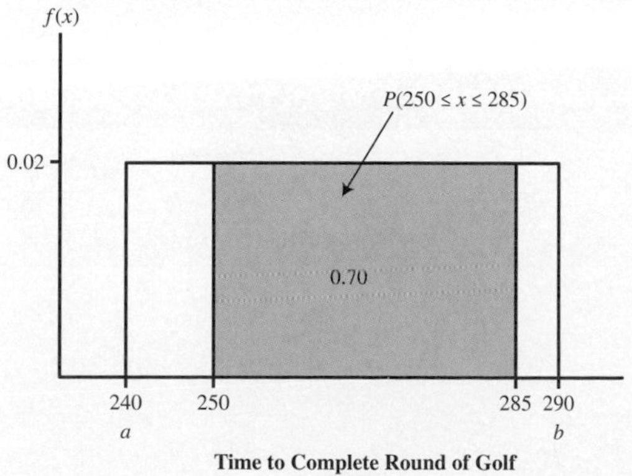

What happens if we try to calculate the probability that the next round will take exactly 250 minutes? For this example, both x_1 and x_2 equal 250. Using Equation 6.7, we have

The probability that a continuous random variable will equal an exact value, such as 250 in this example, will always be equal to zero.

$$P(x_1 \leq x \leq x_2) = \frac{x_2 - x_1}{b - a}$$

$$P(250 \leq x \leq 250) = \frac{250 - 250}{290 - 240} = \frac{0}{50} = 0$$

No, I didn't make a mistake here. This result is consistent with the statement made earlier in the chapter that we can discuss only the probability of a particular interval occurring for continuous distributions. The probability of arriving at an exact value for these types of distributions will always be equal to zero.

The managers of the Deerfield course have a goal that 80% of the rounds played on the course will be completed within 4 hours and 30 minutes (270 minutes). Is this goal being met under the current uniform distribution? To answer this question, we need to find the value of x_2 in Equation 6.7 that covers 80% of the area under the distribution. This is also known as the 80th percentile of the distribution. Figure 6.29 shows this graphically.

FIGURE 6.29 The 80th Percentile of a Continuous Uniform Distribution

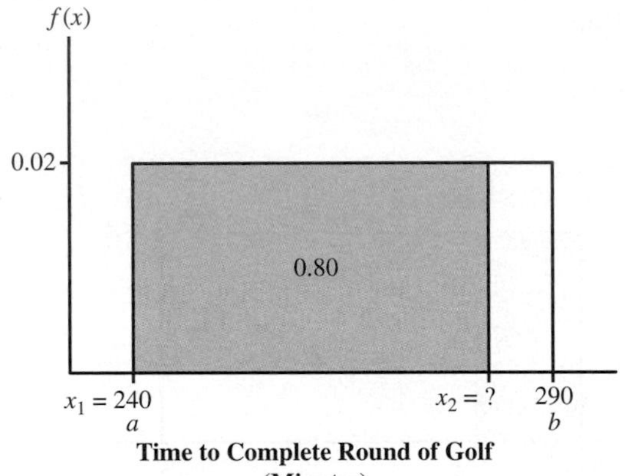

Recall that percentiles were introduced in Chapter 3 and represent the approximate percentage of values that are below the value of interest.

I'll rearrange Equation 6.7 in terms of x_2, knowing that $x_1 = 240$ and $b - a = 290 - 240 = 50$.

$$P(x_1 \leq x \leq x_2) = \frac{x_2 - x_1}{b - a} = 0.80$$

$$\frac{x_2 - 240}{50} = 0.80$$

$$x_2 = (0.80)(50) + 240 = 280 \text{ minutes}$$

Eighty percent of the rounds will be completed within 4 hours and 40 minutes (280 minutes). Because this value exceeds 270 minutes, the goal set by Deerfield's managers is not being met. Perhaps they need to consider making the course easier to speed up the pace of play. (Sounds like a great idea to me.)

The formulas for calculating the mean and standard deviation of the uniform continuous probability distribution are shown in Equations 6.8 and 6.9.

Formula 6.8 for the Mean of the Continuous Uniform Distribution

$$\mu = \frac{a + b}{2}$$

Formula 6.9 for the Standard Deviation of the Continuous Uniform Distribution

$$\sigma = \frac{b - a}{\sqrt{12}}$$

The mean and standard deviation for our Deerfield example are as follows:

$$\mu = \frac{a + b}{2} = \frac{240 + 290}{2} = 265$$

$$\sigma = \frac{b - a}{\sqrt{12}} = \frac{290 - 240}{\sqrt{12}} = \frac{50}{3.46} = 14.45$$

According to our distribution, the average time to complete a round of golf at Deerfield is 265 minutes with a standard deviation of 14.45 minutes.

The next Your Turn section will give you the opportunity to test your uniform probability distribution skills.

YOUR TURN #7

Suppose the actual flight times for American Airlines nonstop flights between Philadelphia and Orlando follows the uniform probability distribution. Assume the minimum flight time between these two cities is 140 minutes and the maximum time is 170 minutes.

a. Determine the probability that the next flight will take less than 145 minutes.
b. Determine the probability that the next flight will take between 148 and 165 minutes.
c. Suppose American Airlines has a goal that 75% of the flights will require less than 165 minutes to complete. Is this goal being met under the current probability distribution?
d. Calculate the mean and standard deviation for this distribution.

Answers can be found on ▶ **page 287**

6.4 Section Problems

Basic Skills

6.29 A random variable follows the continuous uniform distribution between 20 and 50.

a. Calculate the following probabilities for the distribution:
1. $P(x \leq 25)$
2. $P(x \leq 30)$
3. $P(x \leq 45)$
4. $P(x = 28)$

b. What are the mean and standard deviation of this distribution?

6.30 A random variable follows the continuous uniform distribution between 60 and 95.

a. Calculate the following probabilities for the distribution:
1. $P(x > 63)$
2. $P(x > 70)$
3. $P(x > 88)$
4. $P(x = 75)$

b. What are the mean and standard deviation of this distribution?

6.31 A random variable follows the continuous uniform distribution between 20 and 120.

a. Calculate the following probabilities for the distribution:
1. $P(40 \leq x \leq 60)$
2. $P(55 \leq x \leq 100)$
3. $P(80 \leq x \leq 110)$

b. What are the mean and standard deviation of this distribution?

6.32 A random variable follows the continuous uniform distribution between 130 and 300.

a. Calculate the following probabilities for the distribution:
1. $P(180 \leq x \leq 260)$
2. $P(130 \leq x \leq 200)$
3. $P(x > 150)$

b. What are the mean and standard deviation of this distribution?

Applications

6.33 The time required for housekeeping to clean a hotel room for the next customer varies between 25 and 45 minutes and follows the continuous uniform distribution.

- **a.** Calculate the value of $f(x)$.
- **b.** What are the mean and standard deviation for this distribution?
- **c.** What is the probability that the next room will require exactly 30 minutes to clean?
- **d.** What is the probability that the next room will require less than 32 minutes to clean?
- **e.** What is the probability that the next room will require more than 36 minutes to clean?
- **f.** What is the probability that the next room will require between 28 and 34 minutes to clean?
- **g.** What time represents the 70th percentile of this distribution?

6.34 Assume the time required to pass through security at a particular airport follows the continuous uniform distribution with a minimum time of 5 minutes and maximum time of 30 minutes.

- **a.** Calculate the value of $f(x)$.
- **b.** What are the mean and standard deviation for this distribution?
- **c.** What is the probability that the next passenger will require less than 25 minutes to pass through security?
- **d.** What is the probability that the next passenger will require more than 20 minutes to pass through security?
- **e.** What is the probability that the next passenger will require between 8 and 15 minutes to pass through security?
- **f.** What time represents the 75th percentile of this distribution?

6.35 The commute time to work for a particular employee follows a continuous uniform distribution with a minimum time of 10 minutes and maximum time of 22 minutes.

- **a.** Calculate the value of $f(x)$.
- **b.** What are the mean and standard deviation for this distribution?
- **c.** What is the probability that the employee's next commute to work will require less than 12.5 minutes?
- **d.** What is the probability that the employee's next commute to work will require more than 14.5 minutes?
- **e.** What is the probability that the employee's next commute to work will require between 11 and 20 minutes?
- **f.** What commute time represents the 40th percentile of this distribution?

6.36 A vending machine located in a local office dispenses coffee that varies from 7.4 to 8.2 ounces. The volume of coffee dispensed follows a continuous uniform distribution.

- **a.** Calculate the value of $f(x)$.
- **b.** What are the mean and standard deviation for this distribution?
- **c.** What is the probability that the next cup of coffee will contain more than 8.0 ounces of coffee?
- **d.** What is the probability that the next cup of coffee will contain exactly 7.5 ounces of coffee?
- **e.** What is the probability that the next cup of coffee will contain less than 8.1 ounces of coffee?
- **f.** What is the probability that the next cup of coffee will contain between 7.5 and 8.0 ounces of coffee?
- **g.** What volume represents the 15th percentile of this distribution?

CHAPTER 6 Summary

- Continuous random variables are outcomes that take on any numerical value in an interval, including numbers with decimal points.
  - The probability that a continuous random variable equals a specific value is always equal to zero.
- A normal probability distribution has the following characteristics:
  - The distribution is bell-shaped and symmetrical around the mean.
  - Because the shape of the distribution is symmetrical, the mean and median are the same value.
  - Random variables around the mean, where the curve is the tallest, have a higher likelihood of occurring than values toward the ends of the distribution, where the curve is lower.
  - The total area under the curve is always equal to 1.0.
  - Because the distribution is symmetrical around the mean, the area to the left of the mean equals 0.5 as does the area to the right of the mean.
  - The left and right ends of the distribution extend indefinitely, never quite touching the horizontal axis.
- A smaller standard deviation results in a skinnier curve that's tighter and taller around the mean.
- A larger σ (standard deviation) makes for a fatter curve that's more spread out and not as tall.
- The normal distribution's *z*-score determines the number of standard deviations that a particular value, *x*, is from the mean.
- In general, *z*-scores follow a normal distribution with $\mu = 0$ and $\sigma = 1$.
- The *z*-scores for a normal distribution
  - are negative for values of *x* that are less than the distribution mean.
  - are positive for values of *x* that are more than the distribution mean.
  - are zero at the mean of the distribution.
- According to the empirical rule, if a distribution follows a bell-shape, symmetrical curve centered around the mean, approximately 68%, 95%, and 99.7% of the values will fall within one, two, and three standard deviations above and below the mean respectively.
- We can use the normal probability distribution to approximate a binomial probability distribution if $np \geq 5$ and $nq \geq 5$.
  - The continuity correction factor allows us to approximate the binomial distribution with a normal distribution by adding and subtracting the value 0.5 to the interval of interest.
- The exponential probability distribution is a continuous distribution that is commonly used to measure the time between events of interest such as the time between customer arrivals or the time between failures in a business process.
- The exponential distribution is the continuous counterpart of the discrete Poisson distribution from Chapter 5.
  - For example, if a random variable follows the exponential distribution with an average time between arrivals of 5 minutes $(\mu = 5)$, then the same random variable also follows the Poisson distribution with a mean of 0.2 customers per minute $(\lambda = 0.2)$.
- With a continuous uniform distribution, the probability of any interval in the distribution is equal to any other interval with the same width.

CHAPTER 6 Key Terms

Continuity correction factor. A factor that allows us to approximate a binomial distribution using the normal distribution by adding and subtracting the value 0.5 to the interval of interest.

Continuous random variables. Outcomes that take on any numerical value in an interval as a result of conducting an experiment.

Continuous uniform probability density function. The mathematical expression that describes the shape of the continuous uniform probability distribution.

Continuous uniform probability distribution. A distribution in which the probability of any interval occurring is equal to any other interval with the same width.

Empirical rule. A rule that states that approximately 68%, 95%, and 99.7% of a distribution's data values will fall within one, two, and three standard deviations above and below the mean, respectively, if the distribution is symmetrical and bell shaped.

Exponential cumulative distribution function. Used to calculate the probability that a random variable that follows the exponential distribution is less than a specific value.

Exponential probability density function. The mathematical expression that describes the shape of the exponential probability distribution.

Exponential probability distribution. A continuous distribution that is commonly used to measure the time between events of interest, such as the time between customer arrivals or the time between failures in a business process.

Normal probability density function. The mathematical expression that describes the shape of the normal probability distribution.

Normal probability distribution. A continuous distribution that is bell shaped and symmetrical around its mean.

Standard normal distribution. A normal distribution with $\mu = 0$ and $\sigma = 1$.

Uniform cumulative distribution function. Used to calculate the probability that a random variable that follows the uniform distribution is between two specific values.

***z*-score.** Determines the number of standard deviations a particular value, *x*, is from the mean of its distribution.

CHAPTER 6 Equations

6.2 Normal Probability Distributions (pp 250–269)

Formula 6.1 for the Normal Probability Density Function

$$f(x) = \frac{1}{\sigma\sqrt{2\pi}} e^{-(1/2)[(x-\mu)/\sigma]^2}$$

Formula 6.2 for the z-score

$$z = \frac{x - \mu}{\sigma}$$

6.3 Exponential Probability Distributions (pp 269–273)

Formula 6.3 for the Exponential Probability Density Function

$$f(x) = \lambda e^{-\lambda x}$$

Formula 6.4 for the Exponential Cumulative Distribution Function

$$P(x \le a) = 1 - e^{-a\lambda}$$

Formula 6.5 for the Standard Deviation of the Exponential Distribution

$$\sigma = \mu = \frac{1}{\lambda}$$

6.4 Uniform Probability Distributions (pp 273–278)

Formula 6.6 for the Continuous Uniform Probability Density Function

$$f(x) = \frac{1}{b - a} \quad \text{if } a \le x \le b$$

$$f(x) = 0 \quad \text{otherwise}$$

Formula 6.7 for the Uniform Cumulative Distribution Function

$$P(x_1 \le x \le x_2) = \frac{x_2 - x_1}{b - a}$$

Formula 6.8 for the Mean of the Continuous Uniform Distribution

$$\mu = \frac{a + b}{2}$$

Formula 6.9 for the Standard Deviation of the Uniform Distribution

$$\sigma = \frac{b - a}{\sqrt{12}}$$

CHAPTER 6 Problems

6.37 According to the National Association of Childcare Resources and Referral Agencies, the average cost of care for an infant in a child-care center in Delaware was $8,769 a year. Assume this cost follows a normal distribution with a standard deviation of $925.

a. What is the probability that a randomly selected child-care center in Delaware costs
1. more than $8,000 per year for infant care?
2. more than $9,000 per year for infant care?
3. between $8,500 and $9,500 per year for infant care?
b. Use Excel or PHStat to confirm the answers in part a.
c. Determine the rate a child-care center that wishes to be in the 60th percentile in the state of Delaware should charge for an infant.

6.38 The average U.S. monthly cable bill in 2012 has been reported to be $86. Assume monthly cable bills follow a normal distribution with a standard deviation of $9.50.

a. What is the probability that a randomly selected bill will be
1. less than $80?
2. less than $90?
3. exactly $85?
4. between $75 and $95?
b. Use Excel or PHStat to confirm the answers in part a.
c. Which monthly cable bill represents the 75th percentile?

6.39 Assume that the number of miles a particular brand of tire lasts before it needs to be replaced follows a normal distribution with a mean of 45,600 miles and a standard deviation of 5,800 miles.

a. What is the probability that the next tire of this brand sold will last
1. more than 36,000 miles before it needs to be replaced?
2. less than 42,000 miles before it needs to be replaced?
3. between 45,000 and 55,000 miles before it needs to be replaced?
b. Use Excel or PHStat to confirm the answers in part a.
c. What is the mileage that 90% of the tires of this brand will survive before needing to be replaced?

6.40 Assume the room rate for a three-star hotel in Paris follows a normal distribution with a mean of 175 euros and a standard deviation of 16 euros.

a. What is the probability that a randomly selected three-star hotel has a room rate of
1. less than 195 euros?
2. more than 180 euros?
3. exactly 170 euros?
4. between 150 and 182 euros?
b. Use Excel or PHStat to confirm the answers in part a.
c. A particular hotel would like to set its rate so that only 20% of the hotels in Paris will have lower rates. What room rate should the hotel set?

6.41 On weeknights, the average number of hours of sleep per night adults 55–84 years of age get is 7.0. Assume this random variable follows a normal distribution with a standard deviation of 1.1 hours.

a. What is the probability that a randomly selected adult from this age group will get
1. more than 6.0 hours of sleep tonight?
2. less than 5.0 hours of sleep tonight?
3. between 6.3 and 8.0 hours of sleep tonight?
4. between 5.6 and 6.5 hours of sleep tonight?
b. Use Excel or PHStat to confirm the answers in part a.
c. How many hours of sleep will an adult in this age group get if they are in the 35th percentile?

6.42 Assume the selling prices of homes in a particular community follow a normal distribution with a mean of $285,700 and a standard deviation of $46,100. Determine the range of selling prices in this community that includes

a. one standard deviation around the mean.
b. two standard deviations around the mean.
c. three standard deviations around the mean.

6.43 TomTom, the producer of GPS devices, reported that the fastest drivers in the nation are in Mississippi. In Mississippi, interstate drivers average 70.1 miles per hour. Assume that the speed of cars traveling on Mississippi's interstates follows the normal distribution with a standard deviation of 7.2 miles per hour.

a. What is the probability that a randomly selected car on a Mississippi interstate is traveling
   1. faster than 65 miles per hour?
   2. slower than 72 miles per hour?
   3. between 60 and 66 miles per hour?
   4. between 78 and 85 miles per hour?
b. Confirm the answers to part a with Excel or PHStat.
c. What average speed should I drive if I want to travel faster than 70% of the cars on the interstate?

6.44 According to the Organisation for Economic Co-operation and Development (OECD), South Koreans worked an average of 2,090 hours per year in 2011 (compared with 1,787 for workers in the United States). Assume this random variable follows a normal distribution with a standard deviation of 420 hours.

a. What is the probability that a randomly selected South Korean worked
   1. less than 1,800 hours?
   2. between 2,000 and 2,200 hours?
   3. between 1,200 and 1,600 hours?
   4. between 2,300 and 2,500 hours?
b. Confirm the answers to part a using Excel or PHStat.
c. How many hours will a South Korean work if he or she is in the 90th percentile in terms of the hours an average Korean works?

6.45 In a recent, *USA Today* article titled *Consumers Are Caught in a Sugar Battle,* Americans consume an average of 22.2 teaspoons of sugar per day. Assume daily sugar consumption follows the normal distribution with a standard deviation of 6.5 teaspoons.

a. What is the probability that a randomly selected American will consume
   1. more than 25 teaspoons of sugar today?
   2. between 20 and 27 teaspoons of sugar today?
   3. between 10 and 18 teaspoons of sugar today?
   4. between 28 and 35 teaspoons of sugar today?
b. Confirm the answers to part a with Excel or PHStat.
c. How many teaspoons of sugar will a person consume today if he or she is in the 65th percentile?

6.46 According to the U.S. Labor Department, average weekly wages in February 2013 were $822. Assume weekly wages in the United States follow the normal distribution with a standard deviation of $190.

a. What is the probability that a randomly selected worker in the United States earned
   1. less than $900 per week?
   2. between $800 and $920 per week?
   3. between $550 and $700 per week?
   4. between $750 and $1,100 per week?
b. Confirm the answers to part a with Excel or PHStat.
c. What weekly wage will a person earn if he or she is in the 45th percentile?

6.47 The RAD Construction Company has been awarded a contract with the state of Delaware to replace a bridge on Pike Creek Road. Based on experience with previous projects, RAD feels the project completion time follows a normal distribution with a mean of 92 days and a standard deviation of 9 days. RAD anticipates the net profit for completing the project is $125,000. If the company completes the project in less than 84 days, it will receive an additional $20,000 bonus from the state. If it takes longer than 106 days to complete the project, the state of Delaware will penalize RAD $15,000. What is RAD's expected profit for the project?

6.48 Pew Research Center surveyed adults who were 18–64 years old and had their own children under age 18 living in their household in 2011 on the amount of time spent on various activities. The results indicated that dads spent an average of 10 hours per week doing housework (compared to 18 hours per week for moms). Assume the hours per week doing housework follows the normal probability distribution with a standard deviation of 3.2 hours per week and that these statistics still hold true.

a. What is the probability that a randomly selected dad from this group spent
   1. less than 11 hours doing housework this week?
   2. more than 12 hours doing housework this week?
   3. between 7 and 9 hours doing housework this week?
   4. between 8 and 15 hours doing housework this week?
b. Use Excel or PHStat to confirm the answers in part a.
c. How many of hours of housework will a dad in this group perform if he is in the 70th percentile?

6.49 Pew Research Center surveyed adults that were 18–64 years old and had their own children under age 18 living in their household in 2011 on the amount of time spent on various activities. The results indicated that moms spent an average of 21 hours per week doing paid work (compared to 37 hours per week for dads). Assume the hours per week doing paid work follows the normal probability distribution with a standard deviation of 6.7 hours per week and that these statistics still hold true.

a. What is the probability that a randomly selected mom from this group spent
   1. less than 18 hours doing paid work this week?
   2. more than 18 hours doing paid work this week?
   3. between 23 and 30 hours doing paid work this week?
   4. between 11 and 19 hours doing paid work this week?
b. Use Excel or PHStat to confirm the answers in part a.
c. How many of hours of paid work will a mom in this group perform if she is in the 20th percentile?

6.50 The recent economic recession caused a plunge in new cars sales from 2008 to 2010. This trend resulted in a significant shortage of used cars during the next few years which, in turn, pushed up used car prices. Suppose that the average price of a 5-year-old used car is $16,230 with a standard deviation of $4,740. Assume that the price of a 5-year-old used car follows the normal probability distribution.

a. What is the probability that a randomly selected 5-year-old car costs
  1. less than $18,500?
  2. more than $11,300?
  3. between $10,000 and $14,000?
  4. between $12,500 and $17,000?

b. Use Excel or PHStat to confirm the answers in part a.

c. What is the cost of a 5-year-old car in the 90th percentile?

6.51 In an effort to hold colleges accountable for the benefits of a degree, legislation has been recently proposed to require institutions to provide prospective students with salary information for graduates. The state of Virginia has traditionally published starting salary data for their graduating students. For example, the average salary of James Madison University (JMU) students who have recently earned a bachelor's degree was reported to be $35,224. Assume the starting salary for a recent JMU graduate follows the normal probability distribution with a standard deviation of $5,070.

a. What is the probability that a randomly selected JMU graduate from this class had a starting salary
  1. less than $40,000?
  2. more than $38,000?
  3. between $24,000 and $32,000?
  4. between $30,000 and $40,000?

b. Use Excel or PHStat to confirm the answers in part a.

c. What starting salary of a JMU graduating student from this class is in the 75th percentile?

6.52 Automotive dealerships have made recent efforts to reduce the amount of time required to purchase a car. One strategy is to use the Internet to streamline the process by providing prospective buyers with car information. According to J.D. Powers, the average number of minutes to negotiate a deal to purchase a car at the dealership was 60.3 minutes in 2012. Assume the number of minutes to negotiate a deal follows the normal probability distribution with a standard deviation of 17.9 minutes and that these statistics still hold true.

a. What is the probability that a random customer spent
  1. less than 30 minutes negotiating a deal?
  2. more than 45 minutes negotiating a deal?
  3. between 50 and 90 minutes negotiating a deal?
  4. between 65 and 85 minutes negotiating a deal?

b. Use Excel or PHStat to confirm the answers in part a.

c. How many minutes of negotiating are in the 35th percentile?

6.53 In spite an unemployment rate of 26% and an economy in crisis, 70% of Spaniards responded that they were in favor of keeping the euro rather than returning to the peseta and the national currency in 2012. A random sample of 32 Spaniards was selected. Use the normal approximation to the binomial distribution to answer the following:

a. Calculate the mean and standard deviation for this distribution.

b. What is the probability that 20 or more Spaniards from this sample are in favor of retaining the euro?

c. What is the probability that exactly 22 Spaniards from this sample are in favor of retaining the euro?

d. What is the probability that 15, 16, 17, 18, or 19 Spaniards from this sample are in favor of retaining the euro?

e. What is the probability that less than 24 Spaniards from this sample are in favor of retaining the euro?

6.54 According to Leichtman Research Group, 69% of U.S. households had at least one HDTV in 2012. A random sample of 20 U.S. homes was selected. Use the normal approximation to the binomial distribution to answer the following:

a. Calculate the mean and standard deviation for this distribution.

b. What is the probability that 12 or more households own at least one HDTV?

c. What is the probability that exactly 16 households own at least one HDTV?

d. What is the probability that 11, 12, or 13 households own at least one HDTV?

e. What is the probability that 18 or 19 households own at least one HDTV?

6.55 A process produces strings of Christmas tree lights that historically have experienced a defective rate of 4%. A customer has placed an order for 150 strings of lights. Use the normal approximation to the binomial distribution to answer the following:

a. Calculate the mean and standard deviation for this distribution.

b. What is the probability that less than 2 strings in this order will be defective?

c. What is the probability that exactly 7 strings in this order will be defective?

d. What is the probability that 3, 4, or 5 strings in this order will be defective?

e. What is the probability that 8, 9, or 10 strings in this order will be defective?

6.56 A recent survey conducted by the Allstate Foundation reported that 68% of teens admitted to texting while driving. A random sample of 40 teens is selected. Use the normal approximation to the binomial distribution to answer the following:

a. Calculate the mean and standard deviation for this distribution.

b. What is the probability that less than 29 teens of the 40 admit to texting while driving?

c. What is the probability that exactly 24 teens of the 40 admit to texting while driving?
d. What is the probability that more than 32 teens of the 40 admit to texting while driving?
e. What is the probability that 26, 27, or 28 teens of the 40 admit to texting while driving?

6.57 Much of the NCAA men's basketball tournament, otherwise known as March Madness, takes place during the workweek. According to CouponCabin.com, 34% of employed adults who plan to watch at least one game plan to watch tournament games from work in 2013. A random sample of 50 employed adults who plan to watch at least one tournament game was selected. Use the normal approximation to the binomial distribution to answer the following:

a. Calculate the mean and standard deviation for this distribution.
b. What is the probability that more than 19 adults from this sample will watch March Madness at work?
c. What is the probability that exactly 15 adults from this sample will watch March Madness at work?
d. What is the probability that less than 23 adults from this sample will watch March Madness at work?
e. What is the probability that 12, 13, 14, 15, 16, or 17 adults from this sample will watch March Madness at work?

6.58 According to the U.S. Census Bureau, 47.5% of the U.S. population lives in the Eastern Time Zone. A random sample of 50 U.S. residents is selected. Use the normal approximation to the binomial distribution to answer the following:

a. Calculate the mean and standard deviation for this distribution.
b. What is the probability that less than 20 people from the sample live in the Eastern Time Zone?
c. What is the probability that exactly 27 people from the sample live in the Eastern Time Zone?
d. What is the probability that more than 22 people from the sample live in the Eastern Time Zone?
e. What is the probability that 26, 27, or 28 people from the sample live in the Eastern Time Zone?

6.59 The average number of days that a house was on the market in Austin, Texas, in January 2013 was 71 days. Assume the time on the market follows an exponential probability distribution.

a. What is the probability that a randomly selected house will be on the market less than 50 days?
b. What is the probability that a randomly selected house will be on the market between 70 and 100 days?
c. What is the probability that a randomly selected house will be on the market exactly 80 days?
d. Use Excel to verify the results from parts a and b.
e. What is the standard deviation for this distribution?

6.60 During a recent men's college basketball season, the Villanova Wildcats averaged 22.1 personal fouls per 40-minute game. Assume the time between personal fouls follows an exponential distribution.

a. What is the probability that the next personal foul committed by Villanova will occur within the first minute of a game?
b. What is the probability that the next personal foul committed by Villanova will occur between the first 2 and 4 minutes of a game?
c. What is the probability that the next personal foul committed by Villanova will occur more than 3 minutes after the start of a game?
d. Use Excel to verify the results from parts a and b.
e. What is the standard deviation for this distribution?

6.61 Patients arrive at the emergency room for a local hospital at an average rate of 6.5 per hour. Assume the time between patient arrivals follows an exponential distribution.

a. What is the probability that the next patient will arrive in the emergency room within the next 3 minutes?
b. What is the probability that the next patient will arrive in the emergency room between the next 10 and 15 minutes?
c. What is the probability that the next patient will arrive in the emergency room after the next 12 minutes?
d. What is the probability that the next patient will arrive in the emergency room in exactly 12 minutes?
e. Use Excel to verify the results from parts a and b.
f. What is the standard deviation for this distribution?

6.62 A busy intersection in the state of Delaware averages a traffic accident every 32 days. Assume the time between accidents follows an exponential distribution.

a. What is the probability that the next accident will occur within the next 10 days?
b. What is the probability that the next accident will occur between the next 15 and 25 days?
c. What is the probability that the next accident will occur after the next 40 days?
d. Use Excel to verify the results from parts a and b.
e. What is the standard deviation for this distribution?

6.63 Suppose the time between hits on an e-commerce Web site follows the exponential distribution with a mean time of 2.7 minutes.

a. What is the probability that next hit on the Web site will occur within the next 5 minutes?
b. What is the probability that next hit on the Web site will occur within the next 2 to 6 minutes?
c. What is the probability that next hit on the Web site will occur after the next 3 minutes?
d. Use Excel to verify the results from parts a, b, and c.
e. What is the standard deviation for this distribution?

6.64 The optical department at Costco serves customers on a first-come-first-serve basis. Suppose the time between customer arrivals follows the exponential distribution. Historical data indicates that customers arrive at an average rate of 10.8 per hour.

a. What is the probability that next customer will arrive within the next 3 minutes?
b. What is the probability that next customer will arrive within the next 6 to 12 minutes?
c. What is the probability that next customer will arrive after the next 10 minutes?
d. Use Excel to verify the results from parts a, b, and c.
e. What is the standard deviation for this distribution?

6.65 Suppose a number of months before your car battery needs to be replaced follow the exponential distribution with a mean of 50.0 months.

a. What is the probability that your car battery will need to be replaced within 24 months?
b. What is the probability that your car battery will need to be replaced within 30 to 60 months?
c. What is the probability that your car battery will need to be replaced after 84 months?
d. Use Excel to verify the results from parts a, b, and c.
e. What is the standard deviation for this distribution?

6.66 Orange Lake Resort is a major vacation destination near Orlando, Florida, adjacent to the Disney theme parks. Because the property consists of 1,450 acres of land, Orange Lake provides shuttle buses for visitors who need to travel within the resort. Suppose the wait time for a shuttle bus follows the uniform distribution with a minimum time of 30 seconds and a maximum time of 9.0 minutes.

a. What is the probability that a visitor will need to wait more than 3 minutes for the next shuttle?
b. What is the probability that a visitor will need to wait less than 5.5 minutes for the next shuttle?
c. What is the probability that a visitor will need to wait between 4 and 8 minutes for the next shuttle?
d. Calculate the mean and standard deviation for this distribution.
e. Orange Lake has a goal that 80% of the time, the wait for the shuttle will be less than 6 minutes. Is this goal being achieved?

6.67 Precision Doors is an organization that installs new garage doors on residential homes. Suppose the installation time for a residence follows the uniform distribution with a minimum time of 190 minutes and a maximum time of 370 minutes.

a. What is the probability that an installation will require less than 4 hours to complete?
b. What is the probability that an installation will require more than 5 hours to complete?
c. What is the probability that an installation will require between 250 and 350 minutes to complete?
d. Calculate the mean and standard deviation for this distribution.
e. Precision Door has a goal that 80% of the time, the installation time for a residence will be less than 6 hours. Is this goal being achieved?

6.68 Suppose the time to deliver a pizza after an order for one is placed on a local restaurant's Web site follows a uniform distribution with a minimum time of 4 minutes and a maximum time of 18 minutes.

a. Determine the probability that the next delivery will require less than 12 minutes.
b. Determine the probability that the next delivery will require between 6 and 10 minutes.
c. Determine the probability that the next delivery will require more than 7 minutes.
d. Determine the probability that the next delivery will require exactly 15 minutes.
e. Calculate the mean and standard deviation for this distribution.

6.69 Aircraft turnaround time is defined as the time required to prepare an aircraft for its next flight after arriving at a terminal. Assume that United Airlines' turnaround time follows a uniform distribution with a minimum time of 24 minutes and a maximum time of 56 minutes.

a. Determine the probability that the next United Airlines aircraft will require less than 30 minutes to turn around.
b. Determine the probability that the next United Airlines aircraft will require between 30 and 40 minutes to turn around.
c. Determine the probability that the next United Airlines aircraft will require more than 40 minutes to turn around.
d. Calculate the mean and standard deviation for this distribution.
e. United Airlines wants aircraft turnaround times to be less than 50 minutes 90% of the time. Is this goal being achieved?

6.70 While waiting for an order to arrive from its supplier (known as the *lead time*), the golf-department manager at a local Dick's Sporting Goods store will sell an average of 60 boxes of Titleist golf balls. Assume the demand during the lead time for the balls follows a normal distribution with a standard deviation of 12 boxes. Determine the reorder point that will ensure the store a 95% probability that it will have enough inventory of golf balls until the next order arrives.

CHAPTER 6 Solutions to Your Turn

YOUR TURN #1

a. $z_{800} = \dfrac{x - \mu}{\sigma} = \dfrac{800 - 930}{140} = -0.93$

$P(x \le 800) = P(z \le -0.93) = 0.1762$

b. $z_{1,000} = \dfrac{x - \mu}{\sigma} = \dfrac{1,000 - 930}{140} = 0.50$

$P(x \le 1,000) = P(z \le 0.50) = 0.6915$

c. $P(x = 900) = 0$ because x is a continuous random variable.

d. The station will not run out of inventory if demand during the lead time is less than or equal to 1,200 gallons. We need to calculate $P(x \le 1,200)$.

$z_{1,200} = \dfrac{x - \mu}{\sigma} = \dfrac{1,200 - 930}{140} = 1.93$

$P(x \le 1,200) = P(z \le 1.93) = 0.9732$

e. Find the closest value to 0.90 in the body of Table 6.2. This will be 0.8997 in row 1.2 and column 0.08.

$z = \dfrac{x - \mu}{\sigma}$

$x = \mu + z\sigma$

$x = 930 + (1.28)(140) = 930 + 179.2 = 1,109.2$ gallons

YOUR TURN #2

a. $x = \mu \pm z\sigma$

$x = 39.2 + (1)(3.7) = 42.9$

$x = 39.2 - (1)(3.7) = 35.5$

b. $x = \mu \pm z\sigma$

$x = 39.2 + (2)(3.7) = 46.6$

$x = 39.2 - (2)(3.7) = 31.8$

c. $x = \mu \pm z\sigma$

$x = 39.2 + (3)(3.7) = 50.3$

$x = 39.2 - (3)(3.7) = 28.1$

YOUR TURN #3

a. $z_{11.9} = \dfrac{x - \mu}{\sigma} = \dfrac{11.9 - 10.7}{0.8} = 1.50$

$z_{9.8} = \dfrac{x - \mu}{\sigma} = \dfrac{9.8 - 10.7}{0.8} = -1.13$

$P(9.8 \le x \le 11.9) = 0.9332 - 0.1292 = 0.8040$

b. $z_{12.1} = \dfrac{x - \mu}{\sigma} = \dfrac{12.1 - 10.7}{0.8} = 1.75$

$z_{11} = \dfrac{x - \mu}{\sigma} = \dfrac{11 - 10.7}{0.8} = 0.38$

$P(11 \le x \le 12.1) = 0.9599 - 0.6480 = 0.3119$

c. $z_{10.3} = \dfrac{x - \mu}{\sigma} = \dfrac{10.3 - 10.7}{0.8} = -0.50$

$z_{9.7} = \dfrac{x - \mu}{\sigma} = \dfrac{9.7 - 10.7}{0.8} = -1.25$

$P(9.7 \le x \le 10.3) = 0.3085 - 0.1056 = 0.2029$

YOUR TURN #4

a. NORM.DIST(7, 5, 3, TRUE) = 0.7475

b. NORM.DIST(0, 5, 3, TRUE) = 0.0478

c. Using PHStat (see at right) = 0.2782

	A	B	C	D	E
1	Normal Probabilities				
2					
3	Common Data				
4	Mean	5			
5	Standard Deviation	3			
6				Probability for a Range	
7				From X Value	1
8				To X Value	4
9				Z Value for 1	-1.333333
10				Z Value for 4	-0.333333
11				P(X<=1)	0.0912
12				P(X<=4)	0.3694
13				P(1<=X<=4)	0.2782
14					

YOUR TURN #5

$n = 60 \quad p = 0.10 \quad q = 0.90$

$\mu = np = (60)(0.10) = 6.0$

$\sigma = \sqrt{npq} = \sqrt{(60)(0.1)(1 - 0.1)} = \sqrt{5.4} = 2.32$

a. Less than 5 includes 0, 1, 2, 3, and 4. Add 0.5 to 4 for continuity factor.

$$z_{4.5} = \frac{x - \mu}{\sigma} = \frac{4.5 - 6.0}{2.32} = -0.65$$

$P(x < 5) = P(z < -0.65) = 0.2578$

b. Subtract 0.5 from 6 and add 0.5 to 9 for continuity factor.

$$z_{5.5} = \frac{x - \mu}{\sigma} = \frac{5.5 - 6.0}{2.32} = -0.22$$

$$z_{9.5} = \frac{x - \mu}{\sigma} = \frac{9.5 - 6.0}{2.32} = 1.51$$

$P(6 \le x \le 9) = P(5.5 \le x \le 9.5) = P(-0.22 \le z \le 1.51)$

$P(-0.22 \le z \le 1.51) = 0.9345 - 0.4129 = 0.5216$

c. Nine or more includes 9, 10, 11, . . . ,60. Subtract 0.5 from 9 for continuity factor.

$$z_{8.5} = \frac{x - \mu}{\sigma} = \frac{8.5 - 6.0}{2.32} = 1.08$$

$P(x \ge 9) = P(z \ge 1.08) = 1.0 - 0.8599 = 0.1401$

YOUR TURN #6

$$\lambda = \frac{32.2 \text{ shots per game}}{60 \text{ minutes per game}} = 0.537 \text{ shots per minute}$$

$$\mu = \frac{1}{\lambda} = \frac{1}{0.537} = 1.86 \text{ minutes per shot}$$

a1. $P(x \le a) = 1 - e^{-a\lambda}$

$P(x \le 1) = 1 - e^{-(1)(0.537)}$

$P(x \le 1) = 1 - e^{-0.537} = 1 - 0.5845 = 0.4155$

a2. $P(2 \le x \le 3) = P(x \le 3) - P(x \le 2)$

$P(x \le 3) = 1 - e^{-(3)(0.537)} = 1 - e^{-1.611}$

$= 1 - 0.1997 = 0.8003$

$P(x \le 2) = 1 - e^{-(2)(0.537)} = 1 - e^{-1.074}$

$= 1 - 0.3416 = 0.6584$

$P(2 \le x \le 3) = 0.8003 - 0.6584 = 0.1419$

b. $P(x \le 1) = \text{EXPON.DIST}(1, 0.537, \text{TRUE}) = 0.4155$

$P(x \le 3) = \text{EXPON.DIST}(3, 0.537, \text{TRUE}) = 0.8003$

$P(x \le 2) = \text{EXPON.DIST}(2, 0.537, \text{TRUE}) = 0.6584$

c. $\sigma = \mu = 1.86$ minutes per shot

YOUR TURN #7

$x_1 = 140 \quad x_2 = 170$

$$P(x_1 \le x \le x_2) = \frac{x_2 - x_1}{b - a}$$

a. $P(140 \le x \le 145) = \dfrac{145 - 140}{170 - 140} = \dfrac{5}{30} = 0.167$

b. $P(148 \le x \le 165) = \dfrac{165 - 148}{170 - 140} = \dfrac{17}{30} = 0.567$

c. $P(x_1 \le x \le x_2) = \dfrac{x_2 - x_1}{b - a} = 0.75$

$$\frac{x_2 - 140}{170 - 140} = 0.75$$

$x_2 = (0.75)(30) + 140 = 162.5$ minutes

Because 162.5 minutes is less than 165 minutes, the goal of management is being met.

d. $\mu = \dfrac{a + b}{2} = \dfrac{140 + 170}{2} = 155$ minutes

$$\sigma = \frac{b - a}{\sqrt{12}} = \frac{170 - 140}{\sqrt{12}} = \frac{30}{3.46} = 8.67 \text{ minutes}$$

CHAPTER

7

Sampling and Sampling Distributions

IN THIS CHAPTER, YOU WILL LEARN TO:

- Distinguish between the different types of probability sampling.
- Identify the limitations of nonprobability sampling.
- Calculate sampling errors.
- Identify the sources of nonsampling errors.
- Use the sampling distribution of the mean.
- Understand the importance of the Central Limit Theorem.
- Use the sampling distribution of the proportion.
- Use the finite population correction factor.

CHAPTER 7 MAP

Stats in Practice: Super Bowl XLVII Takes the Trophy: Most Watched Telecast Ever!

That's right. At the time of this printing, the Baltimore Ravens' 34-31 victory over the San Francisco 49ers for the NFL Championship on February 3, 2013, in New Orleans, Louisiana was the most watched broadcast in television history with a total audience of 164.1 million viewers. The previous record holder was the 2011 Super Bowl, a game in which the Green Bay Packers defeated the Pittsburgh Steelers in front of 162.9 million total viewers. In fact, the top five most-watched broadcasts are the last five Super Bowls which attests to the popularity of the NFL.

When considering these facts one might ask, "How do they know that 164.1 million people watched the 2013 Super Bowl? I watched the game and nobody counted me." To answer this important question, we need to explore the topic of statistical sampling. Back in Chapter 1, we defined a population as representing all possible outcomes or measurements of interest and a sample as a subset of a population. Nielson Media Research, a company in the sampling business, provides TV networks and advertisers with information about the sizes of television viewing audiences across the nation by surveying 5,000 of the 129 million households there are in the United States. Participating households are selected very carefully so that they are representative of the entire U.S. population. Each person in these households is provided with a "people meter," which is a small box the individual uses to indicate when he or she starts and stops watching a TV program. Based on the results of this relatively small sample, Nielsen can develop an accurate estimate of the viewing habits of the entire country.

The information Nielsen collects plays a critical role in the rates that TV networks charge advertisers to run commercials during programs. Generally, the larger a program's audience is, the more the commercials aired during the show cost advertisers. For example, a 30-second commercial for the top-rated 2013 Super Bowl cost $3.8 million.

In addition to knowing how many viewers are watching a program, advertisers also want to know *who* is watching. The people meters keep track of both the ages and genders of the viewers. For example, Nielsen's data shows that the number of male viewers of Super Bowls have traditionally exceeded the number of female viewers. This helps explain why you see so many more beer commercials during the Super Bowl, than say, advertisements for perfume. The opposite holds true with the Olympics TV audience where the majority of viewers are typically female. Figure 7.1 shows the gender breakdown for Super Bowl XLV and the 2010 Winter Olympics.

FIGURE 7.1 Percentage of Super Bowl XLV and 2010 Winter Olympic Viewers by Gender

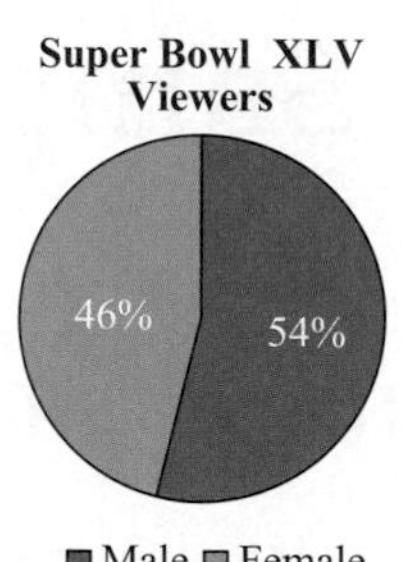

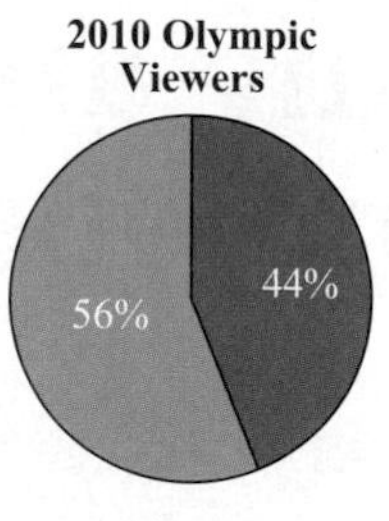

7.1 Why Sample?

A **population** represents all possible subjects of interest.
A **sample** is a subset of a population.

Back in Chapter 1, we introduced the concept of a population and a sample. A **population** refers to all possible subjects that are of interest to us in a particular study. The term **sample** refers to a portion of the population that is representative of the population from which it was selected. In the previous Stats in Practice example, *population* is defined as every television viewer and the sample consists of all the households that possess a Nielsen people meter.

Why not just measure the whole population rather than rely on only a sample? That's a very good question! Depending on the circumstances, measuring an entire population could be very expensive or just plain impossible. Let's use a quality control example in business. Suppose the target for salt content set by Kellogg's for my Cheez-It crackers is 1%. Higher or lower salt content would have a negative impact on the taste of the product.

Stats in Practice: Age Does Matter

Attracting viewers from the coveted 18–49 age group will also boost advertising revenue. For example, commercial time for *American Idol* during the 2012 season cost $340,825 per 30-second spot. *Dancing with the Stars*, which has about the same size viewing audience as *Idol*, commands only $160,466 per commercial. The difference is explained by the average age of the viewers, which is under 50 for *Idol* and over 50 for *Dancing*. The reasoning is that we over-50-year-old consumers are more set in our ways and are not as easily influenced by advertising as you "young-uns."

How does Kellogg's know that its target is being achieved for all of the Cheez-Its produced today? Well, it's not practical to check the salt content of every cracker coming off the production line because any cracker tested would not be fit for sale to the consumer. A better solution would be to routinely select a small, but representative, sample and test its salt content. These sample results would be used to determine if the process was producing satisfactory crackers. More specifically, we can use the salt content from the sample to draw conclusions about the salt content of the entire production process, which, in this case, is the population. By gathering enough representative data, we can *infer* what is happening overall. That's the whole concept of inferential statistics in one paragraph!

Even if we could feasibly measure the entire population, to do so would often be a waste of time and money—resources businesses consider very valuable these days. If a sample is selected properly and the analysis performed correctly, this information can be used to make an accurate assessment of the entire population. There is very little added benefit to continue beyond the sample and measure everything.

One example where a sampling decision was recently made occurred at Goldey-Beacom College, where I currently teach. I am a member of the Academic Honor Code Committee, which launched a project to gather information about the attitudes our college students have toward academic integrity. It would have been possible to ask every student at our college to respond to the survey, but it was actually unnecessary with the availability of inferential statistics. The committee eventually made the intelligent decision to sample only a portion of the students to infer the attitudes of the larger population. Based on our sample, we concluded that the majority of students at our college took academic integrity very seriously.

There are, however, risks involved with making decisions based on sampling. By sampling, we expose ourselves to errors that could lead to poor decisions. As we will see later in the chapter, we can quantify the probability of these errors occurring. As you will see later in this textbook, these probabilities are often small enough to still make sampling worthwhile.

7.2 Types of Sampling

There are many options available for gathering samples from a population. The two basic types that we will discuss in this chapter are probability and nonprobability sampling.

Probability Sampling

A **probability sample** is a sample in which each member of the population has a known, nonzero, chance of being selected for the sample.

A **probability sample** is a sample in which each member of the population has a known, non-zero, chance of being selected for the sample. However, this does not necessarily mean that every member has the same chance of being selected. With probability sampling, we have the ability to perform a variety of inferential statistical tests that will allow us to draw reliable conclusions about the population. These tests are the focus of many of the remaining chapters in this textbook.

There are five main types of probability sampling techniques statisticians use: simple random, systematic, stratified, cluster, and resampling. I will discuss each of the techniques in the following sections.

Simple Random Sampling

A **simple random sample** is a sample in which every member of the population has an equal chance of being chosen.

A **simple random sample** is a sample in which every member of the population has an equal chance of being chosen. One way to ensure this occurs is to use the sampling tool in Excel's Data Analysis ToolPak (Windows version). Unfortunately, this sampling procedure is not available on Excel for Mac. To demonstrate, let's go back to the academic integrity survey at my school. Suppose I want to draw a simple random sample of 10 students out of 1,800 total students to participate in the survey. In Figure 7.2, Column A of the Excel file titled **GBC Students.xlsx** shows the student ID numbers for each of the 1,800 students. The numbers are sorted in ascending order. (I have hidden Rows 13 through 1,796 to conserve space.) To select 10 students at random for the sample, I take the following steps:

1. Open the Excel file **GBC Students.xlsx**.
2. Select **Data** > **Data Analysis**.
3. In the Data Analysis dialog box, select **Sampling** and click **OK**.
4. In the Sampling dialog box, click on the text box for **Input Range:** and select Cells A1:A1800 as shown in Figure 7.2.
5. Select **Random** under Sampling Method.
6. In the **Number of Samples:** text box, type **10**.
7. Click on the text box for **Output Range:** select Cell C1, and click **OK**.

Sampling without replacement means that once a member of the population is selected to be part of the sample, it is not returned to the population. Therefore that member cannot be chosen again in the sample.

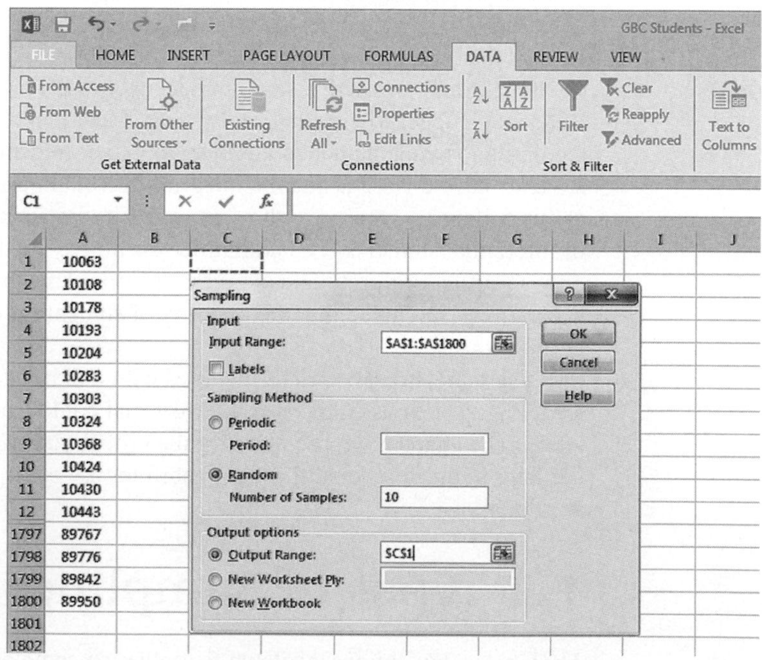

FIGURE 7.2
Using Excel to Generate a Simple Random Sample

Column C in Figure 7.3 (on the next page) provides us with the simple random sample of 10 students from the population.

FIGURE 7.3
Finished Simple Random Sample

	A	B	C	D
1	10063		55516	
2	10108		63282	
3	10178		68399	
4	10193		16568	
5	10204		36320	
6	10283		19301	
7	10303		15054	
8	10324		28914	
9	10368		59625	
10	10424		39182	
11	10430			
12	10443			
1797	89767			
1798	89776			
1799	89842			
1800	89950			
1801				

The student with ID Number 55516 would be the first member in my sample, followed by ID Number 63282, and so forth. This technique ensures that all 1,800 students have the same chance of being selected for the survey. Also, be advised that Excel's random sampling tool uses sampling *with replacement*. This means that after a member of the population has been selected for the sample, he or she is placed back into the population and can be chosen again for the same sample. Therefore, it is possible that a student could be selected more than once for the sample. If this is undesirable, accommodations can be made to replace the duplicated member in the sample.

Systematic Sampling

In **systematic sampling,** every kth member of the population is chosen for the sample. The value of k is determined by dividing the size of the population (N) by the size of the sample (n).

Another way to ensure that samples are selected randomly is to use **systematic sampling**. This technique results in selecting every kth member of the population being in your sample. Every second member could be selected, or every third member, and so on. (Remember in your physical education classes when players were counted off in a line and placed in teams? Systematic sampling is similar.)

But how do you know which value of k to choose? The value of k, the systematic sampling constant, is determined using Equation 7.1.

Formula 7.1 for the Systematic Sampling Constant

$$k = \frac{N}{n}$$

where

N = Size of the population
n = Size of the sample

Using my academic integrity survey, with a population of 1,800 students and a sample of 10,

$$k = \frac{N}{n} = \frac{1{,}800}{10} = 180$$

From a listing of the entire population, I would choose every 180th student to be included in the sample. Excel can also do this for you with the sampling tool I just introduced:

1. Using the **GBC Student.xlsx** file with a blank Column C, select **Periodic** in the **Sampling** dialog box, as shown in Figure 7.4 on the next page.
2. In the **Period:** text box, type in the value for k, which is 180.
3. Click on the text box for **Output Range:**, and select Cell C1, and click **OK.**

FIGURE 7.4
Using Excel to Generate a Systematic Sample

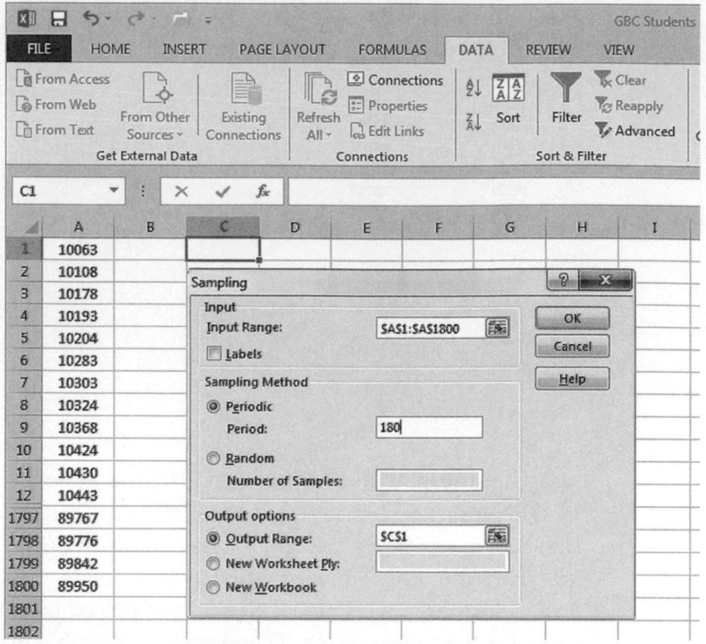

Column C in Figure 7.5 provides us with the systematic sample of 10 students from the population. This list includes the 180th student in our list, followed by the 360th student, and so forth.

FIGURE 7.5
Finished Systematic Sample

	A	B	C	D
1	10063		18106	
2	10108		25275	
3	10178		32980	
4	10193		41519	
5	10204		49923	
6	10283		57575	
7	10303		65938	
8	10324		74231	
9	10368		82200	
10	10424		89950	
11	10430			
12	10443			
1797	89767			
1798	89776			
1799	89842			
1800	89950			
1801				

Generating a systematic sample is easier to do manually than generating a simple random sample. For example, if 500 students walk into a classroom building during the first hour of school, and I need a sample of 100 students, using Equation 7.1, I can easily figure out what k is: $k = 500/100$, or 5. I could then select every fifth student arriving in the morning to participate in the survey. Systematic sampling is better than just randomly selecting students walking by because I could have a bias toward selecting some students rather than others (for example, students I know from my classes).

One concern about systematic sampling is **periodicity**, which is a pattern in the population that is consistent with the value of *k*.

One concern about systematic sampling is **periodicity,** which is a pattern in the population that is consistent with the value of k. For instance, let's say I'm conducting a survey on campus asking students how many hours they study during the week and I select every fourth week to collect my data. Because we are on an eight-week semester schedule at Goldey-Beacom, every fourth week could end up being either a midterm week or a finals week, which would result in a higher number of study hours than normal (or at least I would hope so). The presence of periodicity can result in a sample that is not representative of the entire population. When using systematic sampling, care must be taken to ensure that periodicity does not impact the collection of your data.

Finally, the starting point for systematic sampling does not need to be the first data value. We can randomly choose the starting position and proceed by counting down k values from this point to choose our sample.

Recall that you learned in Chapter 4 that two events are considered to be mutually exclusive if they cannot occur at the same time during an experiment.

When choosing a **stratified sample**, we divide the population into mutually exclusive groups, or strata, and randomly sample from each of those groups. The strata are based on important variables that can have an impact on the data collected and the results that are achieved.

Stratified Sampling

In **stratified sampling,** we divide the population into mutually exclusive groups, or strata, and randomly sample from each of those groups. For example, suppose we want our academic integrity sample to mirror the proportion of freshmen, sophomore, junior, and senior students in the overall college population and that we would like to select a sample size of 100 students. Because freshmen comprise 30% of the student population our sample of 100 students should contain 30 freshmen. Likewise, because sophomores comprise 22% of the student population our sample of 100 students should contain 22 sophomores. The same logic applies to juniors and seniors. Table 7.1 shows the number of freshmen, sophomores, juniors, and seniors required and calculates the size of each stratum in our sample based on its percentage relative to the population. We can then apply the simple random or systematic sampling methods to select the students from each group.

TABLE 7.1 | STRATIFIED SAMPLING FOR THE ACADEMIC INTEGRITY SURVEY

STRATA	SIZE (PERCENT) OF POPULATION	SAMPLE
Freshmen	540 (30%)	$0.30 \times 100 = 30$
Sophomore	396 (22%)	$0.22 \times 100 = 22$
Junior	504 (28%)	$0.28 \times 100 = 28$
Senior	360 (20%)	$0.20 \times 100 = 20$
Total	**1,800 (100%)**	**100**

Why would we go through the trouble of using stratified sampling versus simple random or systematic sampling? Suppose seniors, in general, take academic integrity much more seriously than freshmen do. Also, suppose that we used systematic sampling, and, by chance, 40% of our sample consisted of seniors. Remember, seniors account for only 20% of the student body. If we use our sample to draw conclusions about the attitudes of the population, we may be led to believe our students take academic integrity much more seriously than they really do.

We used stratified sampling because we felt that the class the students belonged to—whether they were freshman, sophomores, juniors, or seniors—was an important factor in how they would respond to our survey. This helps ensure that the sample is representative of the overall population.

Cluster sampling involves dividing the population into mutually exclusive groups, or clusters, that are each representative of the population and then randomly selecting clusters to form the final sample. These clusters are often selected based on geography to help simplify the sampling process.

The purpose of cluster sampling is to make the sampling process more economical. The purpose of stratified sampling is to make the sampling process more accurate.

Cluster Sampling

Clusters are defined as mutually exclusive groups, each which is representative of the population. **Cluster sampling** involves randomly selecting clusters to be part of the final sample. These clusters are often selected based on geography to help simplify the sampling process. Using the academic integrity survey as an example, the clusters could be defined as classrooms in use at certain times of the day. We would randomly choose different classrooms to participate in the survey. We could then include every student in the classroom as a participant in the survey or use simple random sampling within the classroom to select students.

My students often confuse strata and clusters. The members of a specific stratum all have something in common, such as each student being a freshman from my previous example. As a result, strata tend to be homogeneous collections, each with a certain characteristic of interest. Clusters, on the other hand, are "mini-subsets" of the larger population and therefore tend to be a melting pot of various characteristics. For example, a particular classroom (cluster) could have a mixture of freshman, sophomores, juniors, or seniors.

Cluster sampling is often used to test-market new products. Test-market cities are identified, and individual customers within those locations are sampled for their opinions about these products. Cluster sampling can be a cost-effective way to collect a probability sample if performed carefully to ensure that the sample is representative of the population.

Stats in Practice: Which City Best Represents the American Consumer? The Winner is Albany, N.Y.

Companies that are looking to test their product or services in the American marketplace would like to choose a location that best represents the typical U.S. consumer. To help identify these locales, Acxiom Corporation has ranked the populations in the top 150 Metropolitan Statistical Areas (MSAs) based on how closely they mirror the American consumer. At the top of this list is Albany, New York.

"Albany has almost the same proportion of consumers as is found in the nation as a whole—from people just leaving home or school, buying a home, raising kids, approaching retirement, launching the kids out of the house, to being fully retired," said Acxiom's Tiffany Weatherly, who supervised the research for this project.

The following MSAs made the top 10 as far as being the most representative of the U.S. consumer:

1. Albany, N.Y.
2. Rochester, N.Y.
3. Greensboro, N.C.
4. Birmingham, Ala.
5. Syracuse, N.Y.
6. Charlotte, N.C.
7. Nashville, Tenn.
8. Eugene, Ore.
9. Wichita, Kans.
10. Richmond, Va.

Companies would also be interested in knowing which locations to avoid conducting test markets due to the lack of suitability of the local population. The following list is the bottom 10 MSAs according to Acxiom.

1. El Paso, Tex.
2. Columbia, Mo.
3. Tallahassee, Fla.
4. Brownsville, Tex.
5. Provo, Utah
6. Ocala, Fla.
7. McAllen, Tex.
8. Honolulu, Hawaii
9. San Francisco, Calif.
10. New York City, N.Y.

Based on: Jonathan Portis, "Which American City Provides The Best Consumer Test Market?" *Acxiom Corporation News Release*, May 24, 2004, http://www.businesswire.com/news/home/20040524005650/en/American-City-Consumer-Test-Market-Mirror-America.

This Statistics in Practice demonstrates the use of cluster sampling in the marketplace.

Resampling*

Resampling is a statistical technique where many samples are repeatedly drawn from a population.

The **bootstrap method** involves using computer software to extract many samples with replacement in order to estimate a parameter of the population, such as a mean or proportion.

Resampling is a statistical technique where many samples are repeatedly drawn from an available population. A specific type of resampling technique is known as the **bootstrap method**, developed by Bradley Efron, a faculty member in Stanford University's Department of Statistics. Bootstrapping involves using computer software to extract many samples with replacement in order to estimate a certain parameter of the population, such as a mean or proportion.

To demonstrate the bootstrap method, consider the following simple example. Suppose the manager at a particular Walmart location would like to estimate the proportion of female shoppers at her store. She randomly selects 100 transactions and discovers that 58 of them were transacted with female customers. We now know that the sample proportion is 58% female, but the population proportion of female shoppers is still unknown.

In an Excel file, we can populate cells A1 to A58 with the number "1" to represent the female shoppers. Cells A59 through A100 would contain the number "0" for the men. Using

*This content is optional. Special thanks to Dr. Sunil Sapra from California State University for recommending the inclusion of this topic.

Excel's Sampling tool in Data Analysis, shown in Figure 7.2, we can generate a random sample of size 100 and calculate the proportion of female shoppers for this sample. Using bootstrapping software to assist us, we can repeat this sampling process, say 10,000 times or more (otherwise known as resampling). Some of these sample proportions of female shoppers will be less than 58%, whereas others will be more than 58%. We now have a range of proportions that will provide us an idea of where the true population proportion lies based on our original sample of 100 shoppers. This concept is related to confidence intervals, which will be discussed at great length in Chapter 8. Remember, Excel's random sampling tool uses sampling *with replacement*. This means that after a member of the population has been selected for the sample, he or she is placed back into the population and can be chosen again as part of the same sample. This is an important feature of bootstrapping.

As you can see in this example, the bootstrap method can be applied to estimate parameters such as the population proportion, mean, median, or variance. Bootstrapping can also be used to estimate the standard deviation of a sample mean or proportion and is not limited by underlying assumptions that are necessary to conduct many statistical analyses.

Nonprobability Sampling

A **nonprobability sample** is a sample in which the probability of a population member being selected for the sample is not known.

A **nonprobability sample** is a sample in which the probability of a population member being selected for the sample is not known. A common type of nonprobability sample is a **convenience sample**.

A convenience sample is used when members of the population are chosen to become part of the sample simply because they are easily accessible. This type of sampling is useful when you are simply trying to gather some general information about the population. For example, suppose you would like some quick feedback from your customers about a new bakery product you've recently developed. Sending out free samples and having customers who happen to enter your store rate the product would be an example of a convenience sample. In most cases, it would not be appropriate to use these data to perform inferential statistics like we would with probability sampling.

For example, if I would like some student feedback on this textbook, I could select my current statistics classes as my sample. This would be a convenience sample because it is most likely not representative of all of the students in the nation who read statistics textbooks; therefore, I need to be very careful with interpreting the results.

This is especially true because the students in my classes might be telling me what I wanted to hear in an effort to pass my course!

One of the most common types of convenience samples is an Internet poll. Most individuals who participate in Internet polls have very little statistical training. They are impressed when they see thousands of responses recorded in real time and tend to believe the results. What they fail to see, however, is that this is a convenience sample, and that often the conductor of the poll has very little control over who participates in it. Generally, anyone with an Internet connection is eligible to participate, and people can respond to the survey multiple times by re-accessing the poll on a different day or from a different browser or computer. Of course, this reduces the credibility of the results. Suffice it to say, a sampling technique that gives you no control over who participates in your survey does not qualify as probability sampling.

According to my father-in-law, Lindsay Greenplate, who was 12 years old during this election, there was a rumor that Roosevelt did not fly while campaigning because he was afraid of "Landon". I did not make this up.

Stats in Practice: Sampling in Presidential Races

Back in Chapter 1, I discussed one of the most famous convenience samples in history that caused much embarrassment for the poll takers. During the 1936 U.S. presidential race, the *Literary Digest,* which had correctly predicted the previous five presidential winners, predicted that Alf Landon would win the election over the actual winner, Franklin D. Roosevelt. The problem was that the *Digest* conveniently drew its sample from phone books and automobile registrations. People with phones and cars in 1936 tended to be wealthier Republicans and were not representative of the entire voting population. Even though the *Digest* randomly selected names from these sources, they did not choose them from the proper population. In comparison, a 1968 Gallup poll used a probability sample to predict that Richard Nixon would receive 43% of the votes for the 1968 presidential election when in fact he won 42.9%. This Gallup poll was based on a sample size of only 2,000 people, whereas the disastrous 1936 *Literary Digest* poll sampled 2,000,000 people. Probability samples rule when conducted properly!

Beware of convenience sampling. Because no effort is made to ensure the sample is representative of the population, the results based on this type of sample are unreliable.

Try your hand with this next Your Turn section to make sure you understand the difference between the sampling techniques we have discussed.

YOUR TURN #1

Identify the type of sampling technique for each of the following:

a. The first Monday of each month, I ask my customers who come to my store to fill out a satisfaction survey.

b. I randomly select four stores in a mall and ask each customer in those stores about his or her opinion of the latest health care legislation.

c. I position myself on a busy intersection of a city street and ask people what their opinions are of a local sports team.

d. Sixty percent of the students attending my college are female. I construct a random sample that consists of 60% females from the student population to ask what their opinions are of the college's food service.

e. Using computer software, I randomly select 20 employees to participate in a job satisfaction survey.

Answers can be found on ▶ **page 329**

7.3 Sampling and Nonsampling Errors

So far in this chapter, I realize I've been ranting about the marvels of sampling and how life on this planet could not exist as we know it today without this wonderful tool statisticians (sort of) invented. Maybe I'm exaggerating slightly, but sampling is a pretty cool idea that has made our lives a little better. However, I also tell my students that there is no free lunch in statistics because the benefits of sampling come with a cost. When we rely on relatively small samples to draw conclusions about larger populations, we expose ourselves to sampling errors (cue the scary music).

Parameters are values that describe some characteristic of a population, such as its mean or median.

Statistics are values calculated from a sample, such as the sample's mean or median.

Before discussing the details of sampling errors, I need to introduce two new terms: parameters and statistics. **Parameters** are values that describe some characteristic of a population, such as its mean or median. For the most part, parameters are unknown because we rarely observe or measure an entire population. **Statistics** are values calculated from a sample, such as the mean or the median. Statistics are used to estimate the value of a parameter. It is common practice, for example, to use the sample mean (a statistic) to estimate the value of the population mean (a parameter).

Sampling error of the sample mean is defined as the difference between the sample statistic and the population parameter.

Because a statistic is based on just a portion of the population, it would be unreasonable to expect the sample mean and population mean to be the same. The difference between these two values is known as the **sampling error of the sample mean**. The formula for the sampling error is shown in Equation 7.2.

Formula 7.2 for the Sampling Error of the Sample Mean

$$\text{Sampling Error} = \bar{x} - \mu$$

where

$\bar{x} =$ The sample mean
$\mu =$ The population mean

To demonstrate sampling errors and how they typically behave, consider the following example. Suppose I'm teaching a small, graduate-level statistics class composed of 10 students with the following ages.

24 33 28 41 38 30 24 33 37 32

If I consider this class my population, the population mean can be found using Equation 3.2 from Chapter 3.

$$\mu = \frac{\sum_{i=1}^{N} x_i}{N} = \frac{24 + 33 + 28 + \cdots + 37 + 32}{10} = \frac{320}{10} = 32.0$$

The average age of my class is 32.0 years old, which is my population parameter. Next, I would like to draw a random sample consisting of two students to estimate this parameter. I realize we already know the value of the parameter, but I ask you to play along and humor me. The method to my madness will become obvious soon.

Let's say the random sample consists of the first two students ($n = 2$) in our previous list. They are ages 24 and 33. The sample mean can be found using Equation 3.1 from Chapter 3:

$$\bar{x} = \frac{\sum_{i=1}^{n} x_i}{n} = \frac{24 + 33}{2} = 28.5$$

I use Equation 7.2 to calculate my sampling error:

$$\text{Sampling Error} = \bar{x} - \mu = 28.5 - 32.0 = -3.5$$

My sample statistic is 3.5 years below the population parameter due to the negative sampling error. Positive sampling errors would be the result of sample means greater than the population mean. Now, suppose I gather another random sample of two students, which happen to be the last two students in my original list of 10. They are ages 37 and 32. This sample mean is found to be

$$\bar{x} = \frac{\sum_{i=1}^{n} x_i}{n} = \frac{37 + 32}{2} = 34.5$$

I use Equation 7.2 again to calculate my latest sampling error.

$$\text{Sampling Error} = \bar{x} - \mu = 34.5 - 32.0 = 2.5$$

This sample statistic is 2.5 years above the population parameter. This illustrates the first lesson about sampling errors: They can differ from one sample to the next. Sampling errors can also be positive or negative, depending on whether they are above or below the population mean.

Sampling errors can differ from one sample to the next. Sampling errors can also be positive or negative.

In the previous examples, I used a sample size of two students. What happens when I increase the sample size to, say, $n = 5$? If this random sample consists of the first five students in my original list, my new sample mean becomes

$$\bar{x} = \frac{\sum_{i=1}^{n} x_i}{n} = \frac{24 + 33 + 28 + 41 + 38}{5} = 32.8$$

This results in a sampling error given as follows:

$$\text{Sampling Error} = \bar{x} - \mu = 32.8 - 32.0 = 0.8$$

Obviously, this latest sample provides a much better estimate of the actual average age of my statistics class. In general, we expect larger sample sizes to provide smaller corresponding sampling errors. It's important to note, though, that a larger sample size will not guarantee you a smaller sampling error for every sample selected. For example, if my random sample of five happens to include the five oldest students in the class, the sample average and corresponding sampling error would be

$$\bar{x} = \frac{\sum_{i=1}^{n} x_i}{n} = \frac{41 + 38 + 37 + 33 + 33}{5} = 36.4$$

$$\text{Sampling Error} = \bar{x} - \mu = 36.4 - 32.0 = 4.4$$

Increasing the sample size tends to decrease the sampling error. However, there is no guarantee that a particular sampling error will be smaller with a larger sample size.

The error from this sample is larger than both errors from my examples with a sample size of two students. Larger samples simply increase the likelihood that the sampling error will be smaller, but with statistical sampling, there are few guarantees.

Now, in most statistical settings, the population parameter is not known because it is often not feasible to observe or measure the entire population. Therefore, we will rarely know what the actual sampling error will be for a particular sample that we select. However, in upcoming chapters, I will show you how to determine what the probability is of sampling errors occurring. Stay tuned!

Nonsampling errors occur as a result of issues such as ambiguous survey questions, questions that lead respondents to a certain "correct" answer, and data collection errors.

Before we wrap up this section, I feel compelled to mention that sampling errors are not the only pitfall you can encounter with statistics. **Nonsampling errors** occur for a variety of reasons. A common source is survey questions that are ambiguous in the eyes of the respondents, which results in their not answering the questions in a reliable manner. Other survey questions can be written in a way that leads the respondent to certain "correct" answers, which will influence the conclusions.

Data collection errors also fall into the category of nonsampling errors. A data collection error occurs when a person responsible for recording the information being collected as part of a survey makes an input error. Or a measurement device could be faulty, such as a scale that weighs a box of cereal. Unlike sampling errors, nonsampling errors cannot be reduced by simply increasing the size of the sample. Reducing nonsampling errors requires a thorough analysis of the survey's design and how the data are collected.

The following Your Turn section will test your sampling error skills using the stock market.

YOUR TURN #2

Suppose you have an investment portfolio that consists of 16 stocks that have closed today with the following stock prices.

\$21	\$24	\$36	\$23	\$26	\$31	\$26	\$28
\$17	\$30	\$34	\$27	\$21	\$36	\$48	\$33

Calculate the sampling error if the sample includes the following stocks:

a. the first two stocks (\$21, \$24)
b. the first four stocks (\$21, \$24, \$36, \$23)
c. the first six stocks (\$21, \$24, \$36, \$23, \$26, \$31)

What conclusions can be drawn about sample size and sample error for this population?

Answers can be found on ▶ **page 329**

7.3 Section Problems

Applications

7.1 Suppose the average grade point average (GPA) for the undergraduate student population at Goldey-Beacom College is 3.10. The following list is a random sample of the GPAs of five students from the college. Calculate the sampling error.

2.45 3.76 3.48 2.81 3.34

7.2 Jeff Bollinger of Prudential Realtors has 20 residential listings under contract. The following table shows the number of days each of these 20 houses has been on the market as of today.

20	21	2	17	35	21	40	54	52	24
40	53	46	10	42	11	37	62	21	76

a. Calculate the mean for this population.
b. Calculate the sampling error using the first five homes in the first row as your sample.
c. Calculate the sampling error using all 10 homes in the first row as your sample.
d. How does increasing the sample size affect the sampling error?
e. Using a sample size of 5, what is the largest sampling error that can be observed from this population?

7.3 The following table shows the total points scored in the 16 National Football League games played during Week 1 of the 2012 season.

41	62	64	50	47	33	49	72
76	40	52	36	26	50	57	36

a. Calculate the mean for this population.
b. Calculate the sampling error using the first four games in the first row as your sample.
c. Calculate the sampling error using all eight games in the first row as your sample.
d. How does increasing the sample size affect the sampling error?
e. Using a sample size of 4, what is the largest sampling error that can be observed from this population?

7.4 Avis rental car in Whittier, Alaska, currently has 15 rental cars on its lot, each with the following mileage:

19,871	11,483	18,519	10,977	8,325
6,514	14,394	6,225	4,702	11,145
4,768	16,329	15,094	13,317	19,537

a. Calculate the mean for this population.
b. Calculate the sampling error using the five cars in the first row as your sample.
c. Calculate the sampling error using the 10 cars in the first two rows as your sample.
d. How does increasing the sample size affect the sampling error?

7.5 The Excel file titled **states.xlsx** contains the median income in 2011 for all 50 states and the District of Columbia.

a. Use Excel to draw a simple random sample consisting of four states, and then calculate the sampling error for the sample.
b. Use Excel to draw a simple random sample consisting of eight states, and then calculate the sampling error for the sample.
c. Use Excel to draw a simple random sample consisting of 12 states, and then calculate the sampling error for the sample.
d. Compare the sampling error for parts a, b, and c and explain the reason for the differences.

7.6 The Excel file titled **verizon.xlsx** contains daily revenues for the past 350 business days earned from cell phone accessories (Bluetooth headsets, memory cards, and so on) sold at a local Verizon retail store in Delaware.

a. Use Excel to draw a systematic sample consisting of 10 days, and then calculate the sampling error for the sample.
b. Use Excel to draw a systematic sample consisting of 25 days, and then calculate the sampling error for the sample.
c. Use Excel to draw a systematic sample consisting of 50 days, and then calculate the sampling error for the sample.
d. Compare the sampling error for parts a, b, and c and explain the reason for the differences.
e. What problems might be encountered with the sample obtained in part c?

7.4 The Central Limit Theorem

According to the **Central Limit Theorem**, sample means from samples of sufficient size, drawn from any population, will be normally distributed.

I can't overemphasize the importance of the CLT. We will rely on this behavior of sample means over and over again throughout the rest of this book.

When my students encounter the word *theorem,* I often see that glassy-eyed look that tells me their minds are wandering off to some faraway place. But believe me when I tell you that the Central Limit Theorem (CLT) is the "mother of all theorems" and is worthy of your attention. The **Central Limit Theorem** states that the sample means of large-sized samples will be normally distributed regardless of the shape of their population distributions. Without this gem, the field of statistics would probably have never made the cut as a required course for many college students. So you might as well learn about the real reason you are reading this book today.

The best way to describe the CLT is with the following example. My wife, Deb, and I are going out to dinner at a moderately priced restaurant (I am a teacher, after all) that offers the four types of entrées shown in Table 7.2 on the next page. If an entrée from this list is randomly selected, there is a 25% probability that it will cost $12. The same probability holds true for the price of the three other entrées. The graph of this probability distribution is shown in Figure 7.6, also on the next page.

TABLE 7.2 | Entrees, Their Prices, and the Probability of Their Being Randomly Selected

ENTRÉE TYPE	PRICE ($)	PROBABILITY OF BEING RANDOMLY SELECTED
Vegetarian (V)	12	0.25
Chicken (C)	14	0.25
Fish (F)	16	0.25
Steak (S)	18	0.25

FIGURE 7.6 Probability Distribution for Four Randomly Selected Entrée Choices

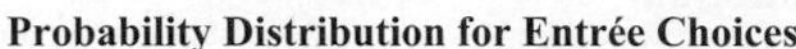

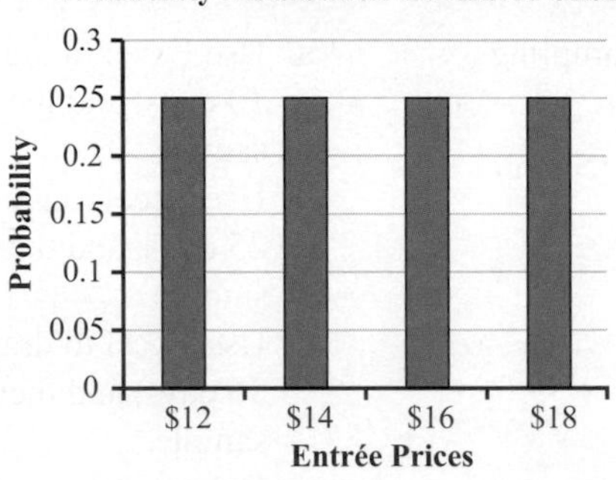

Because Table 7.2 includes all the entrée types that are available to choose from, these data would be considered a population. The mean of this population is found using Equation 5.1:

$$\mu = \sum_{i=1}^{N} x_i P(x_i)$$

$$\mu = (\$12)(0.25) + (\$14)(0.25) + (\$16)(0.25) + (\$18)(0.25)$$

$$\mu = \$3.00 + \$3.50 + \$4.00 + \$4.50$$

$$\mu = \$15.00$$

In other words, the mean price for this population is $15. Next, I want to calculate the standard deviation of this population using Table 7.3 and Equation 5.4.

TABLE 7.3 | Calculating the Standard Deviation for the Population of Entrée Prices

x_i	x_i^2	$P(x_i)$	$x_i^2\,P(x_i)$
12	144	0.25	36
14	196	0.25	49
16	256	0.25	64
18	324	0.25	81
		Total	**= 230**

$$\sum_{i=1}^{N} x_i^2 P(x_i) = 230$$

This calculates the variance of a discrete probability distribution.

$$\sigma^2 = \left(\sum_{i=1}^{N} x_i^2 P(x_i)\right) - \mu^2$$

$$\sigma^2 = 230 - (15)^2 = 230 - 225 = 5$$

$$\sigma = \sqrt{\sigma^2} = \sqrt{5} = \$2.24$$

To summarize so far, we have described a population with the following parameters:

$$\mu = \$15.00$$
$$\sigma = \$2.24$$

Now I'll introduce you to the wonders of the Central Limit Theorem. Suppose Deb and I each randomly select our entrées. (In reality, I'd *never* do this. I'd be so disappointed if I were stuck with the vegetarian entrée. Fish dishes make me nervous, too. Combine the two scenarios, and I would have a 50% chance of walking out hungry.) What are all the possible meal combinations Deb and I could end up with if we both randomly selected our meals? Table 7.4 shows the entrée prices for all possible 16 combinations. The top-left entry of 12, 12 represents the combination of both Deb and me (Bob) selecting a vegetarian entrée (V), each costing \$12. The entry directly to the right of this one (12, 14) shows the cost of me choosing the vegetarian entrée (V), which costs \$12, and Deb choosing a chicken entrée (C), which costs \$14—and so on through the rest of the table. My entrées are highlighted in yellow and Deb's are highlighted in blue.

TABLE 7.4 | POSSIBLE ENTRÉE COMBINATIONS (IN \$)

	DEB (V)	DEB (C)	DEB (F)	DEB (S)
Bob (V)	12, 12	12, 14	12, 16	12, 18
Bob (C)	14, 12	14, 14	14, 16	14, 18
Bob (F)	16, 12	16, 14	16, 16	16, 18
Bob (S)	18, 12	18, 14	18, 16	18, 18

What we have essentially done here is show all the possibilities of selecting a simple random sample of size 2 ($n = 2$) with replacement from this population. The term *with replacement* refers to the fact that Deb and I can both select the same entrée. Sampling *without replacement* means that if Deb selected vegetarian, then I would have to choose one of the other three entrees.

Next, I calculate the sample average for each pair of entrées selected in Table 7.4. All 16 averages are shown in Table 7.5. For example, if I choose chicken and Deb chooses vegetarian (the second entry in the first column in Table 7.4), then the sample average is

$$\bar{x} = \frac{\$14 + \$12}{2} = \$13$$

This value is shown as the second entry in the first column of Table 7.5.

TABLE 7.5 | THE POPULATION OF AVERAGE PRICES FOR TWO ENTRÉES RANDOMLY SELECTED BY DEB AND BOB (IN \$)

	DEB (V)	DEB (C)	DEB (F)	DEB (S)
Bob (V)	12	13	14	15
Bob (C)	13	14	15	16
Bob (F)	14	15	16	17
Bob (S)	15	16	17	18

Each value in this table represents a sample average for the pair of values shown in Table 7.4. This value is the average of 14 and 12.

Finally, I construct frequency and relative frequency distributions of the sample averages from Table 7.5. They are shown in Table 7.6 on the next page.

2/16 = 0.125

TABLE 7.6 | FREQUENCY AND RELATIVE FREQUENCY DISTRIBUTIONS FOR TABLE 7.5: AVERAGE ENTRÉE PRICES

SAMPLE AVERAGE $\bar{x}_i$	FREQUENCY	RELATIVE FREQUENCY $P(\bar{x}_i)$
\$12	1	0.0625
\$13	2	0.125
\$14	3	0.1875
\$15	4	0.25
\$16	3	0.1875
\$17	2	0.125
\$18	1	0.0625
Total	**16**	**1.00**

The **sampling distribution of the mean** describes the pattern that sample averages tend to follow when randomly drawn from a population.

The distribution shown in Table 7.6 has a very special name—the **sampling distribution of the mean**. This table describes the pattern that sample averages tend to follow when randomly drawn from a population. Figure 7.7 shows this distribution graphically.

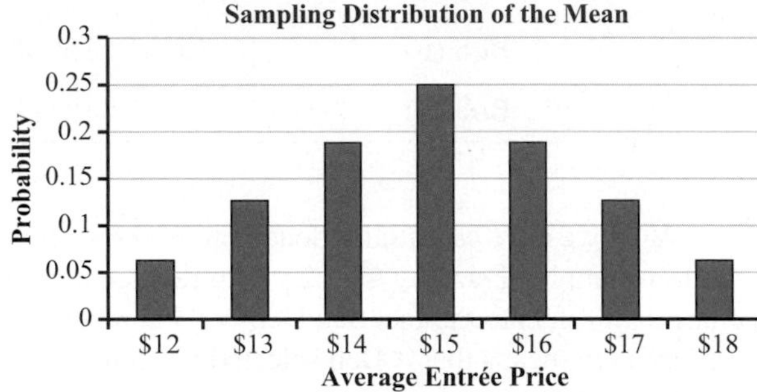

FIGURE 7.7 The Sampling Distribution of the Mean: Average Entrée Prices

Now compare the shape of the sampling distribution of the mean with the population probability distribution in Figure 7.6. Even though the population distribution was uniform (all four entrées had a 25% chance of being randomly selected), the sample means distribution tends to be bell-shaped and symmetrical around the population's mean (\$15), which resembles the normal probability distribution from Chapter 6. This is because the sample mean of \$15 has four different ways to occur, as Table 7.7, which replicates Table 7.6, shows.

TABLE 7.7 | SAMPLE MEANS FOR ENTRÉE PRICES

	DEB (V)	DEB (C)	DEB (F)	DEB (S)
Bob (V)	12	13	14	15
Bob (C)	13	14	15	16
Bob (F)	14	15	16	17
Bob (S)	15	16	17	18

By contrast, the sample means of \$12 and \$18 each appear only once in our sampling distribution.

In general, the CLT tells us the following: For any population distribution, with a sufficiently large sample, the sample means will be normally distributed. In most cases, sample sizes of 30 or larger will result in sample means being normally distributed, regardless of the shape of the population distribution. If the population happens to follow the normal probability distribution, the sample means will also be normally distributed, regardless of the size of the samples.

We can verify the mean of the population by calculating the mean of the sample means, or $\mu_{\bar{x}}$, using Table 7.6:

$$\mu_{\bar{x}} = \sum_{i=1}^{N} \bar{x}_i P(\bar{x}_i)$$

$$\mu_{\bar{x}} = (\$12)(0.0625) + (\$13)(0.125) + (\$14)(0.1875) + (\$15)(0.25) + (\$16)(0.1875) + (\$17)(0.125) + (\$18)(0.0625)$$

$$\mu_{\bar{x}} = \$0.75 + \$1.625 + \$2.625 + \$3.75 + \$3.00 + \$2.125 + \$1.125$$

$$\mu_{\bar{x}} = \$15.00$$

Notice that I distinguish between the two different means.

μ = The population mean

$\mu_{\bar{x}}$ = The mean of the sample means

Because of sampling error, the mean of the sample means ($\mu_{\bar{x}}$) may not always be equal to the population mean (μ). They are equal in this example because we included every possible sample mean from the population using $n = 2$.

It is not a coincidence that $\mu = \mu_{\bar{x}} = \$15.00$. The average of many sample means drawn from a particular population should be very close or equal to the population mean, as we have seen with my entrée example.

Bear with me for one last important point. Let's calculate the standard deviation for the sample means, or $\sigma_{\bar{x}}$, using Table 7.6. I will once again rely on Equation 5.4, substituting $\bar{x}$ for x and $\mu_{\bar{x}}$ for μ. Table 7.8 shows the necessary calculations.

TABLE 7.8 | Standard Deviation Calculations for the Sample Means: Average Entrée Prices

$\bar{x}_i$	$\bar{x}_i^2$	$P(\bar{x}_i)$	$\bar{x}_i^2 P(\bar{x}_i)$
12	144	0.0625	9
13	169	0.125	21.125
14	196	0.1875	36.75
15	225	0.25	56.25
16	256	0.1875	48
17	289	0.125	36.125
18	324	0.0625	20.25
			Total = 227.5

$$\sum_{i=1}^{N} \bar{x}_i^2 P(\bar{x}_i) = 227.5$$

$$\sigma_{\bar{x}}^2 = \left(\sum_{i=1}^{N} \bar{x}_i^2 P(\bar{x}_i) \right) - \mu_{\bar{x}}^2$$

$$\sigma_{\bar{x}}^2 = 227.5 - (15)^2 = 227.5 - 225 = 2.5$$

$$\sigma_{\bar{x}} = \sqrt{\sigma_{\bar{x}}^2} = \sqrt{2.5} = \$1.58$$

In other words, the standard deviation for the sample means is \$1.58. Notice that I distinguish between the two different standard deviations.

σ = The population standard deviation, which measures the variation around the population mean.

$\sigma_{\bar{x}}$ = The standard deviation of the sample means, which measures the average variation around the mean of the sample means for all samples of size n. This is also known as the **standard error of the mean**.

The higher the standard error of the mean, the more variation you will notice from one sample mean to the next as they are drawn from the population.

Let's stop for a minute to summarize what we have found so far.

POPULATION	SAMPLE MEANS
$\mu = \$15.00$	$\mu_{\bar{x}} = \$15.00$
$\sigma = \$2.24$	$\sigma_{\bar{x}} = \$1.58$

If we know the population standard deviation, σ, we can calculate the standard error of the mean, $\sigma_{\bar{x}}$, using Equation 7.3.

The **standard error of the mean** is the sample mean standard deviation, which measures the average variation around the mean of the sample means.

Formula 7.3 for the Standard Error of the Mean

$$\sigma_{\bar{x}} = \frac{\sigma}{\sqrt{n}}$$

where

$\sigma =$ The population standard deviation
$n =$ The sample size

This is a very important equation that you will see much of in the upcoming chapters. Let's put it to work in our entrée example.

$$\sigma_{\bar{x}} = \frac{\sigma}{\sqrt{n}} = \frac{\$2.24}{\sqrt{2}} = \$1.58$$

In our example, $n = 2$ because we randomly selected two entrees way back in Table 7.4 to construct our sampling distribution. Equation 7.3 gives us the same result that we obtained using Table 7.8 and Equation 5.4, but with a lot less work!

Let's take this time to summarize what we have learned so far:

- The sample means for a population that follows the normal distribution will also be normally distributed, regardless of the size of the samples.
- If the population does not follow the normal probability distribution, the CLT tells us that the sample means will be normally distributed with a sufficiently large sample size. In most cases, sample sizes of 30 or larger will result in sample means being normally distributed, regardless of the shape of the population distribution.

$$\mu = \mu_{\bar{x}}$$

$$\sigma_{\bar{x}} = \frac{\sigma}{\sqrt{n}}$$

These properties unlock many statistical procedures that have made significant contributions to decision making. The following section will demonstrate how we can put the CLT to work in the business world. But first, I encourage you to check your understanding of the theorem by trying to solve the next Your Turn problem.

YOUR TURN #3

Debbie and Katie are planning a visit to the Elegant Day Spa where they will each randomly choose one of the following three services that are offered.

Service	Cost
Facial (F)	$40
Pedicure (P)	$30
Manicure (M)	$20

Define the population as the three services and a sample of size two as the service that Debbie chooses and the service that Katie chooses.

a. Identify the frequency distribution for the population.
b. Identify the frequency distribution for all combinations of sample means for Debbie and Katie choosing a service.

c. Verify that the population mean and mean of all possible sample means are equal.
d. Calculate the standard error of the mean two different ways, first using Equation 5.4 and then with Equation 7.3.

Answers can be found on ▶ **pages 329–330**

Putting the Central Limit Theorem to Work

The purpose of this section is to convince you that the CLT is an extremely useful tool worthy of all the praise that I have bestowed on it. To illustrate, I'll use data from a 2012 Pew Research Center study, which discovered that U.S. teenagers send and receive an average of 60 text messages a day. I know little or nothing about the probability distribution for this population and, therefore, cannot answer the following question: What is the probability that a randomly selected teenager will send and receive more than 69 text messages today?

However, using the CLT, I *can* answer the following question: What is the probability that a randomly selected sample of 30 teenagers will average more than 69 text messages today (sent and received).

With this sufficiently large sample $(n \geq 30)$, I can answer the second question because I know that my sample averages will follow a normal probability distribution with the following mean:

$$\mu_{\bar{x}} = \mu = 60$$

My next step is to calculate the standard error of the mean, $\sigma_{\bar{x}}$, using Equation 7.3. However, this equation requires me to know σ, the population standard deviation, which is not always available. There are techniques available to estimate σ that we will investigate in later chapters. In the meantime, for our text messaging example, we'll assume that we have evidence to conclude that the population standard deviation equals 36 text messages per day. We can now calculate the standard error of the mean using Equation 7.3.

$$\sigma = 36$$
$$n = 30$$
$$\sigma_{\bar{x}} = \frac{\sigma}{\sqrt{n}} = \frac{36}{\sqrt{30}} = \frac{36}{5.48} = 6.57$$

To calculate our normal probability, I need to rely on the z-score for sample means shown in Equation 7.4.

Formula 7.4 for the z-Score for the Sample Mean

$$z_{\bar{x}} = \frac{\bar{x} - \mu_{\bar{x}}}{\sigma_{\bar{x}}}$$

where

$\bar{x}$ = Sample mean
$\mu_{\bar{x}}$ = Mean of the sample means
$\sigma_{\bar{x}}$ = Standard error of the mean

This equation is a variation of the z-score that was discussed in Chapter 6. In this sample mean version of the z-score:

- $\bar{x}$ replaces x
- $\sigma_{\bar{x}}$ replaces σ
- $\mu_{\bar{x}}$ replaces μ

Using Equation 7.4, the z-score for $\bar{x} = 69$ is

$$z_{69} = \frac{\bar{x} - \mu_{\bar{x}}}{\sigma_{\bar{x}}} = \frac{69 - 60}{6.57} = 1.37$$

A common mistake that some of my students make is to use σ rather than $\sigma_{\bar{x}}$ in Equation 7.4. Be careful not to be one of these unfortunate statistics!

In other words, the sample mean of 69 is 1.37 standard deviations to the right of the mean for the sampling distribution, $\mu_{\bar{x}}$, and is shown in Figure 7.8.

FIGURE 7.8
The Sampling Distribution of the Mean: Text Messages Example

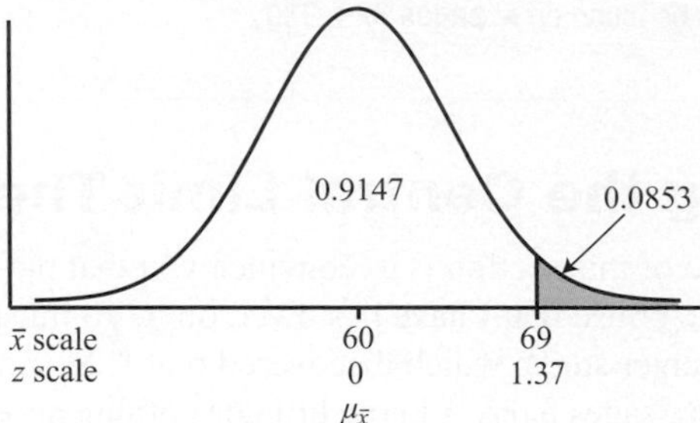

Using Table 4 in Appendix A, I find that the area to the left of $z = 1.37$ equals 0.9147. Therefore,

$$P(\bar{x} > 69) = P(z > 1.37) = 1.0 - 0.9147 = 0.0853$$

The shaded area in Figure 7.8 shows us that the probability that our sample of 30 teenagers will average more than 69 text messages a day is 8.5%. What I find remarkable is that we know this without any information about the population probability distribution. Call me a nerd, but I think this is so cool. Companies like Verizon and AT&T can use this information to help them design pricing levels for service plans for their younger customers.

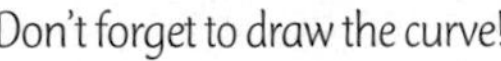

Before moving on, please try your hand at the next Your Turn problem to be sure you understand the CLT.

YOUR TURN #4

According to the U.S. Labor Department, the average hourly wage for private-sector production and non-supervisory workers was \$20.04 in February 2013. Assume the standard deviation for this population is \$6.00 per hour. A random sample of 35 workers from this group was selected. What is the probability that the mean for this sample is less than \$19.00?

Answer can be found on ▶ **page 330**

Using the Central Limit Theorem to Test Claims

But wait—there's more. The CLT can also be used to verify the validity of claims made by individuals or organizations. For example, let's say I make the claim that my average drive of a golf ball while teeing off is equal to a whopping 240 yards in length (picture Deb looking at me doubtfully). You see, Deb has proofread all of my statistics chapters and knows how to put my claim to the test. She can do so by randomly sampling 45 of my drives to satisfy the CLT requirement (we have no knowledge of the shape of the population distribution). Suppose the average drive from this sample is 233 yards, and the standard deviation for my driving population is 20 yards. Is there enough evidence to support my claim?

On the surface, you might be led to believe that, because 233 yards is less than 240, my claim is not supported. However, the mean of 233 yards is based on a sample. We know from earlier in the chapter that a sampling error occurs when a sample is used to estimate a population parameter. The sample mean does not have to equal 240 to support my claim; it can be slightly lower and still suffice. However, to answer this question thoroughly, Deb needs to employ the CLT. Her goal is to determine the probability of observing a sample mean of 233 yards or less, given that the sampling distribution mean (which we assume equals the population mean) is truly 240 yards. Sit back and watch her go to work.

First, Deb sets up our sampling distribution by assuming the mean does equal 240 yards. Even though we don't know if this claim is true at this point, we assume it is in order to test my claim.

$$\mu_{\bar{x}} = \mu = 240 \text{ yards}$$

Next, Deb calculates the standard error of the mean:

$$\sigma = 20 \text{ yards}$$
$$n = 45$$
$$\sigma_{\bar{x}} = \frac{\sigma}{\sqrt{n}} = \frac{20}{\sqrt{45}} = \frac{20}{6.71} = 2.98$$

Now, Deb calculates the z-score for $\bar{x} = 233$:

$$z_{233} = \frac{\bar{x} - \mu_{\bar{x}}}{\sigma_{\bar{x}}} = \frac{233 - 240}{2.98} = -2.35$$

Finally, she calculates the probability that the sample mean will be less than or equal to 233 yards if the actual sampling distribution mean equals 240 yards. I'm calculating the probability that my sample mean is less than 233 yards because 233 yards is less than my claim of 240 yards. Had my sample mean been greater than 240 yards, I would have calculated the probability that my sample mean is greater than 240 yards. Using Table 3 in Appendix A, we have

$$P(\bar{x} \leq 233) = P(z \leq -2.35) = 0.0094$$

This probability is shown graphically in the shaded region in Figure 7.9.

FIGURE 7.9
The Sampling Distribution of the Mean: Golf Example

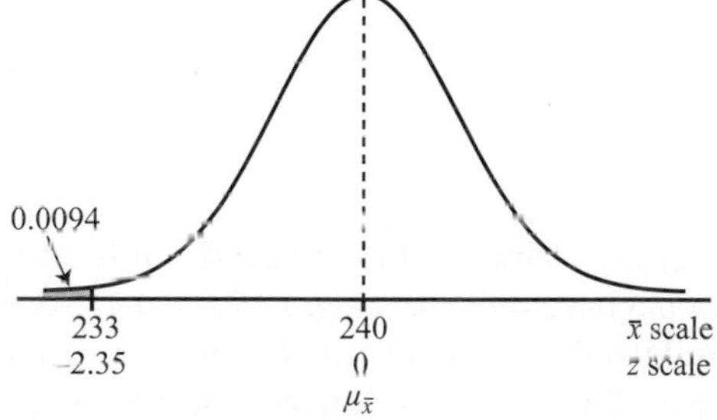

A sample mean between the values of $\bar{x}_L$ and $\bar{x}_u$ would support my claim!

This is bad news for me. If the true population mean for my drives (my average drive) is indeed 240 yards as I claimed, there is less than a 1% chance that Deb would have been able to collect a sample with a mean of 233 or less. It's more likely that my true population mean is somewhat less than 240 yards. It looks like I hit the ball farther in my mind's eye than I actually do on the golf course.

So far, we have discovered that my sample mean of 233 yards did not support my claim that my average drive was 240 yards. What sample mean would support my claim? Obviously, it would need to be closer to 240 yards than 233, so sample means slightly above 240 yards $(\bar{x}_U)$ and below 240 yards $(\bar{x}_L)$ would suffice. The shaded region in Figure 7.10 on the next page shows how we find these two values. Most statisticians would agree that these values can be identified in the symmetrical interval that includes 95% of the sample means if the true population mean was 240 yards.

FIGURE 7.10
Ninety-Five Percent of the Sample Means: Golf Example

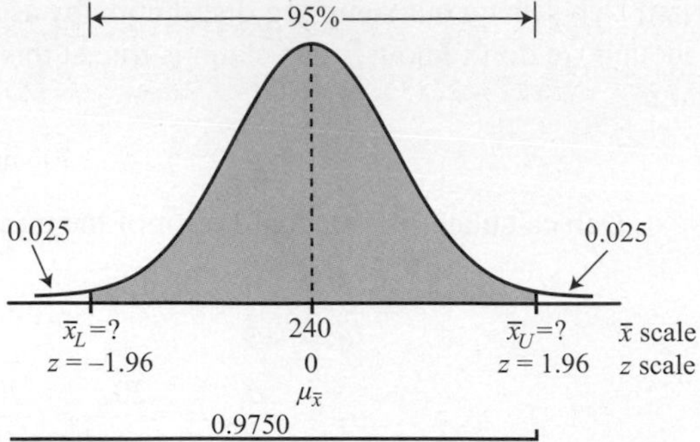

To find $\bar{x}_U$ and $\bar{x}_L$, we need to identify the z-scores that define the shaded region in Figure 7.10. If our 95% region is in the center of the sampling distribution, we have 2.5% of the area to the right of the shaded region and 2.5% of the area to the left.

This means that the area to the left of $\bar{x}_U$ is $0.95 + 0.025 = 0.975$, which is shown in Figure 7.10. We then search Table 4 in Appendix A to find the value in the body of the table closest to 0.975, which happens to be $z = 1.96$. We want to find the sample mean that is 1.96 standard deviations to the right of 240. Because the sampling distribution is symmetrical and the 95% region is in the middle of the curve, the z-score that corresponds to $\bar{x}_L$ is -1.96. In other words, we are also looking for the sample mean that is 1.96 standard deviations to the left of 240 yards. We do this by rearranging Equation 7.4 in terms of $\bar{x}$, as follows:

$$z = \frac{\bar{x} - \mu_{\bar{x}}}{\sigma_{\bar{x}}}$$

$$\bar{x}_U = \mu_{\bar{x}} + z\sigma_{\bar{x}}$$

$$\bar{x}_U = 240 + (1.96)(2.98) = 245.8 \text{ yards}$$

$$\bar{x}_L = \mu_{\bar{x}} - z\sigma_{\bar{x}}$$

$$\bar{x}_L = 240 + (-1.96)(2.98) = 234.2 \text{ yards}$$

To satisfy my claim that I average 240 yards off of the tee, the sample average of 45 drives would have to be between 234.2 and 245.8 yards. If the sample average is below 234.2 yards, I would have evidence that my population mean is less than 240 yards. A sample mean above 245.8 yards would indicate my average drive exceeds 240 yards.

In the next section, we will explore the effect sample size has on the sampling distribution. But before we get there, be sure to test the claim made by Kellogg's in the following Your Turn problem.

YOUR TURN #5

The CLT can be used in a quality control setting, such as a process that fills boxes with cereal. Suppose Kellogg's claims that the average weight for a box of Frosted Flakes is 18 ounces. To make sure that the filling process is working properly, a sample of 30 boxes is selected and found to have a mean of 18.2 ounces. Historical records show that the standard deviation of the filling process is 0.32 ounces.

a. Is the Frosted Flakes filling process working as Kellogg's claims?

b. Identify the symmetrical interval that includes 95% of the sample means if the true population mean is 18 ounces.

Answers can be found on ▶ **page 330**

The Effect of the Sample Size on the Sampling Distribution

Earlier in this chapter, I mentioned that sample size plays an important role in the CLT. As we increase the size of our samples, the standard error of the mean becomes smaller, which in turn reduces the sampling error. Let's return to my debunked claim of averaging 240 yards with my drives on the golf course. (Thanks a lot, Deb.) Using $\sigma = 20$ yards, $n = 45$ (the sample size), and Equation 7.3, we found the standard error of the mean to be $\sigma_{\bar{x}} = 2.98$ yards. Figure 7.11 shows the impact of increasing the sample size from 45 to 100.

FIGURE 7.11 The Effect Changing the Sample Size Has on the Sampling Distribution: Golf Example

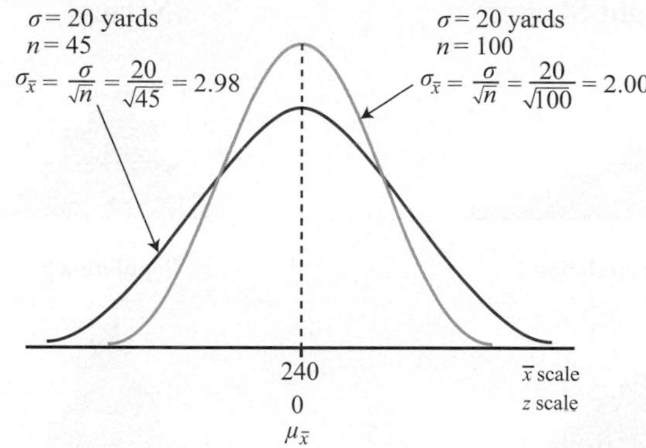

With a larger sample size the standard error is reduced, which results in the sample means having more of a tendency to crowd around the mean of the distribution.

Increasing the sample size to 100 changes the shape of the sampling distribution. The standard error of the mean drops from 2.98 to 2.00, causing the distribution to be taller and narrower, as shown in Figure 7.11. With a larger sample size the standard error is reduced, resulting in the sample means having more of a tendency to crowd around the mean of the distribution, which in this case is 240. We can see this by calculating the interval that will contain 95% of the sample means for $n = 100$.

$$\bar{x}_U = \mu_{\bar{x}} + z\sigma_{\bar{x}}$$
$$\bar{x}_U = 240 + (1.96)(2.00) = 243.9 \text{ yards}$$
$$\bar{x}_L = \mu_{\bar{x}} - z\sigma_{\bar{x}}$$
$$\bar{x}_L = 230 + (-1.96)(2.00) = 236.1 \text{ yards}$$

Table 7.9 compares these results to the interval calculated earlier for $n = 45$. As you can see, the interval of sample means for $n = 100$ is narrower than the one for $n = 45$.

TABLE 7.9 | INTERVALS THAT CONTAIN 95% OF SAMPLE MEANS WHEN THE SAMPLE SIZE CHANGES FROM 45 TO 100: GOLF EXAMPLE

n	$\bar{x}_L$	$\bar{x}_U$
45	234.2	245.8
100	236.1	243.9

Increasing the sample size also effectively reduces the sampling error, which we defined as $\bar{x} - \mu$ earlier in Equation 7.2. Think of it this way: As you gradually increase the sample size until it eventually becomes the population size, the sample means will approach the population mean. If the entire population is "sampled," the mean of that sample is the population mean. This is known as a **census**. Once the entire population is measured, then $\bar{x} = \mu$, which makes the sampling error equal to zero. I can summarize this as follows:

A **census** is the process of recording information from the entire population of interest.

As $n \rightarrow N$

Then $\bar{x} \rightarrow \mu$

Eventually $\bar{x} = \mu$

Making $\bar{x} - \mu = 0$ (Sampling Error)

In most cases, sampling is still the preferred approach over a census (unless you are the U.S. government). When the U.S. government counts the population of the country, it tries to count everyone—even people who are hard to find, such as the homeless. However, for most people and organizations, populations are usually too large to measure or not completely accessible. This concept demonstrates that sample size can be used to control the inherent errors that can occur when relying on a sample to describe a larger population.

The shape of the distribution of the population will also affect the shape of the sampling distribution, as will the size of the sample. Figure 7.12 shows the histograms of three populations, along with their corresponding sampling distributions.

FIGURE 7.12 Population Distributions and Their Corresponding Sampling Distributions (for Three Different-Sized Samples)

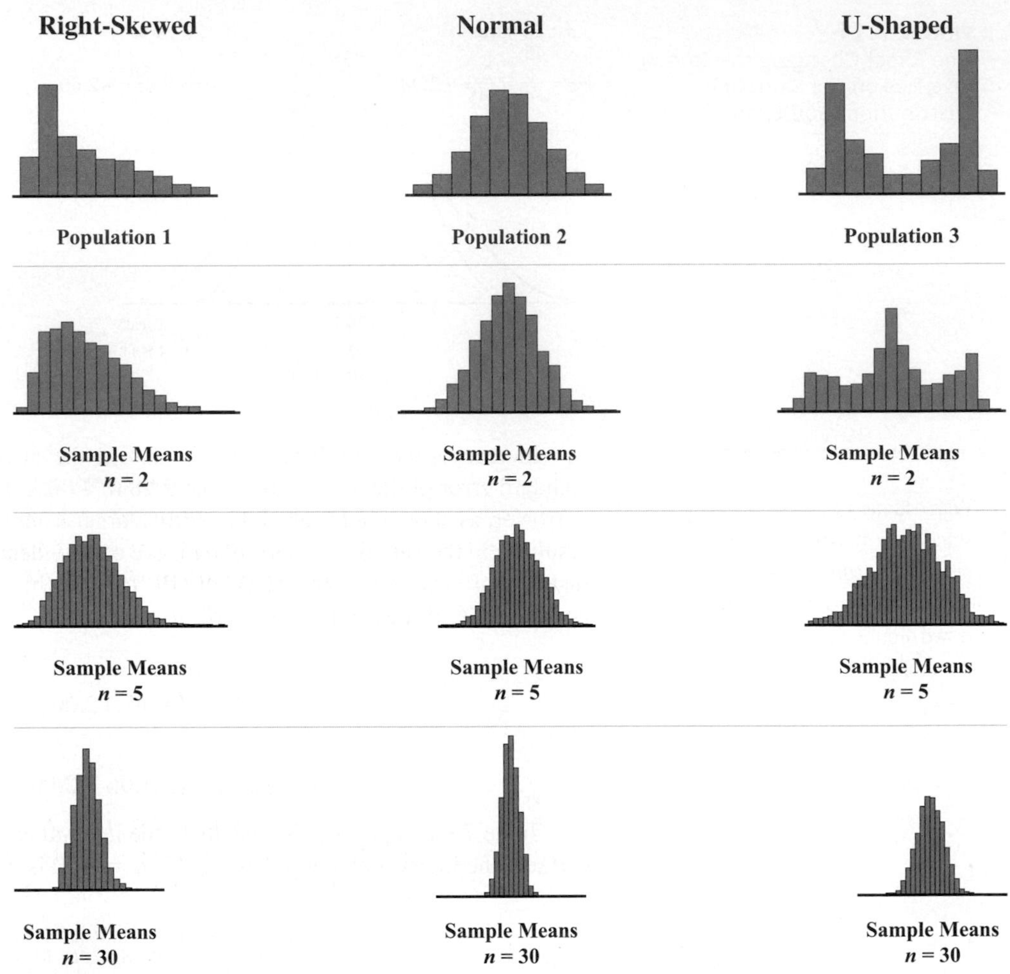

In all three cases, the sampling distribution for $n = 30$ can be described as having the shape of the normal distribution, which is taller and narrower than the distributions with smaller sample sizes. You can also see that the normally distributed population in the middle column has a normal sampling distribution for all sample sizes. The same can't be said for Populations 1 and 3, which obviously are not normal. Figure 7.12 visually shows that when samples are large enough, their means follow a normal distribution regardless of the shape of a population's distribution. This is what the CLT predicts.

I hope I have convinced you of the usefulness of the CLT. If I were your instructor, you'd be seeing all sorts of exam questions on this topic, so give the next Your Turn problem a try.

YOUR TURN #6

The fuel consumption for the 2013 Toyota Prius was rated by the U.S. Environmental Protection Agency (EPA) to average 48 miles per gallon (MPG) for combined city and highway driving. Assume the population standard deviation is 7 MPG. Determine the interval that will contain 95% of the sample means for a sample size of

a. 40 cars
b. 80 cars

Answers can be found on ▶ **page 330**

The Sampling Distribution of the Mean with a Finite Population

Up to this point in the chapter, we have assumed that all of the samples have been selected from a very large, or infinite, population. In these cases, the proportion of the sample size to the population size, n/N, is very small. By contrast, when the population is smaller, or finite, this proportion can be much larger. When sampling from a smaller population when the proportion n/N is greater than 5%, I recommend making an adjustment to the standard error of the mean calculation using Equation 7.5. So, for example, if our population consisted of 100 people and we were sampling more than 5 of them, we would adjust the standard error of the mean using Equation 7.5.

Formula 7.5 for the Standard Error of the Mean (Finite Population)

$$\sigma_{\bar{x}} = \frac{\sigma}{\sqrt{n}}\sqrt{\frac{N-n}{N-1}}$$

When the proportion of sample size to population size, n/N, is greater than 5%, the finite population correction factor is used to adjust the standard error of the mean.

where

σ = Population standard deviation
n = Sample size
N = Population size

The term $\sqrt{\frac{N-n}{N-1}}$ in Equation 7.5 is known as the **finite population correction factor**.

Finite population correction factor
A factor used to adjust the standard error of the mean or proportion when the proportion of sample size to population size, n/N, is greater than 5%.

To illustrate sampling from a finite population, consider Sum-R-Fun, a Delaware pool service company that has 100 residential customers. Historically, Sum-R-Fun's customers have given the company an average rating for customer service of 7.2 on a scale of 1–10 with a standard deviation of 0.7. However, a recent sample of 40 customers led to an average rating of 7.5 for the company. Is there any evidence that the average customer service rating for the entire customer base is different from 7.2? In other words, does the 7.5 rating indicate that if *all* customers were surveyed, the firm's average customer rating might be higher than 7.2? That would suggest that the company's customers were becoming more satisfied. Or, perhaps the higher 7.5 rating is just a result of sampling error. Let's find out which it is.

Because 40 out of 100 customers were sampled, the proportion $n/N = 40/100 = 40\%$. This value is greater than 5%, so this would be considered sampling from a finite population, requiring the use of Equation 7.5.

$$\sigma_{\bar{x}} = \frac{\sigma}{\sqrt{n}}\sqrt{\frac{N-n}{N-1}} = \frac{0.7}{\sqrt{40}}\sqrt{\frac{100-40}{100-1}}$$

$$\sigma_{\bar{x}} = \frac{0.7}{6.32}\sqrt{\frac{60}{99}} = (0.111)\sqrt{0.606}$$

$$\sigma_{\bar{x}} = (0.111)(0.778) = 0.086$$

We now calculate the z-score for $\bar{x} = 7.5$:

$$z_{7.5} = \frac{\bar{x} - \mu_{\bar{x}}}{\sigma_{\bar{x}}} = \frac{7.5 - 7.2}{0.086} = 3.49$$

Using Table 4 in Appendix A, we have

$$P(z \le 3.49) = 0.9998$$

However, we are looking for

$$P(z > 3.49) = 1 - 0.9998 = 0.0002$$

There is only a very small probability (0.02%) that a sample mean of 7.5 or greater could have occurred if the true population mean were 7.2. Therefore, it appears the population mean is greater than 7.2. Apparently, the customer service at Sum-R-Fun has improved recently.

I'm sure you're asking why we need a different standard error formula for finite populations. For an explanation, look at Table 7.10, which shows the standard errors for Sum-R-Fun when samples sizes of 40, 60, 80, and 100 are used. Note that a sample size of 100 is considered a census because the population consists of 100 customers.

The first column in Table 7.10 is the sample size. The second column shows the standard error without the correction factor, which assumes our population is very large (infinite) when compared to the size of the sample. The third column shows the finite population correction factor for each sample size amounts. The last column shows the standard error for each sample size with the correction factor included.

TABLE 7.10 | SAMPLING ERRORS FOR SUM-R-FUN'S SAMPLE SIZES WHEN THE FINITE POPULATION EQUALS 100 ($N = 100$)

SAMPLE SIZE	STANDARD ERROR	FINITE CORRECTION FACTOR	STANDARD ERROR WITH FINITE CORRECTION FACTOR
n	$\sigma_{\bar{x}} = \frac{\sigma}{\sqrt{n}}$	$\sqrt{\frac{N - n}{N - 1}}$	$\sigma_{\bar{x}} = \frac{\sigma}{\sqrt{n}}\sqrt{\frac{N - n}{N - 1}}$
40	0.111	0.778	0.086
60	0.090	0.636	0.057
80	0.078	0.449	0.035
100	0.07	0	0

Recall our sampling-error discussion in the previous section. We learned that as the sample size approaches the population size, the sampling error approaches zero. When the sample mean equals the population mean there is no variation between the two. In other words, $\sigma_{\bar{x}}$ should be equal to zero. However, look at the second column in Table 7.10: As n goes to 100, the standard error only drops to 0.07. This is because the standard error equation in the second column assumes the population is infinite. The finite population correction factor comes to our rescue. When $n = N$, the correction factor equals zero, resulting in a corrected standard error also equaling zero.

We use the correction factor to reduce the standard error because the sampling error is lower for a finite population.

In general, the correction factor reduces the standard error to reflect the fact that the sampling error is lower for a finite population. If you use the infinite population standard error in the second column when the population is finite, you'll be exaggerating your sampling error and adversely affecting your probability calculations.

What happens to the finite correction factor when the population size becomes much larger when compared to the sample size? Let's plug in a population size of 10,000 with a sample size of 30 to find out:

$$N = 10{,}000 \quad n = 30$$

$$\sqrt{\frac{N - n}{N - 1}} = \sqrt{\frac{10{,}000 - 30}{10{,}000 - 1}} = \sqrt{\frac{9{,}970}{9{,}999}} = \sqrt{0.997} = 0.998 \approx 1.0$$

As the calculations show, for an infinite population where n/N is less than 5%, the correction factor is close to 1.0, essentially dropping out of the standard error calculation. The next Your Turn problem demonstrates the finite population concept in an effort to save my job.

YOUR TURN #7

My college requires instructors to have an average approval rating of 9.0 on a scale of 1–10 from student evaluations as a condition for employment. This current semester, I have 120 students, of whom 30 completed the evaluation. My average score on the evaluation was 8.8. Historical data have indicated that the standard deviation for student evaluations in the college is 3.2. My dean has scheduled a meeting with me today to discuss my future employment with the college. Can you help me save my job?

Answer can be found on ▶ **page 331**

Rating data used in the Your Turn #7 example is technically ordinal data which we defined in Chapter 1 as data that are rank-ordered with no assurance that the differences between the ranks are uniform. We have no certainty that the difference between a rating score of 5 and 6 is identical to the difference between a rating score of 8 and 9. Because of the ambiguity of the intervals, it's not proper to calculate the mean and standard deviation of ordinal data. However, it is common practice to assume that rating data used in this Your Turn are close enough to interval data which allows calculations of the mean and standard deviation (which we do perform in this example). Just be aware that some people in the world of statistics take offense at such liberties!

7.4 Section Problems

Basic Skills

7.7 For a population with a mean equal to 150 and a standard deviation equal to 30, calculate the standard error of the mean for a sample size of

a. 10
b. 30
c. 50

7.8 For a normal population with a mean equal to 80 and a standard deviation equal to 15, determine the probability of observing a sample mean of 85 or less from a sample of size 10.

7.9 For a population that is left skewed with a mean of 24 and a standard deviation equal to 15, determine the probability of observing a sample mean of 23 or more from a sample of size 32.

7.10 Identify the symmetrical interval that includes 95% of the sample means for a population with a mean equal to 45 and a standard deviation equal to 9 using a sample size of 36.

7.11 Consider a population of 250 with a mean of 60 and a standard deviation equal to 23. What is the probability of obtaining a sample mean of 62 or less with a sample size of 45?

Applications

7.12 According to the National Association of Theater Owners, the average price for a movie in the United States in 2012 was \$7.96. Assume the population standard deviation is \$0.50 and that a sample of 30 theaters was randomly selected.

a. Calculate the standard error of the mean.
b. What is the probability that the sample mean will be less than \$7.75?
c. What is the probability that the sample mean will be less than \$8.10?
d. What is the probability that the sample mean will be more than \$8.20?

7.13 Iron Hill Café is a full-service restaurant in Columbus, Ohio, which is owned and managed by John Stevens. The number of minutes that diners spend at the table has a major impact on the profitability of the restaurant. Suppose the average number of minutes that diners spend at a table for dinner at the Iron Hill Café is 93 minutes with a standard deviation of 17 minutes. Assume the number of minutes diners spend at their table follows the normal probability distribution. Calculate the probability that the average number of minutes that diners spend at their table for dinner will be less than 100 minutes

a. using a sample size of 10 tables.
b. using a sample size of 20 tables.
c. using a sample size of 30 tables.
d. Explain the difference in these probabilities.

7.14 According to Travel and Leisure, the average hotel price in the Miami, Florida, was \$156 per night in 2012. Assume the population standard deviation is \$26.00 and that a random sample of 35 hotels was selected.

a. Calculate the standard error of the mean.
b. What is the probability that the sample mean will be less than \$160?
c. What is the probability that the sample mean will be more than \$163?
d. What is the probability that the sample mean will be between \$147 and \$151?

7.15 Researchers at the University of California, San Diego, found that a person in the United States spent an average of 5 hours a day watching TV. Assume the population standard deviation is 1.6 hours per day. A sample of 32 people averaged 5.3 hours of television viewing per day. Does this result support the findings of the study?

7.16 A study conducted by TomTom found that Hawaii had the slowest state highway drivers in the country. The drivers traveled at an average speed of 52.7 miles per hour (MPH). Assume the population standard deviation is 6.0 MPH.

a. What is the probability that a sample of 30 of the drivers will have a sample mean less than 51 MPH?
b. What is the probability that a sample of 45 of the drivers will have a sample mean less than 51 MPH?
c. What is the probability that a sample of 60 of the drivers will have a sample mean less than 51 MPH?
d. Explain the difference in these probabilities.

7.17 According to a recent survey by the National Retail Federation, men spent an average of \$135.35 on Valentine's Day gifts (compared with \$72.28 for women). Assume the standard deviation for this population is \$40 and that it is normally distributed. A random sample of 10 men who celebrate Valentine's Day was selected.

a. Calculate the standard error of the mean.
b. What is the probability that the sample mean will be less than \$125?
c. What is the probability that the sample mean will be more than \$140?
d. What is the probability that the sample mean will be between \$120 and \$160?
e. Identify the symmetrical interval that includes 95% of the sample means if the true population mean is \$135.35.

7.18 With higher unemployment rates for young adults, an increasing number of parents are providing some form of financial support for their adult children. According to a 2013 Harris poll, parents of 18- to 35-year-old children spend an average of \$108 per month for their offspring's phone, music, video and remote Web services. Assume the population standard deviation for this financial support is \$33 per month. A random sample of 31 adults with 18- to 35-year-old children was selected and was found to have an average of \$91 per month for this type of financial support.

a. Does this sample provide support for the conclusions of the Harris poll?
b. Identify the symmetrical interval that includes 95% of the sample means if the true population mean is \$108 per month.

7.19 The weight of NFL players has increased steadily, gaining up to 1.5 lbs per year since 1942. According to ESPN, the average weight of a National Football League (NFL) player is now 252.8 lbs. Assume the population standard deviation is 25 lbs. A random sample of 38 NFL players was selected.

a. Calculate the standard error of the mean.
b. What is the probability that the sample mean will be less than 246 lbs?
c. What is the probability that the sample mean will be more than 249 lbs?
d. What is the probability that the sample mean will be between 254 and 258 lbs?
e. Identify the symmetrical interval that includes 95% of the sample means if the true population mean is 252.8 lbs.

7.20 A local pizza shop claims its average home delivery time is 30 minutes. A sample of 40 deliveries had a sample average of 33 minutes. Assume the population standard deviation for the shop's deliveries is 6.5 minutes.

a. Is there support for the shop's claim using the criteria that were previously discussed?
b. Identify the symmetrical interval that includes 95% of the sample means if the true population mean is 30 minutes.

7.21 According to the Organisation for Economic Co-operation and Development (OECD), adults in the United States worked an average of 1,787 hours in 2011. Assume the population standard deviation is 400 hours and that a random sample of 50 U.S. adults was selected.

a. Calculate the standard error of the mean.
b. What is the probability that the sample mean will be more than 1,800 hours?
c. What is the probability that the sample mean will be between 1,750 and 1,780 hours?
d. Would a sample mean of 1,825 hours support the claim made by the OECD?
e. Identify the symmetrical interval that includes 95% of the sample means if the true population mean is 1,787 hours.

7.22 One semester I had a total of 80 students in my statistics classes. The average score for the class on the last exam I administered was 85.4 with a standard deviation of 4.9. A random sample of 32 students was selected.

a. Calculate the standard error of the mean.
b. What is the probability that the sample mean will be less than 87?
c. What is the probability that the sample mean will be more than 86?
d. What is the probability that the sample mean will be between 84.5 and 86.5?

7.23 Newark College has 240 full-time employees who are currently covered under the school's health care plan. The average out-of-pocket cost for the employees on the plan is $1,880 with a standard deviation of $515. Newark College is performing an audit of its health care plan and has randomly selected 30 employees to analyze their out-of-pocket costs.

a. Calculate the standard error of the mean.
b. What is the probability that the sample mean will be less than $1,825?
c. What is the probability that the sample mean will be more than $1,840?
d. What is the probability that the sample mean will be between $1,900 and $1,950?

7.24 The Excel file titled **NBA.xlsx** contains frequency distribution of the heights of the players in the National Basketball Association during a recent season.

a. Calculate the mean and standard deviation of this population.
b. What is the probability that a sample mean of 45 players will be less than 78 in.?
c. What is the probability that a sample mean of 45 players will be more than 79.5 in.?
d. What is the probability that a sample mean of 45 players will be between 78.5 and 80 in.?

7.5 The Sampling Distribution of the Proportion

Up to this point in the chapter, we have focused our attention on sample means and how they behave in a sampling distribution. However, there are times when we are counting observations in a sample and need to rely on the sample percentage rather than the sample mean. I'll use the following hypothetical example to demonstrate. Suppose that CBS, the network that broadcasted the 2013 Super Bowl, estimated that 45% of the U.S. households would tune into the game when they established the cost of a 30-second commercial before the big event. Also, suppose that Coca-Cola, one of the game's advertisers, wanted to verify this claim independently. After the game, Coca-Cola randomly selected 200 households and found that 84 of them watched the Super Bowl. Based on this sample, can Coca-Cola validate the claim made by CBS?

To answer this question, we need to recognize that we are dealing with the binomial probability distribution discussed in Chapter 5, where we count the number of success (x) in a certain number of trials (n). In Chapter 6 we learned that we can use the normal distribution to approximate the binomial distribution if the following conditions are met:

$$np \geq 5$$
$$n(1 - p) \geq 5$$

In these equations, the variable p represents the population proportion. In our Coca-Cola example, we set $p = 0.45$ because CBS claimed that the percentage of households (population) that would watch the Super Bowl is 45%. Using $n = 200$, the condition required to use the normal distribution is satisfied because

$$np = (200)(0.45) = 90 \geq 5$$
$$n(1 - p) = (200)(1 - 0.45) = 110 \geq 5$$

We can determine the sample proportion, $\bar{p}$, using Equation 7.6.

Formula 7.6 for the Sample Proportion

$$\bar{p} = \frac{x}{n}$$

where

$x =$ The number of observations of interest in the sample (successes)
$n =$ Sample size (trials)

For the Coca-Cola example, the sample proportion is

$$\bar{p} = \frac{x}{n} = \frac{84}{200} = 0.42$$

The **sampling distribution of the proportion** describes the pattern that sample proportions tend to follow when randomly drawn from a population.

The standard deviation for this distribution, σ_p, is known as the **standard error of the proportion**.

If Coca-Cola had collected many random samples from the U.S. household population, each with a size 200, and calculated the sample proportion for each of them, the distribution of sample proportions would follow the normal distribution. This is known as the **sampling distribution of the proportion**. The average of these sample proportions should be very close to p, the proportion of the entire population. The sampling distribution of the proportion describes the pattern that sample proportions tend to follow when randomly drawn from a population.

The standard deviation for this distribution, σ_p, is known as the **standard error of the proportion** and is shown in Equation 7.7. This equation is analogous to the standard error of the mean from the previous section.

Formula 7.7 for the Standard Error of the Proportion

$$\sigma_p = \sqrt{\frac{p(1-p)}{n}}$$

where

$p =$ Population proportion
$n =$ Sample size

Let's apply this equation to the Coca-Cola example:

$$\sigma_p = \sqrt{\frac{p(1-p)}{n}} = \sqrt{\frac{(0.45)(1-0.45)}{200}}$$

$$\sigma_p = \sqrt{\frac{0.2475}{200}} = \sqrt{0.001238} = 0.0352$$

To calculate our normal probability, we need to employ the z-score for sample proportions as shown in Equation 7.8.

Formula 7.8 for the z-score for the Sample Proportion

$$z_p = \frac{\bar{p} - p}{\sigma_p}$$

where

$\bar{p} =$ Sample proportion
$p =$ Population proportion
$\sigma_p =$ Standard error of the proportion

This equation is a variation of the z-score for sample means that we used earlier in this chapter. In this sample proportion version of the z-score:

- $\bar{p}$ replaces $\bar{x}$
- σ_p replaces $\sigma_{\bar{x}}$
- p replaces μ

Using Equation 7.8, the z-score for $\overline{p} = 0.42$ is

$$z_{0.42} = \frac{\overline{p} - p}{\sigma_p} = \frac{0.42 - 0.45}{0.0352} = -0.85$$

Our sample proportion of 0.42 is 0.85 standard deviations to the left of the population proportion that is claimed to be true by CBS, p, and is shown in Figure 7.13.

FIGURE 7.13 The Sampling Distribution of the Proportion for the Coca-Cola Example

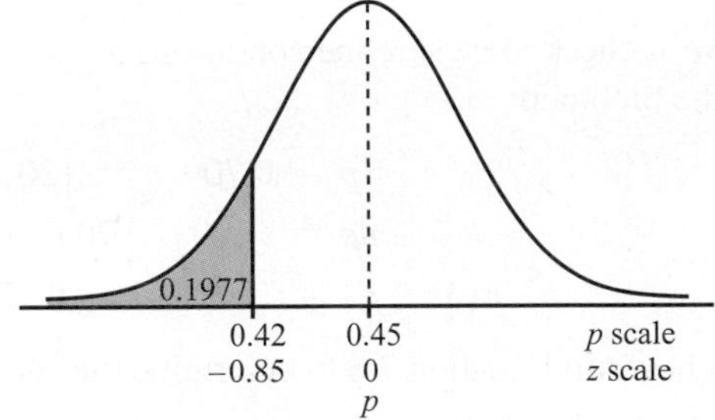

Using Table 3 in Appendix A, we find that the area to the left of $z = -0.85$ is

$$P(\overline{p} \leq 0.42) = P(z \leq -0.85) = 0.1977$$

The shaded area in Figure 7.13 shows us the probability that 84 or fewer households watched the 2013 Super Bowl from any sample of 200 is nearly 20%. This probability assumes that the true population proportion is 0.45, as CBS claimed. From a statistician's perspective, 20% is high enough to support CBS's claim. As we will learn in the next chapter, if this percentage had been, say, 5% or less, Coca-Cola would have some evidence that the true population proportion was most likely less than 0.45.

The following Your Turn problem will give you a chance to test your newly found proportion skills.

YOUR TURN #8

A 2012 survey of adults 18 years and older reported that 34% have texted while driving. A random sample of 125 adults was selected. What is the probability that 36 or more people from this sample send text messages while they drive?

Answer can be found on ▶ **page 331**

The Sampling Distribution of the Proportion with a Finite Population

If the ratio of n/N is greater than 5%, the population correction factor, $\sqrt{\frac{N-n}{N-1}}$, needs to be included in the standard error of the proportion, as shown in Equation 7.9.

Formula 7.9 for the Standard Error of the Proportion (Finite Population)

$$\sigma_p = \sqrt{\frac{p(1-p)}{n}}\sqrt{\frac{N-n}{N-1}}$$

where

p = Population proportion
n = Sample size
N = Population size

The reasoning for using this standard error of the proportion is the same as for using the standard error of the mean. The correction factor reduces the standard error to reflect the fact that the sampling error is lower for a finite population.

I'll use the following example to illustrate this technique. Goldey-Beacom College is graduating 770 students this year and claims that 70% of its graduates have landed full-time jobs in fields related to their majors. To test this claim, 120 students are randomly surveyed, and 97 had indeed found jobs in fields related to their majors. Is the college's claim accurate?

First, we'll check to be sure the conditions are met using the normal distribution to approximate the binomial:

$$p = 0.70 \quad n = 120$$
$$np = (120)(0.70) = 84 \geq 5$$
$$n(1 - p) = (120)(1 - 0.70) = 36 \geq 5$$

We can now use Equation 7.6 to determine the sample proportion.

$$\bar{p} = \frac{x}{n} = \frac{97}{120} = 0.808$$

Because 120 out of 770 students were sampled, the proportion $n/N = 120/770 = 16\%$. This value is greater than 5%, which is considered sampling from a finite population and thus requires the use of Equation 7.9:

$$\sigma_p = \sqrt{\frac{p(1-p)}{n}}\sqrt{\frac{N-n}{N-1}} = \sqrt{\frac{(0.70)(1-0.70)}{120}}\sqrt{\frac{770-120}{770-1}}$$

$$\sigma_p = \sqrt{\frac{0.21}{120}}\sqrt{\frac{650}{769}} = \sqrt{0.00175}\sqrt{0.8453}$$

$$\sigma_p = (0.0418)(0.9194) = 0.0384$$

When the proportion of sample size to population size, n/N, is greater than 5%, the finite population correction factor is used to adjust the standard error of the proportion.

We now calculate the z-score for $\bar{p} = 0.808$: using Equation 7.8:

$$z_{0.808} = \frac{\bar{p} - p}{\sigma_p} = \frac{0.808 - 0.70}{0.0384} = 2.81$$

Using Table 4 in Appendix A, we calculate the probability that the sample proportion will be more than or equal to 0.808 if the actual population proportion is 0.70:

$$P(\bar{p} \geq 0.808) = P(z \geq 2.81) = 1.0 - 0.9975 = 0.0025$$

There is a very small probability (0.0025) that a sample proportion of 0.808 or more will be observed if the true population proportion is 0.70. Therefore, it appears the actual population proportion is more than 0.70. Apparently, according to this sample, the percentage of graduating students employed in a field related to their major is actually greater than 70%.

One last note: Back in Chapter 6, we used the continuity correction factor, which allows us to approximate the binomial distribution with the normal distribution by adding and subtracting the value 0.5 to the interval of interest. This factor is not used in this chapter because the sample size and number of successes observed for these types of problems are large enough to make the correction insignificant in the probability calculations. Therefore, the continuity correction factor will not be needed for the remaining problems in this chapter.

Try this last Your Turn problem to wrap up your sampling distribution skills.

YOUR TURN #9

Crossan Pointe is a housing development in Delaware with 96 homes. It is believed that 75% of these homes are up to date with paying their annual community dues for maintenance and snow removal. A random sample of 50 homes was selected, and it was found that 31 had paid their dues. Is there enough evidence to support the claim that 75% of the houses are up to date with their dues?

Answer can be found on ▶ **page 331**

7.5 Section Problems

Basic Skills

7.25 For a population with a proportion equal to 0.30, calculate the standard error of the proportion for the following sample sizes:

a. 50
b. 100
c. 150

7.26 A sample of 125 is drawn from a population with a proportion equal to 0.65. Determine the probability of observing

a. 80 or fewer successes.
b. 82 or fewer successes.
c. 75 or more successes.

7.27 A sample of 150 is drawn from a population with a proportion equal to 0.40. Determine the probability of observing

a. between 50 and 54 successes.
b. between 55 and 62 successes.
c. between 53 and 70 successes.

7.28 A sample of 150 is drawn from a population with a proportion equal to 0.40 and a population size of 400. Determine the probability of observing

a. between 50 and 54 successes.
b. between 55 and 62 successes.
c. between 53 and 70 successes.

Applications

7.29 Generation Y has been defined as those individuals who were born between 1981 and 1991. A recent survey by the National Foundation for Credit Counseling found that 58% of the young adults in Generation Y pay their monthly bills on time. Suppose we take a random sample of 200 people from Generation Y.

a. Calculate the standard error of the proportion.
b. What is the probability that 125 or fewer will pay their monthly bills on time?
c. What is the probability that 100 or fewer will pay their monthly bills on time?
d. What is the probability that 120 or more will pay their monthly bills on time?
e. What is the probability that between 112 and 122 of them will pay their monthly bills on time?

7.30 First-time buyers are very important to the housing market because these buyers allow existing homeowners to "move up" into their next home. According to the National Association of Realtors, 31% of U.S. homes sold in November 2012 were purchased by first-time buyers. A random sample of 175 people who just purchased homes is selected.

a. Calculate the standard error of the proportion.
b. What is the probability that less than 58 of them are first-time buyers?
c. What is the probability that more than 62 of them are first-time buyers?
d. What is the probability that more than 52 of them are first-time buyers?
e. What is the probability that between 44 and 50 of them are first-time buyers?

7.31 According to the Pew Internet & American Life Project, 73% of U.S. teens aged 12–17 used social networks. A random sample of 130 teenagers from this age group was selected.

a. Calculate the standard error of the proportion.
b. What is the probability that less than 75% of the teens from this sample used social networks?
c. What is the probability that between 70% and 80% of the teens from this sample used social networks?
d. What impact would changing the sample size to 200 teens have on the results of parts a, b, and c?

7.32 The Social Media and Personal Responsibility Survey found that 69% of parents are "friends" with their children on Facebook. A random sample of 140 parents was selected.

a. Calculate the standard error of the proportion.
b. What is the probability that 100 or more parents from this sample are "friends" with their children on Facebook?
c. What is the probability that between 96 and 105 parents from this sample are "friends" with their children on Facebook?
d. If 81 parents responded that they are "friends" with their children on Facebook, does this result support the findings of the Social Media and Personal Responsibility Survey?

7.33 OnCampus Research recently reported that 46% of college students aged 18–24 would spend their spring breaks relaxing at home. A sample of 155 college students was selected.

a. Calculate the standard error of the proportion.
b. What is the probability that less than 40% of the college students from the sample spent their spring breaks relaxing at home?
c. What is the probability that more than 50% of the college students from the sample spent their spring breaks relaxing at home?
d. What is the probability that between 48% and 58% of the college students from the sample spent their spring breaks relaxing at home?

7.34 According to the National Retail Federation, 36% of taxpayers used computer software to do their taxes for the 2012 tax year. A sample of 125 taxpayers was selected.

a. Calculate the standard error of the proportion.
b. What is the probability that less than 30% of the taxpayers from the sample used computer software to do their taxes?

c. What is the probability that between 28% and 40% of the taxpayers from the sample used computer software to do their taxes?

d. What impact would changing the sample size to 225 taxpayers have on the results of parts a, b, and c?

7.35 Pike Creek Golf Club currently has 375 members who pay annual dues to play golf on the course. Historical records show that 38% of the members use the course at least once a week during the summer season. To verify this, a random sample of 100 members was selected.

a. Calculate the standard error of the proportion.

b. What is the probability that 32 or more members from the sample used the course at least once a week?

c. What is the probability that between 30 and 40 members from the sample used the course at least once a week?

d. If 50 members from the sample used the course at least once a week, does this support the historical records of course usage?

7.36 At Goldey-Beacom College, 56% of employees carry dependent family members on their health insurance plans. Currently, there are 200 employees working for the college. A random sample of 50 employees is selected.

a. What is the probability that less than 60% of the sample carries dependent family members on their health insurance plan?

b. Answer the question in part a using sample sizes of 100 and 150. Explain the differences in these probabilities.

c. Answer the question in part a without the finite correction factor. Explain the differences in these probabilities.

7.37 Managers at a local AT&T Wireless retail center have a goal that 75% of the center's customers will have to wait less than 5 minutes for service. The Excel file named **AT&T.xlsx** shows the wait times of a random sample of 160 customers in minutes. Use Excel's COUNTIF function to count the number of successes. Does this sample provide evidence that management's goal is being achieved?

CHAPTER 7 Summary

- A population represents all possible outcomes or measurements of interest.
- A sample as a subset of a population.
- If a sample is selected properly, and the data from the sample is collected correctly, we can use this information to make a very accurate assessment of the entire population.
- Probability sampling describes the process where each member in the population has a known, nonzero, chance of being selected for a sample.
- The four probability sampling techniques are defined as follows:
  - A simple random sample is a sample in which every member of the population has an equal chance of being chosen.
  - Systematic sampling involves selecting every *k*th member of the population to be part of your sample.
    - One concern about systematic sampling is *periodicity*, which is a pattern in the population that is consistent with the value of *k*.
  - In stratified sampling, we divide the population into mutually exclusive groups, or strata, and randomly sample from each of these groups.
  - Cluster sampling involves dividing the population into mutually exclusive groups, or clusters, and then selecting a simple random sample from these clusters to form the final sample.
- *Nonprobability sampling* refers to a sampling practice where the probability of a population member being selected for the sample is not known.
  - Convenience sampling is a type of nonprobability sampling that is used when members of the population are chosen to become part of the sample simply because they are easily accessible.
    - One of the most common types of convenience sampling is an Internet poll
- Parameters are values that describe some characteristic of a population, such as the mean or the median.
- Statistics are values that are calculated from a sample, such as the mean or the median.
- The difference between a statistic and a parameter is known as the sampling error.
  - In general, we expect larger sample sizes to provide smaller corresponding sampling errors.
- Nonsampling errors occur when survey questions are ambiguous in the eyes of the respondents, which results in their not answering them in a reliable manner.
  - Unlike sampling errors, nonsampling errors cannot be reduced by simply increasing the size of the sample.
- The sampling distribution of the mean describes the pattern that sample averages tend to take on when randomly drawn from a population.
- The sample mean standard deviation is also known as the standard error of the mean.
- The Central Limit Theorem states that for any population distribution, the sample means will be normally distributed if the samples are large enough.
  - In most cases, sample sizes of 30 or larger will result in sample means being normally distributed regardless of the shape of the population distribution.
- When a sample size is larger, the standard error is reduced, which results in the sample means having more of a tendency to crowd around the mean of the distribution.

- When the proportion of sample size to population size, n/N, is greater than 5%, the finite population correction factor is used to adjust the standard error of the mean.
  - In general, the correction factor reduces the standard error to reflect the fact that the sampling error is lower for a finite population.
- The sampling distribution of the proportion describes the pattern that sample proportions tend to take on when randomly drawn from a population.
- Proportions follow the binomial distribution, but we can use the normal distribution to approximate the binomial probability distribution if $np \geq 5$ and $n(1 - p) \geq 5$.
- The standard deviation for sampling distribution of the proportion distribution is known as the standard error of the proportion.
- When the proportion of sample size to population size, n/N, is greater than 5%, the finite population correction factor is used to adjust the standard error of the proportion.

CHAPTER 7 Key Terms

Bootstrap method. Using computer software to extract many samples with replacement in order to estimate a parameter of the population.

Census. The process of recording information from the entire population of interest.

Central Limit Theorem. States that sample means from samples of sufficient size, drawn from any population, will be normally distributed.

Cluster sample. A simple random sample of groups, or clusters, of the population often based on geography.

Convenience sample. A sample in which the members of the population are chosen to become part of the sample simply because they are easily accessible.

Finite population correction factor. A factor used to adjust the standard error of the mean or proportion when the proportion of sample size to population size, n/N, is greater than 5%.

Nonprobability sample. A sample in which the probability of a population member being selected for the sample is not known.

Nonsampling errors. Errors that occur as a result of problems such as data collection mistakes, ambiguous survey questions, and questions that lead respondents to certain "correct" answers.

Parameters. Values that describe some characteristic of a population, such as the mean or the median.

Periodicity. A pattern in the population that is consistent with the value of k in systematic sampling.

Probability sample. A sample in which each member in the population has a known, nonzero chance of being selected for the sample.

Resampling. A statistical technique where many samples are repeatedly drawn from a population.

Sampling distribution of the mean. The distribution pattern that sample averages tend to follow when the samples are randomly drawn from a population.

Sampling distribution of the proportion. The distribution pattern that sample proportions tend to follow when the samples are randomly drawn from a population.

Sampling error of the sample mean. The difference between the sample mean and the population mean.

Simple random sample. A sample in which every member of the population has an equal chance of being chosen.

Standard error of the mean. The standard deviation of sample means, which measures the average variation around the mean of the sample means.

Standard error of the proportion. The standard deviation of sample proportions, which measures the average variation around the mean of the sample proportions.

Statistics. Values that are calculated from a sample, such as the mean or the median.

Stratified sample. A sample in which the population is divided into mutually exclusive groups, or strata, and randomly drawn from each of these groups.

Systematic sample. A sample in which every kth member of the population is chosen, with the value of k being equal to N/n.

CHAPTER 7 Equations

7.2 Types of Sampling (pp 291–298)

Formula 7.1 for the Systematic Sampling Constant

$$k = \frac{N}{n}$$

7.3 Sampling and Nonsampling Errors (pp 298–301)

Formula 7.2 for the Sampling Error of the Sample Mean

$$\text{Sampling Error} = \bar{x} - \mu$$

7.4 The Central Limit Theorem (pp 301–317)

Formula 7.3 for the Standard Error of the Mean

$$\sigma_{\bar{x}} = \frac{\sigma}{\sqrt{n}}$$

Formula 7.4 for the z-Score for the Sample Mean

$$z_{\bar{x}} = \frac{\bar{x} - \mu_{\bar{x}}}{\sigma_{\bar{x}}}$$

Formula 7.5 for the Standard Error of the Mean (Finite Population)

$$\sigma_{\bar{x}} = \frac{\sigma}{\sqrt{n}}\sqrt{\frac{N - n}{N - 1}}$$

7.5 The Sampling Distribution of the Proportion (pp 317–322)

Formula 7.6 for the Sample Proportion

$$\bar{p} = \frac{x}{n}$$

Formula 7.7 for the Standard Error of the Proportion

$$\sigma_p = \sqrt{\frac{p(1 - p)}{n}}$$

Formula 7.8 for the z-Score for the Sample Proportion

$$z_p = \frac{\bar{p} - p}{\sigma_p}$$

Formula 7.9 for the Standard Error of the Proportion (Finite Population)

$$\sigma_p = \sqrt{\frac{p(1 - p)}{n}}\sqrt{\frac{N - n}{N - 1}}$$

CHAPTER 7 Problems

7.38 According to FedSmith.com, the average salary for a federal employee in 2012 was $74,804. Assume the population standard deviation is $15,300. A random sample of 34 federal employees is selected.

a. What is the probability that the sample mean will be less than $70,000?

b. What is the probability that the sample mean will be more than $74,000?

c. What is the probability that the sample mean will be between $76,000 and $81,000.

7.39 According to the Bureau of Labor Statistics, the unemployment rate for workers aged 20 to 24 in February 2013 was 13.1%. Consider a random sample of 110 workers from this age group.

a. What is the probability that 20 or fewer will be unemployed?

b. What is the probability that 15 or fewer will be unemployed?

c. What is the probability that between 10 and 16 of them will be unemployed?

7.40 One of Super Giant's grocery stores in Pennsylvania sells, on average, 1,120 cases of Pepsi products a week with a standard deviation of 146 cases. Josh Nelson, who is the Pepsi account manager for this store, receives a bonus if the store's weekly sales over a four-week period during the month average more than 1,200 cases.

a. What is the probability that Josh will receive a bonus next month?
b. What assumptions are needed to answer part a?

7.41 According to the Beverage Marketing Corporation, the per capita consumption of bottled water in the United States is 2.3 gallons per month. Assume the standard deviation for this population is 0.75 gallons per month. Consider a random sample of 36 people.

a. What is the probability that the sample mean will be less than 2.1 gallons per month?
b. What is the probability that the sample mean will be more than 2.2 gallons per month?
c. Identify the symmetrical interval that includes 95% of the sample means if the true population mean is 2.3 gallons per month.

7.42 It is commonly known that approximately 10% of the population is left-handed. Nike Golf would like to estimate the proportion of left-handed golfers in order to plan the schedule of golf club production. Assume Nike collected a sample of 200 golfers.

a. What is the probability that more than 12% of the golfers in the sample are left-handed?
b. What is the probability that less than 14% of the golfers in the sample are left-handed?
c. What is the probability that between 6% and 9% of the golfers in the sample are left-handed?
d. Suppose the sample that Nike collected had nine left-handed golfers. What conclusions should Nike draw about the population of left-handed golfers?

7.43 According to AAA, regular gasoline averaged $3.68 per gallon in the United States in March 2013. Assume the standard deviation for gasoline prices is $0.12 per gallon. A random sample of 30 service stations was selected.

a. What is the probability that the sample mean will be less than $3.66?
b. What is the probability that the sample mean will be more than $3.63?
c. What is the probability that the sample mean will be between $3.62 and $3.72?
d. Suppose the sample mean is $3.75. Does this result support the findings of AAA? Explain your answer.

7.44 Generation Y has been defined as those individuals who were born between 1981 and 1991. According to the Project on Student Debt, Generation Y students graduating from college averaged $23,200 in debt. Assume the standard deviation for debt is $7,500 per student.

a. What is the probability that the sample mean will be less than $24,000 for a sample size of 30 students?
b. Identify the symmetrical interval that includes 95% of the sample means if the true population mean is $23,200 per student.
c. Answer the question in part a for a sample size of 60. Explain the differences in these two probabilities.

7.45 The *Journal of American College Health* found that 56.4% of college students who lived in coed dormitories consumed alcohol weekly (compared with 26.5% who lived in single-sex dormitories). A random sample of 160 students who live in coed dormitories was selected.

a. What is the probability that more than 50% of the students in the sample consume alcohol weekly?
b. What is the probability that less than 65% of the students in the sample consume alcohol weekly?
c. What impact would changing the sample size to 100 students have on the results in part a?
d. Identify the symmetrical interval that includes 95% of the sample proportions with a sample size of 160 if the true population proportion of students in coed dormitories who consume alcohol weekly is 56.4%.

7.46 A certain unnamed statistics teacher needs to grade 90 exams. The teacher claims that exams require an average of 12 minutes to grade with a standard deviation of 3 minutes. A random sample of 15 exams is selected.

a. What is the probability that the sample mean will be more than 11 minutes per exam?
b. What is the probability that the sample mean will be more than 12.5 minutes per exam?
c. Suppose the sample mean is 10 minutes. Is the teacher's claim valid according to this sample?
d. What assumptions need to be made in this problem?

7.47 Shortly after the major oil spill in the Gulf of Mexico that occurred in April 2010 due to an explosion on an oil rig, a Rasmussan Poll found that 23% of respondents were against offshore drilling for oil. In an effort to confirm these results, an environmental group randomly selected 200 adults and asked them their opinions about offshore drilling.

a. What is the probability that 40 or more people from this sample are against offshore drilling for oil?
b. What is the probability that 50 or more people from the sample are against offshore drilling for oil?
c. If 62 people in the sample indicated that they are against offshore drilling for oil, what conclusions can the environmental group make?

7.48 Many homeowners rely on handymen to perform small jobs, such as repairs or maintenance, around their residence. According to HomeAdvisor Inc., the average cost for a handyman project is $460. Assume the population standard deviation is $95. A random sample of 30 handyman projects was selected.

a. What is the probability that the sample mean will be less than $475?
b. What is the probability that the sample mean will be between $450 and $465?
c. Identify the symmetrical interval that includes 95% of the sample means if the true population mean is $460 per project.
d. Suppose the sample mean was $411. Does this result support the findings of HomeAdvisor Inc.?

7.49 In an effort to reduce health care costs, many companies are encouraging their employees to walk more. According to the Medicine & Science in *Sports & Exercise Journal*, Americans take an average of 5,117 steps per day. Assume the population standard deviation is 2,200 steps per day. Jim Powers is the manager of a retail store that employs 230 people and has provided each of them with a pedometer which counts the number of steps taken per day. He chooses a random sample of 45 employees and records the number of steps they walked yesterday. Assume the employee population is representative of the U.S. population.

a. What is the probability that the sample mean is less than 5,800 steps per day?
b. What is the probability that the sample mean is more than 4,800 steps per day?
c. What is the probability that the sample mean is between 4,600 and 5,000 steps per day?

7.50 According to the Bureau of Labor Statistics, the average workweek for an adult in the United States in February 2013 was 34.5 hours. Assume the population standard deviation for the number of hours worked per week is 5.0 hours. A random sample of 30 U.S. adults worked an average of 35.1 hours last week.

a. Do the results from this sample support the claim by the Bureau of Labor Statistics?
b. Identify the symmetrical interval that includes 95% of the sample means if the true population mean is 34.5 hours per week.

7.51 The "sandwich generation" is defined as adults who are financially supporting their children while providing care for their aging parents. The number of adults in this category has increased recently with higher unemployment rates, especially for young adults. Financial burdens carried by this generation can have major implications on their retirement plans. A 2012 study from the Pew Research Center reported that 15% of adults aged 40–59 belong to the sandwich generation. A random sample of 135 adults from this age group was selected.

a. What is the probability that 16 or more adults from this sample belong to the sandwich generation?
b. What is the probability that 24 or more adults from this sample belong to the sandwich generation?
c. What is the probability that between 14 and 25 adults from this sample belong to the sandwich generation?

7.52 According to the Graduate Management Admission Council, the average starting salary for an MBA graduate in the class of 2011 was $85,854. Assume the population standard deviation for starting MBA salaries was $11,700. A random sample of 40 MBA graduates from the class of 2011 was selected.

a. What is the probability that the sample mean is less than $88,000?
b. What is the probability that the sample mean is more than $81,000?
c. What is the probability that the sample mean is between $83,000 and $85,000?
d. Suppose the sample mean was $87,400. Does this result support the findings of Graduate Management Admission Council?

7.53 Urban planners will use electronic traffic counters to count the number of vehicles that travel on a specific road. This information can be used to identify roads that need to be improved or expanded based on traffic needs. Suppose that, from historical studies, Duncan Road in Kent County averages 2,165 vehicles per day with a standard deviation of 485 vehicles per day. A traffic counter was used on this road on 33 days that were randomly selected.

a. What is the probability that the sample mean is less than 2,000 vehicles per day?
b. What is the probability that the sample mean is more than 2,200 vehicles per day?
c. What is the probability that the sample mean is between 2,100 and 2,300 vehicles per day?
d. Suppose the sample mean was 2,400 vehicles per day. Does this result support the stated population mean for this road?

7.54 Some employers are offering their employees a Consumer-Directed Health Plan (CDHP) where the employer provides employees with a sum of money from which employees can purchase their health plan from an online marketplace. The concept is based on the belief that employees will behave more efficiently as consumers spending their own money. According to Aon Hewitt, 39% of employees who had the option chose a CDHP as their insurance plan. Boscov's is a retail store that employs 286 people and offered a CDHP as a health insurance option. A random sample of 42 employees was selected.

a. What is the probability that 15 or fewer employees from this sample chose the CDHP?
b. What is the probability that 18 or more employees from this sample chose the CDHP?
c. What is the probability that between 17 and 22 employees from this sample chose the CDHP?

7.55 Negative equity is defined as a situation where the mortgage on a property is more than the market value of the property. During the recent financial crisis, market values of most homes declined resulting in an increase in the proportion of homes with negative equity. This, in turn, led to an increase in home foreclosures. According to CoreLogic, 52.4% of home mortgages in Nevada during the fourth quarter of 2012 had negative equity. A random sample of 210 home mortgages was randomly selected.

a. What is the probability that 50% or less of this sample has negative equity?
b. What is the probability that 57% or more of this sample has negative equity?
c. What is the probability that between 49% and 55% of this sample has negative equity?
d. Suppose that 130 home mortgages from this sample have negative equity? Does this result support the claim made by CoreLogic?

7.56 According to Catalyst, 14.3% executive positions in Fortune 500 companies are occupied by women in 2012. A random sample of 180 Fortune 500 executives was selected.

a. What is the probability that 20% or less of this sample were women?
b. What is the probability that 18% or more of this sample were women?
c. What is the probability that between 10% and 15% of this sample were women?
d. Suppose that 29 executives from this sample were women? Does this result support the claim made by Catalyst?

7.57 According to the Department of Transportation, the average licensed driver travels 1,123 miles per month in his or her vehicle. Assume the population standard deviation is 341 miles per month. Determine the interval that will contain 95% of the sample means for a sample size of

a. 30 drivers
b. 45 drivers
c. 60 drivers
d. Explain the differences in these probabilities.

7.58 Obtaining a driver's license at the earliest eligible age has been a teenage ritual that appears to be fading. A study performed by the University of Michigan Transportation Research Institute recently found that 30% U.S. teenagers between the ages of 17 to 19 did not possess a driver's license. A random sample of 140 17- to 19-year-old teenagers was selected.

a. What is the probability that 45 or fewer teenagers of this sample had not obtained a driver's license?
b. What is the probability that 50 or more teenagers of this sample had not obtained a driver's license?
c. What is the probability that between 35 and 40 teenagers had not obtained a driver's license?
d. Suppose that 28 teenagers from this sample had not obtained a driver's license? Does this result support the findings reported by the University of Michigan Transportation Research Institute?

7.59 Suppose I am employed at a college in which 62% of the student population is female. I am currently teaching statistics to 135 students this semester. I would like to select 50 students randomly from this group to participate in one of my research projects.

a. What is the probability that 30 or more students in my sample will be female?
b. What is the probability that 27 or more students in my sample will be female?
c. What is the probability that between 28 and 36 of the students in my sample will be female?
d. Which of the four probability sampling procedures would be most appropriate if gender was an important factor in the research?

7.60 Quality control programs will often establish control limits that are three standard errors above and below a target mean for a process. A sample is taken from the process, and if the sample mean is within the control limits the process is deemed satisfactory. A process is designed to fill bottles with 16 ounces of soda with a standard deviation of 0.5 ounces.

a. Determine the control limits above and below the mean for this process using a sample size of 30.
b. What percentage of sample means would you expect to fall within these limits if the process is operating satisfactorily?

7.61 The National Center for Health Statistics reported that 34% of Americans were obese recently. The Center for Disease Control estimated that obese people spent an average of $1,429 more for medical goods and services than non-obese people. Obesity is determined using a formula called body mass index (BMI), which is calculated using the following formula:

$$\text{BMI} = \frac{\text{Weight(lbs)} \times 703}{(\text{Height(inches)})^2}$$

A person with a BMI of 25 to 29 is classified as overweight, 30 to 40 as obese, and 40 or more as morbidly obese. The Excel file named **BMI.xlsx** lists the height and weight of a sample of 80 adults. Does this sample support the findings that 34% of the population is obese?

7.62 Wawa Corporation operates 570 convenient food stores in Delaware, Maryland, New Jersey, Pennsylvania, and Virginia. Suppose the company's managers have a goal that customer satisfaction is to average at least 8.0 on a scale of 1–10. A random sample of 60 stores was selected, and the average customer satisfaction level for these stores was 7.75. Assume the historical standard deviation of satisfaction scores is 0.9. Is the goal set by the managers being achieved?

CHAPTER 7 Solutions to Your Turn

YOUR TURN #1

a. Systematic sampling
b. Cluster sampling
c. Convenience sampling
d. Stratified sampling
e. Simple random sampling

YOUR TURN #2

$$\mu = \frac{\sum_{i=1}^{N} X_i}{N} = \frac{\$21 + \$24 + \cdots + \$48 + \$33}{16}$$

$$= \frac{\$461}{16} = \$28.8$$

a. $\bar{x} = \frac{\sum_{i=1}^{n} x_i}{n} = \frac{\$21 + \$24}{2} = \$22.5$

Sampling Error $= \bar{x} - \mu = \$22.5 - \$28.8 = -\$6.3$

b. $\bar{x} = \frac{\sum_{i=1}^{n} x_i}{n} = \frac{\$21 + \$24 + \$36 + \$23}{4} = \$26.0$

Sampling Error $= \bar{x} - \mu = \$26.0 - \$28.8 = -\$2.8$

c. $\bar{x} = \frac{\sum_{i=1}^{n} x_i}{n} = \frac{\$21 + \$24 + \$36 + \$23 + \$26 + \$31}{6}$

$= \$26.8$

Sampling Error $= \bar{x} - \mu = \$26.8 - \$28.8 = -\$2.0$

The sampling error decreases as the sample size increases.

YOUR TURN #3

a. Population frequency distribution:

Service	Cost ($)	Frequency	Probability
Facial (F)	40.0	1	0.3333
Pedicure (P)	30.0	1	0.3333
Manicure (M)	20.0	1	0.3333
Total		**3**	**1.00**

b. Possible sample combinations:

	Katie (F)	Katie (P)	Katie (M)
Debbie (F)	$40, $40	$40, $30	$40, $20
Debbie (P)	$30, $40	$30, $30	$30, $20
Debbie (M)	$20, $40	$20, $30	$20, $20

Sample means:

	Katie (F)	Katie (P)	Katie (M)
Debbie (F)	$40	$35	$30
Debbie (P)	$35	$30	$25
Debbie (M)	$30	$25	$20

Frequency distribution of sample means:

Sample Average $\bar{x}_i$($)	Frequency	Relative Frequency $P(\bar{x}_i)$
20	1	0.1111
25	2	0.2222
30	3	0.3333
35	2	0.2222
40	1	0.1111
Total	**9**	**1.00**

c. $\mu = \sum_{i=1}^{N} x_i P(x_i)$

$\mu = (\$40)(0.3333) + (\$30)(0.3333) + (\$20)(0.3333)$

$\mu = \$30$

$\mu_{\bar{x}} = \sum_{i=1}^{n} \bar{x}_i P(\bar{x}_i)$

$\mu_{\bar{x}} = (\$20)(0.1111) + (\$25)(0.2222) + (\$30)(0.3333) + (\$35)(0.2222) + (\$40)(0.1111)$

$\mu_{\bar{x}} = \$30$

d. Population standard deviation table:

x_i	x_i^2	$P(x_i)$	$x_i^2 P(x_i)$
20	400	0.3333	133.32
30	900	0.3333	299.97
40	1,600	0.3333	533.28
		Total =	**966.57**

$$\sum_{i=1}^{N} x_i^2 P(x_i) = 966.57$$

$$\sigma^2 = \left(\sum_{i=1}^{N} x_i^2 P(x_i)\right) - \mu^2$$

$$\sigma^2 = 966.57 - (30)^2 = 966.57 - 900 = 66.57$$

$$\sigma = \sqrt{\sigma^2} = \sqrt{66.57} = \$8.16$$

Standard error of the mean table:

$\bar{x}_i$	$\bar{x}_i^2$	$P(\bar{x}_i)$	$\bar{x}_i^2 P(\bar{x}_i)$
20	400	0.1111	44.440
25	625	0.2222	138.875
30	900	0.3333	299.970
35	1,225	0.2222	272.195
40	1,600	0.1111	177.760
		Total =	**933.240**

$$\sum_{i=1}^{n} \bar{x}_i^2 P(\bar{x}_i) = 933.24$$

$$\sigma_{\bar{x}}^2 = \left(\sum_{i=1}^{n} \bar{x}_i^2 P(\bar{x}_i)\right) - \mu_{\bar{x}}^2$$

$$\sigma_{\bar{x}}^2 = 933.24 - (30)^2 = 933.24 - 900 = 33.24$$

$$\sigma_{\bar{x}} = \sqrt{\sigma_{\bar{x}}^2} = \sqrt{33.24} = \$5.77$$

$$\sigma_{\bar{x}} = \frac{\sigma}{\sqrt{n}} = \frac{\$8.16}{\sqrt{2}} = \$5.77$$

YOUR TURN #4

$\mu_{\bar{x}} = \mu = \$20.04$

$\sigma = \$6.00$

$n = 35$

$$\sigma_{\bar{x}} = \frac{\sigma}{\sqrt{n}} = \frac{\$6.00}{\sqrt{35}} = \frac{\$6.00}{5.92} = \$1.014$$

$$z_{19} = \frac{\bar{x} - \mu_{\bar{x}}}{\sigma_{\bar{x}}} = \frac{\$19.00 - \$20.04}{\$1.014} = -1.03$$

$$P(\bar{x} < \$19.00) = P(z < -1.03) = 0.1515$$

YOUR TURN #5

a. $\mu_{\bar{x}} = 18$ ounces

$\sigma = 0.32$ ounces

$n = 30$

$$\sigma_{\bar{x}} = \frac{\sigma}{\sqrt{n}} = \frac{0.32}{\sqrt{30}} = \frac{0.32}{5.48} = 0.058$$

$$z_{18.2} = \frac{\bar{x} - \mu_{\bar{x}}}{\sigma_{\bar{x}}} = \frac{18.2 - 18}{0.058} = 3.45$$

$$P(z \geq 3.45) = 1.0 - 0.9997 = 0.0003$$

Because this probability of obtaining a sample mean of 18.2 ounces or more if the true population mean is 18 ounces is only 0.0003, there is little evidence to support the 18-ounce average. It appears the filling process is putting too much cereal in the boxes.

b. $\bar{x}_U = \mu_{\bar{x}} + z\sigma_{\bar{x}}$

$\bar{x}_U = 18 + (1.96)(0.058) = 18.11$ ounces

$\bar{x}_L = \mu_{\bar{x}} - z\sigma_{\bar{x}}$

$\bar{x}_L = 18 - (1.96)(0.058) = 17.89$ ounces

YOUR TURN #6

a. $\mu_{\bar{x}} = 48$ MPG

$\sigma = 7$ MPG

$n = 40$

$$\sigma_{\bar{x}} = \frac{\sigma}{\sqrt{n}} = \frac{7}{\sqrt{40}} = \frac{7}{6.32} = 1.11$$

$\bar{x}_U = \mu_{\bar{x}} + z\sigma_{\bar{x}}$

$\bar{x}_U = 48 + (1.96)(1.11) = 50.2$ MPG

$\bar{x}_L = \mu_{\bar{x}} - z\sigma_{\bar{x}}$

$\bar{x}_L = 48 - (1.96)(1.11) = 45.8$ MPG

b. $\mu_{\bar{x}} = 48$ MPG

$\sigma = 7$ MPG

$n = 80$

$$\sigma_{\bar{x}} = \frac{\sigma}{\sqrt{n}} = \frac{7}{\sqrt{80}} = \frac{7}{8.94} = 0.78$$

$\bar{x}_U = \mu_{\bar{x}} + z\sigma_{\bar{x}}$

$\bar{x}_U = 48 + (1.96)(0.78) = 49.5$ MPG

$\bar{x}_L = \mu_{\bar{x}} - z\sigma_{\bar{x}}$

$\bar{x}_L = 48 - (1.96)(0.78) = 46.5$ MPG

YOUR TURN #7

$$\frac{n}{N} = \frac{30}{120} = 0.25 > 0.05$$

$$\sigma_{\bar{x}} = \frac{\sigma}{\sqrt{n}}\sqrt{\frac{N-n}{N-1}} = \frac{3.2}{\sqrt{30}}\sqrt{\frac{120-30}{120-1}}.$$

$$= (0.584)(\sqrt{0.756}) = 0.507$$

$$z_{8.8} = \frac{\bar{x} - \mu_{\bar{x}}}{\sigma_{\bar{x}}} = \frac{8.8 - 9.0}{0.507} = -0.39$$

$$P(\bar{x} \leq 8.8) = P(z \leq -0.39) = 0.3483$$

There is a 34.8% chance of observing a sample mean of 8.8 or less with an actual population mean of 9.0. This probability is too high to claim the population mean is less than 9.0. The reason my sample mean is less than 9.0 is due to sampling error.

YOUR TURN #8

$$\bar{p} = \frac{x}{n} = \frac{36}{125} = 0.288$$

$$np = (125)(0.34) = 42.5 \geq 5$$

$$n(1-p) = (125)(1-0.34) = 82.5 \geq 5$$

$$\sigma_p = \sqrt{\frac{p(1-p)}{n}} = \sqrt{\frac{(0.34)(1-0.34)}{125}} = \sqrt{\frac{0.2244}{125}}$$

$$= \sqrt{0.001795} = 0.0424$$

$$z = \frac{\bar{p} - p}{\sigma_p} = \frac{0.288 - 0.34}{0.0424} = -1.23$$

$$P(p \geq 0.288) = P(z \geq -1.23) = 0.8907$$

There is an 89% chance that a sample of 125 will contain more than 36 who drive while they text.

YOUR TURN #9

$$p = 0.75 \quad n = 50 \quad N = 96$$

$$n/N = \frac{50}{96} = 0.51 > 0.05$$

$$\bar{p} = \frac{x}{n} = \frac{31}{50} = 0.62$$

$$np = (50)(0.75) = 37.5 \geq 5$$

$$n(1-p) = (50)(1-0.75) = 12.5 \geq 5$$

$$\sigma_p = \sqrt{\frac{p(1-p)}{n}}\sqrt{\frac{N-n}{N-1}} = \sqrt{\frac{(0.75)(1-0.75)}{50}}\sqrt{\frac{96-50}{96-1}}$$

$$\sigma_p = \sqrt{\frac{0.1875}{50}}\sqrt{\frac{46}{95}} = \sqrt{0.00375}\sqrt{0.4842}$$

$$\sigma_p = (0.0612)(0.6958) = 0.0426$$

$$z_{0.62} = \frac{\bar{p} - p}{\sigma_p} = \frac{0.62 - 0.75}{0.0426} = -3.05$$

$$P(p \leq 0.62) = P(z \leq -3.05) = 0.0011$$

There is a very small probability that a sample proportion of 0.62 or less will be observed if the true population proportion is 0.75. Therefore, it appears the population proportion is less than 0.75 and there is no supporting evidence with this sample that 75% of the homes are up to date with their annual dues.

CHAPTER

8

Confidence Intervals

IN THIS CHAPTER, YOU WILL LEARN TO:

- Calculate and interpret a confidence interval for a population mean.
- Understand the meaning of the margin of error.
- Understand the impact of changing the confidence level for a confidence interval.
- Use the Student's t-distribution to determine a confidence interval.
- Calculate and interpret a confidence interval for a population proportion.
- Determine the sample size required to obtain a specific margin of error.
- Calculate a confidence interval for a finite population.

CHAPTER 8 MAP

Stats in Practice: The BLS Reports That the Unemployment Rate Fell—Or Maybe Rose

An economic statistic that the business community watches very closely each month is the national unemployment rate which is reported by the federal government's Bureau of Labor Statistics (BLS). Because the population of the U.S. workforce is very large, BLS relies on a sample each month to estimate the unemployment rate for the entire economy. For example, the BLS reported that the unemployment rate dropped from 7.92% in January 2013 to 7.74% in February, which provided encouragement that the health of the economy was improving. But what many people who read this statistic don't realize is that there is a level of uncertainty associated with this figure. As it turns out, based on their sample of the workforce, the government was 90% confident that the actual U.S. unemployment rate in February 2013 was between 7.54% and 7.94%. In other words, the unemployment rate may have actually increased from 7.92% in January to 7.94% in February. The government can't say for sure that there was a decrease in unemployment between these two months.

What I am describing here is known as a 90% confidence interval around the estimated unemployment rate of 7.74% in February 2013. As we will learn in this chapter, the uncertainty as to whether unemployment actually rose or fell is not a failure on the part of the BLS, but the nature of the beast fondly known as statistics. Because the reported rate of 7.74% is based on a sample taken from the labor force population, it is only an estimate and subject to sampling error which was discussed in Chapter 7. In this chapter, you will learn how to construct and interpret confidence intervals and, as a result, be able to understand the nuances of reports such as the one described in this section.

Now that you have learned how to collect a random sample and how sample means and sample proportions behave under certain conditions, you are ready to put those samples to work using confidence intervals. One of the most important roles that statistics plays in today's world is to gather information from a sample and then use that information to make a statement about the population from which it was chosen. We are using the sample as an estimate for the population. But just how good of an estimate is the sample providing us? As the previous Stats in Practice indicates, the answer to this question is a very important one. The concept of confidence intervals will allow us to arrive at an answer.

8.1 Point Estimates

A **point estimate** is a single value that best describes the population of interest. The most common point estimates are the sample mean and the sample proportion.

The simplest estimate of a population is a **point estimate**, the most common of which are the sample mean and the sample proportion. A point estimate is a single value that best describes the population of interest.

I fear my wife has been kidnapped and secretly replaced by a Deb lookalike who is completely addicted to QVC, one of the home-shopping channels. No one and no room in our household has escaped the products Deb has found on her new favorite television channel. She has purchased stuff for the car, the kitchen floor, the dog, her skin, her hair, and my back (an inversion table that she wants me to hang upside down on like a bat!).

Suddenly "Diamonique Week" has become a major holiday in our household. I'm not really sure what Diamonique actually is, but I suspect it is "available for a limited time only." Whenever I turn on any television in the house, the channel always seems to be set to a very convincing home-shopping channel–type person pleading with me to "Call now! Only three left!" I have no idea what the person is selling, but I find myself looking for the phone.

Anyway, let's say HSN, one of QVC's competitors, would like to estimate the average dollar value for a QVC customer. To start, we need to collect a random sample of QVC customer orders, the process for which was discussed in Chapter 7. If my sample mean were \$129.20, I could use that as my point estimate for the entire population of QVC customers.

Point estimates are easy to calculate but do not provide any information about their accuracy.

The advantage of a point estimate is that it is easy to calculate and easy to understand. The disadvantage is that I have no information concerning the accuracy of this estimate. Remember how in Chapter 7 we discussed the fact that it is not realistic to assume that the sample mean from one sample will equal the population mean? Every random sample is subject to sampling error, which is the difference between the sample mean and population mean.

To deal with this uncertainty, we can use an interval estimate. An interval estimate provides a range of values that best describes the population. Next, we will look at the most common type of interval estimate, the confidence interval.

8.2 Calculating Confidence Intervals for the Mean when the Standard Deviation (σ) of a Population Is Known

A **confidence interval for the mean** is an interval estimate around a sample mean that provides us with a range of where the true population mean lies.

A **confidence interval for the mean** is an interval estimate around a sample mean that provides us with a range of where the true population mean lies. In reality, the true population mean is rarely known, so the confidence interval is often the only evidence we have for the average of the population.

In this section, we will focus on a case in which our sample size is at least 30 ($n \geq 30$). This allows us to use the properties of the Central Limit Theorem from Chapter 7. Recall that the Central Limit Theorem states that regardless of the shape of a population distribution, its sample means will follow the normal distribution for sample sizes of 30 or greater. We will also assume in this section that the population standard deviation, σ (sigma), is known. However, in reality, the standard deviation is often unknown. Think about it: In Chapter 3, you learned that you need to know the mean in order to calculate the standard deviation. (Sigma measures the average variation of the data from the mean.) Later in this chapter, you will learn how to construct a confidence interval when sigma is unknown. In the meantime, we'll assume we know the population standard deviation.

A **confidence level** is defined as the probability that the interval estimate will include the population parameter of interest, such as a mean or a proportion.

To develop an interval estimate for the population of interest, we need to learn about confidence levels. The Stats in Practice at the beginning of this chapter stated that the government was 90% certain that the unemployment rate for February 2013 was somewhere between 7.54% and 7.94%. In this example, the value 90% represents the **confidence level,** which is defined as the probability that the interval estimate will include the population parameter of interest, such as a mean or proportion. Typically, confidence levels are set by the statistician at 90% or 95% and will occasionally go as high as 99%. I'll discuss the impact these confidence levels have on the confidence interval later in the chapter.

Now we are ready to delve into the confidence interval calculations. Remember from Chapter 7 we learned that the variation in a sample mean, which we called the standard error of the mean and denoted by $\sigma_{\bar{x}}$, could be found using Equation 8.1.

Formula 8.1 for the Standard Error of the Mean

$$\sigma_{\bar{x}} = \frac{\sigma}{\sqrt{n}}$$

where

$\sigma =$ The population standard deviation
$n =$ The sample size

Let's say we want to construct a confidence interval for the average order size of the QVC customer based on my sample mean of $129.20 with a 90% confidence level. To determine this interval, we need two more pieces of information: the sample size and the population standard deviation. Suppose my sample mean was based on the data from 32 orders. In other words, $n = 32$. (I can't help but wonder how many of these orders are from Deb.) Also, we'll assume the population standard deviation is equal to $40.60 ($\sigma = 40.60$). In Chapter 13, we will discuss how to test for a population standard deviation.

We can now calculate the standard error of the mean for our home-shopping example using Equation 8.1 as follows:

$$\sigma_{\bar{x}} = \frac{\sigma}{\sqrt{n}} = \frac{\$40.60}{\sqrt{32}} = \frac{\$40.60}{5.66} = \$7.173$$

Figure 8.1 shows the sampling distribution of the mean (Another Chapter 7 topic—I hope you were paying attention!) for the home-shopping example. This distribution has the following parameters:

$$\mu_{\bar{x}} = \text{The mean of the sample means}$$

$$\sigma_{\bar{x}} = \text{The standard deviation of the sample means}$$

I use the subscript $\alpha/2$ for the critical z-score to indicate that the total area for alpha is split in half on each side of the sampling distribution.

The shaded region represents the area in which we expect to observe 90% of the sample means gathered from the home-shopping population when the size of each of sample is 32. We need to find the critical z-score, $z_{\alpha/2}$, that corresponds to the boundaries of the shaded region by observing that the total area to the left of the right-hand boundary is $0.90 + 0.05 = 0.95$. The variable α is known as the **significance level** and represents the nonshaded (white) areas under the curve in Figure 8.1. For a 90% confidence level, $\alpha = 1 - 0.90 = 0.10$, which leaves each nonshaded area equal to 0.05. The significance level will be discussed in more detail later in this chapter. To find the value of $z_{\alpha/2}$, go to Table 4 in Appendix A and search for the value in the body of the table closest to 0.95. You'll find 0.9495 in the 1.6 row and 0.04 column and 0.9505 in the 0.05 column. Our critical z-score is halfway between these values, which tells us $z_{\alpha/2} = z_{0.05} = 1.645$ on the right side of the mean. This same critical z-score to the left of the mean will be designated $-z_{\alpha/2} = -z_{0.05} = -1.645$ as seen in Figure 8.1. This is the critical z-score for all 90% confidence intervals.

FIGURE 8.1
Critical z-Scores for a 90% Confidence Interval

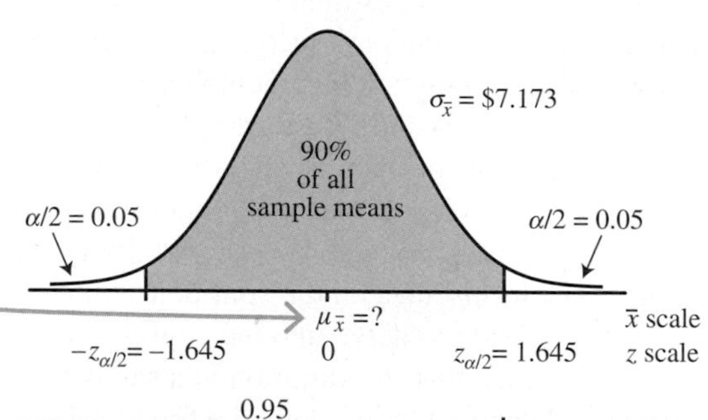

We learned in Chapter 7 that we expect the population mean, μ, to be equal to the mean of the sample means, $\mu_{\bar{x}}$. Both are unknown in Figure 8.1.

Notice that the mean of the sampling distribution in Figure 8.1 is unknown. This is because the population mean for the QVC order size is unknown to us because we have observed only one sample so far. The purpose of generating a confidence interval is to provide an estimate for the value of the population mean.

The confidence interval for the mean has an upper confidence limit ($UCL_{\bar{x}}$) and a lower confidence limit ($LCL_{\bar{x}}$). The upper and lower limits describe the range in which we have some degree of confidence that the actual population mean lies. Equations 8.2 and 8.3 show the formulas for calculating the upper and lower limits for a confidence interval for a particular sample mean.

Formulas 8.2 and 8.3 for the Confidence Interval for the Mean (σ Known)

$$UCL_{\bar{x}} = \bar{x} + z_{\alpha/2}\sigma_{\bar{x}}$$

$$LCL_{\bar{x}} = \bar{x} - z_{\alpha/2}\sigma_{\bar{x}}$$

where

$\bar{x} =$ The sample mean
$z_{\alpha/2} =$ The critical z-score
$\sigma_{\bar{x}} =$ The standard error of the mean

We are now ready to calculate the 90% confidence interval for the average order size of QVC customers using Equations 8.2 and 8.3. First, we start with the upper limit:

$$UCL_{\bar{x}} = \bar{x} + z_{\alpha/2}\sigma_{\bar{x}}$$
$$UCL_{\bar{x}} = (\$129.20) + (1.645)(\$7.173)$$
$$UCL_{\bar{x}} = \$129.20 + \$11.80 = \$141.00$$

Now, we calculate the lower limit:

$$LCL_{\bar{x}} = \bar{x} - z_{\alpha/2}\sigma_{\bar{x}}$$
$$LCL_{\bar{x}} = (\$129.20) - (1.645)(\$7.173)$$
$$LCL_{\bar{x}} = \$129.20 - \$11.80 = \$117.40$$

Based on our sample mean of $129.20, we are 90% confident that the average order size for the population of QVC customers is between $117.40 and $141.00. We can express this interval as ($117.40, $141.00). I need to keep this information from Deb lest she feels it her duty to keep her home-shopping orders in line with this confidence interval.

Be sure and try this next Your Turn problem to test your understanding of how to construct a confidence interval.

YOUR TURN #1

A sample of 35 luxury hotels in the United States had an average room rate of $247.80 per night. Using this sample, construct a 90% confidence interval to estimate the average room rate per night for luxury hotels in the United States assuming the population standard deviation is $39 per night.

Answer can be found on ▶ **page 378**

Calculating the Margin of Error

Margin of error The width of the confidence interval between a sample mean or a proportion and its upper limit and or its lower limit.

Figure 8.2 shows our 90% home-shopping confidence interval and identifies the **margin of error**, $ME_{\bar{x}}$. The margin of error is the width of the interval between a sample mean and its upper limit *or* between a sample mean and its lower limit. This confidence interval can be expressed as $129.20 plus *or* minus $11.80, which is the margin of error.

FIGURE 8.2
The Margin of Error for the Home-Shopping Example

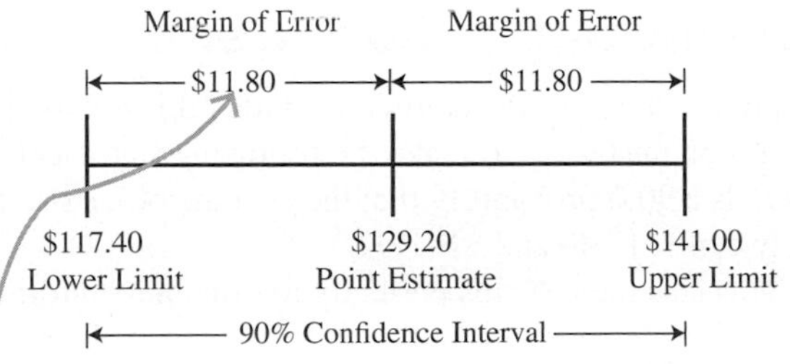

A margin of error represents the width of the confidence interval between a sample mean and its upper limit or between a sample mean and its lower limit. Notice that the confidence interval is symmetrical around the sample mean.

In general, the margin of error for a confidence interval for the mean can be found using Equation 8.4.

Formula 8.4 for the Margin of Error for a Confidence Interval for the Mean

$$ME_{\bar{x}} = z_{\alpha/2}\sigma_{\bar{x}}$$

For our home-shopping example, the margin of error is calculated as follows:

$$ME_{\bar{x}} = z_{\alpha/2}\sigma_{\bar{x}} = (1.645)(\$7.173) = \$11.80$$

For a particular confidence level, say 90%, a smaller margin of error provides a more precise estimate than a larger margin of error. We can lower the margin of error while maintaining our 90% confidence level by simply increasing our sample size from its current value of 32. To illustrate, let's assume our sample mean of \$129.20 was obtained using a sample size of 50. The margin of error for this sample size is as follows:

$$\sigma_{\bar{x}} = \frac{\sigma}{\sqrt{n}} = \frac{\$40.60}{\sqrt{50}} = \frac{\$40.60}{7.07} = \$5.74$$

$$ME_{\bar{x}} = z_{\alpha/2}\sigma_{\bar{x}} = (1.645)(\$5.74) = \$9.44$$

The margin of error decreased from \$11.80 to \$9.44 when we increased the sample size from 32 to 50. As a result, our new and improved 90% confidence interval becomes the following:

Increasing the sample size while keeping the confidence level constant will reduce the margin of error, resulting in a narrower (more precise) confidence interval.

$$UCL_{\bar{x}} = \$129.20 + \$9.44 = \$138.64$$

$$LCL_{\bar{x}} = \$129.20 - \$9.44 = \$119.76$$

As you can see, increasing the sample size from 32 to 50 changes our 90% confidence interval from (\$117.40, \$141.00) to (\$119.76, \$138.64). This new interval is a more precise (narrower) estimate of the average order size for the QVC population. Hopefully, this makes sense to you. A larger sample size provides more information about our population, which, in turn, provides a more precise estimate of the true population mean.

It will be worth your while to spend a minute with this next Your Turn problem to test your margin-of-error skills.

YOUR TURN #2

A random sample of notebook computers currently on the market has an average price of \$507. Assume the standard deviation for the population of notebooks is \$63. Calculate a 90% confidence interval and the margin of error for this sample if the sample size were the following:

a. 30 notebooks

b. 60 notebooks

c. What impact does increasing sample size have on the precision of these estimates?

Answers can be found on ▶ **page 378**

Interpreting a Confidence Interval

The interpretation of the confidence interval is not as simple as you might think it would be. A common mistake is to make the following statement, which, for the record, is *not* true: "There is a 90% probability that the average order size for the population of QVC customers is between \$117.40 and \$141.00."

This statement seems perfectly reasonable. Unfortunately, it cannot be supported with our confidence interval calculations. To fully explain what a confidence interval means, we need to take additional random samples from the QVC population, each with a size of 32, and calculate their sample means. Table 8.1 shows the first sample we collected at the start of this chapter, along with nine additional random samples and their sample means.

An important point that needs to be made here is that each sample taken from the population has its own confidence interval, as shown in Table 8.1. Notice that each of these samples has the same margin of error (\$11.80) because the sample size and population standard deviation are unchanged for each of them and they all represent a 90% confidence level.

Figure 8.3 shows the sampling distribution for the home-shopping example along with the 10 confidence intervals from the samples in Table 8.1. For demonstration purposes, let's assume the average order size from the QVC population is known and is \$125 (μ = \$125); it is represented by the green line in Figure 8.3. The position of the confidence intervals for the 10 samples is shown below this distribution.

Notice that every sample has its own confidence interval centered on the sample mean.

TABLE 8.1 | SAMPLE MEANS FROM THE QVC POPULATION

			90% CONFIDENCE INTERVAL	
SAMPLE	SAMPLE MEAN (\$)	MARGIN OF ERROR (\$)	LOWER LIMIT (\$)	UPPER LIMIT (\$)
1	129.20	11.80	117.40	141.00
2	132.00	11.80	120.20	143.80
3	117.50	11.80	105.70	129.30
4	128.20	11.80	116.40	140.00
5	108.80	11.80	97.00	120.60
6	130.10	11.80	118.30	141.90
7	117.90	11.80	106.10	129.70
8	120.10	11.80	108.30	131.90
9	133.80	11.80	122.00	145.60
10	119.00	11.80	107.20	130.80

FIGURE 8.3
Ten Confidence Intervals for the Home-Shopping Population

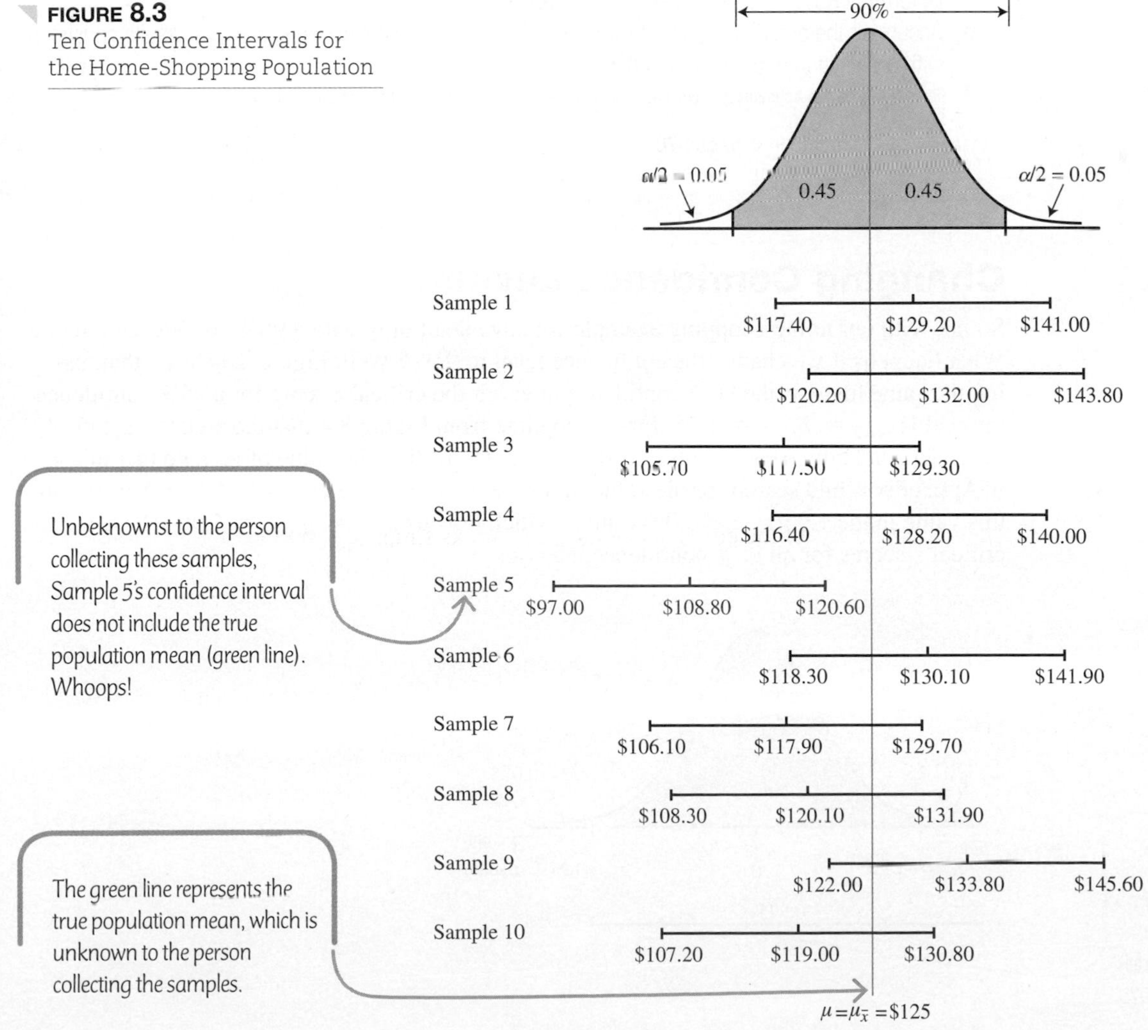

Unbeknownst to the person collecting these samples, Sample 5's confidence interval does not include the true population mean (green line). Whoops!

The green line represents the true population mean, which is unknown to the person collecting the samples.

The definition of a 90% confidence interval is that we expect that close to 90% of a large number of sample means drawn from a population will produce confidence intervals that include that population's mean.

Notice that our first random sample from the beginning of the chapter (Sample 1 in Figure 8.3) has a 90% confidence interval that includes the actual population mean, $\mu = \$125$, because the green line cuts through it. This interval correctly established a range of values that included the average order size of the QVC population. Now, look at the confidence interval for Sample 5. If this had been our random sample, we would state that we were 90% confident that the average order size for the QVC population is between \$97.00 and \$120.60, which, without us knowing it, would be untrue because $\mu = \$125$. The lesson here is that there is no guarantee that every confidence interval will include the population mean. As a matter of fact, Table 8.3 shows us that 9 out of 10 sample means have confidence intervals that include the population mean. This is the definition of a 90% confidence interval. We expect that close to 90% of a large number of sample means drawn from a population will produce confidence intervals that include that population's mean. However, this does not mean that we are guaranteed that 9 out of every 10 intervals will include the population mean. The same can be said for 95% and 99% confidence intervals.

Test your understanding of this interpretation of a confidence interval using the following Your Turn problem.

YOUR TURN #3

Suppose the Princeton Tavern in Avalon, New Jersey, would like to estimate the average wait time for a table for customers arriving for dinner on a Saturday night. Assume the population standard deviation for wait time is 4.1 minutes. Five random samples, each consisting of 30 wait times, were selected with the following sample means, in minutes:

12.4 11.3 13.1 13.7 12.7

a. Determine 80% confidence intervals for each sample.

b. Assuming the actual average wait time for all customers is 13 minutes, are your results consistent with a definition of an 80% confidence interval?

Hint: Use Table 4 in Appendix A to convince yourself that $z_{\alpha/2} = 1.28$ for an 80% confidence level.

Answers can be found on ▶ **page 378**

Changing Confidence Levels

So far, with our home-shopping example we have dealt only with a 90% confidence interval. What happens if we change the confidence level to 95%? Well, Figure 8.4 shows that, using the same logic as the 90% confidence interval, the critical z-score for a 95% confidence interval is $z_{\alpha/2} = z_{0.025} = 1.96$. First, recognize from Figure 8.4 that the area to the left of the right-hand boundary is $0.95 + 0.025 = 0.975$. To find the value of $z_{\alpha/2}$, go to Table 4 in Appendix A and search for the value in the body of the table closest to 0.975. You'll find this value in the 1.9 row and 0.06 column, which tells us $z_{\alpha/2} = z_{0.025} = 1.96$. These are the critical z-scores for all 95% confidence intervals.

FIGURE 8.4
Critical z-Scores for a 95% Confidence Interval

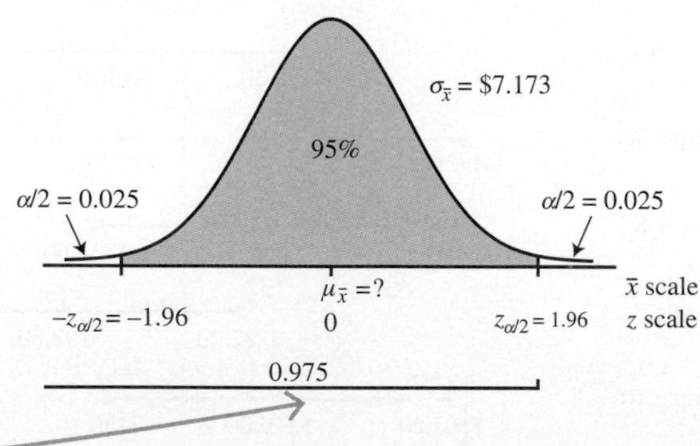

The area to the left of $z_{\alpha/2} = 1.96$ equals the entire shaded region (0.95) plus the small unshaded region in the left tail (0.025), which totals to 0.975.

Because there is a 95% probability that any given confidence interval will contain the true population mean in our current example, we have a 5% chance that it won't. As mentioned earlier, this 5% value is known as the **significance level**, α (known as alpha), which is represented by the total white area in both tails of Figure 8.4. Notice that this 5% area is split in half between both tails of the sampling distribution.

The **significance level**, α, represents the probability that any given confidence interval will not contain the true population mean.

The confidence level of an interval is a complement to the significance level. For example, the significance level for a 90% confidence interval is 10%, and the significance level for a 99% confidence interval is 1%. In general, a $100 \times (1 - \alpha)\%$ confidence interval has a significance level equal to α. We will revisit the significance level in more detail in later chapters.

Observe that the standard error for the mean in Figure 8.4 remains at $\sigma_{\bar{x}} = \$7.173$ for our 95% confidence interval because the sample size and population standard deviation are unchanged from their original values of 32 and $40.72, respectively. Our 95% confidence interval for a sample mean of $129.20 is determined as follows:

$$UCL_{\bar{x}} = \bar{x} + z_{\alpha/2}\sigma_{\bar{x}}$$
$$UCL_{\bar{x}} = (\$129.20) + (1.96)(\$7.173)$$
$$UCL_{\bar{x}} = \$129.20 + \$14.06 = \$143.26$$

$$LCL_{\bar{x}} = \bar{x} - z_{\alpha/2}\sigma_{\bar{x}}$$
$$LCL_{\bar{x}} = (\$129.20) - (1.96)(\$7.173)$$
$$LCL_{\bar{x}} = \$129.20 - \$14.06 = \$115.14$$

Notice that the 95% confidence interval is wider than the 90% interval. In order to be more confident that we have "caught" the true population mean, we need to expand the confidence interval from ($117.40, $141.00) to ($115.14, $143.26).

Finally, let's take a look at the 99% confidence interval for our home-shopping sample using Figure 8.5.

FIGURE 8.5
Critical z-Scores for a 99% Confidence Interval

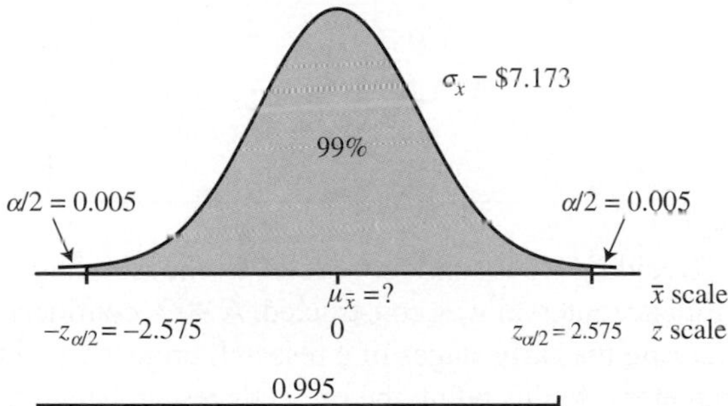

The value 0.995 $(0.99 + 0.005)$ is halfway between the 0.7 and 0.8 columns in the 2.5 row in Table 4 from Appendix A. The critical z-score for our 99% confidence level is therefore $z_{\alpha/2} = z_{0.005} = 2.575$. These are the critical z-scores for all 99% confidence intervals.

Our 99% confidence interval for a sample mean of $129.20 with a sample size of 32 and sigma equal to $40.60 is found as follows:

$$UCL_{\bar{x}} = \bar{x} + z_{\alpha/2}\sigma_{\bar{x}}$$
$$UCL_{\bar{x}} = (\$129.20) + (2.575)(\$7.173)$$
$$UCL_{\bar{x}} = \$129.20 + \$18.47 = \$147.67$$

$$LCL_{\bar{x}} = \bar{x} - z_{\alpha/2}\sigma_{\bar{x}}$$
$$LCL_{\bar{x}} = (\$129.20) - (2.575)(\$7.173)$$
$$LCL_{\bar{x}} = \$129.20 - \$18.47 = \$110.73$$

The margin of error for the 99% confidence interval ($18.47) is the largest of the three intervals at which we have looked. It also results in the widest (least precise) estimate for the population mean. We are 99% confident that the average order size for the QVC population is ($110.73, $147.67). This is noticeably wider than our 90% confidence interval of ($117.40, $141.00), which has a margin of error of just $11.80.

As this example shows, when you are choosing a confidence level that is most appropriate given a specific sample size, you have a tradeoff to consider. You can have more confidence that our interval includes the actual population mean, but this interval will be wider and less precise. If you desire a narrower, more precise interval, this will result in a lower confidence level, meaning you are less certain that you have caught the actual population mean. In other words, in the second case, you need a bigger target to be more confident that you actually hit the population mean. Figure 8.6 illustrates this trade-off.

FIGURE 8.6
A Confidence Level Trade-Off: Home-Shopping Example

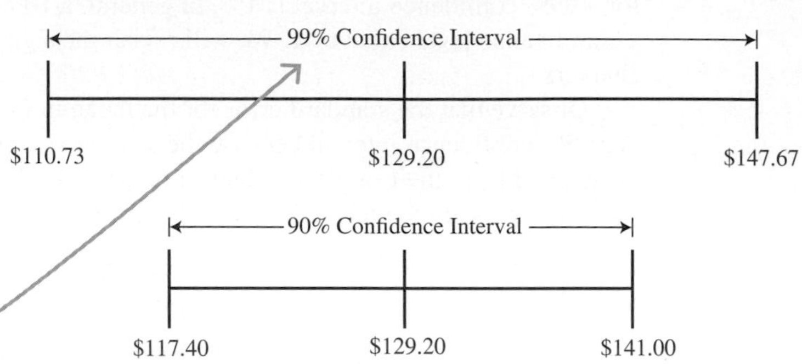

Increasing the confidence level with all else staying constant results in a wider, less precise confidence interval. In order to be more confident that our interval has "caught" the true population mean, we need a wider "net".

Table 8.2 summarizes the critical z-scores for the most common confidence intervals used in statistics.

TABLE 8.2 | CRITICAL Z-SCORES FOR VARIOUS CONFIDENCE INTERVALS

CONFIDENCE LEVEL	SIGNIFICANCE LEVEL	CRITICAL Z-SCORE
$100 \times (1 - \alpha)\%$	$100 \times (\alpha)\%$	$z_{\alpha/2}$
80	20	$z_{0.10} = 1.28$
90	10	$z_{0.05} = 1.645$
95	5	$z_{0.025} = 1.96$
98	2	$z_{0.01} = 2.33$
99	1	$z_{0.005} = 2.575$

Deciding what confidence level to choose often depends on the purpose for which the confidence interval was constructed. A 90% confidence interval might be more appropriate during the early stages of a research project when little is known about the population's parameters. At this point, the project's researchers might still be gauging the parameters, so less precision is needed. The 95% confidence interval is a "workhorse" in the field of statistics and is seen far more than any other confidence level. A 99% confidence interval is often used in scientific or medical research when making a wrong conclusion about a population parameter is very costly. We will discuss the types of errors that can occur in Chapter 9.

Here's another Your Turn problem to help you practice determining confidence intervals for various confidence levels.

YOUR TURN #4

The crisis in the housing market during the most recent economic recession led to lower vacancy rates in the apartment industry. This, in turn, has resulted in an increase in monthly rents for apartments. Suppose a random sample of 40 apartments had an average rent of $1,090. Assume the standard deviation for the population of apartment rents is $260.

a. Determine the 80% confidence interval for this sample.
b. Determine the 95% confidence interval for this sample.
c. Determine the 98% confidence interval for this sample.
d. Explain the differences in these confidence intervals.

Answers can be found on ▶ **page 378**

Putting Confidence Intervals to Work in Businesses

Businesses can use confidence intervals to test the claims made about a product or service. For example, *PC World's* Test Center recently claimed that the talk-time battery life of the current iPhone averaged 5 hours 38 minutes (338 minutes). To validate this claim, suppose we measured the talk time of 35 iPhones and found the sample average to be 324.6 minutes. Assume the standard deviation of iPhone talk time in general is 32 minutes. Does our sample agree with the findings of *PC World*?

To answer this question, let's construct a 95% confidence interval around the mean of this sample. First, we'll start with the standard error of the mean calculation:

$$\sigma_{\bar{x}} = \frac{\sigma}{\sqrt{n}} = \frac{32}{\sqrt{35}} = \frac{32}{5.92} = 5.41$$

Remember, for a 95% confidence interval $z_{\alpha/2} = z_{0.025} = \pm 1.96$. So, the upper and lower limits for our interval are as follows:

$$UCL_{\bar{x}} = \bar{x} + z_{\alpha/2}\sigma_{\bar{x}}$$
$$UCL_{\bar{x}} = (324.6) + (1.96)(5.41) = 335.2$$
$$LCL_{\bar{x}} = \bar{x} - z_{\alpha/2}\sigma_{\bar{x}}$$
$$LCL_{\bar{x}} = (324.6) - (1.96)(5.41) = 314.0$$

If this confidence interval had included the claimed average of 338 minutes, our sample would have validated the results of PC World.

According to our sample, we are 95% confident that the true average talk time of the 3G iPhone is within the interval (314.0, 335.2). Because this interval does not include the claimed average of 338 minutes, our sample does not validate the results of *PC World*'s Test Center. To ensure you grasp this important concept, work the problem in the following Your Turn involving a claim made by the Environmental Protection Agency (EPA).

YOUR TURN #5

Suppose the EPA claimed that the average fuel economy for passenger vehicles in the United States was 20.3 miles per gallon (mpg). To test this claim, a sample of 34 passenger vehicles was randomly selected and their fuel economy was carefully measured. The average fuel economy for this sample was 21.2 mpg. Assume the population standard deviation for passenger vehicle fuel economy is 3.9 mpg. Using a 98% confidence interval, test the validity of the EPA's claim.

Answer can be found on ▶ **page 379**

Using Excel and PHStat to Determine Confidence Intervals for the Mean (Sigma Known)

Excel has a pretty cool built-in function that calculates the margin of error for confidence intervals. The CONFIDENCE.NORM function has the following characteristics:

=CONFIDENCE.NORM (alpha, standard_dev, size)

where

alpha = The significance level of the confidence interval
standard_dev = The standard deviation of the population
size = Sample size

The NORM prefix for this function indicates that sigma is known and that we are using the normal distribution to determine the critical z-score for this interval. We can use the CONFIDENCE.NORM function to calculate the margin of error for the 90% confidence interval for our original home-shopping example, where $\alpha = 0.1$, $\sigma = 40.60$, and $n = 32$.

=CONFIDENCE.NORM(0.1, 40.6, 32) = 11.81

The value 11.81 represents the margin of error in our confidence interval. Notice that this margin of error is slightly different from the one we calculated earlier (11.80) due to the rounding of numbers. Excel uses many more decimal places in the calculations than we do manually. This sure beats using tables and square root functions on a calculator!

PHStat has the ability to also construct the confidence intervals, using the following steps:

1. Go to **Add-Ins > PHStat > Confidence Intervals > Estimate for the Mean, sigma known**, as shown in Figure 8.7.

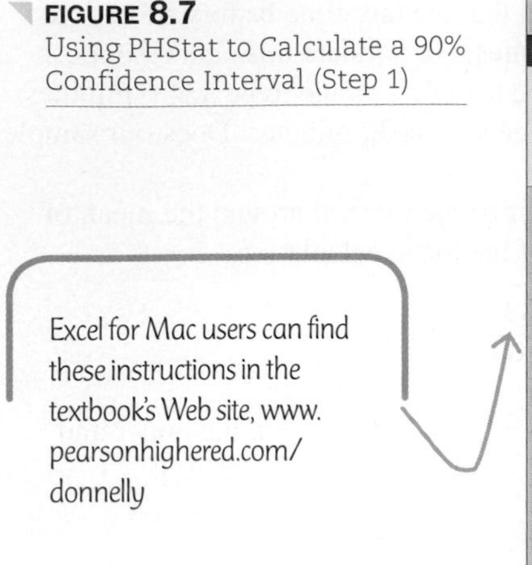

FIGURE 8.7 Using PHStat to Calculate a 90% Confidence Interval (Step 1)

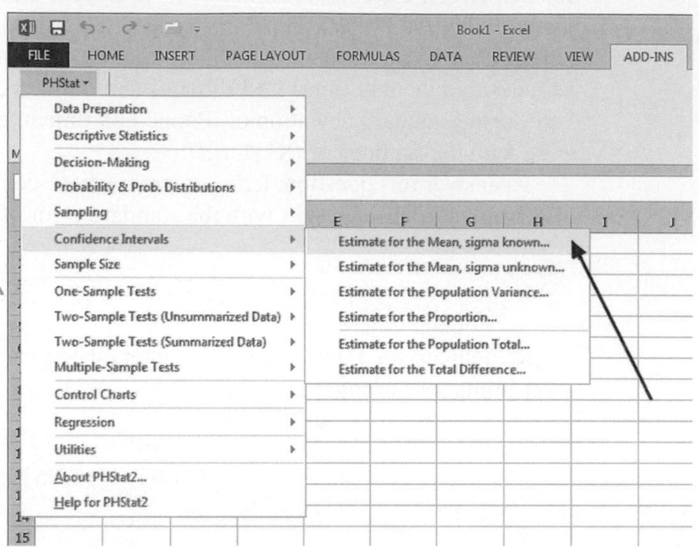

2. Fill in the "Data" and "Input Options" values in the **Estimate for the Mean, sigma known** dialog box as shown in Figure 8.8. Click **OK**.

FIGURE 8.8 Using PHStat to Calculate a Confidence Interval (Step 2)

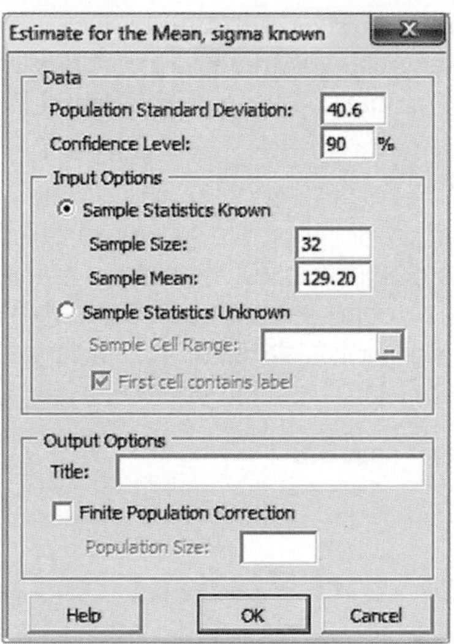

What is the result? The 90% confidence interval is shown in the yellow cells in Figure 8.9. Notice that these values are slightly different from the 90% confidence interval we calculated manually ($117.40, $141.00). Again, this is due to rounding differences. Also, PHStat shows the margin of error as the "Interval Half Width" in Cell B12.

FIGURE 8.9 Using PHStat to Calculate a 90% Confidence Interval (Final Result)

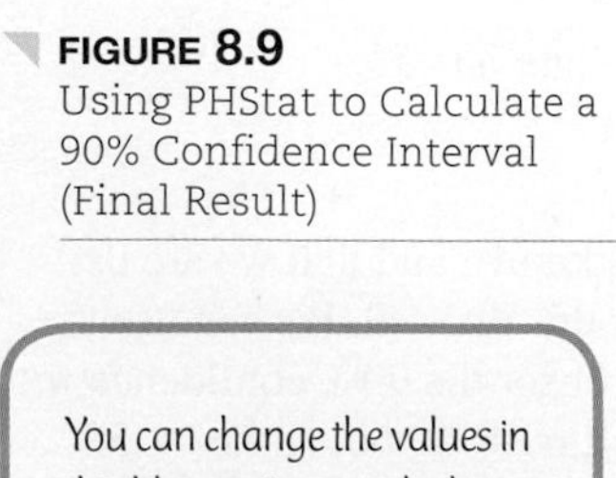

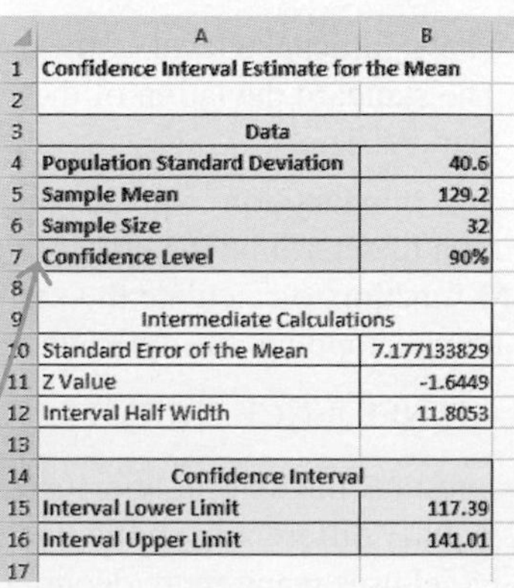

	A	B
1	Confidence Interval Estimate for the Mean	
2		
3	Data	
4	Population Standard Deviation	40.6
5	Sample Mean	129.2
6	Sample Size	32
7	Confidence Level	90%
8		
9	Intermediate Calculations	
10	Standard Error of the Mean	7.177133829
11	Z Value	-1.6449
12	Interval Half Width	11.8053
13		
14	Confidence Interval	
15	Interval Lower Limit	117.39
16	Interval Upper Limit	141.01
17		

I know it always looks easy when I do all the work, so I encourage you to test your Excel skills with this next Your Turn problem.

YOUR TURN #6

A random sample of 45 public colleges and universities averaged $8,650 in tuition and fees during the 2012–2013 academic year. Assume the population standard deviation is $1,490.

a. Use Excel to calculate the margin of error for a 99% confidence interval for this sample.
b. Use PHStat to construct a 99% confidence interval for this sample.

Answers can be found on ▶ **page 379**

Calculating Confidence Intervals for the Mean with Small Samples when the Standard Deviation (σ) of a Population Is Known

So far, all of our examples in this chapter have dealt with sample sizes of 30 or more. As you know from Chapter 7, under these conditions sample means tend to follow the normal probability distribution regardless of the shape of the population. But what happens when the sample size is less than 30, assuming sigma (the population standard deviation) is still known? Well, we can no longer rely on the Central Limit Theorem to bail us out. To construct a confidence interval under these conditions, the population *must* be normally distributed. Later in this textbook, we will discuss a procedure to determine if the population data do, or do not, follow the normal distribution. However, if we do know that the population is normally distributed, and we are using a sample size that is smaller than 30, the procedure to construct a confidence interval when sigma is known is identical to the process already discussed.

When the sample size is less than 30 and sigma is known, the population must be normally distributed to calculate a confidence interval.

I'll use the following example to illustrate this procedure. Rising consumer credit card debt over the past several years has had economists concerned about the financial health of many U.S. households. Suppose a random sample of 15 households had an average credit card debt of $8,150. We will make the following assumptions for this example:

- The population standard deviation for household credit card debt is $2,970.
- The population of household credit card debt follows the normal probability distribution.

Let's construct a 99% confidence interval around this mean to estimate the average credit card debt for the population of U.S. households. First, we'll start with the standard error of the mean calculation using Equation 8.1.

$$\sigma_{\bar{x}} = \frac{\sigma}{\sqrt{n}} = \frac{\$2{,}970}{\sqrt{15}} = \frac{\$2{,}970}{3.87} = \$767.44$$

Remember, for a 99% confidence interval, $z_{\alpha/2} = 2.575$. So, the upper and lower limits for our interval are:

$$UCL_{\bar{x}} = \bar{x} + z_{\alpha/2}\sigma_{\bar{x}}$$
$$UCL_{\bar{x}} = (\$8{,}150) + (2.575)(\$767.44) = \$10{,}126.16$$

$$LCL_{\bar{x}} = \bar{x} - z_{\alpha/2}\sigma_{\bar{x}}$$
$$LCL_{\bar{x}} = (\$8{,}150) - (2.575)(\$767.44) = \$6{,}173.84$$

We are 99% confident that the true average credit card debt for a U.S. household is between $6,173.84 and $10,126.16. If you think this is a pretty wide confidence interval, I'd have to agree with you. There are two factors contributing to this—(1) A smaller sample size results in a relatively high standard error of the mean; (2) in order to be 99% confident that we have "caught" the population mean, we need a wider "net" when compared to a 90% confidence interval.

Take a look at this next Your Turn problem, which will test a claim made by Procter & Gamble about laundry (one of my favorite topics—picture Deb raising her eyebrows as she reads this).

YOUR TURN #7

Procter & Gamble, a major manufacturer of household products including laundry detergent, estimates that the average household does 25 loads of laundry per month. A random sample of 18 households averaged 22.8 loads per month. Assume the population standard deviation is 6.1 loads per month.

a. Construct a 95% confidence interval around this sample mean.
b. What assumptions must you make to perform this procedure?
c. Does this result support the Procter & Gamble estimate?

Answers can be found on ▶ **page 379**

8.2 Section Problems

Basic Skills

8.1 Construct a 90% confidence interval to estimate the population mean using the following data:

$\bar{x} = 75 \quad \sigma = 20 \quad n = 36$

8.2 Construct a 99% confidence interval to estimate the population mean using the following data:

$\bar{x} = 45 \quad \sigma = 30 \quad n = 40$

8.3 Construct a 95% confidence interval to estimate the population mean with $\bar{x} = 110$ and $\sigma = 30$ for the following sample sizes:

a. $n = 30$
b. $n = 45$
c. $n = 60$

8.4 Construct a 98% confidence interval to estimate the population mean with $\bar{x} = 60$ and $\sigma = 12$ for the following sample sizes:

a. $n = 35$
b. $n = 45$
c. $n = 55$

8.5 Determine the margin of error for a confidence interval to estimate the population mean with $n = 35$ and $\sigma = 40$ for the following confidence levels:

a. 90%
b. 95%
c. 96%

8.6 Determine the margin of error for an 80% confidence interval to estimate the population mean with $\sigma = 50$ for the following sample sizes:

a. $n = 30$
b. $n = 45$
c. $n = 60$

8.7 Construct a 90% confidence interval to estimate the population mean using the following data:

$\bar{x} = 85 \quad \sigma = 20 \quad n = 10$

What assumptions need to be made to construct this interval?

8.8 Construct a 99% confidence interval to estimate the population mean using the following data:

$\bar{x} = 60 \quad \sigma = 17 \quad n = 12$

What assumptions need to be made to construct this interval?

Applications

8.9 Banking fees have received much attention during the recent economic recession as banks look for ways to recover from the crisis. A sample of 30 customers paid an average fee of $12.55 per month on their interest-bearing checking accounts. Assume the population standard deviation is $1.75.

a. Construct a 95% confidence interval to estimate the average fee for the population.
b. What is the margin of error for this interval?

8.10 The average selling price of BlackBerry smartphones purchased by a random sample of 35 customers was $311. Assume the population standard deviation was $35.

a. Construct a 90% confidence interval to estimate the average selling price in the population with this sample.
b. What is the margin of error for this interval?

8.11 A random sample of 40 taxpayers with adjusted gross incomes of between $100,000 and $200,000 was drawn. These taxpayers claimed an average of $9,922 in medical expenses for the year. Assume the population standard deviation for these deductions was $2,400. Construct confidence intervals to estimate the average deduction for the population with the following levels of significance:

a. 2%
b. 5%
c. 10%

8.12 The caloric consumption of 32 American adults was measured and found to average 2,157. Assume the population standard deviation is 260 calories per day. Construct confidence intervals to estimate the mean number of calories consumed per day for the American population with the following confidence levels:

a. 95%
b. 99%
c. 92%

8.13 Suppose Apple claims that the average wait time for a customer calling the Apple Care support line is 175 seconds. A random sample of 40 customers had an average wait time of 187 seconds. Assume the population standard deviation for wait time is 50 seconds.

a. Using a 95% confidence interval, does this sample support Apple's claim?
b. Verify your results with Excel.

8.14 The cost of ink cartridges for inkjet printers can be substantial over the life of a printer. Printer manufacturers publish the number of pages that can be printed from an ink cartridge in an effort to attract customers. HP claims that the C6615DN 25mL black print cartridge will yield an average of 495 pages. To test this claim, an independent lab measured the page count of 45 C6615DN cartridges and found the average page count to be 488.9. Assume the standard deviation for this population is 45 pages.

a. Using a 95% confidence interval, does this sample support HP's claim?
b. Verify your results with Excel.

8.15 Golf cart attendants at a local country club often receive tips from golfers they assist with their golf clubs. To help recruit new employees, the country club would like to determine the average tips per day an attendant earns. A sample of 16 attendants averaged $42.60 per day in tips. Assume the population standard deviation for daily tips is $9.00.

a. Construct a 98% confidence interval to estimate the average daily tips for an attendant.
b. What assumption needs to be made for this procedure?
c. Verify your results with Excel.

8.16 Toyota Motor Corporation developed the Scion car model to appeal to young consumers. Toyota claims the average age of a Scion driver is 26 years old. Suppose a random sample of 18 Scion drivers was drawn, and the average age of the drivers was found to be 27.5 years. Assume the standard deviation for the age of scion drivers is 2.3 years.

a. Construct a 95% confidence interval to estimate the average age of a Scion driver.
b. Does this result lend support to Toyota's claim?
c. What assumption needs to be made for this procedure?
d. Verify your results with Excel.

8.3 Calculating Confidence Intervals for the Mean when the Standard Deviation (σ) of a Population Is Unknown

Up until now, we have assumed that sigma, the population standard deviation, was known to us. However, most of the time, we have no knowledge of this value. Under these circumstances, we substitute s, the sample standard deviation, for sigma. Because we have complete information about our sample, the sample standard deviation can always be calculated using the following equation, which was introduced in Chapter 3 and is shown again here as Equation 8.5.

When the population standard deviation is unknown, we substitute s, the sample standard deviation, in its place to calculate the standard error.

Formula 8.5 for the Sample Standard Deviation

$$s = \sqrt{\frac{\sum_{i=1}^{n}(x_i - \bar{x})^2}{n - 1}}$$

where

$\bar{x}$ = The sample mean
n = The sample size (number of data values)
$(x_i - \bar{x})$ = The difference between each data value and the sample mean

We can also use Excel to calculate this value for us by using the STDEV.S function, which was also described in Chapter 3.

If you believe this simple substitution sounds too good to be true, I'd have to tell you that you're correct. As I have mentioned before, there's no free lunch in statistics. When substituting s for σ, we can no longer rely on the normal distribution to provide the critical z-score for the confidence interval. Instead, I need to introduce you to the Student's t-distribution (named to honor you, the Student). It is discussed next.

Using the Student's *t*-Distribution

The **Student's *t*-distribution** is used in place of the normal probability distribution when the sample standard deviation, s, is used in place of the population standard deviation, σ.

The **degrees of freedom** are the number of values that are free to vary given that certain information, such as the sample mean, is known.

The **Student's *t*-distribution**, or simply t-distribution, is a continuous probability distribution with the following properties:

- It is bell-shaped and symmetrical around the mean.
- The shape of the curve depends on the **degrees of freedom** (df), which refer to the number of values that are free to vary. When dealing with the sample mean, the degrees of freedom are equal to $n - 1$.
- The area under the curve is equal to 1.0.
- The t-distribution is flatter and wider than the normal distribution. The critical score for the t-distribution is therefore higher than the critical z-score for the same confidence level. This results in wider (less precise) confidence intervals when using the t-distribution. Consider this the cost of not knowing the population standard deviation and using the sample standard deviation in its place.
- The t-distribution is actually a family of distributions. As the number of degrees of freedom increases, the shape of the t-distribution becomes similar to the normal distribution, as shown in Figure 8.10. With more than 100 degrees of freedom (a sample size of more than 100), the two distributions are practically identical.

FIGURE 8.10
The Student's t-Distribution vs. the Normal Distribution

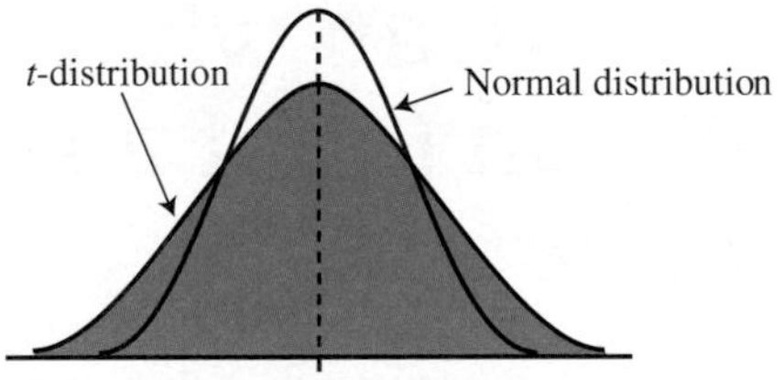

t-distribution
Normal distribution

When substituting s for σ, we can no longer rely on the normal distribution to provide the critical z-score for the confidence interval. Instead, we rely on the Student's t-distribution.

Students often struggle with the concept of degrees of freedom, which represent the number of remaining free choices you have after something has been decided, such as the sample mean (which always will be known). Recall that when dealing with a known sample mean, we said that the degrees of freedom are equal to $n - 1$ (the sample size minus 1). Suppose, for example, that I know that my sample size of $n = 3$ has a mean of 10, which is a value that I can easily calculate. I can then vary only two values because $n - 1 = 3 - 1 = 2$. After I set those two values, I have no control over the third value because my sample mean must be 10. So, for this sample, I have two degrees of freedom.

To demonstrate, let's say the two values that I do know in my sample are 14 and 12. Knowing that my sample mean is 10, the third value in my sample has no freedom. It must be 4, as follows:

If we know that our sample of size 3 has a sample mean equal to 10, then we also know that the sum of our sample must be 30 because $30/3 = 10$. If the first two values (14 and 12) sum to 26, then the third value must equal 4 $(30 - 26 = 4)$.

$$\bar{x} = \frac{14 + 12 + 4}{3} = 10$$

Therefore, when constructing a confidence interval for the mean without knowing the population standard deviation, the t-distribution will always have $n - 1$ degrees of freedom.

When we use the *t*-distribution, we need to assume that the population of interest follows the normal probability distribution. However, suppose your sample size isn't perfectly distributed but is slightly skewed to one side. As your sample size gets larger, it becomes less critical for you to assume that the population is normally distributed, even though you substituted s for σ. This is due to the fact that the shape of the *t*-distribution becomes similar to the normal distribution as the sample size increases. However, for small sample sizes, assuming that the population is normally distributed is critical to your accurately calculating confidence intervals. However, this assumption is not as critical when s is substituted for σ if the following two conditions exist:

- The sample size is larger than 30.
- The shape of the distribution is not very skewed to one side.

This is due to the fact that the shape of the *t*-distribution becomes similar to the normal distribution as the sample size increases. However, when the sample size is small, you must be able to correctly assume that the population follows the normal distribution. To simplify matters, I will assume the population of interest follows the normal distribution throughout this section.

To show how confidence intervals are calculated using the Student's *t*-distribution, let's use the following example. My friend, Dr. Gregg, is a successful chiropractor who needs to treat on average at least 90 patients a week to meet his financial goals for his business. Table 8.3 shows the number of patients per week during 18 randomly selected weeks as does the Excel file **chiropractor.xlsx**. Is there enough evidence with these data to conclude that Dr. Gregg averages at least 90 patients a week in general? To answer this question, I'm going to construct a 95% confidence interval around the mean of our sample.

TABLE 8.3 | NUMBER OF PATIENTS PER WEEK AT DR. GREGG'S OFFICE

116	83	89
87	81	109
114	123	102
131	96	74
109	106	118
78	91	98

We first need to calculate the sample mean ($\bar{x}$) and sample standard deviation (s) for our data. Using Excel's AVERAGE and STDEV.S functions with our sample, we have the following:

$$\bar{x} = 100.3 \text{ patients treated per week}$$

$$s = 16.6 \text{ patients treated per week}$$

Next, we need to calculate the standard error of the mean. However, because sigma is unavailable to us, we calculate the approximate standard error of the mean, $\hat{\sigma}_{\bar{x}}$, using s in Equation 8.6.

I have placed a "hat" symbol over σ to indicate that this is an approximation of the standard error of the mean.

Formula 8.6 for the Approximate Standard Error of the Mean

$$\hat{\sigma}_{\bar{x}} = \frac{s}{\sqrt{n}}$$

where

$\hat{\sigma}_{\bar{x}}$ = The approximate standard error of the mean
s = The sample standard deviation
n = The sample size

For our Dr. Gregg example, the approximate standard error of the mean is calculated as follows:

William Gosset (1876–1937) developed the Student's t-distribution while he was working for the Guinness Brewing Company in Ireland. He published his findings using the pseudonym "Student" because Guinness had a company policy prohibiting employees from publishing papers.

$$\hat{\sigma}_{\bar{x}} = \frac{s}{\sqrt{n}} = \frac{16.6}{\sqrt{18}} = 3.92 \text{ patients treated per week}$$

Our next step is to identify the critical t-score for a confidence interval, $t_{\alpha/2}$, which is analogous to the critical z-score from earlier in the chapter. One way to do this is to refer to Table 5 in Appendix A, which lists critical t-scores for specific confidence levels and degrees of freedom from 1 to 100.

To determine the value of $t_{\alpha/2}$ for this example, I need to calculate the number of degrees of freedom (*df*). Because $n = 18$, I have $n - 1 = 17$ degrees of freedom. This value identifies the appropriate row in Table 8.4, which is an excerpt from Table 5 in Appendix A. To identify the appropriate column in the table, I need to find the confidence level we are looking for, which in this case is 0.95. The intersection of this row and the 0.950 Conf Lev column leads me to $t_{\alpha/2} = t_{0.025} = 2.110$, which is highlighted in red in Table 8.4.

TABLE 8.4 | EXCERPT OF CRITICAL T-SCORES SHOWN IN APPENDIX A

1 TAIL	0.200	0.100	0.050	0.025	0.010	0.005
2 TAIL	0.400	0.200	0.100	0.050	0.020	0.010
CONF LEV	0.600	0.800	0.900	0.950	0.980	0.990
df						
1	1.376	3.078	6.314	12.706	31.821	63.657
2	1.061	1.886	2.920	4.303	6.965	9.925
3	0.978	1.638	2.353	3.182	4.541	5.841
4	0.941	1.533	2.132	2.776	3.747	4.604
5	0.920	1.476	2.015	2.571	3.365	4.032
6	0.906	1.440	1.943	2.447	3.143	3.707
7	0.896	1.415	1.895	2.365	2.998	3.499
8	0.889	1.397	1.860	2.306	2.896	3.355
9	0.883	1.383	1.833	2.262	2.821	3.250
10	0.879	1.372	1.812	2.228	2.764	3.169
11	0.876	1.363	1.796	2.201	2.718	3.106
12	0.873	1.356	1.782	2.179	2.681	3.055
13	0.870	1.350	1.771	2.160	2.650	3.012
14	0.868	1.345	1.761	2.145	2.624	2.977
15	0.866	1.341	1.753	2.131	2.602	2.947
16	0.865	1.337	1.746	2.120	2.583	2.921
17	0.863	1.333	1.740	2.110	2.567	2.898
18	0.862	1.330	1.734	2.101	2.552	2.878
19	0.861	1.328	1.729	2.093	2.539	2.861
20	0.860	1.325	1.725	2.086	2.528	2.845

Generally, when we use the t-distribution, we need to assume that the population of interest follows the normal probability distribution.

Figure 8.11 shows the sampling distribution for the mean and the critical t-scores for Dr. Gregg.

FIGURE 8.11
Critical t-Scores for a 95% Confidence Interval When df = 17

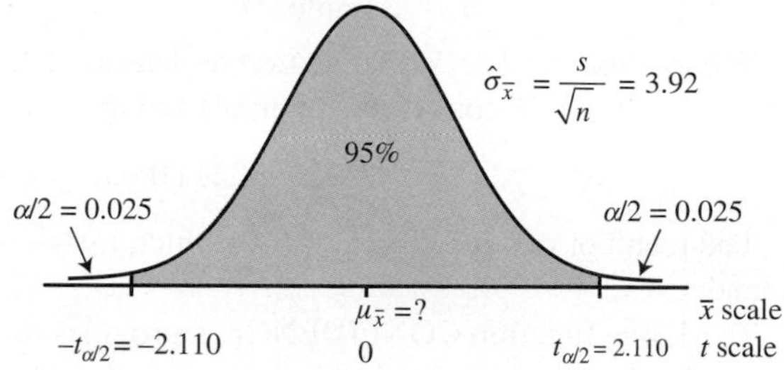

We are now ready to construct our confidence interval for the mean using Equations 8.7 and 8.8 for the upper and lower limits, respectively.

Formulas 8.7 and 8.8 for the Confidence Interval for the Mean (σ Unknown)

$$UCL_{\bar{x}} = \bar{x} + t_{\alpha/2}\hat{\sigma}_{\bar{x}}$$
$$LCL_{\bar{x}} = \bar{x} - t_{\alpha/2}\hat{\sigma}_{\bar{x}}$$

where

$\bar{x}$ = The sample mean
$t_{\alpha/2}$ = The critical t-score
$\hat{\sigma}_{\bar{x}}$ = The approximate standard error of the mean

The upper limit for my 95% confidence interval can be found using Equation 8.5:

$$UCL_{\bar{x}} = \bar{x} + t_{\alpha/2}\hat{\sigma}_{\bar{x}}$$
$$UCL_{\bar{x}} = 100.3 + (2.110)(3.92)$$
$$UCL_{\bar{x}} = 100.3 + 8.27 = 108.57$$

The margin of error for this confidence interval is 8.27.

The lower limit for my 95% confidence interval can be found using Equation 8.6:

$$LCL_{\bar{x}} = \bar{x} + t_{\alpha/2}\hat{\sigma}_{\bar{x}}$$
$$LCL_{\bar{x}} = 100.3 - (2.110)(3.92)$$
$$LCL_{\bar{x}} = 100.3 - 8.27 = 92.03$$

According to our results, Dr. Gregg is 95% confident that the true population mean for the number of patients he treats per week is between 92.03 and 108.57. Because this entire interval exceeds 90 patients per week, it appears that Dr. Gregg's financial goals are being met.

The properties of confidence intervals using the t-distribution are the same for those constructed using the normal distribution:

- Increasing the confidence level will result in a wider (less precise) confidence interval.
- Increasing the sample size will result in a narrower (more precise) confidence interval.
- The margin of error equals $t_{\alpha/2}\hat{\sigma}_{\bar{x}}$.

Using Excel and PHStat to Determine Confidence Intervals for the Mean (Sigma Unknown)

Another way to determine the critical t-score for a confidence interval is with Excel's T.INV.2T function, which has the following characteristics:

=T.INV.2T (alpha, degrees of freedom)

where

alpha (α) = The significance level of the confidence interval
degrees of freedom = $n - 1$
n = Sample size

WE can use the T.INV.2T function to determine the critical t-score for Dr. Gregg when $\alpha = 0.05$ (for a 95% confidence interval) and $df = 17$.

$$=\text{T.INV.2T}(0.05, 17) = 2.110$$

The result of this function is 2.110, which matches the value determined from Table 5 in Appendix A.

The Excel function CONFIDENCE.T provides the margin of error for a confidence interval for the mean when the population standard deviation is unknown. This function has the following characteristics:

$$=\text{CONFIDENCE.T}(\text{alpha, standard\_dev, size})$$

where

alpha = The significance level of the confidence interval
standard_dev = The standard deviation of the sample
size = Sample size

The T prefix for this function indicates that we are using the student's t-distribution to determine the critical t-score for this interval. We can use the CONFIDENCE.T function to calculate the margin of error for the 95% confidence interval for Dr. Gregg's example where $\alpha = 0.05$, $s = 16.6$, and $n = 18$.

$$=\text{CONFIDENCE.T}(0.05, 16.6, 18) = 8.25$$

The value 8.25 represents the margin of error for our confidence interval. This value is slightly different than the margin of error from our manual calculations (8.27) because of rounding differences.

PHStat also has the ability to construct the confidence interval for the mean when sigma is unknown, using the following steps. Excel for Mac users can find these instructions on the textbook's Web site (www.pearsonhighered.com/donnelly).

1. Go to **Add-Ins > PHStat > Confidence Intervals > Estimate for the Mean, sigma unknown**, as seen previously in Figure 8.7.
2. Fill in the **Estimate for the Mean, sigma unknown** dialog box using information from our Dr. Gregg example as shown in Figure 8.12. Click **OK**.

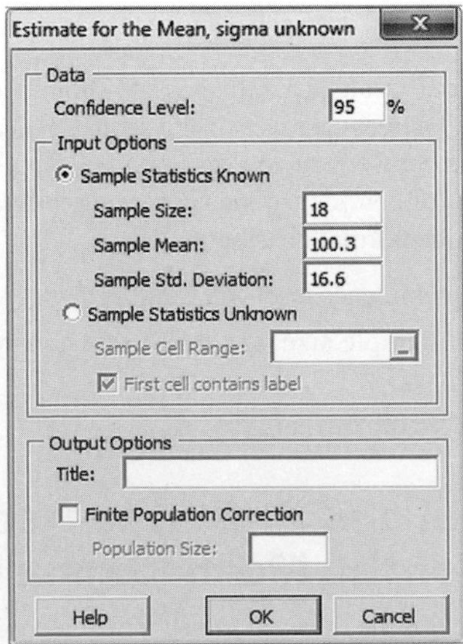

FIGURE 8.12
Using PHStat to Calculate a 95% Confidence Level (Step 2)

The 95% confidence interval is shown in the yellow cells in Figure 8.13. Notice that these values are slightly different from the 95% confidence interval we calculated manually (92.03, 108.57). Again, this is due to rounding differences.

FIGURE 8.13
Using PHStat to Calculate a 95% Confidence Interval (Final Result)

	A	B
1	**Confidence Interval Estimate for the Mean**	
2		
3	Data	
4	**Sample Standard Deviation**	16.6
5	**Sample Mean**	100.3
6	**Sample Size**	18
7	**Confidence Level**	95%
8		
9	Intermediate Calculations	
10	Standard Error of the Mean	3.912657523
11	Degrees of Freedom	17
12	*t* Value	2.1098
13	Interval Half Width	8.2550
14		
15	**Confidence Interval**	
16	**Interval Lower Limit**	92.05
17	**Interval Upper Limit**	108.55
18		

This particular topic requires practice to master, so don't miss this opportunity to construct a confidence interval for a golfer's scores in the next Your Turn section.

YOUR TURN #8

A certain statistics author would like you to construct a 90% confidence interval for the following random sample of golf scores for a particular course he plays so that he can figure out his true (population) average score for the course. (I recommend using Excel to calculate the sample mean with =AVERAGE and the standard deviation with =STDEV.S).

95 92 95 99 92 84 95 94 95 86

Answer can be found on ▶ **page 379**

8.3 Section Problems

Basic Skills

8.17 Construct a 90% confidence interval to estimate the population mean using the following data:

$\bar{x} = 25 \quad s = 5.2 \quad n = 21$

What assumptions need to be made about this population?

8.18 Construct a 95% confidence interval to estimate the population mean using the following data:

$\bar{x} = 38 \quad s = 8.5 \quad n = 25$

What assumptions need to be made about this population?

8.19 Construct a 98% confidence interval to estimate the population mean when $\bar{x} = 60$ and $s = 12.2$ for the following sample sizes:

a. $n = 20$
b. $n = 40$
c. $n = 60$

8.20 Construct an 80% confidence interval to estimate the population mean when $\bar{x} = 125$ and $s = 32$ for the following sample sizes.

a. $n = 30$
b. $n = 60$
c. $n = 90$

8.21 Determine the margin of error for a confidence interval to estimate the population mean with $n = 20$ and $s = 16$ for the following confidence levels:

a. 80%
b. 90%
c. 99%

8.22 Determine the margin of error for a 95% confidence interval to estimate the population mean when $s = 40$ for the following sample sizes:

a. $n = 10$
b. $n = 30$
c. $n = 50$

Applications

8.23 With a capacity of 6,300 people, Royal Caribbean's Oasis of the Seas is the world's largest cruise ship. The average beer consumption over 15 randomly selected seven-day cruises on the ship was 81,740 bottles with a sample standard deviation of 4,590 bottles. Royal Caribbean would like to estimate the average beer consumption to plan its beer inventory levels on future cruises. (The ship certainly doesn't want to run out of beer in the middle of the ocean!)

a. Construct a 95% confidence interval to estimate the average beer consumption per cruise.
b. Verify this interval using Excel.
c. What assumptions need to be made about this population?

8.24 A random sample of 21 NCAA Division I men's basketball games during a recent season had an average attendance of 5,038 with a sample standard deviation of 1,755.

a. Construct a 90% confidence interval to estimate the average attendance of an NCAA men's basketball game during the 2009–2010 season.
b. Verify this interval using Excel.
c. What assumptions need to be made about this population?

8.25 The U.S. air traffic control system handled an average of 47,529 flights during 30 randomly selected days. The standard deviation for this sample is 6,210 flights per day.

a. Construct a 99% confidence interval to estimate the average number of flights per day handled by the system.
b. Suppose the current system can safely handle 50,000 flights per day. What conclusions can be drawn with these results?
c. Verify this interval using Excel.
d. What assumptions need to be made about this population?

8.26 The following data show the number of hours per day 12 adults spent in front of screens watching television-related content:

1.3 4.9 4.2 4.8 7.6 6.9 5.4 2.2 5.3 1.8
2.4 8.3

a. Construct a 95% confidence interval to estimate the average number of hours per day adults spend in front of screens watching television-related content.
b. Verify this interval using Excel.
c. What assumptions need to be made about this population (other than the fact the people in it are watching too much television)?

8.27 According to Expedia.com, workers in Italy lead the world in paid vacation days, averaging 42 days per year. The following data show the number of paid vacation days for a random sample of 20 Italian workers. These data can also be found in the Excel file titled **paid vacation.xlsx**.

48 40 30 58 20 40 55 70 20 41
30 30 60 35 25 37 15 30 64 55

a. Construct a 95% confidence interval to estimate the average number of paid vacation days for Italian workers.
b. Do the results from this sample validate Expedia.com's findings?
c. Verify this interval using Excel.
d. What assumptions need to be made about this population?

8.28 AAA reported that the average price of regular gasoline in Pennsylvania was $3.65 per gallon. The following data show the price per gallon of regular gasoline for 15 randomly selected stations in the state. These data can also be found in the Excel file titled **PA gas prices.xlsx**.

$3.73 $3.59 $3.74 $3.65 $3.71
$3.73 $3.51 $3.71 $3.61 $3.64
$3.58 $3.46 $3.64 $3.74 $3.58

a. Construct a 90% confidence interval to estimate the average price per gallon of gasoline in the state.
b. Do the results from this sample validate AAA's findings?
c. Verify this interval using Excel.
d. What assumptions need to be made about this population?

8.4 Calculating Confidence Intervals for Proportions

The confidence interval for the proportion is an interval estimate around a sample proportion that provides us with a range of where the true population proportion lies.

We can also estimate the proportion of a population by constructing a confidence interval from a sample. As you might recall from Chapter 7, proportion data follow the binomial distribution, which can be approximated by the normal distribution under the following conditions:

$$np \geq 5 \quad \text{and} \quad n(1 - p) \geq 5$$

where

p = The probability of a success in the population
n = The sample size

Suppose the home-shopping channel would like to estimate the proportion of customers who are female in order to improve the channel's advertising effectiveness. Let's say that from a random sample of 175 customers, 116 were female. In Chapter 7, we learned that we can calculate the sample proportion, $\bar{p}$, using Equation 8.9.

Formula 8.9 for the Sample Proportion

$$\bar{p} = \frac{x}{n}$$

where

x = The number of observations of interest in the sample (successes)
n = The sample size

Our sample proportion then becomes as follows:

$$\bar{p} = \frac{x}{n} = \frac{116}{175} = 0.663$$

To estimate the population proportion of female shoppers, I need to construct a 99% confidence interval around this sample proportion. To do so, we need to call on the standard error of the proportion from Chapter 7, which is shown again as Equation 8.10. Recall that this value measures the average variation around the mean of the sample proportions taken from this population of home-shopping customers.

Formula 8.10 for the Standard Error of the Proportion

$$\sigma_p = \sqrt{\frac{p(1-p)}{n}}$$

where

p = The population proportion
n = The sample size

There's extra credit for anyone who can see a problem arising here. Our challenge is that we are trying to estimate p, the population proportion, but we need a value for p to set up the confidence interval. Our solution: Approximate the standard error by using the sample proportion, $\bar{p}$, as a substitute for the population proportion, p, as shown in Equation 8.11.

I have placed a "hat" symbol over σ to indicate that this is an approximation of the standard error of the proportion.

We can approximate the standard error of the proportion by substituting the sample proportion, $\bar{p}$, for the population proportion, p.

Formula 8.11 for the Approximate Standard Error of the Proportion

$$\hat{\sigma}_p = \sqrt{\frac{\bar{p}(1-\bar{p})}{n}}$$

where

$\bar{p}$ = The sample proportion
n = The sample size

Using Equation 8.11 on our home-shopping sample, we have the following:

$$\hat{\sigma}_p = \sqrt{\frac{\bar{p}(1-\bar{p})}{n}} = \sqrt{\frac{(0.663)(1-0.663)}{175}} = \sqrt{\frac{(0.663)(0.337)}{175}}$$

$$\hat{\sigma}_p = \sqrt{\frac{0.223}{175}} = \sqrt{0.001274} = 0.0357$$

Equations 8.12 and 8.13 show the upper and lower limits for a confidence interval for a particular sample proportion.

Formulas 8.12 and 8.13 for the Confidence Interval for a Proportion

$$UCL_p = \bar{p} + z_{\alpha/2}\hat{\sigma}_p$$
$$LCL_p = \bar{p} - z_{\alpha/2}\hat{\sigma}_p$$

This is the same critical z-score found in Table 4 in Appendix A. For this problem it can be found in Table 8.2.

where

$\bar{p}$ = The sample proportion
$z_{\alpha/2}$ = The critical z-score
$\hat{\sigma}_p$ = The approximate standard error of the proportion

We are now ready to calculate the 99% **confidence interval for the proportion** of female home-shopping customers using Equations 8.12 and 8.13. According to Table 8.2, our critical z-score for a 99% confidence interval is $z_{\alpha/2} = 2.575$. First, we start with the upper limit:

$$UCL_p = \bar{p} + z_{\alpha/2}\hat{\sigma}_p$$
$$UCL_p = 0.663 + (2.575)(0.0357)$$
$$UCL_p = 0.663 + 0.092 = 0.755$$

Now, we calculate the lower limit:

$$LCL_p = \bar{p} - z_{\alpha/2}\hat{\sigma}_p$$
$$LCL_p = 0.663 - (2.575)(0.0357)$$
$$LCL_p = 0.663 - 0.092 = 0.571$$

Based on our sample proportion of 0.663, we are 99% confident that the proportion of female shoppers is between 0.571 and 0.755. Deb must be in there somewhere!

This interval—0.571 to 0.755—may seem fairly wide to you. I would agree. Because we want to be 99% confident of capturing the population proportion, we need a wide interval, which leads to the next topic, the margin of error.

Confidence intervals for the proportion have a margin of error similar to what we discussed earlier in the chapter for sample means. The proportion margin of error, ME_p, represents the width of the confidence interval between the sample proportion and its upper limit *or* between the sample proportion and its lower limit. The formula for calculating the proportion margin of error is shown in Equation 8.14.

Formula 8.14 for the Margin of Error for a Confidence Interval for the Proportion

$$ME_p = z_{\alpha/2}\hat{\sigma}_p$$

The proportion margin of error, ME_p, represents the width of the confidence interval between the sample proportion and its upper limit or between the sample proportion and its lower limit.

For our sample proportion of female shoppers, the margin of error is calculated as follows:

$$ME_p = z_{\alpha/2}\hat{\sigma}_p = (2.575)(0.0357) = 0.092$$

A large margin of error translates to a less precise estimate of the true population proportion, and vice versa. The following statement shows how the margin of error is often reported: "The president of the United States has a 46% approval rating ±3%." In this example, the confidence interval is (0.43, 0.49), and the margin of error is 3%. In most cases, the confidence level of such a statement would be 95%.

Using PHStat to Determine Confidence Intervals for a Proportion

PHStat has the ability to construct confidence intervals for the proportion using the following steps. Excel for Mac users can find these instructions on the textbook's Web site.

1. Go to **Add-Ins > PHStat > Confidence Intervals > Estimate for the Proportion**, as seen previously in Figure 8.7.
2. Fill in the **Estimate for the Proportion** dialog box using our female home shopper example as shown in Figure 8.14. Click **OK**.

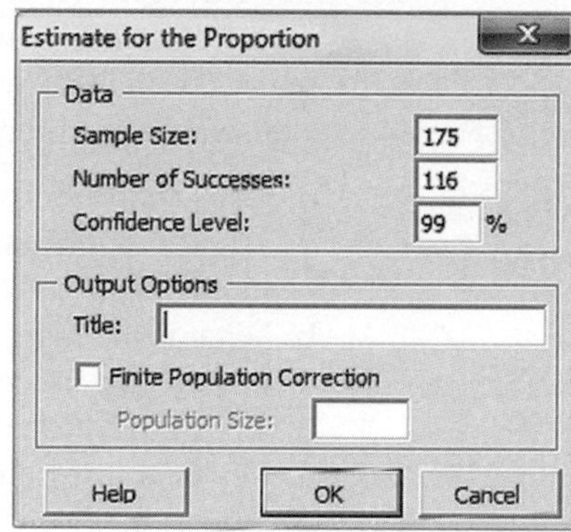

FIGURE 8.14 Using PHStat to Calculate a 99% Confidence Interval for a Proportion (Step 2)

The 99% confidence interval is shown in the yellow cells in Figure 8.15. Notice that these values are slightly different from the 99% confidence interval we calculated manually (0.571, 0.755). Again, this is due to rounding differences.

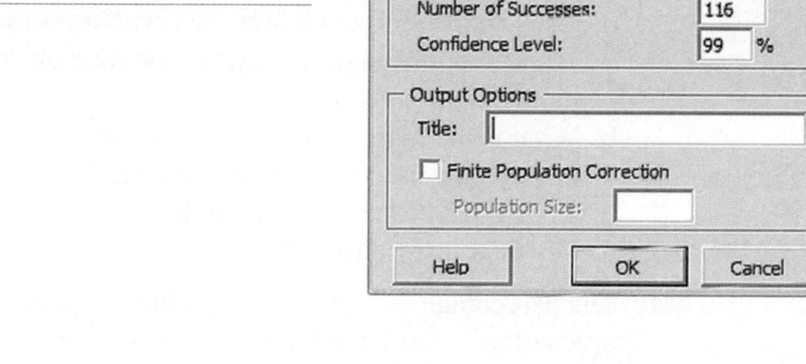

	A	B
1	**Confidence Interval Estimate for the Proportion**	
2		
3	**Data**	
4	**Sample Size**	175
5	**Number of Successes**	116
6	**Confidence Level**	99%
7		
8	Intermediate Calculations	
9	Sample Proportion	0.662857143
10	Z Value	-2.5758
11	Standard Error of the Proportion	0.0357
12	Interval Half Width	0.0920
13		
14	**Confidence Interval**	
15	**Interval Lower Limit**	**0.5708**
16	**Interval Upper Limit**	**0.7549**
17		

FIGURE 8.15 Using PHStat to Calculate a 99% Confidence Interval for a Proportion (Final Result)

Make sure you know how to calculate this type of confidence interval before you move on to the next section.

YOUR TURN #9

During the most recent economic recession, the auto industry relied heavily on 0% financing to entice customers to purchase cars. Edmunds.com estimated that 22.4% of car deals involved 0% financing. A random sample of 500 financed car deals found that 98 of them used 0% financing.

a. Construct a 98% confidence interval around this sample proportion. Does it support the findings of Edmunds.com?
b. Calculate the margin of error for this interval.
c. Verify your results using PHStat.

Answers can be found on ▶ **page 380**

8.4 Section Problems

Basic Skills

8.29 Construct a 90% confidence interval to estimate the population proportion with a sample proportion equal to 0.36 and a sample size equal to 125.

8.30 Construct a 95% confidence interval to estimate the population proportion with a sample proportion equal to 0.60 and a sample size equal to 150.

8.31 Determine the margin of error for a confidence interval to estimate the population proportion for the following confidence levels with a sample proportion equal to 0.40 and $n = 100$:

a. 90%
b. 95%
c. 97%

8.32 Determine the margin of error for a 95% confidence interval to estimate the population proportion with a sample proportion equal to 0.70 for the following sample sizes:

a. $n = 125$
b. $n = 200$
c. $n = 250$

Applications

8.33 The U.S. Department of Education reported that in 2007, 67% of students enrolled in college or a trade school within 12 months of graduating from high school. In 2013, a random sample of 160 individuals who graduated from high school 12 months prior was selected. From this sample, 102 students were found to be enrolled in college or a trade school.

a. Construct a 90% confidence interval to estimate the actual proportion of students enrolled in college or a trade school within 12 months of graduating from high school in 2013.
b. What is the margin of error for this sample?
c. Based on this sample, is there any evidence that this proportion has changed since 2007?
d. Verify your results with PHStat.

8.34 The IRS reported that 81% of individual tax returns were filed electronically in 2012. A random sample of 225 tax returns from 2013 was selected. From this sample, 176 were filed electronically.

a. Construct a 95% confidence interval to estimate the actual proportion of taxpayers who filed electronically in 2013.
b. What is the margin of error for this sample?
c. Is there any evidence that this proportion has changed since 2012 based on this sample?
d. Verify your results with PHStat.

8.35 The percentage of high school graduates applying to multiple colleges has been increasing over the past several years. According to the National Association for College Admission Counseling, 29% of high school students applied to seven or more colleges in 2011. A random sample of 350 high school graduates in 2013 was selected and 84 of them applied to seven or more colleges.

a. Construct a 90% confidence interval to estimate the actual proportion of high school graduates that applied to seven or more colleges in 2013.
b. What is the margin of error for this sample?
c. Is there evidence that this proportion has changed since 2011 based on this sample?
d. Verify your results with PHStat.

8.36 Although Germany has one of the healthiest economies in the euro zone, it has one of the lowest homeownership rates in Europe. According to ECD, the German homeownership rate was 44% in 2011 (compared to 66% in the United States). Suppose, from a random sample of 270 households in Germany in 2014, 127 were occupied by the owners of the residence.

a. Construct a 98% confidence interval to estimate the actual proportion of households in Germany that are occupied by their owners in 2014.
b. What is the margin of error for this sample?
c. Is there evidence that this proportion has changed since 2011 based on this sample?
d. Verify your results with PHStat.

8.37 According to the Centers for Disease Control and Prevention, 20.6% of the U.S. population smoked in 2008. In 2014, a random sample of 650 Americans was selected; 108 of whom smoked.

a. Construct a 90% confidence interval to estimate the actual proportion of people who smoked in the United States in 2014.

b. What is the margin of error for this sample?

c. Is there any evidence that this proportion has changed since 2008 based on this sample?

d. Verify your results with PHStat.

8.5 Determining the Sample Size

The focus of this chapter has been to calculate a confidence interval and a margin of error for a population based on the following information:

- The confidence level
- The sample size
- The standard deviation

In this section, we're going to reverse this procedure by calculating the sample size needed to achieve a specific margin of error, given the following information:

- The confidence level
- The population standard deviation

Recall that you learned earlier in the chapter that increasing the sample size, holding all else constant, reduces the margin of error and provides a narrower, more precise, confidence interval.

This is a very handy procedure because, often, one of the first questions that a statistician is faced with is to choose the size of the sample. On the one hand, because sampling can be a costly procedure, a sample that is larger than necessary is wasteful. On the other hand, a sample that is too small will not be precise enough. We will first examine the process of selecting an adequate sample size using the sample mean. We will then do the same using the sample proportion.

Calculating the Sample Size to Estimate a Population Mean

To show how a sample size is calculated to estimate a population's mean, let's rely on the following example. From 2007 until 2011, AT&T benefited by being the exclusive carrier of Apple's most successful product, the iPhone. However, the agreement between the two companies has also created network capacity problems for AT&T because iPhone users tend to use data-heavy applications such as video streaming and Web browsing. One estimate concluded that just 3% of AT&T's customers tie up 40% of the carrier's bandwidth. It is believed that the average iPhone customer uses 1,350 megabytes (MB) of data each month.

To respond to this situation, AT&T eliminated its unlimited data plans in 2010. To establish a price plan for data usage, suppose that AT&T would like to use a sample to estimate the average monthly data usage of its cell phone customers. Let's say AT&T wants to know the sample size needed to provide a 95% confidence interval around a sample mean with a margin of error of ±75 MB of data per month. Figure 8.16 illustrates the precision that AT&T wants.

FIGURE 8.16
AT&T's Desired Confidence Interval

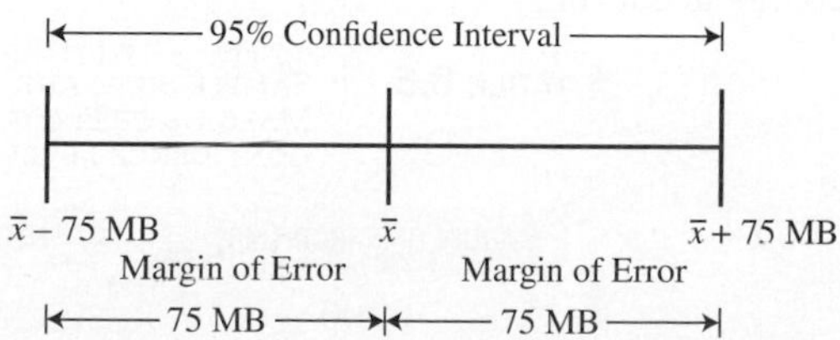

To determine the sample size AT&T needs, we need to return to Equation 8.4, which we used to calculate the margin of error when constructing a confidence interval around a sample mean:

$$ME_{\bar{x}} = z_{\alpha/2}\sigma_{\bar{x}}$$

We also determined the standard error of the mean using Equation 8.1:

$$\sigma_{\bar{x}} = \frac{\sigma}{\sqrt{n}}$$

We can combine these two equations, which will result in the following expression for the margin of error:

$$ME_{\bar{x}} = z_{\alpha/2}\frac{\sigma}{\sqrt{n}}$$

Performing some minor algebra, we have the following:

$$\sqrt{n} = \frac{z_{\alpha/2}\sigma}{ME_{\bar{x}}}$$

By squaring both sides of the equation, we have our required sample size formula, as Equation 8.15 shows.

Formula 8.15 for the Sample Size Needed to Estimate a Population Mean

$$n = \frac{(z_{\alpha/2})^2\sigma^2}{(ME_{\bar{x}})^2}$$

We are almost ready to inform AT&T how large of a sample it needs, but we need one more piece of information—the population standard deviation. For this example, we'll assume that, through past experience, AT&T feels that $\sigma = 400$ MB per month. This value represents the average variation of data usage around the mean of the sampling distribution.

Now, for the moment we all have been waiting for (or at least the moment I have been waiting for; it's nearly 3:00 A.M. as I'm writing this, and I'm running out of energy! Where are my Cheez-Its?). We know from earlier in the chapter, $z_{\alpha/2} = 1.96$ for a 95% confidence interval. Using Equation 8.15, we have the following:

$$n = \frac{(z_{\alpha/2})^2\sigma^2}{(ME_{\bar{x}})^2} = \frac{(1.96)^2(400)^2}{(75)^2} = \frac{(3.842)(160{,}000)}{5{,}625} = 109.3 \approx 110$$

We have found that AT&T should sample 110 customers to estimate the average data usage for all of its customers. This sample will provide AT&T with a 95% confidence level that the true average data usage will be within ± 75 MB of the sample mean.

Notice that in the previous calculation, I rounded up to 110 instead of down to 109, even though my result was closer to 109. I advise you to always round up with your sample size because if you round down, you will not achieve the desired margin of error. It's best to consider the stated margin of error as a minimum requirement. A smaller sample size results in a larger margin of error for a given confidence level. Table 8.5 demonstrates this concept using a 95% confidence level.

TABLE 8.5 | SAMPLE SIZES AND ASSOCIATED MARGINS OF ERROR FOR A 95% CONFIDENCE LEVEL: AT&T EXAMPLE

MARGIN OF ERROR (MB)	REQUIRED SAMPLE SIZE
100	62
75	110
50	246

Notice in Equation 8.15, the margin of error term is squared in the denominator. This squared term causes the required sample size calculation to increase by a factor of four when $ME_{\bar{x}}$ is reduced by half.

Table 8.5 shows that to achieve a smaller margin of error (a more precise confidence interval) a larger sample size is needed. Reducing the margin of error by half (from 100 MB to 50 MB) causes the required sample size to increase fourfold (from 62 to 246).

Earlier in this section I casually mentioned that AT&T estimated that $\sigma = 400$ MB, which is a measure of the variation of data usage from one customer to the next. In reality, this value may not be known. In this case, there are ways to estimate the population standard deviation such as by selecting a pilot sample, which is a small sample from the population. We can then use the standard deviation, s, from the pilot sample as an estimate for sigma.

You might recall that we substituted s for σ earlier in the chapter. As a result, we used the Student's t-distribution in place of the normally distributed critical z-score. Unfortunately, we can't use the t-distribution to determine the sample size. That's because we need the sample size to determine the degrees of freedom, which are used to look up the critical t-score. Fortunately, this is not a major issue when sample sizes are fairly large, as they are with our AT&T example. Remember, the shape of the t-distribution becomes very close to the normal distribution with larger sample sizes.

Using PHStat to Calculate the Sample Size for a Population Mean

You can use PHStat to calculate the sample size by taking the following steps. Excel for Mac users can find these instructions on the textbook's Web site.

1. Go to **Add-Ins > PHStat > Sample Size > Determination for the Mean**, as shown in Figure 8.17.

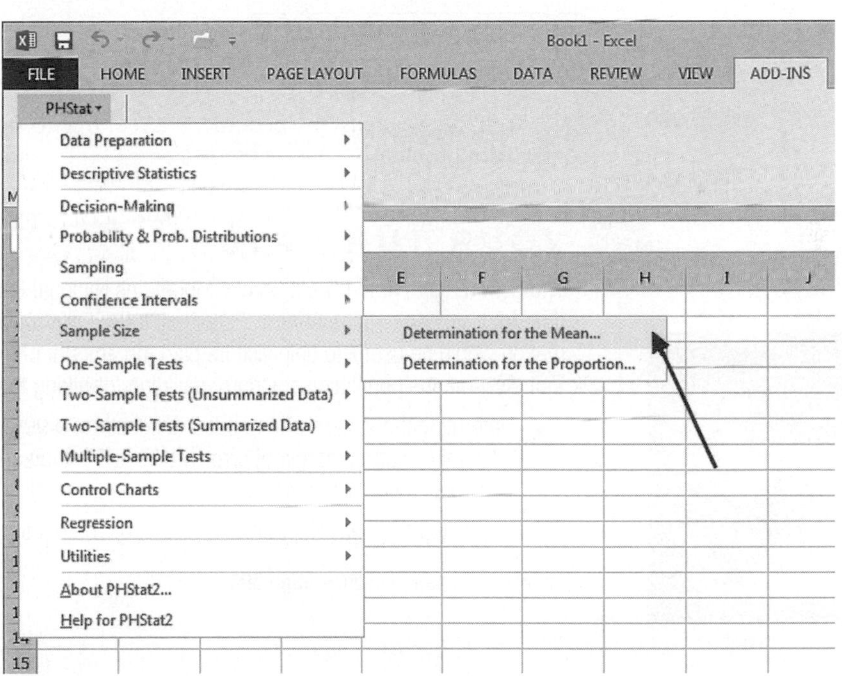

FIGURE 8.17 Using PHStat to Calculate the Sample Size for the Mean with a 95% Confidence Level (Step 1)

2. Fill in the **Sample Size Determination for the Mean** dialog box as shown in Figure 8.18 on the next page. Click **OK**.

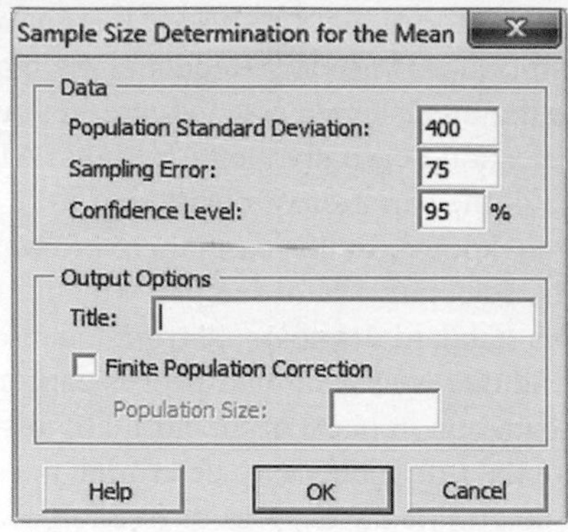

FIGURE 8.18 Using PHStat to Calculate the Sample Size for the Mean with a 95% Confidence Level (Step 2)

The required sample size for AT&T is shown in Cell B13 in Figure 8.19. This matches the result we calculated manually.

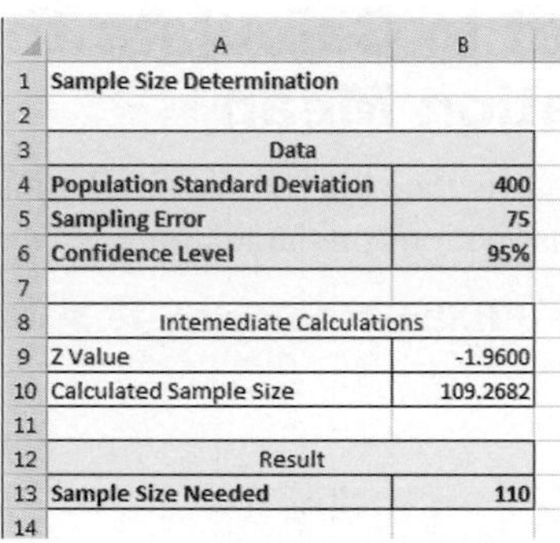

	A	B
1	**Sample Size Determination**	
2		
3	Data	
4	**Population Standard Deviation**	400
5	**Sampling Error**	75
6	**Confidence Level**	95%
7		
8	Intemediate Calculations	
9	Z Value	-1.9600
10	Calculated Sample Size	109.2682
11		
12	Result	
13	**Sample Size Needed**	110
14		

FIGURE 8.19 Using PHStat to Calculate the Sample Size for the Mean with a 95% Confidence Level (Final Result)

Well, it's way past my bedtime, but feel free to stay up and try your hand at this next Your Turn problem.

YOUR TURN #10

The park rangers at the Great Smoky Mountains National Park would like to estimate the mean hiking time for visitors along the Abrams Falls trail, a five-mile roundtrip trek from the parking area. This information would be useful to help visitors plan the amount of time they need to allocate in order to hike the trail. Assume the population standard deviation for hiking the trail is 32 minutes.

a. Determine the sample size needed to construct a 90% confidence interval to estimate the mean hiking time with a margin of error within ± 5 minutes.

b. Verify this result using PHStat.

Deb and I hiked this beautiful trail in June 2010. The photo on the left is a picture I took of Abrams Falls.

Answers can be found on ▶ **page 380**

Calculating the Sample Size Needed to Estimate a Population Proportion

We can use the same logic from the previous section to determine the sample size to estimate a population proportion. To demonstrate this procedure, I'll rely on the following example. A growing number of households are managing their finances without any type of bank account due to frustrations with banking fees and overdraft penalties. Suppose Bank of America, which has concerns about this trend, would like to know the sample size needed to construct a 98% confidence interval to estimate the proportion of households who do not own a checking account within 5% of the actual value. Figure 8.20 illustrates the precision that Bank of America is looking for.

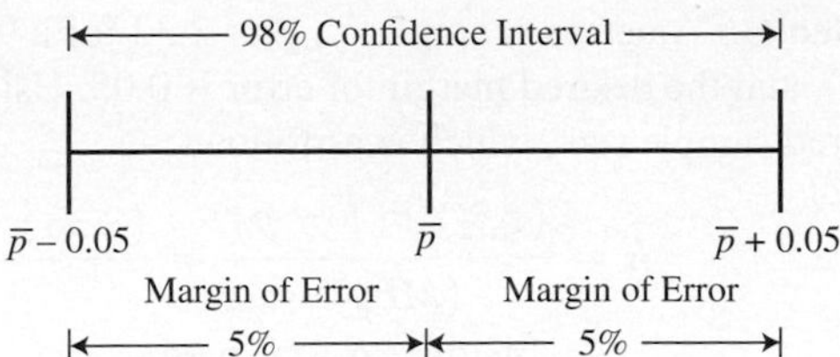

FIGURE 8.20 Bank of America's Desired Confidence Interval

To determine the sample size needed by Bank of America, we need to start with Equation 8.14. Recall that we used it to calculate the margin of error when constructing a confidence interval around a sample proportion.

$$ME_p = z_{\alpha/2}\hat{\sigma}_p$$

We also need the approximate standard error of the proportion from Equation 8.11:

$$\hat{\sigma}_p = \sqrt{\frac{\bar{p}(1 - \bar{p})}{n}}$$

As before, we combine these two equations, which results in the following expression for the margin of error for a proportion:

$$ME_p = z_{\alpha/2}\sqrt{\frac{\bar{p}(1 - \bar{p})}{n}}$$

Once again, we rearrange this equation as follows:

$$\sqrt{n} = \frac{z_{\alpha/2}\sqrt{\bar{p}(1 - \bar{p})}}{ME_p}$$

By squaring both sides of the equation, we have our required sample size formula, as shown in Equation 8.16.

Formula 8.16 for the Sample Size Needed to Estimate the Population Proportion

$$n = \frac{(z_{\alpha/2})^2 \bar{p}(1 - \bar{p})}{(ME_p)^2}$$

Maybe you noticed that we have a little problem here. In order to calculate the required sample size to estimate p, the population proportion, we need to know $\bar{p}$, the sample proportion. We have two solutions for this problem:

1. Select a pilot sample and use the sample proportion, $\bar{p}$, in Equation 8.16.
2. If it is not possible to select a pilot sample, set $\bar{p} = 0.5$ for Equation 8.16. I'll explain the reason for this choice shortly.

Let's assume that Bank of America collected a pilot sample of 50 households and found that six did not own a checking account. The sample proportion of households without a checking account would therefore be as follows:

$$\bar{p} = \frac{6}{50} = 0.12$$

For our Bank of America example, $z_{\alpha/2} = 2.33$ for a 98% confidence interval (see Table 8.2), and the desired margin of error is 0.05. Using Equation 8.16, we can calculate our required sample size, which is as follows:

$$n = \frac{(z_{\alpha/2})^2\bar{p}(1-\bar{p})}{(ME_p)^2} = \frac{(2.33)^2(0.12)(1-0.12)}{(0.05)^2}$$

$$n = \frac{(5.429)(0.12)(0.88)}{(0.0025)} = 229.3 \approx 230$$

Bank of America should sample 230 customers to construct a 98% confidence interval to estimate the proportion of households without checking accounts with a margin of error of 5%.

If a pilot sample is not available, I recommended setting $\bar{p} = 0.5$ to calculate the required sample size. The reasoning is this: If we don't have a value for $\bar{p}$, setting it equal to 0.50 provides the most conservative estimate for a sample size. By conservative, I mean a sample size that is at least large enough to satisfy the margin-of-error requirement. I sense some of you scratching your head with this one, so let me demonstrate. Table 8.6 shows the effect that values of $\bar{p}$ have on the sample sizes for our Bank of America example.

TABLE 8.6 | THE EFFECT OF $\bar{p}$ ON BANK OF AMERICA'S SAMPLE SIZES

$\bar{p}$	$\bar{p}(1-\bar{p})$	n
0.12	0.1056	230
0.25	0.1875	408
0.50	0.2500	543
0.75	0.1875	408

If a pilot sample is not available, I recommended setting $\bar{p} = 0.5$ to calculate the required sample size. Doing so provides us with the largest (most conservative) sample size needed to achieve a desired margin of error.

As shown in Table 8.6, using $\bar{p} = 0.5$ maximizes the term $\bar{p}(1-\bar{p})$, which maximizes the sample size. By choosing a sample size of 543 customers, Bank of America can be assured that its margin of error will be no larger than 5% in its efforts to estimate the proportion of households without checking accounts.

Using PHStat to Calculate the Sample Size for a Population Proportion

PHStat can perform the sample size calculation using the following steps. Excel for Mac users can find these instructions on the textbook's Web site.

1. Go to **Add-Ins > PHStat > Sample Size > Determination for the Proportion**, as seen back in Figure 8.17.
2. Fill in the **Sample Size Determination for the Proportion** dialog box as shown in Figure 8.21. Click **OK**.

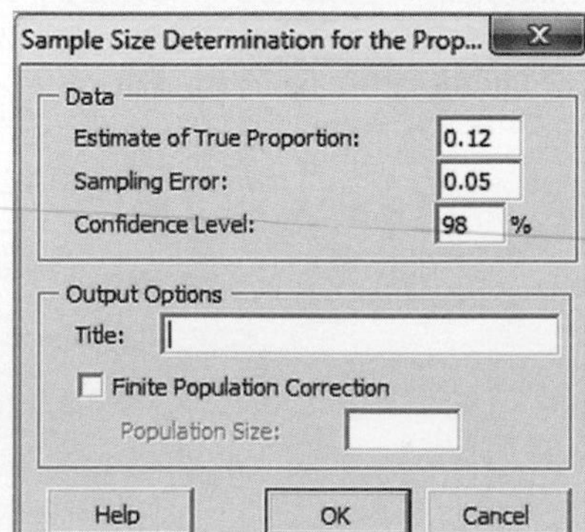

FIGURE 8.21 Using PHStat to Calculate the Sample Size for a Population Proportion (Step 2)

The required sample size for Bank of America is shown in Cell B13 in Figure 8.22. This value is slightly different from the result we calculated manually due to rounding differences.

FIGURE 8.22
Using PHStat to Calculate the Sample Size for a Population Proportion (Final Result)

	A	B
1	Sample Size Determination	
2		
3	Data	
4	Estimate of True Proportion	0.12
5	Sampling Error	0.05
6	Confidence Level	98%
7		
8	Intermediate Calculations	
9	Z Value	-2.3263
10	Calculated Sample Size	228.5984
11		
12	Result	
13	Sample Size Needed	229
14		

The following Your Turn problem allows you to practice a sample size calculation to estimate a population proportion.

YOUR TURN #11

The most recent economic recession has had a dramatic impact on the proportion of Americans who own their own homes. The federal government would like to estimate this proportion for the entire U.S. population.

a. A pilot sample of 60 Americans found that 42 were homeowners. Determine the sample size required to construct a 95% confidence interval to estimate the proportion of homeowners when the margin of error equals 6%.
b. Determine the sample size required to construct a 95% confidence interval to estimate the proportion of homeowners when the margin of error equals 6% and there is no pilot sample.
c. Verify the result from part a with PHStat.

Answers can be found on ▶ page 380

8.5 Section Problems

Basic Skills

8.38 Determine the sample size needed to construct a 90% confidence interval to estimate the population mean when $\sigma = 75$ and the margin of error equals 12.

8.39 Determine the sample size needed to construct a 95% confidence interval to estimate the population mean when $\sigma = 40$ and the margin of error equals 6.

8.40 Determine the sample size needed to construct a 95% confidence interval to estimate the population mean for the following margins of error when $\sigma = 80$:

a. 10
b. 15
c. 20

8.41 Determine the sample size needed to construct a 99% confidence interval to estimate the population proportion when $p = 0.40$ and the margin of error equals 5%.

8.42 Determine the sample size needed to construct a 90% confidence interval to estimate the population proportion when $p = 0.65$ and the margin of error equals 6%.

8.43 Determine the sample size needed to construct a 95% confidence interval to estimate the population proportion for the following sample proportions when the margin of error equals 4%:

a. $p = 0.30$
b. $p = 0.40$
c. $p = 0.50$

Applications

8.44 Determine the sample size needed to construct a 95% confidence interval to estimate the average GPA for the student population at Wilmington College with a margin of error equal to 0.2. Assume the standard deviation of the

GPA for the student population is 1.0. Verify your result using PHStat.

8.45 Michelin Tires would like to estimate the average tire life of its Latitude Tour tire in terms of how many miles it lasts. Determine the sample size needed to construct a 98% confidence interval with a margin of error equal to 2,000 miles. Assume the standard deviation for the tire life of this particular brand is 8,000 miles. Verify your result using PHStat.

8.46 Herr Foods, a producer of a variety of salty snacks, would like to estimate the average weight of a bag of BBQ potato chips produced during the filling process at its Nottingham, Pennsylvania, plant. Determine the sample size needed to construct a 95% confidence interval with a margin of error equal to 0.005 ounces. Assume the standard deviation for the potato chip filling process is 0.02 ounces. Verify your result using PHStat.

8.47 The state of New Jersey would like to estimate the proportion of voters who intend to participate in the upcoming statewide elections. A pilot sample of 50 voters found that 36 of them intended to vote in the election. Determine the additional number of voters that need to be sampled to construct a 95% interval with a margin of error equal to 0.05 to estimate the proportion. Verify your result using PHStat.

8.48 Red Fire Grill would like to estimate the proportion of tips that exceed 18% of its dinner bills. Without any knowledge of the population proportion, determine the sample size needed to construct a 90% interval with a margin of error of no more than 4% to estimate the proportion. Verify your result using PHStat.

8.49 Suppose Christiana Hospital would like to estimate the proportion of patients who feel that physicians who care for them always communicated effectively when discussing their medical care. A pilot sample of 40 patients found that 33 reported that their physician communicated effectively. Determine the additional number of patients that need to be sampled to construct a 95% confidence interval with a margin of error equal to 3% to estimate this proportion. Verify your result using PHStat.

8.6 Calculating Confidence Intervals for Finite Populations

So far in this chapter, we have assumed that all of the populations we sampled from were very large and were considered to be infinite in size. But what if the population is finite? A finite population is defined when the following condition exists:

$$\frac{n}{N} > 0.05$$

where

$n =$ The sample size
$N =$ The population size

Chapter 7 discussed the impact that finite populations have on sampling distributions for the mean and the proportion. We discovered that a finite population overestimates the standard error. When determining a confidence interval with a finite population, we need to adjust the standard error by using the same finite population correction factor used in Chapter 7 and shown in Equation 8.17.

Formula 8.17 for the Finite Population Correction Factor

$$\sqrt{\frac{N - n}{N - 1}}$$

If we fail to use this correction factor with a finite population, our calculated confidence interval will be wider than it should be. Applying this factor to our confidence interval equations from earlier in the chapter results in the equations that follow.

Formulas 8.18 and 8.19 for the Confidence Interval for the Mean of a Finite Population (σ Known)

$$UCL_{\bar{x}} = \bar{x} + z_{\alpha/2}\sigma_{\bar{x}}\left(\sqrt{\frac{N-n}{N-1}}\right)$$

$$LCL_{\bar{x}} = \bar{x} - z_{\alpha/2}\sigma_{\bar{x}}\left(\sqrt{\frac{N-n}{N-1}}\right)$$

Remember that $\sigma_{\bar{x}} = \frac{\sigma}{\sqrt{n}}$.

Formulas 8.20 and 8.21 for the Confidence Interval for the Mean of a Finite Population (σ Unknown)

$$UCL_{\bar{x}} = \bar{x} + t_{\alpha/2}\,\hat{\sigma}_{\bar{x}}\left(\sqrt{\frac{N-n}{N-1}}\right)$$

$$LCL_{\bar{x}} = \bar{x} - t_{\alpha/2}\,\hat{\sigma}_{\bar{x}}\left(\sqrt{\frac{N-n}{N-1}}\right)$$

Remember that $\hat{\sigma}_{\bar{x}} = \frac{s}{\sqrt{n}}$.

We substitute s for σ.

Formulas 8.22 and 8.23 for the Confidence Interval for a Proportion of a Finite Population

$$UCL_p = \bar{p} + z_{\alpha/2}\hat{\sigma}_p\left(\sqrt{\frac{N-n}{N-1}}\right)$$

$$LCL_p = \bar{p} - z_{\alpha/2}\hat{\sigma}_p\left(\sqrt{\frac{N-n}{N-1}}\right)$$

I'll demonstrate this procedure with the following example. Researchers at the University of Tennessee found that Americans walked an average of 5,117 steps per day. (Incidentally, Australians averaged 9,695, and the Swiss averaged 9,650 steps per day! We need to start walking more. Of course, this is easy to say as I sit here typing.) Suppose the administration at the University of Georgia's Terry College of Business performed a similar study using the college's student population of 1,600 business students. The number of steps per day was measured from a sample of 100 students. The sample mean was found to be 5,530 steps per day, and the sample standard deviation was 1,480 steps per day. Let's calculate a 95% confidence interval to estimate the average number of steps per day taken by the student population. We can also see how the Terry College students compare to the national average reported by the researchers at the University of Tennessee.

Because we are estimating a population mean but do not know what the population standard deviation is, we'll use Equations 8.20 and 8.21. This example would be considered a finite population because

$$\frac{n}{N} = \frac{100}{1{,}600} = 0.0625 > 0.05$$

These equations use the sample standard deviation to estimate the population standard deviation. As a result, we use the *t*-distribution to calculate the confidence interval.

Using Equation 8.17, our finite population correction factor is as follows:

$$\sqrt{\frac{N-n}{N-1}} = \sqrt{\frac{1{,}600-100}{1{,}600-1}} = \sqrt{\frac{1{,}500}{1{,}599}} = \sqrt{0.9381} = 0.9686$$

We can then use Equation 8.6 to calculate the approximate standard error of the mean:

$$\hat{\sigma}_{\bar{x}} = \frac{s}{\sqrt{n}} = \frac{1{,}480}{\sqrt{100}} = 148 \text{ steps per day}$$

The critical t-score is found in Table 5 in Appendix A, with $n - 1 = 100 - 1 = 99$ df in the column for a 95% confidence interval. The result is $t_{\alpha/2} = 1.984$. We're now ready to plug these values into Equations 8.20 and 8.21 as follows:

$$UCL_{\bar{x}} = \bar{x} + t_{\alpha/2}\hat{\sigma}_{\bar{x}}\left(\sqrt{\frac{N-n}{N-1}}\right)$$

$$UCL_{\bar{x}} = 5{,}530 + (1.984)(148)(0.9686)$$

$$UCL_{\bar{x}} = 5{,}530 + 284.4 = 5{,}814.4 \text{ steps per day}$$

$$LCL_{\bar{x}} = \bar{x} - t_{\alpha/2}\hat{\sigma}_{\bar{x}}\left(\sqrt{\frac{N-n}{N-1}}\right)$$

$$LCL_{\bar{x}} = 5{,}530 - (1.984)(148)(0.9686)$$

$$LCL_{\bar{x}} = 5{,}530 - 284.4 = 5{,}245.6 \text{ steps per day}$$

We are 95% confident that the average number of steps per day taken by the students at the University of Georgia is between 5,245.6 and 5,814.4. Because this range does not include the average of 5,117 steps reported in the Tennessee study, it appears that the University of Georgia students are walking more than the national average.

We can verify these results by using PHStat and taking the following steps:

1. Go to **Add-Ins > PHStat > Confidence Intervals > Estimate for the Mean, sigma unknown**, as seen in Figure 8.7.
2. Using the information from our walking example, fill in the **Estimate for the Mean, sigma unknown** dialog box as shown in Figure 8.23. Be sure to check the **Finite Population Correction** box and enter the **Population Size**. Click **OK**.

FIGURE 8.23 Using PHStat to Calculate a 95% Confidence Interval for a Finite Population

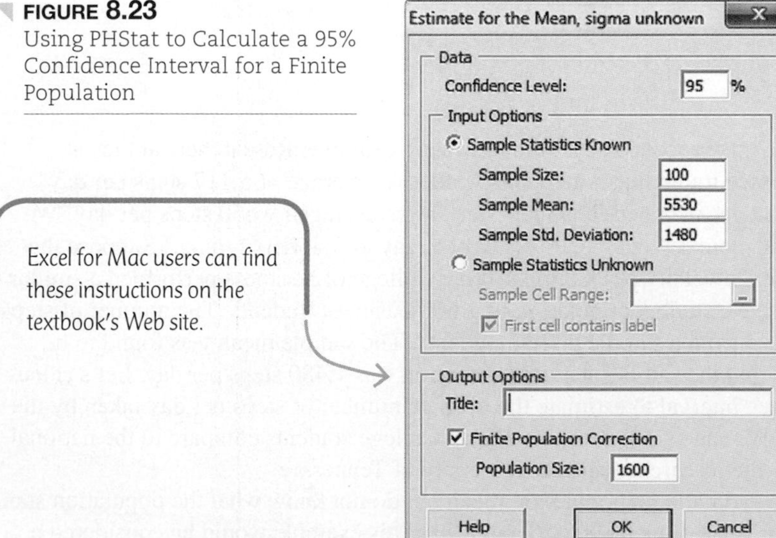

Figure 8.24 shows our results, which match what we found using Equations 8.20 and 8.21. Notice that PHStat also provides the results for the confidence interval without the correction factor. This confirms the point I made earlier. Without the correction factor, the calculated confidence interval will be overestimated and wider than it should be.

FIGURE 8.24
Using PHStat to Calculate a 95% Confidence Interval for a Finite Population (Final Result)

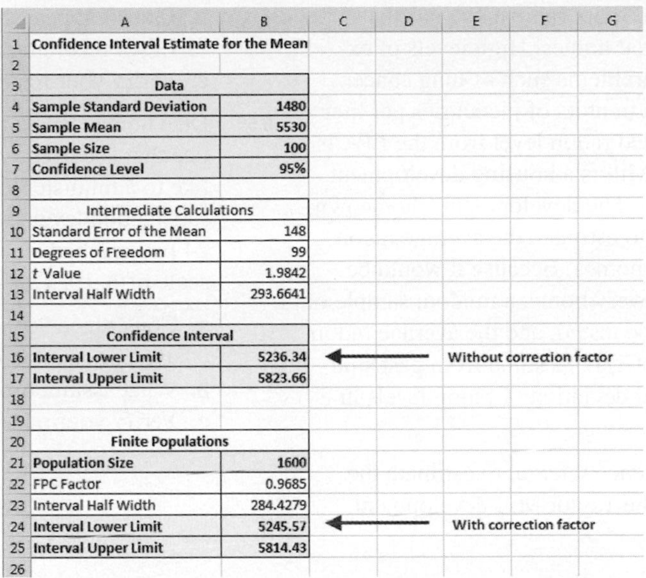

	A	B
1	Confidence Interval Estimate for the Mean	
2		
3	Data	
4	Sample Standard Deviation	1480
5	Sample Mean	5530
6	Sample Size	100
7	Confidence Level	95%
8		
9	Intermediate Calculations	
10	Standard Error of the Mean	148
11	Degrees of Freedom	99
12	t Value	1.9842
13	Interval Half Width	293.6641
14		
15	Confidence Interval	
16	Interval Lower Limit	5236.34
17	Interval Upper Limit	5823.66
18		
19		
20	Finite Populations	
21	Population Size	1600
22	FPC Factor	0.9685
23	Interval Half Width	284.4279
24	Interval Lower Limit	5245.57
25	Interval Upper Limit	5814.43
26		

I promise this will be the last Your Turn problem I will torture you with (for this chapter). Take advantage of the opportunity to construct a confidence interval for a proportion for a finite population.

YOUR TURN #12

Michael Smith is running to become the state representative for the 12th District in Delaware. The district has 700 registered voters. Michael sampled 120 of these voters and found that 72 were planning on voting for him.

a. Construct a 95% confidence interval around this sample proportion.
b. Verify your results using PHStat.
c. Can Michael feel confident that he will receive the majority of votes on Election Day?

Answers can be found on ▶ **page 381**

8.6 Section Problems

Basic Skills

8.50 Construct a 90% confidence interval to estimate the population mean using the following data:

$\bar{x} = 70 \quad \sigma = 20 \quad n = 40 \quad N = 400$

8.51 Construct a 99% confidence interval to estimate the population mean using the following data:

$\bar{x} = 22 \quad s = 4.5 \quad n = 20 \quad N = 180$

8.52 Construct a 95% confidence interval to estimate the population proportion using the following data:

$x = 22 \quad n = 75 \quad N = 500$

Applications

8.53 The University of Delaware would like to estimate the proportion of fans who purchase concessions at the first basketball game of the new season. The basketball facility has a capacity of 3,500 people and is routinely sold out. It was discovered that a total of 260 fans out of a random sample of 400 purchased concessions during the game.

a. Construct a 95% confidence interval to estimate the proportion of fans who purchased concessions during the game.
b. Verify your results using PHStat.

8.54 Radon is a colorless and odorless radioactive gas that can accumulate in residential homes. High levels of exposure can lead to health problems such as lung cancer. Radon levels are measured in units of picocuries per liter (pCi/L). The recommended radon level from the EPA is less than 4 pCi/L. Taylor Mill is a housing development with 105 residential homes. The development's homeowners association would like to estimate the average radon level in the development's homes. Because it would be too expensive to measure every home, a random sample of 32 homes was selected to be tested, and the average radon level was found to be 1.4 pCi/L. Assume from past studies, the population standard deviation of radon levels in homes is 0.5 pCi/L.

a. Construct a 95% confidence interval to estimate the average radon level in the Taylor Mill development.

b. Does it appear the average radon level is below the EPA's recommendation?

c. Verify your results using PHStat.

8.55 Dr. Thomas Bilski is a primary care physician with a practice that is currently serving 280 patients. Dr. Bilski would like to administer a survey to his patients to measure their satisfaction levels with his practice. A random sample of 24 patients had an average satisfaction score of 8.4 on a scale of 1–10. The sample standard deviation was 1.9.

a. Construct a 90% confidence interval to estimate the average satisfaction score for Dr. Bilski's practice.

b. What assumption needs to be made for this analysis?

c. Verify your results with PHStat.

CHAPTER 8 Summary

- A point estimate is a single value that best describes the population of interest, such as the sample mean or sample proportion.
  - The advantage of a point estimate is that it is easy to calculate and easy to understand.
  - The disadvantage of a point estimate is that we have no information about the accuracy of the estimate.
- A confidence interval for the mean is an interval estimate around a sample mean that provides us with a range of where the true population mean lies.
- A confidence level is defined as the probability that the interval estimate will include the population parameter of interest, such as a mean or a proportion.
- The confidence interval for the mean has an upper limit $(UL_{\bar{x}})$ and a lower limit $(LL_{\bar{x}})$ that describe the range where we have some degree of confidence that the actual population mean lies.
- The margin of error represents the width of the confidence interval between the sample mean and its upper limit *or* its lower limit.
  - Increasing the sample size while keeping the confidence level constant will reduce the margin of error, resulting in a narrower (more precise) confidence interval.
- For a 90% confidence interval, we expect 90% of the sample means drawn from a population to include that population's mean.
  - The same can be said for a 95% confidence interval and a 99% confidence interval.
- The significance level, α, represents the probability that any given confidence interval will *not* contain the true population mean.
- When the population standard deviation is unknown, we substitute s, the sample standard deviation, in its place.
  - When substituting s for σ, we rely on the Student's t-distribution to construct a confidence interval.
  - The t-distribution relies on degrees of freedom, which are the number of values that are free to be varied given that certain information, such as the sample mean, is known.
  - When we use the t-distribution, we need to assume that the population of interest follows the normal probability distribution.
- When constructing a confidence interval to estimate the population proportion, we can approximate the standard error of the proportion by substituting the sample proportion, $\bar{p}$, for the population proportion, p.
  - Proportion data follow the binomial distribution, which can be approximated by using the normal distribution when $np \geq 5$ and $n(1 - p) \geq 5$.
  - The proportion margin of error, ME_p, represents the width of the confidence interval between the sample proportion and the upper limit of the interval *or* the lower limit of the interval.
- The sample size needed to achieve a specific margin of error can be calculated for a confidence interval for the mean or proportion.
  - The calculation requires the confidence level and population standard deviation to be known or estimated.
  - A smaller margin of error (a more precise confidence interval) can be achieved with a larger sample size.
- In order to calculate the required sample size to estimate, p, the population proportion, we need to know $\bar{p}$, the sample proportion.
  - We can find a value for $\bar{p}$ by calculating the proportion of a pilot sample or, if a pilot sample is not available, by setting $\bar{p} = 0.5$.
  - Setting $\bar{p} = 0.5$ provides us with the most conservative sample size needed to achieve a specific margin of error.

CHAPTER 8 Key Terms

Confidence interval for the mean. An interval estimate around a sample mean that provides us with a range of where the true population mean lies.

Confidence interval for the proportion. An interval estimate around a sample proportion that provides us with a range of where the true population proportion lies.

Confidence level. The probability that the interval estimate will include the population parameter of interest, such as a mean or proportion.

Degrees of freedom. The number of values that are free to vary given that certain information, such as the sample mean, is known.

Margin of error. The width of the confidence interval between a sample mean or a proportion and its upper limit and or its lower limit.

Point estimate. A single value that best describes the population of interest, with the sample mean and sample proportion being the most common.

Significance level (α). A variable that represents the probability that any given confidence interval will not contain the true population mean or proportion.

Student's *t*-distribution. The probability distribution used in place of the normal distribution to calculate a confidence interval when the sample standard deviation, s, is used in place of the population standard deviation, σ.

CHAPTER 8 Equations

8.2 Calculating Confidence Intervals for the Mean when the Standard Deviation (σ) of a Population Is Known (pp 335–347)

Formula 8.1 for the Standard Error of the Mean

$$\sigma_{\bar{x}} = \frac{\sigma}{\sqrt{n}}$$

Formulas 8.2 and 8.3 for the Confidence Interval for the Mean (σ Known)

$$UCL_{\bar{x}} = \bar{x} + z_{\alpha/2}\sigma_{\bar{x}}$$
$$LCL_{\bar{x}} = \bar{x} - z_{\alpha/2}\sigma_{\bar{x}}$$

Formula 8.4 for the Margin of Error for a Confidence Interval for the Mean

$$ME_{\bar{x}} = z_{\alpha/2}\sigma_{\bar{x}}$$

8.3 Calculating Confidence Intervals for the Mean when the Standard Deviation (σ) of a Population Is Unknown (pp 347–354)

Formula 8.5 for the Sample Standard Deviation

$$s = \sqrt{\frac{\sum_{i=1}^{n}(x_i - \bar{x})^2}{n - 1}}$$

Formula 8.6 for the Approximate Standard Error of the Mean

$$\hat{\sigma}_{\bar{x}} = \frac{s}{\sqrt{n}}$$

Formulas 8.7 and 8.8 for the Confidence Interval for the Mean (σ Unknown)

$$UCL_{\bar{x}} = \bar{x} + t_{\alpha/2}\hat{\sigma}_{\bar{x}}$$
$$LCL_{\bar{x}} = \bar{x} - t_{\alpha/2}\hat{\sigma}_{\bar{x}}$$

8.4 Calculating Confidence Intervals for Proportions (pp 354–359)

Formula 8.9 for the Sample Proportion

$$\bar{p} = \frac{x}{n}$$

Formula 8.10 for the Standard Error of the Proportion

$$\sigma_p = \sqrt{\frac{p(1-p)}{n}}$$

Formula 8.11 for the Approximate Standard Error of the Proportion

$$\hat{\sigma}_p = \sqrt{\frac{\bar{p}(1-\bar{p})}{n}}$$

Formulas 8.12 and 8.13 for the Confidence Interval for a Proportion

$$UCL_p = \bar{p} + z_{\alpha/2}\hat{\sigma}_p$$
$$LCL_p = \bar{p} - z_{\alpha/2}\hat{\sigma}_p$$

Formula 8.14 for the Margin of Error for a Confidence Interval for the Proportion

$$ME_p = z_{\alpha/2}\hat{\sigma}_p$$

8.5 Determining the Sample Size (pp 359–366)

Formula 8.15 for the Sample Size Needed to Estimate a Population Mean

$$n = \frac{(z_{\alpha/2})^2\sigma^2}{(ME_{\bar{x}})^2}$$

Formula 8.16 for the Sample Size Needed to Estimate the Population Proportion

$$n = \frac{(z_{\alpha/2})^2\bar{p}(1-\bar{p})}{(ME_p)^2}$$

8.6 Calculating Confidence Intervals for Finite Populations (pp 366–370)

Formula 8.17 for the Finite Population Correction Factor

$$\sqrt{\frac{N-n}{N-1}}$$

Formulas 8.18 and 8.19 for the Confidence Interval for the Mean of a Finite Population (σ Known)

$$UCL_{\bar{x}} = \bar{x} + z_{\alpha/2}\sigma_{\bar{x}}\left(\sqrt{\frac{N-n}{N-1}}\right)$$
$$LCL_{\bar{x}} = \bar{x} - z_{\alpha/2}\sigma_{\bar{x}}\left(\sqrt{\frac{N-n}{N-1}}\right)$$

Formulas 8.20 and 8.21 for the Confidence Interval for the Mean of a Finite Population (σ Unknown)

$$UCL_{\bar{x}} = \bar{x} + t_{\alpha/2}\hat{\sigma}_{\bar{x}}\left(\sqrt{\frac{N-n}{N-1}}\right)$$

$$LCL_{\bar{x}} = \bar{x} - t_{\alpha/2}\hat{\sigma}_{\bar{x}}\left(\sqrt{\frac{N-n}{N-1}}\right)$$

Formulas 8.22 and 8.23 for the Confidence Interval for a Proportion of a Finite Population

$$UCL_p = \bar{p} + z_{\alpha/2}\hat{\sigma}_p\left(\sqrt{\frac{N-n}{N-1}}\right)$$

$$LCL_p = \bar{p} - z_{\alpha/2}\hat{\sigma}_p\left(\sqrt{\frac{N-n}{N-1}}\right)$$

TABLE 8.7 | A Summary of Confidence Intervals for One Population

TYPE	POPULATION	σ_1, σ_2	CONFIDENCE INTERVAL	EQUATIONS
Mean	Infinite	Known	$UCL_{\bar{x}} = \bar{x} + z_{\alpha/2}\left(\frac{\sigma}{\sqrt{n}}\right)$	8.2
			$LCL_{\bar{x}} = \bar{x} - z_{\alpha/2}\left(\frac{\sigma}{\sqrt{n}}\right)$	8.3
Mean	Infinite	Unknown	$UCL_{\bar{x}} = \bar{x} + t_{\alpha/2}\left(\frac{s}{\sqrt{n}}\right)$	8.7
			$LCL_{\bar{x}} = \bar{x} - t_{\alpha/2}\left(\frac{s}{\sqrt{n}}\right)$	8.8
Proportion	Infinite	Not applicable	$UCL_p = \bar{p} + z_{\alpha/2}\sqrt{\frac{\bar{p}(1-\bar{p})}{n}}$	8.12
			$LCL_p = \bar{p} - z_{\alpha/2}\sqrt{\frac{\bar{p}(1-\bar{p})}{n}}$	8.13
Mean	Finite	Known	$UCL_{\bar{x}} = \bar{x} + z_{\alpha/2}\left(\frac{\sigma}{\sqrt{n}}\right)\left(\sqrt{\frac{N-n}{N-1}}\right)$	8.18
			$LCL_{\bar{x}} = \bar{x} - z_{\alpha/2}\left(\frac{\sigma}{\sqrt{n}}\right)\left(\sqrt{\frac{N-n}{N-1}}\right)$	8.19
Mean	Finite	Unknown	$UCL_{\bar{x}} = \bar{x} + t_{\alpha/2}\left(\frac{s}{\sqrt{n}}\right)\left(\sqrt{\frac{N-n}{N-1}}\right)$	8.20
			$LCL_{\bar{x}} = \bar{x} - t_{\alpha/2}\left(\frac{s}{\sqrt{n}}\right)\left(\sqrt{\frac{N-n}{N-1}}\right)$	8.21
Proportion	Finite	Not applicable	$UCL_p = \bar{p} + z_{\alpha/2}\sqrt{\frac{\bar{p}(1-\bar{p})}{n}}\left(\sqrt{\frac{N-n}{N-1}}\right)$	8.22
			$LCL_p = \bar{p} - z_{\alpha/2}\sqrt{\frac{\bar{p}(1-\bar{p})}{n}}\left(\sqrt{\frac{N-n}{N-1}}\right)$	8.23

CHAPTER 8 Problems

8.56 According to the Bureau of Labor Statistics, the average hourly wage in the United States was $22.57 in May 2010. To confirm this wage, a random sample of 36 hourly workers was selected during the month. The average wage for this sample was $21.32. Assume the standard deviation of wages for the country is $4.30.

a. Are the results of this sample consistent with the claim made by the Bureau of Labor Statistics using a 95% confidence interval?
b. What is the margin of error for this sample?
c. Verify your result using Excel.

8.57 On June 2, 2010, major league pitcher Armando Galarraga of the Detroit Tigers lost his bid for a perfect game when umpire Jim Joyce incorrectly called a runner safe at first base with two outs in the ninth inning. (A perfect game occurs when a pitcher faces 27 batters without any opposing players reaching base during the game. Only 18 perfect games have been pitched in the last 110 years of baseball.) This unfortunate incident led to an outcry for baseball to expand its use of instant replay so that umpires have the option of reversing incorrect calls. A *USA Today*/Gallup poll after this event found that 78% of baseball fans were in favor of expanding the use of instant replay in Major League Baseball. Suppose the size of this sample was 600 people.

a. Estimate the true proportion of baseball fans in favor of expanded replay using a 95% confidence interval.
b. What is the margin of error for this sample?
c. Verify your result using PHStat.

8.58 One provision of the Affordable Care Act, commonly known as Obamacare, requires insurance plans pay for breast-feeding support for mothers, such as consultations and breast pumps. According to the CDC, 48% of mothers were breast-feeding their six-month-old babies in 2012. Suppose Humana Health Insurance would like to estimate the proportion of mothers who breast-fed their children at six months in 2014. A random sample of 210 mothers with six-month-old babies was selected of which 119 were breast-feeding.

a. Construct a 95% confidence interval to estimate the actual proportion of mothers with six-month-old babies that were breast-feeding in 2014.
b. What is the margin of error for this sample?
c. Is there evidence that this proportion has changed since 2012 based on this sample?
d. Verify your results with PHStat.

8.59 The following data show the costs charged by a tax preparation service for a random sample of 15 tax returns. These data can also be found in the Excel file titled **tax prep costs.xlsx**.

$135	$120	$150	$110	$90
$115	$130	$200	$180	$200
$140	$150	$100	$75	$70

a. Using a 98% confidence interval, estimate the average cost of the service for preparing a tax return for a customer.
b. What is the margin of error for this sample?
c. Verify your result using Excel.
d. What assumptions are necessary for this analysis?

8.60 Airline companies recognize that empty seats represent lost revenues that can never be recovered. To avoid losing revenues, the companies often book more passengers than there are available seats. Then, when a flight experiences fewer no-shows than expected, some passengers are "bumped" from their flights (are denied boarding). Incentives are provided to encourage passengers to give up their reserved seat voluntarily, but occasionally some passengers are involuntarily bumped from the flight. Obviously, these incidents can reflect poorly on customer satisfaction. Suppose Southwest Airlines would like to estimate the true proportion of involuntarily bumped passengers across all domestic flights in the industry. In a pilot sample of 55 domestic passengers, 5 were involuntarily bumped from their flights.

a. Determine the sample size needed to construct a 98% confidence interval with a margin of error no more than 5% to estimate the true proportion of involuntarily bumped passengers.
b. Verify your result using PHStat.

8.61 The makers of compact fluorescent light bulbs (CFL) claim the bulbs use 75% less energy and last 10 times longer than incandescent bulbs. A 16-watt CFL (equivalent to a 60-watt incandescent) has a rated lifetime of 8,000 hours. To test this claim, a random sample of 50 CFLs was drawn, and the average life of a bulb was determined to be 7,960 hours. Assume the standard deviation for the life of CFL bulbs is 240 hours.

a. Does this sample provide enough evidence to support the claim that CFLs average 8,000 hours with 95% confidence?
b. What is the margin of error for this sample using a 95% confidence interval?
c. Verify your result using Excel.

8.62 Aetna, a major health insurance company, would like to estimate the average wait time for a patient seeking emergency room services. A random sample of 33 emergency room patients had an average wait time of 222 minutes with a sample standard deviation of 76 minutes. Determine the confidence interval to estimate the average wait time for the following confidence levels:

a. 90%
b. 95%
c. 99%
d. How does the confidence level impact the precision of the estimate?
e. What assumptions need to be made in conjunction with this analysis?

8.63 Certain advertisers would like to estimate the proportion of viewers who spend the majority of their television time watching alone. The consensus is that this percentage has been increasing over the years due to the increased number of television sets in U.S. households.

a. Determine the sample size needed to construct a 90% confidence interval with a margin of error no more than 5% to estimate the true proportion of viewers who watch television alone.
b. What impact would a pilot sample that showed that 38% of viewers spend the majority of their television time watching alone have on your results?
c. Verify your results using PHStat.

8.64 The Department of Labor would like to estimate the average weekly wages for U.S. adults with a margin of error equal to $20. Determine the sample sizes needed to construct a confidence interval for this estimate using the following confidence levels. Assume the population standard deviation for the weekly wage is $160.

a. 90%
b. 95%
c. 98%
d. Explain why the confidence level affects the sample size needed to obtain a particular margin of error.

8.65 To design a new advertising campaign, Volkswagen would like to estimate the proportion of drivers of the new VW Beetle who are women. In a random sample of 250 Beetle owners, 140 of them were women.

a. Construct a 95% confidence interval to estimate this proportion.
b. What is the margin of error for this sample?
c. Verify your results using PHStat.

8.66 Much of the recent euro currency crisis that struck Europe was attributed to the economy of Greece. George Papandreou, Greece's prime minister, claimed that corruption was at the heart of the crisis. Transparency International is a global civil organization that reports on worldwide corruption. The organization's research indicated that the average bribe to a public service in Greece in 2013 was $1,596. To validate these findings, a random sample of 20 private sector transactions in 2013 was taken and each person was asked to report the amount of any bribe. The data are as follows and can also be found in the Excel file titled **bribes.xlsx**.

$0	$0	$3,100	$0	$1,100
$0	$1,800	$2,350	$2,800	$1,900
$0	$2,000	$2,300	$3,000	$2,800
$0	$2,000	$250	$2,350	$2,750

a. Construct a 95% confidence interval with these data to estimate the average bribe to a public service in 2013.
b. Do these results validate the findings of Transparency International?
c. What is the margin of error for this sample?
d. Why is this margin of error so large?
e. Verify your results using Excel.

8.67 Verizon Wireless would like to estimate the average number of text messages received by American teenagers per month. A random sample of 60 teenaged customers was selected. The sample average was 2,272 messages per month, and the sample standard deviation was 953 messages per month. Construct confidence intervals with the following confidence levels:

a. 90%
b. 95%
c. 99%
d. Verify your results using PHStat.

8.68 GMAC reported that 85% of drivers incorrectly answered a question asking them what they are supposed to do when approaching a yellow light. (The correct answer is slow down and proceed through the light only if it is safe to do so. But I'm sure you already knew that.) To verify this surprising result, 330 drivers in a random sample were asked the same question. From this sample, 274 answered incorrectly. Using a 90% confidence interval, are the results reported by GMAC validated?

8.69 The U.S. Census Bureau would like to estimate the average annual contributions to charity by the members of Generation Y (people born in the United States in the years 1981 through 1991). The following data show the annual contributions to charity for a random sample of 18 individuals in this age group. These data can also be found in the Excel file titled **contributions.xlsx**.

$25	$270	$60	$750	$415	$595
$390	$450	$400	$160	$192	$155
$200	$460	$650	$510	$330	$225

a. Construct a 95% confidence interval with these data to estimate the average annual contributions to charity for this age group.
b. What is the margin of error for this sample?
c. Verify your results using Excel.

8.70 A recent trend in the auto financing market is an increase in the length of new car loans. According to Experian, 11% of new car loans in 2009 were between 73 and 84 months in length. Suppose a random sample of 260 new cars loans in 2014 was selected and found to have 47 that were between 73 and 84 months in length.

a. Construct a 90% confidence interval to estimate the actual proportion of new car loans that are between 73 and 84 months in length in 2014.
b. What is the margin of error for this sample?
c. Is there evidence that this proportion has changed since 2009 based on this sample?
d. Verify your results with PHStat.

8.71 In 2010, Bank of America reported that 7.1% of its credit card holders were at least 30 days overdue on their monthly payments. In 2014, a random sample of 450 credit card customers found that 20 were at least 30 days overdue on their monthly payments. Using a 90% confidence interval, can you conclude that the proportion of delinquent card holders changed since 2010?

8.72 Travelocity would like to estimate the current average domestic airfare. The following data show the airfares for 24 randomly selected tickets for travel within the United States. These data can also be found in the Excel file titled **domestic airfares.xlsx**.

$356	$275	$371	$384	$457	$326
$414	$367	$362	$286	$104	$136
$320	$244	$370	$215	$322	$409
$303	$489	$251	$361	$337	$265

a. Construct a 99% confidence interval with these data to estimate the average domestic airfare.
b. What is the margin of error for this sample?
c. Verify your results using Excel.

8.73 Using a 90% confidence level, the U.S. Department of Labor would like to estimate the average weekly hours worked by private employees in the United States who are adults. Assume the standard deviation for the number of hours worked is seven hours. Determine the sample sizes needed to construct this confidence interval using the following margins of error:

a. 2 hours
b. 1 hour
c. 30 minutes
d. Explain why the margin of error affects the sample size needed to obtain a particular confidence level.

8.74 Michael Smith is running to become the state representative for the 12th District in Delaware. The district has 310 registered Republican voters. In an effort to plan his campaign strategy, Michael would like to estimate the average age of a Republican voter in the district. Following a random sample of 27 registered Republicans, the average age of voters was found to be 38.7 years with a sample standard deviation equal to 6.8 years.

a. Construct a 95% confidence interval to estimate the average age of registered Republicans in the 12th District.
b. What assumption needs to be made for this analysis?
c. Verify your results using PHStat.

8.75 A local church has a congregation composed of 362 members. The church's administrators would like to find out how the congregation would react if the church moved its 11:00 A.M. service to 10:00 A.M. A random sample of 115 members was drawn, 46 of whom were in favor of the change.

a. Construct a 95% confidence interval to estimate the proportion of members in the congregation in favor of the time change.
b. What conclusions can be made based on these results?
c. Verify your results using PHStat.

8.76 Clear Bags is an online company that sells a variety of protective bags for photo, art, and stationery products that are placed on display. Currently, its customer database consists of 872 individuals who place at least one order per year. Clear Bags would like to estimate the proportion of their customer base that is 35 years or younger. From a random sample of 240 customers, 77 were found to be 35 years or younger.

a. Construct a 95% confidence interval to estimate the actual proportion of Clear Bags customers who are 35 years or younger.
b. What is the margin of error for this sample?
c. Verify your results with PHStat.

8.77 The manager at an automobile dealership would like to estimate the average satisfaction score from the 915 customers who purchased a car or truck last year. The company goal is to achieve an average satisfaction score of at least 80 on a scale of 0–100. A random sample of 80 customers had an average satisfaction score of 82.7 and a sample standard deviation of 6.7.

a. Construct a 95% confidence interval to estimate the actual average satisfaction score from last year's customers.
b. Based on this sample, can the manager conclude that the company goal has been achieved?
c. Verify your results with PHStat.

8.78 The Excel file labeled **Lowes.xlsx** lists the receipt total for 350 randomly selected customers for the home improvement chain Lowe's.

a. Use these data to construct a 95% confidence interval to estimate the average receipt total for a Lowe's customer.
b. What is the margin of error for this sample?
c. Verify your results using Excel.

8.79 The Hawaii Island Chamber of Commerce collects ocean temperature data to help promote tourism for local businesses. The Excel file titled **Hawaii ocean temps.xlsx** lists daily ocean temperatures for the past 125 days.

a. Use these data to construct a 90% confidence interval to estimate the average ocean temperature for Hawaii.
b. What is the margin of error for this sample?
c. Verify your results with Excel.

CHAPTER 8 Solutions to Your Turn

YOUR TURN #1

$$\sigma_{\bar{x}} = \frac{\sigma}{\sqrt{n}} = \frac{\$39}{\sqrt{35}} = \frac{\$39}{5.92} = \$6.59$$

$$UCL_{\bar{x}} = \bar{x} + z_{\alpha/2}\sigma_{\bar{x}}$$
$$UCL_{\bar{x}} = (\$247.80) + (1.645)(\$6.59)$$
$$UCL_{\bar{x}} = \$247.80 + \$10.84 = \$258.64$$

$$LCL_{\bar{x}} = \bar{x} + z_{\alpha/2}\sigma_{\bar{x}}$$
$$LCL_{\bar{x}} = (\$247.80) - (1.645)(\$6.59)$$
$$LCL_{\bar{x}} = \$247.80 - \$10.84 = \$236.96$$

We are 90% confident that the average room rate for luxury hotels in the United States during the first quarter of 2010 is between \$236.96 and \$258.64.

YOUR TURN #2

a. $\sigma_{\bar{x}} = \frac{\sigma}{\sqrt{n}} = \frac{\$63}{\sqrt{30}} = \frac{\$63}{5.48} = \$11.50 \lim_{x \to \infty}$

$$ME_{\bar{x}} = z_{\alpha/2}\sigma_{\bar{x}} = (1.645)(\$11.50) = \$18.92$$
$$UCL_{\bar{x}} = \$507 + \$18.92 = \$525.92$$
$$LCL_{\bar{x}} = \$507 - \$18.92 = \$488.08$$

b. $\sigma_{\bar{x}} = \frac{\sigma}{\sqrt{n}} = \frac{\$63}{\sqrt{60}} = \frac{\$63}{7.75} = \$8.13$

$$ME_{\bar{x}} = z_{\alpha/2}\sigma_{\bar{x}} = (1.645)(\$8.13) = \$13.37$$

$$UCL_{\bar{x}} = \$507 + \$13.37 = \$520.37$$
$$LCL_{\bar{x}} = \$507 - \$13.37 = \$493.63$$

c. Increasing the sample size from 30 to 60 reduces the margin of error from \$11.50 to \$8.13, which reduces the confidence interval. This provides a more precise estimate of the average price of a notebook in the population of notebook computers.

YOUR TURN #3

a. To find the critical z-score for an 80% confidence interval, we need to recognize that the area to the left of the right-hand boundary is $0.80 + 0.10 = 0.90$. After searching Table 4 in Appendix A for the value in the body of the table closest to 0.90, you'll find 0.8997 in the 1.2 row and 0.08 column, resulting in $z_{\alpha/2} = 1.28$.

$$\sigma_{\bar{x}} = \frac{\sigma}{\sqrt{n}} = \frac{4.1}{\sqrt{30}} = \frac{4.1}{5.48} = 0.748$$

$$ME_{\bar{x}} = z_{\alpha/2}\sigma_{\bar{x}} = (1.28)(0.748) = 0.957$$

			Confidence Interval	
Sample	Sample Mean	Margin of Error	Lower Limit	Upper Limit
1	12.4	0.957	11.44	13.36
2	11.3	0.957	10.34	12.26
3	13.1	0.957	12.14	14.06
4	13.7	0.957	12.74	14.66
5	12.7	0.957	11.74	13.66

b. These results are consistent with the definition of an 80% confidence interval. Four out of five (80%) random samples have confidence intervals that include the population mean of 13 minutes. The confidence interval for the second sample does not include this population mean.

YOUR TURN #4

a. $\sigma_{\bar{x}} = \frac{\sigma}{\sqrt{n}} = \frac{\$260}{\sqrt{40}} = \frac{\$260}{6.32} = \$41.14$

$$UCL_{\bar{x}} = \bar{x} + z_{\alpha/2}\sigma_{\bar{x}}$$
$$UCL_{\bar{x}} = (\$1,090) + (1.28)(\$41.14) = \$1,142.66$$
$$LCL_{\bar{x}} = \bar{x} - z_{\alpha/2}\sigma_{\bar{x}}$$
$$LCL_{\bar{x}} = (\$1,090) - (1.28)(\$41.14) = \$1,037.34$$

b. $UCL_{\bar{x}} = \bar{x} + z_{\alpha/2}\sigma_{\bar{x}}$

$$UCL_{\bar{x}} = (\$1,090) + (1.96)(\$41.14) = \$1,170.63$$
$$LCL_{\bar{x}} = \bar{x} - z_{\alpha/2}\sigma_{\bar{x}}$$
$$LCL_{\bar{x}} = (\$1,090) - (1.96)(\$41.14) = \$1,009.37$$

c. $UCL_{\bar{x}} = \bar{x} + z_{\alpha/2}\sigma_{\bar{x}}$

$$UCL_{\bar{x}} = (\$1,090) + (2.33)(\$41.14) = \$1,185.86$$
$$LCL_{\bar{x}} = \bar{x} - z_{\alpha/2}\sigma_{\bar{x}}$$
$$LCL_{\bar{x}} = (\$1,090) - (2.33)(\$41.14) = \$994.14$$

d. Increasing the confidence level from 80% to 98% increases the size of the confidence interval. If the sample size is held constant, the only way to increase the likelihood of capturing the population mean is to increase the width of the confidence interval.

YOUR TURN #5

$$\sigma_{\bar{x}} = \frac{\sigma}{\sqrt{n}} = \frac{3.9}{\sqrt{34}} = \frac{3.9}{5.83} = 0.669$$

For a 98% confidence interval, $z_{\alpha/2} = 2.33$.

$$UCL_{\bar{x}} = \bar{x} + z_{\alpha/2}\sigma_{\bar{x}}$$
$$UCL_{\bar{x}} = (21.2) + (2.33)(0.669) = 22.8$$

$$LCL_{\bar{x}} = \bar{x} - z_{\alpha/2}\sigma_{\bar{x}}$$
$$LCL_{\bar{x}} = (21.2) - (2.33)(0.669) = 19.6$$

We are 98% confident that the average fuel economy for passenger vehicles in the United States is between 19.6 and 22.8 mpg. Because the interval does include the claimed fuel economy of 20.3, this sample does support the EPA's statement.

YOUR TURN #6

a. =CONFIDENCE.NORM(0.01, 1490, 45) = 572.13

b.

	A	B
1	**Confidence Interval Estimate for the Mean**	
2		
3	**Data**	
4	**Population Standard Deviation**	1490
5	**Sample Mean**	8650
6	**Sample Size**	45
7	**Confidence Level**	99%
8		
9	Intermediate Calculations	
10	Standard Error of the Mean	222.1160858
11	Z Value	-2.5758
12	Interval Half Width	572.1331
13		
14	**Confidence Interval**	
15	**Interval Lower Limit**	8077.87
16	**Interval Upper Limit**	9222.13
17		

We are 99% confident that the average tuition fees for public colleges and universities during the 2012–2013 academic year is between $8,077.87 and $9,222.13.

YOUR TURN #7

$$\sigma_{\bar{x}} = \frac{\sigma}{\sqrt{n}} = \frac{6.1}{\sqrt{18}} = \frac{6.1}{4.24} = 1.44$$

For a 95% confidence interval, $z_{\alpha/2} = 1.96$.

a. $UCL_{\bar{x}} = \bar{x} + z_{\alpha/2}\sigma_{\bar{x}}$

$UCL_{\bar{x}} = (22.8) + (1.96)(1.44) = 25.6$

$LCL_{\bar{x}} = \bar{x} - z_{\alpha/2}\sigma_{\bar{x}}$

$LCL_{\bar{x}} = (22.8) - (1.96)(1.44) = 20.0$

We are 95% confident that the average household does between 20.0 and 25.6 loads of laundry per month.

b. The population must be normally distributed because the sample size is less than 30.

c. Because the 95% confidence interval includes 25 loads per month, this sample does support the claim made by Procter & Gamble.

YOUR TURN #8

$\bar{x} = 92.7$

$s = 4.52$

$n = 10$

$$\hat{\sigma}_{\bar{x}} = \frac{s}{\sqrt{n}} = \frac{4.52}{\sqrt{10}} = 1.43$$

$df = n - 1 = 10 - 1 = 9$

$t_{\alpha/2} = 1.833$ from Table 5 in Appendix A (90% CI)

$$UCL_{\bar{x}} = \bar{x} + t_{\alpha/2}\hat{\sigma}_{\bar{x}}$$
$$UCL_{\bar{x}} = 92.7 + (1.833)(1.43)$$
$$UCL_{\bar{x}} = 92.7 + 2.62 = 95.3$$
$$LCL_{\bar{x}} = \bar{x} - t_{\alpha/2}\,\hat{\sigma}_{\bar{x}}$$
$$LCL_{\bar{x}} = 92.7 - (1.833)(1.43)$$
$$LCL_{\bar{x}} = 92.7 - 2.62 = 90.1$$

We are 90% confident that the statistic author's actual golf average is between 90.1 and 95.3.

YOUR TURN #9

a. $\bar{p} = \dfrac{x}{n} = \dfrac{98}{500} = 0.196$

$$\hat{\sigma}_p = \sqrt{\frac{\bar{p}(1 - \bar{p})}{n}} = \sqrt{\frac{(0.196)(1 - 0.196)}{500}}$$

$$= \sqrt{0.000315} = 0.0177$$

$$UCL_p = \bar{p} + z_{\alpha/2}\hat{\sigma}_p$$

$$UCL_p = 0.196 + (2.33)(0.0177) = 0.237$$

$$UCL_p = \bar{p} - z_{\alpha/2}\hat{\sigma}_p$$

$$UCL_p = 0.196 - (2.33)(0.0177) = 0.155$$

We are 98% confident that the proportion of car deals financed with 0% financing is between 0.155 and 0.237. Because 0.224 is within this confidence interval, the sample does support the findings of Edmunds.com.

b. $ME_p = z_{\alpha/2}\hat{\sigma}_p = (2.33)(0.0177) = 0.041$

c.

	A	B
1	**Confidence Interval Estimate for the Proportion**	
2		
3	Data	
4	**Sample Size**	500
5	**Number of Successes**	98
6	**Confidence Level**	98%
7		
8	Intermediate Calculations	
9	Sample Proportion	0.196
10	Z Value	-2.3263
11	Standard Error of the Proportion	0.0178
12	Interval Half Width	0.0413
13		
14	Confidence Interval	
15	**Interval Lower Limit**	0.1547
16	**Interval Upper Limit**	0.2373
17		

YOUR TURN #10

a. $n = \dfrac{(z_{\alpha/2})^2\sigma^2}{(ME_{\bar{x}})^2} = \dfrac{(1.645)^2(32)^2}{(5)^2}$

$$= \frac{(2.706)(1{,}024)}{(25)} = 110.84 \approx 111$$

The park service should sample the time of 111 hikers using this trail.

b.

	A	B
1	**Sample Size Determination**	
2		
3	Data	
4	**Population Standard Deviation**	32
5	**Sampling Error**	5
6	**Confidence Level**	90%
7		
8	Intemediate Calculations	
9	Z Value	-1.6449
10	Calculated Sample Size	110.8191
11		
12	Result	
13	**Sample Size Needed**	111
14		

YOUR TURN #11

a. $\bar{p} = \dfrac{42}{60} = 0.70$

$$n = \frac{(z_{\alpha/2})^2\bar{p}(1 - \bar{p})}{(ME_p)^2} = \frac{(1.96)^2(0.70)(1 - 0.70)}{(0.06)^2}$$

$$n = \frac{(3.842)(0.7)(0.3)}{(0.0036)} = 224.1 \approx 225$$

With the pilot sample, the government should sample 225 Americans to estimate the proportion of homeowners or an additional $225 - 60 = 165$ homeowners.

b. Set $\bar{p} = 0.5$

$$n = \frac{(z_{\alpha/2})^2\bar{p}(1 - \bar{p})}{(ME_p)^2} = \frac{(1.96)^2(0.50)(1 - 0.50)}{(0.06)^2}$$

$$n = \frac{(3.842)(0.5)(0.5)}{(0.0036)} = 266.8 \approx 267$$

Without a pilot sample, the government should sample 267 Americans to estimate the proportion of homeownership.

c.

	A	B
1	**Sample Size Determination**	
2		
3	Data	
4	**Estimate of True Proportion**	0.7
5	**Sampling Error**	0.06
6	**Confidence Level**	95%
7		
8	Intermediate Calculations	
9	Z Value	-1.9600
10	Calculated Sample Size	224.0851
11		
12	Result	
13	**Sample Size Needed**	225
14		

YOUR TURN #12

a. $\frac{n}{N} = \frac{120}{700} = 0.171 > 0.05$

$$\sqrt{\frac{N-n}{N-1}} = \sqrt{\frac{700-120}{700-1}} = \sqrt{\frac{580}{699}}$$
$$= \sqrt{0.8298} = 0.9109$$
$$\bar{p} = \frac{x}{n} = \frac{72}{120} = 0.60$$
$$\hat{\sigma}_p = \sqrt{\frac{\bar{p}(1-\bar{p})}{n}} = \sqrt{\frac{(0.60)(1-0.60)}{120}}$$
$$= \sqrt{\frac{0.24}{120}} = \sqrt{0.002} = 0.0447$$
$$UCL_p = \bar{p} + z_{\alpha/2}\hat{\sigma}_p\left(\sqrt{\frac{N-n}{N-1}}\right)$$
$$UCL_p = 0.60 + (1.96)(0.0447)(0.9109)$$
$$UCL_p = 0.60 + 0.0798 = 0.6798$$
$$LCL_p = \bar{p} - z_{\alpha/2}\hat{\sigma}_p\left(\sqrt{\frac{N-n}{N-1}}\right)$$
$$LCL_p = 0.60 - (1.96)(0.0447)(0.9109)$$
$$LCL_p = 0.60 - 0.0798 = 0.5202$$

We are 95% confident that the proportion of voters who will vote for Michael Smith is between 0.5202 and 0.6798.

b.

	A	B
1	**Confidence Interval Estimate for the Proportion**	
2		
3	Data	
4	**Sample Size**	120
5	**Number of Successes**	72
6	**Confidence Level**	95%
7		
8	Intermediate Calculations	
9	Sample Proportion	0.6
10	Z Value	-1.9600
11	Standard Error of the Proportion	0.0447
12	Interval Half Width	0.0877
13		
14	**Confidence Interval**	
15	**Interval Lower Limit**	0.5123
16	**Interval Upper Limit**	0.6877
17		
18		
19	**Finite Populations**	
20	**Population Size**	700
21	FPC Factor	0.9109
22	Interval Half Width	0.0798
23	**Interval Lower Limit**	0.5202
24	**Interval Upper Limit**	0.6798
25		

c. Because both the upper and lower limits for this confidence interval exceed 50%, Michael is 95% confident that he will receive the majority of the votes.

Hypothesis Testing for a Single Population

IN THIS CHAPTER, YOU WILL LEARN TO:

- State the null and alternative hypothesis.
- Distinguish between a one-tail and a two-tail hypothesis test.
- Understand the difference between a Type I and Type II error.
- Understand the role that the significance level plays on the hypothesis test.
- Perform a hypothesis test for the population mean and population proportion.
- Calculate and interpret a *p*-value for a hypothesis test.
- Calculate and interpret the power for a hypothesis test.

CHAPTER 9 MAP

In Chapter 8 we learned how to estimate a population parameter such as a mean using a sample and a confidence interval. Now let's move on to the heart and soul of inferential statistics: hypothesis testing.

A **hypothesis** is an assumption about a population parameter such as a mean or a proportion.

In the statistical world, a **hypothesis** is an assumption about a specific population parameter, such as a mean, a proportion, or a standard deviation. One thing we statisticians like to do is to make an assumption about the value of a population parameter, collect a sample from that population, measure the sample, and declare, in a scholarly manner, whether the sample supports the original assumption. This, in a nutshell, is what hypothesis testing is all about. It will, however, require both this and the next chapter to explain exactly how to do this. The focus of this chapter is to test an assumption about a single population mean or population proportion. After we've mastered this technique, Chapter 10 will address hypothesis testing for two populations.

Today's business environment is full of examples that deal with hypothesis testing, such as the following:

- Bank fees have come under scrutiny lately as financial institutions have struggled to recover losses due to the recent economic recession. Prior to the recession, the fees charged by banks for late credit card payments averaged \$40. A government agency would like to test the hypothesis that the fees now average more than \$40.
- The industry that promotes compact fluorescent light (CFL) bulbs claims the bulbs use 75% less energy and last 10 times longer than incandescent bulbs. An independent lab would like to test this claim using hypothesis testing.
- A recent *Wall Street Journal* article titled "Does the Internet Make You Smarter or Dumber?" posed the possibility that online activities turn us into shallow thinkers. The article cited a statistic claiming that the average time an American spends looking at a Web page is 56 seconds. A researcher at a local university would like to test this claim using a hypothesis test.

Hypothesis testing is one of the most widely used procedures in statistics today. As you'll see in this chapter, special care must be taken to set up the proper test and to draw the proper conclusions. First, I'll provide you with an introduction to hypothesis testing, and then we'll discuss tests for the population mean and the population proportion.

9.1 An Introduction to Hypothesis Testing

The purpose of this section is to discuss how to set up a proper hypothesis test, which begins with establishing the null and alternative hypotheses.

Stating the Hypothesis

The **null hypothesis**, denoted by H_0, represents the status quo and involves stating the belief that the population parameter is $\leq$, $=$, or $\geq$ a specific value.

Every hypothesis test has both a null hypothesis and an alternative hypothesis. The **null hypothesis**, denoted by H_0, represents the status quo and involves stating the belief that the population parameter is $\leq$ (less than or equal to), $=$, or $\geq$ (greater than or equal to) a specific value. (Recall from Chapter 1 that we define a parameter as data that describe a characteristic about a population such as a mean or proportion.) The null hypothesis is believed to be true unless there is overwhelming evidence to the contrary.

The **alternative hypothesis**, denoted by H_1, represents the opposite of the null hypothesis and is believed to be true if the null hypothesis is found to be false.

The **alternative hypothesis**, denoted by H_1, represents the opposite of the null hypothesis and is believed to be true if the null hypothesis is found to be false. The alternative hypothesis always states that the population parameter is $>$ (greater than), $\neq$ (not equal to), or $<$ (less than) a specific value.

You need to be careful how you state the null and alternative hypotheses. Your decision will depend on the nature of the test and the motivation of the person conducting it. Suppose the purpose of the test is to determine if the population mean is equal to a specific value, which is what we would want to test based on our previous *Wall Street Journal* article. We would then assign this statement as the null hypothesis, which results in the following equation:

$$H_0: \mu = 56 \text{ seconds (status quo)}$$

In this example, we are assuming the status quo is that Internet users spend an average time of 56 seconds on a Web page. As a result, this statement is assigned to the null hypothesis.

The alternative hypothesis reflects the opposite condition, that the average time is not equal to 56 seconds.

$$H_1: \mu \neq 56 \text{ seconds}$$

A hypothesis statement can be used only with a population parameter (such as μ), not a sample statistic (such as $\bar{x}$). The following statements would *not* be appropriate:

$$H_0: \bar{x} = 56 \text{ seconds}$$
$$H_1: \bar{x} \neq 56 \text{ seconds}$$

These are not appropriate because we can calculate the sample mean or sample proportion. Therefore, there is no need to perform a hypothesis test to make a statement about sample statistics. The purpose of hypothesis statements is to draw a conclusion about the population parameters for which we do not have complete knowledge.

Often, hypothesis testing is performed by researchers who want to prove that their discoveries are an improvement over current products or procedures. Suppose Edalight Company, a producer of CFL bulbs, claims that a new bulb it has developed has an average lifetime that exceeds the current industry average of 8,000 hours. To test this claim, Edalight would set up this hypothesis test as follows:

$$H_0: \mu \leq 8{,}000 \text{ hours (status quo)}$$
$$H_1: \mu > 8{,}000 \text{ hours (manufacturer's claim)}$$

Note that the alternative hypothesis was used to represent the claim that Edalight wants to prove statistically. Because of this, the alternative hypothesis is also known as the research hypothesis. It represents the position the researcher wants to establish. The 8,000-hour average, which is presumed to be true prior to Edalight's new product, is considered the status quo and is assigned to the null hypothesis.

Notice that, even though the status quo states that the average bulb life is equal to 8,000 hours, we write the null hypothesis as $H_0: \mu \leq 8{,}000$ rather than $H_0: \mu = 8{,}000$. Quite honestly, either statement would be acceptable. In this text, I chose to use the $\leq$ convention. However, some textbooks use the $=$ convention. To each his own.

Table 9.1 shows the three valid combinations of the null and alternative hypotheses using the claim that we are testing from the *Wall Street Journal* article as an example.

Notice that the equal sign is always associated with the null hypothesis and is never seen in the alternative hypothesis.

TABLE 9.1 | VALID COMBINATIONS FOR THE NULL AND ALTERNATIVE HYPOTHESES: WALL STREET JOURNAL EXAMPLE

NULL	$H_0: \mu = 56$	$H_0: \mu \geq 56$	$H_0: \mu \leq 56$
ALTERNATIVE	$H_1: \mu \neq 56$	$H_1: \mu < 56$	$H_1: \mu > 56$

The alternative hypothesis (H_1) is associated only with the signs $\neq$, $<$, and $>$. As a result, the null hypothesis (H_0) is only expressed in terms of $=$, $\geq$, and $\leq$.

Two-Tail Hypothesis Tests

Two-tail hypothesis test. A test in which the alternative hypothesis is expressed as $\neq$.

A **two-tail hypothesis test** is used whenever the alternative hypothesis is expressed as $\neq$. Our *Wall Street Journal* example has the following null and alternative hypotheses:

$$H_0: \mu = 56$$
$$H_1: \mu \neq 56$$

This is considered a two-tail test because the alternative hypothesis is stated as $H_1: \mu \neq 56$. We are making the assumption here that $\mu = 56$ unless our sample mean is a lot higher or a lot lower than 56. This test is shown graphically in Figure 9.1.

FIGURE 9.1
An Example of a Two-Tail Hypothesis Test

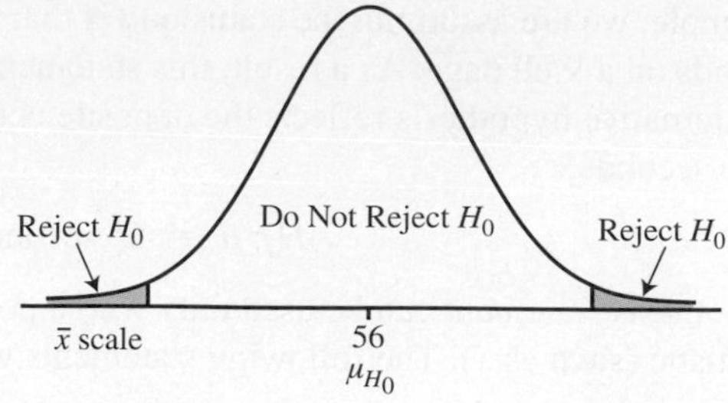

The curve in Figure 9.1 represents the sampling distribution of the mean for the number of seconds an American looks at a Web page. The mean of the population, which is assumed to be 56 seconds according to the null hypothesis, is the mean of the sampling distribution and is designated by μ_{H_0}.

The procedure for a two-tail hypothesis test is as follows:

- Collect a sample of size n, and calculate the sample mean. For this example, our sample would be used to calculate the mean viewing time per Web page.
- Plot the sample mean on the x-axis of the sampling distribution curve shown in Figure 9.1.
- If the sample mean falls within the white region in Figure 9.1, we do not reject H_0. That is, we do not have enough evidence to support H_1, the alternative hypothesis, which states that the population mean is not equal to 56 seconds.
- If the sample mean falls in either shaded region, otherwise known as the rejection regions, we reject H_0. That is, we have enough evidence to support H_1, which results in our belief that the true population mean is not equal to 56 seconds.

Because there are two rejection regions in Figure 9.1, we have a two-tail hypothesis test. We will discuss how to determine the boundaries for the rejection regions shortly.

One-Tail Hypothesis Tests

The **one-tail hypothesis test** is used when the alternative hypothesis is stated as $<$ or $>$.

A **one-tail hypothesis test** involves the alternative hypothesis stated as $<$ or $>$. Edalight Company's claim that its new CFL bulb has an average lifetime that *exceeds* the current industry average lends itself to a one-tail hypothesis test. Recall that the company claims that their new bulb's average lifetime exceeds 8,000 hours. The null and alternate hypothesis can therefore be expressed as follows:

$$H_0: \mu \leq 8{,}000 \text{ hours}$$
$$H_1: \mu > 8{,}000 \text{ hours}$$

This test is shown graphically in Figure 9.2.

FIGURE 9.2
An Example of a One-Tail (Upper Tail) Hypothesis Test

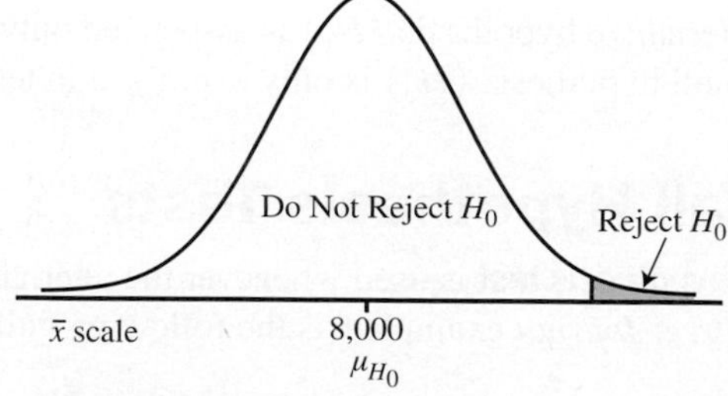

Here, there is only one rejection region, which is the shaded area on the right tail of the sampling distribution. We follow the same procedure outlined for the two-tail test and plot the sample mean, which represents the average life of a new CFL bulb. Two possible scenarios exist:

1. If the sample mean falls within the white region, we do not reject H_0. That is, we do not have enough evidence to support H_1, the alternative hypothesis. Our conclusion is that we have no evidence that the average life of the new CFL bulb exceeds 8,000 hours.
2. If the sample mean falls in the shaded region, we reject H_0. That is, we have enough evidence to support H_1, which supports Edalight's claim that the average life of the new CFL bulb exceeds 8,000 hours.

The Logic of Hypothesis Testing

The only two statements we can make about the null hypothesis are that we

- reject it.
- do not reject it.

The null hypothesis can never be accepted. The only two options available are to (1) reject the null hypothesis or (2) fail to reject the null.

The reason we are limited to these two conclusions is because hypothesis testing relies on "proof by contradiction." That is, we assume the null hypothesis is true and attempt to disprove it by finding evidence to the contrary. By using this strategy, we can only conclude that the null hypothesis *may* be true, but we do not have enough evidence to say the null hypothesis *is* true with certainty. Because of this limitation, we can never accept the null hypothesis. The most we can say is that we do not have enough evidence to reject the null.

We can use the analogy of the legal system to illustrate this point further. Because the U.S. court system assumes a person is innocent until proven guilty, the hypothesis test is formulated as follows:

$$H_0\text{: The defendant is innocent (status quo)}$$
$$H_1\text{: The defendant is guilty}$$

The two conclusions the court system is capable of are as follows:

1. Reject the null hypothesis → The defendant is guilty
2. Fail to reject the null hypothesis → The defendant is not guilty

If the members of a jury find a defendant "not guilty," they are not saying the defendant is innocent. Rather, they are saying that there is not enough evidence to prove guilt. A "not guilty" verdict is failing to reject the null hypothesis. Concluding that a defendant is innocent is a much stronger statement than determining that the defendant is not guilty. However, the court system does not have the capability to conclude innocence, which would be accepting the null hypothesis. In conclusion, there are two things you should *never* do:

1. Run with a sharp object in your hand. (Once a parent, always a parent.)
2. Accept the null hypothesis.

Summary on Setting up Hypothesis Statements

I need to be honest with you—setting up the appropriate hypothesis statements is a topic with which many students struggle. In an effort to help you with this important procedure, I have provided the following points to summarize what we have learned so far about hypothesis tests.

If the purpose of the hypothesis test is to establish that a population parameter is equal to or not equal to a specific value, the null hypothesis is always assigned to the equality statement, leaving the "not equal to" statement for the alternative hypothesis. For example, suppose the White House would like to test the hypothesis that President Obama's approval rating will change from the previous month's 48% based on how he has handled the most recent debt crisis. Here, we are testing for the population proportion, p, which results in the following hypothesis statement:

$$H_0: p = 0.48$$
$$H_1: p \neq 0.48$$

Because the alternative hypothesis does not specify a particular direction (the White House is only testing for a *change* in approval rating rather than specifically for an increase or decrease), we are employing a two-tail test.

Hypothesis tests are frequently used in research studies. Normally, researchers would like to prove that something they developed is different from the status quo. In this situation, the status quo is assigned to the null hypothesis, and the condition the researcher hopes to prove is left to the alternative (or research) hypothesis. For instance, suppose the average battery life of a 14-in. laptop is 3.0 hours. Our company has just developed a new type of battery that it claims has an average battery life greater than 3.0 hours. To test this claim, we use the following hypothesis statements:

This is an upper (right) tail hypothesis test because the alternative hypothesis is stated as >3.0.

$$H_0: \mu \leq 3.0 \text{ hours (status quo)}$$
$$H_1: \mu > 3.0 \text{ hours (research claim)}$$

In this example, we are interested in specifically testing for an *increase* in battery life, which dictates the use of a one-tail hypothesis test. Here, merely claiming that the battery life is different from 3.0 hours (a two-tail test) would not be very impressive to consumers!

Quality control is another area that has benefited from hypothesis testing. Here, the *null hypothesis* refers to a process operating in a satisfactory state, which would be the status quo. The alternative hypothesis takes the stance that the process is not behaving as it should and needs some sort of attention. For example, suppose a glass manufacturer has a particular product whose average thickness needs to be 4.0 mm. If the average is more *or* less than 4.0 mm, the product is not acceptable. We can use the following hypothesis statements for this application:

This is a two-tail hypothesis test because the alternative hypothesis is stated as not equal to 4.0.

$$H_0: \mu = 4.0 \text{ mm (process is satisfactory)}$$
$$H_1: \mu \neq 4.0 \text{ mm (process is not satisfactory)}$$

Because a process average either greater or less than 4.0 mm is unacceptable, this is an example of a two-tail test.

Hypothesis testing can also be used in an attempt to prove a particular point of view. As a user of hypothesis testing, you would assign the alternative hypothesis to establish the point of view you favor. For example, Roger Goodell, the commissioner of the NFL, has claimed that the majority of fans favor expanding the NFL schedule from 16 to 18 regular season games. The NFL players' union, which is not in favor of this expansion, would like to refute the commissioner's claim with the following hypothesis test:

This is a lower (left) tail hypothesis test because the alternative hypothesis is stated as <0.50.

$$H_0: p \geq 0.50 \text{ (the commissioner's claim)}$$
$$H_1: p < 0.50 \text{ (the position the players union wants to establish)}$$

As you can see, this is also an example of a one-tail test. The players' union wants specifically to establish that the proportion of NFL fans who favor an 18-game schedule is *less than* 50%.

To summarize, notice that in all of the above examples, the focus is placed on establishing the alternative hypothesis. I recommend starting with stating the alternative hypothesis and then setting up the null hypothesis in the opposite direction. Because setting up the statements is such an important step in hypothesis testing, my point of view is that it would be really beneficial for you to try this next Your Turn problem. I shouldn't need a hypothesis test to prove it!

YOUR TURN #1

Identify the null and alternative hypotheses for each of the following scenarios:

1. In an effort to increase the number of people who file their returns electronically, suppose the Internal Revenue Service (IRS) launches a promotional campaign on the benefits of this filing method. As a follow-up to the campaign's effectiveness, the IRS would like to test if the proportion of people who plan to be "e-filers" for the next tax season will exceed 70%.
2. To plan properly for equipment and services during the upcoming year, Comcast would like to test the hypothesis that the average number of televisions in the homes of its customers is equal to 2.9.
3. The federal government would like to determine the effectiveness of a recent tax-break program for first-time home buyers. Prior to the tax break, the average time period a house was on the market was 60 days. The government would like to test the claim that the current average time on the market is less than 60 days.

Answers can be found on ▶ **page 432**

Now that we have covered the basics of hypothesis testing, we need to consider errors that can occur due to sampling.

Recall that in Chapter 7 we defined sampling error as the difference between the sample mean and the mean of the population from which it is drawn.

The Difference Between Type I and Type II Errors

Remember that the purpose of a hypothesis test is to verify the validity of a claim about a population based on a single sample. Because we are relying on a sample, we expose ourselves to the risk that our conclusions about the population will be wrong because of a sampling error. For example, perhaps the null hypothesis is true, but we have been unfortunate enough to draw a sample that's not really representative of the population. Or, perhaps the sample is too small or the survey poorly designed. There are many circumstances that can result in a faulty conclusion.

Let's use the previous CFL bulb example to illustrate these errors. Suppose that Edalight's sample falls within the "Reject H_0" region of Figure 9.2. That is, according to the sample, the average life of the new bulb exceeded 8,000 hours. But what if the true population mean is actually much less than 8,000 hours? This can occur primarily because of sampling error, which I discussed in Chapter 7. The type of error where we reject H_0 when, in reality, it's true is known as a **Type I error**. The probability of making a Type I error is known as α. This is the same α that we introduced in Chapter 8, which we defined as the **level of significance**. As the tester of a hypothesis, you decide on the risk level, or α, you are willing to accept if you incorrectly reject the null hypothesis.

A **Type I error** occurs when the null hypothesis is rejected when, in reality, it is true. The probability of making a Type I error is known as α, the **level of significance**.

Generally, those performing hypothesis tests select values of α ranging from 0.01 (1%) to 0.10 (10%). Which level you select depends on how critical it is that you don't make a Type I error. For example, if Edalight is very concerned about making the mistake of claiming its CFL bulb has an average life that exceeds 8,000 hours when, in reality, it doesn't, it would choose a smaller value of α, such as 0.01. Whatever value of α is chosen, it should be determined before the data are gathered.

We also can experience another type of error with hypothesis testing. Let's say the CFL bulb sample falls within the "Do Not Reject H_0" region of Figure 9.2. That is, according to the sample, there is no evidence that the average life of the new CFL bulbs exceeds 8,000 hours. But what if the true population mean is actually much more than 8,000 hours? The type of error where we do not reject H_0 when, in reality, it's false is known as a **Type II error**. The probability of making a Type II error is known as β. As we will see later in the chapter, the value of β will depend on the value of α that is selected.

A **Type II error** occurs when we fail to reject the null hypothesis when, in reality, it is not true. The probability of making a Type II error is known as β.

Table 9.2 summarizes the two types of hypothesis errors.

TABLE 9.2 | DECISION RULES FOR THE TWO TYPES OF HYPOTHESIS TEST ERRORS

	H_0 IS ACTUALLY TRUE	H_0 IS ACTUALLY FALSE
We Reject H_0	Type I Error $P(\text{Type I Error}) = \alpha$	Correct Outcome
We Do Not Reject H_0	Correct Outcome	Type II Error $P(\text{Type II Error}) = \beta$

Let's return to our glass manufacturer example to highlight the difference between Type I and Type II errors. Recall that it produces a glass product whose average thickness needs to be 4.0 mm. If the process average is more or less than 4.0 mm, the product is not acceptable. We used the following hypothesis statements for this application:

$$H_0\colon \mu = 4.0 \text{ mm (process is satisfactory)}$$
$$H_1\colon \mu \neq 4.0 \text{ mm (process is not satisfactory)}$$

A Type I error is known as the **producer's risk** because, when it occurs in quality control settings, the producer is looking for a problem in its process that does not exist.

A Type II error is known as the **consumer's risk** because, when it occurs in quality control settings, the customer is getting a product from a process that is not performing properly.

A Type I error would occur if we reject the null hypothesis and conclude that there is a problem with the process, when in fact the process is working fine. In other words, we conclude that the average glass thickness is not equal to 4.0 mm when, in reality, it is equal to 4.0 mm. We call a Type I error the **producer's risk** because, when it occurs in quality control settings, the producer is looking for a problem in its process that does not exist. That is, the producer is rejecting a good product.

A Type II error would occur if we failed to reject the null hypothesis and concluded that the process was working fine when, in reality, the process was having a bad day. Here, we concluded that the average glass thickness was equal to 4.0 mm when it actually was not. We call a Type II error the **consumer's risk** because, when it occurs in quality control settings, the customer is getting product from a process that is not performing properly.

With hypothesis testing, we decide on a value for α before we collect the sample. Once α has been set, the value of β can be calculated, a method we will discuss later in this chapter. Ideally, we would like the values of α and β to be as small as possible. However, for a given sample size, reducing the value of α will result in an increase in the value of β. The opposite also holds true. The only way to reduce both α and β simultaneously is to increase the sample size. Once the sample size has been increased to the size of the population, the values of α and β will approach 0. However, as we discussed in Chapter 7, this is not a recommended strategy because measuring the entire population is either impractical or too costly.

9.2 Hypothesis Testing for the Population Mean When σ Is Known

The first case of hypothesis testing involves a one-tail test where the population standard deviation, σ, is known. As you learned in Chapter 8, this value is often unknown but can be estimated. We'll address such a case in a later section of this chapter.

When σ is known, we need to consider two different scenarios:

1. If our sample size is small $(n < 30)$, to conduct a hypothesis test the population must follow the normal distribution.
2. If our sample size is large $(n \geq 30)$, we know from the Central Limit Theorem that the sampling distribution follows the normal distribution. When this is the scenario, we have no restrictions on the population distribution.

In the following sections, we'll examine both a one-tail hypothesis test and a two-tail hypothesis test.

An Example of a One-Tail Hypothesis Test for the Population Mean (When σ Is Known)

To illustrate a one-tail hypothesis test when the standard deviation of a population is known, I'll use Edalight's claim that its new CFL bulb has an average life that exceeds 8,000 hours. Suppose the average life of a random sample of 36 of the new bulbs is 8,120 hours. Assume that the population standard deviation for the life of CFL bulbs is 500 hours. The following seven steps describe the hypothesis testing procedure.

Remember, a one-tail hypothesis test is used when the alternative hypothesis is stated as < or >.

Step 1: Identify the null and alternative hypotheses.

$$H_0: \mu \leq 8{,}000 \text{ hours}$$
$$H_1: \mu > 8{,}000 \text{ hours}$$

Step 2: Set a value for the significance level, α.

As mentioned earlier, the level of significance represents the probability of making a Type I error. A Type I error occurs when we reject the null hypothesis but it is actually true. For this example, I'll set $\alpha = 0.05$, which is a common value used in hypothesis testing. Later, I'll discuss the impact this choice has on the results.

If our sample size is 30 or more, we know from the Central Limit Theorem (as we learned in Chapter 7) that the sample mean follows the normal distribution regardless of the population's probability distribution.

Step 3: Determine the appropriate critical value.

Because the standard deviation of the population is known, the z-score is the appropriate choice of a critical value to use in this case. This is consistent with the method used in Chapter 8 to construct confidence intervals under similar conditions. The critical z-score identifies the rejection regions that were shown in Figures 9.1 and 9.2.

Because this is a one-tail test and the alternative hypothesis is $H_1: \mu > 8{,}000$, the entire area for $\alpha = 0.05$ is placed on the right side (upper tail) of the sampling distribution and is shown in the shaded area in Figure 9.3. We find the critical z-score, z_α, by looking for the closest value to 0.95 in Table 4 in Appendix A. This value is found in the *1.6* row, halfway between 0.9495 in the *0.04* column and 0.9505 in the *0.05* column, which tells us that $z_\alpha = 1.645$.

FIGURE 9.3
The Critical z-Score for a One-Tail Hypothesis Test When $\alpha = 0.05$

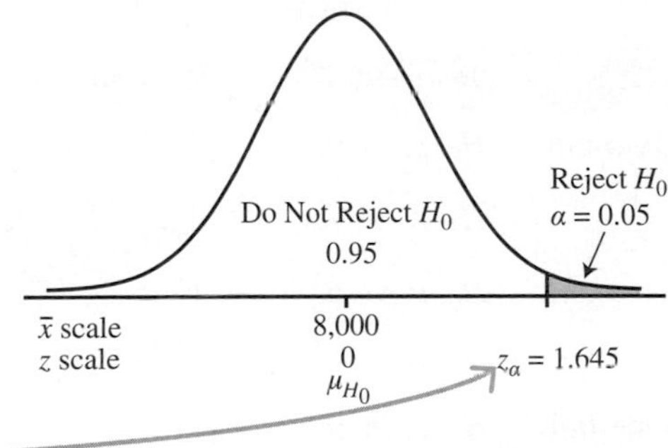

I use the notation z_α to refer to the critical z-score for a one-tail hypothesis test because the area associated with α is on one side of the distribution.

Step 4: Calculate the appropriate test statistic.

Because σ is known, the appropriate test statistic is the z-test statistic, which was introduced in Chapter 8. The z-test statistic, $z_{\bar{x}}$, represents the number of standard deviations between the sample mean and μ_{H_0}, the population mean in the null hypothesis scenario. By contrast, the critical z-score, z_α determined in Step 3, is based on the significance level, α, and determines the boundary for the rejection region. The z-test statistic can be found using Equation 9.1.

Formula 9.1 for the z-Test Statistic for a Hypothesis Test for the Population Mean (When σ Is Known)

$$z_{\bar{x}} = \frac{\bar{x} - \mu_{H_0}}{\dfrac{\sigma}{\sqrt{n}}}$$

where

$z_{\bar{x}}$ = The z-test statistic
$\bar{x}$ = The sample mean
μ_{H_0} = The mean of the sampling distribution, which is assumed to be true for the null hypothesis
σ = The standard deviation of the population
n = The sample size

Using Equation 9.1 for our CFL bulb example, our z-test statistic is as follows:

$$z_{\bar{x}} = \frac{\bar{x} - \mu_{H_0}}{\dfrac{\sigma}{\sqrt{n}}} = \frac{8{,}120 - 8{,}000}{\dfrac{500}{\sqrt{36}}} = \frac{120}{83.33} = 1.44$$

Step 5: Compare the z-test statistic ($z_{\bar{x}}$) with the critical z-score (z_α).

This comparison is used to decide whether to reject or fail to reject the null hypothesis. To do so, we use the decision rules shown in Table 9.3. The term $|z_{\alpha/2}|$ means the "absolute value of the critical z-score." In other words, if the value is negative, it is made positive. So, for instance, $|-1.645|$ simply equals 1.645. Likewise, the term $|z_{\bar{x}}|$ means the "absolute value of the z-test statistic." So, for instance, $|1.44|$ simply equals 1.44.

TABLE 9.3 | Decision Rules for Hypothesis Tests When Comparing the z-Test Statistic ($z_{\bar{x}}$) with the Critical z-Score (z_α)

TEST	HYPOTHESIS	CONDITION		CONCLUSION
Two-tail	$H_0: \mu = \mu_0$	$|z_{\bar{x}}| > |z_{\alpha/2}|$	→	Reject H_0
	$H_1: \mu \neq \mu_0$	$|z_{\bar{x}}| \leq |z_{\alpha/2}|$	→	Do not reject H_0
One-tail	$H_0: \mu \leq \mu_0$	$z_{\bar{x}} > z_\alpha$	→	Reject H_0
(upper)	$H_1: \mu > \mu_0$	$z_{\bar{x}} \leq z_\alpha$	→	Do not reject H_0
One-tail	$H_0: \mu \geq \mu_0$	$z_{\bar{x}} < -z_\alpha$	→	Reject H_0
(lower)	$H_1: \mu < \mu_0$	$z_{\bar{x}} \geq -z_\alpha$	→	Do not reject H_0

Be sure to distinguish between the z-test statistic and the critical z-score. The z-test statistic, $z_{\bar{x}}$, represents the number of standard deviations between the sample mean and μ_{H_0}, the population mean according to the null hypothesis. The critical z-score, z_α, is based on the significance level, α, and determines the boundary for the rejection region.

In our CFL bulb example, which is a one-tail (upper) test, $z_{\bar{x}} = 1.44$ and $z_\alpha = 1.645$. Because $1.44 \leq 1.645$, we come to the "do not reject H_0" conclusion (highlighted in yellow in Table 9.3). Figure 9.4 illustrates this finding.

FIGURE 9.4
Comparing the z-Test Statistic with the Critical z-Score

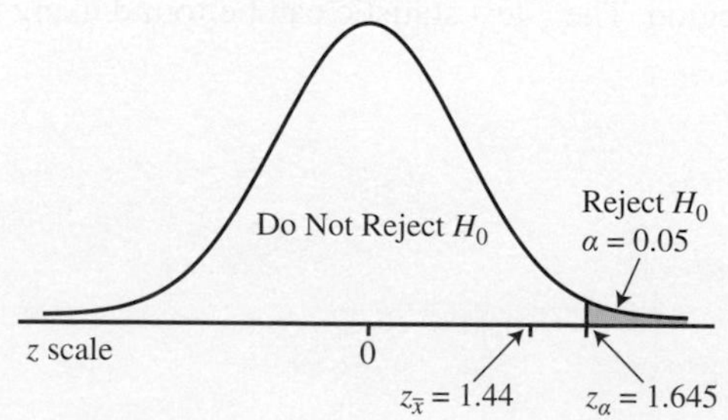

Step 6: (Final Step): State your conclusions.

Now, for the most important step—we need to state our conclusions. Sadly, I have students who make wonderful progress getting to this point only to stumble at the finish line by making an erroneous statement. It's best to go back to step 1 and reread the original hypotheses. In this example, the null hypothesis (H_0) took the position that the new CFL bulbs have an average life of 8,000 hours or less. By failing to reject the null hypothesis, the correct conclusion is as follows:

I recommend rereading the hypothesis statements before drawing your final conclusions.

"According to our sample of 36 new CFL bulbs, we do not have enough evidence to support Edalight's claim that the average life of these bulbs exceeds 8,000 hours."

Because we cannot accept the null hypothesis, we are not saying that the average life of the bulbs is actually 8,000 hours or less. Our evidence indicates that it *might* be 8,000 hours or less, but we do not have enough evidence to confirm this with any degree of certainty.

I'll also have students incorrectly claim that, because the sample mean is 8,120 hours, we have enough evidence to conclude that we can reject the null hypothesis and validate Edalight's claim that the average life is greater than 8,000 hours. However, we must remember that this mean is based on a sample of 36 bulbs and is subject to sampling error. In order to have enough evidence to reject the null hypothesis with a sample size of 36 bulbs, we would need a sample mean greater than 8,120 hours.

Just because this sample mean is greater than the hypothesized mean of 8,000 hours, it does not allow us to reject the null hypothesis.

I also have one last reminder concerning sample size. Because we sampled more than 30 bulbs, the Central Limit Theorem allows us to perform this procedure with no restrictions on the population distribution. Had our sample size been less than 30, we would have needed the population to be normally distributed to perform this procedure.

If your instructor is anything like me, you can bet on getting an exam question similar to the next Your Turn problem. So do yourself a favor and spend some time practicing your hypothesis testing skills before moving on to the next topic.

YOUR TURN #2

Lindsay is the manager at a local Ruby Tuesday restaurant and has implemented changes to her operation to reduce the average wait time for a table between 6:00 P.M. and 8:00 P.M. on Saturday night to less than 20 minutes. A random sample of 45 wait times on Saturday night had a mean of 18.3 minutes. Lindsay knows from past experience that the standard deviation of wait times is 5.0 minutes. Follow the steps in the previous section to determine if Lindsay's changes have reduced average wait time to less than 20 minutes using $\alpha = 0.05$.

Hint: Because this is a one-tail (lower) test, the rejection region is on the left side of the sampling distribution. For $\alpha = 0.05$, the critical z-score is therefore $-z_\alpha = -1.645$. You're welcome!

Answer can be found on ▶ **page 432**

The *p*-Value Approach to Hypothesis Testing: One-Tail Tests

In the previous section, we learned how to use the critical z-score to draw a conclusion for the hypothesis test. This section introduces another approach to deciding whether to reject the null hypothesis. The ***p*-value** is the probability of observing a sample mean at least as extreme as the one selected for the hypothesis test, assuming the null hypothesis is true. For this reason, the p-value is sometimes referred to as the **observed level of significance**. I know this may sound like a lot of mumbo jumbo right now, but an illustration using our CFL bulb example will help make this concept clearer.

The **observed level of significance** is the probability of observing a sample mean at least as extreme as the one selected for the hypothesis test, assuming the null hypothesis is true. It is also known as the ***p*-value**.

The average life of a bulb in our sample was 8,120 hours, which we saw represented a z-test statistic of $z_{\bar{x}} = 1.44$ using Equation 9.1. The p-value represents the probability of obtaining a sample mean of 8,120 hours or greater if the true population mean is 8,000 hours. If this probability is very low, then it is doubtful that the true population mean really is 8,000 hours. The *p*-value is therefore as follows:

$$P(\bar{x} > 8{,}120) = P(z_{\bar{x}} > 1.44) = 1.0 - 0.9251 = 0.0749$$

This *p*-value is the shaded area in the right tail of the sampling distribution shown in Figure 9.5.

FIGURE 9.5
Using the *p*-Value Approach for a One-Tail Hypothesis Test

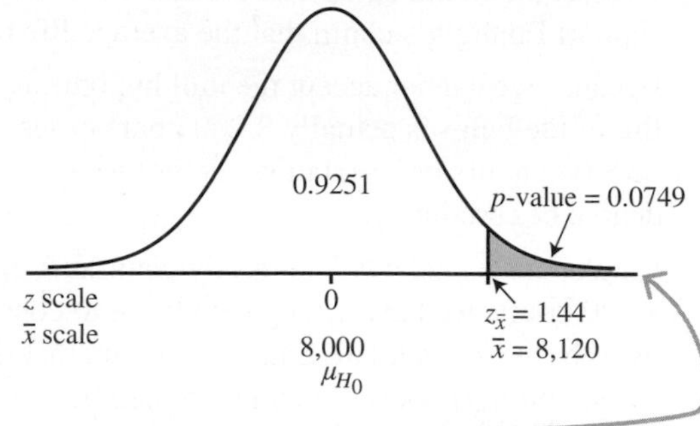

Because this is a one-tail (upper) test, the *p*-value is the area to the right of the test statistic, $z_{\bar{x}}$.

Excel's NORM.S.DIST function that we discussed in Chapter 6 can also be used to determine the *p*-value. Recall that this function has the following characteristics:

=NORM.S.DIST(*z*, cumulative)

When we set the value *z* to the test statistic and cumulative = TRUE, this function returns the area to the left of the test statistic as follows:

=NORM.S.DIST(1.44, TRUE) = 0.9251

Because our *p*-value is the area to the right of the test statistic, we subtract 0.9251 from 1.0 as seen in Figure 9.5.

What do we do with this value? We can draw our hypothesis conclusion by comparing the *p*-value with α, the level of significance, as shown in Table 9.4.

TABLE 9.4 | Decision Rules for Hypothesis Tests Using the p-Value

CONDITION		CONCLUSION
p-Value $\geq \alpha$	→	Do not reject H_0
p-Value $< \alpha$	→	Reject H_0

If the *p*-value is less than α, there is little chance of observing the sample mean from the population on which it is based if the null hypothesis were actually true. We therefore reject the null hypothesis under this condition. The opposite conclusion is made when the *p*-value equals or exceeds the value of α. In our CFL bulb example, the *p*-value = 0.0749 and $\alpha = 0.05$. Because the *p*-value exceeds the value of α, our conclusion is "do not reject H_0," which is consistent with our findings in the previous section. The *p*-value approach should always match the results you get using the critical *z*-score previously discussed.

The *p*-value can also be described as the confidence you have that your null hypothesis is correct.

Another way to describe this *p*-value is to say, in a very academic tone, "Our results are significant at the 0.0749 level." This means that as long as the value of α is 0.0749 or larger, we will reject H_0. Most researchers report *p*-values when summarizing their findings. The smaller the *p*-value, the more confident researchers will be about rejecting the null hypothesis, which will make them very happy. Remember, the alternative hypothesis usually supports the claim the researcher is attempting to establish. Under these conditions, a rejection of the null hypothesis is a successful research result. Low *p*-values are a thing of beauty in this type of setting.

The p-value we just calculated pertains to a one-tail test. Calculating the p-value for a two-tail hypothesis test is slightly different-I'll show you how to do that in the next section. Also note that we can calculate only the p-value directly when we are using z-scores with the normal distribution. We need a slightly different approach when using the Student's t-distribution for our hypothesis test, which is a topic we'll discuss later in this chapter.

In this section, I have shown you two approaches to choose from in order to decide whether to reject the null hypothesis:

1. The p-value approach
2. The critical value approach

Before I turn you loose on the next Your Turn problem, let's quickly summarize how we applied hypothesis testing to our CFL bulb example:

Step 1: Identify the null and alternative hypotheses.

$$H_0: \mu \leq 8{,}000 \text{ hours}$$
$$H_1: \mu > 8{,}000 \text{ hours}$$

Step 2: Set a value for the significance level, α.
In our CFL bulb example, $\alpha = 0.05$.

Step 3: Determine the appropriate critical value.
For a one-tail test with $\alpha = 0.05$, $z_\alpha = 1.645$.

Step 4: Calculate the appropriate test statistic.
Using Equation 9.1,

$$z_{\bar{x}} = \frac{\bar{x} - \mu_{H_0}}{\dfrac{\sigma}{\sqrt{n}}} = \frac{8{,}120 - 8{,}000}{\dfrac{500}{\sqrt{36}}} = \frac{120}{83.33} = 1.44$$

Step 5: Compare the z-test statistic ($z_{\bar{x}}$) with the critical z-score (z_α).
Because $1.44 < 1.645$, we come to the "do not reject H_0" conclusion.

Note: The p-value approach can be used in place of Step 5. The p-value for the CFL bulb example is calculated as follows:

$$P(\bar{x} > 8{,}120) = P(z_{\bar{x}} > 1.44) = 1.0 - 0.9251 = 0.0749$$

Or because $0.0749 > 0.05$ (our value for α), we come to the "do not reject H_0" conclusion.

Step 6: State your conclusions.
According to our sample of 36 new CFL bulbs, we do not have enough evidence to support Edalight's claim that the average life of these bulbs exceeds 8,000 hours.

The next Your Turn problem will give you a chance to try this procedure using our Ruby Tuesday problem.

YOUR TURN #3

Re-solve the Ruby Tuesday problem described in Your Turn #2 using the p-value approach to test Lindsay's efforts to conclude that the average wait time for a table is less than 20 minutes using $\alpha = 0.05$.

Hint: Because this is a one-tail (lower) test, the p-value is the area to the *left* of the test statistic, $z_{\bar{x}}$.

Answer can be found on ▶ **page 432**

An Example of a Two-Tail Hypothesis Test for the Population Mean (When σ Is Known)

Because we are investigating if the amount of time equals 56 seconds (not more than or less than 56 seconds), this is a two-tail test.

To illustrate a two-tail hypothesis test when σ is known, I'll use the statistic in the *Wall Street Journal* article claiming that the average time an American spends looking at a Web page is 56 seconds. A researcher at a local university would like to test this claim using a hypothesis test. Suppose a sample of 60 Internet users spent an average of 47.3 seconds looking at a Web page. Assume that the standard deviation for this population is estimated to be 32 seconds based on previous research.

We will apply the six steps outlined in the previous section to conduct this two-tail hypothesis test.

Step 1: Identify the null and alternative hypotheses.

$$H_0: \mu = 56$$
$$H_1: \mu \neq 56$$

Remember, a two-tail hypothesis test is used when the alternative hypothesis is being stated as $\neq$. Because we are testing the hypothesis that the population mean equals 56 seconds, this premise is assigned as the null hypothesis.

Step 2: Set a value for the significance level, α.

For this example, we set $\alpha = 0.05$. Remember, this value needs to be chosen by the person performing the hypothesis test at the beginning of the procedure.

Step 3: Determine the appropriate critical values.

Because this is a two-tail test, the area for $\alpha = 0.05$ is split evenly between the right and left sides of the sampling distribution; it is shown as the shaded areas in Figure 9.6. Because we are splitting the area for α into two equal parts, I'll refer to the corresponding critical z-score as $z_{\alpha/2}$ (rather than z_α for a one-tail test). Each rejection region in this figure has an area equal to $0.05/2 = 0.025$. That leaves an area of 0.95 in the white region labeled "Do Not Reject H_0." A two-tail hypothesis test has two critical z-scores, one on each end of the sampling distribution. We find the critical z-score, $-z_{\alpha/2}$, on the left side of the distribution by looking for the closest value to 0.025 in Table 3 from Appendix A. You'll find 0.025 in the *−1.9* row and *0.06* column, which tells us that $-z_{\alpha/2} = -1.96$ on the left side of the distribution. Because the sampling distribution is symmetrical, the critical z-score on the right side of the distribution also equals 1.96, as you can see in Figure 9.6.

FIGURE 9.6
The Critical z-Score for a Two-Tail Hypothesis Test When $\alpha = 0.05$

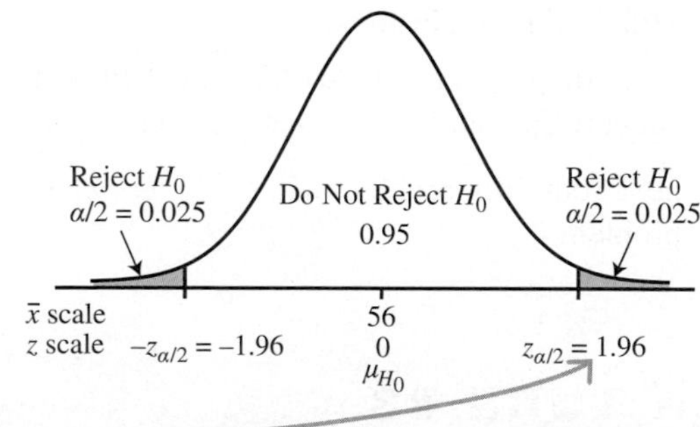

The total area to the left of $z_{\alpha/2}$ is $0.95 + 0.025 = 0.975$.

Step 4: Calculate the appropriate test statistic.

Using Equation 9.1 with our Web page example, our z-test statistic is calculated as follows:

$$\bar{x} = 47.3 \quad \mu_{H_0} = 56 \quad \sigma = 32 \quad n = 60$$

$$z_{\bar{x}} = \frac{\bar{x} - \mu_{H_0}}{\frac{\sigma}{\sqrt{n}}} = \frac{47.3 - 56}{\frac{32}{\sqrt{60}}} = \frac{-8.7}{4.13} = -2.11$$

Step 5: Compare the z-test statistic $(z_{\bar{x}})$ with the critical z-score $(z_{\alpha/2})$.

Because our z-test statistic, $z_{\bar{x}}$, is negative (-2.11), we use the rejection region on the left side of the sampling distribution where the critical z-score is $-z_{\alpha/2} = -1.96$. Taking the absolute value of each, we have $|z_{\bar{x}}| = 2.11$, which is greater than $|z_{\alpha/2}| = 1.96$. According to Table 9.3, we reject the null hypothesis. Figure 9.7 illustrates this finding.

FIGURE 9.7
Comparing the z-Test Statistic with the Critical z-Score in a Two-Tail Hypothesis Test

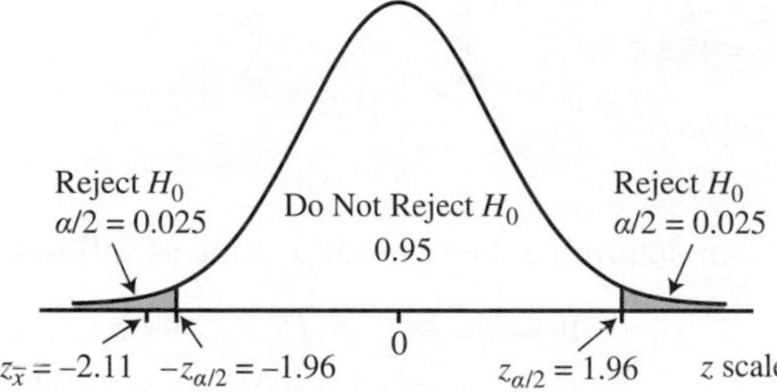

Step 6: State your conclusions.

Important reminder: When performing a hypothesis test using a sample from the population, we would never have enough evidence to conclude that the population mean equals 56 seconds because this would be accepting the null hypothesis which is *never* allowed. We have only two options for our hypothesis test conclusions:

1. Reject the null hypothesis and conclude that the average time spent looking at a Web page is not equal to 56 seconds.
2. Fail to reject the null hypothesis and conclude that we do not have enough evidence to state that the average time spent looking at a Web page is not equal to 56 seconds.

Because we are rejecting the null hypothesis in this example, we have support for the alternative hypothesis that claims the average time spent looking at a Web page is not equal to 56 seconds.

The following Your Turn problem gives you a chance to tackle a two-tail hypothesis.

YOUR TURN #4

Kellogg's has a process for filling boxes of Frosted Flakes cereal with 18 ounces of product when it is operating properly. Too much product in the box is wasteful to Kellogg's, whereas too little product can lead to customer complaints. To determine if the filling process is performing as it should, a random sample of 40 boxes was examined, and the average weight of a box was found to be 18.06 ounces. Historically, the filling process has a standard deviation of 0.25 ounces. Follow the six steps for conducting a two-tail hypothesis test to determine if the filling process is operating properly, using $\alpha = 0.05$.

Answer can be found on ▶ **page 432**

The *p*-Value Approach to Hypothesis Testing: Two-Tail Tests

We previously defined the p-value as the probability of observing a sample mean at least as extreme as the one selected for the hypothesis test assuming the null hypothesis is true. I demonstrated the p-value approach with a one-tail test. The two-tail case is slightly different and is explained in this section using the Web page example.

In this example, our sample has an average of 47.3 seconds, which, using Equation 9.1, gave us a z-test statistic of $z_{\bar{x}} = -2.11$. Because this is a two-tail hypothesis test, the p-value is the area to the left of $z_{\bar{x}} = -2.11$ plus the area to the right of $z_{\bar{x}} = 2.11$, as shown in Figure 9.8.

FIGURE 9.8
Using the p-Value Approach for a Two-Tail Hypothesis Test

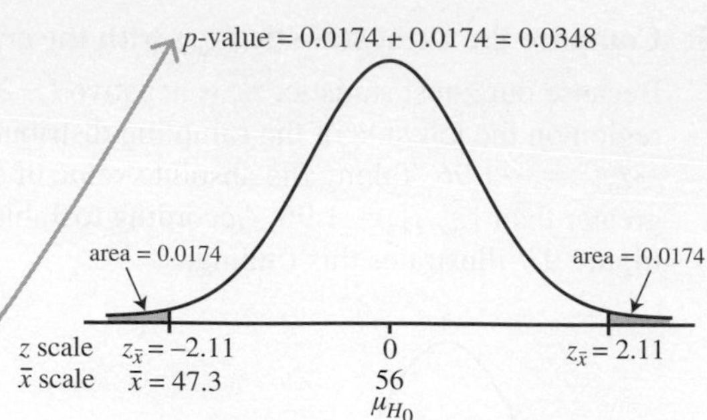

Because we have a two-tail test, the p-value is the sum of both shaded regions.

To find the area associated with $z_{\bar{x}} < -2.11$, go to Table 3 in Appendix A. This area can be found in the -2.1 row and 0.01 column (0.0174). Because we have a two-tail test, we double this area to obtain our p-value.

We can determine the two-tail p-value as follows:

$$p\text{-value} = 2 \times P(\bar{x} < 47.3) = 2 \times P(z_{\bar{x}} < -2.11)$$
$$p\text{-value} = (2)(0.0174) = 0.0348$$

Once again we can also rely on Excel's NORM.S.DIST function to help determine the p-value for our two-tail test:

=NORM.S.DIST(−2.11, TRUE) = 0.0174

Remember, this function always provides the area to the left of the test statistic which is the shaded region on the left side of Figure 9.8. To find our p-value, we still need to multiply 0.0174 by 2.

Based on our results, there is a 3.48% chance that we will collect a sample with a mean in the shaded regions in Figure 9.8 if the real population mean is 56 seconds. According to Table 9.4, because our p-value $= 0.0348$ is less than $\alpha = 0.05$, we reject the null hypothesis and conclude that the average time spent looking at a Web page is not equal to 56 seconds. Our results are significant at the 0.0348 level.

The following Your Turn problem reviews the two-tail p-value procedure by revisiting the Frosted Flakes hypothesis test.

YOUR TURN #5

Perform a hypothesis test using the p-value approach with the data from the Frosted Flakes example in Your Turn #4.

Answer can be found on ▶ **page 433**

The Role α Plays in Hypothesis Testing

For all the examples in this chapter, I have just stated a value for α, the level of significance. Remember, α represents the probability of making a Type I error, which is incorrectly rejecting the null hypothesis when, in reality, the null hypothesis is true. I'm sure you're wondering what impact changing the value of α will have on the hypothesis test. Great question!

Changing α essentially changes the critical z-score in the hypothesis test, which, in turn, changes the rejection region in the sampling distribution. Table 9.5 shows the critical z-scores (z_α or $z_{\alpha/2}$) for various values of α. These values can be found using Tables 3 and 4 in Appendix A in the manner described earlier in this chapter.

Recall that we saw the critical z-scores for a two-tail hypothesis test in Table 9.5 back in Chapter 8 when we discussed confidence intervals. That's because a confidence interval corresponds to a two-tail hypothesis test. In fact, some of the questions that we addressed in Chapter 8 were really two-tail hypothesis tests in disguise!

To demonstrate the effect that the value we choose for α has on the hypothesis test, I'll use the following example. Suppose that I am making a claim that the average grade for a

TABLE 9.5 | Critical z-Scores for Various Alphas

ALPHA (α)	TAIL	CRITICAL Z-SCORE
0.01	One	2.33
0.01	Two	2.575
0.02	One	2.05
0.02	Two	2.33
0.05	One	1.645
0.05	Two	1.96
0.10	One	1.28
0.10	Two	1.645

person using this textbook will be higher than an 87. (I'm not *really* making this claim, so don't get too excited!) I would state the hypothesis test as follows:

$$H_0: \mu \leq 87$$
$$H_1: \mu > 87$$

As a textbook author, it would be in my best interest if I could reject H_0, which would validate my claim that the average grade for a reader will be higher than 87. I can help my chances of this happening by choosing a fairly high value for α, say 0.10. Using Table 9.5, I can see this corresponds to a critical z-score of 1.28, because we are using the upper (right) tail of a one-tail hypothesis test.

To test my claim, I randomly select 32 students who used my book and determined that their average grade was 88.9. Let's say that σ, the population standard deviation, is 7.0. Using Equation 9.1, we calculate the z-test statistic as follows:

$$z_{\bar{x}} = \frac{\bar{x} - \mu_{H_0}}{\frac{\sigma}{\sqrt{n}}} = \frac{88.9 - 87}{\frac{7.0}{\sqrt{32}}} = \frac{1.9}{1.24} = 1.53$$

According to Figure 9.9, I have achieved my goal of rejecting H_0 because the z-test statistic is within the shaded region. My book appears to have done the trick!

FIGURE 9.9
A One-Tail Hypothesis Test When $\alpha = 0.10$

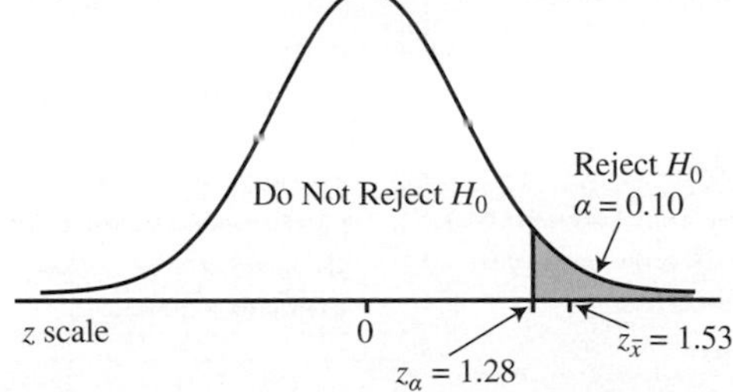

However, I must admit that I chose a pretty "wimpy" value of $\alpha = 0.10$ to increase my chances of proving my claim. In this case, I am willing to accept a 10% chance of claiming my book helped students attain an average greater than 87 when in fact it did not (a Type I error). A more impressive test would be to set α lower, say, $\alpha = 0.01$. Now that's truly significant, as far as I am concerned. According to Table 9.5, this level of significance corresponds to a critical z-score of 2.33. Figure 9.10 shows the impact of this change.

As you can see, to my horror, the shaded region no longer includes my z-test statistic of 1.53. Therefore, I do not reject H_0 and cannot claim the average grade of those using my book exceeds an 87. I have also reduced my chance of making a Type I error to 1%. In general, a hypothesis test that rejects H_0 is most impressive with a low value of α.

FIGURE 9.10
A One-Tail Hypothesis Test When $\alpha = 0.01$

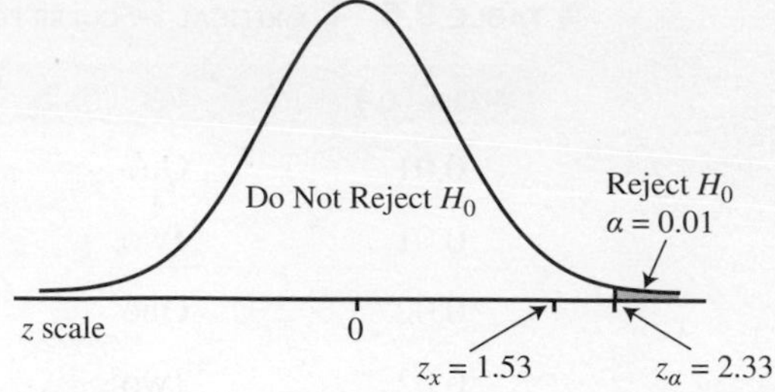

The question is, which value of α should I report? One way to resolve the issue is simply to report the *p*-value of the test statistic and let others decide on the significance of your work. For my grade example, the *p*-value is calculated as follows:

$$P(\bar{x} > 88.9) = P(z_{\bar{x}} > 1.53) = 1.0 - 0.9370 = 0.0630$$

Most published research studies use the *p*-value approach when reporting their findings.

If the true average grade of students who use my book is an 87 or less (the null hypothesis), then there is a 6.3% chance of seeing a sample mean of more than 88.9. Because this probability is relatively high (compared with an α of 0.05 or 0.01), many will view this as lack of evidence that students who use my book will have an average grade higher than 87.

Next on our agenda is to turn some of this work over to PHStat.

Using PHStat to Perform a Hypothesis Test for the Population Mean (When σ Is Known)

PHStat has the capability to perform a hypothesis test for the mean when σ is known. I'll demonstrate this procedure using my statistics grade example. Excel for Mac users can go to the textbook's Web site, www.pearsonhighered.com/donnelly, for these instructions.

1. Go to **Add-Ins > PHStat > One-Sample Tests > Z Test for the Mean, sigma known,** as shown in Figure 9.11A.

FIGURE 9.11A
Calculating the z-Test Statistic for the Population Mean Using PHStat: σ Known (Step 1)

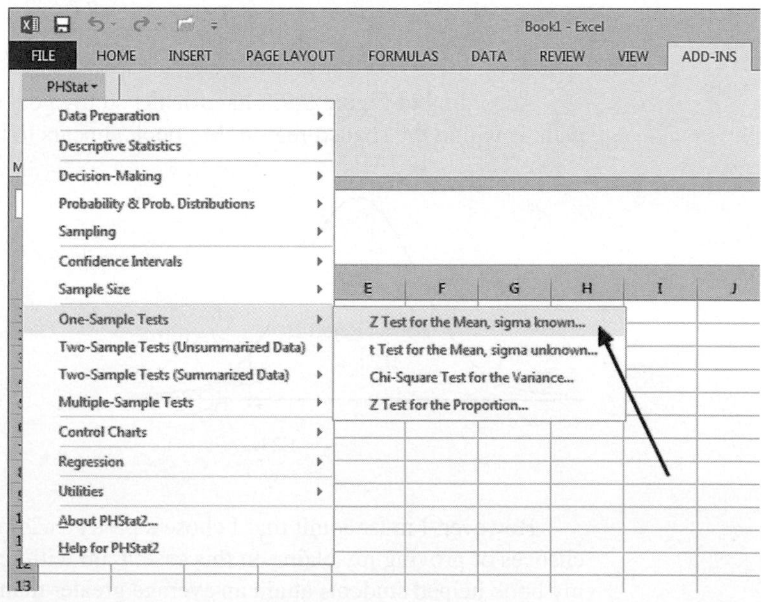

2. Fill in the **Z Test for the Mean, sigma known** dialog box as shown in Figure 9.11B. Click **OK**. Notice that I chose to set the level of significance, α, to 0.05.

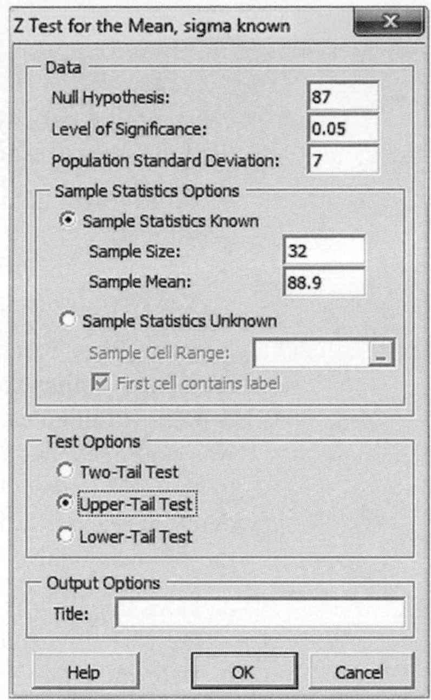

FIGURE 9.11B Calculating the z-Test Statistic for the Population Mean Using PHStat: σ Known (Step 2)

Figure 9.11C shows the output for this hypothesis test. Using $\alpha = 0.05$, we do not reject the null hypothesis because the z-test statistic, $z_{\bar{x}}$, equals 1.53.

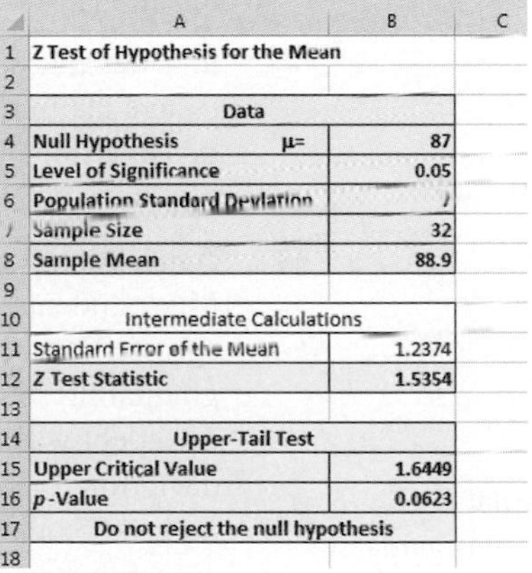

	A	B	C
1	Z Test of Hypothesis for the Mean		
2			
3	Data		
4	Null Hypothesis μ=	87	
5	Level of Significance	0.05	
6	Population Standard Deviation	7	
7	Sample Size	32	
8	Sample Mean	88.9	
9			
10	Intermediate Calculations		
11	Standard Error of the Mean	1.2374	
12	Z Test Statistic	1.5354	
13			
14	Upper-Tail Test		
15	Upper Critical Value	1.6449	
16	p-Value	0.0623	
17	Do not reject the null hypothesis		
18			

FIGURE 9.11C Calculating the z-Test Statistic for the Population Mean Using PHStat: σ Known (Final Result)

This result blows up my claim that students using my textbook have an average grade more than an 87. The following Your Turn problem will give you a chance to put PHStat to work.

YOUR TURN #6

The Institute for College Access and Success reported that the average student debt incurred by 2011 graduates of four-year colleges was $26,500. Suppose a sample of 45 students who graduated from college in 2014 was selected, and it was found that their debt averaged $27,800. Using $\alpha = 0.10$ and a population standard deviation of $7,500, perform a hypothesis test to determine if the average student debt changed from 2011 to 2014 using PHStat.

Answer can be found on ▶ page 433

9.2 Section Problems

Basic Skills

9.1 Calculate the p-value for the following conditions and determine whether to reject the null hypothesis:

a. one-tail test, $z_{\bar{x}} = 1.50$, and $\alpha = 0.05$
b. one-tail test, $z_{\bar{x}} = -2.25$, and $\alpha = 0.02$
c. two-tail test, $z_{\bar{x}} = 2.10$, and $\alpha = 0.05$
d. two-tail test, $z_{\bar{x}} = -1.37$, and $\alpha = 0.10$

9.2 Calculate the p-value for the following conditions and determine whether to reject the null hypothesis:

a. one-tail test, $z_{\bar{x}} = 1.46$, and $\alpha = 0.10$
b. one-tail test, $z_{\bar{x}} = -2.48$, and $\alpha = 0.01$
c. two-tail test, $z_{\bar{x}} = -1.92$, and $\alpha = 0.01$
d. two-tail test, $z_{\bar{x}} = 2.76$, and $\alpha = 0.02$

9.3 Consider the following hypotheses:

$$H_0: \mu \leq 50$$
$$H_1: \mu > 50$$

Given that $\bar{x} = 52$, $\sigma = 12$, $n = 36$, and $\alpha = 0.05$, answer the following questions:

a. What conclusion should be drawn?
b. Determine the p-value for this test.

9.4 Consider the following hypotheses:

$$H_0: \mu = 120$$
$$H_1: \mu \neq 120$$

Given that $\bar{x} = 111$, $\sigma = 26$, $n = 40$, and $\alpha = 0.05$, answer the following questions:

a. What conclusion should be drawn?
b. Determine the p-value for this test.

Applications

9.5 Suppose the University of Memphis advertises that its average class size is 35 students or less. A student organization is concerned that budget cuts have led to increased class sizes and would like to test this claim. A random sample of 38 classes was selected, and the average class size was found to be 36.9 students. Assume that the standard deviation for class size at the college is eight students. Using $\alpha = 0.05$, answer the following questions:

a. Does the student organization have enough evidence to refute the college's claim?
b. Determine the p-value for this test.
c. Verify your results using PHStat.

9.6 Suppose the coffee industry claimed that the average U.S. adult drinks 1.7 cups of coffee per day. To test this claim, a random sample of 34 adults was selected, and their average coffee consumption was found to be 1.95 cups per day. Assume the standard deviation of daily coffee consumption per day is 0.5 cups. Using $\alpha = 0.10$, answer the following questions:

a. Is the coffee industry's claim supported by this sample?
b. Determine the p-value for this test.
c. Verify your results using PHStat.

9.7 Season's Pizza recently hired additional drivers and as a result now claims that its average delivery time for orders is under 45 minutes. A sample of 30 customer deliveries was examined, and the average delivery time was found to be 42.3 minutes. Historically, the standard deviation for delivery time is 11.6 minutes. Using $\alpha = 0.05$, answer the following questions:

a. Does this sample provide enough evidence to refute the delivery time claim made by Season's Pizza?
b. Determine the p-value for this test.
c. Verify your results using PHStat.

9.8 Bob's Sporting Goods believes the average age of its customers is 40 or less. A random sample of 60 customers was surveyed, and the average customer age was found to be 42.7 years. Assume the standard deviation for customer age is 8.0 years. Using $\alpha = 0.02$, answer the following questions:

a. Does this sample provide enough evidence to refute the age claim made by Bob's Sporting Goods?
b. Determine the p-value for this test.
c. Verify your results using PHStat.

9.9 According to the government-lending institution Sallie Mae, students graduating from college have an average credit card debt of $4,100. A random sample of 50 graduating seniors was selected, and their average credit card debt was found to be $4,360. Assume the standard deviation for student credit card debt is $1,200. Using $\alpha = 0.05$, answer the following questions:

a. Does this sample provide enough evidence to challenge the findings by Sallie Mae?
b. Determine the p-value for this test.
c. Verify your results using PHStat.

9.10 Zingo's Grocery store claims that customers spend an average of 5 minutes waiting for service at the store's deli counter. A random sample of 45 customers was timed at the deli counter, and the average service time was found to be 5.5 minutes. Assume the standard deviation is 1.7 minutes per customer. Using $\alpha = 0.02$, answer the following questions:

a. Does this sample provide enough evidence to counter the claim made by Zingo's management?
b. Determine the p-value for this test.
c. Verify your results using PHStat.

9.3 Hypothesis Testing for the Population Mean When σ Is Unknown

Up to this point in the chapter, we assumed that σ, the population standard deviation, was known. Quite honestly, in most hypothesis testing applications, this is not the case. Think about it—if we knew the population standard deviation, we most likely will also know the population mean, which is the purpose of this hypothesis test. We handle this in the same manner used in Chapter 8. We substitute the sample standard deviation, s, in place of σ. The sample standard deviation will always be available to us once we have collected the sample. When doing so, we use the Student's t-distribution for the test statistic rather than the normal distribution.

When we use the t-distribution, we need to assume that the population of interest follows the normal probability distribution. As your sample size gets larger and if the shape of the population is not very skewed to one side, the assumption that the population is normally distributed is not as critical when s is substituted for σ. This is due to the fact that the shape of the t-distribution becomes similar to the normal distribution as the sample size increases. For small sample sizes under these conditions, however, you must be able to assume that the population is normally distributed. To simplify matters, I will assume the population of interest follows the normal distribution throughout this section. We'll first look at the one-tail hypothesis test and then move on to the two-tail version.

An Example of a One-Tail Hypothesis Test for the Population Mean (When σ Is Unknown)

To demonstrate hypothesis testing for the mean when σ is unknown, I'll rely on the following example. Many of us suffer from phobias that we struggle with through life, such as the fear of spiders, snakes, heights, or even clowns. I can handle most of these things without much anxiety. Recently, however, I have developed an irrational fear (at least according to my wife, Deb) of a seemingly innocent process. I have learned to avoid this setting like the plague lest I have a complete breakdown. I am, of course, talking about the self-serve check out system at my local grocery store.

I'm convinced the evil person who designed this system decided to play a nasty practical joke on innocent people like me. When the system first appeared in the store, I felt sure I could handle it. After all, I have a good education, and I like to embrace new technology. It didn't take long to realize I was way out of my league. After scanning the first few items, I attempted to place the bag of groceries into my cart. Wrong move. I was sternly instructed by a mechanical voice out of nowhere to "return the items to the bagging area" as if they were stolen goods. After several unsuccessful attempts to remove my groceries, a light not unlike those used on emergency response vehicles started flashing at the top of the stand. This triggered the arrival of the "self-serve police," who, in reality, was a teenaged employee whose lack of seniority banished him to assisting victims like me who haven't discovered the well-kept secret of how to remove their scanned items from the bagging area. Shaking his head in disgust, the employee pushed a few buttons, which finally stopped the system from yelling at me.

After setting off the mean voice and flashing lights a second time, I finally admitted defeat. I put all my yet-to-be-paid-for groceries back into my cart and proceeded on my "walk of shame" past all the customers who had lined up behind me toward the safety of the nearest human cashier. My publisher won't permit me to print what the mean mechanical voice had to say about this move, but, I assure you, it wasn't pleasant. After other failed attempts to run the gauntlet of the self-serve checkout system, I figured I had experienced enough psychological trauma to last a lifetime. The self-serve police have seen the last of Bob Donnelly.

Suppose this self-serve checkout system was a pilot that was used to test the feasibility of installing future systems at other store locations for Piggly Wiggly, which is a large grocery chain. Currently, the average total time to check out with a cashier is 5 minutes. Piggly Wiggly has decided that if the average self-serve checkout time in the pilot system is less than 5 minutes, additional self-serve systems should be installed to ease the burden on human cashiers. To test this premise, the checkout times of 12 randomly selected self-serve shoppers were recorded (I assume by the self-serve police). The times are shown in Table 9.6.

TABLE 9.6 | CHECKOUT TIMES FOR SELF-SERVE CUSTOMERS (MINUTES)

3.3	1.3	2.8	4.6	5.5	3.4
5.0	5.1	3.1	4.5	6.0	5.8

To perform this hypothesis test, I'll use the following seven steps:

Step 1: Identify the null and alternative hypotheses.

This is a lower one-tail (lower) test because we are interested in proving that the average time is less than 5 minutes.

$$H_0: \mu \geq 5 \text{ minutes (status quo)}$$

$$H_1: \mu < 5 \text{ minutes}$$

Step 2: Set a value for the significance level, α.

For this procedure, the level of significance still represents the probability of making a Type I error, where we reject the null hypothesis but it is actually true. For this example, we set $\alpha = 0.05$.

Step 3: Determine the appropriate critical value.

Because we are using the sample standard deviation in place of the population standard deviation, the *t*-distribution is used to determine the rejection boundaries. In other words, instead of using the critical *z*-score, the appropriate critical value to use in this case is the critical *t*-score, t_α (for a one-tail test). Table 9.7 shows an excerpt of Table 5 in Appendix A, which lists these values.

TABLE 9.7 | EXCERPT OF CRITICAL T-SCORES SHOWN IN TABLE 5 IN APPENDIX A

1 TAIL	0.200	0.100	0.050	0.025	0.010	0.005
2 TAIL	0.400	0.200	0.100	0.050	0.020	0.010
CONF LEV	0.600	0.800	0.900	0.950	0.980	0.990
df						
1	1.376	3.078	6.314	12.706	31.821	63.657
2	1.061	1.886	2.920	4.303	6.965	9.925
3	0.978	1.638	2.353	3.182	4.541	5.841
4	0.941	1.533	2.132	2.776	3.747	4.604
5	0.920	1.476	2.015	2.571	3.365	4.032
6	0.906	1.440	1.943	2.447	3.143	3.707
7	0.896	1.415	1.895	2.365	2.998	3.499
8	0.889	1.397	1.860	2.306	2.896	3.355
9	0.883	1.383	1.833	2.262	2.821	3.250
10	0.879	1.372	1.812	2.228	2.764	3.169
11	0.876	1.363	1.796	2.201	2.718	3.106
12	0.873	1.356	1.782	2.179	2.681	3.055

To find our critical t-score, we locate the column associated with $\alpha = 0.05$ for a one-tail test and the row that corresponds to $n - 1$ degrees of freedom, where $n =$ the sample size. Because we have recorded the times of 12 customers, we have 11 degrees of freedom for this example. The yellow highlights in Table 9.7 indicate that $t_\alpha = 1.796$.

We can also obtain our critical t-score for a one-tail test using Excel's T.INV function which has the following characteristics:

$$= \text{T.INV}(\alpha, \text{degrees\_of\_freedom})$$

Because this function returns the left-tail critical t-score, we need to take the absolute value of the result. For our checkout time example, we have

$$= |\text{T.INV}(0.05,11)| = |-1.796| = 1.796$$

Step 4: Calculate the appropriate test statistic.

The t-test statistic is the calculated t-score that was introduced in Chapter 8 and is shown in Equation 9.2.

Formula 9.2 for the t-Test Statistic for the Hypothesis Test for the Population Mean (When σ Is Unknown)

$$t_{\bar{x}} = \frac{\bar{x} - \mu_{H_0}}{\frac{s}{\sqrt{n}}}$$

Because we are using the sample standard deviation to replace the unknown population standard deviation, we rely on the t-distribution for this test.

where

$t_{\bar{x}} =$ The t-test statistic for the sample mean
$\bar{x} =$ The sample mean
$\mu_{H_0} =$ The mean of the sampling distribution, which is assumed to be true for the null hypothesis
$s =$ The standard deviation of the sample
$n =$ The sample size

To use Equation 9.2, we need to calculate the sample mean and sample standard deviation. We can either use Equation 3.1 on page 79 and Equation 3.7 on page 94 to calculate these manually or rely on Excel's AVERAGE and STDEV.S functions introduced in Chapter 3. I vote for Excel, which provides us with the following results:

$$\bar{x} = 4.2 \text{ minutes} \qquad s = 1.42 \text{ minutes}$$

$$t_{\bar{x}} = \frac{\bar{x} - \mu_{H_0}}{\frac{s}{\sqrt{n}}} = \frac{4.2 - 5}{\frac{1.42}{\sqrt{12}}} = \frac{-0.8}{0.410} = -1.95$$

Step 5: Compare the t-test statistic ($t_{\bar{x}}$) with the critical t-score (t_α).

Applying the same logic that we used in Table 9.3 for a one-tail (lower) test, $t_{\bar{x}} = -1.95$ and $-t_\alpha = -1.796$. Because $-1.95 < -1.796$, we come to the "reject H_0" conclusion. Figure 9.12 illustrates this finding.

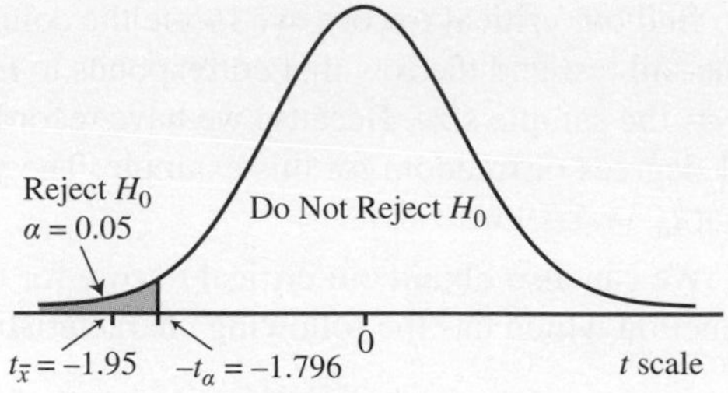

FIGURE 9.12
Comparing the t-Test Statistic with the Critical t-Score

Step 6: State your conclusions.

Rejecting the null indicates that we have support for the alternative hypothesis, H_1: $\mu < 5$ minutes. Therefore, we can conclude that the average self-serve checkout time in the pilot system is less than 5 minutes. It looks like I'm going to be seeing more of these psychological torture devices in the near future.

Remember, we do have an important assumption to keep in mind for this example—that the population follows the normal probability distribution. I will introduce a method in Chapter 12 to test for this assumption. If we find the population is not normally distributed, we can increase our sample size to more than 30, which is where the *t*-distribution can be approximated by the normal distribution.

Estimating the *p*-Value Using the Student's *t*-Distribution

One limitation we are faced with when using the *t*-distribution for hypothesis testing is that we can no longer determine a precise *p*-value using Table 5 in Appendix A, as we did using the normal distribution. This is due to the fact that the structure of the *t*-table in Table 5 depends on the sample size (or degrees of freedom). However, no need to fret. We can still approximate the *p*-value when using the *t*-distribution, as shown in Table 9.8.

TABLE 9.8 | EXCERPT OF CRITICAL T-SCORES FROM TABLE 5 IN APPENDIX A

P-VALUE IS IN THIS RANGE (between 0.050 and 0.025)

1 TAIL	0.200	0.100	0.050	0.025	0.010	0.005
2 TAIL	0.400	0.200	0.100	0.050	0.020	0.010
CONF LEV	0.600	0.800	0.900	0.950	0.980	0.990
df						
1	1.376	3.078	6.314	12.706	31.821	63.657
2	1.061	1.886	2.920	4.303	6.965	9.925
3	0.978	1.638	2.353	3.182	4.541	5.841
4	0.941	1.533	2.132	2.776	3.747	4.604
5	0.920	1.476	2.015	2.571	3.365	4.032
6	0.906	1.440	1.943	2.447	3.143	3.707
7	0.896	1.415	1.895	2.365	2.998	3.499
8	0.889	1.397	1.860	2.306	2.896	3.355
9	0.883	1.383	1.833	2.262	2.821	3.250
10	0.879	1.372	1.812	2.228	2.764	3.169
11	0.876	1.363	1.796	2.201	2.718	3.106
12	0.873	1.356	1.782	2.179	2.681	3.055

$|t_{\bar{x}}| = 1.95$

Recall that our t-test statistic, $t_{\bar{x}}$, is equal to -1.95. We need to find the critical t-scores that bracket $|t_{\bar{x}}| = |-1.95| = 1.95$ along the $n - 1 = 12 - 1 = 11$ row in Table 5 from Appendix A. Table 9.8 shows these values as 1.796 and 2.201, which are highlighted in yellow. To find the corresponding p-values, we go to the **1 Tail** row and find *0.025* and *0.05*, also highlighted in yellow.

According to Table 9.8, the p-value for our hypothesis test is between 0.025 and 0.05. Even though we don't have a precise p-value, using $\alpha = 0.05$ we can still reject the null hypothesis.

If we need a precise p-value for our one-tail (lower) hypothesis test, we can use Excel's T.DIST function which has the following characteristics:

= T.DIST(x, degrees_of_freedom, cumulative)

When we set x to our test statistic ($t_{\bar{x}}$) and cumulative = TRUE, this function provides the area to the left of $t_{\bar{x}} = -1.95$ which equals the p-value as follows:

= T.DIST(−1.95, 11, TRUE) = 0.0386

As you can see, this p-value is between 0.025 and 0.05 as we just concluded from Table 9.8.

The following Your Turn problem provides you the opportunity to perform a one-tail (upper) test. To determine a precise p-value for the right side of the t-distribution, we can use Excel's T.DIST.RT function which has the following characteristics:

= T.DIST.RT(x, degrees_of_freedom)

The RT prefix indicates this is a "right tail" function.

YOUR TURN #7

Recently, the average driving distance of PGA golfers was found to be 284 yards. Suppose I designed a new golf ball that I claim will increase the distance to more than 290 yards. To test my new invention, I randomly selected 15 pro golfers to hit a drive with the ball. The distances in yards for each drive are as follows:

270	295	326	294	284
295	278	308	290	283
288	314	278	280	310

a. To test my claim, follow the steps we just discussed and construct a hypothesis test using $\alpha = 0.10$.

b. Identify the range for the p-value.

c. Use Excel to determine the precise p-value.

Answers can be found on ▶ **page 433**

An Example of a Two-Tail Hypothesis Test for the Population Mean (When σ Is Unknown)

The two-tail hypothesis test with an unknown σ follows the same six steps as in the previous one-tail example. To demonstrate, let's test the claim made by Nielsen that the average American watches 34.5 hours of television per week. The number of hours of television that 10 people watch during a week was recorded; the results are shown in Table 9.9.

TABLE 9.9 | NUMBER OF HOURS OF TELEVISION WATCHED BY 10 PEOPLE PER WEEK

30	64	49	40	21	58	9	43	39	43

I'll perform this hypothesis test using the following six steps:

Because we are testing the claim that the population mean is equal to 34.5 hours per week of television watching, this statement needs to be assigned to the null hypothesis. The alternative hypothesis can never have an equal sign.

Step 1: Identify the null and alternative hypotheses.

$$H_0: \mu = 34.5 \text{ hours (status quo)}$$
$$H_1: \mu \neq 34.5 \text{ hours}$$

Step 2: Set a value for the significance level, α.

Let's raise the bar for this hypothesis test and set $\alpha = 0.02$.

Step 3: Determine the appropriate critical value.

Because this is a two-tail test, the area associated with α is split in two. Therefore, we use $t_{\alpha/2}$ to represent the critical t-score.

We can find our critical t-score highlighted in blue in Table 9.8. Locate the column associated with $\alpha = 0.02$ for a two-tail test and the row that corresponds to $10 - 1 = 9$ degrees of freedom because 10 is our sample size. Table 9.8 indicates that $t_{\alpha/2} = 2.821$. Remember, the two-tail test has a critical score on either side of the sampling distribution.

We can also rely on Excel's T.INV.2T function that was introduced in Chapter 8 to determine the critical t-scores for our two-tail test as follows:

$$= \text{T.INV.2T}(\alpha, \text{degrees\_of\_freedom})$$
$$= \text{T.INV.2T}(0.02, 9) = 2.821$$

Step 4: Calculate the appropriate test statistic.

After we use Excel to calculate the sample mean $(\bar{x})$ and sample standard deviation (s) from the data in Table 9.9, we can then use Equation 9.3 to find our t-test statistic.

$$\bar{x} = 39.6 \text{ hours} \quad s = 16.4 \text{ hours}$$

$$t_{\bar{x}} = \frac{\bar{x} - \mu_{H_0}}{\frac{s}{\sqrt{n}}} = \frac{39.6 - 34.5}{\frac{16.4}{\sqrt{10}}} = \frac{5.1}{5.19} = 0.98$$

Step 5: Compare the t-test statistic $(t_{\bar{x}})$ with the critical t-score $(t_{\alpha/2})$.

Using the logic shown in Table 9.3 for a two-tail test, $|t_{\bar{x}}| = 0.98$ and $|t_{\alpha/2}| = 2.821$. Because $0.98 < 2.821$, we do not reject H_0. Figure 9.13 illustrates this finding.

FIGURE 9.13
Comparing the t-Test Statistic with the Critical t-Score

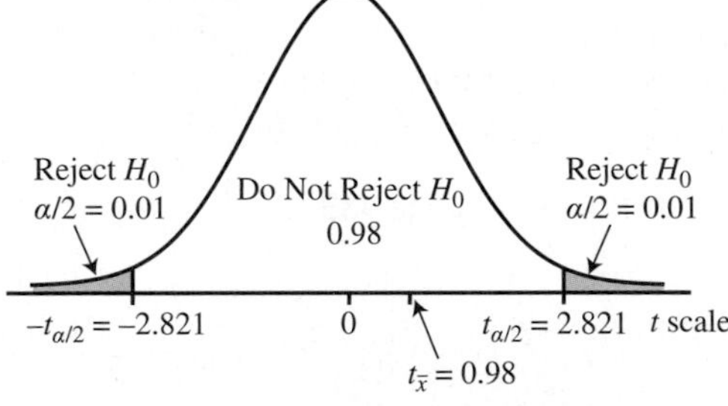

Many students jump to the conclusion that based on these results the average number of viewing hours per week in the population equals 34.5. This is an incorrect statement because it accepts the null hypothesis.

Step 6: State your conclusions.

Failing to reject the null hypothesis indicates that we do not have support for the alternative hypothesis, $H_1: \mu \neq 34.5$ hours. However, we need to exercise caution here. We cannot conclude that the average number of hours equals 34.5 because that would be accepting the null hypothesis. We can only say that we have no evidence to conclude that the average does not equal 34.5 hours.

Using PHStat and Excel for a Hypothesis Test for the Population Mean (When σ Is Unknown)

PHStat can also provide hypothesis testing for the mean when the standard deviation of a population is unknown. I'll demonstrate this procedure using the television viewing example in the previous section.

1. Type the data values from Table 9.9 into Cells A1 to A10 of a spreadsheet (see Figure 9.14A).
2. Go to **Add-Ins > PHStat > One-Sample Tests > t Test for the Mean, sigma unknown,** as seen in Figure 9.11A.
3. Fill in the **t Test for the Mean, sigma unknown** dialog box as shown in Figure 9.14A. Click OK.

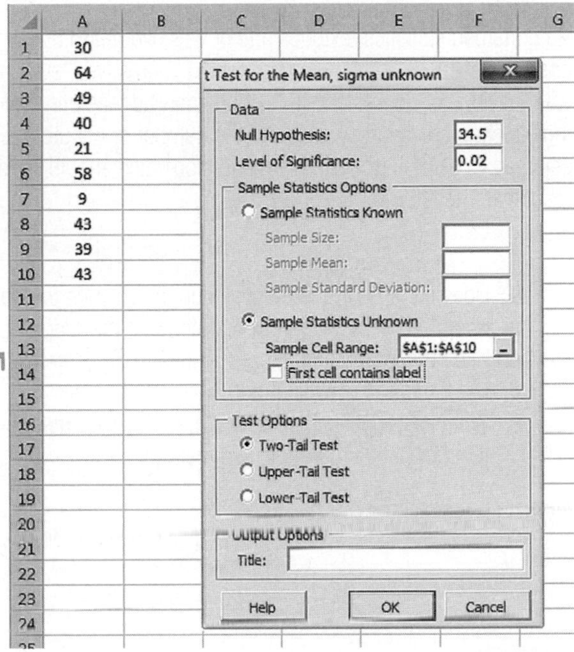

FIGURE 9.14A Calculating the t-Test Statistic for the Mean Using PHStat: σ Unknown

Excel for Mac users can go to the textbook's Web site for these instructions.

Figure 9.14B shows the output for this hypothesis test. Using $\alpha = 0.02$, we do not reject the null hypothesis because the t-test statistic, $t_{\bar{x}}$, equals 0.98.

	A		B
1	t Test for Hypothesis of the Mean		
2			
3	Data		
4	Null Hypothesis	μ=	34.5
5	Level of Significance		0.02
6	Sample Size		10
7	Sample Mean		39.6
8	Sample Standard Deviation		16.39918697
9			
10	Intermediate Calculations		
11	Standard Error of the Mean		5.1859
12	Degrees of Freedom		9
13	t Test Statistic		0.9834
14			
15	Two-Tail Test		
16	Lower Critical Value		-2.8214
17	Upper Critical Value		2.8214
18	p-Value		0.3511
19	Do not reject the null hypothesis		
20			

FIGURE 9.14B Calculating the t-Test Statistic for the Mean Using PHStat: σ Unknown (Final Result)

Notice that PHStat reports a p-value of 0.3511 in Cell B18. Because this p-value $> \alpha$, we can also come to the conclusion not to reject the null hypothesis.

We can also use Excel's T.DIST.2T function to determine the p-value for a two-tail test using the t-distribution as follows:

$$= \text{T.DIST.2T}(x, \text{degrees\_of\_freedom},)$$

When we set $x = |t_{\bar{x}}|$, this function provides the area to the left of $t_{\bar{x}} = -0.98$ plus the area to the right of $t_{\bar{x}} = 0.98$ which equals the p-value as follows:

$$= \text{T.DIST.2T}(0.98, 9) = 0.3527$$

This p-value is slightly different than the p-value provided by PHStat in Figure 9.14B (0.3511) because of rounding.

We'll wrap up this section with one more Your Turn problem to be sure you understand how to perform the t-test on your next exam.

YOUR TURN #8

An unnamed statistics textbook author was overheard by his wife saying that he spends an average of one hour each weekend doing household chores (yes, even authors have their to-do lists). The author's wife, having her doubts about this and knowledgeable in hypothesis testing as a result of her proofreading his chapters, secretly recorded the number of minutes he spent doing his chores over 11 randomly selected weekends (the clipboard and stopwatch should have caught my, I mean his, attention). The results are as follows:

70 22 54 57 56 47 12 60 43 10 56

a. Does the author's wife have enough evidence to challenge his claim using $\alpha = 0.05$?
b. Using Table 5 in Appendix A, determine the range for the p-value and state your conclusion.
c. Use PHStat to validate these results and to determine the p-value for this test.
d. Use Excel to determine the p-value for this test.
e. What assumptions need to be made by the author's wife to perform this analysis (other than that her husband likes to exaggerate)?

Answers can be found on ▶ **page 434**

9.3 Section Problems

Basic Skills

9.11 Determine the critical t-scores for each of the following conditions:

a. one-tail test, $\alpha = 0.05$, and $n = 21$
b. two-tail test, $\alpha = 0.02$, and $n = 10$
c. two-tail test, $\alpha = 0.05$, and $n = 28$
d. two-tail test, $\alpha = 0.01$, and $n = 40$

9.12 Consider the following hypotheses:

$$H_0: \mu \geq 65$$
$$H_1: \mu < 65$$

Given that $\bar{x} = 58.8$, $s = 10.4$, $n = 25$, and $\alpha = 0.05$, answer the following questions:

a. What conclusion should be drawn?
b. Use PHStat to determine the p-value for this test.

9.13 Consider the following hypotheses:

$$H_0: \mu = 140$$
$$H_1: \mu \neq 140$$

Given that $\bar{x} = 148.1$, $s = 37.5$, $n = 20$, and $\alpha = 0.02$, answer the following questions:

a. What conclusion should be drawn?
b. Use PHStat to determine the p-value for this test.

9.14 Consider the following hypotheses and sample data, and then answer the following questions using $\alpha = 0.05$.

$$H_0: \mu \leq 16$$
$$H_1: \mu > 16$$

19 19 12 18 22 21 14 21 17 15

a. What conclusion should be drawn?
b. Use PHStat to determine the p-value for this test.

9.15 Consider the following hypotheses and sample data, and then answer the following questions using $\alpha = 0.05$.

$$H_0: \mu = 10$$
$$H_1: \mu \neq 10$$

8	9	9	8	6	7	10	10
12	7	5	9	10	9	10	

a. What conclusion should be drawn?
b. Use PHStat to determine the p-value for this test.

Applications

9.16 During the winter of 2012–2013, the average utility bill for Delaware residents was $186 per month. A random sample of 40 customers was selected during the winter of 2013–2014, and the average bill was found to be $178.10 with a sample standard deviation of $22.40.

a. Using $\alpha = 0.05$, does this sample provide enough evidence to conclude that the average utility bill in Delaware was lower in the winter of 2013–2014 than it was in the winter of 2012–2013?
b. Does changing the value of α from 0.05 to 0.01 affect your conclusion? Why or why not?
c. Use PHStat to validate these results and to determine the p-value for this test.

9.17 Suppose the average size of a new house built in a certain county in 2010 was 2,272 square feet. A random sample of 25 new homes built in this county was selected in 2014. The average square footage was 2,190, with a sample standard deviation of 225 square feet.

a. Using $\alpha = 0.02$, does this sample provide enough evidence to conclude that the average house size of a new home in the county has changed since 2010?
b. Estimate the p-value for this test using Table 5 in Appendix A.
c. Determine the precise p-value for this test using Excel.
d. Use PHStat to validate these results.

9.18 According to BIGresearch, holiday shoppers spent an average of $373 over the Thanksgiving weekend in 2008. The following data show the amount spent by a random sample of holiday shoppers during the same weekend in 2014:

$427	$274	$370	$238	$222	$215
$360	$434	$387	$395	$323	$63
$415	$429	$377	$279		

a. Test the hypothesis that that shoppers spent less than an average of $373 over the Thanksgiving weekend in 2014 using $\alpha = 0.05$.
b. Estimate the p-value for this test using Table 5 in Appendix A.
c. Determine the precise p-value for this test using Excel.
d. Use PHStat to validate these results.

9.19 According to the market research firm NPD Group, Americans ate an average of 211 meals in restaurants in 2001. The following data show the number of meals eaten in restaurants as determined from a random sample of Americans in 2014:

212	128	197	344	143	79	180	313	57	200
161	320	90	224	266	284	231	322	200	173

a. Using $\alpha = 0.05$, test the hypothesis that the number of meals eaten at restaurants by Americans has not changed since 2001.
b. Estimate the p-value for this test using Table 5 in Appendix A.
c. Determine the precise p-value for this test using Excel.
d. Use PHStat to validate these results.
e. What assumptions need to be made to perform this analysis?

9.20 Fannie Mae is a government-sponsored organization that was established in 1938 after the Depression to provide local banks with money from the federal government to be used for residential mortgages in an effort to increase homeownership rates. As lending standards have tightened during the most recent housing market crisis, credit scores for borrowers of approved mortgages have increased. In 2012, the average credit score for loans that were purchased by Fannie Mae was 766. A random sample of 35 mortgages recently purchased by Fannie Mae was selected, and it was found that the average credit score was 771 with a sample standard deviation of 21.

a. Using $\alpha = 0.05$, is there enough evidence from this sample to conclude that the average credit score for mortgages purchased by Fannie Mae has increased since 2012?
b. Estimate the p-value for this test using Table 5 in Appendix A.
c. Determine the precise p-value for this test using Excel.
d. Use PHStat to validate these results.
e. What assumptions need to be made to perform this analysis?

9.21 In 2008, the online travel agency Travelocity reported that summer travelers booked their airline reservations an average of 73.3 days in advance. A random sample of 40 summer travelers in 2014 was selected, and the number of days travelers booked their airline reservations in advance was recorded. These data can be found in the Excel file titled **Travelocity.xlsx.**

a. Perform a hypothesis test using $\alpha = 0.05$ to determine if the average number of days reservations are booked in advance has changed since 2008.
b. Estimate the p-value for this test using Table 5 in Appendix A.
c. Determine the precise p-value for this test using Excel.
d. Use PHStat to validate these results.

9.4 Hypothesis Testing for the Proportion of a Population

There are situations where we are interested in testing the claim about the population proportion rather than the mean. For example, we might perform a hypothesis test to determine the proportion of citizens who intend to vote for the Democratic candidate in an upcoming election. As you might recall from Chapter 7, proportion data follow the binomial distribution, which can be approximated by the normal distribution under the following conditions:

$$np \geq 5 \quad \text{and} \quad n(1 - p) \geq 5$$

where

p = The probability of a success in the population
n = The sample size

We also learned in Chapter 7 that we can calculate the sample proportion, $\bar{p}$, using Equation 9.3.

Formula 9.3 for the Sample Proportion

$$\bar{p} = \frac{x}{n}$$

where

x = The number of observations of interest in the sample (successes)
n = The sample size

If these conditions are satisfied, our test statistic is found using Equation 9.4.

Formula 9.4 for the z-Test Statistic for a Hypothesis Test for the Proportion

$$z_p = \frac{\bar{p} - p_{H_0}}{\sqrt{\dfrac{p_{H_0}(1 - p_{H_0})}{n}}}$$

where

z_p = The z-test statistic for the proportion
$\bar{p}$ = The sample proportion
p_{H_0} = The population proportion, which is assumed to be true in the null hypothesis
n = The sample size

In the following section, I'll demonstrate a one-tail hypothesis for the proportion.

An Example of a One-Tail Hypothesis Test for the Proportion

In January 2011, the French government passed legislation requiring that at least 40% of corporate board members of large companies to be female within six years. Large companies are defined as those having more than 500 employees or revenues over 50 million euros. A survey performed by Corporate Women Directors International in 2013 found that 25% of corporate board members in large French companies were women (compared to 21% in the United States). Suppose the French government would like to test the hypothesis that the proportion of female board members is currently more than the reported 25% in 2013 due to the current legislation. Out of a random sample of 240 French board members, 73 were found to be women. We'll test this hypothesis with $\alpha = 0.05$.

Hypothesis tests for the proportion follow the same six steps discussed earlier in the chapter:

Because we are testing if the proportion of female board members is currently more than 25%, this is an example of a one-tail (upper) test.

Step 1: Identify the null and alternative hypotheses.

$$H_0: p \leq 0.25 \text{ (status quo)}$$
$$H_1: p > 0.25$$

Notice that the hypotheses statements in this example are expressed in terms of p rather than μ.

Step 2: Set a value for the significance level, α.

For this example, we will set $\alpha = 0.05$.

Step 3: Determine the appropriate critical value.

Because proportion data tend to follow the binomial distribution, which we can approximate with the normal distribution, we can use Table 9.5 to determine the critical z-score. A one-tail test with $H_1: p > 0.25$ and $\alpha = 0.05$ results in $z_\alpha = 1.645$.

Step 4: Calculate the appropriate test statistic.

Equation 9.4 provides our test statistic for this procedure. However, for this example, we first need to calculate the sample proportion using Equation 9.3:

Notice that $p_{H_0} = 0.25$ because we are assuming that the status quo (that corporate boards are 25% female) has not changed until we have evidence otherwise.

$$\bar{p} = \frac{x}{n} = \frac{73}{240} = 0.304$$

$$z_p = \frac{\bar{p} - p_{H_0}}{\sqrt{\frac{p_{H_0}(1 - p_{H_0})}{n}}} = \frac{0.304 - 0.25}{\sqrt{\frac{0.25(1 - 0.25)}{240}}}$$

$$z_p = \frac{0.054}{\sqrt{0.000781}} = \frac{0.054}{0.0279} = 1.94$$

Step 5: Compare the z-test statistic (z_p) with the critical z-score (z_α).

Using the same logic as that outlined in Table 9.3 for a one tail (upper) test, $z_p = 1.94$ and $z_\alpha = 1.645$. Because $1.94 > 1.645$, we reject H_0. Figure 9.15 illustrates this finding.

FIGURE 9.15 Comparing the z-Test Statistic with the Critical z-Score

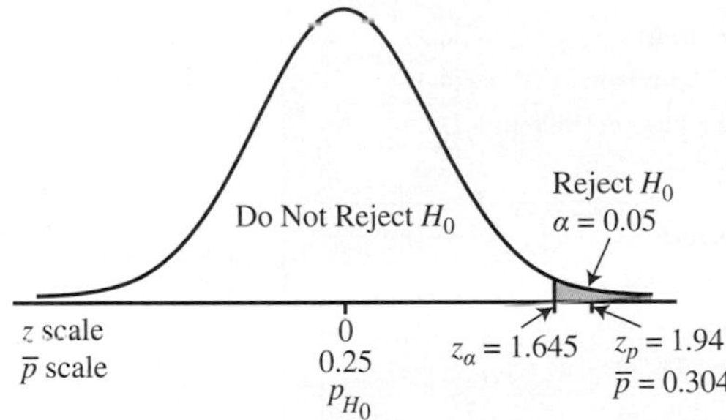

Step 6: State your conclusions.

Rejecting the null indicates that we have support for the alternative hypothesis, $H_1: p > 0.25$. Therefore, we can conclude that the proportion of female board members in France has increased beyond 25%.

The *p*-Value Approach to Hypothesis Testing for the Proportion

The p-value procedure for the hypothesis test for proportions is identical to the procedure for the mean when the population standard deviation is known. For our French boardroom example (a one-tail test), the p-value is the probability of obtaining a sample proportion higher than 0.304 if the true population proportion is 0.25. Therefore, the p-value is as follows:

$$P(\bar{p} > 0.304) = P(z_p > 1.94) = 1.0 - 0.9738 = 0.0262$$

This p-value is represented by the shaded area in the right tail of the sampling distribution shown in Figure 9.16 because we have a one-tail (upper) hypothesis test.

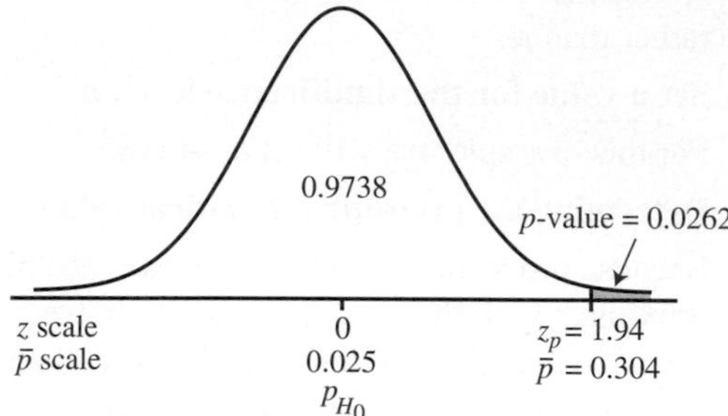

FIGURE 9.16
Using the p-Value for a One-Tail Hypothesis Test for the Proportion

Because the p-value $= 0.0262$, which is less than $\alpha = 0.05$, we reject the null hypothesis.

Using PHStat and Excel for Hypothesis Testing for the Proportion

PHStat provides a way of testing a hypothesis for the proportion. I'll demonstrate this procedure using the French boardroom example:

1. Go to **Add-Ins > PHStat > One-Sample Tests > Z Test for the Proportion,** as seen in Figure 9.11A.
2. Fill in the **Z Test for the Proportion** dialog box as shown in Figure 9.17A. Click **OK**.

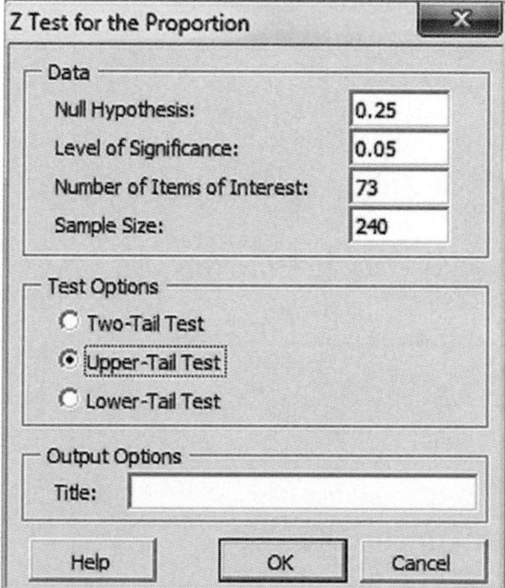

FIGURE 9.17A
Calculating the z-Test Statistic for the Proportion Using PHStat

Figure 9.17B shows the output for this hypothesis test. Using $\alpha = 0.05$, we reject the null hypothesis because the z-test statistic, z_p, equals 1.94. The slight differences between our results from the previous section and the numbers displayed in Figure 9.17B are due to rounding in the calculations. Excel uses many more decimal places in the calculations than I do manually.

FIGURE 9.17B
Calculating the z-Test Statistic for the Proportion Using PHStat (Final Result)

	A	B
1	**Z Test of Hypothesis for the Proportion**	
2		
3	**Data**	
4	**Null Hypothesis** $\pi =$	**0.2500**
5	**Level of Significance**	**0.05**
6	**Number of Items of Interest**	**73**
7	**Sample Size**	**240**
8		
9	Intermediate Calculations	
10	Sample Proportion	0.304166667
11	Standard Error	0.0280
12	**Z Test Statistic**	**1.9379**
13		
14	**Upper-Tail Test**	
15	**Upper Critical Value**	**1.6449**
16	***p*-Value**	**0.0263**
17	**Reject the null hypothesis**	
18		

Notice that PHStat reports a p-value of 0.0263 in Cell B16. Because this p-value $< \alpha$, we reject the null hypothesis.

We can also use Excel's NORM.S.DIST function to help us determine the p-value for this example as follows:

$$= 1.0 - \text{NORM.S.DIST}(1.94, \text{TRUE})$$
$$= 1.0 - 0.9738 = 0.0262$$

We'll wrap up this section with one more Your Turn problem to be sure you understand how to perform hypothesis testing for the proportion.

YOUR TURN #9

A Ewing Marion Kauffman Foundation survey found that 42% of small-business owners in the United States were firstborn in their family. To test this report, a random sample of 150 small-business owners was taken, and 54 of them were found to be firstborn.

a. Perform a hypothesis test using $\alpha = 0.01$ to examine if this proportion has changed recently using the sample data.
b. Calculate the p-value for this sample using the tables in Appendix A and state your conclusion.
c. Determine the p-value for this test using Excel.
d. Confirm these results using PHStat.

Answers can be found on ▶ **pages 434–435**

9.4 Section Problems

Basic Skills

9.22 Calculate the p-value for the following conditions and determine whether to reject the null hypothesis:

a. one-tail (lower) test, $z_p = -1.36$, and $\alpha = 0.05$
b. one-tail (upper) test, $z_p = 1.28$, and $\alpha = 0.10$
c. two-tail test, $z_p = 2.29$, and $\alpha = 0.05$
d. two-tail test, $z_p = -0.90$, and $\alpha = 0.01$

9.23 Calculate the p-value for the following conditions and determine whether to reject the null hypothesis:

a. one-tail (upper) test, $z_p = 2.15$, and $\alpha = 0.10$
b. one-tail (lower) test, $z_p = -0.66$, and $\alpha = 0.05$
c. two-tail test, $z_p = -1.69$, and $\alpha = 0.05$
d. two-tail test, $z_p = 1.44$, and $\alpha = 0.02$

9.24 Consider the following hypotheses:

$$H_0: p \leq 0.24$$
$$H_1: p > 0.24$$

Given that $\overline{p} = 0.277$, $n = 130$, and $\alpha = 0.05$, answer the following questions:

a. What conclusion should be drawn?
b. Determine the p-value for this test.

9.25 Consider the following hypotheses:

$$H_0: p = 0.69$$
$$H_1: p \neq 0.69$$

Given that $\bar{p} = 0.606$, $n = 160$, and $\alpha = 0.05$, answer the following questions:

a. What conclusion should be drawn?
b. Determine the p-value for this test.

Applications

9.26 An increased number of U.S. colleges have been using online resources such as Facebook and Google to research applicants. According to Kaplan Test Prep, 26% of admissions officers indicated that they visited an applying student's social networking page in 2012. A random sample of 100 admissions officers was recently selected and it was found that 35 of them visit the social networking sites of students applying to their college. Using $\alpha = 0.05$, answer the following questions:

a. Does this sample provide support for the hypothesis that the proportion of admissions officers who visit an applying student's social networking page has increased since 2012?
b. Determine the p-value for this test.
c. Use PHStat to validate these results.

9.27 Consumers with credit scores below 600 have a very difficult time getting approved for car or mortgage loans. In 2012, 24% of Americans had a credit score below 600. Due to the recent financial crisis, the federal government is concerned that this proportion has increased. To test this hypothesis, a random sample of 250 Americans was chosen in 2014. From this sample, 67 people had credit scores less than 600. Using $\alpha = 0.10$, answer the following questions:

a. Does this sample provide support for the government's concern that the proportion of Americans with credit scores below 600 has increased since 2012?
b. Determine the p-value for this test.
c. Verify your results using PHStat.

9.28 A 2010 survey by CarMD.com found that 64% of vehicle owners avoided automotive maintenance and repairs. Suppose Sears Automotive would like to perform a hypothesis test to challenge this finding. From a random sample of 170 vehicle owners that was recently taken, it was found that 103 avoid maintenance and repairs. Using $\alpha = 0.02$, answer the following questions:

a. Based on this sample, can we conclude that the proportion of vehicle owners who avoid maintenance has changed since 2010?
b. Determine the p-value for this test.
c. Verify your results using PHStat.

9.29 Recently, the number of airline companies that offer in-flight Wi-Fi service to passengers has increased. However, it is estimated that only 10% of the passengers who have Wi-Fi available to them are willing to pay for it. Suppose Gogo, the largest provider of airline Wi-Fi service, would like to test this hypothesis by randomly sampling 125 passengers and asking them if they would be willing to pay \$4.95 for 90 minutes of onboard Internet access. Suppose that 20 passengers indicated they would use this service. Using $\alpha = 0.05$, answer the following questions:

a. Based on this sample, can we conclude that the proportion of airline passengers willing to pay for onboard Wi-Fi service is different than 10%?
b. Determine the p-value for this test.
c. Verify your results using PHStat.

9.30 The Eurozone consists of 17 European countries that use the euro as their common currency. The European debt crisis, which began in 2009, made it difficult for some Eurozone countries to repay their government debt. A national poll in 2013 indicated that 26% of Germans felt that exiting the Eurozone would be good for Germany. A random sample of 360 Germans was recently selected, and it was found that 72 felt that leaving the Eurozone would be good for Germany. Using $\alpha = 0.01$, answer the following questions:

a. Does this sample provide support for the hypothesis that the proportion of Germans who feel leaving the Eurozone would be good for Germany has decreased since 2013?
b. Determine the p-value for this test.
c. Use PHStat to validate these results.

9.31 The number of long-term unemployed, defined as those out of work for more than 27 weeks, has been a detriment to the recent economic recovery. In 2013, 40% of the unemployed had been out of work for more than 27 weeks. Government policy makers feel that this percentage has declined recently as the job market has improved. To test this theory, a random sample of 300 unemployed people was selected, and it was found that 112 were unemployed for longer than 27 weeks. Using $\alpha = 0.10$, answer the following questions:

a. Based on this sample, can the federal government conclude that the percentage of unemployed who have been out of work for more than 27 weeks has recently decreased?
b. Determine the p-value for this test.
c. Use PHStat to validate these results.
d. Comment on the value of alpha chosen for this test.

9.5 Type II Errors

So far in this chapter, we have performed each hypothesis test by setting a value for α, which is the probability of making a Type I error with our conclusion. Recall that a Type I error occurs when the null hypothesis is true and our sample mean or proportion falls into the "reject the null hypothesis" region. We can also be guilty of a Type II error, which occurs when the null hypothesis is really false and we fail to reject it. The probability of a Type II error is known as β.

Once we set the value for α, the value for β becomes fixed for a constant sample size, n. In this section, we will discover that the values for α and β are inversely related for a constant sample size. As one is raised, the other becomes smaller, and vice versa. In most cases, it is desirable to have small probabilities for α and β for our hypothesis test. The only way to lower the probability of both errors at the same time is to increase the size of the sample.

Calculating the Probability of Type II Errors Occurring (Population Mean Case)

I'll use the following example to show you how to calculate β for a specific value of α for a hypothesis test for the population mean. The Nissan Leaf is a five-door, 100% electric car that began selling in the United States in 2011. During the car's development, Nissan predicted that a fully charged battery would give the Leaf an average driving range of 100 miles. Suppose that Nissan had a recent breakthrough in battery technology that resulted in a claim that the average range of the new batteries would now exceed 100 miles. To test this claim, a random sample of 50 cars equipped with the new technology was selected to have their driving ranges measured. We will assume the population standard deviation for the driving range for these cars is 12 miles. For this hypothesis test, I'll set $\alpha = 0.05$.

Because Nissan would like to prove the average range of the Leaf exceeds 100 miles, this is an example of a one-tail (upper) test. Therefore, the null and alternative hypotheses are stated as follows:

$$H_0: \mu \leq 100 \text{ miles (status quo)}$$
$$H_1: \mu > 100 \text{ miles (research claim)}$$

The **critical sample mean,** $\bar{x}_\alpha$, is the sample mean that marks the boundary of the rejection region when testing for a population mean.

At this point, I need to introduce the **critical sample mean**, $\bar{x}_\alpha$, which is the sample mean that marks the boundary of the rejection region. We are referring to the same boundary shown in Figure 9.15 in the previous section and simply using a different form of measurement—the sample mean rather than the z-score. Equation 9.5 shows how to calculate this value.

Formula 9.5 for The Critical Sample Mean for a Hypothesis Test for the Population Mean (When σ Is Known)

$$\bar{x}_\alpha = \mu_{H_0} \pm (z_\alpha)\left(\frac{\sigma}{\sqrt{n}}\right)$$

We use the plus sign in this equation when we need the critical sample mean on the right side of the sampling distribution and the negative sign when $\bar{x}_\alpha$ is on the left side of the distribution.

Because we have a one-tail (upper) test, we use the plus sign in Equation 9.5 to calculate the critical sample mean:

$$\bar{x}_\alpha = \mu_{H_0} + (z_\alpha)\left(\frac{\sigma}{\sqrt{n}}\right)$$

$$\bar{x}_\alpha = 100 + (1.645)\left(\frac{12}{\sqrt{50}}\right) = 102.8 \text{ miles}$$

If our sample mean exceeds 102.8 miles, we can reject the null hypothesis and conclude the new technology results in a driving range that averages more than 100 miles per charge as Nissan claims.

Let's look at two different scenarios. First, suppose that our sample mean from the 50 cars has an average driving range that exceeds 102.8 miles. If I were a Nissan executive,

When we decide to reject the null hypothesis, there is always the chance, with probability equal to α, that we are wrong! In the Nissan Leaf example, α is the probability of concluding that the average driving distance does exceed 100 miles when, in fact, it does not exceed 100 miles.

I'd pop the champagne cork and celebrate. However, being a statistician, I'd realize there is a 5% chance $(\alpha = 0.05)$ that my conclusion is wrong. This would happen if, in fact, the population average does not exceed 100 miles, resulting in a Type I error.

Now suppose that the sample mean for the 50 cars was an average driving range of less than 102.8 miles. This result would lead us not to reject the null hypothesis and conclude that the new technology was a dud. But before we put the champagne away, we need to ask ourselves, "What is the probability that our conclusions are wrong?" What we're looking for here is β, the probability of our failing to reject the null hypothesis when, in fact, we should be rejecting it and celebrating the success of our improved driving range. This erroneous conclusion is defined as a Type II error.

When we decide not to reject the null hypothesis, there is always the chance, with probability equal to β, that our conclusions are wrong. In the Nissan Leaf example, β is the probability of concluding the average driving distance does not exceed 100 miles when, in fact, it does exceed 100 miles.

As you can see, the β calculation is made under the premise that the null hypothesis is not true for a specific population mean and should be rightfully rejected. In other words, the new battery technology is actually effective, with an average range exceeding 100 miles. Therefore, the value of β depends on the actual value of μ, the population mean (the average range of the new batteries). Even though we don't know μ, we can still calculate the value of β for a specific population mean.

Let's say, hypothetically, that the new batteries are effective and that the population has an average range of 105 miles. What is the probability of mistakenly concluding that the new batteries are not effective (β)? This error will occur if our sample mean for this population is less than 102.8 miles. Figure 9.18 illustrates this scenario. Don't let this figure intimidate you—I'll break it down into bite-size pieces!

FIGURE 9.18
β Calculation When $\mu = 105$ Miles

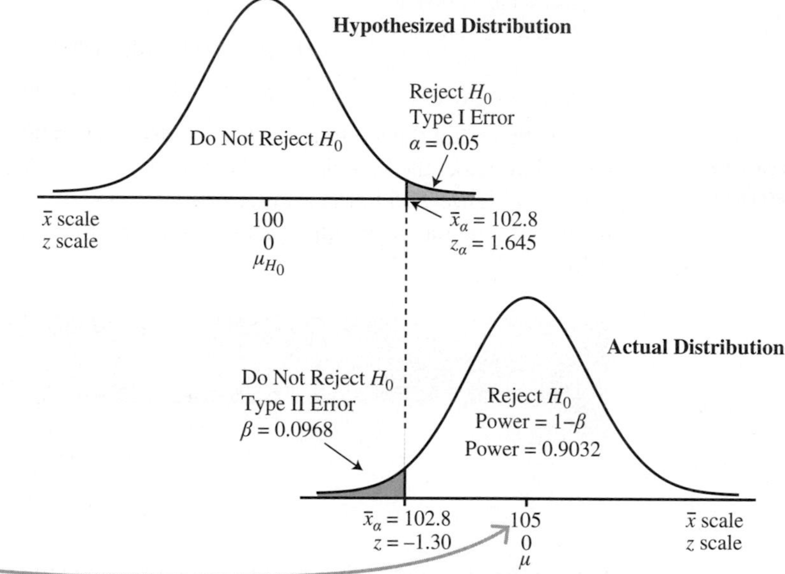

The value of β is based on an assumed value of μ, the actual population mean.

The top half of Figure 9.18 is nothing new. You've seen this curve many times in this chapter. It's simply the sampling distribution for the null hypothesis, which in this case claims the population mean equals 100 miles. The top curve also shows the critical mean (102.8) that we just calculated using Equation 9.5. The probability of making a Type I error is shaded in orange.

The dotted line between the two curves represents the position of the critical mean, which marks the rejection regions in both graphs. If our sample mean is to the left of this line, we do not reject the null. If our mean is to the right, we reject the null hypothesis. Remember, the new batteries are effective, so rejecting the null is the correct hypothesis decision, and failing to reject the null is a Type II error.

The bottom curve in Figure 9.18 represents the sampling distribution of the actual population with a mean equal to 105 miles. What is the chance of seeing a sample mean from our 50 cars that is less than 102.8 miles if the actual population mean equals 105 miles? This probability is β and is found in the green-shaded region in the bottom half of Figure 9.18. We find this area using Equation 9.1 and Table 3 in Appendix A.

$$z = \frac{\bar{x}_\alpha - \mu}{\frac{\sigma}{\sqrt{n}}} = \frac{102.8 - 105}{\frac{12}{\sqrt{50}}} = \frac{-2.2}{1.697} = -1.30$$

$$\beta = P(\bar{x}_\alpha \leq 102.8) = P(z \leq -1.30) = 0.0968$$

If the true population mean equals 105 miles, there is a 9.68% chance that we will not recognize that the new batteries are effective. This probability is based on setting $\alpha = 0.05$ and randomly sampling 50 cars.

The **power** of the hypothesis test is the probability of it correctly rejecting the null hypothesis.

The **power** of a hypothesis test is the probability of it correctly rejecting the null hypothesis. The power is found using Equation 9.6.

Formula 9.6 for the Power of a Hypothesis Test

$$\text{Power} = 1 - \beta$$

The power of this hypothesis test is then as follows:

$$\text{Power} = 1 - 0.0968 = 0.9032$$

In other words, if the true population mean equals 105 miles and we set $\alpha = 0.05$, we have a 90.32% chance of correctly concluding that the new batteries are effective. This value is also shown in the bottom curve in Figure 9.18.

What happens to β if the actual population mean is 106 miles rather than 105? Figure 9.19 shows the effect of this change.

FIGURE 9.19
β Calculation When $\mu = 106$ Miles

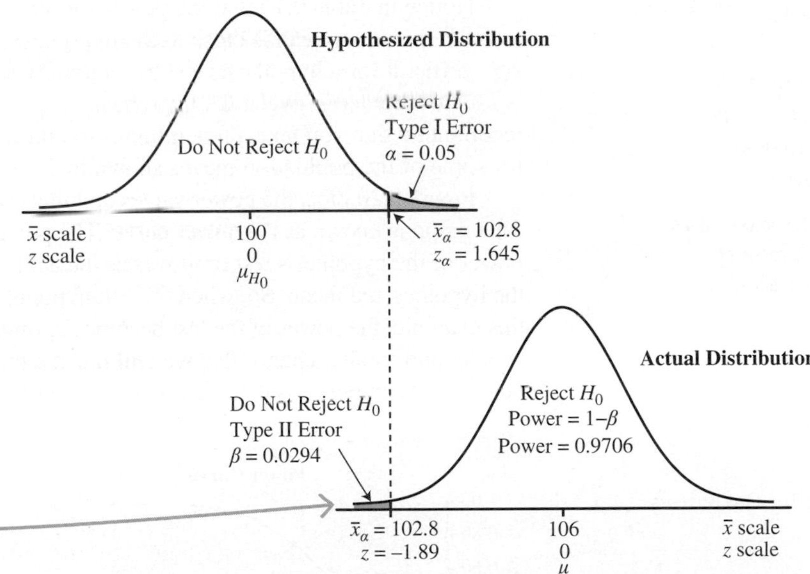

Shifting this actual distribution to the right in this example makes the green-shaded region smaller. This smaller shaded region means the value of β is smaller (there is less chance of making a Type II error).

The top hypothesized distribution is unchanged from the last figure. However, the actual distribution shown in the bottom curve has shifted slightly to the right, reflecting the population mean moving from 105 to 106 miles. β is the probability of obtaining a sample mean of 102.8 miles or less from a population with a mean of 106 miles. The β and power calculations are shown as follows:

$$z = \frac{\bar{x}_\alpha - \mu}{\frac{\sigma}{\sqrt{n}}} = \frac{102.8 - 106}{\frac{12}{\sqrt{50}}} = \frac{-3.2}{1.697} = -1.89$$

$$\beta = P(\bar{x}_\alpha \leq 102.8) = P(z \leq -1.89) = 0.0294$$

$$\text{Power} = 1 - \beta = 1 - 0.0294 = 0.9706$$

As the true population mean moves away from the hypothesized mean, the power of the test increases because it is easier to correctly reject the null hypothesis.

If the true population mean equals 106 miles, we now have a 97.06% chance of correctly concluding that the new batteries are effective. In other words, as the true population mean moves away from the hypothesized mean of 100 miles, the power of the test increases and β decreases. This is due to the fact that it is easier to correctly reject the null when the true population mean is much different from the hypothesized mean. Table 9.10 shows the power that corresponds to various population means for the battery example.

TABLE 9.10 | THE POWER THAT CORRESPONDS TO VARIOUS POPULATION MEANS: BATTERY EXAMPLE

ACTUAL POPULATION MEAN, μ	Z-SCORE	POWER $1-\beta$
100	1.65	0.0495
101	1.06	0.1446
102	0.47	0.3192
103	−0.12	0.5478
104	−0.71	0.7611
105	−1.30	0.9032
106	−1.89	0.9706
107	−2.47	0.9932
108	−3.06	0.9989
109	−3.65	0.9999

When the true population mean is very close to the hypothesized mean, the power of the test becomes very small because it is very difficult for the hypothesis test to accurately reject the null hypothesis.

Notice in Table 9.10 that the power for this hypothesis test is very low when the actual population mean is close to the hypothesized mean of 100 miles. Typically, it is very difficult for a hypothesis test to accurately reject the null hypothesis when there is little difference between the hypothesized and actual population mean. I strongly recommend that you take a few minutes to confirm that you can calculate the power for some of the population means shown in Table 9.10.

The **power curve** plots the power values of a hypothesis test over a range of corresponding population means.

Figure 9.20 plots the power values and their corresponding population means. This graph is known as the **power curve**. The power curve helps you visualize how the power of the hypothesis test improves as the actual population mean moves away from the hypothesized mean. So, when the actual population mean increases mile-wise, as in this example, the power of the test becomes stronger and stronger. As a result, there is a smaller and smaller chance that we will make a mistake by failing to reject the null hypothesis (the hypothesis that the driving range of a Nissan Leaf is 100 miles or less).

FIGURE 9.20

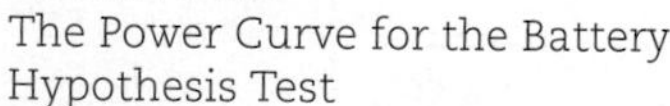

The Power Curve for the Battery Hypothesis Test

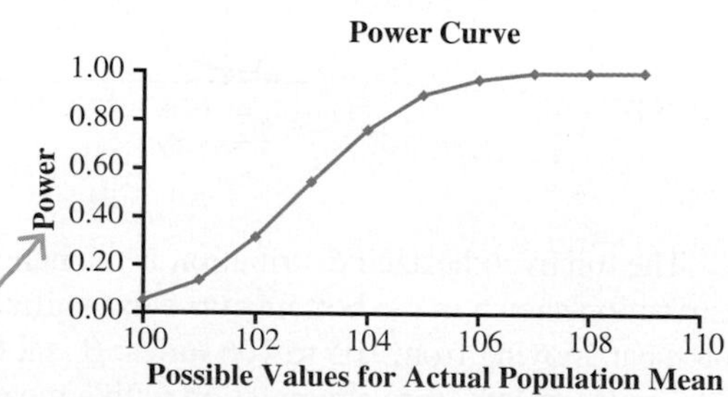

This power curve is based on $H_0 \leq 100$ miles, $\alpha = 0.05$, $n = 50$ cars, and $\sigma = 12$ miles.

The Effect of α on β

So far in this section we have kept the value of α at 0.05 and then proceeded to calculate β. What happens if we decide to reduce the chance of making a Type I error by lowering α to 0.01? Well, as I preached in an earlier chapter, there are no free lunches in statistics. Reducing α without increasing the sample size will cause β to increase. I'll demonstrate this pattern by changing α from 0.05 seen in Figure 9.19 to 0.01.

Let's calculate β for the following conditions:

$$H_0: \mu \leq 100 \text{ miles}$$
$$H_1: \mu > 100 \text{ miles}$$
$$\mu = 106 \quad n = 50 \quad \alpha = 0.01$$

The β and power calculations are as follows:

$$\bar{x}_\alpha = \mu_{H_0} + (z_\alpha)\left(\frac{\sigma}{\sqrt{n}}\right)$$

$$\bar{x}_\alpha = 100 + (2.33)\left(\frac{12}{\sqrt{50}}\right) = 104 \text{ miles}$$

$$z = \frac{\bar{x}_\alpha - \mu}{\frac{\sigma}{\sqrt{n}}} = \frac{104 - 106}{\frac{12}{\sqrt{50}}} = \frac{-2.0}{1.697} = -1.18$$

$$\beta = P(\bar{x}_\alpha \leq 104) = P(z \leq -1.18) = 0.1190$$
$$\text{Power} = 1 - \beta = 1 - 0.1190 = 0.8810$$

Figure 9.21 shows the impact on β when reducing α to 0.01 in our hypothesis test.

FIGURE 9.21
β Calculation When $\mu = 106$ Miles and $\alpha = 0.01$

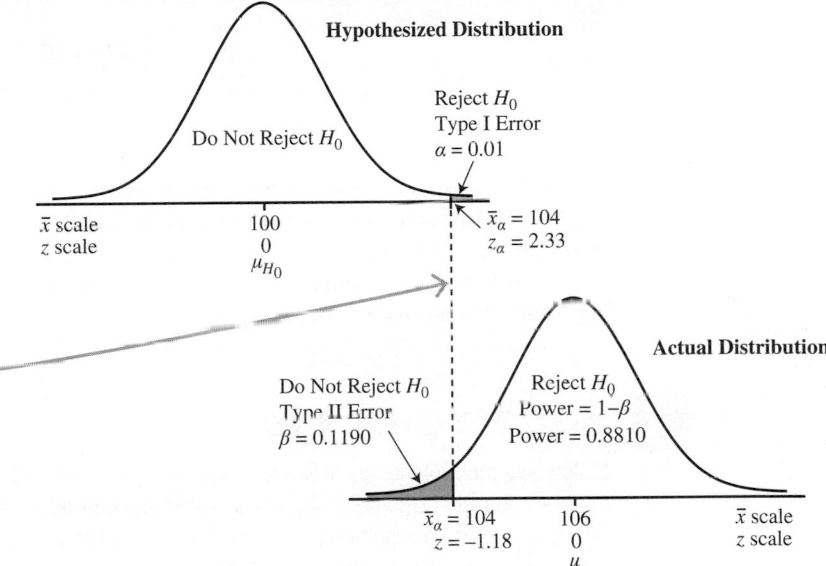

Notice that the dotted line indicating the boundary for the rejection region has shifted to the right, with the critical sample mean, $\bar{x}_\alpha$, moving from 102.8 to 104 miles. Both distributions are in the same position as shown in Figure 9.19 because the hypothesized population mean (100) and actual population mean (106) have not changed. Shifting this dotted line to the right has reduced the orange-shaded area in the hypothesized distribution (top curve), which lowers α from 0.05 to 0.01. This shift has also increased the green-shaded area in the actual distribution (bottom curve), which raises β from 0.0294 to 0.1190. By lowering our chance of making a Type I error (α), we have increased our chance of making a Type II error (β). You can see this visually in the graph. Lowering α made the "do not reject H_0" area in the lower graph bigger. Consequently, there is a greater chance that we will make a Type II mistake and fail to reject the null hypothesis—the hypothesis that the driving range of a battery is 100 miles or less.

How does one choose between the tradeoff of making a Type I error or Type II error? Well, one approach is to consider the cost of each error. In our Nissan Leaf example, a Type I error (with a probability equal to α) occurs when Nissan claims that the new batteries average more than 100 miles per charge when, in fact, they do not. The cost of this error would be disappointed consumers who don't experience the mileage they expect with fully charged batteries. By contrast, a Type II error (with a probability equal to β) occurs when Nissan concludes that the new batteries do not exceed an average of 100 miles per charge when, in fact, they do. The cost of this error could be the lost opportunity to promote the battery's actual performance and potentially lose market share to competing electric cars. Nissan needs to consider the cost of these outcomes when deciding on an acceptable α and the resulting β.

Another approach would be for Nissan to set α to 0.05 (which is very common) and then reduce the level of β by increasing the sample size. Increasing the sample size makes both sampling distributions in Figure 9.21 narrower, which will reduce the shaded areas that represent α and β.

Probability of Type II Errors for Population Proportions

The **critical sample proportion**, p_α, is the sample proportion that marks the boundary of the rejection region when testing for a population proportion.

Our Nissan Leaf example focused on determining the probability of a Type II error when testing for a population mean. The procedure for calculating the probability of a Type II error when testing for a population proportion is the same with one exception—we need to replace the critical sample mean with the **critical sample proportion**, p_α, which is shown in Equation 9.7.

Formula 9.7 for the Critical Proportion for a Hypothesis Test for the Proportion

$$p_\alpha = p_{H_0} \pm (z_\alpha)\sqrt{\frac{p_{H_0}(1 - p_{H_0})}{n}}$$

We use the plus sign in this equation when we need the critical sample proportion on the right side of the sampling distribution and the negative sign when p_α is on the left side of the distribution.

Calculating power can be a little tricky, so I encourage you to take the time to try this last Your Turn problem to see if you get it.

YOUR TURN #10

Historically, the average age of Buick owners has been reported to be 61 years old. Suppose, in an effort to attract younger customer, Buick has invested in a new advertising campaign and would like to test its effectiveness with a hypothesis test. A random sample of 41 new Buick owners was selected. Assume the standard deviation for the age of Buick owners is 10.0 years. Compute the power of this hypothesis test using $\alpha = 0.10$ and assuming the actual population mean is 60.0 years.

Consider the following hints:

- Because this is a one-tail (lower) test, use the negative sign in Equation 9.5 when calculating the critical sample mean.
- Because this is a one-tail (lower) test, the "reject the null" region will be on the left side of the dotted line shown in Figure 9.21.
- The hypothesized distribution will be to the right of the actual distribution, which is the reverse of Figure 9.21.

Answer can be found on ▶ **page 435**

9.5 Section Problems

Basic Skills

9.32 Consider the following hypotheses:

$$H_0: \mu \leq 30$$
$$H_1: \mu > 30$$

Given that $\sigma = 6$, $n = 42$, and $\alpha = 0.05$, calculate β for each of the following conditions:

a. $\mu = 31$
b. $\mu = 32$

9.33 Consider the following hypotheses:

$$H_0: \mu \geq 75$$
$$H_1: \mu < 75$$

Given that $\sigma = 15$, $n = 36$, and $\alpha = 0.01$, calculate β for each of the following conditions:

a. $\mu = 73$
b. $\mu = 66$

9.34 Consider the following hypotheses:

$$H_0: p \geq 0.72$$
$$H_1: p < 0.72$$

Given that $n = 100$ and $\alpha = 0.05$, calculate β for each of the following conditions.

a. $p = 0.66$
b. $p = 0.62$

9.35 Consider the following hypotheses:

$$H_0: p \leq 0.15$$
$$H_1: p > 0.15$$

Given that $n = 150$ and $\alpha = 0.10$, calculate β for each of the following conditions.

a. $p = 0.16$
b. $p = 0.22$

9.36 Consider the following hypotheses:

$$H_0: \mu = 120$$
$$H_1: \mu \neq 120$$

Given that $\sigma = 27$, $n = 60$, and $\alpha = 0.05$, calculate β for each of the following conditions:

a. $\mu = 131$
b. $\mu = 115$

Hint: For a two-tail hypothesis test, β is the area between the critical means under the actual distribution, as shown in the following figure.

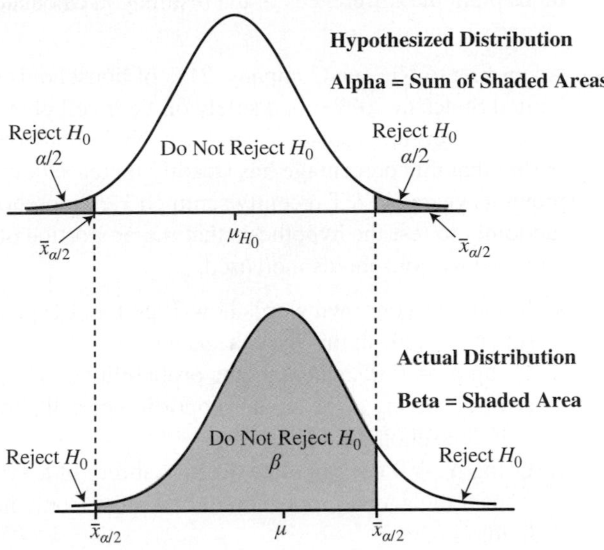

Applications

9.37 The average retirement age for French citizens in 2009 was reported to be 58.7 years according to the Organization for Economic Co-operation and Development, an international group dedicated to promoting trade and economic growth. With the French pension system operating with a deficit, a bill was introduced by the government during the summer of 2010 to raise the minimum retirement age from 60 to 62. Suppose a survey of 40 retiring French citizens was recently taken to investigate whether the bill has raised the average age at which people actually retire. Assume the standard deviation of the retirement age is 5 years. Using $\alpha = 0.05$, answer the following questions:

a. Explain in your own words how Type I and Type II errors can occur in this hypothesis test.
b. Calculate the probability of a Type II error occurring if the actual population age is 60 years old.
c. Calculate the probability of a Type II error occurring if the actual population age is 61.5 years old.

9.38 The crisis in the real estate market caused the listing prices of homes in areas such as Orlando, Florida, to fall from previous years. A real estate office would like to sample 50 new listings randomly to test the hypothesis that the current listing price average is less than $243,000, the average in the previous year. Assume the standard deviation for the price of homes in this market is $45,000.

a. Explain in your own words how Type I and Type II errors can occur in this hypothesis test.
b. Using $\alpha = 0.10$, calculate the probability of a Type II error occurring if the actual average listing is $225,000.

c. Using $\alpha = 0.05$, calculate the probability of a Type II error occurring if the actual average listing is \$225,000.
d. Explain the differences in the results you calculated in parts b and c.

9.39 According to Nielsen Company, 21% of households in the United States in 2009 relied solely on their cell phones for phone service instead of landlines. Nielsen also reported that this percentage has steadily increased over the previous years. AT&T recently sampled 125 households randomly to test the hypothesis that the proportion of cell phone–only households increased.

a. Explain in your own words how Type I and Type II errors can occur in this hypothesis test.
b. Using $\alpha = 0.05$, calculate the probability of a Type II error occurring if the actual proportion of cell phone–only households is 0.30.
c. Using $\alpha = 0.01$, calculate the probability of a Type II error if the actual proportion of cell phone–only households is 0.30.
d. Explain the differences in the results you calculated in parts b and c.

9.40 The Dome restaurant in Delaware is under new management. While under the previous management, 15% of the customers rated their dining experiences as "unsatisfactory." The restaurant's current managers would like to test their belief that this percentage is now lower due to new training procedures. Suppose 75 customers were randomly chosen and asked to rate their dining experiences. Using $\alpha = 0.05$, answer the following questions:

a. Explain in your own words how Type I and Type II errors can occur in this hypothesis test.
b. Calculate the probability of a Type II error occurring if the actual proportion of unsatisfied customers is 11%.
c. Calculate the probability of a Type II error occurring if the actual proportion of unsatisfied customers is 6%.

9.41 According to the Bureau of Labor, the average American aged 15 years or older gets 8 hours and 23 minutes (503 minutes) of sleep per night. To test if this average has changed recently, a random sample of 55 Americans aged 15 years and older was selected, and the number of minutes they slept recorded. Assume the standard deviation of hours of sleep is 60 minutes. Using $\alpha = 0.02$, answer the following questions:

a. Explain in your own words how Type I and Type II errors can occur in this hypothesis test.
b. Calculate the probability of a Type II error given the actual average hours of sleep is 524 minutes.
c. Calculate the probability of a Type II error given the actual average hours of sleep is 500 minutes.

9.42 *Contact rate* is defined as the percentage of plate appearances by Major League Baseball players that the ball is put in play (as opposed to striking out). Historically, the Major League average has been 80%. Suppose we want to test that this rate has not changed recently by randomly selecting 250 plate appearances by players and recording the percentage of players that put the ball in play. Using $\alpha = 0.05$, answer the following questions:

a. Explain in your own words how Type I and Type II errors can occur in this hypothesis test.
b. Calculate the probability of a Type II error occurring if the actual contact rate is 77%.
c. Calculate the probability of a Type II error occurring if the actual contact rate is 88%.

CHAPTER 9 Summary

- A hypothesis is an assumption about a population parameter such as a mean or a proportion.
- The null hypothesis, denoted by H_0, represents the status quo and involves stating the belief that the mean of the population is $\leq$, $=$, or $\geq$ a specific value.
    - The null hypothesis is believed to be true unless there is overwhelming evidence to the contrary.
- The alternative hypothesis, denoted by H_1, represents the opposite of the null hypothesis and holds true if the null hypothesis is found to be false.
    - The alternative hypothesis always states the mean of the population is $<$, $\neq$, or $>$ a specific value.
- The null hypothesis can never be accepted. The only two options available are to
    - reject the null.
    - fail to reject the null.
- A two-tail hypothesis test is used whenever the alternative hypothesis is expressed as $\neq$.
- A one-tail hypothesis test is used when the alternative hypothesis is stated as $<$ or $>$ with the rejection area on the same side as the inequality points.
- A Type I error occurs when the null hypothesis is rejected when, in reality, it is true.
    - The probability of making a Type I error is known as α, the level of significance.
- A Type II error occurs when the null hypothesis is not rejected when, in reality, it is not true.
    - The probability of making a Type II error is known as β.
- When constructing a hypothesis test for the mean when a population's standard deviation (σ) is known, we use the normal distribution to determine the critical value, which identifies the rejection region for the null hypothesis.
- The p-value is the probability of observing a sample mean at least as extreme as the one selected for the hypothesis test, assuming the null hypothesis is true.
    - The p-value is sometimes referred to as the observed level of significance.
    - If the p-value is greater than alpha, we do not reject the null. Otherwise we reject the null.
- To construct a hypothesis test for the mean when a population's standard deviation is unknown, we substitute the sample standard deviation, s, in place of σ and use the Student's t-distribution to determine the critical value for the hypothesis test with $n - 1$ degrees of freedom.
- Proportion data follow the binomial distribution, which can be approximated by the normal distribution when $np \geq 5$ and $n(1 - p) \geq 5$.
    - We can, therefore, use the normal distribution tables in Appendix A to determine the critical value for the population proportion.
    - The p-value for this hypothesis test can also be found directly in Appendix A in the same manner as testing for the mean with sigma known.
- Once we set the value for α, the value for β becomes fixed.
- The values for α and β are inversely related for a constant sample size.
- The only way to lower the probability of both errors at the same time is to increase the size of the sample.
- The power of the hypothesis test, $1 - \beta$, is defined as the probability of correctly rejecting the null hypothesis.
- As the true population mean moves away from the hypothesized mean, the power of the test increases because it is easier to correctly reject the null when the true population mean is much different than the hypothesized mean.
- The power curve plots the power values of a hypothesis test over a range of corresponding population means.

CHAPTER 9 Key Terms

Alpha. The probability of rejecting the null hypothesis when, in reality, it is true.

Alternative hypothesis. Designated H_1, this hypothesis represents the opposite of the null hypothesis and holds true if the null hypothesis is found to be false. The alternative hypothesis always states the population parameter is $<$, $\neq$, or $>$ a specific value.

Beta. The probability of failing to reject the null hypothesis when, in reality, it is not true.

Consumer's risk. A Type II error is known as the consumer's risk when it occurs in quality control settings, because the customer is getting a product from a process that is not performing properly.

Critical sample mean, $\bar{x}_\alpha$. The sample mean that marks the boundary of the rejection region.

Critical sample proportion, p_α. The sample proportion that marks the boundary of the rejection region when testing for a population proportion.

Hypothesis. An assumption about a population parameter such as a mean or a proportion.

Level of significance. The probability of making a Type I error, α.

Null hypothesis. Designated H_0, this hypothesis represents the status quo and involves stating the belief that the population parameter is $\leq$, $=$, or $\geq$ a specific value and is always associated with the equal sign.

Observed level of significance. The probability of observing a sample mean at least as extreme as the one selected for the hypothesis test, assuming the null hypothesis is true. The observed level of significance is also known as the p-value.

One-tail hypothesis test. A test in which the alternative hypothesis is stated as $<$ or $>$.

One-tail (lower) hypothesis test. A test in which the alternative hypothesis is stated as $<$.

One-tail (upper) hypothesis test. A test in which the alternative hypothesis is stated as $>$.

***p*-value.** The probability of observing a sample mean at least as extreme as the one selected for the hypothesis test, assuming the null hypothesis is true.

Power curve. A curve that plots the power values of a hypothesis test over a range of corresponding population means.

Power. The probability that a hypothesis test will correctly reject the null hypothesis.

Producer's risk. A Type I error is known as the producer's risk when it occurs in quality control settings, because the producer is looking for a problem in its process that does not exist.

Two-tail hypothesis test. A test in which the alternative hypothesis is expressed as $\neq$.

Type I error. An error that occurs when the null hypothesis is rejected when, in reality, it is true. The probability of making a Type I error is known as α, the level of significance.

Type II error. An error that occurs when the null hypothesis is not rejected when, in reality, it is not true. The probability of making a Type II error is known as β.

CHAPTER 9 Equations

9.2 Hypothesis Testing for the Population Mean When σ Is Known (pp 390–402)

Formula 9.1 for the z-test Statistic for a Hypothesis Test for the Population Mean (When σ Is Known)

$$z_{\bar{x}} = \frac{\bar{x} - \mu_{H_0}}{\dfrac{\sigma}{\sqrt{n}}}$$

9.3 Hypothesis Testing for the Population Mean When σ Is Unknown (pp 390–402)

Formula 9.2 for the t-test Statistic for the Hypothesis Test for the Population Mean (When σ Is Unknown)

$$t_{\bar{x}} = \frac{\bar{x} - \mu_{H_0}}{\dfrac{s}{\sqrt{n}}}$$

9.4 Hypothesis Testing for the Proportion of a Population (pp 403–411)

Formula 9.3 for the Sample Proportion

$$\bar{p} = \frac{x}{n}$$

Formula 9.4 for the z-test Statistic for a Hypothesis Test for the Proportion

$$z_p = \frac{\bar{p} - p_{H_0}}{\sqrt{\dfrac{p_{H_0}(1 - p_{H_0})}{n}}}$$

Formula 9.5 for the Critical Sample Mean for a Hypothesis Test for the Population Mean (When α Is Known)

$$\bar{x}_\alpha = \mu_{H_0} \pm (z_\alpha)\left(\frac{\sigma}{\sqrt{n}}\right)$$

9.5 Type II Errors (pp 412–416)

Formula 9.6 for the Power of a Hypothesis Test

$$\text{Power} = 1 - \beta$$

Formula 9.7 for the Critical Proportion for a Hypothesis Test for the Proportion

$$p_\alpha = p_{H_0} \pm (z_\alpha)\sqrt{\frac{p_{H_0}(1 - p_{H_0})}{n}}$$

A Summary of Hypothesis Tests for One Population

TYPE	σ	TEST STATISTIC	EQUATION
Mean	Known	$z_{\bar{x}} = \dfrac{\bar{x} - \mu_{H_0}}{\dfrac{\sigma}{\sqrt{n}}}$	9.1
Mean	Unknown	$t_{\bar{x}} = \dfrac{\bar{x} - \mu_{H_0}}{\dfrac{s}{\sqrt{n}}}$	9.2
Proportion	Not applicable	$z_p = \dfrac{\bar{p} - p_{H_0}}{\sqrt{\dfrac{p_{H_0}(1 - p_{H_0})}{n}}}$	9.4

CHAPTER 9 Problems

9.43 According to Hotels.com, the average room rate for a New York City hotel was $204 in 2011. Suppose the Chamber of Commerce of New York City would like to test if this rate has changed recently by randomly sampling 40 room rates. The mean of this sample was found to be $212.30. Assume the population standard deviation is $35. Using $\alpha = 0.05$, answer the following.

a. State the null and alternative hypothesis.

b. What conclusions can be drawn for this test?

c. Determine the p-value for this test and interpret its meaning.
d. Verify your results using PHStat.

9.44 According to comScore, Apple's smartphone operating system controlled 39% of the U.S. smartphone market in February 2013. Suppose Apple believes that this market share will increase due to recent advertising campaign. To test this hypothesis, a random sample of 275 smartphone users was selected, 126 of whom owned smartphones using Apple's operating system. Using $\alpha = 0.05$, answer the following.

a. State the null and alternative hypothesis.
b. Based on this sample, what conclusions can be drawn for this test?
c. Determine the p-value for this test and interpret its meaning.
d. Verify your results using PHStat.

9.45 In April 2013, President Obama's approval rating was 52%. Suppose the White House staff was concerned that the rating had fallen due to the administration's handling of the government's debt crisis during the summer of 2013. Let's say that out of a random sample of 300 adults, 144 approved of President Obama's performance during the summer of 2013. Using $\alpha = 0.05$, answer the following questions.

a. State the null and alternative hypothesis.
b. Based on this sample, what conclusions can be drawn for this test?
c. Determine the p-value for this test and interpret its meaning.
d. Verify your results using PHStat
e. How would the conclusions be affected if the White House chose to use $\alpha = 0.10$ rather than $\alpha = 0.05$.

9.46 Recently, Seasons Pizza has begun receiving complaints from customers about the amount of time they wait for their pizza deliveries. To address this issue, Seasons made some operational changes and added more delivery people to its staff. The restaurant would now like to test the hypothesis that the average delivery time is less than 30 minutes. The following data represent a random sample of delivery times:

23	24	23	36	30	40	34	24	28	29	15	27

Using $\alpha = 0.10$, answer the following:

a. State the null and alternative hypotheses.
b. Does this sample provide enough evidence to support Season's delivery claim?
c. Estimate the p-value for this test using Table 5 in Appendix A.
d. Determine the precise p-value for this test using Excel.
e. Use PHStat to validate these results.
f. What motivation might Season's Pizza have with choosing $\alpha = 0.10$?
g. What assumptions need to be made to perform this analysis?

9.47 According to the *Journal of the American Medical Association*, resident doctors worked an average of 59.3 hours per week at hospitals from 2006 to 2008. The Accreditation Council for Graduate Medical Education, which certifies residency programs in hospitals, has developed a plan to reduce the long hours resident doctors work. To investigate the plan's effectiveness, a random sample of the hours worked per week by 20 resident doctors was recently selected. They are as follows:

53	57	52	65	70	51	55	61	49	61
54	64	44	57	55	60	53	61	51	56

Using $\alpha = 0.05$, answer the following:

a. State the null and alternative hypotheses.
b. Does this sample provide enough evidence to suggest that the new residency plan is effective?
c. Estimate the p-value for this test using Table 5 in Appendix A.
d. Determine the precise p-value for this test using Excel.
e. Use PHStat to validate these results.
f. What assumptions need to be made to perform this analysis?

9.48 In July 2010, a survey conducted by Webroot, a software security firm, found that 32% of the respondents use the same passwords for all of the social networking Web sites they log on to (which, by the way, is not the best idea). Suppose a follow-up survey was recently conducted to investigate if the proportion had changed. Out of a random sample of 225 Internet users, it was found that 86 used the same password for all their social networking Web sites. Using $\alpha = 0.10$, answer the following:

a. State the null and alternative hypotheses.
b. What conclusions can be made about the proportion of Internet users who maintain the same passwords for all the social networking sites to which they log on?
c. Determine the p-value for this test and interpret its meaning.
d. Verify your results using PHStat.

9.49 A *Wall Street Journal* article reported that 15 of the 30 NBA teams have employees whose sole responsibility is to analyze data. The information compiled by these "statheads" is then used to help make decisions during games, for the draft, and to evaluate potential trades. At the time of the article's writing, the 15 teams had played a total of 962 games and had won 570 of them.

a. Using $\alpha = 0.01$, can it be concluded that teams who employ "statheads" (I confess I am not really thrilled with this word) have an advantage over those teams that do not?
b. Verify your results using PHStat.
c. What concerns might you have with using a hypothesis test in this situation?

9.50 According to Fidelity Investments, the average 401(k) account balance was $77,300 in 2013. To test if this average has recently changed, suppose a sample of 30 401(k) plans was recently selected, and it was found that the average 401(k) balance was $85,200. Assume the population standard deviation is $21,000. Using $\alpha = 0.02$, answer the following:

a. State the null and alternative hypothesis.
b. What conclusions can be made about the current average balance of 401(k) accounts?
c. Determine the p-value for this test and interpret its meaning.
d. Verify your results using PHStat.
e. If $\alpha = 0.05$ had been used rather than $\alpha = 0.02$, would the conclusions differ? Comment on this choice of alpha.

9.51 Smart meters are a special type of electrical meter that monitors the usage of electricity and communicates that information back to the utility company. According to the Energy Information Administration, 26.5% of homes in the United States were equipped with smart meters in 2011. To test if this percentage has changed, a random sample of 200 U.S. residences was recently selected, and it was found that 59 of them were equipped with smart meters. Using $\alpha = 0.05$, answer the following:

a. State the null and alternative hypothesis.
b. Based on this sample, do we have enough evidence to conclude that the percentage of homes in the United States equipped with smart meters has changed since 2011?
c. Determine the p-value for this test and interpret its meaning.
d. Verify your results using PHStat.

9.52 Suppose the Department of Transportation would like to test the hypothesis that the average gasoline consumption per car in the United States is 6 liters per day. (We're going metric here.) The following data represent the number of liters used per day for 25 randomly selected cars. These data can also be found in the Excel file labeled **liters.xlsx**.

9.2	2.9	12.0	2.4	5.3
16.4	6.1	7.6	9.6	1.3
9.4	8.9	6.7	11.9	9.0
11.3	6.6	9.3	4.6	7.2
6.1	10.7	0.4	6.6	5.4

Using $\alpha = 0.02$, answer the following:

a. State the null and alternative hypotheses.
b. What conclusions can be drawn based on this sample?
c. Estimate the p-value for this test using Table 5 in Appendix A.
d. Determine the precise p-value for this test using Excel.
e. Use PHStat to validate these results.
f. What assumptions need to be made to perform this analysis?

9.53 A growing number of younger employees have been participating in their company's retirement plans in recent years. According to Vanguard Group, 44% of employees under the age of 25 were making contributions to their 401(k) plans in 2011 (compared to just 27% in 2003). A random sample of 340 employees under the age of 25 was recently selected, and it was found that 167 of them made contributions to their 401(k) plans this year.

a. Using $\alpha = 0.01$, perform a hypothesis test to determine if the percentage of employees under the age of 25 who have made contributions to their 401(k) plan is more than 44%.
b. Determine the p-value for this test and interpret its meaning.
c. Verify your results using PHStat.
d. How would the conclusions be affected if you chose to use $\alpha = 0.05$ rather than $\alpha = 0.01$.

9.54 According to Pew Research Center surveys, 12% of American adults did not own a cell phone in 2012. Suppose Verizon Wireless would like to test if this percentage has recently changed. A recent random sample of 280 American adults was selected, and it was found that 29 of them did not own a cell phone. Using $\alpha = 0.10$, answer the following:

a. State the null and alternative hypothesis.
b. Based on this sample, what conclusions can Verizon Wireless make about this population?
c. Determine the p-value for this test and interpret its meaning.
d. Verify your results using PHStat.

9.55 According to a Staples/Decision Analyst survey conducted in 2013, full-time small-business owners in the United States worked an average of 50.4 hours per week. A recent random sample of 60 full-time small-business owners was selected, and it was found that they worked an average of 48.6 hours last week with a sample standard deviation of 11.4 hours.

a. Using $\alpha = 0.05$, is there enough evidence from this sample to conclude that the average number of hours that full-time small-business owners work per week is different than 50.4 hours?
b. Estimate the p-value for this test using Table 5 in Appendix A.
c. Determine the precise p-value for this test using Excel.
d. Use PHStat to validate these results.

9.56 U.S. cell phone customers reportedly sent an average of 700 text messages per month in 2012, which is lower than previous years. Suppose AT&T would like to test the hypothesis that the average number of text messages per month has declined since 2012. A recent random sample of 75 U.S. cell phone users was selected and the number of text messages sent last month was recorded. These data can be found in the Excel file titled **text messages.xlsx**. Using $\alpha = 0.05$, answer the following:

a. State the null and alternative hypothesis.
b. Based on this sample, what conclusions can AT&T make about this population?
c. Estimate the p-value for this test using Table 5 in Appendix A.
d. Determine the precise p-value for this test using Excel.
e. Use PHStat to validate these results.

9.57 Security experts are raising concerns about hackers targeting smartphones, as owners store more personal and financial information on the devices. In 2012, it was estimated that 7% of smartphone users were victims of malicious attacks on their mobile devices. A random sample of 190 smartphone owners was recently selected, and it was found that 17 had experienced attacks on their devices. Using $\alpha = 0.05$, answer the following:

a. Based on this sample, can we conclude that the percentage of smartphone owners who have had their devices hacked has changed since 2012?
b. Determine the p-value for this test and interpret its meaning.
c. Verify your results using PHStat.

9.58 During 2012, the average monthly bill for digital cable in the United States was $86 according to research firm Centris. Suppose Comcast would like to test the hypothesis that the average monthly bill is higher than $86 this year. A random sample of 52 households was chosen. Assume the standard deviation of monthly cable bills in the country is $17.

a. Explain in your own words how a Type I and Type II error can occur in this hypothesis test.
b. Using $\alpha = 0.01$, compute the probability of a Type II error occurring if the actual average monthly cable bill is $92.
c. Using $\alpha = 0.05$, compute the probability of a Type II error occurring if the actual average monthly cable bill is $92.
d. Explain the differences in the results you calculated in parts b and c.

9.59 The average wait time on the phone for taxpayers calling the IRS in 2012 was 1,080 seconds. Suppose (if you can use your imagination) that the IRS made operational changes in an effort to reduce wait times during 2013. To test the effectiveness of these changes, a random sample of 50 phone calls was selected and the wait time of each call was recorded. Assume the standard deviation for the wait time is 250 seconds.

a. Explain in your own words how Type I and Type II errors can occur in this hypothesis test.
b. Using $\alpha = 0.02$, calculate the probability of a Type II error occurring if the actual average wait time per call is 1,014 seconds.
c. Using $\alpha = 0.02$, calculate the probability of a Type II error occurring if the actual average wait time per call is 960 seconds.
d. Explain the differences in the results you calculated in parts b and c.

9.60 Suppose the average operating time per charge for a 6-volt laptop battery is currently 4.0 hours. Let's say SWET Electronic Technology claims it has developed a new 6-volt battery that has an average charge life that exceeds 4.0 hours. To test the effectiveness of this new technology, a random sample of 45 batteries was selected and the operating time per charge for each battery was recorded. Assume the standard deviation is 0.7 hours.

a. Explain in your own words how Type I and Type II errors can occur in this hypothesis test.
b. Using $\alpha = 0.05$, calculate the probability of a Type II error occurring if the average operating time per charge is actually 4.4 hours.
c. Using $\alpha = 0.01$, calculate the probability of a Type II error occurring if the average operating time per charge is actually 4.4 hours.
d. Explain the differences in the results you calculated in parts b and c.

9.61 According to the U.S. Department of Labor, 12.3% of the U.S. workforce was unionized in 2009. This percentage has declined steadily since the end of World War II, when more than a third of U.S. workers belonged to a union. Suppose the department would like to test the hypothesis that the proportion of union workers decreased in 2014 by randomly sampling 160 employees.

a. Explain in your own words how Type I and Type II errors can occur in this hypothesis test.
b. Using $\alpha = 0.05$, calculate the probability of a Type II error if the actual proportion of unionized employees in the workforce is 10%.
c. Using $\alpha = 0.05$, calculate the probability of a Type II error if the actual proportion of unionized employees in the workforce is 5%.
d. Explain the differences in the results you calculated in parts b and c.

9.62 Suppose the Real Estate Commission for the state of Delaware would like to test the hypothesis that the average number of days a home is on the market in New Castle County is 60 days. To test this hypothesis, 32 homes sold during the year were selected and the number of days that the homes were on the market was recorded. Assume the standard deviation for the time on the market is 25 days.

a. Explain in your own words how Type I and Type II errors can occur in this hypothesis test.
b. Using $\alpha = 0.05$, calculate the probability of a Type II error occurring if the actual average time for a house on the market is 54 days.

c. Using $\alpha = 0.05$, calculate the probability of a Type II error occurring if the actual average time for a house on the market is 78 days.
d. Explain the differences in the results you calculated in parts b and c.

9.63 Small businesses are viewed by many as the backbone of the U.S. economy. Small-business owners are often described as entrepreneurs, requiring a variety of skills in order to be successful. A 2013 survey of small-business owners found that the average age was 40 years. Suppose the Small Business Administration (SBA), which is a government agency that provides support to small businesses, would like to test the hypothesis that the average age of such businesses is now greater than 40 years. The Excel file labeled **SBA.xlsx** shows the ages of a recent sample of 100 small-business owners. Using $\alpha = 0.05$, answer the following:

a. Perform a hypothesis test to determine if the average age of a small-business owner exceeds 40 years.
b. Estimate the p-value for this test using Table 5 in Appendix A.
c. Determine the precise p-value for this test using Excel.
d. Use PHStat to validate these results.

9.64 Small businesses (See Problem 9.63) are viewed by many as the backbone of the U.S. economy. Small-business owners are often described as entrepreneurs, requiring a variety of skills in order to be successful. A 2013 survey of small-business owners found that 47% had a college degree beyond a bachelor's degree. Suppose the Small Business Administration (SBA), which is a government agency that provides support to small businesses, would like to test the hypothesis that the percentage of small-business owners with more than a bachelor's degree is different than 47%. The Excel file labeled **SBA.xlsx** shows the college degrees of a recent sample of 100 small-business owners. Using $\alpha = 0.05$, answer the following:

a. Perform a hypothesis test to determine the percentage of small-business owners with more than a bachelor's degree is different than 47%. You can use the following Excel function to count the number of small-business owners with more than a bachelor's degree in the data file:

= COUNTIF(B2:B101, "Yes")

b. Determine the p-value for this test and interpret its meaning.
c. Verify your results using PHStat.

9.65 A *Wall Street Journal* article discussed the impact that the recent economic downturn has had on the job market for clergy. Many churches have reduced or frozen the salaries and benefits for their clergy because donations from churchgoers have declined. The article reported that the average salary for an associate pastor with 10 years of experience is $64,000. Suppose that to investigate whether this average has changed recently, the National Association of Church Business Administration conducted a salary survey of pastors. The results can be found in the Excel file labeled **Pastor.xlsx**. Using PHStat with $\alpha = 0.05$, answer the following:

a. State the null and alternative hypotheses.
b. Do these data provide enough evidence to conclude that the average pastor salary has changed?
c. Estimate the p-value for this test using Table 5 in Appendix A.
d. Determine the precise p-value for this test using Excel.
e. Use PHStat to validate these results.

9.66 Recently, cell phone companies have been heavily investing in the African continent. With only half of its population owning a phone, Nigeria is considered a market that has much potential for growth. However, recent competition has driven prices for cell phones down in the country. It has been reported that the average monthly revenue earned per customer in Nigeria has been falling steadily since 2006 and is currently at $11. Vodafone, a U.K. cell phone company, has hired you to assist in the decision to enter the Nigerian market. If there is statistical evidence that the average monthly revenue is less than $11, Vodafone will choose not to invest in this market; otherwise, the company will invest. The Excel file labeled **Nigeria.xlsx** contains the monthly revenue from a random sample of 65 Nigerian mobile phone customers. Using PHStat with $\alpha = 0.05$, answer the following:

a. State the null and alternative hypotheses.
b. Based on this sample, what recommendations will you provide Vodafone?
c. Estimate the p-value for this test using Table 5 in Appendix A.
d. Determine the precise p-value for this test using Excel.
e. Use PHStat to validate these results.

CHAPTER 9 Solutions to Your Turn

YOUR TURN #1

1. $H_0: p \leq 0.70$ (the status quo)

   $H_1: p > 0.70$ (what the IRS hopes for)

   This is a one-tail test because the IRS would like to test that its campaign influenced *more* people to file electronically.

2. $H_0: \mu = 2.9$ (the status quo)

   $H_1: \mu \neq 2.9$

   Comcast is only testing that the average number of television sets per household is equal to 2.9. The company has no interest in knowing if this value is greater than or less than 2.9. Therefore, this is a two-tail test.

3. $H_0: \mu \geq 60$ days (status quo)

   $H_1: \mu < 60$ days (what the government hopes for)

   When the effect of a change in a process, such as a new tax-break program, is being measured, we are determining whether the status quo has been disrupted. The claim against the status quo is then assigned to the alternative hypothesis. This is a one-tail hypothesis test because we are interested in determining if the average number of days on the market is *less* than 60.

YOUR TURN #2

Step 1: Identify the null and alternative hypotheses.

Because Lindsay hopes to conclude that the average wait time is less than 20 minutes, we state the alternative hypothesis as $H_1: \mu < 20$.

$H_0: \mu \geq 20$

$H_1: \mu < 20$ (what Lindsay hopes to conclude)

Step 2: Set a value for the significance level, α.

$\alpha = 0.05$

Step 3: Determine the appropriate critical score.

Because this is a one-tail (lower) test, $-z_\alpha = -1.645$.

Step 4: Calculate the appropriate test statistic.

$$z_{\bar{x}} = \frac{\bar{x} - \mu_{H_0}}{\frac{\sigma}{\sqrt{n}}} = \frac{18.3 - 20}{\frac{5.0}{\sqrt{45}}} = \frac{-1.7}{0.745} = -2.28$$

Step 5: Compare the *z*-test statistic $(z_{\bar{x}})$ to the critical *z*-score (z_α).

Because $z_{\bar{x}} = -2.28$ is less than $-z_\alpha = -1.645$, we reject the null hypothesis according to Table 9.3 for a one-tail (lower) test.

Step 6: State your conclusions.

Because we can reject the null hypothesis, our sample of 45 wait times supports the conclusion that the average time customers wait for a table on Saturday night is less than 20 minutes.

YOUR TURN #3

$\bar{x} = 18.3 \quad \alpha = 0.05 \quad \mu_{H_0} = 20 \quad \sigma = 5.0 \quad n = 45$

$$z_{\bar{x}} = \frac{\bar{x} - \mu_{H_0}}{\frac{\sigma}{\sqrt{n}}} = \frac{18.3 - 20}{\frac{5.0}{\sqrt{45}}} = \frac{-1.7}{0.745} = -2.28$$

$$p\text{-value} = P(\bar{x} < 18.3) = P(z_{\bar{x}} < -2.28) = 0.0113$$

Because *p*-value $< \alpha$, we reject the null hypothesis. Our sample of 45 wait times supports the conclusion that the average wait time for a table is less than 20 minutes on Saturday night.

YOUR TURN #4

Step 1: Identify the null and alternative hypotheses.

$H_0: \mu = 18$ (status quo)

$H_1: \mu \neq 18$

The normal condition for this process is to average 18 ounces per box. This position is assigned the null hypothesis.

Step 2: Set a value for the significance level, α.

For this example, we set $\alpha = 0.05$.

Step 3: Determine the appropriate critical values.

Because this is a two-tail test with $\alpha = 0.05$, $z_{\alpha/2} = 1.96$ on the right side of the distribution and $-z_{\alpha/2} = -1.96$ on the left.

Step 4: Calculate the appropriate test statistic.

Using Equation 9.1,

$\bar{x} = 18.06 \quad \mu_{H_0} = 18 \quad \sigma = 0.25 \quad n = 40$

$$z_{\bar{x}} = \frac{\bar{x} - \mu_{H_0}}{\frac{\sigma}{\sqrt{n}}} = \frac{18.06 - 18}{\frac{0.25}{\sqrt{40}}} = \frac{0.06}{0.0395} = 1.52$$

Step 5: Compare the critical *z*-score $(z_{\alpha/2})$ with the z-test statistic $(z_{\bar{x}})$.

Because our *z*-test statistic, $z_{\bar{x}}$, is positive (1.52), we use the rejection region on the right side of the sampling distribution with its positive critical *z*-score (1.96). Taking the absolute value of each, we have $|z_{\bar{x}}| = 1.52$, which is less than $|z_\alpha| = 1.96$. According to Table 9.3 for a two-tail test, we do not reject the null hypothesis.

Step 6: State your conclusions.

We conclude that we have no evidence that the filling process is working improperly. Therefore, no corrective action needs to be taken. Note that we are *not* saying that the process is operating properly.

YOUR TURN #5

$\bar{x} = 18.06 \quad \alpha = 0.05 \quad \mu_{H_0} = 18 \quad \sigma = 0.25 \quad n = 40$

$$z_{\bar{x}} = \frac{\bar{x} - \mu_{H_0}}{\frac{\sigma}{\sqrt{n}}} = \frac{18.06 - 18}{\frac{0.25}{\sqrt{40}}} = \frac{0.06}{0.0395} = 1.52$$

$$p\text{-value} = 2 \times P(\bar{x} > 18.06) = 2 \times P(z_{\bar{x}} > 1.52)$$

$$p\text{-value} = (2)(0.0643) = 0.1286$$

Because p-value $\geq \alpha$, we do not reject H_0. We conclude that we have no evidence that the filling process is working improperly. Therefore, no corrective action needs to be taken.

YOUR TURN #6

H_0: $\mu = \$26{,}500$ (status quo)
H_1: $\mu \neq \$26{,}500$

The p-value $= 0.2449$ and $\alpha = 0.10$. Because the p-value $\geq \alpha$, we do not reject the null hypothesis. We conclude that we have no evidence that the average student debt has changed between 2011 and 2014.

	A		B	C
1	Z Test of Hypothesis for the Mean			
2				
3	Data			
4	Null Hypothesis	μ=	26500	
5	Level of Significance		0.1	
6	Population Standard Deviation		7500	
7	Sample Size		45	
8	Sample Mean		27800	
9				
10	Intermediate Calculations			
11	Standard Error of the Mean		1118.0340	
12	Z Test Statistic		1.1628	
13				
14	Two-Tail Test			
15	Lower Critical Value		-1.6449	
16	Upper Critical Value		1.6449	
17	p-Value		0.2449	
18	Do not reject the null hypothesis			
19				

YOUR TURN #7

a)

Step 1: Identify the null and alternative hypotheses.

H_0: $\mu \leq 290$ yards
H_1: $\mu > 290$ yards (my new ball claim)

Because I am claiming the performance of my golf ball is better than the current ball, my claim is assigned to the alternative hypothesis.

Step 2: Set a value for the significance level, α.

For this example, we set $\alpha = 0.10$.

Step 3: Determine the appropriate critical value.

To find our critical t-score, we locate the column associated with $\alpha = 0.10$ for a one-tail test and the row that corresponds to $15 - 1 = 14$ degrees of freedom in Table 5 in Appendix A. Because the rejection region is on the right side of the sampling distribution, $t_\alpha = 1.345$.

Step 4: Calculate the appropriate test statistic.

After we use Excel to calculate the sample mean and sample standard deviation from the data, we can then use Equation 9.2 to find our t-test statistic:

$\bar{x} = 293.5$ yards $\quad s = 14.8$ yards

$$t_{\bar{x}} = \frac{\bar{x} - \mu_{H_0}}{\frac{s}{\sqrt{n}}} = \frac{293.5 - 290}{\frac{14.8}{\sqrt{15}}} = \frac{3.5}{3.82} = 0.92$$

Step 5: Compare the t-test statistic ($t_{\bar{x}}$) with the critical t-score (t_α).

Applying the same logic that we used in Table 9.3 for a one-tail (upper) test, $t_{\bar{x}} = 0.92$ and $t_\alpha = 1.345$. Because $0.92 < 1.345$, we do not reject H_0.

Step 6: State your conclusions.

Failing to reject the null hypothesis means we do not have enough evidence to justify my claim that PGA golfers will average more than 290 yards using my ball. Even though my sample average exceeds 290 yards, it is too close to this value to justify my claim. Oh well, back to the drawing board!

b) The p-value is between 0.10 and 0.20. Using $\alpha = 0.10$, we fail to reject the null hypothesis.

c) $= \text{T.DIST.RT}(0.92, 14) = 0.1866$

YOUR TURN #8

a)

Step 1: Identify the null and alternative hypotheses.

H_0: $\mu = 60$ minutes

H_1: $\mu \neq 60$ minutes

Because we are testing the claim that the population mean is equal to 60 minutes, this statement needs to be assigned to the null hypothesis. The alternative hypothesis can never have an equal sign.

Step 2: Set a value for the significance level, α.

We set $\alpha = 0.05$.

Step 3: Determine the appropriate critical value.

Using Table 5 in Appendix A, we look in the two-tail 0.05 column and the row that corresponds to $11 - 1 = 10$ degrees of freedom, which gives us $t_{\alpha/2} = 2.228$.

Step 4: Calculate the appropriate test statistic.

Use the AVERAGE and STDEV.S functions in Excel to find the sample mean and sample standard deviation. Using those values in Equation 9.2, we can then find our *t*-test statistic.

$\bar{x} = 44.27$ minutes $\quad s = 20.4$ minutes

$$t_{\bar{x}} = \frac{\bar{x} - \mu_{H_0}}{\frac{s}{\sqrt{n}}} = \frac{44.27 - 60}{\frac{20.4}{\sqrt{11}}} = \frac{-15.73}{6.15} = -2.56$$

Step 5: Compare the t-test statistic ($t_{\bar{x}}$) with the critical *t*-score ($t_{\alpha/2}$).

Using the logic shown in Table 9.3 for a two-tail test, $|t_{\bar{x}}| = 2.56$ and $|t_{\alpha/2}| = 2.228$. Because $2.56 > 2.228$, we reject H_0.

Step 6: State your conclusions.

a) Rejecting the null indicates that we have support for the alternative hypothesis, H_1: $\mu \neq 60$ minutes. Therefore, we can conclude that the average amount of time this author works on chores over the weekend is not equal to 60 minutes. It appears from our sample mean of 44.27 minutes that his average time is less than 60 minutes.

b) The *p*-value ranges between 0.02 and 0.05. With $\alpha = 0.05$, we reject the null hypothesis.

c) The *p*-value $= 0.0285$, which is less than $\alpha = 0.05$. Therefore, we reject the null hypothesis, which is consistent with our previous conclusion.

	A		B	C
1	t Test for Hypothesis of the Mean			
2				
3	Data			
4	Null Hypothesis	μ=	60	
5	Level of Significance		0.05	
6	Sample Size		11	
7	Sample Mean		44.27272727	
8	Sample Standard Deviation		20.40142598	
9				
10	Intermediate Calculations			
11	Standard Error of the Mean		6.1513	
12	Degrees of Freedom		10	
13	t Test Statistic		-2.5568	
14				
15	Two-Tail Test			
16	Lower Critical Value		-2.2281	
17	Upper Critical Value		2.2281	
18	p-Value		0.0285	
19	Reject the null hypothesis			
20				

d) $= \text{T.DIST.2T}(2.56,10) = 0.0284$

Notice that we use the absolute value of -2.56 in this function.

e) Because σ is unknown and the sample size is less than 30, the population needs to be normally distributed to perform this test.

YOUR TURN #9

a)

Step 1: Identify the null and alternative hypotheses.

H_0: $p = 0.42$ (status quo)

H_1: $p \neq 0.42$

Step 2: Set a value for the significance level, α.

For this example, we set $\alpha = 0.01$.

Step 3: Determine the appropriate critical value.

Using Table 9.5 to determine the critical *z*-score, a two-tail test with $\alpha = 0.01$ results in $z_{\alpha/2} = 2.575$.

Step 4: Calculate the appropriate test statistic.

$$\bar{p} = \frac{x}{n} = \frac{54}{150} = 0.36$$

$$z_p = \frac{\bar{p} - p_{H_0}}{\sqrt{\frac{p_{H_0}(1 - p_{H_0})}{n}}} = \frac{0.36 - 0.42}{\sqrt{\frac{0.42(1 - 0.42)}{150}}}$$

$$z_p = \frac{-0.06}{\sqrt{0.001624}} = \frac{-0.06}{0.0403} = -1.49$$

Step 5: Compare the *z*-test statistic (z_p) to the critical *z*-score ($z_{\alpha/2}$).

Using the same logic outlined in Table 9.3 for a two-tail test, $|z_p| = 1.49$ and $|z_{\alpha/2}| = 2.575$. Because $1.49 \leq 2.575$, we do not reject H_0.

Step 6: State your conclusions.

Failing to reject the null indicates that we do not have support for the alternative hypothesis, H_1: $p \neq 0.42$. Therefore, we cannot conclude that the proportion of U.S. small-business owners that are firstborn in their family is different than 42%.

b) $p\text{-value} = 2 \times P(\bar{p} \leq 0.36) = 2 \times P(z_p \leq -1.49)$

$p\text{-value} = 2 \times (0.0681) = 0.1362$

Because the p-value $= 0.1362 \geq \alpha = 0.01$, we do not reject the null hypothesis.

c) $= 2 \times \text{NORM.S.DIST}(-1.49, \text{TRUE})$
$= 2(0.0681) = 0.1362$

d)

	A	B
1	Z Test of Hypothesis for the Proportion	
2		
3	Data	
4	Null Hypothesis π =	0.4200
5	Level of Significance	0.01
6	Number of Items of Interest	54
7	Sample Size	150
8		
9	Intermediate Calculations	
10	Sample Proportion	0.36
11	Standard Error	0.0403
12	Z Test Statistic	-1.4889
13		
14	Two-Tail Test	
15	Lower Critical Value	-2.5758
16	Upper Critical Value	2.5758
17	p-Value	0.1365
18	Do not reject the null hypothesis	
19		

YOUR TURN #10

The null and alternative hypotheses are stated as follows:

$$H_0: \mu \geq 61 \text{ (status quo)}$$
$$H_1: \mu < 61$$

Next, we need to calculate the critical mean using Equation 9.5.

$$\bar{x}_\alpha = \mu_{H_0} - (z_\alpha)\left(\frac{\sigma}{\sqrt{n}}\right)$$

$$\bar{x}_\alpha = 61 - (1.28)\left(\frac{10}{\sqrt{41}}\right) = 59.0$$

Because this is a lower tail test (H_1: $\mu < 61$), we reject the null hypothesis if our sample mean is less than 59 years old. Because the true population mean equals 60.0 according to the problem description, we should reject the null hypothesis. Beta is the probability of getting a sample mean greater than 59.0 from a population whose true mean is 60.0.

$$z = \frac{\bar{x}_\alpha - \mu}{\frac{\sigma}{\sqrt{n}}} = \frac{59.0 - 60.0}{\frac{10}{\sqrt{41}}} = \frac{-1}{1.562} = -0.64$$

$$\beta = P(\bar{x}_\alpha > 59.0) = P(z > -0.64) = 1.0 - 0.2611 = 0.7389$$
$$\text{Power} = 1 - \beta = 1 - 0.7389 = 0.2611$$

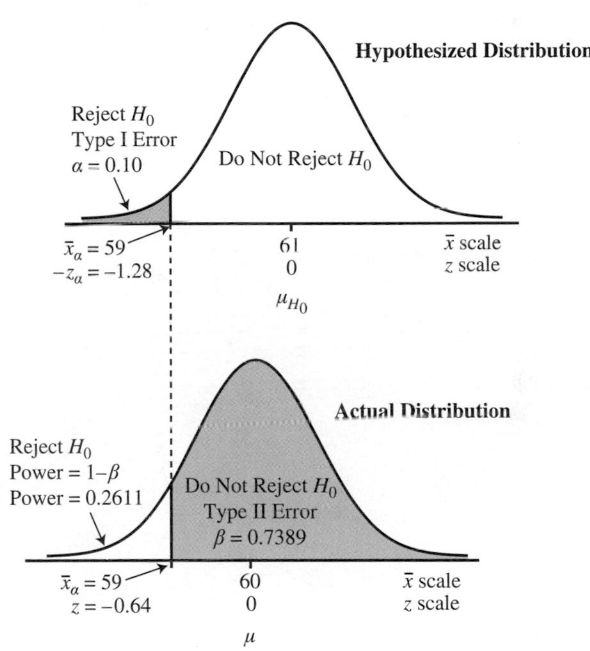

The power is fairly low because the hypothesized mean (61.0) is close to the actual mean (60.0). In other words, it's more difficult to properly reject the null when the true population mean is very close to the hypothesized mean.

CHAPTER

10

Hypothesis Tests Comparing Two Populations

IN THIS CHAPTER, YOU WILL LEARN TO:

- Compare the means of two populations when the population standard deviations are known using independent samples.
- Compare the means of two populations when the population standard deviations are unknown using independent samples.
- Compare the means of two populations when the population standard deviations are unknown using dependent samples.
- Use a confidence interval to compare two population means or two population proportions.
- Test a population difference other than zero.

CHAPTER 10 MAP

Now that you have mastered the art of one-sample hypothesis testing, it's time to step it up a notch and tackle the case of two-sample testing. Quite frankly, it's not that big of a notch. You can apply many of the techniques you learned in Chapter 9 to this chapter. I hope you were paying attention!

You may recall that after Apple released the iPhone 4 in 2010, there were a significant number of complaints by consumers that the phones were dropping calls. The issue was eventually traced back to the antenna design used in the device, and the controversy was quickly dubbed "antenna-gate." The situation also led to a debate about whether the rate of dropped iPhone calls differed on AT&T's network as compared to Verizon's network.

One way to resolve this debate would be to apply a two-sample hypothesis test to determine if there was a significant difference in the dropped call rates in the two populations. Each network could be sampled by making test calls at randomly selected locations. The proportion of dropped calls would be calculated for each network, and a two-sample hypothesis test would tell us if the two population proportions are significantly different. (Sound familiar?)

If my home were selected as a test site, I can almost guarantee a dropped call would occur because I live in a near-dead zone when it comes to cell phone reception. When my cell phone rings and I am home, I routinely race up the stairs to the front bedroom and hang out the window because it's the only way I can get a signal. For a while, our neighbors feared they had a writer living in their midst who was ready to make a suicidal, second-story leap.

Your author, as he risks his life taking a call from Deb. "Of course, dear. I wouldn't dream of playing golf until Chapter 10 is done." (Pay no attention to my golf attire.)

The business world is full of examples like the following that rely on comparing two populations:

- The U.S. government would like to investigate if a difference exists between the average salary of federal workers and that of their private-sector counterparts who hold the same types of jobs.
- A major bank would like to determine if the proportion of customers who do their banking online differs between older and younger customers.
- A consumer group would like to investigate whether running the air conditioner with the windows up on a specific car model reduces the car's gas mileage compared with not using the air conditioner with the windows down.

We will look at these examples, as well as others, as we explore comparing two populations throughout this chapter. You'll find that the topics in this chapter are similar to those found in Chapter 9.

- We'll start with the simplest hypothesis test, where we compare means when the population standard deviations are assumed to be known.
- As we discussed in Chapters 8 and 9, the population standard deviation is not always available. To handle this situation, we will use the sample standard deviation to approximate the population standard deviation and will rely on the Student's t-distribution. (Sound familiar? I sure hope so.)

- We will also investigate the case in which the two samples are related to each other (we'll call these dependent samples). You'll be happy to hear that this relationship actually simplifies the hypothesis testing procedure.
- We'll wrap up this chapter as we did the last by comparing the proportions for two different populations.

As you can see, we have a lot to cover in this chapter, so let's get started.

10.1 Comparing Two Population Means with
- Independent Samples
- Known Population Standard Deviations (σ_1 and σ_2)

To answer the questions posed in the previous section, we need to explore a new sampling distribution. This one has the fanciest name of them all—the sampling distribution for the difference in means (cue screeching violins as dramatic background music that raises the hair on the back of your neck). To illustrate this distribution and settle your nerves, consider the federal workers example that was just mentioned and look at Figure 10.1.

FIGURE 10.1
The Sampling Distribution for the Difference in Two Population Means

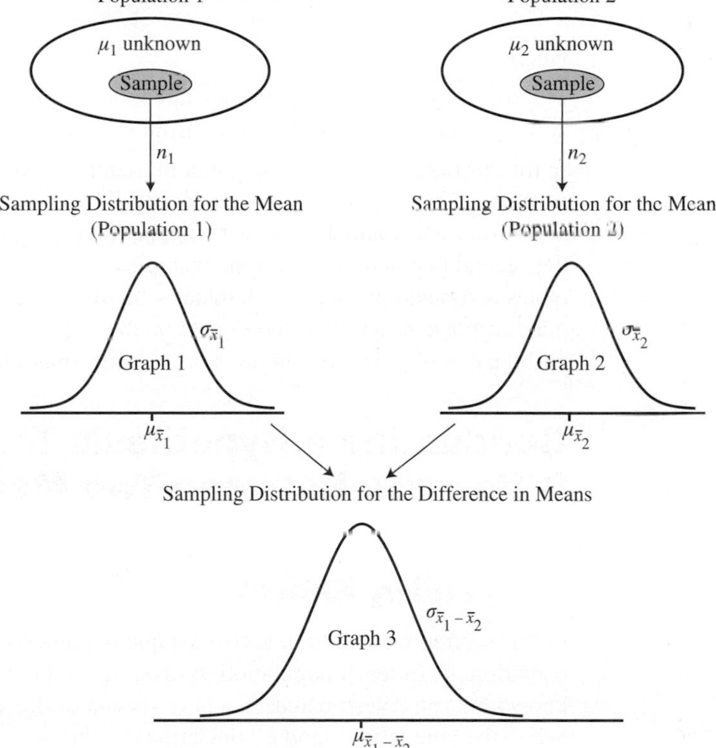

I'll arbitrarily make the federal workers Population 1 and the private-sector workers Population 2. Graph 1 in Figure 10.1 shows the sampling distribution for the salaries of the federal workers from a randomly selected sample of size n_1. As long as $n_1 \geq 30$, this sampling distribution will follow the normal probability distribution with a mean equal to $\mu_{\bar{x}_1}$ due to the Central Limit Theorem described in Chapter 7. Graph 2 represents the same information for the private-sector salaries.

Graph 3 in Figure 10.1 shows the distribution that represents the difference from all possible combinations of the sample means between the federal and private-sector salaries. This graph is known as the **sampling distribution for the difference in means**. The mean of this distribution is denoted as $\mu_{\bar{x}_1-\bar{x}_2}$ and is found using Equation 10.1.

The **sampling distribution for the difference in means** is the result of subtracting the sampling distribution for the mean of one population from the sampling distribution for the mean of a second population.

Formula 10.1 for the Mean of the Sampling Distribution for the Difference in Means

$$\mu_{\bar{x}_1 - \bar{x}_2} = \mu_{\bar{x}_1} - \mu_{\bar{x}_2}$$

where

$\mu_{\bar{x}_1}$ = The mean of the sampling distribution from Population 1
$\mu_{\bar{x}_2}$ = The mean of the sampling distribution from Population 2

In other words, the mean of the distribution in Graph 3 is the difference between the means shown in Graphs 1 and 2. Throughout this chapter, the subscript $\bar{x}_1 - \bar{x}_2$ represents the difference in the sample means of Populations 1 and 2.

The **standard error of the difference between two means** describes the variation in the difference between two sample means.

The standard deviation for Graph 3 is known as the **standard error of the difference between two means**. It describes the variation in the difference between two sample means and is found using Equation 10.2.

Formula 10.2 for the Standard Error of the Difference Between Two Means

$$\sigma_{\bar{x}_1 - \bar{x}_2} = \sqrt{\frac{\sigma_1^2}{n_1} + \frac{\sigma_2^2}{n_2}}$$

where

σ_1 and σ_2 = The standard deviations for Populations 1 and 2
n_1 and n_2 = The sample sizes from Populations 1 and 2

In this section, we are assuming that the samples from the two populations are **independent samples**. When samples are independent of one another, the results you observe when sampling from one population have no impact on the results you observe when sampling from the second population. Here's an example of two independent samples: Randomly selected males and randomly selected females who own iPads are asked their age. The age of each male respondent will have no impact on the age of any female respondent. Now before you pull the rest of your hair out, let's put this information to work in the next section.

Conducting a Hypothesis Test to Compare the Difference Between Two Means with

- **Independent Samples**
- **σ_1 and σ_2 Known**

In this section we will look at two-sample hypothesis tests when we know the standard deviation, σ, for each population. As you learned in Chapter 8, these values are often unknown but can be estimated. In a later section of this chapter, we will estimate these values. When the population standard deviations are known, we need to consider two different scenarios:

If we are sampling from a normal distribution, then our sampling distribution will also be normally distributed regardless of the sample size.

1. If our sample size is small $(n < 30)$, this hypothesis test requires that the population follow the normal distribution.
2. If our sample size is large $(n \geq 30)$, we know from the Central Limit Theorem that the sampling distribution follows the normal distribution. With this scenario, we have no restrictions on the population distribution.

To illustrate a hypothesis test when the standard deviation for each population is known, I'll use our earlier example where the U.S. government would like to investigate if a difference exists between the average salaries of federal workers and their private-sector counterparts. A random sample of 35 federal jobs that also exist in the private sector had an average salary of \$66,700. A random sample of 32 similar-type private-sector jobs had an average salary of \$60,400. Assume the population standard deviations for the federal and private-sector salaries are \$12,000 and \$11,000, respectively. Using $\alpha = 0.05$, can we conclude that there is a difference between federal and private-sector salaries for these two populations?

The two-sample hypothesis test steps that follow are very similar to the steps we learned for the one-sample tests in Chapter 9.

Step 1: Identify the null and alternative hypotheses.

This is a two-tail test because we are only testing if there is a difference in salary means, not if the mean of one population is either higher or lower than the mean of the other. The null hypothesis, H_0, for this two-tail test states that there is no difference between the average salaries of private-sector and federal employees. Another way to express this is that the difference between the two population means is equal to zero. The alternative hypothesis, H_1, is that there is indeed a difference in the average salaries of these two populations.

Clearly defining each population before stating your hypothesis can help you avoid confusion later in the analysis.

Always clearly define your populations at the outset of a test. I'll define Population 1 and 2 as follows:

Population 1 = Federal worker salaries
Population 2 = Private-sector salaries

This assignment is arbitrary and clearly defining it at the start eliminates any confusion later in the analysis.

Because the purpose of the test is to determine if a difference exists between private and federal salaries, this is a two-tail test. Had we been investigating if federal employees had higher salaries, it would be a one tail (upper) test.

The hypotheses statement for this example is as follows:

$$H_0: \mu_1 - \mu_2 = 0 \text{ (no difference in private and federal salaries)}$$
$$H_1: \mu_1 - \mu_2 \neq 0 \text{ (private and federal salaries are different)}$$

Step 2: Set a value for the significance level, α.

As we did for hypothesis testing for a single population (Chapter 9), the value of α should be chosen before we test the data. For our salary example, we have chosen $\alpha = 0.05$.

Step 3: Calculate the appropriate test statistic.

The test statistic for a difference between population means with σ_1 and σ_2 both known is shown in Equation 10.3.

Formula 10.3 for the z-Test Statistic for a Hypothesis Test for the Difference Between Two Means (σ_1 and σ_2 Known)

$$z_{\bar{x}} = \frac{(\bar{x}_1 - \bar{x}_2) - (\mu_1 - \mu_2)_{H_0}}{\sigma_{\bar{x}_1 - \bar{x}_2}}$$

where

$(\mu_1 - \mu_2)_{H_0}$ = The hypothesized difference in population means
$\sigma_{\bar{x}_1 - \bar{x}_2}$ = The standard error of the difference between two means
$\bar{x}_1 - \bar{x}_2$ = The difference in sample means between Populations 1 and 2

First, we'll calculate the standard error of the difference between the two means using Equation 10.2 as follows:

$$\sigma_{\bar{x}_1 - \bar{x}_2} = \sqrt{\frac{\sigma_1^2}{n_1} + \frac{\sigma_2^2}{n_2}} = \sqrt{\frac{12{,}000^2}{35} + \frac{11{,}000^2}{32}}$$

$$\sigma_{\bar{x}_1 - \bar{x}_2} = \sqrt{4{,}114{,}285.7 + 3{,}781{,}250} = \$2{,}809.90$$

The term $(\mu_1 - \mu_2)_{H_0}$ refers to the hypothesized difference between the two population means. Because the null hypothesis is testing that there is no difference between means, this term is 0.

Now we are ready to calculate the z-test statistic using Equation 10.3:

$$z_{\bar{x}} = \frac{(\bar{x}_1 - \bar{x}_2) - (\mu_1 - \mu_2)_{H_0}}{\sigma_{\bar{x}_1 - \bar{x}_2}} = \frac{(\$66{,}700 - \$60{,}400_1) - (0)_{H_0}}{\$2{,}809.90}$$

$$z_{\bar{x}} = \frac{(\$66{,}700 - \$60{,}400) - (0)_{H_0}}{\$2{,}809.90} = \frac{\$6{,}300}{\$2{,}809.90} = 2.24$$

Step 4: Determine the appropriate critical value.

Remember, our critical value defines the rejection region for the null hypothesis. The test statistic shown in Equation 10.3 follows the normal probability distribution. For your convenience, I have provided Table 10.1 which shows the critical z-scores for various levels of alphas taken from the standard normal table.

Remember from Chapter 9, I use the notation $Z_{\alpha/2}$ to refer to the critical z-score for a two-tail hypothesis test because the area associated with α is split in half on each side of the distribution.

TABLE 10.1 | CRITICAL Z-SCORES FOR VARIOUS ALPHAS

ALPHA (α)	TAIL	CRITICAL Z-SCORE
0.01	One	2.33
0.01	Two	2.575
0.02	One	2.05
0.02	Two	2.33
0.05	One	1.645
0.05	Two	1.96
0.10	One	1.28
0.10	Two	1.645

For a two-tail test with $\alpha = 0.05$, our critical z-scores are set to $z_{\alpha/2} = 1.96$.

Step 5: Compare the z-test statistic $(z_{\bar{x}})$ with the critical z-score $(z_{\alpha/2})$

This comparison is used to decide whether to reject or fail to reject the null hypothesis. To do so, we use the following decision rules that were introduced in Chapter 9 and are shown in Table 10.2.

TABLE 10.2 | DECISION RULES FOR HYPOTHESIS TESTS WHEN COMPARING THE Z-TEST STATISTIC AND CRITICAL Z-SCORE

TEST	HYPOTHESIS	CONDITION		CONCLUSION
Two-tail	$H_0: \mu = \mu_0$	$\lvert z_{\bar{x}}\rvert > \lvert z_{\alpha/2}\rvert$	$\rightarrow$	Reject H_0
	$H_1: \mu \neq \mu_0$	$\lvert z_{\bar{x}}\rvert \leq \lvert z_{\alpha/2}\rvert$	$\rightarrow$	Do not reject H_0
One-tail	$H_0: \mu \leq \mu_0$	$z_{\bar{x}} > z_\alpha$	$\rightarrow$	Reject H_0
(upper)	$H_1: \mu > \mu_0$	$z_{\bar{x}} \leq z_\alpha$	$\rightarrow$	Do not reject H_0
One-tail	$H_0: \mu \geq \mu_0$	$z_{\bar{x}} < -z_\alpha$	$\rightarrow$	Reject H_0
(lower)	$H_1: \mu < \mu_0$	$z_{\bar{x}} \geq -z_\alpha$	$\rightarrow$	Do not reject H_0

In our salary example, which is a two-tail test, $\lvert z_{\bar{x}}\rvert = 2.24$ and $\lvert z_{\alpha/2}\rvert = 1.96$. Because $2.24 > 1.96$, we come to the "reject H_0" conclusion. In other words, we cannot say that there is no difference between the average salaries of the two populations. Figure 10.2 illustrates this finding. Notice that $z_{\bar{x}}$ is in the shaded "Reject H_0" region.

FIGURE 10.2
Comparing the z-Test Statistic with the Critical z-Score

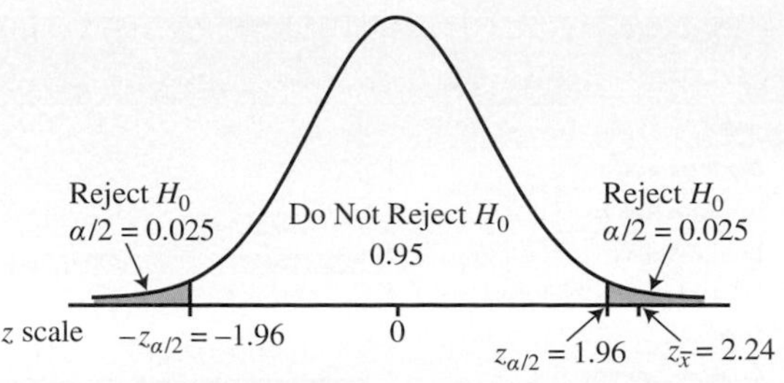

Step 6: Calculate the *p*-value.

In Chapter 9, we learned that the *p*-value is the probability of observing a sample mean at least as extreme as the one selected for the hypothesis test, assuming the null hypothesis is true. We can also apply this concept to our two-sample hypothesis test.

The two-tail *p*-value for our salary example is calculated as follows:

$$p\text{-value} = 2 \times P(z_{\bar{x}} > 2.24)$$
$$p\text{-value} = (2)(1 - 0.9875) = (2)(0.0125) = 0.025$$

The total area of the two shaded regions in Figure 10.3 represents this *p*-value.

FIGURE 10.3
The *p*-Value for a Two-Tail Hypothesis Test

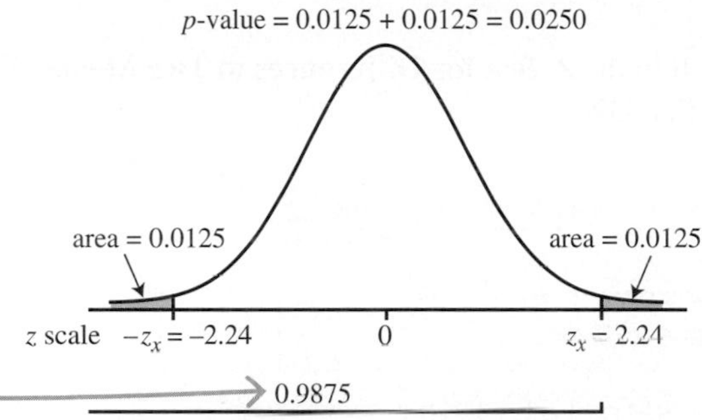

To find the area associated with $z_{\bar{x}} > 2.24$, we first need to find the area for $z_{\bar{x}} \le 2.24$. Using Table 4 in Appendix A, we determine that this area equals 0.9875. Therefore, $z_{\bar{x}} > 2.24 = 1.0 - 0.9875 = 0.0125$.

Using Table 10.3, we can compare the *p*-value to α when deciding to reject or not to reject the null hypothesis.

TABLE 10.3 | Decision Rules for Hypothesis Tests Using the p-Value

CONDITION	CONCLUSION
p-value $\ge \alpha \rightarrow$	Do not reject H_0
p-value $< \alpha \rightarrow$	Reject H_0

According to Table 10.3, because our *p*-value $= 0.025$ is less than $\alpha = 0.05$, we reject the null hypothesis.

Step 7: State your conclusions.

Our final step in this process is to conclude that, by rejecting the null hypothesis, we have support for the alternative hypothesis. According to these two samples, we have evidence to conclude that the average federal salary is not equal to the average private-sector counterpart. After looking at these sample averages, I need to send my résumé to Uncle Sam.

Using PHStat for a Hypothesis Test Comparing the Difference Between Two Means with

- **Independent Samples**
- **σ_1 and σ_2 Known**

We can perform this same procedure using PHStat by taking the following steps. Excel for Mac users can find these instructions on the textbook's Web site.

1. Go to **Add-Ins > PHStat > Two-Sample Tests (Summarized Data) > Z Test for Differences in Two Means**, as shown in Figure 10.4A.

FIGURE 10.4A
Conducting a Hypothesis Test to Compare the Difference Between Means Using PHStat: Independent Samples, σ_1 and σ_2 Known (Step 1)

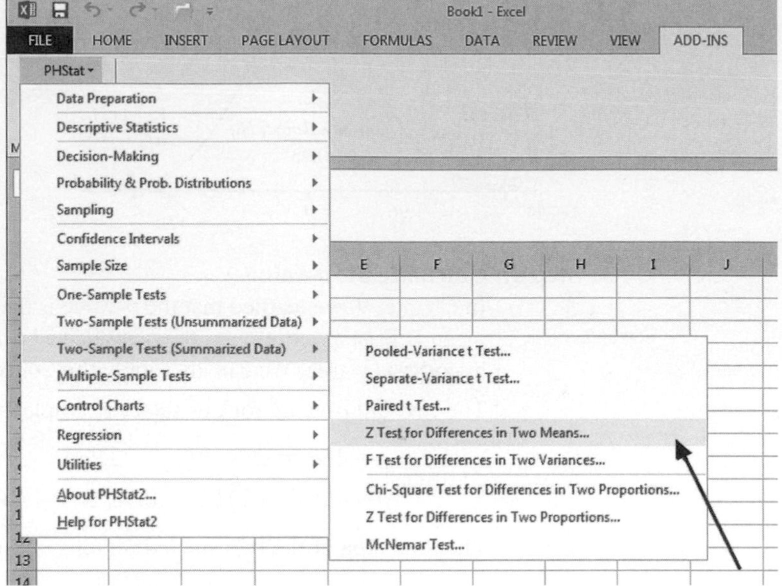

2. Fill in the ***Z* Test for Differences in Two Means** dialog box as shown in Figure 10.4B. Click **OK**.

FIGURE 10.4B
Conducting a Hypothesis Test to Compare the Difference Between Means Using PHStat: Independent Samples, σ_1 and σ_2 Known (Step 2)

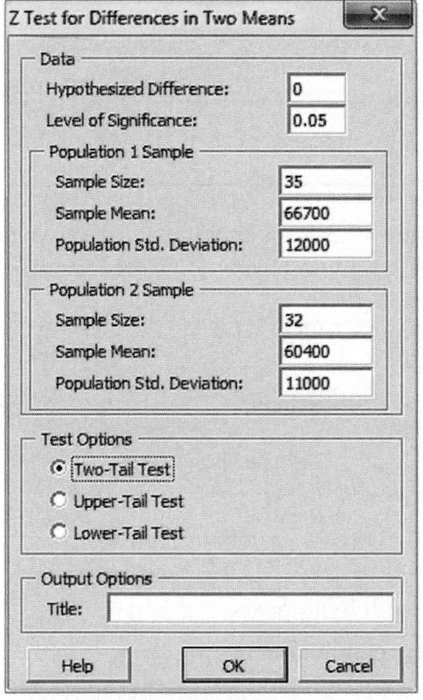

Figure 10.4C shows the output for this hypothesis test, which matches the results we obtained manually.

FIGURE 10.4c
Conducting a Hypothesis Test to Compare the Difference Between Means Using PHStat: Independent Samples, σ_1 and σ_2 Known (Final Result)

	A	B	C
1	**Z Test for Differences in Two Means**		
2			
3	**Data**		
4	**Hypothesized Difference**	0	
5	**Level of Significance**	0.05	
6	**Population 1 Sample**		
7	**Sample Size**	35	
8	**Sample Mean**	66700	
9	**Population Standard Deviation**	12000	
10	**Population 2 Sample**		
11	**Sample Size**	32	
12	**Sample Mean**	60400	
13	**Population Standard Deviation**	11000	
14			
15	Intermediate Calculations		
16	Difference in Sample Means	6300	
17	Standard Error of the Difference in Means	2809.9	
18	Z-Test Statistic	2.242073	
19			
20	Two-Tail Test		
21	**Lower Critical Value**	-1.95996	
22	**Upper Critical Value**	1.959964	
23	***p*-Value**	0.024957	
24	**Reject the null hypothesis**		
25			

Enough of watching me do all the work. The following Your Turn problem will give you a chance to see what you have learned so far in this chapter.

YOUR TURN #1

Major League Baseball officials (and many fans) have been concerned about the lengths of games recently, particularly playoff games. Suppose the officials would like to test the hypothesis that the mean length of a playoff game is longer than the mean length of a regular season game. A random sample of 30 playoff games over the past 10 years had an average length of 189.3 minutes. A random sample of 32 regular season games over the past 10 years had an average length of 175.8 minutes. Assume the standard deviations of the playoff and regular season games are 25 and 21 minutes, respectively. Using $\alpha = 0.02$, can we conclude that playoff games are longer, on average, than regular season games? Follow the seven steps from the previous section and verify your results with PHStat.

Answers can be found on ▶ **page 494**

Using a Confidence Interval to Compare the Difference Between Two Means with

- **Independent Samples**
- **σ_1 and σ_2 Known**

In Chapter 8, I introduced you to the concept of the confidence interval for the mean, which is an interval estimate around a sample mean. A confidence interval provides us with an idea of where the true population mean lies. We can extend this concept to estimate the interval around the difference between two sample means. Doing so will give us an idea of where the true difference in the population means lies.

Our sample size requirement still stands. That is, both sample sizes need to be 30 or more to use the Central Limit Theorem. Under these circumstances, there are no restrictions on the shape of the population distribution because our sampling distribution will be normal with large sample sizes. With smaller sample sizes, the populations need to be normally distributed.

The formulas for determining the upper and lower limits for the confidence interval for the difference between two means are shown in Equations 10.4 and 10.5.

Formulas 10.4 and 10.5 for the Confidence Interval for the Difference in the Means of Two Independent Populations (σ_1 and σ_2 Known)

$$UCL_{\bar{x}_1 - \bar{x}_2} = (\bar{x}_1 - \bar{x}_2) + z_{\alpha/2}\sigma_{\bar{x}_1 - \bar{x}_2}$$
$$LCL_{\bar{x}_1 - \bar{x}_2} = (\bar{x}_1 - \bar{x}_2) - z_{\alpha/2}\sigma_{\bar{x}_1 - \bar{x}_2}$$

where

$UCL_{\bar{x}_1 - \bar{x}_2}$ = The upper limit for the confidence interval
$LCL_{\bar{x}_1 - \bar{x}_2}$ = The lower limit for the confidence interval
$\sigma_{\bar{x}_1 - \bar{x}_2}$ = The standard error of the difference between two means (Equation 10.2)

Because they involve both upper and lower limits, all confidence intervals have two tails.

Let's construct a 95% confidence interval to estimate the true difference between the average salaries of federal and private-sector employees. We can use Table 10.1 to find the appropriate critical z-score by identifying the row that contains 0.05 as the value for $\alpha(1 - 0.95)$ and two as the number of tails. Thus, our critical z-score is $z_{\alpha/2} = 1.96$ for this interval. From the previous section, we know the following:

$$\bar{x}_1 = \$66{,}700 \qquad \bar{x}_2 = \$60{,}400 \qquad \sigma_{\bar{x}_1 - \bar{x}_2} = \$2{,}809.90$$

Plugging these values into Equations 10.4 and 10.5 provides us with the desired confidence interval:

When the confidence interval does not include zero, we have support that a significant difference between population means does exist. When the interval does include zero, we have no such support.

$$UCL_{\bar{x}_1 - \bar{x}_2} = (\bar{x}_1 - \bar{x}_2) + z_{\alpha/2}\sigma_{\bar{x}_1 - \bar{x}_2}$$
$$UCL_{\bar{x}_1 - \bar{x}_2} = (\$66{,}700 - \$60{,}400) + (1.96)(\$2{,}809.90)$$
$$UCL_{\bar{x}_1 - \bar{x}_2} = \$6{,}300 + \$5{,}507.40 = \$11{,}807.40$$

$$LCL_{\bar{x}_1 - \bar{x}_2} = (\bar{x}_1 - \bar{x}_2) - z_{\alpha/2}\sigma_{\bar{x}_1 - \bar{x}_2}$$
$$LCL_{\bar{x}_1 - \bar{x}_2} = (\$66{,}700 - \$60{,}400) - (1.96)(\$2{,}809.90)$$
$$LCL_{\bar{x}_1 - \bar{x}_2} = \$6{,}300 - \$5{,}507.40 = \$792.60$$

Our 95% confidence interval is (\$792.60, \$11,807.40). This means we are 95% confident that the difference between the average salary of federal and private-sector workers is between \$792.60 and \$11,807.40.

Notice that this confidence interval does not include \$0. This is important (hint: now is a good time to focus) because it provides supporting evidence that the true difference in the population means is not equal to zero. This is consistent with our previous conclusion to reject the null hypothesis.

When comparing two means, a negative value for the difference implies that the mean of the first group is less than the mean of the second group, on average. Likewise, a positive value implies the opposite.

To further clarify, let's pretend for a moment that the confidence interval in our salary example was $(-\$792.60, \$11{,}807.40)$. Remember, we defined Population 1 as federal workers and Population 2 as private-sector workers. When $\mu_1 - \mu_2$ (the difference in population means) is positive, federal workers have a higher average salary. When $\mu_1 - \mu_2$ is negative, private-sector workers have a higher average salary. If our confidence interval extends from a negative difference to a positive difference, we would not have enough evidence to say the difference can't be equal to zero. In other words, we would have been unable to reject the null hypothesis.

In this section, we have covered the "base case" of hypothesis testing for comparing two population means. That is, the two samples used in our example were independent of one another and both population standard deviations were known. Under these conditions, our sample test statistic follows the normal probability distribution. Tables 10.12 and 10.13 at the end of the chapter provide a summary of equations for this section. Take a crack at the next Your Turn problem to be sure you are confident with your new confidence interval procedure.

YOUR TURN #2

Construct a 90% confidence interval to estimate the difference in average game lengths between playoff and regular season games in Major League Baseball using the data from Your Turn #1.

Answer can be found on ▶ **page 495**

10.1 Section Problems

Basic Skills

10.1 Consider the following hypothesis statement using $\alpha = 0.05$ and data from two independent samples:

$$H_0: \mu_1 - \mu_2 = 0$$
$$H_1: \mu_1 - \mu_2 \neq 0$$
$$\bar{x}_1 = 237 \quad \bar{x}_2 = 218$$
$$\sigma_1 = 54 \quad \sigma_2 = 63$$
$$n_1 = 42 \quad n_2 = 35$$

a. Calculate the appropriate test statistic and interpret the result.
b. Calculate the p-value and interpret the result.
c. Verify your results using PHStat.

10.2 Consider the following hypothesis statement using $\alpha = 0.10$ and data from two independent samples:

$$H_0: \mu_1 - \mu_2 \leq 0$$
$$H_1: \mu_1 - \mu_2 > 0$$
$$\bar{x}_1 = 86 \quad \bar{x}_2 = 78$$
$$\sigma_1 = 24 \quad \sigma_2 = 18$$
$$n_1 = 50 \quad n_2 = 55$$

a. Calculate the appropriate test statistic and interpret the result.
b. Calculate the p-value and interpret the result.
c. Verify your results using PHStat.

10.3 Consider the following hypothesis statement using $\alpha = 0.01$ and data from two independent samples:

$$H_0: \mu_1 - \mu_2 \geq 0$$
$$H_1: \mu_1 - \mu_2 < 0$$
$$\bar{x}_1 = 122 \quad \bar{x}_2 = 139$$
$$\sigma_1 = 39 \quad \sigma_2 = 33$$
$$n_1 = 40 \quad n_2 = 45$$

a. Calculate the appropriate test statistic and interpret the result.
b. Calculate the p-value and interpret the result.
c. Verify your results using PHStat.

10.4 Consider the following data from two independent samples. Construct a 95% confidence interval to estimate the difference in population means.

$$\bar{x}_1 = 24 \quad \bar{x}_2 = 21$$
$$\sigma_1 = 6 \quad \sigma_2 = 5$$
$$n_1 = 38 \quad n_2 = 32$$

10.5 Consider the following data from two independent samples. Construct a 90% confidence interval to estimate the difference in population means.

$$\bar{x}_1 = 46 \quad \bar{x}_2 = 53$$
$$\sigma_1 = 10 \quad \sigma_2 = 12$$
$$n_1 = 30 \quad n_2 = 36$$

Business Applications

10.6 The following data show the average monthly utility bills for a random sample of households in Baltimore and for a random sample of households in Houston. (The bills include phone, television, Internet, electricity, and natural gas.)

	Baltimore	Houston
Sample mean	\$390.44	\$359.52
Sample size	33	36
Population standard deviation	\$64	\$58

a. Perform a hypothesis test using $\alpha = 0.05$ to determine if there is a difference between the mean utility bills in these two cities.
b. Determine the p-value and interpret the results.
c. Verify your results using PHStat.

10.7 Suppose the Bureau of Labor Statistics would like to investigate if the average retirement age for a worker in Japan is higher than the average retirement age for a worker in the United States. A random sample of 30 retired U.S. workers had an average retirement age of 64.6 years. A random sample of 30 retired Japanese workers had an average retirement age of 67.5 years. Assume the population standard deviation for the retirement age in the United States is 4.0 years and for Japan is 4.5 years.

a. Perform a hypothesis test using $\alpha = 0.05$ to determine if the average retirement age in Japan is higher than it is in the United States.
b. Determine the p-value and interpret the results.
c. Verify your results using PHStat.

10.8 Walmart has an interest in monitoring the average back-to-school spending for grade-school students year to year. The following table shows the average back-to-school spending of households randomly sampled in 2013 and 2014 along with the population standard deviations and sample sizes for each sample.

	2013	2014
Sample mean	\$606.40	\$548.72
Sample size	35	38
Population standard deviation	\$160	\$150

a. Perform a hypothesis test using $\alpha = 0.10$ to determine if the average household back-to-school spending in 2013 was different than it was in 2014.
b. Determine the p-value and interpret the results.
c. Verify your results using PHStat.

10.9 Expedia.com would like to estimate the difference between the average rental price of a car with an automatic transmission and the average rental price of a car with a manual transmission at London's Heathrow airport. A random sample of 50 cars with an automatic transmission had an average weekly rental of \$405.80. A random sample of 36 cars with manual transmission had an average weekly rental of \$339.20. Assume the population standard deviation for weekly rentals of cars with automatic transmissions is \$23 and for manual transmission is \$26.

a. Construct a 95% confidence interval to estimate the difference in the average cost of a one-week rental between these two types of cars at Heathrow.

b. Based on the results from part a, can you conclude that a difference exists in the average rental price of the two types of cars?

10.10 Salary data from two random samples of high school teachers from Pennsylvania and Ohio are as follows. Also shown are the population standard deviations for these populations.

	Pennsylvania	Ohio
Sample mean	\$53,289	\$49,945
Sample size	40	46
Population standard deviation	\$6,433	\$7,012

a. Construct a 90% confidence interval to estimate the difference in the average salaries of the high school teachers in these two states.

b. Based on the results from part a, can you conclude that a difference exists in the average salaries?

10.2 Comparing Two Population Means with

- Independent Samples
- Unknown Population Standard Deviations (σ_1 and σ_2)

When population standard deviations are not known to us (σ_1 *and* σ_2), we use the sample standard deviations (s_1 *and* s_2) in their place. When we make this substitution, we rely on the *t*-distribution to conduct the hypothesis test.

When the population standard deviations are not known to us, which is a common situation, we substitute the sample standard deviations in their place. This substitution affects the hypothesis test in two ways:

1. The Student's *t*-distribution is used in place of the normal distribution to identify the rejection region.
2. Both populations need to be normally distributed unless both sample sizes are 30 or larger.

If the populations are not normally distributed, the *t*-distribution can still be used to identify the rejection region if both sample sizes are 30 or more. This is because the shape of the *t*-distribution approaches the normal distribution as the sample size increases.

We have two cases to consider in this chapter when the population standard deviations are unknown:

- Case 1: The population variances are equal $(\sigma_1^2 = \sigma_2^2)$.
- Case 2: The population variances are not equal $(\sigma_1^2 \neq \sigma_2^2)$.

In Chapter 13, I will demonstrate a technique to test whether population variances are equal or not. Until then, we will just assume one way or the other.

Conducting a Hypothesis Test to Compare the Difference Between Two Means with

- **Independent Samples**
- **σ_1 and σ_2 Unknown**
- **Equal Population Variances**

The health care industry often uses two-sample hypothesis testing for research. For instance, studies have been done to investigate the effects of stimulation on the brain development of rats. (I guess the logic being that what's good for rats can't be all that bad for us humans.)

Suppose that two samples were randomly selected from the same rat population. The rats in the first sample—we'll call these the "lucky rats"—were surrounded with every luxury a rat could imagine. I can envision a country club atmosphere, complete with a golf course (and tiny golf carts), tennis courts, and a five-star restaurant where our lucky rats could feast on imported cheese and French wine while they discuss the state of the rat economy.

The second sample, whom we'll call the "less fortunate rats," didn't have it quite so good. These poor critters were locked in a barren cage and forced to eat imitation cheese from a can and watch reruns of reality television shows. Animal rights activists protested against this experiment, claiming the involuntary eating of imitation cheese is inhumane.

After the rats spent three months in each of these environments, the size of their brains were measured (by weight) to gauge its development. (I'll spare you the details as to how this was done, but I will tell you that Harvey the Rat mysteriously failed to show for his 8:00 A.M. tee time. His group went off without him.) Table 10.4 summarizes the gruesome findings.

TABLE 10.4 | SUMMARIZED DATA FROM THE RAT EXPERIMENT

POPULATION	AVERAGE BRAIN WEIGHT IN GRAMS	SAMPLE STANDARD DEVIATION	SAMPLE SIZE
	$\bar{x}$	s	n
Lucky rats	2.6	0.6	20
Less-fortunate rats	2.1	0.8	25

Because the sample sizes are less than 30, we need to assume that the brain weights in these two populations both follow the normal probability distribution.

Suppose the researchers would like to establish that more stimulation would lead to larger brain weight using $\alpha = 0.05$. For this hypothesis test, we need to assume that the two samples are independent of each other. In other words, the brain weights of the lucky rats have no effect on the brain weights of the less-fortunate rats.

I'll use the following steps to demonstrate the hypothesis testing procedure:

Step 1: Identify the null and alternative hypotheses.

I'll start by defining each population as follows:

Population 1 = lucky rats
Population 2 = less-fortunate rats

If we reverse the definitions for the populations, the signs for the null and alternative hypotheses would also be reversed and we would have a lower tail test. Either case would be acceptable.

The hypotheses statement for this example is as follows:

H_0: $\mu_1 - \mu_2 \leq 0$ (Pop 1 has brains that are less than or equal to Pop 2 in weight)
H_1: $\mu_1 - \mu_2 > 0$ (Pop 1 has brains that are greater than Pop 2 in weight)

where

μ_1 = The mean brain weight of the lucky rat population
μ_2 = The mean brain weight of the less-fortunate rat population

This is a one-tail (upper) test because the researchers are investigating whether Population 1 has an average brain size larger than Population 2, as stated in the alternative hypothesis, H_1 (also known as the research hypothesis).

Step 2: Set a value for the significance level, α.

For our rat-brain research, we decided to use $\alpha = 0.05$.

Step 3: Calculate the appropriate test statistic.

The test statistic for a difference between population means with σ_1 and σ_2 both unknown, but assumed to be equal, is shown in Equation 10.6. We will discuss the case of unequal variances in the next section.

Formula 10.6 for the t-Test Statistic for a Hypothesis Test for the Difference Between Two Means (σ_1 and σ_2 Unknown but Equal)

$$t_{\bar{x}} = \frac{(\bar{x}_1 - \bar{x}_2) - (\mu_1 - \mu_2)_{H_0}}{\sqrt{s_p^2\left(\frac{1}{n_1} + \frac{1}{n_2}\right)}}$$

where

$(\mu_1 - \mu_2)_{H_0}$ = The hypothesized difference in population means

s_p^2 = The pooled variance (see Equation 10.7)

The **pooled variance** is the weighted average of two sample variances drawn from two populations.

The **pooled variance** is simply the weighted average of two sample variances drawn from two populations. The pooled variance, s_p^2, can be found using Equation 10.7.

Formula 10.7 for the Pooled Variance

$$s_p^2 = \frac{(n_1 - 1)s_1^2 + (n_2 - 1)s_2^2}{(n_1 - 1) + (n_2 - 1)}$$

where

s_1^2 = The variance of the sample from Population 1

s_2^2 = The variance of the sample from Population 2

n_1 and n_2 = The sample size from Population 1 and 2

Using the data from Table 10.4 for our rat example, the pooled variance is calculated as follows:

$$s_p^2 = \frac{(n_1 - 1)s_1^2 + (n_2 - 1)s_2^2}{(n_1 - 1) + (n_2 - 1)}$$

$$s_p^2 = \frac{(20 - 1)(0.6)^2 + (25 - 1)(0.8)^2}{(20 - 1) + (25 - 1)} = \frac{(19)(0.36) + (24)(0.64)}{19 + 24} = 0.5163$$

I recommend carrying the pooled variance calculation out to four decimal places to avoid rounding errors in your end result.

Applying this to Equation 10.6, our t-test statistic is calculated as follows:

$$t_{\bar{x}} = \frac{(\bar{x}_1 - \bar{x}_2) - (\mu_1 - \mu_2)_{H_0}}{\sqrt{s_p^2\left(\frac{1}{n_1} + \frac{1}{n_2}\right)}}$$

$$t_{\bar{x}} = \frac{(2.6 - 2.1) - (0)}{\sqrt{(0.5163)\left(\frac{1}{20} + \frac{1}{25}\right)}} = \frac{0.5 - 0}{\sqrt{(0.5163)(0.09)}} = \frac{0.5}{0.2156} = 2.32$$

Sometimes my students confuse s_1 with s_1^2. The term s_1 represents the sample standard deviation taken from Population 1. The term s_1^2 represents the sample variance taken from Population 1, which is simply the square of the standard deviation.

Step 4: Determine the appropriate critical value.

The test statistic shown in Equation 10.6 follows the Student t-distribution with $n_1 + n_2 - 2$ degrees of freedom. Degrees of freedom (*df*) were introduced in Chapter 8 for the confidence interval estimation. For the rat example, we have the following:

Recall that the degrees of freedom for a one-sample test introduced in Chapter 9 is n–1.

$$df = n_1 + n_2 - 2 = 20 + 25 - 2 = 43$$

Using Table 5 in Appendix A for a one-tail (upper) test with 43 degrees of freedom and $\alpha = 0.05$, our critical t-score is $t_\alpha = 1.681$.

Step 5: Compare the t-test statistic ($t_{\bar{x}}$) with the critical t-score (t_α).

This comparison is used to decide whether to reject or fail to reject the null hypothesis. To do so, we use the following decision rules that were introduced in Chapter 9 and are shown in Table 10.5.

TABLE 10.5 | Decision Rules for Hypothesis Tests When Comparing the t-Test Statistic and Critical t-Score

TEST	HYPOTHESIS	CONDITION		CONCLUSION
Two-tail	$H_0: \mu = \mu_0$	$\lvert t_{\bar{x}} \rvert > \lvert t_{\alpha/2} \rvert$	$\rightarrow$	Reject H_0
	$H_1: \mu \neq \mu_0$	$\lvert t_{\bar{x}} \rvert \leq \lvert t_{\alpha/2} \rvert$	$\rightarrow$	Do not reject H_0
One-tail	$H_0: \mu \leq \mu_0$	$t_{\bar{x}} > t_\alpha$	$\rightarrow$	Reject H_0
(upper)	$H_1: \mu > \mu_0$	$t_{\bar{x}} \leq t_\alpha$	$\rightarrow$	Do not reject H_0
One-tail	$H_0: \mu \geq \mu_0$	$t_{\bar{x}} < -t_\alpha$	$\rightarrow$	Reject H_0
(lower)	$H_1: \mu < \mu_0$	$t_{\bar{x}} \geq -t_\alpha$	$\rightarrow$	Do not reject H_0

In our rat example, which is a one-tail (upper) test, $t_{\bar{x}} = 2.32$ and $t_\alpha = 1.681$. Because $2.32 > 1.681$, we reject the null hypothesis according to the decision rules shown in Table 10.5. Figure 10.5 shows that $t_{\bar{x}}$ is clearly in the shaded "Reject H_0" region.

FIGURE 10.5
Comparing the t-Test Statistic with the Critical t-Score

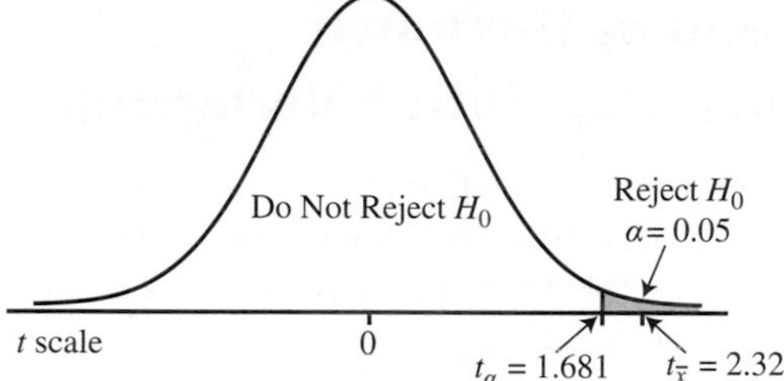

Step 6: Approximate the *p*-value

Recall from Chapter 9 the limitation we are faced with when using the *t*-distribution for hypothesis testing: We can no longer determine a precise *p*-value as we did using the normal distribution. This is because the structure of the *t*-table in Appendix A relies on the sample size (or degrees of freedom). However, we can still approximate the *p*-value when using the *t*-distribution, as Table 10.6 shows.

Recall that our *t*-test statistic, $t_{\bar{x}}$, is equal to 2.32. We need to find the critical *t*-scores that bracket $t_{\bar{x}} = 2.32$ along the $n - 1 = 44 - 1 = 43$ row in Table 5 from Appendix A. Table 10.6 shows these values to be 2.017 and 2.416, and they are highlighted in yellow. To find the corresponding *p*-values, we go to the **1 Tail** row and find *0.025* and *0.010*, also highlighted in yellow.

TABLE 10.6 | Excerpt of Critical t-Scores Shown in Table 5 in Appendix A

				p-VALUE IS IN THIS RANGE		
1 Tail	0.200	0.100	0.050	0.025 ↓	0.010	0.005
2 Tail	0.400	0.200	0.100	0.050	0.020	0.010
Conf Lev	0.600	0.800	0.900	0.950	0.980	0.990
df						
41	0.850	1.303	1.683	2.020	2.421	2.701
42	0.850	1.302	1.682	2.018	2.418	2.698
43	0.850	1.302	1.681	2.017 ↑	2.416	2.695
44	0.850	1.301	1.680	2.015	2.414	2.692
				$t_{\bar{x}} = 2.32$		

According to Table 10.6, the p-value for our hypothesis test is between 0.010 and 0.025. Even though we don't have a precise p-value, because $\alpha = 0.05$ is above this range, we can reject the null hypothesis.

Step 7: State your conclusions.

Rejecting the null hypothesis means we have support for the alternative hypothesis. According to these two samples, we have evidence to conclude that the average brain size of the lucky rat population is larger than the average size of the less-fortunate rat population.

The results of our rat study can greatly improve the lives of many. When your spouse or significant other catches you sneaking off to the golf course on Saturday morning with chores left unfinished, you can tell him or her with a straight face that you are just trying to improve your mind. We now have the statistics to support you. But be warned, you might develop a sore neck with all of that extra brain weight you are carrying around.

Using a Confidence Interval to Compare the Difference Between Two Means with

- **Independent Samples**
- **σ_1 and σ_2 Unknown**
- **Equal Population Variances**

We can also develop a confidence interval around the difference between the sample means to estimate the true difference in the populations when we don't know the population standard deviations. The formulas for determining the upper and lower limits for this confidence interval are shown in Equations 10.8 and 10.9.

Formulas 10.8 and 10.9 for the Confidence Interval for the Difference Between the Means of Two Independent Populations (σ_1 and σ_2 Unknown and Equal)

$$UCL_{\bar{x}_1-\bar{x}_2} = (\bar{x}_1 - \bar{x}_2) + t_{\alpha/2}\sqrt{s_p^2\left(\frac{1}{n_1} + \frac{1}{n_2}\right)}$$

$$LCL_{\bar{x}_1-\bar{x}_2} = (\bar{x}_1 - \bar{x}_2) - t_{\alpha/2}\sqrt{s_p^2\left(\frac{1}{n_1} + \frac{1}{n_2}\right)}$$

Let's construct a 95% confidence interval to estimate the true difference between the average brain weights of our two rat populations. Using Table 5 in Appendix A for a 95% confidence interval and $df = 43$, our critical t-score is $t_{\alpha/2} = 2.017$. In the previous section, we identified the following values:

$$\bar{x}_1 = 2.6 \qquad n_1 = 20$$
$$\bar{x}_2 = 2.1 \qquad n_2 = 25 \qquad s_p^2 = 0.5163$$

Using these values in Equations 10.8 and 10.9, we have our limits for the 95% confidence interval for the sample data from Table 10.4:

$$UCL_{\bar{x}_1-\bar{x}_2} = (\bar{x}_1 - \bar{x}_2) + t_{\alpha/2}\sqrt{s_p^2\left(\frac{1}{n_1} + \frac{1}{n_2}\right)}$$

$$UCL_{\bar{x}_1-\bar{x}_2} = (2.6 - 2.1) + (2.017)\sqrt{(0.5163)\left(\frac{1}{20} + \frac{1}{25}\right)}$$

$$UCL_{\bar{x}_1-\bar{x}_2} = (0.5) + (2.017)\sqrt{0.0465} = 0.5 + 0.4349 = 0.9349$$

$$LCL_{\bar{x}_1-\bar{x}_2} = (\bar{x}_1 - \bar{x}_2) - t_{\alpha/2}\sqrt{s_p^2\left(\frac{1}{n_1} + \frac{1}{n_2}\right)}$$

$$LCL_{\bar{x}_1-\bar{x}_2} = (2.6 - 2.1) - (2.017)\sqrt{(0.5163)\left(\frac{1}{20} + \frac{1}{25}\right)}$$

$$LCL_{\bar{x}_1-\bar{x}_2} = (0.5) - (2.017)\sqrt{0.0465} = 0.5 - 0.4349 = 0.0651$$

Our 95% confidence interval is (0.0651, 0.9349). This means we are 95% confident that the difference between the average brain weight of the two rat populations is between 0.0651 grams and 0.9349 grams. The fact that this interval does not include zero provides more evidence that there is a difference in average brain weights between these two populations.

One comment needs to be made when comparing the results of confidence intervals to hypothesis tests. A confidence interval is analogous to a two-tail hypothesis test because both will use the same identical critical value ($z_{\alpha/2}$ or $t_{\alpha/2}$) for a specific level of α. Recall from Chapter 8 that the confidence level for a confidence interval is described as $(1 - \alpha) \times 100\%$. For example, $\alpha = 0.05$ corresponds to a $(1 - 0.05) \times 100\% = 95\%$ confidence interval. Therefore, a two-tail hypothesis test and the corresponding confidence interval will always provide the same conclusions.

However, this may not be true for a one-tail hypothesis test and the corresponding confidence interval because the critical values will not be the same. Notice in our rat experiment example, the critical value for the one-tail hypothesis test was $t_\alpha = 1.681$ while the critical value for the corresponding confidence interval was $t_\alpha = 2.017$. Because the confidence interval has a higher critical value, there could be an instance when the hypothesis test rejects the null and the confidence interval fails to reject the null. In this case, the confidence interval requires stronger evidence to reject the null than the corresponding one-tail hypothesis test.

Using PHStat and Excel for a Hypothesis Test Comparing the Difference Between Two Means with

- **Independent Samples**
- **σ_1 and σ_2 Unknown**
- **Equal Population Variances**

PHStat refers to this procedure as a pooled-variance *t*-test, which can be performed by taking the following steps. Excel for Mac users can find these instructions on the textbook's web site.

1. Go to **Add-Ins** > **PHStat** > **Two-Sample Tests (Summarized Data)** > **Pooled-Variance t Test,** as can be seen in Figure 10.4A.
2. Fill in the **Pooled-Variance t Test** dialog box as shown in Figure 10.6A. Click **OK.**

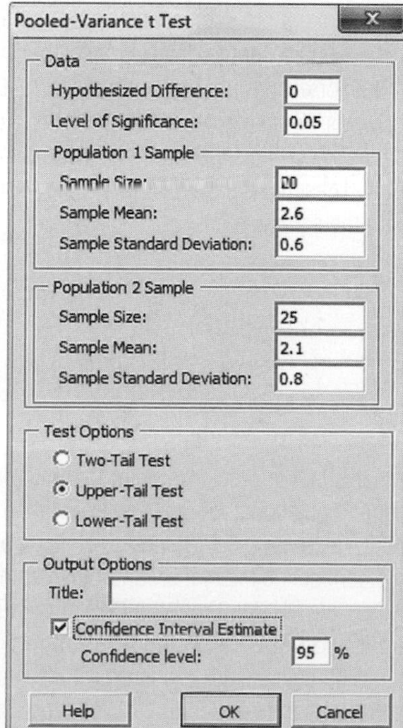

FIGURE 10.6A Conducting a Hypothesis Test to Compare the Difference Between Means Using PHStat: Independent Samples, σ_1 and σ_2 Unknown, and Equal Population Variances (Step 2)

Figure 10.6B shows the output for this hypothesis test, which matches the results we obtained manually.

FIGURE 10.6B Conducting a Hypothesis Test to Compare the Difference Between Means: Independent Samples, σ_1 and σ_2 Unknown, and Equal Population Variances (Final Result)

	A	B	C	D	E
1	**Pooled-Variance *t* Test for the Difference Between Two Means**				
2	(assumes equal population variances)				
3	**Data**			**Confidence Interval Estimate**	
4	**Hypothesized Difference**	0		**for the Difference Between Two Means**	
5	**Level of Significance**	0.05			
6	**Population 1 Sample**			**Data**	
7	**Sample Size**	20		**Confidence Level**	95%
8	**Sample Mean**	2.6			
9	**Sample Standard Deviation**	0.6		Intermediate Calculations	
10	**Population 2 Sample**			Degrees of Freedom	43
11	**Sample Size**	25		*t* Value	2.0167
12	**Sample Mean**	2.1		Interval Half Width	0.4347
13	**Sample Standard Deviation**	0.8			
14				**Confidence Interval**	
15	Intermediate Calculations			**Interval Lower Limit**	0.0653
16	Population 1 Sample Degrees of Freedor	19		**Interval Upper Limit**	0.9347
17	Population 2 Sample Degrees of Freedor	24			
18	Total Degrees of Freedom	43			
19	Pooled Variance	0.516279			
20	Standard Error	0.2156			
21	Difference in Sample Means	0.5			
22	***t* Test Statistic**	2.3196			
23					
24	**Upper-Tail Test**				
25	**Upper Critical Value**	1.6811			
26	***p*-Value**	0.0126			
27	**Reject the null hypothesis**				
28					

Notice that the p-value reported in Figure 10.6B is consistent with our findings using Table 10.6. Here we concluded that the p-value was in the interval between 0.01 and 0.025.

Notice that Cell B26 in Figure 10.6B shows that the *p*-value $= 0.0126$. Because this value is less than $\alpha = 0.05$, we have evidence to reject the null hypothesis. Also, the 95% confidence interval that we calculated in the previous section is shown in Cells E15 and E16.

We can also rely on Excel's T.DIST.RT function that provides a *p*-value for a one-tail (upper) test, which was introduced in Chapter 9:

$$=\text{T.DIST.RT}(x, \text{degrees\_ of\_ freedom})$$
$$=\text{T.DIST.RT}(2.32, 43) = 0.0126$$

Try this next Your Turn problem to help me win an argument with my significant other.

YOUR TURN #3

My wife and I have had an ongoing "discussion" about the quickest route to take traveling the 80 miles from our home in Wilmington, Delaware, to Avalon, New Jersey, where we like to visit for weekends during the summer. Deb prefers a more scenic, back-road route, with lots of annoying turns. My favorite course is on a major road where I get to drive 75 miles per hour. The travel time has been recorded for a random sample of trips for each route and is shown here. Deb has gone as far as accusing me of foul play by driving slower when we take her route. I'm counting on you to help me win this argument. (I don't win many, so please don't disappoint me.) Assume the population variances for the travel time on each route are equal. These data can be found in the Excel file titled **travel time.xlsx**. I suggest using Excel to calculate the sample statistics.

Deb's route:

100 115 109 112 107 111 112 119 93 126

Bob's route:

99 110 104 112 94 86 120 105 115 93 117 114

a. Perform a hypothesis test to prove my claim that my route takes less travel time than Deb's, using $\alpha = 0.05$. Define Population 1 as Bob and Population 2 as Deb.

b. Approximate the *p*-value using Table 5 in Appendix A, and interpret the results.

c. Construct a 95% confidence interval around these sample data.

d. Verify your results using PHStat. From the PHStat menu in Figure 10.4A, choose **Two-Sample Tests (Unsummarized Data) > Pooled-Variance t-Test**.

e. Determine the *p*-value using Excel and interpret the results.

f. What assumption needs to be made to validate these results?

Answers can be found on ▶ **pages 495–496**

Conducting a Hypothesis Test Comparing the Difference Between Two Means with

- **Independent Samples**
- **σ_1 and σ_2 Unknown**
- **Unequal Population Variances**

There are many situations in which the population variances are not equal or we simply cannot verify that they are equal. Under these conditions, the procedure from the previous section changes slightly. To illustrate, let's use the following example.

A consumer group would like to investigate if there is a difference in fuel economy for the following two scenarios using $\alpha = 0.05$.

1. Traveling in a particular car model with the air conditioning on and the windows up during the summer
2. Traveling in the same car model with the air conditioning off and the windows down during the summer

Running the air conditioner causes the engine to work harder, which will decrease the fuel economy. However, driving the car with the windows down increases drag—especially at a higher speed—which also reduces the fuel economy.

To collect data for this test, 10 randomly selected drivers were asked to drive a 2010 Nissan Maxima with the air conditioning on and the windows up using one full tank of gas on the highway. Eleven drivers were asked to do the same, but with the air conditioning off and the windows down. The data are shown in Table 10.7 and can also be found in the Excel file **Maxima.xlsx**. Assume that we have no information about the population variances and therefore cannot assume that they are equal.

TABLE 10.7 | Fuel Economy Data

POPULATION 1 (AIR CONDITIONING ON, WINDOWS UP)					
24.2	26.1	28.8	30.1	24.6	
29.1	28.2	27.4	28.3	27.9	
POPULATION 2 (AIR CONDITIONING OFF, WINDOWS DOWN)					
23.0	21.7	32.7	20.7	31.1	19.6
26.5	21.1	20.6	27.2	26.8	

I'll use the following steps to demonstrate the hypothesis testing procedure where the population variances are not equal.

Step 1: Identify the null and alternative hypotheses.

I start by defining each population as follows:

Population 1 = Air conditioning on, windows up
Population 2 = Air conditioning off, windows down

The hypotheses statements for this example are as follows:

$$H_0: \mu_1 - \mu_2 = 0 \text{ (Fuel economy of the 2 populations are the same)}$$
$$H_1: \mu_1 - \mu_2 \neq 0 \text{ (Fuel economy of the 2 populations are different)}$$

Because we are merely testing for a difference in population means, rather than if one population is greater than the other, this is a two-tail hypothesis test.

where

μ_1 = The average fuel economy from Population 1
μ_2 = The average fuel economy from Population 2

Step 2: Set a value for the significance level, α.

The difference in fuel economy for these two scenarios will be tested using $\alpha = 0.05$.

Step 3: Calculate the appropriate test statistic.

The test statistic for a difference between population means with σ_1 and σ_2 both unknown and not equal is shown in Equation 10.10.

Formula 10.10 for the t-Test Statistic for a Hypothesis Test for the Difference Between Two Means (σ_1 and σ_2 Unknown and Unequal)

$$t_{\bar{x}} = \frac{(\bar{x}_1 - \bar{x}_2) - (\mu_1 - \mu_2)_{H_0}}{\sqrt{\left(\frac{s_1^2}{n_1} + \frac{s_2^2}{n_2}\right)}}$$

We can use Excel to calculate the following sample statistics for our example:

$$\bar{x}_1 = 27.47 \quad s_1 = 1.931 \quad n_1 = 10$$
$$\bar{x}_2 = 24.64 \quad s_2 = 4.500 \quad n_2 = 11$$

Applying this to Equation 10.10, our t-test statistic is calculated as follows:

$$t_{\bar{x}} = \frac{(\bar{x}_1 - \bar{x}_2) - (\mu_1 - \mu_2)_{H_0}}{\sqrt{\left(\frac{s_1^2}{n_1} + \frac{s_2^2}{n_2}\right)}}$$

$$t_{\bar{x}} = \frac{(27.47 - 24.64) - 0}{\sqrt{\left(\frac{(1.931)^2}{10} + \frac{(4.5)^2}{11}\right)}} = \frac{2.83}{\sqrt{0.3729 + 1.8409}} = \frac{2.83}{1.488} = 1.90$$

Step 4: Determine the appropriate critical value.

The test statistic shown in Equation 10.10 follows the Student t-distribution, with degrees of freedom found using Equation 10.11.

Formula 10.11 for the Degrees of Freedom for the t-Distribution When Testing for the Difference Between Two Means (σ_1 and σ_2 Unknown and Unequal)

$$df = \frac{\left(\frac{s_1^2}{n_1} + \frac{s_2^2}{n_2}\right)^2}{\frac{\left(\frac{s_1^2}{n_1}\right)^2}{n_1 - 1} + \frac{\left(\frac{s_2^2}{n_2}\right)^2}{n_2 - 1}}$$

We can simplify matters here by showing the following terms, which were calculated using Equation 10.10:

$$\frac{s_1^2}{n_1} = \frac{(1.931)^2}{10} = 0.3729 \qquad \frac{s_2^2}{n_2} = \frac{(4.50)^2}{11} = 1.8409$$

Let's take our time and plug these values into Equation 10.11:

$$df = \frac{\left(\frac{s_1^2}{n_1} + \frac{s_2^2}{n_2}\right)^2}{\frac{\left(\frac{s_1^2}{n_1}\right)^2}{n_1 - 1} + \frac{\left(\frac{s_2^2}{n_2}\right)^2}{n_2 - 1}} = \frac{(0.3729 + 1.8409)^2}{\frac{(0.3729)^2}{10 - 1} + \frac{(1.8409)^2}{11 - 1}}$$

$$df = \frac{(2.2138)^2}{\frac{(0.1391)}{9} + \frac{3.3889}{10}} = \frac{4.9009}{0.0155 + 0.3389} = 13.8 \approx 13$$

Always round down the degrees of freedom value found using Equation 10.11. This makes it more challenging to reject the null hypothesis, which is a more conservative approach.

To obtain the most conservative hypothesis test, the degrees of freedom from Equation 10.11 should always be rounded down. This provides us with a larger critical t-score, which makes it more challenging to reject the null hypothesis. If you round the previous calculation up, you could end up rejecting the null hypothesis when, in fact, the null should not be rejected. This is a Type I error, which was discussed in Chapter 9. Using Table 5 in Appendix A for a two-tail test, $df = 13$, and $\alpha = 0.05$, our critical t-score is $t_{\alpha/2} = 2.160$.

Step 5: Compare the t-test statistic $(t_{\bar{x}})$ with the critical t-score $(t_{\alpha/2})$.

In our fuel economy example, which is a two-tail test, $|t_{\bar{x}}| = 1.90$ and $|t_{\alpha/2}| = 2.16$. Because $1.90 < 2.16$, we fail to reject the null hypothesis according to the decision rules shown in Table 10.5. Figure 10.7 shows $t_{\bar{x}}$ in the "Do Not Reject H_0" region.

FIGURE 10.7 Comparing the t-Test Statistic with the Critical t-Score

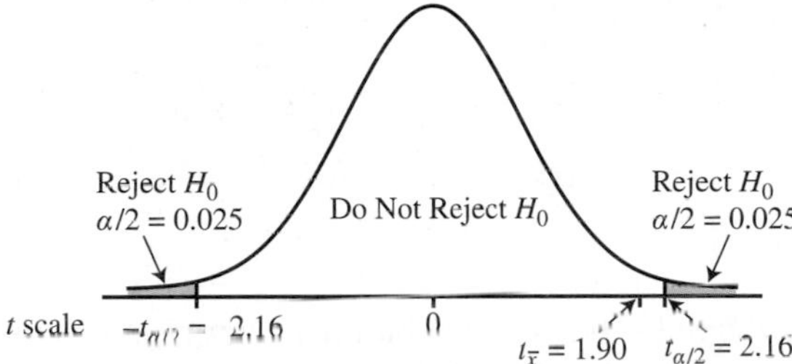

Step 6: Approximate the p-value.

Using Table 5 in Appendix A, go to the row with degrees of freedom equal to 13 and find the values that bracket $t_{\bar{x}} = 1.90$. These values are 1.771 and 2.160. Going to the **2 Tail** row, we find that the p-value is between 0.05 and 0.10. Because $\alpha = 0.05$ is outside of this range, we fail to reject the null hypothesis.

Step 7: State your conclusions.

Failing to reject the null hypothesis means we do not have support for the alternative hypothesis. According to these two samples, there is not enough evidence to claim a difference in fuel economy between these populations.

When in doubt about your assumption that the population variances are equal, the best strategy is to proceed with the unequal variances test. (Better to be safe than sorry!) Even if the population variances turn out to be equal, this procedure will still provide accurate results. On the other hand, if you incorrectly assume population variances are equal, your results may not be reliable.

Using Excel for a Hypothesis Test Comparing the Difference Between Two Means with

- **Independent Samples**
- **σ_1 and σ_2 Unknown**
- **Unequal Population Variances**

Excel's Data Analysis Tools (Windows only) can perform a variety of two-sample hypothesis tests, including the case in which population variance are unequal. However, this Excel

Excel for Mac users can perform this procedure with PHStat and can find instructions on the textbook's online resources.

procedure requires having the raw data available as seen in Table 10.7 in our fuel economy example using the following steps:

1. Enter the fuel economy data values in Columns A and B as shown in Figure 10.8A, or open the Excel file **Maxima.xlsx**.
2. Go to **Data** and click on **Data Analysis** on the right side of the ribbon as shown in Figure 10.8A. This opens the **Data Analysis** dialog box.
3. Select ***t*-Test: Two-Sample Assuming Unequal Variances**. Click **OK**.

FIGURE 10.8A
Conducting a Hypothesis Test to Compare the Difference Between Two Means Using Excel: Independent Samples, σ_1 and σ_2 Unknown, and Unequal Population Variances (Steps 1–3)

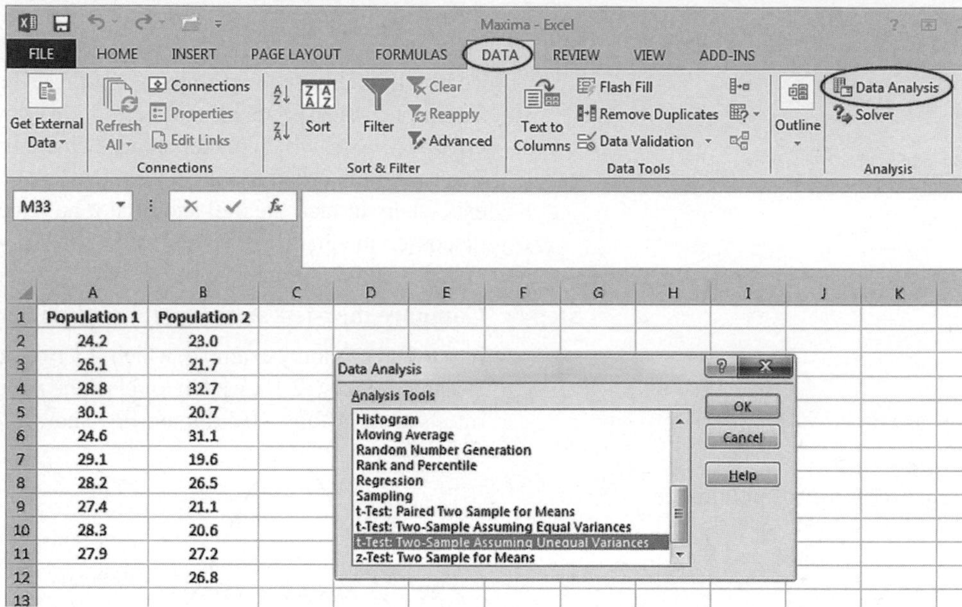

4. Fill in the **t-Test: Two-Sample Assuming Unequal Variances** dialog box as shown in Figure 10.8B. Click **OK**.

FIGURE 10.8B
Conducting a Hypothesis Test to Compare the Difference Between Two Means Using Excel: Independent Samples, σ_1 and σ_2 Unknown, and Unequal Population Variances (Step 4)

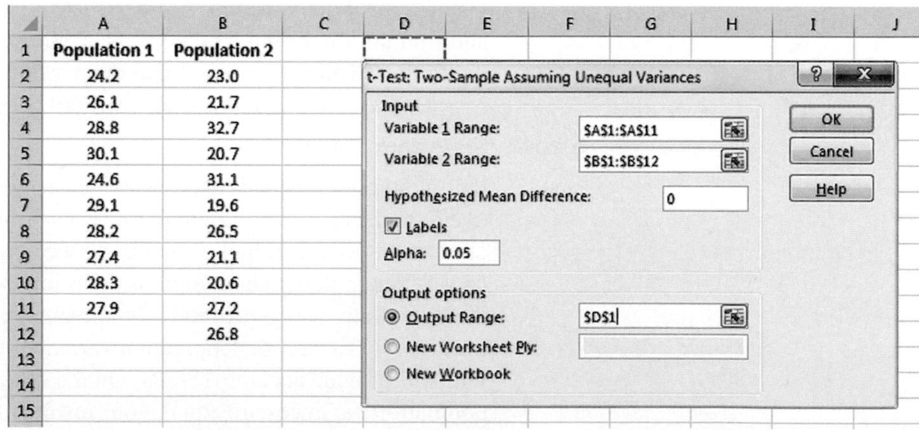

Figure 10.8C shows Excel's output for the fuel economy example.

FIGURE 10.8C
Conducting a Hypothesis Test to Compare the Difference Between Two Means Using Excel: Independent Samples, σ_1 and σ_2 Unknown, and Unequal Population Variances (Final Result)

	A	B	C	D	E	F
1	Population 1	Population 2		t-Test: Two-Sample Assuming Unequal Variances		
2	24.2	23.0				
3	26.1	21.7			*Population 1*	*Population 2*
4	28.8	32.7		Mean	27.47	24.63636364
5	30.1	20.7		Variance	3.729	20.24854545
6	24.6	31.1		Observations	10	11
7	29.1	19.6		Hypothesized Mean Difference	0	
8	28.2	26.5		df	14	
9	27.4	21.1		t Stat	1.904526432	
10	28.3	20.6		P(T<=t) one-tail	0.038797843	
11	27.9	27.2		t Critical one-tail	1.761310136	
12		26.8		P(T<=t) two-tail	0.077595685	
13				t Critical two-tail	2.144786688	
14						

Excel provides results for both a one-tail and a two-tail hypothesis. The two-tail output in Figure 10.8C is circled in red. Note that Excel rounds the degrees of freedom up from 13.8 to 14, which I advised against doing earlier in the chapter. Maybe somebody from Microsoft needs to take a business statistics class!

PHStat can also perform this procedure with unsummarized data using the following steps:

1. Go to **Add-Ins > PHStat > Two-Sample Tests (Unsummarized Data) > Separate-Variance t Test** . . . , as seen back in Figure 10.4A.
2. Fill in the **Separate-Variance t Test** dialog box in the same manner as seen in Figure 10.6A. Click **OK**.

Finally, we can use Excel's T.DIST.2T function to determine the precise p-value for our fuel economy example as follows:

$$=\text{T.DIST.2T}(x, \text{degrees\_of\_freedom})$$
$$=\text{T.DIST.2T}(1.90, 13) = 0.0798$$

This result is consistent with the p-value range of 0.05 to 0.10 found earlier. The slight difference between this result and the one found in Figure 10.8C (0.0776) is due to Excel using 14 degrees of freedom (rather than 13) and rounding that test statistic value to 1.90.

The following Your Turn problem gives you a chance to perform this type of hypothesis test to try out your skills.

YOUR TURN #4

Sprint would like to investigate if women average more minutes per month talking on their cell phones than men. The following data show the number of minutes per month a random sample of men and women talked on their phones. Assume the population variances for the number of minutes per month by men and women are not equal. These data can be found in the Excel file titled **Sprint.xlsx**. I suggest using Excel to calculate the sample statistics.

Men (Population 1)

314	324	288	561	295
299	319	367	207	333

Women (Population 2)

492	803	476	370	525
317	625	373	263	367

a. Perform a hypothesis test to test this claim using $\alpha = 0.01$.
b. If you perform this analysis correctly, you will fail to reject the null hypothesis. Can you explain the cause of this result in spite of the large difference in sample means?
c. Validate your results using Excel's Data Analysis.
d. Identify the precise p-value and interpret the result.
e. What assumption needs to be made to validate these results?

Answers can be found on ▶ **pages 496–497**

Testing a Difference Other Than Zero

So far in this chapter, all the examples tested whether or not there was any difference between two populations. There are situations, however, where we want to test whether the difference exceeds a certain value. For example, suppose the manager at a Ruby Tuesday restaurant would like to see if the type of music played in the restaurant affects the average bill incurred per person. The theory is that slower-paced music will influence patrons to stay longer and spend more compared with faster-paced music. Table 10.8 shows the average bill per person during evenings when the music was fast-paced vs. slow-paced, along with the sample sizes and standard deviations.

TABLE 10.8 | SUMMARIZED DATA FOR RUBY TUESDAY

POPULATION	SLOW MUSIC	FAST MUSIC
Sample mean	\$45.90	\$39.25
Sample standard deviation	\$5.60	\$5.20
Sample size	23	19

The manager would like to perform a hypothesis test to determine if the average bill per person when slow music was played exceeded by more than \$3.00 the average bill per person when fast music was played. We'll assume the population variances are equal and use $\alpha = 0.05$.

This is a one-tail (upper) test because the manger is testing to see if bills are larger for slow music when compared with fast music. If the manager were merely testing for a difference in bills between the two types of music, we would use a two-tail test.

I'll define Population 1 as slow music and Population 2 as fast music, resulting in the following hypothesis statement:

$$H_0\colon \mu_1 - \mu_2 \le \$3.00 \text{ (Bills for slow music average \$3.00 or less than fast)}$$
$$H_1\colon \mu_1 - \mu_2 > \$3.00 \text{ (Bills for slow music average \$3.00 more than fast)}$$

Use Equation 10.7 to calculate the pooled variance:

$$s_p^2 = \frac{(n_1 - 1)s_1^2 + (n_2 - 1)s_2^2}{(n_1 - 1) + (n_2 - 1)}$$

$$s_p^2 = \frac{(23 - 1)(5.60)^2 + (19 - 1)(5.20)^2}{(23 - 1) + (19 - 1)} = \frac{(22)(31.36) + (18)(27.04)}{22 + 18} = 29.4160$$

Applying this to Equation 10.6, our t-test statistic is calculated as follows:

Because we are testing to determine if the slow music bill averages \$3.00 more than the fast music bill, we need to reduce the t-statistic by \$3.00.

$$t_{\bar{x}} = \frac{(\bar{x}_1 - \bar{x}_2) - (\mu_1 - \mu_2)_{H_0}}{\sqrt{s_p^2\left(\frac{1}{n_1} + \frac{1}{n_2}\right)}}$$

$$t_{\bar{x}} = \frac{(45.90 - 39.25) - (3.00)}{\sqrt{(29.416)\left(\frac{1}{23} + \frac{1}{19}\right)}} = \frac{6.65 - 3.00}{\sqrt{(29.4160)(0.0961)}} = \frac{3.65}{1.681} = 2.17$$

Because we are assuming equal variances for this test, the degrees of freedom are as follows:

$$df = n_1 + n_2 - 2 = 23 + 19 - 2 = 40$$

Using Table 5 in Appendix A for a one-tail (upper) test, $df = 40$, and $\alpha = 0.05$, our critical t-score is $t_\alpha = 1.684$. Because $t_{\bar{x}} = 2.17 > t_\alpha = 1.684$, we reject the null hypothesis according to the decision rules shown in Table 10.5. By rejecting the null hypothesis, we can conclude that the average bill when slow music is played exceeds by more than \$3.00 the average bill when fast music is played.

Using PHStat to Test for a Difference Other Than Zero

Because Excel's Data Analysis Tools does not handle summarized data, I'll demonstrate how to analyze the Ruby Tuesday example with PHStat using the following steps. Excel for Mac users can refer to the textbook's Web site for instructions on this procedure.

1. Go to **Add-Ins** > **PHStat** > **Two-Sample Tests (Summarized Data)** > **Pooled-Variance t Test…**, as seen in Figure 10.4A.
2. Fill in the **Pooled-Variance t Test** dialog box as shown in Figure 10.9A, including the hypothesized difference of $3.00. Click **OK**.

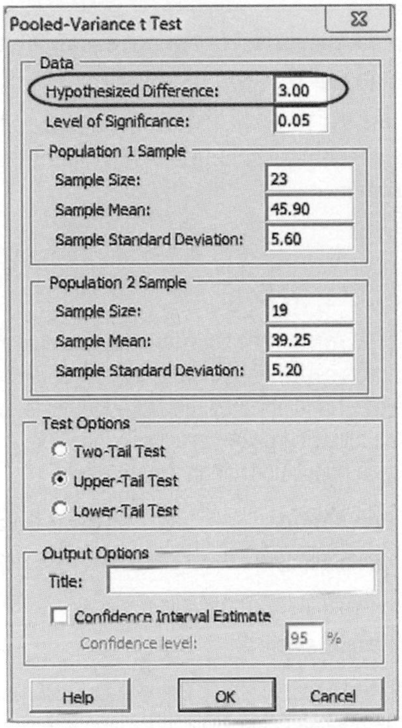

FIGURE 10.9A Testing for a Difference Other Than Zero Using PHStat (Steps 1 and 2)

Pooled-Variance t Test

Data
Hypothesized Difference: 3.00
Level of Significance: 0.05

Population 1 Sample
Sample Size: 23
Sample Mean: 45.90
Sample Standard Deviation: 5.60

Population 2 Sample
Sample Size: 19
Sample Mean: 39.25
Sample Standard Deviation: 5.20

Test Options
Two-Tail Test
Upper-Tail Test
Lower-Tail Test

Output Options
Title:
Confidence Interval Estimate
Confidence level: 95 %

Help OK Cancel

Figure 10.9B shows the output for this hypothesis test, which matches the results we obtained manually.

FIGURE 10.9B Testing for a Difference Other Than Zero Using PHStat (Final Result)

	A	B
1	Pooled-Variance *t* Test for the Difference Between Two Means	
2	(assumes equal population variances)	
3	Data	
4	Hypothesized Difference	3
5	Level of Significance	0.05
6	Population 1 Sample	
7	Sample Size	23
8	Sample Mean	45.9
9	Sample Standard Deviation	5.6
10	Population 2 Sample	
11	Sample Size	19
12	Sample Mean	39.25
13	Sample Standard Deviation	5.2
14		
15	Intermediate Calculations	
16	Population 1 Sample Degrees of Freedom	22
17	Population 2 Sample Degrees of Freedom	18
18	Total Degrees of Freedom	40
19	Pooled Variance	29.4160
20	Standard Error	1.6814
21	Difference in Sample Means	6.6500
22	*t* Test Statistic	2.1708
23		
24	Upper-Tail Test	
25	Upper Critical Value	1.6839
26	*p*-Value	0.0180
27	Reject the null hypothesis	
28		

In this section, I demonstrated testing for a mean other than zero when the population standard deviation was unknown. This type of hypothesis test can also be performed for the case where the population standard deviation is known, which was discussed previously in Section 10.1. You will also have the opportunity to test for a difference other than zero when working with population proportions later in the chapter.

We've covered a lot in this section, so let's quickly summarize what we've learned. We have been focusing on hypothesis testing using independent samples when the population standard deviations were unknown. We handled this condition by using the sample standard deviations to approximate the population standard deviations. As a result, the sample test statistic followed the Student's t-distribution. There are two scenarios to consider under this case:

1. When the population variances are equal, we used the pooled variance to calculate the test statistic.
2. When the population variances are not equal, we used Equation 10.11 to determine the number of degrees of freedom in order to identify the critical value.

Tables 10.12 and 10.13 at the end of the chapter provide a summary of equations for this section. Using these techniques, help me solve another hypothesis test involving Deb in this next Your Turn problem.

YOUR TURN #5

On our weekend trips to Avalon (see Your Turn #3), Deb always makes me wait until we get to New Jersey to buy gas. She is certain that the gas in New Jersey is at least $0.20 per gallon less expensive than in it is in Delaware. Undeterred by my last hypothesis-testing setback (again, see Your Turn #3), I bravely collected the following price-per-gallon data from a random selection of gas stations in both states. Assume that the population variances are equal.

Population	Delaware	New Jersey
Sample mean	$3.75	$3.52
Sample standard deviation	$0.12	$0.15
Sample size	13	10

a. Perform a hypothesis test to check Deb's claim using $\alpha = 0.05$.
b. Approximate the p-value using Appendix A and interpret the results.
c. Validate your results using PHStat.
d. Identify the precise p-value from the PHStat output and interpret the results.
e. What assumption needs to be made to validate these results?

Answers can be found on ▶ **page 497**

10.2 Section Problems

Basic Skills

10.11 Consider the following hypothesis statement using $\alpha = 0.05$ and data from two independent samples. Assume the population variances are equal and the populations are normally distributed.

$$H_0: \mu_1 - \mu_2 = 0$$
$$H_1: \mu_1 - \mu_2 \neq 0$$
$$\bar{x}_1 = 14.3 \qquad \bar{x}_2 = 12.8$$
$$s_1 = 2.7 \qquad s_2 = 3.3$$
$$n_1 = 20 \qquad n_2 = 18$$

a. Calculate the appropriate test statistic and interpret the result.
b. Approximate the p-value using Table 5 in Appendix A and interpret the results.
c. Determine the precise p-value using Excel.
d. Verify your results using PHStat.

10.12 Consider the following hypothesis statement using $\alpha = 0.05$ and data from two independent samples. Assume the population variances are equal and the populations are normally distributed.

$$H_0: \mu_1 - \mu_2 \le 10$$
$$H_1: \mu_1 - \mu_2 > 10$$
$$\bar{x}_1 = 76.3 \quad \bar{x}_2 = 61.5$$
$$s_1 = 18.4 \quad s_2 = 18.7$$
$$n_1 = 16 \quad n_2 = 20$$

a. Calculate the appropriate test statistic and interpret the result.
b. Approximate the p-value using Table 5 in Appendix A and interpret the results.
c. Determine the precise p-value using Excel.
d. Verify your results using PHStat.

10.13 Consider the following hypothesis statement using $\alpha = 0.05$ and data from two independent samples. Assume the population variances are not equal and the populations are normally distributed.

$$H_0: \mu_1 - \mu_2 = 0$$
$$H_1: \mu_1 - \mu_2 \ne 0$$
$$\bar{x}_1 = 114.7 \quad \bar{x}_2 = 122.0$$
$$s_1 = 24.6 \quad s_2 = 14.3$$
$$n_1 = 14 \quad n_2 = 20$$

a. Calculate the appropriate test statistic and interpret the result.
b. Approximate the p-value using Table 5 in Appendix A and interpret the results.
c. Determine the precise p-value using Excel.
d. Verify your results using PHStat.

10.14 Consider the following hypothesis statement using $\alpha = 0.10$ and data from two independent samples. Assume the population variances are not equal and the populations are normally distributed.

$$H_0: \mu_1 - \mu_2 \ge 0$$
$$H_1: \mu_1 - \mu_2 < 0$$
$$\bar{x}_1 = 144.0 \quad \bar{x}_2 = 156.3$$
$$s_1 = 16.8 \quad s_2 = 27.0$$
$$n_1 = 27 \quad n_2 = 21$$

a. Calculate the appropriate test statistic and interpret the result.
b. Approximate the p-value using Table 5 in Appendix A and interpret the results.
c. Determine the precise p-value using Excel.
d. Verify your results using PHStat.

10.15 Consider the following data from two independent samples with equal population variances. Construct a 95% confidence interval to estimate the difference in population means. Assume the population variances are equal and that the populations are normally distributed.

$$\bar{x}_1 = 37.2 \quad \bar{x}_2 = 32.5$$
$$s_1 = 8.9 \quad s_2 = 9.3$$
$$n_1 = 15 \quad n_2 = 16$$

10.16 Consider the following data from two independent samples with equal population variances. Construct a 90% confidence interval to estimate the difference in population means. Assume the population variances are equal and that the populations are normally distributed.

$$\bar{x}_1 = 68.7 \quad \bar{x}_2 = 75.1$$
$$s_1 = 12.5 \quad s_2 = 11.8$$
$$n_1 = 10 \quad n_2 = 14$$

Applications

10.17 The Transportation Security Administration would like to compare the average amount of time it takes passengers to pass through airport security at Philadelphia versus Orlando during peak times. A random sample of 25 travelers in Philadelphia spent an average of 14.6 minutes to pass through airport security with a sample standard deviation of 5.8 minutes. A random sample of 27 travelers in Orlando spent an average of 11.5 minutes to pass through airport security with a sample standard deviation of 4.9 minutes.

a. Perform a hypothesis test using $\alpha = 0.05$ to determine if the average time to pass through security in Philadelphia is more than the average time to pass through security in Orlando. Assume the population variances for time through security at these two locations are equal.
b. Approximate the p-value using Table 5 in Appendix A and interpret the results.
c. Determine the precise p-value using Excel.
d. Verify your results using PHStat.
e. What assumptions need to be made in order to perform this procedure?

10.18 The following table shows the average hourly wage rates for day-care centers from the Northeast and Midwest regions of the United States based on two random samples:

	Northeast	Midwest
Sample mean	\$9.60	\$8.60
Sample standard deviation	\$1.25	\$1.20
Sample size	26	31

a. Perform a hypothesis test using $\alpha = 0.05$ to determine if the average hourly wage for day-care workers in the Northeast is \$0.50 per hour higher than day-care workers in the Midwest. Assume the population variances for wage rates in each region are equal.
b. Approximate the p-value using Table 5 in Appendix A and interpret the results.
c. Determine the precise p-value using Excel.
d. Verify your results using PHStat.
e. What assumptions need to be made in order to perform this procedure?

10.19 The following table shows the results of two random samples that measured the average number of minutes per charge for AA Lithium-ion (Li-ion) rechargeable batteries versus Nickel–Metal Hydride (NiMH) rechargeable batteries:

	Li-ion	NiMH
Sample mean	96.5	82.9
Sample standard deviation	6.5	11.2
Sample size	14	18

a. Perform a hypothesis test using $\alpha = 0.10$ to determine if the average number of minutes per charge differs between these two battery types. Assume the population variances for the number of minutes per charge are not equal.
b. Approximate the p-value using Table 5 in Appendix A and interpret the results.
c. Determine the precise p-value using Excel.
d. Verify your results using PHStat.
e. What assumptions need to be made in order to perform this procedure?

10.20 Suppose a student organization at the University of Illinois collected data for a study involving class sizes from different departments. A random sample of 11 classes in the business department had an average size of 38.1 students with a sample standard deviation of 10.6 students. A random sample of 12 classes in the engineering department had an average size of 32.6 students with a sample standard deviation of 13.2 students.

a. Perform a hypothesis test using $\alpha = 0.05$ to determine if the average class size differs between these departments. Assume the population variances for the number of students per class are not equal.
b. Approximate the p-value using Table 5 in Appendix A and interpret the results.
c. Determine the precise p-value using Excel.
d. Verify your results using PHStat.
e. What assumptions need to be made in order to perform this procedure?

10.21 An online travel agent who specializes in cruises wanted to compare the cost of cruising to different destinations on various cruise lines. The following random sample data show the average cost of a seven-day cruise in a standard room to Alaska vs. the average cost of a seven-day cruise in a standard room to the Caribbean. Assume the population variances for cruise fares for these destinations are equal.

	Alaska	Caribbean
Sample mean	\$994	\$925
Sample standard deviation	\$135	\$128
Sample size	9	12

a. Construct a 95% confidence interval to estimate the difference between the average rates of cruising to Alaska vs. cruising to the Caribbean.
b. What conclusions can be made about the difference in rates between these destinations?
c. What assumptions need to be made in order to perform this procedure?

10.22 The following table shows the average number of words understood by later-born and first-born one-year-old children from two random samples. Assume the population variances of the number of words understood are equal.

	Later-Born	First-Born
Sample mean	430.2	552.0
Sample standard deviation	130.8	133.7
Sample size	12	12

a. Construct a 98% confidence interval to estimate the difference between the average number of words understood by first-born and later-born one-year-old children.
b. What conclusions can be made about the difference between the two populations?
c. What assumptions need to be made in order to perform this procedure?

10.3 Hypothesis Testing with Dependent Samples

Up to this point, all of the samples that we have used in the chapter have been independent samples. Samples are independent if they are not related in any way to each other. By contrast, with **dependent samples**, each observation from one sample is related to an observation from the other sample.

With **dependent samples**, each observation from one sample is related to an observation from the other sample.

A classic example of a dependent sample would be a weight-loss study. Each person is weighed at the beginning (Population 1) and end (Population 2) of the program. The change in weight of each person is calculated by subtracting each of the Population 2 weights from each of the Population 1 weights. In other words, each observation from Population 1 is matched to an observation in Population 2. The hypothesis test that deals with dependent samples is known as a **matched-pair test** because, as you will see in this section, we match up the two related observations from each population in our analysis.

A hypothesis test using dependent samples is known as a **matched-pair test**.

Recall the Maxima example described in Table 10.7. Because different cars were used in each population, the samples were independent. However, if the fuel economy had been measured for the same car under both conditions, the samples would have been considered dependent.

Other examples of matched-pair tests include the following scenarios:

- The test-preparation company Kaplan would like to measure the effectiveness of its MCAT review course for students applying to medical school. Each student is given a pretest before the course, which is then compared with the student's posttest score after having taken the course.
- Citibank would like to test the effectiveness of a promotional campaign designed to encourage customers to use its credit cards. The credit card balances of selected customers before and after the promotion are compared.
- Pfizer would like to test the effectiveness of Lipitor, its cholesterol medication. Cholesterol levels of patients before and after the medication is prescribed are compared.

Conducting a Hypothesis Test to Compare the Difference Between Two Means with Dependent Samples

Hypothesis tests for dependent samples are tested differently than those for independent samples. To demonstrate this technique, I'll use the following example. Rockstar is an energy drink distributed by PepsiCo and sold in grocery stores. Josh is a PepsiCo account manager for nine different stores and is responsible for product sales and inventory. Josh would like to test the hypothesis that placing the product on the ends of aisles results in more sales than placing the product on middle-aisle shelves, using $\alpha = 0.05$. For each of his nine stores, Josh displayed the Rockstar inventory on the end of an aisle for one week and then on a middle-aisle shelf for another week. Table 10.9 shows the number of units of Rockstar sold in each aisle location at each of the nine stores. The data can also be found in the Excel file **Rockstar.xlsx**.

TABLE 10.9 | ROCKSTAR WEEKLY SALES

STORE	1	2	3	4	5	6	7	8	9
End aisle	64	54	126	97	37	74	117	90	81
Middle aisle	72	41	100	62	40	60	122	62	78

I hope you recognize this as an example of two dependent samples. (I envision you looking at me quizzically.) Take the first two data points, 64 and 72. They are related to each other because they both were recorded from Store 1 and are, therefore, considered a matched pair. The same logic can be used for the other eight pairs of sales data from Stores 2 through 9.

As with our previous examples, we need to define our populations:

Population 1: End-aisle sales

Population 2: Middle-aisle sales

The choice for assigning populations here is completely arbitrary. I could have easily reversed these assignments. However, once they are made, be sure to use them consistently throughout the analysis.

I'll use the following steps to walk you through the t-test for matched pairs using $\alpha = 0.05$.

Step 1: Calculate the matched-pair differences.

The matched-pair difference in our Rockstar example is found by subtracting the middle-aisle sales from the end-aisle sales for each store using Equation 10.12.

Formula 10.12 for the Matched-Pair Difference

$$d = x_1 - x_2$$

where

d = The matched-pair difference

x_1 and x_2 = The matched-pair values from Populations 1 and 2, respectively

Because I chose to assign end-aisle sales as Population 1, a positive value of d represents a store where end-aisle sales exceeded middle-aisle sales, which Josh hopes to conclude.

Table 10.10 shows the matched-pair difference calculations for the Rockstar example.

Be sure to keep track of the positive and negative values for the matched-pair differences for the next step.

TABLE 10.10 | MATCHED-PAIR DIFFERENCES FOR ROCKSTAR

END AISLE	MIDDLE AISLE	*d*
64	72	−8
54	41	+13
126	100	+26
97	62	+35
37	40	−3
74	60	+14
117	122	−5
90	62	+28
81	78	+3

Step 2: Calculate the mean and standard deviation of the matched-pair differences.

The mean of the matched-pair differences, $\bar{d}$, can be found using Equation 10.13.

Formula 10.13 for the Mean of the Matched-Pair Differences

$$\bar{d} = \frac{\sum_{i=1}^{n} d_i}{n}$$

where

$\bar{d}$ = The mean of the matched-pair differences

d_i = The ith matched-pair difference

n = The number of matched-pair differences

Plugging the data from Table 10.7 into Equation 10.13 provides the following result:

Our average difference would be negative if the middle-aisle displays averaged more sales than end-aisle. This is based on how we defined Populations 1 and 2 at the beginning.

$$\bar{d} = \frac{\sum_{i=1}^{n} d_i}{n} = \frac{(-8)+13+26+35+(-3)+14+(-5)+28+3}{9} = \frac{103}{9} = 11.44$$

This tells us that across the nine stores, end-aisle displays average 11.44 more unit sales per week than middle-aisle displays. Next, we calculate the standard deviation of the matched-pair differences. Here we can use either Equation 10.14 or Equation 10.15, which is the short-cut version of Equation 10.14. These equations were first introduced back in Chapter 3.

Formulas 10.14 and 10.15 for the Standard Deviation of the Matched-Pair Differences

$$s_d = \sqrt{\frac{\sum_{i=1}^{n}(d_i - \bar{d})^2}{n-1}}$$

or

$$s_d = \sqrt{\frac{\sum_{i=1}^{n} d_i^2 - \frac{\left(\sum_{i=1}^{n} d_i\right)^2}{n}}{n-1}}$$

where

s_d = The standard deviation of the matched-pair differences

Table 10.11 shows the calculations using Equation 10.15.

TABLE 10.11 | STANDARD DEVIATION CALCULATIONS FOR MATCHED-PAIR DIFFERENCES: ROCKSTAR EXAMPLE

d_i	d_i^2
−8	64
13	169
26	676
35	1,225
−3	9
14	196
−5	25
28	784
3	9
Sum of the differences:	**Sum of the squared differences:**
$\sum_{i=1}^{9} d_i = 103$	$\sum_{i=1}^{9} d_i^2 = 3{,}157$
Squared sum of the differences: $\left(\sum_{i=1}^{9} d_i\right)^2 = (103)^2 = 10{,}609$	

Now, carefully plug the values from Table 10.11 into Equation 10.15. Note that $n = 9$ because we have nine matched pairs (stores) in our sample.

$$s_d = \sqrt{\frac{\sum_{i=1}^{n} d_i^2 - \frac{\left(\sum_{i=1}^{n} d_i\right)^2}{n}}{n-1}} = \sqrt{\frac{3{,}157 - \frac{10{,}609}{9}}{9-1}} = \sqrt{\frac{3{,}157 - 1{,}178.78}{8}} = 15.73$$

You can also use Excel to calculate the mean (=AVERAGE) and the standard deviation (=STDEV.S) for the matched-pair differences.

Step 3: Identify the null and alternative hypotheses.

Here's the beauty of the matched-pair *t*-test. Instead of performing a two-sample test comparing the end-aisle and middle-aisle sales, the matched-pair test uses a one-sample test on the matched-pair differences. In the Rockstar example, if the mean population difference is positive, we have support that the end-aisle sales are higher than the middle-aisle sales. Conversely, if this difference is negative, we have evidence that the middle-aisle sales are higher than the end-aisle sales.

Because Josh would like to test whether the end-aisle sales are higher, the hypotheses statement for this example is as follows:

The matched-pair test uses a one-sample hypothesis test on the matched-pair differences.

H_0: $\mu_d \leq 0$ (End-aisle sales are less than or equal to middle-aisle sales)

H_1: $\mu_d > 0$ (End-aisle sales are higher than middle-aisle sales)

where

μ_d = The population mean matched-pair difference

If the end-aisle population mean is greater than the middle-aisle population mean, then μ_d will be greater than zero. This is because Equation 10.12 has defined the matched-pair difference as Population 1 (end-aisle) minus Population 2 (middle-aisle). Therefore, we have a one-tail (upper) test with this example.

Step 4: Set a value for the significance level, α.

In the opening description for this example, we set $\alpha = 0.05$. Remember to choose this value *before* beginning the analysis.

Step 5: Calculate the appropriate test statistic.

The test statistic for our matched-pair difference is shown in Equation 10.16.

Formula 10.16 for the t-Test Statistic for a Matched-Pair Hypothesis Test for the Mean

$$t_{\bar{x}} = \frac{\bar{d} - (\mu_d)_{H_0}}{\dfrac{s_d}{\sqrt{n}}}$$

where

$(\mu_d)_{H_0}$ = The population mean matched-pair difference from the null hypothesis

Applying the results from steps 1 and 2 to Equation 10.16, our *t*-test statistic is calculated as follows:

Because the null hypothesis states there is no difference in the average sales between end-aisle and middle-aisle displays, this value is zero.

$$t_{\bar{x}} = \frac{\bar{d} - (\mu_d)_{H_0}}{\dfrac{s_d}{\sqrt{n}}} = \frac{11.44 - 0}{\dfrac{15.73}{\sqrt{9}}} = \frac{11.44}{5.24} = 2.18$$

Step 6: Determine the appropriate critical value.

Because the sample standard deviation, s_d, was used in place of the unknown population standard deviation, the test statistic shown in Equation 10.16 follows the Student *t*-distribution with $n - 1$ degrees of freedom. For our Rockstar example, $df = n - 1 = 9 - 1 = 8$.

Using Table 5 in Appendix A for a one-tail (upper) test, $df = 8$, and $\alpha = 0.05$, our critical *t*-score is $t_\alpha = 1.860$.

Step 7: Compare the *t*-test statistic ($t_{\bar{x}}$) with the critical *t*-score (t_α).

In our Rockstar example, which is a one-tail (upper) test, $t_{\bar{x}} = 2.18$ and $t_\alpha = 1.860$. Because $2.18 > 1.860$, we reject the null hypothesis according to the decision rules shown in Table 10.5. Figure 10.10 illustrates this finding. Notice that $t_{\bar{x}}$ is in the "Reject H_0" region.

FIGURE 10.10
Comparing the t-Test Statistic with the Critical t-Score

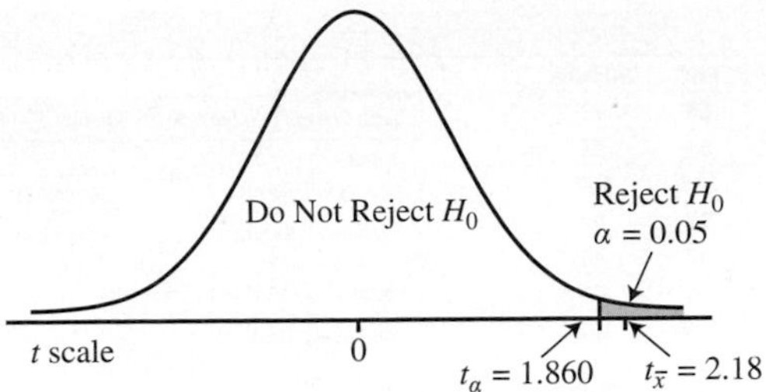

Step 8: Approximate the *p*-value.

Using Table 5 in Appendix A, go to the row in which $df = 8$ and find the values that bracket $t_{\bar{x}} = 2.18$. These values are 1.860 and 2.306. Going to the **1 Tail** row, we find that the *p*-value is between 0.025 and 0.050. Because $\alpha = 0.05$ is within this range, we can reject the null hypothesis.

Step 9: State your conclusions.

By rejecting the null hypothesis, we have enough evidence to conclude that the average weekly sales from end-aisle displays are greater than those for middle-aisle displays. These results should encourage Josh to convince the store managers to display his Rockstar inventory at the end of aisles rather than in the middle.

Using Excel for a Hypothesis Test Comparing the Difference Between Two Means with Dependent Samples

Excel for Mac users can perform this procedure with PHStat and can find instructions on the textbook's online resources.

Excel's Data Analysis Tools (Windows only) can also perform the hypothesis test comparing the difference between two means when working with dependent samples. However, this Excel procedure requires having the raw data available as seen in Table 10.9 in our Rockstar weekly sales example using the following steps:

1. Enter the Rockstar sales data in Columns A through C as shown in Figure 10.11A, or open the Excel file **Rockstar.xlsx**.
2. Go to **Data** and click on **Data Analysis** on the right side of the ribbon, as shown in Figure 10.11A. This opens the **Data Analysis** dialog box.
3. Select **t-Test: Paired Two Sample for Means**. Click **OK**.

FIGURE 10.11A
Conducting a Hypothesis Test Comparing the Difference Between Means Using Excel: Dependent Samples (Steps 1–3)

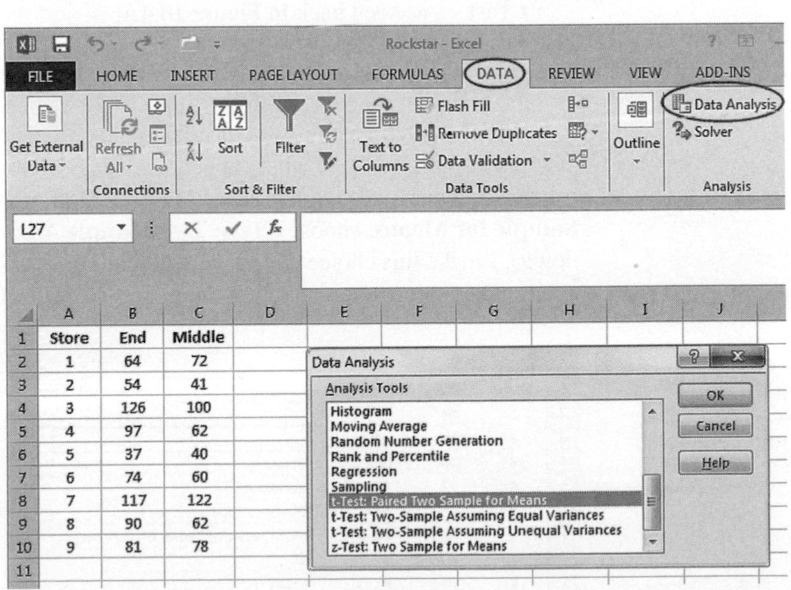

4. Fill in the **t-Test: Paired Two Sample for Means** dialog box as shown in Figure 10.11B. Click **OK**.

FIGURE 10.11B Conducting a Hypothesis Test Comparing the Difference Between Means Using Excel: Dependent Samples (Step 4)

	A	B	C
1	Store	End	Middle
2	1	64	72
3	2	54	41
4	3	126	100
5	4	97	62
6	5	37	40
7	6	74	60
8	7	117	122
9	8	90	62
10	9	81	78

t-Test: Paired Two Sample for Means

- Input
  - Variable 1 Range: `$B$1:$B$10`
  - Variable 2 Range: `$C$1:$C$10`
  - Hypothesized Mean Difference: 0
  - ☑ Labels
  - Alpha: 0.05
- Output options
  - ◉ Output Range: `$E$1`
  - ○ New Worksheet Ply:
  - ○ New Workbook
- OK / Cancel / Help

Figure 10.11C shows the Data Analysis output for the Rockstar sales example.

FIGURE 10.11C Conducting a Hypothesis Test Comparing the Difference Between Means Using Excel: Dependent Samples (Final Result)

	A	B	C	D	E	F	G
1	Store	End	Middle		t-Test: Paired Two Sample for Means		
2	1	64	72				
3	2	54	41			*End*	*Middle*
4	3	126	100		Mean	82.22222222	70.77777778
5	4	97	62		Variance	830.9444444	704.4444444
6	5	37	40		Observations	9	9
7	6	74	60		Pearson Correlation	0.841809771	
8	7	117	122		Hypothesized Mean Difference	0	
9	8	90	62		df	8	
10	9	81	78		t Stat	2.183350326	
11					P(T<=t) one-tail	0.030272709	
12					t Critical one-tail	1.859548038	
13					P(T<=t) two-tail	0.060545418	
14					t Critical two-tail	2.306004135	
15							

Notice that the *p*-value for this test is shown in Cell E11 and is equal to 0.03027 (circled in red). Because this value is less than $\alpha = 0.05$, we reject the null hypothesis. This value is also consistent with the *p*-value approximation between 0.025 and 0.05 when using Table 5 in Appendix A.

PHStat can also perform this procedure with unsummarized data using the following steps:

1. Go to **Add-Ins > PHStat > Two-Sample Tests (Unsummarized Data) > Paired t Test**…, as seen back in Figure 10.4A.
2. Fill in the **Paired t Test** dialog box in the same manner as seen back in Figure 10.6A. Click **OK**.

What would happen if we considered the end-aisle data to be independent of the middle-aisle data? Well, let's see what happens. It's easy enough to check with Excel by going back to your original Rockstar data file. In Figure 10.11A, rather than select ***t*-Test: Paired Two Sample for Means**, choose ***t*-Test: Two-Sample Assuming Unequal Variances** (two choices down). I make this choice due to the fact that I have no information indicating that the variances are equal. After completing the dialog box, you'll get the results shown in Figure 10.12.

FIGURE 10.12 Conducting a Hypothesis Test Comparing the Difference Between Means: Independent Samples (Final Result)

	A	B	C	D	E	F	G
1	Store	End	Middle		t-Test: Two-Sample Assuming Unequal Variances		
2	1	64	72				
3	2	54	41			*End*	*Middle*
4	3	126	100		Mean	82.22222222	70.77777778
5	4	97	62		Variance	830.9444444	704.4444444
6	5	37	40		Observations	9	9
7	6	74	60		Hypothesized Mean Difference	0	
8	7	117	122		df	16	
9	8	90	62		t Stat	0.876207111	
10	9	81	78		P(T<=t) one-tail	0.196941249	
11					t Critical one-tail	1.745883676	
12					P(T<=t) two-tail	0.393882497	
13					t Critical two-tail	2.119905299	
14							

The p-value for this test, shown in Cell F10, is 0.1969, which is greater than $\alpha = 0.05$. According to this test, we now fail to reject the null hypothesis! What the heck happened? Notice that there is a fair amount of variability in the sales data between the stores. For instance, the sales in Store 3 seem to be much larger than that in Store 5 when you look at Figure 10.12. This high variability within each sample makes it more challenging to find evidence that one population has a larger mean than another. This, in turn, makes it more difficult to reject the null hypothesis. This can be visualized by looking at Equation 10.10, which is one of our test statistics for independent samples.

High variability within each sample (high values for s_1 and/or s_2) results in a lower value for t subscript $\bar{x}$. This, in turn, makes it less likely that we will reject H_0.

$$t_{\bar{x}} = \frac{(\bar{x}_1 - \bar{x}_2) - (\mu_1 - \mu_2)_{H_0}}{\sqrt{\left(\frac{s_1^2}{n_1} + \frac{s_2^2}{n_2}\right)}}$$

As the values for s_1 and s_2 get larger (more variability), the test statistic, $t_{\bar{x}}$, becomes closer to zero, which is in the "Do Not Reject H_0" region shown in Figure 10.10. When we treat these two samples as independent, the high variability from store to store makes it more difficult for $t_{\bar{x}}$ to land in the "Reject H_0" region.

By treating these samples as matched pairs and taking their differences, we reduce the effect of the variability from store to store. This provides us with a more powerful hypothesis test. If Josh had just randomly collected independent end-aisle and middle-aisle data without recording the stores that they came from, he might have had no evidence to conclude that end-aisle outsold middle-aisle positions. By using the matched-pair–dependent samples, Josh was able to reject the null hypothesis and make an important discovery. Think about this the next time you pass an end-aisle display at the grocery store.

One last important point needs to be made. In this example, we had small sample sizes and used the sample standard deviations in place of the unknown population standard deviations. Under these conditions, the matched-pair differences need to follow the normal probability distribution. However, if we have 30 or more matched pairs, this requirement can be relaxed because of the Central Limit Theorem.

Unfortunately, this is no time for you to relax. Try this dependent-sample Your Turn problem while the technique is still fresh in your mind.

YOUR TURN #6

Suppose in my spare time I developed a new golf ball that I claimed increased a golfer's driving distance from the tee by more than 15 yards. To test my claim, I had eight golfers hit my golf ball and also hit their own golf ball. The distance in yards for each ball by each golfer is shown in the following table and can be found in the Excel file titled **driving distance.xlsx**.

Golfer	1	2	3	4	5	6	7	8
My ball	201	228	256	233	248	255	239	220
Their ball	204	213	231	241	223	226	212	186

a. Perform a hypothesis test to test this claim using $\alpha = 0.10$.
b. Approximate the p-value using Table 5 in Appendix A and interpret the results.
c. Validate your results using Excel's Data Analysis.
d. Identify the p-value using Excel and interpret the results.
e. What assumption needs to be made to validate these results?

Answers can be found on ▶ **pages 498–499**

Using a Confidence Interval to Compare the Difference Between Two Means with Dependent Samples

Confidence intervals can also be constructed around the mean of a matched-pair difference, $\bar{d}$, when working with dependent samples. The upper and lower limits for this interval can be found using Equations 10.17 and 10.18, respectively.

Formulas 10.17 and 10.18 for the Confidence Interval for the Difference Between the Means of Dependent Samples

$$UCL_{\bar{d}} = \bar{d} + t_{\alpha/2}\frac{s_d}{\sqrt{n}}$$

$$LCL_{\bar{d}} = \bar{d} - t_{\alpha/2}\frac{s_d}{\sqrt{n}}$$

where

$UCL_{\bar{d}}$ = The upper limit for the confidence interval
$LCL_{\bar{d}}$ = The lower limit for the confidence interval

Let's construct a 90% confidence interval to estimate the true matched-pair difference between the end-aisle and middle-aisle sales for Rockstar energy drink. Using Table 5 in Appendix A for a 90% confidence interval and $df = n - 1 = 9 - 1 = 8$, our critical t-score is $t_{\alpha/2} = 1.860$. In the previous section, we identified the following values:

$$\bar{d} = 11.44 \qquad s_d = 15.73 \qquad n = 9$$

Using these values in Equations 10.17 and 10.18, we have our limits for the 90% confidence interval:

$$UCL_{\bar{d}} = \bar{d} + t_{\alpha/2}\frac{s_d}{\sqrt{n}}$$

$$UCL_{\bar{d}} = 11.44 + (1.860)\frac{15.73}{\sqrt{9}} = 11.44 + 9.75 = 21.19$$

$$LCL_{\bar{d}} = \bar{d} - t_{\alpha/2}\frac{s_d}{\sqrt{n}}$$

$$LCL_{\bar{d}} = 11.44 - (1.860)\frac{15.73}{\sqrt{9}} = 11.44 - 9.75 = 1.69$$

Our 90% confidence interval is (1.69, 21.19). This means we are 90% confident that the difference between the sales for the end-aisle and middle-aisle locations is between 1.69 and 21.19 units per week. The fact that this interval does not include zero provides more evidence that the difference between these two locations is not equal to zero.

This next Your Turn problem will give you a chance to construct a confidence interval around two dependent samples.

YOUR TURN #7

Construct a 95% confidence interval around the mean of the matched-pair difference using the golf ball data shown in Your Turn #6. Interpret the results.

Answers can be found on ▶ **page 499**

To summarize, this section considered the case in which the samples are dependent on one another and are also known as matched pairs—that is, each observation from one sample is related to an observation from the other sample. This two-sample hypothesis test is reduced to a one-sample test by taking the difference of the matched pairs. Tables 10.12 and 10.13 at the end of the chapter provide a summary of equations for this section.

10.3 Section Problems

Basic Skills

10.23 The following two samples were collected as matched pairs:

Pair	**1**	**2**	**3**	**4**	**5**	**6**	**7**
Sample 1	5	6	9	4	6	7	8
Sample 2	4	2	6	6	5	9	6

a. State the null and alternative hypotheses to test if a difference in means exists between the populations represented by Samples 1 and 2.
b. Calculate the appropriate test statistic and interpret the results of the hypothesis test using $\alpha = 0.05$.
c. Approximate the *p*-value using Table 5 in Appendix A and interpret the result.
d. Verify your results using Excel's Data Analysis. Mac users can rely on PHStat for this procedure.
e. Identify the *p*-value from Excel and interpret the result.
f. What assumptions need to be made in order to perform this procedure?

10.24 The following two samples were collected as matched pairs:

Pair	**1**	**2**	**3**	**4**	**5**	**6**
Sample 1	7	6	9	5	6	8
Sample 2	4	2	6	6	1	8

a. State the null and alternative hypotheses to test if the population represented by Sample 1 has a higher mean than the population represented by Sample 2.
b. Calculate the appropriate test statistic and interpret the results of the hypothesis test using $\alpha = 0.05$.
c. Approximate the *p*-value using Table 5 in Appendix A and interpret the result.
d. Verify your results using Excel's Data Analysis. Mac users can rely on PHStat for this procedure.
e. Identify the *p*-value from Excel and interpret the result.
f. What assumptions need to be made in order to perform this procedure?

10.25 The following two samples were collected as matched pairs:

Pair	**1**	**2**	**3**	**4**	**5**	**6**	**7**	**8**
Sample 1	8	4	6	9	9	7	9	8
Sample 2	4	2	6	6	1	8	1	4

a. State the null and alternative hypotheses to test if the population represented by Sample 1 has a mean that is 2.0 units higher than the population represented by Sample 2.
b. Calculate the appropriate test statistic and interpret the results of the hypothesis test using $\alpha = 0.10$.
c. Approximate the *p*-value using Table 5 in Appendix A and interpret the result.
d. Verify your results using Excel's Data Analysis. Mac users can rely on PHStat for this procedure.
e. Identify the *p*-value from Excel and interpret the result.
f. What assumptions need to be made in order to perform this procedure?

10.26 The following two samples were collected as matched pairs:

Pair	**1**	**2**	**3**	**4**	**5**	**6**	**7**
Sample 1	8	4	6	9	9	7	9
Sample 2	4	2	6	5	1	8	1

a. Construct a 95% confidence interval to estimate the difference in means between the populations from which Samples 1 and 2 were drawn.
b. What conclusions can be made based on these results?

10.27 The following two samples were collected as matched pairs:

Pair	**1**	**2**	**3**	**4**	**5**	**6**	**7**	**8**
Sample 1	8	4	6	9	9	7	9	8
Sample 2	5	7	6	5	6	9	7	6

a. Construct a 90% confidence interval to estimate the difference in means between the populations from which Samples 1 and 2 were drawn.
b. What conclusions can be made based on these results?

Applications

10.28 Swype is an input technique for touch-screen devices that allows users to input a word by sliding a finger from letter to letter. The user's finger is only removed from the keyboard between words. The following table shows the typing speeds of 10 individuals who were measured typing using both methods. These data can also be found in the Excel file **Swype.xlsx**.

Person	**1**	**2**	**3**	**4**	**5**	**6**	**7**	**8**	**9**	**10**
Swype	48	52	42	36	53	40	37	32	54	46
Traditional	40	45	36	27	44	40	42	38	46	37

a. Perform a hypothesis test using $\alpha = 0.05$ to determine if the average typing speed using these two input methods is different.
b. Approximate the p-value using Table 5 in Appendix A and interpret the result.
c. Verify your results using Excel's Data Analysis. Mac users can rely on PHStat for this procedure.
d. Identify the p-value using Excel and interpret the result.
e. What assumptions need to be made in order to perform this procedure?

10.29 The MCAT is a standardized test used by medical schools in the admissions process. The scale of this exam ranges from 3 to 45. A new type of review course for the MCAT was developed by a training company. The following table shows MCAT scores for nine students before and after taking the review course. These data can also be found in the Excel file **MCAT.xlsx**.

Student	**1**	**2**	**3**	**4**	**5**	**6**	**7**	**8**	**9**
Before	26	21	20	31	18	33	25	23	30
After	28	26	17	34	20	31	26	22	32

a. Perform a hypothesis test using $\alpha = 0.05$ to determine if the average MCAT score is higher for students after the review course when compared with before the course.
b. Approximate the p-value using Table 5 in Appendix A and interpret the result.
c. Verify your results using Excel. Mac users can rely on PHStat for this procedure.
d. Identify the p-value using Excel and interpret the result.
e. What assumptions need to be made in order to perform this procedure?

10.30 A new weight-loss program claims that participants will lose an average of more than 10 lbs after completing it. The following table shows the weights of eight individuals before and after the program. These data can also be found in the Excel file **weight loss.xlsx**.

Person	**1**	**2**	**3**	**4**	**5**	**6**	**7**	**8**
Before	227	214	207	186	203	198	243	190
After	202	194	194	172	195	180	231	192

a. Perform a hypothesis test using $\alpha = 0.10$ to determine if the average weight loss was more than 10 lbs for participants in the weight-loss program.
b. Approximate the p-value using Table 5 in Appendix A and interpret the result.
c. Construct an 80% confidence interval to estimate the average weight loss for individuals in the program. Interpret the results.
d. Verify your results using Excel's Data Analysis. Mac users can rely on PHStat for this procedure.
e. Identify the p-value using Excel and interpret the result.
f. What assumptions need to be made in order to perform this procedure?

10.31 The following table shows the golf scores of nine people before and after a lesson given by the golf professional at Pike Creek Golf Club. These data can also be found in the Excel file **lessons.xlsx**.

Golfer	**1**	**2**	**3**	**4**	**5**	**6**	**7**	**8**	**9**
Before lesson	96	88	94	86	102	90	100	90	99
After lesson	88	81	95	79	95	85	101	85	95

a. Using $\alpha = 0.05$, test the professional's claim that the average golfer will lower his or her score by more than two strokes after a lesson.
b. Approximate the p-value using Table 5 in Appendix A and interpret the result.
c. Construct a 90% confidence interval to estimate the average reduction in golf scores after the lesson. Interpret the results.
d. Verify your results using Excel's Data Analysis. Mac users can rely on PHStat for this procedure.
e. Identify the p-value using Excel and interpret the result.
f. What assumptions need to be made in order to perform this procedure?

10.4 Comparing Two Population Proportions with Independent Samples

Now that we have exhausted every conceivable hypothesis test for comparing population means (and yes, I am exhausted), it's time to move on to proportions, which will wrap up this chapter. There are many interesting applications in which a hypothesis test can be used to compare two population proportions, such as the following:

- An insurance company would like to know if the proportion of young male drivers who have car accidents differs from the proportion of young female drivers who have car accidents.

- A bank would like to compare the proportion of young customers to the proportion of older customers who pay their bills online.

Recall that we discussed the single sample test for a proportion in Chapter 9. This section expands that concept by demonstrating the two-population scenario, which is illustrated in Figure 10.13.

FIGURE 10.13 The Sampling Distribution for the Difference in Population Proportions

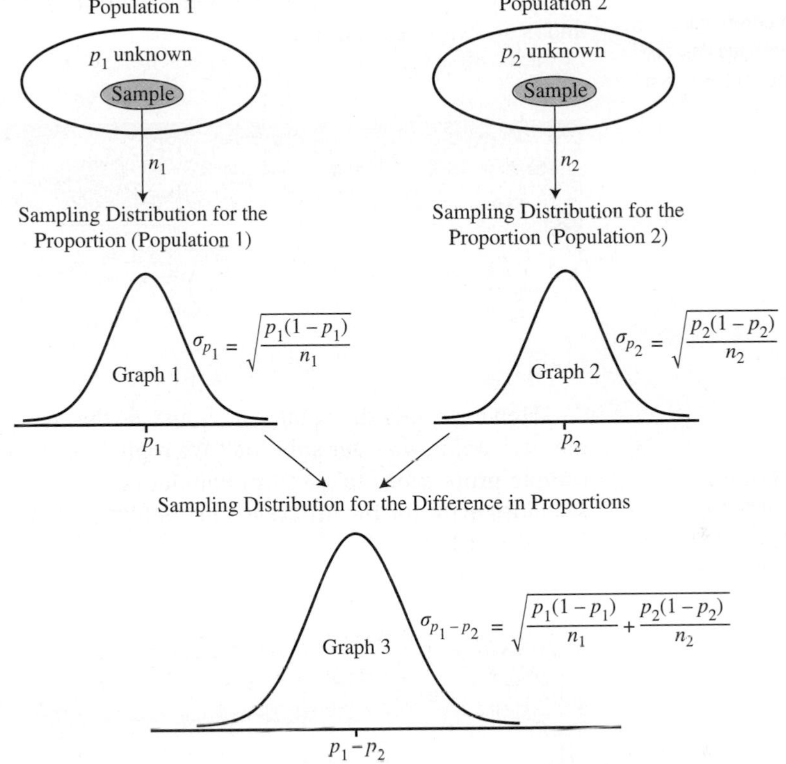

To demonstrate this technique, let's use the following example. The recent economic downturn has had a negative impact on the nation's homeownership rate, which is found by dividing the number of owner-occupied housing units by the total number of housing units. Suppose the government would like to compare this rate in the northeastern United States to the rate in the southeastern United States. A random sample of 150 southeastern homes was drawn, and it was found that 105 were owner-occupied. A random sample of 125 northeastern homes was drawn, and it was found that 80 were owner-occupied. I'll assign the populations as follows:

As before, the choice of assigning populations is arbitrary.

Population 1: Southeast
Population 2: Northeast

Figure 10.13 uses the following notation:

p_1 = The true proportion of owner-occupied homes in the Southeast
p_2 = The true proportion of owner-occupied homes in the Northeast
$\bar{p}_1$ = The sample proportion of owner-occupied homes in the Southeast
$\bar{p}_2$ = The sample proportion of owner-occupied homes in the Northeast
n_1 = The sample size from the southeastern population
n_2 = The sample size from the northeastern population

Graphs 1 and 2 in Figure 10.13 show the sampling distribution for the proportion for each of the two populations. We examined these scenarios in Chapter 9. The mean and standard deviation (also known as the standard error) for each distribution are indicated as well. Nothing new here.

The **sampling distribution for the difference in proportions** is the result of subtracting one sampling distribution for the proportion from a second sampling distribution for the proportion.

The **standard error of the difference between population proportions** describes the variation in the difference between two sample proportions.

Graph 3 is where we break new ground. Here I show the **sampling distribution for the difference in proportions**. This new distribution is the result of subtracting one sampling distribution for the proportion from a second sampling distribution for the proportion. What we are doing is similar to what we did at the start of this chapter when we estimated population means. A key equation in this figure is the standard deviation, of this new distribution, which is known as the **standard error for the difference in population proportions** and is shown in Equation 10.19.

Formula 10.19 for the Standard Error for the Difference in Population Proportions

$$\sigma_{p_1 - p_2} = \sqrt{\frac{p_1(1 - p_1)}{n_1} + \frac{p_2(1 - p_2)}{n_2}}$$

The **approximate standard error of the difference between population proportions** uses $\bar{p}_1$ and $\bar{p}_2$ to estimate the values of p_1 and p_2 when determining the standard deviation.

However, it is the values of p_1 and p_2 that we are trying to estimate because they are unknown. Our solution? We replace p_1 and p_2 with $\bar{p}_1$ and $\bar{p}_2$, which are the sample proportions taken from Populations 1 and 2. Doing so gives us the **approximate standard error for the difference in population proportions**, $\hat{\sigma}_{p_1 - p_2}$, which is shown in Equation 10.20.

Formula 10.20 for the Approximate Standard Error for the Difference in Population Proportions

$$\hat{\sigma}_{p_1 - p_2} = \sqrt{\frac{\bar{p}_1(1 - \bar{p}_1)}{n_1} + \frac{\bar{p}_2(1 - \bar{p}_2)}{n_2}}$$

Let's put this equation to work. First, we need to calculate the sample proportions, as follows:

$$\bar{p}_1 = \frac{x_1}{n_1} = \frac{105}{150} = 0.70 \qquad \bar{p}_2 = \frac{x_2}{n_2} = \frac{80}{125} = 0.64$$

where

x_1 and x_2 = The number of owner-occupied homes from the southeastern and northeastern samples, respectively

Plugging these values into Equation 10.20, we have the approximate standard error for the difference in proportions:

I suggest taking the standard error of the difference between population proportion calculations out to six decimal places to avoid rounding errors. I know this is a pain, but I'm trying to save you more pain later on!

$$\hat{\sigma}_{p_1 - p_2} = \sqrt{\frac{\bar{p}_1(1 - \bar{p}_1)}{n_1} + \frac{\bar{p}_2(1 - \bar{p}_2)}{n_2}}$$

$$\hat{\sigma}_{p_1 - p_2} = \sqrt{\frac{(0.70)(1 - 0.70)}{150} + \frac{(0.64)(1 - 0.64)}{125}}$$

$$\hat{\sigma}_{p_1 - p_2} = \sqrt{0.001400 + 0.001843} = \sqrt{0.003243} = 0.056947$$

Keep this value handy because we will need it in the next section.

Notice that the shapes of all three sampling distributions in Figure 10.13 appear to resemble the normal probability distribution. As you might recall from Chapter 7, proportion data follow the binomial distribution, which can be approximated by the normal distribution if we have relatively large sample sizes. In this section, we will assume our sample sizes are large enough to meet this requirement.

We are now ready to start comparing these two populations. We'll begin with a look at constructing a confidence interval and then wrap up this chapter with one last hypothesis test.

Using a Confidence Interval to Compare the Difference Between Two Proportions

Had our population definitions been reversed, this value would be −0.06, which would also be perfectly acceptable.

Our point estimate for the difference between population proportions is simply the difference between the sample proportions, $\bar{p}_1 - \bar{p}_2$. In our example, the estimate for the difference in homeownership rates between the Southeast and Northeast is as follows:

$$\bar{p}_1 - \bar{p}_2 = 0.70 - 0.64 = 0.06$$

We can construct a confidence interval around this point estimate using Equations 10.21 (upper limit) and 10.22 (lower limit).

Formulas 10.21 and 10.22 for the Confidence Interval for the Difference Between Two Proportions

$$UCL_{p_1-p_2} = (\bar{p}_1 - \bar{p}_2) + z_{\alpha/2}\hat{\sigma}_{p_1-p_2}$$
$$LCL_{p_1-p_2} = (\bar{p}_1 - \bar{p}_2) - z_{\alpha/2}\hat{\sigma}_{p_1-p_2}$$

where

$UCL_{p_1-p_2}$ = The upper limit for the confidence interval
$LCL_{p_1-p_2}$ = The lower limit for the confidence interval
$\hat{\sigma}_{p_1-p_2}$ = The approximate standard error of the difference between two proportions (Equation 10.20)

Let's construct a 95% confidence interval to estimate the true difference between the homeownership rates between the Southeast and Northeast. We can use Table 10.1 to find the appropriate critical z-score by identifying the row with an α value of 0.05 and two tails (remember, all confidence intervals have two tails). Our critical z-score is set at $z_{\alpha/2} = 1.96$ for this interval. From the previous section, we know that $\hat{\sigma}_{p_1-p_2} = 0.056947$. Putting Equations 10.21 and 10.22 to work results in the following:

$$UCL_{p_1-p_2} = (\bar{p}_1 - \bar{p}_2) + z_{\alpha/2}\hat{\sigma}_{p_1-p_2}$$
$$UCL_{p_1-p_2} = 0.06 + (1.96)(0.056947) = 0.172$$

$$UCL_{p_1-p_2} = (\bar{p}_1 - \bar{p}_2) - z_{\alpha/2}\hat{\sigma}_{p_1-p_2}$$
$$LCL_{p_1-p_2} = 0.06 - (1.96)(0.056947) = -0.052$$

Our 95% confidence interval is $(-0.052, 0.172)$. This means we are 95% confident that the difference in homeownership rates between the Southeast and Northeast is between −5.2% and 17.2%. The −5.2% simply refers to the possibility that the homeownership rate in the Northeast (Population 2) is 5.2% larger than the rate in the Southeast (Population 1). Because this confidence interval does include 0%, we have no evidence that the homeownership rates are different between these two sections of the country.

Conducting a Hypothesis Test to Compare the Difference Between Two Proportions

When performing a hypothesis test for the difference between two proportions, the null hypothesis assumes that the populations have equal proportions $(p_1 = p_2)$. Therefore, we have three possible hypotheses statements:

Two-Tail	One-Tail	One-Tail
$H_0: p_1 - p_2 = 0$	$H_0: p_1 - p_2 \leq 0$	$H_0: p_1 - p_2 \geq 0$
$H_1: p_1 - p_2 \neq 0$	$H_1: p_1 - p_2 > 0$	$H_0: p_1 - p_2 < 0$

Suppose the government would like to perform a hypothesis test to decide whether there is enough evidence to conclude that there is a difference in homeownership rates between the Southeast and Northeast using $\alpha = 0.05$. I will demonstrate this procedure using the following steps.

Step 1: Identify the null and alternative hypotheses.

Because we are testing for a difference in rates rather than testing if one section is greater than the other, we have the following two-tail hypothesis statement:

$H_0: p_1 - p_2 = 0$ (No difference in ownership rates between regions)

$H_1: p_1 - p_2 \neq 0$ (Ownership rates are different between regions)

Because the government is testing only for a difference in ownership rates (rather than if one region has a greater rate than the other), this is a two-tail test.

where

p_1 = The true proportion of owner-occupied homes in the Southeast

p_2 = The true proportion of owner-occupied homes in the Northeast

Step 2: Set a value for the significance level, α.

For this example, we had set $\alpha = 0.05$.

Step 3: Calculate the appropriate test statistic.

When we assume that $p_1 = p_2$ with the null hypothesis, we can estimate the overall proportion between the two populations using Equation 10.23. This is known as the pooled estimate of the overall proportion, $\hat{p}$. This is analogous to the pooled variance for a difference in means that we used earlier in the chapter when we assumed the population variances were equal.

Formula 10.23 for the Pooled Estimate for the Overall Proportion

$$\hat{p} = \frac{x_1 + x_2}{n_1 + n_2}$$

This is simply a weighted average of the two sample proportions taken from the populations. Using our homeownership data, we have the following:

$$\hat{p} = \frac{x_1 + x_2}{n_1 + n_2} = \frac{105 + 80}{150 + 125} = \frac{185}{275} = 0.673$$

Our estimate of the homeownership rate of both sections combined is 67.3%.

We can now calculate the test statistic for a difference between population proportions, z_p, using Equation 10.24.

Formula 10.24 for the z-Test Statistic for a Hypothesis Test for the Difference Between Two Proportions

$$z_p = \frac{(\bar{p}_1 - \bar{p}_2) - (p_1 - p_2)_{H_0}}{\sqrt{\hat{p}(1 - \hat{p})\left(\frac{1}{n_1} + \frac{1}{n_2}\right)}}$$

The term $(p_1 - p_2)_{H_0}$ refers to the hypothesized difference between the two population proportions. When the null hypothesis is testing that there is no difference between population proportions, then the term $(p_1 - p_2)_{H_0}$ is set to 0.

where

$(p_1 - p_2)_{H_0}$ = The hypothesized difference in population proportions

Our test statistic for the homeownership example is as follows:

$$z_p = \frac{(\bar{p}_1 - \bar{p}_2) - (p_1 - p_2)_{H_0}}{\sqrt{\hat{p}(1-\hat{p})\left(\frac{1}{n_1} + \frac{1}{n_2}\right)}} = \frac{(0.70 - 0.64) - (0)}{\sqrt{(0.673)(1 - 0.673)\left(\frac{1}{150} + \frac{1}{125}\right)}}$$

$$z_p = \frac{0.06}{\sqrt{(0.673)(0.327)0.014667}} = \frac{0.06}{\sqrt{0.003228}} = \frac{0.06}{0.056815} = 1.06$$

Step 4: Determine the appropriate critical value.

Because the test statistic in Equation 10.24 follows the normal distribution, we can use Table 10.1 to determine the critical value, $z_{\alpha/2}$. For a two-tail test with $\alpha = 0.05$, our critical z-score is $z_{\alpha/2} = 1.96$.

Step 5: Compare the z-test statistic (z_p) with the critical z-score ($z_{\alpha/2}$).

In our homeownership example, which is a two-tail test, $|z_p| = 1.06$ and $|z_{\alpha/2}| = 1.96$. Because $1.06 < 1.96$, we fail to reject the null hypothesis. Figure 10.14 illustrates this finding. Notice that z_p is in the "Do Not Reject H_0" region.

FIGURE 10.14
Comparing the z-Test Statistic with the Critical z-Score.

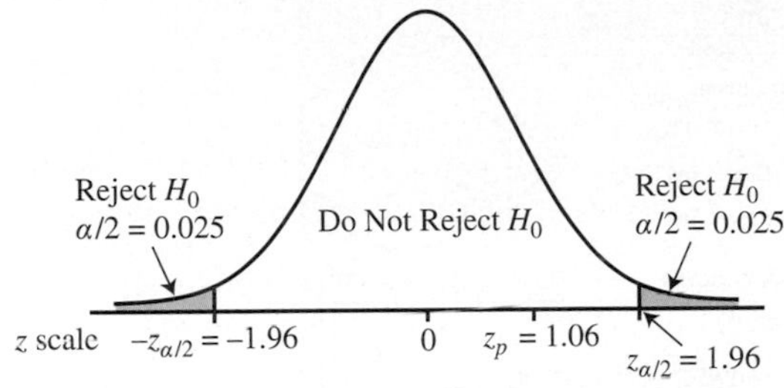

Step 6: Calculate the p-value.

The two-tail p-value for our homeownership example is as follows:

$$p\text{-value} = 2 \times P(z_p > 1.06)$$
$$p\text{-value} = (2)(1 - 0.8554) = (2)(0.1446) = 0.2892$$

The total area of the two shaded regions in Figure 10.15 represents this p-value.

FIGURE 10.15
The p-Value for a Two-Tail Hypothesis Test

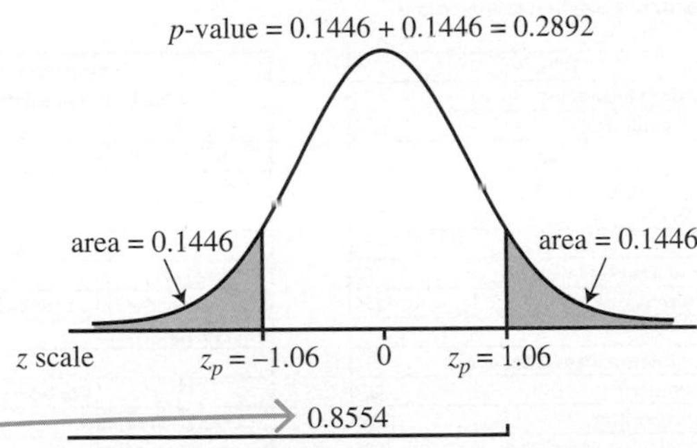

To find the area associated with $z_p > 1.06$, we first need to find the area for $z_p \le 1.06$. Using Table 4 in Appendix A, we determine that this area equals 0.8554. Therefore, $z_p > 1.06 = 1.0 - 0.8554 = 0.1446$.

Because our p-value $= 0.2892$ and is greater than $\alpha = 0.05$, we fail to reject the null hypothesis.

Step 7: State your conclusions.

By failing to reject the null hypothesis, we conclude that we do not have enough evidence to support the alternative hypothesis, $H_1: p_1 - p_2 \neq 0$. We cannot conclude that the homeownership rates are different when comparing the southeastern with the northeastern part of the country. This result is consistent with the confidence interval we previously constructed.

Using PHStat to Compare Two Population Proportions

Now it's time to turn these procedures over to PHStat, using the following steps. Excel for Mac users can find these instructions on the textbook's web site.

1. Go to **Add-Ins** > **PHStat** > **Two-Sample Tests (Summarized Data)** > **Z Test for Differences in Two Proportions**, as seen in Figure 10.4A.
2. Fill in the **Z Test for Differences in Two Proportions** dialog box as shown in Figure 10.16A. Click **OK**.

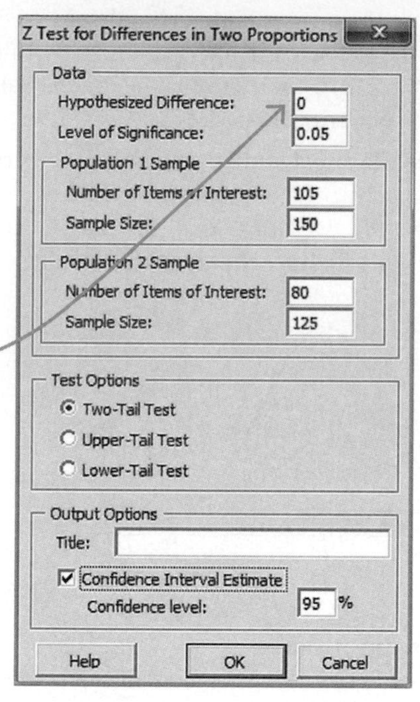

FIGURE 10.16A Conducting a Hypothesis Test Using PHStat to Compare the Difference Between Two Proportions (Steps 1 and 2)

If we wanted to test for a difference other than zero as we did earlier in the chapter, we would input that value here.

Figure 10.16B shows the output for this hypothesis test, including the confidence interval, which matches the results we obtained manually.

FIGURE 10.16B Conducting a Hypothesis Test Using PHStat to Compare the Difference Between Two Population Proportions (Final Result)

	A	B	C	D	E
1	Z Test for Differences in Two Proportions				
2					
3	Data			Confidence Interval Estimate	
4	Hypothesized Difference	0		of the Difference Between Two Proportions	
5	Level of Significance	0.05			
6	Group 1			Data	
7	Number of Items of Interest	105		Confidence Level	95%
8	Sample Size	150			
9	Group 2			Intermediate Calculations	
10	Number of Items of Interest	80		Z Value	-1.9600
11	Sample Size	125		Std. Error of the Diff. between two Proporti	0.0569
12				Interval Half Width	0.1116
13	Intermediate Calculations				
14	Group 1 Proportion	0.7		Confidence Interval	
15	Group 2 Proportion	0.64		Interval Lower Limit	-0.0516
16	Difference in Two Proportions	0.06		Interval Upper Limit	0.1716
17	Average Proportion	0.6727			
18	Z Test Statistic	1.0559			
19					
20	Two-Tail Test				
21	Lower Critical Value	-1.9600			
22	Upper Critical Value	1.9600			
23	*p*-Value	0.2910			
24	Do not reject the null hypothesis				
25					

Once again we can also rely on Excel's NORM.S.DIST function to help determine the *p*-value for our two-tail test:

$$=\text{NORM.S.DIST}(1.06, \text{TRUE}) = 0.8554$$

Remember, this function always provides the area to the left of the test statistic. Our p-value is double the area to the right of the test statistic, $z_p = 1.06$, which is

$$p\text{-value} = (2)(1.0 - 0.8554) = (2)(0.1446) = 0.2892$$

As you can see, this result matches what we observed in Figure 10.15. The slight difference between this value and the one seen in Cell B23 in Figure 10.16B is due to rounding.

In this final section, we compared two population proportions. Proportions follow the binomial probability distribution, which can be approximated with the normal distribution under the proper conditions. The standard error for the test statistic, shown as Equation 10.20, uses the sample proportions as an estimate for the population proportions. Tables 10.12 and 10.13 at the end of the chapter provide a summary of equations for this section. Why don't you apply this technique to this last Your Turn problem to wrap up your understanding of Chapter 10?

YOUR TURN #8

Bank of America would like to test the hypothesis that a higher percentage of younger customers use online banking compared with older customers. In a survey of 80 customers under the age of 40, it was found that 68 of them used online banking for the majority of their services. From a group of 100 customers 40 years and older, 72 used online banking for the majority of their services.

a. Using $\alpha = 0.05$ and following the seven steps outlined in this section, perform a hypothesis test to test the claim that a higher proportion of younger customers use online banking.

b. Construct a 95% confidence interval around these sample data.

c. Verify your results using PHStat.

Answers can be found on ▶ **pages 499–500**

Stats in Practice: Using Hypothesis Testing for Good Student Discounts

Liberty Mutual Insurance Company is the fifth largest insuror of automobiles and homes in the United States. As a result, the company relies heavily on statistics as a tool to determine the premiums its policyholders pay. For example, Liberty Mutual provides drivers with zero to six years of driving experience a 10% discount on collision coverage if they qualify as good students. A good student is defined as anyone enrolled in high school or college who maintains a GPA of at least 3.0. Do good students have fewer accidents when compared with other young drivers who do not qualify as good students?

To answer this question, the following data were taken from a single state during 2009 for policyholders with zero to six years of driving experience:

We'll set up the following hypothesis test using $\alpha = 0.05$ with good students as Population 1 and the others as Population 2.

	Number of Policyholders	Number of Accidents	Proportion
Good students	1,207	167	0.138
Others	4,963	799	0.161

Step 1: Identify the null and alternative hypotheses.

H_0: $p_1 - p_2 \geq 0$ (Good students have an equal or higher proportion of accidents)

H_1: $p_1 - p_2 < 0$ (Good students have a lower proportion of accidents)

(continued)

Using PHStat, we come up with the following results shown in Figure 10.17.

FIGURE 10.17

	A	B
1	Z Test for Differences in Two Proportions	
2		
3	Data	
4	Hypothesized Difference	0
5	Level of Significance	0.05
6	Group 1	
7	Number of Items of Interest	167
8	Sample Size	1207
9	Group 2	
10	Number of Items of Interest	799
11	Sample Size	4963
12		
13	Intermediate Calculations	
14	Group 1 Proportion	0.138359569
15	Group 2 Proportion	0.160991336
16	Difference in Two Proportions	-0.02263177
17	Average Proportion	0.1566
18	Z Test Statistic	-1.9406
19		
20	Lower-Tail Test	
21	Lower Critical Value	-1.6449
22	p-Value	0.0262
23	Reject the null hypothesis	
24		

Step 2: Set a value for the significance level, α.

For this analysis, we'll use $\alpha = 0.05$.

Step 3: Identify the appropriate test statistic.

According to our PHStat output, $z_p = -1.94$

Step 4: Determine the appropriate critical value.

According to our PHStat output, $-z_\alpha = -1.645$.

Step 5: Compare the z-test statistic (z_p) with the critical z-score (z_α).

Because $z_p = -1.94 < -z_\alpha = -1.645$, we reject the null hypothesis.

Step 6: Identify the p-value.

According to our PHStat output, the p-value $= 0.0262$. Because this values is less than $\alpha = 0.05$, we reject the null hypothesis.

Step 7: State your conclusions.

Based on this sample, we can conclude that good students have fewer accidents than other drivers in this age group from this particular state. This analysis supports Liberty Mutual's decision to provide a discount to young drivers who are good students.

Special thanks to Liberty Mutual for providing this material.

10.4 Section Problems

Basic Skills

10.32 Consider the following hypothesis statement using $\alpha = 0.10$ and the following data from two independent samples:

$$H_0: p_1 - p_2 \geq 0$$
$$H_1: p_1 - p_2 < 0$$
$$x_1 = 60 \qquad x_2 = 72$$
$$n_1 = 150 \qquad n_2 = 160$$

a. Calculate the appropriate test statistic and interpret the result.
b. Calculate the p-value and interpret the result.
c. Verify your results using PHStat.

10.33 Consider the following hypothesis statement using $\alpha = 0.02$ and the following data from two independent samples:

$$H_0: p_1 - p_2 \leq 0.20$$
$$H_1: p_1 - p_2 > 0.20$$
$$x_1 = 190 \qquad x_2 = 118$$
$$n_1 = 225 \qquad n_2 = 200$$

a. Calculate the appropriate test statistic and interpret the result.
b. Calculate the p-value and interpret the result.
c. Verify your results using PHStat.

10.34 Consider the following hypothesis statement using $\alpha = 0.05$ and the following data from two independent samples:

$$H_0: p_1 - p_2 = 0$$
$$H_1: p_1 - p_2 \neq 0$$
$$x_1 = 18 \qquad x_2 = 24$$
$$n_1 = 85 \qquad n_2 = 105$$

a. Calculate the appropriate test statistic and interpret the result.
b. Calculate the p-value and interpret the result.
c. Verify your results using PHStat.

10.35 Consider the following data from two independent samples. Construct a 90% confidence interval to estimate the difference in population proportions.

$$x_1 = 46 \qquad x_2 = 48$$
$$n_1 = 90 \qquad n_2 = 80$$

10.36 Consider the following data from two independent samples. Construct a 90% confidence interval to estimate the difference in population proportions.

$$x_1 = 92 \qquad x_2 = 76$$
$$n_1 = 130 \qquad n_2 = 150$$

Applications

10.37 Economists theorize that the recent recession has affected men more than women because men are typically employed in industries that have been hit hardest by the recession, such as manufacturing and construction. Women, on the other hand, are typically employed in services such as health care and education, which are considered more recession resistant. A sample of 175 men and a sample of 140 women were drawn. Eighteen in the group of men were unemployed; 12 in the group of women were unemployed.

a. Perform a hypothesis test using $\alpha = 0.05$ to determine if the unemployment rate for men is higher than the rate for women.

b. Determine the p-value and interpret the results.

c. Verify your results using PHStat.

10.38 A major challenge for retailers like Best Buy is "showrooming" which describes customers who browse through their stores and then make their purchase from an online competitor. In an effort to measure the volume of showrooming, Best Buy observes the percentage of customers who leave their stores with a purchase. Suppose Best Buy would like to investigate if the percentage of women who leave the store with a purchase is higher than the percentage of men. A random sample of 170 female shoppers was selected and it was found that 73 left the store with a purchase. A random sample of 150 male shoppers was selected and it was found that 56 left the store with a purchase.

a. Perform a hypothesis test with $\alpha = 0.10$ to determine if the percentage of women who leave the store with a purchase is higher than the percentage of men.

b. Determine the p-value and interpret the results.

c. Verify your results using PHStat.

10.39 People are considered obese when they are approximately 30 lbs over their healthy weight. Obesity can increase the risk of heart disease and diabetes, which could add to the cost of the health care system. Two random samples of adults were selected. The individuals in one of the samples lacked high school diplomas. The individuals in the other sample held college degrees. The number of people sampled and the obese individuals from each sample are as follows:

No High School Diploma	College Degree
$x_1 = 70$	$x_2 = 37$
$n_1 = 205$	$n_2 = 180$

a. Perform a hypothesis test using $\alpha = 0.05$ to determine if the proportion of obese individuals without high school diplomas differs from the proportion of obese individuals who have college degrees.

b. Determine the p-value and interpret the results.

c. Verify your results using PHStat.

10.40 Office occupancy in a city is an indication of the economic health of the region in which it is located. A random sample of 165 offices in Boston was selected and it was found that 24 were vacant. A random sample of 145 offices in Chicago was selected and it was found that 17 were vacant.

a. Construct a 95% confidence interval to estimate the difference in vacancy rates between these two cities. What conclusions can be made?

b. Verify your results using PHStat.

10.41 Passing the ball between two players during a soccer game is a critical skill for the success of a team. A random sample of passes made by the English and German teams in a recent World Cup was drawn, and the number of successful passes in each sample was counted. The data are as follows:

Germany	England
$x_1 = 69$	$x_2 = 71$
$n_1 = 76$	$n_2 = 91$

a. Construct a 90% confidence interval to estimate the difference in accuracy between the German and English passes. What conclusions can be made?

b. Verify your results using PHStat.

CHAPTER 10 Summary

- The sampling distribution for the difference in means is the result of subtracting one sampling distribution for the mean from a second sampling distribution for the mean.
- The standard error of the difference between two means describes the variation in the sampling distribution for $\bar{x}_1 - \bar{x}_2$.
- Two samples are independent of one another when the results observed when sampling from one population have no effect on the results observed when sampling from the other population.
- When constructing a hypothesis test for the difference in means when the standard deviations of two populations are known, we use the normal distribution to determine the critical value that identifies the rejection region for the null hypothesis.
- We can also use the *p*-value to determine the conclusion for a hypothesis test.
- Confidence intervals can be constructed around the difference between two sample means to estimate where the true difference in population means lies.
  - When the confidence interval for the difference between two means does not include zero, we have supporting evidence that a difference between the population means does exist.
  - When the confidence interval for the difference between two means includes zero, we do not have supporting evidence that a difference between the population means exists.
- When the population standard deviations are not known to us, we substitute the sample standard deviations in their place.
  - When doing so, the Student's *t*-distribution is used in place of the normal distribution to identify the rejection region.
  - Under this scenario, both populations need to be normally distributed.
  - However, if the populations are not normally distributed, the *t*-distribution can still be used to identify the rejection region if both sample sizes are 30 or more.
  - When the population variances are equal, the pooled variance is used to calculate the test statistic.
    - The corresponding critical value uses $n_1 + n_2 - 2$ degrees of freedom.
    - When the population variances are not equal, the degrees of freedom for the critical value are determined using Equation 10.11.
- With dependent samples, the observation from one of the samples is related to a corresponding observation from the other sample.
- A hypothesis test using dependent samples is known as a matched-pair test.
- Rather than treat each sample independently, the difference between each matched pair is calculated. This difference is then treated as a one-sample hypothesis test.
- Using matched-pair tests, when possible, reduces the effect of variability within each sample, which results in a more powerful hypothesis test.
- Many business decisions involve comparing two population proportions rather than population means.
- The sampling distribution for the difference in proportions is the result of subtracting one sampling distribution for the proportion from a second sampling distribution for the proportion.
- The standard error of the difference between population proportions describes the variation in the sampling distribution for $p_1 - p_2$.
- As you might recall from Chapter 7, proportion data follow the binomial distribution and can be approximated by the normal distribution for a relatively large sample size.

CHAPTER 10 Key Terms

Approximate standard error of the difference between population proportions. Uses $\overline{p}_1$ and $\overline{p}_2$ to describe the variation in the sampling distribution for $\overline{p}_1 - \overline{p}_2$.

Dependent samples. Samples in which the results observed when sampling from one population correspond to the results observed when sampling from the second sample.

Independent samples. Samples in which the results observed when sampling from one population have no effect on the results observed when sampling from the second population.

Matched-pair test. A hypothesis test for means using dependent samples.

Pooled variance. A weighted average of two sample variances using the number of degrees of freedom for each sample as the weights.

Sampling distribution for the difference in means. The result of subtracting one sampling distribution for the mean from a second sampling distribution for the mean.

Sampling distribution for the difference in proportions. The result of subtracting one sampling distribution for the proportion from a second sampling distribution for the proportion.

Standard error of the difference between two means. A value that describes the variation in the sampling distribution for $\overline{x}_1 - \overline{x}_2$.

Standard error of the difference between population proportions. A value that describes the variation in the sampling distribution for $\overline{p}_1 - \overline{p}_2$.

CHAPTER 10 Equations

10.1 Comparing Two Population Means with (pp 439–448)

- Independent Samples
- Known Population Standard Deviations (σ_1 and σ_2)

Formula 10.1 for the Mean of the Sampling Distribution for the Difference in Means

$$\mu_{\overline{x}_1 - \overline{x}_2} = \mu_{\overline{x}_1} - \mu_{\overline{x}_2}$$

Formula 10.2 for the Standard Error of the Difference Between Two Means

$$\sigma_{\overline{x}_1 - \overline{x}_2} = \sqrt{\frac{\sigma_1^2}{n_1} + \frac{\sigma_2^2}{n_2}}$$

Formula 10.3 for the z-Test Statistic for a Hypothesis Test for the Difference Between Two Means (σ_1 and σ_2 Known)

$$z_{\overline{x}} = \frac{(\overline{x}_1 - \overline{x}_2) - (\mu_1 - \mu_2)_{H_0}}{\sigma_{\overline{x}_1 - \overline{x}_2}}$$

Formulas 10.4 and 10.5 for the Confidence Interval for the Difference in the Means of Two Independent Populations (σ_1 and σ_2 Known)

$$UCL_{\overline{x}_1 - \overline{x}_2} = (\overline{x}_1 - \overline{x}_2) + z_{\alpha/2}\sigma_{\overline{x}_1 - \overline{x}_2}$$
$$LCL_{\overline{x}_1 - \overline{x}_2} = (\overline{x}_1 - \overline{x}_2) - z_{\alpha/2}\sigma_{\overline{x}_1 - \overline{x}_2}$$

10.2 Comparing Two Population Means with (pp 448–464)

- Independent Samples
- Unknown Population Standard Deviations (σ_1 and σ_2)

Formula 10.6 for the t-Test Statistic for a Hypothesis Test for the Difference Between Two Means (σ_1 and σ_2 Unknown but Equal)

$$t_{\bar{x}} = \frac{(\bar{x}_1 - \bar{x}_2) - (\mu_1 - \mu_2)_{H_0}}{\sqrt{s_p^2\left(\frac{1}{n_1} + \frac{1}{n_2}\right)}}$$

Formula 10.7 for the Pooled Variance

$$s_p^2 = \frac{(n_1 - 1)s_1^2 + (n_2 - 1)s_2^2}{(n_1 - 1) + (n_2 - 1)}$$

Formulas 10.8 and 10.9 for the Confidence Interval for the Difference Between the Means of Two Independent Populations (σ_1 and σ_2 Unknown and Equal)

$$UCL_{\bar{x}_1 - \bar{x}_2} = (\bar{x}_1 - \bar{x}_2) + t_{\alpha/2}\sqrt{s_p^2\left(\frac{1}{n_1} + \frac{1}{n_2}\right)}$$

$$LCL_{\bar{x}_1 - \bar{x}_2} = (\bar{x}_1 - \bar{x}_2) - t_{\alpha/2}\sqrt{s_p^2\left(\frac{1}{n_1} + \frac{1}{n_2}\right)}$$

Formula 10.10 for the t-Test Statistic for a Hypothesis Test for the Difference Between Two Means (σ_1 and σ_2 Unknown and Unequal)

$$t_{\bar{x}} = \frac{(\bar{x}_1 - \bar{x}_2) - (\mu_1 - \mu_2)_{H_0}}{\sqrt{\left(\frac{s_1^2}{n_1} + \frac{s_2^2}{n_2}\right)}}$$

Formula 10.11 for the Degrees of Freedom for the t-Distribution When Testing for the Difference Between Two Means (σ_1 and σ_2 Unknown and Unequal)

$$df = \frac{\left(\frac{s_1^2}{n_1} + \frac{s_2^2}{n_2}\right)^2}{\frac{\left(\frac{s_1^2}{n_1}\right)^2}{n_1 - 1} + \frac{\left(\frac{s_2^2}{n_2}\right)^2}{n_2 - 1}}$$

10.3 Hypothesis Testing with Dependent Samples (pp 464–474)

Formula 10.12 for the Matched-Pair Difference

$$d = x_1 - x_2$$

Formula 10.13 for the Mean of the Matched-Pair Differences

$$\bar{d} = \frac{\sum_{i=1}^{n} d_i}{n}$$

Formulas 10.14 and 10.15 for the Standard Deviation of the Matched-Paired Differences

$$s_d = \sqrt{\frac{\sum_{i=1}^{n}(d_i - \bar{d})^2}{n-1}} \quad \text{or} \quad s_d = \sqrt{\frac{\sum_{i=1}^{n} d_i^2 - \frac{\left(\sum_{i=1}^{n} d_i\right)^2}{n}}{n-1}}$$

Formula 10.16 for the t-Test Statistic for a Matched-Pair Hypothesis Test for the Mean

$$t_{\bar{x}} = \frac{\bar{d} - (\mu_d)_{H_0}}{\frac{s_d}{\sqrt{n}}}$$

Formulas 10.17 and 10.18 for the Confidence Interval for the Difference Between the Means of Dependent Samples

$$UCL_{\bar{d}} = \bar{d} + t_{\alpha/2}\frac{s_d}{\sqrt{n}}$$
$$LCL_{\bar{d}} = \bar{d} - t_{\alpha/2}\frac{s_d}{\sqrt{n}}$$

10.4 Comparing Two Population Proportions with Independent Samples (pp 474–483)

Formula 10.19 for the Standard Error for the Difference in Population Proportions

$$\sigma_{p_1-p_2} = \sqrt{\frac{p_1(1-p_1)}{n_1} + \frac{p_2(1-p_2)}{n_2}}$$

Formula 10.20 for the Approximate Standard Error for the Difference in Population Proportions

$$\hat{\sigma}_{p_1-p_2} = \sqrt{\frac{\bar{p}_1(1-\bar{p}_1)}{n_1} + \frac{\bar{p}_2(1-\bar{p}_2)}{n_2}}$$

Formulas 10.21 and 10.22 for the Confidence Interval for the Difference Between Two Proportions

$$UCL_{p_1-p_2} = (\bar{p}_1 - \bar{p}_2) + z_{\alpha/2}\hat{\sigma}_{p_1-p_2}$$
$$LCL_{p_1-p_2} = (\bar{p}_1 - \bar{p}_2) - z_{\alpha/2}\hat{\sigma}_{p_1-p_2}$$

Formula 10.23 for the Pooled Estimate for the Overall Proportion

$$\hat{p} = \frac{x_1 + x_2}{n_1 + n_2}$$

Formula 10.24 for the z-Test Statistic for a Hypothesis Test for th e Difference Between Two Proportions

$$z_p = \frac{(\bar{p}_1 - \bar{p}_2) - (p_1 - p_2)_{H_0}}{\sqrt{\hat{p}(1-\hat{p})\left(\frac{1}{n_1} + \frac{1}{n_2}\right)}}$$

TABLE 10.12 | A Summary of Hypothesis Tests for Comparing Two Populations

TYPE	SAMPLE	σ_1, σ_2	TEST STATISTIC	OTHER REQUIRED EQUATIONS
Mean	Independent samples	Known	$z_{\bar{x}} = \frac{(\bar{x}_1 - \bar{x}_2) - (\mu_1 - \mu_2)_{H_0}}{\sigma_{\bar{x}_1 - \bar{x}_2}}$	$\sigma_{\bar{x}_1 - \bar{x}_2} = \sqrt{\frac{\sigma_1^2}{n_1} + \frac{\sigma_2^2}{n_2}}$
Mean	Independent samples	Unknown and equal	$t_{\bar{x}} = \frac{(\bar{x}_1 - \bar{x}_2) - (\mu_1 - \mu_2)_{H_0}}{\sqrt{s_p^2\left(\frac{1}{n_1} + \frac{1}{n_2}\right)}}$	$s_p^2 = \frac{(n_1 - 1)s_1^2 + (n_2 - 1)s_2^2}{(n_1 - 1) + (n_2 - 1)}$ $df = n_1 + n_2 - 2$
Mean	Independent samples	Unknown and unequal	$t_{\bar{x}} = \frac{(\bar{x}_1 - \bar{x}_2) - (\mu_1 - \mu_2)_{H_0}}{\sqrt{\left(\frac{s_1^2}{n_1} + \frac{s_2^2}{n_2}\right)}}$	$df = \frac{\left(\frac{s_1^2}{n_1} + \frac{s_2^2}{n_2}\right)^2}{\frac{\left(\frac{s_1^2}{n_1}\right)^2}{n_1 - 1} + \frac{\left(\frac{s_2^2}{n_2}\right)^2}{n_2 - 1}}$
Mean	Dependent samples	Unknown	$t_{\bar{x}} = \frac{\bar{d} - (\mu_d)_{H_0}}{\frac{s_d}{\sqrt{n}}}$	$s_d = \sqrt{\frac{\sum_{i=1}^{n} d_i^2 - \frac{\left(\sum_{i=1}^{n} d_i\right)^2}{n}}{n - 1}}$
Proportion	Independent samples	Not applicable	$z_p = \frac{(\bar{p}_1 - \bar{p}_2) - (p_1 - p_2)_{H_0}}{\sqrt{\hat{p}(1 - \hat{p})\left(\frac{1}{n_1} + \frac{1}{n_2}\right)}}$	$\hat{p} = \frac{x_1 + x_2}{n_1 + n_2}$

TABLE 10.13 | A Summary of Confidence Intervals for Comparing Two Populations

TYPE	SAMPLE	σ_1, σ_2	CONFIDENCE INTERVAL	EQUATIONS
Mean	Independent samples	Known	$UCL_{\bar{x}_1 - \bar{x}_2} = (\bar{x}_1 - \bar{x}_2) + z_{\alpha/2}\sigma_{\bar{x}_1 - \bar{x}_2}$ $LCL_{\bar{x}_1 - \bar{x}_2} = (\bar{x}_1 - \bar{x}_2) - z_{\alpha/2}\sigma_{\bar{x}_1 - \bar{x}_2}$	10.4 10.5
Mean	Independent samples	Unknown	$UCL_{\bar{x}_1 - \bar{x}_2} = (\bar{x}_1 - \bar{x}_2) + t_{\alpha/2}\sqrt{s_p^2\left(\frac{1}{n_1} + \frac{1}{n_2}\right)}$ $LCL_{\bar{x}_1 - \bar{x}_2} = (\bar{x}_1 - \bar{x}_2) - t_{\alpha/2}\sqrt{s_p^2\left(\frac{1}{n_1} + \frac{1}{n_2}\right)}$	10.8 10.9
Mean	Dependent samples	Unknown	$UCL_{\bar{d}} = \bar{d} + t_{\alpha/2}\frac{s_d}{\sqrt{n}}$ $LCL_{\bar{d}} = \bar{d} - t_{\alpha/2}\frac{s_d}{\sqrt{n}}$	10.17 10.18
Proportion	Independent samples	Not applicable	$UCL_{p_1 - p_2} = (\bar{p}_1 - \bar{p}_2) + z_{\alpha/2}\hat{\sigma}_{p_1 - p_2}$ $UCL_{p_1 - p_2} = (\bar{p}_1 - \bar{p}_2) - z_{\alpha/2}\hat{\sigma}_{p_1 - p_2}$	10.21 10.22

CHAPTER 10 Problems

10.42 The federal government has become concerned about the default rates of loans made to students who attend for-profit schools. Two random samples of student loans were collected: one from students at for-profit schools and another from students at nonprofit schools. The following data show the sample sizes and the number of loans in each sample that defaulted:

For-Profit	Nonprofit
$x_1 = 23$	$x_2 = 7$
$n_1 = 220$	$n_2 = 200$

a. Perform a hypothesis test using $\alpha = 0.05$ to determine if the proportion of for-profit loans that default is larger than the proportion of loans for nonprofit schools that default.
b. Determine the p-value and interpret the results.
c. Construct a 95% confidence interval to estimate the difference in the proportion of loans in default at these two types of schools.
d. Verify your results using PHStat.

10.43 Baggage fees charged by airlines have received much attention recently as the industry has looked for ways to increase revenue without directly increasing fares. American Airlines would like to investigate if the average number of bags checked per flight fell after the company implemented fees for checking them. The following table shows the average numbers of checked bags per flight for a random sample of Boeing 737 domestic flights both before and after the fees were implemented. The population standard deviations and sample sizes are also indicated.

	Before	After
Sample mean	111.9	109.7
Sample size	42	50
Population standard deviation	10.7	9.4

a. Perform a hypothesis test using $\alpha = 0.10$ to determine if the average number of checked bags decreased after the checked-baggage fees were administered.
b. Determine the p-value and interpret the results.
c. Construct a 90% confidence interval to estimate the difference in the average number of checked bags per flight before and after the fees were implemented.
d. Verify your results using PHStat.

10.44 A survey asked respondents how many online "friends" they have on networking sites such as Facebook. The following table presents the average number of friends for men and women along with the sample standard deviations and sample sizes. Assume the population variances for the number of friends per person are not equal.

	Men	Women
Sample mean	178.3	144.6
Sample size	26	23
Sample standard deviation	72.3	56.9

a. Using $\alpha = 0.05$, perform a hypothesis test to determine if the men average 10 more online friends than the women.
b. Approximate the p-value using Table 5 in Appendix A and interpret the result.
c. Determine the precise p-value using Excel and interpret the results.
d. Verify your results using PHStat.
e. What assumptions need to be made in order to perform this procedure?

10.45 During the recent decline in the housing market, it appeared that the average size of a newly constructed house fell. To investigate this trend, the square footages of a random sample of houses built in 2010 were compared to houses built in 2014. A random sample of 45 homes built in 2010 had a sample mean of 2,462.3 square feet and a sample standard deviation of 760.8 square feet. A random sample of 40 homes built in 2014 had a sample mean of 2,257.0 square feet and a sample standard deviation of 730.2 square feet. Assume that the population variances for the square footages of houses built in these two years are equal.

a. Using $\alpha = 0.05$, perform a hypothesis test to determine if the average home constructed in 2010 was larger than a home built in 2014.
b. Construct a 95% confidence interval to estimate the average difference in the square footages of new homes constructed in these two years. Interpret your result.
c. Determine the precise p-value using Excel and interpret the results.
d. Verify your results using PHStat.
e. What assumptions need to be made in order to perform this procedure?

10.46 The recent financial crisis in Europe has resulted in high unemployment rates in some European Union countries. A recent survey of 120 adults from Greece found that 34 were currently unemployed. A corresponding survey of 135 adults from Spain found that 33 were currently unemployed.

a. Perform a hypothesis test with $\alpha = 0.02$ to determine if the percentage of unemployed adults in Greece is different than the percentage of unemployed adults in Spain.
b. Determine the p-value and interpret the results.
c. Determine the 98% confidence interval to estimate the difference in the proportion of unemployed workers between these two countries.
d. Verify your results using PHStat.

10.47 Small-business owners play a major role in the welfare of today's economy. This particular segment has a reputation for working long hours during the week. Suppose the Small Business Administration (SBA), a federal agency charged with supporting small businesses, would like to test the hypothesis that full-time small-business owners average more than 5 hours per week at work when compared to part-time small-business owners. A random sample of 15 full-time owners averaged 51.9 hours per week with a sample standard deviation of 5.5 hours per week. A random sample of 12 part-time owners averaged 41.5 hours per week with a sample standard deviation of 5.2 hours per week. Assume the population variances for hours worked per week for both groups are equal.

a. Using $\alpha = 0.05$, perform this hypothesis test for the SBA.

b. Approximate the p-value using Table 5 in Appendix A and interpret the results.

c. Construct a 95% confidence interval to estimate the average difference in hours worked per week between these two groups. Interpret your result.

d. Determine the precise p-value using Excel and interpret the results.

e. Verify your results using PHStat.

f. What assumptions need to be made in order to perform this procedure?

10.48 McDonald's would like to compare the wait times its drive-through customers experience vs. the wait times its customers using the restaurants' inside counters experience. The following data represent the wait times, in minutes, randomly selected customers in the two types of groups experienced. These data can also be found in the Excel file **wait times.xlsx.** Assume the population variances for the wait times for both locations are equal.

Drive-Through		Inside Counter	
3.2	1.7	3.0	1.7
5.0	4.0	2.8	5.0
0.9	4.9	3.4	1.9
6.4	3.0	3.3	4.5
3.6	3.2	2.4	5.9
3.5	3.4	4.5	4.0
3.9	6.3	1.1	3.3
3.3	0.0	2.0	2.8
2.1	3.3	0.0	5.3
		4.9	2.4

a. Using $\alpha = 0.05$, perform a hypothesis test to determine if the average wait time differs for customers in these two locations.

b. Approximate the p-value using Table 5 in Appendix A and interpret the result.

c. Construct a 95% confidence interval to estimate the average difference in wait time between these locations. Interpret your result.

d. Verify your results using PHStat or Excel.

e. Identify the p-value using Excel and interpret the result.

f. What assumptions need to be made in order to perform this procedure?

10.49 The on-time performances of flights in the airline industry are an important measurement that can help attract customers. The following data show the number of late flights from random samples taken from United Airlines and Southwest Airlines:

United	Southwest
$x_1 = 130$	$x_2 = 119$
$n_1 = 175$	$n_2 = 140$

a. Perform a hypothesis test using $\alpha = 0.05$ to determine if the on-time performances of these two airlines are different.

b. Determine the p-value and interpret the results.

c. Construct a 95% confidence interval to estimate the difference in the on-time performances of these two airlines.

d. Verify your results using PHStat.

10.50 Pfizer would like to test the effectiveness of a new cholesterol medication it has recently developed. To test the effectiveness, the LDL cholesterol level of 12 randomly selected individuals was measured before and after they took the medication. The data are shown as follows and can be found in the Excel file **cholesterol.xlsx**.

Person	Before	After	Person	Before	After
1	187	144	7	184	105
2	196	146	8	185	104
3	184	117	9	212	138
4	180	104	10	206	125
5	208	114	11	192	120
6	203	135	12	175	121

a. Using $\alpha = 0.01$, perform a hypothesis test to determine if the average LDL level is more the 50 points lower for patients who have taken the new medication.

b. Approximate the p-value using Table 5 in Appendix A and interpret the result.

c. Construct a 99% confidence interval to estimate the average difference in LDL levels for people before and after they take the medication.

d. Verify your results using Excel.

e. Identify the p-value using Excel and interpret the result.

f. What assumptions need to be made in order to perform this procedure?

10.51 The new health care plan that the federal government recently implemented has caused people to become concerned that a shortage of primary care physicians, particularly in under-served rural areas, will occur. Random samples of patient visits to primary care physicians in both rural and urban areas were selected. The number of days the patients had to wait for an appointment was recorded. The summarized data for each sample are shown in the following table:

	Rural	Urban
Sample mean	11.7	8.6
Sample size	32	30
Population standard deviation	5.0	3.5

a. Perform a hypothesis test using $\alpha = 0.01$ to determine if the average number of days patients in urban areas waited to see their primary care physicians differs from the average number of days patients in rural areas waited.

b. Determine the p-value and interpret the results.

c. Construct a 99% confidence interval to estimate the difference in the average number of days patients in urban areas waited to see their primary care physicians vs. the average number of days patients in rural areas waited.

d. Verify your results using PHStat.

10.52 The airline industry measures fuel efficiency by calculating how many miles one seat can travel, whether occupied or not, on one gallon of jet fuel. The following data show the fuel economy, in miles per seat, for 15 randomly selected flights on Delta and US Airways. These data can also be found in the Excel file **fuel efficiency.xlsx**. Assume the population variances for the fuel efficiency for these two airlines are not equal.

Delta			US Airways		
82.1	68.4	52.7	60.8	68.3	77.2
58.8	52.0	71.4	76.4	71.4	63.0
60.0	59.6	44.9	58.9	72.1	81.1
57.9	67.6	55.9	68.6	63.1	83.5
45.2	61.0	86.7	58.2	73.3	69.0

a. Perform a hypothesis test using $\alpha = 0.05$ to determine if the average fuel efficiency differs between the two airlines.

b. Approximate the p-value using Table 5 in Appendix A and interpret the result.

c. Verify your results using PHStat or Excel.

d. Identify the p-value using Excel and interpret the result.

e. What assumptions need to be made in order to perform this procedure?

10.53 Recent attention has been given to the percentage of successful free throws that resulted in points made in men's college basketball and the number of dribbles the shooter takes prior to the free throw. Samples of players who dribbled twice and players who dribbled four times before making free throws were randomly collected, and the number in both groups that was successful recorded:

Two Dribbles	Four Dribbles
$x_1 = 79$	$x_2 = 112$
$n_1 = 120$	$n_2 = 145$

a. Perform a hypothesis test using $\alpha = 0.10$ to determine if the proportion of successful free throws differs when players take two vs. four dribbles before shooting.

b. Determine the p-value and interpret the results.

c. Construct a 90% confidence interval to estimate the difference in the proportion of successful free throws when players take two vs. four dribbles before shooting.

d. Verify your results using PHStat.

10.54 Low-profile tires are automobile tires that have a short sidewall height, which is the distance between the tire rim and the road. These tires provide better performance at the expense of gas mileage. The Ford Taurus was chosen to measure the effect these tires have on gas mileage. Ten cars of this model were selected, and the gas mileage obtained on one tank of gas was measured with standard tires. Low-profile tires were then installed on the same cars. Using the same drivers, the gas mileage was again recorded. The results are shown as follows and can be found in the Excel file **low profile.xlsx**. Assume the population variances are equal.

Car	Standard	Low Profile	Car	Standard	Low Profile
1	21.5	22.4	6	26.5	19.0
2	22.3	20.1	7	25.5	19.7
3	25.6	24.0	8	19.5	16.2
4	19.3	19.5	9	23.9	21.4
5	22.3	21.7	10	22.9	22.4

a. Using $\alpha = 0.05$, perform a hypothesis test to determine if the average gas mileage obtained using standard tires is higher than the average gas mileage obtained using low-profile tires.

b. Approximate the p-value using Appendix A and interpret the result.

c. Construct a 90% confidence interval to estimate the average difference in gas mileage obtained using these two types of tires. Interpret the results.

d. Verify your results using Excel or PHStat.

e. Identify the p-value using Excel and interpret the result.

f. What assumptions need to be made in order to perform this procedure?

10.55 In Major League Baseball, the umpire behind the plate uses his best judgment to decide if a pitch is within the strike zone or outside of the strike zone. The age-old question is whether the strike zone for the batter in the National League is different from the strike zone in the American League. One way to address this question is to compare the percentage of called third strikes in the two leagues. The logic is that a batter who looks at a called third strike without swinging believed the pitch was outside the strike zone when the umpire considered the pitch within the strike zone. To test this hypothesis, a random sample of plate appearances from each league was selected and the number of called third strikes was counted. The data are as follows:

American	National
$x_1 = 46$	$x_2 = 37$
$n_1 = 170$	$n_2 = 160$

a. Perform a hypothesis test with $\alpha = 0.10$ to determine if the proportion of called third strikes differs between the two leagues.
b. Determine the p-value and interpret the results.
c. Construct a 90% confidence interval to estimate the difference in the proportion of called third strikes between the two leagues.
d. Verify your results using PHStat.

10.56 Brand loyalty in the automotive industry can be measured by the percentage of brand owners who purchase again. Suppose Cars.com would like to investigate if there is a difference in brand loyalty between Chevrolet and Buick owners. A random sample of 160 Chevrolet owners found that 68 had previously owned a Chevrolet. A random sample of 150 Buick owners found that 76 had previously owned a Buick.

a. Using $\alpha = 0.05$, perform this hypothesis test for Cars.com.
b. Construct a 95% confidence interval to estimate the difference in the proportion of owners who purchased the same brand of car for these two populations. Interpret your result.
c. Determine the p-value and interpret the results.
d. Verify your results using PHStat.

10.57 According to the Institute for College Access & Success, the average student-loan debt for the most recent class of students from Pennsylvania is \$9,000 more than the average for students in California. To test this claim, the following data were collected from random samples. Assume the population variances for the student-loan debt for these two states are equal.

	Pennsylvania	California
Sample mean	\$29,959	\$18,879
Sample size	20	20
Sample standard deviation	\$8,000	\$7,000

a. Using $\alpha = 0.05$, perform a hypothesis test to investigate the claim of the Institute for College Access & Success.
b. Approximate the p-value using Table 5 in Appendix A and interpret the results.
c. Construct a 95% confidence interval to estimate the average difference in the student-loan debt between these two states. Interpret your result.
d. Determine the precise p-value using Excel and interpret the results.
e. Verify your results using PHStat.
f. What assumptions need to be made in order to perform this procedure?

10.58 Past research has shown that Millennials, defined as those in the 18–34 age group, are more willing to provide personal information online to a company in exchange for something in return when compared to older individuals. To verify these reports, a random sample of 200 Millennials was selected and it was found that 112 responded that they would share their location in order to receive deals from nearby businesses. A random sample of 200 individuals older than 34 years was selected and 84 responded in the same manner.

a. Using $\alpha = 0.02$, perform a hypothesis test to investigate if Millennials are more willing to share personal information online when compared to older individuals.
b. Construct a 98% confidence interval to estimate the difference in the proportion of people willing to share personal information online for these two populations. Interpret your result.
c. Determine the p-value and interpret the results.

10.59 Many homeowners rely on handymen to perform small jobs, such as repairs or maintenance, around their residence. According to HomeAdvisor Inc., the average cost for a handyman project in Atlanta is more than the average cost for a project in Chicago. To test this claim, a random sample of 32 handyman projects in Atlanta was selected, and it was found that the average cost was \$437 with a sample standard deviation of \$83. A random sample of 36 handyman projects in Chicago was selected, and it was found that the average cost was \$411 with a sample standard deviation of \$62. Assume the population variances for the cost of handyman projects for these two cities are not equal.

a. Using $\alpha = 0.05$, perform a hypothesis test for the HomeAdvisor claim.
b. Approximate the p-value using Table 5 in Appendix A and interpret the results.
c. Determine the precise p-value using Excel and interpret the results.
d. Verify your results using PHStat.
e. What assumptions need to be made in order to perform this procedure?

10.60 In January 2011, the French government passed legislation requiring that within six years at least 40% of corporate board members of large companies be female. Large companies are defined as those having more than 500 employees or revenues over 50 million euros. Suppose the Corporate Women Directors International (CWDI) would like to test the hypothesis that the proportion of women on corporate boards of French companies is more than 5% higher than the proportion of women on boards of U.S. companies. From a random sample of 240 French board members, 73 were found to be women. From a random sample of 225 U.S. board members, 40 were found to be women.

a. Using $\alpha = 0.10$, perform this hypothesis test for the CWDI.
b. Construct a 90% confidence interval to estimate the difference in the proportion of women board members for these two countries. Interpret your result.
c. Determine the p-value and interpret the results.
d. Verify your results using PHStat.

10.61 *Negative equity* (also known as being "underwater") refers to a scenario where the market value of a residence is worth less than the outstanding balance on the mortgage for that home. Suppose the Federal Housing Administration (FHA), which is the government agency charged with supporting the home financing market, would like to test the hypothesis that the proportion of home mortgages with negative equity in Florida is more than 10% higher than the national proportion. A random sample of 180 mortgages from Florida found that 67 were underwater. A random sample of 190 mortgages across the United States found that 42 were underwater.

a. Using $\alpha = 0.05$, perform this hypothesis test for the FHA.
b. Construct a 95% confidence interval to estimate the difference in the proportion of underwater mortgages for these two populations. Interpret your result.
c. Determine the p-value and interpret the results.
d. Verify your results using PHStat.

10.62 Retailers pay close attention to holiday sales during the Thanksgiving weekend each year. To monitor these sales, a random sample of shoppers was selected in 2012 and again in 2013. The amount of money each shopper spent in stores and on Web sites was recorded. These data can be found in the Excel file **holiday sales.xlsx**. Assume that the population variances for the amounts spent during this weekend in the two years are equal.

a. Using $\alpha = 0.10$, perform a hypothesis test to determine if the average amounts spent on holiday shopping during this weekend differ between the two years.
b. Approximate the p-value using Table 5 in Appendix A and interpret the results.
c. Construct a 90% confidence interval to estimate the average difference in the amounts spent by holiday shoppers between the two years. Interpret your result.
d. Verify your results using PHStat or Excel.
e. Identify the p-value and interpret the result.
f. What assumptions need to be made in order to perform this procedure?

10.63 Citibank, which has a major credit card division, has instituted a promotion designed to encourage its customers to increase their current credit card usage. To test the effectiveness of this promotion, Citibank monitored the monthly credit card balances of 25 customers before and after the promotion was launched. The results can be found in the Excel file **Citibank 1.xlsx**.

a. Using $\alpha = 0.05$, perform a hypothesis test to determine if the average credit card balance was higher after the promotion than before the promotion.
b. Construct a 90% confidence interval to estimate the average difference in a customer's credit card balance before and after the promotion.
c. Verify your results using Excel or PHStat.
d. Identify the p-value and interpret the result.
e. What assumptions need to be made in order to perform this procedure?

10.64 Citibank, which has a major credit card division, has designed a promotion that the firm hopes will encourage its customers to increase their current credit card usage. To test the effectiveness of the promotion, Citibank monitored the monthly balances of 25 customers who were informed of the promotion and the monthly balances of 25 customers who were not aware of it. Assume the population variance for the credit card balances are equal. The results can be found in the Excel file **Citibank 2.xlsx**.

a. Using $\alpha = 0.05$, perform a hypothesis test to determine if the average credit card balance is higher for customers aware of the promotion than it was for customers unaware of the promotion.
b. Construct a 90% confidence interval to estimate the average difference in credit card balance before and after the promotion.
c. Verify your results using PHStat.
d. Identify the p-value and interpret the result.
e. What assumptions need to be made in order to perform this procedure?

10.65 The Excel file **golf scores.xlsx** contains a random sample of golf scores from two highly competitive sons of a certain statistics author. Each son claims he is the better golfer. Assume the population variances for each son's golf score are equal.

a. Perform a hypothesis test using $\alpha = 0.05$ to determine if there is a difference in the average golf score between the two sons.
b. Determine the p-value and interpret the results.
c. Construct a 95% confidence interval to estimate the difference in the average golf score between these two sons.
d. Verify your results using PHStat or Excel.

10.66 Coke would like to perform a blind taste test of its cola vs. the cola from its biggest competitor, Pepsi. To conduct this test, 24 individuals were randomly selected, asked to taste one unmarked cola, and to rate it on a scale of 1–10. The individuals were then asked to do the same for the other unmarked cola. The results are shown in the Excel file **taste test.xlsx**.

a. Using $\alpha = 0.10$, perform a hypothesis test to determine if a difference exists between the average scores for these two colas.

b. Construct a 90% confidence interval to estimate the average difference in scores between these two colas.

c. Verify your results using Excel or PHStat.

d. Identify the p-value and interpret the result.

e. What assumptions need to be made in order to perform this procedure?

CHAPTER 10 Solutions to Your Turn

YOUR TURN #1

Step 1: Identify the null and alternative hypotheses.

Population 1 = Playoff games

Population 2 = Regular season games

H_0: $\mu_1 - \mu_2 \leq 0$ (playoff games are not longer)

H_1: $\mu_1 - \mu_2 > 0$ (playoff games are longer)

This is a one-tail test because we are testing that playoff games are longer than regular season games. There is a direction in the test.

Step 2: Set a value for the significance level, α.

$$\alpha = 0.02$$

Step 3: Determine the appropriate critical value.

Using Table 10.1, a one-tail test using $\alpha = 0.02$ has a critical z-score, z_α, equal to 2.05.

Step 4: Calculate the appropriate test statistic.

$$\sigma_{\bar{x}_1 - \bar{x}_2} = \sqrt{\frac{\sigma_1^2}{n_1} + \frac{\sigma_2^2}{n_2}} = \sqrt{\frac{25^2}{30} + \frac{21^2}{32}}$$

$$\sigma_{\bar{x}_1 - \bar{x}_2} = \sqrt{20.83 + 13.78} = 5.88 \text{ minutes}$$

$$z_{\bar{x}} = \frac{(\bar{x}_1 - \bar{x}_2) - (\mu_1 - \mu_2)_{H_0}}{\sigma_{\bar{x}_1 - \bar{x}_2}}$$

$$= \frac{(189.3 - 175.8) - (0)_{H_0}}{5.88}$$

$$z_{\bar{x}} = \frac{(13.5) - (0)}{5.88} = 2.30$$

Step 5: Compare the z-test statistic ($z_{\bar{x}}$) with the critical z-score (z_α).

In our Major League Baseball example, which is a one-tail (upper) test, $z_{\bar{x}} = 2.30$ and $z_\alpha = 2.05$. Because 2.30 > 2.05, we come to the "Reject H_0" conclusion.

Step 6: Calculate the p-value.

The one-tail p-value for our example is as follows:

$$p\text{-value} = P(z_{\bar{x}} > 2.30) = (1 - 0.9893) = 0.0107$$

According to Table 10.3, because our p-value $= 0.0107$ is less than $\alpha = 0.05$, we reject the null hypothesis.

Step 7: State your conclusions.

Rejecting the null hypothesis means we have support for the alternative hypothesis. According to these two samples, we have evidence to support that the average playoff game is longer than the average regular season game.

	A	B
1	Z Test for Differences in Two Means	
2		
3	Data	
4	Hypothesized Difference	0
5	Level of Significance	0.02
6	Population 1 Sample	
7	Sample Size	30
8	Sample Mean	189.3
9	Population Standard Deviation	25
10	Population 2 Sample	
11	Sample Size	32
12	Sample Mean	175.8
13	Population Standard Deviation	21
14		
15	Intermediate Calculations	
16	Difference in Sample Means	13.5
17	Standard Error of the Difference in Means	5.883416
18	Z-Test Statistic	2.294585
19		
20		
21	Upper-Tail Test	
22	Upper Critical Value	2.053749
23	p-Value	0.010878
24	Reject the null hypothesis	
25		

YOUR TURN #2

According to Table 10.1, for $\alpha = 0.10$ and two tails, $z_{\alpha/2} = 1.645$.

$$\bar{x}_1 = 189.3 \quad \bar{x}_2 = 175.8 \quad \sigma_{\bar{x}_1-\bar{x}_2} = 5.88$$

$$UCL_{\bar{x}_1-\bar{x}_2} = (\bar{x}_1 - \bar{x}_2) + z_{\alpha/2}\sigma_{\bar{x}_1-\bar{x}_2}$$
$$UCL_{\bar{x}_1-\bar{x}_2} = (189.3 - 175.8) + (1.645)(5.88) = 23.17 \text{ minutes}$$

$$LCL_{\bar{x}_1-\bar{x}_2} = (\bar{x}_1 - \bar{x}_2) - z_{\alpha/2}\sigma_{\bar{x}_1-\bar{x}_2}$$
$$LCL_{\bar{x}_1-\bar{x}_2} = (189.3 - 175.8) - (1.645)(5.88) = 3.83 \text{ minutes}$$

Because the confidence interval does not include zero, we reject the null hypothesis.

YOUR TURN #3

a)

Step 1: Identify the null and alternative hypotheses.

Population 1 = Bob's route

Population 2 = Deb's route

H_0: $\mu_1 - \mu_2 \geq 0$ (Bob's route is equal to or takes more time than Deb's)

H_1: $\mu_1 - \mu_2 < 0$ (Bob's route takes less time than Deb's)

where

μ_1 = The mean time for Bob's route

μ_2 = The mean time for Deb's route

This is a one-tail (lower) test because the question is asking if Bob's route takes less time than Deb's.

Step 2: Set a value for the significance level, α.

$$\alpha = 0.05$$

Step 3: Calculate the appropriate test statistic.

$$\bar{x}_1 = 105.8 \text{ minutes} \qquad s_1 = 10.7883 \text{ minutes} \qquad n_1 = 12$$
$$\bar{x}_2 = 110.4 \text{ minutes} \qquad s_2 = 9.2400 \text{ minutes} \qquad n_2 = 10$$

$$s_p^2 = \frac{(n_1 - 1)s_1^2 + (n_2 - 1)s_2^2}{(n_1 - 1) + (n_2 - 1)}$$

$$s_p^2 = \frac{(12 - 1)(10.7883)^2 + (10 - 1)(9.2400)^2}{(12 - 1) + (10 - 1)}$$

$$s_p^2 = \frac{(11)(116.3874) + (9)(85.3776)}{(11) + (9)} = 102.4330$$

$$t_{\bar{x}} = \frac{(\bar{x}_1 - \bar{x}_2) - (\mu_1 - \mu_2)_{H_0}}{\sqrt{s_p^2\left(\frac{1}{n_1} + \frac{1}{n_2}\right)}}$$

$$t_{\bar{x}} = \frac{(105.8 - 110.4) - (0)}{\sqrt{(102.4330)\left(\frac{1}{12} + \frac{1}{10}\right)}}$$

$$= \frac{-4.6 - 0}{\sqrt{(102.4330)(0.1833)}} = \frac{-4.6}{4.333} = -1.06$$

Step 4: Determine the appropriate critical value.

Using Table 5 in Appendix A for a one-tail test, $df = n_1 + n_2 - 2 = 12 + 10 - 2 = 20$, and $\alpha = 0.05$, our critical t-score is $-t_\alpha = -1.725$.

Step 5: Compare the t-test statistic $(t_{\bar{x}})$ with the critical t-score (t_α).

In this example, which is a one-tail (lower) test, $t_{\bar{x}} = -1.06$ and $-t_\alpha = -1.725$. Because $-1.06 > -1.725$, we fail to reject the null hypothesis according to the decision rules shown in Table 10.5.

Step 6: State your conclusions.

Failing to reject the null hypothesis means we do not have support for the alternative hypothesis. According to these two samples, we do not have evidence to conclude that Bob's route is faster than Deb's. I have been foiled again by my beloved statistics (and my wife).

b) Using Table 5 in Appendix A, go to the row in which $df = 20$ and find the values that bracket $|t_{\bar{x}}| = |-1.06| = 1.06$. These values are 0.860 and 1.325. Going to the **1 Tail** row, the p-value is between 0.10 and 0.20. With $\alpha = 0.05$, we fail to reject the null hypothesis.

c) Using Table 5 in Appendix A for a 95% confidence interval and $df = 20$, our critical t-score is $t_{\alpha/2} = 2.086$. Using Equations 10.8 and 10.9, our limits for the 95% confidence interval are as follows:

$$UCL_{\bar{x}_1-\bar{x}_2} = (\bar{x}_1 - \bar{x}_2) + t_{\alpha/2}\sqrt{s_p^2\left(\frac{1}{n_1} + \frac{1}{n_2}\right)}$$

$$UCL_{\bar{x}_1-\bar{x}_2} = (105.8 - 110.4) + (2.086)\sqrt{(102.4294)\left(\frac{1}{12} + \frac{1}{10}\right)}$$

$$UCL_{\bar{x}_1-\bar{x}_2} = (-4.6) + (2.086)\sqrt{18.7787}$$
$$= -4.6 + 9.04 = 4.44 \text{ minutes}$$

$$LCL_{\bar{x}_1-\bar{x}_2} = (\bar{x}_1 - \bar{x}_2) - t_{\alpha/2}\sqrt{s_p^2\left(\frac{1}{n_1} + \frac{1}{n_2}\right)}$$

$$LCL_{\bar{x}_1-\bar{x}_2} = (105.8 - 110.4) - (2.086)\sqrt{(102.4294)\left(\frac{1}{12} + \frac{1}{10}\right)}$$

$$LCL_{\bar{x}_1-\bar{x}_2} = (-4.6) - (2.086)\sqrt{18.7787}$$
$$= -4.6 - 9.04 = -13.64 \text{ minutes}$$

Our 95% confidence interval is $(-13.64, 4.44)$. This means we are 95% confident that the difference between the average travel time in the two routes is between −13.64 minutes and 4.44 minutes. The fact that this interval does include zero provides more evidence that there is not a difference in the average travel times of the two routes.

d)

	A	B	C	D	E
1	**Pooled-Variance *t* Test for the Difference Between Two Means**				
2	(assumes equal population variances)				
3	**Data**			**Confidence Interval Estimate**	
4	**Hypothesized Difference**	0		**for the Difference Between Two Means**	
5	**Level of Significance**	0.05			
6	**Population 1 Sample**			**Data**	
7	**Sample Size**	12		**Confidence Level**	95%
8	**Sample Mean**	105.75			
9	**Sample Standard Deviation**	10.78825		Intermediate Calculations	
10	**Population 2 Sample**			Degrees of Freedom	20
11	**Sample Size**	10		*t* Value	2.0860
12	**Sample Mean**	110.4		Interval Half Width	9.0395
13	**Sample Standard Deviation**	9.24001			
14				**Confidence Interval**	
15	Intermediate Calculations			**Interval Lower Limit**	-13.6895
16	Population 1 Sample Degrees of Freedor	11		**Interval Upper Limit**	4.3895
17	Population 2 Sample Degrees of Freedor	9			
18	Total Degrees of Freedom	20			
19	Pooled Variance	102.4325			
20	Standard Error	4.3335			
21	Difference in Sample Means	-4.65			
22	***t* Test Statistic**	-1.0730			
23					
24	**Lower-Tail Test**				
25	**Lower Critical Value**	-1.7247			
26	***p*-Value**	0.1480			
27	**Do not reject the null hypothesis**				
28					

e) $=\text{T.DIST}(-1.06, 20, \text{TRUE}) = 0.1509$ (This function is used for a one-tail lower test.)

f) Because the sample standard deviations are being used to approximate the population standard deviations, the populations must be normally distributed.

YOUR TURN #4

a)

Step 1: Identify the null and alternative hypotheses.

Population 1 = Men

Population 2 = Women

H_0: $\mu_1 - \mu_2 \geq 0$ (men use the same or more minutes than women)

H_1: $\mu_1 - \mu_2 < 0$ (men use less minutes than women)

With the populations defined, we have a lower-tail test. If we reverse the definitions, we would have an upper-tail test. Either case is acceptable.

Step 2: Set a value for the significance level, α.

$$\alpha = 0.01$$

Step 3: Calculate the appropriate test statistic.

We can use Excel to calculate the following sample statistics for our example:

$$\bar{x}_1 = 330.7 \qquad s_1 = 90.8149 \qquad n_1 = 10$$

$$\bar{x}_2 = 461.1 \qquad s_2 = 161.2255 \qquad n_2 = 10$$

Applying this to Equation 10.10, our *t*-test statistic is as follows:

$$t_{\bar{x}} = \frac{(\bar{x}_1 - \bar{x}_2) - (\mu_1 - \mu_2)_{H_0}}{\sqrt{\left(\frac{s_1^2}{n_1} + \frac{s_2^2}{n_2}\right)}}$$

$$t_{\bar{x}} = \frac{(330.7 - 461.1) - 0}{\sqrt{\left(\frac{(90.8149)^2}{10} + \frac{(161.2255)^2}{10}\right)}}$$

$$= \frac{-130.4}{\sqrt{824.7346 + 2{,}599.3662}} = \frac{-130.4}{58.5158} = -2.23$$

Step 4: Determine the appropriate critical value.

We can simplify using Equation 10.11 by calculating the following terms:

$$\frac{s_1^2}{n_1} = \frac{(90.8149)^2}{10} = 824.7346$$

$$\frac{s_2^2}{n_2} = \frac{(161.2255)^2}{10} = 2,599.3662$$

We then plug these values into Equation 10.11:

$$df = \frac{\left(\frac{s_1^2}{n_1} + \frac{s_1^2}{n_1}\right)^2}{\frac{\left(\frac{s_1^2}{n_1}\right)^2}{n_1 - 1} + \frac{\left(\frac{s_2^2}{n_2}\right)^2}{n_2 - 1}} = \frac{(824.7346 + 2{,}599.3662)^2}{\frac{(824.7346)^2}{10 - 1} + \frac{(2{,}599.3662)^2}{10 - 1}}$$

$$df = \frac{(3{,}424.1008)^2}{\frac{(680{,}187.1604)^2}{9} + \frac{(6{,}756{,}704.6417)^2}{9}}$$

$$df = \frac{11{,}724{,}466.2886}{75{,}576.3512 + 750{,}744.9602} = 14.2 \approx 14$$

Using Table 5 in Appendix A for a one-tail (lower) test, $df = 14$, and $\alpha = 0.01$, our critical *t*-score is $-t_\alpha = -2.624$.

Step 5: Compare the *t*-test statistic ($t_{\bar{x}}$) with the critical *t*-score (t_α).

For this example, which is a one-tail (lower) test, $t_{\bar{x}} = -2.23$ and $-t_\alpha = -2.624$. Because $-2.23 > -2.624$, we fail to reject the null hypothesis according to the decision rules shown in Table 10.5.

Step 6: Approximate the p-value.

The p-value is between 0.01 and 0.025.

Step 7: State your conclusions.

Failing to reject the null hypothesis means we do not have support for the alternative hypothesis. According to these two samples, there is not enough evidence to claim that women average more minutes talking on their cell phones than men.

b) This result may seem surprising because the sample average for the women (461.1 minutes) is so much larger than the sample average for the men (330.7 minutes). The following three reasons make it more challenging to reject the null hypothesis:

1. Using a low $\alpha (\alpha = 0.01)$
2. Having small sample sizes $(n_1 = 10, n_2 = 10)$
3. Having high sample standard deviations relative to the sample means $(s_1 = 90.8, s_2 = 161.2)$

c)

D	E	F
t-Test: Two-Sample Assuming Unequal Variances		
	Men	*Women*
Mean	330.7	461.1
Variance	8247.344444	25993.65556
Observations	10	10
Hypothesized Mean Difference	0	
df	14	
t Stat	-2.228457581	
P(T<=t) one-tail	0.021376841	
t Critical one-tail	2.624494068	
P(T<=t) two-tail	0.042753682	
t Critical two-tail	2.976842734	

d) Because the p-value $= 0.0214$ (see Cell E10 in previous figure) is greater than $\alpha = 0.01$, we fail to reject the null hypothesis.

e) Because the sample sizes are less than 30, and the population standard deviations are unknown, the population needs to be normally distributed.

YOUR TURN #5

a) I'll define Population 1 as Delaware (DE) stations and Population 2 as New Jersey (NJ) stations, resulting in the following hypothesis statement:

H_0: $\mu_1 - \mu_2 \leq \$0.20$

H_1: $\mu_1 - \mu_2 > \$0.20$ (DE gas is more than \$0.20 per gallon than NJ gas)

Use Equation 10.7 to calculate the pooled variance:

$$s_p^2 = \frac{(n_1 - 1)s_1^2 + (n_2 - 1)s_2^2}{(n_1 - 1) + (n_2 - 1)}$$

$$s_p^2 = \frac{(13 - 1)(0.12)^2 + (10 - 1)(0.15)^2}{(13 - 1) + (10 - 1)}$$

$$= \frac{(12)(0.0144) + (9)(0.0225)}{12 + 9} = 0.01787$$

Applying this to Equation 10.6, our t-test statistic is as follows:

$$t_{\bar{x}} = \frac{(\bar{x}_1 - \bar{x}_2) - (\mu_1 - \mu_2)_{H_0}}{\sqrt{s_p^2\left(\frac{1}{n_1} + \frac{1}{n_2}\right)}}$$

$$t_{\bar{x}} = \frac{(3.75 - 3.52) - (0.20)}{\sqrt{(0.01787)\left(\frac{1}{13} + \frac{1}{10}\right)}}$$

$$= \frac{0.23 - 0.20}{\sqrt{(0.01787)(0.1769)}} = \frac{0.03}{0.0562} = 0.53$$

For this test, the degrees of freedom are calculated as follows:

$$df = n_1 + n_2 - 2 = 13 + 10 - 2 = 21$$

Using Table 5 in Appendix A for a one-tail (upper) test, $df = 21$, and $\alpha = 0.05$, our critical t-score is $t_\alpha = 1.721$. Because $t_{\bar{x}} = 0.53 < t_\alpha = 1.721$, we fail to reject the null hypothesis according to the decision rules shown in Table 10.5. By failing to reject the null hypothesis, we do not have enough evidence to conclude that New Jersey gas averages at least \$0.20 per gallon less than Delaware. Yes, I finally win!

b) Using Table 5 in Appendix A, go to the row in which $df = 21$ and find the values that bracket $t_{\bar{x}} = 0.53$. The lowest value in this row is 0.859 in the first column. Going to the **1 Tail** row, the p-value is more than 0.20. With $\alpha = 0.05$, we fail to reject the null hypothesis.

c)

	A	B
1	Pooled-Variance *t* Test for the Difference Between Two Means	
2	(assumes equal population variances)	
3	Data	
4	Hypothesized Difference	0.2
5	Level of Significance	0.05
6	Population 1 Sample	
7	Sample Size	13
8	Sample Mean	3.75
9	Sample Standard Deviation	0.12
10	Population 2 Sample	
11	Sample Size	10
12	Sample Mean	[illegible]
13	Sample Standard Deviation	0.15
14		
15	Intermediate Calculations	
16	Population 1 Sample Degrees of Freedom	12
17	Population 2 Sample Degrees of Freedom	9
18	Total Degrees of Freedom	21
19	Pooled Variance	0.0179
20	Standard Error	0.0562
21	Difference in Sample Means	0.2300
22	*t* Test Statistic	0.5335
23		
24	Upper-Tail Test	
25	Upper Critical Value	1.7207
26	*p*-Value	0.2996
27	Do not reject the null hypothesis	
28		

d) Because the p-value $= 0.2996$ (see Cell B26 in the previous figure) is greater than $\alpha = 0.05$, we fail to reject the null hypothesis.

e) Because the sample sizes are less than 30 and the population standard deviations are unknown, we can't rely on the Central Limit Theorem to come to our rescue. Therefore, the population needs to be normally distributed.

YOUR TURN #6

a)

Step 1: Calculate the matched-pair differences.

Population 1 = My ball
Population 2 = Their ball

My Ball	Their Ball	d
201	204	−3
228	213	15
256	231	25
233	241	−8
248	223	25
255	226	29
239	212	27
220	186	34

Step 2: Calculate the mean and the standard deviation of the matched-pair differences.

$$\bar{d} = \frac{\sum_{i=1}^{n} d_i}{n}$$

$$= \frac{(-3) + 15 + 25 + (-8) + 25 + 29 + 27 + 34}{8}$$

$$= \frac{144}{8} = 18.0$$

d_i	d_i^2
−3	9
15	225
25	625
−8	64
25	625
29	841
27	729
34	1,156

Sum of the differences: $\sum_{i=1}^{9} d_i = 144$

Sum of the squared differences: $\sum_{i=1}^{9} d_i^2 = 4{,}274$

Squared sum of the differences: $\left(\sum_{i=1}^{9} d_i\right)^2 = (144)^2 = 20{,}736$

$$s_d = \sqrt{\frac{\sum_{i=1}^{n} d_i^2 - \frac{\left(\sum_{i=1}^{n} d_i\right)^2}{n}}{n-1}}$$

$$= \sqrt{\frac{4{,}274 - \frac{20{,}736}{8}}{8-1}}$$

$$= \sqrt{\frac{4{,}274 - 2{,}592}{7}} = 15.5$$

Step 3: Identify the null and alternative hypotheses.

$H_0: \mu_d \leq 15$

$H_1: \mu_d > 15$ (My ball averages 15 yards more than theirs)

Step 4: Set a value for the significance level, α.

$$\alpha = 0.10$$

Step 5: Calculate the appropriate test statistic.

$$t_{\bar{x}} = \frac{\bar{d} - (\mu_d)_{H_0}}{\frac{s_d}{\sqrt{n}}} = \frac{18.0 - 15}{\frac{15.5}{\sqrt{8}}} = \frac{3.0}{5.48} = 0.55$$

Step 6: Determine the appropriate critical value.

Using Table 5 in Appendix A for a one-tail (upper) test, $df = n - 1 = 8 - 1 = 7$, and $\alpha = 0.10$, our critical t-score is $t_\alpha = 1.415$.

Step 7: Compare the t-test statistic $(t_{\bar{x}})$ with the critical t-score (t_α).

In our golf example, which is a one-tail (upper) test, $t_{\bar{x}} = 0.55$ and $t_\alpha = 1.415$. Because $0.55 < 1.415$, we fail to reject the null hypothesis according to the decision rules shown in Table 10.5.

Step 8: Approximate the p-value.

See the answer to part b following.

Step 9: State your conclusions.

By failing to reject the null hypothesis, we do not have enough evidence to conclude that my golf ball increases golfers' driving distances by more than 15 yards. Back to the drawing board again!

b) Using Table 5 in Appendix A, go to the row in which $df = 7$ and find the values that bracket $t_{\bar{x}} = 0.55$. The lowest value in this row is 0.896 in the first column. Going to the **1 Tail** row, we find that the p-value is more than 0.20. Because $\alpha = 0.10$ is outside this range, we fail to reject the null hypothesis.

c)

	A	B	C	D	E	F
1	My Ball	Their Ball		t-Test: Paired Two Sample for Means		
2	201	204				
3	228	213			*My Ball*	*Their Ball*
4	256	231		Mean	235	217
5	233	241		Variance	351.4285714	294.2857143
6	248	223		Observations	8	8
7	255	226		Pearson Correlation	0.630349237	
8	239	212		Hypothesized Mean Difference	15	
9	220	186		df	7	
10				t Stat	0.547396823	
11				P(T<=t) one-tail	0.300557351	
12				t Critical one-tail	1.414923928	
13				P(T<=t) two-tail	0.601114702	
14				t Critical two-tail	1.894578605	
15						

d) Because the *p*-value $= 0.3005$ (see Cell E11 in the previous figure) and is greater than $\alpha = 0.10$, we fail to reject the null hypothesis.

e) Because the sample sizes are less than 30 and the population standard deviations are unknown, the matched-pair differences need to follow the normal probability distribution.

YOUR TURN #7

Using Table 5 in Appendix A for a 95% confidence interval and $df = n - 1 = 8 - 1 = 7$, our critical *t*-score is $t_{\alpha/2} = 2.365$. In the previous Your Turn section, we identified the following values:

$$\bar{d} = 18.0 \qquad s_d = 15.5 \qquad n = 8$$

Using these values in Equations 10.17 and 10.18, we have our limits for the 95% confidence interval:

$$UCL_{\bar{d}} = \bar{d} + t_{\alpha/2}\frac{s_d}{\sqrt{n}}$$

$$UCL_{\bar{d}} = 18.0 + (2.365)\frac{15.5}{\sqrt{8}} = 18.0 + 12.96 = 30.96$$

$$LCL_{\bar{d}} = \bar{d} - t_{\alpha/2}\frac{s_d}{\sqrt{n}}$$

$$LCL_{d} = 18.0 - (2.365)\frac{15.5}{\sqrt{8}} = 18.0 - 12.96 = 5.04$$

Our 95% confidence interval is (5.04, 30.96). This means we are 95% confident that the difference between the distance using my golf ball and their golf balls is between 5.04 and 30.96 yards. The fact that this interval does include less than 15 yards places doubt on my claim and is consistent with the conclusion not to reject the null hypothesis. There is no proof my golf ball averages more than 15 yards farther off the tee than their golf balls. Back to the drawing board again!

YOUR TURN #8

a)

Step 1: Identify the null and alternative hypotheses.

Because we are testing that one group has a higher proportion of online customers than the other group, we have the following one-tail (upper) hypothesis statement:

H_0: $p_1 - p_2 \leq 0$ (proportion of younger is equal to or less than older)

H_1: $p_1 - p_2 > 0$ (proportion of younger is more than older)

where

$p_1 =$ The true proportion of younger online customers

$p_2 =$ The true proportion of older online customers

Step 2: Set a value for the significance level, α.

$$\alpha = 0.05$$

Step 3: Calculate the appropriate test statistic.

$$\hat{p} = \frac{x_1 + x_2}{n_1 + n_2} = \frac{68 + 72}{80 + 100} = 0.778$$

$$\bar{p}_1 = \frac{x_1}{n_1} = \frac{68}{80} = 0.85 \quad \bar{p}_2 = \frac{x_2}{n_2} = \frac{72}{100} = 0.72$$

$$z_p = \frac{(\bar{p}_1 - \bar{p}_2) - (p_1 - p_2)_{H_0}}{\sqrt{\hat{p}(1 - \hat{p})\left(\frac{1}{n_1} + \frac{1}{n_2}\right)}}$$

$$= \frac{(0.85 - 0.72) - (0)_{H_0}}{\sqrt{(0.778)(1 - 0.778)\left(\frac{1}{80} + \frac{1}{100}\right)}}$$

$$z_p = \frac{0.13}{\sqrt{(0.778)(0.222)(0.0225)}}$$

$$= \frac{0.13}{\sqrt{0.003886}} = \frac{0.13}{0.062338} = 2.09$$

Step 4: Determine the appropriate critical value.

Using Table 10.1, for a one-tail test using $\alpha = 0.05$ our critical z-score is $z_\alpha = 1.645$.

Step 5: Compare the z-test statistic (z_p) with the critical z-score (z_α).

In our online banking example, which is a one-tail (upper) test, $z_p = 2.09$ and $z_\alpha = 1.645$. Because $2.09 > 1.645$, we reject the null hypothesis.

Step 6: Calculate the p-value.

The one-tail p-value for our example is as follows:

$$p\text{-value} = P(z_p > 2.09) = 1.0 - 0.9817 = 0.0183$$

Because our p-value $= 0.0183$ and is less than $\alpha = 0.05$, we reject the null hypothesis, according to Table 10.3.

Step 7: State your conclusions.

By rejecting the null hypothesis, we conclude that we do have enough evidence to support the alternative hypothesis, $H_1: p_1 - p_2 > 0$. Therefore, we conclude that the proportion of younger customers who use online banking is greater than the proportion of older customers.

b)

$$\hat{\sigma}_{p_1-p_2} = \sqrt{\frac{\bar{p}_1(1-\bar{p}_1)}{n_1} + \frac{\bar{p}_2(1-\bar{p}_2)}{n_2}}$$

$$\hat{\sigma}_{p_1-p_2} = \sqrt{\frac{(0.85)(1-0.85)}{80} + \frac{(0.72)(1-0.72)}{100}}$$

$$\hat{\sigma}_{p_1-p_2} = \sqrt{0.001594 + 0.002016}$$

$$= \sqrt{0.003610} = 0.060083$$

$$UCL_{p_1-p_2} = (\bar{p}_1 - \bar{p}_2) + Z_{\alpha/2}\hat{\sigma}_{p_1-p_2}$$

$$UCL_{p_1-p_2} = (0.85 - 0.72) + (1.96)(0.060083)$$

$$= 0.13 + 0.11776 = 0.2478$$

$$LCL_{p_1-p_2} = (\bar{p}_1 - \bar{p}_2) - Z_{\alpha/2}\hat{\sigma}_{p_1-p_2}$$

$$LCL_{p_1-p_2} = (0.85 - 0.72) - (1.96)(0.060083)$$

$$= 0.13 - 0.11776 = 0.0122$$

We are 95% confident that the true difference between the proportion of younger and older online customers is between 1.22% and 24.78%. Because this interval does not contain zero, we conclude that the proportion of younger customers who use online banking is different from the proportion of older customers who use online banking.

c)

	A	B	C	D	E
1	**Z Test for Differences in Two Proportions**				
2					
3	**Data**			**Confidence Interval Estimate**	
4	**Hypothesized Difference**	0		**of the Difference Between Two Proportions**	
5	**Level of Significance**	0.05			
6	**Group 1**			**Data**	
7	**Number of Items of Interest**	68		**Confidence Level**	95%
8	**Sample Size**	80			
9	**Group 2**			Intermediate Calculations	
10	**Number of Items of Interest**	72		Z Value	-1.9600
11	**Sample Size**	100		Std. Error of the Diff. between two Proporti	0.0601
12				Interval Half Width	0.1178
13	Intermediate Calculations				
14	Group 1 Proportion	0.85		**Confidence Interval**	
15	Group 2 Proportion	0.72		**Interval Lower Limit**	**0.0122**
16	Difference in Two Proportions	0.13		**Interval Upper Limit**	**0.2478**
17	Average Proportion	0.7778			
18	**Z Test Statistic**	**2.0846**			
19					
20	**Upper-Tail Test**				
21	**Upper Critical Value**	1.6449			
22	***p*-Value**	0.0186			
23	**Reject the null hypothesis**				
24					

CHAPTER 11

Analysis of Variance (ANOVA) Procedures

IN THIS CHAPTER, YOU WILL LEARN TO:

- Test for a difference between the means of three or more populations using one-way ANOVA.
- Test for a difference between the means of three or more populations with a blocking factor using randomized block ANOVA.
- Understand the benefits of incorporating a blocking factor with analysis of variance.
- Examine the effects two factors have on the means of three or more populations using two-way ANOVA.
- Test for the interaction between the two main factors with two-way ANOVA.
- Perform multiple comparison tests for all three ANOVA techniques.

CHAPTER 11 MAP

Analysis of variance (ANOVA) is a technique used to conduct a hypothesis test to compare three or more population means simultaneously.

In Chapter 9, we learned how to perform a hypothesis test to estimate a single-population parameter such as a mean or a proportion. Chapter 10 extended this concept to estimate the difference between two population parameters. This chapter will take hypothesis testing an additional step by comparing three or more population means using a technique known as the **analysis of variance (ANOVA)**. This procedure is so special that it even has its own acronym: ANOVA. Sounds like the title of an awesome sci-fi movie. (*ANOVA: Revenge of the Aliens*. Coming to a theater near you!)

This technique has many useful business applications such as determining the following:

- If the average amount of time spent per month on Facebook differs between various age groups
- If the average airfare for round-trip flights from Philadelphia to Paris differs between airlines
- If the average number of sales calls per day differs between sales representatives

Let's start the chapter with the following example. Recently, the CFI Group, a firm that studies customer satisfaction, conducted a survey to measure how satisfied customers were with several smartphones. Table 11.1 shows the average satisfaction scores reported by the firm from a sample of users.

TABLE 11.1 | AVERAGE SATISFACTION SCORES FOR SMARTPHONES

POPULATION	PHONE	AVERAGE SCORE
1	iPhone	83
2	Android	77
3	BlackBerry	73
4	Nokia	66

We can employ an ANOVA procedure to test if we have enough evidence from this sample to conclude whether the satisfaction scores from these populations of smartphone users are truly different from one another. In other words, the purpose of the ANOVA procedure is to determine whether the variation in satisfaction scores is due to the type of smartphone or simply to randomness. To do so, we need to identify the factors and levels in the analysis. A **factor** in an ANOVA test describes the cause of the variation in the data. In this example, the factor would be the smartphones, which cause various degrees of satisfaction with their users. A **level** in an ANOVA test describes a category within the factor of interest. For our example, we have four levels because we have satisfaction scores from four different smartphone models.

A **factor** in an ANOVA test describes the cause of the variation in the data.

A **level** in an ANOVA test describes a category within the factor of interest.

The analysis of variance technique comes in three different flavors, which are known as designs. Each design organizes the data in a manner conducive to the type of analysis that is desired; the designs are as follows:

- One-way ANOVA. The one-way ANOVA design is the simplest of the three designs and compares the means of different levels of one factor. Comparing the satisfaction levels of four different smartphone brands is an example of this procedure. Think of a one-way ANOVA as the vanilla of ANOVA—the most basic of the procedures but very reliable.
- Randomized block ANOVA. The randomized block ANOVA design is a variation of the one-way ANOVA where we use matched samples in a similar way to the matched pairs in Chapter 10. For example, suppose we believe that the size of the monthly smartphone bill influenced the satisfaction score. We could then group customers with similar bills together within each brand. This design allows us to block out the variation in scores due to the size of the bill for each brand. Doing so may allow us to detect differences in satisfaction scores between brands that may not be evident if we had used the one-way ANOVA design. I would describe this procedure as the mint chocolate chip flavor (my personal favorite) of ANOVA—a bit fancier than the one-way method.

- Two-way ANOVA. The two-way ANOVA design compares the means from different levels using two factors. For example, this method allows us to look for differences in satisfaction scores between smartphone brands (the first factor) and differences in satisfaction scores between education level of the user (the second factor) simultaneously. I would compare this procedure to bacon ice cream (yes, this does exist) because the two-way ANOVA is a more exotic and complicated flavor of ANOVA when compared with the two previous types.

Each of these procedures relies on the following set of assumptions:

- Each of the populations being compared follows the normal probability distribution.
- The observations must be independent of one another.
- The populations being compared have equal variances.
- The observations are either interval or ratio data.

Recall that interval data exhibit differences between values are meaningful. Ratio data have all the properties of interval data, with the added benefit of a true zero point.

For the remainder of this chapter, we will assume these conditions have been met. Later in this text, we will discuss methods to verify that we have normal populations and equal variances. We're now ready to examine our first ANOVA procedure.

11.1 One-Way ANOVA: Examining the Effect a Single Factor Has on the Means of Populations

A **one-way ANOVA** is used when we are looking at the influence that one factor has on the data values.

A **one-way ANOVA** is used when we are looking at the influence that one factor has on the data values. Consider the smartphone example in the previous section. Suppose Table 11.2 shows the satisfaction scores for individual users of each phone. These data can also be found in the file **smartphones.xlsx**.

TABLE 11.2 | Individual Satisfaction Scores for Four Smartphones

IPHONE	ANDROID	BLACKBERRY	NOKIA
87	71	66	65
85	82	74	69
78	75	79	67
82	80		63

An ANOVA test allows us to have unequal sample sizes.

Because smartphones are the only factor that influences satisfaction scores in Table 11.2, this is an example of a one-way ANOVA. The following steps will illustrate this technique.

Step 1: Identify the null and alternative hypotheses.

Here's some good news for you. The null hypothesis for every ANOVA procedure states that all the population means are equal. The alternative hypothesis, therefore, claims that not all population means are equal. For our smartphone example, we have the following:

This is a whole lot easier than trying to figure out if we have a one-tail or two-tail test. Be grateful for small favors!

$$H_0: \mu_1 = \mu_2 = \mu_3 = \mu_4$$
$$H_1: \text{Not all } \mu\text{s are equal}$$

By rejecting the null hypothesis, we are concluding that a difference in population means truly exists (that is, that the users of some smartphones generate higher mean satisfaction scores than others). As with one- and two-sample hypothesis testing from the previous chapters, we need to set our level of significance when using an ANOVA. For this example, I'll set the probability of making a Type I error at $\alpha = 0.05$.

In this example, a Type I error happens when we conclude there is a difference in the satisfaction scores among the groups of smartphone users when, in reality, there is no difference in the population means.

Step 2: Calculate the sample means ($\bar{x}$) and grand mean ($\bar{\bar{x}}$).

The sample mean calculations for our smartphone data from Table 11.2 are shown in Table 11.3.

TABLE 11.3 | SAMPLE DATA FOR THE SATISFACTION SCORES FOR THE SMARTPHONES

	IPHONE	ANDROID	BLACKBERRY	NOKIA	TOTAL
	87	71	66	65	
	85	82	74	69	
	78	75	79	67	
	82	80		63	
Total	332	308	219	264	1,123
Size	4	4	3	4	15
Mean	83.0	77.0	73.0	66.0	74.87

Be careful not to simply average the four sample means to calculate the grand mean when the sample sizes are not equal. Don't calculate the grand mean of the smartphone data by adding 83, 77, 73, and 66 and then simply dividing by 4. Rather, divide the total score (1,123) by the total number of scores (15).

The mean scores for each smartphone can be found by taking the average of each column in Table 11.3.

$$\bar{x}_1 = \frac{\text{Sum of iphone scores}}{n_1} = \frac{332}{4} = 83.0$$

$$\bar{x}_2 = \frac{\text{Sum of Android scores}}{n_2} = \frac{308}{4} = 77.0$$

$$\bar{x}_3 = \frac{\text{Sum of BlackBerry scores}}{n_3} = \frac{219}{3} = 73.0$$

$$\bar{x}_4 = \frac{\text{Sum of Nokia scores}}{n_4} = \frac{264}{4} = 66.0$$

We also need to determine the grand mean, $\bar{\bar{x}}$, which is the average of all the smartphone scores in Table 11.3. The equation for calculating the grand mean is as follows:

$$\bar{\bar{x}} = \frac{\text{Sum of all scores}}{\text{Total number of scores}} = \frac{1{,}123}{15} = 74.87$$

Here is the question we are pondering: Are these four sample means far enough from one another to justify a claim that the population means from which they were drawn are significantly different using $\alpha = 0.05$? Let's find out!

Step 3: Calculate the total sum of squares (SST) and mean square total (MST).

The **total sum of squares (*SST*)** measures the amount of variation between each data value and the grand mean.

To answer this question, we need to find the **total sum of squares (*SST*)**, which measures the amount of variation between each data value and the grand mean. Figure 11.1 shows the *SST* graphically for our smartphone example.

Each circle in Figure 11.1 represents one specific satisfaction score from Table 11.2. The red horizontal line indicates the grand mean for all 15 scores ($\bar{\bar{x}} = 74.87$). The length of each arrow represents the variation between each score and the grand mean. Longer arrows in Figure 11.1 indicate a larger value for the *SST*. Equations 11.1 and 11.2 show how to calculate the *SST*. Both equations will provide the same result, but using Equation 11.2 requires fewer computations and is the one that I will use.

FIGURE 11.1
The Total Sum of Squares (SST) for the Smartphone Data

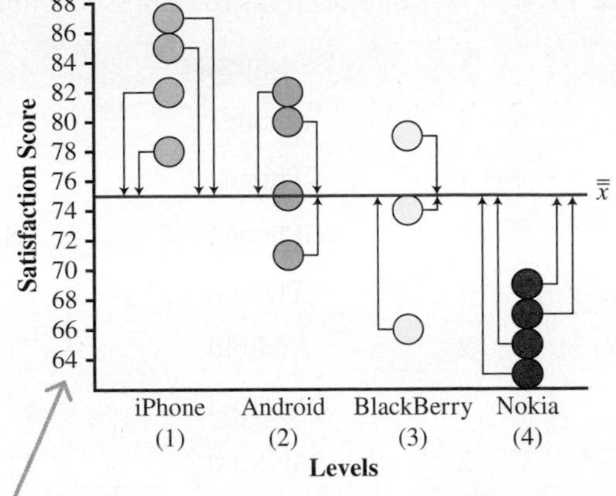

Students often wonder why we call a procedure that compares means an analysis of variance. As you can see in Figure 11.1, we are examining variances to see if the average scores are different. More on this later!

Notice the connection between Figure 11.1 and Equation 11.1. The arrows in the figure represent the difference between x_{ij} and the grand mean, $\bar{\bar{x}}$.

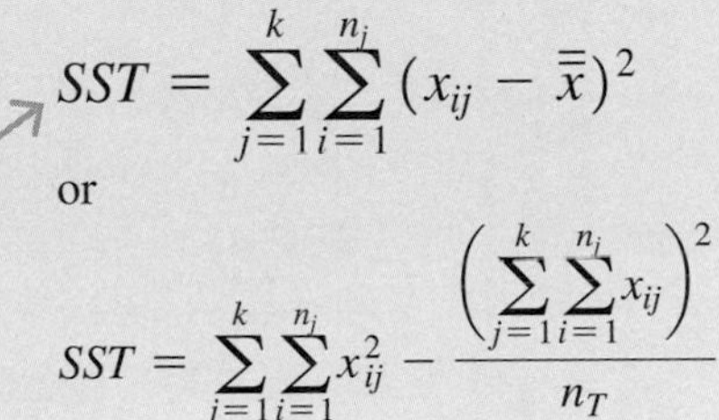

Formulas 11.1 and 11.2 for the Total Sum of Squares (SST)

$$SST = \sum_{j=1}^{k}\sum_{i=1}^{n_j}(x_{ij} - \bar{\bar{x}})^2$$

or

$$SST = \sum_{j=1}^{k}\sum_{i=1}^{n_j}x_{ij}^2 - \frac{\left(\sum_{j=1}^{k}\sum_{i=1}^{n_j}x_{ij}\right)^2}{n_T}$$

where

SST = The total sum of squares
x_{ij} = The ith value in the jth population
$\bar{\bar{x}}$ = The grand mean of all the data values
n_j = The sample size from the jth population
n_T = The total number of data values
k = The number of populations being compared

Even though Equation 11.1 looks simpler than Equation 11.2, it requires more effort when using a hand calculator. If you are using Excel, however, Equation 11.1 is more manageable.

Some of you may be freaking out over the looks of these equations, so let's call a time-out and break these bad boys down. Table 11.4 shows the corresponding data values for various subscripts of i (the row in Table 11.3) and j (the column). For example, x_{11} $(i = 1, j = 1)$ refers to the first iPhone score in the first column (87), whereas x_{21} $(i = 2, j = 1)$ refers to the second iPhone score (85) in the same column. The first Android score (71) is assigned to x_{12} $(i = 1, j = 2)$, which is the first score in the second column. To use Equation 11.2, we sum up all 15 data values $(n_T = 15)$ and also sum the square of all the data values.

We plug these two values into Equation 11.2, as follows:

$$SST = \sum_{j=1}^{k}\sum_{i=1}^{n_j}x_{ij}^2 - \frac{\left(\sum_{j=1}^{k}\sum_{i=1}^{n_j}x_{ij}\right)^2}{n_T} = 84{,}909 - \frac{(1{,}123)^2}{15}$$

$$SST = 84{,}909 - 84{,}075.27 = 833.73$$

Notice that in Table 11.4, $j = 1$ for the iPhone scores, $j = 2$ for the Android scores, $j = 3$ for the BlackBerry scores, and $j = 4$ for the Nokia scores.

TABLE 11.4 | SST Calculations for the Smartphone Data

i	j	SMARTPHONE	X_{ij}	X_{ij}^2
1	1	iPhone	87	7,569
2	1	iPhone	85	7,225
3	1	iPhone	78	6,084
4	1	iPhone	82	6,724
1	2	Android	71	5,041
2	2	Android	82	6,724
3	2	Android	75	5,625
4	2	Android	80	6,400
1	3	BlackBerry	66	4,356
2	3	BlackBerry	74	5,476
3	3	BlackBerry	79	6,241
1	4	Nokia	65	4,225
2	4	Nokia	69	4,761
3	4	Nokia	67	4,489
4	4	Nokia	63	3,969
			$\sum_{j=1}^{k}\sum_{i=1}^{n_j} x_{ij} = 1{,}123$	$\sum_{j=1}^{k}\sum_{i=1}^{n_j} x_{ij}^2 = 84{,}909$

For those of you who prefer Equation 11.1, Figure 11.2 shows the *SST* calculation using Excel.

FIGURE 11.2
Using Excel to Calculate the SST

	A	B	C	D
1	x_{ij}	$\bar{\bar{x}}$	$(x_{ij} - \bar{\bar{x}})$	$(x_{ij} - \bar{\bar{x}})^2$
2	87	74.87	12.13	147.14
3	85	74.87	10.13	102.62
4	78	74.87	3.13	9.80
5	82	74.87	7.13	50.84
6	71	74.87	-3.87	14.98
7	82	74.87	7.13	50.84
8	75	74.87	0.13	0.02
9	80	74.87	5.13	26.32
10	66	74.87	-8.87	78.68
11	74	74.87	-0.87	0.76
12	79	74.87	4.13	17.06
13	65	74.87	-9.87	97.42
14	69	74.87	-5.87	34.46
15	67	74.87	-7.87	61.94
16	63	74.87	-11.87	140.90
17				
18			Total	833.73

The **mean square total (*MST*)** is simply another term for the variance of the sample data. It is found by dividing the total sum of squares (*SST*) by $n_T - 1$.

The **mean square total (*MST*)**, which can be found using Equation 11.3, is derived from the *SST* and is simply another term for the variance of the sample data. The denominator in this equation is the degrees of freedom for the data set, which equals $n_T - 1$.

Formula 11.3 for the Mean Square Total (MST)

$$MST = \frac{\text{Total sum of squares}}{n_T - 1} = \frac{SST}{n_T - 1}$$

In Chapter 8, we learned that degrees of freedom are the number of values that are free to be varied given that information, such as the sample mean, is known.

where

MST = The mean square total
SST = The total sum of squares
n_T = The total number of data values

For our smartphone example, the mean square total (MST) is calculated as follows:

$$MST = \frac{SST}{n_T - 1} = \frac{833.73}{15 - 1} = 59.55$$

If the null hypothesis is true (and we assume it is unless we find evidence to believe otherwise), all of the levels being compared (smartphone brand) are drawn from the same population with a mean equal to μ and variance equal to σ^2. Under these circumstances, the MST would be a good estimate for the population variance, σ^2. We'll revisit this point later in the chapter.

Remember that the null hypothesis assumes that all population means are equal.

We've covered a lot of material so far in this chapter, and now would be a good time to try your hand at starting your own ANOVA procedure with this Your Turn problem.

YOUR TURN #1

Pretzel Guys is a retail establishment that bakes hand-rolled pretzels on site for its customers. A key step in the pretzel-baking process is to ensure that a consistent-size pretzel is hand-rolled by each employee. To test for consistency, a random sample of four pretzels made by each employee was weighed. The weights of each pretzel in ounces are shown in the following table for each employee and can be found in the Excel file **pretzel.xlsx**.

Jane (1)	Tom (2)	Jason (3)
2.5	2.1	3.3
2.7	2.9	2.8
2.2	2.2	3.7
2.6	2.4	3.0

a. State the null and alternative hypotheses.
b. Calculate the sample means and grand mean.
c. Calculate the total sum of squares (*SST*).
d. Calculate the mean square total (*MST*).

Answers can be found on ▶ **page 568**

Step 4: Partition the total sum of squares (*SST*) into the sum of squares between (*SSB*) and the sum of squares within (*SSW*).

As Figure 11.3 shows, the total sum of squares (*SST*) can be divided into two components:

1. The sum of squares between (*SSB*)
2. The sum of squares within (*SSW*)

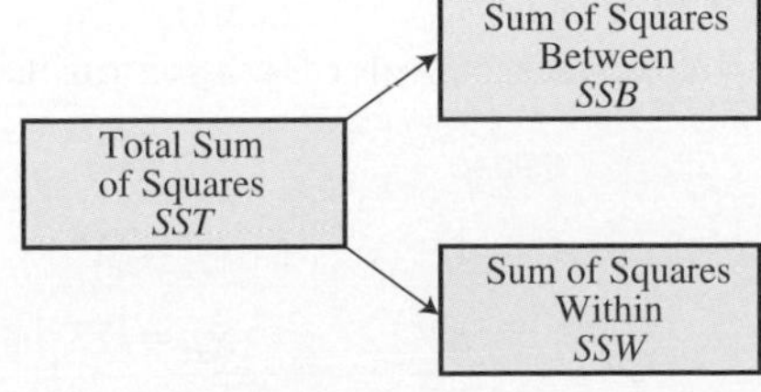

FIGURE 11.3
Partitioning the Total Sum of Squares (SST) for a One-Way ANOVA

Equation 11.4 shows the mathematical relationship for this partitioning.

Formula 11.4 for the Partitioning of the Total Sum of Squares (SST) for a One-Way ANOVA

$$SST = SSB + SSW$$

Figure 11.4 illustrates the *SSB* using our smartphone example.

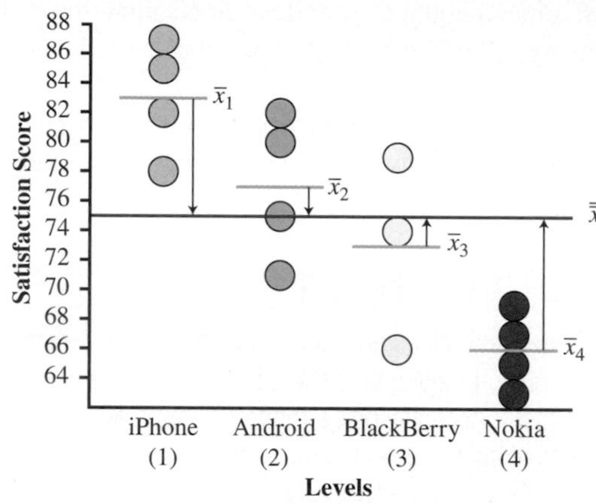

FIGURE 11.4 The Sum of Squares Between (SSB) for the Smartphone Data

The first component, the **sum of squares between (*SSB*)**, measures the variation between each sample mean and the grand mean of the data.

The first component, the **sum of squares between (*SSB*)**, measures the variation between each sample mean and the grand mean as shown by the arrows in this figure. The mean of each sample is shown by a green horizontal line, whereas the grand mean of all 15 scores is indicated by the red line. The length of each arrow represents the variation between each sample mean and the grand mean. A longer arrow in Figure 11.4 indicates a larger value for the *SSB*. The *SSB* can be calculated using Equation 11.5.

Formula 11.5 for the Sum of Squares Between (SSB)

$$SSB = \sum_{j=1}^{k} n_j(\bar{x}_j - \bar{\bar{x}})^2$$

where

SSB = The sum of squares between
$\bar{x}_j$ = The sample mean from the *j*th population
$\bar{\bar{x}}$ = The grand mean of all the data values
n_j = The sample size from the *j*th population
k = The number of populations being compared

For our smartphone example, we have already determined that $\bar{\bar{x}} = 74.87$ and $k = 4$. Tables 11.3 and 11.4 provide us with the remaining sample data needed for this equation. For your convenience, I've summarized this information in Table 11.5.

TABLE 11.5 | SUMMARIZED SAMPLE DATA FOR THE SMARTPHONES EXAMPLE

	IPHONE	ANDROID	BLACKBERRY	NOKIA
	$j = 1$	$j = 2$	$j = 3$	$j = 4$
$\bar{x}_j$	$\bar{x}_1 = 83$	$\bar{x}_2 = 77$	$\bar{x}_3 = 73$	$\bar{x}_4 = 66$
n_j	$n_1 = 4$	$n_2 = 4$	$n_3 = 3$	$n_4 = 4$

Applying this data to Equation 11.5, we have the formula:

$$SSB = \sum_{j=1}^{k} n_j(\bar{x}_j - \bar{\bar{x}})^2$$

$$SSB = n_1(\bar{x}_1 - \bar{\bar{x}})^2 + n_2(\bar{x}_2 - \bar{\bar{x}})^2 + n_3(\bar{x}_3 - \bar{\bar{x}})^2 + n_4(\bar{x}_4 - \bar{\bar{x}})^2$$

$$SSB = (4)(83 - 74.87)^2 + (4)(77 - 74.87)^2 + (3)(73 - 74.87)^2 + (4)(66 - 74.87)^2$$

$$SSB = (4)(8.13)^2 + (4)(2.13)^2 + (3)(-1.87)^2 + (4)(-8.87)^2$$

$$SSB = 264.40 + 18.16 + 10.50 + 314.72$$

$$SSB = 607.78$$

Remember that squaring a negative number has a positive result.

The **mean square between (*MSB*)** provides an estimate for the population variance, σ^2, if the null hypothesis is true. It is found by dividing the sum of squares between (*SSB*) by $k - 1$.

The **mean square between (*MSB*)**, which can be found using Equation 11.6, provides a second estimate for the population variance, σ^2, if the null hypothesis is true. The denominator in this equation is the degrees of freedom for the *SSB*, which equals $k - 1$.

Formula 11.6 for the Mean Square Between (MSB)

$$MSB = \frac{\text{Sum of squares between}}{k - 1} = \frac{SSB}{k - 1}$$

Recall that the MST provided us with our first estimate of the population variance.

where

MSB = The mean square between
SSB = The sum of squares between
k = The number of populations being compared

Putting Equation 11.6 to work with our smartphone example, the mean square between is calculated as following:

$$MSB = \frac{SSB}{k - 1} = \frac{607.78}{4 - 1} = 202.59$$

Last, but not least, we can determine the sum of squares within (*SSW*) with the help of Figure 11.5.

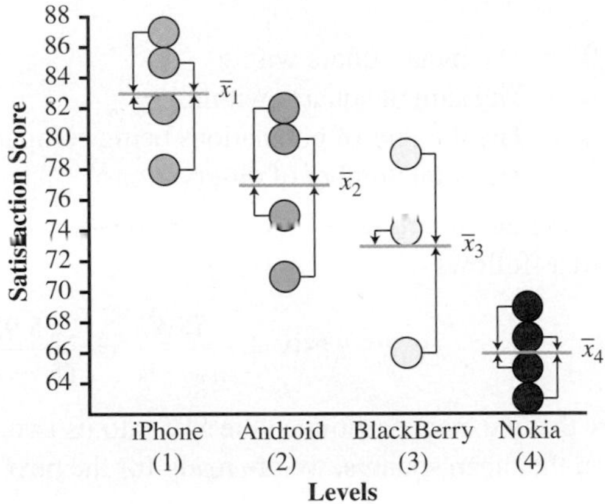

FIGURE 11.5 The Sum of Squares Within (SSW) for the Smartphone Data

The **sum of squares within (*SSW*)** measures the variation within each sample.

The **sum of squares within (*SSW*)** measures the variation within each sample, as shown by the arrows in Figure 11.5. Longer arrows in Figure 11.5 indicate a larger value for the sum of squares within (*SSW*). The sum of squares within (*SSW*) can be calculated using Equation 11.7 or Equation 11.8.

Formulas 11.7 and 11.8 for the Sum of Squares Within (SSW)

$$SSW = \sum_{j=1}^{k}\sum_{i=1}^{n_j}(x_{ij} - \bar{x}_j)^2$$

or

$$SSW = SST - SSB$$

where

SSW = The sum of squares within
SST = The total sum of squares
SSB = The sum of squares between
x_{ij} = The ith value in the jth population
$\bar{x}_j$ = The sample mean from the jth population
n_j = The sample size from the jth population
k = The number of populations being compared

I'll use Equation 11.8 to determine the *SSW* because it is a much easier calculation than Equation 11.7 (I'm sure you'll agree):

$$SSW = SST - SSB$$

$$SSW = 833.73 - 607.78 = 225.95$$

The **mean square within (*MSW*)** provides another estimate for the population variance, σ^2. It is found by dividing the sum of squares within (*SSW*) by $n_T - k$.

In addition to the mean square total (*MST*) and mean square between (*MSB*), the **mean square within (*MSW*)** provides a third estimate for the population variance, σ^2. The *MSW* can be found using Equation 11.9. The denominator in this equation is the degrees of freedom for the sum of squares within, which equals $n_T - k$.

Unlike the MST and MSB, the mean square within (MSW) provides a good estimate of the population variance whether or not the null hypothesis is true.

Formula 11.9 for the Mean Square Within (MSW)

$$MSW = \frac{\text{Sum of squares within}}{n_T - k} = \frac{SSW}{n_T - k}$$

where

MSW = The mean square within
SSW = The sum of squares within
k = The number of populations being compared
n_T = The total number of observations

Plugging our smartphone values into Equation 11.9, the mean square within (*MSW*) is calculated as follows:

$$MSW = \frac{SSW}{n_T - k} = \frac{225.95}{15 - 4} = 20.54$$

Now that we have partitioned the *SST* into its two components (the *SSB* and *SSW*) and calculated the mean squares, we are ready for the next step.

Step 5: Calculate the appropriate test statistic.

The *F*-test statistic, which was named after the British statistician Ronald Fisher, is the appropriate test statistic to use for a one-way ANOVA. Equation 11.10 shows how to calculate the *F*-test statistic for a one-way ANOVA.

Formula 11.10 for the F-Test Statistic for a One-Way ANOVA

$$F_{\bar{x}} = \frac{MSB}{MSW}$$

Using our mean square values from the last step, the calculated *F*-score, $F_{\bar{x}}$, is as follows:

$$F_{\bar{x}} = \frac{MSB}{MSW} = \frac{202.59}{20.54} = 9.86$$

An ANOVA table is a convenient way to summarize and present the results of the ANOVA procedure. Table 11.6 shows the format and the equations for an ANOVA table.

TABLE 11.6 | ONE-WAY ANOVA EQUATIONS: A SUMMARY

SOURCE	SUM OF SQUARES	DEGREES OF FREEDOM	MEAN SUM OF SQUARES	F
Between	SSB	$k - 1$	$MSB = \frac{SSB}{k-1}$	$F_{\bar{x}} = \frac{MSB}{MSW}$
Within	SSW	$n_T - k$	$MSW = \frac{SSW}{n_T - k}$	
Total	SST	$n_T - 1$		

Table 11.7 summarizes the results of the smartphone ANOVA.

TABLE 11.7 | SUMMARY TABLE FOR THE SMARTPHONE DATA

SOURCE	SUM OF SQUARES	DEGREES OF FREEDOM	MEAN SUM OF SQUARES	F
Between	607.78	3	202.59	9.86
Within	225.95	11	20.54	
Total	833.73	14		

As I mentioned in the previous step, both the *MSB* and the *MSW* provide reasonable estimates for the population variance, σ^2. Because the null hypothesis assumes all of the samples are drawn from the same population, we would expect the *MSB* and the *MSW* to be very close to one another if the null hypothesis was, in fact, true. This would be evident by a critical *F*-score close to 1.0.

If the null hypothesis is not true because the population means are different, we would expect the *MSB* to be larger than the *MSW*, causing the critical *F*-score to exceed 1.0. To illustrate this point, refer to Figure 11.4. Under these conditions, the sample means would be even farther apart from one another than they currently are in the figure, resulting in even longer arrows to the grand mean. This, in turn, would elevate the values of both the *SSB* and the *MSB* while leaving the values for the *SSW* and the *MSW* relatively unaffected.

Step 6: Determine the appropriate critical value.

The test statistic shown in Equation 11.10 follows a new distribution known as the *F*-distribution, which is shown in Figure 11.6. As you can see, this distribution is right-skewed, with the rejection region in the right tail. The ANOVA *F*-test is always a one-tail (upper) hypothesis test, as shown in Figure 11.6. The critical value, F_α, can be found in Table 6 in Appendix A. The *F*-distribution has two types of degrees of freedom, D_1 and D_2, which correspond to the degrees of freedom for the sum of squares between *SSB* and the sum of squares within *SSW* as follows:

$$D_1 = k - 1$$
$$D_2 = n_T - k$$

FIGURE 11.6
The F-Distribution

Remember, an ANOVA procedure always uses a one-tail hypothesis test to compare population means.

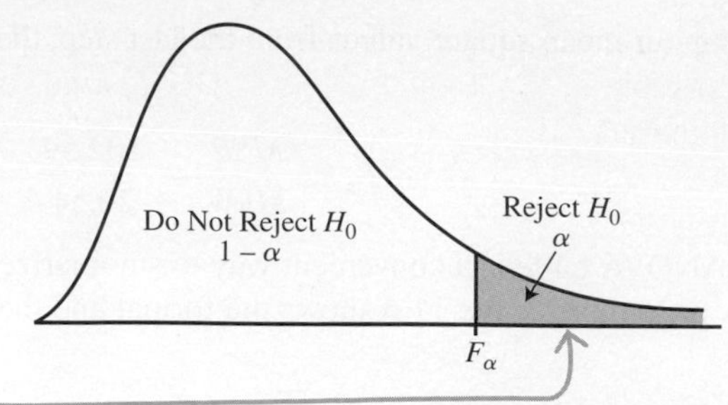

Table 11.8 shows an excerpt from Table 6 in Appendix A, with the following smartphone data:

$$D_1 = k - 1 = 4 - 1 = 3$$
$$D_2 = n_T - k = 15 - 4 = 11$$

TABLE 11.8 | EXCERPT FROM TABLE 6 IN APPENDIX A AREA IN THE RIGHT TAIL OF DISTRIBUTION = 0.05

					D_1					
D_2	1	2	3	4	5	6	7	8	9	10
1	161.448	199.500	215.707	224.583	230.162	233.986	236.768	238.883	240.543	241.882
2	18.513	19.000	19.164	19.247	19.296	19.330	19.353	19.371	19.385	19.396
3	10.128	9.552	9.277	9.117	9.013	8.941	8.887	8.845	8.812	8.786
4	7.709	6.944	6.591	6.388	6.256	6.163	6.094	6.041	5.999	5.964
5	6.608	5.786	5.409	5.192	5.050	4.950	4.876	4.818	4.772	4.735
6	5.987	5.143	4.757	4.534	4.387	4.284	4.207	4.147	4.099	4.060
7	5.591	4.737	4.347	4.120	3.972	3.866	3.787	3.726	3.677	3.637
8	5.318	4.459	4.066	3.838	3.687	3.581	3.500	3.438	3.388	3.347
9	5.117	4.256	3.863	3.633	3.482	3.374	3.293	3.230	3.179	3.137
10	4.965	4.103	3.708	3.478	3.326	3.217	3.135	3.072	3.020	2.978
11	4.844	3.982	3.587	3.357	3.204	3.095	3.012	2.948	2.896	2.854

According to Table 11.8, the critical value for our smartphone ANOVA with $\alpha = 0.05$ and degrees of freedom equal to 3 and 11 is $F_\alpha = 3.587$ (highlighted in yellow).

We can also obtain the critical F-score for our ANOVA procedure using Excel's F.INV.RT function, which has the following characteristics:

$$=\text{F.INV.RT}\ (\alpha, D_1, D_2)$$
$$=\text{F.INV.RT}\ (0.05, 3, 11) = 3.587$$

Step 7: Compare the F-test statistic ($F_{\bar{x}}$) with the critical F-score (F_α).

This comparison is used to decide whether to reject or fail to reject the null hypothesis. To do so, we use the decision rules shown in Table 11.9.

TABLE 11.9 | DECISION RULES FOR ANOVA

CONDITION		CONCLUSION
$F_{\bar{x}} \le F_\alpha$	→	Do not reject H_0
$F_{\bar{x}} > F_\alpha$	→	Reject H_0

Because $F_{\bar{x}} = 9.86$ and is greater than $F_{\alpha} = 3.587$, we reject the null hypothesis according to Table 11.9. We can see this graphically in Figure 11.7. The test statistic, $F_{\bar{x}}$, is clearly in the shaded rejection region.

FIGURE 11.7
Comparing the F-Test Statistic with the Critical F-Score for the Smartphone Example

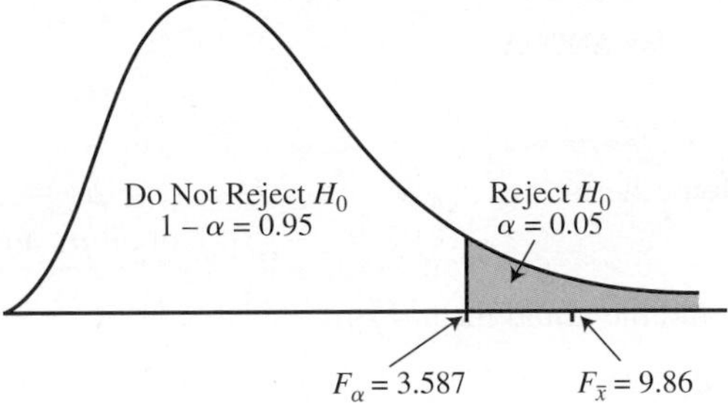

Step 8: State your conclusions.

It's been a while since we've seen our hypothesis statement, so let's restate it:

$$H_0: \mu_1 = \mu_2 = \mu_3 = \mu_4$$
$$H_1: \text{Not all } \mu\text{s are equal}$$

By rejecting the null hypothesis, we have evidence that not all of the four population means are equal. In other words, it appears that the owners of some smartphone brands are more satisfied with their phones than owners of other brands. At this point, however, we don't have enough information to decide which populations have significantly different satisfaction scores. We'll tackle that task in a later section.

An analysis of variance compares the variance between samples to the variance within those samples to determine if the means of the populations are different.

I have two final comments to wrap up this section. First, you may have wondered at the beginning of this chapter why we call a procedure that compares population means an "analysis of variance." Hopefully by now you realize that to test our hypothesis, an ANOVA compares two types of variances: the variance between samples and the variance within those samples. This is necessary because we are simultaneously comparing more than two sample means.

This leads me to my second point. I have had some insightful students ask me why don't we just use the two-sample *t*-test that we learned in Chapter 10 to compare these population means two at a time. Great question! For one thing, this would result in many more calculations than an ANOVA procedure requires because every possible pair of sample means would have to be tested. For instance, with our smartphone example with four sample means, we would have six separate *t*-tests to perform in order to examine all possible combinations.

More importantly, performing six individual *t*-tests increases our probability of a Type I error to a level that is much higher than the desired $\alpha = 0.05$ that we set for the ANOVA procedure. If each *t*-test had a 95% chance of correctly not rejecting the null hypothesis, then according to our multiplication rule for independent events (Chapter 4), the probability of all six *t*-tests correctly not rejecting the null is as follows:

By performing six individual *t*-tests, we increase the probability of a Type I error to a level that is much higher than the desired $\alpha = 0.05$.

$$(0.95)(0.95)(0.95)(0.95)(0.95)(0.95) = 0.735$$

That means the probability of making at least one Type I error for these six *t*-tests is approximately the following:

$$1 - 0.735 = 0.265$$

Obviously, 26.5% is a lot higher than the 5% chance of a Type I error with our ANOVA procedure. This is because the ANOVA procedure compares all four population means simultaneously instead of two at a time.

I use the term *approximately* to describe the 26.5% chance of making a Type I error because these six events are not completely independent. This is due to the fact that some of the comparisons share the same sample mean. However, the point still stands: An ANOVA test is much more effective than multiple *t*-tests when comparing three or more population means. You can take that to the bank!

Because we have covered so much material in this section, I thought it would be helpful to summarize the eight steps of a one-way ANOVA in Table 11.10.

TABLE 11.10 | SUMMARY OF STEPS FOR A ONE-WAY ANOVA

STEP	DESCRIPTION	PROCEDURE
1	Identify the null and alternative hypotheses.	$H_0: \mu_1 = \mu_2 = \ldots = \mu_k$ H_1: Not all μs are equal
2	Calculate the sample means $(\bar{x})$ and the grand mean $(\bar{\bar{x}})$.	
3	Calculate the total sum of squares (SST). Calculate the mean square total (MST).	$SST = \sum_{j=1}^{k}\sum_{i=1}^{n_j} x_{ij}^2 - \frac{\left(\sum_{j=1}^{k}\sum_{i=1}^{n_j} x_{ij}\right)^2}{n_T}$ (11.2) $MST = \frac{SST}{n_T - 1}$ (11.3)
4	Partition the total sum of squares (SST) into the sum of squares between (SSB) and the sum of squares within (SSW). Calculate the corresponding mean squares.	$SSB = \sum_{j=1}^{k} n_j(\bar{x}_j - \bar{\bar{x}})^2$ (11.5) $MSB = \frac{SSB}{k - 1}$ (11.6) $SSW = SST - SSB$ (11.8) $MSW = \frac{SSW}{n_T - k}$ (11.9)
5	Calculate the appropriate test statistic.	$F_{\bar{x}} = \frac{MSB}{MSW}$ (11.10)
6	Determine the appropriate critical value.	Critical value, F_α, is found in Table 6 in Appendix A with degrees of freedom: $D_1 = k - 1$ $D_2 = n_T - k$
7	Compare the F-test statistic $(F_{\bar{x}})$ with the critical F-score (F_α).	$F_{\bar{x}} \le F_\alpha \rightarrow$ Do not reject H_0 $F_{\bar{x}} > F_\alpha \rightarrow$ reject H_0
8	State your conclusions.	

Using Excel for a One-Way ANOVA

www.pearsonhighered.com/donnelly

We can use Excel's Data Analysis to perform a one-way ANOVA procedure for our smartphone example by taking the following steps. Students with Excel for Mac can go to the textbook's Web site for instructions to perform one-way ANOVA using PHStat.

1. Either open the Excel file **smartphones.xlsx** or enter the satisfaction score data values in Columns A, B, C, and D as shown in Figure 11.8A.
2. Go to **Data** and click on **Data Analysis** on the right side of the ribbon, as shown in Figure 11.8A. This opens the **Data Analysis** dialog box.
3. Select **ANOVA: Single Factor**. Click **OK**.

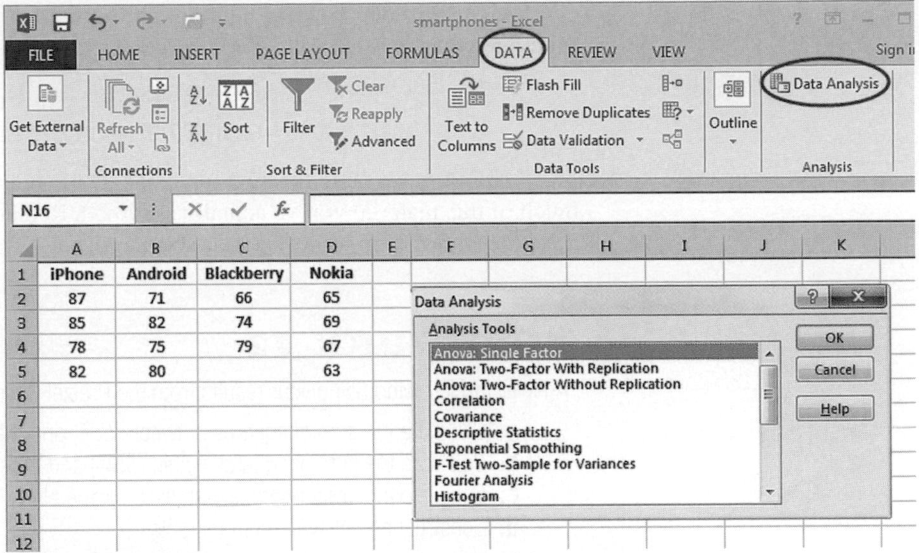

FIGURE 11.8A Conducting a One-Way ANOVA Test Using Excel (Steps 1–3)

4. Fill in the **ANOVA: Single Factor** dialog box as shown in Figure 11.8B. Click **OK**.

	A	B	C	D
1	iPhone	Android	Blackberry	Nokia
2	87	71	66	65
3	85	82	74	69
4	78	75	79	67
5	82	80		63

Anova: Single Factor
Input
Input Range: $A$1:$D$5
Grouped By: Columns / Rows
Labels in first row
Alpha: 0.05
Output options
Output Range: $F$1
New Worksheet Ply:
New Workbook
OK Cancel Help

FIGURE 11.8B Conducting a One-Way ANOVA Test Using Excel (Step 4)

Figure 11.8C shows the ANOVA output for the smartphone example, which matches our results from the previous section.

	A	B	C	D	E	F	G	H	I	J	K	L
1	iPhone	Android	Blackberry	Nokia		Anova: Single Factor						
2	87	71	66	65								
3	85	82	74	69		SUMMARY						
4	78	75	79	67		*Groups*	*Count*	*Sum*	*Average*	*Variance*		
5	82	80		63		iPhone	4	332	83	15.33333		
6						Android	4	308	77	24.66667		
7						Blackberry	3	219	73	43		
8						Nokia	4	264	66	6.666667		
9												
10												
11						ANOVA						
12						*Source of Variation*	*SS*	*df*	*MS*	*F*	*P-value*	*F crit*
13						Between Groups	607.7333	3	202.5778	9.85998	0.001887	3.587434
14						Within Groups	226	11	20.54545			
15												
16						Total	833.7333	14				
17												

FIGURE 11.8C Conducting a One-Way ANOVA Test Using Excel (Final Result)

Notice that the p-value reported in Cell K13 shown in Figure 11.8C equals 0.001887. This value represents the probability of obtaining a critical F-score of 9.86 or more if the population means are truly equal. Because this p-value is less than $\alpha = 0.05$, we reject the null hypothesis and conclude that the average scores in these populations are not equal.

We can also obtain the p-value for our ANOVA procedure using Excel's F.DIST.RT function, which has the following characteristics:

$$=\text{F.DIST.RT}\,(F_{\bar{x}}, D_1, D_2)$$
$$=\text{F.DIST.RT}\,(9.86, 3, 11) = 0.0019$$

Before I move on to the next topic, it's that magical time where you get to find out how much of this material you've actually absorbed. Remember, it always looks easy when I do it, so take a few minutes to work on this next Your Turn problem.

YOUR TURN #2

Answer the following using your results from the Pretzel Guys problem described in Your Turn #1.

a. Calculate the sum of squares between (*SSB*) and the mean square between (*MSB*).
b. Calculate the sum of squares within (*SSW*) and the mean square within (*MSW*).
c. Calculate the appropriate test statistic for the ANOVA procedure.
d. Construct an ANOVA summary table.
e. Using $\alpha = 0.05$, can you conclude that there is a difference in the average weight of the pretzels made by the three employees?
f. Verify your results with Excel.

Answers can be found on ▶ **pages 568–569**

Multiple Comparisons: Comparing Pairs of Population Means (One-Way ANOVA)

The **Tukey–Kramer Multiple Comparison Test for One-Way ANOVA** allows us to examine each pair of sample means and to conclude whether their respective population means differ for one-way ANOVA.

As mentioned in the previous section, rejecting the null hypothesis with an ANOVA test allows us to conclude that a difference exists between the population means. At this point, however, we are not able to state which populations differ. To do so, we need to rely on the **Tukey–Kramer Multiple Comparison Test for One-Way ANOVA**, which allows us to examine each pair of sample means and to conclude whether their respective population means differ.

The hypothesis statement for this procedure is

$$H_0: \mu_i = \mu_j$$
$$H_1: \mu_i \neq \mu_j$$

for every combination of population pairs being compared from the original ANOVA procedure. We also set our significance level, α, based on the acceptable probability of a Type I error. We'll apply this multiple comparison method to the smartphone example from the previous section, using $\alpha = 0.05$ with the following steps.

> An ANOVA procedure only tests to see if population means are different. To find out which means are different, we need to perform a multiple comparison test.

Step 1: Calculate the absolute sample mean differences.

When we have k sample means to compare, we have

$$\frac{k(k-1)}{2}$$

pairs of sample means. In the smartphone example, $k = 4$, so we have $4(3)/2 = 6$ pairs of sample means. The following pairs are samples:

1 and 2	2 and 3
1 and 3	2 and 4
1 and 4	3 and 4

Because the Tukey-Kramer multiple comparisons procedure tests only for a difference between population means (rather than one being greater than another), we calculate the absolute value of the difference between sample means, as follows:

$$|\bar{x}_1 - \bar{x}_2| = |83 - 77| = |6| = 6$$
$$|\bar{x}_1 - \bar{x}_3| = |83 - 73| = |10| = 10$$
$$|\bar{x}_1 - \bar{x}_4| = |83 - 66| = |17| = 17$$
$$|\bar{x}_2 - \bar{x}_3| = |77 - 73| = |4| = 4$$
$$|\bar{x}_2 - \bar{x}_4| = |77 - 66| = |11| = 11$$
$$|\bar{x}_3 - \bar{x}_4| = |73 - 66| = |7| = 7$$

If the differences between any two sample means are negative, the absolute value of that difference is positive.

Step 2: Calculate the Tukey–Kramer critical range.

The Tukey–Kramer critical range, $CR_{i,j}$, is calculated for each of the sample pairs by comparing the means from samples i and j using Equation 11.11.

Formula 11.11 for the Tukey-Kramer Critical Range

$$CR_{i,j} = Q_\alpha \sqrt{\frac{MSW}{2}\left(\frac{1}{n_i} + \frac{1}{n_j}\right)}$$

where

$CR_{i,j}$ = The critical range for comparing sample i to sample j
Q_α = The critical value from the studentized range table (Appendix A, Table 7)
MSW = The mean square within
n_i = The sample size from sample i
n_j = The sample size from sample j

The critical value for the Tukey–Kramer critical range is found in Table 7 in Appendix A based on the desired significance level and the following two degrees of freedom:

$$D_1 = k$$
$$D_2 = n_T - k$$

Be sure not to confuse this D_1 with the D_1 for the ANOVA procedure described on page 511 which equals $k - 1$.

Table 11.11 shows an excerpt from Table 7 using the following smartphone data:

$$D_1 = k = 4$$
$$D_2 = n_T - k = 15 - 4 = 11$$

TABLE 11.11 | EXCERPT FROM THE STUDENTIZED RANGE TABLE: CRITICAL VALUES (Q_α) OF THE STUDENTIZED RANGE (0.05 LEVEL)

	D_1								
D_2	2	3	4	5	6	7	8	9	10
1	17.97	26.98	38.32	37.08	40.41	43.12	45.40	47.36	49.07
2	6.09	8.33	9.80	10.88	11.74	12.44	13.03	13.54	13.99
3	4.50	5.91	6.82	7.50	8.04	8.48	8.85	9.18	9.46
4	3.93	5.04	5.76	6.29	6.71	7.05	7.35	7.60	7.83
5	3.64	4.60	5.22	5.67	6.03	6.33	6.58	6.80	6.99
6	3.46	4.34	4.90	5.30	5.63	5.90	6.12	6.32	6.49
7	3.34	4.16	4.68	5.06	5.36	5.61	5.82	6.00	6.16
8	3.26	4.04	4.53	4.89	5.17	5.40	5.60	5.77	5.92
9	3.20	3.95	4.41	4.76	5.02	5.24	5.43	5.59	5.74
10	3.15	3.88	4.33	4.65	4.91	5.12	5.30	5.46	5.60
11	3.11	3.82	4.26	4.57	4.82	5.03	5.20	5.35	5.49

According to Table 11.11, the critical value for our smartphone ANOVA with $\alpha = 0.05$ and degrees of freedom equal to 4 and 11 is $Q_\alpha = 4.26$ (highlighted in yellow).

Let's begin this procedure by comparing the difference between the iPhone mean (sample 1) and the Android mean (sample 2). We need the following data from our one-way ANOVA results found earlier:

$$MSW = 20.54 \quad n_1 = 4 \quad n_2 = 4$$

Using Equation 11.11, the Tukey–Kramer critical range for comparing samples 1 and 2 is calculated as follows:

$$CR_{1,2} = Q_\alpha \sqrt{\frac{MSW}{2}\left(\frac{1}{n_1} + \frac{1}{n_2}\right)}$$

$$CR_{1,2} = (4.26)\sqrt{\frac{20.54}{2}\left(\frac{1}{4} + \frac{1}{4}\right)} = (4.26)\sqrt{(10.27)(0.50)}$$

$$CR_{1,2} = (4.26)(2.266) = 9.65$$

The critical range for comparing the difference between the iPhone mean (sample 1) and the BlackBerry mean (sample 3) using $n_1 = 4$ and $n_3 = 3$ is calculated as follows:

$$CR_{1,3} = Q_\alpha \sqrt{\frac{MSW}{2}\left(\frac{1}{n_1} + \frac{1}{n_3}\right)}$$

$$CR_{1,3} = (4.26)\sqrt{\frac{20.54}{2}\left(\frac{1}{4} + \frac{1}{3}\right)} = (4.26)\sqrt{(10.27)(0.5833)}$$

$$CR_{1,3} = (4.26)(2.448) = 10.43$$

Table 11.12 shows the critical ranges for all six pairs of smartphones.

If the size for each sample is the same for the one-way ANOVA, the critical range for all pairs would be the same.

TABLE 11.12 | CRITICAL RANGES FOR THE SMARTPHONE EXAMPLE

COMPARING SAMPLES		CRITICAL RANGE
i	*j*	
1	2	9.65
1	3	10.43
1	4	9.65
2	3	10.43
2	4	9.65
3	4	10.43

Step 3: State your conclusions.

The hypothesis for multiple comparisons of sample means was stated as

$$H_0: \mu_i = \mu_j$$
$$H_1: \mu_i \neq \mu_j$$

for every combination of sample pairs from the original ANOVA procedure. Table 11.13 shows the decision rules for determining whether we can reject the null hypothesis.

TABLE 11.13 | DECISION RULES FOR COMPARING PAIRS OF POPULATION MEANS

CONDITION		CONCLUSION
$\lvert \bar{x}_i - \bar{x}_j \rvert \leq CR_{ij}$	→	Do not reject H_0
$\lvert \bar{x}_i - \bar{x}_j \rvert > CR_{ij}$	→	Reject H_0

The logic behind these rules is as follows: If the absolute difference between two sample means is large enough to be greater than the critical range, we have enough evidence to conclude the population means are different (so we reject the null). If the absolute difference between two sample means is *not* large enough to be greater than the critical range, we do *not* have enough evidence to conclude the population means are different (so we do not reject the null).

Table 11.14 shows these decision rules being applied to the six pairs of samples.

TABLE 11.14 | DECISION TABLE FOR COMPARING PAIRS OF POPULATION MEANS: SMARTPHONE EXAMPLE

$\lvert \bar{x}_i - \bar{x}_j \rvert$	$CR_{i,j}$	DECISION
$\lvert \bar{x}_1 - \bar{x}_2 \rvert = 6$	9.65	6 < 9.65; population means are not different
$\lvert \bar{x}_1 - \bar{x}_3 \rvert = 10$	10.43	10 < 10.43; population means are not different
$\lvert \bar{x}_1 - \bar{x}_4 \rvert = 17$	9.65	17 > 9.65; population means are different
$\lvert \bar{x}_2 - \bar{x}_3 \rvert = 4$	10.43	4 < 10.43; population means are not different
$\lvert \bar{x}_2 - \bar{x}_4 \rvert = 11$	9.65	11 > 9.65; population means are different
$\lvert \bar{x}_3 - \bar{x}_4 \rvert = 7$	10.43	7 < 10.43; population means are not different

If the absolute difference between two sample means is large enough to be greater than the Tukey–Kramer critical range, we have enough evidence to conclude that the population means are different (we should reject the null hypothesis).

From these results, we can conclude that the average score for the iPhone (sample 1) is higher than the average score for Nokia (sample 4). The average score for the Android (sample 2) is also higher than the average score for Nokia (sample 4). There is not enough evidence to conclude that any other pairs are significantly different at the $\alpha = 0.05$ level.

This leads me to my next point. The advantage of using the Tukey–Kramer multiple comparisons procedure is that the probability of making a Type I error (5% when we set $\alpha = 0.05$) applies to all possible combinations of sample pairs. In other words, we have a 5% chance that we will draw the wrong conclusion for at least one of the sample pairs. This 5% value is known as the **experiment-wide error rate**. Compare this value to the approximate 26.5% chance of making an error that we derived earlier in the chapter when performing six individual *t*-tests for our smartphone data.

The **experiment-wide error rate** is the probability of committing a Type I error for at least one pair of population means being compared.

Using PHStat to Perform Multiple Comparisons between Population Means

We can perform the Tukey–Kramer multiple comparisons procedure using PHStat by taking the following steps. Excel for Mac users can find instructions for this procedure on the textbook's Web site.

1. Open the Excel file **smartphones.xlsx** or enter the satisfaction score data values in Columns A, B, C, and D as shown back in Figure 11.8A.
2. Go to **Add-Ins > PHStat > Multiple-Sample Tests > One-Way ANOVA**, as shown in Figure 11.9A.

FIGURE 11.9A Conducting a Multiple Comparisons Test Using PHStat (Step 2)

smartphone - Excel
FILE HOME INSERT PAGE LAYOUT FORMULAS DATA REVIEW VIEW ADD-INS
PHStat
Data Preparation
Descriptive Statistics
Decision-Making
Probability & Prob. Distributions
Sampling
Confidence Intervals
Sample Size
One-Sample Tests
Two-Sample Tests (Unsummarized Data)
Two-Sample Tests (Summarized Data)
Multiple-Sample Tests
Control Charts
Regression
Utilities
About PHStat...
Help for PHStat
Chi-Square Test...
Kruskal-Wallis Rank Test...
Levene Test...
One-Way ANOVA...
Two-Way ANOVA with replication...

3. Fill in the **One-Way ANOVA** dialog box as shown in Figure 11.9B. Click **OK**.

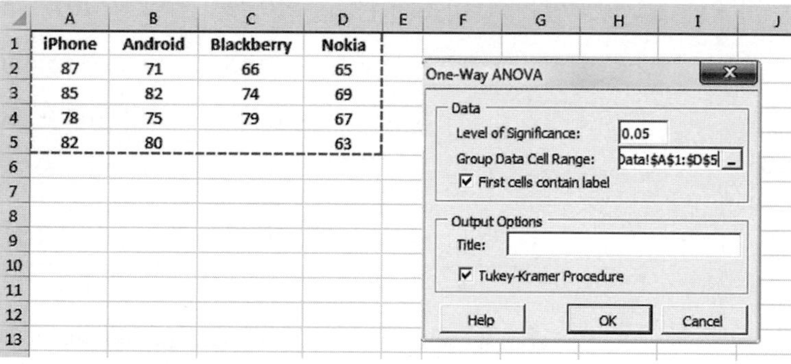

FIGURE 11.9B Conducting a Multiple Comparisons Test Using PHStat (Step 3)

4. A pop-up message will appear saying, "Look up Q Statistic and enter value in Cell B15." Click **OK**.

Figure 11.9C shows the output for the multiple comparison tests, which matches the results we obtained manually after the critical value for the studentized range (4.26) is inserted in Cell B15.

FIGURE 11.9C Conducting a Multiple Comparisons Test Using PHStat (Final Result)

Tukey-Kramer Multiple Comparisons

Group	Sample Mean	Sample Size	Comparison	Absolute Difference	Std. Error of Difference	Critical Range	Results
1: iPhone	83	4	Group 1 to Group 2	6	2.266354702	9.6547	Means are not different
2: Android	77	4	Group 1 to Group 3	10	2.447942859	10.428	Means are not different
3: Blackberry	73	3	Group 1 to Group 4	17	2.266354702	9.6547	Means are different
4: Nokia	66	4	Group 2 to Group 3	4	2.447942859	10.428	Means are not different
			Group 2 to Group 4	11	2.266354702	9.6547	Means are different
			Group 3 to Group 4	7	2.447942859	10.428	Means are not different

Other Data	
Level of significance	0.05
Numerator d.f.	4
Denominator d.f.	11
MSW	20.54545
Q Statistic	4.26

For this next Your Turn, let's return to the pretzel example from the previous Your Turns to help you practice the multiple comparison procedure.

YOUR TURN #3

Using the data and results from Your Turn #1 and #2, perform the Tukey–Kramer multiple comparisons procedure using $\alpha = 0.05$ to identify which employees have average pretzel weights that are different. Verify your results with PHStat.

Answers can be found on ▶ page 569

11.1 Section Problems

Basic Skills

11.1 Consider the following partially completed one-way ANOVA summary table:

Source	Sum of Squares	Degrees of Freedom	Mean Sum of Squares	F
Between		4		
Within	60			
Total	76	24		

a. Complete the remaining entries in the table.
b. How many population means are being tested?
c. Using $\alpha = 0.05$, what conclusions can be made concerning the population means?

11.2 Consider the following data collected from three independent populations:

Sample 1	Sample 2	Sample 3
10	20	7
14	17	15
7	14	9
11	21	17

a. Calculate the total sum of squares (*SST*).
b. Partition the total sum of squares (*SST*) into its two components.
c. Using $\alpha = 0.05$, what conclusions can be made concerning the population means?

11.3 Using the data from Problem 11.2, determine which means are different using $\alpha = 0.05$.

11.4 Consider the following partially completed one-way ANOVA summary table:

Source	Sum of Squares	Degrees of Freedom	Mean Sum of Squares	F
Between	50			
Within		20		
Total	150	22		

a. Complete the remaining entries in the table.
b. How many population means are being tested?
c. Using $\alpha = 0.01$, what conclusions can be made concerning the population means?

11.5 Consider the following data collected from four independent populations:

Sample 1	Sample 2	Sample 3	Sample 4
3	14	21	8
8	9	15	3
6	13	16	13
5		14	

a. Calculate the total sum of squares (*SST*).
b. Partition the total sum of squares (*SST*) into its two components.
c. Using $\alpha = 0.01$, what conclusions can be made about the population means?

11.6 Using the data from Problem 11.5, determine which means are different using $\alpha = 0.01$.

Applications

11.7 The Federal Aviation Administration (FAA) would like to determine if the average number of minutes that a plane departs late differs between airports in Philadelphia, Orlando, and Chicago. The following data were collected from randomly selected flights and indicate the number of minutes that each plane was behind schedule at its departure. These data can also be found in the Excel file **FAA.xlsx**.

Philadelphia	Orlando	Chicago
12	8	33
0	19	10
27	0	41
34	10	51
12	13	30

a. Perform a one-way ANOVA using $\alpha = 0.05$ to determine if there is a difference in the average lateness of the flights from these three airports.
b. If warranted, perform a multiple comparison test to determine which pairs are different using $\alpha = 0.05$.
c. Verify your results with Excel or PHStat.

11.8 The following table indicates the driving distance, in yards, from a random sample of drives for the pro golfers

Phil Mickelson, Tiger Woods, and Jim Furyk. These data can also be found in the Excel file **MWF.xlsx.**

Mickelson	Woods	Furyk
290	311	266
295	290	265
288	297	285
327	286	279
		280

a. Perform a one-way ANOVA using $\alpha = 0.05$ to determine if there is a difference in the average driving distances of these three players.
b. If warranted, perform a multiple comparison test to determine which pairs are different using $\alpha = 0.05$.
c. Verify your results with Excel or PHStat.

11.9 The following data show the number of pounds of bananas sold per week at the Avalon Grocery store when the banana display was positioned in the produce, milk, and cereal sections of the store. These data can also be found in the Excel file **bananas.xlsx**.

Produce	Milk	Cereal
62	39	27
40	19	52
61	32	53
54	56	50
	38	

a. Perform a one-way ANOVA using $\alpha = 0.05$ to determine if there is a difference in the average number of pounds of bananas sold per week in these three locations.
b. If warranted, perform a multiple comparison test to determine which pairs are different using $\alpha = 0.05$.
c. Verify your results with Excel or PHStat.

11.10 Avis Rent A Car maintains a fleet of low-mileage cars for its customer base. Suppose that Avis would like to promote the fact that its cars have a lower average mileage than that of its competitors in an advertising campaign. To support this claim, Avis has collected the following mileage data from a random sample of rental cars from its own fleet and the fleets of three competitors. Hint: To help make the calculations more manageable, consider converting the mileage into thousands of miles (for example, 13,100 = 13.1). These data can also be found in the Excel file **Avis.xlsx**.

Avis	Hertz	National	Enterprise
13,100	15,900	15,300	14,500
7,800	11,400	21,800	20,000
10,400	5,600	18,100	17,400
14,600	10,100	12,800	24,800
8,600	16,000	20,500	16,300

a. Using $\alpha = 0.05$, determine if there is a difference in the average mileage between these four companies.
b. Using $\alpha = 0.05$, determine if there is evidence to support the claim made by Avis.
c. Verify your results with Excel or PHStat.

11.11 A consumer group would like to compare the satisfaction ratings of three fast-food restaurants: McDoogles, Burger Queen, and Windys. A random sample of satisfaction scores on a scale of 1–20 was collected from customers at each restaurant. These data can also be found in the Excel file **fast food.xlsx**. The scores are as follows:

McDoogles	Burger Queen	Windys
14	16	18
13	19	14
12	14	16
10	12	11
12	18	16
	17	15
	16	

a. Perform a one-way ANOVA using $\alpha = 0.05$ to determine if there is a difference in the average satisfaction scores for the three restaurants.
b. If warranted, perform a multiple comparison test to determine which pairs are different using $\alpha = 0.05$.
c. Verify your results with Excel or PHStat.

11.12 The following table shows the weight of randomly selected packages shipped by FedEx, UPS, and DHL. These data can also be found in the Excel file **package weight.xlsx**.

FedEx		UPS		DHL	
13.7	9.8	0.7	20.2	13.0	4.0
11.9	5.3	5.7	6.1	7.7	2.0
2.8	14.8	22.8	12.5	8.6	3.7
4.1	1.6	0.4	11.6	7.2	9.8

a. Perform a one-way ANOVA using $\alpha = 0.05$ to determine if there is a difference in the average package weights shipped by these three delivery companies.
b. If warranted, perform a multiple comparison test to determine which pairs are different using $\alpha = 0.05$.
c. Verify your results with Excel or PHStat.

11.13 Recently, Las Vegas has seen increased competition from Singapore and Macau (China) for customers in the casino resort industry. One measurement of success is the average length of stay by visitors. The following data show the number of days a random sample of visitors stayed at each location. These data can also be found in the Excel file **casinos.xlsx**.

Singapore	Macau	Las Vegas
7	2	3
4	4	6
4	3	3
3	1	4
7	1	5

a. Perform a one-way ANOVA using $\alpha = 0.05$ to determine if the average length of stay of visitors was different for the three locations.
b. If warranted, perform a multiple comparison test to determine which pairs are different using $\alpha = 0.05$.
c. Verify your results with Excel or PHStat.

11.14 Suppose a manager at a local Domino's Pizza would like to determine if the average time it takes to deliver a pizza and return to the store differs for the four employees who make the deliveries. The following data show a random sample of the delivery times for each driver. These data can also be found in the Excel file **Dominos.xlsx**.

Driver 1	Driver 2	Driver 3	Driver 4
40	16	27	21
32	9	24	7
28	13	13	34
29	22	9	14
40		10	

a. Using $\alpha = 0.05$, determine if the manager has enough evidence to conclude there is a difference in the delivery times of the four drivers.
b. If warranted, perform a multiple comparison test to determine which pairs are different using $\alpha = 0.05$.
c. Verify your results with Excel or PHStat.

11.2 Randomized Block ANOVA: Examining the Effects of a Single Factor by Blocking a Second Factor

In the previous section, the order in which the smartphone satisfaction scores were presented had no bearing on the results. For example, if we rearranged the BlackBerry scores from 66-74-79 to 74-79-66 in the third column of Table 11.2, the ANOVA results would be unchanged. However, there are situations where the order in which the data are presented does have an impact on the analysis. Consider the following example.

Tony is an area manager for Procter and Gamble (P&G), a company that provides a variety of household products sold in many retail stores. Tony is responsible for three P&G representatives who make sales calls to store managers to service their product needs. Table 11.15 shows the number of sales calls the three reps made last week for each weekday. The data can also be found in the Excel file **sales.xlsx**.

TABLE 11.15 | Sales Calls Made by the P&G Representatives

	SALES REPRESENTATIVES		
DAY	DAN	AMY	BETH
Monday	5	8	8
Tuesday	4	7	4
Wednesday	6	8	7
Thursday	6	7	5
Friday	4	5	3

Tony would like to know if there is a difference in the average number of calls made per day by these three sales reps. At first glance, this appears to be a straightforward one-way ANOVA problem like we saw in the previous section (obviously it's not because I've introduced a new topic, but bear with me for a minute.) In the previous section, we were comparing average scores for each phone. Here we will compare average sales for each representative. Let's perform a one-way ANOVA with Excel using $\alpha = 0.05$. The results are shown in Figure 11.10.

FIGURE 11.10
A One-Way ANOVA Test for the P&G Sales Call Example

	A	B	C	D	E	F	G
1	Anova: Single Factor						
2							
3	SUMMARY						
4	*Groups*	*Count*	*Sum*	*Average*	*Variance*		
5	Dan	5	25	5	1		
6	Amy	5	35	7	1.5		
7	Beth	5	27	5.4	4.3		
8							
9							
10	ANOVA						
11	*Source of Variation*	*SS*	*df*	*MS*	*F*	*P-value*	*F crit*
12	Between Groups	11.2	2	5.6	2.470588	0.126307	3.885294
13	Within Groups	27.2	12	2.266667			
14							
15	Total	38.4	14				
16							

Because the p-value (0.126) is more than α (0.05), we conclude that there is no difference in the average number of sales calls made per day by these three reps.

According to Figure 11.10, Dan averages 5.0 calls per day, Amy averages 7.0 calls per day, and Beth averages 5.4 calls per day. Because the p-value in Cell F12 equals 0.126, which is more than $\alpha = 0.05$, we fail to reject the null hypothesis. Using one-way ANOVA, Tony concludes that, based on the data from these three samples, there is no difference in the average number of sales calls made per day by these three reps.

However (I hope you see this coming), the order in which the sales calls have been recorded is important and has meaning because each value represents a different day of the week. The first row of data in Table 11.15 is linked together because it represents the number of sales calls made on Monday by each employee. The same logic holds true for the other four rows. For example, if we rearranged the order of Dan's sales calls, we would also have to do the same for Amy and Beth's sales calls to ensure the proper data value is assigned to the proper weekday. This dependency across the rows is analogous to the situation from Chapter 10 in which two samples were matched pairs. When we have this kind of structure with more than two populations, the appropriate procedure to test the difference in population means is known as a **randomized block ANOVA**.

A **randomized block ANOVA** incorporates a blocking factor to account for variation outside of the main factor in hopes of increasing the likelihood of detecting a variation due to the main factor.

The levels of the **blocking factor** are known as **blocks**.

With a randomized block ANOVA, we have added a second factor to the procedure. The main factor is the sales reps, of which there are three levels (Dan, Amy, and Beth). Tony would like to determine if this main factor has an effect on the average number of sales calls made per week. However, by arranging the data according to weekday, we have introduced a second factor, which is known as the **blocking factor**. The levels of the blocking factor (specific weekdays) are known as **blocks**. The purpose of the blocking factor is to remove some of the variability in the sales calls associated with the weekday, which may allow us to better detect any differences due to the main factor (the sales reps). That is what we are truly interested in knowing. For instance, if the average number of calls on Friday is less than Monday's average (perhaps one or more of the reps began the weekend early), a randomized block ANOVA might do a better job at detecting a difference in the average number of calls made by the three employees than a one-way ANOVA. Let's give it a try!

Step 1: Identify the null and alternative hypotheses.

The hypothesis statement for a randomized block ANOVA is identical to that for the one-way case discussed in the previous section:

The three population means in the null hypothesis pertain to the three employees' sales calls.

$$H_0: \mu_1 = \mu_2 = \mu_3$$
$$H_1: \text{Not all } \mu\text{s are equal}$$

For this example, I'll set the probability of making a Type I error to $\alpha = 0.05$.

Step 2: Calculate the factor means, the block means, and the grand mean $(\bar{\bar{x}})$.

The mean calculations for our sales call data from Table 11.15 are shown in Table 11.16. Notice that I calculated the means for both the columns (the factors, or sales reps) and the rows (the blocks, or weekday).

TABLE 11.16 | SAMPLE DATA FOR THE P&G SALES CALLS

WEEKDAY	DAN	AMY	BETH	BLOCK TOTAL	BLOCK MEAN
Monday	5	8	8	21	7.0
Tuesday	4	7	4	15	5.0
Wednesday	6	8	7	21	7.0
Thursday	6	7	5	18	6.0
Friday	4	5	3	12	4.0
Factor total	25	35	27	87	
Factor mean	5.0	7.0	5.4		

With a randomized block ANOVA, the size of each sample needs to be the same.

Once again, we need to find our grand mean, $\bar{\bar{x}}$, which is the sum of all the data divided by the total number of data points, n_T, in Table 11.16. This represents the overall average number of sales calls made per day by these three reps.

The variable n_T represents the total number of observations. For the sales call example, we have 15 data values (3 employees multiplied by 5 days), so $n_T = 15$.

$$\bar{\bar{x}} = \frac{\text{Sum of all data values}}{n_T} = \frac{87}{15} = 5.8$$

Step 3: Calculate the total sum of squares (*SST*).

The total sum of squares (*SST*) for a randomized block ANOVA is calculated the same way as it is for a one-way ANOVA. We'll again use Equation 11.2 to determine the *SST* with the help from the calculations in Table 11.17.

TABLE 11.17 | SST CALCULATIONS FOR THE P&G SALES CALLS

i	j	EMPLOYEE	x_{ij}	x_{ij}^2
1	1	Dan	5	25
2	1	Dan	4	16
3	1	Dan	6	36
4	1	Dan	6	36
5	1	Dan	4	16
1	2	Amy	8	64
2	2	Amy	7	49
3	2	Amy	8	64
4	2	Amy	7	49
5	2	Amy	5	25
1	3	Beth	8	64
2	3	Beth	4	16
3	3	Beth	7	49
4	3	Beth	5	25
5	3	Beth	3	9
			$\sum_{j=1}^{k}\sum_{i=1}^{n_j} x_{ij} = 87$	$\sum_{j=1}^{k}\sum_{i=1}^{n_j} x_{ij}^2 = 543$

Notice that in Table 11.17, $j = 1$ for Dan, $j = 2$ for Amy, and $j = 3$ for Beth.

We plug these two values into Equation 11.2 as follows:

$$SST = \sum_{j=1}^{k}\sum_{i=1}^{n_j} x_{ij}^2 - \frac{\left(\sum_{j=1}^{k}\sum_{i=1}^{n_j} x_{ij}\right)^2}{n_T} = 543 - \frac{(87)^2}{15}$$

$$SST = 543 - 504.6 = 38.4$$

The mean square total (*MST*) is found using Equation 11.3, as follows:

$$MST = \frac{SST}{n_T - 1} = \frac{38.4}{15 - 1} = 2.74$$

Before we move on to the next step in a randomized block ANOVA, this would be a good time to stop and catch our breath with a Your Turn exercise. This one will give you an opportunity to start a randomized block ANOVA problem and learn about mystery shopping at the same time.

YOUR TURN #4

Many retail establishments use mystery shoppers to provide managers with feedback on how well their service employees perform. A mystery shopper is a person who is hired to pose as a typical customer and complete a report that rates various aspects of his or her shopping experience. The following table shows mystery shopper ratings for the cleanliness of three retail stores on a scale of 1–20. These data can also be found in the Excel file **mystery.xlsx.** Each shopper rated all three stores.

Shopper	Walmart	Starbucks	The Gap
1	12	17	13
2	16	18	17
3	14	17	17
4	18	20	19

a. State the null and alternative hypotheses.
b. Calculate the factor, block, and grand means.
c. Calculate the total sum of squares (*SST*).
d. Calculate the mean square total (*MST*).

Answers can be found on ▶ **page 570**

Step 4: Partition the total sum of squares (*SST*) into the sum of squares between (*SSB*), the sum of squares block (*SSBL*), and the sum of squares error (*SSE*).

The total sum of squares (*SST*) for the randomized block ANOVA is partitioned into the following three sums of squares:

1. Sum of squares between (*SSB*)
2. Sum of squares block (*SSBL*)
3. Sum of squares error (*SSE*)

Equation 11.12 shows the relationship between these sums of squares.

Remember that k represents the number of populations being tested. In the sales call example, we have three employees, so $k = 3$.

Formula 11.12 for the Partitioning of the Total Sum of Squares (SST) for a Randomized Block ANOVA

$$SST = SSB + SSBL + SSE$$

The sum of squares between (*SSB*), which is found using Equation 11.5, has the same meaning as it does for a one-way ANOVA. For our sales call example, we have already determined that $\bar{\bar{x}} = 5.8$ and $k = 3$. Table 11.16 provides us with the remaining sample data needed for this equation. For your convenience, Table 11.18 summarizes this information.

TABLE 11.18 | SUMMARIZED SAMPLE DATA FOR THE P&G SALES CALLS

	DAN	AMY	BETH
	$j = 1$	$j = 2$	$j = 3$
$\bar{x}_j$	$\bar{x}_1 = 5.0$	$\bar{x}_2 = 7.0$	$\bar{x}_3 = 5.4$
n_j	$n_1 = 5$	$n_2 = 5$	$n_3 = 5$

Applying these data to Equation 11.5, we have the following:

$$SSB = \sum_{j=1}^{k} n_j(\bar{x}_j - \bar{\bar{x}})^2$$
$$SSB = n_1(\bar{x}_1 - \bar{\bar{x}})^2 + n_2(\bar{x}_2 - \bar{\bar{x}})^2 + n_3(\bar{x}_3 - \bar{\bar{x}})^2$$
$$SSB = (5)(5.0 - 5.8)^2 + (5)(7.0 - 5.8)^2 + (5)(5.4 - 5.8)^2$$
$$SSB = (5)(-0.8)^2 + (5)(1.2)^2 + (5)(-0.4)^2$$
$$SSB = (5)(0.64) + (5)(1.44) + (5)(0.16)$$
$$SSB = 11.2$$

The mean square between (*MSB*) is again found using Equation 11.6:

$$MSB = \frac{SSB}{k - 1} = \frac{11.2}{3 - 1} = 5.6$$

The **sum of squares block (*SSBL*)** measures the variation between the block means and the grand mean.

Next, we'll see that Equation 11.13 introduces the **sum of squares block (*SSBL*)**, which measures the variation between the block means and the grand mean.

Formula 11.13 for the Sum of Squares Block (SSBL)

$$SSBL = k\sum_{i=1}^{b}(\bar{x}_i - \bar{\bar{x}})^2$$

where

$SSBL$ = The sum of squares block
$\bar{x}_i$ = The sample mean from the *i*th block
$\bar{\bar{x}}$ = The grand mean of all the data values
b = The number of blocks
k = The number of populations being compared

Remember, for our sales call example, the blocks are the weekdays, which means that $b = 5$. Table 11.19 summarizes the data shown in Table 11.16 that is needed for Equation 11.13.

TABLE 11.19 | SUMMARIZED BLOCK SAMPLE DATA FOR THE P&G SALES CALLS

	MONDAY	TUESDAY	WEDNESDAY	THURSDAY	FRIDAY
	$i = 1$	$i = 2$	$i = 3$	$i = 4$	$i = 5$
$\bar{x}_i$	$\bar{x}_1 = 7$	$\bar{x}_2 = 5$	$\bar{x}_3 = 7$	$\bar{x}_4 = 6$	$\bar{x}_5 = 4$

Applying these data to Equation 11.5, we have the following:

$$SSBL = k\sum_{i=1}^{b}(\bar{x}_i - \bar{\bar{x}})^2$$
$$SSBL = (3)\left[(\bar{x}_1 - \bar{\bar{x}})^2 + (\bar{x}_2 - \bar{\bar{x}})^2 + (\bar{x}_3 - \bar{\bar{x}})^2 + (\bar{x}_4 - \bar{\bar{x}})^2 + (\bar{x}_5 - \bar{\bar{x}})^2\right]$$
$$SSBL = (3)\left[(7 - 5.8)^2 + (5 - 5.8)^2 + (7 - 5.8)^2 + (6 - 5.8)^2 + (4 - 5.8)^2\right]$$
$$SSBL = (3)[(1.2)^2 + (-0.8)^2 + (1.2)^2 + (0.2)^2 + (-1.8)^2]$$
$$SSBL = (3)[(1.44) + (0.64) + (1.44) + (0.04) + (3.24)]$$
$$SSBL = (3)[6.80] = 20.4$$

The **mean square block (*MSBL*)** represents the variance associated with the sum of squares block (*SSBL*).

The **mean square block (*MSBL*)** is found using Equation 11.14.

Formula 11.14 for the Mean Square Block (MSBL)

$$MSBL = \frac{\text{Sum of squares block}}{b - 1} = \frac{SSBL}{b - 1}$$

Using our sales call results, we have the following:

$$MSBL = \frac{SSBL}{b - 1} = \frac{20.4}{5 - 1} = 5.1$$

The mean square block (*MSBL*) represents the variance associated with the sum of squares block. If the average number of sales calls per day was the same for each weekday, the mean square block (*MSBL*) value would be zero.

The **sum of squares error (*SSE*)** represents the random variation in the data not attributed to either the main factor or the blocking factor.

The last component of the total sum of squares (*SST*) is the **sum of squares error (*SSE*)**, which represents the random variation in the sales call data that is attributed to neither the employee nor the weekday. The *SSE* can be determined using Equation 11.15.

Formula 11.15 for the Sum of Squares Error (SSE) for Randomized Block ANOVA

$$SSE = SST - (SSB + SSBL)$$

Using our previous results, we have the following:

$$SSE = SST - (SSB + SSBL)$$
$$SSE = 38.4 - (11.2 + 20.4) = 38.4 - 31.6 = 6.8$$

Finally, the **mean square error (*MSE*)** represents the variance associated with the *SSE* and can be found using Equation 11.16.

Formula 11.16 for the Mean Square Error (MSE) for Randomized Block ANOVA

The **mean square error (*MSE*)** represents the variance associated with the sum of squares error (*SSE*).

$$MSE = \frac{\text{Sum of squares error}}{(b - 1)(k - 1)} = \frac{SSE}{(b - 1)(k - 1)}$$

Using our sales call results, we have the following:

$$MSE = \frac{SSE}{(b - 1)(k - 1)} = \frac{6.8}{(5 - 1)(3 - 1)} = 0.85$$

Now that we have partitioned the *SST* into its three components and calculated the mean squares, we are ready for the test statistic.

Step 5: Calculate the main factor test statistic.

The main factor test statistic for a randomized block ANOVA is used to determine if a difference in population means exists; it is shown in Equation 11.17.

Formula 11.17 for Main Factor F-Test Statistic for a Randomized Block ANOVA

$$F_{\bar{x}} = \frac{MSB}{MSE}$$

Using our mean square values from the previous step, the calculated F-score, $F_{\bar{x}}$, is calculated as follows:

$$F_{\bar{x}} = \frac{MSB}{MSE} = \frac{5.6}{0.85} = 6.59$$

Step 6: Determine the appropriate critical value.

The main factor test statistic shown in Equation 11.17 follows the F-distribution with the following degrees of freedom:

$$D_1 = k - 1$$
$$D_2 = (b - 1)(k - 1)$$

Using our P&G sales call data, the degrees of freedom are as follows:

$$D_1 = k - 1 = 3 - 1 = 2$$
$$D_2 = (b - 1)(k - 1) = (5 - 1)(3 - 1) = 8$$

According to Table 11.8, the critical value for our sales call ANOVA using $\alpha = 0.05$ and degrees of freedom equal to 2 and 8 is $F_\alpha = 4.459$.

We can also obtain this critical F-score using Excel's F.INV.RT function as follows:

=F.INV.RT (0.05, 2, 8) = 4.459

Step 7: Compare the F-test statistic ($F_{\bar{x}}$) with the critical F-score (F_α).

Because $F_{\bar{x}} = 6.59$, which is greater than $F_\alpha = 4.459$, we reject the null hypothesis according to the decision rules shown back in Table 11.9. We can see this graphically in Figure 11.11.

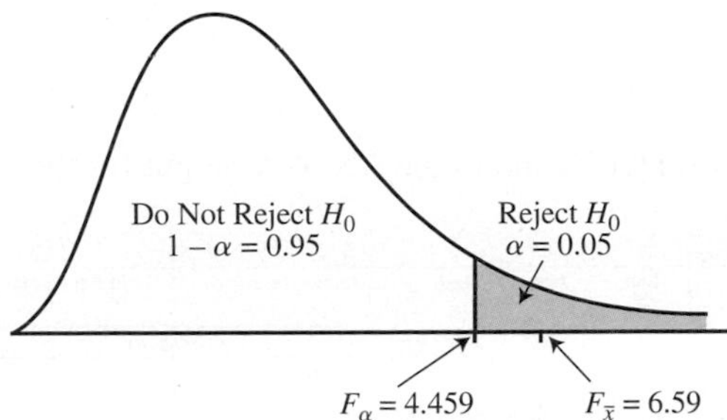

FIGURE 11.11 Comparing the F-Test Statistic with the Critical F-Score for the P&G Sales Call Example

Step 8: State your conclusions.

By rejecting the null hypothesis, we can conclude that not all of the three population means are equal. Tony can conclude that some employees average more sales calls per week than others.

Now, hold on 1 minute. Didn't we just conclude that there was no difference in average calls per week with our one-way ANOVA (see Figure 11.10)? Before we solve this mystery, allow me to demonstrate how to perform a randomized block ANOVA with Excel.

Using Excel to Perform a Randomized Block ANOVA

Excel's Data Analysis can perform a randomized block ANOVA procedure for us. Using the sales call data, we take the following steps. Those of you with Excel for Mac can go to the textbook's Web site for instructions to perform one-way ANOVA using PHStat.

1. Open the Excel file **sales.xlsx** or enter the sales call data values in Columns A, B, C, and D as shown in Figure 11.12A.
2. Go to **Data** and click on **Data Analysis** on the right side of the ribbon as shown in Figure 11.12A. This opens the **Data Analysis** dialog box.
3. Select **ANOVA: Two Factor Without Replication**. Click **OK**.

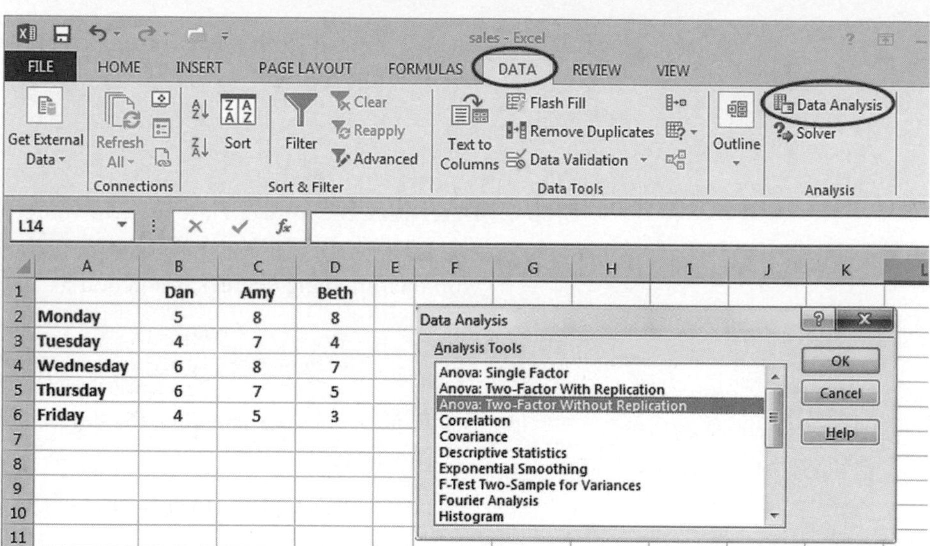

FIGURE 11.12A Conducting a Randomized Block ANOVA Test Using Excel (Steps 1–3)

4. Fill in the **ANOVA: Two Factor Without Replication** dialog box as shown in Figure 11.12B. Click **OK**.

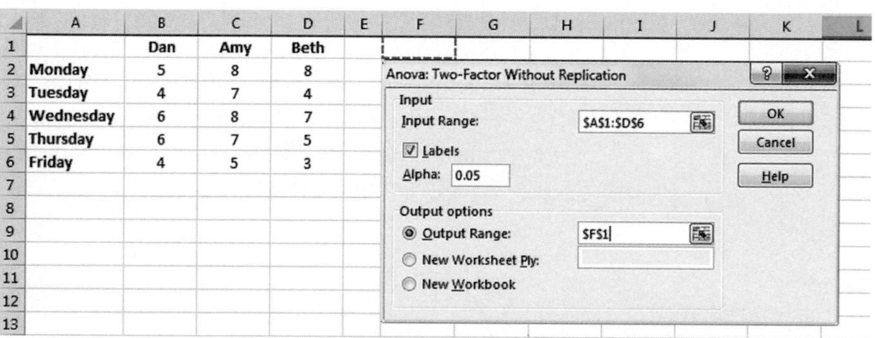

FIGURE 11.12B Conducting a Randomized Block ANOVA Test Using Excel (Step 4)

5. Figure 11.12C shows the ANOVA output for the sales call example.

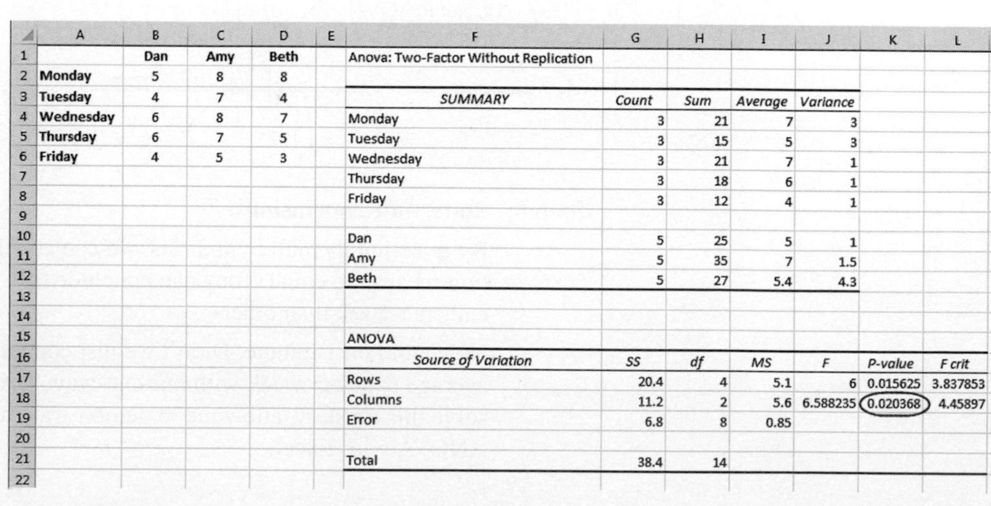

	Dan	Amy	Beth
Monday	5	8	8
Tuesday	4	7	4
Wednesday	6	8	7
Thursday	6	7	5
Friday	4	5	3

Anova: Two-Factor Without Replication

SUMMARY	Count	Sum	Average	Variance
Monday	3	21	7	3
Tuesday	3	15	5	3
Wednesday	3	21	7	1
Thursday	3	18	6	1
Friday	3	12	4	1
Dan	5	25	5	1
Amy	5	35	7	1.5
Beth	5	27	5.4	4.3

ANOVA

Source of Variation	SS	df	MS	F	P-value	F crit
Rows	20.4	4	5.1	6	0.015625	3.837853
Columns	11.2	2	5.6	6.588235	0.020368	4.45897
Error	6.8	8	0.85			
Total	38.4	14				

FIGURE 11.12C Conducting a Randomized Block ANOVA Test Using Excel (Final Result)

The "Sources of Variation" section in Figure 11.12C shows the different variables we have discussed, but they are labeled slightly differently in Excel:

- Rows = Blocking variation (*SSBL*, *MSBL*)
- Columns = Between variation (*SSB*, *MSB*)
- Error = Error variation (*SSE*, *MSE*)

To determine if a difference exists in the means of the populations, we focus our attention on the "Columns" source of variation found in Row 18 in Figure 11.12C. The *p*-value in Cell K18 is 0.020368 and is less than $\alpha = 0.05$. Therefore, we reject the null hypothesis and conclude that a difference does exist in the average sales calls made per week between these three employees. In other words, the probability of observing an *F*-test statistic greater than 6.588235 if the null hypothesis is true is only 0.020368, which is less than the $\alpha = 0.05$ significance level we set for ourselves.

We can also obtain the *p*-value for this ANOVA procedure using Excel's F.DIST.RT function as follows:

=F.DIST.RT (6.59, 2, 8) = 0.0204

To Block or Not to Block: That Is the Question

Now, back to our mystery. Why did our one-way ANOVA tell us there was no difference in the average number of sales calls made by the employees, whereas the randomized block ANOVA confirmed there *was* a difference? To answer this question, let's investigate the impact of the blocking factor on the hypothesis test. In doing so, we need to decide whether the blocking factor (in this case, the weekday) helped or hindered our analysis. Take a look at Figure 11.13, which illustrates the partitioning of the total sum of squares (*SST*) for both the one-way and randomized block ANOVA.

FIGURE 11.13 Further Partitioning the Total Sum of Squares (SST) for a Randomized Block ANOVA

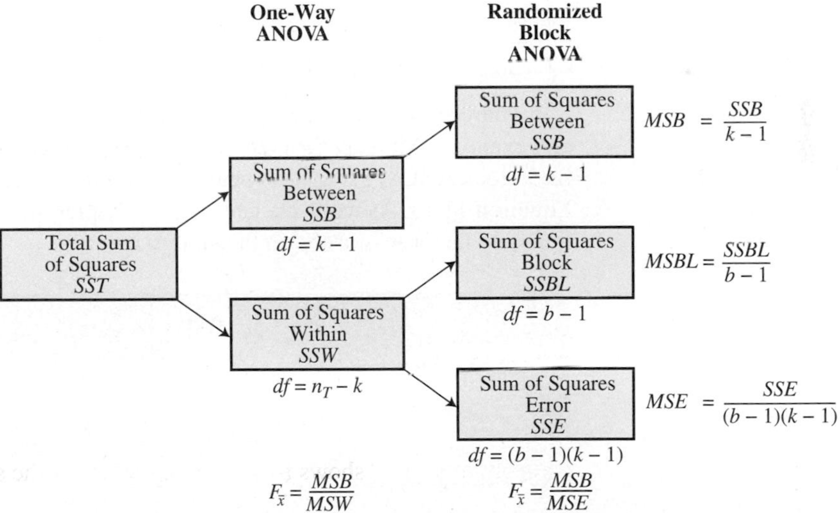

With a one-way ANOVA, we will have a greater chance of rejecting the null hypothesis when more variation in the data is due to the *SSB* rather than the *SSW*. Notice in Figure 11.13 with a randomized block ANOVA, the *SSW* is further partitioned into the *SSBL* and the *SSE*. As more variation in the data is explained by the *SSBL* for given values of *k* and *b*

→ less is attributed to the *SSE*,

→ which makes the $MSE = \dfrac{SSE}{(b-1)(k-1)}$ smaller,

→ which makes the test statistic, $F_{\bar{x}} = \dfrac{MSB}{MSE}$, larger,

→ which increases the likelihood of rejecting the null hypothesis $(\text{when } F_{\bar{x}} > F_{\alpha})$.

To illustrate this point, take a look at Table 11.20, which compares these two ANOVAs using the sales call example.

See Figure 11.10 for these values.

TABLE 11.20 | COMPARING THE SALES CALL DATA USING A ONE-WAY ANOVA VS. A RANDOMIZED BLOCK ANOVA

	ONE-WAY ANOVA	RANDOMIZED BLOCK ANOVA
Test statistic	$F_{\bar{x}} = \dfrac{MSB}{MSW}$	$F_{\bar{x}} = \dfrac{MSB}{MSE}$
	$F_{\bar{x}} = \dfrac{5.6}{2.27} = 2.47$	$F_{\bar{x}} = \dfrac{5.6}{0.85} = 6.59$
Critical value	3.885	4.459
Decision	Fail to reject null hypothesis	Reject null hypothesis

Although our primary reason for performing ANOVA was to compare average sales between employees, testing the significance of the blocking factor tells us whether blocking was effective.

As you can see, the test statistic for the randomized block ANOVA has a smaller denominator (0.85) than the one-way ANOVA (2.27) because the blocking factor, weekday, has removed some of the variation. In this example, the blocking factor was effective because it resulted in rejecting the null hypothesis. In other words, we were able to tell that the days of the week were masking the result—that the representatives weren't really making the same number of calls per week. When the blocking was not used (in our one-way ANOVA calculations), we did not detect a difference in sales calls and failed to reject the null hypothesis.

We can take this question of whether to block one step further by testing the significance of the blocking factor. With our sales call example, we have the following hypotheses:

$$H_0: \mu_{BL1} = \mu_{BL2} = \mu_{BL3} = \mu_{BL4} = \mu_{BL5}$$
$$H_1: \text{Not all } \mu_{BL}\text{s are equal}$$

where

$\mu_{BLi} =$ The population mean for the *ith* block

There are five means in this null hypothesis because there are five blocks in the sales call example (Monday through Friday). The blocking factor test statistic for the randomized block ANOVA is used to determine if a difference in block means exists; it is shown in Equation 11.18. As we'll see later in this chapter, this information can help us decide if the blocking factor was useful in the analysis.

Formula 11.18 for Blocking Factor F-Test Statistic for a Randomized Block ANOVA

$$F_{BL} = \frac{MSBL}{MSE}$$

Using our mean square values from Figure 11.12C, the calculated *F*-score for the blocking factor, F_{BL}, is as follows:

$$F_{BL} = \frac{MSBL}{MSE} = \frac{5.1}{0.85} = 6.0$$

The blocking factor test statistic shown in Equation 11.18 follows the *F*-distribution with the following degrees of freedom:

$$D_1 = b - 1$$
$$D_2 = (b - 1)(k - 1)$$

Using our sales call data, the blocking degrees of freedom are as follows:

$$D_1 = b - 1 = 5 - 1 = 4$$
$$D_2 = (b - 1)(k - 1) = (5 - 1)(3 - 1) = 8$$

Because blocking was effective in the sales call example (it led to a different result than that obtained with the one-way ANOVA procedure), the randomized block ANOVA is the appropriate procedure to use.

According to Table 11.8, the blocking critical value for our sales call ANOVA using $\alpha = 0.05$ and degrees of freedom equal to 4 and 8 is $F_\alpha = 3.838$. Because $F_{BL} = 6.0$ is greater than $F_\alpha = 3.838$, we reject the null hypothesis according to the decision rules shown in Table 11.9. By rejecting the blocking null hypothesis, we have evidence that the blocking factor was effective and that it belongs in our final analysis.

In terms of the sales call example, this conclusion means that the weekday appears to influence the number of sales calls made. This can also be verified by looking back at Figure 11.12C and observing that the p-value for the blocking factor, found in Cell K17, is equal to 0.0156, which is less than $\alpha = 0.05$. In other words, on some weekdays there is a higher or lower number of sales calls across all three employees. This is why we failed to reject the null hypothesis for the sales call example using a one-way ANOVA and were able to reject the null hypothesis using a randomized block ANOVA.

I do have a note of caution at this point. If one of the objectives of the ANOVA procedure is to test specifically for a difference in the means of the blocks—that is, if the goal is to consider the blocks as a main factor—the randomized block ANOVA would not be the appropriate procedure. Rather, the two-way ANOVA test, which is discussed later in the chapter, would be the procedure of choice.

The ANOVA table for the randomized block procedure, which is shown in Table 11.21, looks slightly different from that for the one-way ANOVA example.

TABLE 11.21 | RANDOMIZED BLOCK ANOVA EQUATIONS: A SUMMARY

SOURCE	SUM OF SQUARES	DEGREES OF FREEDOM	MEAN SUM OF SQUARES	F
Between	SSB	$k - 1$	$MSB = \frac{SSB}{k - 1}$	$F_{\bar{x}} = \frac{MSB}{MSE}$
Block	$SSBL$	$b - 1$	$MSBL = \frac{SSBL}{b - 1}$	$F_{BL} = \frac{MSBL}{MSE}$
Error	SSE	$(b - 1)(k - 1)$	$MSE = \frac{SSE}{(b - 1)(k - 1)}$	
Total	SST	$n_T - 1$		

Table 11.22 summarizes the results of the sales call randomized block ANOVA.

TABLE 11.22 | RANDOMIZED BLOCK ANOVA SUMMARY TABLE FOR THE P&G SALES CALL DATA

SOURCE	SUM OF SQUARES	DEGREES OF FREEDOM	MEAN SUM OF SQUARES	F
Between	11.2	2	5.6	6.59
Block	20.4	4	5.1	6.0
Error	6.8	8	0.85	
Total	38.4	14		

If you decide to use the randomized block ANOVA and fail to reject the null hypothesis for the main factor, it's important to investigate the effectiveness of the blocks by looking at the p-value for the "Rows" source of variation in Excel. If blocking is not effective, it will result in your failing to reject the null hypothesis for the blocking factor. So, including it in the final analysis could result in inflating the probability of a Type II error (failing to find a difference in the means when one really exists). In a sense, the blocking factor, because it is ineffective, is masking the true difference in the means of the main factor. In this case, you should redo the analysis by conducting a one-way ANOVA. The following is a quick example.

A certain unnamed statistics author likes to humiliate himself on a regular basis by playing golf with his two sons, who like to remind him constantly how much better they are on the golf course than he is (in spite of the fact that he always pays for the rounds). To investigate these claims, I—I mean the unnamed author—recorded the last four rounds of golf played by all three players at four different courses. The scores are shown in Table 11.23.

TABLE 11.23 | Golf Scores

COURSE	AUTHOR	BRIAN	JOHN
1	90	83	85
2	84	85	86
3	90	83	82
4	90	85	80

Because each row in Table 11.23 represents a different golf course, a randomized block ANOVA would appear to be the analysis of choice. Figure 11.14 shows these results using Excel.

FIGURE 11.14
Randomized Block ANOVA Results for the Golf Scores

	A	B	C	D	E	F	G	H	I	J	K	L
1	Course	Author	Brian	John		Anova: Two-Factor Without Replication						
2	1	90	83	85								
3	2	84	85	86		SUMMARY	Count	Sum	Average	Variance		
4	3	90	83	82		1	3	258	86	13		
5	4	90	85	80		2	3	255	85	1		
6						3	3	255	85	19		
7						4	3	255	85	25		
8												
9						Author	4	354	88.5	9		
10						Brian	4	336	84	1.333333		
11						John	4	333	83.25	7.583333		
12												
13												
14						ANOVA						
15						Source of Variation	SS	df	MS	F	P-value	F crit
16						Rows	2.25	3	0.75	0.087379	0.964384	4.757063
17						Columns	64.5	2	32.25	3.757282	0.087508	5.143253
18						Error	51.5	6	8.583333			
19												
20						Total	118.25	11				
21												

Further evidence that the blocking factor is not effective can be found by looking at the block means in Figure 11.14. The average scores for each of the four courses (86, 85, 85, and 85) don't vary much at all. It does not appear the different courses have much influence on the golf scores.

Because the p-value for the main factor (golfer) in Cell K17 is 0.087508 and is greater than $\alpha = 0.05$, we fail to reject the null hypothesis. In other words, there is no evidence to support the claims that the sons are better golfers than their poor, broke dad. However, because we used a randomized block ANOVA and failed to reject the null hypothesis, there is a chance that the blocking factor is masking any true difference in the main factor means.

Figure 11.14 provides us with some evidence that the blocking factor was not effective in this analysis. The p-value for the blocking factor (course) can be found in Cell K16 and is equal to 0.964384. Because this value is greater than $\alpha = 0.05$, we fail to reject the null hypothesis, which means the blocking factor is not carrying its weight in the problem and should be removed from the analysis. In fact, if you look at the average scores in Cells I4 through I7, you will see that the different courses don't have much effect on the scores of the golfers. Thus, the blocking factor is ineffective. To do the analysis properly, we should perform a one-way ANOVA to be sure the blocking factor is not covering up the difference between the golfers' average scores.

Figure 11.15 shows the one-way ANOVA results from Excel for the golf score example.

FIGURE 11.15
One-Way ANOVA Results for the Golf Scores

	A	B	C	D	E	F	G	H	I	J	K	L
1	Course	Author	Brian	John		Anova: Single Factor						
2	1	90	83	85								
3	2	84	85	86		SUMMARY						
4	3	90	83	82		Groups	Count	Sum	Average	Variance		
5	4	90	85	80		Author	4	354	88.5	9		
6						Brian	4	336	84	1.333333		
7						John	4	333	83.25	7.583333		
8												
9												
10						ANOVA						
11						Source of Variation	SS	df	MS	F	P-value	F crit
12						Between Groups	64.5	2	32.25	5.4	0.02878	4.256495
13						Within Groups	53.75	9	5.972222			
14												
15						Total	118.25	11				
16												

Notice that the p-value in Cell K12 is now equal to 0.02878, which is less than $\alpha = 0.05$.

Our final conclusion, to this author's chagrin, is to reject the null hypothesis for the main factor. It appears that there is a difference in the average golf scores of these three players. To spare his pride, it looks like this author needs to keep this chapter away from his sons.

Use the following steps as a guide to answer the question, "To block or not to block?"

1. If a blocking factor seems appropriate for a particular analysis, begin with a randomized block ANOVA design.
2. If the main factor is significant, reject the null hypothesis and proceed with your conclusions.
3. If the main factor with the randomized block design is not significant, proceed to test the main factor with the one-way ANOVA design.

A randomized block ANOVA should not be used to test the significance of the blocking factor. Under these circumstances, use a two-way ANOVA, which is discussed later in this chapter.

As long as the main factor is statistically significant, there is no concern about the significance of the blocking factor. Remember, the purpose of using the randomized block design is to reduce the variability due to the blocking factor. If there is an interest in investigating the significance of the blocking factor, the randomized block ANOVA is not the appropriate design. Rather, a two-way ANOVA design, which can test the significance of two main factors, should be employed. We'll discuss the two-way ANOVA procedure later in this chapter.

Table 11.24 provides a summary of the steps required to test the main factor using a randomized block ANOVA design.

TABLE 11.24 | SUMMARY OF STEPS FOR A RANDOMIZED BLOCK ANOVA

STEP	DESCRIPTION	PROCEDURE
1	Identify the null and alternative hypotheses.	H_0: All μs are equal H_1: Not all μs are equal
2	Calculate the factor means, the block means, and the grand mean ($\bar{\bar{x}}$).	
3	Calculate the total sum of squares (SST).	$SST = \sum_{j=1}^{k}\sum_{i=1}^{n_j} x_{ij}^2 - \frac{\left(\sum_{j=1}^{k}\sum_{i=1}^{n_j} x_{ij}\right)^2}{n_T}$ (11.2) $MST = \frac{SST}{n_T - 1}$ (11.3)
4	Partition the total sum of squares (SST) into the sum of squares between (SSB), the sum of squares block ($SSBL$), and the sum of squares error (SSE). Calculate the corresponding mean squares.	$SSB = \sum_{j=1}^{k} n_j(\bar{x}_j - \bar{\bar{x}})^2$ (11.5) $MSB = \frac{SSB}{k - 1}$ (11.6) $SSBL = k\sum_{i=1}^{b}(\bar{x}_i - \bar{\bar{x}})^2$ (11.13) $MSBL = \frac{SSBL}{b - 1}$ (11.14) $SSE = SST - (SSB + SSBL)$ (11.15) $MSE = \frac{SSE}{(b - 1)(k - 1)}$ (11.16)

(continued)

TABLE 11.24 | SUMMARY OF STEPS FOR A RANDOMIZED BLOCK ANOVA (CONTINUED)

STEP	DESCRIPTION	PROCEDURE
5	Calculate the main factor test statistic.	$F_{\bar{x}} = \dfrac{MSB}{MSE}$ (11.17)
6	Determine the appropriate critical value.	Critical value, F_α, is found in Table 6 in Appendix A with degrees of freedom: $D_1 = k - 1$, $D_2 = (b - 1)(k - 1)$
7	Compare the F-test statistic $(F_{\bar{x}})$ with the critical F-score (F_α).	$F_{\bar{x}} \le F_\alpha \rightarrow$ Do not reject H_0; $F_{\bar{x}} > F_\alpha \rightarrow$ Reject H_0
8	State your conclusions.	

This next Your Turn problem will give you the chance to finish the randomized block procedure on the mystery shopper example.

YOUR TURN #5

Answer the following using your results from the mystery shopper problem described in Your Turn #4.

- **a.** Calculate the sum of squares between (*SSB*) and the mean square between (*MSB*).
- **b.** Calculate the sum of squares block (*SSBL*) and the mean square block (*MSBL*).
- **c.** Calculate the sum of squares error (*SSE*) and the mean square error (*MSE*).
- **d.** Calculate the main factor test statistic for the ANOVA procedure.
- **e.** Using $\alpha = 0.05$, can you conclude there is a difference in the average cleanliness scores of the three stores?
- **f.** Does the blocking factor appear to be effective?
- **g.** Construct an ANOVA summary table.
- **h.** Verify your results with Excel.

Answers can be found on ▶ **pages 570–571**

Multiple Comparisons: Comparing Pairs of Populations Mean (Randomized Block ANOVA)

Tukey–Kramer Multiple Comparison Test for Randomized Block ANOVA allows us to examine each pair of sample means and to conclude whether their respective population means differ for randomized block ANOVA.

There are several different procedures to choose from when making multiple comparisons for a randomized block ANOVA. I'll demonstrate the **Tukey–Kramer Multiple Comparison Test for Randomized Block ANOVA** using the P&G sales call example. This procedure is very similar to the one-way procedure discussed earlier in the chapter when we were looking at the smartphone data.

Step 1: Calculate the absolute sample mean differences.

With $k = 3$ populations (employees) being compared, we have $3(2)/2 = 3$ pairs of sample means. The pairs are made up of the following samples:

1 and 2 1 and 3 2 and 3

Using data from Table 11.16, we have the following:

$$|\bar{x}_1 - \bar{x}_2| = |5.0 - 7.0| = |-2.0| = 2.0$$
$$|\bar{x}_1 - \bar{x}_3| = |5.0 - 5.4| = |-0.4| = 0.4$$
$$|\bar{x}_2 - \bar{x}_3| = |7.0 - 5.4| = |1.6| = 1.6$$

Step 2: Calculate the critical range.

The critical range for comparing pairs for a randomized block ANOVA, *CR*, is used to determine if the difference between a pair of sample means is large enough to conclude that the population means are significantly different. The formula for the *CR* for a randomized block ANOVA is shown as Equation 11.19.

Formula 11.19 for the Critical Range for a Randomized Block ANOVA

$$CR = Q_{\alpha}\sqrt{\frac{MSE}{b}}$$

where

CR = The critical range for comparing two sample means
Q_{α} = The critical value from the studentized range table (Appendix A, Table 7)
MSE = The mean square error
b = The number of blocks

The critical value, Q_{α}, is found in Table 7 in Appendix A. The value is based on our desired significance level and the following two degrees of freedom:

$$D_1 = k$$
$$D_2 = (b - 1)(k - 1)$$

Using the P&G sales call data with $k = 3$ employees and $b = 5$ weekdays, the degrees of freedom are as follows:

$$D_1 = k = 3$$
$$D_2 = (b - 1)(k - 1) = (5 - 1)(3 - 1) = 8$$

Using Table 7 in Appendix A with $\alpha = 0.05$, the critical value is $Q_{\alpha} = 4.04$. The critical range for the P&G sales call example can be found with Equation 11.19. Recall from Table 11.22 that the $MSE = 0.85$.

$$CR = Q_{\alpha}\sqrt{\frac{MSE}{b}} = (4.04)\sqrt{\frac{0.85}{5}} = (4.04)(0.4123) = 1.67$$

Step 3: State your conclusions.

We can use the decision rules in Table 11.13 to determine which pairs of population means are different. Table 11.25 shows these decision rules being applied to the three pairs of samples.

TABLE 11.25 | DETERMINING WHICH POPULATION MEANS ARE DIFFERENT IN THE SALES CALL EXAMPLE

$\lvert \bar{x}_i - \bar{x}_j \rvert$	*CR*	DECISION
$\lvert \bar{x}_1 - \bar{x}_2 \rvert = 2.0$	1.67	$2.0 > 1.67$; means are different
$\lvert \bar{x}_1 - \bar{x}_3 \rvert = 0.4$	1.67	$0.4 < 1.67$; means are not different
$\lvert \bar{x}_2 - \bar{x}_3 \rvert = 1.6$	1.67	$1.6 < 1.67$; means are not different

According to Table 11.25, we can conclude that a difference exists between the average number of weekly sales calls made by Dan (1) vs. Amy (2). There is no evidence that the other two pairs of employees (Dan and Beth, and Amy and Beth) have different means based on these data.

In this next Your Turn section, try the multiple comparison technique on the mystery shopper problem on which you have been working.

YOUR TURN #6

Using the data and results from Your Turn #4 and #5, perform the Tukey–Kramer multiple comparisons procedure using $\alpha = 0.05$ to identify which stores have average cleanliness scores that are different from one another.

Answer can be found on ▶ page 571

11.2 Section Problems

Basic Skills

11.15 Consider the following partially completed randomized block ANOVA summary table:

Source	Sum of Squares	Degrees of Freedom	Mean Sum of Squares	*F*
Between		2		
Block	105	7		
Error	42			
Total	183	23		

a. Complete the remaining entries in the table.
b. How many population means are being tested?
c. Using $\alpha = 0.05$, what conclusions can be made about the population means?
d. Was blocking effective? Why or why not?

11.16 Consider the following data collected for a randomized block ANOVA:

Block	Sample 1	Sample 2	Sample 3
1	8	4	3
2	5	4	3
3	6	2	1
4	13	9	5

a. Calculate the total sum of squares (*SST*).
b. Partition the total sum of squares (*SST*) into its three components.
c. Using $\alpha = 0.05$, what conclusions can be made about the population means?
d. Was blocking effective? Why or why not?

11.17 Using the data from Problem 11.16, determine which means are different from one another using $\alpha = 0.05$.

11.18 Consider the following partially completed randomized block ANOVA summary table:

Source	Sum of Squares	Degrees of Freedom	Mean Sum of Squares	*F*
Between	72			6.0
Block	168		28.0	
Error		18		
Total	312	27		

a. Complete the remaining entries in the table.
b. How many population means are being tested?
c. Using $\alpha = 0.05$, what conclusions can be made concerning the population means?
d. Was blocking effective? Why or why not?

11.19 Consider the following data collected for a randomized block ANOVA.

Block	Sample 1	Sample 2	Sample 3	Sample 4
1	5	5	10	8
2	4	4	8	4
3	4	3	8	1
4	3	5	8	4
5	4	3	3	2

a. Calculate the total sum of squares (*SST*).
b. Partition the total sum of squares (*SST*) into its three components.
c. Using $\alpha = 0.05$, what conclusions can be made about the population means?
d. Was blocking effective? Why or why not?

11.20 Using the data from Problem 11.19, determine which means are different using $\alpha = 0.05$.

Applications

11.21 Suppose Gatorade has developed four new drink flavors and would like to conduct a taste test to collect data on customers' preferences. Six people were asked to sample and rate each flavor on a scale of 1–20. The data are as follows and can be found in the file **Gatorade.xlsx**.

Person	Flavor 1	Flavor 2	Flavor 3	Flavor 4
1	19	20	12	17
2	18	17	17	18
3	17	18	16	19
4	13	19	12	14
5	10	13	7	18
6	13	12	11	16

a. Using $\alpha = 0.05$, what conclusions can be made about the preference for the four flavors?
b. Was blocking effective? Why or why not?
c. If warranted, determine which pairs of flavors were different from one another using $\alpha = 0.05$.
d. Verify your results with Excel.

11.22 Suppose the Environmental Protection Agency (EPA) would like to investigate the impact that octane has on gas mileage. The following table shows the gas mileage for six cars that were driven 1,000 miles with three different grades of gasoline: 87, 89, and 93 octane. The gas mileage was recorded for each octane level. Each car was tested with all three gasoline grades. These data can also be found in the file **octane.xlsx**.

Car	87 Octane	89 Octane	93 Octane
Maxima	22.6	23.3	23.0
Focus	28.0	29.6	30.1
Accord	22.6	22.1	23.3
Sonata	28.6	29.1	29.4
Camry	24.1	27.7	26.0
Jetta	30.0	29.4	30.7

a. Using $\alpha = 0.05$, does the octane level appear to have an effect on the gas mileage?
b. Was blocking effective? Why or why not?
c. If warranted, determine which pairs of octanes were different using $\alpha = 0.05$.
d. Verify your results with Excel.

11.23 The superintendent of the Red Clay School District is concerned about the sick time taken by teachers and administrators. More specifically, she would like to know if there is a difference in the number of hours of sick time taken when comparing the days of the week. To investigate this, seven random weeks were selected during the school year, and the total "sick hours" taken by all employees each day were recorded. The hours are shown in the following table and can be found in the file **sick hours.xlsx**.

Week	Mon	Tues	Wed	Thurs	Fri
1	17	29	24	19	24
2	23	24	18	23	27
3	26	22	22	22	30
4	22	26	20	27	32
5	30	28	21	20	33
6	36	17	21	22	32
7	21	22	21	21	25

a. Using $\alpha = 0.05$, does there appear to be a difference in the number of sick hours taken during the days of the week?
b. Was blocking effective? Why or why not?
c. If warranted, determine which pairs of days were different using $\alpha = 0.05$.
d. What might account for some of these differences?
e. Verify your results with Excel.

11.24 Suppose *Golf Magazine* would like to do an article comparing the driving distances of various golf balls. Eight golfers were asked to hit Top Flite, Pinnacle, and Titleist golf balls with their drivers. The distance for each shot was measured in yards and is as follows. The file **golf balls.xlsx** also contains these data.

Golfer	Top Flite	Pinnacle	Titleist
1	217	202	205
2	228	270	228
3	226	237	224
4	214	257	249
5	236	274	267
6	229	252	230
7	241	242	237
8	233	242	230

a. Using $\alpha = 0.05$, does there appear to be a difference in the driving yardage of the balls?
b. Was blocking effective? Why or why not?
c. If warranted, determine which pairs of balls were different using $\alpha = 0.05$.
d. Verify your results with Excel.

11.25 Avon Products has a 24-hour distribution facility in Newark, Delaware, that fulfills orders for the cosmetic maker's sales representatives. Orders are filled in one of three distribution lines. Random business days were selected, and the number of orders processed for each line over 4-hour intervals was recorded. The data are as follows and can also be found in the file **Avon.xlsx**.

Interval	Line 1	Line 2	Line 3
7:00 A.M.–11:00 A.M.	1,313	1,254	1,279
11:00 A.M.–3:00 P.M.	1,118	1,093	1,395
3:00 P.M.–7:00 P.M.	1,276	1,227	1,190
7:00 P.M.–11:00 P.M.	1,096	988	1,210
11:00 P.M.–3:00 A.M.	1,050	1,244	1,114
3:00 A.M.–7:00 A.M.	1,239	1,202	1,036

a. Using $\alpha = 0.05$, does there appear to be a difference in the number of orders processed by the lines?
b. Was blocking effective? Why or why not?
c. If warranted, determine which pairs of lines were different using $\alpha = 0.05$.
d. Verify your results with Excel.

11.26 Bagel Boys is a chain that sells New York–style bagels at three locations. The owner of the chain would like to investigate if there is a difference in the number of bagels sold per day at each location. A random week was selected, and the number of bagels sold each day at each location was recorded. The data are as follows and can also be found in the file **bagels.xlsx**.

Day	Store 1	Store 2	Store 3
Monday	156	140	130
Tuesday	169	182	131
Wednesday	157	177	139
Thursday	135	151	132
Friday	158	139	146
Saturday	170	213	145
Sunday	175	188	171

a. Using $\alpha = 0.05$, does there appear to be a difference in the number of bagels sold per day by the three stores?
b. Was blocking effective? Why or why not?
c. If warranted, determine which pairs of stores were different using $\alpha = 0.05$.
d. Verify your results with Excel.

11.27 Warehouse clubs such as Costco, BJ's, and Sam's Club compete with traditional supermarkets by advertising lower prices to customers who are willing to pay a membership fee and purchase in bulk quantities. Suppose a consumer group would like to investigate if warehouse clubs have different average prices than traditional supermarkets. Data in the Excel file **warehouse.xlsx** show the price of 11 grocery items from a supermarket and three warehouse clubs.

a. Choose the most appropriate ANOVA procedure using $\alpha = 0.05$ to determine if a difference exists in the average price of these items at the four stores?
b. Was blocking effective? Why or why not?
c. If warranted, determine which pairs of stores were different using $\alpha = 0.05$.
d. Verify your results with Excel.

11.3 Two-Way ANOVA: Examining the Effects Two Factors Have on the Means of Populations

So far in this chapter, we have considered a one-way ANOVA, which examines the effect that one main factor has on the observed data. I then introduced a randomized block ANOVA, which uses a blocking factor to reduce some of the variation in hopes of improving our chances of discovering a difference in the population means due to the main factor.

A **two-way ANOVA** is a procedure in which we examine the simultaneous effect that two main factors have on the observed data.

Now that we have mastered both the one-way and randomized block ANOVA procedures, I'll wrap up this chapter with **two-way ANOVA**. A two-way ANOVA examines the simultaneous effect that two main factors have on the observed data. To demonstrate a two-ANOVA technique, let's use the following example.

Recently, there was an article in *USA Today* titled "U.S. Fliers Pay Much More Than Europeans." The article reported that transatlantic round-trip flights originating in the United States cost considerably more than the same flights originating in Europe. To investigate this phenomenon, I personally gathered the data shown in Table 11.26 which displays round-trip airfares between Chicago and London for three different airlines originating in both cities. These data can also be found in the Excel file **airfares.xlsx**.

TABLE 11.26 | ROUND-TRIP AIRFARE DATA FOR FLIGHTS BETWEEN CHICAGO AND LONDON

	UNITED AIRLINES ($)	AIR FRANCE ($)	BRITISH AIRWAYS ($)
Flights originated in Chicago	1,063	1,314	1,442
	1,299	1,493	1,413
	995	1,443	1,063
	1,299	1,577	1,442
	1,406	1,314	1,575
Flights originated in London	1,015	1,374	1,603
	856	977	1,531
	802	1,043	1,079
	850	1,070	807
	935	1,428	870

With a two-way ANOVA test, we need to identify two main factors from our data. The convention that I'll use in this section is to assign Factor A to the levels associated with the columns in Table 11.26, of which there are three airlines (United Airlines, Air France, and British Airways). Factor B will be assigned to the levels associated with the rows in Table 11.26, which is the city from which the round-trip flight originated—either Chicago or London. Each of these factors has the potential to contribute variability to the airfares. The purpose of our two-way ANOVA procedure is to simultaneously measure the impact that *both* of these factors have on the price of a trip. More specifically, we are interested in answering the following two questions:

1. Do the average airfares for round-trip flights between the two cities differ among the three airlines? (In other words, is there a difference between the Factor A means?)
2. Do the round-trip airfares differ among the airlines depending on whether the flights originated in London or Chicago? (In other words, is there a difference between the Factor B means)?

A **cell** in a two-way ANOVA is a specific combination of one level from Factor A and one level from Factor B.

Replications represent the number of data values assigned to each cell in a two-way ANOVA table.

The top half of Table 11.26 displays, for each airline, five airfares for flights that originated in Chicago, flew to London, and returned to Chicago. The bottom half of the table shows matched airfares for the same days for flights that originated in London, flew to Chicago, and returned to London. A **cell** in a two-way ANOVA is a specific combination of one level from Factor A and one level from Factor B. Table 11.26 shows a total of six cells $(3 \times 2 = 6)$ because Factor A (the airline companies) has three levels and Factor B has two levels (Chicago-originated flights and London-originated flights). The five airfares in the United Airlines cell for flights originating in Chicago are known as **replications** because we have five observations for the same level of both factors. The procedure that I will demonstrate requires the same number of replications to occur in each cell.

It is not advisable to perform the two-way ANOVA procedure manually because of the number of calculations required. Instead, I will rely on Excel to provide the ANOVA results.

Using Excel for a Two-Way ANOVA

Excel's Data Analysis can perform a two-way ANOVA procedure for our airfare example. Those of you with Excel for Mac can go to the textbook's Web site for instructions to perform two-way ANOVA using PHStat.

1. Either open Excel file **airfares.xlsx** or enter the airfare data values in Columns A, B, C, and D as Figure 11.16A shows.
2. Go to **Data** and click on **Data Analysis** on the right side of the ribbon as shown in Figure 11.16A. This opens the **Data Analysis** dialog box.
3. Select **ANOVA: Two-Factor with Replication**. Click **OK**.

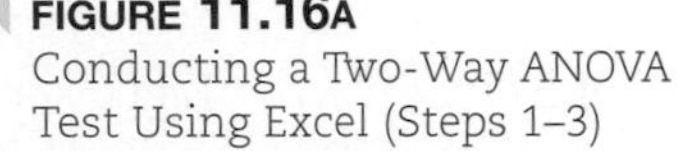

FIGURE 11.16A Conducting a Two-Way ANOVA Test Using Excel (Steps 1–3)

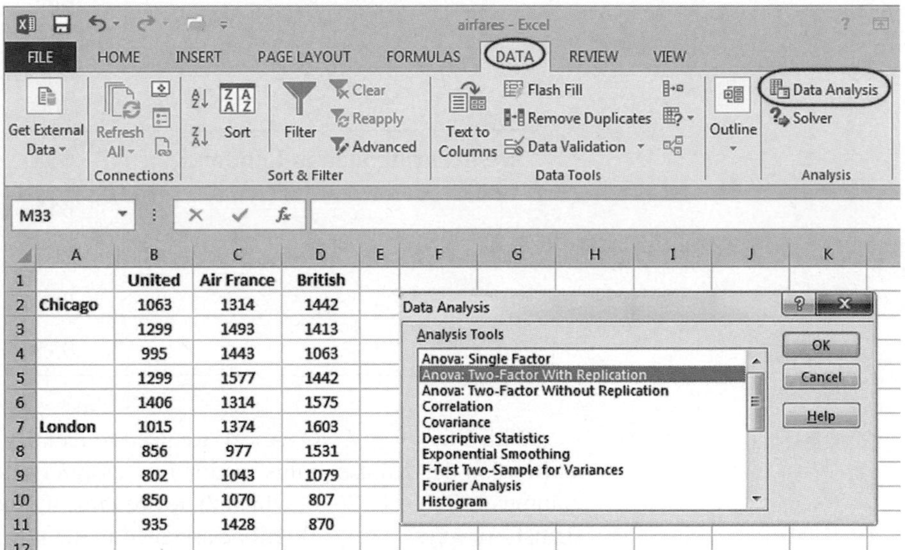

4. Fill in the **ANOVA: Two-Factor with Replication** dialog box as shown in Figure 11.16B. The **Rows per sample:** input refers to the number of replications per cell, which in our airfare example is 5. Click **OK**.

FIGURE 11.16B Conducting a Two-Way ANOVA Test Using Excel (Step 4)

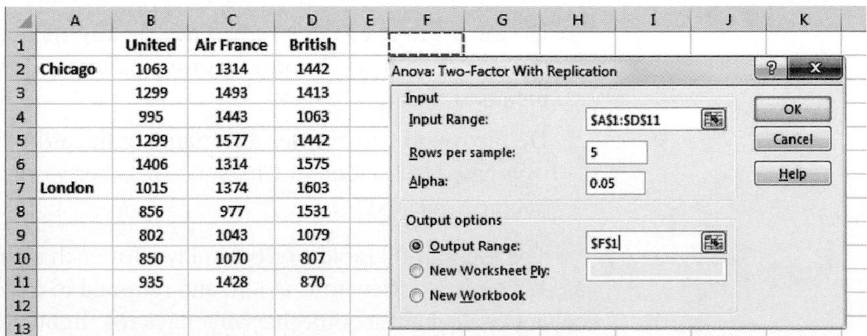

Figure 11.16C shows the two-way ANOVA output for the airfare example. How the output is derived will be explained in the next section.

FIGURE 11.16C
Conducting a Two-Way ANOVA Test Using Excel (Final Result)

	A	B	C	D	E	F	G	H	I	J	K	L
1		United	Air France	British		Anova: Two-Factor With Replication						
2	Chicago	1063	1314	1442								
3		1299	1493	1413		SUMMARY	United	Air France	British	Total		
4		995	1443	1063		*Chicago*						
5		1299	1577	1442		Count	5	5	5	15		
6		1406	1314	1575		Sum	6062	7141	6935	20138		
7	London	1015	1374	1603		Average	1212.4	1428.2	1387	1342.533		
8		856	977	1531		Variance	30515.8	13160.7	36761.5	32357.55		
9		802	1043	1079								
10		850	1070	807		*London*						
11		935	1428	870		Count	5	5	5	15		
12						Sum	4458	5892	5890	16240		
13						Average	891.6	1178.4	1178	1082.667		
14						Variance	7034.3	42801.3	136885	72905.81		
15												
16						*Total*						
17						Count	10	10	10			
18						Sum	10520	13033	12825			
19						Average	1052	1303.3	1282.5			
20						Variance	45275.7778	42205.3444	89309.83			
21												
22												
23						ANOVA						
24						*Source of Variation*	*SS*	*df*	*MS*	*F*	*P-value*	*F crit*
25						Sample	506480.133	1	506480.1	11.37482	0.002521	4.259677
26						Columns	389048.6	2	194524.3	4.368738	0.024099	3.402826
27						Interaction	16004.0667	2	8002.033	0.179714	0.836623	3.402826
28						Within	1068634.4	24	44526.43			
29												
30						Total	1980167.2	29				
31												

In the Excel output, Factor A corresponds to the "Columns" source of variation, whereas Factor B data can be found in the "Sample" source of variation.

The Mean Sum of Squares for a Two-Way ANOVA

The logic behind a two-way ANOVA is similar to the ANOVA topics we have already covered. Figure 11.17 shows the partitioning of the total sum of squares (*SST*) for two-way ANOVA, which still represents the total variation for all of the data values.

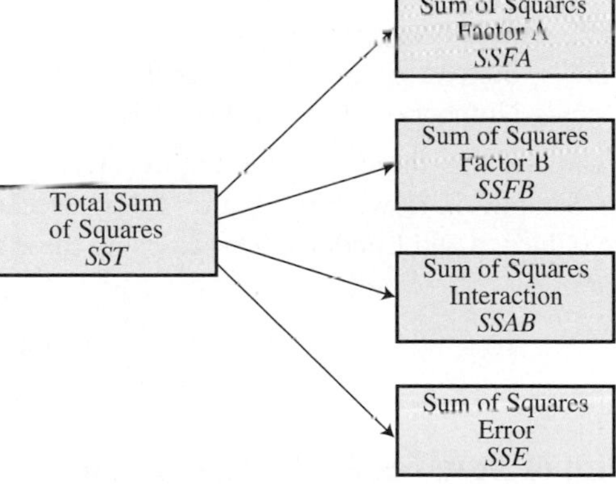

FIGURE 11.17
Partitioning the Total Sum of Squares (SST) in a Two-Way ANOVA

As you can see in Figure 11.17, the total sum of squares (*SST*) is partitioned into the following four sums of squares:

1. Sum of squares Factor A (*SSFA*)
2. Sum of squares Factor B (*SSFB*)
3. Sum of squares interaction (*SSAB*)
4. Sum of squares error (*SSE*)

Each of these will be discussed in the following sections.

The Sum of Squares for Factor A (*SSFA*)

The **sum of squares for Factor A (*SSFA*)** measures the variation between the Factor A means and the grand mean for all the data.

The **sum of squares for Factor A (*SSFA*)** measures the variation between the Factor A means (airlines) and the grand mean for all of the data. Using Equation 11.20, we utilize the *SSFA* to determine the **mean sum of squares for Factor A (*MSFA*)**.

Formula 11.20 for the Mean Sum of Squares for Factor A (MSFA)

$$MSFA = \frac{\text{Sum of squares factor A}}{a - 1} = \frac{SSFA}{a - 1}$$

where

$MSFA$ = The mean sum of squares for Factor A
$SSFA$ = The sum of squares for Factor A
a = The number of levels for Factor A

We can find these values in Figure 11.16C. The variation due to Factor A is labeled as "Columns" in Row 26 in Figure 11.16C. Because we have three airlines in our data, $a = 3$.

$$MSFA = \frac{SSFA}{a - 1} = \frac{389{,}048.6}{3 - 1} = 194{,}524.3$$

The Sum of Squares for Factor B ($SSFB$)

The **sum of squares for Factor B (*SSFB*)** measures the variation between the Factor B means and the grand mean for all the data.

The **sum of squares for Factor B (*SSFB*)** measures the variation between the Factor B means (flight-origination city) and the grand mean for all of the data. We use the *SSFB* to determine the **mean sum of squares for Factor B (*MSFB*)** using Equation 11.21.

Formula 11.21 for the Mean Sum of Squares for Factor B (MSFB)

$$MSFB = \frac{\text{Sum of squares factor B}}{b - 1} = \frac{SSFB}{b - 1}$$

where

$MSFB$ = Mean sum of squares for Factor B
$SSFB$ = Sum of squares for Factor B
b = Number of levels for Factor B

We can also find these values in Figure 11.16C. The variation due to Factor B is labeled as "Sample" in Row 25 in Figure 11.16C. Because we have two cities in which flights originate (Chicago and London), $b = 2$. Using these values in Equation 11.21, we get the following:

$$MSFB = \frac{SSFB}{b - 1} = \frac{506{,}480.1}{2 - 1} = 506{,}480.1$$

The Sum of Squares for Interaction of Factors A and B ($SSAB$)

The **sum of squares interaction (*SSAB*)** represents the variation due to the effect that Factor A has on Factor B, or vice versa.

Because we are examining the simultaneous effect of Factors A and B on the airline fares, we have to consider any interaction between the two factors themselves that could contribute to some of the variation in airfares. The **sum of squares interaction (*SSAB*)** represents the variation due to the effect that Factor A has on Factor B, or vice versa.

For example, if airfares were consistently lower for flights originating in London on United Airlines and Air France, but the same flights were consistently higher for British Airways, we would observe an interaction between Factors A and B. This is because the airfares for a level in Factor A (British Airways) have been influenced by a level in Factor B (London).

We'll discuss interaction in more detail in another section of this chapter. In the meantime, all you need to know for the time being is that, if interaction between Factors A and B is present, we cannot rely on the validity of the ANOVA results to measure the effect the factors have on the data. In other words, interaction causes headaches and we hope not to see it in our analysis.

The sum of squares for the interaction of Factors A and B is used to determine the **mean sum of squares for interaction of Factors A and B (*MSAB*)**, which can be found using Equation 11.22.

Formula 11.22 for the Mean Sum of Squares for Interaction of Factors A and B (MSAB)

$$MSAB = \frac{SSAB}{(a-1)(b-1)}$$

where

$MSAB$ = The mean sum of squares for interaction of Factors A and B
$SSAB$ = The sum of squares for interaction of Factors A and B

The **mean sum of squares for interaction of Factors A and B (*MSAB*)** is found by dividing the sum of squares interaction (SSAB) by $(a-1)(b-1)$

Again, we can find these values in Figure 11.16C in the "Interaction" source of variation found in Row 27 in Figure 11.16C. Using these values in Equation 11.22, we get the following:

$$MSAB = \frac{SSAB}{(a-1)(b-1)} = \frac{16{,}004.1}{(3-1)(2-1)} = 8{,}002.0$$

The Sum of Squares for Error (*SSE*)

The **sum of square error (*SSE*)** for two-way ANOVA represents the variation in the data that's left over after we have removed the variation from Factor A, Factor B, and the interaction from Factors A and B.

The **sum of squares error (*SSE*)** is the variation in the data that's left over after we have removed the variation from the following:

- Factor A
- Factor B
- The interaction from Factors A and B

The **mean square error (*MSE*)** for two-way ANOVA is found by dividing the sum of squares error (*SSE*) by $n_T - (ab)$.

In other words, the *SSE* represents the randomness in the data that is not accounted for by any factor or interaction between the factors. We use *SSE* to determine the **mean square error (*MSE*)** for two-way ANOVA using Equation 11.23.

Formula 11.23 for the Mean Squares Error (MSE) for a Two-Way ANOVA

$$MSE = \frac{SSE}{n_T - (ab)}$$

where

MSE = The mean square error
SSE = The sum of squares error
n_T = The total number of data values

We can also find these values in Figure 11.16C in the "Within" source of variation (see Row 28). Because each airline has 10 airfares (five replications from each originating city) and we have three airlines, we have a total of 30 data values $(n_T = 30)$. Using these values in Equation 11.23, we get the following:

$$MSE = \frac{SSE}{n_T - (ab)} = \frac{1{,}068{,}634.4}{30 - (3)(2)} = \frac{1{,}068{,}634.4}{30 - 6} = 44{,}526.4$$

Multiplying the number of replications (5) by the number of airlines $(a = 3)$ by the number of cities $(b = 2)$ results in the total number of observations $(n_T = 30)$.

Interpreting the Output for a Two-Way ANOVA

We are now ready to put all of these mean sum of squares together to determine if the population means of the airfares are different from one another.

Step 1: Test for interaction between Factors A and B.

We perform this test first because if we do find that interaction exists, we are stopped in our tracks when it comes to using a two-way ANOVA. The presence of interaction interferes with the interpretation of the impact of Factors A and B on the population means. I'll conduct all of the hypothesis tests using $\alpha = 0.05$. The hypothesis statement for the interaction is as follows:

The null hypothesis for interaction is always that Factors A and B do not interact.

H_0: Factors A and B do not interact

H_1: Factors A and B do interact

The test statistic for the interaction hypothesis is shown as Equation 11.24.

Formula 11.24 for the Interaction Test Statistic

$$F_{AB} = \frac{MSAB}{MSE}$$

After failing to reject the null hypothesis that tests for interaction, we can proceed testing for Factors A and B. Had we rejected the null hypothesis for interaction, the test for Factors A and B would be unreliable.

Using our results from the previous section, we have the following:

$$F_{AB} = \frac{MSAB}{MSE} = \frac{8{,}002.0}{44{,}526.4} = 0.18$$

The p-value in Cell K27 in Figure 11.16C equals 0.8366. This value represents the probability of observing an F-statistic greater than 0.18 if the null hypothesis were true. Because this probability is more than $\alpha = 0.05$, we fail to reject the null hypothesis. We do not have enough evidence to conclude that interaction between Factors A and B exists. We can now move on to the next step and test the effect that each main factor (each airline and each city from which the flights originate) has on our conclusion.

Step 2: Test for Factor A.

Factor A is defined as the airlines. Using the following hypothesis statement, we can now test if the airline means are different.

This alternative hypothesis is testing to determine if the average airfares for United Airlines, Air France, and British Airways are different.

H_0: $\mu_{A1} = \mu_{A2} = \mu_{A3}$

H_1: Not all Factor A means are equal

where

μ_{Ai} = The population mean for the *ith* level of Factor A

The test statistic for the Factor A hypothesis is shown in Equation 11.25.

Formula 11.25 for the Factor A Test Statistic

$$F_A = \frac{MSFA}{MSE}$$

Using our results from the previous section, we have the following:

$$F_A = \frac{MSFA}{MSE} = \frac{194{,}524.3}{44{,}526.4} = 4.37$$

The p-value, which is shown in Cell K26 in Figure 11.16C and which equals 0.0241, represents the probability of observing an F-statistic greater than 4.37 if the null hypothesis is true. Because this probability is much less than $\alpha = 0.05$, we can reject the null hypothesis. In other words, we have enough evidence to conclude that the average airfares for round-trip flights between Chicago and London do differ among the three airlines. The average airfares can be found in Cells G19, H19, and I19 for United Airlines, Air France, and British Airways, respectively, in Figure 11.16C and are summarized in Table 11.27.

TABLE 11.27 | AVERAGE AIRFARE BY AIRLINE

AIRLINE	AVERAGE AIRFARE ($)
United Airlines	1,052.00
Air France	1,303.30
British Airways	1,282.50

Step 3: Test for Factor B.

Factor B is defined as the originating city for a round-trip flight. We can now make the following hypothesis statement to test if the Factor B means are different:

This alternative hypothesis is testing to determine if the average airfares for flights originating in Chicago and London are different.

$$H_0: \mu_{B1} = \mu_{B2}$$

$$H_1: \text{Not all Factor B means are equal}$$

where

$\mu_{Bi} =$ The population mean for the *ith* level of Factor B

The test statistic for the Factor B hypothesis is shown as Equation 11.26.

Formula 11.26 for the Factor B Test Statistic

$$F_B = \frac{MSFB}{MSE}$$

Using our results from the previous section, we have the following:

$$F_B = \frac{MSFB}{MSE} = \frac{506{,}480.1}{44{,}526.4} = 11.37$$

The p-value in Cell K25 in Figure 11.16C equals 0.0025. It represents the probability of observing an F-statistic greater than 11.37 if the null hypothesis is true. Because this probability is much less than $\alpha = 0.05$, we can again reject the null hypothesis. In other words, we have enough evidence to conclude that the average airfares for flights originating in Chicago are different from those originating in London. These average airfares can be found in Cell J7 for Chicago and Cell J13 for London in Figure 11.16C. Table 11.28 summarizes the averages for the two cities.

TABLE 11.28 | AVERAGE AIRFARE BY ORIGINATING CITY

CITY	AVERAGE AIRFARE ($)
Chicago	1,342.53
London	1,082.67

It appears that across all three airlines, flights originating in Chicago are much more expensive than those starting in London. Apparently, the *USA Today* article was accurate.

Step 4: Summarize the results in an ANOVA table.

Table 11.29 is a summary table for the two-way ANOVA procedure.

TABLE 11.29 | Two-Way ANOVA Summary Table

SOURCE	SUM OF SQUARES	DEGREES OF FREEDOM	MEAN SUM OF SQUARES	F
B	$SSFB$	$b - 1$	$MSFB = \frac{SSFB}{b - 1}$	$F_B = \frac{MSFB}{MSE}$
A	$SSFA$	$a - 1$	$MSFA = \frac{SSFA}{a - 1}$	$F_A = \frac{MSFA}{MSE}$
AB	$SSAB$	$(a - 1)(b - 1)$	$MSAB = \frac{SSAB}{(a - 1)(b - 1)}$	$F_{AB} = \frac{MSAB}{MSE}$
Error	SSE	$n_T - (a)(b)$	$MSE = \frac{SSE}{n_T - (a)(b)}$	
Total	SST	$n_T - 1$		

Table 11.30 summarizes the results of the airfare two-way ANOVA.

TABLE 11.30 | Two-Way ANOVA Summary Table for the Airfare Data

SOURCE	SUM OF SQUARES	DEGREES OF FREEDOM	MEAN SUM OF SQUARES	F
Factor B	506,480.1	1	506,480.1	11.37
Factor A	389,048.6	2	194,524.3	4.37
Interaction	16,004.1	2	8,002.0	0.18
Error	1,068,634.4	24	44,526.4	
Total	1,980,167.2	29		

It's time for me to take a break and turn this over to you so you can try your own two-way ANOVA problem.

YOUR TURN #7

Katie is a regional manager for Target and is responsible for the performance of three New Jersey stores located in Gloucester, Deptford, and Voorhees. Katie has read some research about the impact that environmental scents have on customers' perceptions. To investigate this phenomenon, Katie made arrangements for each store to be scented with lavender for a period of time and then with citrus for another period of time. Customers were surveyed on a scale of 1–20 about their overall impressions of the stores during these periods. Data were also collected when the stores were unscented. The following table shows these results, which can also be found in the file **target.xlsx**.

	Lavender	Citrus	Unscented
Gloucester	13	18	12
	16	20	16
	19	15	15
	16	18	15
Deptford	15	17	14
	12	17	9
	14	14	12
	13	17	13

(continued)

	Lavender	Citrus	Unscented
Voorhees	11	15	15
	19	16	16
	15	20	11
	16	18	12

a. Perform a two-way ANOVA using Excel to test the effects Factor A (the scent or lack of it) and Factor B (the location) have on the perceptions of customers, along with any interaction of the two factors.
b. Construct an ANOVA summary table for this problem.
c. State your conclusions using $\alpha = 0.05$.

Answers can be found on ▶ **page 572**

Revisiting Interaction

Earlier in this chapter, we discussed the issue of interaction between the two main factors in a two-way ANOVA. The best way to explain interaction is through an interaction plot that displays the relationship between the factors. Let's start this section by using Excel to show how to construct this plot for our airfare example:

Excel for Mac users can find these instructions on the textbook's Web site.

1. Open the Excel file **airfares.xlsx** or enter the airfare data values in Cells A1 through D11 as shown in Figure 11.18.
2. Calculate the mean for each of the six cells as shown in Cells B15 through D16 in Figure 11.18. For example, Cell B15 shows the average airfare for the five flights originating in Chicago with United Airlines. Cell B15 has the Excel formula =AVERAGE(B2:B6). Repeat this calculation for the remaining five cells.
3. Calculate the difference between the cell means for each airline. For example, Cell B18 has the formula = (B15 − B16). Repeat this calculation for Cells C18 and D18.
4. Highlight Cells A14 through D16 as shown in Figure 11.18.
5. Go to **Insert** and click on **Line** on the middle of the ribbon as shown in Figure 11.18.
6. Select **Line with Markers** as shown in Figure 11.18.

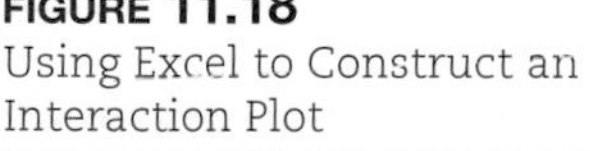

FIGURE 11.18
Using Excel to Construct an Interaction Plot

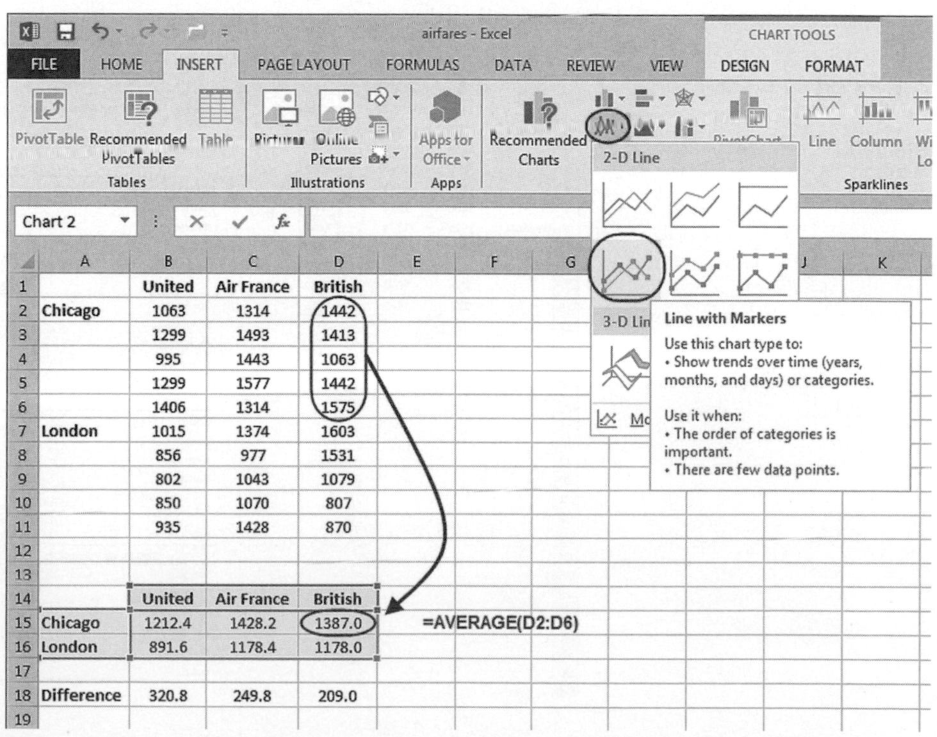

	A	B	C	D
1		United	Air France	British
2	Chicago	1063	1314	1442
3		1299	1493	1413
4		995	1443	1063
5		1299	1577	1442
6		1406	1314	1575
7	London	1015	1374	1603
8		856	977	1531
9		802	1043	1079
10		850	1070	807
11		935	1428	870
12				
13				
14		United	Air France	British
15	Chicago	1212.4	1428.2	1387.0
16	London	891.6	1178.4	1178.0
17				
18	Difference	320.8	249.8	209.0
19				

Figure 11.19 shows the resulting interaction plot for our airfare data.

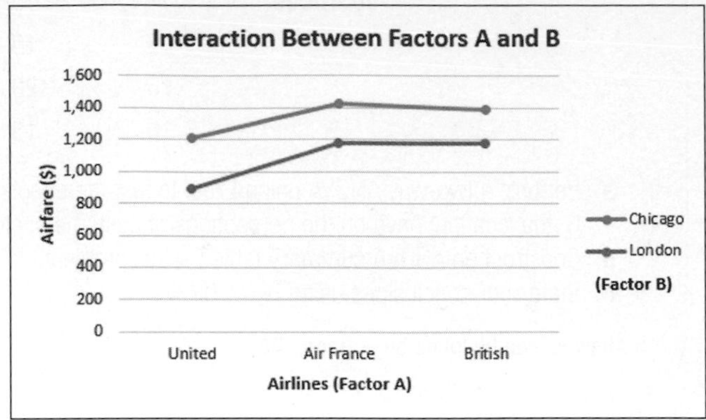

FIGURE 11.19
An Interaction Plot for the Airfare Example (No Interaction)

The orange line in Figure 11.19 plots the average airfare for each airline for one level in Factor B (flights originating in London). The blue line represents the average airfare for each airline for the other level in Factor B (flights originating in Chicago). The distance between these two lines represents the average difference in airfare between flights originating in Chicago and London that was calculated in Row 18 in Figure 11.18. You saw in Figure 11.18 that the difference ranges from $209 for British Airways to $320.80 for United Airlines. Figure 11.19 shows this result visually: The average airfare is more expensive when a flight originates in Chicago, regardless of which airline we examine.

The fact that the two lines in the figure are close to being parallel to one another indicates that there is little or no interaction between Factors A and B. In other words, it does not matter which airline we examine. The average airfare across the three airlines will always be higher for flights originating from Chicago. In general, there is no interaction between Factors A and B when the data values for each level of one factor behave in the same fashion across all levels of the other factor.

Figure 11.19 shows an instance in which there was little or no interaction between Factors A and B. But what does interaction look like when it does occur, you might be wondering? I'm glad you asked. To illustrate the presence of interaction, I'm going to rearrange the airfare data by swapping the two sets of cells for British Airways shown in Figure 11.20 (the cells in the red boxes). In this new spreadsheet, the Chicago flights are still more expensive for United Airlines and Air France. However, the London flights are now more expensive for British Airways.

FIGURE 11.20
A Two-Way ANOVA with Interaction

	A	B	C	D	E	F	G	H	I	J	K	L
1		United	Air France	British		Anova: Two-Factor With Replication						
2	Chicago	1063	1314	1603								
3		1299	1493	1531		SUMMARY	United	Air France	British	Total		
4		995	1443	1079		*Chicago*						
5		1299	1577	807		Count	5	5	5	15		
6		1406	1314	870		Sum	6062	7141	5890	19093		
7	London	1015	1374	1442		Average	1212.4	1428.2	1178	1272.867		
8		856	977	1413		Variance	30515.8	13160.7	136885	64726.27		
9		802	1043	1063								
10		850	1070	1442		*London*						
11		935	1428	1575		Count	5	5	5	15		
12						Sum	4458	5892	6935	17285		
13						Average	891.6	1178.4	1387	1152.333		
14						Variance	7034.3	42801.3	36761.5	68931.24		
15												
16						*Total*						
17						Count	10	10	10			
18						Sum	10520	13033	12825			
19						Average	1052	1303.3	1282.5			
20						Variance	45275.78	42205.3444	89309.83			
21												
22												
23						ANOVA						
24						*Source of Variation*	*SS*	*df*	*MS*	*F*	*P-value*	*F crit*
25						Sample	108962.1	1	108962.1	2.447134	0.130831	4.259677
26						Columns	389048.6	2	194524.3	4.368738	0.024099	3.402826
27						Interaction	413522.1	2	206761	4.643557	0.019734	3.402826
28						Within	1068634	24	44526.43			
29												
30						Total	1980167	29				
31												

Allow me to restate the hypothesis statement for the interaction of Factors A and B.

H_0: Factor A and B do not interact

H_1: Factor A and B do interact

The *p*-value for the interaction of factors (shown in Cell K27) is now 0.0197. Because this value is less than $\alpha = 0.05$, we reject the null hypothesis and conclude that interaction between Factors A and B exists. Figure 11.21 shows the interaction plot for the revised data.

FIGURE 11.21
An Interaction Plot for the Airfare Example (Interaction Present)

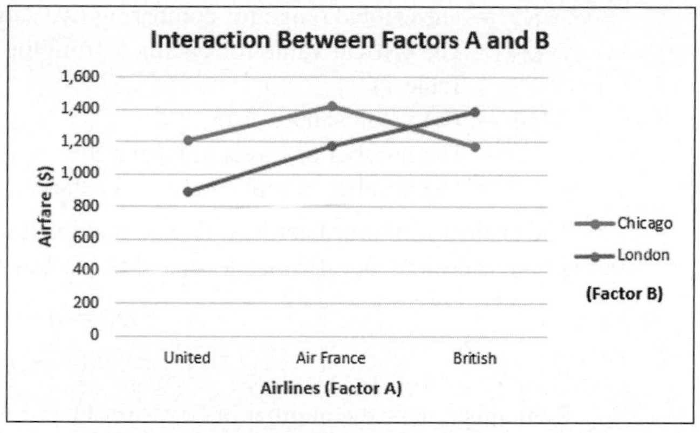

Notice now that the orange and blue lines intersect one another, which is an indication that interaction is present between the two main factors. Here, the more expensive originating city depends on which airline you are considering. A Chicago origination is more expensive on United and Air France. However, a London origination is now more expensive on British Airways. Intersecting lines like the ones we see in Figure 11.21 suggest the presence of interaction between Factors A and B. Interaction is present because the pattern that the more expensive flights originate in Chicago does not hold true across all airlines. Under these circumstances, the conclusions from testing Factor A and Factor B with a two-way ANOVA can be unreliable.

Just because lines cross in Figure 11.21 does not mean that interaction in the populations exists. The plot in Figure 11.21 is based on a sample that is subject to sampling error. The *p*-value in Figure 11.20 is the deciding factor for interaction in the populations.

When interaction is present, however, all is not lost. Another option would be to perform a one-way ANOVA for Factor A for each level of Factor B, or vice versa. For example, we could perform a one-way ANOVA to see if there is a difference in the mean airfares of the airlines for flights originating in Chicago. We could then repeat this analysis for flights originating in London.

YOUR TURN #8

Construct an interaction plot for Factors A and B using the data shown in Your Turn #7. Hint: There will be three horizontal lines in this plot.

Answer can be found on ▶ **page 572**

Multiple Comparisons: Comparing Pairs of Population Means (Two-Way ANOVA)

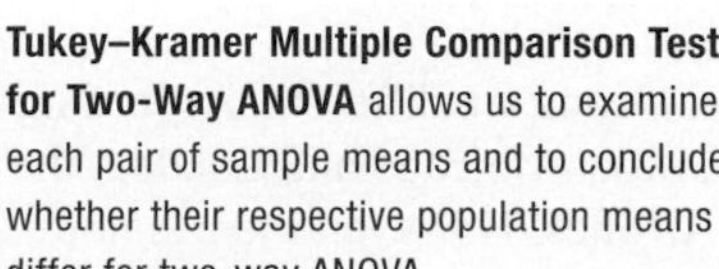

Tukey–Kramer Multiple Comparison Test for Two-Way ANOVA allows us to examine each pair of sample means and to conclude whether their respective population means differ for two-way ANOVA.

When interaction between Factors A and B is not present and we have found that a difference in means does exist with either factor, we can perform the **Tukey–Kramer Multiple Comparison Test for Two-Way ANOVA** (now, that's a mouthful). This test is very similar to the previous comparison tests that we've already encountered. We'll compare the absolute difference in sample means from our original airfare example (without interaction) with a critical range to determine which means are different.

First, we'll calculate the critical range for Factor A, CR_A, using Equation 11.27.

Formula 11.27 for the Critical Range for Factor A

$$CR_A = Q_A\sqrt{\frac{MSE}{br}}$$

where

CR_A = The critical range for comparing two sample means for Factor A
Q_A = The critical value for Factor A from the studentized range table (Appendix A, Table 7)
MSE = The mean square error
b = The number of levels in Factor B
r = The number of replications in each cell

The critical value for Factor A, Q_A, is found in Table 7 in Appendix A. The value is based on our desired significance level and the following two degrees of freedom:

$$D_1 = a$$
$$D_2 = ab(r - 1)$$

Remember, a = the number of levels for Factor A. Using the airfare data with $a = 3$ airlines, $b = 2$ cities, and $r = 5$ replications per cell, the degrees of freedom are as follows:

$$D_1 = a = 3$$
$$D_2 = ab(r - 1) = (3)(2)(5 - 1) = 24$$

Using $\alpha = 0.05$, Table 7 in Appendix A shows that the critical value is $Q_A = 3.53$. Recalling that $MSE = 44{,}526.4$ as shown in Figure 11.16C, the critical range for the airfare example can be found with Equation 11.27:

$$CR_A = Q_A\sqrt{\frac{MSE}{br}} = (3.53)\sqrt{\frac{44{,}526.4}{(2)(5)}} = (3.53)(66.73) = 235.6$$

Table 11.27 summarizes the Factor A means for each airline. Using these data, Table 11.31 compares the absolute differences in the sample means with the critical value and states the decision. Note that United Airlines = Sample 1, Air France = Sample 2, and British Airways = Sample 3.

TABLE 11.31 | DETERMINING WHICH SAMPLE MEANS ARE DIFFERENT FOR FACTOR A

$\lvert\bar{x}_i - \bar{x}_j\rvert$	CR_A	DECISION
$\lvert\bar{x}_1 - \bar{x}_2\rvert = \lvert 1{,}052.0 - 1{,}303.3\rvert = 251.3$	235.6	$251.3 > 235.6$; means are different
$\lvert\bar{x}_1 - \bar{x}_3\rvert = \lvert 1{,}052.0 - 1{,}282.5\rvert = 230.5$	235.6	$230.5 < 235.6$; means are not different
$\lvert\bar{x}_2 - \bar{x}_3\rvert = \lvert 1{,}303.3 - 1{,}282.5\rvert = 20.8$	235.6	$20.8 < 235.6$; means are not different

If $\lvert\bar{x}_i - \bar{x}_j\rvert > CR_A$, we can conclude that the population means are different. According to Table 11.31, we can conclude that for round-trip flights between Chicago and London, the average airfare for Air France is higher than it is for United Airlines. However, there is not enough evidence to claim there is a difference in the round-trip airfares between United Airlines and British Airways and between Air France and British Airways.

Next, we'll calculate the critical range for Factor B, CR_B, using Equation 11.28.

Formula 11.28 for the Critical Range for Factor B

$$CR_B = Q_B\sqrt{\frac{MSE}{ar}}$$

where

CR_B = The critical range for comparing two sample means for Factor B
Q_B = The critical value for Factor B from the studentized range table (Appendix A, Table 7)
MSE = The mean square error
a = The number of levels in Factor A
r = The number of replications in each cell

The critical value for Factor B, Q_B, is found in Table 7 from Appendix A. The value is based on our desired significance level and the following two degrees of freedom:

$$D_1 = b$$
$$D_2 = ab(r - 1)$$

Using the airfare data with $a = 3$ airlines, $b = 2$ cities, and $r = 5$ replications per cell, the degrees of freedom are as follows:

$$D_1 = b = 2$$
$$D_2 = ab(r - 1) = (3)(2)(5 - 1) = 24$$

Using $\alpha = 0.05$, Table 7 in Appendix A shows that the critical value is $Q_B = 2.92$. With $MSE = 44{,}526.4$, the critical range for the airfare example can be found using Equation 11.28:

$$CR_B = Q_B\sqrt{\frac{MSE}{ar}} = (2.92)\sqrt{\frac{44{,}526.4}{(3)(5)}} = (2.92)(54.48) = 159.08$$

Normally, we would not bother performing a multiple comparison test for a factor with only two levels, such as Factor B in our airfare example, because there is only one pair of sample means to examine: the mean fare for flights originating from Chicago and the mean fare for flights originating from London. However, I'll perform the test in this instance to provide you with an example of how to proceed (you're very welcome). Table 11.28 provides us with sample means for the two levels in Factor B. Using these data, Table 11.32 compares the absolute difference in the sample means with the critical value and states the decision.

TABLE 11.32 | DETERMINING WHICH SAMPLE MEANS ARE DIFFERENT FOR FACTOR B

$\lvert\bar{x}_i - \bar{x}_j\rvert$	CR_B	DECISION
$\lvert\bar{x}_1 - \bar{x}_2\rvert = \lvert 1{,}342.5 - 1{,}082.7\rvert = 259.8$	159.08	$259.8 > 159.08$; means are different

Table 11.32 simply confirms what we already knew. Round-trip airfares between Chicago and London are significantly cheaper if the flight originates in London rather than Chicago. Who would have guessed?

Take advantage of this last Your Turn problem to make sure you understand how to perform multiple comparisons with a two-way ANOVA.

YOUR TURN #9

Using the data from Your Turn #7, perform a multiple comparison test to see if there is difference in the means of the populations. Then state your conclusions.

Answers can be found on ▶ **page 573**

11.3 Section Problems

Basic Skills

11.28 Consider the following partially completed two-way ANOVA summary table:

Source	Sum of Squares	Degrees of Freedom	Mean Sum of Squares	F
Factor A	100	2		
Factor B		2		
Interaction	60			
Error	450	45		
Total	730	53		

a. Complete the remaining entries in the table.
b. How many replications are present for each cell?
c. Using $\alpha = 0.05$, is there significant interaction between Factors A and B?
d. Using $\alpha = 0.05$, are the Factor A means different?
e. Using $\alpha = 0.05$, are the Factor B means different?

11.29 Consider the following data collected for a two-way ANOVA:

	Factor A		
Factor B	**Level 1**	**Level 2**	**Level 3**
Level 1	9	31	29
	18	20	31
	31	22	35
Level 2	21	22	34
	23	27	33
	13	21	23

a. Using $\alpha = 0.05$, is there significant interaction between Factors A and B?
b. Using $\alpha = 0.05$, are the Factor A means different?
c. Using $\alpha = 0.05$, are the Factor B means different?

11.30 Using the data from Problem 11.29, determine which means are different using $\alpha = 0.05$, when warranted.

11.31 Consider the following partially completed two-way ANOVA summary table:

Source	Sum of Squares	Degrees of Freedom	Mean Sum of Squares	F
Factor A		3	30.0	
Factor B	20			2.0
Interaction		6	7.0	1.4
Error		72		
Total				

a. Complete the remaining entries in the table.
b. How many replications are present for each cell?
c. Using $\alpha = 0.05$, is there significant interaction between Factors A and B?
d. Using $\alpha = 0.05$, are the Factor A means different?
e. Using $\alpha = 0.05$, are the Factor B means different?

11.32 Consider the following data collected for a two-way ANOVA:

	Factor A		
Factor B	**Level 1**	**Level 2**	**Level 3**
Level 1	8	9	10
	6	12	28
	14	19	24
Level 2	28	31	25
	10	21	36
	16	19	33
Level 3	39	40	38
	33	28	37
	23	40	31

a. Using $\alpha = 0.05$, is there significant interaction between Factors A and B?
b. Using $\alpha = 0.05$, are the Factor A means different?
c. Using $\alpha = 0.05$, are the Factor B means different?

11.33 Using the data from Problem 11.32, determine which means are different using $\alpha = 0.05$, when warranted.

Applications

11.34 Suppose the Robert H. Smith School of Business at the University of Maryland would like to compare the starting salaries for both men and women who graduated with different majors. The following data show starting salaries for random students from the most recent graduating class. These data can also be found in the file **starting salaries.xlsx**.

	Majors		
	Finance ($)	**Marketing ($)**	**Accounting ($)**
Women	45,400	41,700	52,600
	46,200	44,600	40,900
	48,100	41,400	47,000
	46,200	46,100	53,700
Men	49,200	43,900	44,000
	50,300	42,100	50,500
	43,100	43,700	45,300
	53,300	39,600	47,300

a. Using $\alpha = 0.05$, is there significant interaction between Factor A and Factor B (major and gender)?
b. Using a two-way ANOVA and $\alpha = 0.05$, does the major have an effect on a person's starting salary?
c. Using a two-way ANOVA and $\alpha = 0.05$, does gender have an effect on a person's starting salary?
d. If warranted, determine which means are significantly different using $\alpha = 0.05$.
e. Construct an interaction plot for the major and gender factors.

11.35 The recent *Wall Street Journal* article titled "The Power of a Gentle Nudge" cited a Stanford University study that researched the motivation of people to exercise. Participants were placed in one of three groups. After stating an exercise program, people in the first group received a phone call every three weeks from a trained health educator to ask about their exercise programs and encourage them to continue exercising. A second group received the same call from an automated system. The third group did not receive a call. The number of minutes spent exercising per week was recorded at the beginning of the program, after six months, and after one year. Suppose the following table provides data from this study. These data can also be found in the file **exercise.xlsx**.

	Type of Advice		
	Human Advice	**Automated Advice**	**No Advice**
At the beginning	93	64	68
	99	65	56
	118	106	64
	89	117	102
After six months	119	198	106
	167	242	97
	141	115	151
	121	166	74
After one year	104	186	144
	212	250	128
	173	140	101
	193	185	125

a. Using $\alpha = 0.05$, is there significant interaction between the type of advice and the length of the exercise program?
b. Using a two-way ANOVA and $\alpha = 0.05$, does the type of advice have an effect on the number of minutes the groups exercised per week?
c. Using a two-way ANOVA and $\alpha = 0.05$, does the length of the exercise program (the length of time since it began) have an effect on the number of minutes the groups exercised per week?
d. If warranted, determine which means are significantly different using $\alpha = 0.05$.
e. Construct an interaction plot for the type of advice and length of the exercise program (the length of time since it began).

11.36 Urban traffic congestion throughout the world has been increasing in recent years, especially in developing countries. The following table shows the number of minutes that randomly selected drivers spent stuck in traffic in various cities on both weekdays and weekends. The data for this problem can also be found in the file **traffic.xlsx**.

	City			
	Beijing	**New Delhi**	**Mexico City**	**New York**
Weekday	89	44	56	53
	74	113	81	65
	119	65	81	38
	67	76	99	42
	94	97	122	51
Weekend	80	81	35	30
	87	26	86	39
	69	104	75	44
	71	79	66	44
	58	77	36	42

a. Using $\alpha = 0.05$, is there significant interaction between the city and time of the week?
b. Using a two-way ANOVA and $\alpha = 0.05$, does the city have an effect on the amount of time stuck in traffic?
c. Using a two-way ANOVA and $\alpha = 0.05$, does the time of the week have an effect on the amount of time stuck in traffic?
d. If warranted, determine which means are significantly different using $\alpha = 0.05$.
e. Construct an interaction plot for the city and the time of the week.

11.37 A credit score is a numerical value between 300 and 850 that measures a person's creditworthiness. The following table shows the credit scores for randomly selected individuals from Texas, Pennsylvania, California, and Florida, who are grouped according to their ages. These data can also be found in the file **credit scores.xlsx**.

	State			
	TX	**PA**	**CA**	**FL**
20–39 years old	619	736	663	681
	671	607	506	632
	614	727	717	713
	517	794	574	620
40–59 years old	691	775	708	574
	700	645	728	697
	641	767	666	677
	639	669	716	629
60+ years old	766	743	756	765
	663	737	675	698
	672	718	696	795
	661	788	692	730

a. Using $\alpha = 0.05$, is there significant interaction between the state and age of the individual?
b. Using a two-way ANOVA and $\alpha = 0.05$, does the state have an effect on the person's credit score?

c. Using a two-way ANOVA and $\alpha = 0.05$, does the age group of the individual have an effect on their credit score?
d. If warranted, determine which means are significantly different using $\alpha = 0.05$.
e. Construct an interaction plot for the state and the age group.

11.38 Movie theater ticket prices have been increasing to accommodate the demand for movies formatted in 3D. The following data show the prices for adult tickets for three different movie formats in three different cities. These data can also be found in the file **ticket prices.xlsx**.

	Format		
	2D ($)	**3D ($)**	**IMAX 3D ($)**
New York	11	18	22
	11	19	13
	13	15	22
	11	15	19
	7	20	19
Atlanta	10	17	16
	11	14	19
	12	14	20
	11	16	15
	13	15	15
Dallas	5	14	16
	7	13	17
	8	11	14
	10	17	16
	8	12	15

a. Using $\alpha = 0.05$, is there significant interaction between the city and the movie format?
b. Using a two-way ANOVA and $\alpha = 0.05$, does the city have an effect on the cost of a movie?
c. Using a two-way ANOVA and $\alpha = 0.05$, does the movie format have an effect on the cost of a movie?
d. If warranted, determine which means are significantly different using $\alpha = 0.05$.
e. Construct an interaction plot for the city and the movie format.

11.39 The following table shows the retirement ages for a random sample of retirees from four different countries according to their genders. These data can also be found in the file **retirement.xlsx**.

	Country			
	Mexico	**Japan**	**United States**	**France**
Women	66	62	60	57
	73	65	62	70
	77	66	56	48
	74	65	67	51
	63	64	60	56
	78	60	66	56
Men	76	69	64	59
	67	64	68	63
	79	66	57	58
	76	67	72	59
	71	68	68	65
	69	75	57	59

a. Using $\alpha = 0.05$, is there significant interaction between the country and the gender?
b. Using a two-way ANOVA and $\alpha = 0.05$, does the country have an effect on the retirement age?
c. Using a two-way ANOVA and $\alpha = 0.05$, does the gender of the retiree have an effect on the retirement age?
d. Using $\alpha = 0.05$, if warranted, determine which means are significantly different.
e. Construct an interaction plot for country and gender.

CHAPTER 11 Summary

- An analysis of variance is a technique for performing a hypothesis test to compare three or more population means simultaneously.
- A factor in an ANOVA describes the cause of variation in the data.
- A level in ANOVA describes a category within the factor.
- To accurately conduct an analysis of variance the following set of assumptions must be made:
  - Each of the populations being compared must follow the normal probability distribution.
  - The populations being compared must have an equal variance.
  - The observations must be independent of one another. In other words, one data value can have no influence on other data values.
  - The observations must be either interval or ratio data.
- The null hypothesis for every ANOVA procedure states that all the population means are equal.
- The alternative hypothesis, therefore, claims that not all of the population means are equal.
- A one-way ANOVA is used when we are looking at the influence that one factor has on the data values.
  - The total sum of squares (*SST*) measures the amount of variation between each data value and the grand mean.
    - The mean square total (*MST*) is derived from the *SST* and is simply another term for the variance of the sample data.
  - The total sum of squares can be divided into the sum of squares between (*SSB*) and the sum of squares within (*SSW*).
  - The sum of squares between measures the variation between each sample mean and the grand mean of the data.
    - The mean square between (*MSB*) provides an estimate for the population variance, σ^2, if the null hypothesis is true.
  - The sum of squares within (*SSW*) measures the variation between each data value and the corresponding sample mean.
    - The mean square within (*MSW*) provides another estimate for the population variance, σ^2.
    - If the null hypothesis is true, we would expect the values for *MSB* and *MSW* to be close to one another.
    - If the null hypothesis is not true, we would expect the value of *MSB* to be larger than the value of *MSW*, causing the *F*-test statistic to exceed 1.0.
- The Tukey-Kramer multiple comparisons procedure allows us to examine each pair of sample means and to conclude whether their respective population means differ.
  - If the absolute difference between two sample means is large enough to be greater than the Tukey-Kramer critical range, we have enough evidence to conclude the population means are different.
  - The experiment-wide error rate is the probability of committing a Type I error for at least one pair of population means being compared.
- Randomized block ANOVA incorporates a blocking factor to account for any variation outside of the main factor in hopes of increasing the likelihood of detecting variation due to the main factor.
- The levels of the blocking factor are known as blocks.
- With randomized block ANOVA, the size of each sample needs to be the same.

- The total sum of squares *(SST)* for the randomized block ANOVA is partitioned into the following three sums of squares:
  - Sum of squares between (*SSB*)
  - Sum of squares block (*SSBL*)
  - Sum of squares error (*SSE*)
- The sum of squares between (*SSB*) measures the variation between each sample mean and the grand mean of the data.
- The sum of squares block (*SSBL*) measures the variation between the block means and the grand mean.
- The sum of squares error (*SSE*) represents the random variation in the data not attributed to either the main factor or the blocking factor.
- Use the following steps as a guide to decide whether to include a blocking factor in your final analysis.
  - If a blocking factor seems appropriate for a particular analysis, start off with a randomized block ANOVA procedure.
  - If you reject the null hypothesis for the main factor, proceed with your conclusions.
  - If you fail to reject the null hypothesis for the main factor with the randomized block ANOVA, redo the analysis with a one-way ANOVA.
- If the null hypothesis for the randomized block ANOVA is rejected, we can identify which population means are different by using the Tukey-Kramer multiple comparisons procedure for randomized block ANOVA.
- Two-way ANOVA is a procedure used to examine the simultaneous effect that two main factors (known as Factor A and Factor B) have on the observed data.
- A cell in a two-way ANOVA is a specific combination of one level from Factor A and one level from Factor B.
- Replications represent the number of data values assigned to each cell in the two-way ANOVA table.
- The procedure used in this textbook requires that the same number of replications occur in each cell.
- Because we are examining the simultaneous effect of Factors A and B with two-way ANOVA, we have to consider any interaction between Factors A and B that could be contributing to some of the variation in the data.
- The total sum of squares for two-way ANOVA is partitioned into the following four sums of squares:
  - Sum of squares Factor A (*SSFA*)
  - Sum of squares Factor B (*SSFB*)
  - Sum of squares interaction (*SSAB*)
  - Sum of squares error (*SSE*)
- The sum of squares for Factor A *(SSFA)* measures the variation between the Factor A means and the grand mean for all the data.
- The sum of squares for Factor B *(SSFB)* measures the variation between the Factor B means and the grand mean for all the data.
- The sum of squares interaction (*SSAB*) represents the variation due to the effect that Factor A has on Factor B or vice versa.

- An interaction plot displays the relationship between Factors A and B.
- Lines on the interaction plot that are relatively parallel are evidence that no interaction between the main factors exists.
- By contrast, intersecting lines are evidence that interaction does exist between the factors. In general, there is no interaction between Factors A and B when the data values for each level of one factor behave in the same fashion across all levels of the other factor.
- If we can reject the null hypothesis for either main factor, we can use the Tukey-Kramer Multiple Comparison Test for Two-Way ANOVA to identify which means are different.

CHAPTER 11 Key Terms

Analysis of variance (ANOVA). A technique used to perform a hypothesis test to compare three or more population means simultaneously.

Blocking factor. A factor used to account for variations outside of the main factor in hopes of increasing the likelihood of detecting variations due to the main factor in a randomized block ANOVA.

Blocks. The levels of the blocking factor in a randomized block ANOVA.

Cell. A specific combination of one level from Factor A and one level from Factor B in a two-way ANOVA.

Experiment-wide error rate. The probability of committing a Type I error for at least one pair of population means being compared.

Factor. The cause of variation in the data for an ANOVA procedure.

Level. A category within the factor of interest for an ANOVA procedure.

Mean square between (*MSB*). A value that provides an estimate for the population variance, σ^2, if the null hypothesis is true. It is found by dividing the sum of squares between (*SSB*) by $k - 1$.

Mean square block (*MSBL*). Is found by dividing the sum of squares block (*SSBL*) by $b - 1$.

Mean square error for randomized block ANOVA (*MSE*). Is found by dividing the sum of squares error (*SSE*) by $(b - 1)(k - 1)$.

Mean square error for two-way ANOVA (*MSE*). Is found by dividing the sum of squares error (*SSE*) by $n_T - (ab)$.

Mean square total (*MST*). A value derived from the *SST*, it is simply another term for the variance of the sample data. It is found by dividing the total sum of squares (*SST*) by $n_T - 1$.

Mean square within (*MSW*). A value that provides an estimate for the population variance, σ^2. It is found by dividing the sum of squares within (*SSW*) by $n_T - k$.

Mean sum of squares for Factor A (*MSFA*). Is found by dividing the sum of squares for Factor A (*SSFA*) by $a - 1$.

Mean sum of squares for Factor B (*MSFB*). Is found by dividing the sum of squares for Factor B (*SSFB*) by $b - 1$.

Mean sum of squares for interaction of Factors A and B (*MSAB*). Is found by dividing the sum of squares interaction (*SSAB*) by $(a - 1)(b - 1)$.

One-way ANOVA. The type of ANOVA used when we are looking at the influence that one factor has on the data values.

Randomized block ANOVA. An ANOVA procedure that incorporates a blocking factor to account for variations outside of the main factor in hopes of increasing the likelihood of detecting variations due to the main factor.

Replications. The number of data values assigned to each cell in a two-way ANOVA table.

Sum of squares between (*SSB*). A value that measures the variation between each sample mean and the grand mean of the data.

Sum of squares block (*SSBL*). A value that measures the variation between the block means and the grand mean.

Sum of squares error (*SSE*). A value that represents the random variation in the data not attributed to either the main factor or the blocking factor.

Sum of squares for Factor A (*SSFA*). A value that measures the variation between the Factor A means and the grand mean for all of the data.

Sum of squares for Factor B (*SSFB*). A value that measures the variation between the Factor B means and the grand mean for all of the data.

Sum of squares interaction (*SSAB*). A value that measures the variation of the means of populations due to the effect that Factor A has on Factor B, or vice versa.

Sum of squares within (*SSW*). A value that measures the variation between each data value and the corresponding sample mean.

Total sum of squares (*SST*). A value that measures the amount of variation between each data value and the grand mean.

Tukey–Kramer Multiple Comparison Test for One-Way ANOVA. Allows us to examine each pair of sample means and to conclude whether their respective population means differ for one-way ANOVA.

Tukey–Kramer Multiple Comparison Test for Randomized Block ANOVA. Allows us to examine each pair of sample means and to conclude whether their respective population means differ for randomized block ANOVA.

Tukey–Kramer Multiple Comparison Test for Two-Way ANOVA. Allows us to examine each pair of sample means and to conclude whether their respective population means differ for two-way ANOVA.

Two-way ANOVA. A procedure used to examine the simultaneous effect that two main factors have on the observed data.

CHAPTER 11 Equations

11.1 One-Way ANOVA: Examining the Effect a Single Factor Has on the Means of Populations (pp 503–523)

Formulas 11.1 and 11.2 for the Total Sum of Squares (SST)

$$SST = \sum_{j=1}^{k}\sum_{i=1}^{n_j}(x_{ij} - \bar{\bar{x}})^2$$

or

$$SST = \sum_{j=1}^{k}\sum_{i=1}^{n_j}x_{ij}^2 - \frac{\left(\sum_{j=1}^{k}\sum_{i=1}^{n_j}x_{ij}\right)^2}{n_T}$$

Formula 11.3 for the Mean Square Total (MST)

$$MST = \frac{\text{Total sum of squares}}{n_T - 1} = \frac{SST}{n_T - 1}$$

Formula 11.4 for the Partitioning of the Total Sum of Squares (SST) for a One-Way ANOVA

$$SST = SSB + SSW$$

Formula 11.5 for the Sum of Squares Between (SSB)

$$SSB = \sum_{j=1}^{k}n_j(\bar{x}_j - \bar{\bar{x}})^2$$

Formula 11.6 for the Mean Square Between (MSB)

$$MSB = \frac{\text{Sum of squares between}}{k - 1} = \frac{SSB}{k - 1}$$

Formulas 11.7 and 11.8 for the Sum of Squares Within (SSW)

$$SSW = \sum_{j=1}^{k}\sum_{i=1}^{n_j}(x_{ij} - \bar{x}_j)^2$$

or

$$SSW = SST - SSB$$

Formula 11.9 for the Mean Square Within (MSW)

$$MSW = \frac{\text{Sum of squares within}}{n_T - k} = \frac{SSW}{n_T - k}$$

Formula 11.10 for the F-Test Statistic for a One-Way ANOVA

$$F_{\bar{x}} = \frac{MSB}{MSW}$$

Formula 11.11 for the Tukey–Kramer Critical Range

$$CR_{i,j} = Q_{\alpha}\sqrt{\frac{MSW}{2}\left(\frac{1}{n_i} + \frac{1}{n_j}\right)}$$

11.2 Randomized Block ANOVA: Examining the Effects of a Single Factor by Blocking a Second Factor (pp 523–540)

Formula 11.12 for the Partitioning of the Total Sum of Squares (SST) for a Randomized Block ANOVA

$$SST = SSB + SSBL + SSE$$

Formula 11.13 for the Sum of Squares Block (SSBL)

$$SSBL = k\sum_{i=1}^{b}(\bar{x}_i - \bar{\bar{x}})^2$$

Formula 11.14 for the Mean Square Block (MSBL)

$$MSBL = \frac{\text{Sum of squares block}}{b - 1} = \frac{SSBL}{b - 1}$$

Formula 11.15 for the Sum of Squares Error (SSE) for a Randomized Block ANOVA

$$SSE = SST - (SSB + SSBL)$$

Formula 11.16 for the Mean Square Error (MSE) for Randomized Block ANOVA

$$MSE = \frac{\text{Sum of squares error}}{(b - 1)(k - 1)} = \frac{SSE}{(b - 1)(k - 1)}$$

Formula 11.17 for the Main Factor F-Test Statistic for a Randomized Block ANOVA

$$F_{\bar{x}} = \frac{MSB}{MSE}$$

Formula 11.18 for the Blocking Factor F-Test Statistic for a Randomized Block ANOVA

$$F_{BL} = \frac{MSBL}{MSE}$$

Formula 11.19 for the Critical Range for a Randomized Block ANOVA $CR = Q_\alpha \sqrt{\frac{MSE}{b}}$

11.3 Two-Way ANOVA: Examining the Effects Two Factors Have on the Means of Populations (pp 540–556)

Formula 11.20 for the Mean Sum of Squares for Factor A (MSFA) $MSFA = \frac{\text{Sum of squares factor A}}{a - 1} = \frac{SSFA}{a - 1}$

Formula 11.21 for the Mean Sum of Squares for Factor B (MSFB) $MSFB = \frac{\text{Sum of squares factor B}}{b - 1} = \frac{SSFB}{b - 1}$

Formula 11.22 for the Mean Sum of Squares for Interaction of Factors A and B (MSAB) $MSAB = \frac{SSAB}{(a - 1)(b - 1)}$

Formula 11.23 for the Mean Square Error (MSE) for Two-way ANOVA $MSE = \frac{SSE}{n_T - (ab)}$

Formula 11.24 for the Interaction Test Statistic $F_{AB} = \frac{MSAB}{MSE}$

Formula 11.25 for the Factor A Test Statistic $F_A = \frac{MSFA}{MSE}$

Formula 11.26 for the Factor B Test Statistic $F_B = \frac{MSFB}{MSE}$

Formula 11.27 for the Critical Range for Factor A $CR_A = Q_A \sqrt{\frac{MSE}{br}}$

Formula 11.28 for the Critical Range for Factor B $CR_B = Q_B \sqrt{\frac{MSE}{ar}}$

CHAPTER 11 Problems

11.40 A critical factor in the successful operation in today's hospital system is the effective staffing of emergency room (ER) personnel. In an effort to examine this issue, Wilmington Hospital would like to determine if the average number of emergency room visits differs over the three 8-hour shifts during the day. The following table shows the number of ER visits for randomly selected 8-hour shifts. These data can also be found in the Excel file **ER.xlsx**.

7:00 A.M.–3:00 P.M.	3:00 P.M.–11:00 P.M.	11:00 P.M.–7:00 A.M.
41	25	15
32	67	11
26	24	26
26	31	10
40	53	23

a. Perform a one-way ANOVA using $\alpha = 0.05$ to determine if there is a difference in the average number of ER visits during the three shifts.
b. If warranted, perform a multiple comparison test to determine which pairs are different using $\alpha = 0.05$.
c. Can you recommend a more effective way to collect these data that would enhance this analysis?
d. Verify your results with Excel or PHStat.

11.41 Television advertisers base their investment decisions regarding the promotion of their products and services on demographic information about television viewers. The age of the viewers is a key factor in this process. The following table shows the number of hours that a random sample of individuals watched television during the week. The individuals are grouped according to their ages. These data can also be found in the Excel file **advertisers.xlsx**.

18–24	25–34	35–49	50–64
39	41	44	49
14	40	19	33
15	33	27	33
17	35	36	39
20	21	49	71

a. Perform a one-way ANOVA using $\alpha = 0.05$ to determine if there is a difference in the average number of hours per week of television viewing by the four age groups.
b. If warranted, perform a multiple comparison test to determine which pairs are different using $\alpha = 0.05$.
c. Verify your results with Excel or PHStat.

11.42 Because most National Football League games are sold out, the secondary market, in which people resell their tickets, is very active during the season. The following table shows the price for secondary market tickets to the games of four NFL teams. These data can also be found in the Excel file **NFL tickets.xlsx**.

Green Bay Packers ($)	New Orleans Saints ($)	Indianapolis Colts ($)	New York Jets ($)
213	197	170	197
190	198	152	151
185	216	165	184
188	199	166	188
214	220	165	182

a. Perform a one-way ANOVA using $\alpha = 0.05$ to determine if there is a difference in the average ticket prices for the four NFL teams.
b. If warranted, perform a multiple comparison test to determine which pairs are different using $\alpha = 0.05$.
c. Verify your results with Excel or PHStat.

11.43 Budget shortfalls in many states during the most recent recession placed a strain on education resources. One area that receives much attention from both parents and administrators is the number of students per teacher. Suppose the U.S. Department of Education would like to compare this ratio in kindergartens for schools in California, Delaware, Nevada, and Georgia. The following data show the number of kindergarten students in randomly selected classrooms in these four states. These data can also be found in the Excel file **kindergarten.xlsx**.

CA	DE	NV	GA
26	21	30	14
21	23	35	15
23	31	22	15
25	33	29	21
26	18	31	16
12	25	39	15

a. Perform a one-way ANOVA using $\alpha = 0.05$ to determine if the average number of students in kindergarten classes is different in the four states.
b. If warranted, perform a multiple comparison test to determine which pairs are different using $\alpha = 0.05$.
c. Verify your results with Excel or PHStat.

11.44 The following table shows the selling price of a random sample of residential homes, in thousands of dollars, at three beach communities in New Jersey. The homes are categorized by the real estate firm that is listing the home. These data can also be found in the Excel file **beach.xlsx**.

Real Estate Firm	Avalon ($)	Stone Harbor ($)	Sea Isle City ($)
Prudential	550	700	500
Re/Max	625	840	500
Diller	775	1,070	620
Fox	900	1,350	1,100
Century 21	1,500	1,600	800

a. Using $\alpha = 0.05$ and the real estate firm as a blocking factor, test to see if a difference exists in the average selling prices of homes in the three communities.
b. If warranted, determine which pairs of communities are different using $\alpha = 0.05$.
c. Verify your results with Excel or PHStat.
d. Was the blocking factor effective? Why or why not?

11.45 Suppose *Consumer Reports* would like to conduct a study comparing the prices of televisions made by different manufacturers. The following data show the prices of a random sample of televisions for various screen sizes. These data can also be found in the Excel file **Consumer Reports.xlsx**.

Size	LG ($)	Panasonic ($)	Samsung ($)	Insignia ($)
32"	450	450	600	450
37"	700	1,000	1,000	600
42"	1,000	750	600	500
46"	1,300	700	1,300	900
50"	1,600	1,400	1,300	700
55"	1,900	1,500	2,200	1,100

a. Using a one-way ANOVA and $\alpha = 0.05$, test to see if a difference exists in the average prices of the brands.
b. Using a randomized block ANOVA and $\alpha = 0.05$, test to see if a difference exists in the average prices of the brands.
c. If warranted, determine which pairs of television brands are different using $\alpha = 0.05$.
d. Verify your results with Excel.
e. Explain the differences in the results from parts a and b.

11.46 Mike is a restaurant owner and has read about the effect that music can have on the amount of time that customers stay at their tables for dinner. To test this effect, Mike made arrangements to play slow-paced music at his establishment on a busy Saturday night and recorded the time that customers at the randomly selected tables spent in the restaurant during five months of the year. Mike did the same on subsequent Saturday nights with fast-paced music and no music. The following data show the amount of the time, in minutes, for the observed tables. These data can also be found in the Excel file **music.xlsx**.

Month	No Music	Low Music	Fast Music
January	60	76	64
March	120	128	115
May	98	110	111
August	73	82	70
October	136	138	142

a. Test to determine if a difference exists between the different types of music using a one-way ANOVA with $\alpha = 0.05$.
b. If the results in part a indicate that there is no difference between types of music, what additional steps should be taken to test the difference in means for each category of music?
c. If warranted, determine which pairs of music categories are different using $\alpha = 0.05$.
d. Verify your results with Excel.

11.47 Suppose Scotts Lawn Care would like to test the effectiveness of four new grass fertilizers that it has developed. Each fertilizer is applied to identical-size sections of grass, and after a period of time the sections of grass are mowed. The weight of the grass clippings are used to measure the effectiveness of the fertilizer. To control for variations in soil and ambient conditions, each fertilizer was applied to five different lawns, which can act as a blocking factor. The pounds of grass clippings for each sample are shown in the following table. These data can also be found in the Excel file **fertilizer.xlsx**.

	FERT 1	FERT 2	FERT 3	FERT 4
Lawn 1	10	12	8	10
Lawn 2	9	13	11	11
Lawn 3	9	9	13	9
Lawn 4	7	10	9	12
Lawn 5	5	13	12	10

a. Using a randomized block ANOVA and $\alpha = 0.05$, does there appear to be a difference in the effectiveness of the four fertilizers?
b. If the answer to part a is no, what additional steps should be taken to test the difference in the population means of each fertilizer?
c. If warranted, determine which pairs of fertilizers were different using $\alpha = 0.05$.
d. Verify your results with Excel.

11.48 You have been assigned to test the hypothesis that the average number of hours worked per week by employees differs between the United States, China, and Sweden. The following data show the number of hours that a random sample of employees worked last week in each country. These data can also be found in the Excel file **employee hours.xlsx**.

United States	Sweden	China
34	28	43
41	34	51
38	25	40
31	33	34

a. Perform a one-way ANOVA using $\alpha = 0.05$ to determine if a difference exists in the average number of hours that an employee works per week between these countries.

b. If appropriate, perform a multiple comparison test to determine which pairs are different using $\alpha = 0.05$.

c. Verify your results using Excel or PHStat.

11.49 One area that fast-food restaurants compete with one another is with the service time for the drive-through window. The following data show the drive-through service times, in minutes, for a random sample of customers at three fast-food chains. These data can also be found in the Excel file **drive through service.xlsx**.

McDonald's	Wendy's	Burger King
3.1	0.8	2.5
3.7	2.8	3.1
2.3	1.2	3.0
3.6	2.5	2.6
3.3	2.0	3.3
5.0	2.1	2.9

a. Perform a one-way ANOVA using $\alpha = 0.01$ to determine if a difference exists in the average drive-through service time between these three restaurants.

b. If appropriate, perform a multiple comparison test to determine which pairs are different using $\alpha = 0.01$.

c. Verify your results using Excel or PHStat.

11.50 The following data show customer satisfaction scores, on a scale of 1–20, for a chain of hair salons at three different locations during specific days of the week. The manager would like to investigate if a difference exists in satisfaction scores between these locations. These data can also be found in the Excel file **hair salon.xlsx**.

	Locations		
Day	Midway	Towson	Dover
Monday	13	14	12
Wednesday	14	15	10
Friday	16	15	14
Saturday	16	18	17
Sunday	17	20	14

a. Perform a randomized block ANOVA using $\alpha = 0.05$ to test if a difference exists in satisfaction scores between these three locations.

b. Perform a hypothesis test using $\alpha = 0.05$ to determine if the blocking factor was effective.

c. If appropriate, perform a multiple comparison test to determine which pairs are different using $\alpha = 0.05$.

d. Verify your results with Excel.

11.51 The data in the following table represent the number of days that a random sample of homes in four price ranges were on the market before being sold for three different competing real estate companies in a local area. You have been assigned to test the hypothesis that the average number of days that a home is on the market differs between these three real estate companies. It is believed that the selling price of the home could be an effective blocking factor for this test. These data can also be found in the Excel file **housing market.xlsx**.

	Company		
Selling Price	Century 21	Re/Max	Weichert
Under $300,000	37	18	86
$300,000 to under $400,000	41	44	71
$400,000 to under $500,000	46	63	59
$500,000 to under $600,000	38	67	72

a. Perform a randomized block ANOVA using $\alpha = 0.05$ to test if a difference exists in the number of days a home is on the market between these three companies. Also, perform any other procedures that are necessary to complete this analysis.

b. If appropriate, perform a multiple comparison test to determine which main factor pairs are different using $\alpha = 0.05$.

c. Verify your results with Excel.

11.52 Some research has indicated that diet programs may be more effective when the dieter reports their weight-loss progress publically to others. A consumer group organization would like to compare the average weight-loss for those that report their progress to those that do not report. This group would also like to study the effectiveness of three different diets. Diet 1 focuses on reducing carbohydrate intake, Diet 2 focuses on controlling calorie intake and Diet 3 focuses on reducing fat intake. The following data represent the weight-loss, in pounds, for individuals under each factor. These data can also be found in the Excel file **diet reports.xlsx**.

	Diet 1	Diet 2	Diet 3
No report	6	4	2
	10	13	7
	6	5	0
	5	4	3
	5	8	6
	6	8	1
Report	9	13	15
	15	15	14
	13	16	4
	8	9	11
	3	12	5
	10	13	4

a. Using $\alpha = 0.05$, is there a significant interaction between the type of diet and the reporting status of the individual?

b. Using a two-way ANOVA and $\alpha = 0.05$, does the reporting status have an effect on the weight loss experienced by the individual?

c. Using a two-way ANOVA and $\alpha = 0.05$, does the type of diet have an effect on the weight loss experienced by the individual?

d. If warranted, determine which diets have means that are significantly different using $\alpha = 0.05$.

e. Construct an interaction plot for the reporting status and the type of diet.

11.53 The Department of Labor (DoL) would like to investigate if there is a difference in the average number of hours worked per week by employees in the United States, China, and Sweden. DoL would also like to test if the age of the employee impacts the average number of hours worked per week. The following data show the number of hours that a random sample of employees worked last week in each country along with their age group. These data can also be found in the Excel file **DOL.xlsx**.

Age Group	United States	Sweden	China
30 to under 40	40	36	38
	35	27	41
	43	37	45
	37	27	34
	36	31	46
40 to under 50	26	39	53
	34	28	49
	31	30	41
	35	29	34
	34	23	44
50 to under 60	39	51	43
	41	38	38
	38	39	39
	34	30	36
	37	30	49

a. Using $\alpha = 0.05$, is there a significant interaction between the age group and the country of the individual?

b. Using a two-way ANOVA and $\alpha = 0.05$, does the age group have an effect on the average number of weeks worked by the individual?

c. Using a two-way ANOVA and $\alpha = 0.05$, does the country have an effect on the average number of weeks worked by the individual?

d. If warranted, determine which means are significantly different using $\alpha = 0.05$.

e. Construct an interaction plot for the age group and the country

11.54 A possible contributor to rising health care costs in the United States is obesity, which is currently determined using a formula called body mass index (BMI). This index is calculated using the following formula:

$$\text{BMI} = \frac{\text{Weight(lbs)} \times 703}{(\text{Height(in.)})^2}$$

A person with a BMI of 25 to 29 is classified as overweight, 30 to 40 as obese, and 40 or more as morbidly obese. A random sample of individuals was selected from Michigan, Florida, Utah, and New York, and their BMI measurements were taken. The gender of each person was also noted. These data can be found in the file **BMI by state.xlsx**.

a. Using $\alpha = 0.05$, is there significant interaction between the gender and the state?

b. Using a two-way ANOVA and $\alpha = 0.05$, does the state in which the person resides have an effect on his or her BMI level?

c. Using a two-way ANOVA and $\alpha = 0.05$, does a person's gender have an effect on his or her BMI level?

d. If warranted, determine which means are significantly different using $\alpha = 0.05$.

e. Construct an interaction plot for the gender and the state.

11.55 Suppose the Department of Energy would like to compare residential utility bills for different cities in the United States. A random sample of households was selected, and their utility bills for the month were recorded. The number of bedrooms in the houses was also noted. These data can also be found in the file **utility bills.xlsx**.

a. Using $\alpha = 0.05$, is there significant interaction between the number of bedrooms and the city?
b. Using a two-way ANOVA and $\alpha = 0.05$, does the number of bedrooms have an effect on the average monthly utility bill?
c. Using a two-way ANOVA and $\alpha = 0.05$, does the city have an effect on the average monthly utility bill?
d. If warranted, determine which means are significantly different using $\alpha = 0.05$.
e. Construct an interaction plot for the number of bedrooms and the city.

11.56 Suppose Bank of America developed a credit card promotion to entice its customers to increase the balances on their credit cards. To test the effectiveness of different ways of communicating this promotion, Bank of America sent the promotion to some customers through e-mail, sent it to other customers through traditional mail, and did not send it to other customers. A random sample of customers from each group was selected, and their credit card balances following the promotion period were recorded. These data can be found in the file **credit card promotion.xlsx**.

a. Perform a one-way ANOVA using $\alpha = 0.05$ to determine if there is a difference in the average credit card balances of these three groups.
b. If warranted, perform a multiple comparison test to determine which pairs are different using $\alpha = 0.05$.
c. What conclusions can be drawn about the effectiveness of communicating the promotion?
d. Verify your results with Excel and PHStat2.

11.57 Suppose the National Center for Education Statistics would like to investigate the effect that the education level for high school teachers and the state that employs them have on their salaries. Excel file **high school salaries.xlsx** contains salaries for a random sample of high school teachers from Colorado, Kansas, Minnesota, and Nebraska. The educational level for these teachers is also indicated in the file.

a. Using $\alpha = 0.05$, is there significant interaction between the education level and the state?
b. Does the education level of the teacher have an effect on his or her salary?
c. Using a two-way ANOVA and $\alpha = 0.05$, does the state that employs the teacher have an effect on his or her salary?
d. If warranted, determine which means are significantly different using $\alpha = 0.05$.
e. Construct an interaction plot for the education level and the state.

11.58 Suppose the American Association of Retired Persons (AARP) would like to test if a difference exists in the average 401(k) balance between people in different age groups. A random sample of individuals in the 50–59, 60–69, and 70 or older was selected and their 401(k) balance was recorded. These 401(k) balances, in thousands of dollars, can be found in the Excel file **AARP.xlsx**.

a. Using $\alpha = 0.05$, test to determine if a difference exists in the average 401(k) balance between these three age groups.
b. If appropriate, perform a multiple comparison test to determine which pairs are different using $\alpha = 0.05$.

11.59 Many homeowners rely on handymen to perform small jobs, such as repairs or maintenance, around their residence. According to HomeAdvisor Inc., the average cost for a handyman project varies substantially between the cities of New York, Chicago, Denver, and Atlanta. To test this claim, a random sample of handyman projects from each city was selected and can be found in the Excel file **handyman.xlsx**.

a. Using $\alpha = 0.01$, test to determine if a difference exists in the average cost of handyman projects in these four cities.
b. If appropriate, perform a multiple comparison test to determine which pairs are different using $\alpha = 0.01$.

CHAPTER 11 Solutions to Your Turn

YOUR TURN #1

a. H_0: $\mu_1 = \mu_2 = \mu_3$
H_1: Not all μs are equal

b. $\bar{x}_1 = \dfrac{10}{4} = 2.5 \quad \bar{x}_2 = \dfrac{9.6}{4} = 2.4 \quad \bar{x}_3 = \dfrac{12.8}{4} = 3.2$

$\bar{\bar{x}} = \dfrac{32.4}{12} = 2.7$

c. Using Equation 11.2 for *SST*, we have the following:

i	*j*	Employee	x_{ij}	x_{ij}^2
1	1	Jane	2.5	6.25
2	1	Jane	2.7	7.29
3	1	Jane	2.2	4.84
4	1	Jane	2.6	6.76
1	2	Tom	2.1	4.41
2	2	Tom	2.9	8.41
3	2	Tom	2.2	4.84
4	2	Tom	2.4	5.76
1	3	Jason	3.3	10.89
2	3	Jason	2.8	7.84
3	3	Jason	3.7	13.69
4	3	Jason	3.0	9.0

$$\sum_{j=1}^{k}\sum_{i=1}^{n_j} x_{ij} = 32.4 \qquad \sum_{j=1}^{k}\sum_{i=1}^{n_j} x_{ij}^2 = 89.98$$

$$SST = \sum_{j=1}^{k}\sum_{i=1}^{n_j} x_{ij}^2 - \frac{\left(\sum_{j=1}^{k}\sum_{i=1}^{n_j} x_{ij}\right)^2}{n_T} = 89.98 - \frac{(32.4)^2}{12}$$

$$SST = 89.98 - 87.48 = 2.50$$

Using Equation 11.1 for *SST*, we have the following:

	A	B	C	D
1	x_{ij}	$\bar{\bar{x}}$	$\left(x_{ij} - \bar{\bar{x}}\right)$	$\left(x_{ij} - \bar{\bar{x}}\right)^2$
2	2.5	2.7	-0.2	0.04
3	2.7	2.7	0.0	0.00
4	2.2	2.7	-0.5	0.25
5	2.6	2.7	-0.1	0.01
6	2.1	2.7	-0.6	0.36
7	2.9	2.7	0.2	0.04
8	2.2	2.7	-0.5	0.25
9	2.4	2.7	-0.3	0.09
10	3.3	2.7	0.6	0.36
11	2.8	2.7	0.1	0.01
12	3.7	2.7	1.0	1.00
13	3.0	2.7	0.3	0.09
14				
15			Total	2.50
16				

d. $MST = \dfrac{SST}{n_T - 1} = \dfrac{2.50}{12 - 1} = 0.227$

YOUR TURN #2

a. $SSB = \sum_{j=1}^{k} n_j(\bar{x}_j - \bar{\bar{x}})^2$

$SSB = n_1(\bar{x}_1 - \bar{\bar{x}})^2 + n_2(\bar{x}_2 - \bar{\bar{x}})^2 + n_3(\bar{x}_3 - \bar{\bar{x}})^2$

$SSB = (4)(2.5 - 2.7)^2 + (4)(2.4 - 2.7)^2 + (4)(3.2 - 2.7)^2$

$SSB = (4)(-0.2)^2 + (4)(-0.3)^2 + (4)(0.5)^2$

$SSB = (4)(0.04) + (4)(0.09) + (4)(0.25)$

$SSB = 0.16 + 0.36 + 1.00$

$SSB = 1.52$

$MSB = \dfrac{SSB}{k - 1} = \dfrac{1.52}{3 - 1} = 0.76$

b. $SSW = SST - SSB$

$SSW = 2.50 - 1.52 = 0.98$

$MSW = \dfrac{SSW}{n_T - k} = \dfrac{0.98}{12 - 3} = 0.109$

c. $F_{\bar{x}} = \dfrac{MSB}{MSW} = \dfrac{0.76}{0.109} = 6.97$

d.

Source	Sum of Squares	Degrees of Freedom	Mean Sum of Squares	*F*
Between	1.52	2	0.76	6.97
Within	0.98	9	0.109	
Total	2.50	11		

e. $D_1 = k - 1 = 3 - 1 = 2$

$D_2 = n_T - k = 12 - 3 = 9$

$\alpha = 0.05$

Using Table 6 in Appendix A, $F_\alpha = 4.256$. Because $F_{\bar{x}} = 6.97$ is greater than $F_\alpha = 4.256$, we reject the null hypothesis according to Table 11.9. There appears to be a difference in the average weight of the pretzels between these three employees. Management should consider investigating this discrepancy.

f.

	A	B	C	D	E	F	G	H	I	J	K
1	Jane	Tom	Jason		Anova: Single Factor						
2	2.5	2.1	3.3								
3	2.7	2.9	2.8		SUMMARY						
4	2.2	2.2	3.7		Groups	Count	Sum	Average	Variance		
5	2.6	2.4	3		Jane	4	10	2.5	0.046666667		
6					Tom	4	9.6	2.4	0.126666667		
7					Jason	4	12.8	3.2	0.153333333		
8											
9											
10					ANOVA						
11					Source of Variation	SS	df	MS	F	P-value	F crit
12					Between Groups	1.52	2	0.76	6.979591837	0.014783842	4.256494729
13					Within Groups	0.98	9	0.108888889			
14											
15					Total	2.5	11				
16											

Because the *p*-value in Cell J12 equals 0.01478 and is less than $\alpha = 0.05$, we reject the null hypothesis and conclude that the average weights of pretzels made by these employees are not equal.

YOUR TURN #3

Step 1: Calculate the sample mean differences.

In the pretzel example, $k = 3$, so we have $3(2)/2 = 3$ pairs of sample means. The following pairs are samples:

1 and 2   1 and 3   2 and 3

$$|\bar{x}_1 - \bar{x}_2| = |2.5 - 2.4| = |0.1| = 0.1$$
$$|\bar{x}_1 - \bar{x}_3| = |2.5 - 3.2| = |-0.7| = 0.7$$
$$|\bar{x}_2 - \bar{x}_3| = |2.4 - 3.2| = |-0.8| = 0.8$$

Step 2: Calculate the Tukey–Kramer critical range.

The critical value from the studentized range table (Appendix A, Table 7), using $\alpha = 0.05$, $D_1 = k = 3$, and $D_2 = n_T - k = 12 - 3 = 9$, is $Q_\alpha = 3.95$.

Because the sample sizes are equal (each employee has four pretzel weights), the critical range, $CR_{i,j}$, for each pair of samples is the same. Using Equation 11.11 with $MSW = 0.109$, we have the following:

$$CR_{i,j} = Q_\alpha \sqrt{\frac{MSW}{2}\left(\frac{1}{n_i} + \frac{1}{n_j}\right)}$$

$$CR_{i,j} = (3.95)\sqrt{\frac{0.109}{2}\left(\frac{1}{4} + \frac{1}{4}\right)}$$

$$= (3.95)\sqrt{(0.0545)(0.50)}$$

$$CR_{i,j} = (3.95)(0.1651) = 0.652$$

Step 3: Draw your conclusion.

$\lvert\bar{x}_i - \bar{x}_j\rvert$	CR_{ij}	Decision
$\lvert\bar{x}_1 - \bar{x}_2\rvert = 0.1$	0.652	Means are not different
$\lvert\bar{x}_1 - \bar{x}_3\rvert = 0.7$	0.652	Means are different
$\lvert\bar{x}_2 - \bar{x}_3\rvert = 0.8$	0.652	Means are different

From these results, we can conclude that the average pretzel weight for Jane is lower than the average weight for Jason (samples 1 and 3). Tom's average pretzel weight is also lower than Jason's (samples 2 and 3). There is not enough evidence to conclude that Jane's and Tom's weights are significantly different at the $\alpha = 0.05$ level.

	A	B	C	D	E	F	G	H	I
1	Tukey-Kramer Multiple Comparisons								
2									
3		Sample	Sample			Absolute	Std. Error	Critical	
4	Group	Mean	Size		Comparison	Difference	of Difference	Range	Results
5	1: Jane	2.5	4		Group 1 to Group 2	0.1	0.164991582	0.6517	Means are not different
6	2: Tom	2.4	4		Group 1 to Group 3	0.7	0.164991582	0.6517	Means are different
7	3: Jason	3.2	4		Group 2 to Group 3	0.8	0.164991582	0.6517	Means are different
8									
9	Other Data								
10	Level of significance	0.05							
11	Numerator d.f.	3							
12	Denominator d.f.	9							
13	MSW	0.108889							
14	Q Statistic	3.95							
15									

YOUR TURN #4

a. H_0: $\mu_1 = \mu_2 = \mu_3$
H_1: Not all μs are equal

b.

Shopper	Wal	Star	Gap	Block Total	Block Mean
1	12	17	13	42	14.0
2	16	18	17	51	17.0
3	14	17	17	48	16.0
4	18	20	19	57	19.0
Factor total	60	72	66	198	
Factor mean	15.0	18.0	16.5		

$$\bar{\bar{x}} = \frac{198}{12} = 16.5$$

c. Using Equation 11.2 for *SST*, we have the following:

i	*j*	Company	x_{ij}	x_{ij}^2
1	1	Walmart	12	144
2	1	Walmart	16	256
3	1	Walmart	14	196
4	1	Walmart	18	324
1	2	Starbucks	17	289
2	2	Starbucks	18	324
3	2	Starbucks	17	289
4	2	Starbucks	20	400
1	3	The Gap	13	169
2	3	The Gap	17	289
3	3	The Gap	17	289
4	3	The Gap	19	361

$$\sum_{j=1}^{k}\sum_{i=1}^{n_j} x_{ij} = 198 \quad \sum_{j=1}^{k}\sum_{i=1}^{n_j} x_{ij}^2 = 3{,}330$$

$$SST = \sum_{j=1}^{k}\sum_{i=1}^{n_j} x_{ij}^2 - \frac{\left(\sum_{j=1}^{k}\sum_{i=1}^{n_j} x_{ij}\right)^2}{n_T} = 3{,}330 - \frac{(198)^2}{12}$$

$$SST = 3{,}330 - 3{,}267 = 63.0$$

Using Equation 11.1 for *SST*, we have the following:

	A	B	C	D
1	x_{ij}	$\bar{\bar{x}}$	$(x_{ij} - \bar{\bar{x}})$	$(x_{ij} - \bar{\bar{x}})^2$
2	12	16.5	-4.5	20.25
3	16	16.5	-0.5	0.25
4	14	16.5	-2.5	6.25
5	18	16.5	1.5	2.25
6	17	16.5	0.5	0.25
7	18	16.5	1.5	2.25
8	17	16.5	0.5	0.25
9	20	16.5	3.5	12.25
10	13	16.5	-3.5	12.25
11	17	16.5	0.5	0.25
12	17	16.5	0.5	0.25
13	19	16.5	2.5	6.25
14				
15			Total	63.00
16				

d. $$MST = \frac{SST}{n_T - 1} = \frac{63}{12 - 1} = 5.73$$

YOUR TURN #5

a. $$SSB = \sum_{j=1}^{k} n_j(\bar{x}_j - \bar{\bar{x}})^2$$

$$SSB = n_1(\bar{x}_1 - \bar{\bar{x}})^2 + n_2(\bar{x}_2 - \bar{\bar{x}})^2 + n_3(\bar{x}_3 - \bar{\bar{x}})^2$$

$$SSB = (4)(15.0 - 16.5)^2 + (4)(18.0 - 16.5)^2 + (4)(16.5 - 16.5)^2$$

$$SSB = (4)(-1.5)^2 + (4)(1.5)^2 + (4)(0)^2$$

$$SSB = (4)(2.25) + (4)(2.25) + (4)(0)$$

$$SSB = 18.0$$

$$MSB = \frac{SSB}{k - 1} = \frac{18.0}{3 - 1} = 9.0$$

b. $$SSBL = k\sum_{i=1}^{b}(\bar{x}_i - \bar{\bar{x}})^2$$

$$SSBL = (3)[(\bar{x}_1 - \bar{\bar{x}})^2 + (\bar{x}_2 - \bar{\bar{x}})^2 + (\bar{x}_3 - \bar{\bar{x}})^2 + (\bar{x}_4 - \bar{\bar{x}})^2]$$

$$SSBL = (3)[(14 - 16.5)^2 + (17 - 16.5)^2 + (16 - 16.5)^2 + (19 - 16.5)^2]$$

$$SSBL = (3)[(-2.5)^2 + (0.5)^2 + (-0.5)^2 + (2.5)^2]$$

$$SSBL = (3)[(6.25) + (0.25) + (0.25) + (6.25)]$$

$$SSBL = (3)[13.0] = 39.0$$

$$MSBL = \frac{SSBL}{b - 1} = \frac{39.0}{4 - 1} = 13.0$$

c. $SSE = SST - (SSB + SSBL)$

$$SSE = 63.0 - (18.0 + 39.0) = 63.0 - 57.0 = 6.0$$

$$MSE = \frac{SSE}{(b-1)(k-1)} = \frac{6.0}{(4-1)(3-1)} = 1.0$$

d. $F_{\bar{x}} = \frac{MSB}{MSE} = \frac{9.0}{1.0} = 9.0$

e. $D_1 = k - 1 = 3 - 1 = 2$

$$D_2 = (b-1)(k-1) = (4-1)(3-1) = 6$$

According to Table 11.8, the critical value with $\alpha = 0.05$ and degrees of freedom equal to 2 and 6 is $F_\alpha = 5.143$. Because $F_{\bar{x}} = 9.0$, which is greater than $F_\alpha = 5.143$, we reject the null hypothesis according to the decision rules shown in Table 11.9. By rejecting the null hypothesis, we can conclude that not all of the three population means are equal. The average cleanliness scores of the three stores are different.

f. $F_{BL} = \frac{MSBL}{MSE} = \frac{13.0}{1.0} = 13.0$

$$D_1 = b - 1 = 4 - 1 = 3$$

$$D_2 = (b-1)(k-1) = (4-1)(3-1) = 6$$

According to Table 11.8, the critical value with $\alpha = 0.05$ and degrees of freedom equal to 3 and 6 is $F_\alpha = 4.757$. Because $F_{BL} = 13.0$, which is greater than $F_\alpha = 4.757$, we reject the null hypothesis and conclude that blocking was effective.

g.

Source	Sum of Squares	Degrees of Freedom	Mean Sum of Squares	F
Between	18.0	2	9.0	9.0
Block	39.0	3	13.0	13.0
Error	6.0	6	1.0	
Total	63.0	11		

h.

	A	B	C	D	E	F	G	H	I	J	K	L
1	Shopper	Walmart	Starbucks	The Gap		Anova: Two-Factor Without Replication						
2	1	12	17	13								
3	2	16	18	17		SUMMARY	Count	Sum	Average	Variance		
4	3	14	17	17		1	3	42	14	7		
5	4	18	20	19		2	3	51	17	1		
6						3	3	48	16	3		
7						4	3	57	19	1		
8												
9						Walmart	4	60	15	6.666667		
10						Starbucks	4	72	18	2		
11						The Gap	4	66	16.5	6.333333		
12												
13												
14						ANOVA						
15						Source of Variation	SS	df	MS	F	P-value	F crit
16						Rows	39	3	13	13	0.004919	4.757063
17						Columns	18	2	9	9	0.015625	5.143253
18						Error	6	6	1			
19												
20						Total	63	11				
21												

YOUR TURN #6

Step 1: Calculate the absolute sample mean differences.

With $k = 3$ populations (stores) being compared, we have $3(2)/2 = 3$ pairs of sample means. The following pairs are samples:

1 and 2 1 and 3 2 and 3

$$|\bar{x}_1 - \bar{x}_2| = |15.0 - 18.0| = |-3.0| = 3.0$$

$$|\bar{x}_1 - \bar{x}_3| = |15.0 - 16.5| = |-1.5| = 1.5$$

$$|\bar{x}_2 - \bar{x}_3| = |18.0 - 16.5| = |1.5| = 1.5$$

Step 2: Calculate the critical range for a randomized block ANOVA.

With $b = 4$ blocks (shoppers),

$$D_1 = k = 3$$

$$D_2 = (b-1)(k-1) = (4-1)(3-1) = 6$$

Using Table 7 in Appendix A and $\alpha = 0.05$, the critical value is $Q_\alpha = 4.34$. Recalling that $MSE = 1.0$ from Your Turn #5, we have the following:

$$CR = Q_\alpha \sqrt{\frac{MSE}{b}} = (4.34)\sqrt{\frac{1.0}{4}} = (4.34)(0.50) = 2.17$$

Step 3: Draw your conclusion.

$\lvert\bar{x}_i - \bar{x}_j\rvert$	CR	Decision
$\lvert\bar{x}_1 - \bar{x}_2\rvert = 3.0$	2.17	Means are different
$\lvert\bar{x}_1 - \bar{x}_3\rvert = 1.5$	2.17	Means are not different
$\lvert\bar{x}_2 - \bar{x}_3\rvert = 1.5$	2.17	Means are not different

According to these results, we can conclude that a difference exists between the cleanliness of Walmart (1) and Starbucks (2). There is no evidence that the other two pairs of stores have different means based on these data.

YOUR TURN #7

a.

	A	B	C	D	E	F	G	H	I	J	K	L
1		Lavender	Citrus	Unscented		Anova: Two-Factor With Replication						
2	Gloucester	13	18	12								
3		16	20	16		SUMMARY	Lavender	Citrus	Unscented	Total		
4		19	15	15		*Gloucester*						
5		16	18	15		Count	4	4	4	12		
6	Deptford	15	17	14		Sum	64	71	58	193		
7		12	17	9		Average	16	17.75	14.5	16.08333		
8		14	14	12		Variance	6	4.25	3	5.537879		
9		13	17	13								
10	Voorhees	11	15	15		*Deptford*						
11		19	16	16		Count	4	4	4	12		
12		15	20	11		Sum	54	65	48	167		
13		16	18	12		Average	13.5	16.25	12	13.91667		
14						Variance	1.666667	2.25	4.666666667	5.719697		
15												
16						*Voorhees*						
17						Count	4	4	4	12		
18						Sum	61	69	54	184		
19						Average	15.25	17.25	13.5	15.33333		
20						Variance	10.91667	4.916667	5.666666667	8.424242		
21												
22						*Total*						
23						Count	12	12	12			
24						Sum	179	205	160			
25						Average	14.91667	17.08333	13.33333333			
26						Variance	6.265152	3.537879	4.787878788			
27												
28												
29						ANOVA						
30						*Source of Variation*	*SS*	*df*	*MS*	*F*	*P-value*	*F crit*
31						Sample	29.05556	2	14.52777778	3.017308	0.065664	3.354131
32						Columns	85.05556	2	42.52777778	8.832692	0.001119	3.354131
33						Interaction	1.444444	4	0.361111111	0.075	0.989213	2.727765
34						Within	130	27	4.814814815			
35												
36						Total	245.5556	35				
37												

b.

Source	Sum of Squares	Degrees of Freedom	Mean Sum of Squares	*F*
Factor B	29.06	2	14.53	3.02
Factor A	85.06	2	42.53	8.83
Interaction	1.44	4	0.36	0.08
Error	130	27	4.81	
Total	245.56	35		

Note that Factor A in the previous table refers to "Columns" in Excel's ANOVA output and Factor B corresponds to "Sample" in Excel.

c. Interaction hypothesis: Fail to reject the null because the *p*-value equals 0.989 (Cell K33), which is greater than $\alpha = 0.05$. Because there is no interaction between Factors A and B, we can test them individually.

Factor A hypothesis: Reject the null hypothesis because the *p*-value equals 0.001119 (Cell K32), which is less than $\alpha = 0.05$. It appears that there is a difference in the overall impression of the stores based on the scents.

Factor B hypothesis: Fail to reject the null hypothesis because the *p*-value equals 0.065664 (Cell K31), which is more than $\alpha = 0.05$. There is not enough evidence to conclude that the impression scores are different for the locations.

YOUR TURN #8

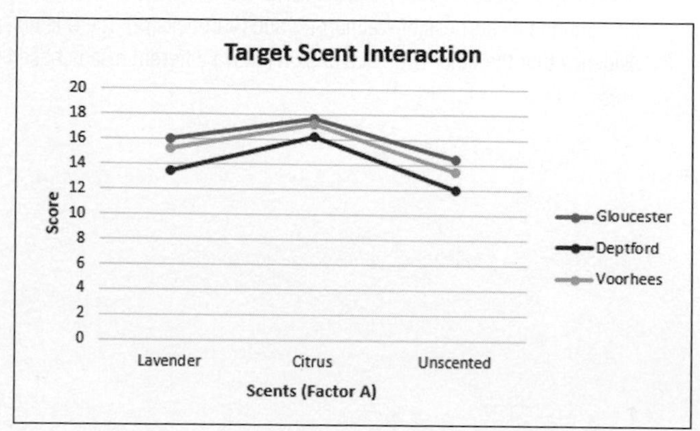

Because the three lines do not intersect, there is no evidence of interaction between Factor A (scent) and Factor B (location).

YOUR TURN #9

Your Turn #7 concludes that there was a difference in Factor A means, but not Factor B. Therefore, multiple comparisons are carried out only for Factor A. Using the Target data with $a = 3$ scents, $b = 3$ locations, and $r = 4$ replications per cell, the degrees of freedom for the Factor A critical value, CR_A, are as follows:

$$D_1 = b = 3$$
$$D_2 = ab(r - 1) = (3)(3)(4 - 1) = 27$$

Using Table 7 in Appendix A and $\alpha = 0.05$, the critical value is approximately $Q_A = 3.51$ (halfway between $D_2 = 24$ and 30). Note that $MSE = 4.815$ (Excel Cell I34 from Your Turn #7).

$$CR_A = Q_A\sqrt{\frac{MSE}{br}} = (3.51)\sqrt{\frac{4.815}{(3)(4)}}$$
$$= (3.51)(0.6334) = 2.22$$

Factor A means for each scent can be found in Excel Cells G25, H25, and I25 from Your Turn #7. Note that Lavender = Sample 1, Citrus = Sample 2, and Unscented = Sample 3.

$\lvert\bar{x}_i - \bar{x}_j\rvert$	CR_A	**Decision**
$\lvert\bar{x}_1 - \bar{x}_2\rvert = \lvert 14.92 - 17.08\rvert = 2.16$	2.22	Means are not different
$\lvert\bar{x}_1 - \bar{x}_3\rvert = \lvert 14.92 - 13.33\rvert = 1.59$	2.22	Means are not different
$\lvert\bar{x}_2 - \bar{x}_3\rvert = \lvert 17.08 - 13.33\rvert = 3.75$	2.22	Means are different

We can conclude that the average citrus scores are higher than the average unscented scores. There is not enough evidence to claim a difference in the lavender and unscented scores, or the average lavender and citrus scores.

Chi-Square Tests

IN THIS CHAPTER, YOU WILL LEARN TO:

- Test for a difference in two or more population proportions.
- Determine if observed frequencies follow a discrete probability distribution.
- Determine if observed frequencies follow a Poisson probability distribution.
- Determine if observed frequencies follow a binomial probability distribution.
- Determine if observed frequencies follow a normal probability distribution.
- Test the independence of two categorical variables.

CHAPTER 12 MAP

Stats in Practice: Quadrophobia: The Fear of the Number 4

Imagine examining the financial statements of thousands of U.S. firms with the sole purpose of recording the last digit of the quarterly earnings per share (EPS). It would be reasonable to expect that you would observe roughly the same number of occurrences of each digit from 0 to 9. However, when this very task was performed by Stanford University's Joseph Grundfest and Nadya Malenko on nearly half a million earnings reports over a 27-year period, a surprising result was discovered. When the authors calculated earnings per share down to the tenth of a cent and then rounded to the nearest cent, they found the digit "4" occurred far less than the expected 10%. The values "2" and "3" were also underrepresented in the sample. Figure 12.1 summarizes the findings as a relative frequency distribution.

FIGURE 12.1
The Relative Frequency Distribution for the Final Digits in Earnings-per-Share Reports

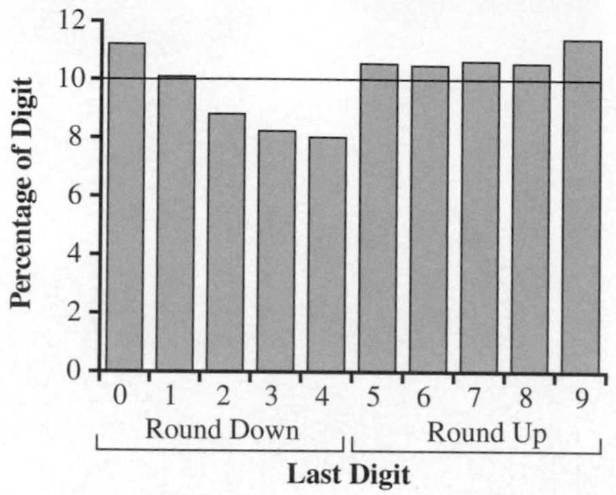

Reported EPSs that appear in a firm's financial statements are rounded to the nearest cent. For example, 16.4 cents would be rounded down to 16 cents, whereas 16.5 cents would be rounded up to 17 cents. It is therefore beneficial for firms to arrive at an EPS that ends in 0.5 cents or greater in order to round up.

If the tenth-of-a-cent place digit in the EPS reports were truly random, we would expect the percentage for each of the 10 digits from zero through nine to be close to 10%. The Stanford University authors concluded that there is an extremely low probability of the results shown in Figure 12.1 occurring merely by chance. It is more likely firms are manipulating their earnings results through accounting practices. Missing a company's EPS expectations, even by a cent, can have financial ramifications for the firm's managers. Sounds like some companies may be cooking the books (at least a little)!

Grundfest and Malenko coined the term *quadrophobia* to describe the apparent aversion of firms to report their earnings per share with the number "4" as the final digit. After reading this chapter, you will be able to calculate the probability of the number "4" appearing only 8% of the time on financial reports. Then you can decide for yourself how prevalent the phenomenon of quadrophobia is.

Based on: "Quadrophobia: Strategic Rounding of EPS Data," by Joseph Grundfest and Nadya Malenko, Stanford University, October 2009.

The previous three chapters have focused on different types of hypothesis testing. In Chapter 9 we learned how to perform a test for a single population mean or proportion. We then compared two population means or proportions in Chapter 10. In Chapter 11 we compared three or more population means.

In this chapter we will learn a series of hypothesis-testing techniques that rely on a new probability distribution known as the **chi-square distribution**. With this distribution we can do the following:

The **chi-square distribution** is used to compare two or more population proportions, perform a goodness-of-fit test, and test two categorical variables for independence.

- Compare two or more population proportions. For example, we can decide if there is a difference in the proportions of Democrats, Republicans, and Independent voters who are in favor of the new health care plan.

- Perform a goodness-of-fit test to determine if data follow a particular probability distribution, such as the normal distribution
- Test two categorical variables for independence. With this procedure, we can determine if the education level of a consumer has an impact on the model of car he or she purchases.

We'll start this chapter off with a chi-square technique that allows us to compare two or more population proportions.

12.1 Comparing Two or More Population Proportions

To introduce the technique to compare two or more population proportions, I'll rely on the following example. The writer of a recent article in *Bloomberg BusinessWeek*[1] stated that "on Wall Street, Monday is the best day of the week." So what do you think? Is this true? The information was based on the number of days the S&P 500 index increased and decreased by weekday over the course of a six-month period. Table 12.1 shows the number of times the market was up and the number of times the market was down for each day of the week along with the total number of observations for each. The last column in the table shows the proportion, or percentage, of days the index increased on each weekday. The statement in the article is based on the fact that on 80% of Mondays in this sample there was an increase in the S&P 500 index. This was a higher percentage of "up" days than any other day of the week experienced.

The **observed frequencies**, f_o, refer to the sample data collected from a population of interest.

The term f_o in Table 12.1 refers to the **observed frequencies**. We are interested in determining if the proportion of "up" days truly differs across days of the week for the S&P index, which would provide support for the claim made by the *BusinessWeek* article. In other words, do we have enough evidence from this sample to support the writer's statement that Mondays have more "up" days than the rest of the week as a general rule? Does the information present a real pattern we could rely on as investors to make decisions? Let's go to work!

TABLE 12.1 | THE PERFORMANCE OF THE S&P 500 BY WEEKDAY

DAY	UP DAYS f_o	DOWN DAYS f_o	TOTAL DAYS	PROPORTION OF UP DAYS
Monday	20	5	25	$20/25 = 0.80$
Tuesday	15	11	26	$15/26 = 0.58$
Wednesday	17	9	26	$17/26 = 0.65$
Thursday	14	11	25	$14/25 = 0.56$
Friday	12	11	23	$12/23 = 0.52$
Total	78	47	125	

Step 1: Identify the null and alternative hypotheses.

The hypothesis statement for this test is very similar to the one-way ANOVA from Chapter 11. For the S&P 500 example, it is as follows:

$$H_0: p_1 = p_2 = p_3 = p_4 = p_5$$
$$H_1: \text{Not all } p\text{s are equal}$$

[1] "Wall Street Loves Mondays," *Bloomberg BusinessWeek*, April 12, 2010; http://www.businessweek.com

Lowering α without changing the sample size will increase β, the probability of a Type II error (failing to reject a null hypothesis that should be rejected). This happens when we conclude there is no difference in the proportion of "up" days among the weekdays when, in reality, there is a difference.

where

p_i = The proportion of "up" days for the ith day of the week

As with our previous hypothesis tests, we need to identify our significance level, which is the probability of committing a Type I error. For this example, I'll set the significance level to $\alpha = 0.05$. Had we chosen a lower value for α, say 0.01, we would reduce our chances of incorrectly rejecting the null hypothesis. In other words, we would be less likely to conclude there is a difference in the proportion of "up" days among the weekdays, when in reality, there is no difference in the population proportions for the S&P index.

Step 2: Calculate the expected frequencies.

The **expected frequencies**, f_e, refer to the frequencies that are most likely to occur if the null hypothesis is true.

In this step, we calculate the **expected frequencies**, which are the frequencies that are most likely to occur if the null hypothesis is true. We are assuming that the proportions are equal for each weekday because, like rolling a die, that is what we would expect to see if the number of "up" days were purely random. Consequently, we need to calculate the overall proportion, $\hat{p}$, of "up" days. From Table 12.1, we recorded a total of 78 "up" days from a total of 125 days. This results in the following overall proportion:

$$\hat{p} = \frac{78}{125} = 0.624$$

In other words, 62.4% of the days during the period were "up" days. This proportion represents our estimate for each value of p_1 through p_5 under the null hypothesis. We would expect this proportion to hold true for each weekday. We use this proportion to calculate the expected frequency of "up" days, f_e, for each weekday by multiplying $\hat{p}$ by the values in the "Total Days" column in Table 12.1. Table 12.2 shows these calculations.

TABLE 12.2 | CALCULATING THE EXPECTED FREQUENCIES OF "UP" DAYS

DAYS	$\hat{p}$	TOTAL DAYS	EXPECTED FREQUENCIES OF UP DAYS, f_e
Monday	0.624	25	15.6
Tuesday	0.624	26	16.22
Wednesday	0.624	26	16.22
Thursday	0.624	25	15.6
Friday	0.624	23	14.35

Expected frequencies do not have to be integers because they represent only theoretical values. On the other hand, observed frequencies (total days) must be integers, because they are countable items.

We also need to calculate the expected frequencies of the occurrence of "down" days. We can do this by subtracting the expected frequencies of "up" days from the total days shown in Table 12.3.

TABLE 12.3 | CALCULATING THE EXPECTED FREQUENCIES OF "DOWN" DAYS

DAYS	TOTAL DAYS	EXPECTED FREQUENCIES OF UP DAYS, f_e	EXPECTED FREQUENCIES OF DOWN DAYS, f_e
Monday	25	15.6	9.4
Tuesday	26	16.22	9.78
Wednesday	26	16.22	9.78
Thursday	25	15.6	9.4
Friday	23	14.35	8.65

The chi-square test requires that each expected frequency be equal to or greater than five.

The chi-square test requires that each expected frequency be equal to or greater than five. This requirement ensures that the chi-square test statistic (shown in Step 3) follows the chi-square distribution (to be introduced in Step 4). Looking at Tables 12.2 and 12.3, it appears that the lowest frequency is 8.65. Consequently, this requirement is met. (Later in the chapter, we'll examine how to handle the situation when this requirement is not met.)

Step 3: Calculate the chi-square test statistic, χ^2.

The test statistic for the chi-square test for two or more proportions is shown in Equation 12.1.

Formula 12.1 for the Chi-Square Test Statistic

$$\chi^2 = \sum \frac{(f_o - f_e)^2}{f_e}$$

where

χ^2 = The chi-square test statistic
f_o = The observed frequencies
f_e = The expected frequencies if the null hypothesis is true

The logic of the chi-square test statistic is as follows:

The null hypothesis states that the proportion of "up" days is the same for each day of the week.

- If the observed frequencies are close to the expected frequencies, the term $(f_o - f_e)^2$ in Equation 12.1 will be small. This will result in a smaller chi-square test statistic, which increases the likelihood that there is support for the null hypothesis.
- If the observed frequencies are far apart from the expected frequencies, the term $(f_o - f_e)^2$ in Equation 12.1 will be large. This will result in a larger chi-square test statistic, which increases the likelihood of our rejecting the null hypothesis.

Table 12.4 assists us with these calculations. Columns 1 and 2 are the observed and expected frequencies from Table 12.1, 12.2, and 12.3. The remaining columns were determined as follows:

Column 3 = Column 1 minus Column 2
Column 4 = Column 3 squared
Column 5 = Column 4 divided by Column 2

TABLE 12.4 | CALCULATING THE CHI-SQUARE TEST STATISTIC

DAY	(1) f_o	(2) f_e	(3) $(f_o - f_e)$	(4) $(f_o - f_e)^2$	(5) $\frac{(f_o - f_e)^2}{f_e}$
Monday–up	20	15.6	4.4	19.36	1.24
Monday–down	5	9.4	−4.4	19.36	2.06
Tuesday–up	15	16.22	−1.22	1.49	0.09
Tuesday–down	11	9.78	1.22	1.49	0.15
Wednesday–up	17	16.22	0.78	0.61	0.04
Wednesday–down	9	9.78	−0.78	0.61	0.06
Thursday–up	14	15.6	−1.6	2.56	0.16
Thursday–down	11	9.4	1.6	2.56	0.27
Friday–up	12	14.35	−2.35	5.52	0.38
Friday–down	11	8.65	2.35	5.52	0.64
Total					$\chi^2 = \sum \frac{(f_o - f_e)^2}{f_e} = 5.09$

If the null hypothesis is true ($\hat{p}$ is close to the same value for each day of the week), we would expect the chi-square test statistic to be close to zero. Think about it: Under these conditions, the values for f_o and f_e would be very close, making the difference between these values almost zero. On the other hand, if our test statistic is very large, we have evidence that the null hypothesis is not true. Stay tuned!

Step 4: Determine the chi-square critical value, χ^2_α.

The test statistic shown in Equation 12.1 follows a new distribution—the chi-square distribution shown in Figure 12.2. As you can see, this distribution is right-skewed, and the rejection region lies in the right tail. The chi-square test for proportions is always a one-tail (upper) hypothesis test as shown in Figure 12.2. This is because the chi-square statistic in Equation 12.1 will increase (move toward the right tail) under either of the following scenarios:

- When observed frequencies are less than expected frequencies
- When observed frequencies are more than expected frequencies

This is a result of the squared difference of observed and expected frequencies, $(f_o - f_e)^2$, in the numerator of Equation 12.1.

The chi-square distribution has degrees of freedom (*df*) equal to

$$df = k - 1$$

where k equals the number of categories. In the S&P 500 example, the categories are the weekdays, so $k = 5$.

FIGURE 12.2
The Chi-Square Distribution

Do Not Reject H_0
$1 - \alpha$
Reject H_0
α
χ^2_α
Critical Score

The rejection region for a chi-square test for two or more proportions is always in the right tail of the distribution.

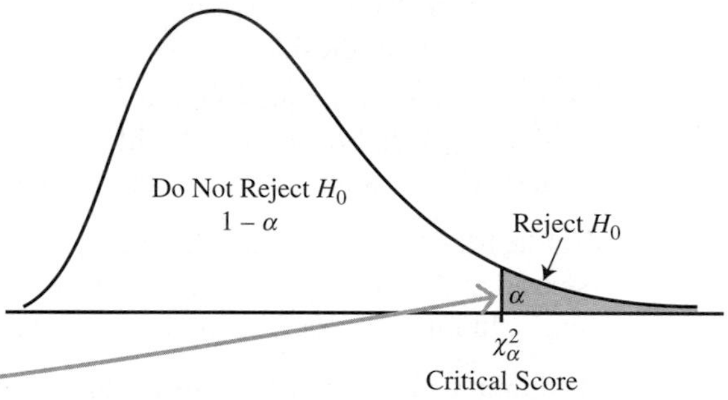

The critical value for the chi-square distribution, χ^2_α, can be found in Table 8 in Appendix A. An excerpt from this table is shown in Table 12.5.

TABLE 12.5 | Excerpt of Chi-Square Critical Values

	AREA IN RIGHT TAIL OF DISTRIBUTION									
df	**0.995**	**0.99**	**0.975**	**0.95**	**0.90**	**0.10**	**0.05**	**0.025**	**0.01**	**0.005**
1			0.001	0.004	0.016	2.706	3.841	5.024	6.635	7.879
2	0.010	0.020	0.051	0.103	0.211	4.605	5.991	7.378	9.210	10.597
3	0.072	0.115	0.216	0.352	0.584	6.251	7.815	9.348	11.345	12.838
4	0.207	0.297	0.484	0.711	1.064	7.779	9.488	11.143	13.277	14.860
5	0.412	0.554	0.831	1.145	1.610	9.236	11.070	12.833	15.086	16.750
6	0.676	0.872	1.237	1.635	2.204	10.645	12.592	14.449	16.812	18.548

For our S&P 500 example, we have $k - 1 = 5 - 1 = 4$ degrees of freedom. Using the $\alpha = 0.05$ column, Table 12.5 indicates that our critical value is $\chi^2_\alpha = \chi^2_{0.05} = 9.488$ (highlighted in red).

Another way to determine the critical chi-square score is with Excel's CHISQ.INV.RT function, which has the following characteristics:

$$=\text{CHISQ.INV.RT (alpha, degrees\_of\_freedom)}$$

where

$$\begin{aligned} \text{alpha} &= \text{The significance level, } \alpha \\ \text{degrees\_of\_freedom} &= k - 1 \\ k &= \text{The number of categories} \end{aligned}$$

For our S&P 500 example, we have

$$=\text{CHISQ.INV.RT}(0.05, 4) = 9.488$$

which matches the value from Table 12.5.

Step 5: Compare the test statistic (χ^2) with the critical value (χ^2_α).

This comparison is used to decide whether to reject or fail to reject the null hypothesis. To do so, we use the decision rules shown in Table 12.6.

TABLE 12.6 | DECISION RULES FOR THE CHI-SQUARE TEST

CONDITION		CONCLUSION
$\chi^2 \le \chi^2_\alpha$	$\longrightarrow$	Do not reject H_0
$\chi^2 > \chi^2_\alpha$	$\longrightarrow$	Reject H_0

Because $\chi^2 = 5.09$, which is less than $\chi^2_\alpha = 9.488$, we fail to reject the null hypothesis according to Table 12.6. We can see this graphically in Figure 12.3. The test statistic, χ^2, is clearly in the white "Do Not Reject" region.

FIGURE 12.3
Comparing the Chi-Square Test Statistic with the Chi-Square Critical Score for the S&P 500 Example

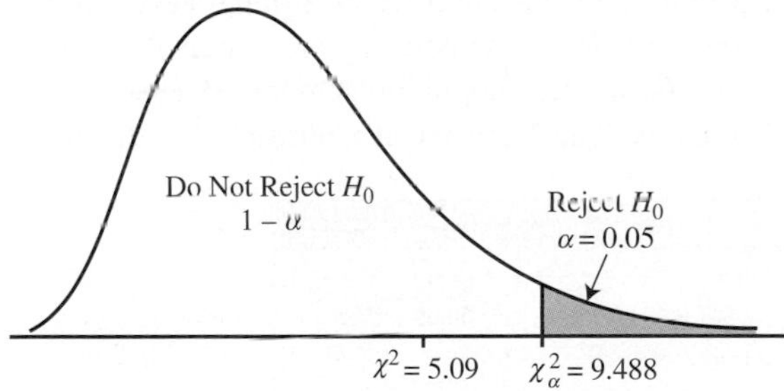

Step 6: State your conclusions.

Recall that our hypothesis statement was as follows:

$$H_0: p_1 = p_2 = p_3 = p_4 = p_5$$
$$H_1: \text{Not all } p\text{s are equal}$$

Be careful here not to make the common mistake of accepting the null hypothesis and claiming that the proportions of "up" days for each day of the week are equal. Because our conclusions are based only on a sample from the population, we do not have enough evidence to claim the population proportions are equal.

By failing to reject the null hypothesis, we do not have enough evidence to conclude the population proportions are different. Notice that this is *not* consistent with the claim by the *BusinessWeek* article that "Monday is the best day of the week" for the S&P 500 index. I hope that you agree with me that this statement has little statistical merit but sounds convincing coming from a well-known publication such as *BusinessWeek*. After all, if it's in print, it must be true!

As tempting as it is to believe *BusinessWeek* and alter our investment strategy, we just don't have enough evidence to confirm the publication's claim because we failed to reject the null hypothesis. This *BusinessWeek* article is guilty of using a sample to make an erroneous conclusion about a population. This is a great example of the benefits of statistics in the business world. Now aren't you glad you're reading this chapter?

Using PHStat to Compare Two or More Proportions

You can also use PHStat for Windows to compare two or more proportions by taking the following steps. Excel for Mac users can go the the textbook's Web site for these instructions. (www.pearsonhighered.com/donnelly)

1. Go to **Add-Ins** > **PHStat** > **Multiple-Sample Tests** > **Chi-Square Test**, as shown in Figure 12.4A.

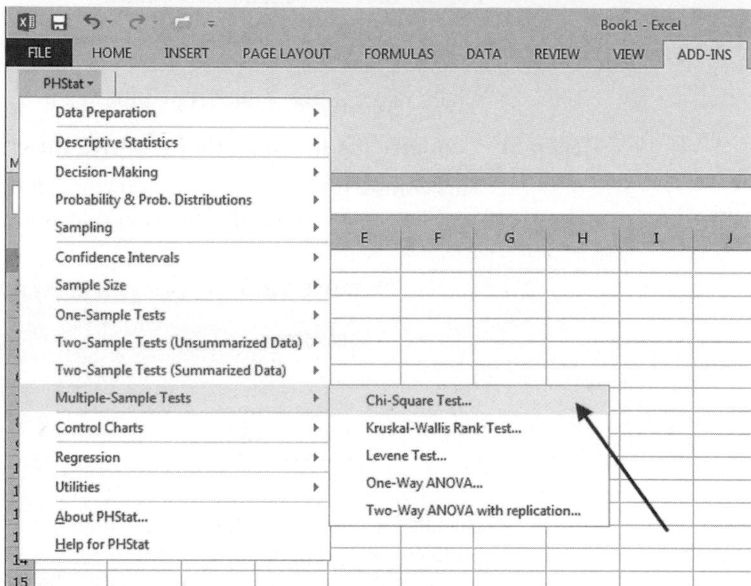

FIGURE 12.4A
Using PHStat to Compare Two or More Proportions (Step 1)

2. Fill in the values in the **Chi-Square Test** dialog box as shown in Figure 12.4B. Notice that in PHStat, the columns are assigned to the categories being tested. Because we are comparing five populations in the S&P example, the **Number of Rows** = 5 in the dialog box. The **Number of Columns** = 2 for the "up" and "down" days. Click **OK**.

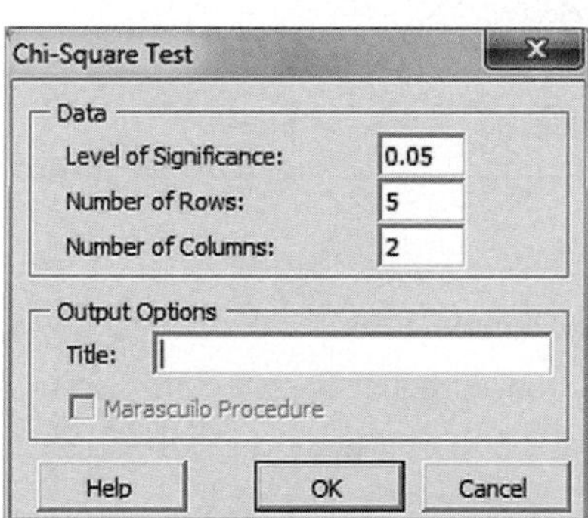

FIGURE 12.4B
Using PHStat to Compare Two or More Proportions (Step 2)

3. You will be presented with a spreadsheet that contains a PHStat User Note in a text box. After reading the note, hit the **Delete** key to remove it.
4. Enter the observed frequencies and labels from Table 12.1 into the top blue-shaded table (circled in red) as shown in Figure 12.4C.

FIGURE 12.4C
Using PHStat to Compare Two or More Proportions (Final Result)

	A	B	C	D	E	F	G
1	**Chi-Square Test**						
2							
3	**Observed Frequencies**						
4		Column variable				Calculations	
5	**Row variable**	**C1**	**C2**	**Total**		fo-fe	
6	**R1**	**20**	**5**	25		4.4	-4.4
7	**R2**	**15**	**11**	26		-1.224	1.224
8	**R3**	**17**	**9**	26		0.776	-0.776
9	**R4**	**14**	**11**	25		-1.6	1.6
10	**R5**	**12**	**11**	23		-2.352	2.352
11	**Total**	**78**	**47**	**125**			
12							
13	Expected Frequencies						
14		Column variable					
15	Row variable	C1	C2	Total		(fo-fe)^2/fe	
16	R1	15.6	9.4	25		1.241026	2.059574
17	R2	16.224	9.776	26		0.092343	0.15325
18	R3	16.224	9.776	26		0.037116	0.061597
19	R4	15.6	9.4	25		0.164103	0.27234
20	R5	14.352	8.648	23		0.385445	0.639674
21	Total	78	47	125			
22							
23	**Data**						
24	**Level of Significance**	**0.05**					
25	Number of Rows	5					
26	Number of Columns	2					
27	Degrees of Freedom	4					
28							
29	**Results**						
30	**Critical Value**	**9.487729**					
31	**Chi-Square Test Statistic**	**5.10647**					
32	**p-Value**	**0.276546**					
33	**Do not reject the null hypothesis**						
34							
35	***Expected frequency assumption***						
36	***is met.***						
37							

The results of the chi-square analysis are shown in the yellow-shaded table in Figure 12.4C. Notice that the chi-square test statistic in Cell B31 (5.10647) is slightly different from the 5.09 value that we previously calculated. This discrepancy is due to rounding differences because Excel uses many more decimal places than we did when performing this analysis. Cell B32 shows our old friend the *p*-value, which represents the probability of observing a value for our test statistic, χ^2, greater than 5.10647 if the null hypothesis is true. This is shown graphically in Figure 12.5.

FIGURE 12.5
The *p*-Value for the S&P 500 Example

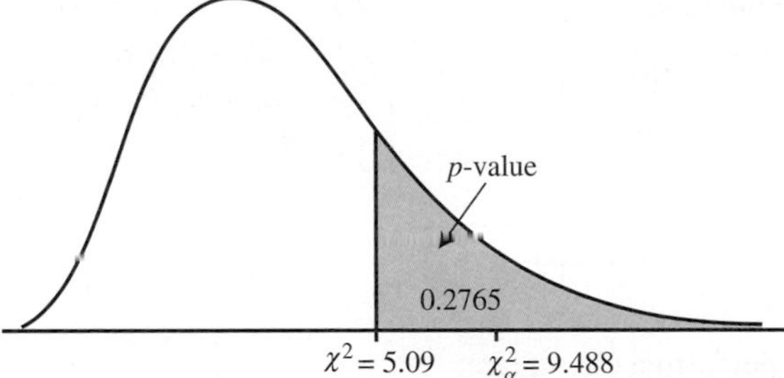

Because our *p*-value $= 0.2765$, which is greater than $\alpha = 0.05$, we fail to reject the null hypothesis.

We can use Excel's CHISQ.DIST.RT function to determine the *p*-value for our chi-square test statistic, which has the following characteristics:

$$=\text{CHISQ.DIST.RT}(x, \text{degrees\_of\_freedom})$$

When we set x to our test statistic (χ^2), this function provides the area to the right of $\chi^2 = 5.09$, which equals the *p*-value as follows:

$$=\text{CHISQ.DIST.RT}(5.09, 4) = 0.2782$$

The slight difference between this value and the one shown in Figure 12.5 (0.2765) is due to rounding.

While I've got you excited about the chi-square test for proportions, take a few minutes to work on this Your Turn problem.

YOUR TURN #1

A *Wall Street Journal* article titled "When Icing the Kicker Can Backfire[2]" discussed the strategy of calling time-out just before a kicker in the NFL is about to try a field goal in the last 2 minutes of a game. The theory is that making the kicker wait the extra time will make him more nervous and increase the chances of him missing the field goal. This strategy is known as "icing the kicker." The *Wall Street Journal* article relied on field goal data collected from games since 2000. The following table shows this data for field goal attempts from 51 yards and longer:

Time-Out Called	Field Goals Made	Field Goals Missed	Total	Proportion Made
No	23	31	54	$23/54 = 0.426$
Yes (icing)	14	11	25	$14/25 = 0.560$
Total	37	42	79	

From this sample, notice that a higher proportion of field goals are made when the "icing the kicker" strategy is employed. The *Wall Street Journal* article concludes by implying that icing the kicker may have the *opposite* effect and actually improve the kicker's chances of making the field goal.

a. Using $\alpha = 0.05$, comment on the validity of this article's conclusion.
b. Determine the *p*-value using Excel and interpret its meaning.
c. Verify your results with PHStat.

Answers can be found on ▶ **pages 619–620**

[2]"When Icing the Kicker Can Backfire," *Wall Street Journal*, September 22, 2010; http://online.wsj.com

12.1 Section Problems

Basic Skills

12.1 Consider the following observed frequencies:

Population	Yes	No
A	20	18
B	10	12

Calculate the expected frequency for each observed frequency.

12.2 Using the data from Problem 12.1, perform a chi-square test using $\alpha = 0.05$ to determine if the proportion of "Yes" observations differs between Populations A and B.

12.3 Consider the following observed frequencies:

Population	Yes	No
A	10	22
B	16	26
C	17	9

Calculate the expected frequency for each observed frequency.

12.4 Using the data from Problem 12.3, perform a chi-square test using $\alpha = 0.05$ to determine if the proportion of "Yes" observations differs among Populations A, B, and C.

Applications

12.5 An important statistic that the Bureau of Labor Statistics (BLS) tracks is the percentage of Americans between the ages of 25 and 54 who are currently working. Suppose a random sample of 100 men in this age group as selected and it was found that 83 were currently working. A similar sample of 100 women was selected and it was discovered that 70 were working.

a. Using $\alpha = 0.05$, can we conclude that the proportion of men in this age group who are working differs from the proportion of women who are working?
b. Determine the *p*-value for the chi-square test statistic using Excel and interpret its meaning.
c. Confirm your results using PHStat.

12.6 The federal government would like to determine if the proportion of households without health insurance coverage differs with household income. Suppose the following data were collected from 700 randomly selected households.

Household Income	Health Insurance Yes	No
Less than $25,000	57	21
$25,000 to $49,999	142	41
$50,000 to $74,999	205	36
$75,000 or more	180	18

a. Using $\alpha = 0.01$, perform a chi-square test to determine if the proportion of households without health insurance differs by income bracket.
b. Confirm your results with PHStat.
c. Interpret the meaning of the p-value from PHStat.
d. How does income appear to impact the likelihood that a household has insurance coverage?

12.7 A survey asked Democrats, Republicans, and Independent voters what the most important message is to send to Congress. One of the most popular responses for all three groups was to "focus on the economy." The number of respondents, the messages they want sent, and their party affiliations are shown in the following table:

Message	Democrat	Republican	Independent
Focus on economy	55	61	59
Other	95	114	61
Total	150	175	120

a. Using $\alpha = 0.05$, perform a chi-square test to determine if the proportion of voters who responded "focus on the economy" differs among the three groups of voters.
b. Determine the p-value using Excel and interpret its meaning.
c. Confirm your results with PHStat.
d. How does party affiliation appear to affect the likelihood that a voter will choose the "focus on the economy" message to send to Congress?

12.8 An increase in the number of skin cancer cases has raised the awareness of the importance on wearing sunscreen for protection. Suppose the Skin Cancer Foundation surveyed 75 men and found that 35 had not applied sunscreen in the past 12 months. A random sample of 80 women found that 23 had not applied sunscreen during the past year.

a. Using $\alpha = 0.01$, can we conclude that the proportion of men who have not applied sunscreen during the past year is different than the proportion of women?
b. Determine the p-value for the chi-square test statistic using Excel and interpret its meaning.
c. Confirm your results using PHStat.

12.2 Determining If Observed Frequencies Follow a Known Probability Distribution

The chi-square **goodness-of-fit test** is used to decide if observed frequencies follow a known probability distribution

The next chi-square technique we'll discuss is known as a **goodness-of-fit test**. The test helps us to decide if the observed frequencies follow a known probability distribution. In the following sections, we will test for a general discrete distribution as well as binomial, Poisson, and normal distributions. (Yes, I know. These distributions seem like the creatures in the movie *Zombieland*: They just keep coming back. However, unlike zombies, I promise you they are quite useful.)

Testing for a Discrete Probability Distribution

We'll start off our discussion of the goodness-of-fit test by using the chi-square distribution to test if a set of observed frequencies follows a predetermined discrete frequency distribution. For example, a local Bank of America branch has a drive-through window for teller transactions. The bank's managers believe that the weekly demand for services through this window follows the probability distribution shown in Table 12.7. For instance, it is thought that 20% of the weekly volume occurs on Monday. This table also shows the number of daily customers using this window during a randomly selected week, which represents the observed frequencies, f_o.

TABLE 12.7 | The Probability Distribution and Demand for Drive-Through Service

WEEKDAY	PROBABILITY	DAILY DEMAND, f_o
Monday	0.20	58
Tuesday	0.10	21
Wednesday	0.10	27
Thursday	0.15	20
Friday	0.25	71
Saturday	0.20	43
Total	1.00	240

We would like to perform a chi-square test to determine if the observed frequencies shown in Table 12.7 provide enough evidence to conclude, using $\alpha = 0.10$, that the overall demand pattern follows the stated probabilities. This information is useful in assisting management with planning and staffing decisions. I'll do so with the following steps:

The null hypothesis for a chi-square goodness-of-fit test always states that the stated distribution is followed.

Step 1: Identify the null and alternative hypotheses.

The null hypothesis for this test is that weekly demand does follow the stated probability distribution. The hypothesis statement is therefore as follows:

H_0 : Weekly demand follows the stated probability distribution

H_1 : Weekly demand does not follow the stated probability distribution

Step 2: Calculate the expected frequencies.

For the Bank of America example, the expected frequencies represent the daily demand that will occur if the stated probabilities describe the demand pattern. We calculate the expected frequencies, f_e, by multiplying the total weekly demand (240) by the probability for each day of the week. These calculations are shown in Table 12.8.

TABLE 12.8 | Calculating the Expected Frequencies Demanded for Drive-Through Service

DAY	PROBABILITY	TOTAL DEMAND	EXPECTED FREQUENCIES DEMANDED, f_e
Monday	0.20	240	48
Tuesday	0.10	240	24
Wednesday	0.10	240	24
Thursday	0.15	240	36
Friday	0.25	240	60
Saturday	0.20	240	48
Total	1.00		240

If you do the math correctly, the total expected frequency should equal the total demand. In this example, the values for both are 240.

All of the chi-square tests in this section also require that each expected frequency be 5 or more. As you can see, this requirement is satisfied in Table 12.8.

Step 3: Calculate the chi-square test statistic, χ^2.

We'll use Equation 12.1 again, with the help of Table 12.9, to calculate the chi-square test statistic.

TABLE 12.9 | CALCULATING THE CHI-SQUARE TEST STATISTIC

DAY	f_o	f_e	$(f_o - f_e)$	$(f_o - f_e)^2$	$\frac{(f_o - f_e)^2}{f_e}$
Monday	58	48	10	100	2.08
Tuesday	21	24	−3	9	0.38
Wednesday	27	24	3	9	0.38
Thursday	20	36	−16	256	7.11
Friday	71	60	11	121	2.02
Saturday	43	48	−5	25	0.52
Total			$\chi^2 = \sum\frac{(f_o - f_e)^2}{f_e}$		= 12.49

A true null hypothesis would result in the observed and expected frequencies being very close to one another. This, in turn, would cause the test statistic, χ^2, to be close to zero. A large test statistic would increase the likelihood of rejecting the null hypothesis.

Step 4: Determine the chi-square critical value, χ^2_α.

The chi-square goodness-of-fit test has the following degrees of freedom:

$$df = k - m - 1$$

where

$m =$ The number of parameters estimated from the sample in the hypothesis statement

$k =$ The number of categories

The next section provides an example of when you will need to calculate the sample mean in order to determine the expected frequencies.

For our Bank of America example, we are not estimating any population parameters, such as the mean or standard deviation, with the sample. Therefore, $m = 0$. This example does have six categories (one for each day of the workweek), so $k = 6$. As a result, our chi-square critical value has $k - m - 1 = 6 - 0 - 1 = 5$ degrees of freedom. If we go to the $\alpha = 0.10$ column in Table 12.5, we'll find that $\chi^2_\alpha = 9.236$.

Step 5: Compare the test statistic (χ^2) with the critical value (χ^2_α.)

Because $\chi^2 = 12.49$ and this is more than $\chi^2_\alpha = 9.236$, we reject the null hypothesis according to Table 12.6. We can see this graphically in Figure 12.6 which shows the test statistic, χ^2, in the shaded rejection region.

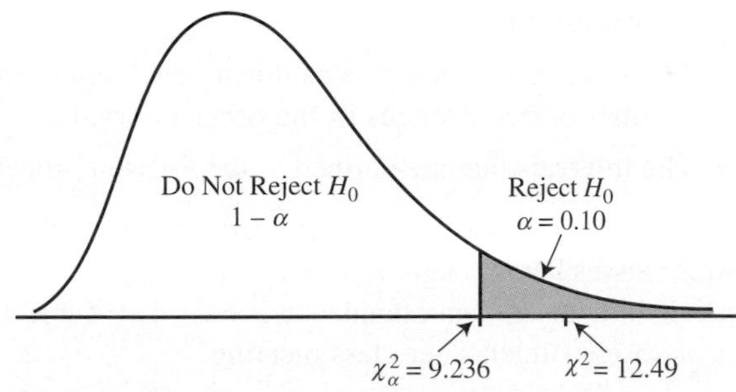

FIGURE 12.6 Comparing the Chi-Square Test Statistic with the Chi-Square Critical Score for the Drive-Through Service Example

Step 6: Determine the p-value.

We can use Excel's CHISQ.DIST.RT function to determine the p-value for this chi-square test statistic:

=CHISQ.DIST.RT (12.49, 5) = 0.0287

Because the p-value $= 0.0287$ and is less than $\alpha = 0.05$, we can reject the null hypothesis.

Step 7: State your conclusions.

By rejecting the null hypothesis, we conclude that the true probability distribution for weekly demand does not follow the stated distribution shown in Table 12.7. For instance, it appears that the observed demand for Thursday was much lower than the distribution predicted.

The following Your Turn problem will give you a chance to try your hand at a goodness-of-fit test.

YOUR TURN #2

A college professor claims that her intended grade distribution is shown in the following table. The table also shows the actual grade distribution from the most recent semester for the 120 students in her classes.

Grade	Intended Percentage	Actual Number of Students
A	20	36
B	25	27
C	40	42
D	10	9
F	5	6
Total	100	120

Using $\alpha = 0.05$, use this semester's data to test the faculty member's claim.

Answer can be found on ▶ **page 620**

Testing for a Poisson Distribution

We can also perform a chi-square hypothesis test to determine if observed data follow a Poisson distribution. Recall from Chapter 5 that a **Poisson process** has the following characteristics:

- The experiment consists of counting the number of occurrences of an event over a period of time, area, distance, or any other type of measurement.
- The mean of the Poisson distribution has to be the same for each equal interval of measurement.
- The number of occurrences during each equal interval has to be independent of the number of occurrences in the other intervals.
- The intervals that are defined in the Poisson process cannot be overlapping.

I'll use the following example to demonstrate this procedure. Suppose there are five statistics classes being taught this semester at Averett University. The classes meet three times a week, and the student attendance is recorded. Table 12.10 shows the frequency of the number of absent students per class meeting.

TABLE 12.10 | FREQUENCY OF THE NUMBER OF ABSENT STUDENTS PER CLASS

NUMBER OF ABSENT STUDENTS PER CLASS MEETING, X	FREQUENCY, f_o
0	22
1	38
2	39
3	29
4	15
5	5
6	2
Total	150

For instance, of the 150 class meetings, there were 22 in which no students were absent.

Suppose the Registrar's Office would like to perform a hypothesis test to determine if the number of absent students per class follows the Poisson distribution using $\alpha = 0.05$. Knowing the probability that a certain number of students will be absent could be used to implement attendance policies.

Recall from Chapter 5 that there is no limit to the number of occurrences for a Poisson process. In other words, the value for x in Table 12.10 has no upper limit. Obviously, we have a finite number of students in these classes (fortunately for the instructor); but the class size is so much larger than the typical number of absent students (fortunately for the instructor again); we can assume this process could follow the Poisson distribution.

I'll demonstrate this technique using the following steps:

Step 1: Identify the null and alternative hypotheses.

The null hypothesis for this test is that the number of students absent per class meeting follows the Poisson probability distribution. The hypothesis statement is therefore as follows:

The hypothesis for this absent-student example is testing only to determine that the data follow a Poisson distribution. This is opposed to testing for a Poisson distribution with a specific mean. There's a big difference between the two as you will later see.

H_0 : The number of absent students follows the Poisson distribution

H_1 : The number of absent students does not follow the Poisson distribution

Step 2: Calculate the expected frequencies.

To calculate the expected frequencies, we need to find the Poisson probabilities for each number of absent students in Table 12.10. Recall from Chapter 5 that the Poisson probabilities can be calculated using Equation 12.2.

Formula 12.2 for the Poisson Probability Distribution

$$P(x) = \frac{\lambda^x e^{-\lambda}}{x!}$$

where

$x =$ The number of occurrences of interest over the interval
$\lambda =$ The mean number of occurrences over the interval
$e =$ The mathematical constant 2.71828
$P(x) =$ The probability of exactly x occurrences over the interval

In this example, the interval is a class meeting, and the random variable x represents the number of absent students for each class meeting.

We also need λ, the mean of the Poisson distribution, to calculate our probabilities. Notice that the mean of the distribution was not specified in the hypothesis statement. Because of this, we need to calculate the mean for the data in Table 12.10 and use it to estimate the mean for the Poisson distribution. In Chapter 3, you learned how to calculate the mean of a frequency distribution. The formula is repeated in Equation 12.3.

Formula 12.3 for the Mean of a Frequency Distribution

$$\lambda = \frac{\sum_{i=1}^{k}(x_i f_i)}{\sum_{i=1}^{k} f_i}$$

Using the values from Table 12.10, we have the following:

$$\lambda = \frac{\sum_{i=1}^{k}(x_i f_i)}{\sum_{i=1}^{k} f_i} = \frac{(0)(22) + (1)(38) + (2)(39) + (3)(29) + (4)(15) + (5)(5) + (6)(}{22 + 38 + 39 + 29 + 15 + 5 + 2}$$

Based on our sample, the average number of students absent per class meeting is 2.0

$$\lambda = \frac{300}{150} = 2.0 \text{ students per class meeting}$$

We now have enough information to generate our Poisson probabilities for each value of x, the number of absent students. We can do so using one of four methods:

1. Equation 12.2
2. Excel's POISSON.DIST(x, λ, False) function
3. The Poisson probability table found in Table 2 in Appendix A
4. Guess and hope for the best (*not* recommended)

Table 12.11 shows an excerpt from Appendix A with the appropriate column highlighted in yellow.

TABLE 12.11 | EXCERPT FROM TABLE 2 IN APPENDIX A (POISSON PROBABILITIES)

x	1.10	1.20	1.30	1.40	1.50	1.60	1.70	1.80	1.90	2.00
0	0.3329	0.3012	0.2725	0.2466	0.2231	0.2019	0.1827	0.1653	0.1496	0.1353
1	0.3662	0.3614	0.3543	0.3452	0.3347	0.3230	0.3106	0.2975	0.2842	0.2707
2	0.2014	0.2169	0.2303	0.2417	0.2510	0.2584	0.2640	0.2678	0.2700	0.2707
3	0.0738	0.0867	0.0998	0.1128	0.1255	0.1378	0.1496	0.1607	0.1710	0.1804
4	0.0203	0.0260	0.0324	0.0395	0.0471	0.0551	0.0636	0.0723	0.0812	0.0902
5	0.0045	0.0062	0.0084	0.0111	0.0141	0.0176	0.0216	0.0260	0.0309	0.0361
6	0.0008	0.0012	0.0018	0.0026	0.0035	0.0047	0.0061	0.0078	0.0098	0.0120
7	0.0001	0.0002	0.0003	0.0005	0.0008	0.0011	0.0015	0.0020	0.0027	0.0034
8	0.0000	0.0000	0.0001	0.0001	0.0001	0.0002	0.0003	0.0005	0.0006	0.0009
9	0.0000	0.0000	0.0000	0.0000	0.0000	0.0000	0.0001	0.0001	0.0001	0.0002

To calculate the expected frequencies for each number of absent students, we need to multiply each highlighted probability by the total number of class meetings recorded (150). Table 12.12 shows these calculations.

TABLE 12.12 | CALCULATING THE EXPECTED FREQUENCIES OF ABSENT STUDENTS

NUMBER OF ABSENT STUDENTS, X	POISSON PROBABILITIES	CLASSES	TOTAL EXPECTED FREQUENCIES
0	0.1353	150	20.30
1	0.2707	150	40.61
2	0.2707	150	40.61
3	0.1804	150	27.06
4	0.0902	150	13.53
5	0.0361	150	5.42
6 or more	0.0165	150	2.48

Remember, there is no upper limit to the number of occurrences with an interval using the Poisson distribution. Theoretically, we can have an infinite number of students absent from class on a given day. I don't like the sound of that!

Because we never had more than six students absent per class meeting, I combined the probabilities of six, seven, eight, and nine students from Table 12.11, as follows:

$$P(6 \text{ or more students absent}) = 0.0120 + 0.0034 + 0.0009 + 0.0002 = 0.0165$$

Also, notice that the expected frequency of six or more students being absent is only 2.48 instances, which is less than 5. Remember that the chi-square test requires each expected frequency to be 5 or more. To accommodate this requirement, we need to combine "5" and "6 or more" events to "5 or more," as shown in Table 12.13.

TABLE 12.13 | COMBINING THE EVENTS "5" AND "6 OR MORE"

NUMBER OF ABSENT STUDENTS, X	OBSERVED FREQUENCIES, f_o	EXPECTED FREQUENCIES, f_e
0	22	20.30
1	38	40.61
2	39	40.61
3	29	27.06
4	15	13.53
5 or more	7	7.90

Every expected frequency in Table 12.13 is now at least 5.

Step 3: Calculate the chi-square test statistic, χ^2.

We'll use Equation 12.1, with the help of Table 12.14, again to calculate the chi-square test statistic.

The closer f_o is to f_e, the smaller the chi-square test statistic will be. This reduces the chance of rejecting the null hypothesis.

TABLE 12.14 | Calculating the Chi-Square Test Statistic

Students Absent	f_o	f_e	$(f_o - f_e)$	$(f_o - f_e)^2$	$\frac{(f_o - f_e)^2}{f_e}$
0	22	20.30	1.70	2.89	0.14
1	38	40.61	−2.61	6.81	0.17
2	39	40.61	−1.61	2.59	0.06
3	29	27.06	1.94	3.76	0.14
4	15	13.53	1.47	2.16	0.16
5 or more	7	7.90	−0.90	0.81	0.10
Total					$\chi^2 = \sum\frac{(f_o - f_e)^2}{f_e} = 0.77$

Step 4: Determine the chi-square critical value, χ^2_α.

Recall from the previous section that the chi-square goodness-of-fit test has $k - m - 1$ degrees of freedom. Table 12.14 has six categories (0, 1, 2, 3, 4, 5 or more), so $k = 6$. In this example, $m = 1$ because we have to estimate the mean number of students absent in the population (the number absent in all of the statistics classes at Averett University) using the mean number of students absent in our sample. Again, this is because the hypothesis statement did not specify a population mean, λ, to be tested. Instead, with this test, we are simply trying to see if the observed data follow a Poisson distribution without λ being specified. Therefore, we have $k - m - 1 = 6 - 1 - 1 = 4$ degrees of freedom for our chi-square distribution. Essentially, having to estimate the mean from our sample has cost us 1 degree of freedom.

When we go to the $\alpha = 0.05$ column in Table 12.5 with 4 degrees of freedom, we find that $\chi^2_\alpha = 9.488$.

Step 5: Compare the test statistic (χ^2) with the critical value (χ^2_α).

Because $\chi^2 = 0.77$ and this is less than $\chi^2_\alpha = 9.488$, we fail to reject the null hypothesis according to Table 12.6.

Step 6: Determine the *p*-value.

$$p\text{-value} = \text{CHISQ.DIST.RT}\ (0.77, 4) = 0.9424$$

Because the p-value $= 0.9424$ and is greater than $\alpha = 0.05$, we fail to reject the null hypothesis.

Step 7: State your conclusions.

By failing to reject the null hypothesis, the assumption that the number of absent students per class meeting follows the Poisson distribution cannot be rejected. This leads to an interesting point (at least for me). I have been harping for quite some time now on the dangers of *accepting* the null hypothesis. When I put on my statistician's hat, I cannot state that the number of absent students follows the Poisson distribution (cannot accept the null hypothesis). However, Averett University has a *business* decision to make here, which is to (a) use the Poisson distribution to assist in developing an attendance policy or (b) not to use the Poisson distribution. When I put on my businessperson's hat, the results of this hypothesis test lead me to choose option a, which is to use the Poisson distribution in this case. I know this might seem like a contradiction, but choosing to use the Poisson distribution in this example is the appropriate business decision. I say this because there is more evidence supporting the use of the Poisson distribution than there is to not use it.

Use this Your Turn opportunity to sharpen your Poisson skills.

YOUR TURN #3

Each chapter that I write for this textbook is sent to my Development Editor, Amy Ray, who has the unfortunate task of trying to make sense of what I'm trying to say and fixing it so that it appears I know what I am talking about. I assure you, folks, this is no easy task. One issue that Amy deals with is all my typos. (I am guilty of using the two-finger hunt and peck method of typing.) Suppose the following table shows the frequencies of typos per page for a 120-page manuscript chapter that I just finished:

Typos per Page	Frequency
0	59
1	28
2	23
3	6
4	4

In other words, the chapter had 28 pages that had one typo. Setting $\alpha = 0.10$, use this chapter as your sample to test the hypothesis that the number of typos per page in my entire manuscript follows a Poisson distribution.

Answer can be found on ▶ **page 621**

You may be wondering how to proceed with the chi-square technique when the population mean is specified in the hypothesis statement. This is such a great question that I set up another Your Turn problem for you to work on. Don't worry—I give you some helpful hints along the way.

YOUR TURN #4

Redo Your Turn #3 using the following hypothesis statement:

H_0: The number of typos per page follows the Poisson distribution with $\lambda = 1.5$ per page

H_1: The number of typos per page does not follow the Poisson distribution with $\lambda = 1.5$ per page

Helpful hints: Having the mean specified in the hypothesis statement affects the procedure in three ways:

1. There is no need to calculate the mean from the sample data.
2. The probabilities used to calculate expected frequencies are based on the mean in the hypothesis statement, $\lambda = 1.5$.
3. We set $m = 0$ for the degrees of freedom because we are not relying on the sample mean as an estimate for the population mean.

Other than these changes, the chi-square procedure is the same for both cases. Setting $\alpha = 0.10$, use the sample chapter to test the hypothesis that the number of typos per page in my manuscript follows the stated Poisson distribution.

Answer can be found on ▶ **pages 621–622**

Testing for a Binomial Distribution

We can also perform a chi-square hypothesis test to determine if observed data follow a binomial distribution. Recall from Chapter 5 that a **binomial experiment** has the following characteristics:

- The experiment consists of a fixed number of trials, denoted by n.
- Each trial has only two possible outcomes, a success or a failure.
- The probability of a success (denoted by p) and the probability of a failure (denoted by q) are constant throughout the experiment.
- Each trial is independent of the other trials in the experiment.

I'll demonstrate this particular hypothesis test with the following example. Southwest Airlines operates four flights a day from Philadelphia to Orlando and would like to develop a model to predict the number of late flights per day between these cities. Table 12.15 shows the frequency of late flights per day for 200 randomly selected days. Historically, 20% of Southwest's flights nationwide have been late.

TABLE 12.15 | LATE FLIGHTS PER DAY FOR SOUTHWEST AIRLINES

NUMBER OF LATE FLIGHTS PER DAY	FREQUENCY
0	70
1	78
2	40
3	11
4	1
Total	200

For instance, there were 70 days that none of the four flights from Philadelphia to Orlando was late.

In this section, I would like to investigate if the frequency of late flights follows the binomial distribution with $n = 4$ and $p = 0.20$. In other words, each day consists of four trials (flights) with each trial having a probability of success (late) equal to 20%. I'll use $\alpha = 0.10$ to perform this hypothesis test with the following steps.

Step 1: Identify the null and alternative hypotheses.

The hypothesis statement for this chi-square test is as follows:

H_0: The number of late flights per day follows the binomial distribution with $n = 4$ and $p = 0.2$

H_1: The number of late flights per day does not follow the binomial distribution with $n = 4$ and $p = 0.2$

Back in Chapter 5, we learned that the mean of a binomial distribution is equal to np. The mean for this binomial distribution is therefore $(4)(0.2) = 0.8$. Notice that this mean is specified in the hypothesis statement, which will affect the test in a later step.

Step 2: Calculate the expected frequencies.

To calculate the expected frequencies, we need to find the binomial probabilities for each number of late flights in Table 12.15. The formula for calculating a binomial probability distribution is shown in Equation 12.4. (Recall that you first encountered this equation in Chapter 5.)

Formula 12.4 for the Binomial Probability Distribution

$$P(x, n) = \frac{n!}{(n - x)!x!} p^x q^{n-x}$$

where

$P(x, n) =$ The probability of observing x successes in n trials
$n =$ The number of trials
$x =$ The number of successes
$p =$ The probability of a success
$q =$ The probability of a failure

As with our Poisson example, we can generate the binomial probabilities using one of three methods:

1. Equation 12.4
2. Excel's BINOM.DIST(x, n, p, False) function
3. The binomial probability table found in Table 1 in Appendix A

Table 12.16 shows an excerpt from Table 1 in Appendix A with the appropriate column highlighted in yellow.

TABLE 12.16 | EXCERPT FROM TABLE 1 IN APPENDIX A (BINOMIAL PROBABILITIES)

n	x	0.1	0.15	0.2	0.25	0.3	0.35	0.4	0.45	0.5
4	0	0.6561	0.5220	0.4096	0.3164	0.2401	0.1785	0.1296	0.0915	0.0625
	1	0.2916	0.3685	0.4096	0.4219	0.4116	0.3845	0.3456	0.2995	0.2500
	2	0.0486	0.0975	0.1536	0.2109	0.2646	0.3105	0.3456	0.3675	0.3750
	3	0.0036	0.0115	0.0256	0.0469	0.0756	0.1115	0.1536	0.2005	0.2500
	4	0.0001	0.0005	0.0016	0.0039	0.0081	0.0150	0.0256	0.0410	0.0625

To calculate the expected frequencies for each number of late flights, we need to multiply each highlighted probability by the total number of days recorded (200). Table 12.17 shows these calculations.

TABLE 12.17 | CALCULATING THE EXPECTED FREQUENCIES OF LATE FLIGHTS

If the null hypothesis is true, we would expect to see about 82 days where none of the four daily flights were late from a random sample of 200 days.

NUMBER OF LATE FLIGHTS, X	BINOMIAL PROBABILITIES	TOTAL DAYS	EXPECTED FREQUENCIES
0	0.4096	200	81.92
1	0.4096	200	81.92
2	0.1536	200	30.72
3	0.0256	200	5.12
4	0.0016	200	0.32

Note that the expected frequency of four late flights is only 0.32 instances, which is less than 5. We therefore need to combine the "3" and "4" late-flight events, as shown in Table 12.18.

TABLE 12.18 | COMBINING THE "3" AND "4" LATE-FLIGHT EVENTS

NUMBER OF LATE FLIGHTS, X	OBSERVED FREQUENCIES, f_o	EXPECTED FREQUENCIES, f_e
0	70	81.92
1	78	81.92
2	40	30.72
3–4	12	5.44

Every expected frequency in Table 12.18 is now at least 5.

Step 3: Calculate the chi-square test statistic, χ^2.

We'll use Equation 12.1 again, with the help of Table 12.19, to calculate the chi-square test statistic.

TABLE 12.19 | CALCULATING THE CHI-SQUARE TEST STATISTIC

LATE FLIGHTS	f_o	f_e	$(f_o - f_e)$	$(f_o - f_e)^2$	$\frac{(f_o - f_e)^2}{f_e}$
0	70	81.92	−11.92	142.09	1.73
1	78	81.92	−3.92	15.37	0.19
2	40	30.72	9.28	86.12	2.80
3–4	12	5.44	6.56	43.03	7.91
Total				$\chi^2 = \sum \frac{(f_o - f_e)^2}{f_e}$	= 12.63

Step 4: Determine the chi-square critical value, χ^2_α.

Table 12.19 has four categories $(0, 1, 2, 3\text{–}4)$, so $k = 4$. The mean of the distribution (0.8) was included in the null hypothesis, so we don't need to calculate it using the sample data. As a result, $m = 0$. Therefore, we have $k - m - 1$, or $4 - 0 - 1 = 3$ degrees of freedom for our chi-square distribution. If we go to the $\alpha = 0.10$ column in Table 12.5 with 3 degrees of freedom, we'll find that $\chi^2_\alpha = 6.251$.

If the hypothesis statement back in step 1 had not specified a value for p, we would have to calculate p from our sample. In that case, $m = 1$ and we would have $4 - 1 - 1 = 2$ degrees of freedom.

Step 5: Compare the test statistic (χ^2) with the critical value (χ^2_α).

Because $\chi^2 = 12.63$ and this is greater than $\chi^2_\alpha = 6.251$, we reject the null hypothesis according to Table 12.6.

Step 6: Determine the *p*-value.

$$p\text{-value} = \text{CHISQ.DIST.RT}\,(12.63, 3) = 0.0055$$

Because the p-value = 0.0055 and is less than $\alpha = 0.10$, we reject the null hypothesis.

Step 7: State your conclusions.

By rejecting the null hypothesis, we have no evidence to conclude that the number of late flights per day from Philadelphia to Orlando follows the binomial distribution with $n = 4$ and $p = 0.2$. It appears that Southwest Air needs to develop another model to predict late flights between these locations.

Try your hand at testing for a binomial distribution with this next Your Turn problem.

YOUR TURN #5

Aramis Ramirez is a Major League Baseball player for the Milwaukee Brewers who had a 0.300 batting average during the 2012 season. In other words, 30% of Ramirez's at-bat appearances resulted in base hits that year. During the 2012 season, Ramirez made exactly four plate appearances in each of 84 games. The following table records the frequency of the number of hits during these games:

Number of Hits per Game (Four at Bats)	Frequency
0	21
1	35
2	23
3	5
4	0
Total	**84**

For instance, there were 21 games during the season in which Ramirez batted 4 times but did not get a hit. Using $\alpha = 0.01$, perform a hypothesis test to determine if Ramirez's number of hits per game follows the binomial distribution when $n = 4$ and $p = 0.30$.

Answers can be found on ▶ **pages 622–623**

Testing for a Normal Distribution

Many times in this textbook I have made the assumption that a population is normally distributed. I have also promised to show you how to test that assumption. In this section, I keep that promise. The following example will show you how a chi-square distribution can be used to test if a population follows the normal distribution.

Suppose Texas Christian University (TCU) uses the math SAT scores of incoming freshman to place them in math courses. Table 12.20 shows the math SAT scores for a random sample of 40 incoming freshmen this year. These data can also be found in the Excel file **math SAT scores normal.xlsx.**

TABLE 12.20 | MATH SAT SCORES

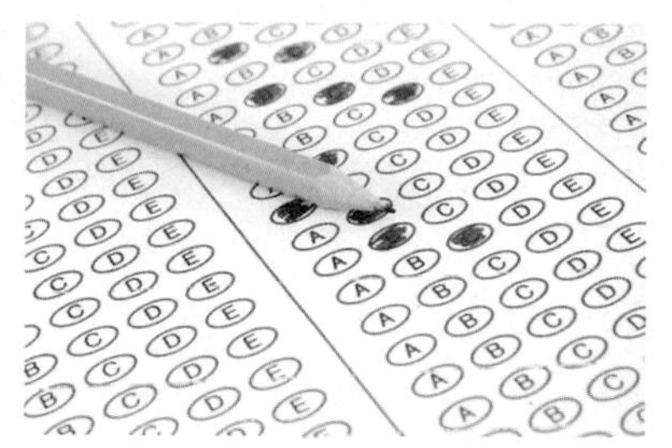

549	656	582	635	606	619	730
570	686	628	627	596	593	647
647	643	731	623	527	649	566
561	537	562	536	663	468	444
620	640	625	624	569	623	548
569	593	590	603	707		

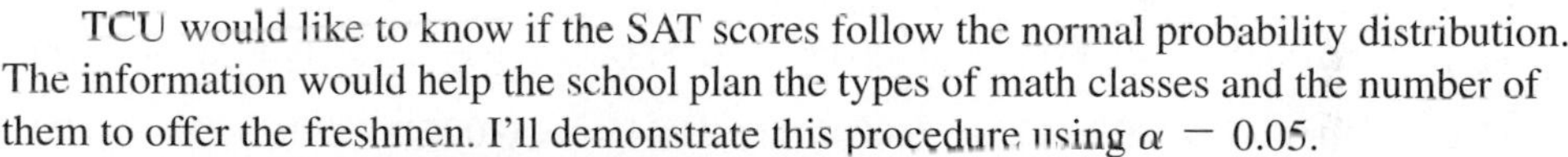

TCU would like to know if the SAT scores follow the normal probability distribution. The information would help the school plan the types of math classes and the number of them to offer the freshmen. I'll demonstrate this procedure using $\alpha = 0.05$.

Step 1: Identify the null and alternative hypotheses.

The null hypothesis for this test is that math SAT scores follow the normal probability distribution. The hypothesis statement is therefore as follows:

H_0: The math SAT scores follow the normal distribution

H_1: The math SAT scores do not follow the normal distribution

Step 2: Calculate the expected frequencies.

Because the mean and standard deviation of the population are not specified in the hypothesis statement, we need to calculate the mean and standard deviation of our sample. Using Excel's =AVERAGE(*data values*) and =STDEV.S(*data values*) functions, we have the following:

$$\bar{x} = 604.8 \qquad s = 60.6$$

Calculating the expected frequencies for a normal distribution is a little more complicated than the procedure we used for the previous discrete distributions. But don't panic—it's not that bad. Because the normal distribution is a continuous distribution rather than a discrete distribution, we need to establish uniform intervals for the continuous data. We then count the frequency of data values within each interval. We are essentially converting the continuous data into a discrete frequency distribution and then proceeding with the same chi-square test with which you are already familiar.

We first need to decide how many intervals we will use for the conversion from continuous to discrete data. I'll start by arbitrarily using six intervals of uniform width across the distribution, as shown in Figure 12.7. This is analogous to the number of categories from the previous examples. I'll discuss this choice later in the section.

As you can see in Figure 12.7, the six intervals are as follows:

$z \leq -2.0$ $-2.0 < z \leq -1.0$ $-1.0 < z \leq 0$

$0 < z \leq 1.0$ $1.0 < z \leq 2.0$ $z > 2.0$

Recall from Chapter 6, the z-scores represent the number of standard deviations from the mean. The width of these intervals is identical, but the areas within the intervals are not. We need to use Tables 3 and Table 4 in Appendix A to find the area of each interval. Table 12.21 shows an excerpt from Table 3 in Appendix A.

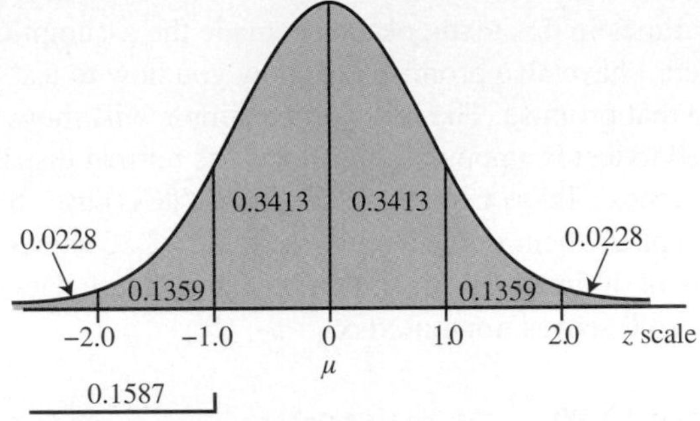

FIGURE 12.7 Dividing the Normal Distribution into Six Intervals

TABLE 12.21 | EXCERPT FROM TABLE 3 IN APPENDIX A (NORMAL DISTRIBUTION)

FIRST DIGIT OF Z	SECOND DIGIT OF Z									
z	0.00	0.01	0.02	0.03	0.04	0.05	0.06	0.07	0.08	0.09
−3.0	0.0013	0.0013	0.0013	0.0012	0.0012	0.0011	0.0011	0.0011	0.0010	0.0010
−2.9	0.0019	0.0018	0.0018	0.0017	0.0016	0.0016	0.0015	0.0015	0.0014	0.0014
−2.8	0.0026	0.0025	0.0024	0.0023	0.0023	0.0022	0.0021	0.0021	0.0020	0.0019
−2.7	0.0035	0.0034	0.0033	0.0032	0.0031	0.0030	0.0029	0.0028	0.0027	0.0026
−2.6	0.0047	0.0045	0.0044	0.0043	0.0041	0.0040	0.0039	0.0038	0.0037	0.0036
−2.5	0.0062	0.0060	0.0059	0.0057	0.0055	0.0054	0.0052	0.0051	0.0049	0.0048
−2.4	0.0082	0.0080	0.0078	0.0075	0.0073	0.0071	0.0069	0.0068	0.0066	0.0064
−2.3	0.0107	0.0104	0.0102	0.0099	0.0096	0.0094	0.0091	0.0089	0.0087	0.0084
−2.2	0.0139	0.0136	0.0132	0.0129	0.0125	0.0122	0.0119	0.0116	0.0113	0.0110
−2.1	0.0179	0.0174	0.0170	0.0166	0.0162	0.0158	0.0154	0.0150	0.0146	0.0143
−2.0	0.0228	0.0222	0.0217	0.0212	0.0207	0.0202	0.0197	0.0192	0.0188	0.0183
−1.9	0.0287	0.0281	0.0274	0.0268	0.0262	0.0256	0.0250	0.0244	0.0239	0.0233
−1.8	0.0359	0.0351	0.0344	0.0336	0.0329	0.0322	0.0314	0.0307	0.0301	0.0294
−1.7	0.0446	0.0436	0.0427	0.0418	0.0409	0.0401	0.0392	0.0384	0.0375	0.0367
−1.68	0.054	0.0537	0.0526	0.0516	0.0505	0.0495	0.0485	0.0475	0.0465	0.0455
−1.5	0.0668	0.0655	0.0643	0.0630	0.0618	0.0606	0.0594	0.0582	0.0571	0.0559
−1.4	0.0808	0.0793	0.0778	0.0764	0.0749	0.0735	0.0721	0.0708	0.0694	0.0681
−1.3	0.0968	0.0951	0.0934	0.0918	0.0901	0.0885	0.0869	0.0853	0.0838	0.0823
−1.2	0.1151	0.1131	0.1112	0.1093	0.1075	0.1056	0.1038	0.1020	0.1003	0.0985
−1.1	0.1357	0.1335	0.1314	0.1292	0.1271	0.1251	0.1230	0.1210	0.1190	0.1170
−1.0	0.1587	0.1562	0.1539	0.1515	0.1492	0.1469	0.1446	0.1423	0.1401	0.1379

For example, to find the area between $-2.0 < z \leq -1.0$, we plug the values we found in Table 12.21 into the following equations:

$$P(-2.0 < z \leq -1.0) = P(z \leq -1.0) - P(z \leq -2.0)$$
$$P(z \leq -1.0) = 0.1587$$
$$P(z \leq -2.0) = 0.0228$$
$$P(-2.0 < z \leq -1.0) = 0.1587 - 0.0228 = 0.1359$$

Excel lovers (which includes me) can use the NORM.S.DIST function introduced in Chapter 6 to determine the area to the left of a z-score as follows:

$$=\text{NORM.S.DIST}(-1.0, \text{TRUE}) = 0.1587$$

We repeat these calculations for the remaining intervals. We are now ready to calculate the expected frequencies for each of these intervals by multiplying the probabilities by the total number of SAT scores (40). Table 12.22 shows these calculations.

TABLE 12.22 | Expected Frequencies for the Six Intervals

INTERVAL	PROBABILITY	TOTAL SCORES	EXPECTED FREQUENCIES
$z \leq -2.0$	0.0228	40	0.91
$-2.0 < z \leq -1.0$	0.1359	40	5.44
$-1.0 < z \leq 0$	0.3413	40	13.65
$0 < z \leq 1.0$	0.3413	40	13.65
$1.0 < z \leq 2.0$	0.1359	40	5.44
$z > 2.0$	0.0228	40	0.91

Having intervals with expected frequencies less than 5 violates a requirement of the chi-square goodness-of-fit test.

For instance, if the TCU SAT scores follow the normal distribution, we would expect less than one score (0.91) out of the 40 scores to be in the interval more than 2.0 standard deviations from the mean $(z > 2.0)$, which is the highest interval of the distribution.

The first and last intervals (highest and lowest intervals) have expected frequencies of less than 5, which occurs because the total number of scores is only 40. To achieve the minimum expected frequencies of 5 for each of the six intervals, we need at least 220 scores, as shown by the following calculation:

$$220 \times 0.0228 = 5.02$$

Because we have only 40 scores, let's reduce the number of intervals to five, as shown in Figure 12.8. As you can see, the five intervals are as follows:

$$z \leq -1.5 \qquad -1.5 < z \leq -0.5 \qquad -0.5 < z \leq 0.5$$
$$0.5 < z \leq 1.5 \qquad z > 1.5$$

FIGURE 12.8
Dividing the Normal Distribution into Five Intervals

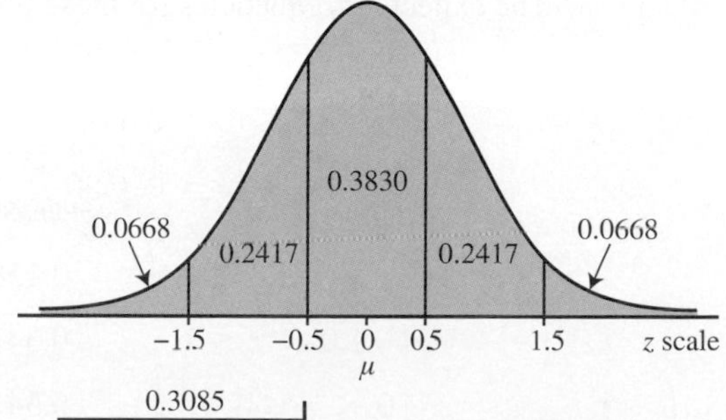

For example, to find the area between $-1.5 < z \le -0.5$, we use the following calculations and Table 3 in Appendix A:

$$P(-1.5 < z \le -0.5) = P(z \le -0.5) - P(z \le -1.5)$$
$$P(-1.5 < z \le -0.5) = 0.3085 - 0.0668 = 0.2417$$

The expected frequencies for these five intervals are found in Table 12.23.

TABLE 12.23 | Expected Frequencies for the Five Intervals

INTERVAL	PROBABILITY	TOTAL SCORES	EXPECTED FREQUENCIES
$z \le -1.5$	0.0668	40	2.67
$-1.5 < z \le -0.5$	0.2417	40	9.67
$-0.5 < z \le 0.5$	0.3830	40	15.32
$0.5 < z \le 1.5$	0.2417	40	9.67
$z > 1.5$	0.0668	40	2.67

Using five intervals, we still have two intervals with expected frequencies of less than 5. To achieve the minimum expected frequencies of 5 using five intervals, we need at least 75 scores, as shown by the following calculation:

$$75 \times 0.0668 = 5.01$$

Let's reduce the number of intervals to four, as shown in Figure 12.9.

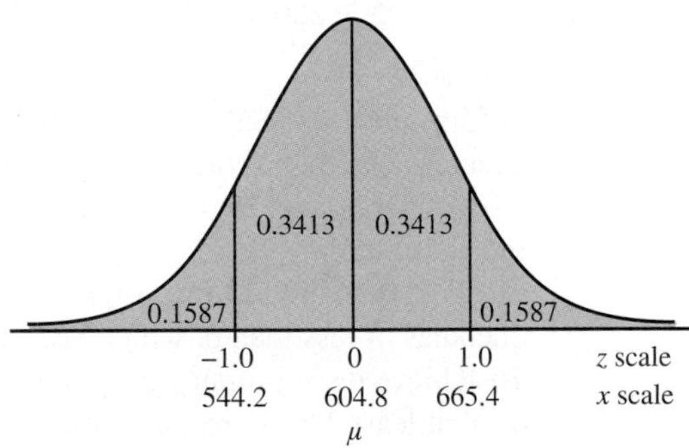

FIGURE 12.9 Dividing the Normal Distribution into Four Intervals

Figure 12.9 also shows the SAT scores that correspond to the z-scores calculated with the following equations:

$$x = \mu + z\sigma$$
$$x = 604.8 + (1.0)(60.6) = 665.4$$
$$x = 604.8 - (1.0)(60.6) = 544.2$$

The expected frequencies for these four intervals are found in Table 12.24.

TABLE 12.24 | Expected Frequencies for the Four Intervals

INTERVAL	PROBABILITY	TOTAL SCORES	EXPECTED FREQUENCIES
$z \le -1.0$	0.1587	40	6.35
$-1.0 < z \le 0$	0.3413	40	13.65
$0 < z \le 1.0$	0.3413	40	13.65
$z > 1.0$	0.1587	40	6.35

Bingo! According to Table 12.24, we've finally achieved our goal of having expected frequencies of at least 5 for each category. It's about time! To achieve the minimum expected frequencies of 5 using four intervals, we need at least 32 scores, as shown by the following calculation:

$$32 \times 0.1587 = 5.08$$

To summarize, Table 12.25 shows the number of data values needed for each interval size. You can use this table for future reference when trying to decide how many intervals to use for your normal distribution hypothesis test (you're welcome).

TABLE 12.25 | NUMBER OF DATA VALUES REQUIRED TO ACHIEVE EXPECTED FREQUENCIES OF AT LEAST 5 PER INTERVAL

INTERVALS PER DISTRIBUTION	REQUIRED NUMBER OF DATA VALUES
Four intervals	Between 32 and 75
Five intervals	Between 75 and 220
Six intervals	More than 220

Step 3: Count the observed frequencies for each interval.

This step is pretty straightforward—simply count the number of SAT scores in each of the four intervals from Figure 12.9. Sorting the Excel file **math SAT scores normal.xlsx** from low to high scores makes this process easier. Table 12.26 shows these results.

There were 14 SAT scores from Table 12.20 between 544.2 and 604.8.

TABLE 12.26 | OBSERVED FREQUENCIES OF THE SAT SCORES

INTERVAL	OBSERVED FREQUENCY
544.2 or less	5
> 544.2 to 604.8	14
> 604.8 to 665.4	17
More than 665.4	4
Total	**40**

The chi-square test has no minimum requirement for the number of observed frequencies for each category. Only the expected frequencies are required to have a minimum of five observations per category.

Step 4: Calculate the chi-square test statistic, χ^2.

We'll use Equation 12.1 again, with the help of Table 12.27, to calculate the chi-square test statistic. The expected frequencies were calculated in Table 12.24.

TABLE 12.27 | CALCULATING THE CHI-SQUARE TEST STATISTIC

INTERVAL	f_o	f_e	$(f_o - f_e)$	$(f_o - f_e)^2$	$\frac{(f_o - f_e)^2}{f_e}$
544.2 or less	5	6.35	−1.35	1.82	0.29
> 544.2 to 604.8	14	13.65	0.35	0.12	0.01
> 604.8 to 665.4	17	13.65	3.35	11.22	0.82
More than 665.4	4	6.35	−2.35	5.52	0.87
Total	**40**	**40**	$\chi^2 = \sum \frac{(f_o - f_e)^2}{f_e}$		= 1.99

Step 5: Determine the chi-square critical value, χ^2_α.

Table 12.27 has four categories, so $k = 4$. Recall that the mean and standard deviation of the population were not specified in the hypothesis statement. Because we have to estimate both using our sample, $m = 2$. Therefore, we have $k - m - 1 = 4 - 2 - 1 = 1$ degree of freedom for our chi-square distribution. Four intervals is the lowest number of k we can use to test normal distributions because this leaves us with only 1 degree of freedom for the chi-square distribution, which is the minimum allowed. In other words, we can't reduce the number of intervals to three for this test because it would result in 0 degree of freedom (a very bad thing). If we go to the $\alpha = 0.05$ column in Table 12.5 with 1 degree of freedom, we'll find that $\chi^2_\alpha = 3.841$.

Because we are estimating both the mean and standard deviation using sample data (two parameters), we set $m = 2$

Step 6: Compare the test statistic (χ^2) with the critical value (χ^2_α).

Because $\chi^2 = 1.99$ and this is less than $\chi^2_\alpha = 3.841$, we fail to reject the null hypothesis according to Table 12.6.

Step 7: Determine the *p*-value.

$$p\text{-value} = \text{CHISQ.DIST.RT}\,(1.99, 1) = 0.1583$$

Because the p-value $= 0.1583$ and is greater than $\alpha = 0.05$, we fail to reject the null hypothesis.

Step 8: State your conclusions.

By failing to reject the null hypothesis, the assumption that the math SAT score follows the normal distribution cannot be rejected. As I mentioned earlier in the chapter, from a statistician's perspective, we cannot accept the null hypothesis and conclude the SAT scores follow the normal distribution. However, from a business perspective we need to choose between (a) using the normal distribution for planning purposes and (b) not using the normal distribution for planning purposes. As a businessperson, the results of this hypothesis test lead me to choose option (a), which is to use the normal distribution in this case. Again, I know this might seem like a contradiction, but choosing to use the normal distribution in this example is the appropriate business decision.

While this procedure is still fresh in your mind, spend a few minutes on this next "normal" Your Turn.

YOUR TURN #6

A credit score measures a person's creditworthiness. The following data show the credit scores of 36 randomly selected adults. The scores are sorted from low to high for your convenience. These data can also be found in the Excel file **credit scores normal.xlsx.**

480	522	549	555	571	576
590	593	596	599	609	618
625	650	651	657	657	658
663	664	677	690	694	705
705	728	740	753	755	762
768	769	769	772	773	787

Use these data to perform a hypothesis test to determine if credit scores follow the normal distribution using $\alpha = 0.10$.

Answer can be found on ▶ **page 623**

12.2 Section Problems

Basic Skills

12.9 Consider the following discrete probability distribution along with observed frequencies for each day of the week:

Weekday	Probability	Observed Frequency, f_o
Monday	0.10	12
Tuesday	0.20	27
Wednesday	0.05	7
Thursday	0.30	40
Friday	0.35	34
Total	**1.00**	**120**

a. Perform a chi-square test using $\alpha = 0.05$ to determine if the observed frequencies follow a discrete probability distribution.

b. Determine the p-value using Excel and interpret its meaning.

12.10 Consider the observed frequency distribution for the following set of random variables:

Random Variable, x	Frequency, f_o
0	17
1	35
2	30
3	15
4 and more	3
Total	**100**

Perform a chi-square test using $\alpha = 0.05$ to determine if the observed frequencies follow the Poisson probability distribution when $\lambda = 1.5$.

12.11 Consider the observed frequency distribution for the following set of random variables:

Random Variable, x	Frequency, f_o
0	23
1	60
2	122
3	83
4	12
Total	**300**

a. Perform a chi-square test using $\alpha = 0.05$ to determine if the observed frequencies follow the binomial probability distribution when $p = 0.50$ and $n = 4$.

b. Determine the p-value using Excel and interpret its meaning.

12.12 Consider the observed frequency distribution for the following set of grouped random variables:

Random Variable, x	Frequency, f_o
Less than 80	10
80 to under 100	14
100 to under 120	19
120 and more	7
Total	**50**

Perform a chi-square test using $\alpha = 0.05$ to determine if the observed frequencies follow the normal probability distribution with $\mu = 100$ and $\sigma = 20$.

Applications

12.13 In 1991, the Consumer Bankruptcy Project conducted a study to determine the education levels of people who declare bankruptcy. The percentages are shown in the following table. Also shown in the table is the observed frequency for these education levels from a random sample of individuals who filed for bankruptcy in 2014.

Education Level	Probability 1991 (%)	Observed Frequency 2014
No high school diploma	21.8	11
High school diploma	31.7	38
Some college	35.1	56
College diploma	8.6	15
Advanced degree	2.8	5
Total	**100**	**125**

a. Using $\alpha = 0.05$, perform a chi-square test to determine if the probability distribution for the education levels of individuals who filed for bankruptcy changed between 1991 and 2014.

b. Determine the p-value using Excel and interpret its meaning.

c. What conclusions can be drawn about the type of individual who filed for bankruptcy in 2014 vs. the type of individual who filed for bankruptcy in 1991?

12.14 The following table shows the U.S. market share for automotive manufacturers in 2013 according to Autodata. Also shown is the frequency of car purchases by manufacturer from a random sample of 220 customers during 2014.

Manufacturer	Market Share 2013 (%)	Frequency 2014
General Motors	18.5	35
Ford Motor	16.5	37
Toyota	13.7	24
Chrysler	12.2	20
Honda	10.2	17
Other	28.9	87
Total		**220**

a. Using $\alpha = 0.10$, perform a chi-square test to determine if the U.S. market share in the automotive industry has changed between 2013 and 2014.

b. Determine the p-value for the chi-square test statistic using Excel and interpret its meaning.

12.15 In an effort to predict customer arrivals better, the Avalon grocery store counted the number of customers who arrived at the store during randomly selected 10-minute intervals. The following table shows these data. For example, there were 12 10-minute intervals in which no customers arrived, and 27 10-minute intervals in which one customer arrived.

Number of Customers Arriving in a 10-Minute Interval	Frequency
0	12
1	27
2	29
3	22
4	12
5	5
6	3
Total	**110**

a. Using $\alpha = 0.05$, perform a chi-square test to determine if the number of customers arriving over a 10-minute interval follows the Poisson probability distribution.

b. Determine the p-value using Excel and interpret its meaning.

12.16 The following data show the number of touchdown passes thrown by quarterback Aaron Rodgers during 40 games in which he played with the Green Bay Packers. These data can also be found in the Excel file **Rodgers.xlsx.**

1	3	0	2	3	2	1	1	0	2
2	3	2	1	2	3	1	1	2	2
2	3	3	2	1	2	3	3	0	3
1	1	2	2	1	3	1	1	2	0

Using $\alpha = 0.05$, perform a chi-square test to determine if the number of touchdown passes thrown per game by Aaron Rodgers follows the Poisson probability distribution when $\lambda = 1.7$.

12.17 Suppose that candidates for a job opening at Citibank interview with four different managers. Each manager independently evaluates each candidate with a "yes" or "no" hiring decision. The following table shows the number of "yes" decisions given the last 90 candidates:

Number of "Yes"	Decisions per Candidate	Frequency
	0	22
	1	36
	2	23
	3	8
	4	1
Total		**90**

a. Using $\alpha = 0.05$, perform a chi-square test to determine if the number of "yes" decisions per candidate follows the binomial probability distribution when the probability of a candidate receiving a "yes" vote is 30%.

b. Determine the p-value using Excel and interpret its meaning.

12.18 Suppose I gave my statistics class a four-question, multiple-choice quiz at the beginning of the semester to measure how well prepared they were for the class. The following table shows the number of students who had 0, 1, 2, 3, and 4 questions correct:

Number of Correct Answers per Student	Frequency
0	4
1	5
2	12
3	9
4	10
Total	**40**

Using $\alpha = 0.05$, perform a chi-square test to determine if the number of correct answers per student follows the binomial probability distribution.

12.19 In Chapter 8 we examined confidence intervals. Recall that to construct a confidence interval for the mean when the population standard deviation is unknown, the population must follow the normal probability distribution. To test this condition, the following data show a random sample of weekly visits by patients to Dr. Gregg's chiropractic office. The data can also be found in the Excel file **Dr. Gregg's office.xlsx.**

110	117	78	114	131	67	105	105	93	118	114	93
91	96	109	114	127	116	112	82	92	100	98	67
100	129	107	105	72	65	131	78	103	81		

a. Using $\alpha = 0.05$, perform a chi-square test to determine if the number of patient visits per week follows the normal probability distribution. Note that $\bar{x} = 100.6$ and $s = 18.7$.

b. Determine the p-value using Excel and interpret its meaning.

12.20 The following data shows the weekly purchases of printers at a particular electronic store. The data can also be found in the Excel file **weekly printer demand.xlsx.**

8	15	12	17	19	12	14	5	8	3	3	15
6	16	15	10	12	17	12	12	6	10	9	10
9	17	8	8	16	6	19	11	3	9	12	7
15	10	14	14	13	10	11	7	17			

Using $\alpha = 0.05$, perform a chi-square test to determine if the number of printers sold per week follows the normal probability distribution. Note that $\bar{x} = 11.2$ and $s = 4.3$.

12.3 Testing the Independence of Two Variables

The **chi-square test of independence** is used to determine if two categorical variables are independent of one another.

You can also use a chi-square distribution test to determine if two categorical variables are independent of one another. This procedure is known as the **chi-square test of independence**. Two variables are independent of one another if changes in the levels of one variable do not affect the levels of the other variable.

Consider the following example. Suppose Best Buy would like to know if the age of a customer affects the brand of digital camera he or she purchases. This information would be used to help design a new promotional campaign. To investigate this relationship, Best Buy collected the data shown in Table 12.28. The data show the frequency with which 150 people, categorized by their age groups, purchased various camera brands. Recall from Chapter 2 that this type of table is known as a contingency table and each observation is known as a cell.

TABLE 12.28 | BEST BUY'S CONTINGENCY TABLE

	CAMERA BRAND			
AGE GROUP	CANON	NIKON	SONY	TOTAL
18–34	30	16	8	54
35–51	22	25	19	66
52 and older	8	9	13	30
Total	60	50	40	150

In this example we have two categorical variables: camera brand and age group. Table 12.28 tells us that 30 customers aged 18–34 purchased Canon cameras. Using the chi-square independence test, we can find out if a pattern exists between the age of customer and the camera brand he or she chooses. We will use $\alpha = 0.05$ for this test.

Step 1: Identify the null and alternative hypotheses.

The null hypothesis for this test is that the two categorical variables are independent of one another. In other words, the age of a customer has no effect on the camera brand he or she purchases. Consequently, there is no relationship between the two variables. The hypothesis statement is therefore as follows:

The null hypothesis for a chi-square test of independence always states that the two variables are independent of one another (there is no relationship between the two variables).

H_0: The camera brand and age of customer are independent of one another

H_1: The camera brand and age of customer are not independent of one another

Step 2: Calculate the expected frequencies.

Again, the expected frequencies are calculated under the assumption that there is no relationship between the two categories (the null hypothesis). As Equation 12.5 shows, we calculate the expected frequencies, f_e, for each cell in the contingency table by multiplying the row total by the column total. This result is then divided by the total number of observations.

Formula 12.5 for the Expected Frequencies for a Contingency Table

$$f_e = \frac{(\text{Row total})(\text{Column total})}{\text{Total number of observations}}$$

For example, to calculate the expected number of customers who purchased a Canon in the 18–34 age group, we need to go back to Table 12.28. The table shows that there were 54 customers in the 18–34 age group and that a total of

60 customers purchased a Canon. Assuming the null hypothesis is true, the expected frequency for this cell is as follows:

$$f_e = \frac{(\text{Row total})(\text{Column total})}{\text{Total number of observations}} = \frac{(18\text{–}34\text{ total})(\text{Canon total})}{150} = \frac{(54)(60)}{150} = 21.6$$

The expected frequency calculations for the remaining cells are shown in Table 12.29.

TABLE 12.29 | EXPECTED FREQUENCIES FOR THE BEST BUY EXAMPLE

	CAMERA BRAND		
AGE GROUP	CANON	NIKON	SONY
18–34	$\frac{(54)(60)}{150} = 21.6$	$\frac{(54)(50)}{150} = 18.0$	$\frac{(54)(40)}{150} = 14.4$
35–51	$\frac{(66)(60)}{150} = 26.4$	$\frac{(66)(50)}{150} = 22.0$	$\frac{(66)(40)}{150} = 17.6$
52 and older	$\frac{(30)(60)}{150} = 12.0$	$\frac{(30)(50)}{150} = 10.0$	$\frac{(30)(40)}{150} = 8.0$

Once again, we need to ensure that the expected frequency for each cell is at least 5 in order to proceed with the chi-square test. If needed, we can combine either rows or columns like we did in previous examples. Fortunately, this is not necessary for this example.

Step 3: Calculate the chi-square test statistic, χ^2.

We'll use Equation 12.1 again, with the help of Table 12.30, to calculate the chi-square test statistic. The expected frequencies are pulled from Table 12.29.

The chi-square test of independence requires that every value in this column of expected frequencies be at least five.

TABLE 12.30 | CALCULATING THE CHI-SQUARE TEST STATISTIC FOR THE BEST BUY EXAMPLE

CELL	f_o	f_e	$(f_o - f_e)$	$(f_o - f_e)^2$	$\frac{(f_o - f_e)^2}{f_e}$
18–34 Canon	30	21.6	8.4	70.56	3.27
18–34 Nikon	16	18.0	−2.0	4.00	0.22
18–34 Sony	8	14.4	−6.4	40.96	2.84
35–51 Canon	22	26.4	−4.4	19.36	0.73
35–51 Nikon	25	22.0	3.0	9.00	0.41
35–51 Sony	19	17.6	1.4	1.96	0.11
52+ Canon	8	12.0	−4.0	16.00	1.33
52+ Nikon	9	10.0	−1.0	1.00	0.10
52+ Sony	13	8.0	5.0	25.00	3.13
Total				$x^2 = \sum \frac{(f_o - f_e)^2}{f_e}$	$= 12.14$

Step 4: Determine the chi-square critical value, χ^2_α.

The chi-square test of independence has the following degrees of freedom:

$$(r - 1)(c - 1)$$

where

$r =$ The number of rows in the contingency table
$c =$ The number of columns in the contingency table

For our Best Buy example, we have three age groups, so $r = 3$. We also have three camera brands, so $c = 3$. This means our chi-square critical value has $(r - 1)(c - 1)$, or $(3 - 1)(3 - 1) = 4$ degrees of freedom. If we go to the $\alpha = 0.05$ column in Table 12.5, we'll find that $\chi^2_\alpha = 9.488$.

Step 5: Compare the test statistic (χ^2) with the critical value (χ^2_α).

Because $\chi^2 = 12.14$ and this is greater than $\chi^2_\alpha = 9.488$, we reject the null hypothesis according to Table 12.6.

Step 6: Determine the *p*-value.

$$p\text{-value} = \text{CHISQ.DIST.RT}(12.14, 4) = 0.0163$$

Because the p-value $= 0.0163$ and is less than $\alpha = 0.05$, we reject the null hypothesis.

Step 7: State your conclusions.

By rejecting the null hypothesis, we have found support that there is a relationship between the age groups of customers and the camera brands they purchase. So, these categorical variables do not appear to be independent of one another. Comparing the observed and expected frequencies in Table 12.30, it seems that younger customers favor Canon cameras. I make this statement based on the fact that Table 12.30 showed 30 customers in this cell when I expected only 21.6 had there been no relationship. (Recall that 21.6 was the expected frequency we calculated.) Using the same logic, older customers appear to be partial to Sony cameras. This information could help Best Buy and the camera manufacturers target different kinds of customers with different kinds of promotional campaigns.

We need to exercise caution when stating the conclusions for a chi-square test of independence. Rejecting the null hypothesis does not allow us to state that one variable causes the other variable to change. We have no proof for that kind of statement. In other words, we can't go so far as to say that the ages of customers *cause* them to choose different camera brands. The chi-square test of independence simply identified that there was a pattern between the age groups and camera brands chosen.

The chi-square test of independence does not allow us to state that one variable causes a change in another variable when the null hypothesis is rejected. The test simply identifies that a pattern exists between the two variables.

Using PHStat to Conduct a Chi-Square Test of Independence

We can use PHStat to perform a chi-square test of independence by taking the following steps. Excel for Mac users can go the textbook's Web site for these instructions.

1. Go to **Add-Ins > PHStat > Multiple-Sample Tests > Chi-Square Test**, which was shown in Figure 12.4A.
2. Fill in the values in the **Chi-Square Test** dialog box as shown in Figure 12.10A. Click **OK**.

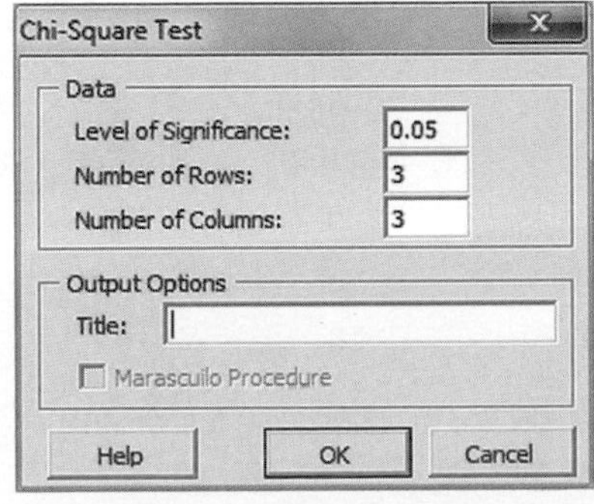

FIGURE 12.10A Using PHStat to Conduct a Chi-Square Test of Independence

3. Hit the **Delete** key to remove the text box with instructions after you have read them.
4. Enter the observed frequencies and labels from Table 12.29 into the top blue-shaded table as shown in Figure 12.10B.

FIGURE 12.10B
Using PHStat to Conduct a Chi-Square Test of Independence (Final Result)

	A	B	C	D	E	F
1	Chi-Square Test					
2						
3	Observed Frequencies					
4		Column variable				
5	Row variable	C1	C2	C3	Total	
6	R1	30	16	8	54	
7	R2	22	25	19	66	
8	R3	8	9	13	30	
9	Total	60	50	40	150	
10						
11	Expected Frequencies					
12		Column variable				
13	Row variable	C1	C2	C3	Total	
14	R1	21.6	18	14.4	54	
15	R2	26.4	22	17.6	66	
16	R3	12	10	8	30	
17	Total	60	50	40	150	
18						
19	Data					
20	Level of Significance	0.05				
21	Number of Rows	3				
22	Number of Columns	3				
23	Degrees of Freedom	4				
24						
25	Results					
26	Critical Value	9.487729				
27	Chi-Square Test Statistic	12.14545				
28	*p*-Value	0.016302				
29	Reject the null hypothesis					
30						

The results of the chi-square analysis are shown in the yellow-shaded table in Figure 12.10B. Notice that the results are consistent with our manual calculations. In addition, Cell B28 shows the p-value, which represents the probability of observing a value for our test statistic, χ^2, greater than 12.14545 if the null hypothesis is true. Because our p-value is less than $\alpha = 0.05$, we reject the null hypothesis and conclude that a relationship does exist between camera brand and the age group of the customer.

YOUR TURN #7

When discussing conditional probabilities in Chapter 5, I used a tennis example involving my wife, Deb. Recall that Deb is an avid tennis player, and we enjoy playing matches against each other. We do, however, have one difference of opinion on the court. Deb likes to have a nice long warm-up session before the game begins, but I want to start keeping score right away. Deb claims that when we rush through the warm-up, she doesn't play as well. After examining the conditional probabilities in Chapter 5, I had to admit there is some evidence supporting Deb's claim. However, I'm not one to take this result sitting down. I demand further evidence. What do you say we just conduct a chi-square test of independence, instead?

Unbeknownst to Deb, I have meticulously collected data from our 50 previous matches. The following table shows the number of wins for each of us categorized by the length of the warm-up period.

	0–10 Minutes	11–20 Minutes	More Than 20 Minutes	Total
Deb wins	5	12	10	27
Bob wins	13	7	3	23
Total	18	19	13	50

a. Using $\alpha = 0.05$ and the chi-square test of independence, determine if warm-up time has an effect on who wins the tennis match.

b. Verify your results with PHStat.

Answers can be found on ▶ **page 624**

Stats in Practice: Using the Chi-Square Test in Health Care

Health Care Associates (HCA) is an organization that employs doctors who, in turn, are contracted to work in hospitals. HCA provides these physicians, known as hospitalists, with their salaries, benefits, and insurance. University Hospital has a contract with HCA to provide physician services for its patients. The following table shows the number of patients seen by six HCA physicians who worked at University Hospital for a particular month. The data are organized by the type of admission, which relates to the complexity of a patient's condition. Level 1 is a relatively simple condition to treat, whereas Level 3 is a very complex condition to treat.

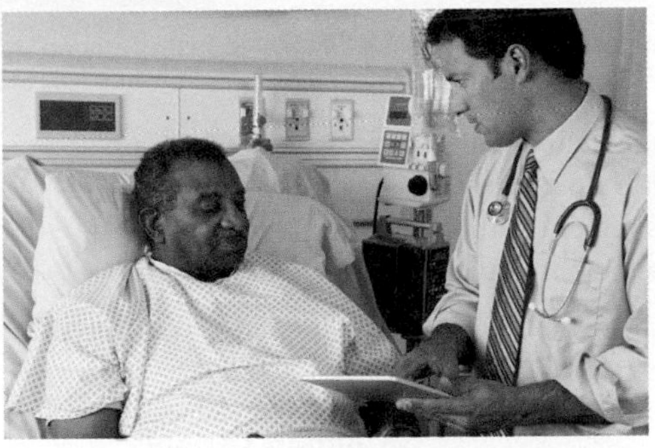

	Physicians					
Admission	**Phy 1**	**Phy 2**	**Phy 3**	**Phy 4**	**Phy 5**	**Phy 6**
Level 1	3	4	9	9	13	8
Level 2	15	8	21	16	13	19
Level 3	45	27	13	16	19	32

Under normal conditions, HCA expects the allocation of patients according to the admission type to be assigned randomly to the physicians. In other words, the admission type and physician should be independent of one another. We can perform a chi-square test of independence to determine if this is, in fact, the case. The following PHStat output (Figure 12.11) provides the results for this hypothesis test using $\alpha = 0.05$.

Because the p value in Cell B28 equals 0.0003, which is less than $\alpha = 0.05$, we reject the null hypothesis. By rejecting the null hypothesis, it appears that the admission type and physician are not independent, which is a cause of concern for HCA management. For example, Physician 1 seems to see many more Level 3 patients (45 vs. 33) and fewer Level 1 patients (3 vs. 10) than are expected if the null hypothesis were true. Insurance companies that are reimbursing HCA for these visits monitor the proportions of the three admission levels to detect if physicians are "upcoding." This term refers to the practice of classifying a Level 1 admission as a Level 2 or 3 in order to increase a medical organization's revenue.[3]

	A	B	C	D	E	F	G	H
1	**Chi-Square Test**							
2								
3				**Observed Frequencies**				
4				**Column variable**				
5	**Row variable**	**Physician 1**	**Physician 2**	**Physician 3**	**Physician 4**	**Physician 5**	**Physician 6**	**Total**
6	**Level 1 Admission**	3	4	9	9	13	8	46
7	**Level 2 Admission**	15	8	21	16	13	19	92
8	**Level 3 Admission**	45	27	13	16	19	32	152
9	**Total**	63	39	43	41	45	59	290
10								
11				Expected Frequencies				
12				Column variable				
13	Row variable	Physician 1	Physician 2	Physician 3	Physician 4	Physician 5	Physician 6	Total
14	Level 1 Admission	9.993103448	6.1862069	6.82068966	6.50344828	7.13793103	9.35862069	46
15	Level 2 Admission	19.9862069	12.3724138	13.6413793	13.0068966	14.2758621	18.7172414	92
16	Level 3 Admission	33.02068966	20.4413793	22.537931	21.4896552	23.5862069	30.9241379	152
17	Total	63	39	43	41	45	59	290
18								
19	**Data**							
20	**Level of Significance**	**0.05**						
21	Number of Rows	3						
22	Number of Columns	6						
23	Degrees of Freedom	10						
24								
25	**Results**							
26	**Critical Value**	**18.30703805**						
27	**Chi-Square Test Statistic**	**32.71642789**						
28	***p*-Value**	**0.000303937**						
29	**Reject the null hypothesis**							
30								

FIGURE 12.11

[3]Special thanks to Kemal Erkan, FACHE, and John Donnelly (Yes, this is my son!) for providing this material.

12.3 Section Problems

Basic Skills

12.21 Consider a contingency table of observed frequencies with three rows and four columns:

a. How many chi-square degrees of freedom are associated with this table?
b. What is the chi-square critical value when $\alpha = 0.05$?
c. What is the chi-square critical value when $\alpha = 0.10$?

12.22 Consider the following contingency table of observed frequencies:

	Column Variable		
Row Variable	**C1**	**C2**	**C3**
R1	9	7	10
R2	10	7	7

a. Identify the null and alternative hypotheses for a chi-square test of independence based on the information in the table.
b. Calculate the expected frequencies for each cell in the contingency table.
c. Calculate the chi-square test statistic.
d. Using $\alpha = 0.05$, state your conclusions.

12.23 Consider the following contingency table of observed frequencies:

	Column Variable		
Row Variable	**C1**	**C2**	**C3**
R1	20	6	18
R2	7	8	11
R3	10	15	5

a. Identify the null and alternative hypotheses for a chi-square test of independence based on the information in the table.
b. Calculate the expected frequencies for each cell in the contingency table.
c. Calculate the chi-square test statistic.
d. Using $\alpha = 0.01$, state your conclusions.
e. Determine the p-value using Excel and interpret its meaning.

Applications

12.24 The following contingency table shows the distribution of grades earned by students taking a midterm exam in an MBA class, categorized by the number of hours the students spent studying for the exam:

	Grade		
Time Spent Studying	**A**	**B**	**C**
Less than 3 hours	4	18	8
3–5 hours	15	14	6
More than 5 hours	18	12	5

a. Using $\alpha = 0.05$, perform a chi-square test to determine if a student's grade on the exam and the hours spent studying for it are independent of one another.
b. What conclusions can be made based on these results?
c. Verify your results using PHStat.

12.25 Suppose Capital One would like to determine if the type of credit card influences the payment status of a customer's account. The following table indicates the card type for 200 randomly selected customers, along with the number of days their payments were overdue:

	Card Type		
Days Overdue	**Standard**	**Gold**	**Platinum**
30 days or less	76	40	30
31–60 days	12	10	7
61 days or more	12	8	5

a. Using $\alpha = 0.05$, perform a chi-square test to determine if the credit card type and payment status are independent of one another.
b. What conclusions can be made based on these results?
c. Determine the p-value using Excel and interpret its meaning.
d. Verify your results using PHStat.

12.26 The following table shows the medal count for the United States, Germany, and Great Britain following the 2012 Summer Olympics in London.

	Medal		
Country	**Gold**	**Silver**	**Bronze**
United States	46	29	29
Germany	11	19	14
Great Britain	29	17	19

a. Using $\alpha = 0.05$, perform a chi-square test to determine if the type of medal and country that earned it are independent of one another.
b. What conclusions can be made based on these results?
c. Determine the p-value for the chi-square test statistic using Excel and interpret its meaning.
d. Verify your results using PHStat.

12.27 Suppose the marketing research firm comScore would like to examine if the social networking site that a person primarily uses is influenced by his or her age. In a randomly drawn sample, 355 social network users were asked which site they primarily visited. These data are presented in the following table along with each person's age group:

Age Group	Facebook	Twitter	LinkedIn
2–17	25	14	3
18–34	100	30	11
35–54	98	18	19
55 and older	27	3	7

a. Using $\alpha = 0.05$, perform a chi-square test to determine if the age group of a social network user and the site he or she primarily visits are independent.
b. What conclusions can be made based on these results?
c. Determine the p-value using Excel and interpret its meaning.
d. Verify your results using PHStat.

CHAPTER 12 Summary

- When comparing two or more proportions, the null hypothesis for the chi-square test states that all population proportions are equal.
- The observed frequencies, f_o, refer to the sample data collected from a population of interest.
    - Observed frequencies must be integers, because they are countable items.
- The expected frequencies, f_e, refer to the frequencies that are most likely to occur if the null hypothesis is true.
    - Expected frequencies do not have to be integers because they represent only theoretical values.
- The chi-square test requires that each expected frequency be 5 or more.
- If the null hypothesis is true, we would expect the chi-square test statistic to be close to zero.
- The test statistic follows the chi-square probability distribution with $k - 1$ degrees of freedom where k equals the number of categories.
- The rejection region for a chi-square test for two or more proportions is always in the right tail of the distribution.
- If the chi-square statistic is greater than the critical value, we reject the null hypothesis.
- The chi-square goodness-of-fit test allows us to determine if our data follow a specific probability distribution. In this chapter, we tested for the following distributions:
    - Discrete
    - Poisson
    - Binomial
    - Normal
- In the goodness-of-fit test, the null hypothesis states that the data follow the stated probability distribution.
    - By contrast, the alternative hypothesis states that the data do not follow the stated probability distribution.
- The chi-square goodness-of-fit test has $k - m - 1$ degrees of freedom where $m =$ the number of parameters estimated from the sample in the hypothesis statement.
    - If a parameter is not specified in the hypothesis statement, the sample statistic must be calculated and used as an estimate for the population parameter.
- A chi-square test can also be used to determine if two categorical variables are independent of one another.
- Two variables are independent of one another if changes in the levels of one variable do not affect the levels of the other variable.
- The null hypothesis for this test is that the two categorical variables are independent of one another.
- The chi-square test of independence has $(r - 1)(c - 1)$ degrees of freedom where $r =$ the number of rows in the contingency table and $c =$ the number of columns in the contingency table.

CHAPTER 12 Key Terms

Chi-square distribution. Used to compare two or more population proportions, perform a goodness-of-fit test, and test two categorical variables for independence.

Chi-square test of independence. A test used to determine if two categorical variables are independent of one another.

Expected frequencies. The frequencies that are most likely to occur if the null hypothesis is true.

Goodness-of-fit test. A chi-square test used to decide if the observed frequencies in a set of data follow a known probability distribution.

Observed frequencies. The sample data collected from a population of interest.

CHAPTER 12 Equations

12.1 Comparing Two or More Population Proportions (pp 577–585)

Formula 12.1 for the Chi-Square Test Statistic

$$\chi^2 = \sum \frac{(f_o - f_e)^2}{f_e}$$

12.2 Determining If Observed Frequencies Follow a Known Probability Distribution (pp 585–604)

Formula 12.2 for the Poisson Probability Distribution

$$P(x) = \frac{\lambda^x e^{-\lambda}}{x!}$$

Formula 12.3 for the Mean of a Frequency Distribution

$$\lambda = \frac{\sum_{i=1}^{k}(x_i f_i)}{\sum_{i=1}^{k} f_i}$$

Formula 12.4 for the Binomial Probability Distribution

$$P(x, n) = \frac{n!}{(n - x)!x!} p^x q^{n-x}$$

12.3 Testing the Independence of Two Variables (pp 605–611)

Formula 12.5 for the Expected Frequencies for a Contingency Table

$$f_e = \frac{(\text{Row total})(\text{Column total})}{\text{Total number of observations}}$$

CHAPTER 12 Problems

12.28 The percentage of students from for-profit institutions who have defaulted on their student loans has received much attention recently. Suppose the following data were collected from a random sample of students who graduated three years ago from various types of institutions with student loans:

	Defaulted on Loan?	
Institution	**Yes**	**No**
Public	9	111
Private	7	143
For-profit	13	67

a. Using $\alpha = 0.05$, perform a chi-square test to determine if the proportion of students who default on their student loans differs by the type of institution.
b. Confirm your results using PHStat.
c. Interpret the meaning of the p-value from PHStat2.
d. How does the type of institution appear to relate to the likelihood of students defaulting on their loans?

12.29 A survey was conducted to determine by age group the number of registered voters who cast ballots during the recent elections. The following data were recorded:

	Did You Vote?	
Age Group	**Yes**	**No**
18–24	18	62
25–34	39	76
35–44	64	76
45–54	54	46
55 and older	82	43

a. Using $\alpha = 0.01$, perform a chi-square test to determine if the proportion of voters who cast ballots during the elections differs among the five age groups of voters.
b. Determine the p-value using Excel and interpret its meaning.
c. Confirm your results using PHStat.
d. How does age appear to relate to the likelihood that a voter will cast a ballot during the elections?

12.30 Major League Baseball (MLB) records a pitcher's contact percentage by dividing the number of times batters make contact with the pitches by the number of times they swing at them. The following data represent a sample of this information for three MLB pitchers during the recent season:

	Number of Pitches	
Pitcher	**Contacts Made**	**Contacts Missed**
Stephen Strasburg, Nationals	134	76
Clayton Kershaw, Dodgers	129	51
Tim Lincecum, Giants	138	52

a. Using $\alpha = 0.05$, perform a chi-square test to determine if the contact percentage differs among these three pitchers.
b. Confirm your results using PHStat.
c. Interpret the meaning of the p-value from PHStat.

12.31 Union membership, as a percentage of the working population, varies from country to country. A number of workers from different countries were randomly surveyed and asked whether they belonged to a union. The data from the survey are as follows:

	Member of Union?	
Country	**Yes**	**No**
France	6	54
United States	6	39
Japan	9	41
Germany	11	44

a. Using $\alpha = 0.05$, perform a chi-square test to determine if the proportion of workers who belong to unions differs among these four countries.
b. Determine the p-value using Excel and interpret its meaning.
c. Confirm your results using PHStat.

12.32 The U.S. Centers for Disease Control and Prevention (CDC) recommends people consume five servings of fruits and vegetables daily. A random sample of adults from various states was asked if they follow these guidelines. The results are as follows:

	Follow the CDC Guidelines?	
State	**Yes**	**No**
Delaware	10	30
Maryland	10	22
New Jersey	13	37
Pennsylvania	8	27

a. Using $\alpha = 0.05$, perform a chi-square test to determine if the proportion of adults who follow the CDC's guidelines differs among the four states.
b. Confirm your results using PHStat.
c. Interpret the meaning of the p-value from PHStat.

12.33 The following table shows the U.S. market share for smartphone manufacturers in 2013 according to the research firm comScore. The table also shows the frequency of purchases of smartphones by brand for a random sample of customers during 2014.

Brand	Market Share 2013 (%)	Observed Frequency 2014
Apple	36.3	20
Samsung	21.0	14
HTC	10.2	4
Motorola	9.1	3
Other	23.4	9
Total	**100**	**50**

a. Using $\alpha = 0.05$, perform a chi-square test to determine if the observed frequencies in the table are consistent with the comScore report.
b. Determine the p-value for the chi-square test statistic using Excel and interpret its meaning.

12.34 The following table shows the distribution of the ages of Ohio voters in a 2008 exit poll conducted by Quinnipiac University. The table also shows the observed frequencies from a random sample of Ohio voters by age group in the 2014 midterm elections.

Age Group	Percentage 2008	Observed Frequency 2014
18–29	17	14
30–44	27	18
45–64	39	73
65 and older	17	35
Total	**100**	**140**

a. Using $\alpha = 0.05$, perform a chi-square test to determine if the ages of voters in Ohio changed from 2008 to 2014.
b. What conclusions about an Ohio voter's age can be made based on this sample?

12.35 A survey conducted by Wakefield Research asked adults what their favorite night to order takeout for dinner was. The results are shown in the following table. Suppose a second survey was conducted asking restaurants about the actual observed frequencies for each night's takeout business. Those numbers are reported in the "Observed Frequency" column.

Night	Wakefield Percentage	Observed Frequency
Monday	7	12
Tuesday	5	12
Wednesday	12	4
Thursday	7	6
Friday	38	59
Saturday	21	20
Sunday	10	12
Total	**100**	**125**

a. Using $\alpha = 0.05$, perform a chi-square test to determine if the observed frequencies confirm the results obtained by Wakefield Research.
b. Determine the p-value using Excel and interpret its meaning.

12.36 In a *Wall Street Journal* article titled "Where to Shoot in the Shootout",[4] data were presented about the direction in which penalty shots were kicked toward soccer goals during all of the World Cups since 1998. The following figure shows these data. For example, a total of 37 penalty shots were directed toward the left corner of the soccer goal, and 25 of them were successful.

25 of 37	12 of 20	30 of 41

a. Using $\alpha = 0.05$, perform a chi-square test to determine if the number of attempted shots differs across all three segments of the soccer goal.
b. Using $\alpha = 0.05$, perform a chi-square test to determine if the proportion of successful shots differs across all three segments of the soccer goal.
c. What conclusions can be made about the strategy for attempted penalty shots in soccer?

12.37 The following table shows the frequency distribution for the number of spam e-mails I've received over the last 75 days:

Number of Spam E-Mails Per Day	Frequency
0	12
1	24
2	19
3	12
4	5
5	2
6	1
Total	**75**

a. Using $\alpha = 0.10$, perform a chi-square test to determine if the number of spam e-mails per day follows the Poisson probability distribution when $\lambda = 1.8$.
b. Determine the p-value using Excel and interpret its meaning.

12.38 The following data show the number of employees who called in sick to a chemical plant during the last 50 days. This data can be found in the Excel file **sick days.xlsx**.

2	1	2	3	2	3	0	3	5	2
4	3	1	0	2	0	5	3	1	1
0	2	4	3	2	4	0	0	0	3
3	2	2	1	3	2	3	2	5	3
2	0	1	2	3	0	2	1	0	2

Using $\alpha = 0.01$, perform a chi-square test to determine if the number of employees calling in sick per day follows the Poisson probability distribution.

[4]"Where to Shoot in the Shootout," *Wall Street Journal*, July 5, 2010.

12.39 Chris is a salesperson who makes five sales calls each day to potential customers. Either the customers make a purchase from Chris or they do not. The following table shows the number of days over the past 400 that Chris had 0, 1, 2, 3, 4, or 5 purchases per day.

Number of Purchases Per Day	Frequency
0	98
1	157
2	106
3	36
4	3
5	0
Total	**400**

a. Using $\alpha = 0.05$, perform a chi-square test to determine if the number of purchases per day follows the binomial probability distribution, with the probability of a customer making a purchase being equal to 25%.

b. Determine the p-value using Excel and interpret its meaning.

12.40 A foursome of golfers plays together routinely. One of the golfers happens to be a statistician who enjoys keeping track of the number of fairways the players hit while teeing off. The following table shows these data for the last 250 holes the golfers have played together:

Number of Fairways Hit Per Hole	Frequency
0	32
1	86
2	88
3	38
4	6
Total	**250**

Using $\alpha = 0.05$, perform a chi-square test to determine if the number of fairways hit per hole follows a binomial probability distribution.

12.41 A particular weight-loss company claims that the average weight a person lost after two weeks on its program is 5 lbs. The following data represent the weight loss of 36 randomly selected adults who have been on the program for two weeks. Negative values represent weight gains (oops!). These data can also be found in the Excel file **normal weight loss.xlsx**.

9	11	6	8	2	−4	7	0	8	10	11	2
4	5	5	7	11	3	4	10	5	5	9	7
7	−1	0	4	1	9	−2	1	7	0	7	3

a. Using $\alpha = 0.05$, perform a chi-square test to determine if the weight loss after two weeks on this program follows a normal probability distribution when $\mu = 5.0$ and $\sigma = 4.0$.

b. Determine the p-value using Excel and interpret its meaning.

12.42 In Chapter 6, I used annual snowfall amounts in Minneapolis from 1884 until 2012 to describe a normal probability distribution. This data can be found in the Excel file **snowfall.xlsx.**

a. Using $\alpha = 0.01$, perform a chi-square test to determine if the data follow a normal probability distribution.

b. Determine the p-value for the chi-square test statistic using Excel and interpret its meaning.

12.43 Suppose the Federal Aviation Administration would like to compare the on-time performances of different airlines on domestic, nonstop flights. The following table shows three different airlines and the frequency of flights that arrived early, on time, and late for each:

Status	Southwest	United Airlines	Delta
Early	20	24	22
On time	60	55	50
Late	25	30	14

a. Using $\alpha = 0.05$, perform a chi-square test to determine if on-time performance and airline are independent of one another.

b. What conclusions can be made based on your results?

c. Determine the p-value using Excel and interpret its meaning.

d. Verify your results using PHStat.

12.44 A political poll asked potential voters if they felt the economy was going to get worse, stay the same, or get better during the next 12 months. The party affiliations of the respondents were also noted. The results are shown in the following table:

	Party Affiliation		
Response	**Democrat**	**Republican**	**Independent**
Get worse	34	30	19
Stay the same	17	22	7
Get better	5	7	9

a. Using $\alpha = 0.01$, perform a chi-square test to determine if voters' responses about the economy and their party affiliations are independent of one another.

b. What conclusions can be made based on your results?

c. Verify your results using PHStat.

12.45 A random sample of 150 new car buyers who purchased Ford, General Motors (GM), and Chrysler models was selected, and their ages were recorded. The following table shows these data:

Age	Ford	GM	Chrysler
20–29	5	11	11
30–39	8	23	7
40–49	16	15	5
50–59	24	15	10

a. Using $\alpha = 0.05$, perform a chi-square test to determine if the age of the buyer and the car brand he or she purchased are independent of one another.
b. What conclusions can be made based on your results?
c. Determine the p-value using Excel and interpret its meaning.
d. Verify your results using PHStat.

12.46 Suppose that General Motors gathers from its dealers information about the percentage of new cars that require warranty work during the first year following their sale. Based on these data, GM then compares the dealerships to monitor any unusual patterns. The following table shows the number of randomly selected cars at five dealerships that required warranty work during the first year following their sale:

	Warranty Work Required	
Dealership	**Yes**	**No**
Aston	7	50
Dover	11	80
Springfield	7	86
Media	8	81
Newark	5	47

a. Using $\alpha = 0.05$, determine if the proportion of new cars requiring warranty work differs across these dealerships.
b. Confirm your results using PHStat.
c. Interpret the meaning of the p-value from PHStat.

12.47 Suppose that Air France would like to determine if the number of lost bags per flight follows the Poisson probability distribution with a mean of 0.7 bags. To test this hypothesis, the following data were collected from 200 randomly selected flights:

Number of Lost Bags per Flight	Frequency
0	106
1	63
2	22
3	4
4	3
5 or more	2

a. Using $\alpha = 0.05$, determine if the number of lost bags per Air France flight follows the Poisson probability distribution when $\lambda = 0.7$.
b. Determine the p-value using Excel and interpret its meaning.

12.48 Suppose that Princess Cruise Lines would like to determine if the satisfaction rating of a customer is related to the number of cruises the person has taken with the company. The following table shows the number of customers who rated their cruises with Princess as Excellent, Good, Average, Fair, or Poor, along with the number of cruises the customers have taken with the company:

	Number of Cruises		
Rating	**1–3**	**4–6**	**7 or More**
Excellent	20	26	25
Good	42	20	20
Average	18	15	12
Fair	10	6	8
Poor	4	7	7

a. Using $\alpha = 0.05$, perform a chi-square test to determine if the number of cruises and a customer's satisfaction rating are independent of one another.
b. What conclusions can be made based on your results?
c. Verify your results using PHStat.

12.49 A Gallup poll conducted in 2011 asked respondents why they would not consider buying a hybrid car for their next purchase. The results are shown in the following table. Suppose Toyota would like to confirm these results with its own survey, so the company asked 300 people the same question. The results of Toyota's survey are also shown in the following table:

Reason	Gallup Poll (%)	Toyota
Too expensive	39	104
Technology not proven	19	50
Inconvenient to use	9	33
Poor performance	8	33
Something else	21	56
No opinion	4	24
Total	**100**	**300**

a. Using $\alpha = 0.05$, determine if the observed frequencies in the Toyota survey are consistent with the results from the Gallup poll.
b. Determine the p-value using Excel and interpret its meaning.

12.50 There has been recent interest in a legislative initiative for laws that ensure paid time off for workers who take sick days. Suppose the Bureau of Labor Statistics (BLS) would like to test if the proportion of workers with paid sick days is influenced by the size of the organization, measured by number of employees. The following table summarizes a random sample of 245 employees by indicating the size of their organization and if they have paid sick days.

	Paid Sick Days	
Number of Employees	**Yes**	**No**
99 or less	47	43
100–499	53	27
500 or more	59	16

a. Using $\alpha = 0.05$, perform a chi-square test to determine if the size of the employee's organization and his or her paid sick days category are independent.
b. Determine the p-value for the chi-square test statistic using Excel and interpret its meaning.
c. Verify your results using PHStat.

12.51. Suppose the Federal Communications Commission would like to compare the percentage of the population with access to broadband Internet between Alaska, California, Virginia, and New Mexico. A random sample of 270 adults from these four states was selected and their Internet availability was recorded. These results are shown in the following table.

	Access to Internet	
State	**Yes**	**No**
Alaska	48	12
California	87	3
Virginia	44	6
New Mexico	60	10

a. Using $\alpha = 0.05$, perform a chi-square test to determine if the percentage of the population without access to broadband Internet between Alaska, California, Virginia, and New Mexico differs.
b. Determine the p-value for the chi-square test statistic using Excel and interpret its meaning.
c. Verify your results using PHStat.

12.52 A survey conducted by Intermedia reported the percentage of work-related emails sent each day of the work week. To verify Intermedia's findings, a random sample of work-related emails was selected and the weekday that it was sent was noted. The following table displays these results.

Weekday	Intermedia Percentage	Sample Frequency
Monday	15	33
Tuesday	23	51
Wednesday	22	48
Thursday	21	42
Friday	19	26
Total	**100**	**200**

a. Using $\alpha = 0.05$, perform a chi-square test to determine if the sample frequencies in the table are consistent with the Intermedia report.
b. Determine the p-value for the chi-square test statistic using Excel and interpret its meaning.

12.53 A particular university includes a capstone course in its MBA program which all graduating students take and covers an overview of topics for their degree. The following contingency table shows the number of students from three different concentrations along with the grade they received in the capstone course.

	Grade		
Concentration	**A**	**B**	**C**
Management	10	20	10
Marketing	30	40	30
Finance	20	40	0

a. Perform a hypothesis test to determine if the concentration of the students and the grade they received in the capstone course are independent variables using $\alpha = 0.01$.
b. Determine the p-value for the chi-square test statistic using Excel and interpret its meaning.
c. Verify your results using PHStat.

12.54 Diller & Fisher is a real estate company that rents vacation properties in an ocean-side community in New Jersey. They believe that the following table represents the probability distribution for the number of bedrooms for rental properties.

Bedrooms	2	3	4	5	6
Probability	0.12	0.28	0.35	0.15	0.10

The number of bedrooms from a random sample of rental properties that Diller & Fisher collected is shown here.

Bedrooms	2	3	4	5	6
Frequency	4	10	27	8	1

a. Using $\alpha = 0.10$, does this sample provide enough evidence to support Diller & Fisher's belief about the probability distribution?
b. Determine the p-value for the chi-square test statistic using Excel and interpret its meaning.

12.55 Sara is a salesperson for Camera's Etc. which is a retailer for high-end digital cameras. Historically, Sara has sold an average of 2.1 extended warranties per day. Data in the Excel file **camera warranty.xlsx** display the number of extended warranties that Sara has sold per day over the past 100 business days.

a. Using $\alpha = 0.10$, perform a chi-square test to determine if the data follow a Poisson probability distribution with $\lambda = 2.1$.

b. Determine the p-value for the chi-square test statistic using Excel and interpret its meaning.

12.56 Spencer is the owner of Island Art, a retail establishment in the beach community of Stone Harbor, New Jersey. He would like to develop a probability model to predict the number of customers who visit his establishment each day during the summer season. The Excel file **Island Art 1.xlsx** shows the number of customers who entered his store over 240 business days during past summer seasons. Using $\alpha = 0.05$, determine if the number of customers per day visiting Island Art follows the normal probability distribution.

12.57 At the beginning of this chapter, the term *quadrophobia* was defined as the apparent aversion that many firms seem to have of arriving at earnings-per-share calculations that end with the digit "4." Here's your chance to investigate the presence of the quadrophobia phenomenon. Suppose you reviewed 1,000 earnings statements from randomly selected companies and found the following frequency distribution for the final digits for earnings per share:

Final Digit	Frequency	Final Digit	Frequency
0	116	5	106
1	100	6	105
2	81	7	106
3	80	8	110
4	80	9	116

a. Using $\alpha = 0.05$, determine if the presence of quadrophobia is evident.

b. Determine the p-value using Excel and interpret its meaning.

CHAPTER 12 Solutions to Your Turn

YOUR TURN #1

a) $H_0: p_1 = p_2$

H_1: Not all ps are equal

$$\hat{p} = \frac{37}{79} = 0.468$$

Time-Out	$\hat{p}$	Total Attempts	Expected Frequencies Made, f_e	Expected Frequencies Missed, f_e
No	0.468	54	25.27	28.73
Yes	0.468	25	11.70	13.30

Time-Out	f_o	f_e	$(f_o - f_e)$	$(f_o - f_e)^2$	$\frac{(f_o - f_e)^2}{f_e}$
No—made	23	25.27	−2.27	5.15	0.20
No—missed	31	28.73	2.27	5.15	0.18
Yes—made	14	11.7	2.3	5.29	0.45
Yes—missed	11	13.3	−2.3	5.29	0.40
Total			$\chi^2 = \sum \frac{(f_o - f_e)^2}{f_e} = 1.23$		

We have $k - 1 = 2 - 1 = 1$ degree of freedom. Using the $\alpha = 0.05$ column, Table 12.5 indicates that our critical value is $\chi^2_\alpha = \chi^2_{0.05} = 3.841$. Because $\chi^2 = 1.23$ is less than $\chi^2_\alpha = 3.841$, we fail to reject the null hypothesis. We have no evidence to conclude that there is a difference in the proportion of field goals made when the kicker is iced vs. not iced. The claim made by the *Wall Street Journal* that icing the kicker backfires is not supported by the statistics.

b) p-value $=$ CHISQ.DIST.RT(1.23, 1) $= 0.2674$. Because this value is greater than alpha, we fail to reject the null hypothesis.

(Continued on next page)

c) Number of rows = 2, Number of columns = 2

	A	B	C	D
1	Chi-Square Test			
2				
3	Observed Frequencies			
4		Column variable		
5	Row variable	C1	C2	Total
6	R1	23	31	54
7	R2	14	11	25
8	Total	37	42	79
9				
10	Expected Frequencies			
11		Column variable		
12	Row variable	C1	C2	Total
13	R1	25.29114	28.70886	54
14	R2	11.70886	13.29114	25
15	Total	37	42	79
16				
17	Data			
18	Level of Significance	0.05		
19	Number of Rows	2		
20	Number of Columns	2		
21	Degrees of Freedom	1		
22				
23	Results			
24	Critical Value	3.841459		
25	Chi-Square Test Statistic	1.233671		
26	p-Value	0.266694		
27	Do not reject the null hypothesis			

YOUR TURN #2

Step 1: Identify the null and alternative hypotheses.

H_0: This faculty's grade distribution follows the stated probability distribution
H_1: This faculty's grade distribution does not follow the stated probability distribution

Step 2: Calculate the expected frequencies.

We calculate the expected frequencies, f_e, by multiplying the total number of students (120) by the probability of each grade being awarded. These calculations are as follows:

Grade	Probability	Total Students	Expected Frequencies Students, f_e
A	0.20	120	24
B	0.25	120	30
C	0.40	120	48
D	0.10	120	12
F	0.05	120	6
Total	1.00		120

Step 3: Calculate the chi-square test statistic, χ^2.

	(1)	(2)	(3)	(4)	(5)
Grade	f_o	f_e	$(f_o - f_e)$	$(f_o - f_e)^2$	$\frac{(f_o - f_e)^2}{f_e}$
A	36	24	12	144	6.00
B	27	30	−3	9	0.30
C	42	48	−6	36	0.75
D	9	12	−3	9	0.75
F	6	6	0	0	0
Total			$\chi^2 = \sum \frac{(f_o - f_e)^2}{f_e} = 7.80$		

Step 4: Determine the chi-square critical value, χ^2_α.

For our grade distribution example, we have five categories (one for each letter grade), so $k = 5$. That means our chi-square critical value has $k - 1 = 5 - 1 = 4$ degrees of freedom. If we go to the $\alpha = 0.05$ column in Table 12.5, we'll find that $\chi^2_\alpha = 9.488$.

Step 5: Compare the test statistic (χ^2) with the critical value (χ^2_α).

Because $\chi^2 = 7.80$ and this is less than $\chi^2_\alpha = 9.488$, we fail to reject the null hypothesis according to Table 12.6.

Step 6: Determine the *p*-value.

$$p\text{-value} = \text{CHISQ.DIST.RT}(7.80, 4) = 0.0992$$

Because the *p*-value $= 0.0992$ and is greater than $\alpha = 0.05$, we fail to reject the null hypothesis.

Step 7: State your conclusions.

Because we failed to reject the null hypothesis, we do not have enough evidence to conclude that the grade distribution is not being followed. However, we cannot conclude that the distribution *is* being followed because that statement would be equivalent to accepting the null hypothesis.

YOUR TURN #3

Step 1: Identify the null and alternative hypotheses.

H_0: Number of typos per page follows the Poission distribution
H_1: Number of typos per page does not follow the Poission distribution

Step 2: Calculate the expected frequencies.

$$\lambda = \frac{\sum_{i=1}^{k}(x_i f_i)}{\sum_{i=1}^{k} f_i}$$

$$= \frac{(0)(59) + (1)(28) + (2)(23) + (3)(6) + (4)(4)}{59 + 28 + 23 + 6 + 4}$$

$$\lambda = \frac{108}{120} = 0.9 \text{ typo per page}$$

Number of Typos, *x*	Poisson Probabilities	Total Pages	Expected Frequencies
0	0.4066	120	48.79
1	0.3659	120	43.91
2	0.1647	120	19.76
3	0.0494	120	5.93
4 or more	0.0134	120	1.61

Because we never had more than four typos per page, I combined the probabilities of four, five, six, and seven typos from Table 2 in Appendix A, as follows:

$$P(4 \text{ or more typos}) = 0.0111 + 0.0020 + 0.0003 + 0.0000 = 0.0134$$

Also, notice that the expected frequency of four or more typos occurring is only 1.61, which is less than 5. To accommodate the 5 or more requirement, we need to combine the "3" and "4 or more" events into a "3 or more" category, as the following table shows:

Number of Typos, *x*	Observed Frequencies, f_o	Expected Frequencies, f_e
0	59	48.79
1	28	43.91
2	23	19.76
3 or more	10	7.54

Step 3: Calculate the chi-square test statistic, χ^2.

Typos	f_o	f_e	$(f_o - f_e)$	$(f_o - f_e)^2$	$\frac{(f_o - f_e)^2}{f_e}$
0	59	48.79	10.21	104.24	2.14
1	28	43.91	−15.91	253.13	5.76
2	23	19.76	3.24	10.50	0.53
3 or more	10	7.54	2.46	6.05	0.80
Total					$\chi^2 = \sum \frac{(f_o - f_e)^2}{f_e} = 9.23$

Step 4: Determine the chi-square critical value, χ^2_α.

This example has four categories (0, 1, 2, and 3 or more), so $k = 4$. In this example, $m = 1$ because we have to estimate the mean of the population (every manuscript page) using the mean number of typos from our sample. Therefore, we have $k - m - 1 = 4 - 1 - 1 = 2$ degrees of freedom for our chi-square distribution.

If we go to the $\alpha = 0.10$ column in Table 12.5 with 2 degrees of freedom, we'll find that $\chi^2_\alpha = 4.605$.

Step 5: Compare the test statistic (χ^2) with the critical value (χ^2_α).

Because $\chi^2 = 9.23$ and this is greater than $\chi^2_\alpha = 4.605$, we reject the null hypothesis according to Table 12.6.

Step 6: Determine the *p*-value.

$$p\text{-value} = \text{CHISQ.DIST.RT}(9.23, 2) = 0.0099$$

Because the *p*-value $= 0.0099$ and is less than $\alpha = 0.10$, we reject the null hypothesis.

Step 7: State your conclusions.

By rejecting the null hypothesis, we cannot support the assumption that the number of typos per page follows the Poisson distribution.

YOUR TURN #4

Step 1: Identify the null and alternative hypotheses.

H_0: Number of typos per page follows the Poission distribution with $\lambda = 1.5$ typos per page
H_1: Number of typos per page does not follow the Poission distribution with $\lambda = 1.5$ typos per page

Step 2: Calculate the expected frequencies.

Because the population mean is specified in the hypothesis statement, we'll use the Poisson probabilities for $\lambda = 1.5$ from Table 2 in Appendix A to calculate expected frequencies.

Number of Typos, *x*	Poisson Probabilities	Total Pages	Expected Frequencies
0	0.2231	120	26.77
1	0.3347	120	40.16
2	0.2510	120	30.12
3	0.1255	120	15.06
4 or more	0.0656	120	7.87

Because we never had more than four typos per page, I combined the probabilities in Table 2 from Appendix A that correspond to the values 4, 5, 6, 7, and 8 in our typos column:

$$P(4 \text{ or more typos}) = 0.0471 + 0.0141 + 0.0035 + 0.0008 + 0.0001 = 0.0656$$

Step 3: Calculate the chi-square test statistic, χ^2.

Typos	f_o	f_e	$(f_o - f_e)$	$(f_o - f_e)^2$	$\frac{(f_o - f_e)^2}{f_e}$
0	59	26.77	32.23	1,038.77	38.80
1	28	40.16	−12.16	147.87	3.68
2	23	30.12	−7.12	50.69	1.68
3	6	15.06	−9.06	82.08	5.45
4 or more	4	7.87	−3.87	14.98	1.90
Total					$\chi^2 = \sum \frac{(f_o - f_e)^2}{f_e} = 51.51$

Step 4: Determine the chi-square critical value, χ^2_α.

This example has five categories (0, 1, 2, 3, 4 or more), so $k = 5$. In this example, $m = 0$ because we did not estimate the mean of the population using the mean number of typos from our sample. Therefore, we have $k - m - 1 = 5 - 0 - 1 = 4$ degrees of freedom for our chi-square distribution.

If we go to the $\alpha = 0.10$ column in Table 12.5 with 4 degrees of freedom, we'll find that $\chi^2_\alpha = 7.779$.

Step 5: Compare the test statistic (χ^2) with the critical value (χ^2_α).

Because $\chi^2 = 51.51$, and this is greater than $\chi^2_\alpha = 7.779$, we reject the null hypothesis according to Table 12.6.

Step 6: Determine the *p*-value.

$$p\text{-value} = \text{CHISQ.DIST.RT}(51.51, 4) = 0.0000$$

Because the *p*-value $= 0.0000$ and is less than $\alpha = 0.10$, we reject the null hypothesis.

Step 7: State your conclusions.

By rejecting the null hypothesis, we conclude that the assumption that the number of typos per page follows the Poisson distribution when $\lambda = 1.5$ does not have support.

YOUR TURN #5

Step 1: Identify the null and alternative hypotheses.

H_0: Number of hits per game follows the binomial distribution with $n = 4$ and $p = 0.3$

H_1: Number of hits per game does not follow the binomial distribution with $n = 4$ and $p = 0.3$

Step 2: Calculate the expected frequencies.

Because the population mean is specified in the hypothesis statement, we'll use the binomial probabilities for $n = 4$ and $p = 0.30$ from Table 1 in Appendix A to calculate the expected frequencies.

Number of Hits, x	Binomial Probabilities	Total Games	Expected Frequencies
0	0.2401	84	20.17
1	0.4116	84	34.57
2	0.2646	84	22.23
3	0.0756	84	6.35
4	0.0081	84	0.68

Note that the expected frequency of four hits per game is only 0.68 instances, which is less than 5. To accommodate the 5 or more requirement, we need to combine the "3" and "4" hits categories to "3–4" as shown in the following table.

Number of Hits, x	Observed Frequencies, f_o	Expected Frequencies, f_e
0	21	20.17
1	35	34.57
2	23	22.23
3–4	5	7.03

Step 3: Calculate the chi-square test statistic, χ^2.

Hits	f_o	f_e	$(f_o - f_e)$	$(f_o - f_e)^2$	$\frac{(f_o - f_e)^2}{f_e}$
0	21	20.17	0.83	0.69	0.034
1	35	34.57	0.43	0.18	0.005
2	23	22.23	0.77	0.59	0.027
3–4	5	7.03	−2.03	4.12	0.586
Total					$\chi^2 = \sum \frac{(f_o - f_e)^2}{f_e} = 0.652$

Step 4: Determine the chi-square critical value, χ^2_α.

This example has four categories (0, 1, 2, 3–4), so $k = 4$. In this example, $m = 0$ because we did not have to estimate the mean of the population from our sample. Therefore, we have $k - m - 1 = 4 - 0 - 1 = 3$ degrees of freedom for our chi-square distribution. If we go to the $\alpha = 0.01$ column in Table 12.5 with 3 degrees of freedom, we'll find that $\chi^2_\alpha = 11.345$.

Step 5: Compare the test statistic (χ^2) to the critical value (χ^2_α).

Because $\chi^2 = 0.652$, and this is less than $\chi^2_\alpha = 11.345$, we fail to reject the null hypothesis according to Table 12.6.

Step 6: Determine the *p*-value.

$$p\text{-value} = \text{CHISQ.DIST.RT}\,(0.652, 3) = 0.8844$$

Because the *p*-value $= 0.8844$ and is less than $\alpha = 0.10$, we fail to reject the null hypothesis.

Step 7: State your conclusions.

By failing to reject the null hypothesis, the assumption that the number of hits per game follows the binomial distribution when $n = 4$ and $p = 0.30$ cannot be rejected.

YOUR TURN #6

Step 1: Identify the null and alternative hypotheses.

H_0: Credit scores follow the normal distribution
H_1: Credit scores do not follow the normal distribution

Step 2: Calculate the expected frequencies.

Using Excel's AVERAGE (*data values*) and STDEV.S (*data values*) functions, we have the following:

$$\bar{x} = 664.7 \qquad s = 81.8$$

According to Table 12.25, with 36 data values we should use four intervals to calculate the expected frequencies for this distribution.

Interval	Probability	Total Scores	Expected Frequencies
$z \le -1.0$	0.1587	36	5.71
$-1.0 < z \le 0$	0.3413	36	12.29
$0 < z \le 1.0$	0.3413	36	12.29
$z > 1.0$	0.1587	36	5.71

The credit scores that correspond to these intervals are as follows:

$$x = \mu + z\sigma$$
$$x = 664.7 + (1.0)(81.8) = 746.5$$
$$x = 664.7 - (1.0)(81.8) = 582.9$$

Step 3: Count the observed frequencies for each interval.

Interval	Frequency
Less than 582.9	6
582.9 to 664.7	14
664.7 to 746.5	7
More than 746.5	9
Total	36

Step 4: Calculate the chi-square test statistic, χ^2.

Interval	f_o	f_e	$(f_o - f_e)$	$(f_o - f_e)^2$	$\frac{(f_o - f_e)^2}{f_e}$
<582.9	6	5.71	0.29	0.08	0.01
$582.9 - 664.7$	14	12.29	1.71	2.92	0.24
$664.7 - 746.5$	7	12.29	−5.29	27.98	2.28
>746.5	9	5.71	3.29	10.82	1.89
Total					$\chi^2 = \sum \frac{(f_o - f_e)^2}{f_e} = 4.42$

Step 5: Determine the chi-square critical value, χ^2_α.

Table 12.27 has four categories, so $k = 4$. In this example, $m = 2$ because we have to estimate both the mean and the standard deviation of the population using our sample. Therefore, we have $k - m - 1 = 4 - 2 - 1 = 1$ degree of freedom for our chi-square distribution. If we go to the $\alpha = 0.10$ column in Table 12.5 with 1 degree of freedom, we'll find that $\chi^2_\alpha = 2.706$.

Step 6: Compare the test statistic (χ^2) with the critical value (χ^2_α).

Because $\chi^2 = 4.42$ and this is more than $\chi^2_\alpha = 2.706$, we reject the null hypothesis according to Table 12.6.

Step 7: Determine the *p*-value.

$$p\text{-value} = \text{CHISQ.DIST.RT}\,(4.42, 1) = 0.0355$$

Because the *p*-value $= 0.0355$ and is less than $\alpha = 0.10$, we reject the null hypothesis.

Step 8: State your conclusions.

By rejecting the null hypothesis, we have no evidence that the population of credit scores follows the normal distribution.

YOUR TURN #7

a)

Step 1: Identify the null and alternative hypotheses.

H_0: There is no relationship between warm-up time and winner of match
H_1: There is a relationship between warm-up time and winner of match

Step 2: Calculate the expected frequencies.

	0–10 Minutes	11–20 Minutes	More Than 20 Minutes
Deb wins	$\frac{(27)(18)}{50} = 9.72$	$\frac{(27)(19)}{50} = 10.26$	$\frac{(27)(13)}{50} = 7.02$
Bob wins	$\frac{(23)(18)}{50} = 8.28$	$\frac{(23)(19)}{50} = 8.74$	$\frac{(23)(13)}{50} = 5.98$

Step 3: Calculate the chi-square test statistic, χ^2.

Cell	f_o	f_e	$(f_o - f_e)$	$(f_o - f_e)^2$	$\frac{(f_o - f_e)^2}{f_e}$
Deb 0–10	5	9.72	−4.72	22.28	2.29
Deb 11–20	12	10.26	1.74	3.03	0.30
Deb 20+	10	7.02	2.98	8.88	1.26
Bob 0–10	13	8.28	4.72	22.28	2.69
Bob 11–20	7	8.74	−1.74	3.03	0.35
Bob 20+	3	5.98	−2.98	8.88	1.48
Total			$\chi^2 = \sum \frac{(f_o - f_e)^2}{f_e}$		$= 8.37$

Step 4: Determine the chi-square critical value, χ^2_α

We have two players, so $r = 2$. We have three warm-up times, so $c = 3$. This means our chi-square critical value has $(r-1)(c-1) = (2-1)(3-1) = 2$ degrees of freedom. If we go to the $\alpha = 0.05$ column in Table 12.5, we'll find that $\chi^2_\alpha = 5.991$.

Step 5: Compare the test statistic (χ^2) with the critical value (χ^2_α).

Because $\chi^2 = 8.37$ and this is greater than $\chi^2_\alpha = 5.991$, we reject the null hypothesis according to Table 12.6.

Step 6: Determine the *p*-value.

$$p\text{-value} = \text{CHISQ.DIST.RT}(8.37, 2) = 0.0152$$

Because the *p*-value $= 0.0152$ and is less than $\alpha = 0.05$, we reject the null hypothesis.

Step 7: State your conclusions.

By rejecting the null hypothesis, we have found support for a relationship between the warm-up time and the winner of the match, so these categorical variables do not appear to be independent of one another. Comparing the observed and expected frequencies, you can see that Deb won 10 matches after warm-ups that exceeded 20 minutes. If the null hypothesis were true, we would expect her to win only 7.02 matches. After short warm-up times, I won 13 matches, but I was expected to win only 8.28. Therefore, there indeed appears to be a relationship between warm-up time and performance when Deb and I play tennis. Darn it! Once again, Deb is right. Boy, does this story have a familiar ring to it.

b)

	A	B	C	D	E
1	Chi-Square Test				
2					
3	Observed Frequencies				
4		Column variable			
5	Row variable	0-10	11-20	20+	Total
6	Deb wins	5	12	10	27
7	Bob wins	13	7	3	23
8	Total	18	19	13	50
9					
10	Expected Frequencies				
11		Column variable			
12	Row variable	0-10	11-20	20+	Total
13	Deb wins	9.72	10.26	7.02	27
14	Bob wins	8.28	8.74	5.98	23
15	Total	18	19	13	50
16					
17	Data				
18	Level of Significance	0.05			
19	Number of Rows	2			
20	Number of Columns	3			
21	Degrees of Freedom	2			
22					
23	Results				
24	Critical Value	5.991465			
25	Chi-Square Test Statistic	8.37417			
26	p-Value	0.01519			
27	Reject the null hypothesis				
28					

CHAPTER

13

Hypothesis Tests for the Population Variance

IN THIS CHAPTER, YOU WILL LEARN TO:

- Use the chi-square distribution to test the variance of a single population.
- Use the F-distribution to compare the variances of two populations.

CHAPTER 13 MAP

The previous four chapters have focused on a variety of hypothesis tests for population means and proportions. In this chapter, we turn our attention to hypothesis testing for the population variance (σ^2). As we have learned, most businesses try to achieve a certain degree of quality control by maintaining acceptable levels of variability. For example, let's consider the temperature inside the refrigerator in your kitchen. Today's refrigerators are designed to maintain an average temperature around 37°F. However, this temperature will vary as the compressor periodically cycles on and off to keep the refrigerator cool. Most refrigerator owners would probably find it acceptable if the inside temperature of their refrigerators averaged 37°F but ranged from 32°F to 42°F. However, many of these same owners would not find it acceptable if the temperature of their refrigerators ranged from 22°F to 52°F. My salad-loving wife, Deb, tends to get very irritated when her lettuce goes through several freeze–thaw cycles and ends up in the trash. If Amana, a major refrigerator manufacturer, performed a hypothesis test to determine only the mean, or average, temperature of its units, the lettuce-freezing scenario could go undetected. Performing a hypothesis test for the temperature variance, as well, would save the day (and Deb's lettuce).

Recall from Chapter 3 that the variance of a data set is a measure of variability around the mean of the data.

The following are other business scenarios in which a hypothesis test for a population variance could be useful:

- Kellogg's would like to ensure that the amount of Frosted Flakes being added to the cereal boxes is within an acceptable range. Too much variability could result in unhappy customers if their boxes aren't a consistent weight, and overfilling the boxes would hurt the profitability of Kellogg's.
- United Medical would like to measure the standard deviation of the time doctors spend with patients. Too much variability results in long wait times for other patients waiting to see the doctor.
- US Airways would like to reduce the variability of its flight times between Paris and Philadelphia. Reducing the variability will allow the company to improve its on-time performance for these flights and other connecting flights.

The lesson here is that testing for the population mean in many business settings tells only half the story. Testing for both the mean and variance can provide a more complete picture of what is happening with a business process so that problems with it can be detected and fixed.

Recall that the standard deviation is simply the square root of the variance.

Notice that we have not mentioned the population standard deviation at this point in the chapter. That's because there is no hypothesis test to measure the standard deviation directly. However, as we will see, we can convert a hypothesis statement about a standard deviation into a variance before performing the required procedure.

In this chapter, we will begin with a hypothesis test for a single population variance. After mastering this procedure, you will learn a procedure that will allow you to compare the variances for two populations.

13.1 Testing the Variance of a Single Population

In Chapter 12, we introduced the chi-square distribution to conduct a variety of hypotheses tests that involved comparing proportions, performing goodness-of-fit tests, and testing for independence. We will once again rely on the chi-square distribution to perform a hypothesis test for a single population variance. We'll consider both one-tail and two-tail tests.

One-Tail Hypothesis Test for a Single Population Variance

I'll start this section by referring back to Chapter 9 and my horrific experience with the new self-serve checkout system being tested at my local grocery store. Suppose the store's managers have decided that if the standard deviation for the time required by self-serve customers to check out is less than 2 minutes, additional self-serve systems should be installed at other locations. A standard deviation of at least 2 minutes would be one indication that some customers (such as your author) struggle with the self-serve system and take much longer to check out than other (normal) customers. To test if new systems should be installed in other stores, the checkout times, in minutes, of 24 randomly selected self-serve shoppers were recorded and are shown in Table 13.1. These data can also be found in the Excel file **checkout times.xlsx.**

TABLE 13.1 | CHECKOUT TIMES FOR 24 SELF-SERVE CUSTOMERS (MINUTES)

4.4	3.9	4.2	4.5	2.3	2.7
4.2	6.0	6.2	6.0	5.0	5.1
1.9	1.8	5.6	4.3	3.6	5.3
4.0	6.1	6.1	3.4	1.3	5.0

Using this sample data, I will conduct a hypothesis test to see if the population standard deviation for the checkout time of customers is less than 2 minutes.

A standard deviation of less than 2.0 minutes converts to a variance that is less than 4.0 minutes squared.

Step 1: Identify the null and alternative hypotheses.

The store's goal is to achieve a standard deviation of less than 2.0 minutes. Because we do not have a procedure to test for the standard deviation directly, we need to convert the standard deviation of 2.0 minutes into a variance by squaring it ($2.0^2 = 4.0$ minutes squared.) This results in the following hypotheses:

H_0: $\sigma^2 \geq 4.0$

H_1: $\sigma^2 < 4.0$ (The goal that the store would like to achieve)

This hypothesis is a one-tail (lower) test because the store would like to prove that the population variance is less than 4.0.

Step 2: Set a value for the significance level, α.

The significance level has the same interpretation for this test as it has had for previous hypotheses tests regarding the mean and proportion. The value of α. represents the probability of a Type I error, which occurs when we reject a null hypothesis that is true. For our self-serve example, a Type I error occurs when we conclude that the population variance is less than 4.0 minutes squared when, in reality, it is 4.0 minutes squared or more. Let's conduct our hypothesis test using $\alpha = 0.05$.

Step 3: Calculate the chi-square test statistic, χ^2.

The test statistic for a one-sample variance test, χ^2, is shown in Equation 13.1.

Formula 13.1 for the Test Statistic for a One-Sample Variance Test

$$\chi^2 = \frac{(n-1)s^2}{\sigma^2}$$

where

χ^2 = The test statistic
s^2 = The sample variance
σ^2 = The population variance expressed in the null hypothesis
n = The sample size

We first need to calculate the sample variance, which can be done in one of two ways. Recall that I introduced the sample variance way back in Chapter 3. The equation for calculating it is repeated here as Equation 13.2.

Formula 13.2 for the Sample Variance

$$s^2 = \frac{\sum_{i=1}^{n} x_i^2 - \frac{\left(\sum_{i=1}^{n} x_i\right)^2}{n}}{n-1}$$

To use this equation we need to sum up the values $\left(\sum x_i\right)$ and sum up the square of the values $\left(\sum x_i^2\right)$ from Table 13.1. These results are as follows:

$$\sum x_i = 4.4 + 3.9 + 4.2 + \cdots + 3.4 + 1.3 + 5.0 = 102.9$$

$$\sum x_i^2 = (4.4)^2 + (3.9)^2 + (4.2)^2 + \cdots + (3.4)^2 + (1.3)^2 + (5.0)^2 = 490.55$$

Recognizing that we have 24 observations in our sample $(n = 24)$, our sample variance, s^2, is as follows:

$$s^2 = \frac{\sum_{i=1}^{n} x_i^2 - \frac{\left(\sum_{i=1}^{n} x_i\right)^2}{n}}{n-1} = \frac{490.55 - \frac{(102.9)^2}{24}}{24-1} = \frac{490.55 - 441.184}{23} = 2.146$$

We can also rely on the Excel function = VAR.S(*data values*) to provide us with this same result.

Now that we have our sample variance, we plug the remaining values into Equation 13.1 to get the following test statistic:

$$\chi^2 = \frac{(n-1)s^2}{\sigma^2} = \frac{(24-1)(2.146)}{4} = 12.34$$

Step 4: Determine the chi-square critical value, χ^2_α.

The test statistic shown in Equation 13.1 follows the chi-square distribution that we introduced in Chapter 12 with $n - 1$ degrees of freedom (*df*). Table 13.2 shows an excerpt from Table 8 in Appendix A, which shows the chi-square critical values. Rows 1 through 22 in this table have been hidden to conserve space.

TABLE 13.2 | EXCERPT OF CHI-SQUARE CRITICAL VALUES

	AREA IN RIGHT TAIL OF DISTRIBUTION									
df	0.995	0.99	0.975	0.95	0.90	0.10	0.05	0.025	0.01	0.005
	(ROWS 1 THROUGH 22 HAVE BEEN HIDDEN)									
23	9.260	10.196	11.689	13.091	14.848	32.007	35.172	38.076	41.638	44.181
24	9.886	10.856	12.401	13.848	15.659	33.196	36.415	39.364	42.980	45.559
25	10.520	11.524	13.120	14.611	16.473	34.382	37.652	40.646	44.314	46.928
26	11.160	12.198	13.844	15.379	17.292	35.563	38.885	41.923	45.642	48.290
27	11.808	12.879	14.573	16.151	18.114	36.741	40.113	43.195	46.963	49.645
28	12.461	13.565	15.308	16.928	18.939	37.916	41.337	44.461	48.278	50.993
29	13.121	14.256	16.047	17.708	19.768	39.087	42.557	45.722	49.588	52.336

This is a lower (left) tail test because the alternative hypothesis, H_1, is expressed as "less than 4.0." This puts the rejection region with area $\alpha = 0.05$ on the left side of the distribution, and leaves 95% of the distribution to the right of the critical value (also known as the right tail). The columns in Table 13.2 are based on the area in the right tail of the distribution, so we look for the column labeled "0.95." We also have $n - 1 = 24 - 1 = 23$ degrees for freedom for this example. According to the Table 13.2, the critical value is $\chi^2_\alpha = \chi^2_{0.95} = 13.091$ (the appropriate row, column, and critical value are highlighted).

We can also use Excel's CHISQ.INV.RT function to determine the chi-square critical value, which has the following characteristics:

=CHISQ.INV.RT(right_tail_area, degrees_of_freedom)

For our checkout time example, we have

=CHISQ.INV.RT(0.95, 23) = 13.091

Step 5: Compare the test statistic (χ^2) with the critical value (χ^2_α).

Figure 13.1 shows the rejection region for the self-serve checkout example along with the critical value and test statistic.

FIGURE 13.1
Comparing the Chi-Square Test Statistic with the Chi-Square Critical Value for the Self-Serve Checkout Example

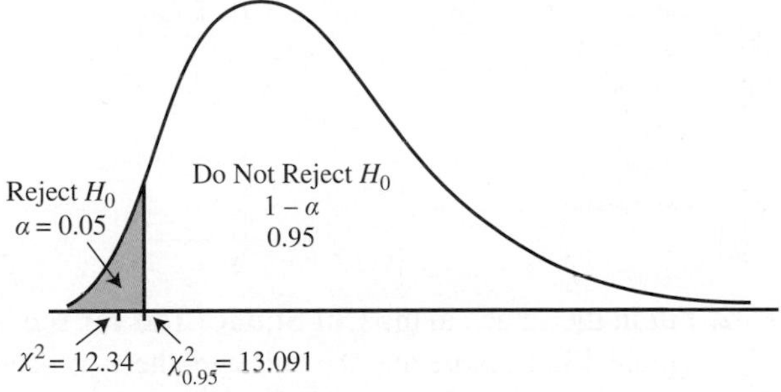

We reject the null hypothesis according to Figure 13.1 because our test statistic, $\chi^2 = 12.34$, is less than $\chi^2_{0.95} = 13.091$ and lies in the shaded rejection region.

Step 6: State your conclusions.

By rejecting the null hypothesis, we have evidence that the population variance for the checkout times is less than 4.0, which translates into a standard deviation of less than 2.0 minutes. Because we have rejected the null hypothesis, the decision should be made to install additional systems in other locations.

The chi-square test for a variance does have an important requirement. The population from which the sample is drawn needs to be normally distributed in order to get valid results. This requirement holds true for any sample size and is fairly rigid. In other words, moderate deviations from a normal population can result in unreliable conclusions about the population variance. Chapter 12 demonstrated a method to test if a population follows the normal probability distribution.

Using PHStat to Test the Variance of a Population

You can use PHStat to perform the chi-square test for a single population variance by taking the following steps. Excel for Mac users can go to the textbook's Web site for these instructions (www.pearsonhighered.com/donnelly).

1. Go to **Add-Ins** > **PHStat** > **One-Sample Tests** > **Chi-Square Test for the Variance**, as shown in Figure 13.2A.

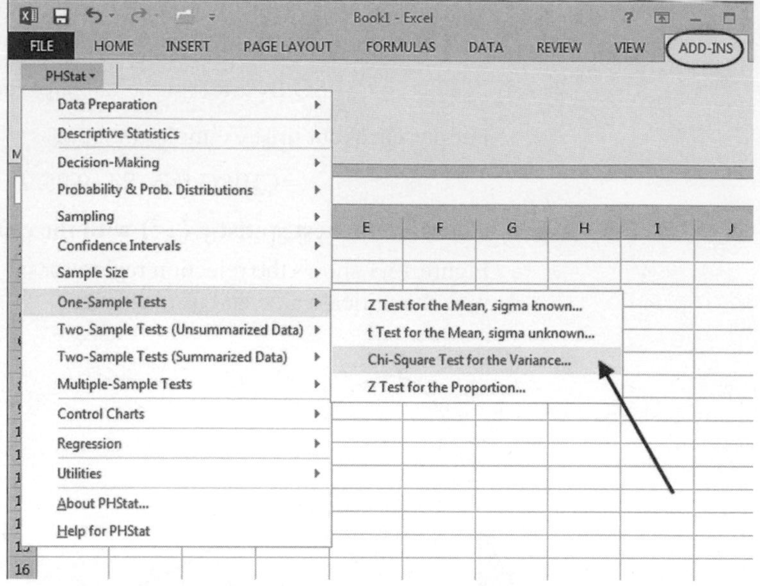

FIGURE 13.2A Using PHStat to Test the Variance of a Population (Step 1)

2. Fill in the values in the **Chi-Square Test for the Variance** dialog box as shown in Figure 13.2B. Note that the null hypothesis is stated as a variance and that the program asks for the sample standard deviation rather than the sample variance. For this example, $s = \sqrt{2.146} = 1.465$. Click **OK.**

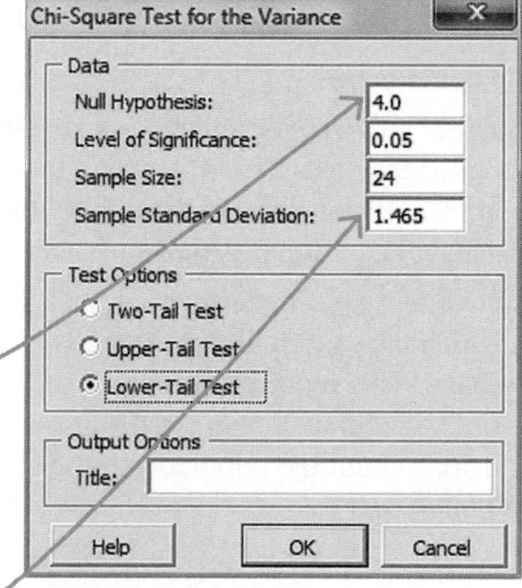

FIGURE 13.2B Using PHStat to Test the Variance of a Population (Step 2)

Be sure to state the null hypothesis as the variance rather than the standard deviation.

Be sure to use the sample standard deviation rather than the sample variance for this input.

Figure 13.2C shows the final results for our variance test.

	A		B
1	**Chi-Square Test of Variance**		
2			
3	**Data**		
4	**Null Hypothesis**	**σ^2=**	**4**
5	**Level of Significance**		**0.05**
6	**Sample Size**		**24**
7	**Sample Standard Deviation**		**1.465**
8			
9	Intermediate Calculations		
10	Degrees of Freedom		23
11	Half Area		0.025
12	**Chi-Square Statistic**		**12.3408**
13			
14	**Lower-Tail Test**		
15	Lower Critical Value		13.0905
16	*p*-Value		0.0351
17	**Reject the null hypothesis**		
18			

FIGURE 13.2C Using PHStat to Test the Variance of a Population (Final Result)

These results are consistent with our manual calculations. Also, note that the *p*-value shown in Cell B16 equals 0.0351. This value represents the probability of seeing a chi-square test statistic less than 12.34 if the null hypothesis is true. Because the *p*-value is less than $\alpha = 0.05$, we reject the null hypothesis.

Take a break from watching me do all the work and try your hand at a variance test in this next Your Turn problem.

YOUR TURN #1

Canon Business Solutions (CBS) is a division of Canon that sells and services Canon copiers to corporate customers (lots of *c* words in this sentence). The length of time a customer waits for a service call when a copier requires maintenance is monitored very closely. Suppose CBS measures, in addition to the average wait time, the standard deviation of the wait times in an effort to provide consistent service. Let's say that CBS has decided that if the standard deviation exceeds 30 minutes, additional service personnel should be hired to reduce the longer wait times.

Suppose CBS collected the wait times for a random sample of 20 service calls and found the sample standard deviation to be 32.4 minutes. (I sense you are grateful I didn't make you calculate the sample standard deviation. Just trying to help you out.)

a. Using $\alpha = 0.10$, determine if CBS needs to hire additional service personnel.
b. Verify your results using PHStat.
c. Interpret the *p*-value.

Hint: Set this up as an upper-tail test.

Answers can be found on ▶ **page 648**

Two-Tail Hypothesis Test for a Single Population Variance

Now that you have mastered the one-tail variance test, let's move on and examine the two-tail procedure with the following example. As we learned in the beginning of the chapter, refrigerator manufacturers design their units to maintain temperatures within a certain range. Too much temperature variation can result in food freezing or spoiling prematurely. Too little temperature variation can lead to higher energy costs because the refrigerator's compressor cycles on and off more often than necessary. Suppose Amana, a major refrigerator manufacturer, has been trying to achieve a standard deviation equal to 4.0°F for a particular model.

To test for this variation under normal operating conditions, the refrigerator was filled to 75% capacity with food and was opened 30 times during an 8-hour day for 10 seconds' duration. Table 13.3 shows the temperature readings recorded during this experiment. These data can also be found in the Excel file **refrigerator.xlsx**.

TABLE 13.3 | TEMPERATURE READINGS (°F)

38.2	37.5	29.7	42.5	43.4	41.5
41.0	41.2	40.0	41.4	39.5	39.8
44.6	42.2	34.9	28.5	38.5	34.7
36.6	37.0	32.0	34.9	36.9	36.6
34.9	35.6	45.6	34.1	45.2	33.5

Using these data and $\alpha = 0.05$, Amana would like to perform a hypothesis test to determine if the standard deviation of the temperature for this particular model is equal to 4.0°F.

Step 1: Identify the null and alternative hypotheses.

Amana's goal is to achieve a standard deviation equal to 4.0°F. This translates into a variance of $4.0^2 = 16.0$ degrees squared. Because we are testing for equality, this is a two-tail test.

Remember, equalities are always expressed in the null hypothesis.

H_0: $\sigma^2 = 16.0$ (This is the goal that Amana would like to achieve)
H_1: $\sigma^2 \neq 16.0$

Step 2: Set a value for the significance level, α.

Amana set $\alpha = 0.05$ for this hypothesis test.

Step 3: Calculate the chi-square test statistic, χ^2.

For this example, I'm going to take the easy way out and use Excel to calculate the sample variance. (I hope you don't mind.) Using the VAR.S function on the data set, I get the following:

$$s^2 = 19.151$$

Using Equation 13.1, our test statistic is as follows:

$$\chi^2 = \frac{(n-1)s^2}{\sigma^2} = \frac{(30-1)(19.151)}{16.0} = 34.71$$

Step 4: Determine the chi-square critical value, χ^2_α.

Because we have a two-tail test, there are two critical values, one in each tail of the chi-square distribution. The area that corresponds to $\alpha = 0.05$ is split evenly $(\alpha/2 = 0.025)$ between the two tails of the distribution.

The left (lower) critical value has an area equal to 0.025 to its left and 0.975 to its right. Look back at Table 13.2 under the "Area in Right Tail of Distribution" $= 0.975$ column and in the degrees of freedom (*df*) row $n - 1 = 30 - 1 = 29$. Here you will find that the left critical value is $\chi^2_\alpha = \chi^2_{0.975} = 16.047$.

The right (upper) critical value has an area equal to 0.025 to its right. In Table 13.2, look for the "Area in Right Tail of Distribution" $= 0.025$ column and the degrees of freedom (*df*) row 29. Here you will find the right critical value is $\chi^2_\alpha = \chi^2_{0.025} = 45.722$. Both of these critical values are shown in Figure 13.3.

Using Excel's CHISQ.INV.RT function, we can confirm the chi-square critical values for our refrigerator example:

=CHISQ.INV.RT(0.975, 29) = 16.047

=CHISQ.INV.RT(0.025, 29) = 45.722

Step 5: Compare the test statistic (χ^2) with the critical value (χ^2_α).

Figure 13.3 graphically illustrates the test statistic and the rejection regions for the refrigerator example.

FIGURE 13.3
Comparing the Chi-Square Test Statistic with the Chi-Square Critical Value for Refrigerator Temperature Example

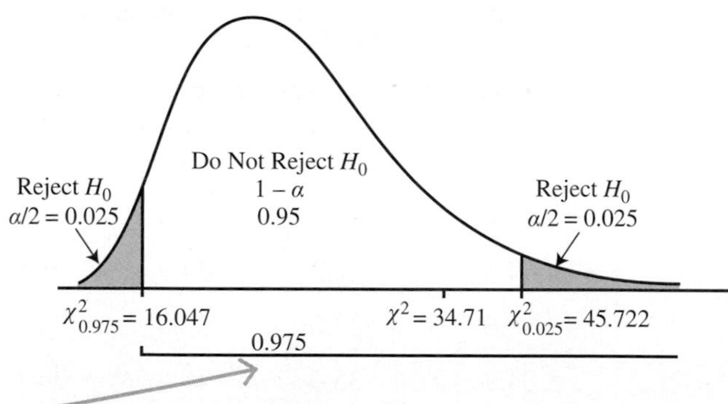

The area to the right of the lower critical value is 0.95 + 0.25 = 0.975. Go to the "0.975" column and *df* = "29" row in Table 13.2 to find the critical value equal to 16.047.

Because $\chi^2 = 34.71$ is between $\chi^2_{0.975} = 16.047$ and $\chi^2_{0.025} = 45.722$, we fail to reject the null hypothesis according to Figure 13.3.

Step 6: State your conclusions.

By failing to reject the null hypothesis, we do not have evidence that the population standard deviation is not equal to 4.0°F. Because we can never accept the null hypothesis, we cannot conclude that the standard deviation for this population equals 4.0°F. However, we have a business decision to make here, which is to (a) decide that the population standard deviation is acceptable (that is, equal to 4.0°F) or (b) decide that the population standard deviation is unacceptable (that is, not equal to 4.0°F). When I put on my businessperson's hat, the results of this hypothesis test lead me to choose option (a) and conclude that the refrigerator design is working properly for this particular model. I know this might seem like a contradiction, but choosing to find support for the null hypothesis in this example is the appropriate business decision.

As I mentioned earlier in the chapter, the people who conduct quality control programs are very interested in the variance of a process because it is a measure of consistency. Generally speaking, more consistency (low variance) is more effective than less consistency (high variance) when dealing with a business process. However, variances that are much lower than expected can be an indication that something has gone wrong, which merits further investigation. One explanation may be that the measuring device has malfunctioned. The following Your Turn problem provides such an example.

YOUR TURN #2

Consider the process at Kellogg's that fills boxes of Frosted Flakes. The target weight of sugary corn flakes per box is set at 18 ounces (makes my mouth water as I write this). Due to the nature of this process, we expect some slight variation in the weights of the boxes. Suppose that historically, when the process was performing as designed, the standard deviation of the weights was 0.15 ounces. To verify that the filling process is currently operating with this variation, 18 randomly selected boxes were weighed on a precision scale and were found to have the following weights. These data can also be found in the Excel file **FF weights.xlsx.**

18.0	18.1	18.0	17.8	18.1	18.1
18.0	18.0	18.0	18.0	17.9	18.0
18.1	17.8	17.8	18.0	17.9	18.0

a. Using $\alpha = 0.10$, determine if the filling process still has a standard deviation equal to 0.15 ounces.
b. Verify your results using PHStat.
c. Interpret the p-value.

Hint: $\sum x_i = 323.6$, $\sum x_i^2 = 5{,}817.78$

Answers can be found on ▶ **page 649**

13.1 Section Problems

Basic Skills

13.1 Consider the following hypothesis statement:

$$H_0: \sigma^2 \geq 5.0$$
$$H_1: \sigma^2 < 5.0$$

State your conclusion given that $s = 1.6$, $n = 32$, and $\alpha = 0.05$.

13.2 Consider the following hypothesis statement:

$$H_0: \sigma^2 \leq 9.0$$
$$H_1: \sigma^2 > 9.0$$

State your conclusion given that $s = 3.4$, $n = 25$, and $\alpha = 0.10$.

13.3 Consider the following hypothesis statement:

$$H_0: \sigma^2 = 12.0$$
$$H_1: \sigma^2 \neq 12.0$$

State your conclusion given that $s = 4.6$, $n = 36$, and $\alpha = 0.05$.

13.4 Consider the following hypothesis statement:

$$H_0: \sigma^2 = 39.0$$
$$H_1: \sigma^2 \neq 39.0$$

State your conclusion given that $s = 6.5$, $n = 40$, and $\alpha = 0.05$.

Applications

13.5 Suppose that on a 100-point test, my goal is for my students' exam scores to have a standard deviation of less than 10 points. A recent sample of 22 exams has a sample standard deviation of 12.1.

a. Test whether my goal was achieved using $\alpha = 0.05$.
b. Verify your results using PHStat.
c. Interpret the p-value obtained from the software.

13.6 Recently, Seasons Pizza was receiving customer complaints about erratic pizza delivery times. To address this issue, Seasons made some operational changes in its restaurant and added more delivery people to its staff. To study the effectiveness of these changes, Seasons would like to test the hypothesis that the standard deviation for the delivery times of its pizzas is less than 12 minutes. The following data represent a random sample of delivery times (in minutes). These data can also be found in the Excel file **pizza delivery times.xlsx.**

23	24	23	36	30	40	34	24	28	29	15	27
17	22	33	30	15	10	12	21	38	35	18	20

a. Using $\alpha = 0.05$, test whether Seasons Pizza's goal was achieved.
b. Verify your results using PHStat.
c. Interpret the p-value obtained from the software.

13.7 Utz Pretzels produces hard pretzels and packages them in 16-ounce bags. However, the size of each pretzel makes it challenging to fill each bag to precisely 16 ounces. When the filling process is working normally, the standard deviation of the bag weights equals 0.25 ounces. To test if this standard deviation is being achieved, the following random sample of pretzel-bag weights was recorded. These data can also be found in the Excel file **Utz pretzel weights.xlsx.**

15.9	15.7	16.4	16.3	15.8	16.0	15.9
16.1	16.2	16.2	16.2	16.4	16.0	16.3
16.3	16.6	16.3	15.8	15.7	16.0	16.5
15.7	15.9	15.7	16.1			

a. Using $\alpha = 0.05$, determine if the filling process is performing normally.
b. Verify your results using PHStat.
c. Interpret the p-value obtained from the software.

13.8 Refrigerator manufacturers design their freezer units to maintain temperatures within a certain range. Too much temperature variation can result in food spoiling due to thawing. Too little temperature variation can cause higher energy costs as the refrigerator's compressor cycles on and off more often than necessary. Suppose Amana, a major refrigerator manufacturer, wants the freezer of a particular model to have a standard deviation equal to 4°F. To test for this variation under normal operating conditions, the freezer was filled to 75% capacity with food and was opened periodically during an 8-hour day for 10 seconds' duration. The following table shows the freezer temperature readings in degrees Fahrenheit that were recorded during this experiment. These data can also be found in the Excel file **freezer temperatures.xlsx.**

6.4	−8.6	−3.8	−1.1	1.1	0.2	1.1
0.7	−0.5	1.0	1.9	1.4	5.9	−7.2
6.9	6.6	6.9	8.1	5.5	6.1	8.2
8.9	6.1	7.0	−0.4	−1.4	−2.6	0.8
0.6	0.2	−2.8	−5.5	6.8	7.3	7.5
2.5	0.2	2.4	−2.9	−3.1		

a. Using $\alpha = 0.05$, test to determine if Amana has achieved its goal.
b. Verify your results using PHStat.
c. Interpret the p-value obtained from the software.

13.2 Comparing the Variances of Two Populations

Back in Chapter 10, we learned about hypothesis tests that compare two population means or two population proportions. One of the t-tests made the assumption that the two population variances were equal. The ANOVA procedure that was covered in Chapter 11 also assumed the two population variances were equal. In this final section of the chapter, we'll examine a technique to validate these variance assumptions while covering both a one-tail case and a two-tail case. As with the single population variance test already discussed, this technique requires that both populations be normally distributed.

Testing the Variances of Two Populations (One-Tail Test)

I'll use the following example to demonstrate a one-tail hypothesis test that compares two population variances. Suppose Ron owns a Taco Bell restaurant that has a single drive-through window. Ron would like to reduce the variability of the service time that customers who use the drive-through experience. To accomplish this, he would like to test a new system that outsources the drive-through orders to a third-party call center. Customers placing orders in the drive-through would be actually talking to a centralized call center that would transfer the order information directly to the restaurant. This would free up employees in the Taco Bell restaurant who normally take the orders. The data in Table 13.4 show the service times, in seconds, for customers using the on-site and outsourced systems. These data can also be found in the Excel file **Taco Bell.xlsx.**

TABLE 13.4 | Taco Bell Drive-Through Service Times (Seconds)

ON-SITE SYSTEM						
105	125	60	184	189	126	211
176	149	79	122	175		
OUTSOURCED SYSTEM						
163	158	153	174	138	140	195
138	189	142	182	138	175	91

Using these data and $\alpha = 0.05$, Ron would like to perform a hypothesis test to determine if the standard deviation of the service times for the outsourced system is less than that of the on-site system.

Step 1: Calculate the variance for each sample.

We can use either Equation 13.2 or Excel's VAR.S function to provide the variance for each sample. For this example, let's use Excel, which gives us the following:

$$s^2_{\text{on-site}} = 2{,}184.93$$
$$s^2_{\text{outsource}} = 744.42$$

Step 2: Identify the null and alternative hypotheses.

When comparing two population variances, always assign the larger sample variance to Population 1 and the smaller sample variance to Population 2.

Population 1 = On-site system
Population 2 = Outsourced system

Ron would like to see if the outsourced system times have a lower variance than the on site system times. The hypothesis statement would then be as follows:

This is a one-tail hypothesis test because we are testing to see if the Population 1 variance is greater than the Population 2 variance.

$$H_0: \sigma_1^2 \le \sigma_2^2$$
$$H_1: \sigma_1^2 > \sigma_2^2 \text{ (Outsource system has lower variance than on-site system)}$$

Step 3: Set a value for the significance level, α.

Ron set $\alpha = 0.05$ for this hypothesis test.

Step 4: Calculate the F-test statistic.

The test statistic for a two-sample variance test, F, is shown in Equation 13.3.

Formula 13.3 for the Test Statistic for a Two-Sample Variance Test

$$F = \frac{s_1^2}{s_2^2}$$

where

F = The test statistic
s_1^2 = The sample variance from Population 1
s_2^2 = The sample variance from Population 2

Always place the larger variance in the numerator in Equation 13.3.

Plugging our sample variances into Equation 13.3 results in the following:

$$F = \frac{s_1^2}{s_2^2} = \frac{2{,}184.93}{744.42} = 2.935$$

Because Population 1 will always have the larger sample variance (because we assigned the variances that way at the outset of the problem), the test statistic from Equation 13.3 will always be greater than 1.0.

Step 5: Determine the critical value, F_{α}.

The test statistic shown in Equation 13.3 follows the F-distribution, which was first introduced in Chapter 11. Recall that this distribution is skewed to the right and has the following degrees of freedom:

$$D_1 = n_1 - 1$$
$$D_2 = n_2 - 1$$

where n_1 and n_2 are the sample sizes from Populations 1 and 2, respectively. Recall there were 12 observations for the on-site system and 14 observations for the outsourced system.

So, for our Taco Bell example, we have the following degrees of freedom:

$$D_1 = n_1 - 1 = 12 - 1 = 11$$
$$D_2 = n_2 - 1 = 14 - 1 = 13$$

The critical value, F_{α}, can be found in Table 6 in Appendix A. An excerpt from this table is shown in Table 13.5. Select the portion of Table 6 in Appendix A labeled "Area in the Right Tail of Distribution = 0.05" (because we set $\alpha = 0.05$ for this hypothesis test). Go to the $D_1 = 11$ column and $D_2 = 13$ row to find $F_{\alpha} = F_{0.05} = 2.635$. This value is highlighted in Table 13.5.

TABLE 13.5 | Excerpt of F-Distribution Critical Values

AREA IN THE RIGHT TAIL OF DISTRIBUTION = 0.05

D_2 \ D_1	11	12	13	14	15	16	17	18	19	20
ROWS 1 THROUGH 11 HAVE BEEN HIDDEN										
12	2.717	2.687	2.660	2.637	2.617	2.599	2.583	2.568	2.555	2.544
13	2.635	2.604	2.577	2.554	2.533	2.515	2.499	2.484	2.471	2.459
14	2.565	2.534	2.507	2.484	2.463	2.445	2.428	2.413	2.400	2.388

We can also obtain the critical F-score for our two-population variance test using Excel's F.INV.RT function, which has the following characteristics:

$$=\text{F.INV.RT}\,(\alpha, D_1, D_2)$$
$$=\text{F.INV.RT}\,(0.05, 11, 13) = 2.635$$

Step 6: Compare the test statistic (F) with the critical value (F_{α}).

Figure 13.4 graphically illustrates the test statistic and the rejection region for the Taco Bell example. Be sure to always set up the hypothesis statement for a right-tail test as the figure shows. In other words, assign H_1 the ">" sign as we did in this example. That way, the rejection region will always be in the right tail of the F-distribution.

Because $F = 2.935$ is more than $F_{\alpha} = 2.635$, we reject the null hypothesis according to Figure 13.4.

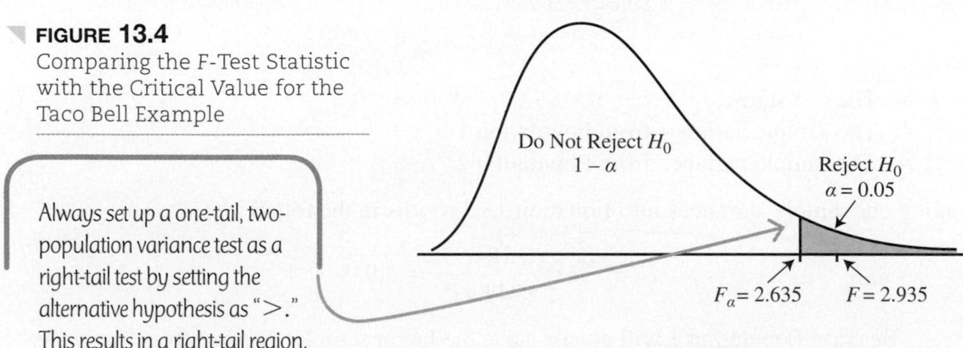

FIGURE 13.4
Comparing the F-Test Statistic with the Critical Value for the Taco Bell Example

Step 7: State your conclusions.

By rejecting the null hypothesis, we have evidence that the variance for Population 2 is less than the variance for Population 1. Ron can conclude that the service times for the outsourced system have less variability than the service times for the on-site system.

A two-population variance test has the same normal distribution requirement as a one-population variance test. Specifically, both populations being compared must be normally distributed to achieve reliable results.

Using Excel to Compare Two Population Variances

We can use Excel's Data Analysis (for Windows users) to conduct our two-population variance test by taking the following steps. Excel for Mac users can go to the textbook's Web site and find instructions for this procedure with PHStat.

1. Either open the Excel file **Taco Bell.xlsx** or enter the service time data values in Columns A and B as shown in Figure 13.5A.
2. Go to **Data** and click on **Data Analysis** on the right side of the ribbon. This opens the **Data Analysis** dialog box.
3. Select **F-Test Two-Sample for Variances.** Click **OK.**

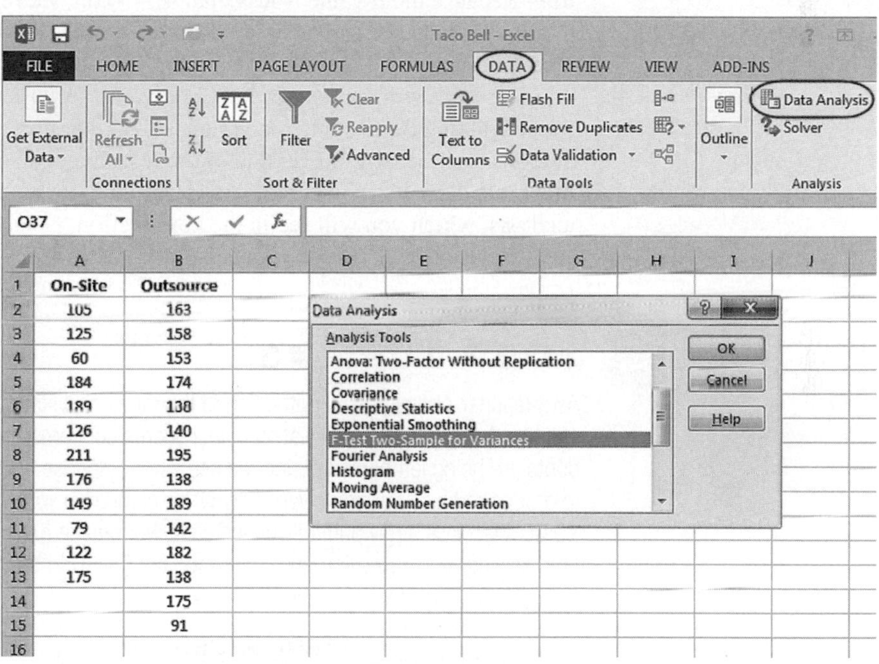

FIGURE 13.5A
Using Excel to Compare Two Population Variances (Steps 1-3)

4. Fill in the **F-Test Two-Sample for Variances** dialog box as shown in Figure 13.5B. Click **OK.**

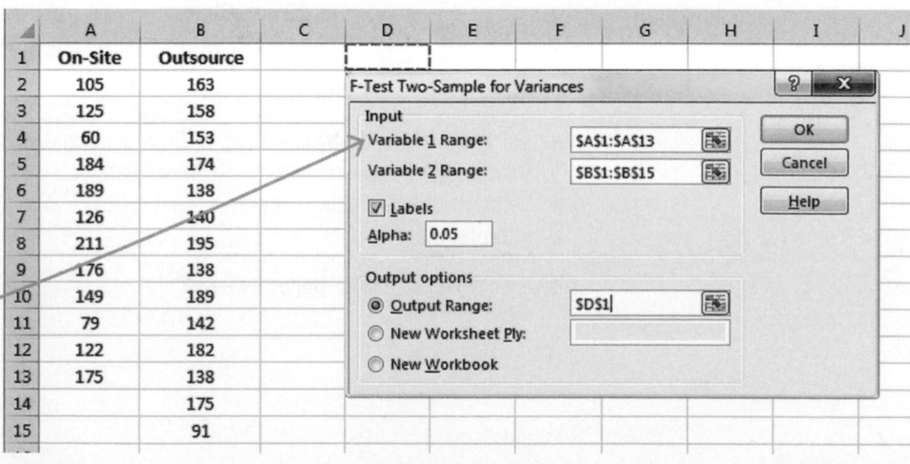

FIGURE 13.5B
Using Excel to Compare Two Population Variances (Step 4)

Place the on-site sample in the "Variable 1 Range" because it has the higher variance of the two samples. You can use Excel's VAR.S function to find the variable with the higher variance.

Figure 13.5C shows the output for our Taco Bell example, which matches our results from the previous section.

FIGURE 13.5C
Using Excel to Compare Two Population Variances (Final Result)

	A	B	C	D	E	F
1	On-Site	Outsource		F-Test Two-Sample for Variances		
2	105	163				
3	125	158			*On-Site*	*Outsource*
4	60	153		Mean	141.75	155.428571
5	184	174		Variance	2184.9318	744.417582
6	189	138		Observations	12	14
7	126	140		df	11	13
8	211	195		F	2.9350889	
9	176	138		P(F<=f) one-tail	0.0342805	
10	149	189		F Critical one-tail	2.6346505	
11	79	142				
12	122	182				
13	175	138				
14		175				
15		91				
16						

Notice that the p-value shown in Cell E9 of Figure 13.5C equals 0.0343. This value represents the probability of obtaining a test statistic of 2.935 or higher if the null hypothesis is true. Because the p-value is less than $\alpha = 0.05$, we reject the null hypothesis and conclude that the variance of the outsourced service times is less than the variance of the on-site service times.

For some strange reason, Excel provides only the results for a one-tail hypothesis test for comparing two population variances. So, we'll use PHStat in the following section to demonstrate the two-tail version of the test. Excel also requires unsummarized (raw) data for this procedure. If we only have summarized data, we'll need to use PHStat to perform this analysis, which you will see in the next section.

Now see what you've learned so far by solving the following Your Turn problem.

YOUR TURN #3

As a teacher, I pay particular attention to the mean and standard deviation of exam scores for my classes. A large standard deviation in test scores concerns me because it is an indication that some students are being left behind during the semester. Suppose I want to investigate if having students work in groups reduces the grade variability when compared with a more traditional lecture format. So, in my 10:00 A.M. class, I rely primarily on lectures, whereas in my 11:00 A.M. class, the students spend more time solving problems in groups. I collected the following data after the first exam. The data can also be found in the Excel file **exam scores.xlsx.**

10:00 A.M. Class

86	83	86	89	89
85	96	99	75	79

11:00 A.M. Class

90	76	73	90	88
89	84	82	78	86

a. Using $\alpha = 0.01$, determine if the 11:00 A.M. class experienced less variability in its exam scores than the 10:00 A.M. class did.

b. Verify your results using Excel.

c. Interpret the p-value.

Answers can be found on ▶ **pages 649–650**

Testing the Variances of Two Populations (Two-Tail Test)

The last thing we will do in this chapter is conduct a two-tail hypothesis test to compare two population variances. We use this test only to investigate whether a difference exists between the two variances rather than to test if one variance is greater than the other. To demonstrate, I'll use the following example.

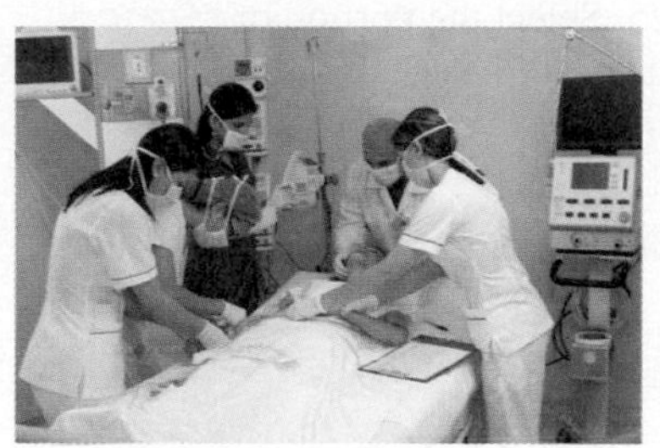

In an effort to control costs, health care insurance companies pay close attention to the length of the hospital stays of their customers. Suppose the health care insurer Blue Cross Blue Shield (BCBS) is interested in studying the difference in the variation in the number of days patients stay at two different hospitals for a specific procedure. A significant difference in the variation of stays at the two hospitals might be something BCBS would want to investigate. Data on the stays of 20 randomly selected patients hospitalized at Christiana Hospital and 20 randomly selected patients hospitalized at Bayhealth Hospital were collected for the same procedure. This information, along with the standard deviations (in days) for each of the two samples, is shown in Table 13.6.

Be very careful when identifying the problem's standard deviation and variance. If I had a nickel for every time students confused them in their calculations, I would have retired long ago!

TABLE 13.6 | VARIATION IN HOSPITAL STAYS

	CHRISTIANA HOSPITAL	BAYHEALTH HOSPITAL
Sample standard deviation	0.92 days	0.71 days
Sample size	20	20

Using these data and $\alpha = 0.05$, BCBS would like to perform a hypothesis test to determine if the standard deviation of the hospital stays differs between Christiana and Bayhealth for this procedure:

Step 1: Calculate the variance for each sample.

Because I so generously provided you with the sample standard deviations in Table 13.6, the sample variances are a straightforward calculation:

$$s^2_{\text{Christiana}} = (0.92)^2 = 0.8464$$
$$s^2_{\text{Bayhealth}} = (0.71)^2 = 0.5041$$

Step 2: Identify the null and alternative hypotheses.

Once again, we assign the larger sample variance to Population 1 and the smaller to Population 2:

$$\text{Population 1} = \text{Christiana}$$
$$\text{Population 2} = \text{Bayhealth}$$

Because BCBS is interested only in examining a difference in population variances, we have the following two-tail test:

This is a two-tail test because we are only testing for a difference in population variances, as opposed to testing if one is greater than the other.

$$H_0: \sigma_1^2 = \sigma_2^2$$
$$H_1: \sigma_1^2 \neq \sigma_2^2 \quad \text{(Population variances are different)}$$

Step 3: Set a value for the significance level, α.

BCBS set $\alpha = 0.05$ for this hypothesis test.

Step 4: Calculate the F-test statistic.

Plugging our sample variances into Equation 13.3 results in the following:

Remember, when comparing two population variances, always place the larger sample variance in the numerator when calculating the F-test statistic.

$$F = \frac{s_1^2}{s_2^2} = \frac{0.8464}{0.5041} = 1.679$$

Step 5: Determine the critical value, F_α.

For our BCBS example,

$$D_1 = n_1 - 1 = 20 - 1 = 19$$
$$D_2 = n_2 - 1 = 20 - 1 = 19$$

Because we have a two-tail test, the area that corresponds to $\alpha = 0.05$ is split evenly $(\alpha/2 = 0.025)$ between the two tails of the distribution. This means that the area in the right tail of the distribution is 0.025. Select the portion of Table 6 in Appendix A labeled "Area in the Right Tail of Distribution $= 0.025$" for this hypothesis test. Go to the $D_1 = 19$ column and $D_2 = 19$ row to find $F_{\alpha/2} = F_{0.025} = 2.526$.

We can also obtain the critical F-score for our two-population variance test using Excel's F.INV.RT function as follows:

$$=\text{F.INV.RT}\,(0.025, 19, 19) = 2.526$$

Step 6: Compare the test statistic (F) with the critical value $(F_\alpha.)$

Figure 13.6 graphically illustrates the test statistic and the rejection region for the BCBS example. Even though this is a two-tail test, we consider only the rejection region on the right side of the distribution. This is because when comparing two population variances, we always assign the sample with the higher variance to the numerator of the test statistic calculation shown in Equation 13.3. Doing so ensures that the test statistic, F, will always be greater than 1.0.

FIGURE 13.6
Comparing the F-Test Statistic with the Critical Value for the Blue Cross Shield Example

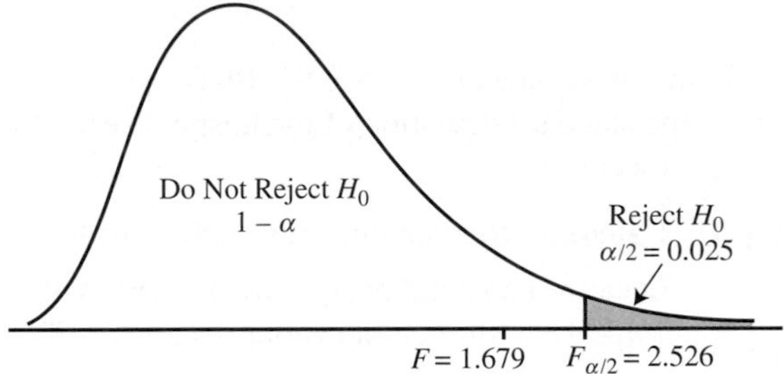

Because $F = 1.679$ and this is less than $F_{\alpha/2} = 2.526$, we fail to reject the null hypothesis.

Step 7: State your conclusions.

By failing to reject the null hypothesis, we do not have evidence that the population variances are different for the two hospitals. We are not, however, saying that the variances for patient stays between the two hospitals are equal. That would be accepting the null hypothesis, which is a very bad thing to do. However, from a business perspective, there does not appear to be any reason to investigate the length of stays at these two hospitals further.

Using PHStat to Compare Two Population Variances

We can use PHStat to compare two population variances by taking the following steps. Excel for Mac users can go to the textbook's Web site for these instructions.

1. Go to **Add-Ins > PHStat > Two-Sample Tests (Summarized Data) > F Test for Differences in Two Variances**, as shown in Figure 13.7A.

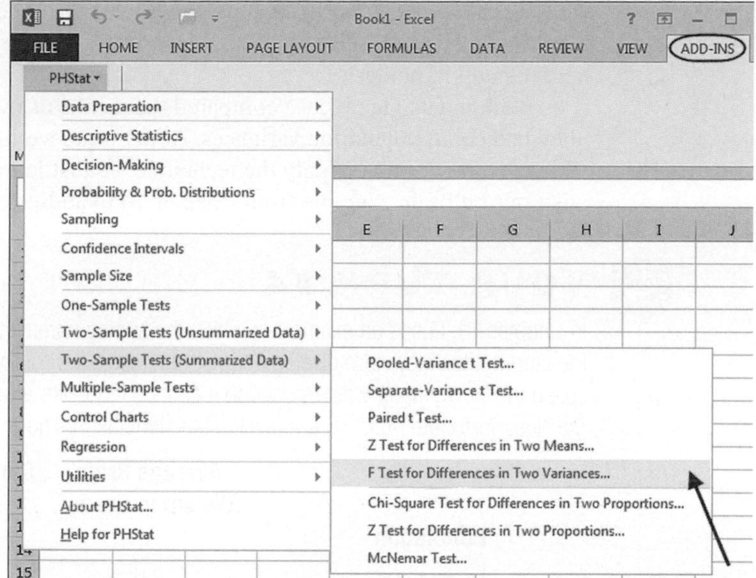

FIGURE 13.7A Using PHStat to Compare Two Population Variances (Step 1)

2. Fill in the values in the **F Test for Differences in Two Variances** dialog box as shown in Figure 13.7B. Note that PHStat asks for the sample variance rather than the sample standard deviation for both populations. Click **OK**.

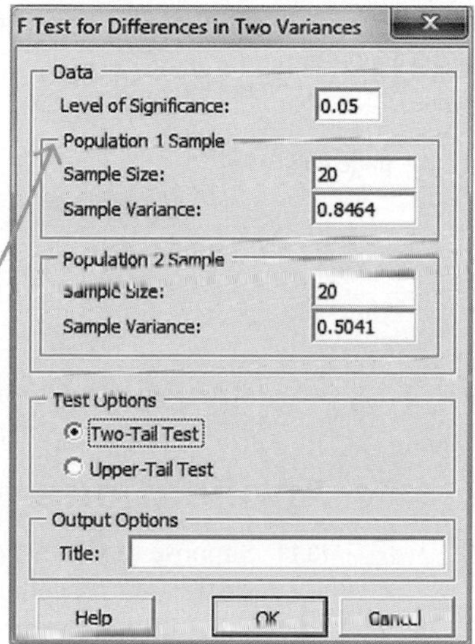

FIGURE 13.7B Using PHStat to Compare Two Population Variances (Step 2)

Be sure to assign the sample with the higher variance as "Population 1" in the dialog box

Figure 13.7C shows the final results for our variance test.

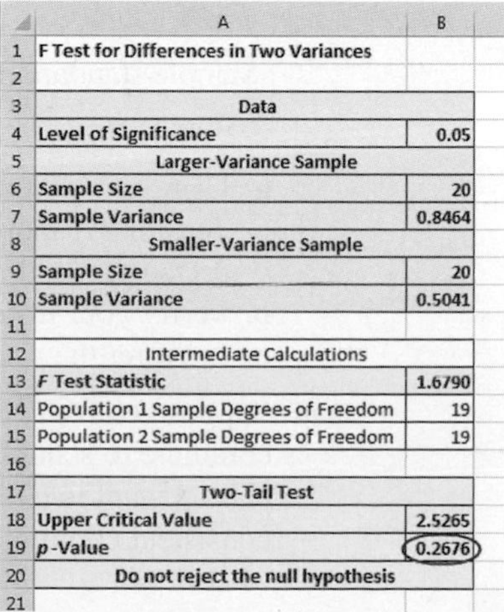

	A	B
1	F Test for Differences in Two Variances	
2		
3	Data	
4	Level of Significance	0.05
5	Larger-Variance Sample	
6	Sample Size	20
7	Sample Variance	0.8464
8	Smaller-Variance Sample	
9	Sample Size	20
10	Sample Variance	0.5041
11		
12	Intermediate Calculations	
13	F Test Statistic	1.6790
14	Population 1 Sample Degrees of Freedom	19
15	Population 2 Sample Degrees of Freedom	19
16		
17	Two-Tail Test	
18	Upper Critical Value	2.5265
19	p-Value	0.2676
20	Do not reject the null hypothesis	
21		

FIGURE 13.7C Using PHStat to Compare Two Population Variances (Final Result)

These results match what we found with our manual calculations. Also, note that the p-value shown in Cell B19 equals 0.2676. Because the p-value is more than $\alpha = 0.05$, we fail to reject the null hypothesis.

Back in Chapter 10, we compared the means of two populations given the condition that they had equal population variances. At the time, we just assumed the condition was true. However, now we can apply the technique we just learned to test this assumption. We'll revisit our rat brain example from Chapter 10 to address this assumption.

YOUR TURN #4

In Chapter 10, I used an example in which the average brain weights of two populations of rats were measured after they were given different amounts of environmental stimulation. The first population, called the "lucky rats," was exposed to a country club–like atmosphere. The second population, called the "less-fortunate rats," received very little stimulation. The following data were presented:

Population	Average Brain Weight in Grams $\bar{x}$	Sample Standard Deviation s	Sample Size n
Lucky rats	2.6	0.6	20
Less-fortunate rats	2.1	0.8	25

We performed a two-sample hypothesis test comparing the population means and found that the average brain weight for the lucky rats was more than the average brain weight for the less-fortunate rats. However, this test required the populations to have equal variances.

a. Using $\alpha = 0.10$, determine if the equal variance assumption holds true.
b. Verify your results using PHStat.
c. Interpret the p-value.

Answers can be found on ▶ **page 650**

13.2 Section Problems

Basic Skills

13.9 Identify the appropriate critical F-score for the following scenarios:

a. $n_1 = 16, n_2 = 10$, and $\alpha = 0.05$.
b. $n_1 = 28, n_2 = 22$, and $\alpha = 0.01$.
c. $n_1 = 15, n_2 = 20$, and $\alpha = 0.10$.

13.10 Consider the following hypothesis statement:

$$H_0: \sigma_1^2 \leq \sigma_2^2$$
$$H_1: \sigma_1^2 > \sigma_2^2$$

State your conclusion given that $s_1 = 18, s_2 = 15, n_1 = 25, n_2 = 20$, and $\alpha = 0.05$.

13.11 Consider the following hypothesis statement:

$$H_0: \sigma_1^2 = \sigma_2^2$$
$$H_1: \sigma_1^2 \neq \sigma_2^2$$

State your conclusion given that $s_1 = 35, s_2 = 30, n_1 = 22, n_2 = 26$, and $\alpha = 0.05$.

13.12 Consider the following hypothesis statement:

$$H_0: \sigma_1^2 = \sigma_2^2$$
$$H_1: \sigma_1^2 \neq \sigma_2^2$$

State your conclusion given that $s_1 = 63, s_2 = 41, n_1 = 25, n_2 = 28$, and $\alpha = 0.05$.

Applications

13.13 Suppose the Transportation Security Administration is investigating procedures at the Atlanta airport to reduce the variability in the amount of time it takes passengers to get through airport security. The following table summarizes sample data collected from two different terminals employing different security procedures:

	Terminal A	Terminal B
Sample standard deviation	8.4 minutes	9.7 minutes
Sample size	15	13

a. Using $\alpha = 0.05$, determine if the procedures at Terminal A more effectively reduce the variability than do the procedures at Terminal B.
b. Verify your results using PHStat.
c. Interpret the p-value obtained from the software.

13.14 Suppose I have two different possible routes for my commute to school. Because I never want to be late for class, I want to choose the route that provides a more consistent commute time. Being a hopeless statistician,

I meticulously drove the first route 21 times and the second route 24 times and calculated the standard deviations for each. The data are as follows:

	Route 1	Route 2
Sample standard deviation	6.5 minutes	10.4 minutes
Sample size	21	24

a. Using $\alpha = 0.05$, determine if Route 1 provides a more consistent commute time than Route 2.
b. Verify your results using PHStat.
c. Interpret the *p*-value obtained from the software.

13.15 Suppose the Goodyear Tire Company developed two new brands of tires and would like to compare the variability of the tire life of the two. Both brands were driven under normal conditions, and random samples of the tires were collected. The following table shows the sample sizes and the standard deviations, in miles, calculated for each sample:

	Brand 1	Brand 2
Sample standard deviation	5,300 miles	3,500 miles
Sample size	20	20

a. Using $\alpha = 0.10$, determine if there is a difference in the variability of the two tire brands.
b. Verify your results using PHStat.
c. Interpret the *p*-value obtained from the software.

13.16 The New Jersey teacher's union would like to see if there is a difference in the variability of the salaries earned by high school teachers in Cape May County as compared with those in Camden County. A random sample of teacher salaries from each county was selected, and the standard deviation of each sample was calculated. The data are as follows:

	Cape May	Camden
Sample size	30	27
Sample standard deviation	\$6,300	\$5,200

a. Using $\alpha = 0.05$, determine if there is a difference in the variability of the salaries for the two populations.
b. Verify your results using PHStat.
c. Interpret the *p*-value obtained from the software.

CHAPTER 13 Summary

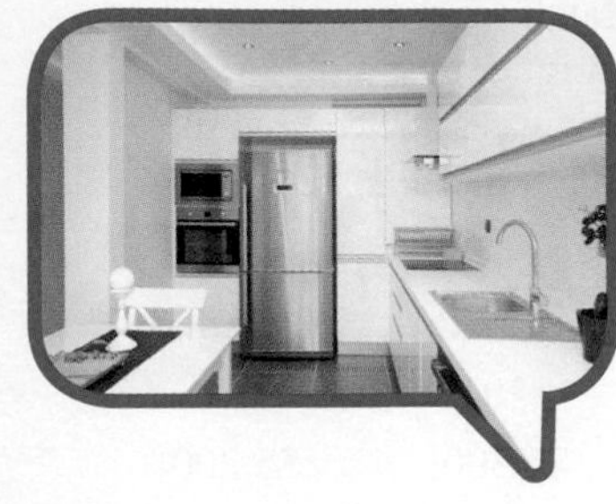

- The chi-square distribution can be used to perform a hypothesis test for a population variance.
- The test statistic follows the chi-square distribution with $n - 1$ degrees of freedom where n equals the sample size from the population of interest.
- The population from which the sample is drawn needs to be normally distributed in order for the tester to get valid results.
- The test statistic for comparing two population variances follows the F-distribution, with $n_1 - 1$ degrees of freedom for the numerator and $n_2 - 1$ degrees of freedom for the denominator.
- To calculate the critical value, the sample size with the larger sample standard deviation should be designated n_1, and the sample size with the smaller sample standard deviation should be designated n_2.
- Be sure to always set up the hypothesis statement for a right-tail test by assigning H_1 the ">" sign.
  - That way, the rejection region will always be on the right side of the F-distribution.
  - This holds true for both one-tail and two-tail tests.
- The populations from which the samples are drawn need to be normally distributed in order for the tester to get valid results.

CHAPTER 13 Equations

13.1 Testing the Variance of a Single Population (pp 626–634)

Formula 13.1 for the Test Statistic for a One-Sample Variance Test

$$\chi^2 = \frac{(n-1)s^2}{\sigma^2}$$

Formula 13.2 for the Sample Variance

$$s^2 = \frac{\sum_{i=1}^{n} x_i^2 - \frac{\left(\sum_{i=1}^{n} x_i\right)^2}{n}}{n-1}$$

13.2 Comparing the Variances of Two Populations (pp 634–643)

Formula 13.3 for the Test Statistic for a Two-Sample Variance Test

$$F = \frac{s_1^2}{s_2^2}$$

CHAPTER 13 Problems

13.17 A high variation in the speed at which cars travel on the interstate can lead to unsafe driving conditions. When some cars are traveling at high speeds and others are traveling at low speeds on the same stretch of highway, the likelihood of an accident increases. Suppose the state of Virginia believes that a standard deviation of more than 7 miles per hour between cars results in an unsafe driving condition. The following speeds, in miles per hour, were clocked on an interstate in Virginia. The data can also be found in the Excel file **interstate speeds.xlsx**.

83	71	77	75	68	59	62	83	57	62	63	77
59	66	66	56	79	69	65	77	60	70	69	69

a. Using $\alpha = 0.05$, test whether an unsafe driving condition exists on this interstate.
b. Verify your results using PHStat.
c. Interpret the *p*-value obtained from the software.

13.18 According to the *Journal of the American Medical Association*, a resident doctor worked an average of 59.3 hours per week during 2006–2008. In 2010, the Accreditation Council for Graduate Medical Education, which certifies residency programs in hospitals, developed a plan to reduce the long hours as well as to reduce the standard deviation of hours the doctors work to less than 8 hours per week. To investigate the plan's effectiveness, a random sample of the hours 20 residents worked per week was selected in 2014. The data are shown in the following table, and can be found in the Excel file **resident hours.xlsx**.

53	57	52	65	70	51	55	61	49	61
54	64	44	57	55	60	53	61	51	56

a. Using $\alpha = 0.05$, determine if the standard deviation of working hours per week is below 8 hours in 2014.
b. Verify your results using PHStat.
c. Interpret the *p*-value obtained from the software.

13.19 Purina produces dog food sold in 40-lb. bags. When the filling process is working properly, the standard deviation for the bag weights is 1.4 ounces. The following data represent a random sample of 30 bags from this process. The data can also be found in the Excel file **Purina dog food.xlsx**.

40	38	42	41	39	42	41	43	41	37
41	39	39	37	40	39	43	41	39	41
42	37	39	40	38	38	37	38	41	39

a. Using $\alpha = 0.05$, determine if the filling process is performing satisfactorily.
b. Verify your results using PHStat.
c. Interpret the *p*-value obtained from the software.

13.20 Low-profile tires are automobile tires that have a short sidewall height, which is the distance between the tire rim and the road. These tires provide better performance at the expense of gas mileage. The Ford Taurus was chosen to measure the effect these tires have on the variability of the car's gas mileage. Ten cars of this model were selected, and the gas mileage each obtained on one tank of gas was measured using standard tires. Low-profile tires were installed on 10 other cars, and the gas mileage was again recorded. The results are shown in the following table and can be found in the Excel file **low profile variance.xlsx**.

Standard		Low-Profile	
21.5	26.5	22.4	19.0
22.3	25.5	20.1	19.7
25.6	19.5	24.0	16.2
19.3	23.9	19.5	21.4
22.3	22.9	21.7	22.4

a. Using $\alpha = 0.05$, determine if there is a difference in the variability of the mileage the two types of tires get.
b. Verify your results using PHStat.
c. Interpret the *p*-value obtained from the software.

13.21 In order that patients don't experience excessive wait times, Aston Medical Center's goal is for the standard deviation for the time doctors spend with their patients to be less than 6.0 minutes. To determine if this goal is being met, a random sample of times the center's doctors spent with their patients was collected. These data can be found in the Excel file **Aston.xlsx**. The times are as follows:

9	11	18	16	18	20	16	15
12	16	23	12	21	19	12	

a. Using $\alpha = 0.10$, determine if the goal set by Aston Medical Center is being met.
b. Verify your results using PHStat.
c. Interpret the *p*-value obtained from the software.

13.22 Pretzel Boys sells hand-rolled pretzels that are prepared by its employees on the premises. Management would like to ensure that the weight of the pretzels rolled by the employees is consistent by ensuring that the standard deviation for the weight of pretzels is less than 0.04 ounces. The following data represent the weights, in ounces, of 12 randomly selected pretzels. These data can be found in the Excel file **Pretzel Boys.xlsx**.

0.38	0.36	0.36	0.38	0.36	0.39
0.32	0.33	0.30	0.33	0.37	0.40

a. Using $\alpha = 0.05$, determine if the standard deviation of the pretzel weights is less than 0.04 ounces.
b. Verify your results using PHStat.
c. Interpret the *p*-value obtained from the software.

13.23 Susan is shopping for a new golf club that will allow her to hit golf balls more consistently. She is considering

Callaway and Nike models. She used a simulator at the golf store to test each club, and the following data were collected. These data can be found in the Excel file **Callaway.xlsx**.

Callaway		Nike	
203	189	199	213
195	206	196	200
207	187	237	188
183	200	177	216
196	212	202	169

a. Using $\alpha = 0.05$, determine if there is a difference in the variance of the driving distance between these two golf clubs.
b. Verify your results using PHStat.
c. Interpret the p-value obtained from the software.
d. Which driver would Susan prefer based on the consistency of its driving distance?

13.24 As a customer-satisfaction consistency measure, Tony's Bistro monitors the size of the tips its waiters receive for serving tables of two customers. The restaurant's manager believes if the standard deviation of these tips exceeds \$3.00, there could be an issue with inconsistent service among the waitstaff. The tips from randomly selected tables with two customers at each table can be found in the Excel file **tips.xlsx** and are shown as follows:

\$17	\$11	\$9	\$12	\$14	\$14	\$15	\$11	\$10
\$9	\$9	\$13	\$10	\$17	\$6	\$13	\$6	\$16

a. Using $\alpha = 0.05$, determine if there is any indication of inconsistent service at Tony's.
b. Verify your results using PHStat.
c. Interpret the p-value obtained from the software.

13.25 Herr Foods, a producer of a variety of salty snacks, performs taste tests to compare how consumers react to its products. A product such as horseradish cheddar chips is considered a polarizing product because it has a very strong taste. Consumers tend to rate the product very high or very low, which results in highly variable taste-test ratings for the product. A more standard product, such as regular tortilla chips, typically receives more consistent ratings. The following table shows how seven customers rated each product on a scale of 1–10. The mean and standard deviation for each type of chip are also shown in the table and can be found in the Excel file **Herr.xlsx**.

	Horseradish Cheddar Chips	Tortilla Chips
	4	8
	10	8
	10	7
	3	8
	10	8
	9	10
	10	7
Mean	**8.0**	**8.0**
Standard deviation	**3.11**	**1.00**

Even though both products have the same average (mean) rating, the horseradish cheddar chip is viewed more positively from a marketing perspective if it has a higher standard deviation.

a. Using $\alpha = 0.05$, determine if the horseradish cheddar chip has a higher variance than the tortilla chip.
b. Verify your results using PHStat.
c. Interpret the p-value obtained from the software.

13.26 American Airlines and Air France both schedule non-stop flights from Paris to Philadelphia. Suppose you are choosing which airline to fly based on the one with more consistent flight times for the route. For each airline, the following table shows the flight times, in hours, of randomly selected flights for the route. These data can be found in the Excel file **Air France.xlsx**.

American Airlines		Air France	
8.4	8.5	6.6	8.0
7.2	8.0	9.3	9.6
7.7	9.5	7.7	9.8
6.6	8.1	7.7	7.5
7.9	6.8	6.9	7.9
8.4	8.4	7.9	

a. Using $\alpha = 0.10$, determine if there is a difference in the variability of the flight times for these two airlines for this route.
b. Verify your results using PHStat.
c. Interpret the p-value obtained from the software.

13.27 To help visitors decide which trails are most appropriate for them to hike, the National Park Service (NPS) rates the difficulty of the trails in the nation's parks. Abrams Falls Trail is a 5-mile trek through Great Smoky Mountains National Park. Suppose the NPS has decided to give Abrams Falls Trail a "moderate" rating if the standard deviation for the time to hike the trail is longer than 30 minutes. The following data represent the hours it took 20 randomly selected people to hike the trail. These data can be found in the Excel file **NPS.xlsx**.

1.4	3.2	2.7	3.4	3.0	3.3	3.5	2.9	2.4	3.9
2.9	3.5	3.2	4.1	4.1	3.4	3.7	3.5	4.0	1.7

a. Using $\alpha = 0.05$, determine if the NPS should give the Abrams Falls Trail a "moderate" rating.
b. Verify your results using PHStat.
c. Interpret the p-value obtained from the software.

13.28 Edalight is a manufacturer of compact fluorescent lights (CFL) bulbs which are fluorescent bulbs designed to be more efficient than traditional incandescent bulbs. In an effort to produce a consistent product, suppose Edalight has a goal that the standard deviation for the life of its CFL bulbs is less than 500 hours. The standard deviation for the life of a random sample of 28 CFL bulbs was found to be 378 hours.

a. Using $\alpha = 0.05$, perform a hypothesis test to determine if Edalight's goal has been achieved.
b. Verify your results using PHStat.
c. Interpret the p-value obtained from the software.

13.29 As smartphones have become more sophisticated, their data usage has increased causing capacity issues with service providers. High variability in data usage among customers can result in slow connections with the cellphone network. Suppose Verizon Wireless would like to test if the standard deviation of monthly data usage for its customers has increased beyond 400 megabytes (MB). A random sample of 25 customers was found to have a standard deviation of 458 MB.

a. Using $\alpha = 0.10$, perform a hypothesis test to determine if the standard deviation for the monthly data usage for Verizon Wireless customers has exceeded 400 MB.
b. Verify your results using PHStat.
c. Interpret the p-value obtained from the software.

13.30 The pH scale measures the amount of alkalinity or acidity in a liquid and ranges from 0 to 14. The ideal pH for a swimming pool is 7.2. A pH that is too high or low can cause discomfort for the swimmers, especially in the eyes. Chemicals need to be added to the water to adjust the pH to the desired level. Fifteen pH readings were taken at the Wilson Community Pool from different locations at 10:00 A.M. this morning. The standard deviation for the pH reading from this sample was 0.45.

a. Using $\alpha = 0.05$, perform a hypothesis test to determine if the standard deviation for the pH readings at 10:00 A.M. equals 0.30.
b. Verify your results using PHStat.
c. Interpret the p-value obtained from the software.

13.31 Suppose a student organization at the University of Illinois would like to test for a difference in class sizes between the business and engineering departments. A random sample of 11 classes in the business department had an average size of 38.1 students with a sample standard deviation of 10.6 students. A random sample of 12 classes in the engineering department had an average size of 32.6 students with a sample standard deviation of 13.2 students.

a. Recall that testing for a difference between two population means requires an assumption about population variances. Perform a hypothesis test using $\alpha = 0.05$ to determine if the population variance for class size is different for these two departments.
b. Verify your results using PHStat.
c. Identify the p-value from part b and interpret the result.

13.32 Traveler's Insurance would like to investigate if the average number of miles driven per month by a male teenage driver exceeds the average number of miles driven per month by a female teenage driver. The following data summarizes the sample statistics for the miles driven per month by each gender.

	Male	Female
Sample mean	685	580
Sample size	23	27
Sample standard deviation	147	102

a. Recall that testing for a difference between two population means requires an assumption about population variances. Perform a hypothesis test using $\alpha = 0.10$ to determine if the population variance for miles driven per month is different for teenage males and teenage females.
b. Verify your results using PHStat.
c. Identify the p-value from part b and interpret the result.

13.33 Bank of New York would like to determine if the average checking account balance for younger customers (under 40 years) is different from the average checking account balance for older customers (40 or more years). These data can be found in the Excel file **checking accounts.xlsx**.

a. Recall that testing for a difference between two population means requires an assumption about population variances. Perform a hypothesis test using $\alpha = 0.05$ to determine if the population variance for the checking account balance of younger customers is greater than the variance of accounts for older customers.
b. Verify your results using Excel or PHStat.
c. Identify the p-value from part b and interpret the result.

13.34 Suppose one of the products manufactured by Pittsburgh Plate and Glass (PPG) is a glass pane that is 3/8 in., thick. One of the quality control measurements is the variability in the thickness of the glass panes. If the standard deviation for the thickness of the glass exceeds 0.01 in., the process is considered out of control and needs to be corrected. The glass thickness, in inches, as measured from a random sample of 25 panes can be found in the Excel file **PPG.xlsx**.

a. Using $\alpha = 0.05$, determine if the process variability is out of control.
b. Verify your results using PHStat.
c. Interpret the p-value obtained from the software.

13.35 The Excel file **golf scores.xlsx** contains a random sample of golf scores for two highly competitive sons of a certain statistics author. Each son claims he is the more consistent golfer.

a. Perform a hypothesis test using $\alpha = 0.05$ to determine if there is a difference in the variability of the two sons' golf scores.
b. Verify your results using PHStat.
c. Interpret the p-value obtained from the software.

13.36 Coke would like to perform a blind taste test between its cola and the cola produced by its biggest competitor, Pepsi. To conduct this test, 24 individuals were randomly selected and asked to taste the Coke product and rate it on a scale of 1–10. Another 24 individuals were asked to taste and rate the Pepsi product on the same scale. The results are shown in the Excel file **taste test variance.xlsx**.

a. Using $\alpha = 0.05$, determine if the variability in the ratings for the Pepsi product is greater than the variability in the ratings for the Coke product.
b. Verify your results using PHStat.
c. Interpret the p-value obtained from the software.

CHAPTER 13 Solutions to Your Turn

YOUR TURN #1

a.

Step 1: Identify the null and alternative hypotheses.

Don't forget to express the hypothesis statement as a variance ($30^2 = 900$).

$$H_0: \sigma^2 \le 900$$
$$H_1: \sigma^2 > 900$$

Step 2: Set a value for the significance level, α.

Set $\alpha = 0.10$ for this hypothesis test.

Step 3: Calculate the chi-square test statistic, χ^2.

Using Equation 13.1 along with $s = 32.4$ and $n = 20$, our test statistic is as follows:

$$\chi^2 = \frac{(n-1)s^2}{\sigma^2} = \frac{(20-1)(32.4)^2}{900} = 22.16$$

Step 4: Determine the chi-square critical value, χ^2_α.

This is a right-tail test because the alternative hypothesis, H_1, is expressed as ">900." This puts the rejection region with the area $\alpha = 0.10$ in the right tail of the distribution. In Table 8 in Appendix A, we look for the column labeled "0.10" and the row labeled $n - 1 = 20 - 1 = 19$ degrees of freedom; the critical value is $\chi^2_\alpha = \chi^2_{0.10} = 27.204$.

Step 5: Compare the test statistic (χ^2) with the critical value (χ^2_α).

The rejection region is to the right of $\chi^2_\alpha = \chi^2_{0.10} = 27.204$. Because $\chi^2 = 22.16$ and this is less than $\chi^2_\alpha = \chi^2_{0.10} = 27.204$, we fail to reject the null hypothesis.

Step 6: State your conclusions.

By failing to reject the null hypothesis, we do not have evidence that the standard deviation of wait times exceeds 30 minutes. Therefore, CBS should not hire additional service personnel.

b.

	A	B
1	Chi-Square Test of Variance	
2		
3	Data	
4	Null Hypothesis σ^2=	900
5	Level of Significance	0.1
6	Sample Size	20
7	Sample Standard Deviation	32.4
8		
9	Intermediate Calculations	
10	Degrees of Freedom	19
11	Half Area	0.05
12	Chi-Square Statistic	22.1616
13		
14	Upper-Tail Test	
15	Upper Critical Value	27.2036
16	p-Value	0.2763
17	Do not reject the null hypothesis	
18		

c. The p-value equals 0.2763, which represents the probability of observing a test statistic greater than 22.16 if the null hypothesis is true. Because this value is greater than $\alpha = 0.10$, we fail to reject the null hypothesis.

YOUR TURN #2

a.

Step 1: Identify the null and alternative hypotheses.

We need to convert a standard deviation of 0.15 ounces to a variance by $(0.15)^2 = 0.0225$. Because we are testing for equality, this is a two-tail test.

$$H_0: \sigma^2 = 0.0225$$
$$H_1: \sigma^2 \neq 0.0225$$

Step 2: Set a value for the significance level, α.

Set $\alpha = 0.10$ for this hypothesis test.

Step 3: Calculate the chi-square test statistic, χ^2.

We have 18 observations in our sample $(n = 18)$, and our sample variance is found by using Equation 13.2:

$$s^2 = \frac{\sum_{i=1}^{n} x_i^2 - \frac{\left(\sum_{i=1}^{n} x_i\right)^2}{n}}{n - 1} = \frac{5{,}817.78 - \frac{(323.6)^2}{18}}{18 - 1}$$

$$= \frac{5{,}817.78 - 5{,}817.61}{17} = 0.010$$

Using Equation 13.1, our test statistic is as follows:

$$\chi^2 = \frac{(n - 1)s^2}{\sigma^2} = \frac{(18 - 1)(0.010)}{0.0225} = 7.56$$

Step 4: Determine the chi-square critical value, χ^2_α.

The area that corresponds to $\alpha = 0.10$ is split evenly $(\alpha/2 = 0.05)$ between the two tails of the distribution.

The left (lower) critical value has an area equal to 0.05 to its left and 0.95 to its right. In Table 8 in Appendix A, we look for the column labeled "0.95" and the row labeled $n - 1 = 18 - 1 = 17$ degrees of freedom; the left critical value is $\chi^2_\alpha = \chi^2_{0.095} = 8.672$.

The right (upper) critical value has an area equal to 0.05 to its right. In Table 8 in Appendix A, we look for the column labeled "0.05" and the row labeled 17 degrees of freedom; the right critical value is $\chi^2_\alpha = \chi^2_{0.05} = 27.587$.

Step 5: Compare the test statistic (χ^2) with the critical value (χ^2_α).

Because $\chi^2 = 7.56$ is lower than $\chi^2_{0.95} = 8.672$ (the left critical value), we reject the null hypothesis.

Step 6: State your conclusions.

By rejecting the null hypothesis, we have evidence that the population standard deviation is not equal to 0.15 ounces. It appears that filling process is experiencing a lower variance than what it normally demonstrates. Either the process is working better than earlier reported or the measurement process is possibly flawed.

b.

	A		B
1	**Chi-Square Test of Variance**		
2			
3	**Data**		
4	**Null Hypothesis**	σ^2=	0.0225
5	**Level of Significance**		0.1
6	**Sample Size**		18
7	**Sample Standard Deviation**		0.1
8			
9	Intermediate Calculations		
10	Degrees of Freedom		17
11	Half Area		0.05
12	**Chi-Square Statistic**		7.5556
13			
14	**Two-Tail Test**		
15	Lower Critical Value		8.6718
16	Upper Critical Value		27.5871
17	*p*-value		0.0248
18	**Reject the null hypothesis**		
19			

c. Because the *p*-value $= 0.0248$ and is less than $\alpha = 0.10$, we reject the null hypothesis.

YOUR TURN #3

a.

Step 1: Calculate the variance for each sample.

Using Excel's VAR.S function, we have the following:

$$s^2_{10:00} = 51.34$$
$$s^2_{11:00} = 37.82$$

Step 2: Identify the null and alternative hypotheses.

When dealing with the comparison of two population variances, assign the larger sample variance to Population 1 and the smaller sample variance to Population 2:

Population 1 = The scores from the 10:00 A.M. class
Population 2 = The scores from the 11:00 A.M. class

$$H_0: \sigma_1^2 \leq \sigma_2^2$$
$$H_1: \sigma_1^2 > \sigma_2^2$$

(11:00 A.M. class has lower variance than 10:00 A.M. class)

Step 3: Set a value for the significance level, α.

Set $\alpha = 0.01$ for this hypothesis test.

Step 4: Calculate the *F*-test statistic.

Plugging our sample variances into Equation 13.3 results in the following:

$$F = \frac{s_1^2}{s_2^2} = \frac{51.34}{37.82} = 1.357$$

Step 5: Determine the critical value, F_α.

For our exam score example, the degrees of freedom are as follows:

$$D_1 = n_1 - 1 = 10 - 1 = 9$$
$$D_2 = n_2 - 1 = 10 - 1 = 9$$

Select the section of Table 6 in Appendix A labeled "Area in the Right Tail of Distribution = 0.01" because we set $\alpha = 0.01$ for this hypothesis test. Go to the $D_1 = 9$ column and $D_2 = 9$ row to find $F_\alpha = F_{0.01} = 5.351$.

Step 6: Compare the test statistic (*F*) with the critical value (F_α).

Because $F = 1.357$ is less than $F_\alpha = 5.351$, we fail to reject the null hypothesis.

Step 7: State your conclusions.

By failing to reject the null hypothesis, we do not have evidence that the variance for the 11:00 A.M. class is less than the variance for the 10:00 A.M. class. It does not appear that working in groups reduces the test-score variability.

b.

	A	B	C	D	E	F
1	10:00	11:00		F-Test Two-Sample for Variances		
2	86	90				
3	83	76			10:00	11:00
4	86	73		Mean	86.7	83.6
5	89	90		Variance	51.344444	37.822222
6	89	88		Observations	10	10
7	85	89		df	9	9
8	96	84		F	1.3575206	
9	99	82		P(F<=f) one-tail	0.3281179	
10	75	78		F Critical one-tail	5.3511289	
11	79	86				
12						

c. The *p*-value reported in Cell E9 equals 0.3281. This value represents the probability of obtaining a calculated *F*-score of 1.358 or higher if the null hypothesis is true. Because this *p*-value is more than $\alpha = 0.01$, we fail to reject the null hypothesis and conclude that working in groups does not reduce test-score variability.

YOUR TURN #4

a.

Step 1: Calculate the variance for each sample.

$$s^2_{\text{lucky}} = (0.6)^2 = 0.36$$
$$s^2_{\text{less fortunate}} = (0.8)^2 = 0.64$$

Step 2: Identify the null and alternative hypotheses.

Once again, we assign the larger sample variance to Population 1 and the smaller sample variance to Population 2.

Population 1 = Less-fortunate rats
Population 2 = Lucky rats

Because we are interested only in examining a difference in population variances, we have the following two-tail test:

H_0: $\sigma_1^2 = \sigma_2^2$

H_1: $\sigma_1^2 \neq \sigma_2^2$ (population variances are different)

Step 3: Set a value for the significance level, α.

Set $\alpha = 0.10$ for this hypothesis test.

Step 4: Calculate the *F*-test statistic.

Plugging our sample variances into Equation 13.3 results in the following:

$$F = \frac{s_1^2}{s_2^2} = \frac{0.64}{0.36} = 1.778$$

Step 5: Determine the critical value, F_α.

For our rat example, we have the following degrees of freedom:

$$D_1 = n_1 - 1 = 25 - 1 = 24$$
$$D_2 = n_2 - 1 = 20 - 1 = 19$$

Because we have a two-tail test, the area that corresponds to $\alpha = 0.10$ is split evenly ($\alpha/2 = 0.05$) between the two tails of the distribution. This means that the area in the right tail of the distribution is 0.05. Select the portion of Table 6 in Appendix A labeled "Area in the Right Tail of Distribution = 0.05" for this hypothesis test. Go to the $D_1 = 24$ column and $D_2 = 19$ row to find $F_{\alpha/2} = F_{0.05} = 2.114$.

Step 6: Compare the test statistic (*F*) with the critical value (F_α).

Because *F* = 1.778 is less than $F_{\alpha/2} = 2.114$, we fail to reject the null hypothesis.

Step 7: State your conclusions.

By failing to reject the null hypothesis, we do not have evidence to conclude that the variances are different for the two rat populations. Even though we cannot accept the null hypothesis and state that the two populations have equal variances, this result provides enough evidence to satisfy the variance requirement for the original test comparing population means.

b. Be sure to assign the less fortunate rats to Population 1.

	A	B
1	F Test for Differences in Two Variances	
2		
3	Data	
4	Level of Significance	0.1
5	Larger-Variance Sample	
6	Sample Size	25
7	Sample Variance	0.64
8	Smaller-Variance Sample	
9	Sample Size	20
10	Sample Variance	0.36
11		
12	Intermediate Calculations	
13	F Test Statistic	1.7778
14	Population 1 Sample Degrees of Freedom	24
15	Population 2 Sample Degrees of Freedom	19
16		
17	Two-Tail Test	
18	Upper Critical Value	2.1141
19	p-Value	0.2041
20	Do not reject the null hypothesis	
21		

c. The *p*-value reported in Cell B19 equals 0.2041. Because this *p*-value is more than $\alpha = 0.10$, we do not have evidence to conclude that the variances are different for the two rat populations.

CHAPTER 14

Correlation and Simple Linear Regression

IN THIS CHAPTER, YOU WILL LEARN TO:

- Distinguish between a dependent and an independent variable.
- Use correlation analysis to measure the strength and direction in a relation between two variables.
- Use the least squares method to determine the slope and intercept of a linear equation that best fits a set of ordered pairs.
- Partition the sum of squares for a dependent and an independent variable.
- Calculate and interpret the coefficient of determination.
- Test the significance of the slope of the regression equation.
- Understand the underlying assumptions for regression analysis.

CHAPTER 14 MAP

Stats in Practice: Beware of Positive Correlation with Your Investments

According to the *Wall Street Journal* article "Why the Math of Correlation Matters" by Jonnelle Marte, the concept of correlation should be a key part of your financial investment strategy. Correlation, in this setting, simply measures the degree to which investment values move together. For example, if the price of Stock A tends to increase whenever the price of Stock B increases, these two investment assets have a positive correlation. This also implies that if the price of Stock B *decreased*, the price of Stock A would also tend to decrease.

What does this mean if you are an investor? It means that if you own investments that are positively correlated with one another, your returns will tend to be very volatile. When the returns are good, they will be very, very good. But when they are bad, they will be horrid.

Generally speaking, investors don't like volatility. It scares them to think they could lose a lot of money quickly. Instead, investors would rather earn moderate, steady returns. According to Cassandra Toroian, president and chief investment officer of Bell Rock Capital LLC, an investment firm based in Rehoboth Beach, Delaware, investors rely on correlation to help smooth out volatility in their portfolio.

On the other end of the scale is negative correlation, which exists when the returns on assets tend to move in opposite directions from one another. For example, if the price of Stock A tends to rise when the price of Stock B falls, these assets exhibit negative correlation. Perfect negative correlation is measured with a value of -1.0. By contrast, perfect positive correlation is measured with a value of $+1.0$. Financial investments that move independently of one another are considered to be uncorrelated, which is represented with a value that is close to zero. This would be observed in financial portfolios that are properly diversified, which is a goal of many investors.

Figure 14.1 shows how various investment assets are correlated with the stock market as a whole (the S&P 500). You can see from this chart that the prices of stocks move in the same direction as the S&P 500. Treasury bills and bonds tend to move in an opposite direction, which is a pattern well known in the financial world.

The bottom line of Marte's *Wall Street Journal* article is that you should rely on correlation to ensure your investment portfolio is properly diversified. What a great reason to master correlations—the topic of this chapter.

FIGURE 14.1
Correlation between the S&P 500 Index and Various Investments Using Excel

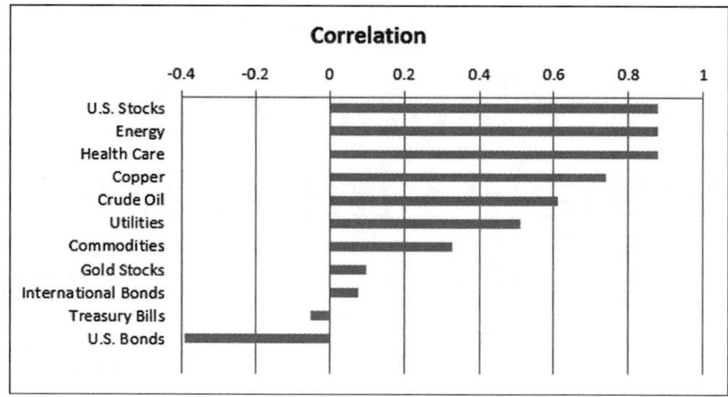

Based on: "Why the Math of Correlation Matters," *Wall Street Journal,* October 4, 2010, http://online.wsj.com.

As a student, have you ever wondered how many hours you need to study to score a grade such as a 90 on your next exam? I know that I did as student back in the Dark Ages. What you are really looking for is the linear relationship between hours of study and exam score. The purpose of this chapter is to explain two techniques that describe such a linear relationship.

The first technique we will use is correlation analysis, which determines the strength and direction of the linear relationship between two variables. We will then perform a hypothesis test to determine if the strength of the linear relationship between hours of study and exam grade is strong enough to be useful.

The second technique we will explore is simple regression, which describes the linear relationship between the two variables using a linear equation. With this equation, we will be able to predict an exam score given a specific number of study hours. Again, we will need to perform hypothesis testing to determine if the results are accurate enough to be useful.

There are many useful applications for simple regression and correlation in the business world. Consider the following examples:

- Century 21 Realtors would like to establish the linear relationship between the living space in a house and its eventual selling price in a particular town.
- A manager at a certain Best Buy store would like to know what effect dropping the price of an HP printer by $10 will have on the demand for the printer the following week.
- The Coca-Cola Company would like to predict the extent to which running a 30-second Super Bowl commercial will improve the sales of Coke.

However, before we begin learning about these procedures, we need to discuss the concept of dependent and independent variables.

14.1 Dependent and Independent Variables

An **independent variable, *x*,** explains the variation (which is a fancy word for change) in another variable, which is called the **dependent variable, *y*.**

An **independent variable, *x*,** explains the variation (which is a fancy word for change) in another variable, which is called the **dependent variable, *y*.** This linear relationship between independent and dependent variables exists only in one direction and is as follows:

$$\text{Independent variable } (x) \rightarrow \text{Dependent variable } (y)$$

For example, in the used car market, the mileage of the car would be the independent variable, and the price of the car would be the dependent variable. As the miles on the car's odometer increases, you would expect the price of the car to decrease.

This linear relationship between the independent and dependent variables does not work in reverse. For example, changing the price of the car will not cause a change in the odometer mileage.

Other examples of independent and dependent variables are shown in Table 14.1.

Exercise caution when deciding which variable is independent and which is dependent. Examine the relationship from both directions to see which one makes the most sense.

TABLE 14.1 | EXAMPLES OF INDEPENDENT AND DEPENDENT VARIABLES

INDEPENDENT VARIABLE		DEPENDENT VARIABLE
The size of a television screen	⟶	The selling price of the television
The number of visitors per day on a Web site	⟶	The amount of sales per day from the Web site
The curb weight of a car	⟶	The car's gas mileage

14.2 Correlation Analysis

The **sample correlation coefficient, *r*,** indicates both the strength and direction of the linear relationship between the independent and dependent variables.

A relationship is linear if the scatter plot of the independent and dependent variables has a straight-line pattern. See Figure 14.2 for an example.

As I mentioned in the start of this chapter, a correlation analysis allows us to measure both the strength and direction of the linear relationship between two variables by calculating the **sample correlation coefficient, *r*.** I first introduced the sample correlation coefficient in Chapter 3 when we used the covariance of two variables for our calculations. In this section, I will demonstrate a different procedure to determine the correlation coefficient. However, the Chapter 3 method can be used in place of the correlation coefficient calculations shown in this section. After r is calculated, you will learn how to perform a hypothesis test to decide if the linear relationship between the two variables is strong enough to be considered statistically significant.

Suppose I would like to investigate the linear relationship between the number of hours students study for a statistics exam and the grades they get for that exam. Table 14.2 shows sample data from six students who were randomly chosen. These data can also be found in the Excel file **exam grades.xlsx.**

TABLE 14.2 | STATISTICS EXAM DATA

STUDENT	HOURS OF STUDY	EXAM GRADE
1	3	86
2	6	95
3	4	92
4	4	83
5	3	78
6	2	79

Call me old fashioned, but I would expect the number of hours studying to affect the grade. Since I envision having your rapt attention at this moment, I'm hoping you agree. The Hours of Study variable is considered the independent variable (x) because we expect that it affects the change in the Exam Grade, which is considered to be the dependent variable (y). Using the data from the previous table, we can create ordered pairs (x, y) of values, such as (3,86) and (6,95).

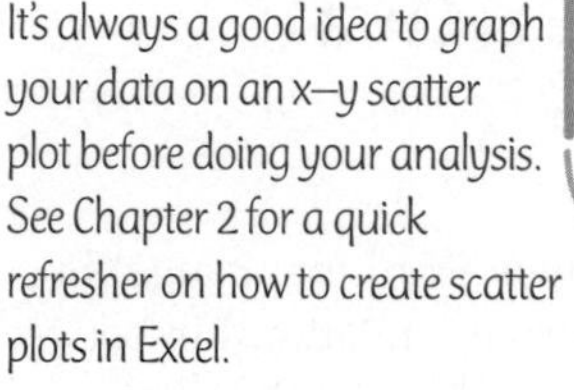

It's always a good idea to graph your data on an x–y scatter plot before doing your analysis. See Chapter 2 for a quick refresher on how to create scatter plots in Excel.

Figure 14.2 shows the scatter plot for the six sets of ordered pairs. Our job in this chapter is to measure the linear relationship between these two variables in terms of both the direction and strength.

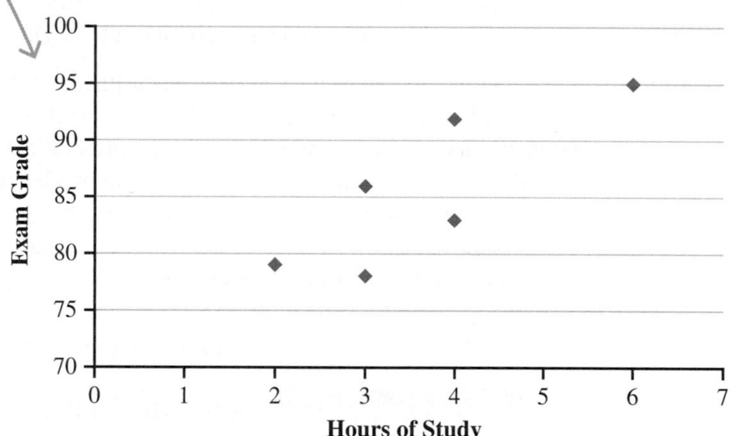

FIGURE 14.2 The Scatter Plot of the Exam Data

The next step in this process is to construct Table 14.3, which will provide you with the values you need for future calculations. The third column in this table is the product of x and y. The fourth and fifth columns are the squares of x and y, respectively.

TABLE 14.3 | A SUMMARY OF THE CALCULATIONS FOR THE EXAM EXAMPLE

HOURS OF STUDY	EXAM GRADE			
x	y	xy	x^2	y^2
3	86	258	9	7,396
6	95	570	36	9,025
4	92	368	16	8,464
4	83	332	16	6,889
3	78	234	9	6,084
2	79	158	4	6,241
$\sum x = 22$	$\sum y = 513$	$\sum xy = 1{,}920$	$\sum x^2 = 90$	$\sum y^2 = 44{,}099$

A correlation analysis requires that the data be either interval data or ratio data. See Chapter 1 for a review of these two data measurement levels.

Every calculation that will be performed in this chapter can be completed using the five summation values shown in Table 14.3 along with the value for n, which represents the number of ordered pairs in the table. For this example, $n = 6$. I call these values "The Six-Number Summary for Correlation and Simple Regression," or SNSCSR for short. I suggest writing them down and putting them somewhere safe, as we will be referring to them throughout the rest of this chapter.

The Sample Correlation Coefficient

We are now ready to calculate the sample correlation coefficient, r, for our exam-grade example using Equation 14.1.

Formula 14.1 for the Sample Correlation Coefficient

$$r = \frac{n\sum xy - (\sum x)(\sum y)}{\sqrt{\left[n\sum x^2 - (\sum x)^2\right]\left[n\sum y^2 - (\sum y)^2\right]}}$$

With $\sum x^2$, we first square each value of x and then add each squared term. With $(\sum x)^2$, we first add each value of x, and then square this result. The answers between the two are very different!

I know from experience that many of my students get that glassy-eyed, deer-caught-in-the-headlights look when I first show them this equation. But there's no need to panic. Pull out your handy-dandy SNSCSR values and simply plug them in, *very carefully*.

$$r = \frac{n\sum xy - (\sum x)(\sum y)}{\sqrt{[n\sum x^2 - (\sum x)^2][n\sum y^2 - (\sum y)^2]}}$$

$$r = \frac{(6)(1{,}920) - (22)(513)}{\sqrt{[(6)(90) - (22)^2][(6)(44{,}099) - (513)^2]}}$$

$$r = \frac{(11{,}520) - (11{,}286)}{\sqrt{[(540) - (484)][(264{,}594) - (263{,}169)]}}$$

$$r = \frac{234}{\sqrt{[56][1{,}425]}} = \frac{234}{\sqrt{79{,}800}} = \frac{234}{282.5} = 0.828$$

What exactly does the r value mean? As I mentioned earlier, the correlation coefficient, r, provides us with both the strength and direction of the linear relationship between an independent variable and a dependent variable. The values of r range from -1.0 to $+1.0$. When r is positive, the linear relationship between x and y is positive. This means that as the value of x increases, the value of y tends to increase. By contrast, when r is negative, the linear relationship between x and y is negative. So, as the value of x increases, the value of y tends to decrease.

The strength of the linear relationship between x and y is measured by how close the sample correlation coefficient is to $+1.0$ or -1.0. Figure 14.3 illustrates the strengths of various correlation coefficients.

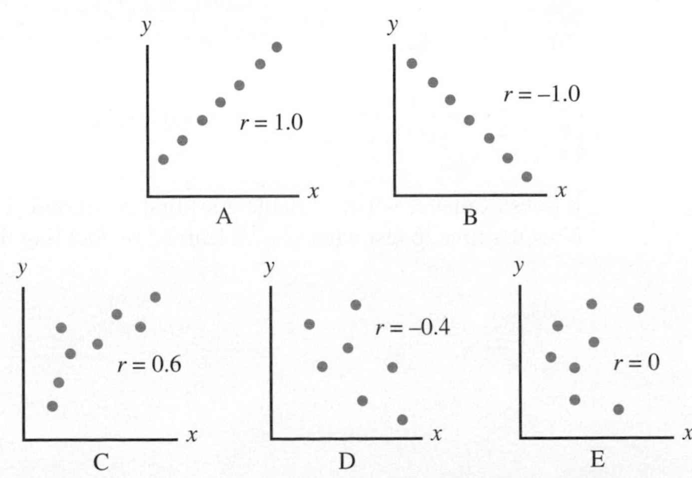

FIGURE 14.3 The Strength and Direction of Various Linear Relationships, along with Their Sample Correlation Coefficients

The correlation coefficient is not a measure of the slopes in Figure 14.3, although it may appear that way after looking at the graphs.

Graph A shows that there is a perfect positive correlation between x and y when $r = +1.0$. We see that the value of y increases at a steady rate as the value of x increases.

Graph B shows a perfect negative correlation between x and y when $r = -1.0$. This is just the opposite of Graph A. The value of y decreases at a constant rate as the value of x increases. This type of perfect correlation shown in Graphs A and B is rarely seen in business settings.

Graph C shows a weaker positive linear relationship between the variables. In this scenario, y tends to increase as x increases, but not necessarily at the steady rate we observed in Graph A. This type of linear relationship might be observed between the variables *advertising* and *sales*. That is, there is a positive correlation between the amount an organization spends on advertising and the sales it makes.

Graph D shows a negative linear relationship between the variables that is slightly weaker than Graph C because the correlation coefficient is closer to zero. Also, you can observe more "scatter" in the data when you compare this with Graph C. In this scenario, y tends to decrease as x increases, but not necessarily at the steady rate we observed in Graph B. Conceivably, this type of linear relationship describes the pattern that variables such as price and demand for many consumer products tend to follow. In other words, when the price of a product rises, people want to buy less of it.

Finally, Graph E shows the case where $r = 0$, which means there is no linear relationship between x and y. As x increases, there appears to be no particular pattern for the values of y.

Because $r = 0.828$ in our example, we have discovered a fairly strong positive linear relationship between Hours of Study and Exam Grade. Those students who studied more tended to have better grades. Just what a teacher wants to hear!

Using Excel to Calculate the Sample Correlation Coefficient

You can use the CORREL Function in Excel to calculate the Sample correlation coefficient. It has the following characteristics:

=CORREL(array1, array2)

where

array1 = The range of data for the first variable
array2 = The range of data for the second variable

Figure 14.4 shows how to calculate the correlation coefficient for the exam-grade example. Cell C1 contains the Excel formula =CORREL (A2:A7,B2:B7), with the result being 0.828.

FIGURE 14.4
Using Excel to Calculate the Correlation Coefficient

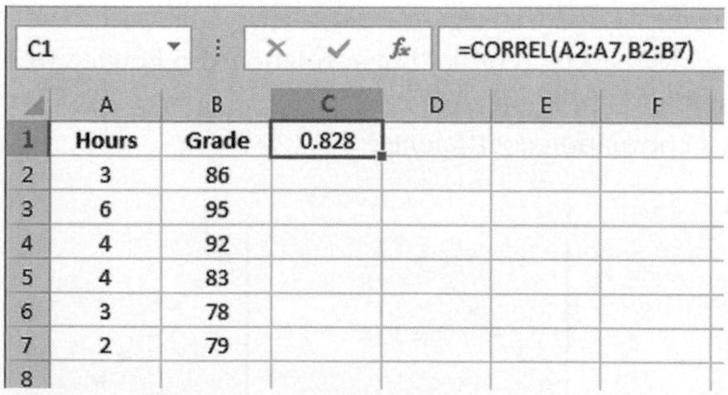

C1 | fx =CORREL(A2:A7,B2:B7)

	A	B	C	D	E	F
1	Hours	Grade	0.828			
2	3	86				
3	6	95				
4	4	92				
5	4	83				
6	3	78				
7	2	79				
8						

It doesn't matter which variable goes first or second. The result will be the same either way. Now it's time to test what you've learned by tackling this next Your Turn problem.

YOUR TURN #1

The Swiss Hiking Federation (SHF) is an organization that is responsible for promoting the safe use of the hiking trail system throughout Switzerland. Trails are clearly marked with signposts and the approximate hiking time to assist individuals with their hiking agenda. Suppose the SHF would like to investigate the linear relationship between the amount of time to hike the Wengen-Kleine Scheidegg trail in the Jungfrau region and the age of the hiker. A random sample of seven hikers on this trail was selected and their age and hiking time, in hours, are shown here. These data can also be found in the Excel file **Wengen.xlsx.**

My wife and I had the pleasure of hiking this beautiful trail in 2012.

Age	Time	Age	Time
24	2.7	26	2.2
32	4.2	53	2.9
47	5.0	38	3.0
40	3.8		

Calculate the sample correlation coefficient for this sample.

Answer can be found on ▶ **page 704**

Conducting a Hypothesis Test to Determine the Significance of the Population Correlation Coefficient

The **population correlation coefficient (ρ)** refers to the correlation between all values of two variables of interest in a population.

The value r that we calculated in the previous section represents the correlation coefficient for a random sample of six students selected from a larger student population. By contrast, the **population correlation coefficient (ρ)** refers to the correlation between all of the students' study hours and the grades they received. Because we have not gathered data on every student who took the exam, we do not know the value of the actual population correlation coefficient. We can, however, perform a hypothesis test to determine if the population correlation coefficient, ρ, is significantly different from zero based on the sample correlation coefficient, r. This test uses the following hypothesis statement:

Remember, a correlation coefficient equal to zero means that there is no linear relationship between x and y.

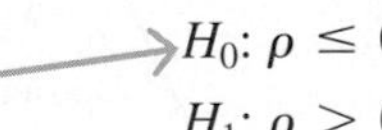

$$H_0: \rho \leq 0$$
$$H_1: \rho > 0$$

If we reject the null hypothesis, we have enough evidence from our sample to conclude that a linear relationship does exists between the hours studied and the exam scores earned by the student population. We are testing for the significance of the population correlation coefficient because we are determining if this value is significantly different from zero. For this test, we will use $\alpha = 0.05$. I am using a one-tail (upper) hypothesis test for this example because my hope is to conclude that the population correlation coefficient is positive (the more you study, the better your grade). The next Your Turn problem will look at the two-tail case of this test.

The test statistic for this hypothesis test uses the Student's t-distribution as shown in Equation 14.2.

Formula 14.2 for the Test Statistic for the Correlation Coefficient

$$t = \frac{r}{\sqrt{\frac{1 - r^2}{n - 2}}}$$

where

$r =$ The sample correlation coefficient
$n =$ The number of ordered pairs

Calculating the test statistics requires the following data from the previous section:

$$r = 0.828 \quad n = 6$$

Plugging these values into Equation 14.2 results in the following test statistic:

$$t = \frac{r}{\sqrt{\frac{1 - r^2}{n - 2}}} = \frac{0.828}{\sqrt{\frac{1 - (0.828)^2}{6 - 2}}} = \frac{0.828}{\sqrt{\frac{1 - 0.6856}{4}}}$$

$$t = \frac{0.828}{\sqrt{\frac{0.3144}{4}}} = \frac{0.828}{\sqrt{0.0786}} = \frac{0.828}{0.2804} = 2.953$$

The critical t-score, t_α, defines the rejection region for this one-tail test. We can find the critical t-score for this test in Table 5 from Appendix A with $n - 2$ degrees of freedom. Because we have grades from six students, there are $6 - 2 = 4$ degrees of freedom for our example. Using $\alpha = 0.05$ for a one-tail test, the critical t-score is found to be $t_\alpha = 2.132$. We can also obtain our critical t-score for a one-tail test using Excel's T.INV function, which was introduced in Chapter 9. We need the absolute value of this function's result because it returns the left-tail area associated with α. For our exam-grade example, our critical t-score is

$$= |\text{T.INV}(0.05, 4)| = |-2.132| = 2.132$$

Because $t = 2.953$ is to the right of $t_\alpha = 2.132$, we reject the null hypothesis and conclude that the population correlation coefficient is greater than zero. Figure 14.5 illustrates this result. We can now conclude that there appears to be a linear relationship between the hours that the population of students studied and their exam scores. This author heaves a sigh of relief. I'm glad to know I didn't write all of the Your Turn questions in this book for no reason!

FIGURE 14.5
Testing the Significance of the Population Correlation Coefficient

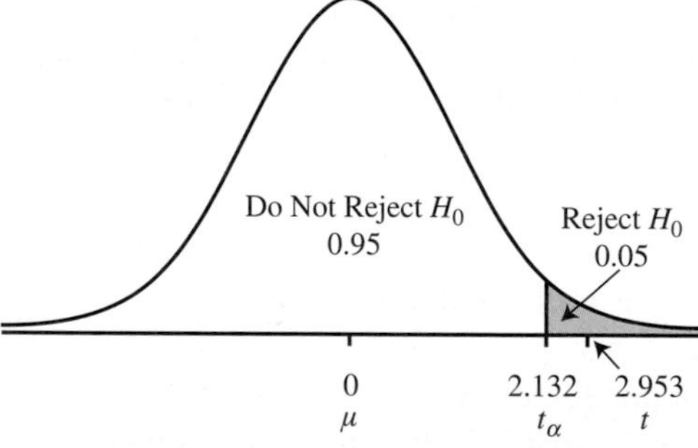

Don't confuse correlation with causation. Correlation simply measures how one variable moves with another. We cannot, however, assume that one variable causes movement in the other variable.

We can determine the p-value for this one-tail (upper) hypothesis test by using Excel's T.DIST.RT function, which was introduced in Chapter 9.

$$p\text{-value} = \text{T.DIST.RT}(2.953, 4) = 0.0209$$

Because this value is less than $\alpha = 0.05$, we can reject the null hypothesis.

In the last example, we set up a one-tail hypothesis test to determine if the population correlation coefficient was greater than zero. We can also conduct a two-tail test to determine if the population correlation coefficient is not equal to zero. Try your hand at a two-tail test for the significance of the correlation coefficient in the following Your Turn problem.

YOUR TURN #2

Test to determine if the population correlation coefficient for the Swiss hiking data from Your Turn #1 is not equal to zero using $\alpha = 0.10$.

Answer can be found on ▶ **page 705**

14.2 Section Problems

Basic Skills

14.1 Consider the following ordered pairs:

x	4	7	2	6	6
y	6	9	5	5	7

Calculate the sample correlation coefficient.

14.2 Perform a hypothesis test with the data from Problem 14.1 to determine if the population correlation coefficient is not equal to zero using $\alpha = 0.05$. What are your conclusions?

14.3 Consider the following ordered pairs:

x	7	6	2	3
y	6	8	9	6

Calculate the sample correlation coefficient.

14.4 Perform a hypothesis test with the data from Problem 14.3 to determine if the population correlation coefficient is less than zero using $\alpha = 0.05$. What are your conclusions?

Applications

14.5 Fair Isaac, the company that developed the credit score model used by most lenders today, would like to examine the linear relationship between the age and credit score of an individual. The following table shows the credit scores and ages of 10 randomly selected people:

Age	Credit Score	Age	Credit Score
36	675	47	790
24	655	35	720
54	760	59	760
28	615	40	685
31	660	42	610

Determine the sample correlation coefficient between a person's age and credit score.

14.6 Using the data from Problem 14.5 and $\alpha = 0.02$, test if the population correlation coefficient between a person's age and credit score is different than zero. What conclusions can you draw?

14.7 Best Buy would like to investigate the linear relationship between the selling price of a Canon PowerShot digital camera and the demand for it. The following table shows the weekly demand for the camera in one particular market along with the corresponding price:

Demand	Price ($)	Demand	Price ($)
16	300	11	340
19	310	12	350
14	320	8	360
13	330		

Determine the sample correlation coefficient between the selling price and the demand for this camera.

14.8 Using $\alpha = 0.10$ and the data from Problem 14.7, test if the population correlation coefficient between the selling price and the demand for the camera is less than zero. What conclusions can you draw?

14.9 The University of Delaware would like to describe the linear relationship between the grade point average (GPA) and the starting monthly salary of a graduate who earned a business degree from the university. The following table shows the monthly starting salaries for eight graduates of the business school along with their corresponding GPAs:

Starting Salary ($)	GPA	Starting Salary ($)	GPA
2,600	3.2	3,000	3.7
2,900	3.4	2,900	4.0
2,500	2.6	2,200	2.5
2,600	3.5	2,400	3.3

Determine the sample correlation coefficient between the starting salary and the GPA of a University of Delaware business graduate.

14.10 Using $\alpha = 0.05$ and the data from Problem 14.9, test if the population correlation coefficient between the starting salary and the GPA of a University of Delaware business graduate is greater than zero. What conclusions can you draw?

14.11 The following table shows the selling prices, in thousands of dollars, and the square footages of seven randomly selected houses recently sold by Century 21 Realtors.

Price ($)	Square Feet	Price ($)	Square Feet
258	2,730	249	2,310
191	1,860	245	2,450
253	2,140	282	2,920
168	2,180		

Determine the sample correlation coefficient between a house's selling price and its square footage.

14.12 Using $\alpha = 0.10$ and the data from Problem 14.11, test the significance of the population correlation coefficient between a house's selling price and its square footage. What conclusions can you draw?

14.3 Simple Linear Regression Analysis

We now know that the correlation coefficient provides us with a measurement describing the strength and direction of the linear relationship between two variables. The next procedure we'll discuss, known as **simple regression analysis**, enables us to describe a straight line that best fits a series of ordered pairs (x, y). As you will see later in this section, having a straight line that describes the linear relationship between the independent (x) and the dependent (y) variable provides some advantages over the correlation coefficient.

The technique of **simple regression analysis** enables us to describe a straight line that best fits a series of ordered pairs (x, y).

An ordered pair is a set of *x* and *y* values that pertains to a specific observation.

This technique is known as simple regression because we are using only one independent variable. Chapter 15 will introduce the multiple regression technique, which includes more than one independent variable.

We begin this procedure by collecting a random sample of ordered pairs from a population of interest. The equation that describes a straight line through our sample of ordered pairs, known as a linear equation, takes the form shown in Equation 14.3.

Formula 14.3 for the Equation Describing a Straight Line through Ordered Pairs

$$\hat{y} = b_0 + b_1 x$$

where

$\hat{y}$ = The predicted value of y given a value of x
x = The independent variable from the sample
b_0 = The sample y-intercept of the straight line
b_1 = The sample slope of the straight line

Figure 14.6 illustrates this concept.

FIGURE 14.6
The Equation for a Straight Line Graphically Illustrated

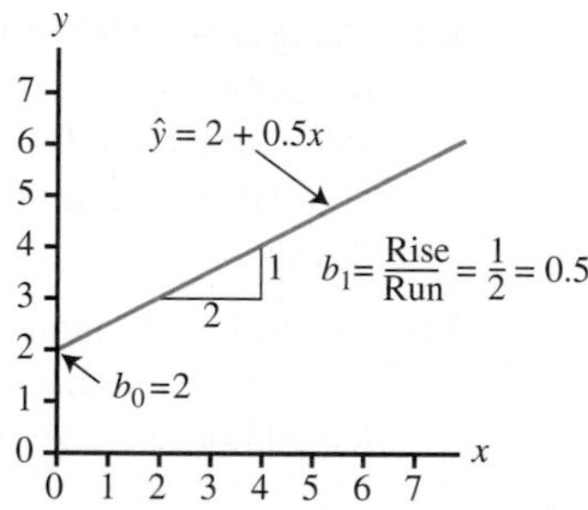

Figure 14.6 shows a line described by the equation $\hat{y} = 2 + 0.5x$. The y-intercept is the point where the line crosses the y-axis (that is, the value of y when x is zero). So in this case, $b_0 = 2$. The slope of the line, b_1, is the ratio of the rise of the line over the run of the line. In this case, $b_1 = 0.5$. A positive slope like the one shown in the figure indicates that the line is rising from left to right. If the slope in Figure 14.6 were negative, the line would move lower as it moved from left to right. If the slope equaled zero, the line would be horizontal, which would mean there is no linear relationship between the independent and the dependent variable. In other words, a change in the value of x would have no discernable effect on the value of y.

So far in this section we have focused our attention on the sample of ordered pairs. However, our real interest lies in the population from which our sample was taken. The simple linear regression model for a population can be described using Equation 14.4.

Formula 14.4 for the Simple Linear Regression Model for a Population

$$y_i = \beta_0 + \beta_1 x_i + \varepsilon_i$$

where

y_i = The ith observation for the dependent variable from the population
β_0 = The population y-intercept
β_1 = The population slope
x_i = The ith observation for the independent variable from the population
ε_i = The residual for the ith observation from the population

Our goal in this chapter is to estimate β_0 and β_1 based on our sample of ordered pairs. The residual in Equation 14.4 can be considered an error term and is discussed in more detail with Equation 14.5.

My students sometimes struggle with the distinction between $\hat{y}$ and y. Figure 14.7 shows six ordered pairs and a line that appears to fit the data described by the equation $\hat{y} = 2 + 0.5x$.

FIGURE 14.7
The Difference between y and ŷ Graphically Illustrated

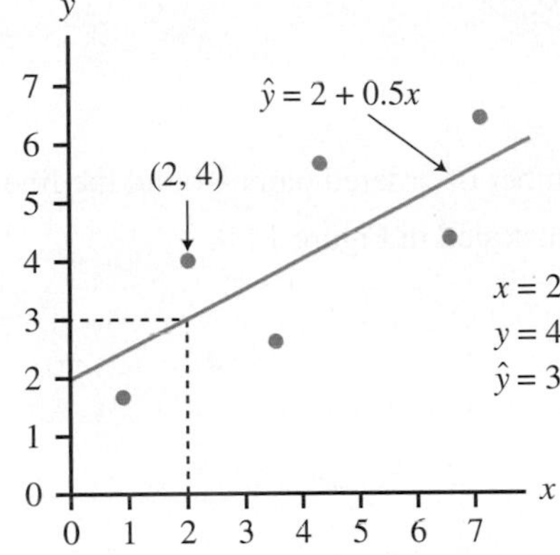

Figure 14.7 shows a data point that corresponds to the ordered pair $x = 2$ and $y = 4$. Notice that the *predicted* value of y, which you can find by looking up the dotted line rising from $x = 2$ and over to the left, is $\hat{y} = 3$. We can verify this using the Equation 14.3 as follows:

$$\hat{y} = 2 + 0.5x = 2 + 0.5(2) = 3$$

The difference between the actual data value and the predicted value is known as the **residual, e_i**.

The value of y represents an actual data point. By contrast, the value of $\hat{y}$ is the predicted value of y using the linear equation, given a value for x. The difference between the actual data value and the predicted value is known as the **residual, e_i**, which is shown in Equation 14.5.

Formula 14.5 for the Residual

$$e_i = y_i - \hat{y}_i$$

where

e_i = The residual of the ith observation in the sample
y_i = The actual value of the dependent variable for the ith data point
$\hat{y}_i$ = The predicted value of the dependent variable for the ith data point

The residual for the data point that corresponds to the ordered pair $x = 2$ and $y = 4$ is therefore as follows:

$$e_i = y_i - \hat{y}_i = 4 - 3 = 1$$

We will revisit the importance of the residual later in this chapter. Our next step is to find the linear equation that best fits a set of ordered pairs.

The Least Squares Method

The **least squares method** is a mathematical procedure used to identify the linear equation that best fits a set of ordered pairs.

The **regression line** is the line that best fits the data.

The **least squares method** is a mathematical procedure used to identify the linear equation that best fits a set of ordered pairs. The line that best fits the ordered pairs is called the **regression line**. The procedure can be used to find the values for b_0 (the y-intercept) and b_1 (the slope of the line). The goal of the least squares method is to minimize the total squared error between the values of y and $\hat{y}$, which provides us with the best fitting line through our data points. The least squares method will minimize the sum of squares error (SSE), which is described in Equation 14.6.

Formula 14.6 for the Sum of Squares Error

$$SSE = \sum_{i=1}^{n} (y_i - \hat{y}_i)^2$$

where

$n =$ The number of ordered pairs around the line that best fits the data

This concept is illustrated in Figure 14.8.

FIGURE 14.8 Minimizing the Sum of Squares Error

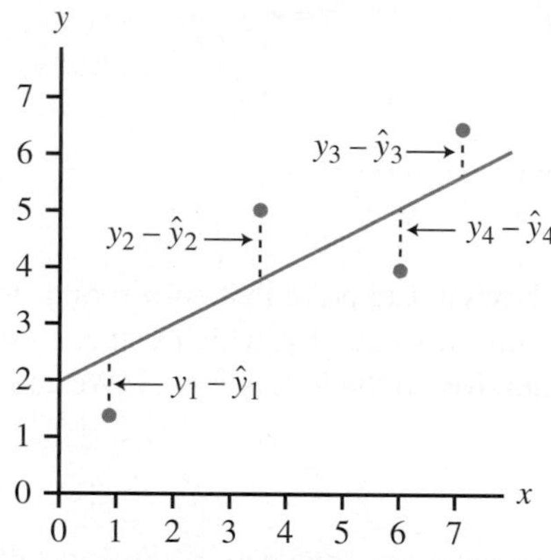

Imagine moving the blue line in Figure 14.8 to a different position. This would cause some of the error terms to get smaller while others would become larger. The least squares method finds the one line position that minimizes the sum of squares error for all of the data points.

According to Figure 14.8, the regression line that best fits the data will minimize the total squared error of the four data points.

As I mentioned earlier, the purpose of the least squares method is to determine the values for b_0 (the y-intercept) and b_1 (the slope) for the regression equation $\hat{y} = b_0 + b_1x$. These values can be obtained in one of three ways:

1. Your instructor has a brain lapse and simply gives you the values.
2. You calculate the values manually using equations.
3. Excel calculates the values.

Counting on the first option is an act of pure desperation known as the "Hail Mary pass" of statistics, which rarely works. (Unless, of course, your name is Doug Flutie. For those of you who are too young to know who Doug Flutie is, go to YouTube and type in "Flutie Hail Mary." Play the video clip and you will see one of the greatest endings of a college football game ever—one in which a Hail Mary pass actually worked. For those of you not named Doug Flutie, I will demonstrate the last two techniques.)

Calculating the Slope and *y*-Intercept Manually

Equations 14.7 and 14.8 can be used to calculate the slope and *y*-intercept, respectively.

Formula 14.7 for the Regression Slope

$$b_1 = \frac{n\sum xy - \left(\sum x\right)\left(\sum y\right)}{n\sum x^2 - \left(\sum x\right)^2}$$

Formula 14.8 for the Regression Intercept

$$b_0 = \frac{\sum y}{n} - b_1\left(\frac{\sum x}{n}\right)$$

Using the SNSCSR values with $n = 6$ for our exam-grade example, which I asked you to put in a safe place earlier in the chapter, we first calculate the slope of the regression equation (b_1) using Equation 14.7:

$$\sum x = 22 \quad \sum y = 513 \quad \sum xy = 1{,}920 \quad \sum x^2 = 90 \quad \sum y^2 = 44{,}099$$

$$b_1 = \frac{n\sum xy - \left(\sum x\right)\left(\sum y\right)}{n\sum x^2 - \left(\sum x\right)^2}$$

$$b_1 = \frac{(6)(1920) - (22)(513)}{(6)(90) - (22)^2}$$

$$b_1 = \frac{11520 - 11286}{540 - 484} = \frac{234}{56} = 4.1786$$

You're probably thinking that carrying these calculations out to four decimal places seems excessive. However, doing so reduces the rounding errors, which is important because we will use these values for calculations later in the chapter. Check with your instructor concerning his or her expectations for rounding.

Once the slope has been determined, use it to calculate the *y*-intercept using Equation 14.8:

$$b_0 = \frac{\sum y}{n} - b_1\left(\frac{\sum x}{n}\right)$$

$$b_0 = \frac{513}{6} - (4.1786)\left(\frac{22}{6}\right)$$

$$b_0 = 85.5 - (4.1786)(3.6667)$$

$$b_0 = 85.5 - 15.3217 = 70.1783$$

The regression equation for the exam score data is therefore as follows:

$$\hat{y} = 70.1783 + 4.1786x$$

What does this regression equation mean for our exam-grade example? Because $b_1 = 4.1786$, we can conclude that each additional hour spent studying is associated with an average increase of 4.1786 points in exam scores. Also, because the slope is positive, increasing the hours of study will result in an increase in the exam score. This result is consistent with the conclusions from the correlation coefficient.

The interpretation for the *y*-intercept requires a little more caution. Technically, the *y*-intercept represents the value of $\hat{y}$ when $x = 0$. For our exam grade example, this represents the grade for a student who studies zero hours, or

$$\hat{y} = 70.1783 + 4.1786(0) = 70.1783$$

The problem with this interpretation is that we have no values from our sample where $x = 0$. This makes our conclusions that a student who does not study will receive an average grade of 70 unreliable. This issue will be discussed in more detail later in the chapter.

What is the predicted exam grade for a student who studies 3.0 hours? If we set $x = 3.0$ in the regression equation, we get the following:

$$\hat{y} = 70.1783 + 4.1786(3.0)$$

$$\hat{y} = 70.1783 + 12.5358 = 82.7 \approx 83$$

The predicted exam score for a student who studies 3.0 hours is an 83. We call this a *point estimate* for the regression equation. A little later, we will investigate the accuracy of this estimate using confidence intervals.

Having a straight line describe the linear relationship between the two variables has some advantages over using the correlation coefficient. First, you can observe the effect that the independent variable has on the dependent variable. For example, if a car dealership has historical data tracking the selling prices of used 2007 Honda Civics with various mileages, the dealership could discover what will happen to the selling price of one of these cars given an increase in its odometer reading. Second, a straight line allows you to predict a specific value for the dependent variable, given a value for the independent variable. With the proper data, for instance, our dealership could predict the selling price for a 2007 Civic with 52,000 miles.

Spend a couple of minutes on the next Your Turn problem to convince yourself that you know what you are doing before moving on. You'll thank me later for not having to throw that Hail Mary pass come exam time!

YOUR TURN #3

Determine the regression equation for the Swiss hiking data from Your Turn #1. Use your results to predict the hiking time for a 36-year-old hiker on Wengen-Kleine Scheidegg trail.

Answers can be found on ▶ **page 705**

Calculating the Slope and *y*-Intercept Using Excel

Now that I have tortured you with those nasty slope/intercept calculations, I'm going to show you an easy way to generate those values using Excel with the following steps. Mac users can go to the textbook's Web site for instructions on how to use PHStat for this procedure (www.pearsonhighered.com/donnelly).

1. Open the Excel file **exam grades.xlsx** or list the two variables, with labels, as Figure 14.9A shows. It doesn't matter which variable goes in which column.
2. Go to the Data tab and select **Data Analysis**, which opens the **Data Analysis** dialog box shown in Figure 14.9A.
3. Scroll down to Regression and click **OK**. This opens the **Regression** dialog box shown in Figure 14.9B.

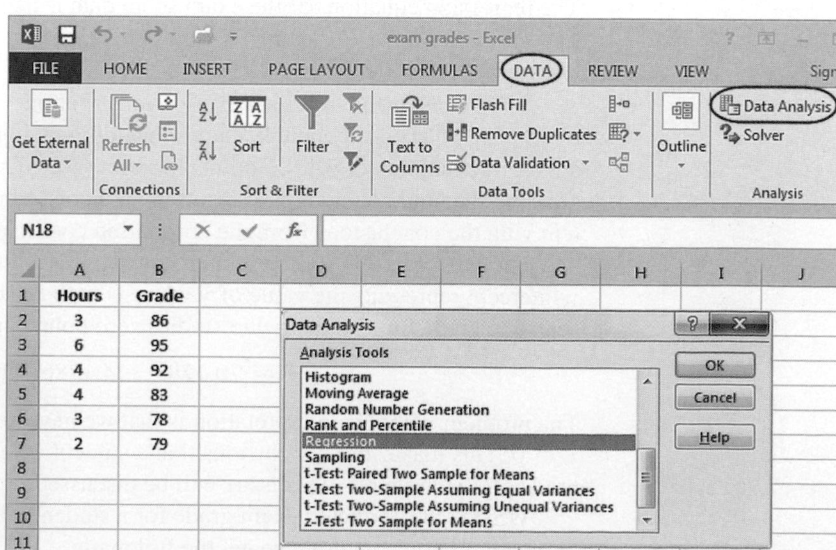

FIGURE 14.9A
Using Excel to Calculate the Slope and y-Intercept (Steps 1–3)

In the Regression dialog box in Figure 14.9B, do the following:

4. Click on the first text box, which is labeled **Input Y Range.**
5. Because our *y* (dependent) variable is Exam Grades, highlight cells B1 to B7, which includes the label "Grade."
6. Click on the second text box, which is labeled **Input X Range.**
7. Highlight cells A1 to A7.
8. Because labels are included in our data range, check the **Labels** box as Figure 14.9B shows.
9. Click on **Output Range**. Then click on the text box to the right, followed by cell D1 in the spreadsheet. This tells Excel where to put the report. Click **OK**.

I recommend including labels in your data range because Excel will then use those labels in the final regression report, which will make the report easier to read.

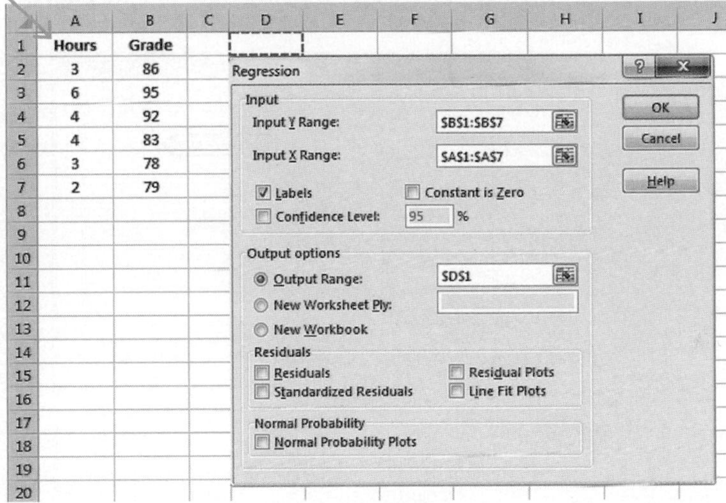

FIGURE 14.9B Using Excel to Calculate the Slope and y-Intercept (Steps 4–9)

Right before your very eyes, every calculation you can possibly dream of (that is, for a regression analysis) magically appears in your spreadsheet, as Figure 14.9C shows. In the bottom left-hand corner, you will find the two values under the "Coefficients" heading circled in red. These are the *y*-intercept and slope values for our regression equation. Notice they are slightly different from what we calculated in the last section. Have no fear—this is simply due to rounding differences. Also, the correlation coefficient *r* that we determined earlier in the chapter is found next to the "Multiple R" label (0.828).

FIGURE 14.9C Using Excel to Calculate the Slope and y-Intercept (Final Result)

D	E	F	G	H	I	J
SUMMARY OUTPUT						
Regression Statistics						
Multiple R	0.828351021					
R Square	0.686165414					
Adjusted R Square	0.607706767					
Standard Error	4.316703438					
Observations	6					
ANOVA						
	df	*SS*	*MS*	*F*	*Significance F*	
Regression	1	162.9642857	162.9643	8.745568	0.041666379	
Residual	4	74.53571429	18.63393			
Total	5	237.5				
	Coefficients	*Standard Error*	*t Stat*	*P-value*	*Lower 95%*	*Upper 95%*
Intercept	70.17857143	5.472420416	12.82405	0.000213	54.98469655	85.372446
Hours	4.178571429	1.412972876	2.957291	0.041666	0.255529805	8.1016131

I just know your curious minds are asking, "What about all those other numbers? When are we going to have to learn about them?" Don't panic—we will be revisiting Figure 14.9C throughout this chapter and explaining what they all mean.

Before we move on, I have one more trick to show you. You can add a regression line and display its corresponding equation in an Excel scatter plot. Use the grade data from the Excel file we just used and construct the scatter plot shown in Figure 14.2. Follow the steps outlined in Chapter 2 on page 62 if you need a refresher.

Once the scatter plot is completed, take the following steps to add the regression line to the graph:

1. Left-click on any of the data points in the scatter plot. This will highlight all the data points in the plot.
2. Right-click on one of the highlighted data points.
3. Left-click on **Add Trendline** in the drop-down menu. This opens the **Format Trendline** dialog box as shown in Figure 14.10.
4. Check the box for **Display Equation on chart.**

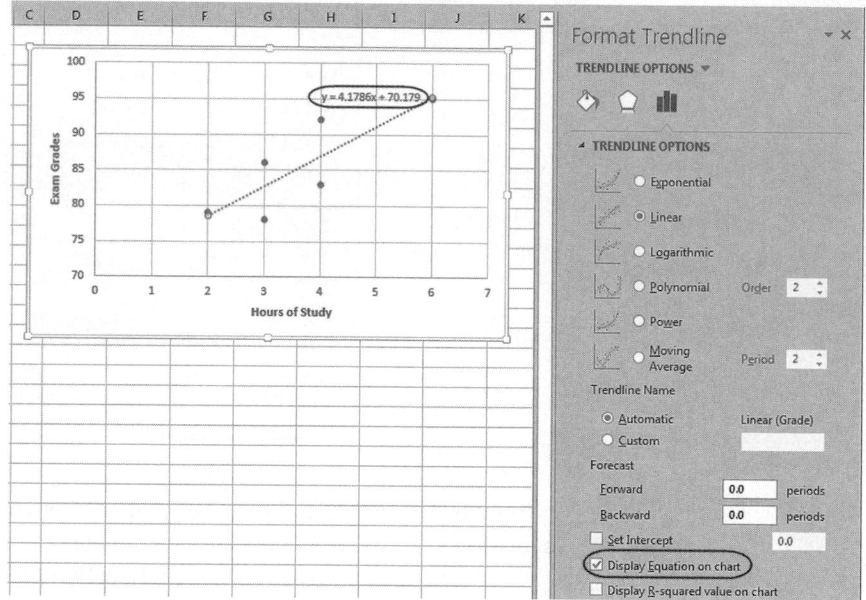

FIGURE 14.10 Inserting a Regression Line through the Data in a Scatter Plot Using Excel

As you can see for yourself, Excel draws the regression line through the data and displays the regression equation right on the scatter plot. Please hold your applause until the end of the chapter.

Partitioning the Sum of Squares

The **total sum of squares (*SST*)** measures the total variation in the dependent variable.

Notice that the exam scores in our example differ among students. This difference is known as variation and is measured by a term known as the **total sum of squares (*SST*)**, which is described by Equation 14.9. Recall that *SST* was first introduced in Chapter 11 and appears here in a slightly different form because we are applying it to a dependent variable. But, rest assured, it has the same meaning.

Formula 14.9 for the Total Sum of Squares (SST)

$$SST = \sum (y - \bar{y})^2$$

where

y = A value of the dependent variable from the sample

$\bar{y}$ = The average value of the dependent variable from the sample

Unfortunately, Equation 14.9 is rather tedious to calculate manually. But don't fret. Equation 14.10 shows a more calculator-friendly version of the *SST* we can use instead.

Formula 14.10 for the Total Sum of Squares (SST), Calculator-Friendly Version

$$SST = \sum y^2 - \frac{\left(\sum y\right)^2}{n}$$

Let's put Equation 14.10 to work with our SNSCSR values from the exam-grade example:

$$\sum y = 513 \quad \sum y^2 = 44{,}099 \quad n = 6$$

$$SST = \sum y^2 - \frac{\left(\sum y\right)^2}{n}$$

$$SST = 44{,}099 - \frac{(513)^2}{6}$$

$$SST = 44{,}099 - 43{,}861.5 = 237.5$$

Simply put, this value measures the squared difference between each exam score and the average exam score for the six students. The bigger the difference is between the scores, the larger the *SST* will be. If all six grades were the same, there would be no variation in *y*, which means the *SST* would equal zero.

Our next step is to partition (or divide) our *SST* value into two portions, the sum of squares regression (*SSR*) and the sum of squares error (*SSE*). (Recall that we discussed the sum of squares error earlier in the chapter but have not yet calculated it.) The linear relationship between the three sums of squares is shown in Equation 14.11.

Formula 14.11 for the Relationship between the SSR and SSE

$$SST = SSR + SSE$$

To explain the difference between the sum of squares regression and the sum of squares error, let's look at the data from our original exam-grade example, which is shown again in Table 14.4.

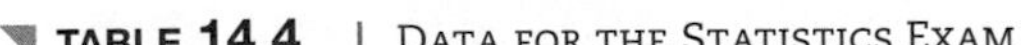

TABLE 14.4 | DATA FOR THE STATISTICS EXAM

STUDENT	HOURS OF STUDY	EXAM GRADE
1	3	86
2	6	95
3	4	92
4	4	83
5	3	78
6	2	79

Notice that Student 2's grade (95) is higher than Student 1's (86). One reason for this difference might be due to the fact that Student 2 studied 6 hours for the exam, whereas Student 1 studied 3 hours. There could also be other reasons for the difference in the scores not accounted for in our example, such as Student 1 missing some classes or not getting enough sleep the night before the exam. (Sound familiar?)

The **sum of squares error (*SSE*)** measures the variation in the dependent variable that is explained by variables other than the independent variable.

The **sum of squares error (*SSE*)** measures the variation in the dependent variable that is due to variables other than the independent variable. In our exam-grade example, class attendance could be an "other" variable. Equation 14.6 describes the *SSE*, but I recommend you use the friendlier version shown in Equation 14.12.

Formula 14.12 for the Sum of Squares Error (SSE), Calculator-Friendly Version

$$SSE = \sum y^2 - b_0 \sum y - b_1 \sum xy$$

This equation requires us to use our SNSCSR values, along with the *y*-intercept (b_0) and the slope (b_1) from the regression equation $\hat{y} = 70.1783 + 4.1786x$ that we calculated in the previous section:

$$\sum y = 513 \quad \sum xy = 1{,}920 \quad \sum y^2 = 44{,}099$$

$$SSE = \sum y^2 - b_0 \sum y - b_1 \sum xy$$

$$SSE = (44{,}099) - (70.1783)(513) - (4.1786)(1{,}920)$$

$$SSE = 44{,}099 - 36{,}001.47 - 8{,}022.91$$

$$SSE = 74.62$$

We now turn our undivided attention to the sum of squares regression.

The **sum of squares regression (*SSR*)** measures the amount of variation in the dependent variable (exam grade) that is explained by the independent variable (hours of study).

The **sum of squares regression (*SSR*)** measures the amount of variation in the dependent variable (exam grades) that is explained by the independent variable (hours of study). Equation 14.13 describes the *SSR*, but I recommend using Equation 14.11 for a simpler calculation.

Formula 14.13 for the Sum of Squares Regression (SSR)

$$SSR = \sum (\hat{y} - \bar{y})^2$$

The values for all three sum of squares should never be negative. If you do calculate a negative number, stop and check for your mistake!

We can rearrange Equation 14.11 as follows to find the *SSR* (remember the $SST = 237.5$):

$$SST = SSR + SSE$$

$$SSR = SST - SSE$$

$$SSR = 237.5 - 74.62 = 162.88$$

In summary, we have partitioned our *SST* in the following manner:

$$SSR = 162.88$$

$$SSE = 74.62$$

$$SST = 237.5$$

We will put the numbers to work in the following sections. However, I sense that you need to show off your newfound skills to partition the sum of squares in the next Your Turn problem. Don't let me stop you!

YOUR TURN #4

Partition the *SST* for the Swiss hiking data from Your Turn #1 into the *SSR* and the *SSE*.

Answer can be found on ▶ **page 705**

Calculating the Sample Coefficient of Determination

The **sample coefficient of determination, R^2,** measures the percentage of the total variation of our dependent variable that is explained by our independent variable from a sample.

The **sample coefficient of determination, R^2**, measures the *percentage* of the total variation of our dependent variable (grade) that is explained by our independent variable (hours of study). We find the coefficient of determination for simple regression using Equation 14.14.

Formula 14.14 for the Sample Coefficient of Determination

$$R^2 = \frac{SSR}{SST}$$

The value of R^2 ranges from 0% to 100%. Higher values of R^2 are more desirable than lower ones because we would like to explain as much of the variation of the dependent variable by the independent variable as possible. As we will see in Chapter 15, low values of R^2 mean that we either are using the wrong independent variable or need additional independent variables to explain the variation in the dependent variable.

Using the results from partitioning the sum of squares for the exam-grade example, we have the following:

$$SSR = 162.88 \quad SST = 237.5$$

$$R^2 = \frac{SSR}{SST} = \frac{162.88}{237.5} = 0.686$$

We can now conclude that 68.6% of the total variation in exam grades can be explained by the hours of study. The value of the coefficient of determination ranges from 0 to 1.0. The higher the value, the stronger the linear relationship between the dependent and independent variables.

I love showing my students shortcuts, so here's one for you. The sample coefficient of determination can also be determined by squaring the sample correlation coefficient, r (which we calculated earlier in the chapter) as follows:

$$R^2 = r^2 = (0.828)^2 = 0.686$$

Conducting a Hypothesis Test to Determine the Significance of the Population Coefficient of Determination

The **population coefficient of determination,** ρ^2, measures for an entire population the percentage of the total variation of a dependent variable that is explained by an independent variable.

The value for R^2 that we calculated in the previous section represents the coefficient of determination for a random sample of six students that was collected from a larger student population. This population has a **population coefficient of determination,** ρ^2, that is unknown because we have not gathered data on every student who took the exam. We can, however, perform a hypothesis test to determine if the population coefficient of determination, ρ^2, is significantly different from zero based on the sample coefficient of determination, R^2. This test uses the following hypothesis statement:

$$H_0: \rho^2 \leq 0$$
$$H_1: \rho^2 > 0$$

Remember, a population coefficient of determination equal to zero means that none of the variation in exam grades is explained by hours of study, which indicates that there is no linear relationship between x and y.

A one-tail (upper) test is appropriate here because the coefficient of determination cannot be negative. If we reject the null hypothesis, we have enough evidence from our sample to conclude that a linear relationship exists between the hours studied and the exam scores in the student population. For this test, we will use $\alpha = 0.05$.

The F-test statistic, which was named after the British statistician Ronald Fisher, is the appropriate test statistic to use for the coefficient of determination. Equation 14.15 shows how to calculate the F-test statistic for this procedure.

Formula 14.15 for the F-Test Statistic for the Coefficient of Determination

$$F = \frac{SSR}{\left(\frac{SSE}{n-2}\right)}$$

We need to plug in the partitioned sum of squares values from earlier in the chapter:

$$SSR = 162.88 \quad SSE = 74.62$$

The calculated F-score for this test is as follows:

$$F = \frac{SSR}{\left(\frac{SSE}{n-2}\right)} = \frac{162.88}{\left(\frac{74.62}{6-2}\right)} = \frac{162.88}{18.66} = 8.73$$

The critical F-score, F_α, identifies the rejection region for the hypothesis test.

The test statistic shown in Equation 14.15 follows the F-distribution, which was introduced in Chapter 11 with ANOVA. The critical value, F_α, can be found in Table 6 in Appendix A. The F-distribution has two types of degrees of freedom, D_1 and D_2, which correspond to the degrees of freedom for the *SSR* and the *SSE*:

$$D_1 = 1$$
$$D_2 = n - 2 = 6 - 2 = 4$$

The degrees of freedom for *SSR* (D_1) always equal 1 because we have only one independent variable with a simple regression. In Chapter 15 (multiple regression), D_1 will equal the number of independent variables and can be greater than 1.

Using $\alpha = 0.05$, the critical F-score found in Table 6 in Appendix A is $F_\alpha = 7.709$. We can also obtain the critical F-score using Excel's F.INV.RT function, which we introduced in Chapter 11, as follows:

$$=\text{F.INV.RT}\,(0.05, 1, 4) = 7.709$$

Because $F = 8.73$ is higher than $F_\alpha = 7.709$, as Figure 14.11 shows, we reject H_0 and conclude that the population coefficient of determination is greater than zero. There appears to be a linear relationship between students' exam grades and their hours of study.

This is a conclusion we should expect because earlier in the chapter we rejected the null hypothesis for the significance test of the correlation coefficient.

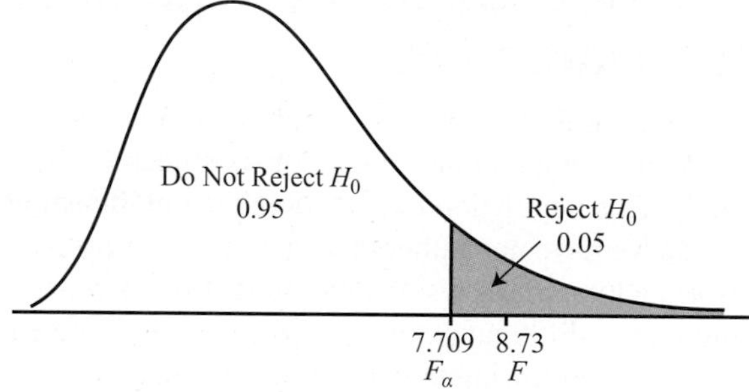

FIGURE 14.11 Testing the Significance of the Population Coefficient of Determination

I promised we would take a closer look at all of the numbers we saw in the Excel output in Figure 14.9C. Figure 14.12 shows these numbers again. The coefficient of determination, R^2, is shown next to the "R Square" label (0.686) under the "Regression Statistics" heading and is circled in red. The sum of squares values that we calculated earlier are shown under the "SS" column heading in the ANOVA table, which is also circled in red. Excel uses the term *residual* instead of *error*. The calculated F-score is shown under the "F" column, and the degrees of freedom, D_1 and D_2, can be found under the "df" column. The slight differences between our calculations and the values seen in Figure 14.12 are due to rounding.

FIGURE 14.12
Regression Output in Excel

SUMMARY OUTPUT

Regression Statistics	
Multiple R	0.828351021
R Square	0.686165414
Adjusted R Square	0.607706767
Standard Error	4.316703438
Observations	6

ANOVA

	df	SS	MS	F	Significance F
Regression	1	162.9642857	162.9643	8.745568	0.041666379
Residual	4	74.53571429	18.63393		
Total	5	237.5			

	Coefficients	Standard Error	t Stat	P-value	Lower 95%	Upper 95%
Intercept	70.17857143	5.472420416	12.82405	0.000213	54.98469655	85.3724463
Hours	4.178571429	1.412972876	2.957291	0.041666	0.255529805	8.101613053

Excel also gives us the p-value for this hypothesis test under the "Significance F" column in the ANOVA table. Recall from Chapter 9 that the p-value represents the area under the distribution to the right and/or left of the calculated test statistic. The p-value for our exam-grade example is shown graphically in Figure 14.13.

FIGURE 14.13
The p-Value for the Exam-Grade Example

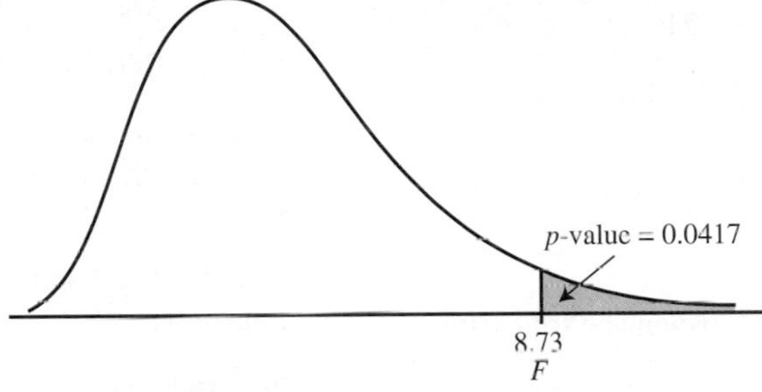

We can also obtain the p-value using Excel's F.DIST.RT function which we introduced in Chapter 11 as follows:

$$=\text{F.DIST.RT}\ (8.73, 1, 4) = 0.0418$$

Because our p-value equals 0.0418, which is less than $\alpha = 0.05$, we can reject the null hypothesis, which stated that there was no linear relationship between hours of study and exam grade. By rejecting this hypothesis, we can conclude that there is evidence that a linear relationship exists between these two variables.

Let's test your understanding of this material before we move on to bigger and better things.

YOUR TURN #5

Calculate the coefficient of determination for the Swiss hiking data from Your Turn #1 and test its significance using $\alpha = 0.10$.

Answers can be found on ▶ **page 705**

14.3 Section Problems

Basic Skills

14.13 Consider the following set of ordered pairs:

x	4	7	2	6	6
y	6	9	5	5	7

a. Calculate the slope and y-intercept for these data.
b. Calculate the total sum of squares (SST).
c. Partition the sum of squares into the SSR and SSE.

14.14 Using the data from Problem 14.13, calculate the sample coefficient of determination and test the significance of the population coefficient of determination using $\alpha = 0.05$.

14.15 Consider the following set of ordered pairs:

x	2	5	3	1
y	5	7	4	2

a. Calculate the slope and y-intercept for these data.
b. Calculate the *SST*.
c. Partition the sum of squares into the *SSR* and *SSE*.

14.16 Using the data from Problem 14.15, calculate the sample coefficient of determination and test the significance of the population coefficient of determination using $\alpha = 0.05$.

Applications

14.17 The following table shows the hot dogs bought from a street vendor over the course of eight days ("Demand"). Also shown is the temperature for each day in degrees Celsius.

Temperature (°C)	Demand	Temperature (°C)	Demand
20	48	7	18
11	30	12	23
23	36	18	42
18	40	21	33

a. Calculate the slope and y-intercept for the linear regression equation for these data.
b. Predict the demand for hot dogs on a day with a temperature of 15°C.
c. Verify your results using Excel.

14.18 Use the data from Problem 14.17 to answer the following questions:

a. Calculate the *SST*.
b. Partition the total sum of squares into the *SSR* and *SSE*.
c. Calculate the sample coefficient of determination.
d. Test the significance of the population coefficient of determination using $\alpha = 0.05$.

14.19 Consider the following partially completed ANOVA summary table:

Source	*df*	*SS*	*MS*	*F*
Regression	1	600		
Residual				
Total	9	1000		

a. Complete the remaining entries in the table.
b. How many ordered pairs are in this sample?
c. Calculate the sample coefficient of determination.
d. Using $\alpha = 0.05$, what conclusions can be made about the population coefficient of determination?

14.20 The following data set shows the entrance exam score (Verbal GMAT) for each of eight MBA students along with his or her grade point average (GPA) upon graduation.

GMAT	GPA	GMAT	GPA
310	3.7	350	4.0
290	3.0	270	3.0
260	3.1	300	3.7
280	3.2	300	3.0

a. Calculate the slope and y-intercept for the linear regression equation for these data.
b. Verify your results using Excel.

14.21 Use the data from Problem 14.20 to answer the following questions:

a. Calculate the *SST*.
b. Partition the *SST* into the *SSR* and *SSE*.
c. Calculate the sample coefficient of determination.
d. Test the significance of the population coefficient of determination using $\alpha = 0.05$.

14.4 Using a Regression to Make a Prediction

As mentioned earlier, we can use our regression equation to predict the grades we would expect students to get based on the number of hours they spend studying. Earlier in the chapter we figured out that a student who studies 3 hours could expect the following grade:

$$\hat{y} = 70.1783 + 4.1786(3.0)$$
$$\hat{y} = 70.1783 + 12.5358 = 82.7 \approx 83$$

What we don't know yet is how reliable our prediction is because we have information only on a sample of students—not the entire population. So, just how accurate is our estimate based on the information we have? To answer this, we need to construct a confidence interval around our predicted exam grade to get a feel for the accuracy of the regression line. Recall from Chapter 8 that confidence intervals provide an estimate of a population parameter based on a sample statistic. In this application, our confidence interval will provide a range of grades students can be confident of achieving if they study for a particular number of hours.

The **standard error of the estimate, s_e,** measures the amount of dispersion of observed data around a regression line.

To construct such an interval, we first need to determine the **standard error of the estimate, s_e,** using Equation 14.16.

Formula 14.16 for the Standard Error of the Estimate

$$s_e = \sqrt{\frac{SSE}{n-2}}$$

The standard error of the estimate measures the amount of dispersion of observed data around a regression line. If the data points are very close to the line, such as in the graph on the left in Figure 14.14, the standard error of the estimate is relatively low. The graph on the right in Figure 14.14 shows a larger standard error because the actual data points are farther from our regression line.

FIGURE 14.14
Comparing Standard Errors of the Estimate

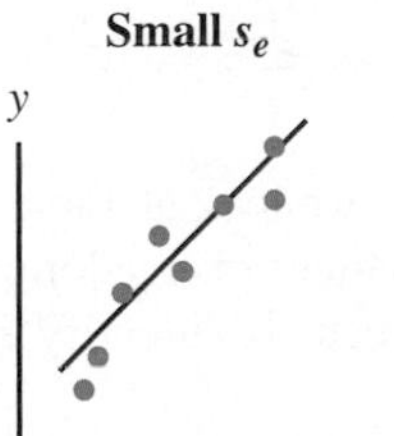

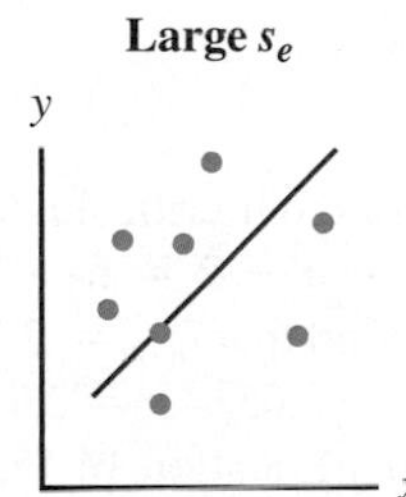

I hope you agree with me when I claim that a smaller standard error of the estimate is more desirable than a larger one. If my regression line is used to estimate the dependent variable (exam grades) given a value for the independent variable (hours of study), it will be more accurate if the data points are close to the line. That's why we call it the standard error of the estimate!

Using our exam-grade data from the previous section and Equation 14.16, the standard error of the estimate is calculated as follows:

$$SSE = 74.62 \qquad n = 6$$

$$s_e = \sqrt{\frac{SSE}{n-2}} = \sqrt{\frac{74.62}{6-2}} = \sqrt{18.66} = 4.32$$

Make a note of this value because we will be using it in future calculations in the chapter. Our next step is to calculate the confidence interval for y (the grade) around an average value of x (the hours of study).

The Confidence Interval for an Average Value of *y* Based on a Value of *x*

Notice that the first student in our sample studied 3 hours and earned a grade of 86. Our regression line predicted this student's grade would be an 83. Now, I hear your curious mind asking, "I wonder what the 95% confidence interval would be for the average exam score for students who studied 3 hours?" Well, you've come to the right place. The answer to your excellent question lies in Equation 14.17.

Formula 14.17 for the Confidence Interval (CI) for an Average Value of y

$$CI = \hat{y} \pm t_{\alpha/2} s_e \sqrt{\frac{1}{n} + \frac{(x - \bar{x})^2}{\left(\sum x^2\right) - \frac{\left(\sum x\right)^2}{n}}}$$

where

$CI =$ The confidence interval for an average value of y
$\hat{y} =$ The predicted exam grade for a student who studies 3 hours
$t_{\alpha/2} =$ The critical t-score from the Student's t-distribution
$s_e =$ The standard error of the estimate
$n =$ The number of ordered pairs
$\bar{x} =$ The average value of x from the sample

Now, before you start regretting your question, let's put this equation to work one step at a time. From previous sections, we have determined the following values:

$$\hat{y} = 82.7 \quad s_e = 4.32 \quad n = 6 \quad \sum x = 22 \quad \sum x^2 = 90$$

We need to calculate the average value of x (hours of study) as follows:

$$\bar{x} = \frac{\sum x}{n} = \frac{22}{6} = 3.667$$

To find our critical t-score, $t_{\alpha/2}$, we look at Table 5 in Appendix A. This procedure has $n - 2 = 6 - 2 = 4$ degrees of freedom. For $\alpha = 0.05$ and a two-tail test, we find that $t_{\alpha/2} = 2.776$. We can also identify this critical score using Excel's $\text{T.INV.2T}(0.05, 4) = 2.776$.

Using Equation 14.17, our confidence interval is calculated as follows:

$$CI = \hat{y} \pm t_{\alpha/2} s_e \sqrt{\frac{1}{n} + \frac{(x - \bar{x})^2}{\left(\sum x^2\right) - \frac{\left(\sum x\right)^2}{n}}}$$

$$CI = 82.7 \pm (2.776)(4.32)\sqrt{\frac{1}{6} + \frac{(3 - 3.667)^2}{90 - \frac{(22)^2}{6}}}$$

$$CI = 82.7 \pm (11.99)\sqrt{0.1667 + \frac{(-0.667)^2}{90 - \frac{(484)}{6}}}$$

$$CI = 82.7 \pm (11.99)\sqrt{0.1667 + 0.0477}$$

$$CI = 82.7 \pm 5.55$$

We can describe this confidence interval with the upper confidence limit (*UCL*) and lower confidence limit (*LCL*), as follows:

$$UCL = 82.7 + 5.55 = 88.3$$
$$LCL = 82.7 - 5.55 = 77.2$$

What does this interval mean? Let's define our population as all of the students who took the statistics exam. Our sample consists of only six of these students. Based on their grades, we predicted that studying 3 hours would result in an exam grade of 82.7. However, because we don't have data on the entire class (population), we can't guarantee that everyone who studies for 3 hours will earn this grade. However, we can say that we are 95% confident that the *average* exam grade earned by all of the students who study 3 hours will be between a 77.2 and an 88.3. Pretty cool, huh? This interval is shown graphically in Figure 14.15.

FIGURE 14.15
A 95% Confidence Interval for x = 3

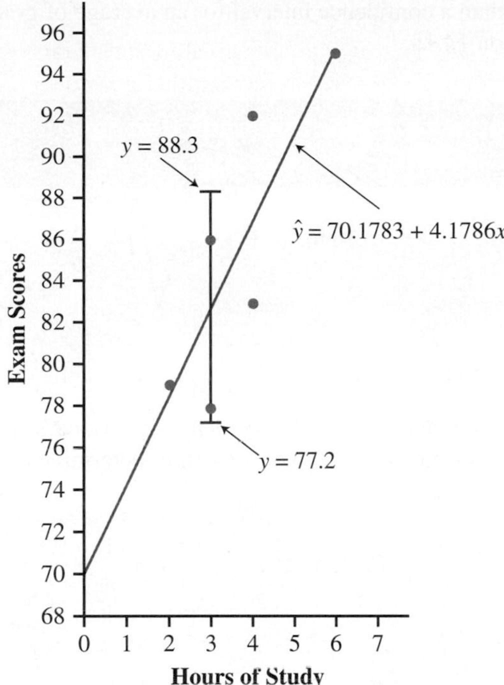

The width of the confidence interval, which is shown in red, changes depending on the value of x (hours of study) that we choose. The width at $x = 3.0$ is as follows:

$$88.3 - 77.2 = 11.1$$

The interval is narrowest at the average value of x in our sample, which is as follows:

$$\overline{x} = \frac{\sum x}{n} = \frac{22}{6} = 3.67$$

As we construct intervals for larger and smaller values of x away from this mean, the interval widens, as Table 14.5 shows.

TABLE 14.5 | CONFIDENCE INTERVALS FOR VARIOUS VALUES OF X (EXAM-GRADE EXAMPLE)

The smallest interval is highlighted in yellow.

X	UPPER LIMIT *UCL*	LOWER LIMIT *LCL*	INTERVAL WIDTH
2.0	86.7	70.4	16.3
3.0	88.3	77.2	11.1
3.67	90.4	80.6	9.8
4.0	92.0	81.8	10.2
5.0	98.2	83.9	14.3

As a result of this effect, our estimate for the average grade is more precise the closer we are to $\overline{x}$.

The Prediction Interval for a Specific Value of *y* Based on a Value of *x*

In the previous section, we constructed a confidence interval for the average grade of *all* students in the population who studied 3 hours. What if you would like to know what the interval of grades are if *you* study 3 hours? This is a different question than the one we answered in the previous section. Here we are looking for a prediction interval for an individual grade rather than a confidence interval for an average of grades. The prediction interval is shown in Equation 14.18.

Formula 14.18 for the Prediction Interval (PI) for a Specific Value of y

$$PI = \hat{y} \pm t_{\alpha/2} s_e \sqrt{1 + \frac{1}{n} + \frac{(x - \bar{x})^2}{\left(\sum x^2\right) - \frac{\left(\sum x\right)^2}{n}}}$$

Notice that this equation is identical to Equation 14.17 except that we add 1 in the square root. Let's use Equation 14.18 to determine our 95% prediction interval if you study for 3.0 hours.

$$PI = \hat{y} \pm t_{\alpha/2} s_e \sqrt{1 + \frac{1}{n} + \frac{(x - \bar{x})^2}{\left(\sum x^2\right) - \frac{\left(\sum x\right)^2}{n}}}$$

$$PI = 82.7 \pm (2.776)(4.32) \sqrt{1 + \frac{1}{6} + \frac{(3 - 3.667)^2}{90 - \frac{(22)^2}{6}}}$$

$$PI = 82.7 \pm (11.99) \sqrt{1 + 0.1667 + \frac{(-0.667)^2}{90 - \frac{(484)}{6}}}$$

$$PI = 82.7 \pm (11.99)\sqrt{1.1667 + 0.0477}$$

$$PI = 82.7 \pm 13.21$$

We can also describe this prediction interval with the upper prediction limit (*UPL*) and lower prediction limit (*LPL*), as follows:

$$UPL = 82.7 + 13.21 = 95.9$$

$$LCL = 82.7 - 13.21 = 69.5$$

As you can see, our prediction interval is much wider (less precise) than our confidence interval from before. Recall from Chapter 7 that sample means have less variation than individual values from which the sample is drawn. Because our prediction interval is estimating a single value, the variation will be much greater than when we are estimating an average grade. If we want a more precise (narrower) estimate for our grade, a larger sample size would help achieve this.

Now that I have tortured you with all these nasty interval calculations, I'll show you how to achieve the same results using PHStat.

Using PHStat to Construct Confidence and Prediction Intervals

PHStat will construct a confidence interval and a prediction interval for our exam-grade example with the following steps. Mac users can go to the textbook's Web site for instructions on this procedure.

1. Open the Excel file **exam grades.xlsx** or enter the grade data shown in Figure 14.16B.
2. Go to **Add-Ins > PHStat > Regression > Simple Linear Regression**, as shown in Figure 14.16A.

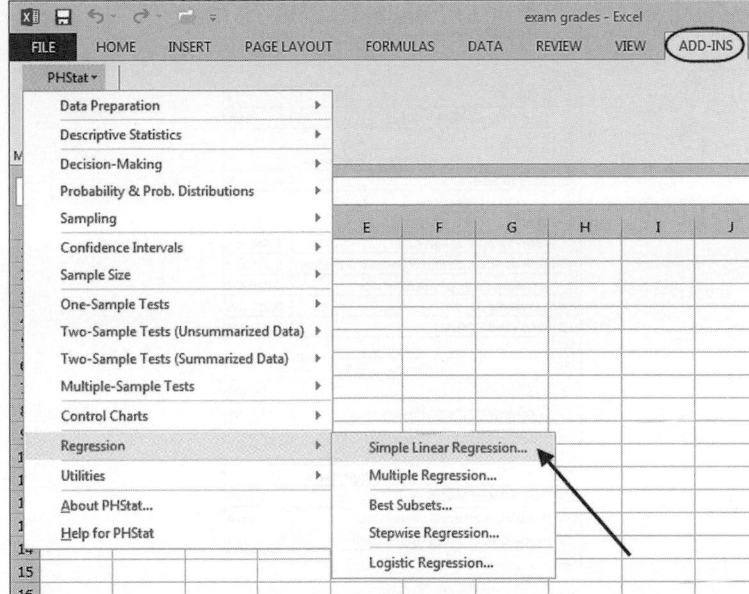

FIGURE 14.16A Using PHStat to Construct Confidence and Prediction Intervals (Steps 1 and 2)

3. Fill in the **Data** section of the **Simple Linear Regression** dialog box as shown in Figure 14.16B. Also fill in the **Output Options** that are circled in red. Click **OK**.

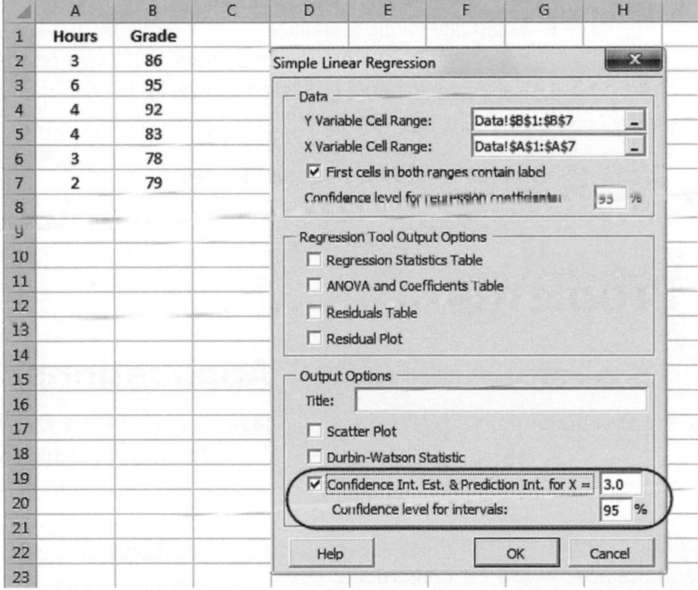

FIGURE 14.16B Using PHStat to Construct Confidence and Prediction Intervals (Step 3)

4. Figure 14.16C shows both the confidence and prediction intervals, which are circled in red. This figure can be found in the **CIEandPI** worksheet created by PHStat. These values match our results from the previous section.

FIGURE 14.16c Using PHStat to Construct Confidence and Prediction Intervals (Final Result)

	A	B
1	Confidence Interval Estimate	
2		
3	Data	
4	X Value	3
5	Confidence Level	95%
6		
7	Intermediate Calculations	
8	Sample Size	6
9	Degrees of Freedom	4
10	t Value	2.776445
11	XBar, Sample Mean of X	3.666667
12	Sum of Squared Differences from XBar	9.333333
13	Standard Error of the Estimate	4.316703
14	h Statistic	0.214286
15	Predicted Y (YHat)	82.71429
16		
17	For Average Y	
18	Interval Half Width	5.5480
19	Confidence Interval Lower Limit	77.1663
20	Confidence Interval Upper Limit	88.2623
21		
22	For Individual Response Y	
23	Interval Half Width	13.2069
24	Prediction Interval Lower Limit	69.5074
25	Prediction Interval Upper Limit	95.92121
26		

Let's see how well you have absorbed the material in this section. Try your hand at calculating confidence and prediction intervals in the next Your Turn problem.

YOUR TURN #6

1. Determine the 80% confidence interval for the average hiking time on the Wengen-Kleine Scheidegg trail for a 40-year-old hiker. Verify your results with PHStat.
2. Determine the 80% prediction interval for the hiking time on the Wengen-Kleine Scheidegg trail for Deb, who is a 40-year-old hiker. Verify your results with PHStat.

Answers can be found on ▶ **pages 705–706**

14.4 Section Problems

Basic Skills

14.22 Consider the following set of ordered pairs:

x	3	6	2	4	4
y	5	6	4	6	2

Assuming that the regression equation is $\hat{y} = 3.045 + 0.409x$ and the $SSE = 9.727$, construct a 95% confidence interval for $x = 5$.

14.23 Using the data in Problem 14.22, construct a 95% prediction interval for $x = 5$.

14.24 Consider the following set of ordered pairs:

x	6	0	4	3	3	1
y	5	2	5	4	2	2

Assuming that the regression equation is $\hat{y} = 1.679 + 0.584x$ and the $SSE = 3.547$, construct a 90% confidence interval for $x = 3$.

14.25 Using the data in Problem 14.24, construct a 90% prediction interval for $x = 3$.

Applications

14.26 As part of a research program for a new cholesterol drug, Johnson Pharmaceuticals would like to investigate the linear relationship between the ages and LDL (low-density lipoprotein) cholesterol levels of men. The following data set shows the ages and LDL cholesterol levels of seven randomly selected men:

Age	Cholesterol	Age	Cholesterol
23	140	42	160
37	177	31	144
26	155	41	210
32	195		

a. Construct a 95% confidence interval to estimate the average LDL cholesterol level of a 30-year-old man.
b. Verify your results with PHStat.

14.27 Use the data in Problem 14.26 to construct a 95% prediction interval to estimate the LDL cholesterol level of a 30-year-old man. Verify your results with PHStat.

14.28 Data in the Excel file **points per game.xlsx** show the number of wins eight teams had during a recent NFL season. Also in this file are the average points each team scored per game during the season.

a. Construct a 90% confidence interval to estimate the average number of wins for teams that scored an average of 21 points a game.

b. Verify your results with PHStat.

14.29 Use the data in Problem 14.28 to construct a 90% prediction interval estimating the number of wins a team that scores an average of 21 points a game will have. Verify your results using PHStat.

14.30 Suppose the Department of Energy would like to investigate the linear relationship between the cost of heating a home during the month of February in the Northeast and the home's square footage. Data for a random sample of 10 homes are as follows:

Heating Cost ($)	Square Footage	Heating Cost ($)	Square Footage
330	2,400	450	2,600
290	2,400	330	2,200
300	2,000	390	3,100
260	2,200	330	2,500
310	2,300	370	2,900

a. Construct a 90% confidence interval to estimate the average cost in February to heat a Northeast home that is 2,400 square feet.

b. Verify your results with PHStat.

14.31 Use the data in Problem 14.30 to construct a 90% prediction interval to estimate the cost in February to heat a Northeast home that is 2,400 square feet. Verify your results using PHStat.

14.5 Testing the Significance of the Slope of the Regression Equation

Remember, the slope, b_1, represents how much we expect exam grades to change (y) when we change the hours of study (x) by 1 hour.

The last set of procedures we'll examine in this chapter is to test the significance of the slope of the regression equation. Figure 14.17 shows exam-grade data for another group of students, along with the regression line that best fits the data. Notice that this regression line is horizontal. A horizontal line has a slope that is equal to zero, as the figure shows. I'd be very surprised if interpreting the meaning of a slope of zero didn't appear in your next exam (you can count on it in my classes), so let's take a minute to examine what it means in our example.

FIGURE 14.17
Interpreting a Slope Equal to Zero

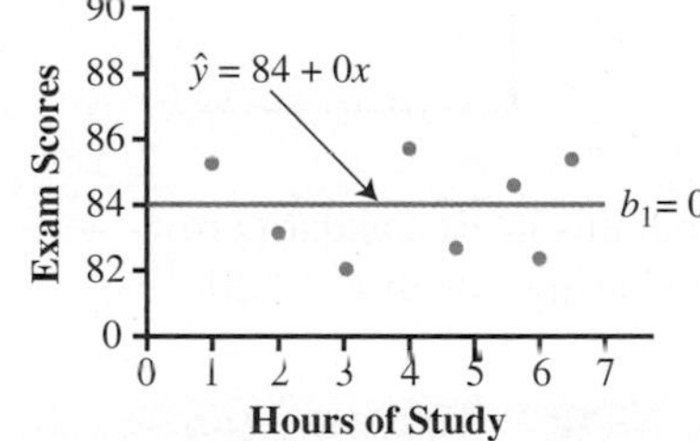

According to Figure 14.17, the regression equation is $\hat{y} = 84 + 0x$. This means that for any value of x, $\hat{y}$ will always equal 84. No matter how much a student studies, the predicted exam grade is 84 because the slope equals zero. Under these circumstances, we can conclude there is no linear relationship between the dependent and independent variables. Increasing your hours of study will not increase your exam grade. This would be very unsettling for me as a teacher.

In our original exam-grade example, the value $b_1 = 4.1786$ represents the regression slope for a random sample of six students that was collected from a larger student population. This population has a regression slope, β_1, that is unknown because we have not gathered data on every student who took the exam. We can, however, perform a hypothesis test to determine if the population regression slope, β_1, is significantly different from zero based on the sample regression slope, b_1. This test uses the following hypothesis statement:

When the slope of a population regression line β_1, equals zero, we conclude that there is no linear relationship between the dependent and independent variables.

H_0: $\beta_1 = 0$ (There is no linear relationship between hours of study and exam score)

H_1: $\beta_1 \neq 0$ (There is a linear relationship between hours of study and exam score)

If we have enough evidence from our sample to reject the null hypothesis, we can conclude that there is a significant linear relationship between the dependent and the independent variables.

The test statistic for this hypothesis test uses the *t*-distribution and is shown in Equation 14.19.

Formula 14.19 for the t-Test Statistic for the Regression Slope

$$t = \frac{b_1 - \beta_1}{s_b}$$

where

b_1 = The sample regression slope
β_1 = The population regression slope from the null hypothesis
s_b = The standard error of the slope

If you are anything like my students, I imagine that you are getting sick of all these standard errors, but bear with me one last time. The **standard error of the slope, s_b**, measures how consistent the slope of the regression equation, b_1, would be if several sets of samples from the population were selected and the regression equation were derived for each of them. Each sample selected from the population will most likely have a different value for the slope, b_1. The $64,000 question is how close will these slopes be to one another?

Figure 14.18 shows the effect of small and large standard errors of slopes. Each of the three regression lines shown in the two graphs represents a separate sample taken from the population. A smaller standard error of the slope increases the likelihood that we can establish a significant linear relationship between our two variables.

FIGURE 14.18
Comparing Small and Large Standard Errors of Slopes

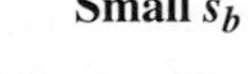

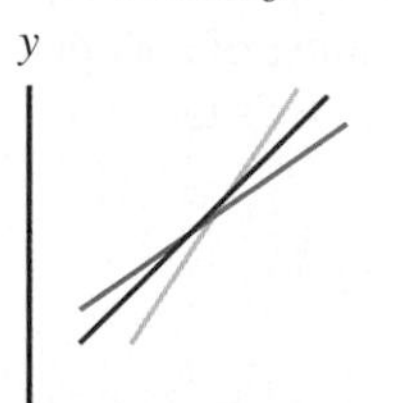

Large s_b

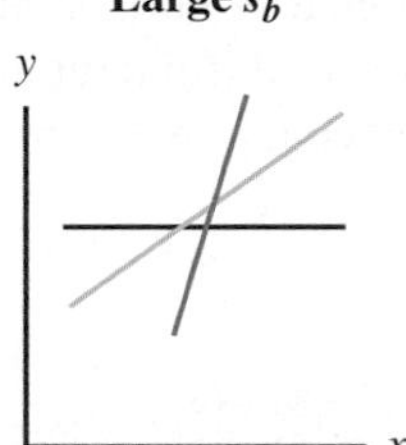

Enough talk about this latest standard error—let's calculate! The standard error of the slope, s_b, can be found using Equation 14.20.

Formula 14.20 for the Standard Error of a Slope

$$s_b = \frac{s_e}{\sqrt{\sum x^2 - n(\bar{x})^2}}$$

To calculate s_b, we need to use the following data from earlier in the chapter:

$$\bar{x} = 3.667 \quad \sum x^2 = 90 \quad n = 6 \quad s_e = 4.32$$

The calculations for the standard error of the slope are as follows:

$$s_b = \frac{s_e}{\sqrt{\sum x^2 - n(\bar{x})^2}} = \frac{4.32}{\sqrt{90 - (6)(3.667)^2}}$$

$$s_b = \frac{4.32}{\sqrt{90 - (6)(13.447)}} = \frac{4.32}{\sqrt{90 - 80.682}} = \frac{4.32}{3.053} = 1.42$$

Now we can finally calculate our test statistic for the hypothesis test, using the following data:

β_1 is set to zero because the null hypothesis claims $\beta_1 = 0$.

$$b_1 = 4.1786 \quad \beta_1 = 0$$

$$t = \frac{b_1 - \beta_1}{s_b} = \frac{4.1786 - 0}{1.42} = 2.94$$

To find our critical t-score, $t_{\alpha/2}$, for this hypothesis test, we look at Table 5 in Appendix A. This test also has $n - 2 = 6 - 2 = 4$ degrees of freedom. For $\alpha = 0.05$ and a two-tail test, the critical t-score is $t_{\alpha/2} = 2.776$. Because $t = 2.94$ is higher than $t_{\alpha/2} = 2.776$, we reject the null hypothesis and conclude that the population regression slope is not equal to zero. This result provides support that a linear relationship exists between the hours that students studied and their exam grades. Figure 14.19 illustrates this hypothesis test.

FIGURE 14.19 Testing the Significance of the Slope of the Regression Equation

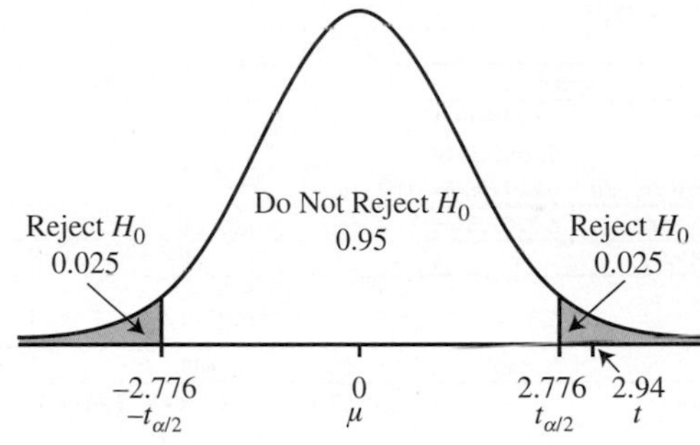

We can determine the p-value for this two-tail hypothesis test by using Excel's T.DIST.2T function which was introduced in Chapter 9.

$$p\text{-value} = \text{T.DIST.2T}(2.94, 4) = 0.0424$$

Because this value is less than $\alpha = 0.05$, we can reject the null hypothesis.

OK, I realize I'm pushing my luck here, but I have one final topic to close out this example. Recall that $b_1 = 4.1786$ is the slope for only the six students from our sample and that the actual population slope, β_1, is unknown. We can develop a 95% confidence interval for β_1 using our sample with Equation 14.21.

For this example, the population consists of all the students who took the exam.

Formula 14.21 for the Confidence Interval for the Population Slope

$$CI = b_1 \pm t_{\alpha/2} s_b$$

The critical t-score, $t_{\alpha/2}$, for this 95% confidence interval uses $n - 2 = 6 - 2 = 4$ degrees of freedom. Looking at Table 5 in Appendix A, we find that this results in $t_{\alpha/2} = 2.776$.

Recalling that $s_b = 1.41$, the confidence interval calculation using Equation 14.21 is shown as follows:

$$CI = b_1 \pm t_{\alpha/2} s_b = 4.1786 \pm (2.776)(1.42)$$

$$CI = 4.1786 \pm 3.942$$

We can describe this confidence interval with the upper confidence limit (UCL) and lower confidence limit (LCL) as follows:

If this confidence interval included zero, we would have some evidence that β_1 could be equal to zero, which would indicate that there may not be a linear relationship between our two variables. Fortunately, zero is not in our confidence interval, so be sure and study for that next exam!

$$UCL = 4.1786 + 3.942 = 8.121$$

$$LCL = 4.1786 - 3.942 = 0.237$$

Based on our sample of six students, we are 95% confident that the true population slope is between 0.237 and 8.121 exam points. In other words, we are 95% sure that every additional hour of study will increase your exam grade somewhere between 0.237 and 8.121 points.

Because this confidence interval does not include zero, we have supporting evidence to conclude that there is a linear relationship between the hours that students studied and their exam grades.

One last look at the regression output in Excel shown in Figure 14.20 shows that the standard error of the estimate (s_e) is 4.32. It is found under the "Regression Statistics" heading and is circled in red. In the very last row of the ANOVA table in this figure, we find the standard error of the slope (s_b). It equals 1.41 and appears under the "Standard Error" column in the red box. The calculated t-score, 2.96, is located under the "t Stat" column, whereas the 95% confidence interval for the slope (0.256, 8.102) can be seen under the "Lower 95%" and "Upper 95% columns, respectively. The slight discrepancies from our manual calculations are due to rounding differences.

FIGURE 14.20 The Excel Output for the Significance of the Slope of the Regression Equation

	A	B	C	D	E	F	G
1	SUMMARY OUTPUT						
2							
3	*Regression Statistics*						
4	Multiple R	0.828351021					
5	R Square	0.686165414					
6	Adjusted R Square	0.607706767					
7	Standard Error	4.316703438					
8	Observations	6					
9							
10	ANOVA						
11		*df*	*SS*	*MS*	*F*	*Significance F*	
12	Regression	1	162.9642857	162.9643	8.745568	0.041666379	
13	Residual	4	74.53571429	18.63393			
14	Total	5	237.5				
15							
16		*Coefficients*	*Standard Error*	*t Stat*	*P-value*	*Lower 95%*	*Upper 95%*
17	Intercept	70.17857143	5.472420416	12.82405	0.000213	54.98469655	85.3724463
18	Hours	4.178571429	1.412972876	2.957291	0.041666	0.255529805	8.101613053
19							

Also, Excel provides the p-value for the significance test of the slope, which equals 0.0417. Because we have a two-tail hypothesis test, this value represents the area to the right of $t = 2.96$ plus the area to the left of $t = -2.96$. We can determine the area to the right of $t = 2.96$ with Excel's T.DIST.RT function which is shown graphically in Figure 14.21:

$$=\text{T.DIST.RT}(2.96, 4) = 0.0208$$

FIGURE 14.21 The p-Value for the Exam-Grade Example

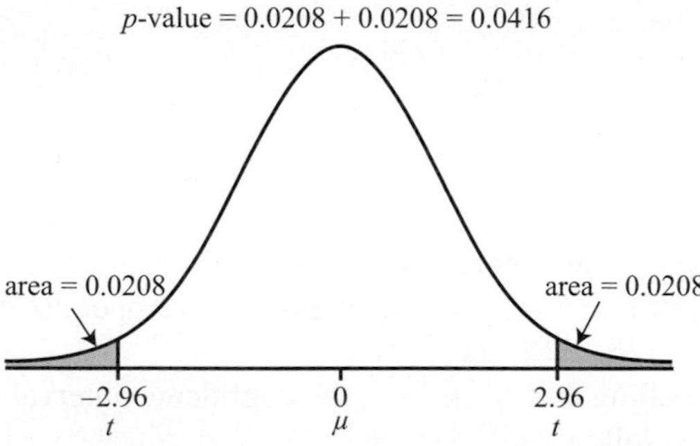

Because our p-value equals 0.0416 and is less than $\alpha = 0.05$, we can reject the null hypothesis.

Notice that the p-value for the F-test that we performed in Section 14.3 and the t-test are identical. This occurs because we have only one independent variable (hours of study) in our regression model. When we consider more than one independent variable in Chapter 15, this will no longer be the case.

My students sometimes tell me how easy it looks when they watch me solve a problem and then find themselves struggling when they're on their own. Avoid any surprises during your next exam: Practice what you just learned by solving the following Your Turn problem.

YOUR TURN #7

Using $\alpha = 0.10$, test the significance of the slope for the Swiss hiking data from Your Turn #1. Provide a 90% confidence interval for the population slope and interprets its meaning.

Answers can be found on ▶ page 706

14.5 Section Problems

Basic Skills

14.32 Consider the following set of ordered pairs:

x	3	6	2	4	4
y	5	8	4	6	5

Assuming that the regression equation is $\hat{y} = 1.886 + 0.977x$ and that the $SSE = 0.7955$, test to determine if the slope is not equal to zero using $\alpha = 0.05$.

14.33 Using the data in Problem 14.32, construct a 95% confidence interval for the slope.

14.34 Consider the following set of ordered pairs:

x	6	0	4	3	3	1
y	5	2	5	4	5	6

Assuming that the regression equation is $\hat{y} = 3.693 + 0.285x$ and that the $SSE = 7.650$, test to determine if the slope is not equal to zero using $\alpha = 0.10$.

14.35 Using the data in Problem 14.34, construct a 90% confidence interval for the slope.

Applications

14.36 The Human Resource Department at Neumann University would like to examine the linear relationship between a faculty member's performance rating (measured on a scale of 1–20) and his or her annual salary increase. The following table shows these data for eight randomly selected faculty members and can also be found in the Excel file **Neumann.xlsx**.

Rating	Increase ($)	Rating	Increase ($)
16	2,400	15	2,000
18	2,500	15	2,600
12	1,800	17	2,000
13	1,700	16	1,900

a. Construct a scatter plot for these data using Excel.
b. Using $\alpha = 0.05$, determine if the slope for the regression equation is statistically significant.

14.37 Using the data in Problem 14.36, construct a 95% confidence interval for the regression slope.

14.38 Wilmington University is concerned about the presence of grade inflation, which is defined as an increase in the average GPA of the institution's students over time without a comparable increase in academic standards. To investigate this phenomenon, the average GPA for the student body was recorded over the past 11 years. The data are as follows and can also be found in the Excel file **grade inflation.xlsx**.

Year	GPA	Year	GPA
1	3.08	7	3.08
2	2.87	8	3.00
3	2.96	9	3.19
4	2.85	10	3.15
5	2.99	11	3.15
6	3.04		

a. Construct a scatter plot for these data using Excel.
b. Using $\alpha = 0.05$, determine if the slope for the regression equation is statistically significant.
c. What conclusions can be drawn about grade inflation over this time period?

14.39 Using the data in Problem 14.38, construct a 95% confidence interval for the regression slope.

14.40 Suppose the Internet retailer Buy.com would like to investigate the linear relationship between the amount of time in minutes a purchaser spends on its Web site and the amount of money he or she spends on an order. The following table shows the data from a random sample of 12 customers and can also be found in the Excel file **Buy.com.xlsx.**

Time	Order Size ($)	Time	Order Size ($)
18	69	5	58
13	26	37	365
26	94	6	127
23	199	36	160
2	49	24	75
14	38	9	250

a. Construct a scatter plot for these data using Excel.
b. Using $\alpha = 0.05$, determine if the slope for the regression equation is statistically significant.
c. What conclusions can be drawn about a purchaser's time on the Web site and his or her order size?

14.41 Using the data in Problem 14.40, construct a 95% confidence interval for the regression slope.

14.6 Assumptions for Regression Analysis

In order for the results from regression analysis to be reliable, certain key assumptions need to hold true. As you can see from this chapter, Excel provides a very convenient way to construct a line that best fits the data and then describe that line with a linear equation. The convenience of Excel, however, can cause uninformed individuals to misuse it to generate a regression line without considering these assumptions which may lead to unreliable conclusions. (I am not referring to you, of course.) The purpose of this section is to discuss the following four assumptions that linear regression analysis is based upon:

1. The relationship between the independent variable and the dependent variable is linear.
2. The residuals exhibit no patterns across values for the independent variable.
3. The variation of the dependent variable is the same across all values for the independent variable, which is known as homoscedasticity.
4. The residuals follow the normal probability distribution.

Each of these assumptions will be explained using the following example. Suppose Canon, a manufacturer of business copiers, would like to perform a regression analysis to identify the linear relationship between the year-to-date (YTD) maintenance costs and the age of a particular brand of copy machine. This information would be useful to Canon when it's designing maintenance contracts for its customers. The Excel file **Canon copier 1.xlsx** contains the YTD maintenance costs along with the age of 30 Canon copiers up to four years old. The Excel file **Canon copier 2.xlsx** contains the data for the same 30 copiers along with 27 additional copiers up to seven years old. The scatter plots for both files are shown in Figure 14.22A and Figure 14.22B, respectively.

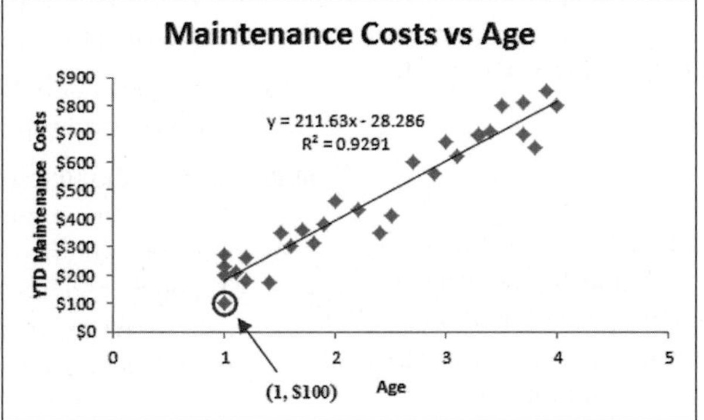

FIGURE 14.22A Scatter Plots for the Year-to-Date Maintenance Cost Example from Canon copier 1.xlsx Using Excel

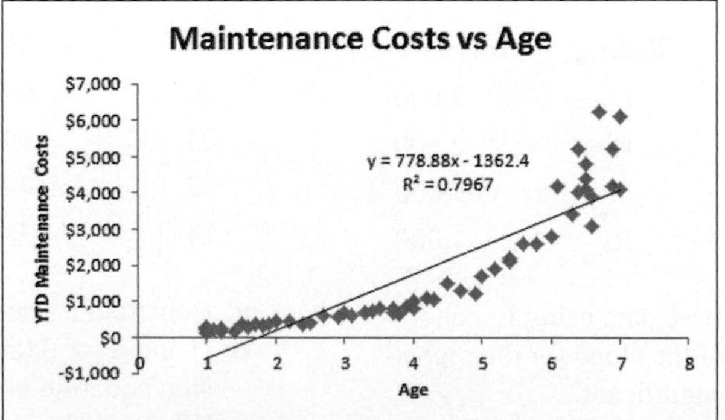

FIGURE 14.22B Scatter Plots for the Year-to-Date Maintenance Cost Example from Canon copier 2.xlsx Using Excel

Graph A appears to meet the linear assumption for a regression analysis. Graph B does not meet this requirement.

The first assumption of a regression analysis is that the relationship between the independent and dependent variables is linear. The data in Graph A, which plots the costs of copiers up to four years of age, does appear somewhat linear. The data straddle the red regression line, and the points above and below the line are evenly dispersed. The same can't be said for the scatter plot in Graph B, which also includes the older copiers. It appears that the maintenance costs increase at a faster rate for copiers that are six and seven years old when compared with newer copiers. Let's see how this nonlinear pattern affects our regression results.

The regression equations and the R^2 for both data sets are statistically significant at $\alpha = 0.05$. Let's calculate the predicted YTD maintenance costs for a one-year-old copier using both regression equations:

$$\text{Graph A: } \hat{y} = -28.286 + 211.63(1) = \$183.34$$
$$\text{Graph B: } \hat{y} = -1{,}362.4 + 778.88(1) = -\$583.52$$

The predicted YTD maintenance costs from Graph A seem reasonable, but the costs from Graph B certainly do not. Notice that all of the data points in Graph B are above the red regression line for one-year-old copiers. The same pattern holds true for most copiers that are six to seven years old. Even though these regression results are statistically significant, Graph B does a very poor job at predicting costs for copiers on either end of the scatter plot.

The next assumptions for regression analysis involve residuals, which I introduced earlier in the chapter with Equation 14.4. The residual for each ordered pair is the difference between the actual and the predicted values of the dependent variable using the regression equation. Let's calculate the residual for the first ordered pair in Graph A. I've circled this data point in Figure 14.22A, which shows that the YTD maintenance costs for a one-year-old copier are \$100. We just determined that the predicted YTD maintenance costs for this copier is \$183.34. Using Equation 14.4, the residual for this ordered pair is as follows:

This residual is negative because the predicted costs are higher than the actual costs. Residuals will be positive when the predicted costs are lower than the actual.

$$e_i = y_i - \hat{y}_i = \$100 - \$183.34 = -\$83.34$$

Excel will generate a residual plot for each ordered pair in the data set. I'll demonstrate this procedure using the data from Graph A with the following steps:

1. Open the Excel file **Canon copier 1.xlsx**.
2. Go to **Data > Data Analysis**, as shown earlier in Figure 14.9A.
3. Select **Regression** from **Data Analysis** and click **OK**.
4. Fill in the **Regression** dialog box as shown in Figure 14.23 and click **OK**.

FIGURE 14.23
Residual Plots in the Regression Dialog Box Using Excel

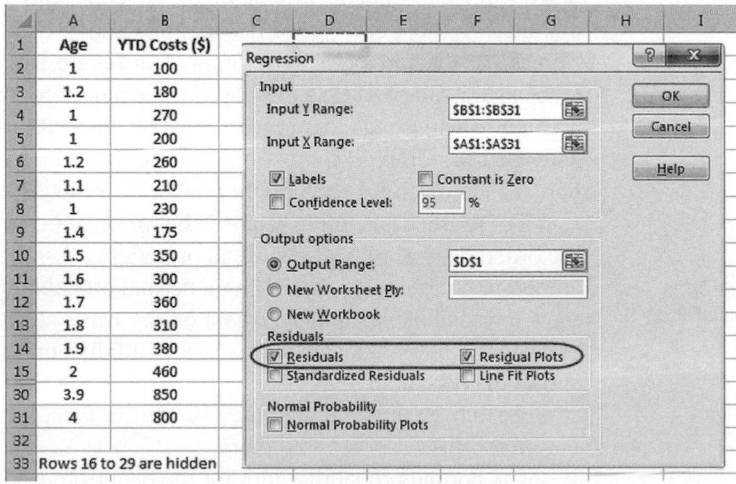

Graph A in Figure 14.24 shows us the residual plot for the data set with newer copiers. Repeat the previous steps with the second data set that includes older copiers to generate Graph B in this figure.

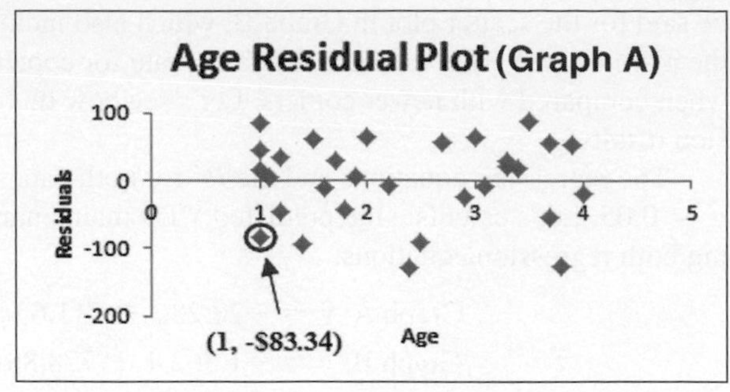

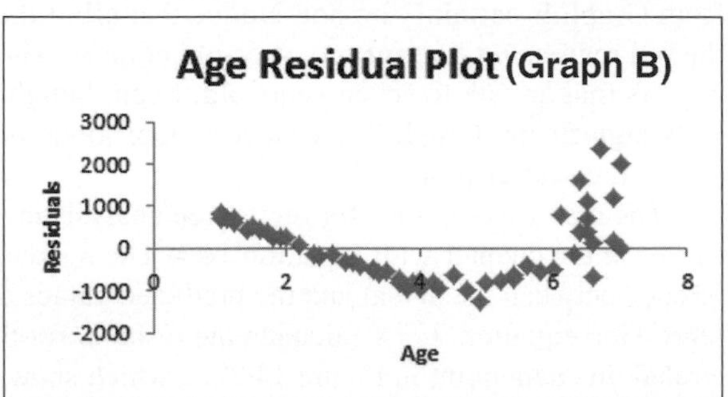

FIGURE 14.24 Residual Plots for the Year-to-Date Maintenance Cost Example Using Excel

I've circled the residual for the first ordered pair that we just calculated to show you how this plot is generated. Notice that this residual matches what we just calculated ($-\$83.35$). All of the data points below the horizontal line represent negative residuals, whereas the points above the line are positive residuals.

The second assumption of a regression analysis is that the residuals exhibit no patterns across values for the independent (age) variable. Graph A in Figure 14.24 appears to meet this requirement, with the data points evenly dispersed around the horizontal axis. We can't say the same for Graph B: Notice that the residuals in this graph are consistently positive for copiers one to two years old, negative for copiers two to six years old, and positive again for copiers six to seven years old. Not a pretty sight for a residual plot!

Homoscedasticity is a regression assumption that states that the variation of the dependent variable is the same across all values for the independent variable.

The third assumption a regression analysis depends on is known as **homoscedasticity**, which states that the variation of the dependent variable (costs) is the same across all values for the independent variable (age). We can again rely on the residual plot to see if this condition is satisfied. A good residual plot shows data points having roughly the same variation across the horizontal axis. Graph A in Figure 14.24 appears to meet this requirement. Once again, Graph B fails the test. For the newer copiers, the residuals are very close to one another, whereas the older copiers have residuals that are more dispersed. This pattern indicates that the Graph B regression equation will more accurately predict the costs for newer copiers and much less accurately predict the costs for older copiers.

A **normal probability plot** is used to verify if data follows the normal probability distribution by graphing the data on the *y*-axis and the *z*-scores for the data on the *x*-axis.

The fourth assumption required by linear regression analysis is that the residuals from the ordered pairs follow the normal probability distribution. We can investigate if this assumption holds true by inspecting a **normal probability plot**, which graphs the residuals on the *y*-axis and the residuals' *z*-score on the *x*-axis. If the residuals follow the normal probability distribution, the data in this plot will fall approximately on a straight line. Figure 14.25 shows the normal probability plot for the Cannon Copier 1 data, which appears to follow a straight line. Based on this figure, we can confirm that the residuals follow a normal distribution for this set of ordered pairs.

The normal probability plot for the data from Cannon Copier 2 is not shown here but also has a straight line pattern. See the textbook's Web site for instructions on how to construct a normal probability plot. Finally, if you inspect Figure 14.23, you will see an option in Excel's regression procedure to generate a normal probability plot. However, this option, for some strange reason, generates a plot for the dependent variable rather than the residuals which tells us nothing about this fourth regression assumption.

Hopefully, you now understand the risk related to performing a regression analysis without examining the assumptions on which the method depends. Even though both regression

FIGURE 14.25
Normal Probability Plot

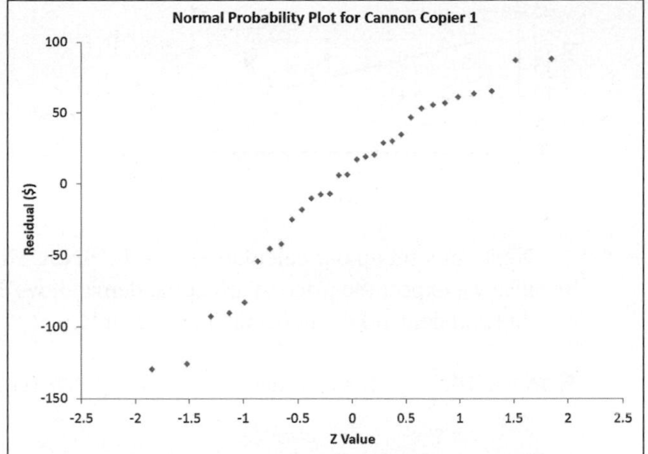

Always examine both the scatter and residual plots for violations of the assumptions on which a regression analysis depends.

equations that we examined were statistically significant, the data set from Graph B violated all three assumptions. As a result, the predicted maintenance costs from this regression equation proved to be very unreliable. An important rule to follow when performing a regression analysis is always to examine both the scatter and residual plots for violations of these assumptions.

14.7 A Simple Regression Example with a Negative Correlation

Both of the examples from the previous sections involved a positive linear relationship between the dependent and independent variables. This section will provide a nice review of the material we have covered so far, but this time, there will be a negative linear relationship between the variables. Let's now look at the following example and see what happens.

Before Circuit City declared bankruptcy in 2010, a product manager wanted to investigate the linear relationship between the price of a new HP DeskJet printer and the demand for it. Every two weeks the price was increased by $5, and the demand at a particular store was recorded.

Table 14.6 shows the results. These data can also be found in the Excel file **printer demand.xlsx**. (Because I am an electronic gadget freak, I mourned for days after finding out Circuit City was going out of business. My wife finally gave me a worried look and asked if I was all right. I wailed, not unlike Brandi in the movie *Observe and Report*, "Physically yes, but psychologically? No!" She looked at me with concern, as she often does.)

TABLE 14.6 | PRICE OF AND DEMAND DATA FOR AN HP PRINTER

PRICE ($)	DEMAND
70	18
75	23
80	10
85	16
90	17
95	15
100	5

Figure 14.26 shows the scatter plot for the data. As you would expect, there appears to be a general downward trend in the demand for the printer as its price increases, which indicates there's a negative linear relationship between the two variables.

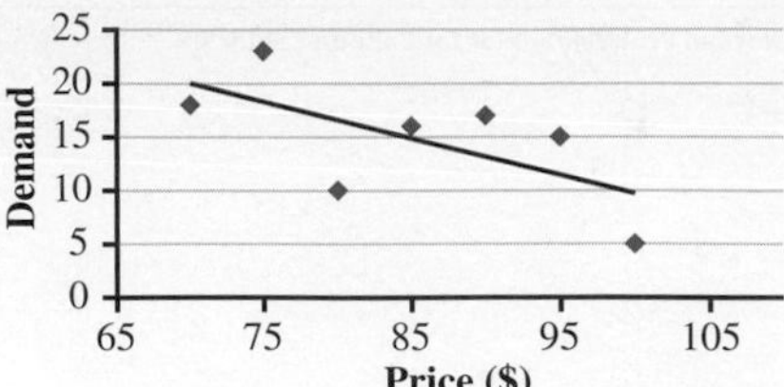

FIGURE 14.26
The Scatter Plot for the HP Printer Example

Next, let's set up our calculations for the SNSCSR values from the data in Table 14.7. Because we expect the price to affect the demand, we'll make the price the independent (x) variable and demand the dependent (y) variable.

TABLE 14.7 | THE SNSCSR VALUES FOR THE PRINTER EXAMPLE

PRICE X	DEMAND Y	XY	X^2	Y^2
70	18	1,260	4,900	324
75	23	1,725	5,625	529
80	10	800	6,400	100
85	16	1,360	7,225	256
90	17	1,530	8,100	289
95	15	1,425	9,025	225
100	5	500	10,000	25
$\sum x = 595$	$\sum y = 104$	$\sum xy = 8,600$	$\sum x^2 = 51,275$	$\sum y^2 = 1,748$

The Sample Correlation Coefficient

Using the SNSCSR numbers from Table 14.7 along with $n = 7$, we can calculate the sample correlation coefficient using Equation 14.1:

$$r = \frac{n\sum xy - (\sum x)(\sum y)}{\sqrt{[n\sum x^2 - (\sum x)^2][n\sum y^2 - (\sum y)^2]}}$$

$$r = \frac{(7)(8{,}600) - (595)(104)}{\sqrt{[(7)(51{,}275) - (595)^2][(7)(1{,}748) - (104)^2]}}$$

$$r = \frac{-1{,}680}{\sqrt{[4{,}900][1{,}420]}} = \frac{-1{,}680}{\sqrt{6{,}958{,}000}} = \frac{-1{,}680}{2{,}637.80} = -0.637$$

Both final terms in the denominator under the square root sign (4,900 and 1,420) must always be positive. If either value is negative, stop and find your mistake. Trying to take the square root of a negative number causes your calculator to freak out!

Notice that the sample correlation coefficient, r, is negative due to the fact that the price of and the demand for the printer tend to move in opposite directions when we look at our sample data. As one goes up, the other tends to go down.

We'll use the following hypothesis statement to test the significance of the population correlation coefficient. Let's set $\alpha = 0.10$ for this example:

$$H_0: \rho = 0$$
$$H_1: \rho \neq 0$$

The test statistic for this hypothesis test is found using Equation 14.2:

$$t = \frac{r}{\sqrt{\frac{1 - r^2}{n - 2}}} = \frac{-0.637}{\sqrt{\frac{1 - (-0.637)^2}{7 - 2}}} = \frac{-0.637}{\sqrt{\frac{1 - 0.4058}{5}}} = -1.85$$

Remember, when you square −0.637, the result is a positive 0.4058.

Using Table 5 in Appendix A with $df = n - 2 = 7 - 2 = 5$ and $\alpha = 0.10$ for a two-tail test, we find that the critical t-score is $t_{\alpha/2} = 2.015$. Because $|t| = 1.85$ and is less than

$|t_{\alpha/2}| = 2.015$, we do not reject the null hypothesis and cannot conclude that the population correlation coefficient is not equal to zero. Figure 14.27 illustrates the results of this hypothesis test. According to our sample, we do not have enough evidence to conclude that we have a linear relationship between the price of and the demand for this HP printer. One reason for this result may be the fact that we have only seven data points in this regression analysis. Performing this analysis again with a larger set of data could very well provide the statistically significant linear relationship that we would expect to see.

FIGURE 14.27 Testing the Significance of the Correlation Coefficient (HP Printer Example)

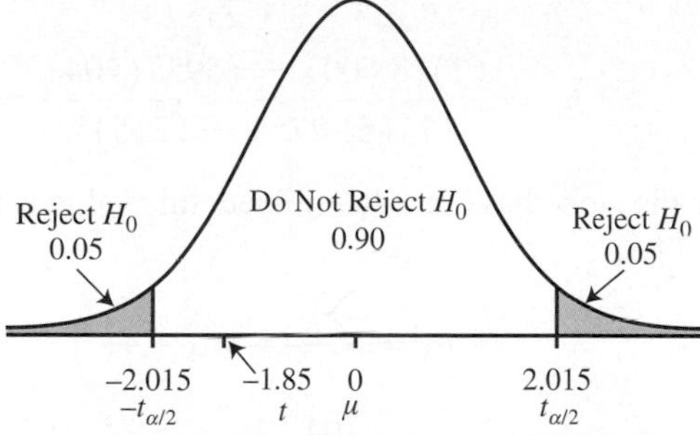

Even though we have discovered that there is no linear relationship between price and demand for this printer, we'll continue with this example in the following sections for demonstration purposes. Try your hand at the following Your Turn problem to test your newfound skills.

YOUR TURN #8

At the time of this writing, I have been in a long-term relationship of nearly 40 years that is just not working anymore. I have tried countless times to end it but to no avail. Every April for as long as I can remember, I have high hopes that things will be better this year. By May, disappointment starts to settle in. By July, I am completely depressed. By September, I don't even care anymore.

Then comes the long off-season when I forget the pain and disappointment of the past year, and then the cycle repeats itself once again. I am of course talking about my love/hate relationship with those basement-dwelling Pittsburgh Pirates, a baseball team that has not had a winning season since 1992. I long for the glory days when, as a young boy, I watched Roberto Clemente throw out runners at home plate from deep in the outfield and Willie Stargell hit massive upper-deck home runs in Forbes Field. I guess I'm just an eternal optimist or a glutton for punishment as I endure one losing season after another with no end in sight. There must be something seriously wrong with me.

If an effort to wake up from this eternal nightmare, the Pittsburgh Pirates front office is investigating the linear relationship between the team's wins and the average number of runs the pitchers give up per game (ERA, or earned run average) during the season. The following table shows these data for eight teams for a recent Major League Baseball season. Notice that Pittsburgh has the fewest wins and gave up the most runs per game. Once again, I rest my case. These data can also be found in the Excel file **earned run average.xlsx**.

Team	Wins	ERA
Pittsburgh	57	5.0
Arizona	65	4.8
Washington	69	4.1
Los Angeles	80	4.0
Philadelphia	97	3.7
Chicago	75	4.2
Miami	80	4.1
Oakland	81	3.6

Calculate the correlation coefficient for the two variables in the table and test its significance using $\alpha = 0.01$.

Answers can be found on ▶ **pages 706–707**

Calculating the Slope and *y*-Intercept Manually

Next, I am going to calculate the slope and *y*-intercept manually for the HP printer example using the SNSCSR values calculated in the previous section with $n = 7$. The slope is found using Equation 14.7:

$$\sum x = 595 \quad \sum y = 104 \quad \sum xy = 8{,}600 \quad \sum x^2 = 51{,}275 \quad \sum y^2 = 1{,}748$$

$$b_1 = \frac{n\sum xy - (\sum x)(\sum y)}{n\sum x^2 - (\sum x)^2}$$

$$b_1 = \frac{(7)(8{,}600) - (595)(104)}{(7)(51{,}275) - (595)^2} = \frac{-1{,}680}{4{,}900} = -0.3429$$

Once the slope has been determined, this value is used to calculate the *y*-intercept with Equation 14.8:

Remember, subtracting a negative number is the same as adding a positive number, as seen in the *y*-intercept equation.

$$b_0 = \frac{\sum y}{n} - b_1\left(\frac{\sum x}{n}\right)$$

$$b_0 = \frac{104}{7} - (-0.3429)\left(\frac{595}{7}\right)$$

$$b_0 = 14.857 - (-0.3429)(85) = 44.00$$

The regression equation for the HP printer data is as follows:

$$\hat{y} = 44 - 0.3429x$$

Because $b_1 = -0.3429$, or is negative, we can conclude that every one-dollar increase in the price will decrease the demand by an average of 0.3429 printers. (Conversely, decreasing the price will result in an increase in the printers' demand.) This result is consistent with the negative correlation coefficient.

What is the predicted demand for the printer when its price is \$87? By setting $x = 87$ in the regression equation, we have the following:

$$\hat{y} = 44 - 0.3429(87)$$

$$\hat{y} = 44 - 29.83 = 14.17 \approx 14 \text{ printers}$$

The predicted demand for an \$87 price is 14 printers over the two-week period.

Now I'm going to turn it over to you to lend a hand to those poor Pittsburgh Pirates.

YOUR TURN #9

Determine the regression equation for the Major League Baseball example from Your Turn #8. Use your results to predict the number of wins for the Pittsburgh Pirates if their pitchers give up an average of 4.2 runs per game next year.

Answers can be found on ▶ **page 707**

Partitioning the Sum of Squares for a Negative Correlation

Our next step in the HP printer example is to partition the sum of squares using our SNSCSR values starting with the *SST*, which I find using Equation 14.10:

$$\sum y = 104 \quad \sum y^2 = 1{,}748 \quad n = 7$$

$$SST = \sum y^2 - \frac{(\sum y)^2}{n}$$

$$SST = 1{,}748 - \frac{(104)^2}{7} = 202.857$$

Now we calculate the *SSE* using Equation 14.12:

$$b_0 = 44 \quad b_1 = -0.3429 \quad \sum xy = 8{,}600$$
$$SSE = \sum y^2 - b_0 \sum y - b_1 \sum xy$$
$$SSE = (1{,}748) - (44)(104) - (-0.3429)(8{,}600)$$
$$SSE = 1{,}748 - 4{,}576 + 2{,}948.94 = 120.94$$

Lastly, we calculate the *SSR* using Equation 14.11:

$$SST = SSR + SSE$$
$$SSR = SST - SSE$$
$$SSR = 202.857 - 120.94 = 81.917$$

In summary, we have partitioned our *SST* in the following way:

$$SSR = 81.917$$
$$SSE = 120.94$$
$$SST = 202.857$$

OK, back to our (my) favorite baseball team.

YOUR TURN #10

Partition the *SST* for the Major League Baseball example from Your Turn #8 into the *SSR* and the *SSE*.

Answer can be found on ▶ **page 707**

Calculating the Sample Coefficient of Determination

To calculate the sample coefficient of determination for our HP printer example, we need the following data and Equation 14.14:

$$SSR = 81.917 \qquad SST = 202.857$$

$$R^2 = \frac{SSR}{SST} = \frac{81.917}{202.857} = 0.404$$

We have concluded that 40.4% of the total variation in demand for the printer can be explained by the price. The next question we tackle is to see if this percentage is statistically significant.

Let's check if the 40.4% total variation is statistically significant using $\alpha = 0.10$:

$$H_0: \rho^2 = 0$$
$$H_1: \rho^2 > 0$$

Using the necessary data and Equation 14.15, the calculated *F*-score for this test is as follows:

$$SSR = 81.917 \qquad SSE = 120.94$$

$$F = \frac{SSR}{\left(\frac{SSE}{n-2}\right)} = \frac{81.917}{\left(\frac{120.94}{7-2}\right)} = \frac{81.917}{24.19} = 3.39$$

The degrees of freedom for the critical *F*-score are as follows:

$$D_1 = 1$$
$$D_2 = n - 2 = 7 - 2 = 5$$

Using $\alpha = 0.10$, the critical *F*-score in Table 6 in Appendix A is $F_\alpha = 4.060$. Because $F = 3.39$ is lower than $F_\alpha = 4.060$, we fail to reject H_0 and find that there is not enough evidence to conclude the coefficient of determination is greater than zero. There does not appear to be support that a linear relationship exists between the price of the HP printer and its demand. Figure 14.28 illustrates the results of this hypothesis test.

FIGURE 14.28
Testing the Significance of the Coefficient of Determination (HP Printer Example)

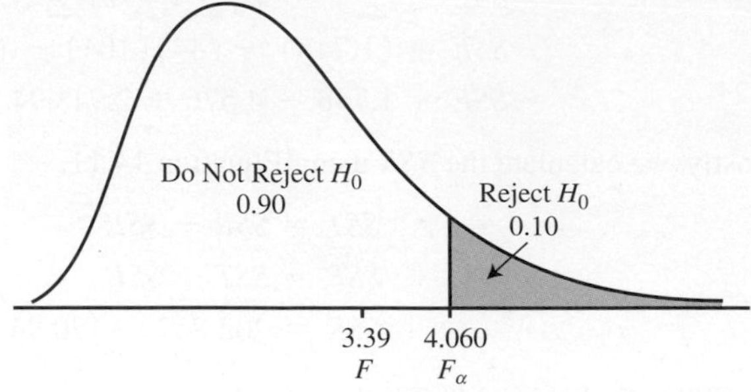

We'll move on to the confidence interval for the regression line after a brief commercial break. (In case you didn't catch on, this is your cue to solve the following Your Turn problem.)

YOUR TURN #11

Calculate the coefficient of determination for the Major League Baseball example from Your Turn #8 and test its significance using $\alpha = 0.01$.

Answers can be found on ▶ **page 707**

Calculating Confidence and Prediction Intervals for a Negative Correlation

Remember, 15.5 printers represent only the predicted demand using our sample of seven price levels. The demand for the "printer population" at $83 is unknown and will be estimated with our soon-to-be-found confidence interval. Patience!

Suppose we are interested in calculating a 90% confidence interval for the demand of the HP printer when the price is $83. We first calculate the demand for the $83 price using our regression equation:

$$\hat{y} = 44 - 0.3429x$$

$$\hat{y} = 44 - 0.3429(83) = 15.5 \text{ printers}$$

Next we need to calculate the standard error of the estimate, s_e, using the following data along with Equation 14.16:

$$SSE = 120.94 \qquad n = 7$$

$$s_e = \sqrt{\frac{SSE}{n-2}} = \sqrt{\frac{120.94}{7-2}} = \sqrt{24.188} = 4.92$$

We also need the average price from our sample, using the SNSCSR value $\sum x = 595$.

$$\bar{x} = \frac{\sum x}{n} = \frac{595}{7} = \$85$$

To find our critical t-score, $t_{\alpha/2}$, for a 90% confidence interval, we look at Table 5 in Appendix A. This procedure has $n - 2 = 7 - 2 = 5$ degrees of freedom, so for a two-tail and $\alpha = 0.10$, $t_{\alpha/2} = 2.015$.

We can finally determine our 90% confidence interval (thanks for your patience) for the demand of the printer when the price is $83 using the previous results, our SNSCSR value $\sum x^2 = 51{,}275$, and Equation 14.17:

$$CI = \hat{y} \pm t_{\alpha/2}s_e\sqrt{\frac{1}{n} + \frac{(x-\bar{x})^2}{\left(\sum x^2\right) - \frac{\left(\sum x\right)^2}{n}}}$$

$$CI = 15.5 \pm (2.015)(4.92)\sqrt{\frac{1}{7} + \frac{(83 - 85)^2}{51{,}275 - \frac{(595)^2}{7}}}$$

$$CI = 15.5 \pm (9.91)\sqrt{0.1429 + \frac{(-2)^2}{51{,}275 - \frac{(354{,}025)}{7}}}$$

$$CI = 15.5 \pm (9.91)\sqrt{0.1429 + 0.0057}$$

$$CI = 15.5 \pm 3.8$$

$$UCL = 15.5 + 3.8 = 19.3$$

$$LCL = 15.5 - 3.8 = 11.7$$

We are 90% confident that the average weekly demand for the printer when its price is $83 is between 12 and 19 printers.

The 90% prediction interval for printer demand with an $83 price is found using Equation 14.18:

$$PI = \hat{y} \pm t_{\alpha/2}s_e\sqrt{1 + \frac{1}{n} + \frac{(x - \bar{x})^2}{\left(\sum x^2\right) - \frac{\left(\sum x\right)^2}{n}}}$$

$$PI = 15.5 \pm (2.015)(4.92)\sqrt{1 + \frac{1}{7} + \frac{(83 - 85)^2}{51{,}275 - \frac{(595)^2}{7}}}$$

$$PI = 15.5 \pm (9.91)\sqrt{1 + 0.1429 + \frac{(-2)^2}{51{,}275 - \frac{(354{,}025)}{7}}}$$

$$PI = 15.5 \pm (9.91)\sqrt{1.1429 + 0.0057}$$

$$PI = 15.5 \pm 10.6$$

$$UPL = 15.5 + 10.6 = 26.1$$

$$LPL = 15.5 - 10.6 = 4.9$$

We have learned that if we set our HP printer price to $83, we are 90% confident that the demand for it during the two-week period will be between 5 and 26 printers.

Enough of watching me do all the work. Here's your chance to show off your skills with this next Your Turn problem.

YOUR TURN #12

Using the data from Your Turn #8, determine the 90% confidence and prediction intervals for the number of games that a Major League Baseball team will win if it gives up 4.7 runs per game during the year.

Answer can be found on ▶ **page 708**

Testing the Significance of the Regression of a Slope with a Negative Correlation

Since your instructor could very well ask you to test the significance of the regression slope in your next exam (I certainly would), let's go through this procedure for our HP printer example using $\alpha = 0.10$. The hypothesis statement for this test is as follows:

Remember, the slope for our HP printer sample is $b_1 = -0.3429$. If the true population slope, β_1, were actually equal to zero, we would conclude that there is no linear relationship between the price of and the demand for the printer.

H_0: $\beta_1 = 0$ (There is no linear relationship between price and demand)

H_1: $\beta_1 \neq 0$ (There is a linear relationship between price and demand)

To kick this test off, we first need to calculate the standard error of the slope, s_b, using Equation 14.20 along with the following values:

$$\bar{x} = \$85 \quad \sum x^2 = 51{,}275 \quad n = 7 \quad s_e = 4.92$$

$$s_b = \frac{s_e}{\sqrt{\sum x^2 - n(\bar{x})^2}} = \frac{4.92}{\sqrt{51{,}275 - (7)(85)^2}} = 0.186$$

Remember, β_1 is set to zero because the null hypothesis claims that $\beta_1 = 0$.

Now we can calculate our test statistic for the hypothesis test using Equation 14.19 and the following data:

$$b_1 = -0.3429 \quad \beta_1 = 0$$

$$t = \frac{b_1 - \beta_1}{s_b} = \frac{-0.3429 - 0}{0.186} = -1.84$$

Using Table 5 in Appendix A with $df = n - 2 = 7 - 2 = 5$ and $\alpha = 0.10$ for a two-tail test, the critical t-score is found to be $t_{\alpha/2} = 2.015$. Because $|t| = 1.84$ and is less than $|t_{\alpha/2}| = 2.015$, we fail to reject the null hypothesis and cannot conclude that the population regression slope is not equal to zero. There does not appear to be a significant linear relationship between the price of and the demand for the HP printer. Figure 14.29 illustrates this hypothesis test.

FIGURE 14.29
Testing the Significance of the Regression of the Slope (HP Printer Example)

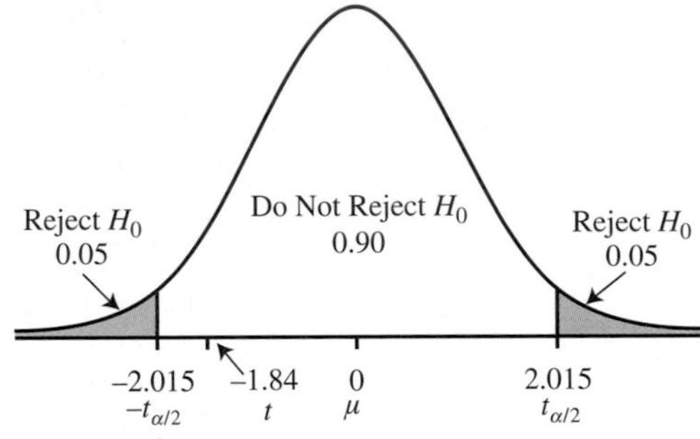

Finally, let's use a 90% confidence interval around the sample slope of $b_1 = -0.3429$ to estimate the true population slope. Again, our critical t-score for a 90% confidence interval and 5 degrees of freedom is $t_{\alpha/2} = 2.015$. We calculate the confidence interval using Equation 14.21:

$$CI = b_1 \pm t_{\alpha/2}s_b = -0.3429 \pm (2.015)(0.186)$$
$$CI = b_1 \pm t_{\alpha/2}s_b = -0.3429 \pm 0.3748$$
$$UCL = -0.3429 + 0.3748 = 0.0319$$
$$LCL = -0.3429 - 0.3748 = -0.7177$$

Because this confidence interval does include zero, we have supporting evidence to conclude that there is no linear relationship between the price of and the demand for this HP printer.

Based on our sample of prices and the demand for the printer, we are 90% confident that the true population slope is between −0.7177 and 0.0319. In other words, we are 90% sure that every additional dollar in the price could affect the demand by increasing it by 0.0319 printers or decreasing it by 0.7177 printers or anything in between.

I know that you're tired (come to think of it, so am I), but let's solve one more problem for my Pirates. They really need your help.

YOUR TURN #13

Using $\alpha = 0.01$, test the significance of the slope for the Major League Baseball example from Your Turn #8. Provide a 99% confidence interval for the population slope.

Answers can be found on ▶ **page 708**

14.7 Section Problems

Basic Skills

14.42 Consider the following set of ordered pairs:

x	5	2	3	3	7	5
y	4	8	6	5	1	6

a. Calculate the correlation coefficient.
b. Using $\alpha = 0.05$, perform a hypothesis test to determine if the population correlation coefficient is less than zero.

14.43 Answer the following questions using the data from Problem 14.42:

a. Calculate the slope and the y-intercept for the regression equation.
b. Calculate the *SST*.
c. Partition the *SST* into the *SSR* and the *SSE*.

14.44 Answer the following questions using the data from Problem 14.42:

a. Calculate the coefficient of determination.
b. Using $\alpha = 0.05$, test the significance of the population coefficient of determination.

14.45 Answer the following questions using the data from Problem 14.42:

a. Construct a 95% confidence interval for an average value of y given that $x = 4$.
b. Construct a 95% prediction interval for y given that $x = 4$.

14.46 Answer the following questions using the data from Problem 14.42:

a. Using $\alpha = 0.05$, test for the significance of the regression slope.
b. Construct a 95% confidence interval for the population slope.

Applications

14.47 Suppose the Environmental Protection Agency (EPA) would like to investigate the linear relationship between the engine size of sedans and the miles per gallon (MPG) they get. Data from the Excel file **engine size.xlsx** show the engine size in cubic liters and rated miles per gallon for a selection of sedans.

a. Construct a scatter plot for these data.
b. Calculate the slope and the y-intercept for the regression equation.
c. Provide an interpretation for the value of the slope.
d. Predict the MPG for a sedan with a 3.0-liter engine.
e. Calculate the *SST*.
f. Partition the *SST* into the *SSR* and the *SSE*.

14.48 Answer the following questions using the data from Problem 14.47:

a. Calculate the coefficient of determination.
b. Using $\alpha = 0.05$, test the significance of the population coefficient of determination.
c. Construct a 95% confidence interval for the average MPG of a 2.5-cubic liter engine.
d. Construct a 95% prediction interval for the MPG of a 2.5-cubic liter engine.

14.49 Answer the following questions using the data from Problem 14.47:

a. Using $\alpha = 0.05$, test for the significance of the regression slope.
b. Construct a 95% confidence interval for the population slope.
c. What conclusions about engine size and MPG can be drawn from these results?

14.50 Comcast's customer service department asks its customers to rate their over-the-phone service on a scale of 1–20 immediately after their service has been completed. The company then matches each customer's rating with the number of minutes the person waited on hold. The following table shows the ratings and number of minutes on hold for 10 randomly selected customers. These data can also be found in the Excel file **hold.xlsx**.

Minutes	Rating	Minutes	Rating
4	15	2	16
8	13	10	14
0	18	3	20
5	10	8	14
6	14	4	13

a. Construct a scatter plot for these data.
b. Calculate the slope and the y-intercept for the regression equation.
c. Provide an interpretation for the value of the slope.
d. Calculate the *SST*.
e. Partition the *SST* into the *SSR* and *SSE*.

14.51 Answer the following questions using the data from Problem 14.50:

a. Calculate the coefficient of determination.
b. Using $\alpha = 0.05$, test the significance of the population coefficient of determination.
c. Construct a 90% confidence interval for the average customer rating from customers who are on hold for 5 minutes.
d. Construct a 90% prediction interval for the customer rating from a customer who is on hold for 5 minutes.

14.52 Answer the following questions using the data from Problem 14.50:

a. Using $\alpha = 0.05$, test for the significance of the regression slope.
b. Construct a 95% confidence interval for the population slope.
c. What conclusions about customer rating and time on hold can be drawn from these results?

14.53 Suppose *Consumer Reports* would like to investigate the linear relationship between the battery life, in hours, and the screen size, in diagonal inches, of a laptop computer. The following table shows a random sample of eight laptops and the battery life and corresponding screen size of each. These data can also be found in the Excel file **battery life.xlsx**.

Battery Life	Screen Size	Battery Life	Screen Size
3.6	15.6	3.1	14.0
3.7	17.3	4.1	13.3
4.2	14.5	4.5	11.6
4.0	12.1	3.9	13.1

a. Construct a scatter plot for these data.
b. Calculate the slope and the y-intercept for the regression equation.
c. Provide an interpretation for the value of the slope.
d. Predict the battery life for a laptop with a 14.5-in. screen size.
e. Calculate the SST.
f. Partition the SST into the SSR and SSE.

14.54 Answer the following questions using the data from Problem 14.53:

a. Calculate the coefficient of determination.
b. Using $\alpha = 0.05$, test the significance of the population coefficient of determination.
c. Construct a 95% confidence interval for the average battery life for a laptop with a 14-in. screen.
d. Construct a 95% prediction interval for the battery life for a laptop with a 14-in. screen.

14.55 Answer the following questions using the data from Problem 14.53:

a. Using $\alpha = 0.05$, test the significance of the regression slope.
b. Construct a 95% confidence interval for the population slope.
c. What conclusions about battery life and screen size can be drawn from these results?

14.8 Some Final (but Very Important) Thoughts

Now that you are prepared to go out and dazzle the world with your newfound regression skills, I need to impart some wisdom regarding the potential pitfalls you may encounter.

The first pitfall involves using the regression equation to predict values for the dependent variable beyond the range of the data. In the exam-grade example from earlier in the chapter, the number of hours that the six students studied ranged from two to six. What if we tried to use the regression equation that we derived from these data to predict the exam score for a student who studied 20 hours?

$$\hat{y} = 70.1783 + 4.1786(20) = 154 \text{ (Wow!)}$$

Assuming most exam scores are based on 100 points, this answer obviously doesn't make any sense unless you have a very generous teacher with a very generous exam curve. Because our data did not extend beyond 6 hours of studying, we really don't know how exam scores will be affected beyond that range. As you can see, results under these circumstances can be of questionable value.

The second pitfall involves the nature of the linear relationship between the independent and dependent variables. Just because the linear relationship between the variables is statistically significant doesn't prove that independent variable actually caused the change in the dependent variable. To prove causation, you need to have evidence that one variable is causing the other to move, which regression and correlation alone do not provide. For example, if our ordered pairs were the left and right shoe sizes of people, we would expect a very high correlation. This is not the result of one foot causing the other foot to be a certain size. These two variables just tend to move together naturally—unless, of course, you are me, who has to suffer through life with a left foot that is bigger than the right. Oh well, we all have our burdens to bear.

CHAPTER 14 Summary

- An independent variable x explains the variation (the change) in a dependent variable y.
- The relationship between independent and dependent variables exists only in one direction, $x \rightarrow y$.
- A correlation coefficient (r) indicates both the strength and direction of the linear relationship between an independent and dependent variable.
  - The values of r range from -1.0, a strong negative linear relationship, to $+1.0$, a strong positive linear relationship.
  - When $r = 0$, there is no linear relationship between the variables x and y.
- We can perform a hypothesis test to determine if the population correlation coefficient, ρ, is significantly different from zero based on the sample correlation coefficient, r.
  - If we reject the null hypothesis, we have enough evidence from our sample to conclude that a linear relationship does exist between the two variables.
- The least squares method is a mathematical procedure used to identify the linear equation that best fits a set of ordered pairs.
  - The procedures involve finding values for b_0, the y-intercept, and b_1, the slope.
  - The value of y represents an actual data point, whereas the value of $\hat{y}$ is the predicted value of y using the linear equation, given a value for x.
- The difference in the values of the dependent variable is known as variation and is measured by a term known as the total sum of squares *(SST)*.
- The sum of squares regression (*SSR*) measures the amount of variation in a dependent variable explained by an independent variable.
- The sum of squares error (*SSE*) measures the variation in a dependent variable that is explained by variables *other than* the independent variable.
- The coefficient of determination, R^2, measures the percentage of the total variation of a dependent variable explained by an independent variable.
  - A coefficient of determination equal to zero means that there is no linear relationship between the variables.
  - The coefficient of determination is the square of the correlation coefficient.
- A regression equation provides a point estimate for a dependent variable, given the value of an independent variable.
- The standard error of the estimate, s_e, measures the amount of dispersion of the observed data around the regression line.
  - If the data points are very close to the line, the standard error of the estimate is relatively low.
- We can construct a confidence interval for an average value of y based on a value of x or a prediction interval for an individual value of y based on a value of x.
- We can perform a hypothesis test to determine if the population slope, β_1, is equal to zero.
  - If we fail to reject the null hypothesis, we can conclude that there is no linear relationship between the dependent and independent variables.
- The standard error of the slope, s_b, measures how consistent the slope of a regression equation, b_1, would be if several sets of samples from the population were selected and the regression equation were derived for each of them.
- We can construct a confidence interval for the regression slope to provide an estimate for the possible values for β_1.
  - If the confidence interval includes zero, we have some evidence that β_1 could be equal to zero, which indicates that there may not be a linear relationship between the independent and dependent variables.

- The following assumptions must hold true for a regression analysis in order for it to provide reliable results.
  - The relationship between the independent variable and the dependent variable is linear.
  - The residuals exhibit no patterns across values for the independent variable.
  - The variation of the dependent variable is the same across all values for the independent variable, which is known as homoscedasticity.
  - The residuals follow the normal probability distribution.
- Caution must be exercised when using the regression equation to predict values outside of the range of the sample data from which the equation was derived.
- Also, just because the linear relationship between the variables is statistically significant doesn't prove that independent variable actually caused the change in the dependent variable.

CHAPTER 14 Key Terms

Dependent variable, y. A variable that is explained by the independent variable, x.

Homoscedasticity. A regression assumption that states that the variation of a dependent variable is the same across all values of an independent variable.

Independent variable, x. A variable that explains the variation in the dependent variable, y.

Least squares method. A mathematical procedure used to identify the linear equation that best fits a set of ordered pairs. The procedure involves finding values for b_0, the y-intercept, and b_1, the slope.

Normal probability plot. Used to verify if data follow the normal probability distribution by graphing the data on the y-axis and the z-scores for the data on the x-axis.

Population coefficient of determination, ρ^2. Measures the percentage of total variation of the dependent variable that is explained by the independent variable from the population.

Population correlation coefficient, ρ. A coefficient that refers to the correlation between all values of two variables of interest in a population.

Regression line. The line created by a regression analysis that best fits the data.

Residual, e_i. The difference between the actual data value and the predicted value.

Sample Coefficient of determination, R^2. A coefficient that measures the percentage of the total variation of a dependent variable that is explained by an independent variable.

Sample Correlation coefficient, r. A coefficient that indicates both the strength and direction of a linear relationship between independent and dependent variables from a sample.

Simple regression analysis. A technique that allows us to describe a straight line that best fits a series of ordered pairs (x, y).

Standard error of the estimate, s_e. A value that measures the amount of dispersion of observed data around a regression line.

Standard error of the slope, s_b. A value that measures how consistent the slope of a regression equation, b, would be if several sets of samples from the population were selected and the regression equation were derived for each of them.

Sum of squares error (SSE). A value that measures the variation in a dependent variable that is explained by variables *other than* an independent variable.

Sum of squares regression (SSR). A value that measures the amount of variation in a dependent variable that is explained by an independent variable.

Total sum of squares (SST). A value that measures the variation in the values of a dependent variable.

CHAPTER 14 Equations

14.2 Correlation Analysis (pp 653–659)

Formula 14.1 for the Sample Correlation Coefficient

$$r = \frac{n\sum xy - \left(\sum x\right)\left(\sum y\right)}{\sqrt{\left[n\sum x^2 - \left(\sum x\right)^2\right]\left[n\sum y^2 - \left(\sum y\right)^2\right]}}$$

Formula 14.2 for the Test Statistic for the Correlation Coefficient

$$t = \frac{r}{\sqrt{\frac{1 - r^2}{n - 2}}}$$

14.3 Simple Regression Analysis (pp 660–672)

Formula 14.3 for Equation Describing a Straight Line through Ordered Pairs

$$\hat{y} = b_0 + b_1 x$$

Formula 14.4 for the Simple Linear Regression Model for a Population

$$y_i = \beta_0 + \beta_1 x_i + \varepsilon_i$$

Formula 14.5 for the Residual

$$e_i = y_i - \hat{y}_i$$

Formula 14.6 for the Sum of Squares Error

$$SSE = \sum_{i=1}^{n} (y_i - \hat{y}_i)^2$$

Formula 14.7 for the Regression Slope

$$b_1 = \frac{n\sum xy - \left(\sum x\right)\left(\sum y\right)}{n\sum x^2 - \left(\sum x\right)^2}$$

Formula 14.8 for the Regression Intercept

$$b_0 = \frac{\sum y}{n} - b_1\left(\frac{\sum x}{n}\right)$$

Formula 14.9 for the Total Sum of Squares (SST)

$$SST = \sum (y - \bar{y})^2$$

Formula 14.10 for the Total Sum of Squares (SST), Calculator-Friendly Version

$$SST = \sum y^2 - \frac{\left(\sum y\right)^2}{n}$$

Formula 14.11 for the Relationship between the SSR and the SSE

$$SST = SSR + SSE$$

Formula 14.12 for the Sum of Squares Error (SSE), Calculator-Friendly Version

$$SSE = \sum y^2 - b_0 \sum y - b_1 \sum xy$$

Formula 14.13 for the Sum of Squares Regression (SSR)

$$SSR = \sum(\hat{y} - \bar{y})^2$$

Formula 14.14 for the Sample Coefficient of Determination

$$R^2 = \frac{SSR}{SST}$$

Formula 14.15 for the F-Test Statistic for the Coefficient of Determination

$$F = \frac{SSR}{\left(\dfrac{SSE}{n - 2}\right)}$$

14.4 Using a Regression to Make a Prediction (pp 672–679)

Formula 14.16 for the Standard Error of the Estimate

$$s_e = \sqrt{\frac{SSE}{n - 2}}$$

Formula 14.17 for the Confidence Interval (CI) for an Average Value of y

$$CI = \hat{y} \pm t_{\alpha/2}s_e \sqrt{\frac{1}{n} + \frac{(x - \bar{x})^2}{\left(\sum x^2\right) - \dfrac{\left(\sum x\right)^2}{n}}}$$

Formula 14.18 for the Prediction Interval (PI) for a Specific Value of y

$$PI = \hat{y} \pm t_{\alpha/2}s_e \sqrt{1 + \frac{1}{n} + \frac{(x - \bar{x})^2}{\left(\sum x^2\right) - \dfrac{\left(\sum x\right)^2}{n}}}$$

14.5 Testing the Significance of the Slope of the Regression Equation (pp 679–683)

Formula 14.19 for the t-Test Statistic for the Regression Slope

$$t = \frac{b_1 - \beta_1}{s_b}$$

Formula 14.20 for the Standard Error of a Slope

$$s_b = \frac{s_e}{\sqrt{\sum x^2 - n(\bar{x})^2}}$$

Formula 14.21 for the Confidence Interval for the Population Slope

$$CI = b_1 \pm t_{\alpha/2}s_b$$

CHAPTER 14 Problems

14.56 As a measure of productivity, Verizon Wireless records the number of customers each of its retail employees activates weekly. An activation is defined as either a new customer signing a cell phone contract or an existing customer renewing a contract. The following table shows the number of weekly activations for eight randomly selected employees along with their job-satisfaction levels rated on a scale of 1–10 (10 = Most satisfied). These data can also be found in the Excel file **activations.xlsx**.

Activations	Satisfaction	Activations	Satisfaction
36	8.0	19	6.1
25	7.9	28	7.0
40	8.5	33	8.2
38	9.0	25	7.7

a. Construct a scatter plot for these data.
b. Calculate the slope and the y-intercept for the regression equation.
c. Provide an interpretation for the value of the slope.
d. Predict the number of activations next week for an employee with a satisfaction level of 7.5.
e. Calculate the SST.
f. Partition the SST into the SSR and the SSE.
g. Verify your results using Excel.

14.57 Answer the following questions using the data from Problem 14.56:
a. Calculate the correlation coefficient for this sample.
b. Using $\alpha = 0.01$, test to determine if the population correlation coefficient is not equal to zero.
c. What conclusions can be made based on these results?

14.58 Answer the following questions using the data from Problem 14.56:
a. Calculate the coefficient of determination.
b. Using $\alpha = 0.01$, test the significance of the population coefficient of determination.
c. Construct a 99% confidence interval for the average number of activations made by an employee with a job-satisfaction score of 8.0.
d. Construct a 99% prediction interval for the number of activations made by an employee with a job-satisfaction score of 8.0.
e. Verify your results with PHStat.

14.59 Answer the following questions using the data from Problem 14.56:
a. Using $\alpha = 0.01$, test for the significance of the regression slope.
b. Construct a 99% confidence interval for the population slope.
c. What conclusions about the number of weekly activations and job satisfaction can be drawn from these results?
d. Verify your results using Excel.

14.60 The American Board of Family Medicine would like to investigate the theory that a mother's shoe size can be used to predict an infant's birth weight in pounds. The following table records a random sample of the shoe sizes of 10 mothers and the birth weights of their infants. These data can also be found in the Excel file **ABFM.xlsx**.

Shoe Size	Weight	Shoe Size	Weight
7.5	7.2	8.0	6.9
8.0	7.8	8.5	9.2
9.0	8.0	7.5	6.5
8.5	9.4	8.0	9.1
8.5	7.7	9.0	9.8

a. Construct a scatter plot for these data.
b. Calculate the slope and the y-intercept for the regression equation.
c. Provide an interpretation for the value of the slope.
d. Predict the infant weight for a mother with an 8.5 shoe size.
e. Calculate the SST.
f. Partition the SST into the SSR and the SSE.

14.61 Answer the following questions using the data from Problem 14.60:
a. Calculate the correlation coefficient for this sample.
b. Using $\alpha = 0.10$, test to determine if the population correlation coefficient is greater than zero.
c. What conclusions can be made based on these results?

14.62 Answer the following questions using the data from Problem 14.60:
a. Calculate the coefficient of determination.
b. Using $\alpha = 0.10$, test the significance of the population coefficient of determination.
c. Construct a 90% confidence interval for the average birth weight for a maternal shoe size of 8.5.
d. Construct a 90% prediction interval for the birth weight for a maternal shoe size of 8.5.

14.63 Answer the following questions using the data from Problem 14.60:
a. Using $\alpha = 0.10$, test for the significance of the regression slope.
b. Construct a 90% confidence interval for the population slope.
c. What conclusions about the maternal shoe size and birth weight can be drawn from these results?
d. Verify your results using Excel.

14.64 Zagat surveys airline customers on a 30-point satisfaction scale measuring comfort, service, and food for both domestic and international flights. The Excel file **Zagat.xlsx** contains survey results that were recently collected showing the average scores for various airlines.

a. Calculate the correlation coefficient for this sample.
b. Using $\alpha = 0.01$, perform a hypothesis test to determine if the correlation coefficient is greater than zero.
c. What conclusions can be drawn based on these results?

14.65 A regional manager at Acme Markets would like to develop a model to predict weekly sales of pet food based on the shelf space. The following table shows the data collected from nine randomly selected stores and can also be found in the Excel file **Acme.xlsx**.

Shelf Space (Feet)	Sales ($100)	Shelf Space (Feet)	Sales ($100)
2	3	2	4
3	3	4	5
4	6	5	7
6	14	5	10
5	12		

a. Construct a scatter plot for these data.
b. Calculate the slope and the *y*-intercept for the regression equation.
c. Provide an interpretation for the value of the slope.
d. Predict the weekly sales based on four feet of shelf space.
e. Calculate the *SST*.
f. Partition the *SST* into the *SSR* and the *SSE*.

14.66 Answer the following questions using the data from Problem 14.65:
a. Calculate the correlation coefficient for this sample.
b. Using $\alpha = 0.05$, perform a hypothesis test to determine if the correlation coefficient is greater than zero.
c. What conclusions can be drawn based on these results?

14.67 Answer the following questions using the data from Problem 14.65:
a. Calculate the coefficient of determination.
b. Using $\alpha = 0.05$, test the significance of the population coefficient of determination.
c. Construct a 95% confidence interval for the average sales from 4.0 feet of shelf space.
d. Construct a 95% prediction interval for the sales from 4.0 feet of shelf space.
e. Verify your results from parts c and d with PHStat.

14.68 Answer the following questions using the data from Problem 14.65:
a. Using $\alpha = 0.05$, test for the significance of the regression slope.
b. Construct a 95% confidence interval for the population slope.
c. What conclusions about the shelf space and sales can be drawn from these results?
d. Verify your results using Excel.

14.69 Suppose I recorded the attendance of my students in a recent statistics class because I wanted to investigate the linear relationship between the number of classes they missed and their final grades. The following table shows these data for a random sample of nine students and can also be found in the Excel file **missed classes.xlsx**.

Missed Classes	Final Grade	Missed Classes	Final Grade
4	74	2	84
6	79	0	90
1	93	5	86
4	70	2	95
0	96		

a. Construct a scatter plot for these data.
b. Calculate the slope and the *y*-intercept for the regression equation.
c. Provide an interpretation for the value of the slope.
d. Predict the final grade for a student who missed five classes.
e. Calculate the *SST*.
f. Partition the *SST* into the *SSR* and the *SSE*.
g. Verify your results using Excel.

14.70 Answer the following questions using the data from Problem 14.69:
a. Calculate the correlation coefficient for this sample.
b. Using $\alpha = 0.05$, perform a hypothesis test to determine if the correlation coefficient is less than zero.
c. What conclusions can be drawn based on these results?

14.71 Answer the following questions using the data from Problem 14.69:
a. Calculate the coefficient of determination.
b. Using $\alpha = 0.05$, test the significance of the population coefficient of determination.
c. Construct a 95% confidence interval for the average grade of students who missed two classes.
d. Construct a 95% prediction interval for the grade of a student who missed two classes.
e. Verify your results from parts c and d with PHStat.

14.72 Answer the following questions using the data from Problem 14.69:
a. Using $\alpha = 0.05$, test for the significance of the regression slope.
b. Construct a 95% confidence interval for the population slope.
c. What conclusions about missed classes and final grade can be drawn from these results?
d. Verify your results using Excel.

14.73 Suppose GNC, a vitamin and supplement supplier, would like to investigate the relationship between the size of an order and the age of the customer who ordered it. This information could allow GNC to target its promotions to specific age groups. The following table shows the ages for seven randomly selected customers along with their most recent order sizes in dollars. This data can also be found in the Excel file **GNC.xlsx**.

Age	Order Size ($)	Age	Order Size ($)
41	54	29	15
26	30	49	25
34	22	38	85
54	63		

a. Construct a scatter plot for these data.
b. Calculate the correlation coefficient for this sample.
c. Using $\alpha = 0.05$, perform a hypothesis test to determine if the population correlation coefficient is greater than zero?
d. What conclusions can be drawn based on these results?

14.74 Answer the following questions based on the data from Problem 14.73.
a. Calculate the slope and the y-intercept for the regression equation.
b. Predict the order size of a 32-year-old customer.
c. Provide an interpretation for the value of the slope.
d. Calculate the total sum of squares.
e. Partition the total sum of squares into the SSR and SSE.
f. Verify your results using Excel.

14.75 Answer the following questions based on the data from Problem 14.73.
a. Calculate the coefficient of determination.
b. Test the significance of the population coefficient of determination using $\alpha = 0.05$.
c. Construct a 95% confidence interval for the average order size for a 40-year-old customer.
d. Construct a 95% prediction interval for the order size for Rick, who is a 40-year-old customer.
e. Verify your results from parts c and d with PHStat.

14.76 Answer the following questions based on the data from Problem 14.73.
a. Test for the significance of the regression slope using $\alpha = 0.05$.
b. Construct a 95% confidence interval for the population slope.
c. What conclusions about the order size and customer's age can be drawn from these results?
d. Verify your results using Excel.

14.77 A Buick dealership would like to develop a regression model that would predict the number of cars sold per month by a dealership employee based on the employee's number of years of sales experience. The following regression output was developed based on a random sample of employees.

Anova		
	df	*SS*
Regression	1	84.72068376
Residual	23	243.1193162
Total	24	327.84
	Coefficients	**Standard Error**
Intercept	7.069059829	1.507676628
Experience	0.601709402	0.212538635

a. Predict the sales next month for an employee with 3.5 years of sales experience.
b. Compute the coefficient of determination and interpret its meaning.
c. Do the sample data provide evidence that the model is useful for predicting average monthly sales for employees based on their sales experience using $\alpha = 0.05$?
d. Construct a 95% confidence interval around the sample slope and interpret its meaning.

14.78 Mike Lynch manages a real estate firm in Myrtle Beach, South Carolina, and would like to construct a model to help him predict the selling price of beach properties for his customers based on the age of the house in years. Mike has collected a random sample of home sales from the area and generated a regression model using Excel, which is shown in the following table. Selling price for homes were recorded in thousands of dollars.

Anova		
	df	*SS*
Regression	1	178208.8925
Residual	28	1797115.274
Total	29	1975324.167
	Coefficients	**Standard Error**
Intercept	859.5990541	142.9768355
Age	−10.2005605	6.121647288

a. Predict the selling price for a 16-year-old home.
b. Compute the coefficient of determination and interpret its meaning.
c. Do the sample data provide evidence that the model is useful for predicting average selling price based on the age of the home using $\alpha = 0.01$?
d. Construct a 98% confidence interval around the sample slope and interpret its meaning.

14.79 Each week during the NCAA men's college basketball season, teams are ranked according to two polls—the AP Poll and the Coach's Poll. Each team's position is determined by the number of points received by the polls. The Excel file **NCAA basketball.xlsx** lists the points 24 teams received for the week of March 11, 2013.

a. Using Excel, calculate the correlation coefficient for this sample.

b. Using $\alpha = 0.05$, perform a hypothesis test to determine if the correlation coefficient is not equal to zero.

c. What conclusions can be drawn about the consistency of these two polls based on these results?

14.80 Suppose Cars.com would like to describe the linear relationship between the odometer mileage of a used 2010 Ford Explorer and its asking price. The Excel file **Explorer.xlsx** contains data for these variables for 40 used 2010 Explorers currently on the market. Use Excel and PHStat to answer the following questions:

a. Construct a scatter plot for these data.

b. Identify the slope and the y-intercept for the regression equation.

c. Provide an interpretation for the value of the slope.

d. Is the linear relationship between mileage and asking price statistically significant using $\alpha = 0.05$?

e. Identify the 95% confidence interval for the slope and interpret the results.

f. Construct a 95% confidence interval for the average asking price for Explorers with 36,000 miles on their odometers.

g. Construct a 95% prediction interval for the asking price for an Explorer with 36,000 miles on its odometer.

14.81 The Excel file **MLB 2012 Payroll.xlsx** contains the total payroll in millions of dollars for each Major League Baseball team at the start of the 2012 season along with the total number of each team's wins at the end of the season. Use Excel and PHStat to answer the following questions:

a. Construct a scatter plot for these data.

b. Identify the slope and the y-intercept for the regression equation.

c. Provide an interpretation for the value of the slope.

d. Is the linear relationship between payroll and wins statistically significant using $\alpha = 0.05$?

e. Identify the 95% confidence interval for the slope and interpret the results.

f. Construct a 95% confidence interval for the average number of wins for teams that have \$100 million payrolls.

g. Construct a 95% prediction interval for the number of wins for a team that has a \$100 million payroll.

CHAPTER 14 Solutions to Your Turn

YOUR TURN #1

Age x	Hours y	xy	x^2	y^2
24	2.7	64.8	576	7.29
32	4.2	134.4	1,024	17.64
47	5.0	235.0	2,209	25.00
40	3.8	152.0	1,600	14.44
26	2.2	57.2	676	4.84
53	2.9	153.7	2,809	8.41
38	3.0	114.0	1,444	9.00
$\sum x = 260$	$\sum y = 23.8$	$\sum xy = 911.1$	$\sum x^2 = 10{,}338$	$\sum y^2 = 86.62$

$$r = \frac{n\sum xy - \left(\sum x\right)\left(\sum y\right)}{\sqrt{\left[n\sum x^2 - \left(\sum x\right)^2\right]\left[n\sum y^2 - \left(\sum y\right)^2\right]}}$$

$$r = \frac{(7)(911.1) - (260)(23.8)}{\sqrt{[(7)(10{,}338) - (260)^2][(7)(86.62) - (23.8)^2]}}$$

$$r = \frac{(6{,}377.7) - (6{,}188)}{\sqrt{[(72{,}366) - (67{,}600)][(606.34) - (566.44)]}}$$

$$r = \frac{189.7}{\sqrt{[4{,}766][39.9]}} = \frac{189.7}{\sqrt{190{,}163.4}} = \frac{189.7}{436.08} = 0.435$$

According to this sample, because the correlation coefficient is greater than zero, it appears that as the hiker's age increases, the hiking time on this trail tend to increase.

YOUR TURN #2

$$H_0: \rho = 0$$
$$H_1: \rho \neq 0$$

$$t = \frac{r}{\sqrt{\frac{1-r^2}{n-2}}} = \frac{0.435}{\sqrt{\frac{1-(0.435)^2}{7-2}}} = \frac{0.435}{\sqrt{\frac{1-0.1892}{5}}}$$

$$t = \frac{0.435}{\sqrt{\frac{0.8108}{5}}} = \frac{0.435}{\sqrt{0.1622}} = \frac{0.435}{0.4027} = 1.08$$

For a one-tail test with $\alpha = 0.10$ and $7 - 2 = 5$ degrees of freedom, $t_\alpha = 1.476$. Because $t = 1.08$ is less than $t_\alpha = 1.476$, we fail to reject the null hypothesis. Based on our sample, the correlation coefficient between the age of a hiker and the hiking time for this trail is not different than zero. In other words, there is no support that a linear relationship exists between the two.

YOUR TURN #3

$$b_1 = \frac{n\sum xy - (\sum x)(\sum y)}{n\sum x^2 - (\sum x)^2}$$

$$b_1 = \frac{(7)(911.1) - (260)(23.8)}{(7)(10{,}338) - (260)^2}$$

$$b_1 = \frac{6{,}377.7 - 6{,}188}{72{,}366 - 67{,}600} = \frac{189.7}{4{,}766} = 0.0398$$

$$b_0 = \frac{\sum y}{n} - b_1\left(\frac{\sum x}{n}\right)$$

$$b_0 = \frac{23.8}{7} - (0.0398)\left(\frac{260}{7}\right)$$

$$b_0 = 3.40 - 1.4783 = 1.9217$$

$$\hat{y} = 1.9217 + 0.0398x$$

$$\hat{y} = 1.9217 + 0.0398(36) = 3.35 \text{ hours}$$

As the hiker's age increases by one year, his or her hiking time tends to increase by an average of 0.0398 hours (or 2.4 minutes) on this trail.

YOUR TURN #4

$$SST = \sum y^2 - \frac{(\sum y)^2}{n}$$

$$SST = 86.62 - \frac{(23.8)^2}{7}$$

$$SST = 86.62 - 80.92 = 5.70$$

$$SSE = \sum y^2 - b_0\sum y - b_1\sum xy$$

$$SSE = (86.62) - (1.9217)(23.8) - (0.0398)(911.1)$$

$$SSE = 86.62 - 45.736 - 36.262 = 4.622$$

$$SSR = SST - SSE$$

$$SSR = 5.70 - 4.622 = 1.078$$

YOUR TURN #5

$$R^2 = \frac{SSR}{SST} = \frac{1.078}{5.70} = 0.189$$

$$R^2 = r^2 = (0.435)^2 = 0.189$$

$$F = \frac{SSR}{\left(\frac{SSE}{n-2}\right)} = \frac{1.078}{\left(\frac{4.622}{7-2}\right)} = \frac{1.078}{0.9244} = 1.17$$

$$D_1 = 1$$

$$D_2 = n - 2 = 7 - 2 = 5$$

$$F_\alpha = 4.060$$

$F < F_\alpha \rightarrow 1.17 < 4.060 \rightarrow$ Do not reject H_0

A hiker's age explains only about 18.9% of the variation in the hiking time on this trail. This percentage is too low to be considered statistically significant.

YOUR TURN #6

$$s_e = \sqrt{\frac{SSE}{n-2}} = \sqrt{\frac{4.622}{7-2}} = \sqrt{0.9244} = 0.961$$

$$\hat{y} = 1.9217 + 0.0398x$$

$$\hat{y} = 1.9217 + 0.0398(40) = 3.51 \text{ hours}$$

$$\bar{x} = \frac{\sum x}{n} = \frac{260}{7} = 37.14$$

$$df = n - 2 = 7 - 2 = 5$$

$$t_{\alpha/2} = 1.476$$

1. Confidence interval:

$$CI = \hat{y} \pm t_{\alpha/2}s_e\sqrt{\frac{1}{n} + \frac{(x-\bar{x})^2}{\left(\sum x^2\right) - \frac{\left(\sum x\right)^2}{n}}}$$

$$CI = 3.51 \pm (1.476)(0.961)\sqrt{\frac{1}{7} + \frac{(40-37.14)^2}{10{,}338 - \frac{(260)^2}{7}}}$$

$$CI = 3.51 \pm (1.418)\sqrt{0.1429 + \frac{(2.86)^2}{10{,}338 - \frac{(67{,}600)}{7}}}$$

$$CI = 3.51 \pm (1.418)\sqrt{0.1429 + 0.0120}$$

$$CI = 3.51 \pm (1.418)\sqrt{0.1549}$$

$$CI = 3.51 \pm 0.558$$

$$UCL = 3.51 + 0.558 = 4.07 \text{ hours}$$

$$LCL = 3.51 - 0.558 = 2.95 \text{ hours}$$

We are 80% confident that the average hiking time for a 40-year-old hiker on the Wengen-Kleine Scheidegg trail is between 2.95 hours and 4.07 hours.

2. Prediction interval:

$$PI = \hat{y} \pm t_{\alpha/2}s_e\sqrt{1 + \frac{1}{n} + \frac{(x-\bar{x})^2}{\left(\sum x^2\right) - \frac{\left(\sum x\right)^2}{n}}}$$

$$PI = 3.51 \pm (1.476)(0.961)\sqrt{1 + \frac{1}{7} + \frac{(40-37.14)^2}{10{,}338 - \frac{(260)^2}{7}}}$$

$$PI = 3.51 \pm (1.418)\sqrt{1 + 0.1429 + \frac{(2.86)^2}{10{,}338 - \frac{(67{,}600)}{7}}}$$

$$PI = 3.51 \pm (1.418)\sqrt{1.1429 + 0.0120}$$

$$PI = 3.51 \pm (1.418)\sqrt{1.1549}$$

$$PI = 3.51 \pm 1.52$$

$$UPL = 3.51 + 1.52 = 5.03 \text{ hours}$$

$$LPL = 3.51 - 1.52 = 1.99 \text{ hours}$$

We are 80% confident that the hiking time for Deb, a 40-year-old hiker on the Wengen-Kleine Scheidegg trail, is between 1.99 hours and 5.03 hours.

YOUR TURN #7

$$H_0: \beta_1 = 0$$

$$H_1: \beta_1 \neq 0$$

$$s_e = 0.961 \quad \sum x^2 = 10{,}338 \quad n = 7 \quad \bar{x} = 37.14$$

$$s_b = \frac{s_e}{\sqrt{\sum x^2 - n(\bar{x})^2}} = \frac{0.961}{\sqrt{10{,}338 - (7)(37.14)^2}}$$

$$s_b = \frac{0.961}{\sqrt{10{,}338 - 9{,}655.657}} = \frac{0.961}{26.122} = 0.0368$$

$$b_1 = 0.0398 \quad \beta_1 = 0$$

$$t = \frac{b_1 - \beta_1}{s_b} = \frac{0.0398 - 0}{0.0368} = 1.08$$

$$t_{\alpha/2} = 2.015$$

$t < t_{\alpha/2} \rightarrow 1.08 < 2.015 \rightarrow$ Do not reject H_0

$$CI = b_1 \pm t_{\alpha/2}s_b = 0.0398 \pm (2.015)(0.0368)$$

$$CI = b_1 \pm t_{\alpha/2}s_b = 0.0398 \pm 0.0742$$

$$UCL = 0.0398 + 0.0742 = 0.114$$

$$LCL = 0.0398 - 0.0742 = -0.0344$$

Notice that this confidence interval for the slope includes zero. Since there is evidence that the population slope could be equal to zero, this is consistent with the conclusion that there is no relationship between a hiker's age and the hiking time for the Wengen-Kleine Scheidegg trail.

YOUR TURN #8

ERA	Wins			
x	*y*	*xy*	x^2	y^2
5.0	57	285.0	25.00	3,249
4.8	65	312.0	23.04	4,225
4.1	69	282.9	16.81	4,761
4.0	80	320.0	16.00	6,400
3.7	97	358.9	13.69	9,409
4.2	75	315.0	17.64	5,625
4.1	80	328.0	16.81	6,400
3.6	81	291.6	12.96	6,561
$\sum x = 33.5$	$\sum y = 604$	$\sum xy = 2{,}493.4$	$\sum x^2 = 141.95$	$\sum y^2 = 46{,}630$

$$r = \frac{n\sum xy - (\sum x)(\sum y)}{\sqrt{[n\sum x^2 - (\sum x)^2][n\sum y^2 - (\sum y)^2]}}$$

$$r = \frac{(8)(2{,}493.4) - (33.5)(604)}{\sqrt{[(8)(141.95) - (33.5)^2][(8)(46{,}630) - (604)^2]}}$$

$$r = \frac{(19{,}947.2) - (20{,}234.0)}{\sqrt{[(1{,}135.6) - (1{,}122.25)][(373{,}040) - (364{,}816)]}}$$

$$r = \frac{-286.8}{331.35} = -0.866$$

$$H_0: \rho = 0$$

$$H_1: \rho \neq 0$$

$$t = \frac{r}{\sqrt{\frac{1 - r^2}{n - 2}}} = \frac{-0.866}{\sqrt{\frac{1 - (-0.866)^2}{8 - 2}}} = \frac{-0.866}{\sqrt{\frac{1 - 0.750}{6}}} = \frac{-0.866}{0.2042} = -4.24$$

$t_{\alpha/2} = 3.707$ for $df = 6$

Reject the null hypothesis. As expected, the more runs a team gives up, the fewer games it will win. This linear relationship is significant because we rejected the null hypothesis.

YOUR TURN #9

$$b_1 = \frac{n\sum xy - (\sum x)(\sum y)}{n\sum x^2 - (\sum x)^2}$$

$$b_1 = \frac{(8)(2{,}493.4) - (33.5)(604)}{(8)(141.95) - (33.5)^2} = \frac{-286.8}{13.35} = -21.4831$$

$$b_0 = \frac{\sum y}{n} - b_1\left(\frac{\sum x}{n}\right)$$

$$b_0 = \frac{604}{8} - (-21.4831)\left(\frac{33.5}{8}\right) = 165.4605$$

$$\hat{y} = 165.4605 - 21.4831x$$

$$\hat{y} = 165.4605 - 21.4831(4.2) = 75.232 \approx 75 \text{ games}$$

If the Pirates can reduce the average number of runs they give up per game by one (make x smaller), the team would expect to win 21.4831, or 21, additional games during the season (make $\hat{y}$ larger). I am not holding my breath.

YOUR TURN #10

$$SST = \sum y^2 - \frac{(\sum y)^2}{n}$$

$$SST = 46{,}630 - \frac{(604)^2}{8}$$

$$SST = 46{,}630 - 45{,}602 = 1{,}028$$

$$SSE = \sum y^2 - b_0\sum y - b_1\sum xy$$

$$SSE = (46{,}630) - (165.4605)(604) - (-21.4831)(2{,}493.4)$$

$$SSE = 46{,}630 - 99{,}938.142 + 53{,}565.962$$

$$SSE = 257.82$$

$$SSR = SST - SSE$$

$$SSR = 1{,}028 - 257.82 = 770.18$$

YOUR TURN #11

$$R^2 = \frac{SSR}{SST} = \frac{770.18}{1{,}028} = 0.749$$

$$F = \frac{SSR}{\left(\frac{SSE}{n - 2}\right)} = \frac{770.18}{\left(\frac{257.82}{8 - 2}\right)} = \frac{770.18}{42.97} = 17.92$$

$$D_1 = 1$$

$$D_2 = n - 2 = 8 - 2 = 6$$

$$F_\alpha = 13.745$$

Reject the null hypothesis. According to our results, 74.9% of the variation in wins can be explained by the average number of runs a team gives up per game. This percentage is high enough to be statistically significant. It looks like in order to add some games to the win column, the Pirates need to find some better pitching next year.

YOUR TURN #12

$$s_e = \sqrt{\frac{SSE}{n-2}} = \sqrt{\frac{257.82}{8-2}} = \sqrt{42.97} = 6.555$$

$$\hat{y} = 165.4605 - 21.4831x$$

$$\hat{y} = 165.4605 - 21.4831(4.7) = 64.49$$

$$\bar{x} = \frac{\sum x}{n} = \frac{33.5}{8} = 4.1875$$

$$df = n - 2 = 8 - 2 = 6$$

$$t_{\alpha/2} = 1.943$$

The 90% confidence interval is calculated as follows:

$$CI = \hat{y} \pm t_{\alpha/2}s_e\sqrt{\frac{1}{n} + \frac{(x-\bar{x})^2}{\left(\sum x^2\right) - \frac{\left(\sum x\right)^2}{n}}}$$

$$CI = 64.49 \pm (1.943)(6.555)\sqrt{\frac{1}{8} + \frac{(4.7-4.1875)^2}{141.95 - \frac{(33.5)^2}{8}}}$$

$$CI = 64.49 \pm (12.74)\sqrt{0.125 + \frac{(0.5125)^2}{141.95 - \frac{(1{,}122.25)}{8}}}$$

$$CI = 64.49 \pm (12.74)\sqrt{0.125 + 0.1573}$$

$$CI = 64.49 \pm 6.77$$

$$UCL = 64.49 + 6.77 = 71.26$$

$$LCL = 64.49 - 6.77 = 57.72$$

We are 90% confident that if a team gives up an average of 4.7 runs per game, it will win an average of between 58 and 71 games during the season.

The 90% prediction interval is calculated as follows:

$$PI = \hat{y} \pm t_{\alpha/2}s_e\sqrt{1 + \frac{1}{n} + \frac{(x-\bar{x})^2}{\left(\sum x^2\right) - \frac{\left(\sum x\right)^2}{n}}}$$

$$PI = 64.49 \pm (1.943)(6.555)\sqrt{1 + \frac{1}{8} + \frac{(4.7-4.1875)^2}{141.95 - \frac{(33.5)^2}{8}}}$$

$$PI = 64.49 \pm (12.74)\sqrt{1 + 0.125 + \frac{(0.5125)^2}{141.95 - \frac{(1{,}122.25)}{8}}}$$

$$PI = 64.49 \pm (12.74)\sqrt{1.125 + 0.1573}$$

$$PI = 64.49 \pm 14.43$$

$$UPL = 64.49 + 14.43 = 78.92$$

$$LPL = 64.49 - 14.43 = 50.06$$

We are 90% confident that a team that gives up an average of 4.7 runs per game will win between 50 and 79 games. I have absolutely no recollection of when the Pirates last won 79 games in a season.

YOUR TURN #13

$$H_0: \beta_1 = 0$$

$$H_1: \beta_1 \neq 0$$

$$s_e = 6.555 \quad \sum x^2 = 141.95 \quad n = 8 \quad \bar{x} = 4.1875$$

$$s_b = \frac{s_e}{\sqrt{\sum x^2 - n(\bar{x})^2}} = \frac{6.555}{\sqrt{141.95 - (8)(4.1875)^2}}$$

$$s_b = \frac{6.555}{\sqrt{141.95 - (8)(17.5352)}} = \frac{6.555}{\sqrt{141.95 - 140.282}} = 5.074$$

$$b_1 = -21.4831 \quad \beta_1 = 0$$

$$t = \frac{b_1 - \beta_1}{s_b} = \frac{-21.4831 - 0}{5.074} = -4.23$$

$$t_{\alpha/2} = 3.707$$

Reject the null hypothesis.

$$CI = b_1 \pm t_{\alpha/2}s_b = -21.4831 \pm (3.707)(5.074)$$

$$CI = b_1 \pm t_{\alpha/2}s_b = -21.4831 \pm 18.809$$

$$UCL = -21.4831 + 18.809 = -2.67$$

$$LCL = -21.4831 - 18.809 = -40.29$$

Notice that this confidence interval for the slope does not include zero. This is consistent with the conclusion that there is a linear relationship between wins and ERAs in Major League Baseball. According to our interval, we are 99% sure that giving up one extra run per game will result in a team losing between 2.67 and 40.29 games during the season. This interval is relatively wide because of the small sample size (8) and the very small value for alpha (0.01).

15

Multiple Regression and Model Building

IN THIS CHAPTER, YOU WILL LEARN TO:

- Develop a multiple regression model using software.
- Interpret the meaning of regression coefficients.
- Interpret the meaning of the multiple coefficient of determination.
- Test the significance of the overall regression model and the individual regression coefficients.
- Use qualitative independent variables in the regression model.
- Identify the presence of multicollinearity in the regression model.
- Develop a regression model using general stepwise method and best subset method.

CHAPTER 15 MAP

Stats in Practice: Using Statistics to Set Used Car Prices

Congratulations! You have just been promoted to the job of used car sales manager for Brandywine Ford, a major car dealership in the Mid-Atlantic area. One of your primary responsibilities is to decide on the asking price for used cars, which have been traded in by customers purchasing new cars. You have just learned that the dealership has acquired a six-year-old Toyota Camry with 76,320 miles in a recent trade-in. What asking price should you set for this used car?

In Chapter 14, we learned about simple regression analysis, where one independent variable is used to describe the variation in a dependent variable. We extend that concept in this chapter to the multiple regression technique, which uses more than one independent variable to explain the variation in the dependent variable of interest. The opening example in this chapter is a perfect application of the multiple regression technique.

In this chapter, we will use a multiple regression model to describe the relationship between independent variables (such as a car's age and mileage) and a dependent variable (such as a car's asking price). We can then use this relationship to help us choose an asking price for the used Toyota Camry.

Multiple regression techniques can be used to make many business decisions, including the following:

- Predicting the volume of natural gas used by a residence based on its size, the thermostat setting, and the temperature outdoors
- Estimating the creditworthiness of potential customers based on their incomes, ages, and education levels
- Predicting the weekly sales volume of a particular product based on its price, the amount of shelf space it's allotted, and the amount of advertising it receives

I do have some good news for you. Because multiple regression calculations are very complex, we will be relying primarily on Excel to generate the output (very few nasty hand calculations). Our focus in this chapter will be to interpret the results of multiple regressions.

15.1 Developing the Multiple Regression Model

As explained at the beginning of the chapter, the multiple regression model is an extension of the simple regression model discussed in Chapter 14. Instead of a single independent variable, we now have the opportunity to incorporate k independent variables to explain the variation in our dependent variable of interest. Remember from Chapter 14 that an **independent variable, *x***, explains the variation in the **dependent variable, *y***. The equation that provides the relationship between the multiple variables for a sample is shown in Equation 15.1.

An **independent variable, *x***, explains the variation (which is a fancy word for change) in the **dependent variable, *y***.

Formula 15.1 for the Multiple Linear Regression Model for a Sample

$$\hat{y} = b_0 + b_1x_1 + b_2x_2 + \cdots + b_kx_k$$

where

$\hat{y}$ = The predicted value of y given values of $x_1, x_2, \ldots, x_k$

$x_1, x_2, \ldots, x_k$ = The independent variables of interest

k = The number of independent variables in our regression model

b_0 = The y-intercept of the regression line

b_1 = The average change in $\hat{y}$ due to a one-unit change in x_1 with $x_2, \ldots, x_k$ constant

b_2 = The average change in $\hat{y}$ due to a one-unit change in x_2 with $x_1, x_3, \ldots, x_k$ constant

b_k = The average change in $\hat{y}$ due to a one-unit change in x_k with $x_1, x_2, \ldots, x_{k-1}$ constant

We will be relying on the same least squares method that was introduced in Chapter 14 which identifies the linear equation that best fits a specific data set. As you can see, Equation 15.1 provides information about relationships between the dependent variable and independent variable for our *sample*. However, our real interest lies in the *population* from which our sample was taken. The multiple linear regression model for a population can be described using Equation 15.2.

Formula 15.2 for the Multiple Linear Regression Model for a Population

$$y = \beta_0 + \beta_1 x_1 + \beta_2 x_2 + \cdots + \beta_k x_k + \varepsilon$$

where

y = The dependent variable from the population
β_0 = The population y-intercept
$\beta_1, \beta_2, \ldots, \beta_k$ = The population slope for the k independent variables
x_1 = The first independent variable from the population
x_2 = The second independent variable from the population
x_k = The kth independent variable from the population
ε = The residual for the dependent variable from the population

Although Excel can perform multiple regression, PHStat provides more functionality for this procedure.

Our goal in this chapter is to estimate the values for $\beta_0, \beta_1, \beta_2, \ldots, \beta_k$ based on our sample which will allow us to make conclusions about our population of interest. In this chapter, I'll rely on PHStat to provide the regression coefficients for each independent variable shown in Equation 15.1 in the following section (as opposed to calculating them manually like we did in Chapter 14—be thankful for small favors). Mac users can find these instructions on the textbook's Web site (www.pearsonhighered.com/donnelly).

Identifying Regression Coefficients

A **regression coefficient** predicts the change in a dependent variable due to a one-unit increase in an independent variable while other variables are held constant.

The procedure for developing a multiple regression model is very similar to the simple regression case discussed in Chapter 14. A **regression coefficient** predicts the change in a dependent variable due to a one-unit increase in an independent variable while other variables are held constant. For example, how much will an extra year's age affect the price of a Toyota Camry? To determine what a regression's coefficients are, let's begin by first collecting sample data related to 20 used Toyota Camrys currently on the market. The data are shown in Table 15.1 and can be found in the Excel file **Used Camrys.xlsx**.

Be sure you understand the difference between y and $\hat{y}$. The variable y represents the value of the dependent variable such as $27,995 for the first car. The variable $\hat{y}$ represents the predicted value for the dependent variable that results from Equation 15.1.

TABLE 15.1 | Asking Prices for 20 Used Toyota Camrys

CAR	PRICE ($)	MILEAGE (MILES)	AGE (YRS)	CAR	PRICE ($)	MILEAGE (MILES)	AGE (YRS)
1	27,995	52,438	2	11	13,899	62,330	4
2	22,500	30,815	7	12	13,500	86,137	4
3	21,490	18,260	5	13	12,999	53,969	5
4	20,400	36,504	3	14	12,500	54,718	9
5	19,495	23,781	3	15	11,600	50,366	5
6	18,700	33,796	7	16	11,400	64,567	7
7	15,995	51,706	3	17	11,295	69,953	4
8	15,000	78,251	5	18	9,995	92,367	6
9	13,990	44,692	4	19	9,995	78,880	8
10	13,900	59,060	5	20	9,600	55,512	8

As you can see from Table 15.1, we have two independent variables in this example, mileage and age, so $k = 2$. This results in the following regression equation:

$$\hat{y} = b_0 + b_1x_1 + b_2x_2$$

We will predict the value for our used Camry by identifying the values for b_0, b_1, and b_2 in this equation by using PHStat:

1. Open the Excel file **Used Camrys.xlsx.**
2. Go to **Add-Ins** > **PHStat** > **Regression** > **Multiple Regression**, as shown in Figure 15.1A.

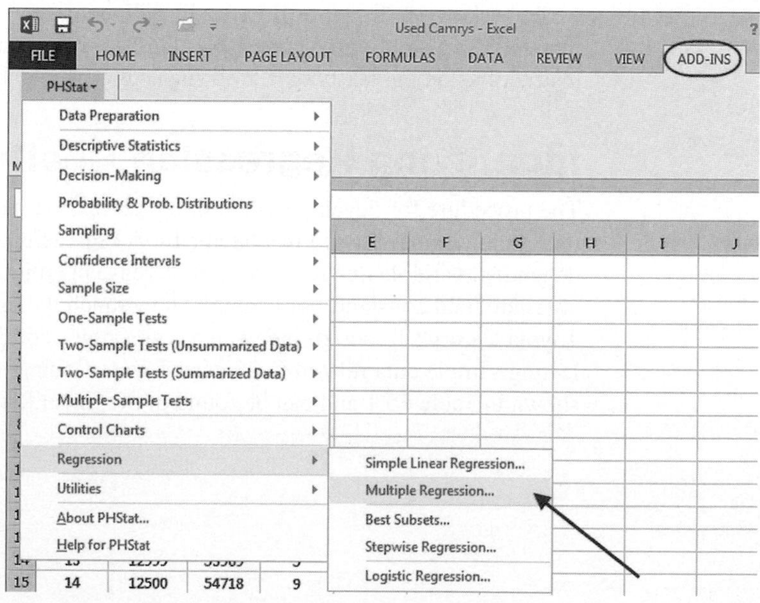

FIGURE 15.1A
Using PHStat for a Multiple Regression (Steps 1 and 2)

In the **Multiple Regression** dialog box, shown in Figure 15.1B, do the following:

3. Click on the first text box, which is labeled **Y Variable Cell Range**.
4. Because our y (dependent) variable is Price, highlight Cells B1 to B21, which includes the label "Price."
5. Click on the second text box, which is labeled **X Variables Cell Range**.

6. Highlight Cells C1 to D21.
7. Because labels were included in our data range, check the **First cells in both ranges contain label**, as Figure 15.1B shows.
8. Check the boxes in the **Regression Tool Output Options** and **Output Options** sections as shown in Figure 15.1B.
9. In the **Confidence level for interval estimates** text box, enter 95. Click **OK**.

FIGURE 15.1B
Using PHStat for a Multiple Regression (Steps 3–9)

	A	B	C	D
1	Car	Price ($)	Mileage	Age
2	1	27995	52438	2
3	2	22500	30815	7
4	3	21490	18260	5
5	4	20400	36504	3
6	5	19495	23781	3
7	6	18700	33796	7
8	7	15995	51706	3
9	8	15000	78251	5
10	9	13990	44692	4
11	10	13900	59060	5
12	11	13899	62330	4
13	12	13500	86137	4
14	13	12999	53969	5
15	14	12500	54718	9
16	15	11600	50366	5
17	16	11400	64567	7
18	17	11295	69953	4
19	18	9995	92367	6
20	19	9995	78880	8
21	20	9600	55512	8

Multiple Regression
Data
Y Variable Cell Range: Data!$B$1:$B$21
X Variables Cell Range: Data!$C$1:$D$21
☑ First cells in both ranges contain label
Confidence level for regression coefficients: 95 %
Regression Tool Output Options
☑ Regression Statistics Table
☑ ANOVA and Coefficients Table
☑ Residuals Table
☑ Residual Plots
Output Options
Title:
☐ Durbin-Watson Statistic
☑ Coefficients of Partial Determination
☑ Variance Inflationary Factor (VIF)
☑ Confidence Interval Estimate & Prediction Interval
Confidence level for intervals: 95 %
Help OK Cancel

PHStat and Excel both require that the independent variables be located in adjacent columns in the spreadsheet as shown in Figure 15.1B.

10. PHStat creates several worksheets for the multiple regression output. The current sheet will be labeled "COMPUTE" and contains the multiple regression results shown in Figure 15.1C.

FIGURE 15.1C
Using PHStat for a Multiple Regression (Final Result)

	A	B	C	D	E	F	G
1	Regression Analysis						
2							
3	*Regression Statistics*						
4	Multiple R	0.7435					
5	R Square	0.5528					
6	Adjusted R Square	0.5002					
7	Standard Error	3489.1291					
8	Observations	20					
9							
10	ANOVA						
11		*df*	*SS*	*MS*	*F*	*Significance F*	
12	Regression	2	255828307.3	127914153.6	10.5071	0.0011	
13	Residual	17	206958369.5	12174021.7			
14	Total	19	462786676.8				
15							
16		*Coefficients*	*Standard Error*	*t Stat*	*P-value*	*Lower 95%*	*Upper 95%*
17	Intercept	28253.0486	2965.0561	9.5287	0.0000	21997.3270	34508.7702
18	Mileage	-0.1422	0.0402	-3.5408	0.0025	-0.2270	-0.0575
19	Age	-986.6639	418.0287	-2.3603	0.0305	-1868.6273	-104.7005

Recording these coefficients to four decimal places may seem like overkill, but doing so will reduce rounding errors later in the chapter.

The coefficients for our regression equation are circled in red in Figure 15.1C. The equation to predict the asking price for used Camrys is therefore as follows:

$$\hat{y} = 28{,}253.0486 - 0.1422x_1 - 986.6639x_2$$

where

x_1 = The mileage
x_2 = The age in years of the used car

Let's look at how to interpret the meaning of these regression coefficients. The mileage coefficient $(b_1 = -0.1422)$ tells us that an additional mile on a used car's odometer will reduce the asking price by an average of \$0.1422. The negative sign for this coefficient means that increasing the mileage will reduce the asking price, which is to be expected. This change assumes that the age of the car stays constant.

The age coefficient $(b_2 = -986.6639)$ tells us that an additional year on the age of a used car will reduce the asking price by an average of \$987. The negative sign for this coefficient means that increasing the age of the car will reduce the asking price, which is also to be expected. This change assumes that the mileage of the car stays constant.

Using the multiple regression equation to predict the dependent variable using values of independent variables outside of the range of the original sample can lead to unreliable results.

Finally, the y-intercept $(b_0 = 28{,}253)$ provides an estimate for the price of a Camry with zero miles and zero years, or essentially a new vehicle. However, because we do not have any observations in our sample with these values of x_1 and x_2, predicting that a new Camry will cost \$28,253 is not a reliable estimate.

The coefficients for the age and the mileage are the result of the software using the least squares method to find the values that minimize $\sum(y - \hat{y})^2$, which is essentially minimizing the squared error (difference) between the actual and predicted dependent variable.

Using the Regression Model to Make Predictions

We're now ready to answer the question posed at the start of this chapter: What should your asking price for the six-year-old Toyota Camry with 76,320 miles be? We need to set $x_1 = 76{,}320$ and $x_2 = 6$ into our used Camry regression equation:

$$\hat{y} = 28{,}253.0486 - 0.1422x_1 - 986.6639x_2$$

$$\hat{y} = 28{,}253.0486 - 0.1422(76{,}320) - 986.6639(6) = \$11{,}480$$

Based on our regression results, the asking price of the recently acquired Camry should be set to \$11,480. I can only imagine how impressed your new boss will be to see this analysis!

We can construct a confidence interval around this asking price to get a sense of the range of asking prices in the market for vehicles with similar ages and mileages. The PHStat output provides this information in the "CIEandPI" worksheet (found by scrolling left to the first worksheet) which we generated in the previous section. The worksheet is shown in Figure 15.2 after using the Delete key to remove the PHStat User Note.

FIGURE 15.2
Confidence and Prediction Intervals Using PHStat

	A	B	C
1	Confidence Interval Estimate and Prediction Interval		
2			
3	Data		
4	Confidence Level	95%	
5		1	
6	Mileage given value	76320	
7	Age given value	6	
8			
9	X'X	20	1098102
10		1098102	6.8E+10
11		104	5818873
12			
13	Inverse of X'X	0.722157	-6.2E-06
14		-6.2E-06	1.33E-10
15		-0.06353	-2E-07
16			
17	X'G times Inverse of X'X	-0.13414	2.68E-06
18			
19	[X'G times Inverse of X'X] times XG	0.113044	
20	t Statistic	2.109816	
21	Predicted Y (YHat)	11476.9	
22			
23	For Average Predicted Y (YHat)		
24	Interval Half Width	2475.06	
25	Confidence Interval Lower Limit	9001.839	
26	Confidence Interval Upper Limit	13951.96	
27			
28	For Individual Response Y		
29	Interval Half Width	7766.364	
30	Prediction Interval Lower Limit	3710.534	
31	Prediction Interval Upper Limit	19243.26	
32			

Recall from Chapter 14 that confidence intervals estimate the range of an average value of the dependent variable (asking price). Prediction intervals estimate the range of one specific value of the dependent variable.

We first need to provide the mileage and age of our vehicle in Cells B6 and B7, which are circled in blue at the top of the worksheet. PHStat then provides us with the predicted asking price ($\hat{y}$) in Cell B21 (circled in green). This value ($11,476.90) is slightly different from our manual calculation ($11,480) because of rounding in the calculations.

Your boss will probably want to know how confident you are that you set the right asking price for the used Camry. Fortunately for you, the answer lies in Figure 15.2. Back in Chapter 14, we learned about confidence and prediction intervals for the dependent variable in a simple regression. We can apply the same concept here. According to Figure 15.2, the 95% confidence interval for the *average* asking price of a six-year-old car with 76,320 miles is $9,002 to $13,952. This interval can be found in Cells B25 and B26 and is circled in red. The 95% prediction interval for the asking price of a *specific* six-year-old car with 76,320 miles is $3,711 to $19,243. This interval can be found in Cells B30 and B31 and is circled in purple. One way to make these intervals smaller (more precise) is to collect a larger sample of used Camrys and to repeat the analysis.

As you can see, our prediction interval is much wider (less precise) than our confidence interval. This is because a sample mean is an average of the variables in the sample; as a result, it's going to vary less than the individual values in the sample. Because our prediction interval is estimating a single value, the variation will be much greater than when we estimate an average asking price. If we want a more precise (narrower) estimate for our asking price, we could gather a larger sample size.

Let's see how much you've learned so far by trying your hand at this Your Turn problem before moving on to the next section.

YOUR TURN #1

The Excel file **MLB 2012 Wins 1.xlsx** lists the number of games each Major League Baseball team won during the 2012 season. The file also provides the average number of runs scored per game (RPG) and the average number of runs given up per game (ERA) for each team.

a. Develop a regression equation to predict the number of games won by a Major League Baseball team based on its RPG and ERA.

b. Interpret the meaning of the regression coefficients.

c. Predict the number of games won for a team that scores an average of 4.0 runs per game and gives up an average of 3.5 runs per game.

d. Construct a 95% confidence interval to estimate the average number of games won by teams described in part c.

e. Construct a 95% prediction interval to estimate the number of games won by a specific team described in part c.

Answers can be found on ▶ **page 761**

15.1 Section Problems

Basic Skills

15.1 Consider the following set of dependent and independent variables. These data can also be found in the Excel file **Prob 151.xlsx.**

y	10	11	15	15	20	24	27	32
x_1	2	5	5	9	7	11	16	20
x_2	16	10	13	10	2	8	7	4

a. Using PHStat, construct a multiple regression model with these data.

b. Interpret the meaning of the values for b_1 and b_2.

c. Provide an estimate for y when $x_1 = 10$ and $x_2 = 12$.

15.2 Consider the following set of dependent and independent variables. These data can also be found in the Excel file **Prob 152.xlsx**.

y	47	42	40	40	31	26	23	18	10
x_1	74	63	78	52	44	47	35	17	15
x_2	22	29	20	17	13	17	8	15	10

a. Using PHStat, construct a multiple regression model with these data.

b. Interpret the meaning of the values for b_1 and b_2.
c. Provide an estimate for y when $x_1 = 50$ and $x_2 = 15$.

15.3 Use the sample data from Problem 15.1 to answer the following questions:

a. Construct a 95% confidence interval for the dependent variable when $x_1 = 7$ and $x_2 = 14$.
b. Interpret the meaning of the interval constructed in part a.
c. Construct a 95% prediction interval for the dependent variable when $x_1 = 7$ and $x_2 = 14$.
d. Interpret the meaning of the interval constructed in part c.

15.4 Use the sample data from Problem 15.2 to answer the following questions:

a. Construct a 90% confidence interval for the dependent variable when $x_1 = 30$ and $x_2 = 20$.
b. Interpret the meaning of the interval constructed in part a.
c. Construct a 90% prediction interval for the dependent variable when $x_1 = 30$ and $x_2 = 20$.
d. Interpret the meaning of the interval constructed in part c.

Applications

15.5 Jersey Shore Realtors would like to develop a regression model to help it set weekly rental rates for beach properties during the summer season in New Jersey. The independent variables for this model are the number of bedrooms a property has, its age in years, and the number of blocks away from the ocean the property is. The data for randomly selected rental properties can be found in the Excel file **Jersey Shore Realtors 1.xlsx**.

a. Construct a regression model using all three independent variables.
b. Interpret the meaning of the regression coefficients.
c. Predict the average weekly rental rate for a four-bedroom house that is 15 years old and three blocks from the ocean.
d. Construct a 95% confidence interval for the average weekly rental rate for a house described in part c. Interpret the meaning of the interval.
e. Construct a 95% prediction interval for the weekly rental rate for a house described in part c. Interpret the meaning of the interval.

15.6 City Hospital would like to develop a regression model to predict the total hospital bill for a patient based on his or her length of stay, the number of days in the hospital's intensive care unit (ICU), and the age of the patient. Data for these variables can be found in the Excel file **City Hospital.xlsx**.

a. Construct a regression model using all three independent variables.
b. Interpret the meaning of the regression coefficients.
c. Predict the average hospital bill for a 53-year-old person hospitalized for three days with no days spent in the ICU.
d. Construct a 95% confidence interval for the average hospital bill for the patient in part c. Interpret the meaning of the interval.
e. Construct a 95% prediction interval for the hospital bill for the patient in part c. Interpret the meaning of the interval.

15.7 A business statistics professor at State College would like to develop a regression model to predict the final exam scores for students based on their current grade point averages (GPAs), the number of hours they studied for the exam, and the number of times they were absent during the semester. The data for these variables can be found in the Excel file **final exam scores 1.xlsx**.

a. Construct a regression model using all three independent variables.
b. Interpret the meaning of the regression coefficients.
c. Predict the average exam score for a student who studied 4.0 hours for the exam, missed two classes during the semester, and has a current GPA of 2.95.
d. Construct a 90% confidence interval for the average exam score for a student who studied 3.0 hours, missed four classes, and has a GPA equal to 3.10.
e. Construct a 90% prediction interval for the exam score for a particular student who studied 3.0 hours, missed four classes, and has a GPA equal to 3.10.
f. Explain the reason for the different intervals in parts d and e.

15.8 A finance executive would like to determine if a relationship exists between the current earnings per share (EPS) of a bank and the following independent variables:

- Total assets ($ billions)
- Previous period's EPS
- Previous period's return on average assets (ROAA)
- Previous period's return on average equity (ROAE)

ROAA measures how effectively assets are utilized, and ROAE measures a firm's profitability. The Excel file **Bank EPS.xlsx** contains these data for several banks.

a. Construct a regression model using all four independent variables.
b. Interpret the meaning of the regression coefficients.
c. Predict the average EPS for a bank that has $2.6 billion in total assets and the following results from the previous period: ROAA = 1.5%, EPS = $1.80, ROAE = 8%.
d. Construct a 95% confidence interval for the average EPS for a bank described in part c. Interpret the meaning of the interval.
e. Construct a 95% prediction interval for the EPS for a bank described in part c. Interpret the meaning of the interval.

15.9 Suppose the athletic director at Villanova University would like to develop a regression model to predict the point differential for games played by the college's men's basketball team. A point differential is the difference between the final points scored by two competing teams.

A positive differential is a win for Villanova, and a negative differential is a loss. For a random sample of games, shown in the Excel file **Villanova basketball 1.xlsx**, the point differential was calculated for Villanova, along with the number of assists, rebounds, turnovers, and personal fouls.

a. Construct a regression model using all four independent variables.
b. Interpret the meaning of the regression coefficients.
c. Predict the average point differential for a game in which Villanova had 12 assists, 32 rebounds, 15 turnovers, and 20 personal fouls.
d. Construct a 95% confidence interval for the average point differential for the game described in part c. Interpret the meaning of the interval.
e. Construct a 95% prediction interval for the point differential for the game described in part c. Interpret the meaning of the interval.
f. Explain the reason for the different intervals in parts d and e.

15.10 Delmarva Power is a utility company that would like to predict the monthly heating bill for a household in Kent County during the month of January. A random sample of households in the county was selected and their January heating bill recorded along with the following variables:

SF: the square footage of the house

Age: the age of the current heating system in years

Temp: the thermostat setting, in degrees Fahrenheit, during the day

The following figure shows the regression output from Excel.

16		Coefficients
17	Intercept	-652.2924
18	SF	0.0904
19	Age	2.0430
20	Temp	10.8250

a. Interpret the meaning of all three regression coefficients.
b. Predict the average January heating bill for a household with 2,850 square feet, with a heating system that is nine years old, and a thermostat set to 72 degrees during the day.

15.11 Comcast would like to develop the ability to predict the monthly cable bill for a customer. A multiple regression model was developed using a random sample of customers using the following independent variables:

TV: the number of televisions in the household

People: the number of people living in the household

Years: the number of years that the household has been a Comcast customer

The following figure shows the regression output from Excel.

16		Coefficients
17	Intercept	39.3247
18	TV	11.9025
19	People	7.3994
20	Years	-0.8577

a. Interpret the meaning of all three regression coefficients.
b. Predict the average cable bill for a household with three televisions, with five people in residence, and six years of being a customer.

15.2 Explaining the Variation of the Dependent Variable

When you examine the asking prices of used Camrys shown in Table 15.1, you will notice that they range from \$9,600 to \$27,995. This variation from car to car could be due to several factors, such as a car's age, mileage, condition, and upgrades such as leather seats. In this section, we will determine how much of this variation is due to the independent variables age and mileage.

The Multiple Coefficient of Determination

In our example, the SST measures the amount of variation of actual used car prices around their mean.

When we discussed the simple regression model back in Chapter 14, you learned about three sums of squares. All three have come back to visit us in this chapter, except now we have multiple independent variables:

- The total sum of squares (*SST*) measures the variation in the dependent variable.
- The sum of squares regression (*SSR*) measures the amount of variation in a dependent variable that is explained by a set of independent variables.

In our example, the *SSR* measures the amount of variation of predicted used car prices around the mean.

- The sum of squares error (*SSE*) measures the variation in a dependent variable that is explained by variables other than a set of independent variables.

We can determine these sums of squares with the following three equations:

Formula 15.3 for the Total Sum of Squares (SST)

$$SST = \sum (y - \bar{y})^2$$

Formula 15.4 for the Sum of Squares Regression (SSR)

$$SSR = \sum (\hat{y} - \bar{y})^2$$

Formula 15.5 for the Sum of Squares Error (SSE)

$$SSE = \sum (y - \hat{y})^2$$

where

y = A value of the dependent variable from the sample
$\hat{y}$ = The predicted value of the dependent variable from the regression model
$\bar{y}$ = The average value of the dependent variable from the sample

Rather than calculate these sums of squares manually, I'm going to cut you a huge break and use PHStat to provide them for us. The *SST* can be partitioned as we did in Chapter 14 according to Equation 15.6.

Formula 15.6 for Partitioning the Total Sum of Squares

$$SST = SSR + SSE$$

We can identify these sums of squares for our used Camry example in the PHStat output that we have already generated. They are found in Cells C12, C13, and C14 (circled in red) in the ANOVA (analysis of variance) section of the "COMPUTE" worksheet, as shown in Figure 15.3.

FIGURE 15.3
The Sums of Squares from the Camry Regression Output Using PHStat

	A	B	C	D	E	F	G
1	**Regression Analysis**						
2							
3	*Regression Statistics*						
4	Multiple R	0.7435					
5	R Square	0.5528					
6	Adjusted R Square	0.5002					
7	Standard Error	3489.1291					
8	Observations	20					
9							
10	**ANOVA**						
11		*df*	*SS*	*MS*	*F*	*Significance F*	
12	Regression	2	255828307.3	127914153.6	10.5071	0.0011	
13	Residual	17	206958369.5	12174021.7			
14	Total	19	462786676.8				
15							
16		*Coefficients*	*Standard Error*	*t Stat*	*P-value*	*Lower 95%*	*Upper 95%*
17	Intercept	28253.0486	2965.0561	9.5287	0.0000	21997.3270	34508.7702
18	Mileage	-0.1422	0.0402	-3.5408	0.0025	-0.2270	-0.0575
19	Age	-986.6639	418.0287	-2.3603	0.0305	-1868.6273	-104.7005
20							

$$R^2 = \frac{SSR}{SST} = \frac{255{,}828{,}307.3}{462{,}786{,}676.8} = 0.5528$$

If all 20 used Camrys in our sample had the same asking price, the *SST* would equal zero.

According to Figure 15.3, the sums of squares are as follows:

$$SSR = 255{,}828{,}307.3$$
$$SSE = 206{,}958{,}369.5$$
$$SST = 462{,}786{,}676.8$$

The **multiple coefficient of determination, R^2**, is the percentage of variation in the dependent variable that is explained by all of the independent variables.

We are now ready to calculate the **multiple coefficient of determination, R^2**—which is the percentage of the variation in the dependent variable (such as a car's asking price) that is explained by all of the independent variables (such as the car's age and mileage)—using Equation 15.7.

Formula 15.7 for the Multiple Coefficient of Determination

$$R^2 = \frac{SSR}{SST}$$

Applying Equation 15.7 to our used Camry example, we have the following:

$$R^2 = \frac{SSR}{SST} = \frac{255{,}828{,}307.3}{462{,}786{,}676.8} = 0.5528$$

In other words, 55.28% of the variation in the asking price for the used Camrys in our sample can be explained by the age and mileage of the car. Figure 15.3 shows this result circled in green in Cell B5. The remaining variation is probably due to other factors that we have not considered, such as the condition of the car or its upgrades. We'll look at how introducing additional variables affects our model later in the chapter.

Testing the Significance of the Overall Regression Model

In this section, we'll use the sums of squares data to decide if the relationship between the independent and dependent variables is statistically significant. In other words, can we use our regression equation $\hat{y} = 28{,}253.0486 - 0.1422x_1 - 986.6639x_2$ to accurately determine the appropriate asking price for the used Camry? Considering this is your first used car appraisal, this is a very good question to answer. Based on our sample of 20 used Camrys, Excel provides us with the following coefficients for the independent variables:

The terms b_1 and b_2 represent the effects that age and mileage have on the price of the 20 used Camrys in the sample.

$$\text{Mileage: } b_1 = -0.1422$$
$$\text{Age: } b_2 = -986.6639$$

Remember, our model predicted that every additional mile on the used car's odometer reduced the asking price by an average of \$0.1422, and every additional year reduced the average asking price by \$987. These coefficients, however, are only estimates of the true population coefficients of all the used Camrys for sale in the market, β_1 and β_2. The terms β_1 and β_2 represent the effects that age and mileage have on the price of every used Camry on the market, which is our population. The terms b_1 and b_2 represent the effects that age and mileage have on the price of the 20 used Camrys in our sample.

The terms β_1 and β_2 represent the effects that age and mileage have on the price of every used Camry in the population.

If the population coefficients β_1 and β_2 are actually equal to zero, then mileage and age would have no effect on the asking price of the car. Therefore, to test the overall significance of our regression equation, we examine the following hypothesis statement:

H_0: $\beta_1 = \beta_2 = 0$ (No relationship between dependent and independent variables)

H_1: At least one $\beta_i \neq 0$ (Relationship exists between dependent and independent variables)

The null hypothesis assumes that no relationship exists between the dependent and independent variables, whereas the alternative hypothesis takes the opposite position. Rejecting the null hypothesis provides support that a relationship *does* exist between the variables, so it's appropriate to use this model to determine the asking price. We'll test our hypothesis using $\alpha = 0.05$.

The **mean square regression** (*MSR*) is found by dividing the sum of squares regression (*SSR*) by the number of independent variables (*k*).

The **mean square error** (*MSE*) is found by dividing the sum of squares error (*SSE*) by $n-k-1$.

We start by calculating the **mean square regression** (*MSR*) and **mean square error** (*MSE*) from our sums of squares using Equations 15.8 and 15.9.

Formula 15.8 for the Mean Square Regression (MSR)

$$MSR = \frac{SSR}{k}$$

Formula 15.9 for the Mean Square Error (MSE)

$$MSE = \frac{SSE}{n-k-1}$$

where

$SSR =$ The sum of squares regression
$SSE =$ The sum of squares error
$n =$ The number of observations in the sample
$k =$ The number of independent variables

The denominators in both of the mean square equations represent the degrees of freedom (*df*) in our model. Adding them together represents the total degrees of freedom for our example, which is always $n - 1$. For example, the *MSR* has two degrees of freedom $(k = 2)$. The *MSE* has $n - k - 1 = 20 - 2 - 1 = 17$ degrees of freedom (remember we have 20 cars in our sample, so $n = 20$). Adding these together results in $2 + 17 = 19$ total degrees of freedom, which is the same result as $n - 1\ (20 - 1)$.

The mean squares for our used Camry example are as follows:

$$MSR = \frac{SSR}{k} = \frac{255{,}828{,}307.3}{2} = 127{,}914{,}153.6$$

$$MSE = \frac{SSE}{n-k-1} = \frac{206{,}958{,}369.5}{20-2-1} = 12{,}174{,}021.7$$

We use the *F*-test to determine the significance of the overall regression model. The *F*-test statistic is shown in Equation 15.10.

Formula 15.10 for the F-Test Statistic for the Overall Regression Model

$$F = \frac{MSR}{MSE}$$

Applying Equation 15.10 to our used Camry example, we have the following:

$$F = \frac{MSR}{MSE} = \frac{127{,}914{,}153.6}{12{,}174{,}021.7} = 10.51$$

This test statistic follows the *F*-distribution with the degrees of freedom we discussed before:

$$D_1 = k = 2$$
$$D_2 = n - k - 1 = 17$$

The critical *F*-score, F_α, identifies the rejection region for the hypothesis test. Using $\alpha = 0.05$, the critical *F*-score found in Table 6 in Appendix A is $F_\alpha = 3.592$.

The F-test does not tell us which of the independent variables in our used-car example are statistically significant. We'll examine another procedure later in the chapter that will test the significance of each independent variable.

Excel also provides the critical F-score with the F.INV.RT function as follows:

$$=\text{F.INV.RT}(\alpha, D_1, D_2)$$

This function is useful when the value of D_2 exceeds 30, which is the highest value found in Table 6. Using this function for our Camry example, we have =F.INV.RT(0.05, 2, 17) = 3.592.

Because $F = 10.51$ is higher than $F_\alpha = 3.592$, we reject H_0 and conclude that at least one of the population coefficients for our independent variables is not equal to zero. In other words, you can indeed use this regression model to determine the asking price for the used Camry. Figure 15.4 illustrates the results of this hypothesis test.

FIGURE 15.4
Testing the Significance of the Used Camry Example Using PHStat

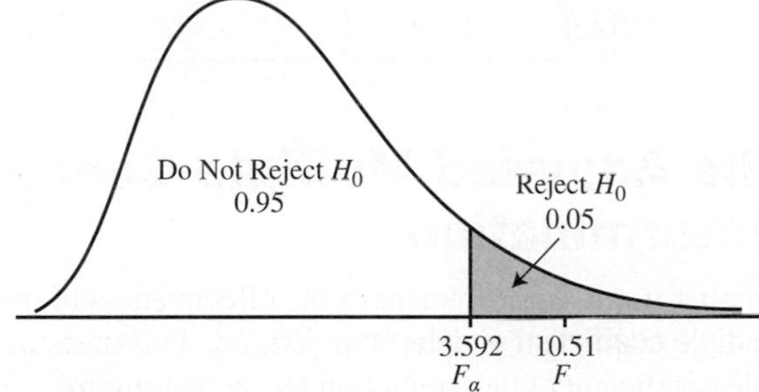

These results can also be identified in the PHStat output that we have already generated. They are circled in red in the ANOVA section in the "COMPUTE" worksheet shown in Figure 15.5.

FIGURE 15.5
The Mean Sums of Squares from the Regression Output: Used Camry Example

	A	B	C	D	E	F	G
1	**Regression Analysis**						
2							
3	*Regression Statistics*						
4	Multiple R	0.7435					
5	R Square	0.5528					
6	Adjusted R Square	0.5002					
7	Standard Error	3489.1291					
8	Observations	20					
9							
10	ANOVA						
11		*df*	*SS*	*MS*	*F*	*Significance F*	
12	Regression	2	255828307.3	127914153.6	10.5071	0.0011	
13	Residual	17	206958369.5	12174021.7			
14	Total	19	462786676.8				
15							
16		*Coefficients*	*Standard Error*	*t Stat*	*P-value*	*Lower 95%*	*Upper 95%*
17	Intercept	28253.0486	2965.0561	9.5287	0.0000	21997.3270	34508.7702
18	Mileage	-0.1422	0.0402	-3.5408	0.0025	-0.2270	[illegible]
19	Age	-986.6639	418.0287	-2.3603	0.0305	-1868.6273	-104.7005
20							

$$R^2 = \frac{SSR}{SST} = \frac{255{,}828{,}307.3}{462{,}786{,}676.8} = 0.5528$$

Cell F12 in Figure 15.5 reports the p-value for this hypothesis test, which is labeled "Significance F." Because this p-value = 0.0011 and is less than $\alpha = 0.05$, we reject the null hypothesis. This result is illustrated in Figure 15.6.

FIGURE 15.6
The p-Value for the Used Camry Example

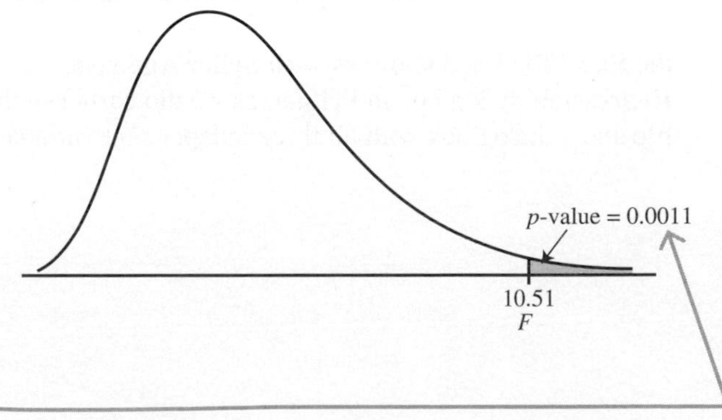

Remember, the p-value represents the probability of obtaining an F-test statistic greater than 10.51 if the null hypothesis were indeed true.

Table 15.2 summarizes the ANOVA calculations that underlie the Excel regression output in Figure 15.5.

TABLE 15.2 | ANOVA SUMMARY CALCULATIONS FOR EXCEL'S REGRESSION OUTPUT

SOURCE	df	SS	MS	F
Regression	k	SSR	$MSR = \frac{SSR}{k}$	$F = \frac{MSR}{MSE}$
Residual	$n - k - 1$	SSE	$MSE = \frac{SSE}{n - k - 1}$	
Total	$n - 1$	SST		

The Adjusted Multiple Coefficient of Determination

The **adjusted multiple coefficient of determination,** R_A^2, modifies, or adjusts, the multiple coefficient of determination by accounting for the number of independent variables and the sample size used to develop a multiple regression model.

Another useful measurement of the effectiveness of the regression model is the **adjusted multiple coefficient of determination,** R_A^2. This measurement modifies, or adjusts, the multiple coefficient of determination by accounting for the number of independent variables and the sample size used to develop the model and is found using Equation 15.11.

Formula 15.11 for the Adjusted Multiple Coefficient of Determination

$$R_A^2 = 1 - \left[(1 - R^2)\left(\frac{n - 1}{n - k - 1}\right)\right]$$

Let's find the adjusted R^2 for our used-car example. Using the data from Figure 15.5, we have the following:

$$R_A^2 = 1 - \left[(1 - R^2)\left(\frac{n - 1}{n - k - 1}\right)\right]$$

$$R_A^2 = 1 - \left[(1 - 0.5528)\left(\frac{20 - 1}{20 - 2 - 1}\right)\right]$$

$$R_A^2 = 1 - [(0.4472)(1.1176)] = 1 - 0.4998 = 0.5002$$

This value is reported in Cell B6 in Figure 15.5.

I'm sure your curious mind is already wondering why we need another R^2 value. Well, in most cases, one of our goals when using a multiple regression is to explain as much of the variation in the dependent variable as possible. Adding additional independent variables to the regression equation will always increase the value of R^2. However, as we will see later in this chapter, not all independent variables are worth including in the regression model.

To illustrate this concept, I've modified our used Camry example by including a third independent variable—the age of people selling their Camrys. These data can be found in the Excel file **Used Camrys with Seller Age.xlsx**. Open this file and go to the **Multiple Regression** dialog box in PHStat, as we did earlier in the chapter. Figure 15.7A shows this file and a dialog box with all three independent variables selected.

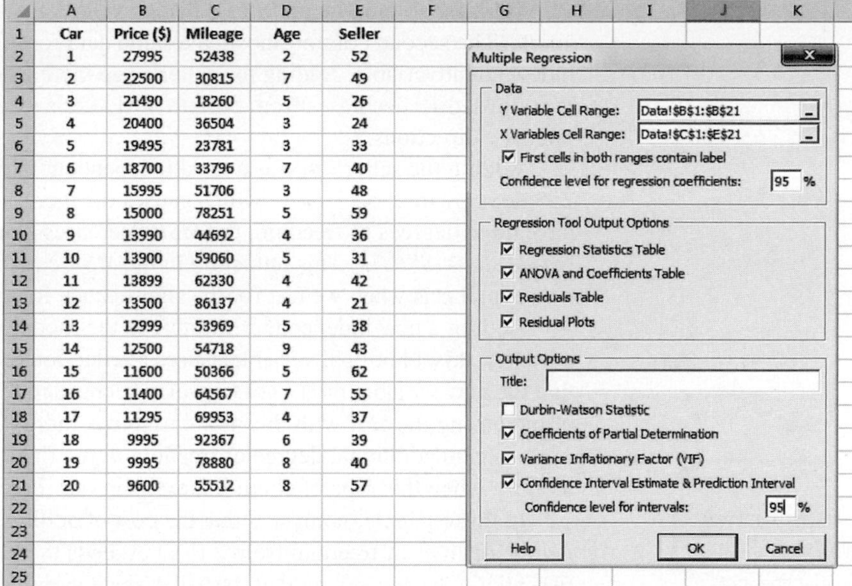

Car	Price ($)	Mileage	Age	Seller
1	27995	52438	2	52
2	22500	30815	7	49
3	21490	18260	5	26
4	20400	36504	3	24
5	19495	23781	3	33
6	18700	33796	7	40
7	15995	51706	3	48
8	15000	78251	5	59
9	13990	44692	4	36
10	13900	59060	5	31
11	13899	62330	4	42
12	13500	86137	4	21
13	12999	53969	5	38
14	12500	54718	9	43
15	11600	50366	5	62
16	11400	64567	7	55
17	11295	69953	4	37
18	9995	92367	6	39
19	9995	78880	8	40
20	9600	55512	8	57

FIGURE 15.7A Using PHStat to Find the Multiple Coefficients of Determination: Used Camrys with Sellers' Ages Example (Step 1)

The PHStat regression output is shown in Figure 15.7B.

Regression Analysis

Regression Statistics	
Multiple R	0.7450
R Square	0.5551
Adjusted R Square	0.4716
Standard Error	3587.3868
Observations	20

ANOVA

	df	SS	MS	F	Significance F
Regression	3	256877169.5	85625723.2	6.6535	0.0040
Residual	16	205909507.3	12869344.2		
Total	19	462786676.8			

	Coefficients	Standard Error	t Stat	P-value	Lower 95%	Upper 95%
Intercept	27616.1414	3777.6910	7.3103	0.0000	19607.7942	35624.4886
Mileage	-0.1434	0.0415	-3.4553	0.0033	-0.2314	-0.0554
Age	-1020.9699	446.2837	-2.2877	0.0361	-1967.0491	-74.8908
Seller	21.1137	73.9577	0.2855	0.7789	-135.6697	177.8971

FIGURE 15.7B Using PHStat to Find the Multiple Coefficients of Determination: Used Camrys with Sellers' Ages Example (Final Result)

Table 15.3 summarizes the multiple coefficients of determination for each example.

TABLE 15.3 | Comparing R^2 for Two Different Regression Models

	MODELS: WITHOUT SELLERS' AGES	MODELS: WITH SELLERS' AGES
Independent variables	2	3
R^2	0.5528	0.5551
Adjusted R^2	0.5002	0.4716
SSR	255,828,307	256,877,170
df	2	3
MSR	127,914,154	85,625,723

Adding the sellers' ages as an independent variable in this example drastically reduces the *MSR*, which makes it more difficult to reject the null hypothesis.

A smaller *MSR* results in a smaller *F*-test statistic. This, in turn, reduces the chance of rejecting the null hypothesis.

The first column in Table 15.3 displays the R^2 data from our original used Camry example. The second column shows the same data for the modified example with the third independent variable. Adding the seller's age increases R^2 from 55.3% to 55.5%. However, the adjusted R^2 decreases from 50% to 47%. Let's examine why these two R^2 values move in opposite directions.

Adding the seller's age as a third independent variable increases the *SSR* from 255,828,307 to 256,877,170, which causes the increase in R^2. However, because we now have three degrees of freedom, the *MSR* decreases from 127,914,154 to 85,625,723 (remember, $MSR = SSR/k$). This reduction in the *MSR* can make it more challenging to reject the null hypothesis when we test for the significance for the overall regression model.

Adding a new independent variable to the model will always increase the R^2 value. If, however, this additional variable causes a reduction in the adjusted R^2, we have evidence that the new variable might not be worth keeping in the model. In other words, the "benefit" of increasing the *SSR* with this new variable is more than offset with the increased "cost" of having an additional degree of freedom in the final model. The adjusted R^2 allows us to identify when this type of condition exists in our regression model.

In this example, it appears that the cost of adding the seller's age to the model (increasing the degrees of freedom from 2 to 3) exceeds the benefit of the increase in the *SSR*. Essentially, we are saying that the seller's age variable is not carrying its weight in the regression model. Therefore, our model would be better served by not including the seller's age variable. We will further examine this issue of whether to include independent variables later in the chapter.

The model confirms what we would logically conclude—that the age of the seller does not affect the selling price of the Camry.

In summary, the adjusted R^2 will always be less than or equal to R^2. If R^2 is very small and there are a relatively large number of independent variables, the adjusted R^2 could be negative. In these cases, simply report the value as zero. The adjusted R^2 value is particularly useful when comparing regression models using the same dependent variable and different numbers of independent variables.

If adding an independent variable results in a reduction in the adjusted R^2, we have evidence that the new variable might not be contributing enough to the explanation of the dependent variable to remain in the model.

Enough of me doing all the work. It's time to test your newly found regression skills on the following Your Turn problem. By the way, you'll notice that some of the Your Turn and chapter problems appear to repeat themselves. Don't worry—I haven't had a brain lapse. These problems use the same data and build on your skills as you learn new concepts.

YOUR TURN #2

The Excel file **MLB 2012 Wins 1.xlsx** lists the number of games each Major League Baseball team won during the 2012 season. This file also provides the average number of runs scored per game (RPG) and the average number of runs given up per game (ERA) for each team.

a. Identify the *SSR*, *SSE*, and *SST* from the Excel output.
b. Calculate the multiple coefficient of determination and interpret its meaning.
c. Test the significance of the overall regression model using $\alpha = 0.01$.
d. Interpret the meaning of the *p*-value from the Excel output.
e. Calculate the adjusted R^2.

Answers can be found on ▶ **page 762**

15.2 Section Problems

Basic Skills

15.12 Consider the following set of dependent and independent variables. These data can also be found in the Excel file **Prob 151.xlsx**.

y	10	11	15	15	20	24	27	32
x_1	2	5	5	9	7	11	16	20
x_2	16	10	13	10	2	8	7	4

a. Using PHStat, identify the *SST*, *SSR*, and *SSE*.
b. Calculate the multiple coefficient of determination.
c. Test the significance of the overall regression model using $\alpha = 0.05$.
d. Interpret the *p*-value for the overall regression model.
e. Calculate the adjusted multiple coefficient of determination.

15.13 Consider the following set of dependent and independent variables. These data can also be found in the Excel file **Prob 153.xlsx**.

y	47	42	40	40	31	26	23	18	10
x_1	74	63	78	52	44	47	35	17	15
x_2	22	29	20	17	13	17	8	15	10

a. Using PHStat, identify the *SST*, *SSR*, and *SSE*.
b. Calculate the multiple coefficient of determination.
c. Test the significance of the overall regression model using $\alpha = 0.10$.
d. Interpret the *p*-value for the overall regression model.
e. Calculate the adjusted multiple coefficient of determination.

15.14 Consider the following ANOVA table for a multiple regression model:

Source	*df*	*SS*	*MS*	*F*
Regression	4	1,600	400	10
Residual	30	1,200	40	
Total	34	2,800		

a. What is the size of this sample?
b. How many independent variables are in this model?
c. Calculate the multiple coefficient of determination.
d. Test the significance of the overall regression model using $\alpha = 0.05$.
e. Calculate the adjusted multiple coefficient of determination.

15.15 Consider the following ANOVA table for a multiple regression model:

Source	*df*	*SS*	*MS*	*F*
Regression	3			
Residual		7,000		
Total	53	9,100		

a. Complete the remaining entries in the table.
b. What is the size of this sample?
c. How many independent variables are in this model?
d. Calculate the multiple coefficient of determination.
e. Test the significance of the overall regression model using $\alpha = 0.05$.
f. Calculate the adjusted multiple coefficient of determination.

Applications

15.16 Squirt Squad is a cleaning service that sends crews to residential homes on either a once-a-month or a twice-a-month schedule, depending on the customer's preference. The owner would like to predict the amount of time, in minutes, required to clean a house based on the square footage of the house, the total number of rooms in the house, the number of bathrooms it has, and the size of the cleaning crew. Data from randomly selected homes can be found in the Excel file **Squirt Squad 1.xlsx**.

a. Construct a regression model using all the independent variables.
b. Calculate the multiple coefficient of determination.
c. Test the significance of the overall regression model using $\alpha = 0.05$.
d. Calculate the adjusted multiple coefficient of determination.

15.17 A finance executive would like to determine if a relationship exists between the current earnings per share (EPS) of a bank and the following independent variables:

- Total assets ($ billions)
- Previous period's EPS
- Previous period's return on average assets (ROAA)
- Previous period's return on average equity (ROAE)

ROAA measures how effectively assets are utilized, and ROAE measures a firm's profitability. The Excel file **Bank EPS.xlsx** contains these data for several banks.

a. Construct a regression model using all three independent variables.
b. Calculate the multiple coefficient of determination.
c. Test the significance of the overall regression model using $\alpha = 0.05$.
d. Calculate the adjusted multiple coefficient of determination.

15.18 Jersey Shore Realtors would like to develop a regression model to help it set weekly rental rates for beach properties during the summer season in New Jersey. The independent variables for this model are the number of bedrooms a property has, its age in years, and the number of blocks away from the ocean it is. The data for randomly selected rental properties can be found in the Excel file **Jersey Shore Realtors 1.xlsx**.

a. Construct a regression model using all three independent variables.
b. Calculate the multiple coefficient of determination.
c. Test the significance of the overall regression model using $\alpha = 0.05$.
d. Calculate the adjusted multiple coefficient of determination.

15.19 A business statistics professor at State College would like to develop a regression model to predict the final exam scores for students based on their current GPAs, the number of hours they studied for the exam, and the number of times they were absent during the semester. The data for these variables can be found in the Excel file **final exam scores 1.xlsx**.

a. Construct a regression model using all three independent variables.
b. Calculate the multiple coefficient of determination.
c. Test the significance of the overall regression model using $\alpha = 0.10$.
d. Calculate the adjusted multiple coefficient of determination.

15.20 City Hospital would like to develop a regression model to predict the total hospital bill for a patient based on his or her length of stay, number of days in the hospital's intensive care unit (ICU), and age of the patient. Data for these variables can be found in the Excel file **City Hospital .xlsx**.

a. Construct a regression model using all three independent variables.
b. Calculate the multiple coefficient of determination.
c. Test the significance of the overall regression model using $\alpha = 0.05$.
d. Calculate the adjusted multiple coefficient of determination.

15.21 Comcast would like to develop the ability to predict the monthly cable bill for a customer. A multiple regression model was developed using a random sample of customers using the following independent variables:

TV: the number of televisions in the household

People: the number of people living in the household

Years: the number of years that the household has been a Comcast customer

The following figure shows the regression output from Excel.

10	ANOVA		
11		*df*	*SS*
12	Regression	3	9526.63
13	Residual	24	7970.33
14	Total	27	17496.96
15			
16		*Coefficients*	*Standard Error*
17	Intercept	39.3247	15.4384
18	TV	11.9025	3.2437
19	People	7.3994	2.7922
20	Years	-0.8577	1.2931

a. Calculate the multiple coefficient of determination.
b. Test the significance of the overall regression model using $\alpha = 0.05$.
c. Calculate the adjusted multiple coefficient of determination.

15.22 Delmarva Power is a utility company that would like to predict the monthly heating bill for a household in Kent County during the month of January. A random sample of households in the county was selected and their January heating bill recorded along with the following variables:

SF: the square footage of the house

Age: the age of the current heating system in years

Temp: the thermostat setting, in degrees Fahrenheit, during the day

The following figure shows the regression output from Excel.

10	ANOVA		
11		*df*	*SS*
12	Regression	3	102454.9381
13	Residual	28	61158.5619
14	Total	31	163613.5000
15			
16		*Coefficients*	*Standard Error*
17	Intercept	-652.2924	322.0966
18	SF	0.0904	0.0210
19	Age	2.0430	1.5089
20	Temp	10.8250	5.0068

a. Calculate the multiple coefficient of determination.
b. Test the significance of the overall regression model using $\alpha = 0.05$.
c. Calculate the adjusted multiple coefficient of determination.

15.3 Inferences about the Independent Variables

In the previous section, we focused on testing the significance of the overall regression model, that is, we included all of the independent variables in the hypothesis test together at one time. In this section, I'll show you how to examine each independent variable separately to make sure that it belongs in the final regression model. We'll also look at confidence intervals for the regression coefficients and interpret their meanings.

A Significance Test for the Regression Coefficients

To demonstrate the technique of testing each independent variable, let's refer to the modified used Camry example from the previous section where I added the age of the seller to the data file. Figure 15.8 shows the regression output with the data of interest circled in red.

FIGURE 15.8
Using PHStat for the Regression Output: Coefficients for the Used Camrys with Sellers' Ages Example

	A	B	C	D	E	F	G
1	Regression Analysis						
2							
3	Regression Statistics						
4	Multiple R	0.7450					
5	R Square	0.5551					
6	Adjusted R Square	0.4716					
7	Standard Error	3587.3868					
8	Observations	20					
9							
10	ANOVA						
11		df	SS	MS	F	Significance F	
12	Regression	3	256877169.5	85625723.2	6.6535	0.0040	
13	Residual	16	205909507.3	12869344.2			
14	Total	19	462786676.8				
15							
16		Coefficients	Standard Error	t Stat	P-value	Lower 95%	Upper 95%
17	Intercept	27616.1414	3777.6910	7.3103	0.0000	19607.7942	35624.4886
18	Mileage	-0.1434	0.0415	-3.4553	0.0033	-0.2314	-0.0554
19	Age	-1020.9699	446.2837	-2.2877	0.0361	-1967.0491	-74.8908
20	Seller	21.1137	73.9577	0.2855	0.7789	-135.6697	177.8971
21							

The regression coefficients from our sample for this model are as follows:

$$\text{Mileage: } b_1 = -0.1434$$
$$\text{Car's age: } b_2 = -1{,}020.9699$$
$$\text{Seller's age: } b_3 = 21.1137$$

The null hypothesis assumes that no relationship exists between the asking price and a used Camry's mileage, whereas the alternative hypothesis takes the opposite position.

We'll start by testing the following hypothesis statement to see if the population mileage coefficient, β_1, is equal to zero:

$$H_0: \beta_1 = 0 \text{ (No relationship exists between asking price and mileage)}$$
$$H_1: \beta_1 \neq 0 \text{ (Relationship exists between asking price and mileage)}$$

Rejecting the null hypothesis provides support that there is a significant relationship between a used Camry's mileage and its asking price. I would like to reject the null hypothesis because I have included independent variables in the model that I think belong there. We'll test our hypothesis using $\alpha = 0.05$.

We use the t-test to determine the significance of this relationship. The general t-test statistic is shown in Equation 15.12.

Formula 15.12 for the t-Test Statistic for the Regression Coefficient

$$t = \frac{b_j - \beta_j}{s_{b_j}}$$

where

b_j = The regression coefficient for the jth independent variable
β_j = The population regression coefficient for the jth independent variable from the null hypothesis
s_{b_j} = The standard error of the regression coefficient for the jth independent variable

The standard error of the regression coefficient for mileage, $s_{b_1} = 0.0415$, is the standard deviation for b_1, the mileage coefficient (Cell C18 in Figure 15.8). For our sample of 20 used Camrys, $b_1 = -0.1434$. However, if we collected additional samples of 20 Camrys, we would expect each sample to have a different value for b_1. The **standard error of the regression coefficient**, s_{b_1}, measures the variation in b_1 among these samples. The larger this variation is, the larger the value of s_{b_1} is.

The **standard error of the regression coefficient,** S_{b_j}, measures the variation in the regression coefficient, b_j, among several samples.

$\beta_1 = 0$ in this equation because the null hypothesis assumes there is no relationship between the independent and dependent variables.

With mileage being our first independent variable ($j = 1$), our t-test statistic from Equation 15.12 and Figure 15.8 is as follows:

$$t = \frac{b_1 - \beta_1}{s_{b_1}} = \frac{-0.1434 - 0}{0.0415} = -3.46$$

The test statistic in Equation 15.12 follows the t-distribution with $n - k - 1$ degrees of freedom. The critical t-score, $t_{\alpha/2}$, identifies the rejection region for this two-tail hypothesis test. Using $\alpha = 0.05$ and $20 - 3 - 1 = 16$ degrees of freedom, the critical t-score found in Table 5 in Appendix A is $t_{\alpha/2} = 2.120$.

Excel also provides the critical t-score for a two-tail test with the T.INV.2T function as follows:

$$=\text{T.INV.2T}(\alpha, df)$$

By rejecting the null hypothesis, we conclude that mileage appears to be a good predictor of the asking price.

Using this function for our Camry example, we have =T.INV.2T(0.05, 16) = 2.120. To use this function with a one-tail test, double the value of α.

Because $t = -3.46$ is lower than $-t_{\alpha/2} = -2.120$, we reject H_0 and conclude that the mileage population coefficient is not equal to zero. In other words, the relationship between a used Camry's mileage and asking price is statistically significant. Figure 15.9 illustrates the results of this hypothesis test.

As is always the case, we reach the same conclusion by looking at the p-value for this hypothesis test. According to Figure 15.8, the p-value in the Mileage row equals 0.00326. Because this value is less than $\alpha = 0.05$, we reject the null hypothesis.

FIGURE 15.9
Testing the Significance of the Mileage Coefficient

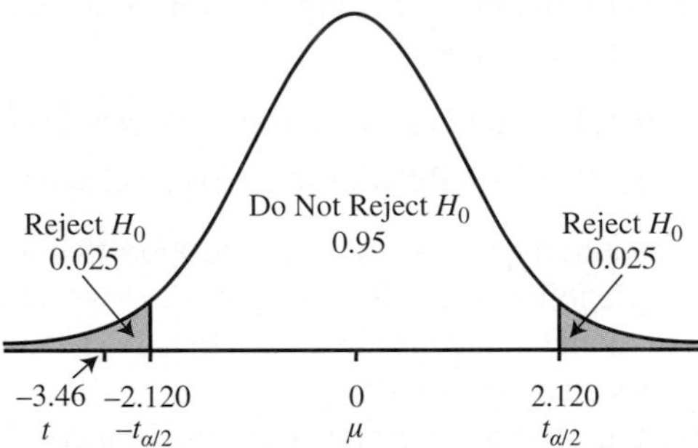

When we examine the second independent variable, the age of the car, we come to the same conclusion. The p-value = 0.03611, which is also less than $\alpha = 0.05$. We conclude that the age of a used Camry is also a good predictor of its asking price.

We get a different story when we look at the third independent variable, the seller's age. Here, the p-value = 0.77894, which is greater than $\alpha = 0.05$. We therefore fail to reject the null hypothesis in this case. Remember, rejecting the null hypothesis means that there is a relationship between the independent and dependent variable. So, *not* rejecting the null hypothesis means we conclude that there isn't a relationship between the two. Because we didn't reject the null hypotheses, we conclude that the seller's age is not a good predictor of the car's asking price. The proper decision would be to remove this independent variable from our regression model.

Use the F-test to determine if the overall regression model is significant and the t-test to examine the significance of the individual independent variables.

Some of my students struggle with the decision of when to use a t-test and when to use an F-test for multiple regression. The F-test is designed to determine if the overall regression model, with all of the independent variables included, is statistically significant. For instance, the F-test in Figure 15.8 shows that the overall regression model for the used Camry example is significant with a p-value equal to 0.00398 (see Cell F12). However, all three independent variables are not statistically significant, as we just discovered. To examine the significance of the individual independent variables, we use the t-test.

Confidence Intervals for the Regression Coefficients

We can also estimate the population coefficients by constructing confidence intervals around the sample coefficients from our regression results. These intervals provide a range to give us a sense as to the values of the true regression slopes and can be found using Equation 15.13.

Formula 15.13 for the Confidence Interval for the Regression Coefficient

$$CI = b_j \pm t_{\alpha/2} s_{b_j}$$

Let's apply this equation to construct a 95% confidence interval to estimate the population mileage coefficient. The critical *t*-score, $t_{\alpha/2}$, for this interval uses $n - k - 1 = 20 - 3 - 1 = 16$ degrees of freedom, as shown in Table 5 in Appendix A, resulting in $t_{\alpha/2} = 2.120$. Recalling that $b_1 = -0.1434$ and $s_{b_1} = 0.0415$, the confidence interval calculation using Equation 15.12 is as follows:

$$CI = b \pm t_{\alpha/2} s_b = -0.1434 \pm (2.120)(0.0415)$$

$$CI = b \pm t_{\alpha/2} s_b = -0.1434 \pm 0.0880$$

$$\text{Upper confidence limit } (UCL) = -0.1434 + 0.0880 = -0.0554$$

$$\text{Lower confidence limit } (LCL) = -0.1434 - 0.0880 = -0.2314$$

If this confidence interval did include zero, we would have some evidence that β could be equal to zero, which indicates that there may not be a relationship between our two variables.

Based on our sample of 20 used Camrys, we are 95% confident that adding an additional mile on the car's odometer will reduce the average asking price between \$0.0554 and \$0.2314. Because this confidence interval does not include zero, we have evidence to conclude that there is a relationship between a used Camry's asking price and the car's mileage.

This confidence interval is also reported in the regression output, which is shown again in Figure 15.10 and is circled in red.

FIGURE 15.10 Using PHStat for Confidence Intervals for the Regression Coefficients: Used Camrys with Sellers' Ages Example

	A	B	C	D	E	F	G
1	**Regression Analysis**						
2							
3	*Regression Statistics*						
4	Multiple R	0.7450					
5	R Square	0.5551					
6	Adjusted R Square	0.4716					
7	Standard Error	3587.3868					
8	Observations	20					
9							
10	ANOVA						
11		*df*	*SS*	*MS*	*F*	*Significance F*	
12	Regression	3	256877169.5	85625723.2	6.6535	0.0040	
13	Residual	16	205909507.3	12869344.2			
14	Total	19	462786676.8				
15							
16		*Coefficients*	*Standard Error*	*t Stat*	*P-value*	*Lower 95%*	*Upper 95%*
17	Intercept	27616.1414	3777.6910	7.3103	0.0000	19607.7942	35624.4886
18	Mileage	-0.1434	0.0415	-3.4553	0.0033	-0.2314	-0.0554
19	Age	-1020.9699	446.2837	-2.2877	0.0361	-1967.0491	-74.8908
20	Seller	21.1137	73.9577	0.2855	0.7789	-135.6697	177.8971
21							

Because zero is included in this confidence interval, the population slope for a seller's age could be equal to zero. We therefore fail to reject the null hypothesis.

Cells F19 and G19 in Figure 15.10 show the 95% confidence interval for the second independent variable, the age of the car. Based on our sample of 20 used Camrys, we are 95% confident that adding an additional year to the car's age will reduce the average asking price by \$74.89 to \$1,967.05. Because this confidence interval does not include zero, we have supporting evidence to conclude that there is a relationship between the age of the car and the asking price.

Finally, Cells F20 and G20 in Figure 15.10 show the 95% confidence interval for the third independent variable, the age of the seller. Based on our sample of 20 used Camrys, we are 95% confident that adding an additional year to the seller's age will result in the average asking price changing from a reduction of \$135.67 to an increase of \$177.90. Notice that zero is included in this interval, which means the true population coefficient for the seller's age could be zero. Based on this result, we fail to reject the null hypothesis and conclude that the seller's age is not a good predictor for asking price.

YOUR TURN #3

The Excel file **MLB 2012 Wins 2.xlsx** lists the number of games each Major League Baseball team won during the 2012 season. This file also shows the average number of runs scored per game (RPG), the average number of runs given up per game (ERA), and the number of errors committed in the field for the year (ERR) for each team. Using the output from PHStat, answer the following questions. (Hint: Be sure to change the "Confidence level for the regression coefficients" to 99% in the **Multiple Regression** dialog box.)

a. Using $\alpha = 0.01$, perform a hypothesis test to determine if including the number of errors committed during the season is a good predictor of games won.

b. Interpret the *p*-value for the ERR independent variable.

c. Construct a 99% confidence interval to estimate the population coefficient for the number of errors committed and interpret its meaning.

d. Comment on the usefulness of including the RPG and ERA independent variables in the model to predict the number of a team's wins.

e. Interpret the meaning of the 99% confidence intervals to estimate the population coefficient for the RPG and ERA.

Answers can be found on ▶ **page 762**

15.3 Section Problems

Basic Skills

15.23 Consider the following set of dependent and independent variables. These data can also be found in the Excel file **Prob 151.xlsx.**

y	10	11	15	15	20	24	27	32
x_1	2	5	5	9	7	11	16	20
x_2	16	10	13	10	2	8	7	4

a. Using PHStat, construct a regression model using both independent variables.

b. Test the significance of each independent variable using $\alpha = 0.05$.

c. Interpret the p-value for each independent variable.

15.24 Consider the following set of dependent and independent variables. These data can also be found in the Excel file **Prob 153.xlsx.**

y	47	42	40	40	31	26	23	18	10
x_1	74	63	78	52	44	47	35	17	15
x_2	22	29	20	17	13	17	8	15	10

a. Using PHStat, construct a regression model using both independent variables.

b. Test the significance of each independent variable using $\alpha = 0.10$.

c. Interpret the p-value for each independent variable.

15.25 Use the data from Problem 15.23 to answer the following questions:

a. Construct a 95% confidence interval for the regression coefficient for x_1 and interpret its meaning.

b. Construct a 95% confidence interval for the regression coefficient for x_2 and interpret its meaning.

15.26 Use the data from Problem 15.24 to answer the following questions:

a. Construct a 90% confidence interval for the regression coefficient for x_1 and interpret its meaning.

b. Construct a 90% confidence interval for the regression coefficient for x_2 and interpret its meaning.

Applications

15.27 Jersey Shore Realtors would like to develop a regression model to help it set weekly rental rates for beach properties during the summer season in New Jersey. The independent variables for this model are the number of bedrooms a property has, its age, and the number of blocks away from the ocean it is. The data for randomly selected rental properties can be found in the Excel file **Jersey Shore Realtors 1.xlsx.**

a. Using PHStat, construct a regression model using all three independent variables.

b. Test the significance of each independent variable using $\alpha = 0.05$.

c. Using p-values, determine which independent variables are significant with $\alpha = 0.05$.

d. Construct a 95% confidence interval for the regression coefficients for the Bedroom variable and interpret the meaning.

e. Using the results from part d, comment on the significance of the Bedroom variable.

15.28 Suppose the athletic director at Villanova University would like to develop a regression model to predict the point differential for games played by the college's men's basketball team. A point differential is the difference between the final points scored by two competing teams. A positive differential is a win for Villanova, and a negative differential is a loss. For a random sample of games, shown in the Excel file **Villanova basketball 1.xlsx**, the point differential was calculated for Villanova, along with the number of assists, rebounds, turnovers, and personal fouls.

a. Using PHStat, construct a regression model using all four independent variables.
b. Test the significance of each independent variable using $\alpha = 0.10$.
c. Interpret the p-value for each independent variable.
d. Construct a 90% confidence interval for the regression coefficients for the Personal Fouls independent variable and interpret the meaning.
e. Using the results from part d, comment on the significance of the Personal Fouls variable.

15.29 City Hospital would like to develop a regression model to predict the total hospital bill for a patient based on his or her length of stay, number of days in the hospital's intensive care unit (ICU), and age of the patient. Data for these variables can be found in the Excel file **City Hospital.xlsx.**

a. Using PHStat, construct a regression model using all three independent variables.
b. Test the significance of each independent variable using $\alpha = 0.05$.
c. Interpret the p-value for each independent variable.
d. Construct a 95% confidence interval for the regression coefficients for the ICU variable and interpret the meaning.
e. Using the results from part d, comment on the significance of the ICU variable.

15.30 A finance executive would like to determine if a relationship exists between the current earnings per share (EPS) of a bank and the following independent variables:

- Total assets ($ billions)
- Previous period's EPS
- Previous period's return on average assets (ROAA)
- Previous period's return on average equity (ROAE)

ROAA measures how effectively assets are utilized, and ROAE measures a firm's profitability. The Excel file **Bank EPS.xlsx** contains these data for several banks.

a. Using PHStat, construct a regression model using all three independent variables.
b. Test the significance of each independent variable using $\alpha = 0.05$.
c. Interpret the p-value for each independent variable.
d. Construct a 95% confidence interval for the regression coefficients for the Previous ROAA variable and interpret the meaning.
e. Using the results from part d, comment on the significance of the Previous ROAA variable.

15.31 Squirt Squad is a cleaning service that sends crews to residential homes on either a once-a-month or a twice-a-month schedule, depending on the customer's preference. The owner would like to predict the amount of time, in minutes, required to clean a house based on the square footage of the house, the total number of rooms in the house, the number of bathrooms it has, and the size of the cleaning crew. Data from randomly selected homes can be found in the Excel file **Squirt Squad 1.xlsx.**

a. Using PHStat, construct a regression model using all independent variables.
b. Test the significance of each independent variable using $\alpha = 0.05$.
c. Interpret the p-value for each independent variable.
d. Construct a 95% confidence interval for the regression coefficients for the Size of Crew variable and interpret the meaning.
e. Using the results from part d, comment on the significance of the Size of Crew variable.

15.32 Comcast would like to develop the ability to predict the monthly cable bill for a customer. A multiple regression model was developed using a random sample of customers using the following independent variables:

TV: the number of televisions in the household

People: the number of people living in the household

Years: the number of years that the household has been a Comcast customer

The following figure shows the regression output from Excel.

10	ANOVA		
11		*df*	*SS*
12	Regression	3	9526.63
13	Residual	24	7970.33
14	Total	27	17496.96
15			
16		*Coefficients*	*Standard Error*
17	Intercept	39.3247	15.4384
18	TV	11.9025	3.2437
19	People	7.3994	2.7977
20	Years	-0.8577	1.2931

a. Test the significance of each independent variable using $\alpha = 0.05$.
b. Construct a 95% confidence interval for each regression coefficient and interpret the meaning.

15.33 Delmarva Power is a utility company that would like to predict the monthly heating bill for a household in Kent County during the month of January. A random sample of households in the county was selected and their January heating bill recorded along with the following variables:

SF: the square footage of the house

Age: the age of the current heating system in years

Temp: the thermostat setting, in degrees Fahrenheit, during the day

The following figure shows the regression output from Excel.

10	ANOVA		
11		*df*	*SS*
12	Regression	3	102454.9381
13	Residual	28	61158.5619
14	Total	31	163613.5000
15			
16		*Coefficients*	*Standard Error*
17	Intercept	-652.2924	322.0966
18	SF	0.0904	0.0210
19	Age	2.0430	1.5089
20	Temp	10.8250	5.0068

a. Test the significance of each independent variable using $\alpha = 0.05$.
b. Construct a 95% confidence interval for each regression coefficient and interpret the meaning.

15.4 Using Qualitative Independent Variables

So far in this chapter, all of the independent variables have been quantitative data, such as age and mileage. However, there may be times when you are interested in using qualitative, or categorical, data in your regression model. Examples of such data would be the gender (male, female) or education level (high school, college) of a person in your data set. To handle such a scenario, we need to create **dummy variables** that take on the values of 0 or 1.

Dummy variables are used to represent qualitative data in a multiple regression model and can take on only the values 0 and 1.

For example, if we would like to include the gender of a respondent in our model, there are only two mutually exclusive possibilities for each instance, male and female. We can create a dummy variable called GENDER that takes on the following values:

$$\text{GENDER} = 0 \text{ if the person is a male}$$
$$\text{GENDER} = 1 \text{ if the person is a female}$$

The choice of assigning a 0 to a male and 1 to a female is completely arbitrary. We treat this dummy variable as a quantitative independent variable and proceed with the analysis as we have done with previous examples.

To demonstrate the use of dummy variables in our regression model, I'll use the following example. Suppose David is a street vendor who sells hot dogs in the city and would like to develop a regression model to help him predict the daily demand for his product in order to improve inventory control. David believes that the three main factors affecting hot-dog demand for a particular day are his price per hot dog, the high temperature during business hours that day, and whether the day falls on a weekday or weekend (many of David's customers are businesspeople). To develop his model, David recorded during 12 randomly selected days the data shown in Table 15.4.

TABLE 15.4 | DATA FOR THE HOT-DOG DEMAND MODEL

DAILY DEMAND	HIGH TEMPERATURE	PRICE ($)	DAY
144	73	1.00	Weekday
90	64	1.00	Weekend
108	73	1.00	Weekday
120	82	1.00	Weekday
54	45	1.20	Weekend
69	54	1.20	Weekday
126	86	1.20	Weekday
99	70	1.20	Weekend
48	73	1.50	Weekend
33	66	1.50	Weekend
90	75	1.50	Weekday
81	61	1.50	Weekday

We first need to create a dummy variable, which I'll call Day, to represent the qualitative categories "weekday" and "weekend." I'll use the following arbitrary assignment for this variable:

$$\text{Day} = 1 \text{ for a weekday}$$
$$\text{Day} = 0 \text{ for a weekend}$$

Which value of the dummy variable that is assigned a 1 and which is assigned a 0 is arbitrary.

These data can be found in the Excel file **hot dog demand.xlsx**. Open this file and go the **Multiple Regression** dialog box in PHStat, as we did earlier in the chapter. Figure 15.11A shows this file and dialog box with all three independent variables selected.

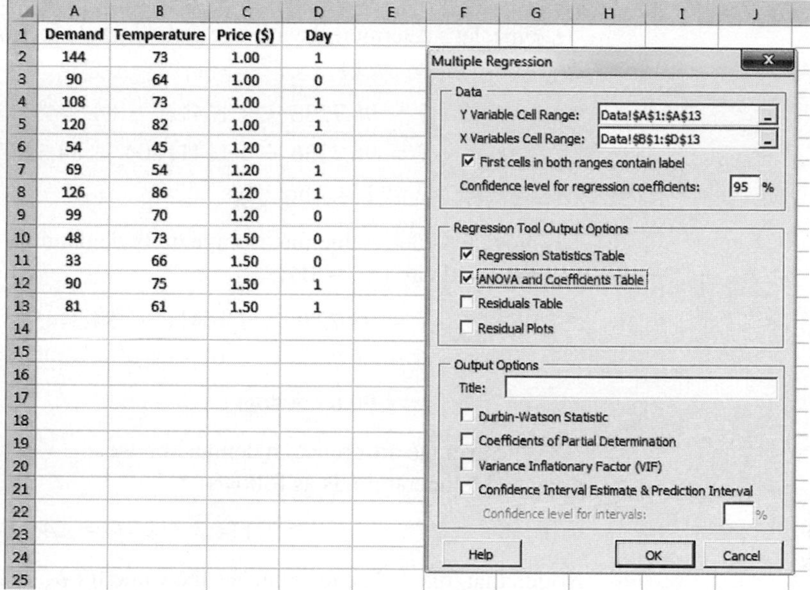

FIGURE 15.11A
Using a Dummy Variable in a Multiple Regression with PHStat (Step 1)

Figure 15.11B shows the regression results for our hot-dog demand model.

FIGURE 15.11B
Using a Dummy Variable in a Multiple Regression with PHStat (Final Result)

Regression Analysis

Regression Statistics	
Multiple R	0.9108
R Square	0.8295
Adjusted R Square	0.7656
Standard Error	16.2041
Observations	12

ANOVA

	df	*SS*	*MS*	*F*	*Significance F*
Regression	3	10220.4191	3406.8064	12.9747	0.0019
Residual	8	2100.5809	262.5726		
Total	11	12321.0000			

	Coefficients	*Standard Error*	*t Stat*	*P-value*	*Lower 95%*	*Upper 95%*
Intercept	98.7236	43.5432	2.2673	0.0531	-1.6873	199.1345
Temperature	1.1641	0.4621	2.5190	0.0359	0.0985	2.2298
Price ($)	-84.3445	23.2308	-3.6307	0.0067	-137.9147	-30.7742
Day	24.1025	10.3807	2.3219	0.0488	0.1645	48.0405

According to Figure 15.11B, the regression equation for our hot-dog model is

$$\hat{y} = 98.7236 + 1.1641x_1 - 84.3445x_2 + 24.1025x_3$$

where

x_1 = High temperature in degrees Fahrenheit
x_2 = The price per hot dog
x_3 = 1 for a weekday and 0 for a weekend

The interpretations for the regression coefficients in this equation are as follows:

$b_1 = 1.1641$: Every additional degree of the daily high temperature results in an average increase of 1.1641 hot dogs sold per day, assuming there is no change in the other two variables.

$b_2 = -84.3445$: Every additional dollar in price results in an average decrease in hot-dog demand of 84.3445, assuming there is no change in the other two variables. In other words, a \$0.10 increase in the price reduces the demand by an average of 8.4 hot dogs per day.

$b_3 = 24.1025$: On average, the weekday demand exceeds the weekend demand by 24.1025 hot dogs per day, assuming there is no change in the other two variables.

The interpretation of the dummy variable coefficient becomes more obvious when we examine the regression equation under the following conditions:

- First, let's determine the average daily demand for hot dogs at a $1.20 price on an 80°F weekday $(x_3 = 1)$:

$$\hat{y} = 98.7236 + 1.1641x_1 - 84.3445x_2 + 24.1025x_3$$
$$\hat{y} = 98.7236 + 1.1641(80) - 84.3445(1.20) + 24.1025(1)$$
$$\hat{y} = 114.7 \text{ hot dogs}$$

- Now, let's determine the average daily demand for hot dogs at a $1.20 price on an 80°F weekend day $(x_3 = 0)$:

$$\hat{y} = 98.7236 + 1.1641x_1 - 84.3445x_2 + 24.1025x_3$$
$$\hat{y} = 98.7236 + 1.1641(80) - 84.3445(1.20) + 24.1025(0)$$
$$\hat{y} = 90.6 \text{ hot dogs}$$

The average difference in demand between a weekday and weekend day, given the same price and temperature, is as follows:

$$114.7 - 90.6 = 24.1 \text{ hot dogs}$$

Notice that this difference matches the value for b_3, which is no coincidence (hold your applause until the end of the chapter).

Because there are only two possible outcomes for the qualitative variable in our hot-dog example, we needed only one dummy variable in our model. However, we do encounter situations in which the qualitative variable has more than two categories. How do we handle this? To answer this question, let's return to our original used Camry example. In addition to the age and mileage of the car, I'm going to add the condition of the car as a variable, with the following three possibilities:

Excellent Good Poor

These data can be found in the Excel file **Used Camrys with Condition.xlsx**. For this example we need two dummy variables, Cond1 and Cond2, as Table 15.5 shows.

TABLE 15.5 | CREATING "USED-CAR CONDITION" DUMMY VARIABLES

	DUMMY VARIABLES	
CONDITION	COND1	COND2
Excellent	0	0
Good	0	1
Poor	1	0

In other words, a used Camry in excellent condition would be assigned a value of zero for both Cond1 and Cond2 dummy variables. Again, the choice of assigning condition levels to a dummy variable set is arbitrary. I could have easily assigned a car in poor condition zeros for both dummy variables.

The pattern of values for qualitative variables with three categories should always be as follows:

$$(0,0),\ (0,1),\ (1,0)$$

The category that is assigned (0,0) is known as the base category, which in this example is the excellent condition. In general, the number of dummy variables used is always one less than the number of categories in the qualitative data.

Figure 15.12A shows our Excel file with the PHStat Multiple Regression dialog box.

FIGURE 15.12A
Using Two Dummy Variables in a Multiple Regression with PHStat (Step 1)

Car	Price ($)	Mileage	Age	Cond1	Cond2	Condition
1	27995	52438	2	0	0	Excellent
2	22500	30815	7	0	0	Excellent
3	21490	18260	5	0	1	Good
4	20400	36504	3	0	1	Good
5	19495	23781	3	0	0	Excellent
6	18700	33796	7	0	1	Good
7	15995	51706	3	0	1	Good
8	15000	78251	5	0	1	Good
9	13990	44692	4	1	0	Poor
10	13900	59060	5	0	1	Good
11	13899	62330	4	1	0	Poor
12	13500	86137	4	0	1	Good
13	12999	53969	5	0	1	Good
14	12500	54718	9	0	1	Good
15	11600	50366	5	1	0	Poor
16	11400	64567	7	0	1	Good
17	11295	69953	4	0	1	Good
18	9995	92367	6	0	1	Good
19	9995	78880	8	1	0	Poor
20	9600	55512	8	0	1	Good

Multiple Regression
Data
Y Variable Cell Range: Data!$B$1:$B$21
X Variables Cell Range: Data!$C$1:$F$21
☑ First cells in both ranges contain label
Confidence level for regression coefficients: 95 %
Regression Tool Output Options
☑ Regression Statistics Table
☑ ANOVA and Coefficients Table
☐ Residuals Table
☐ Residual Plots
Output Options
Title:
☐ Durbin-Watson Statistic
☐ Coefficients of Partial Determination
☐ Variance Inflationary Factor (VIF)
☐ Confidence Interval Estimate & Prediction Interval
Confidence level for intervals: %
Help OK Cancel

Remember, all of the independent variables need to be in adjacent columns in the Excel spreadsheet.

Notice that I have included the qualitative variable, Condition, in this file in Column G and the two corresponding dummy variables, Cond1 and Cond2, in Columns E and F. The red circles illustrate that the qualitative variable is converted into the two dummy variables for each car. Also note that the "X Variable Cell Range" in the dialog box does *not* include the qualitative variable (Condition) but does include both dummy variables (Cond1 and Cond2). Figure 15.12B shows the regression results.

FIGURE 15.12B
Using Two Dummy Variables in a Multiple Regression with PHStat (Final Result)

Regression Analysis

Regression Statistics	
Multiple R	0.8623
R Square	0.7435
Adjusted R Square	0.6751
Standard Error	2813.1132
Observations	20

ANOVA

	df	*SS*	*MS*	*F*	*Significance F*
Regression	4	344082585.2	86020646.3	10.8700	0.0002
Residual	15	118704091.6	7913606.1		
Total	19	462786676.8			

	Coefficients	*Standard Error*	*t Stat*	*P-value*	*Lower 95%*	*Upper 95%*
Intercept	29903.3768	2446.8607	12.2211	0.0000	24688.0166	35118.7371
Mileage	-0.0988	0.0352	-2.8071	0.0133	-0.1738	-0.0238
Age	-762.2102	346.6417	-2.1988	0.0440	-1501.0595	-23.3608
Cond1	-7695.6992	2334.7034	-3.2962	0.0049	-12672.0017	-2719.3968
Cond2	-5637.5586	2022.2392	-2.7878	0.0138	-9947.8595	-1327.2577

According to Figure 15.12B, the regression equation for our used Camry with the condition model is as follows:

$$\hat{y} = 29{,}903.3768 - 0.0988x_1 - 762.2102x_2 - 7{,}695.6992x_3 - 5{,}637.5586x_4$$

where

x_1 = The mileage of the used Camry
x_2 = The age in years of the used Camry
x_3 = The value of Cond1 for the used Camry
x_4 = The value of Cond2 for the used Camry

The interpretations for the regression coefficients in this equation are as follows:

$b_1 = -0.0988$: Every additional mile on the car's odometer will reduce the asking price by an average of \$0.0988, assuming there is no change in the age or condition of the car. We can extrapolate this to mean that every 1,000 miles on the car reduces the average asking price by \$98.80.

$b_2 = -762.2102$: Every additional year on the car's age will reduce the asking price by an average of \$762.21, assuming there is no change in the mileage or condition of the car.

The interpretation of the coefficients for the dummy variables ($b_3 = -7{,}695.6992$ and $b_4 = -5{,}637.5586$) require a little more explanation. Let's start with calculating the average asking price of a used Camry with 47,270 miles that is four years old and in excellent condition ($x_3 = 0, x_4 = 0$). Recall that this is our base category.

$$\hat{y} = 29{,}903.3769 - 0.0988x_1 - 762.2102x_2 - 7{,}695.6992x_3 - 5{,}637.5586x_4$$
$$\hat{y} = 29{,}903.3769 - 0.0988(47270) - 762.2102(4) - 7{,}695.6992(0) - 5{,}637.5586(0)$$
$$\hat{y} = \$22{,}184$$

Now, we'll determine the average asking price of a used Camry with 47,270 miles that is four years old and in good condition ($x_3 = 0, x_4 = 1$):

$$\hat{y} = 29{,}903.3769 - 0.0988x_1 - 762.2102x_2 - 7{,}695.6992x_3 - 5{,}637.5586x_4$$
$$\hat{y} = 29{,}903.3769 - 0.0988(47270) - 762.2102(4) - 7{,}695.6992(0) - 5{,}637.5586(1)$$
$$\hat{y} = \$16{,}547$$

The difference between the average asking price of a used Camry in excellent condition and one in good condition (with the same mileage and age) is as follows:

$$\$22{,}184 - \$16{,}547 = \$5{,}637$$

Recall that this is also the value for b_4, the coefficient for the dummy variable Cond2. Based on the manner in which we set up our dummy variables in Table 15.5, the value for b_4 tells us that a used Camry in good condition is worth, on average, \$5,637 less than the same car in excellent condition (the base category).

How do we interpret the other dummy variable coefficient, b_3? Now we calculate the average asking price of a used Camry with 47,270 miles that is four years old and in poor condition ($x_3 = 1, x_4 = 0$).

$$\hat{y} = 29{,}903.3769 - 0.0988x_1 - 762.2102x_2 - 7{,}695.6992x_3 - 5{,}637.5586x_4$$
$$\hat{y} = 29{,}903.3769 - 0.0988(47270) - 762.2102(4) - 7{,}695.6992(1) - 5{,}637.5586(0)$$
$$\hat{y} = \$14{,}489$$

The difference between the average asking price of a used Camry in excellent condition and one in poor condition (with the same mileage and age) is as follows:

$$\$22{,}184 - \$14{,}489 = \$7{,}695$$

As you can see, that is also the value for b_3, the coefficient for the dummy variable Cond1. Based on the manner in which we set up our dummy variables in Table 15.5, the value for b_3 tells us that a used Camry in poor condition is worth, on average, \$7,695 less than the same car in excellent condition (base category). The lesson here (besides dummy variables) is to take care of your car, a message that I continue to preach to my adult children, with limited success.

The coefficients for the dummy variables reflect the change in the dependent variable when comparing one category of the qualitative variable to the base category (the one with all of zeros). This begs the obvious question, what happens when you have more than three categories in your quantitative variable? Table 15.6 shows a possible set of dummy variables for four car-condition categories.

TABLE 15.6 | CREATING DUMMY VARIABLES FOR FOUR CATEGORIES

	DUMMY VARIABLES		
CONDITION	COND1	COND2	COND3
Excellent	0	0	0
Good	0	0	1
Fair	0	1	0
Poor	1	0	0

Here, again, I'm electing to use the excellent condition to be my base category. The key to the pattern is that no more than one dummy variable can be assigned a 1 for each condition. In other words, the number 1 cannot appear more than once in any row or column in Table 15.6.

To avoid feeling like a "dummy" on your next exam, test your dummy variable skills on this next Your Turn problem.

YOUR TURN #4

The Excel file **MLB 2012 Wins 3.xlsx** lists the number of games each Major League Baseball team won during the 2012 season. This file also provides the average number of runs scored per game (RPG) by each team, the average number of runs it gave up per game (ERA), and whether its stadium had a retractable roof/dome (ROOF).

Perform a regression analysis with PHStat and interpret the effect that a retractable roof or dome had on the number of games a team won during the season.

Answer can be found on ▶ page 763

15.4 Section Problems

Basic Skills

15.34 Consider the following set of dependent and independent variables. The variable x_3 is qualitative with M = Male and F = Female. The quantitative data for this problem can be found in the Excel file **Prob 1534.xlsx**.

y	10	11	15	15	20	24	27	32
x_1	2	5	5	9	7	11	16	20
x_2	16	10	13	10	2	8	7	4
x_3	M	M	F	F	F	M	F	F

a. Using PHStat, construct a regression model using all three independent variables.

b. Interpret the meaning of each of the regression coefficients.

15.35 Consider the following set of dependent and independent variables. The variable x_3 is qualitative with H = High, M = Medium, and L = Low. The quantitative data for this problem can be found in the Excel file **Prob 1535.xlsx**.

y	47	42	40	40	31	26	23	18	10
x_1	74	63	78	52	44	47	35	17	15
x_2	22	29	20	17	13	17	8	15	10
x_3	M	H	H	L	M	H	M	L	L

a. Using PHStat, construct a regression model using all three independent variables.

b. Interpret the meaning of each of the regression coefficients.

Applications

15.36 A business statistics professor at State College would like to develop a regression model to predict the final exam scores for students based on their current GPAs, the number of hours they studied for the exam, the number of times they were absent during the semester, and their genders. The data for these variables can be found in the Excel file **final exam scores 2.xlsx**.

a. Using PHStat, construct a regression model using all of the independent variables.

b. Test the significance of the overall regression model using $\alpha = 0.10$.
c. Interpret the meaning of the regression coefficient for the dummy variable.
d. Using the p-values, identify which independent variables are significant with $\alpha = 0.10$.
e. Construct a regression model using only the significant variables found in part d and predict the average exam score for a student who studied 4.0 hours for the exam, missed two classes during the semester, has a current GPA of 3.45, and is male.

15.37 Squirt Squad is a cleaning service that sends crews to residential homes on either a once-a-month or a twice-a-month schedule, depending on the customer's preference. The owner would like to predict the amount of time required to clean a house based on the square footage of the house, the total number of rooms in the house, the number of bathrooms it has, the size of the cleaning crew, the frequency of the cleaning schedule, and whether the household has children. Data from randomly selected homes can be found in the Excel file **Squirt Squad 2.xlsx**.

a. Using PHStat, construct a regression model using all of the independent variables.
b. Test the significance of the overall regression model using $\alpha = 0.05$.
c. Interpret the meaning of the regression coefficient for the Rooms, Crew, Children, and Frequency variables.
d. Using the p-values, identify which independent variables are significant with $\alpha = 0.05$.
e. Construct a regression model using only the significant variables found in part d and predict the average time to clean a house that has 2,250 square feet, 11 total rooms, 3.5 bathrooms, and no children. This house is cleaned once a month with a crew of four employees.

15.38 Suppose the athletic director at Villanova University would like to develop a regression model to predict the point differential for games played by the college's men's basketball team. A point differential is the difference between the final points scored by two competing teams. A positive differential is a win for Villanova, and a negative differential is a loss. For a random sample of home and away games, the point differential was calculated for Villanova, along with the number of assists, rebounds, turnovers, and personal fouls. The data can be found in the Excel file **Villanova Basketball 2.xlsx**.

a. Using PHStat, construct a regression model using all of the independent variables.
b. Test the significance of the overall regression model using $\alpha = 0.10$.
c. Interpret the meaning of the regression coefficient for the dummy variable.
d. Using the p-values, identify which independent variables are significant with $\alpha = 0.10$.
e. Construct a regression model using only the significant variables found in part d and predict the average point differential for a home game in which Villanova has 8 assists, 37 rebounds, 15 turnovers, and 22 personal fouls.

15.39 Suppose the Bank of Delaware would like to develop a regression model to predict a person's credit score based on his or her age, weekly income, education level (high school, bachelor's degree, graduate degree), and whether he or she owns or rents his or her primary residence. The Excel file **Bank of Delaware 1.xlsx** provides these data for a random sample of customers.

a. Using PHStat, construct a regression model using all of the independent variables.
b. Test the significance of the overall regression model using $\alpha = 0.01$.
c. Interpret the meaning of each of the regression coefficients.
d. Using the p-values, identify which independent variables are significant with $\alpha = 0.01$.
e. Construct a regression model using only the significant variables found in part d and predict the average credit score for a 42-year-old person who earns $1,200 per month, has a bachelor's degree, and owns his or her residence.

15.40 Jersey Shore Realtors would like to develop a regression model to help it set weekly rental rates for beach properties during the summer season in New Jersey. The independent variables for this model are the number of bedrooms a property has, its age, the number of blocks away from the ocean it is, and the rental month (June, July, or August). These data can be found in the Excel file **Jersey Shore Realtors 2.xlsx** for randomly selected rental properties.

a. Using PHStat, construct a regression model using all of the independent variables.
b. Test the significance of the overall regression model using $\alpha = 0.05$.
c. Interpret the meaning of each of the regression coefficients for the dummy variables.
d. Using the p-values, identify which independent variables are significant with $\alpha = 0.05$.
e. Construct a regression model using only the significant variables found in part d and predict the average weekly rental rate during the month of August for a three-bedroom house that is 12 years old and two blocks from the ocean.

15.5 Model Building

In each of the examples in this chapter, the regression models were shown with all the independent variables together. As we will see in this section, it's best to consider the effect of each independent variable on the regression model to decide which combination is most effective. The process of deciding which independent variables should be part of the final regression model is known as **model building**.

Model building is the process of deciding which independent variables should be part of a final regression model.

Remember that correlation was discussed in Chapter 14 as measuring both the strength and direction of the linear relationship between two variables.

Multicollinearity

Independent variables that are highly correlated with each other can cause problems for the multiple regression model. This condition has a special name in statistics—**multicollinearity**. The best way to explain this issue is through a simple example. Table 15.7 shows the weight in pounds of eight men along with their right and left shoe sizes. These data can also be found in the Excel file **shoe size.xlsx**.

Multicollinearity is present in the regression model when independent variables within the model are highly correlated.

TABLE 15.7 | WEIGHT VS. SHOE SIZE

	SHOE SIZE	
WEIGHT	RIGHT	LEFT
160	9	9
168	8	8
172	10.5	10.5
185	10	10
188	11	11.5
196	11	11
200	12	12
204	12	12

First, I'll use PHStat to develop a regression model that predicts a man's weight based on the size of his right shoe. These results are shown in Figure 15.13.

FIGURE 15.13 Predicting a Man's Weight Based on the Size of His Right Shoe Using PHStat

	A	B	C	D	E	F	G
1	Regression Analysis						
2							
3	*Regression Statistics*						
4	Multiple R	0.8771					
5	R Square	0.7694					
6	Adjusted R Square	0.7309					
7	Standard Error	8.3015					
8	Observations	8					
9							
10	ANOVA						
11		*df*	*SS*	*MS*	*F*	*Significance F*	
12	Regression	1	1379.4	1379.4	20.0158	0.0042	
13	Residual	6	413.5	68.9			
14	Total	7	1792.9				
15							
16		*Coefficients*	*Standard Error*	*t Stat*	*P-value*	*Lower 95%*	*Upper 95%*
17	Intercept	79.4647	23.5769	3.3704	0.0150	21.7740	137.1554
18	Right	10.0273	2.2413	4.4739	0.0042	4.5431	15.5116
19							

As you can see, based on the circled *p*-value (Cell E18), which equals 0.0042, the regression model is significant using $\alpha = 0.05$. The regression equation is as follows:

$$\hat{y} = 79.4647 + 10.0273x_1$$

According to our model, each additional shoe size on the right foot will result in an average increase of 10 lbs in weight. This seems reasonable to me.

Now, watch what happens when I include both the right and left shoe-size independent variables together in our regression model, which is shown in Figure 15.14.

FIGURE 15.14
Predicting a Man's Weight Based on the Sizes of Both His Shoes Using PHStat

	A	B	C	D	E	F	G
1	**Regression Analysis**						
2							
3	*Regression Statistics*						
4	Multiple R	0.8783					
5	R Square	0.7714					
6	Adjusted R Square	0.6800					
7	Standard Error	9.0535					
8	Observations	8					
9							
10	ANOVA						
11		*df*	*SS*	*MS*	*F*	*Significance F*	
12	Regression	2	1383.0	691.5	8.4367	0.0250	
13	Residual	5	409.8	82.0			
14	Total	7	1792.9				
15							
16		*Coefficients*	*Standard Error*	*t Stat*	*P-value*	*Lower 95%*	*Upper 95%*
17	Intercept	78.8369	25.8839	3.0458	0.0286	12.3002	145.3736
18	Right	14.2567	20.1684	0.7069	0.5112	-37.5878	66.1011
19	Left	-4.1444	19.6175	-0.2113	0.8410	-54.5728	46.2841
20							

In this model, as you can tell from the circled p-values (Cells E18 and E19), neither independent variable is significant. We also have a rather curious regression equation:

$$\hat{y} = 78.8369 + 14.2567x_1 - 4.1444x_2$$

We suspect the presence of multicollinearity in the model when regression coefficients have the opposite sign from what we would normally expect.

According to this model, each additional shoe size on the left foot will result in an average *decrease* of 4 lbs in weight. This makes no sense to me. What happened?

Looking at Table 15.7, we can see that the right and left shoe sizes tend to move together because they are highly correlated ($r = 0.99$ using Excel). Using both of these variables in our regression model is redundant. Adding the left shoe size as an independent variable provides very little new information to help us predict weight. In fact, this high correlation will often cause some independent variables that should be significant to appear as not being significant. Also, some regression coefficients in the model might appear with the wrong signs. For instance, I wouldn't expect an increase in the left shoe size of a man to predict a *decrease* in his weight. When our regression model behaves in this bizarre manner, we suspect the presence of multicollinearity.

Our shoe size example clearly (I hope) describes the problems that multicollinearity can cause in the model. When multicollinearity is present, detecting which independent variables are statistically significant may not be possible. It is also more difficult to interpret the regression coefficients. Later in this section, I'll show you how to detect the presence of multicollinearity and what to do about it.

However, if the purpose of the regression model is to provide a prediction for the dependent variable, the presence of multicollinearity is not necessarily a problem. Notice in Figure 15.14, the p-value for the significance of the overall regression model is 0.0250 (see Cell F12). Despite the head-scratching coefficients, because the p-value is less than $\alpha = 0.05$ this model can effectively predict the average weight of a man given his right and left shoe sizes.

The presence of multicollinearity can be detected in a regression model using the **variance inflation factor (*VIF*)**.

The presence of multicollinearity can be detected using the **variance inflation factor** (VIF). The formula the *VIF* is shown in Equation 15.14.

Formula 15.14 for the Variance Inflation Factor

$$VIF_j = \frac{1}{1 - R_j^2}$$

where

VIF_j = The variance inflation factor for the jth independent variable

R_j^2 = The coefficient of multiple determination using the jth independent variable as the dependent variable against the remaining independent variables

The variable R_j^2 needs a little explanation. This is the same R^2 we discussed earlier in the chapter, with one twist. We completely ignore the original dependent variable in the data set and focus solely on the independent variables. As an example, consider the following independent variables from earlier in the chapter:

Variable 1: Car's mileage $(j = 1)$
Variable 2: Car's age $(j = 2)$
Variable 3: Seller's age $(j = 3)$

The variable R_1^2 is calculated using the car's mileage as the dependent variable and the car's age and seller's age as the independent variables. Likewise, the variable R_2^2 is calculated using the car's age as the dependent variable and the car's mileage and seller's age as the independent variables. The same pattern holds true for R_3^2.

Suppose we have three independent variables, x_1, x_2, and x_3, in our regression model and we want to determine VIF_1, the factor for the first independent variable, x_1. This requires using x_1 as the dependent variable and performing a regression analysis with x_2 and x_3 as the independent variables. The original dependent variable is ignored for this analysis.

If there is no correlation between the three independent variables in the previous scenario, then $R_1^2 = 0$. Plugging this value into Equation 15.14, we have the following:

$$VIF_1 = \frac{1}{1 - R_1^2} = \frac{1}{1 - 0} = 1.0$$

With the presence of correlation in the previous scenario, R_1^2 would approach 1.0, which in turn will cause VIF_1 to increase. This process would be continued to determine VIF_2 and VIF_3. If any value of VIF_j exceeds 5.0, enough correlation exists between the independent variables to claim that multicollinearity is present in the regression model.

The good news is that PHStat will provide us with the values for VIF_j, which I will demonstrate with the following example. Verizon Wireless records as a measure of productivity the number of weekly cell phone activations each of its retail employees achieves. An activation is defined as either a new customer signing a cell phone contract or an existing customer renewing a contract. Excel file **activations 1.xlsx** provides the number of activations last week for 25 employees, which is our dependent variable; the following are the independent variables:

Exp (x_1): The employee's number of years of experience on the job
Gend (x_2): The gender of the employee, 0 = Male, 1 = Female
Perf (x_3): The performance rating of the employee on a scale of 1–100
Age (x_4): The age of the employee
Salary (x_5): The weekly salary of the employee

PHStat's **Multiple Regression** dialog box is shown for the Excel file in Figure 15.15A. Notice that the **Variance Inflationary Factor** (VIF) box is checked.

FIGURE 15.15A Determining the Variance Inflationary Factors for the Cell Phone Activation Example Using PHStat (Step 1)

	A	B	C	D	E	F
1	Activations	Exp	Gend	Perf	Age	Salary ($)
2	19	1	0	80	27	810
3	20	7	0	76	32	720
4	20	2	0	82	46	960
5	22	5	0	82	35	750
6	23	1	0	80	41	850
7	24	5	1	62	25	680
8	24	4	0	77	22	800
9	25	3	0	78	41	730
10	26	4	0	85	53	900
11	27	6	0	71	39	770
12	27	4	0	87	29	1000
13	27	7	0	74	33	720
14	29	2	0	75	31	780
15	29	6	1	83	38	930
16	30	6	0	81	44	890
17	32	2	0	80	21	800
18	33	8	1	94	47	1040
19	33	6	1	85	40	960
20	35	8	1	92	35	1120
21	36	6	1	88	39	910
22	36	5	1	92	41	1200
23	36	5	1	85	34	1000
24	38	7	1	92	28	1170
25	40	10	0	90	40	1100
26	40	9	1	96	32	1300
27						

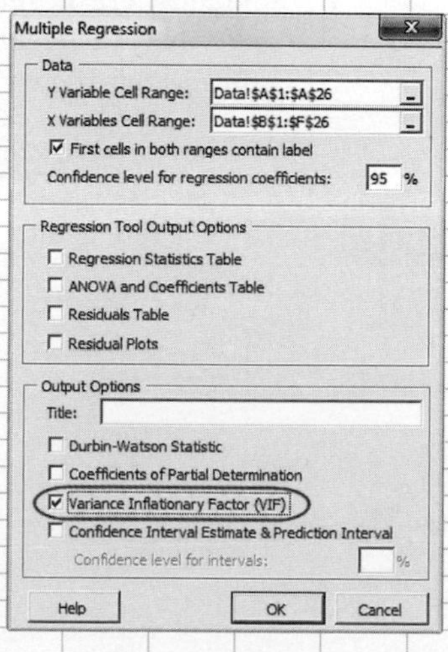

Multiple Regression
Data
Y Variable Cell Range: Data!$A$1:$A$26
X Variables Cell Range: Data!$B$1:$F$26
☑ First cells in both ranges contain label
Confidence level for regression coefficients: 95 %
Regression Tool Output Options
☐ Regression Statistics Table
☐ ANOVA and Coefficients Table
☐ Residuals Table
☐ Residual Plots
Output Options
Title:
☐ Durbin-Watson Statistic
☐ Coefficients of Partial Determination
☑ Variance Inflationary Factor (VIF)
☐ Confidence Interval Estimate & Prediction Interval
Confidence level for intervals: %
Help OK Cancel

After we click **OK**, PHStat creates a worksheet for each independent variable, labeling them X1, X2, and so forth. Figure 15.15B shows the value for VIF_1, the Exp independent variable.

FIGURE 15.15B Determining the Variance Inflationary Factors for the Cell Phone Activation Example Using PHStat (Final Result)

	A	B
1	**Regression Analysis**	
2	Exp and all other X	
3	***Regression Statistics***	
4	Multiple R	0.5398
5	R Square	0.2914
6	Adjusted R Square	0.1497
7	Standard Error	2.2379
8	Observations	25
9	VIF	**1.4113**
10		

We can verify the value of VIF_1 using the data in Figure 15.15B and Equation 15.14:

$$VIF_1 = \frac{1}{1 - R_1^2} = \frac{1}{1 - 0.2914} = 1.41$$

Table 15.8 summarizes the remaining *VIF* values for the activation example.

TABLE 15.8 | VARIANCE INFLATIONARY FACTOR VALUES FOR THE CELL PHONE ACTIVATION EXAMPLE

INDEPENDENT VARIABLE	VIF_j	MULTICOLLINEARITY?
Exp	1.41	No
Gend	1.65	No
Perf	5.30	Yes
Age	1.15	No
Salary	6.07	Yes

Because we have *VIF* values greater than 5.0 in Table 15.8, multicollinearity is present in our model if we use all five independent variables. It appears that the variables Salary and Perf are highly correlated, which makes sense—employees with the higher performance ratings could conceivably have the higher salaries. If you take the time to use Excel's CORREL function with these two variables, you could confirm that $r = 0.889$.

To eliminate the presence of multicollinearity from our activation example, we need to eliminate one or both of the offending independent variables from our model. The analogy I like to use is two misbehaving children who cannot be left in the same room together (something most parents can relate to). I'll start by removing the variable Salary because it has the highest *VIF* in Table 15.8.

Next, I'll repeat the *VIF* procedure with the remaining four independent variables. These results are shown in Table 15.9.

The fact that all four remaining variables in the model have VIFs less than 5.0 is evidence that multicollinearity is not present in the regression model.

TABLE 15.9 | VARIANCE INFLATIONARY FACTOR VALUES FOR THE CELL PHONE ACTIVATION EXAMPLE

INDEPENDENT VARIABLE	VIF_j	MULTICOLLINEARITY?
Exp	1.38	No
Gend	1.43	No
Perf	1.49	No
Age	1.13	No

Because each of these *VIF* values is less than 5.0, it seems I have found a group of "well-behaved" independent variables that get along with one another. Had the *VIF* value for the Perf variable remained over 5.0, I would also remove it from the model and repeat the process again to verify the remaining *VIF* values were acceptable.

Now that we have eliminated multicollinearity by removing unwanted independent variables, we're ready to start building our final model with general stepwise regression. But first, see how well the independent variables in this next Your Turn problem get along together.

YOUR TURN #5

Suppose Arizona State University would like to develop a regression model to identify the factors that contribute to the GPA of MBA students (MBAGPA). The Excel file **MBA GPA.xlsx** provides data for 24 randomly selected MBA students who have recently graduated. The independent variables in this file are as follows:

MGMAT (x_1): The student's math GMAT (entrance exam) score

VGMAT (x_2): The student's verbal GMAT (entrance exam) score

UGGPA (x_3): The student's undergraduate GPA

DEGREE (x_4): A dummy variable that equals 0 for students with business undergraduate degrees and 1 for students with non-business undergraduate degrees

Determine if multicollinearity is present among these independent variables. If it is, take the necessary steps to eliminate it.

Answers can be found on ▶ **page 763**

General Stepwise Regression

Now that we have eliminated the presence of multicollinearity from our independent variables in the cell phone activation example, it's now time to decide which of the remaining independent variables to include in our final regression model. The remaining variables are as follows.

Exp (x_1): The employee's number of years of experience on the job

Gend (x_2): The gender of the employee, $0 =$ Male, $1 =$ Female

Perf (x_3): The employee's performance rating on a scale of 1–100

Age (x_4): The age of the employee

General stepwise regression brings one independent variable at a time into a regression model based on its *p*-value. The "*p*-value to enter" and "*p*-value to remove" values determine the threshold for independent variables joining and leaving the regression model, respectively.

There are several methods to achieve this goal, all of which require the use of a software program such as PHStat. The first selection method we'll examine is known as a **general stepwise regression**, which brings independent variables into the model one at a time using the following steps:

1. Select the independent variable that has the highest correlation with the dependent variable.
2. If this variable is statistically significant, it enters the model.
3. The next variable chosen is the one that explains the largest portion of the unexplained variation in the dependent variable.
4. If this variable is statistically significant, it enters the model.
5. Occasionally, adding a new independent variable will cause the *p*-values of an independent variable already in the model to exceed the value of α. In this case, the independent variable that is no longer statistically significant is removed from the model.
6. This process continues until no remaining independent variables are statistically significant.

General stepwise regression can be performed with our cell phone activation example using PHStat as follows:

1. Open the Excel file **activations 2.xlsx**. This file contains the four independent variables shown in Table 15.9 along with our dependent variable, Activations.
2. Go to **Add-Ins > PHStat > Regression > Stepwise Regression**, as seen in Figure 15.1A.
3. Fill in the **Stepwise Regression** dialog box as shown in Figure 15.16A. The **p value to enter** and **p value to remove** values determine the threshold for independent variables joining and leaving the regression model, respectively.
4. Click **OK**.

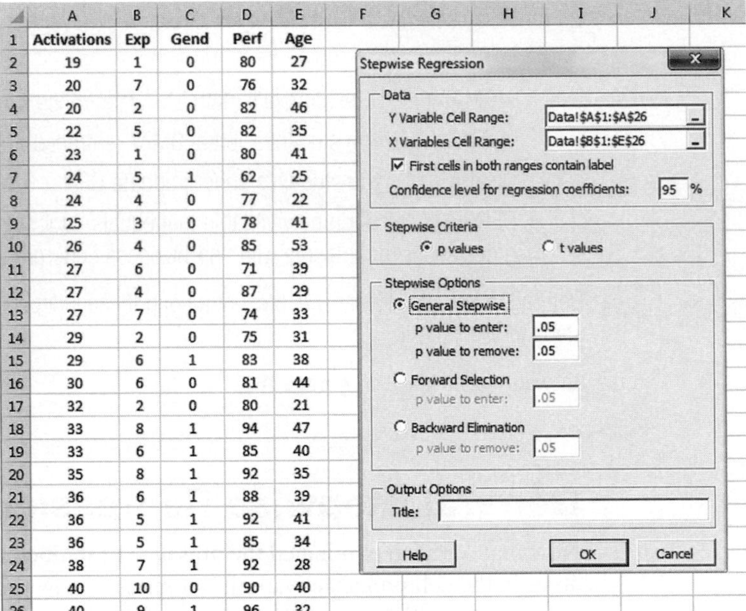

	A	B	C	D	E
1	Activations	Exp	Gend	Perf	Age
2	19	1	0	80	27
3	20	7	0	76	32
4	20	2	0	82	46
5	22	5	0	82	35
6	23	1	0	80	41
7	24	5	1	62	25
8	24	4	0	77	22
9	25	3	0	78	41
10	26	4	0	85	53
11	27	6	0	71	39
12	27	4	0	87	29
13	27	7	0	74	33
14	29	2	0	75	31
15	29	6	1	83	38
16	30	6	0	81	44
17	32	2	0	80	21
18	33	8	1	94	47
19	33	6	1	85	40
20	35	8	1	92	35
21	36	6	1	88	39
22	36	5	1	92	41
23	36	5	1	85	34
24	38	7	1	92	28
25	40	10	0	90	40
26	40	9	1	96	32

FIGURE 15.16A
Using PHStat for a Stepwise Regression (Steps 1–4)

PHStat creates a new worksheet labeled "Stepwise," which displays the results of the stepwise regression. Figure 15.16B shows the first independent variable to be chosen to enter the model, Perf.

FIGURE 15.16B
The First Variable in the Stepwise Regression Model with PHStat

Stepwise Regression Analysis
Table of Results for General Stepwise

Perf entered.

	df	SS	MS	F	Significance F
Regression	1	446.5597	446.5597	19.2338	0.0002
Residual	23	534.0003	23.2174		
Total	24	980.5600			

	Coefficients	Standard Error	t Stat	P-value	Lower 95%	Upper 95%
Intercept	-15.7907	10.3129	-1.5312	0.1394	-37.1245	5.5431
Perf	0.5446	0.1242	4.3856	0.0002	0.2877	0.8015

As you can see, because it has a *p*-value equal to 0.0002, the variable Perf is statistically significant. Figure 15.16C shows the second independent variable to be chosen to enter the model, Exp.

FIGURE 15.16C
The Second Variable in the Stepwise Regression Model with PHStat

15							
16	Exp entered.						
17							
18		*df*	*SS*	*MS*	*F*	*Significance F*	
19	Regression	2	585.3038	292.6519	16.2890	0.0000	
20	Residual	22	395.2562	17.9662			
21	Total	24	980.5600				
22							
23		*Coefficients*	*Standard Error*	*t Stat*	*P-value*	*Lower 95%*	*Upper 95%*
24	Intercept	-9.5712	9.3439	-1.0243	0.3168	-28.9494	9.8069
25	Perf	0.4010	0.1209	3.3182	0.0031	0.1504	0.6516
26	Exp	1.0960	0.3944	2.7789	0.0109	0.2781	1.9139
27							
28	**No other variables could be entered into the model. Stepwise ends.**						
29							

Both independent variables have *p*-values less than 0.05 and therefore stay in the model. The last two independent variables, Gend and Age, were not selected to join the model because their *p*-values would exceed 0.05 had they been included. Our final regression model is as follows:

$$\hat{y} = -9.5712 + 1.0960x_1 + 0.4010x_3$$

where

x_1 = The employee's number of years of experience on the job
x_3 = The employee's performance rating on a scale of 1–100

The interpretations for the regression coefficients in this equation are as follows:

$b_1 = 1.096$: Every additional year of job experience will result in an average increase of 1.096 activations per week, assuming there is no change in the performance rating of the employee.

$b_3 = 0.401$: Every additional point in the employee's performance rating will result in an average increase of 0.401 activations per week, assuming there is no change in the experience of the employee.

Using general stepwise regression will always result in a model in which all of the independent variables are statistically significant. The drawback of using this technique is that by considering only one independent variable at a time, all possible combinations of variables might not be considered when choosing a final model.

In the next section, we'll examine another selection method that does consider all possible combinations. But before we move on, please spend a few minutes with this next Your Turn exercise.

YOUR TURN #6

Perform a general stepwise regression using the remaining variables (without multicollinearity) and data from the Arizona State University **MBA GPA.xlsx** file in Your Turn #5. Use 0.05 as the *p*-values to enter and remove. Interpret the meaning of the regression coefficients for the final model.

Answers can be found on ▶ **pages 763–764**

Best Subsets Regression

A **best subsets regression** examines all combinations of independent variables as possible candidates for the final regression model.

Another technique for selecting the appropriate independent variables for the final model is known as a **best subsets regression**. Rather than selecting variables one at a time, this method will examine all of the combinations of the independent variables as possible candidates for the final regression model. For example, suppose we have three independent variables to consider, x_1, x_2, and x_3. A best subsets regression will consider all combinations of the variables. These combinations are shown in Table 15.10.

TABLE 15.10 | Best-Subset-Regression Combinations for Three Independent Variables

x_1	x_1 and x_2	$x_1, x_2,$ and x_3
x_2	x_1 and x_3	
x_3	x_2 and x_3	

Because it allows only one variable at a time to enter the model, a general stepwise regression might not examine all these particular combinations, which can be a drawback. However, a best subsets regression limits the number of independent variables that can be considered. For k independent variables, there are $2^k - 1$ total combinations of regression models to consider. With three independent variables, we have $2^3 - 1 = 8 - 1 = 7$ total combinations to examine. Therefore, as the number of independent variables increases, the number of combinations expands rather drastically. For example, the best subsets regression procedure in PHStat is limited to examining seven independent variables. If more independent variables need to be considered, a general stepwise regression needs to be used.

To see how a best subsets regression works, let's use the previous cell phone activation data that are free of multicollinearity, and then take the following steps:

1. Open the Excel file **activations 2.xlsx**.
2. Go to **Add-Ins > PHStat > Regression > Best Subsets**, as seen in Figure 15.1A.
3. Fill in the **Best Subsets** dialog box as shown in Figure 15.17A and click **OK**.

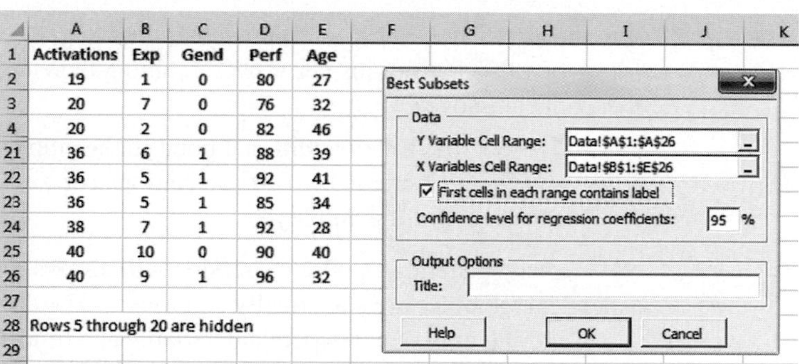

	A	B	C	D	E
1	Activations	Exp	Gend	Perf	Age
2	19	1	0	80	27
3	20	7	0	76	32
4	20	2	0	82	46
21	36	6	1	88	39
22	36	5	1	92	41
23	36	5	1	85	34
24	38	7	1	92	28
25	40	10	0	90	40
26	40	9	1	96	32
27					
28	Rows 5 through 20 are hidden				
29					

FIGURE 15.17A Using PHStat for a Best Subsets Regression (Steps 1–3)

4. PHStat creates several worksheets in the Excel file, one of which is labeled "Best Subsets." Selecting this sheet will display the data shown in Figure 15.17B.

FIGURE 15.17B The Best Subsets Analysis Data with PHStat

	A	B
1	Best Subsets Analysis	
2		
3	Intermediate Calculations	
4	R2T	0.673905
5	1 - R2T	0.326095
6	n	25
7	T	5
8	n - T	20
9		

	Model	Cp	k+1	R Square	Adj. R Square	Std. Error
11	X1	16.0956	2	0.3952	0.3689	5.0780
12	X2	16.7122	2	0.3851	0.3584	5.1200
13	X3	12.4006	2	0.4554	0.4317	4.8184
14	X4	40.1307	2	0.0033	-0.0401	6.5187
15	X1X2	9.5541	3	0.5344	0.4921	4.5553
16	X1X3	5.7224	3	0.5969	0.5603	4.2387
17	X1X4	18.0341	3	0.3962	0.3413	5.1878
18	X2X3	6.5324	3	0.5837	0.5459	4.3075
19	X2X4	18.5849	3	0.3872	0.3315	5.2262
20	X3X4	12.8592	3	0.4805	0.4333	4.8117
21	X1X2X3	3.9862	4	0.6578	0.6089	3.9972
22	X1X2X4	11.5450	4	0.5346	0.4681	4.6618
23	X1X3X4	6.1022	4	0.6233	0.5695	4.1938
24	X2X3X4	7.7902	4	0.5958	0.5381	4.3443
25	X1X2X3X4	5.0000	5	0.6739	0.6087	3.9985

Figure 15.17B shows that four independent variables provide 15 possible combinations to be considered $(2^4 - 1 = 15)$. This figure also shows the adjusted R^2 and the standard

Recall that the adjusted R^2 measures the proportion of variation in the dependent variable that is explained by the independent variables and is adjusted for the number of independent variables and the sample size in the model.

error for each of these regression models. Ideally, we're looking for the subset with the highest adjusted R^2 and lowest standard error. The two models highlighted in yellow are the best candidates based on these criteria.

The best subsets procedure in PHStat assigns the first independent variable in the Excel file as x_1, the second as x_2, and so forth. Based on this convention, we have the following assignments for our activation example:

Exp (x_1): The employee's number of years of experience on the job
Gend (x_2): The gender of the employee, 0 = Male, 1 = Female
Perf (x_3): The employee's performance rating on a scale of 1–100
Age (x_4): The age of the employee

Recall that the standard error measures how well the regression equation fits the sample data.

Notice that the adjusted R^2 for the model using only Age (x_4) in Figure 15.17B (circled in red) is negative. This can occur when the coefficient of determination (R^2) is very low, as it is in Figure 15.17B, or when there are a large number of independent variables in the regression model. Below, I show Equation 15.11 again, which calculates the adjusted R^2. As you can see, the number of independent variables, k, is in the denominator. This makes the adjusted R^2 smaller as k is larger.

$$R_A^2 = 1 - \left[(1 - R^2)\left(\frac{n - 1}{n - k - 1}\right)\right]$$

Figure 15.17B also shows a value known as the C_p statistic, which measures the difference between the true population model and the regression model derived from the sample data. The goal is for the C_p statistic to be less than or equal to $k + 1$, where k equals the number of independent variables. Our highlighted subsets in Figure 15.17B also meet this criterion, which is summarized in Table 15.11

When comparing models with similar adjusted R^2 values, choose the one with the fewer number of independent variables.

TABLE 15.11 | BEST SUBSET CANDIDATES FOR THE CELL PHONE ACTIVATION EXAMPLE

MODEL	C_p	$k + 1$	ADJ R^2
x_1, x_2, x_3	3.99	4	0.6089
x_1, x_2, x_3, x_4	5.00	5	0.6087

Both of these models will provide roughly the same level of performance when predicting the number of weekly cell phone activations for an employee. When faced with such a choice, the more desirable model is the one with fewer independent variables. This results in a final model that requires less data and has a smaller chance of multicollinearity wreaking havoc on the regression. Therefore, using the best subset method, our preferred choice is the model that includes the independent variables x_1, x_2, and x_3.

You can find the regression model for this subset in another worksheet labeled "3X" because this subset is the first one listed in the group of three independent variables in Figure 15.17B. These data are displayed in Figure 15.17C.

FIGURE 15.17C
The Final Best Subsets Regression Model with PHStat

	A	B	C	D	E	F	G	H
1	**Best Subsets Analysis**							
2								
3	*Regression Statistics*			Note:				
4	Multiple R	0.8111		This worksheet does not recalculate.				
5	R Square	0.6578		If regression data changes, rerun procedure				
6	Adjusted R Square	0.6089		to create an updated version of this worksheet.				
7	Standard Error	3.9972						
8	Observations	25						
9								
10	ANOVA							
11		*df*	*SS*	*MS*	*F*	*Significance F*		
12	Regression	3	645.0377	215.0126	13.4574	0.0000		
13	Residual	21	335.5223	15.9773				
14	Total	24	980.5600					
15								
16		*Coefficients*	*Standard Error*	*t Stat*	*P-value*	*Lower 95%*	*Upper 95%*	
17	Intercept	-3.8522	9.2947	-0.4144	0.6827	-23.1817	15.4773	
18	Exp	0.8415	0.3945	2.1329	0.0449	0.0210	1.6619	
19	Gend	3.7355	1.9319	1.9336	0.0668	-0.2821	7.7531	
20	Perf	0.3297	0.1198	2.7519	0.0119	0.0805	0.5788	
21								

According to Figure 15.17C, our final activations regression model is as follows:

$$\hat{y} = -3.8522 + 0.8415x_1 + 3.7355x_2 + 0.3297x_3$$

where

x_1 = The employee's number of years of experience on the job
x_2 = The gender of the employee, 0 = Male, 1 = Female
x_3 = The employee's performance rating on a scale of 1–100

Suppose Verizon would like to use this model to predict the average number of weekly activations for a male employee who has a performance rating of 85 and four years of experience on the job. Our best subset model predicts the following:

$$\hat{y} = -3.8522 + 0.8415x_1 + 3.7355x_2 + 0.3297x_3$$
$$\hat{y} = -3.8522 + 0.8415(4) + 3.7355(0) + 0.3297(85) = 27.5 \text{ activations per week}$$

Notice that the best subsets regression method arrived at a different final model than the general stepwise regression that was discussed earlier. This can occur because the best subsets method will often find a combination of variables that the general stepwise method never examined.

There is also the possibility that the subset with the highest adjusted R^2 might include independent variables that are not statically significant (with p-values greater than α). For instance, the Gend variable in 15.17C has a p-value equal to 0.0668. The model builder might need to decide which is more important—significant independent variables or the highest adjusted R^2. As we saw in Figure 15.17B, there is often more than one appropriate subset from which to choose.

Table 15.12 compares the best subset and general stepwise methods for our cell phone activation example. The adjusted R^2 for the general stepwise method can be found in Row 16 in Figure 15.17B.

TABLE 15.12 | COMPARING THE BEST SUBSET REGRESSION WITH THE GENERAL STEPWISE REGRESSION

MODEL	VARIABLES	ADJ R^2
Best subset	x_1, x_2, x_3	0.6089
General stepwise	x_1, x_3	0.5603

Now that you're an expert on best subset regression, take this time to choose a model in the next Your Turn problem.

YOUR TURN #7

Perform a best subsets regression using the remaining variables (without multicollinearity) and data from the Arizona State University model in Your Turn #5.

a. Select the subset with the highest adjusted R^2.
b. Compare this to the model using the general stepwise approach from Your Turn #6.

Answers can be found on ▶ **page 764**

Other Selection Methods

Forward selection regression brings one independent variable into the model at a time and does not allow any variables to leave once they have entered.

Two additional stepwise regression techniques are available through PHStat that are similar to the general stepwise regression method. The first method is known as **forward selection regression**. This method follows the same steps as the general stepwise method in that it begins with no variables in the model. The forward selection method also uses the "p-value to enter" criterion to determine if an independent variable is eligible to be part of the model. The major difference in these two techniques is that once an independent variable enters the forward selection model, it can never leave (sort of like members of your family). As a result, you may end up with independent variables in the final model that are not statistically significant. You can select this method in PHStat's Stepwise Regression dialog box, which is shown in Figure 15.16A.

Backward elimination regression begins with all of the independent variables in the model. Variables that are not significant leave the model one at a time and are never allowed to return.

Another stepwise method is known as **backward elimination regression**. Here we begin the process with all of the independent variables in the model. Using the "*p*-value to remove" value provided by the user in the dialog box, independent variables are selected to leave the model one at a time. Once an independent variable has been banished from a backward elimination model, it can never come back in a later step (just like the contestants on the TV show *American Idol*). With backward elimination, you can be assured that all the remaining variables will be significantly significant. This method can also be found in PHStat's Stepwise Regression dialog box shown in Figure 15.16A.

Because forward selection and backward elimination are stepwise models that look at the effect of one independent variable at a time, there is no guarantee that the final model will find the group of variables that provides the highest possible adjusted R^2. However, just as with the general stepwise procedure, both these methods can examine a large number of independent variables as possible candidates for the final regression model.

Residual Analysis

The last step of the model building process is to conduct a procedure known as residual analysis. In order for the results from multiple regression analysis to be reliable, certain key assumptions need to hold true. Interpreting regression output without regard to these assumptions may lead to misleading conclusions. These important assumptions are as follows:

1. The residuals for the regression model have a constant variance.
2. The residuals follow the normal probability distribution.
3. The residuals are independent of one another.
4. The relationship between each independent variable and the dependent variable is linear.

A **residual** describes the difference between the actual and predicted values of a dependent variable.

As you can see, the majority of these assumptions focus on the **residuals**, which is just a fancy word statisticians use to describe the difference between the actual and predicted values of the dependent variable. In other words, we can describe the residual as a type of regression error. For example, the first employee in the **activations 2.xlsx** data file had 19 activations with a performance rating of 80, had one year of experience, and was male. Our best subset regression model predicts the following number of activations for this employee:

$$\hat{y} = -3.8522 + 0.8415x_1 + 3.7355x_2 + 0.3297x_3$$

$$\hat{y}_1 = -3.8522 + 0.8415(1) + 3.7355(0) + 0.3297(80) = 23.4 \text{ activations per week}$$

The difference between the actual and predicted activations can be found using Equation 15.15.

Formula 15.15 for the Residual

$$e_i = y_i - \hat{y}_i$$

where

e_i = The residual of the *i*th observation in the sample
y_i = The actual value of the dependent variable for the *i*th data point
$\hat{y}_i$ = The predicted value of the dependent variable for the *i*th data point

The residual for this first employee, using Equation 15.15, is as follows:

$$e_1 = y_1 - \hat{y}_1 = 19 - 23.4 = -4.4$$

In other words, the regression model predicts that the first employee will have 4.4 more activations in a week than he actually had.

Using Excel's Data Analysis ToolPak, we can find the residuals for each observation in our sample. Mac users can find these instructions using PHStat on the textbook's Web site.

I'll demonstrate this procedure using the Excel file **activations 3.xlsx**, which contains the independent variables from the best subset regression model:

1. Open the Excel file **activations 3.xlsx**.
2. Go to **Data > Data Analysis**, as shown in Figure 15.18A.
3. Select **Regression** in the **Data Analysis** dialog box, and click **OK**.

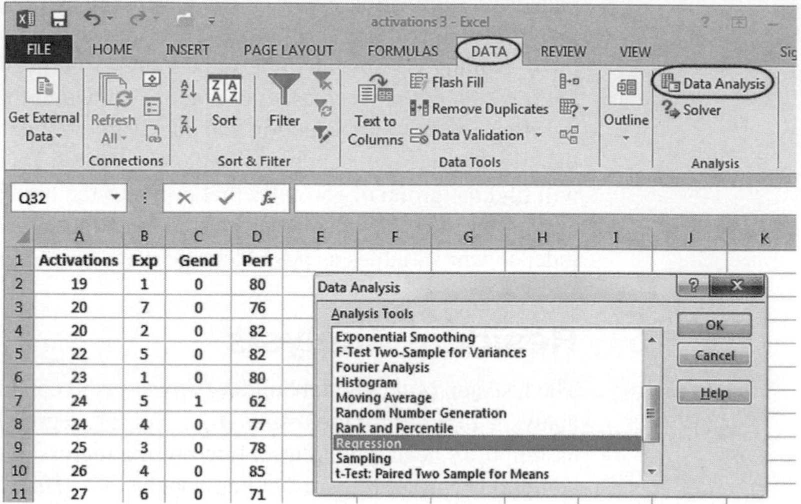

FIGURE 15.18A Residual Analysis Using Excel's Data Analysis Function (Steps 1–3)

4. Fill in the **Regression** dialog box as shown in Figure 15.18B, and click **OK**.

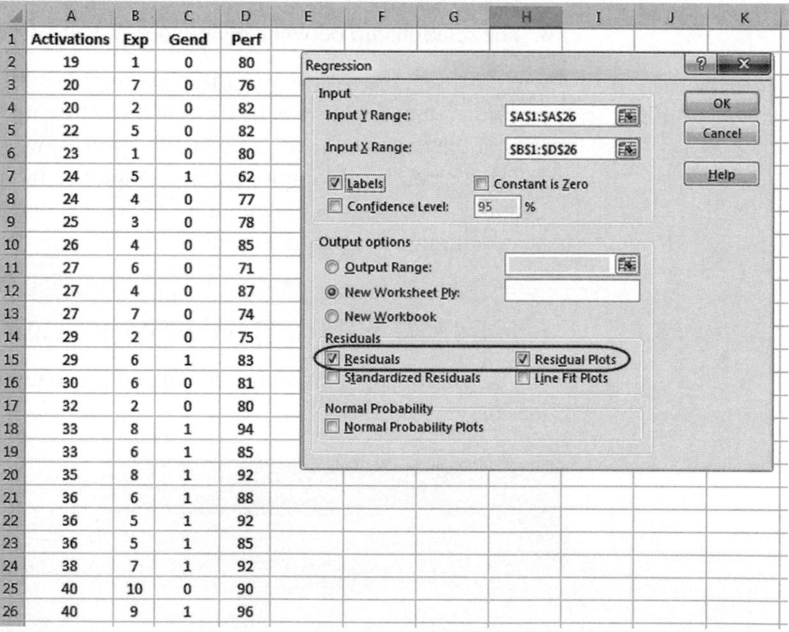

FIGURE 15.18B Residual Analysis Using Excel's Data Analysis Function (Step 4)

Because we checked Residuals in the dialog box, Excel provides a residual output table listing the residual for each observation in our sample. Figure 15.18C shows this output.

FIGURE 15.18C
Residual Analysis Using Excel's Data Analysis Function (Final Result)

24	RESIDUAL OUTPUT		
25			
26	*Observation*	*Predicted Activations*	*Residuals*
27	1	23.4	-4.4
28	2	27.1	-7.1
29	3	24.9	-4.9
30	4	27.4	-5.4
31	5	23.4	-0.4
32	6	24.5	-0.5
33	7	24.9	-0.9
34	8	24.4	0.6
35	9	27.5	-1.5
36	10	24.6	2.4
37	11	28.2	-1.2
38	12	26.4	0.6
39	13	22.6	6.4
40	14	32.3	-3.3
41	15	27.9	2.1
42	16	24.2	7.8
43	17	37.6	-4.6
44	18	33.0	0.0
45	19	36.9	-1.9
46	20	33.9	2.1
47	21	34.4	1.6
48	22	32.1	3.9
49	23	36.1	1.9
50	24	34.2	5.8
51	25	39.1	0.9

Negative residuals indicate that the predicted cell phone activations are more than the actual activations for each employee. Positive residuals reflect the opposite condition. The closer the residuals are to zero, the better the fit of the regression model.

Homoscedasticity states that the variation of the dependent variable is the same across all values of the independent variables.

Our first assumption for the multiple regression model is that the residuals have a constant variance, which is also known as **homoscedasticity,** a term we introduced in Chapter 14. Because we checked Residual Plots in the dialog box, the Excel regression output provides a residual plot for each independent variable so that we can examine if this condition is being met. Figure 15.19 shows the residual plot for the Exp variable.

FIGURE 15.19
Residual Plot for the Exp Variable

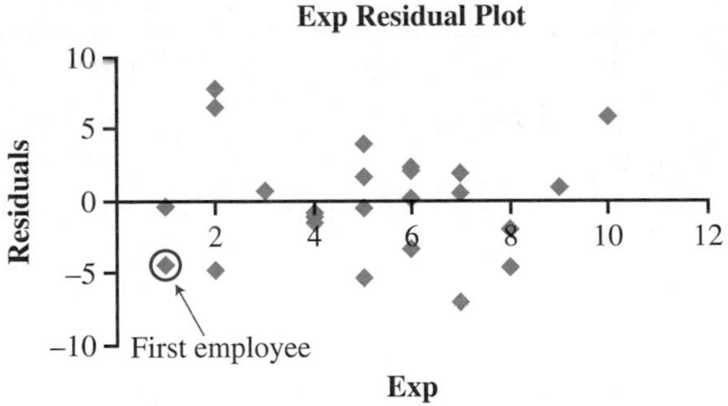

This first employee had 19 activations and the regression model predicted he would have 23.4 activations. The difference is −4.4 activations.

Each point in this plot represents the residual for each employee plotted against the number of years of experience on the job for that employee. Recall that the first employee in our sample has a residual of −4.4 activations. This employee also had one year of experience. The point shown in the red circle in Figure 15.19 corresponds to this employee.

The multiple regression model assumes that the variation in the residuals along the horizontal axis in Figure 15.19 is fairly constant. In other words, the error in the regression model for employees with little experience should not greatly differ from more experienced employees. This condition of constant residual variance across the Exp variable appears to be satisfied as we examine Figure 15.19. Notice that the data points are randomly scattered around the horizontal axis in the residual plot.

I'm sure some of you are wondering how the residual plot would appear if this constant variance condition was not met. Figure 15.20 shows a hypothetical case of such an instance.

FIGURE 15.20
Hypothetical Residual Plot for the Exp Variable

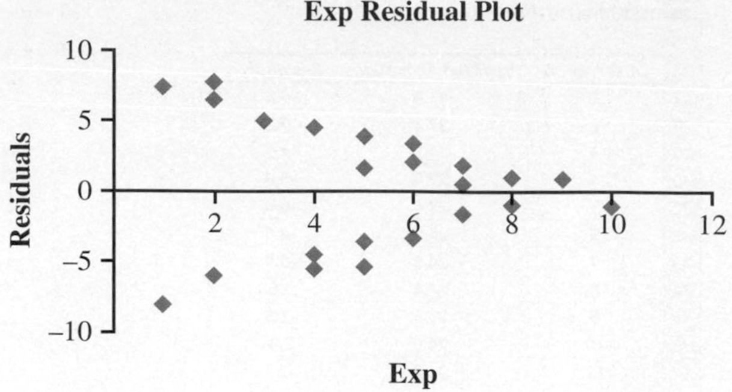

Notice that the regression error is much larger for less experienced employees when compared with those with more experience. I draw this conclusion because the data in Figure 15.20 have residual values closer to zero as we move toward the right side of the horizontal (experience) axis. According to this figure, an employee with 10 years of experience has a residual very close to zero, meaning this model does a good job in predicting activations for more experienced employees. Compare this with the residuals for an employee with two years of experience. As you can see, the prediction errors are farther from zero on this end of the plot. This pattern suggests that this model is more accurate when predicting the number of activations for experienced salespeople when compared with less experienced salespeople. Thus, this residual plot does not appear to satisfy the condition that the residuals have a constant variance.

Figures 15.21 and 15.22 show the residual plots for the other two remaining independent variables from our original example, Perf and Gend. Again, the residual for the first employee (-4.4) from our sample is circled in red in both figures, with a performance rating equal to 80 and a gender dummy variable equal to zero.

FIGURE 15.21
Residual Plot for the Perf Variable

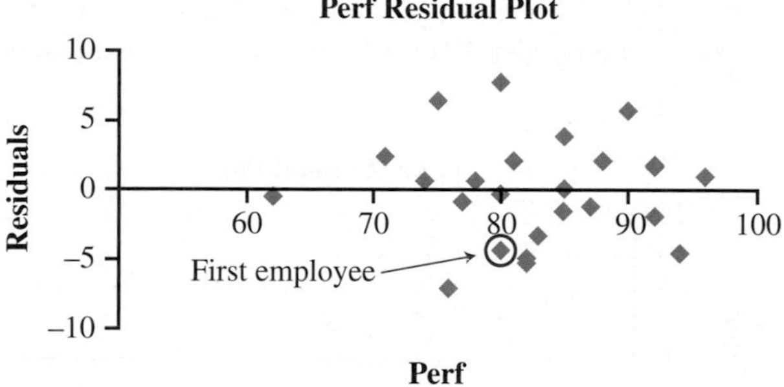

FIGURE 15.22
Residual Plot for the Gend Variable

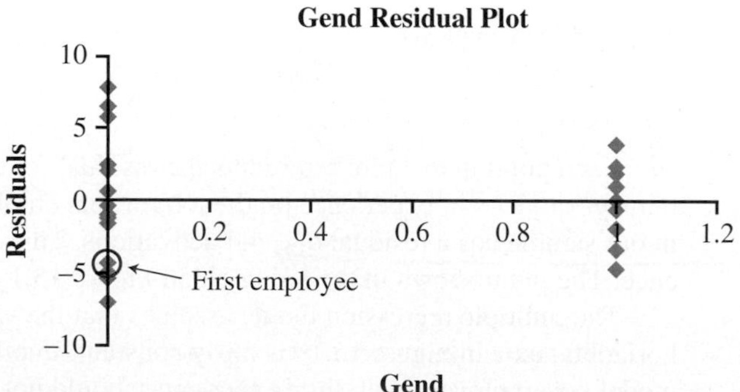

There does not appear to be a blatant violation of the constant variance requirement in either figure, although it does seem that the male employees have a little more error in the regression model than the female employees. You can tell this is so because the points are spread out farther from the *x*-axis for the men than they are for the women.

The second assumption for the multiple regression model is that the residuals follow the normal probability distribution. We can investigate if this assumption holds true by

A **normal probability plot** is used to verify if data follow the normal probability distribution by graphing the data on the *y*-axis and the *z*-scores for the data on the *x*-axis.

inspecting a **normal probability plot**, which graphs the residuals on the *y*-axis and the residuals' *z*-score on the *x*-axis. If the residuals follow the normal probability distribution, the data in this plot will fall approximately on a straight line. Figure 15.23 shows the normal probability plot for the activations data which appears to follow a straight line. Based on this figure, we can confirm that the residuals follow a normal distribution for this data set.

FIGURE 15.23
Normal Probability Plot

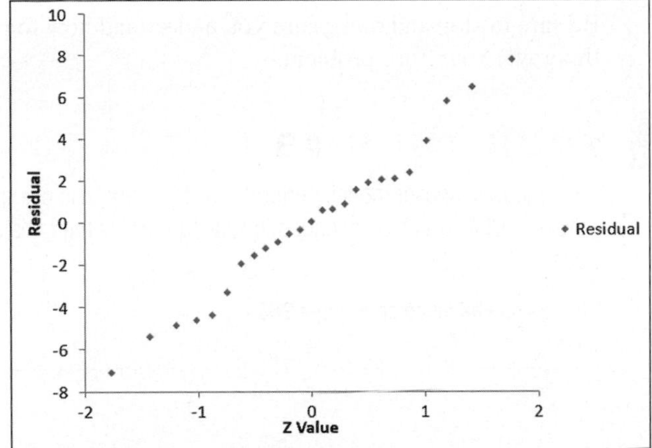

See the textbook's Web site (www.pearsonhighered.com/donnelly) for instructions on how to construct this normal probability plot using PHStat. Also, if you inspect Figure 15.18B, you will see an option in Excel's regression procedure to generate a normal probability plot. However, this option, for some strange reason, generates a plot for the dependent variable which tells us nothing about the distribution of the model's residuals.

The third assumption for the multiple regression model is that the residuals are independent of one another. Essentially, this is saying that the size of the residual for one observation will have no influence on the size of the residual from another observation. Because this phenomenon occurs more commonly using regression analysis as a forecasting technique, I address this assumption in Chapter 16 using the Durbin–Watson statistic.

The fourth assumption for the multiple regression model is that the relationship between each independent variable and the dependent variable is linear. Fortunately for you, testing for this assumption is rather complex and goes beyond the scope of this textbook. Therefore, we will assume that a linear relationship exists between the dependent and each of the independent variables in this chapter.

Model Building Summary

We've covered quite a bit of material in this model building section, so I thought it would be helpful to summarize the procedure in the following steps:

1. If the presence of multicollinearity will cause problems with the regression model, determine the variance inflation factor (*VIF*) for each independent variable using PHStat. Otherwise, proceed to step 2.
   a. If none of the variables have a *VIF* greater than 5.0, proceed to step 2.
   b. If one of the variables has a *VIF* greater than 5.0, remove it from the model and proceed to step 2.
   c. If more than two independent variables have a *VIF* greater than 5.0, remove the variable with the highest *VIF* from the model and go back to step 1.
2. If you have more than seven independent variables remaining in your model, perform a stepwise regression to identify the appropriate regression equation. Otherwise, proceed to step 3.
3. If you have seven or fewer independent variables remaining in your model, perform a best subsets regression to identify all of the possible candidates for the final model.
4. Identify the subsets with the highest adjusted R^2 as possible candidates.

5. Also include as a possible candidate any subset with a C_p less than or equal to $k + 1$.
6. From the list of possible candidates, choose the most appropriate model that performs adequately.
7. All else being equal, choose the model with the fewest number of independent variables.
8. Examine the residual plot for each independent variable included in the final model to ensure that the constant variance of residuals is not violated.

Be sure to stop and make sure you understand how to perform residual analysis with this last (hooray!) Your Turn problem.

YOUR TURN #8

Using the best subset model, perform a residual analysis using the information from the Arizona State University GPA example described in Your Turn #5. Is the constant variance requirement met for this model?

Answers can be found on ▶ page 765

15.5 Section Problems

Basic Skills

15.41 Consider the following set of dependent and independent variables. These data can also be found in the Excel file **Prob 1541.xlsx**.

y	10	11	15	15	20	24	27	32	26	39
x_1	2	5	5	9	7	11	16	20	39	21
x_2	16	10	13	10	2	8	7	4	8	5
x_3	7	15	9	12	18	17	23	20	27	30

Using PHStat, check for the presence of multicollinearity. If multicollinearity is present, take the necessary steps to eliminate it.

15.42 Consider the following set of dependent and independent variables. These data can also be found in the Excel file **Prob 1542.xlsx**.

y	47	42	40	40	31	26	23	18	10	14	6
x_1	74	63	78	52	44	47	35	17	15	20	17
x_2	22	29	20	17	13	17	8	15	10	10	7
x_3	7	15	9	12	18	17	23	20	27	30	33

Using PHStat, check for the presence of multicollinearity. If multicollinearity is present, take the necessary steps to eliminate it.

15.43 Consider the following set of dependent and independent variables. These data can also be found in the Excel file **Prob 1543.xlsx**.

y	64	43	51	49	40	42	23	37	30	27	20
x_1	74	63	78	52	44	47	35	17	15	20	17
x_2	22	29	20	17	13	17	8	15	10	10	7
x_3	24	15	9	38	18	17	5	40	27	30	33

a. Perform a general stepwise regression using $\alpha = 0.05$ for the p-value to enter and to remove independent variables from the regression model.

b. Perform a residual analysis for the model developed in part a to verify that the regression conditions are met.

15.44 Consider the following set of dependent and independent variables. These data can also be found in the Excel file **Prob 1544.xlsx**.

y	64	43	51	49	40	42	23	37	30	27	20
x_1	74	63	78	52	44	47	35	17	15	20	17
x_2	22	29	20	17	13	17	8	15	10	10	7
x_3	24	15	9	38	18	17	5	40	27	30	33
x_4	17	30	25	29	38	30	33	39	44	41	49

a. Perform a best subsets regression and choose the most appropriate model for these data.

b. Perform a residual analysis to verify that the conditions for the model are met.

Applications

15.45 A finance executive would like to determine if a relationship exists between the current earnings per share (EPS) of a bank and the following independent variables:

- Total assets ($ billions)
- Previous period's EPS
- Previous period's return on average assets (ROAA)
- Previous period's return on average equity (ROAE)

ROAA measures how effectively assets are utilized, and ROAE measures a firm's profitability. The Excel file **Bank EPS.xlsx** contains these data for several banks.

a. Using PHStat, check for the presence of multicollinearity.
b. If multicollinearity is present, take the necessary steps to eliminate it.
c. Perform a general stepwise regression using $\alpha = 0.05$ for the p-value to enter and to remove independent variables from the regression model.
d. Identify the regression equation for the model in part c.
e. Perform a residual analysis with the model in part c to verify that the conditions for the model are met.

15.46 A business statistics professor at State College would like to develop a regression model to predict the final exam scores for students based on their current GPAs, the number of hours they studied for the exam, the number of times they were absent during the semester, and their genders. The data for these variables can be found in the Excel file **final exam scores 2.xlsx**.

a. Using PHStat, check for the presence of multicollinearity.
b. If multicollinearity is present, take the necessary steps to eliminate it.
c. Perform a general stepwise regression using $\alpha = 0.10$ for the p-value to enter and to remove independent variables from the regression model.
d. Identify the regression equation for the model in part c.
e. Perform a residual analysis with the model in part c to verify that the conditions for the model are met.

15.47 City Hospital would like to develop a regression model to predict the total hospital bill for a patient based on his or her length of stay, number of days in the hospital's intensive care unit (ICU), and age of the patient. Data for these variables can be found in the Excel file **City Hospital.xlsx**.

a. Using PHStat, check for the presence of multicollinearity.
b. If multicollinearity is present, take the necessary steps to eliminate it.
c. Perform a general stepwise regression using $\alpha = 0.05$ for the p-value to enter and to remove independent variables from the regression model.
d. Identify the regression equation for the model in part c.
e. Perform a residual analysis with the model in part c to verify that the conditions for the model are met.

15.48 Squirt Squad is a cleaning service that sends crews to residential homes on either a once-a-month or a twice-a-month schedule, depending on the customer's preference. The owner would like to predict the amount of time required to clean a house based on the square footage of the house, the total number of rooms in the house, the number of bathrooms it has, the size of the cleaning crew, and whether the household has children. Data from randomly selected homes can be found in the Excel file **Squirt Squad 3.xlsx**.

a. Using PHStat, check for the presence of multicollinearity.
b. If multicollinearity is present, take the necessary steps to eliminate it.
c. Perform a best subsets regression and choose the most appropriate model for these data.
d. Perform a residual analysis with the model in part c to verify that the conditions for the model are met.

15.49 Suppose the athletic director at Villanova University would like to develop a regression model to predict the point differential for games played by the college's men's basketball team. A point differential is the difference between the final points scored by two competing teams. A positive differential is a win for Villanova, and a negative differential is a loss. For a random sample of games, shown in the Excel file **Villanova basketball 1.xlsx**, the point differential was calculated for Villanova, along with the number of assists, rebounds, turnovers, and personal fouls.

a. Using PHStat, check for the presence of multicollinearity.
b. If multicollinearity is present, take the necessary steps to eliminate it.
c. Perform a best subsets regression and choose the most appropriate model for these data.
d. Identify the regression equation for the model in part c.
e. Perform a residual analysis with the model in part c to verify that the conditions for the model are met.

15.50 Suppose the Bank of Delaware would like to develop a regression model to predict a person's credit score based on his or her age, weekly income, and education level (high school diploma, bachelor's degree, graduate degree). The Excel file **Bank of Delaware 2.xlsx** provides these data for a random sample of customers.

a. Using PHStat, check for the presence of multicollinearity.
b. If multicollinearity is present, take the necessary steps to eliminate it.
c. Perform a best subsets regression and choose the most appropriate model for these data.
d. Identify the regression equation for the model in part c.
e. Perform a residual analysis with the model in part c to verify that the conditions for the model are met.

15.51 Jersey Shore Realtors would like to develop a regression model to help the firm set weekly rental rates for beach properties during the summer season in New Jersey. The independent variables for this model will be the size of the property in square feet, the number of bedrooms and bathrooms it has, and its age. These data can be found in the Excel file **Jersey Shore Realtors 3.xlsx** for randomly selected rental properties.

a. Using PHStat, check for the presence of multicollinearity.
b. If multicollinearity is present, take the necessary steps to eliminate it.
c. Perform a best subsets regression and choose the most appropriate model for these data.
d. Identify the regression equation for the model in part c.
e. Perform a residual analysis with the model in part c to verify that the conditions for the model are met.

CHAPTER 15 Summary

- The multiple regression model is an extension of the simple regression model discussed in Chapter 14.
  - Instead of a single independent variable, we now have the opportunity to incorporate k independent variables to explain the variation in our dependent variable of interest.
- A regression coefficient predicts the change in a dependent variable due to a one-unit change in an independent variable with all else being held constant.
- Using the regression equation to predict the dependent variable with values of the independent variable that are outside the range of the original sample can provide unreliable results.
- The difference in the values of the dependent variable is known as variation and is measured by a term known as the total sum of squares (*SST*).
- The sum of squares regression (*SSR*) measures the amount of variation in the dependent variable that is explained by the independent variables.
- The sum of squares error (*SSE*) measures the variation in the dependent variable that is explained by variables other than the independent variables.
- The multiple coefficient of determination, R^2, is the percentage of variation in the dependent variable explained by all of the independent variables.
- The F-test statistic is used to perform a hypothesis test to determine if the overall regression equation is statistically significant.
- The adjusted multiple coefficient of determination, R_A^2, modifies, or adjusts, the multiple coefficient of determination by accounting for the number of independent variables and the sample size used to develop the regression model.
- The t-test statistic is used to perform a hypothesis test to determine if each independent variable in the regression model is statistically significant.
- The standard error of the regression coefficient measures the variation in the regression coefficient, b_i, among several samples.
- If the confidence interval for the regression coefficient includes zero, we have some evidence that β could be equal to zero, which indicates that there may not be a relationship between the dependent and independent variable.
- Dummy variables are used to represent qualitative data in a multiple regression model and can take on only the values 0 and 1.
  - We treat dummy variables as quantitative independent variables and proceed with the regression analysis as usual.
  - In general, the number of dummy variables used is always one less than the number of categories in the qualitative data.
  - The coefficient for a dummy variable reflects the change in the dependent variable when comparing one category of the qualitative variable to the base.

Model building is the process of deciding which independent variables should be part of the final regression model. Independent variables that are highly correlated with each other can cause problems for the multiple regression model. Multicollinearity is present in the regression model when independent variables within the model are highly correlated. However, if the purpose of the regression model is to predict the value of a dependent variable, the presence of multicollinearity is not necessarily a problem. The presence of multicollinearity can be detected using the variance inflation factor (*VIF*). If any value of VIF_j exceeds 5.0, enough correlation exists between the independent variables to claim that multicollinearity is present in the regression model.

A general stepwise regression brings one independent variable at a time into the regression model based on its p-value. The "p-value to enter" and "p-value to remove" values determine the threshold for independent variables joining and leaving the regression model, respectively. A best subsets regression is another model-building method. It examines all combinations of independent variables as possible candidates for the final regression model. When comparing models with similar adjusted R^2 values, choose the one with the fewer number of independent variables. A forward selection regression brings one independent variable into the model at a time and does not allow any variables to leave once they have entered. A backward elimination regression begins with all of the independent variables in the model. Variables that are not significant are then removed from the model one at a time and are never allowed to return.

Residuals describe the difference between the actual and predicted values of a dependent variable. One of the assumptions of the multiple regression model is that the residuals have a constant variance.

CHAPTER 15 Key Terms

Adjusted multiple coefficient of determination, R_A^2. A coefficient that modifies, or adjusts, the multiple coefficient of determination by accounting for the number of independent variables and the sample size used to develop the regression model.

Backward elimination regression. A regression method in which variables that are not significant leave the model one at a time and are never allowed to return.

Best subsets regression. A regression method that examines all combinations of independent variables as possible candidates for the final regression model.

Dependent variable. Assigned as the variable y, it is explained by the independent variables (denoted by x).

Dummy variables. Used to represent qualitative data in a multiple regression model.

Forward selection regression. A regression method that brings one independent variable into the model at a time and does not allow any variables to leave once they have entered.

General stepwise regression. A regression method that brings one independent variable at a time into the regression model based on its p-value. Variables that enter the model may leave in a future step.

Homoscedasticity. A regression model assumption that states that the variation of the dependent variable is the same across all values of the independent variables.

Independent variable. Assigned the variable x, it explains the variation in the dependent variable y.

Mean square error (MSE). Value found by dividing the sum of squares error (SSE) by $n - k - 1$.

Mean square regression (MSR). Value found by dividing the sum of squares regression (SSR) by the number of independent variables (k).

Model building. The process of deciding which independent variables should be part of a final regression model.

Multicollinearity. A condition that occurs when independent variables within the regression model are highly correlated with one another.

Multiple coefficient of determination, R^2. The percentage of variation in a dependent variable explained by a set of independent variables.

Normal probability plot. Used to verify if data follow the normal probability distribution by graphing the data on the y-axis and the z-scores for the data on the x-axis.

Regression coefficient. Predicts the change in a dependent variable due to a one-unit change in an independent variable while holding other variables constant.

Residual. The difference between the actual and predicted values of a dependent variable.

Standard error of the regression coefficient, s_{b_j}. A measure of the variation in the regression coefficient, b_j, among several samples.

Variance inflation factor (VIF). A factor used to detect the presence of multicollinearity in a regression model.

CHAPTER 15 Equations

15.1 Developing the Multiple Regression Model (pp 710–717)

Formula 15.1 for the Multiple Linear Regression Model for a Sample $\hat{y} = b_0 + b_1x_1 + b_2x_2 + \cdots + b_kx_k$

Formula 15.2 for the Multiple Linear Regression Model for a Population $y_i = \beta_0 + \beta_1x_1 + \beta_2x_2 + \cdots + \beta_kx_k + \varepsilon$

15.2 Explaining the Variation of the Dependent Variable (pp 717–726)

Formula 15.3 for the Total Sum of Squares (SST) $SST = \sum(y - \bar{y})^2$

Formula 15.4 for the Sum of Squares Regression (SSR) $SSR = \sum(\hat{y} - \bar{y})^2$

Formula 15.5 for the Sum of Squares Error (SSE) $SSE = \sum(y - \hat{y})^2$

Formula 15.6 for Partitioning the Total Sum of Squares $SST = SSR + SSE$

Formula 15.7 for the Multiple Coefficient of Determination $R^2 = \frac{SSR}{SST}$

Formula 15.8 for the Mean Square Regression (MSR) $MSR = \frac{SSR}{k}$

Formula 15.9 for the Mean Square Error (MSE) $MSE = \frac{SSE}{n - k - 1}$

Formula 15.10 for the F-Test Statistic for the Overall Regression Model $F = \frac{MSR}{MSE}$

Formula 15.11 for the Adjusted Multiple Coefficient of Determination $R_A^2 = 1 - \left[(1 - R^2)\left(\frac{n - 1}{n - k - 1}\right)\right]$

15.3 Inferences about the Independent Variables (pp 726–731)

Formula 15.12 for the *t*-Test Statistic for the Regression Coefficient $t = \frac{b_j - \beta_j}{s_{b_j}}$

Formula 15.13 for the Confidence Interval for the Regression Coefficient $CI = b_j \pm t_{\alpha/2}s_{b_j}$

15.5 Model Building (pp 739–755)

Formula 15.14 for the Variance Inflation Factor

$$VIF_j = \frac{1}{1 - R_j^2}$$

Formula 15.15 for the Residual

$$e_i = y_i - \hat{y}_i$$

CHAPTER 15 Problems

15.52 For one of its clients, a marketing research firm would like to predict the weekly food expenditures for households. The independent variables of interest are the number of individuals living in a household, the number of teenagers in it, and the total household income. Data for these variables from randomly selected households can be found in the Excel file **food expenditures.xlsx**.

a. Construct a regression model using all three independent variables.

b. Interpret the meaning of the regression coefficients.

c. Test the significance of the overall regression model using $\alpha = 0.05$.

d. Predict the average weekly food expenditure for a household with a weekly income of $1,200 and five people, one of whom is a teenager.

e. Construct a 95% confidence interval for the average weekly food expenditure for the household described in part d. Interpret the meaning of the interval.

f. Construct a 95% prediction interval for the weekly food expenditure for the household described in part d. Interpret the meaning of the interval.

g. Test the significance of each independent variable using $\alpha = 0.05$.

h. Construct a 95% confidence interval for the regression coefficients for the teenager variable. Be sure to interpret the meaning of this confidence interval.

i. Construct a regression model using best subsets. Identify the most appropriate regression model for this problem.

15.53 Bob is a statistics textbook author and aspiring photographer who sells his 13 × 19 prints on consignment at Island Art in Stone Harbor, New Jersey (stop in if you are in the area and ask for Spencer). To improve his inventory management, Bob would like to develop a model to predict the number of prints he will sell in a week. The Excel file **Island Art 2.xlsx** provides the following data from a random selection of summer weeks over the past few years: the number of prints sold per week, the price of the prints during the week, the number of prints in inventory at the start of the week, and the season (in-season or off-season).

a. Construct a regression model to predict the average demand for prints during the week using all three independent variables.

b. Interpret the meaning of the regression coefficients from part a.

c. Test the significance of the overall regression model from part a using $\alpha = 0.05$.

d. Show the calculation for the adjusted multiple coefficient of determination for part a.

c. Using p-values, identify which independent variables are significant from the model in part a with $\alpha = 0.05$.

f. Using PHStat, check for the presence of multicollinearity for all three independent variables. If it is present, take the necessary steps to eliminate it.

g. Construct a regression model using a general stepwise regression using the independent variables from part f. Use $\alpha = 0.05$ for the p-value to enter and remove independent variables.

h. Predict the average demand for an in-season week in which Bob has 65 prints in inventory priced at $59 per print using the model developed in part g.

i. Construct a 95% confidence interval for the regression coefficients for the Price variable from part g. Be sure to interpret the meaning of this confidence interval.

j. Perform a residual analysis to verify that the conditions for the regression model are met for the model developed in part g.

15.54 The owner of Soffritto Italian Grill would like to predict the amount of the tip a server receives from dinner customers. From randomly selected tables, the owner has collected the data shown in the Excel file **Sofrittos.xlsx**. The data show the tip, the food bill for the table, the number of diners at the table, the number of minutes the diners were in the restaurant, and whether the meal was on a weekday (Monday through Thursday) or a weekend (Friday through Sunday).

a. Check for the presence of multicollinearity between the independent variables. If it is present, take the necessary steps to eliminate it.
b. Construct a regression model using all the independent variables remaining after part a.
c. Interpret the meaning of the regression coefficients.
d. Test the significance of the overall regression model using $\alpha = 0.02$.
e. Using the p-values, identify which independent variables are significant with $\alpha = 0.02$.
f. Construct a 98% confidence interval for the regression coefficients for the bill variable from part b. Be sure to interpret the meaning of this confidence interval.
g. Construct a regression model using a best subsets regression that predicts the average tip from a table of diners using the independent variables from part b.
h. With the model from part g, predict the average tip for a table of four weekend diners with a total bill of $125 who spent 95 minutes at the table.

15.55 The general manager of a major league baseball team would like to develop a regression model to predict the number of wins during the season by a starting pitcher. The Excel file **MLB pitchers.xlsx** provides the following data on a random sample of starting pitchers from a recent season:

- Wins
- Average walks and hits per innings pitched (WHIP)
- Average strikeouts per nine innings (K/9)
- Average strikeout-to-walk ratio (K/BB)
- Earned run average (ERA)—the average number of earned runs given up per game
- Average pitches per plate appearance (P/PA)
- Average pitches per inning (P/IP)
- The ground-ball-to-fly-ball ratio (G/F)—pitchers who have higher G/F ratios tend to cause batters to hit the ball on the ground rather than the air
- Run support average (RS)—the average number of runs scored by the pitcher's team per start
- Right-handed or left-handed pitcher (R/L)

a. Check for the presence of multicollinearity between the independent variables. If it is present, take the necessary steps to eliminate it.
b. Construct a regression model using a best subsets regression that predicts the average number of wins for a pitcher using the independent variables from part a.
c. Interpret the meaning of the regression coefficients from part b.
d. Construct a 99% confidence interval for the regression coefficients for the run support variable from part b. Be sure to interpret the meaning of this confidence interval.
e. Predict the average number of wins for a left-handed pitcher who averages 1.2 walks and hits per inning, 7.1 strikeouts per game, 3.8 pitches per plate appearances, 15.2 pitches per inning, a ground-ball-to-fly-ball ratio of 0.8, a strikeout-to-walk ratio of 2.5, and an earned run average of 3.6 runs per game and whose team averages 5.3 runs per game during his starts.
f. Perform a residual analysis to verify that the conditions for the regression model are met for the model developed in part b.
g. The general manager would like to add a new starting pitcher to his team's roster. Using the results of this model, should he pursue a pitcher that has a high strikeout-to-walk ratio or a high ground-ball-to-fly-ball ratio? Explain your choice.

15.56 The provost at a major university would like to develop a model to examine the relationship between the salaries of full-time associate professors at the institution and the following independent variables: an associate professor's performance rating on a scale of 1–20, his or her gender, student approval rating on a scale of 0–100%, age, years of teaching experience, and college (arts and sciences, or business). The provost has collected these data from a random sample of associate professors, which can be found in the Excel file **faculty salaries.xlsx**.

a. Check for the presence of multicollinearity between the independent variables. If it is present, take the necessary steps to eliminate it.
b. Construct a regression model using all the independent variables remaining after part a.
c. Interpret the meaning of each of the regression coefficients.
d. Test the significance of the overall regression model using $\alpha = 0.01$.
e. Using the p-values, identify which independent variables are significant with $\alpha = 0.01$.
f. Construct a regression model using a general stepwise regression to predict an associate professor's salary using the independent variables from part b. Use $\alpha = 0.01$ for the p-value to enter and remove independent variables.
g. Predict the salary of a female associate professor in the business college who is 41 years old with 11 years of teaching experience, a performance score of 17, and a student approval rating of 88.3%.
h. Use PHStat to construct a 99% confidence interval for the average salary of an associate professor described in part f using the general stepwise regression results and interpret its meaning.
i. Use PHStat to construct a 99% prediction interval for the salary of an associate professor described in part f using the general stepwise regression results and interpret its meaning.
j. Perform a residual analysis to verify that the conditions for the regression model are met for the model developed in part f.

15.57 You have just completed your business statistics course and are shopping for a laptop computer at Best Buy. To help you with your decision, you decide to construct a regression model to predict the selling price of the laptop. The Excel file **laptops.xlsx** provides the following data for a random sample of laptops on Best Buy's Web site:

- Selling price
- Brand
- Screen size (in.)
- Hard drive size (GB)
- Amount of RAM memory (GB)
- Number of USB ports
- Weight (oz.)

a. Check for the presence of multicollinearity between the independent variables. If it is present, take the necessary steps to eliminate it.

b. Construct a regression model using all the independent variables remaining after part a.

c. Test the significance of the overall regression model from part a using $\alpha = 0.05$.

d. Construct a regression model using best subsets regression to predict the price of a laptop using the independent variables from part b.

e. Interpret the meaning of each of the regression coefficients with the model from part d.

f. Construct a 95% confidence interval for the regression coefficients for the size variable from part d. Be sure to interpret the meaning of this confidence interval.

g. Predict the price of a Toshiba laptop with a 15.6-in. screen, 4 GB of RAM memory, a 500-GB hard drive, and three USB ports that weigh 5.2 ounces.

h. Use PHStat to construct a 95% prediction interval for the laptop described in part g and interpret its meaning.

15.58 Mike Lynch manages a real estate firm in Myrtle Beach, South Carolina, and would like to construct a model to help him predict the selling price of beach properties for his customers. Mike has collected the following data from a random sample of homes that have recently sold: a home's selling price (in $000), asking price (in $000), days on the market, size in square feet, age, number of bedrooms, number of bathrooms, and property setting (golf course, or wooded). These data can be found in the Excel file **Myrtle Beach Homes.xlsx**. Develop a best subsets regression model to predict a home's selling price using $\alpha = 0.01$ for a home that is 18 years old, has been on the market for 57 days, has an asking price of $499,000, with 4 bedrooms, 3.5 bathrooms, 2,800 square feet, and is on a wooded lot. Provide a complete analysis of your findings.

CHAPTER 15 Solutions to Your Turn

YOUR TURN #1

Using PHStat:

a. $\hat{y} = 83.4034 + 17.1673x_1 - 19.1125x_2$

where:

$x_1 = \text{RPG}$

$x_2 = \text{ERA}$

b. Increasing the average runs scored per game by 1.0 will result in a team winning an average of 17.2 more games per season. Increasing the average runs per game given up by 1.0 will result in a team losing an average of 19.1 additional games per season.

c. $\hat{y} = 80.4034 + 17.1673(4.0) - 19.1125(3.5) = 85.2$ wins

d. 83.0 to 87.4 wins

e. 77.9 to 92.4 wins

YOUR TURN #2

a. $SSR = 3{,}822.2$

$SSE = 307.8$

$SST = 4{,}130.0$

b. $R^2 = \frac{SSR}{SST} = \frac{3{,}822.2}{4{,}130.0} = 0.9255$

92.55% of the variation in a team's wins can be explained by the average number of runs it scored per game and the average number of runs it gave up per game.

c. H_0: $\beta_1 = \beta_2 = 0$

H_1: At least one $\beta_i \neq 0$

$$MSR = \frac{SSR}{k} = \frac{3{,}822.2}{2} = 1{,}911.1$$

$$MSE = \frac{SSE}{n - k - 1} = \frac{307.8}{30 - 2 - 1} = 11.4$$

$$F = \frac{MSR}{MSE} = \frac{1{,}911.1}{11.4} = 167.6$$

Using $\alpha = 0.01$, the critical F-score found in Table 6 of Appendix A is $F_\alpha = 5.488$. Because $F = 167.6$ is higher than $F_\alpha = 5.488$, we reject H_0 and conclude that at least one of the population coefficients for our independent variables is not equal to zero. In other words, you can use this regression model to predict the number of wins based on the average number of runs scored and given up per game.

d. $P(F > 167.6) = 0.0000$. Because this p-value is less than $\alpha = 0.01$, we reject the null hypothesis.

e. $R_A^2 = 1 - \left[(1 - R^2)\left(\frac{n-1}{n-k-1}\right)\right]$

$$R_A^2 = 1 - \left[(1 - 0.9255)\left(\frac{30-1}{30-2-1}\right)\right]$$

$$R_A^2 = 1 - [(0.0745)(1.0741)] = 1 - 0.0800 = 0.9200$$

YOUR TURN #3

Note: PHStat provides a 95% confidence interval for the regression coefficients by default. To save space, these two columns have been removed from the following figure.

	A	B	C	D	E	F	G
1	**Regression Analysis**						
2							
3	***Regression Statistics***						
4	Multiple R	0.9621					
5	R Square	0.9256					
6	Adjusted R Square	0.9170					
7	Standard Error	3.4387					
8	Observations	30					
9							
10	**ANOVA**						
11		*df*	*SS*	*MS*	*F*	*Significance F*	
12	Regression	3	3822.5633	1274.1878	107.7584	0.0000	
13	Residual	26	307.4367	11.8245			
14	Total	29	4130.0000				
15							
16		*Coefficients*	*Standard Error*	*t Stat*	*P-value*	*Lower 99%*	*Upper 99%*
17	Intercept	84.4511	11.0440	7.6468	0.0000	53.7630	115.1393
18	RPG	17.0753	1.8561	9.1997	0.0000	11.9178	22.2328
19	ERA	-19.0483	1.3238	-14.3886	0.0000	-22.7269	-15.3697
20	ERR	-0.0091	0.0509	-0.1780	0.8601	-0.1504	0.1323
21							

a. H_0: $\beta_3 = 0$

H_1: $\beta_3 \neq 0$

$$t = \frac{b_1 - \beta_1}{s_{b_1}} = \frac{-0.0091 - 0}{0.0509} = -0.178$$

Using $\alpha = 0.01$ and $30 - 3 - 1 = 26$ degrees of freedom, the critical t-score found in Table 5 in Appendix A is $t_{\alpha/2} = 2.779$. Because $t = -0.178$ is to the right of $-t_{\alpha/2} = -2.779$, we fail to reject H_0 and conclude that the errors population coefficient could be equal to zero. In other words, the relationship between the number of errors committed during the season and the number of wins is not statistically significant. The ERR independent variable should not be included in the final regression model.

b. The ERR $p\text{-value} = 0.8601$, which is greater than $\alpha = 0.01$, so we fail to reject the null hypothesis. We conclude that the number of errors committed during the season is not a good predictor of the number of wins.

c. $CI = b \pm t_{\alpha/2}s_b = -0.0091 \pm (2.779)(0.0509)$

$UCL = -0.0091 + 0.1415 = 0.1324$

$LCL = -0.0091 - 0.1415 = -0.1506$

We are 99% confident that committing an additional error during the season will result in changing the number of average wins per season from a reduction of 0.1506 to an increase of 0.1324. Because this confidence interval includes zero, we have supporting evidence to conclude that there is no relationship between errors and wins.

d. The RPG $p\text{-value} = 0.000$, which is less than $\alpha = 0.01$, so we reject the null hypothesis. We conclude that the number of runs scored per game is a good predictor of the number of wins. The ERA $p\text{-value} = 0.000$, which is less than $\alpha = 0.01$, so we again reject the null hypothesis. We conclude that the number of runs given up per game is a good predictor of the number of wins.

e. We are 99% confident that an additional run scored per game will increase the number of average wins per season by between 11.9 and 22.2 wins. Because this confidence interval does not include zero, we have supporting evidence to conclude that there is a relationship between average runs scored per game and wins. We are 99% confident that giving up one additional run per game will decrease the average wins per season by between 15.4 and 22.7 wins. Because this confidence interval does not include zero, we have supporting evidence to conclude that there is a relationship between average runs given up per game and wins.

YOUR TURN #4

Setting the dummy variable Dome equal to 1 for a team with a roof and zero for no roof, we have the following results:

	A	B	C	D	E	F	G
1	**Regression Analysis**						
2							
3	*Regression Statistics*						
4	Multiple R	0.9690					
5	R Square	0.9391					
6	Adjusted R Square	0.9320					
7	Standard Error	3.1114					
8	Observations	30					
9							
10	ANOVA						
11		*df*	*SS*	*MS*	*F*	*Significance F*	
12	Regression	3	3878.2913	1292.7638	133.5347	0.0000	
13	Residual	26	251.7087	9.6811			
14	Total	29	4130.0000				
15							
16		*Coefficients*	*Standard Error*	*t Stat*	*P-value*	*Lower 95%*	*Upper 95%*
17	Intercept	87.6775	8.6392	10.1488	0.0000	69.9194	105.4357
18	RPG	16.2332	1.6590	9.7850	0.0000	12.8231	19.6433
19	ERA	-18.9774	1.1538	-16.4472	0.0000	-21.3491	-16.6056
20	Dome	-3.3299	1.3833	-2.4073	0.0235	-6.1732	-0.4866
21							

Teams that have a roof average 3.3 fewer wins per year than teams that do not have a roof as long as the other variables stay constant. Note that with a $p\text{-value} = 0.0235$, this dummy variable is statistically significant.

YOUR TURN #5

From PHStat, we have the following:

Independent Variable	VIF_j	Multicollinearity?
MGMAT	8.61	Yes
VGMAT	5.95	Yes
UGGPA	2.73	No
DEGREE	1.37	No

Because the *VIF* value for *MGMAT* is greater than 5.0 and is the highest value in the table, remove it as an independent variable and repeat the process.

Independent Variable	VIF_j	Multicollinearity?
VGMAT	1.21	No
UGGPA	1.42	No
DEGREE	1.21	No

This set of independent variables does not exhibit the presence of multicollinearity.

YOUR TURN #6

Using the set of independent variables that does not exhibit the presence of multicollinearity from Your Turn #5, the first variable to enter the model is UGGPA, as the following figure shows:

	A	B	C	D	E	F	G	H
1	**Stepwise Regression Analysis**							
2	**Table of Results for General Stepwise**							
3								
4	**UGGPA entered.**							
5								
6			*df*	*SS*	*MS*	*F*	*Significance F*	
7		Regression	1	1.0233	1.0233	25.9882	0.0000	
8		Residual	22	0.8663	0.0394			
9		Total	23	1.8896				
10								
11			*Coefficients*	*Standard Error*	*t Stat*	*P-value*	*Lower 95%*	*Upper 95%*
12		Intercept	1.7317	0.3647	4.7489	0.0001	0.9755	2.4880
13		UGGPA	0.5544	0.1088	5.0979	0.0000	0.3289	0.7800

The second and last variable to enter the model is DEGREE, as the following figure shows:

15								
16	DEGREE entered.							
17								
18		df	SS	MS	F	Significance F		
19	Regression	2	1.2086	0.6043	18.6353	0.0000		
20	Residual	21	0.6810	0.0324				
21	Total	23	1.8896					
22								
23		Coefficients	Standard Error	t Stat	P-value	Lower 95%	Upper 95%	
24	Intercept	1.4546	0.3506	4.1486	0.0005	0.7255	2.1838	
25	UGGPA	0.6621	0.1085	6.1029	0.0000	0.4365	0.8877	
26	DEGREE	-0.1959	0.0820	-2.3904	0.0263	-0.3663	-0.0255	
27								
28	No other variables could be entered into the model. Stepwise ends.							
29								

Our final regression model is as follows:

$$\hat{y} = 1.4546 + 0.6621x_3 - 0.1959x_4$$

where

$x_3 =$ The undergraduate GPA of the student

$x_4 =$ A dummy variable that equals 0 for students with undergraduate business degrees and 1 for students with non-business undergraduate degrees

The interpretations for the regression coefficients in this equation are as follows:

$b_3 = 0.6621$: Every additional point in an undergraduate's GPA will result in an average increase of 0.6621 points in his or her MBA GPA, assuming there is no change in the status of the student.

$b_5 = -0.1959$: The MBA GPAs for students with non-business undergraduate degrees are an average of 0.1959 points lower than the MBA GPAs of students with business degrees, assuming there is no change in the undergraduate GPA of a student.

YOUR TURN #7

10	Model	Cp	k+1	R Square	Adj. R Square	Std. Error
11	X1	27.7401	2	0.2773	0.2444	0.2492
12	X2	10.2821	2	0.5416	0.5207	0.1984
13	X3	46.0257	2	0.0004	-0.0450	0.2930
14	X1X2	8.3957	3	0.6004	0.5623	0.1896
15	X1X3	29.4378	3	0.2818	0.2134	0.2542
16	X2X3	5.8049	3	0.6396	0.6053	0.1801
17	X1X2X3	4.0000	4	0.6972	0.6518	0.1691

a. According to the previous figure, the best subset includes all three independent variables, which are highlighted in yellow.

	A	B	C	D	E	F	G
1	Best Subsets Analysis						
2							
3	Regression Statistics						
4	Multiple R	0.8350					
5	R Square	0.6972					
6	Adjusted R Square	0.6518					
7	Standard Error	0.1691					
8	Observations	24					
9							
10	ANOVA						
11		df	SS	MS	F	Significance F	
12	Regression	3	1.3174	0.4391	15.3512	0.0000	
13	Residual	20	0.5721	0.0286			
14	Total	23	1.8896				
15							
16		Coefficients	Standard Error	t Stat	P-value	Lower 95%	Upper 95%
17	Intercept	1.4050	0.3303	4.2534	0.0004	0.7159	2.0940
18	VGMAT	0.0121	0.0062	1.9506	0.0653	-0.0008	0.0251
19	UGGPA	0.5788	0.1105	5.2381	0.0000	0.3483	0.8092
20	DEGREE	-0.1947	0.0770	-2.5290	0.0200	-0.3552	-0.0341

b. The model constructed in Your Turn #6 using a general stepwise regression had only two independent variables, UGGPA (x_2) and DEGREE (x_3). The adjusted R^2 for this model is shown in the figure from part a and is equal to 0.6053 (see Row 16). This is lower than the adjusted R^2 from the best subsets model (0.6518). However, the best subsets model has an independent variable with a *p*-value greater than 0.05: VGMAT.

YOUR TURN #8

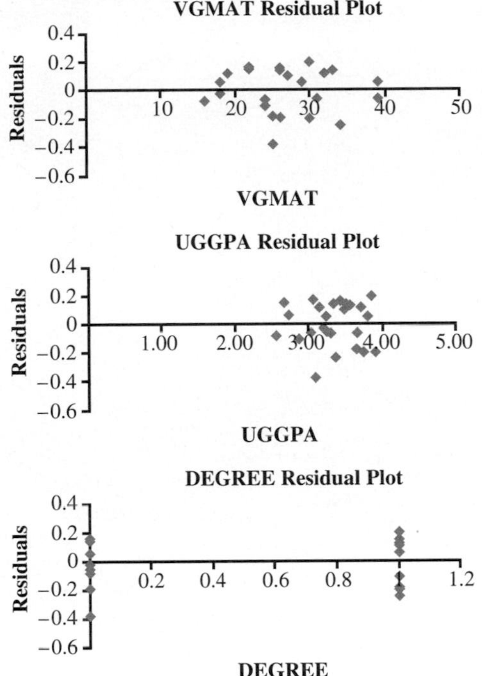

There does not appear to be a blatant violation of the constant variance for the residuals for these independent variables. It is worth noting, however, that the regression error for business degree students $(\text{DEGREE} = 0)$ is greater than it is for non-business degree students $(\text{DEGREE} = 1)$.

Forecasting

IN THIS CHAPTER, YOU WILL LEARN TO:

- Generate a forecast using various moving average techniques.
- Generate a forecast using exponential smoothing with and without a trend component.
- Determine the accuracy of the forecast using mean absolute deviation.
- Generate a forecast using regression analysis.
- Test for the presence of autocorrelation in a time series.
- Generate a forecast using multiplicative decomposition.
- Generate a forecast which uses dummy variables to represent seasonality.

CHAPTER 16 *MAP*

Stats in Practice: Forecasting Car Sales

Congratulations are in order again! Because of your remarkable performance using the multiple regression techniques discussed in Chapter 15, Brandywine Ford, a major car dealership in the Mid-Atlantic area, has promoted you to the position of new car sales manager. One of the primary responsibilities in your new job is to predict, or forecast, the number of new cars that will be sold in the upcoming quarter. This information will be used to decide the number of sales and service personnel that will be needed on staff in the near future. Fortunately, this chapter will provide you with the tools to make such a decision. So if you really want to impress your boss, by all means, read on!

For businesses to be successful in today's competitive environment, they need the foresight to plan ahead for future events. Many business decisions, such as building new facilities or hiring and training new employees, require time to implement. Even near-term business decisions such as ordering inventory and scheduling employees require foresight. To help make these decisions, accurate forecasts are needed to predict future demand and other events. If these forecasts turn out to be inaccurate, the decisions on which they are based have little chance of being helpful to an organization.

Examples of organizations that rely heavily on accurate forecasts are as follows:

- Government agencies: Tax revenues need to be predicted in order to pay for the government spending.
- Utility companies: Because the cost of investing in new facilities is very high and they take time to build, utility companies spend a great deal of time and resources forecasting future energy requirements.
- Financial institutions: Economic data such as interest rates and stock prices play a major role in decision making and need to be predicted with as much accuracy as possible.

Qualitative forecasting is a subjective technique that relies primarily on a knowledgeable person's intuition and judgment to predict future events.

With **quantitative forecasting** historical data and math are used to predict future conditions.

Forecasting techniques can be classified into two broad categories: qualitative and quantitative methods. **Qualitative forecasting** is a subjective technique that relies primarily on a knowledgeable person's intuition and judgment to predict future events. There are many structured techniques available to facilitate this process. By contrast, with **quantitative forecasting** historical data and math are used to predict future events.

In this chapter, we'll examine several different quantitative forecasting techniques available to businesses. We will also learn how to compare the effectiveness of these various methods depending on our data. After all, you want to impress your boss with your statistical talents, don't you?

16.1 Introduction to Forecasting

I'm sure most of you have experienced the frustrations of poor forecasting. As it so happens, I'm writing this chapter on a cold January evening. My favorite weatherman predicted a major snowstorm that would ensure me a "snow day" tomorrow, so I don't have to go to school. I must let you in on a well-kept secret: We faculty enjoy snow days as much as our students do. Much to my chagrin, the storm seems to be petering out this evening with barely an inch of snow on the ground. Oh well, I better start preparing for class tomorrow.

When it comes to business decisions, there is often much more at stake than mistakenly predicting a snow day. Poor decisions due to inaccurate forecasting can lead to careers being damaged and reputations being lost. Speaking of careers, let's return to the original example at the start of the chapter, where you wanted to forecast new car sales for the next quarter. To do so, you will need car sales data from previous quarters, which I provide in Table 16.1. These data can also be found in the Excel file **new car sales.xlsx**.

TABLE 16.1 | New Car Sales for Brandywine Ford

PERIOD	YEAR	QUARTER	SALES	PERIOD	YEAR	QUARTER	SALES
1	2011	1	97	7	2012	3	126
2	2011	2	142	8	2012	4	150
3	2011	3	108	9	2013	1	123
4	2011	4	135	10	2013	2	151
5	2012	1	120	11	2013	3	141
6	2012	2	164	12	2013	4	142

Each data point in a **time series** is associated with a specific point in time.

The data in Table 16.1 are known as a **time series** because each sales data point is associated with a specific point in time. Because time-series forecasting is very common in business, it is the focus of this chapter.

The very first thing that any good forecaster worth his or her weight would do is to construct an XY scatter plot of the data like the one in Figure 16.1. Doing so will provide some visual insights that a table can't. (See Chapter 2 for instructions on how to construct such a plot.) A scatter plot allows us to look at the different components of a time series, which we will discuss in the next section.

FIGURE 16.1
XY Scatter Plot: New Car Sales

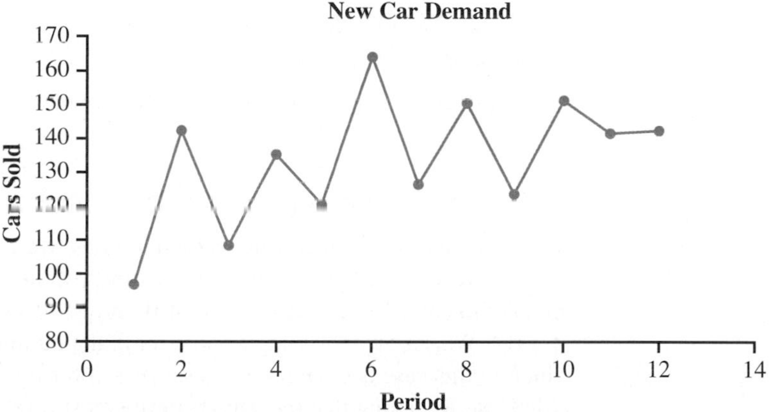

The Components of a Time Series

Any time series could contain one or more of the following types of components:

- Trend
- Seasonal
- Cyclical
- Random

A **trend component** is present in a time series if a general upward or downward movement can be observed in the data.

A **trend component** is present in a time series if a general upward or downward movement can be observed in the data. For example, although the new car demand data in Figure 16.1 jump around, they appear to follow an overall upward trend over the 12-quarter time period. It seems your dealership has experienced sales growth over the last three years.

A **seasonal component** is present in a time series if a consistent pattern in the data can be associated with a calendar.

Our data are said to contain a **seasonal component** if we can detect a consistent pattern that can be associated with the calendar. For example, in Figure 16.1, the second and fourth quarters of each year saw a spike in new car sales, whereas the first and third quarters saw a downturn. Seasonal patterns repeat themselves within a calendar year. Therefore, to observe them, data need to be collected more frequently than on an annual basis. In other words, the seasonal patterns in Figure 16.1 would not be observable if the sales data for the four quarters of each year were lumped together as annual sales. Businesses that are impacted by seasonality, such as tourism, need to consider this component when developing forecasting models.

A **cyclical component** is movement in a time series that results from upward or downward swings in the U.S. or world economy over a period of several years.

A **random component** is defined as the unpredictable movements in a time series that cannot be attributed to either trend, seasonal, or cyclical components.

A **cyclical component** is movement in a time series that results from upward or downward swings in the U.S. or world economy. These patterns tend to extend beyond the one-year pattern of seasonal components. For example, the demand for framing lumber was in a downward cycle during 2007–2010 due to the weak housing market.

Finally, every time series contains a **random component**, which consists of unpredictable movements in the data that cannot be attributed to trend, seasonal, or cyclical components. This component is often referred to as "noise" because it has no detectable pattern.

Some of the forecasting methods discussed in this chapter will attempt to identify these components and use that information to predict future values. We'll start off by learning about a class of forecasting techniques known as smoothing methods.

16.2 Smoothing Forecasting Methods

The goal of the smoothing method category is to average, or smooth out, the random movements in a time series because they are unpredictable. If our forecast is an average of the most recent time-series values, we would expect the random component to "cancel itself out" in the long run. That is, the upward and downward movements attributed to the component would balance out.

Smoothing techniques work best with data that are fairly consistent over time—in other words, data without significant trend, seasonal, or cyclical components. The following forecasting techniques are smoothing methods:

- Simple moving average
- Weighted moving average
- Exponential smoothing
- Exponential smoothing with trend adjustment

Simple Moving Average (*SMA*) Forecast

A **simple moving average** forecast is generated by averaging the most recent p values in a time series.

As the name of this forecasting method implies, we generate a **simple moving average** (*SMA*) forecast by simply averaging the most recent p values in our time series. Let's use this method and Table 16.1 to forecast Brandywine Ford's new car sales for the first quarter of 2014. We start by choosing a value for p, the number of periods to include in our average, which in this case is quarters. Let's set $p = 3$ for this example; we'll discuss this choice a little later. Recalling that the values for the most recent three quarters in Table 16.1 are 151, 141, and 142, we have the following:

$$SMA(p = 3, \text{Quarter \#1, 2014}) = \frac{151 + 141 + 142}{3} = \frac{434}{3} = 144.7 \approx 145$$

Using a three-period *SMA*, the sales forecast for the first quarter in 2014 is 145 cars.

Now, I'm sure your boss would like to know something about the accuracy of this forecast. When Brandywine Ford's sales are tallied following the first quarter of 2014, how close will your forecast be? You can answer your boss's question by applying the three-period *SMA* technique to the historical data shown in Table 16.1. This allows you to calculate the forecasting error for each period by subtracting the historical forecasts from the historical data. The **mean absolute deviation (*MAD*)** is the average forecasting error and can be found using Equation 16.1.

The **mean absolute deviation (*MAD*)** measures the accuracy of a forecast by calculating the average absolute forecasting error per period of historical data.

Formula 16.1 for the Mean Absolute Deviation (MAD)

$$MAD = \frac{\sum |A_t - F_t|}{n}$$

where

MAD = The mean absolute deviation
A_t = The actual value for the time period t
F_t = The forecasted value for the time period t
$A_t - F_t$ = The forecasting error for the time period t
$|A_t - F_t|$ = The absolute value of the forecasting error
n = The number of forecasting errors

Table 16.2 shows the calculations for our three-period *SMA* forecast. We will need them to find the *MAD* for the car sales data.

TABLE 16.2 | DATA AND CALCULATIONS NEEDED TO FIND THE MEAN ABSOLUTE DEVIATION: THREE-PERIOD SIMPLE MOVING AVERAGE FORECAST

The actual car sales for Period 4 is 135, whereas the forecasted car sales for this period is 115.7. Our forecasting error is therefore 135 − 115.7 = 19.3.

PERIOD, t	ACTUAL SALES, A_t	FORECAST SALES, F_t	FORECASTING ERROR, $A_t - F_t$	ABSOLUTE FORECASTING ERROR, $\|A_t - F_t\|$
1	97			
2	142			
3	108			
4	135	115.7	19.3	19.3
5	120	128.3	−8.3	8.3
6	164	121.0	43.0	43.0
7	126	139.7	−13.7	13.7
8	150	136.7	13.3	13.3
9	123	146.7	−23.7	23.7
10	151	133.0	18.0	18.0
11	141	141.3	−0.3	0.3
12	142	138.3	3.7	3.7
				$\sum\|A_t - F_t\| = 143.3$

Let's break this table down one piece at a time. Because $p = 3$, the first historical forecast we can calculate is for Period 4, which we obtained as follows:

$$SMA(p = 3, \text{Period } 4) = \frac{97 + 142 + 108}{3} = \frac{347}{3} = 115.7$$

A common mistake some of my students make is to assign this forecast to Period 3. But recall that the purpose of calculating a forecast is to predict future values with the data you already have. You can see from Table 16.1 that you already have actual sales data for Periods 1, 2, and 3. What you are trying to predict are the sales for Period 4, which you don't know. So, be sure to apply this forecast to the future period, which is Period 4, rather than to Period 3.

We call this method a "moving average" because we drop the oldest value and pick up the most recent value as we move down the historical data. Therefore, to determine the three-period *SMA* forecast for Period 5, we drop the first period (97) and pick up the fourth period (135) in our moving average calculation, which results in the following calculation:

$$SMA(p = 3, \text{Period } 5) = \frac{142 + 108 + 135}{3} = \frac{385}{3} = 128.3$$

The fourth column in Table 16.2 shows the forecasting error, $A_t - F_t$, for each period. For example, we sold 135 cars in the fourth period, and our three-period *SMA* forecast predicted we would sell 115.7 cars. Therefore, our forecast for this quarter was 19.3 cars too low. Similarly, our forecasting error in the fifth period is −8.3, meaning that our forecast was 8.3 cars too high. The last column in Table 16.2 shows the absolute value for this forecasting error, $|A_t - F_t|$, which simply removes the negative sign for any forecasting errors. We use the absolute value when we average the forecasting error for *MAD* because we don't want the positive and negative errors to cancel each other out. This would result in an average error that appears much lower than it should be. Think about it: If the forecasting errors for two periods are +10 and −10, the average error is zero, which is very misleading. Using the absolute value of the errors results in an average error of 10, which is more accurate.

Using the data from Table 16.2, we can calculate the *MAD* for our three-period *SMA* forecast using Equation 16.1:

$$MAD = \frac{\sum |A_t - F_t|}{n} = \frac{143.3}{9} = 15.9$$

For this example, $n = 9$ because we have to average the nine forecasting errors for Periods 4–12 in Table 16.2. What we have learned is that using the three-period *SMA* forecast, we would expect the average forecasting error to be about 16 cars per quarter. It would be up to you and your boss to decide if this average error is acceptable for your forecast. Of course, lower forecasting errors are better than larger ones. I'm sure your boss would prefer your forecast to be off by a dozen cars than by two or three dozen.

Figure 16.2 illustrates the smoothing effect of the *SMA* forecast. The blue line shows the actual data, whereas the red line displays the forecasted values. As you can see, the *SMA* forecast averages out, or "smoothes" the highs and lows of the actual values.

FIGURE 16.2
Three-Period Simple Moving Average Forecast vs. the Actual Data: New Car Sales

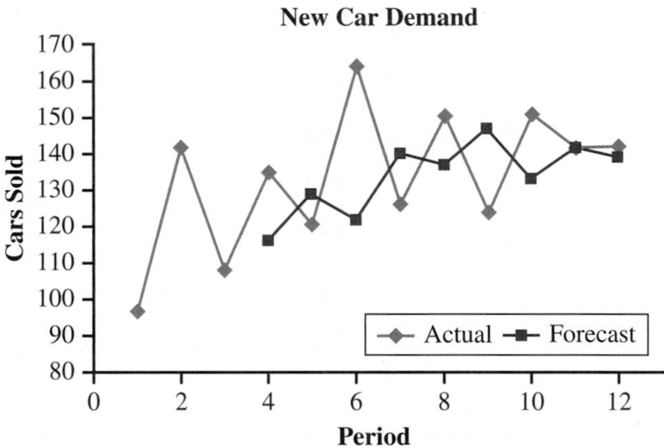

What happens if we choose to use a four-period *SMA* forecast? This would result in a different forecast for the first quarter in 2014, which is the 13th period in our data:

$$SMA(p = 4, \text{Period } 13) = \frac{123 + 151 + 141 + 142}{4} = \frac{557}{4} = 139.3 \approx 139$$

I'm wondering (and I hope you are too) if our four-period *SMA* forecast has the potential to be more accurate in the long run than our three-period forecast that we calculated earlier in the section (145). To answer this question, we need to recalculate our *SMA* forecasts, as shown in Table 16.3.

First, notice that our first historical forecast is now Period 5 because we need the first four periods for the first moving average calculation:

$$SMA(p = 4, \text{Period } 5) = \frac{97 + 142 + 108 + 135}{4} = \frac{482}{4} = 120.5$$

The *MAD* for the four-period *SMA* forecast is calculated as follows:

$$MAD = \frac{\sum |A_t - F_t|}{n} = \frac{89.1}{8} = 11.1$$

All else being equal, choose the forecast with the lower *MAD*.

This average error (11.1) is less than the *MAD* found for the three-period *SMA* forecast (15.9). If you had to choose between these two forecasts, the four-period *SMA* forecast would be preferable because it's *MAD* is lower.

TABLE 16.3 | Data and Calculations Needed to Find the Mean Absolute Deviation: Four-Period Simple Moving Average Forecast

PERIOD, t	ACTUAL SALES, A_t	FORECAST SALES, F_t	FORECASTING ERROR, $A_t - F_t$	ABSOLUTE FORECASTING ERROR, $\|A_t - F_t\|$
1	97			
2	142			
3	108			
4	135			
5	120	120.5	−0.5	0.5
6	164	126.3	37.7	37.7
7	126	131.8	−5.8	5.8
8	150	136.3	13.7	13.7
9	123	140.0	−17.0	17.0
10	151	140.8	10.2	10.2
11	141	137.5	3.5	3.5
12	142	141.3	0.7	0.7
				$\sum \|A_t - F_t\| = 89.1$

Increasing the number of periods in *SMA* provides more smoothing in the forecast. Figure 16.3 shows both the actual (blue line) and the forecasted values (red line) for the four-period *SMA*. Notice that the forecasts in Figure 16.3 are "smoother" than the three period *SMA* forecasts shown in Figure 16.2. By including more periods in our average, the forecast will tend to move less from period to period. We can also describe this forecast as less responsive to changes in the actual data. However, increasing the number of periods in an *SMA* forecast may or may not lower the forecasting error. It simply depends on the historical data.

FIGURE 16.3
Four-Period Simple Moving Average Forecast vs. the Actual Data: New Car Sales

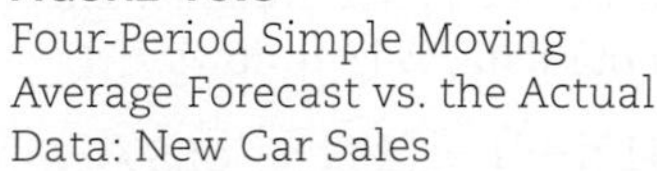

By including more periods in the *SMA*, our forecast will tend to be less volatile, or move less, from period to period. Notice that this red line is flatter than the one shown in Figure 16.2.

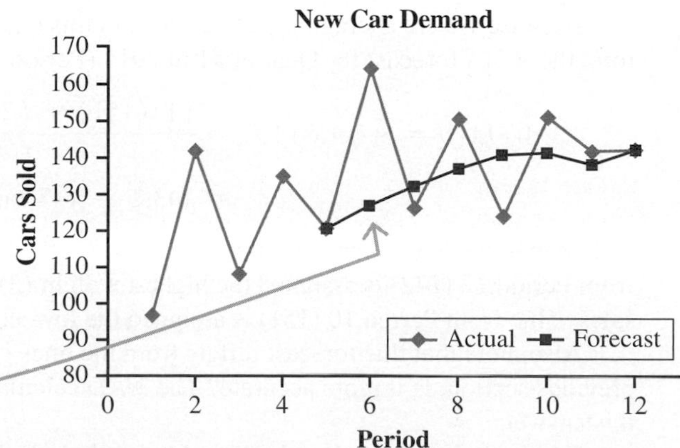

The following Your Turn problem is an opportunity for you to calculate an *SMA* forecast and its *MAD*.

YOUR TURN #1

Suppose a fellow student at your school would like your help in forecasting her GPA for the upcoming fall semester of her senior year. The following table shows this student's GPA for each of the last nine semesters (using a trimester schedule). These data can be found in the Excel file **GPA.xlsx.**

Year	Semester	GPA
Freshman	Fall	2.5
Freshman	Spring	2.2
Freshman	Summer	2.7
Sophomore	Fall	3.0
Sophomore	Spring	2.6
Sophomore	Summer	3.0
Junior	Fall	3.2
Junior	Spring	2.7
Junior	Summer	3.3

a. Calculate a two-period *SMA* for the student's GPA for the fall semester of her senior year.
b. Calculate the *MAD* for this forecast.

Answers can be found on ▶ **page 820**

Weighted Moving Average Forecast

A **weighted moving average** is a smoothing technique in which weights are applied to historical data when generating a forecast.

A variation of the *SMA* method is the **weighted moving average**, *WMA*, which applies weights to the historical data. This allows the forecaster (aka, you) to place more emphasis on certain historical values and less emphasis on others when calculating a forecast. Let's demonstrate this method with our car sales data from Table 16.1 using a three-period *WMA* with the weights 3, 2, and 1.

The convention is to assign the highest weight to the most recent data and the lowest weight to the oldest data. The reasoning is that the most recent data are more relevant, so they should have more of an effect on the forecast. Think about it: Suppose you were the manager of a retail establishment and wanted to forecast next month's sales with a *WMA* technique. You might be inclined to feel that last month's sales volume will have a bigger influence on next month's sales when compared with, say, a month from last year. *WMA* allows us to apply this strategy by assigning a higher weight to the most recent historical data.

Because we are averaging three periods in this example, we need three weights. Therefore, the *WMA* forecast for Quarter #1 in 2014 (Period 13 in our data) is as follows:

$$WMA(p = 3, \text{Period } 13) = \frac{(1)(151) + (2)(141) + (3)(142)}{1 + 2 + 3} = \frac{859}{6}$$
$$= 143.2 \approx 143 \text{ cars}$$

Notice that the denominator for this calculation is the sum of the weights. The sales value from Period 12 (142) is assigned the highest weight (3) because it is the most recent. The sales value from Period 10 (151) is assigned the lowest weight (1) because it is the oldest.

Also, note that this forecast differs from the ones generated with the *SMA* method in the previous section. Is it more accurate? The *MAD* calculations shown in Table 16.4 provide this answer.

The forecast calculations in this table for Periods 4 and 5 are as follows:

The denominator is the sum of the weights for a *WMA* forecast.

$$WMA(p = 3, \text{Period } 4) = \frac{(1)(97) + (2)(142) + (3)(108)}{1 + 2 + 3} = \frac{705}{6} = 117.5$$

$$WMA(p = 3, \text{Period } 5) = \frac{(1)(142) + (2)(108) + (3)(135)}{1 + 2 + 3} = \frac{763}{6} = 127.2$$

TABLE 16.4 | DATA AND CALCULATIONS NEEDED TO DETERMINE THE MEAN ABSOLUTE DEVIATION: THREE-PERIOD WEIGHTED MOVING AVERAGE FORECAST WITH WEIGHTS 3, 2, AND 1

PERIOD, t	ACTUAL SALES, A_t	FORECAST SALES, F_t	FORECASTING ERROR, $A_t - F_t$	ABSOLUTE FORECASTING ERROR, $\lvert A_t - F_t \rvert$
1	97			
2	142			
3	108			
4	135	117.5	17.5	17.5
5	120	127.2	−7.2	7.2
6	164	123.0	41.0	41.0
7	126	144.5	−18.5	18.5
8	150	137.7	12.3	12.3
9	123	144.3	−21.3	21.3
10	151	132.5	18.5	18.5
11	141	141.5	−0.5	0.5
12	142	141.3	0.7	0.7
				$\sum \lvert A_t - F_t \rvert = 137.5$

The denominator for this *MAD* calculation is 9 because we have nine forecasting error terms in the last column in Table 16.4.

The *MAD* for the three-period *WMA* forecast using weights 3, 2, and 1 is calculated as follows:

$$MAD = \frac{\sum |A_t - F_t|}{n} = \frac{137.5}{9} = 15.3$$

This average error is slightly better than that for the three-period *SMA* forecast calculated earlier (15.9) but not as good as that for the four-period *SMA* forecast (11.1). Of course, we can always try another set of weights to see if the *MAD* can be lowered, as well as averaging a different number of periods. The choice of weights is an arbitrary one that involves trial and error to find a set that provides an acceptable forecasting error.

The *SMA* forecast is actually a variation of the *WMA* but with all of the weights being equal.

The moving average techniques we have demonstrated in the chapter can be effective for forecasting one period ahead and require relatively simple calculations. The purpose of these techniques is to remove the noise, or randomness, from a time series when projecting averages for future time periods. However, if the time series exhibits significant trend or seasonal components, this forecasting method has a tendency to lag behind the data, resulting in increased forecasting errors.

Try the following Your Turn problem to see if you understand how to calculate a *WMA*.

YOUR TURN #2

Using the GPA data from Your Turn #1, answer the following questions:

a. Using weights of 2 and 1, calculate a two-period *WMA* for the student's GPA for the fall semester of her senior year.

b. Calculate the *MAD* for this forecast.

c. Which method is the better forecast to use—the *SMA* forecast from Your Turn #1 or this forecast?

Answers can be found on ▶ **page 820**

Exponential Smoothing Forecast

Exponential smoothing adjusts the previous forecast with a portion of the previous period's forecasting error.

One of the more popular forecasting techniques is **exponential smoothing**, which adjusts the previous forecast with a portion of the previous period's forecasting error. Equation 16.2 shows how an exponential smoothing forecast is calculated.

Formula 16.2 for the Exponential Smoothing Forecast

$$F_t = F_{t-1} + \alpha(A_{t-1} - F_{t-1})$$

where

F_t = The forecasted value for period t
A_{t-1} = The actual value for period $t - 1$
F_{t-1} = The forecasted value for period $t - 1$
α = The smoothing factor for the forecast

Don't confuse the value of α used in exponential smoothing with the value of α used in hypothesis testing. Both forecasters and hypothesis testers use α in their calculations, but it has different meanings in each context.

The value of the smoothing factor, α, ranges from 0 to 1 (inclusive) and needs to be chosen in order to calculate a forecast. When the value of α is close to 1, the previous period's forecasting error has a large effect on the current forecast. When the smoothing factor is close to 0, the previous forecasting error has little impact on the current forecast. I'll show how an exponential smoothing forecast is calculated using our car sales data with $\alpha = 0.6$ (more on this choice later).

We will begin by again using Table 16.1, which provides us with only 12 quarters of historical data. Our first forecast will then be for Period 13 $(t = 13)$, and we will use Equation 16.2 to calculate it:

$$F_{13} = F_{12} + \alpha(A_{12} - F_{12})$$

As you can see, in order to calculate a forecast for Period 13, I need a forecast for Period 12, which I don't yet have. The same holds true for calculating a forecast for Period 12: I need the forecast for Period 11. To resolve this issue, we need a starting forecast to "prime the pump" and get things rolling. To do so, I'll make F_1 equal to A_1 (the Period 1 forecast equal to the Period 1 actual sales). Now I can calculate my Period 2 forecast using Equation 16.2:

$$F_2 = F_1 + \alpha(A_1 - F_1)$$
$$F_2 = 97 + (0.6)(97 - 97) = 97$$

We can now calculate the Period 3 forecast as follows:

$$F_3 = F_2 + \alpha(A_2 - F_2)$$
$$F_3 = 97 + (0.6)(142 - 97) = 124.0$$

For good measure, I'll show the calculations for Period 4 for you:

$$F_4 = F_3 + \alpha(A_3 - F_3)$$
$$F_4 = 124.0 + (0.6)(108 - 124.0)$$
$$F_4 = 124.0 - 9.6 = 114.4$$

Notice that the forecasting error is negative for Period 3 $(108 - 124 = -16)$, resulting in a reduction of 9.6 cars in the forecast between Periods 3 and 4 (from 124 to 114.4).

Table 16.5 shows the results of applying Equation 16.2 for Periods 1 through 12. While I'm at it, I also show the *MAD* calculations for each period in this table to investigate the forecasting accuracy (I'm sure you saw that one coming).

Notice that there is no forecasting error for Period 1 in this table because we arbitrarily assigned $F_1 = A_1$ to start the forecasting technique. The first calculated exponentially smoothed forecast is Period 2, which is the first forecasting error shown in Table 16.5.

We're now ready to calculate our forecast for Period 13 (first quarter for 2014) with Equation 16.2.

$$F_{13} = F_{12} + \alpha(A_{12} - F_{12})$$
$$F_{13} = 141.8 + (0.6)(142 - 141.8) = 141.7 \approx 142 \text{ cars}$$

Including a zero forecasting error for Period 1 in Table 16.5 would lower the *MAD* for this forecasting technique. This would make for an unfair comparison to the previous methods that don't have this luxury.

TABLE 16.5 | Exponential Smoothing Forecasts ($\alpha = 0.6$): New Car Sales

PERIOD, t	ACTUAL SALES, A_t	FORECAST SALES, F_t	FORECASTING ERROR, $A_t - F_t$	ABSOLUTE FORECASTING ERROR, $\|A_t - F_t\|$
1	97	97.0	—	—
2	142	97.0	45.0	45.0
3	108	124.0	−16.0	16.0
4	135	114.4	20.6	20.6
5	120	126.8	−6.8	6.8
6	164	122.7	41.3	41.3
7	126	147.5	−21.5	21.5
8	150	134.6	15.4	15.4
9	123	143.8	−20.8	20.8
10	151	131.3	19.7	19.7
11	141	143.1	−2.1	2.1
12	142	141.8	0.2	0.2
				$\sum \|A_t - F_t\| = 209.4$

And finally, the *MAD* for our exponentially smoothed forecast with $\alpha = 0.6$ using Equation 16.1 is calculated as follows:

$$MAD = \frac{\sum |A_t - F_t|}{n} = \frac{209.4}{11} = 19.0$$

How does this compare with our moving average forecasts from earlier in the chapter? The exponentially smoothed forecast has a higher *MAD* than both the *SMA* and *WMA* forecasts for the car sales data we were given in Table 16.1. However, this relationship might not hold true for other data sets. The lesson here is that none of these methods will always provide superior results (a lower *MAD*) across all data sets.

What happens if we change the values for α in this example? Not only will the forecast change, but the *MAD* will either increase or decrease as well. I went to the trouble of calculating the *MAD* for our car sales example for various values of alpha and graphed these values in Figure 16.4 (you're welcome).

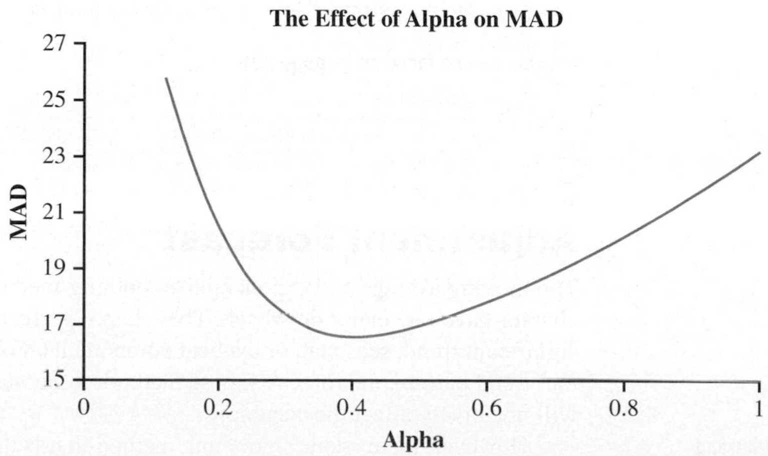

FIGURE 16.4 The Effect of α on the Mean Absolute Deviation: New Car Sales

As you can see from this figure, the *MAD* tends to follow a U-shaped curve across various values of α. Ideally, we would choose a value of α that would minimize the *MAD*, which, according to Figure 16.4, is around $\alpha = 0.35$. Even with this α, the *MAD* is close to 16, which is still higher than the *MAD*s from the moving average forecasts.

How does the value of α affect the forecast? (By the way, these are great questions!) Figure 16.5 shows the actual quarterly sales (black line) as well as forecasted sales using $\alpha = 0.2$ (red line) and $\alpha = 0.8$ (blue line).

FIGURE 16.5
The Effect of α on the Forecast: New Car Sales

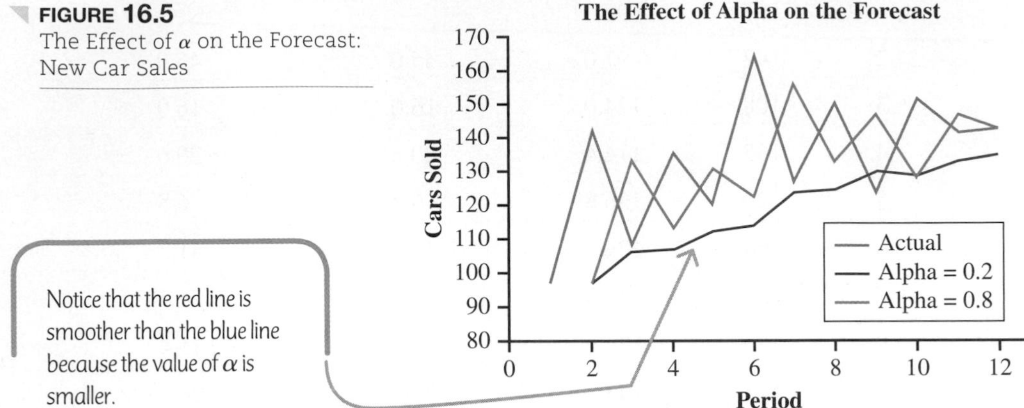

Notice that the red line is smoother than the blue line because the value of α is smaller.

As you can see in this figure, the role of α is similar to that of the number of periods included in a moving average forecast. A larger α tends to make the forecast more responsive to previous forecasts errors, that is, it causes the forecast to jump around from period to period. This is because more of the previous forecasting error is carried forward to the current forecast. The opposite holds true for smaller values of α. The red line shows little response to the changes in the actual data values. The best value for α—the one that will result in the lowest *MAD*—will always depend on the data.

I describe exponential smoothing to my students as a self-correcting forecasting method. If the previous forecast was lower than the actual value (positive error), the new forecast will be higher than the previous forecast. If the previous forecast was higher than the actual value (negative error), the new forecast will be lower than the previous forecast. The amount of this correction is controlled by the size of α. A smaller α results in a smaller correction, whereas a higher α results in a larger correction.

It's time for you to show off your exponential smoothing forecasting skills with this next Your Turn problem.

YOUR TURN #3

Using the GPA data from Your Turn #1, answer the following questions:

a. Use exponential smoothing with $\alpha = 0.4$ to calculate a forecast for the student's GPA in the fall semester of her senior year.

b. Calculate the mean absolute deviation for this forecast.

Answers can be found on ▶ **page 821**

Exponential Smoothing with Trend Adjustment Forecast

The moving average and exponential smoothing methods that we have learned about in this chapter have one major drawback. They do not perform well when the historical data have significant trend, seasonal, or cyclical components. For example, in the presence of a consistent trend pattern, the forecasts these methods generate will lag behind the actual data, which will negatively affect the accuracy.

Exponential smoothing with trend adjustment is a technique that compensates an exponential smoothing forecast for any trend detected in the data.

However, there is one smoothing method that is the exception—**exponential smoothing with trend adjustment**. As its label implies, this technique will modify an exponential smoothing forecast by compensating for any trends detected in the data. The exponential smoothing with trend adjustment forecast for period t, FIT_t, can be calculated using Equations 16.3, 16.4, and 16.5

Formulas 16.3, 16.4 and 16.5 for the Exponential Smoothing with Trend Adjustment Forecast

$$FIT_t = F_t + T_t$$
$$F_t = FIT_{t-1} + \alpha(A_{t-1} - FIT_{t-1})$$
$$T_t = \beta(F_t - F_{t-1}) + (1 - \beta)T_{t-1}$$

where

FIT_t = The forecast including trend for period t
F_t = The exponentially smoothed forecast for period t
T_t = The exponentially smoothed trend for period t
A_{t-1} = The actual value for period $t - 1$
α = The smoothing factor for the forecast
β = The smoothing factor for the trend

Notice that we've added a couple of new terms with this method. The trend adjusted forecast of interest for period t is FIT_t, which is found using Equation 16.3. To get this value, we need both F_t, the exponentially smoothed forecast *without* trend, and T_t, the trend component. In addition to α, the smoothing factor from the previous section, we introduce β, the smoothing factor for the trend component, which, like α, also ranges from 0 to 1.

Equation 16.4 is similar to Equation 16.3, with FIT_{t-1} replacing F_{t-1}. Equation 16.5 calculates the trend adjustment for the current period. You can see that there are two parts to this equation: the most recent trend $(F_t - F_{t-1})$ and the cumulative trend over the entire time series (T_{t-1}). The most recent trend is weighted by β, and the cumulative trend is weighted by $(1 - \beta)$. For a relatively large β (closer to 1.0), the current trend adjustment is more affected by the most recent trend. For a relatively small β (closer to 0), the current trend adjustment is more affected by the cumulative trend over the entire time series. Again, we can use the *MAD* to help us choose the best values of α and β for our time series.

Let's put these equations to work and calculate a trend adjusted, exponentially smoothed forecast for new cars sales using $\alpha = 0.3$ and $\beta = 0.1$. As with the exponential smoothing procedure from the previous section, we need to develop forecasts from the start of the time series in order to calculate a sales forecast for Period 13. We assign values for Period 1 as follows:

$$F_1 = A_1 = 97.0$$
$$T_1 = 0$$
$$FIT_1 = F_1 + T_1 = 97.0$$

Because T_t reflects the overall trend component in the time series up to period t, we need to set this value equal to zero for the first period as a starting point.

For each quarter starting with Period 2 $(t = 2)$, we perform the following three steps, starting with Equation 16.4:

$$F_t = FIT_{t-1} + \alpha(A_{t-1} - FIT_{t-1})$$
$$F_2 = FIT_1 + \alpha(A_1 - FIT_1)$$
$$F_2 = 97.0 + (0.3)(97 - 97.0) = 97.0$$

We then use Equation 16.5 to calculate the trend component for Period 2:

$$T_t = \beta(F_t - F_{t-1}) + (1 - \beta)T_{t-1}$$
$$T_2 = \beta(F_2 - F_1) + (1 - \beta)T_1$$
$$T_2 = (0.1)(97.0 - 97.0) + (1 - 0.1)(0)$$
$$T_2 = 0 + 0 = 0$$

Finally, we call on Equation 16.3 to determine the trend adjusted forecast for Period 2:

$$FIT_t = F_t + T_t$$
$$FIT_2 = F_2 + T_2$$
$$FIT_2 = 97.0 + 0 = 97.0$$

Let's apply these three steps once more to calculate a forecast for Period 3 to help you see the pattern:

$$F_3 = FIT_2 + \alpha(A_2 - FIT_2)$$
$$F_3 = 97.0 + (0.3)(142 - 97.0) = 110.5$$
$$T_3 = \beta(F_3 - F_2) + (1 - \beta)T_2$$
$$T_3 = (0.1)(110.5 - 97.0) + (1 - 0.1)(0)$$
$$T_3 = 1.4 + 0 = 1.4$$
$$FIT_3 = F_3 + T_3$$
$$FIT_3 = 110.5 + 1.4 = 111.9$$

We continue with these calculations with Periods 4 through 12, which I've shown in Table 16.6. Table 16.6 also shows the absolute error, $|A_t - FIT_t|$, for each quarter, which we will need for our *MAD* calculation.

TABLE 16.6 | DATA AND CALCULATIONS NEEDED TO FIND THE MEAN ABSOLUTE DEVIATION: EXPONENTIAL SMOOTHING WITH TREND ADJUSTMENT FORECAST

PERIOD, t	ACTUAL SALES, A_t	SMOOTHED FORECAST, F_t	TREND T_t	FORECAST W/TREND, FIT_t	ABSOLUTE ERROR, $\lvert A_t - FIT_t \rvert$
1	97	97.0	0	97.0	—
2	142	97.0	0	97.0	45.0
3	108	110.5	1.4	111.9	3.9
4	135	110.7	1.3	112.0	23.0
5	120	118.9	2.0	120.9	0.9
6	164	120.6	2.0	122.6	41.4
7	126	135.0	3.2	138.2	12.2
8	150	134.5	2.8	137.3	12.7
9	123	141.1	3.2	144.3	21.3
10	151	137.9	2.6	140.5	10.5
11	141	143.7	2.9	146.6	5.6
12	142	144.9	2.7	147.6	5.6
					$\sum \lvert A_t - FIT_t \rvert = 182.1$

Remember not to include the trend adjusted forecasting error for Period 1 because we did not calculate a forecast for this quarter (some of my students forget this).

At this point, we haven't done any forecasting of car sales for a future quarter. But we're now ready to calculate our trend adjusted forecast for Period 13 (first quarter of 2014) as follows:

$$F_{13} = FIT_{12} + \alpha(A_{12} - FIT_{12})$$
$$F_{13} = 147.6 + (0.3)(142 - 147.6)$$
$$F_{13} = 147.6 - 1.7 = 145.9$$
$$T_{13} = \beta(F_{13} - F_{12}) + (1 - \beta)T_{12}$$
$$T_{13} = (0.1)(144.9 - 143.7) + (1 - 0.1)(2.7)$$
$$T_{13} = 0.1 + 2.4 = 2.5$$
$$FIT_{13} = F_{13} + T_{13}$$
$$FIT_{13} = 145.9 + 2.5 = 148.4 \approx 148 \text{ cars}$$

Using exponential smoothing with trend adjustment, our first quarter 2014 sales forecast is 148 cars. The *MAD* for this forecast is found using Equation 16.1 once again:

$$MAD = \frac{\sum |A_t - FIT_t|}{n} = \frac{182.1}{11} = 16.6$$

The average forecasting error using this method to predict sales with $\alpha = 0.3$ and $\beta = 0.1$ is 16.6 cars.

In this section, we have looked at several different smoothing techniques to forecast car sales for the upcoming quarter. These methods are popular because they can be fairly effective and are relatively straightforward to use. Table 16.7 summarizes the results of each of these techniques using our sales data from Table 16.1.

TABLE 16.7 | SUMMARY OF SMOOTHING FORECASTING METHODS

METHOD	FORECAST	*MAD*
Simple moving average, $p = 3$	145	15.9
Simple moving average, $p = 4$	139	11.1
Weighted moving average, $p = 3$ (3, 2, 1)	143	15.3
Exponential smoothing, $\alpha = 0.6$	142	19.0
Exponential smoothing w/trend, $\alpha = 0.3, \beta = 0.1$	148	16.6

If you were choosing a forecast from the selection in Table 16.7, your best bet is to go with the four-period simple moving average forecast of 139 cars because this method has the lowest *MAD*. However, we can't generalize by concluding that the simple moving average method will always outperform the other smoothing techniques. Using another data set will probably lead to a different recommendation.

Please don't be *MAD* if I ask you to do another exponential smoothing forecast with trend adjustment in this next Your Turn problem.

YOUR TURN #4

Using the GPA data from Your Turn #1, answer the following questions:

a. Use exponential smoothing with trend adjustment and set $\alpha = 0.5$ and $\beta = 0.7$ to calculate a forecast for the student's fall semester GPA for her senior year.

b. Calculate the mean absolute deviation for this forecast.

Answers can be found on ▶ **page 821**

16.2 Section Problems

Basic Skills

16.1 Consider the following time series:

Period	1	2	3	4	5	6	7
Demand	15	12	8	14	19	16	10

a. Forecast the demand for Period 8 using a two-period simple moving average.

b. Calculate the *MAD* for the forecast in part a.

c. Forecast the demand for Period 8 using a three-period simple moving average.

d. Calculate the *MAD* for the forecast in part b.

e. Which forecast would you choose?

16.2 Using the time series shown in Problem 16.1, answer the following questions:

a. Forecast the demand for Period 8 using a three-period weighted moving average with weights 4, 3, and 1, applying 4 to the most recent data and 1 to the oldest data.

b. Calculate the *MAD* for the forecast in part a.

16.3 Consider the following time series:

Period	1	2	3	4	5	6	7	8
Demand	15	24	26	33	20	22	27	20

a. Forecast the demand for Period 9 using exponential smoothing with $\alpha = 0.1$.

b. Calculate the *MAD* for the forecast in part a.

c. Forecast the demand for Period 9 using exponential smoothing with $\alpha = 0.3$.

d. Calculate the *MAD* for the forecast in part c.

e. Which forecast would you choose?

16.4 Using the time series shown in Problem 16.3, answer the following questions:

a. Forecast the demand for Period 9 using exponential smoothing with trend adjustment and setting $\alpha = 0.4$ and $\beta = 0.7$.
b. Calculate the *MAD* for the forecast in part a.

Applications

16.5 Bob is a photographer who sells his 13 × 19 prints on consignment at Island Art in Stone Harbor, New Jersey. Each week during the summer, Bob checks the inventory so that he can replenish the prints that have been sold. The following data show the number of prints sold each week during the last eight weeks:

Week	1	2	3	4	5	6	7	8
Sold	9	12	10	6	9	15	11	7

a. Forecast the demand for Week 9 using a two-period simple moving average.
b. Calculate the *MAD* for the forecast in part a.
c. Forecast the demand for Week 9 using a three-period simple moving average.
d. Calculate the *MAD* for the forecast in part c.
e. Which forecast should you choose?

16.6 The Consumer Price Index (CPI), which is published by the U.S. Bureau of Labor Statistics, is a measurement that reflects changes in consumer prices over time. The following data show the CPI over a 10-year period using 1982 as the base year with the CPI = 100. These data can also be found in the Excel file **CPI.xlsx**.

Year	CPI	Year	CPI
2003	184.0	2008	215.3
2004	188.9	2009	214.5
2005	195.3	2010	218.1
2006	201.6	2011	224.9
2007	207.3	2012	229.6

Based on: U.S. Bureau of Labor Statistics data.

a. Forecast the CPI for 2013 using exponential smoothing with trend adjustment, and set $\alpha = 0.3$ and $\beta = 0.5$.
b. Calculate the *MAD* for the forecast in part a.

16.7 The IRS is actively encouraging individuals to file their taxes electronically in order to increase accuracy and reduce expenses. The following data show the percentage of tax returns filed electronically from 2003 to 2012. These data can also be found in the Excel file **electronic filing.xlsx**.

Year	Percentage	Year	Percentage
2003	40	2008	58
2004	47	2009	67
2005	51	2010	70
2006	54	2011	77
2007	57	2012	78

Based on: IRS data.

a. Forecast the percentage of tax returns that will be electronically filed for 2013 using exponential smoothing with $\alpha = 0.4$.
b. Calculate the *MAD* for the forecast in part a.
c. Forecast the percentage of tax returns that will be electronically filed for 2013 using exponential smoothing with trend adjustment. Set $\alpha = 0.4$ and $\beta = 0.6$.
d. Calculate the *MAD* for the forecast in part c.
e. In which forecast do you have the most confidence? Why?

16.8 The number of viewers for network television shows has a direct effect on the amount of advertising dollars that will be generated. The following data show the number of viewers, in millions, for the final performance of the following seasons of *American Idol*. These data can also be found in the Excel file **American Idol viewers.xlsx**.

Year	Viewers	Year	Viewers
2005	30.3	2010	20.1
2006	31.8	2011	20.6
2007	25.3	2012	14.9
2008	27.1	2013	12.1
2009	23.8		

Based on: Nielsen data.

a. Forecast the number of viewers for *American Idol* for the final performance of the 2014 season using three-period weighted moving average with weights 3, 2, and 1.
b. Calculate the *MAD* for the forecast in part a.
c. Forecast the number of viewers for *American Idol* for the final performance of the 2014 season using exponential smoothing with trend adjustment and setting $\alpha = 0.4$ and $\beta = 0.2$.
d. Calculate the *MAD* for the forecast in part c.
e. In which forecast do you have the most confidence? Why?

16.9 General Motors (GM) is one of the world's largest car and truck manufacturer and employs over 200,000 employees worldwide. In 1970, GM had captured nearly 60% of the U.S. market share. However, due to increased global competition over the past 40 years, GM's market share has eroded to less than 18% in 2012. The following data show GM's U.S. market share from 2004 until 2012. These data can also be found in the Excel file **GM market share.xlsx**.

Year	Market Share (%)	Year	Market Share (%)
2004	26.2	2009	19.7
2005	33.0	2010	18.8
2006	27.3	2011	19.4
2007	22.1	2012	17.9
2008	22.1		

a. Forecast the U.S. market share for GM in 2013 using two-period weighted moving average with weights 3 and 1.

b. Calculate the *MAD* for the forecast in part a.
c. Forecast the U.S. market share for GM in 2013 using exponential smoothing with $\alpha = 0.7$.
d. Calculate the *MAD* for the forecast in part c.
e. Which forecast do you have most confidence in? Why?

16.10 The Independence School is a private grade school that depends on enrollment forecasting to plan for the upcoming school year. The following data show the enrollments for the past several years. These data can also be found in the Excel file **Independence School.xlsx**.

Year	Enrollment	Year	Enrollment
2006	624	2010	630
2007	645	2011	625
2008	659	2012	641
2009	643	2013	656

a. Forecast the 2014 enrollment for the Independence School using four-period simple moving average.
b. Calculate the *MAD* for the forecast in part a.
c. Forecast the 2014 enrollment for the Independence School using exponential smoothing with $\alpha = 0.4$.
d. Calculate the *MAD* for the forecast in part c.
e. In which forecast do you have most confidence? Why?

16.11 The following data show the average prices for flat-panel televisions in the United States over a six-quarter period.

Month	Q1 '11	Q2 '11	Q3 '11	Q4 '11	Q1 '12	Q2 '12
Price ($)	1,108	1,124	1,142	1,130	1,190	1,224

Based on: DisplaySearch data.

a. Forecast the average price of a flat-panel TV in the third quarter of 2012 using a two-period simple moving average.
b. Calculate the *MAD* for the forecast in part a.
c. Forecast the average price of a flat-panel TV in the third quarter of 2012 using a three-period simple moving average.
d. Calculate the *MAD* for the forecast in part b.
e. Which forecast would you choose?

16.12 The Park family would like to prepare next month's family budget by forecasting its family expenses. One item of particular importance is the amount of money spent on food. The following data show the amount of money spent on food for the last 10 months. These data can also be found in the Excel file **food expenditures.xlsx**.

Month	1	2	3	4	5	6	7	8	9	10
Dollars	344	360	294	339	362	340	321	312	364	345

a. Forecast the family's food expenditures next month using a three-period simple moving average.
b. Forecast the family's food expenditures next month using a three-period weighted moving average with weights 0.7, 0.2, and 0.1.
c. Forecast the family's food expenditures next month using exponential smoothing when $\alpha = 0.1$.
d. Which forecast should you choose? Why?

16.3 Forecasting with Regression Analysis

The forecasting methods that rely on smoothing techniques strive to "average out" the random component in the historical time series. As we have discussed, a potential drawback of these techniques is that they perform well under static conditions—that is, when future periods were much like the last. However, these techniques don't perform well with data that are changing, or contain trend or seasonal patterns. Forecasting errors can be relatively high under these conditions. One solution to this problem is to consider using the simple and multiple regression techniques we discussed in Chapters 14 and 15. These methods will often provide better results when trend and/or seasonal components are present.

Trend Projection

In Chapter 14, you learned that a simple linear regression describes a straight line that best fits a series of ordered pairs (x, y), each of which pertains to a single observation. This regression line explains how a change in an independent variable (x) influences a change in a dependent variable (y). In this chapter, we will use this straight line to describe the linear trend component of our time series. Using **trend projection**, we can then "project" this trend line into future periods to develop a forecast for the time series.

Trend projection is a forecasting technique that projects into the future a linear regression equation that best fits the data in a time series.

Figure 16.6 shows the trend projection graphically. The x-axis displays the time period, which, for our car sales data, is quarters. The y-axis displays the forecasted variable, which is number of cars sold per quarter. The blue dots indicate the 12 quarters of car sales data from Table 16.1, and the solid red line represents the regression line that best fits these data. Finally, the dotted red line is the trend projection, which provides us with a forecast for car sales in future quarters.

FIGURE 16.6
Forecasting with a Trend Projection: New Car Sales

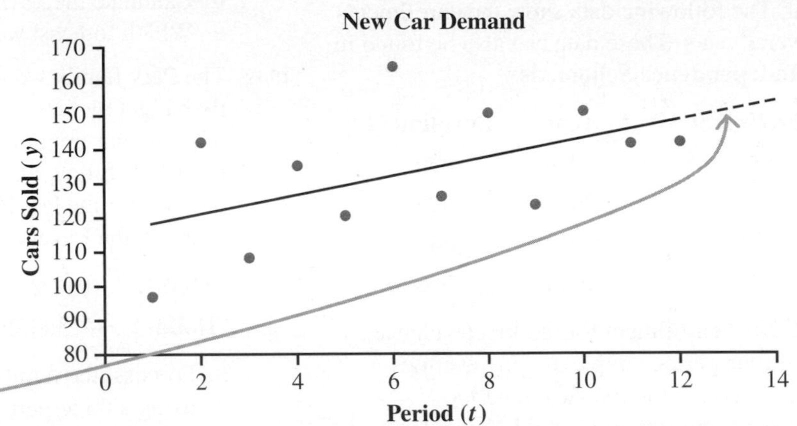

The trend projection method extends the trend line over future periods to determine a forecast. However, the farther into the future a forecast is projected, the less accurate it tends to be.

The equation for the trend projection line takes the form shown in Equation 16.6.

Formula 16.6 for the Trend Projection

$$\hat{y}_t = b_0 + b_1 t$$

where

$\hat{y}_t$ = The forecasted value of y given a value of t
t = The time period
b_0 = The y-intercept of the trend projection line
b_1 = The slope of the trend projection line

The slope of the red line, b_1, in Figure 16.6 measures the rate at which car sales change from one quarter to the next. The y-intercept, b_0, indicates the level of car sales at which the red line crosses the vertical axis. Equations 16.7 and 16.8 can be used to calculate the slope and y-intercept, respectively.

Formula 16.7 for the Trend Projection Slope

$$b_1 = \frac{n\sum ty - \left(\sum t\right)\left(\sum y\right)}{n\sum t^2 - \left(\sum t\right)^2}$$

We first encountered Equations 16.7 and 16.8 in Chapter 14 when we discussed simple regression.

Formula 16.8 for the Trend Projection Intercept

$$b_0 = \frac{\sum y}{n} - b_1\left(\frac{\sum t}{n}\right)$$

Table 16.8 shows the summary calculations needed to calculate the slope and y-intercept for our car sales time series.

TABLE 16.8 | SUMMARY CALCULATIONS FOR A TREND PROJECTION: NEW CAR SALES

PERIOD, t	SALES, y	ty	t^2
1	97	97	1
2	142	284	4
3	108	324	9
4	135	540	16
5	120	600	25
6	164	984	36
7	126	882	49
8	150	1,200	64
9	123	1,107	81
10	151	1,510	100
11	141	1,551	121
12	142	1,704	144
$\sum t = 78$	$\sum y = 1{,}599$	$\sum ty = 10{,}783$	$\sum t^2 = 650$

We first calculate the slope of the trend projection equation, b_1, using Equation 16.7:

$$b_1 = \frac{n\sum ty - \left(\sum t\right)\left(\sum y\right)}{n\sum t^2 - \left(\sum t\right)^2}$$

$$b_1 = \frac{(12)(10{,}783) - (78)(1{,}599)}{(12)(650) - (78)^2}$$

$$b_1 = \frac{129{,}396 - 124{,}722}{7{,}800 - 6{,}084} = \frac{4{,}674}{1{,}716} = 2.7238$$

Once the slope has been determined, we use this value along with Equation 16.8 to calculate the y-intercept, b_0:

$$b_0 = \frac{\sum y}{n} - b_1\left(\frac{\sum t}{n}\right)$$

$$b_0 = \frac{1{,}599}{12} - (2.7238)\left(\frac{78}{12}\right)$$

$$b_0 = 133.25 - (2.7238)(6.5) = 115.5453$$

The regression equation that describes the trend component through our car sales time series data is therefore as follows:

$$\hat{y}_t = 115.5453 + 2.7238t$$

According to this result, sales increase an average of 2.7238 cars per quarter. It looks like business at Brandywine Ford is getting better over time.

We are now ready to generate a forecast using trend projection for Period 13. We do this by substituting 13 for the variable t in our trend equation:

$$\hat{y}_{13} = 115.5453 + 2.7238(13) = 150.95 \approx 151 \text{ cars}$$

Our trend projection forecast for Period 13 sales is 151 cars. Figure 16.7 illustrates this graphically. The green line shows that our projected trend line in Period 13 corresponds to forecasted sales of 151 cars.

FIGURE 16.7
Forecasting with a Trend Projection for Period 13: New Car Sales

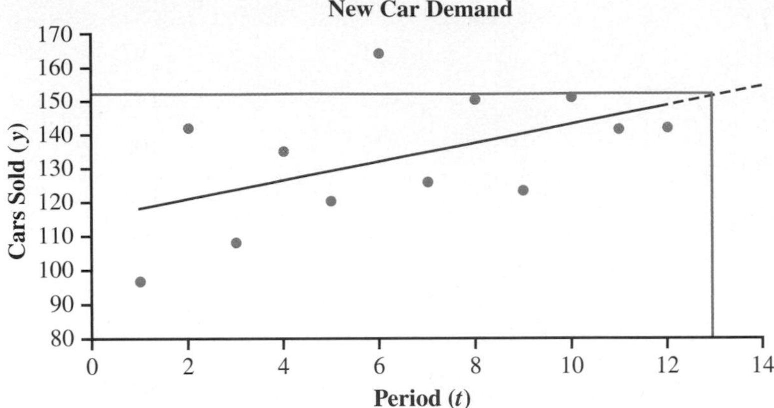

We can also forecast sales for Period 14 if we choose, as follows:

$$\hat{y}_{14} = 115.5453 + 2.7238(14) = 153.68 \approx 154 \text{ cars}$$

However, recall that the further out into the future we project our trend line, the less reliable our forecasted value will be. For example, as I explained earlier in the chapter, we usually give much more credence to tomorrow's weather forecast than we do to the 10th day in a 10-day forecast. Too often I've had my golfing plans spoiled watching what once was a great 10-day forecast turn miserable when the fateful day arrived!

In order to compare the accuracy of this forecasting method with our car sales data to the smoothing methods from earlier in the chapter, we need to return to our friend the *MAD*. We do so by calculating the forecasted car sales for Periods 1 through 12 using the trend equation and then comparing these values with the actual sales. For example, the forecast for Period 1 is found by setting $t = 1$ in the trend equation:

$$\hat{y}_1 = 115.5453 + 2.7238(1) = 118.3$$

Residuals describe the difference between the actual and predicted values of dependent variables in a regression analysis.

Recall that with a regression analysis, the forecasting error is known as the **residual**, which is just a fancy word for the difference between an actual value and a predicted value. The residual can be found using Equation 16.9.

Formula 16.9 for the Residual

$$e_i = y_i - \hat{y}_i$$

where

e_i = The residual of the ith observation in the sample
y_i = The actual value of the dependent variable for the ith data point
$\hat{y}_i$ = The predicted value of the dependent variable for the ith data point

For Period 1, the forecasting error is therefore given as follows:

$$e_1 = y_1 - \hat{y}_1 = 97 - 118.3 = -21.3$$

Our forecast using the trend equation predicted sales that were 21.3 cars higher than the actual sales in Period 1. This forecasting error is shown graphically in Figure 16.8.

FIGURE 16.8
Forecasting Error with a Trend Projection for Period 1: New Car Sales

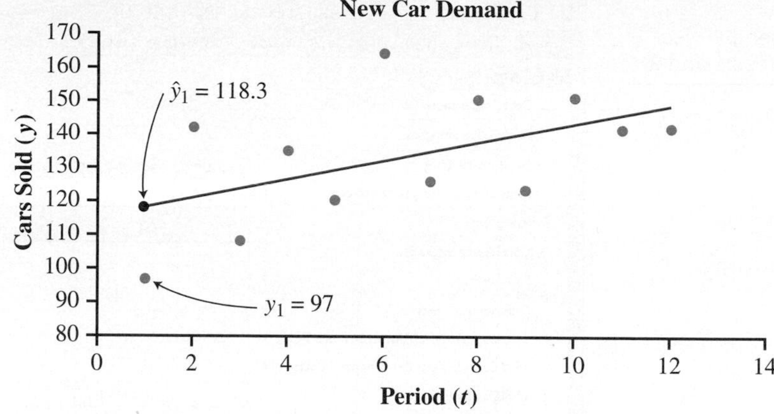

The forecast and forecasting error calculations for the remaining periods are shown in Table 16.9.

TABLE 16.9 | TREND PROJECTION FORECASTS: NEW CAR SALES

PERIOD, t	ACTUAL SALES, y_t	FORECAST SALES, $\hat{y}_t$	FORECASTING ERROR, $y_t - \hat{y}_t$	ABSOLUTE ERROR, $\lvert y_t - \hat{y}_t \rvert$
1	97	118.3	−21.3	21.3
2	142	121.0	21.0	21.0
3	108	123.7	−15.7	15.7
4	135	126.4	8.6	8.6
5	120	129.2	−9.2	9.2
6	164	131.9	32.1	32.1
7	126	134.6	−8.6	8.6
8	150	137.3	12.7	12.7
9	123	140.1	−17.1	17.1
10	151	142.8	8.2	8.2
11	141	145.5	−4.5	4.5
12	142	148.2	−6.2	6.2
				$\sum \lvert y_t - \hat{y}_t \rvert = 165.2$

The *MAD* for our trend projection forecast is therefore as follows:

$$MAD = \frac{\sum |y_t - \hat{y}_t|}{n} = \frac{165.2}{12} = 13.8$$

This forecasting accuracy beats most of the smoothing methods except for the four-period simple moving average, which had a *MAD* equal to 11.1.

Trend Projection with PHStat

We can use PHStat's simple regression function to provide the trend projection equation we calculated manually in the previous section. Excel for Mac users can go to the textbook's Web site for these instructions. (www.pearsonhighered.com/donnelly)

1. Open the Excel file **new car sales.xlsx** or enter the data shown in Figure 16.9B.
2. Go to **Add-Ins** > **PHStat** > **Regression** > **Simple Linear Regression**, as shown in Figure 16.9A.

FIGURE 16.9A
Using PHStat for Trend Projection Forecasting (Steps 1 and 2)

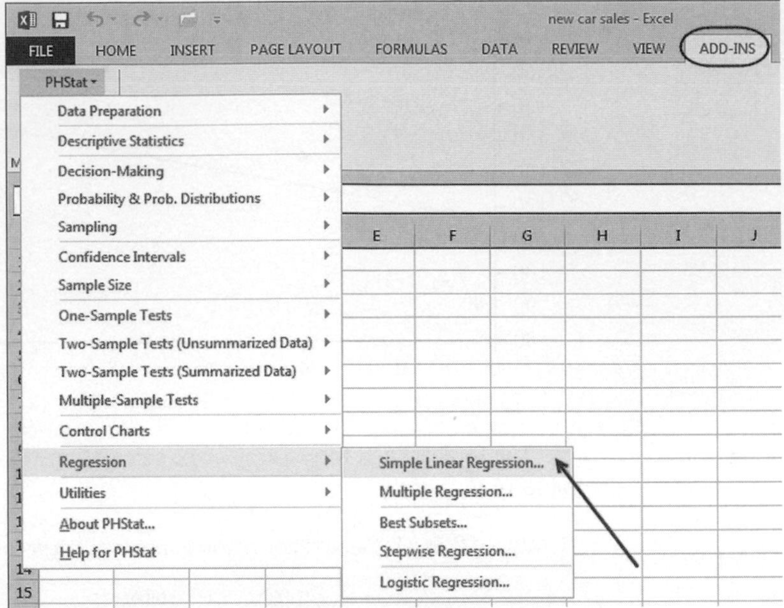

3. Fill in the **Data** section of the **Simple Linear Regression** dialog box as shown in Figure 16.9B. Click **OK**.

FIGURE 16.9B
Using PHStat for Trend Projection Forecasting (Step 3)

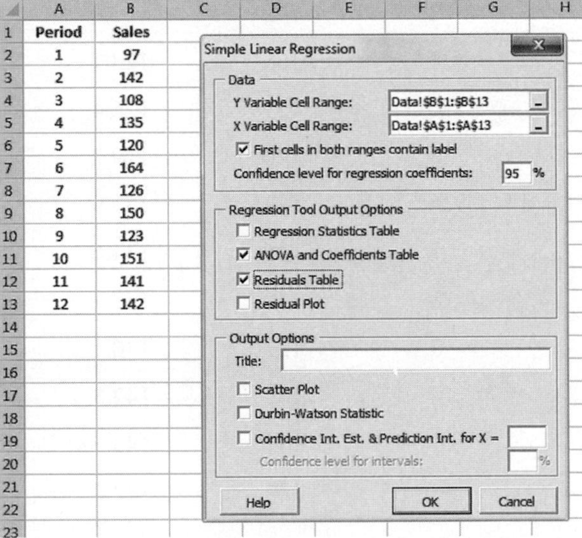

PHStat creates a worksheet labeled "COMPUTE" that contains the regression output shown in Figure 16.9C.

FIGURE 16.9C
Using PHStat for Trend Projection (Final Result)

	A	B	C	D	E	F	G
1	**Simple Linear Regression Analysis**						
2							
3							
4	**ANOVA**						
5		*df*	*SS*	*MS*	*F*	*Significance F*	
6	Regression	1	1060.9108	1060.9108	3.5585	0.0886	
7	Residual	10	2981.3392	298.1339			
8	Total	11	4042.2500				
9							
10		*Coefficients*	*Standard Error*	*t Stat*	*P-value*	*Lower 95%*	*Upper 95%*
11	Intercept	115.5455	10.6268	10.8730	0.0000	91.8674	139.2235
12	Period	2.7238	1.4439	1.8864	0.0859	-0.4934	5.9410
13							

The trend equation coefficients that we calculated manually are circled in red in Figure 16.9C. Also circled in this Figure is the p-value of the independent variable, period, which is 0.0859. If we use $\alpha = 0.05$ for our significance level, we would conclude that there is no relationship between time and car sales. However, because the *MAD* for a trend projection with these data (13.8 using Table 16.9) is one of the lower values we have seen so far in this chapter, this seems like a viable forecasting choice at the moment (more on this later).

PHStat also creates a worksheet labeled "Residuals" that is shown in Figure 16.9D. This output contains the forecasts and forecasting errors (residuals) for Periods 1 through 12, which matches our results in Table 16.9.

FIGURE 16.9D
Using PHStat for Residuals (Final Result)

L30

	A	B	C	D	E
1	Observation	Period	Predicted Y	Sales	Residuals
2	1	1	118.3	97	-21.3
3	2	2	121.0	142	21.0
4	3	3	123.7	108	-15.7
5	4	4	126.4	135	8.6
6	5	5	129.2	120	-9.2
7	6	6	131.9	164	32.1
8	7	7	134.6	126	-8.6
9	8	8	137.3	150	12.7
10	9	9	140.1	123	-17.1
11	10	10	142.8	151	8.2
12	11	11	145.5	141	-4.5
13	12	12	148.2	142	-6.2

Forecasts
Forecasting Errors

The following Your Turn problem will give you the chance to test your trend projection skills.

YOUR TURN #5

Using the GPA data from Your Turn #1, answer the following questions:

a. Use the trend projection technique to calculate a forecast for the student's fall semester GPA for her senior year.

b. Calculate the mean absolute deviation for this forecast.

c. Verify your results using PHStat.

Answers can be found on ▶ **page 822**

Checking for Autocorrelation

The regression model that we have been discussing in this section relies on certain assumptions holding true. One such assumption is that the residuals are independent of one another. I'll use the following example to clarify this concept. Suppose that on the first five quarters of your job as the new car sales manager for Brandywine Ford, you had provided your boss with the forecasts shown in Table 16.10. Also shown are the actual sales and your forecasting errors for each quarter.

TABLE 16.10 | SALES FORECASTS FOR YOUR FIRST FIVE QUARTERS

PERIOD, t	SALES, y_t	FORECAST SALES, $\hat{y}_t$	RESIDUALS, $e_t = y_t - \hat{y}_t$
1	136	116	20
2	155	135	20
3	143	123	20
4	125	105	20
5	132	112	20

Autocorrelation describes the condition when residuals in a regression model are not independent of one another.

The **Durbin–Watson statistic** is used to test for the presence of autocorrelation in a series of residuals.

In Table 16.10, the residuals are not independent of one another. I say this because by knowing the residual for Period 1, I can predict the residual for Period 2. This pattern holds true for other periods as well. The term **autocorrelation** is used to describe this condition when residuals are not independent of one another.

To determine the presence of autocorrelation, we can use the **Durbin–Watson statistic**, *d*, which is shown in Equation 16.10.

Formula 16.10 for the Durbin–Watson Statistic

$$d = \frac{\sum_{t=2}^{n}(e_t - e_{t-1})^2}{\sum_{t=1}^{n} e_t^2}$$

where

d = The Durbin–Watson statistic
$e_t = y_t - \hat{y}_t$ = The residual for period t
n = The number of values in the time series

The Durbin–Watson statistic ranges from 0 to 4:

- A value of 0 indicates perfect positive autocorrelation.
- A value of 2 indicates no autocorrelation.
- A value of 4 indicates perfect negative autocorrelation.

Positive autocorrelation is present when we observe a pattern of positive residuals in succession (such as those shown in Table 16.10) or a pattern of consecutive negative residuals in succession. When this occurs, the consecutive residuals tend to be close to one another, making the numerator in Equation 16.10 relatively small. This, in turn, makes the Durbin–Watson statistic approach zero. Table 16.11 demonstrates the case of perfect positive autocorrelation using the data from Table 16.10, which occurs when the residuals from each period are equal.

TABLE 16.11 | PERFECT POSITIVE AUTOCORRELATION

PERIOD, t	RESIDUAL, e_t	PRIOR RESIDUAL, e_{t-1}	$e_t - e_{t-1}$	$(e_t - e_{t-1})^2$	$(e_t)^2$
1	20				400
2	20	20	0	0	400
3	20	20	0	0	400
4	20	20	0	0	400
5	20	20	0	0	400
			$\sum_{t=2}^{n}(e_t - e_{t-1})^2 = 0$		$\sum_{t=1}^{n} e_t^2 = 2{,}000$

The Durbin–Watson statistic for perfect positive autocorrelation is then as follows:

$$d = \frac{\sum_{t=2}^{n}(e_t - e_{t-1})^2}{\sum_{t=1}^{n} e_t^2} = \frac{0}{2{,}000} = 0$$

Because negative autocorrelation is rarely observed in time series data, the remainder of this chapter will focus only on positive autocorrelation.

Negative autocorrelation is present when the consecutive residuals are far apart from one another, causing the numerator in Equation 16.10 to be relatively large. Because residuals tend to oscillate around zero, large swings in consecutive values tend to alternate between positive and negative signs.

In the case of perfect negative autocorrelation, we see forecasting errors such as 20, −20, 20, and −20. As we subtract the difference between consecutive residuals $(20 - (-20) = 40)$ and square the difference $(40^2 = 1{,}600)$, the numerator in the Durbin–Watson statistic approaches four times the denominator $(20^2) = 400$. As a result, perfect negative autocorrelation is measured with a Durbin–Watson statistic equal to 4, its upper limit. However, this type of residual pattern is not very common in practice.

When calculating the Durbin–Watson statistic from a sample to detect autocorrelation in the population, the value of d is subject to sampling error. To test the presence of autocorrelation in the population, we need to perform a (take a deep breath) hypothesis test. To obtain reliable results for this test, we need a time series that has at least 15 observations. Because our car sales example has only 12 periods of data, I won't test this time series for autocorrelation. Rather, I'll use the following example.

Union membership in the United States over the past 16 years has experienced a general decline. Table 16.12 shows the percentage of the labor force in the United States that belonged to a union over a 16-year period. These data can also be found in the Excel file **union membership.xlsx**.

TABLE 16.12 | Union Membership as a Percentage of the U.S. Labor Force

YEAR	PERIOD	PERCENTAGE	YEAR	PERIOD	PERCENTAGE
1997	1	14.1	2005	9	12.1
1998	2	14.0	2006	10	12.2
1999	3	13.6	2007	11	12.5
2000	4	13.7	2008	12	12.4
2001	5	13.5	2009	13	12.5
2002	6	13.0	2010	14	11.9
2003	7	12.6	2011	15	11.8
2004	8	12.5	2012	16	11.3

A graph of these data is shown in Figure 16.10 and illustrates a decreasing trend component over time. The linear trend line from Excel is shown in red in this figure.

FIGURE 16.10
Union Membership Trend Line

This is considered a one-tail hypothesis test because we are testing only for the presence of positive autocorrelation.

Because negative autocorrelation is rarely seen, we'll focus on the detection of positive autocorrelation. With that in mind, our hypothesis statement becomes the following:

H_0 : No positive autocorrelation is present

H_1 : Positive autocorrelation is present

I'll conduct this one-tail test using $\alpha = 0.05$.

To calculate the Durbin–Watson statistic, I'll rely on PHStat, which provides this value for us. I'll also show you how to calculate it with Excel, using the following steps:

1. Open the Excel file **union membership.xlsx** or enter the data shown in Figure 16.11A.
2. Go to **Add-Ins > PHStat > Regression > Simple Linear Regression**, as shown in Figure 16.9A.
3. Fill in the **Simple Linear Regression** dialog box as shown in Figure 16.11A. Be sure to check the **Durbin–Watson Statistic** in the Output Options area of the dialog box. Click **OK**.

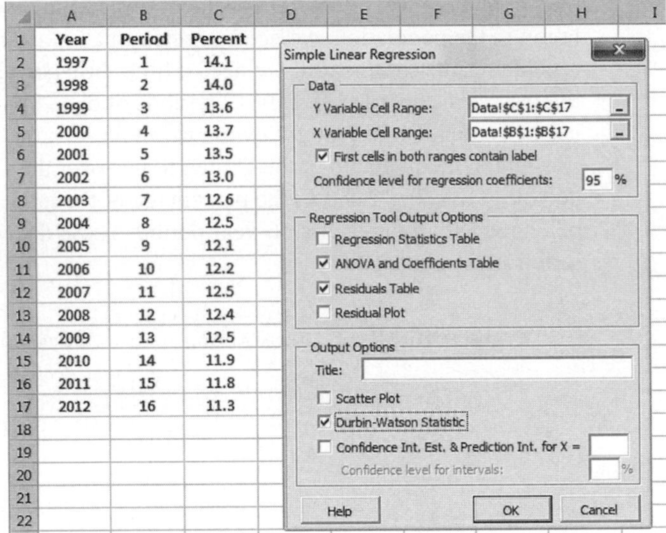

	A	B	C
1	Year	Period	Percent
2	1997	1	14.1
3	1998	2	14.0
4	1999	3	13.6
5	2000	4	13.7
6	2001	5	13.5
7	2002	6	13.0
8	2003	7	12.6
9	2004	8	12.5
10	2005	9	12.1
11	2006	10	12.2
12	2007	11	12.5
13	2008	12	12.4
14	2009	13	12.5
15	2010	14	11.9
16	2011	15	11.8
17	2012	16	11.3

FIGURE 16.11A Using PHStat to Determine the Durbin–Watson Statistic (Steps 1–3)

PHStat creates worksheets labeled "COMPUTE" and "Residuals" that I have combined in Figure 16.11B. I'll use this information to demonstrate how to calculate the Durbin–Watson statistic manually.

FIGURE 16.11B Using PHStat to Determine the Durbin–Watson Statistic (Step 4)

	ANOVA					
5		df	SS	MS	F	Significance F
6	Regression	1	9.2071	9.2071	106.7655	0.0000
7	Residual	14	1.2073	0.0862		
8	Total	15	10.4144			

10		Coefficients	Standard Error	t Stat	P-value	Lower 95%	Upper 95%
11	Intercept	14.1300	0.1540	91.7552	0.0000	13.7997	14.4603
12	Period	-0.1646	0.0159	-10.3327	0.0000	-0.1987	-0.1304

14	Observation	Period	Predicted Y	Percent	Residuals
15	1	1	13.97	14.1	0.13
16	2	2	13.80	14	0.20
17	3	3	13.64	13.6	-0.04
18	4	4	13.47	13.7	0.23
19	5	5	13.31	13.5	0.19
20	6	6	13.14	13	-0.14
21	7	7	12.98	12.6	-0.38
22	8	8	12.81	12.5	-0.31
23	9	9	12.65	12.1	-0.55
24	10	10	12.48	12.2	-0.28
25	11	11	12.32	12.5	0.18
26	12	12	12.16	12.4	0.24
27	13	13	11.99	12.5	0.51
28	14	14	11.83	11.9	0.07
29	15	15	11.66	11.8	0.14
30	16	16	11.50	11.3	-0.20

PHStat also creates a worksheet labeled "Durbin Watson," which contains the value of the Durbin–Watson statistic, as shown in Figure 16.11C.

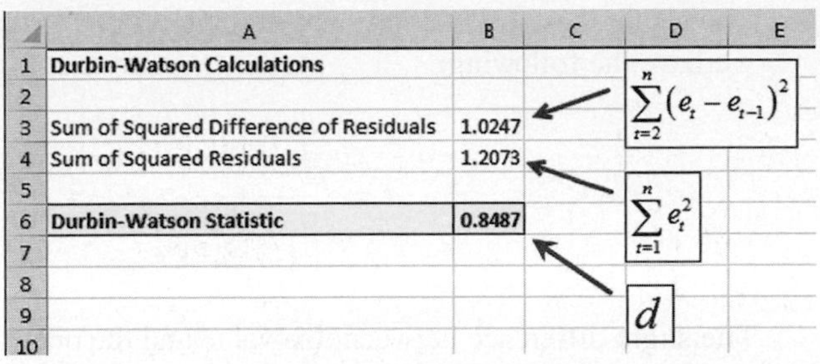

FIGURE 16.11C Using PHStat to Determine the Durbin–Watson Statistic (Final Result)

According to Figure 16.11C, the Durbin–Watson statistic for our union membership time series using Equation 16.10 is therefore as follows:

$$d = \frac{\sum_{t=2}^{n}(e_t - e_{t-1})^2}{\sum_{t=1}^{n} e_t^2} = \frac{1.0247}{1.2073} = 0.849$$

This value can be calculated directly from Excel using the regression output in Figure 16.11C. We'll start with the regression equation for the time series.

$$\hat{y}_t = 14.1300 - 0.1646t$$

Next, I'll calculate the predicted union membership for Period 1 (1997) along with the residual for that year:

$$\hat{y}_1 = 14.1300 - 0.1646(1) = 13.97$$
$$e_1 = y_1 - \hat{y}_1 = 14.1 - 13.97 = 0.13$$

Next, I'll show the same calculations for Period 2 (1998):

$$\hat{y}_2 = 14.1300 - 0.1646(2) = 13.80$$
$$e_2 = y_2 - \hat{y}_2 = 14.0 - 13.80 = 0.20$$

Finally, I'll take the difference in these two residuals and square the result:

$$(e_2 - e_1)^2 = (0.20 - 0.13)^2 = (0.07)^2 = 0.0049$$

I'll repeat these calculations for the remaining years of our time series with the help of Excel (for which we should all be grateful). The results are shown in Figure 16.11D.

FIGURE 16.11D Using Excel to Determine the Durbin–Watson Statistic

	A	B	C	D	E	F	G
1	Period	Percent	Predicted	Residual			
2	t	y_t	$\hat{y}_t$	e_t	e_{t-1}	$(e_t - e_{t-1})^2$	$(e_t)^2$
3	1	14.1	13.97	0.13			0.0181
4	2	14.0	13.80	0.20	0.13	0.0048	0.0397
5	3	13.6	13.64	-0.04	0.20	0.0558	0.0013
6	4	13.7	13.47	0.23	-0.04	0.0720	0.0522
7	5	13.5	13.31	0.19	0.23	0.0014	0.0372
8	6	13.0	13.14	-0.14	0.19	0.1105	0.0203
9	7	12.6	12.98	-0.38	-0.14	0.0565	0.1427
10	8	12.5	12.81	-0.31	-0.38	0.0045	0.0981
11	9	12.1	12.65	-0.55	-0.31	0.0569	0.3010
12	10	12.2	12.48	-0.28	-0.55	0.0708	0.0807
13	11	12.5	12.32	0.18	-0.28	0.2122	0.0326
14	12	12.4	12.15	0.25	0.18	0.0043	0.0601
15	13	12.5	11.99	0.51	0.24	0.0728	0.2599
16	14	11.9	11.83	0.07	0.51	0.1897	0.0055
17	15	11.8	11.66	0.14	0.07	0.0048	0.0193
18	16	11.3	11.50	-0.20	0.14	0.1132	0.0386
19							
20					Total	1.0300	1.2073
21							

Using these calculations and Equation 16.10 to determine the Durbin–Watson statistic, we have the following:

$$d = \frac{\sum_{t=2}^{n}(e_t - e_{t-1})^2}{\sum_{t=1}^{n} e_t^2} = \frac{1.0300}{1.2073} = 0.853$$

The slight difference between this value and the one found using PHStat can be attributed to minor rounding in the calculations.

We need to compare this number with the critical values for the Durbin–Watson test, which can be found in Table 9 in Appendix A. An excerpt of this table is shown in Table 16.13.

TABLE 16.13 | CRITICAL VALUES FOR THE DURBIN–WATSON TEST (α = 0.05)

	$k = 1$		$k = 2$		$k = 3$	
n	d_L	d_U	d_L	d_U	d_L	d_U
15	1.08	1.36	0.95	1.54	0.82	1.75
16	1.10	1.37	0.98	1.54	0.86	1.73
17	1.13	1.38	1.02	1.54	0.90	1.71

The critical values shown in Table 16.13 are for a one-tail test (which we have in our union membership example). The value of k in this table refers to the number of independent variables in the regression model. For our union membership example, there is only one independent variable (period number), so $k = 1$. The value of n refers to the number of observations in our time series, which for this example equals 16. The Durbin–Watson test uses two critical values, d_L and d_U, which for our example are 1.10 and 1.37, respectively (highlighted in yellow). We use the following decision rules to state our conclusions:

- If $d < d_L$, we reject H_0 and conclude that a positive autocorrelation is present.
- If $d_L < d < d_U$, the test is inconclusive.
- If $d > d_U$, we fail to reject H_0 and conclude that no positive autocorrelation is present.

The presence of autocorrelation in our time series could cause us to conclude that the coefficient for our trend line is statistically significant when, in reality, it is not.

Because $d = 0.853 < d_L = 1.10$, we reject H_0 and conclude that a positive autocorrelation exists with our union membership time series. As a result, an important assumption of the regression model is violated in this example.

Time series regression models tend to be particularly susceptible to autocorrelation because the data value from one period can often influence the data value in a later period. The presence of autocorrelation makes the significance test for the regression coefficient unreliable. One possible solution to address autocorrelation would be to identify additional independent variables to add to the model that would help explain the variation in the dependent (forecasted) variable. This would result in a different series of residuals that might not exhibit the pattern of autocorrelation.

Now it's your turn to test a time series for a positive autocorrelation.

YOUR TURN #6

The following table shows the number of permits authorized for new, privately owned housing units, in thousands, in the state of Pennsylvania from 1995 to 2012. These data can also be found in the Excel file **building permits.xlsx.**

Year	Permits	Year	Permits	Year	Permits
1995	36.3	2001	41.4	2007	33.7
1996	37.9	2002	45.1	2008	24.6
1997	39.9	2003	47.4	2009	18.3
1998	41.6	2004	49.7	2010	19.7
1999	42.7	2005	44.5	2011	15.0
2000	41.1	2006	39.1	2012	18.8

Based on: www.census.gov.

a. Use PHStat to test this time series for positive autocorrelation with $\alpha = 0.05$.
b. Verify your Durbin–Watson statistic using Excel.

Answers can be found on ▶ **page 822–823**

16.3 Section Problems

Basic Skills

16.13 Consider the following time series:

Period	1	2	3	4	5	6	7	8
Demand	7	8	7	10	14	16	13	16

a. Using a trend projection, forecast the demand for Period 9.
b. Verify your results using PHStat.
c. Calculate the *MAD* for this forecast.

16.14 Consider the following time series:

Period	1	2	3	4	5	6	7	8
Demand	15	17	14	7	10	12	7	5

a. Using a trend projection, forecast the demand for Period 9.
b. Verify your results with PHStat.
c. Calculate the *MAD* for this forecast.

16.15 Consider the following time series:

Period	Sales	Period	Sales	Period	Sales
1	4	6	10	11	18
2	6	7	12	12	12
3	11	8	13	13	15
4	9	9	10	14	16
5	8	10	12	15	16

a. Use PHStat with $\alpha = 0.05$ to test this time series for positive autocorrelation.
b. Verify your Durbin–Watson statistic using Excel.

16.16 Consider the following time series:

Period	Sales	Period	Sales	Period	Sales
1	37	6	29	11	18
2	30	7	24	12	16
3	22	8	17	13	21
4	28	9	22	14	17
5	25	10	24	15	15

a. Use PHStat and set $\alpha = 0.05$ to test this time series for positive autocorrelation.
b. Verify your Durbin–Watson statistic using Excel.

Applications

16.17 According to the National Association of Theatre Owners, the average U.S. ticket price has been steadily increasing over the past several years. The following data show the average price during an eight-year period. These data can also be found in the Excel file **average ticket price.xlsx**.

Year	Price ($)	Year	Price ($)
2006	6.55	2010	7.89
2007	6.88	2011	7.93
2008	7.18	2012	7.96
2009	7.50	2013	7.94

a. Construct a graph showing the average ticket price over time.
b. Forecast the average ticket price in the United States for 2014 using a trend projection.
c. Calculate the *MAD* for this forecast.

16.18 The size of the audience watching the Super Bowl plays a major role in the price the broadcasting network charges for advertising. The following data show the average number of viewers, in millions, who watched previous Super Bowls, according to Nielsen. These data can also be found in the Excel file **Super Bowl viewers.xlsx**.

Year	Viewers	Year	Viewers
2005	86.0	2010	106.5
2006	90.7	2011	111.0
2007	93.2	2012	111.3
2008	97.5	2013	108.4
2009	98.7		

a. Construct a graph showing the average Super Bowl viewership over time.
b. Forecast the average number of viewers for the 2014 Super Bowl using a trend projection.
c. Calculate the *MAD* for this forecast.

16.19 Steve, who has been working hard to improve his golf game, has seen some improvement in his scores over the summer. He would like to use forecasting to set a goal for his next round. The following data show the scores from his last nine rounds of golf at the course he plays most often.

Round	1	2	3	4	5	6	7	8	9
Score	94	93	90	88	92	89	85	89	88

a. Construct a graph showing Steve's golf scores over time.
b. Forecast Steve's golf score for his next round using a trend projection.
c. Calculate the *MAD* for this forecast.

16.20 The following table shows the number of cell phone minutes used per month on my family plan for the past eight months. These data can also be found in the Excel file **cell phone minutes.xlsx**.

Month	1	2	3	4	5	6	7	8
Minutes	325	355	326	433	390	414	447	440

a. Construct a graph showing the number of minutes used per month on my cell phone account over time.
b. Forecast the number of minutes for next month using a trend projection.
c. Calculate the *MAD* for this forecast.
d. If my family plan includes only 500 minutes per month, in what month am I predicted to exceed these minutes?

16.21 Julie owns 100 shares of Apple stock (lucky her) and is trying to decide how much her portfolio will be worth next month. The data in the Excel file **Apple stock price.xlsx** show the closing price of a share of Apple stock at the end of each month from October 2011 until May 2013.

Based on: BigCharts.com data.

a. Construct a graph showing the Apple stock price over time.
b. Forecast the closing price for Apple stock at the end of June 2013 using a trend projection.
c. Calculate the *MAD* for this forecast.
d. Check for the presence of positive autocorrelation.
e. What concerns should you have using trend projection to forecast with this data.

16.22 Gold has long been a very popular investment choice during times of economic crisis. This has resulted in a significant increase in the price of gold per ounce in recent years. The Excel file **gold prices.xlsx** shows the average price of an ounce of gold from 1992 until 2012.

Based on: data at www.kitco.com.

a. Construct a graph showing the price per ounce of gold over time.
b. Forecast the average price of gold for 2013 using a trend projection.
c. Calculate the *MAD* for this forecast.
d. Check for the presence of positive autocorrelation.
e. Based on these results, does this forecasting method seem appropriate for these data?

16.23 Recently, fixed mortgage rates have been at historical lows due to the housing slowdown. Data in the Excel file **mortgage rates.xlsx** show the average 30-year fixed mortgage rate for the month of December every year between 1989 and 2012, as reported by Freddie Mac.

a. Construct a graph showing the average December mortgage rate over time.
b. Forecast the average December mortgage rate in 2013 using a trend projection.
c. Calculate the *MAD* for this forecast.
d. Check for the presence of positive autocorrelation.
e. What limitations do you foresee with this forecasting method projecting mortgage rates several years into the future?

16.4 Forecasting with Seasonality

Early in the chapter, you learned that a time series could consist of one or more of the following types of components:

- Trend
- Seasonal
- Cyclical
- Random

We've already discussed using the trend component to generate a forecast. In this section we'll investigate the benefit of including a seasonal component in our forecasting method. Recall that a seasonal component is present in a time series if a consistent pattern associated with a calendar can be observed in the data. We'll explore these methods using our new car sales data, which are again shown graphically in Figure 16.12.

FIGURE 16.12
New Car Sales Time Series

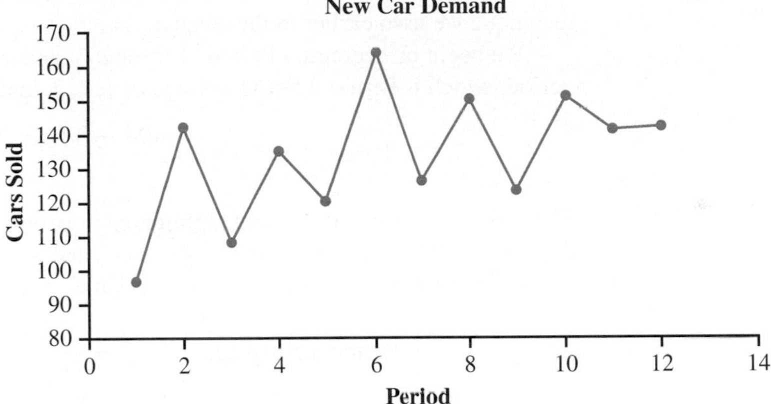

It appears there might be a consistent seasonal pattern in the car sales data. Notice that sales spike upward in the even-numbered quarters (the second and fourth quarters of each year). Perhaps we can use this pattern to our advantage when forecasting future sales. Let's take a look.

Multiplicative Decomposition of a Time Series

Multiplicative decomposition is a technique that multiplies the individual time series components together to generate a forecast.

The first technique that we'll examine attempts to separate the trend and seasonal components of a time series using a method known as decomposition. In this section, we'll decompose the time series we're studying using the **multiplicative decomposition** model described in Equation 16.11.

Formula 6.11 for the Multiplicative Decomposition Model

$$y_t = T_t \times S_t \times R_t$$

where

y_t = The time series value at period t
T_t = The trend component at period t
S_t = The seasonal component at period t
R_t = The random component at period t

Notice that I did not include the cyclical component in Equation 16.11. This is because cyclical patterns, which vary with the economy, often require a longer time frame to identify than our three-year car sales data provide.

To use the multiplicative decomposition technique for a forecast, you need to take the following four steps:

1. Identify the seasonal components.
2. Deseasonalize the original data using the seasonal components.
3. Identify the trend component with the deseasonalized data.
4. Use the trend and seasonal components to forecast future periods.

Identify the Seasonal Components

Earlier in the chapter, you learned that a seasonal component is a consistent pattern in the data that can be associated with a calendar. The number of seasonal components equals the number of seasons within a calendar year. With our new car sales data, we have four quarters for each year, which results in four seasonal components that we need to identify. For example, the first quarter consists of months January through March, the second quarter consists of months April through June, and so on. We start this process by calculating a four-period moving average (because of our four seasons) centered on the original time series data, as Table 16.14 shows. This procedure is not to be confused with the simple moving average technique we used earlier in the chapter.

We begin by averaging Periods 1 through 4 and associating this average with the center period, which is Period 2.5 (the average of 1, 2, 3, and 4 is 2.5). Our results are as follows:

$$\text{Period 2.5 average} = \frac{97 + 142 + 108 + 135}{4} = 120.50$$

These figures are in red text and highlighted in yellow in Table 16.14. As shown in the table, the value 120.5 is halfway between Periods 2 and 3.

Next, we move down one period to calculate the average sales for Period 3.5 as follows:

$$\text{Period 3.5 average} = \frac{142 + 108 + 135 + 120}{4} = 126.25$$

We continue this averaging process for the rest of the time series, stopping at the average for Period 10.5, as shown in green text and highlighted in yellow in Table 16.14.

TABLE 16.14 | DETERMINING THE SEASONAL COMPONENTS OF THE NEW CAR SALES TIME SERIES (STEP 1)

PERIOD	SEASON	Y_t	FOUR-PERIOD MOVING AVERAGE
1	2011-Q1	**97**	
2	2011-Q2	**142**	
			120.50
3	2011-Q3	**108**	
			126.25
4	2011-Q4	**135**	
			131.75
5	2012-Q1	120	
			136.25
6	2012-Q2	164	
			140.00
7	2012-Q3	126	
			140.75
8	2012-Q4	150	
			137.50
9	2013-Q1	**123**	
			141.25
10	2013-Q2	**151**	
			139.25
11	2013-Q3	**141**	
12	2013-Q4	**142**	

This four-period moving average is found by averaging 97, 142, 108, and 135.

Because we have an even number of seasons each year (four), the moving averages are assigned to half-periods (Period 2.5, 3.5, and so forth). This happens because the average of the numbers 1, 2, 3, and 4 is 2.5. As a result, we need an additional step to center each of these averages on whole periods (3, 4, and so on), as Table 16.15 shows. These values are known as **centered moving averages (*CMA*)**. We begin by finding the centered moving average for Period 3, CMA_3, by averaging the results from periods 2.5 and 3.5 as follows:

A **centered moving average** assigns the average value of a set of data points to the center time period.

$$CMA_3 = \frac{120.5 + 126.25}{2} = 123.375$$

These figures are in red text and highlighted in yellow in Table 16.15. We next find the centered moving average for Period 4, CMA_4, as follows:

$$CMA_4 = \frac{126.25 + 131.75}{2} = 129.0$$

The final centered moving average is assigned to Period 10 and is shown in green text and highlighted in yellow in Table 16.15.

TABLE 16.15 | DETERMINING THE SEASONAL COMPONENTS OF THE NEW CAR SALES TIME SERIES (STEP 2)

PERIOD	SEASON	y_t	FOUR-PERIOD MOVING AVERAGE	CENTERED MOVING AVERAGE
1	2011-Q1	97		
2	2011-Q2	142		
			120.50	
3	2011-Q3	108		**123.375**
			126.25	
4	2011-Q4	135		129.000
			131.75	
5	2012-Q1	120		134.000
			136.25	
6	2012-Q2	164		138.125
			140.00	
7	2012-Q3	126		140.375
			140.75	
8	2012-Q4	150		139.125
			137.50	
9	2013-Q1	123		139.375
			141.25	
10	2013-Q2	151		**140.250**
			139.25	
11	2013-Q3	141		
12	2013-Q4	142		

This centered moving average is found by averaging 120.50 and 126.25.

If our time series contained an odd number of seasons, say three, the step shown in Table 16.15 would not have been necessary. This is because the moving averages in Table 16.14 would have already been centered on whole periods. For instance, the result obtained by averaging Periods 1, 2, and 3 would be centered on Period 2.

The purpose of calculating a four-period centered moving average in Table 16.15 is to remove the seasonal component, S_t, from the time series. This occurs due to the fact that our averages include all four seasons. By averaging, we have also removed the random component, R_t, because we expect the random fluctuations to average out over time. Now that we have eliminated the impact of seasonality and randomness, the centered moving average values in Table 16.15 represent the remaining time series component, trend (T_t). We can express this relationship as the following:

$$CMA_t = T_t$$

Recall from Equation 16.11 that our original time series can be described as follows:

$$y_t = T_t \times S_t \times R_t$$

The **ratio-to-moving-average** represents the seasonal and random components in the original time series and is found by dividing the time series value by its centered moving average.

With a little algebra, we have what is known as the **ratio-to-moving-average** (*RMA*), which is shown in Equation 16.12.

Formula 16.12 for the Ratio-to-Moving-Average

$$RMA_t = S_t \times R_t = \frac{y_t}{T_t} = \frac{y_t}{CMA_t}$$

The ratio-to-moving-average represents the seasonal and random components in the original time series. The first ratio-to-moving-average we can calculate is for Period 3 because that is the first centered moving average available from Table 16.15. Using Equation 16.12, we have the following:

$$RMA_3 = \frac{y_3}{CMA_3} = \frac{108}{123.375} = 0.8754$$

These values are shown in red text and highlighted in yellow in Table 16.16. We continue these calculations down the time series until we reach RMA_{10}, as follows:

$$RMA_{10} = \frac{y_{10}}{CMA_{10}} = \frac{151}{140.25} = 1.0766$$

TABLE 16.16 | DETERMINING THE SEASONAL COMPONENTS OF THE NEW CAR SALES TIME SERIES (STEP 3)

PERIOD	SEASON	y_t	FOUR-PERIOD MOVING AVERAGE	CENTERED MOVING AVERAGE	RATIO-TO-MOVING-AVERAGE
1	2011-Q1	97			
2	2011-Q2	142			
			120.50		
3	2011-Q3	**108**		**123.375**	**0.8754**
			126.25		
4	2011-Q4	135		129.000	1.0465
			131.75		
5	2012-Q1	120		134.000	0.8955
			136.25		
6	2012-Q2	164		138.125	1.1873
			140.00		
7	2012-Q3	126		140.375	0.8976
			140.75		

This ratio-to-moving-average is found by dividing 108 by 123.375.

TABLE 16.16 | (CONTINUED)

PERIOD	SEASON	y_t	FOUR-PERIOD MOVING AVERAGE	CENTERED MOVING AVERAGE	RATIO-TO-MOVING-AVERAGE
8	2012-Q4	150		139.125	1.0782
			137.50		
9	2013-Q1	123		139.375	0.8825
			141.25		
10	2013-Q2	151		140.250	1.0766
			139.25		
11	2013-Q3	141			
12	2013-Q4	142			

Notice in Table 16.16 that we have two ratio-to-moving-averages for each season. For example, the two ratio-to-moving-averages for the first quarter are 0.8955, which occurred in 2012 (Period 5), and 0.8825, which occurred in 2013 (Period 9). We also know that these values represent the seasonal and random components of the time series (see Equation 16.12), as follows:

$$RMA_t = S_t \times R_t$$

Seasonal factors are obtained by averaging the ratio-to-moving-averages associated with each season in the time series.

To isolate the seasonal component, S_t, in the preceding expression, we first need to identify a **seasonal factor**, SF_Q (the subscript Q refers to the quarter number), for each quarter by averaging the two ratio-to-moving-averages that are associated with each season, as shown in Table 16.17. By averaging the two periods, we cancel out the random component, R_t, in Equation 16.12.

TABLE 16.17 | DETERMINING THE SEASONAL COMPONENTS FOR THE NEW CAR SALES TIME SERIES (STEP 4)

	QUARTER 1	QUARTER 2	QUARTER 3	QUARTER 4
	0.8955	1.1873	0.8754	1.0465
	0.8825	1.0766	0.8976	1.0782
Average	**0.8890**	**1.1320**	**0.8865**	**1.0624**

The following equation shows how the seasonal factor for Quarter 1, SF_1, is calculated by averaging the ratio-to-moving-averages for Periods 5 and 9 in Table 16.17:

$$SF_1 = \frac{RMA_5 + RMA_9}{2} = \frac{0.8955 + 0.8825}{2} = 0.8890$$

We repeat these calculations for the remaining seasons to obtain the following seasonal factors for Quarters 1, 2, 3, and 4:

$$\begin{aligned} SF_1 &= 0.8890 \text{ (from Periods 5 and 9)} \\ SF_2 &= 1.1320 \text{ (from Periods 6 and 10)} \\ SF_3 &= 0.8865 \text{ (from Periods 3 and 7)} \\ SF_4 &= 1.0624 \text{ (from Periods 4 and 8)} \\ \text{Total} &= 3.9699 \end{aligned}$$

Notice that the sum of the seasonal factors is 3.9699. We need one final adjustment so that our seasonal factors add up to 4, which is the number of seasons in our time series.

Normalized seasonal factors are seasonal factors that are adjusted so that they add up to the number of seasons in the time series.

This process is called normalizing the seasonal factors. It is performed as follows to calculate the **normalized seasonal factors**, NSF_Q, for Quarters 1, 2, 3, and 4:

$$NSF_1 = \frac{4}{3.9699}(SF_1) = (1.0076)(0.8890) = 0.8958$$

$$NSF_2 = \frac{4}{3.9699}(SF_2) = (1.0076)(1.1320) = 1.1406$$

$$NSF_3 = \frac{4}{3.9699}(SF_3) = (1.0076)(0.8865) = 0.8932$$

$$NSF_4 = \frac{4}{3.9699}(SF_4) = (1.0076)(1.0624) = 1.0704$$

$$\text{Total} = 4.0000$$

Because of rounding, this value may be slightly different than the number of seasons.

What do these normalized seasonal factors tell us? It appears that in Quarter 2, the dealership typically experiences a higher volume of car sales than in any other quarter during the year. In fact, we can say that Quarter 2 has about 14% more sales than an average quarter during the year. Quarters 1 and 3 generate lower than average sales when compared with the other quarters. This pattern is consistent with what we observed in Figure 16.12, which showed that in even-numbered quarters sales spiked.

We are now ready to assign our normalized seasonal factors to the seasonal component, S_t, for each period of our time series in Table 16.18.

Quarter 2 averages the highest demand because it has the highest seasonal factor.

TABLE 16.18 | DESEASONALIZING THE NEW CAR SALES TIME SERIES

PERIOD	YEAR	QUARTER	SEASONAL COMPONENT, S_T
1	2011	1	0.8958
2	2011	2	1.1406
3	2011	3	0.8932
4	2011	4	1.0704
5	2012	1	0.8958
6	2012	2	1.1406
7	2012	3	0.8932
8	2012	4	1.0704
9	2013	1	0.8958
10	2013	2	1.1406
11	2013	3	0.8932
12	2013	4	1.0704

I realize we've covered a lot of material in this section. Now is a good time to stop, take a deep breath, and calculate some seasonal components in this next Your Turn before moving on.

YOUR TURN #7

Identify the seasonal components for the GPA data from Your Turn #1. (Hint: There are three seasons, or semesters, in each school year—Fall, Spring, and Summer. You're welcome.)

Answer can be found on ▶ **page 823–824**

Deseasonalize the Time Series

Our next step in the decomposition process is to deseasonalize the original time series. We do this by removing the seasonality from the car sales data using the seasonal components we just computed. Recall from Equation 16.11 that our original time series can be described as the following:

$$y_t = T_t \times S_t \times R_t$$

With a little algebra, we can calculate the deseasonalized sales with Equation 16.13.

Formula 16.13 for the Deseasonalized Time Series

$$T_t \times R_t = \frac{y_t}{S_t}$$

Deseasonalizing the time series removes the effect that the seasonal component has on the data.

For example, the deseasonalized sales for Period 1 would be as follows:

$$\frac{y_1}{S_1} = \frac{97}{0.8958} = 108.3 \text{ cars}$$

In other words, if we remove the effect that the Quarter 1 season has on car sales, we would expect to sell 108 cars that period. We continue with these calculations for the remaining periods to deseasonalize them. The results are shown in Table 16.19.

TABLE 16.19 | Determining the Deseasonalized New Car Sales

PERIOD	YEAR	QUARTER	SALES y_t	SEASONAL, COMPONENT, S_t	DESEASONALIZED SALES
1	2011	1	97	0.8958	108.3
2	2011	2	142	1.1406	124.5
3	2011	3	108	0.8932	120.9
4	2011	4	135	1.0704	126.1
5	2012	1	120	0.8958	133.9
6	2012	2	164	1.1406	143.8
7	2012	3	126	0.8932	141.1
8	2012	4	150	1.0704	140.1
9	2013	1	123	0.8958	137.3
10	2013	2	151	1.1406	132.4
11	2013	3	141	0.8932	157.9
12	2013	4	142	1.0704	132.7

Figure 16.13 shows the effect of deseasonalizing the data. The blue line represents the original time series with seasonality, whereas the red line represents the deseasonalized time series. As you can see, most of the seasonal spikes in the original data have been removed with the deseasonalized data.

Our next goal is to identify the linear trend line through the deseasonalized data using a simple regression.

FIGURE 16.13
Deseasonalized Time Series: New Car Sales

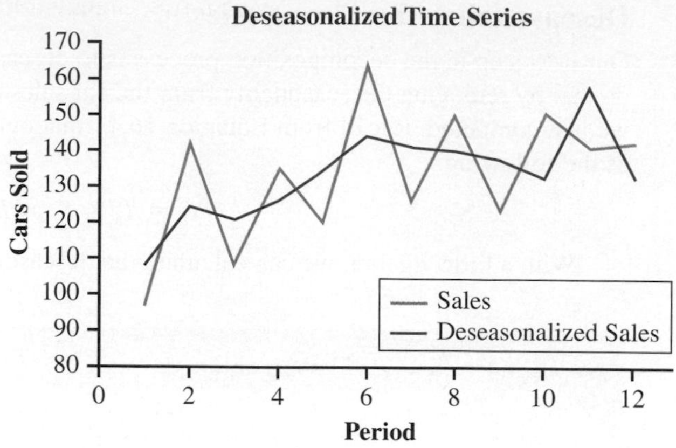

Identify the Trend Component with the Deseasonalized Data

Figure 16.14 shows the deseasonalized data (red line) along with the trend line that best fits these data (green line). The regression equation that describes the green line will act as our trend component for the decomposition forecasting method.

FIGURE 16.14
Deseasonalized Trend Component for the New Car Sales Time Series

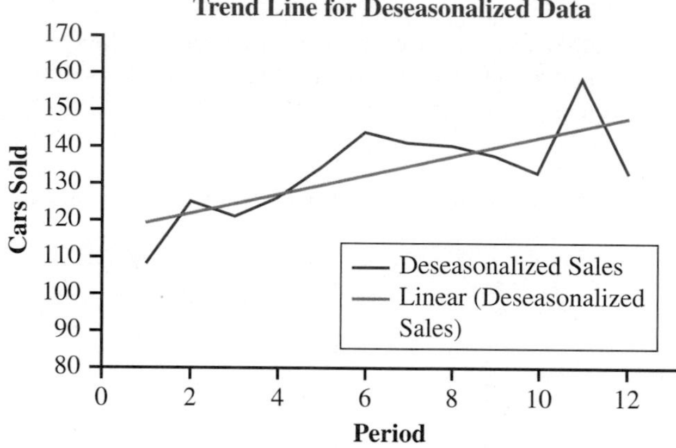

To generate our regression equation for this trend line, we can use either Excel's Data Analysis function or the simple regression function in PHStat. The following steps will demonstrate how PHStat is used for this procedure. Excel for Mac users can find instructions for this procedure on the textbook's Web site.

1. Open the Excel file **deseasonalized car sales.xlsx** or enter the data shown in Figure 16.15A.
2. Go to **Add-Ins > PHStat > Regression > Simple Linear Regression**, as shown in Figure 16.9A.

FIGURE 16.15A
Using PHStat for a Deseasonalized Trend Projection (Steps 1–3)

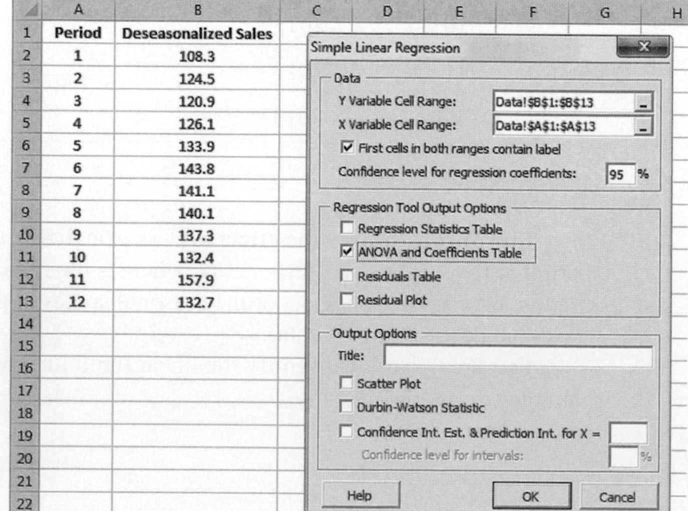

	A	B
1	Period	Deseasonalized Sales
2	1	108.3
3	2	124.5
4	3	120.9
5	4	126.1
6	5	133.9
7	6	143.8
8	7	141.1
9	8	140.1
10	9	137.3
11	10	132.4
12	11	157.9
13	12	132.7

3. Fill in the **Data** section of the **Simple Linear Regression** dialog box as shown in Figure 16.15A. Click **OK**.

Figure 16.15B shows our trend equation in the deseasonalized worksheet labeled "SLR." The regression coefficients are circled in red.

FIGURE 16.15B
Using PHStat for a Deseasonalized Trend Projection (Final Result)

	A	B	C	D	E	F	G
1	**Simple Linear Regression Analysis**						
2							
3							
4	ANOVA						
5		*df*	*SS*	*MS*	*F*	*Significance F*	
6	Regression	1	909.8216	909.8216	10.8544	0.0081	
7	Residual	10	838.2084	83.8208			
8	Total	11	1748.0300				
9							
10		*Coefficients*	*Standard Error*	*t Stat*	*P-value*	*Lower 95%*	*Upper 95%*
11	Intercept	116.8545	5.6347	20.7382	0.0000	104.2996	129.4095
12	Period	2.5224	0.7656	3.2946	0.0071	0.8165	4.2283
13							

Based on these results, our trend component for the deseasonalized car sales data is described with the following linear equation:

$$T_t = 116.8545 + 2.5224t$$

Notice that the p-value for the regression coefficient in Figure 16.15B is equal to 0.008 (in Cell E11), indicating that the Period variable is statistically significant. Normally, this would be an appropriate time to test for the presence of autocorrelation using the Durbin–Watson statistic. However, because we have less than 15 data points in this example, this test cannot be performed. Believe it or not, we are now ready to forecast some car sales. It's about time!

Generate Forecasts with the Trend and Seasonal Components

To generate a sales forecast, F_t, for the upcoming quarter (Period 13) using the multiplicative decomposition method, we use Equation 16.14.

Notice that the random component, R_t, is not part of the forecasting equation. This is because randomness, by definition, cannot be predicted. We also expect the random component to "cancel itself out" over time.

Formula 16.14 for Forecasting with the Multiplicative Decomposition Method

$$F_t = T_t \times S_t$$

Let's start by determining the trend component, T_t, for Period 13 $(t = 13)$ as follows:

$$T_t = 116.8545 + 2.5224t$$
$$T_{13} = 116.8545 + 2.5224(13) = 149.65$$

To find our seasonal component, we need to refer to Table 16.18. Because Period 13 is the first quarter of 2014, $S_1 = 0.8958$. Using Equation 16.14, our sales forecast for the next quarter is calculated as follows:

$$F_{13} = T_{13} \times S_{13} = (149.65)(0.8958) = 134.1 \approx 134 \text{ cars}$$

Because sales are typically lower for Quarter 1 as compared with other quarters, the seasonal component reduced our forecast from 149 to 134 cars.

With the multiplicative decomposition method, we can also forecast additional quarters into the future. For example, Table 16.20 shows how I can generate forecasts for the remaining three quarters of 2014 (Periods 14, 15, and 16).

TABLE 16.20 | FORECASTING WITH MULTIPLICATIVE DECOMPOSITION

PERIOD	YEAR	QUARTER	TREND COMP, T_t	SEASONAL COMPONENT, S_t	SALES FORECAST, F_t
13	2014	1	149.65	0.8958	134
14	2014	2	152.17	1.1406	174
15	2014	3	154.69	0.8932	138
16	2014	4	157.21	1.0704	168

As we discussed earlier in the chapter, be aware that the farther out into the future we project our trend and seasonality components, the less reliable our forecasted value will be. Forecasting errors tend to increase as the time horizon of the forecast increases.

Your boss has to be impressed with your analysis. Looks like somebody might be getting a pay raise. I told you taking statistics was a great idea!

Because multiplicative decomposition requires several steps, I've summarized them for you:

- Identify the seasonal components by calculating the centered moving averages.
- Deseasonalize the original data by dividing the original time series with the seasonal components.
- Identify the trend component by performing a simple regression using the deseasonalized data.
- Use the trend and seasonal components to forecast future periods.

Let's see how much you have learned in this section with the following Your Turn problem.

YOUR TURN #8

Use the results from Your Turn #7 and multiplicative decomposition to forecast for the next three semesters the GPA for the student in Your Turn #1.

Answer can be found on ▶ pages 824–825

Investigate the Accuracy of the Forecast

I hope you saw this next question coming: How accurate is the car sales forecast using multiplicative decomposition compared with the methods discussed previously in the chapter? You know the drill—we need to calculate the *MAD*!

First, I'll calculate the forecasting error for the first period. The trend component, T_t, for Period 1 $(t = 1)$ is as follows:

$$T_t = 116.8545 + 2.5224t$$
$$T_1 = 116.8545 + 2.5224(1) = 119.4$$

According to Table 16.18, the seasonal component for the first quarter of 2010, $S_1 = 0.8958$. Using Equation 16.14, our sales forecast for Period 1 is calculated as follows:

$$F_1 = T_1 \times S_1 = (119.4)(0.8958) = 107.0$$

Our forecasting error is defined as the actual sales value, y_t, minus the forecasted sales value, F_t. For Period 1, our forecasting error is calculated as follows:

$$y_1 - F_1 = 97 - 107.0 = -10.0$$

For the upcoming *MAD* calculation, we take the absolute value of this forecasting error as well as the remaining errors shown in Table 16.21.

TABLE 16.21 | Data and Calculations Needed to Find the Mean Absolute Deviation: Multiplicative Decomposition

Period, t	Sales, y_t	Trend Component, T_t	Seasonal Component, S_t	Sales Forecast, F_y	Absolute Forecasting Error, $\lvert Y_t - F_t \rvert$
1	97	119.4	0.8958	107.0	10.0
2	142	121.9	1.1406	139.0	3.0
3	108	124.4	0.8932	111.1	3.1
4	135	126.9	1.0704	135.8	0.8
5	120	129.5	0.8958	116.0	4.0
6	164	132.0	1.1406	150.6	13.4
7	126	134.5	0.8932	120.1	5.9
8	150	137.0	1.0704	146.6	3.4
9	123	139.6	0.8958	125.1	2.1
10	151	142.1	1.1406	162.1	11.1
11	141	144.6	0.8932	129.2	11.8
12	142	147.1	1.0704	157.5	15.5
					$\sum \lvert y_t - F_t \rvert = 84.1$

The average forecasting error for multiplicative decomposition with our car sales data using *MAD* is therefore as follows:

$$MAD = \frac{\sum \lvert y_t - F_t \rvert}{n} = \frac{84.1}{12} = 7.0$$

Using this method, our average forecasting error is 7.0 cars per quarter. How does this accuracy stack up when compared with the previous methods we've explored in this chapter? Table 16.22 provides a summary of what we've done so far.

TABLE 16.22 | Summary of the Mean Absolute Deviation for Various Forecasting Methods

Method	Sales Forecast	*MAD*
Simple moving average, $p = 3$	145	15.9
Simple moving average, $p = 4$	139	11.1
Weighted moving average, $p = 3$ (3, 2, 1)	143	15.3
Exponential smoothing, $\alpha = 0.6$	142	19.0
Exponential smoothing w/trend, $\alpha = 0.3, \beta = 0.1$	148	16.6
Trend projection	151	13.8
Multiplicative decomposition	134	7.0

As you can see in this table, multiplicative decomposition provides the best results. This is not surprising considering the fact that our car sales time series exhibits patterns of both trend and seasonality and that this last forecasting method is the only one in the table that accounts for both. It's worth noting, however, that one of the more basic methods, four-period simple moving average, also performs very well with this data set. In forecasting, there's no guarantee that a more complicated method will outperform a simpler forecasting technique.

It's time for another Your Turn problem that will give you the opportunity to check the *MAD* for a multiplicative decomposition forecast. Sounds like fun to me!

YOUR TURN #9

Use the results from Your Turn #7 and #8 to calculate the *MAD* for the GPA forecast using multiplicative decomposition.

Answer can be found on ▶ **page 825**

Representing Seasonality with Dummy Variables

Chapter 15 introduced the concept of dummy variables. Dummy variables allowed us to use qualitative variables in the regression model. We can represent seasonality with dummy variables in our regression model as well. Because we have four categories of seasons (first, second, third, and fourth quarters), we need three seasonal dummy variables, which are identified in Table 16.23. For example, SD_1 is the first of three seasonal dummy variables.

Recall from Chapter 15 that we need k − 1 dummy variables when we have k categories in our qualitative variable.

TABLE 16.23 | Creating Dummy Variables to Represent Seasonality

	DUMMY VARIABLES		
SEASON	SD_1	SD_2	SD_3
First quarter	0	0	0
Second quarter	1	0	0
Third quarter	0	1	0
Fourth quarter	0	0	1

I've arbitrarily chosen the first quarter as my base season by assigning a zero value for all three dummy variables in Table 16.23.

Our new data set now includes the following variables:

- Dependent variable: car sales
- Independent variables: time period, seasonal dummy variables (SD_1, SD_2, and SD_3)

Table 16.24 shows the car sales data with dummy variables for this regression model. These data can also be found in the Excel file **car sales dummy.xlsx**.

TABLE 16.24 | New Car Sales Data with Dummy Variables

			SALES,	DUMMY VARIABLES						SALES,	DUMMY VARIABLES		
PERIOD	YEAR	QUARTER	y_t	SD_1	SD_2	SD_3	PERIOD	YEAR	QUARTER	y_t	SD_1	SD_2	SD_3
1	2011	1	97	0	0	0	7	2012	3	126	0	1	0
2	2011	2	142	1	0	0	8	2012	4	150	0	0	1
3	2011	3	108	0	1	0	9	2013	1	123	0	0	0
4	2011	4	135	0	0	1	10	2013	2	151	1	0	0
5	2012	1	120	0	0	0	11	2013	3	141	0	1	0
6	2012	2	164	1	0	0	12	2013	4	142	0	0	1

Our next step is to use PHStat to perform a multiple regression on our car sales data. If you recall from the previous chapter, we have some choices as to what multiple regression method to use with PHStat. I'll use best subsets regression, which examines all combinations of independent variables as possible candidates for the final regression model. Excel for Mac users can find instructions for this procedure on the textbook's Web site.

1. Open the Excel file **car sales dummy.xlsx** or enter the data shown in Figure 16.16A.
2. Go to **Add-Ins > PHStat > Regression > Best Subsets**, as Figure 16.9A shows.
3. Fill in the **Best Subsets** dialog box as Figure 16.16A shows and click **OK**.

FIGURE 16.16A Using PHStat to Forecast Seasonality with Dummy Variables (Steps 1–3)

	A	B	C	D	E
1	Sales	Period	SD_1	SD_2	SD_3
2	97	1	0	0	0
3	142	2	1	0	0
4	108	3	0	1	0
5	135	4	0	0	1
6	120	5	0	0	0
7	164	6	1	0	0
8	126	7	0	1	0
9	150	8	0	0	1
10	123	9	0	0	0
11	151	10	1	0	0
12	141	11	0	1	0
13	142	12	0	0	1
14					

Best Subsets
Data
Y Variable Cell Range: Data!$A$1:$A$13
X Variables Cell Range: Data!$B$1:$E$13
☑ First cells in each range contains label
Confidence level for regression coefficients: 95 %
Output Options
Title:
Help OK Cancel

4. PHStat creates several worksheets in the Excel file, one of which is labeled "Best Subsets." Selecting this sheet will display the data shown in Figure 16.16B.

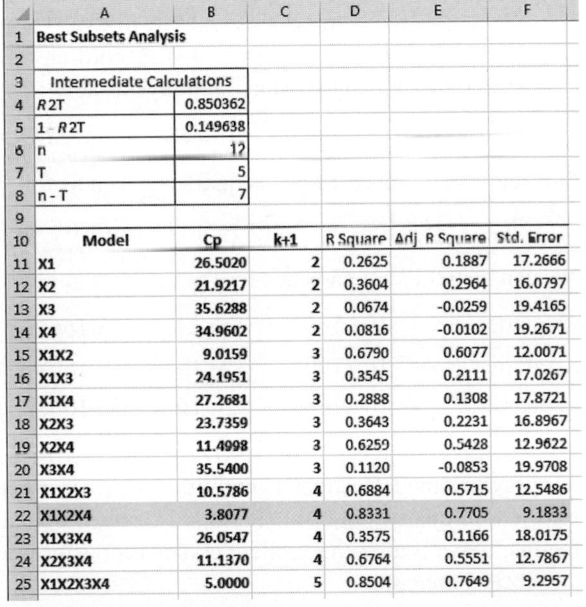

	A	B	C	D	E	F
1	Best Subsets Analysis					
2						
3	Intermediate Calculations					
4	R2T	0.850362				
5	1 - R2T	0.149638				
6	n	12				
7	T	5				
8	n - T	7				
9						
10	Model	Cp	k+1	R Square	Adj. R Square	Std. Error
11	X1	26.5020	2	0.2625	0.1887	17.2666
12	X2	21.9217	2	0.3604	0.2964	16.0797
13	X3	35.6288	2	0.0674	-0.0259	19.4165
14	X4	34.9602	2	0.0816	-0.0102	19.2671
15	X1X2	9.0159	3	0.6790	0.6077	12.0071
16	X1X3	24.1951	3	0.3545	0.2111	17.0267
17	X1X4	27.2681	3	0.2888	0.1308	17.8721
18	X2X3	23.7359	3	0.3643	0.2231	16.8967
19	X2X4	11.4998	3	0.6259	0.5428	12.9622
20	X3X4	35.5400	3	0.1120	-0.0853	19.9708
21	X1X2X3	10.5786	4	0.6884	0.5715	12.5486
22	X1X2X4	3.8077	4	0.8331	0.7705	9.1833
23	X1X3X4	26.0547	4	0.3575	0.1166	18.0175
24	X2X3X4	11.1370	4	0.6764	0.5551	12.7867
25	X1X2X3X4	5.0000	5	0.8504	0.7649	9.2957

FIGURE 16.16B Using PHStat to Forecast Seasonality with Dummy Variables (Step 4)

Figure 16.16B shows that the four independent variables provided 15 possible combinations to be considered $(2^4 - 1 = 15)$. This figure also shows the adjusted R^2 and the standard error for each of these regression models. Ideally, we're looking for the subset with the highest adjusted R^2 and lowest standard error. The model that meets this criterion (X1X2X4) is highlighted in yellow. To find the regression results for this model, go to the worksheet labeled "3X2" because, in the list of models in Figure 16.16B, we are choosing the second model in the group with three independent variables. Figure 16.16C shows these regression results.

FIGURE 16.16C Using PHStat to Forecast Seasonality with Dummy Variables (Final Result)

	A	B	C	D	E	F	G
1	Best Subsets Analysis						
2							
3	Regression Statistics			Note:			
4	Multiple R	0.9127		This worksheet does not recalculate.			
5	R Square	0.8331		If regression data changes, rerun procedure			
6	Adjusted R Square	0.7705		to create an updated version of this worksheet.			
7	Standard Error	9.1833					
8	Observations	12					
9							
10	ANOVA						
11		df	SS	MS	F	Significance F	
12	Regression	3	3367.5833	1122.5278	13.3106	0.0018	
13	Residual	8	674.6667	84.3333			
14	Total	11	4042.2500				
15							
16		Coefficients	Standard Error	t Stat	P-value	Lower 95%	Upper 95%
17	Intercept	104.1667	6.0591	17.1919	0.0000	90.1944	118.1389
18	Period	2.5000	0.7933	3.1513	0.0136	0.6706	4.3294
19	SD1	33.1667	6.4936	5.1076	0.0009	18.1924	48.1409
20	SD3	18.1667	6.6846	2.7177	0.0263	2.7519	33.5814
21							

The average demand for Quarter 2 is 33.1667 cars more than Quarter 1 (the base quarter). Remember, in Table 16.23 we assigned Quarter 2 as $SD_1 = 1$, $SD_2 = 0$, and $SD_3 = 0$.

As you can see in Figure 16.16C, our final model contains the time period and two of the three seasonal dummy variables (SD_1 and SD_3). This model has an adjusted R^2 equal to 77%, and all three independent variables have p-values less than 0.05. The regression equation that we can use for forecasting is therefore as follows:

$$F_t = 104.1667 + 2.5t + 33.1667SD_1 + 18.1667SD_3$$

Once again, this would be an appropriate time to test for the presence of autocorrelation using the Durbin–Watson statistic. However, because we have less than 15 data points in this example, this test cannot be performed.

We're now ready to put this bad boy to work for us by generating a forecast for the first quarter of 2014 (Period 13, so $t = 13$). According to Table 16.23, the first quarter of any year uses the following seasonal dummy variables:

$$SD_1 = 0 \quad SD_3 = 0$$

Our regression forecast for this quarter is then as follows:

$$F_{13} = 104.1667 + 2.5(13) + 33.1667(0) + 18.1667(0) = 136.7 \approx 137 \text{ cars}$$

We can also forecast car sales for the remaining three quarters in 2014 as follows:

$$\text{Second quarter: } F_{14} = 104.1667 + 2.5(14) + 33.1667(1) + 18.1667(0) = 172.3 \approx 172 \text{ cars}$$
$$\text{Third quarter: } F_{15} = 104.1667 + 2.5(15) + 33.1667(0) + 18.1667(0) = 141.7 \approx 142 \text{ cars}$$
$$\text{Fourth quarter: } F_{16} = 104.1667 + 2.5(16) + 33.1667(0) + 18.1667(1) = 162.3 \approx 162 \text{ cars}$$

I'd be remiss not to check the *MAD* for this forecasting method to see how it compares with our previous models, so let's get to it. First, I'll demonstrate how to calculate the forecasts for the four quarters in 2011 (Periods 1 through 4) and then summarize the remaining calculations. Excel is also an excellent choice for performing these calculations.

2011 Forecasts:

$$\text{First quarter } (t = 1): F_1 = 104.1667 + 2.5(1) + 33.1667(0) + 18.1667(0) = 106.7$$
$$\text{Second quarter } (t = 2): F_2 = 104.1667 + 2.5(2) + 33.1667(1) + 18.1667(0) = 142.3$$
$$\text{Third quarter } (t = 3): F_3 = 104.1667 + 2.5(3) + 33.1667(0) + 18.1667(0) = 111.7$$
$$\text{Fourth quarter } (t = 4): F_4 = 104.1667 + 2.5(4) + 33.1667(0) + 18.1667(1) = 132.3$$

Table 16.25 shows the forecasts for the remaining quarters along with the forecasting errors for the *MAD* calculation.

TABLE 16.25 | DATA AND CALCULATIONS NEEDED TO FIND THE MEAN ABSOLUTE DEVIATION: NEW CAR SALES DATA WITH DUMMY VARIABLES

PERIOD, t	ACTUAL SALES, y_t	SALES FORECAST, F_y	FORECASTING ERROR, $y_t - F_t$	ABSOLUTE FORECASTING ERROR, $\lvert y_t - F_t \rvert$
1	97	106.7	−9.7	9.7
2	142	142.3	−0.3	0.3
3	108	111.7	−3.7	3.7
4	135	132.3	2.7	2.7
5	120	116.7	3.3	3.3
6	164	152.3	1.7	11.7
7	126	121.7	4.3	4.3
8	150	142.3	7.7	7.7
9	123	126.7	−3.7	3.7
10	151	162.3	−11.3	11.3
11	141	131.7	9.3	9.3
12	142	152.3	−10.3	10.3
				$\sum \lvert y_t - F_t \rvert = 78.0$

The average forecasting error for multiple regression with seasonal dummy variables is therefore as follows:

$$MAD = \frac{\sum \lvert y_t - F_t \rvert}{n} = \frac{78.0}{12} = 6.5$$

Table 16.26 compares this result with the previous models in the chapter.

TABLE 16.26 | SUMMARY OF THE MEAN ABSOLUTE DEVIATION FOR VARIOUS FORECASTING METHODS

METHOD	FORECAST	*MAD*
Simple moving average, $p = 3$	145	15.9
Simple moving average, $p = 4$	139	11.1
Weighted moving average, $p = 3$ (3, 2, 1)	143	15.3
Exponential smoothing, $\alpha = 0.6$	142	19.0
Exponential smoothing w/trend, $\alpha = 0.3, \beta = 0.1$	148	16.6
Trend projection	151	13.8
Multiplicative decomposition	134	7.0
Regression with seasonal dummy variables	137	6.5

Remember, one forecasting method will not always provide the best forecast. Regression with seasonal dummy variables was the best method for our car sales data but may not be the best choice for another data set.

It looks like the seasonal dummy variable model gets the trophy, at least for this particular data set. Both the multiplicative decomposition and the regression with seasonal dummy variables should perform fairly well if the overall trend is relatively linear and the seasonal patterns are somewhat consistent from year to year. I would recommend you provide your boss with a sales forecast of 137 cars for the first quarter of 2014 by using the seasonal dummy variable model. Good luck with your new job. You're off to a great start!

Before we call it a day, I get to torture you one last time with the following Your Turn problem that tests your understanding of the use of dummy seasonal variables.

YOUR TURN #10

Using a regression with seasonal dummy variables and data from the Excel file **GPA.xlsx**,forecast your fellow student's GPA for the three semesters of her senior year. Also, calculate the *MAD* for this forecasting method.

Answers can be found on ▶ **pages 826**

16.4 Section Problems

Basic Skills

16.24 Consider the following time series:

	Demand		
Quarter	**Year 1**	**Year 2**	**Year 3**
1	6	8	7
2	11	14	15
3	9	10	14
4	5	7	9

a. Forecast the demand for each quarter in Year 4 using multiplicative decomposition.
b. Interpret the meaning of the seasonal components.
c. Calculate the *MAD* for this forecast.

16.25 Consider the following time series:

	Demand		
Quarter	**Year 1**	**Year 2**	**Year 3**
1	31	28	27
2	18	18	15
3	25	22	20
4	14	6	8

a. Forecast the demand for each quarter in Year 4 using multiplicative decomposition.
b. Interpret the meaning of the seasonal components.
c. Calculate the *MAD* for this forecast.

16.26 Using the time series shown in Problem 16.24, answer the following questions:

a. Forecast the demand for each quarter in Year 4 using seasonal dummy variables and a best subsets regression.
b. Interpret the meaning of the coefficients for the seasonal dummy variables.
c. Calculate the *MAD* for this forecast.

16.27 Using the time series shown in Problem 16.25, answer the following questions:

a. Forecast the demand for each quarter in Year 4 using seasonal dummy variables and a best subsets regression.
b. Interpret the meaning of the coefficients for the seasonal dummy variables.
c. Calculate the *MAD* for this forecast.

Applications

16.28 Suppose Bellevue University accepts new students into its program year-round on a tri-semester schedule (Fall, Spring, and Summer). Forecasting future enrollments helps the school ensure it has the proper resources to accommodate the student body. The following data show the number of students who enrolled each semester for the last four academic years. (Year 4 is the most recent year). These data can also be found in the Excel file **Bellevue.xlsx**.

	Enrollment			
Semester	**Year 1**	**Year 2**	**Year 3**	**Year 4**
Fall	267	278	270	274
Spring	75	69	95	81
Summer	24	37	43	55

a. Construct a graph showing the student enrollment over time.
b. Forecast the student enrollment for each semester in Year 5 using seasonal dummy variables and a best subsets regression.
c. Interpret the meaning of the coefficients for the seasonal dummy variables.
d. Calculate the *MAD* for this forecast.

16.29 Answer the following questions using the data from the Excel file **Bellevue.xlsx** described in Problem 16.28.

a. Forecast the student enrollment for each semester in Year 5 using multiplicative decomposition.
b. Interpret the meaning of the seasonal components.
c. Calculate the *MAD* for this forecast.

16.30 Back in the late 1990s, AOL was the dominant Internet provider. It charged an hourly rate for online access. However, AOL was slow to respond to changes in the Internet business model and lost a significant amount of market share. Today, advertising revenue is a major source of income for the company. The following data show the advertising revenue, in millions of dollars, for each quarter over a recent three-year period. These data can also be found in the Excel file **AOL.xlsx**.

	Revenue (million $)		
Quarter	**2010**	**2011**	**2012**
1	346	313	330
2	297	319	338
3	293	318	340
4	332	364	411

a. Construct a graph showing AOL's advertising revenue over time.
b. Forecast the advertising revenue for each quarter in 2013 using multiplicative decomposition.
c. Interpret the meaning of the seasonal components.
d. Calculate the *MAD* for this forecast.
e. What can you conclude about AOL's business outlook for 2013?

16.31 Answer the following questions using the data from the Excel file **AOL.xlsx** described in Problem 16.30:

a. Forecast the advertising revenue for each quarter in 2013 using seasonal dummy variables and a best subsets regression.
b. Interpret the meaning of the coefficients for the seasonal dummy variables.
c. Calculate the *MAD* for this forecast.

16.32 Diamond Shamrock Corporation produces liquid chlorine that it ships to its customers Monday through Friday by truckload and railcar. To improve its scheduling, the company's plant manager would like to develop a forecasting model to predict the tons of chlorine shipped each day for the following week. The following data show the tons of chlorine shipped each day for the past three weeks. These data can also be found in the Excel file **chlorine.xlsx**.

	Tons per Day Shipped		
Day	**Week 1**	**Week 2**	**Week 3**
Monday	177	168	154
Tuesday	130	130	127
Wednesday	136	122	116
Thursday	147	128	138
Friday	192	160	152

a. Construct a graph showing the tons of chlorine shipped over time.
b. Forecast the tons of chlorine shipped each day next week using seasonal dummy variables and a best subsets regression.
c. Interpret the meaning of the coefficients for the seasonal dummy variables.
d. Calculate the *MAD* for this forecast.

16.33 Answer the following questions using the data from the Excel file **chlorine.xlsx** described in Problem 16.32.

a. Forecast the tons of chlorine shipped each day next week using multiplicative decomposition.
b. Interpret the meaning of the seasonal components.
c. Calculate the *MAD* for this forecast.

16.34 The food service at Goldey-Beacom College provides lunch and dinner for the students Monday through Friday. The food-service manager would like to forecast the sales for each day of the following week to ensure she has enough employees staffing the counter. The following data show the daily sales, in dollars, for the last three weeks. These data can also be found in the Excel file **cafeteria.xlsx**.

	Daily Sales ($)		
Day	**Week 1**	**Week 2**	**Week 3**
Monday	657	718	728
Tuesday	563	561	550
Wednesday	726	740	809
Thursday	539	502	523
Friday	530	587	633

a. Construct a graph showing the food service's daily sales over time.
b. Forecast the sales for each day next week using multiplicative decomposition.
c. Interpret the meaning of the seasonal components.
d. Calculate the *MAD* for this forecast.

16.35 Answer the following questions using the data from the Excel file **cafeteria.xlsx** described in Problem 16.34.

a. Forecast the food service's sales for each day next week using seasonal dummy variables and a best subsets regression.
b. Interpret the meaning of the coefficients for the seasonal dummy variables.
c. Calculate the *MAD* for this forecast.

CHAPTER 16 Summary

- Forecasting is used to predict future values and can be classified as either qualitative or quantitative.
    - Qualitative forecasting relies primarily on a knowledgeable person's intuition and judgment to predict future events.
    - Quantitative forecasting uses historical data and math to predict future events.
- Data values that are associated with specific points in time are known as a time series.
- A time series can consist of four different components.
    - A trend component is present in a time series if a general upward or downward movement can be observed in the data.
    - A seasonal component is present in a time series if a consistent pattern in the data can be associated with a calendar.
    - A cyclical component is defined as movement in the time series that is attributed to upward or downward swings in the U.S. or world economy over a period of several years.
    - A random component is defined as the unpredictable movements in the data that cannot be attributed to either the trend, seasonal, or cyclical components.
- A simple moving average forecast is generated by averaging the most recent p data values in our time series.
- The mean absolute deviation (*MAD*) measures a forecast's accuracy by calculating the average absolute forecasting error per period of historical data.
    - All else being equal, you should choose the forecast with the lower *MAD*.
- A weighted moving average is a smoothing technique that allows weights to be applied to the historical data.
- Exponential smoothing is a technique that adjusts the previous forecast with a portion of the previous period's forecasting error.
    - The smoothing factor, α, which ranges from 0 to 1, determines the amount of the previous forecasting error to be used in the current forecast.
    - Larger alphas cause a forecast to jump around more because they make it more responsive to previous forecasting errors.
- Exponential smoothing with trend adjustment is a technique that compensates for any trends detected in the data when exponential smoothing is used to generate a forecast.
    - In addition to α, this method incorporates a smoothing factor for the trend component, β, which also ranges from 0 to 1.
- A trend projection is a forecasting technique that projects into the future the linear regression equation that best fits the data of a time series.
- The x axis displays the time period of the series, whereas the y axis displays the forecasted variable.
- Residuals describe the difference between the actual and predicted values of the dependent variable for a regression analysis.
- When a systematic error, or pattern, is present in the residuals, the forecasting method is not performing adequately and needs to be revised.
    - This pattern of residuals is known as autocorrelation.
- First-order autocorrelation refers to the correlation that exists when the error of the current time period moves in a consistent pattern with the error from the previous period.

- To determine the presence of autocorrelation, we can use the Durbin–Watson statistic which ranges from 0 to 4, with a value of 0 indicating perfect positive autocorrelation, a value of 2 indicating no autocorrelation, and a value of 4 indicating perfect negative autocorrelation.
    - Positive autocorrelation is present when we observe a pattern of positive residuals in succession or a pattern of negative residuals in succession.
    - Negative autocorrelation is present when the consecutive residuals are far apart from one another, resulting in values that tend to alternate between positive and negative signs.
- Multiplicative decomposition is a technique that multiplies the individual time series components together to generate a forecast.
- A seasonal component reflects the influence that a particular season has on a time series.
- A centered moving average assigns the average value of a set of data points to the center time period.
- The ratio-to-moving-average represents the seasonal and random components in the original time series and is found by dividing the time series value by its centered moving average.
- To isolate the seasonal component, S_t, we first need to identify a seasonal factor, SF, for each period in a season by averaging the ratio-to-moving-averages that are associated with each season.
- We then adjust the seasonal factors to normalized seasonal factors, which add up to the number of seasons in the time series.
- The next step of multiplicative decomposition is to deseasonalize the original data by dividing each value in the time series by its corresponding seasonal component.
- We identify the trend component by performing a regression analysis on the deseasonalized time series.
- To make a forecast using the multiplicative decomposition method, the trend component is determined using the regression equation, which is then multiplied by the appropriate seasonal component.
- Seasonality can be represented by dummy variables in a multiple regression, which allows us to use qualitative variables in the regression model.
- The independent variables in the model would be the time period and the $k - 1$ dummy variables, where k equals the number of seasons in the time series.

CHAPTER 16 Key Terms

Autocorrelation. Describes the condition where residuals from a regression model are not independent from one another.

Centered moving average. The average value of a set of data points assigned to the center time period.

Cyclical component. A movement in a time series that is attributed to upward or downward swings in the U.S. or world economy over a time period of several years.

Durbin–Watson statistic. A statistic used to test for the presence of autocorrelation in a series of residuals.

Exponential smoothing. A forecasting method that adjusts the previous forecast with a portion of the previous period's forecasting error.

Exponential smoothing with trend adjustment. A technique that compensates for any trends detected in the data when exponential smoothing is used to generate a forecast.

Mean absolute deviation (*MAD*). A value that measures the accuracy of a forecast by calculating the average absolute forecasting error per period of historical data.

Multiplicative decomposition. A technique that multiplies the individual time series components together to generate a forecast.

Normalized seasonal factors. Seasonal factors that are adjusted so they add up to the number of seasons in a time series.

Qualitative forecasting. A forecasting method that relies primarily on a knowledgeable person's intuition and judgment to predict future events.

Quantitative forecasting. A forecasting method in which historical data and math are used to predict future events.

Random component. The unpredictable movements in a time series that cannot be attributed to the trend, seasonal, or cyclical components.

Ratio-to-moving-average. A value that represents the seasonal and random components in the original time series and that is found by dividing the time series value by its centered moving average.

Residuals. The difference between the actual and predicted values of the dependent variable for a regression analysis.

Seasonal component. A consistent pattern in a time series that can be associated with a calendar.

Seasonal factors. A factor obtained by averaging the ratio-to-moving averages associated with each season in a time series.

Simple moving average. A forecasting technique that averages the most recent p data values in a time series.

Time series. A group of data values associated with specific points in time.

Trend component. A general upward or downward movement of data in a time series.

Trend projection. A forecasting technique that projects into the future the linear regression equation that best fits the data of a time series.

Weighted moving average. A smoothing technique that allows weights to be applied to the historical data used to generate a forecast.

CHAPTER 16 Equations

16.2 Smoothing Methods (pp 770–784)

Formula 16.1 for the Mean Absolute Deviation (MAD)

$$MAD = \frac{\sum |A_t - F_t|}{n}$$

Formula 16.2 for the Exponential Smoothing Forecast

$$F_t = F_{t-1} + \alpha(A_{t-1} - F_{t-1})$$

Formulas 16.3, 16.4 and 16.5 for the Exponential Smoothing with Trend Adjustment Forecast

$$FIT_t = F_t + T_t$$
$$F_t = FIT_{t-1} + \alpha(A_{t-1} - FIT_{t-1})$$
$$T_t = \beta(F_t - F_{t-1}) + (1 - \beta)T_{t-1}$$

16.3 Forecasting with Regression Analysis (pp 784–796)

Formula 16.6 for the Trend Projection

$$\hat{y}_t = b_0 + b_1 t$$

Formula 16.7 for the Trend Projection Slope

$$b_1 = \frac{n\sum ty - (\sum t)(\sum y)}{n\sum t^2 - (\sum t)^2}$$

Formula 16.8 for the Trend Projection Intercept

$$b_0 = \frac{\sum y}{n} - b_1\left(\frac{\sum t}{n}\right)$$

Formula 16.9 for the Residual

$$e_i = y_i - \hat{y}_i$$

Formula 16.10 for the Durbin–Watson Statistic

$$d = \frac{\sum_{t=2}^{n}(e_t - e_{t-1})^2}{\sum_{t=1}^{n} e_t^2}$$

16.4 Forecasting with Seasonality (pp 797–813)

Formula 16.11 for the Multiplicative Decomposition Model

$$y_t = T_t \times S_t \times R_t$$

Formula 16.12 for the Ratio-to-Moving-Average

$$RMA_t = S_t \times R_t = \frac{y_t}{T_t} = \frac{y_t}{CMA_t}$$

Formula 16.13 for the Deseasonalized Time Series

$$T_t \times R_t = \frac{y_t}{S_t}$$

Formula 16.14 for Forecasting with the Multiplicative Decomposition Method

$$F_t = T_t \times S_t$$

CHAPTER 16 Problems

16.36 Deloitte is a firm that conducts an annual survey that gauges consumer spending expectations during the year-end holiday season. The following data show the percentage of respondents who indicated that they would spend less this year on holiday gifts when compared to the previous year. These data can also be found in the Excel file **Deloitte.xlsx**.

Year	Percentage	Year	Percentage
2005	32	2009	51
2006	29	2010	38
2007	41	2011	42
2008	59	2012	37

Based on: Deloitte Annual Holiday Survey.

a. Using a three-period simple moving average, forecast the percentage of holiday shoppers who intend to spend less in 2013.

b. Calculate the *MAD* for the forecast in part a.

c. Using a three-period weighted moving average with the weights 5, 3, and 1, forecast the percentage of holiday shoppers who intend to spend less in 2013.

d. Calculate the *MAD* for the forecast in part c.

e. Which forecast do you have most confidence in?

16.37 Answer the following questions using the data from the Excel file **Deloitte.xlsx** from Problem 16.36.

a. Using exponential smoothing with $\alpha = 0.6$, forecast the percentage of holiday shoppers who intend to spend less in 2013.

b. Calculate the *MAD* for the forecast in part a.

c. Using exponential smoothing with trend adjustment, $\alpha = 0.6$ and $\beta = 0.4$, forecast the percentage of holiday shoppers who intend to spend less in 2013.

d. Calculate the *MAD* for the forecast in part c.

e. Which forecast do you have most confidence in?

16.38 Dave is a manager of a local AT&T Wireless retail store. He would like to forecast the number of customers walking into his retail store per day to improve his staffing decisions. The following data show the number of customers who entered Dave's store during the last eight days. These data can also be found in the Excel file **daily customers.xlsx**.

Day	1	2	3	4	5	6	7	8
Customers	260	243	232	277	270	285	248	254

a. Forecast the number of customers who will visit Dave's store on Day 9 using a three-period simple moving average.
b. Calculate the *MAD* for the forecast in part a.
c. Forecast the number of customers who will visit Dave's store on Day 9 using exponential smoothing with $\alpha = 0.1$.
d. Calculate the *MAD* for the forecast in part c.
e. In which forecast do you have the most confidence?

16.39 Answer the following questions using the data from the Excel file **daily customers.xlsx** described in Problem 16.38:

a. Forecast the number of customers who will visit Dave's store on Day 9 using a two-period weighted moving average with the weights 5 and 2.
b. Calculate the *MAD* for the forecast in part a.
c. Forecast the number of customers who will visit Dave's store on Day 9 using exponential smoothing with trend adjustment and setting $\alpha = 0.1$ and $\beta = 0.3$.
d. Calculate the *MAD* for the forecast in part c.
e. In which forecast do you have the most confidence?

16.40 Grade inflation, which is defined as an increase in the average GPA of an institution over time without a corresponding increase in academic performance, is a concern for many colleges. The presence of grade inflation could be an indication of lowered academic standards over time. Suppose the following data show the average GPA for the student body at Newark College over the past several years. These data can also be found in the Excel file **grade inflation.xlsx**.

Year	GPA	Year	GPA
2006	2.94	2010	2.85
2007	2.82	2011	3.08
2008	2.90	2012	3.15
2009	2.96	2013	3.10

a. Construct a graph showing the average GPA over time at Newark College.
b. Forecast the average GPA for the student body for 2014 using a trend projection.
c. Is there any indication that grade inflation is present at Newark College? Why or why not?

16.41 Newark College (see Problem 16.40) would like to include seasonality in its GPA forecasting model. The average GPA of the study body for each year was broken down into the average GPA by semester (Fall, Spring, Summer) and can be found in the Excel file **grade inflation by semester.xlsx**.

a. Using multiplicative decomposition, forecast the average GPA for the student body for each semester during 2014.
b. Interpret the meaning of the seasonal components.
c. Calculate the *MAD* for this forecast.

16.42 Answer the following questions using the data from the Excel file **grade inflation by semester.xlsx** described in Problem 16.41:

a. Forecast the average GPA for each semester during 2014 using a multiple regression with seasonal dummy variables.
b. Interpret the meaning of the coefficients for the seasonal dummy variables.
c. Calculate the *MAD* for this forecast.

16.43 Cash bonuses paid to financial investment employees were reduced during the 2007 economic recession and have shown signs of rebounding with the recent recovery. The following data show the average cash bonus, in thousands of dollars, for New York City investment employees over an eight-year period. These data can also be found in the Excel file **average bonus.xlsx**.

Year	Average Bonus ($000)	Year	Average Bonus ($000)
2005	149.8	2009	140.6
2006	191.4	2010	139.0
2007	177.8	2011	111.3
2008	100.9	2012	121.9

a. Using a three-period simple moving average, forecast the average cash bonus for a financial investment employee in New York City in 2013.
b. Calculate the *MAD* for the forecast in part a.
c. Using a two-period weighted moving average with the weights 3 and 2, forecast the average cash bonus for a financial investment employee in New York City in 2013.
d. Calculate the *MAD* for the forecast in part c.
e. Which forecast do you have most confidence in?

16.44 Answer the following questions using the data from the Excel file **average bonus.xlsx** from Problem 16.43.

a. Using exponential smoothing with $\alpha = 0.5$, forecast the average cash bonus for a financial investment employee in New York City in 2013.
b. Calculate the *MAD* for the forecast in part a.
c. Using exponential smoothing with trend adjustment, $\alpha = 0.5$ and $\beta = 0.5$, forecast the average cash bonus for a financial investment employee in New York City in 2013.
d. Calculate the *MAD* for the forecast in part c.
e. Which forecast do you have most confidence in?

16.45 Spain's economy has struggled with very high unemployment rates as a result of the Eurozone banking crisis. The following data show the annual unemployment rate over a nine-year period. These data can also be found in the Excel file **Spain unemployment.xlsx**.

Year	Unemployment Rate (%)	Year	Unemployment Rate (%)
2004	10.4	2009	18.0
2005	9.2	2010	20.1
2006	8.1	2011	21.7
2007	8.3	2012	25.0
2008	11.3		

a. Using a three-period weighted moving average with weights 4, 2, and 1, forecast the unemployment rate for Spain in 2013.
b. Calculate the *MAD* for the forecast in part a.
c. Using exponential smoothing with $\alpha = 0.8$, forecast the unemployment rate for Spain in 2013.
d. Calculate the *MAD* for the forecast in part a.
e. Which forecast do you have most confidence in?

16.46 Answer the following questions using the data from the Excel file **Spain unemployment.xlsx** from Problem 16.45.

a. Construct a graph showing the annual unemployment rate for Spain over time.
b. Forecast the unemployment rate for Spain in 2013 using a trend projection.
c. Calculate the *MAD* for the forecast in part b.

16.47 The Great Smoky Mountain National Park on the border of Tennessee and North Carolina is America's most popular national park with more than nine million visitors each year. Suppose the National Park Service would like to forecast the number of visitors to this park in 2013. The Excel file **Great Smoky Mountain.xlsx** contains the number of visitors each year, in millions, to this park from 1997 until 2012.

a. Construct a graph showing the number of visitors each year visiting the Great Smoky Mountain National Park over time.
b. Forecast the number of visitors each year visiting the Great Smoky Mountain National Park in 2013 using a trend projection.
c. Interpret the meaning of the slope for the trend projection forecast.
d. Calculate the *MAD* for the forecast in part b.
e. Check for the presence of autocorrelation in the forecasting model using $\alpha = 0.05$.

16.48 Answer the following questions using the data from the Excel file **Great Smoky Mountain.xlsx** from Problem 16.47.

a. Using a four-period simple moving average, forecast the number of visitors each year visiting the Great Smoky Mountain National Park in 2013.
b. Calculate the *MAD* for the forecast in part a.
c. Using exponential smoothing with $\alpha = 0.7$, forecast the number of visitors each year visiting the Great Smoky Mountain National Park in 2013.
d. Calculate the *MAD* for the forecast in part c.
e. Which forecast do you have most confidence in?

16.49 Toys Unlimited is an online toy store with a product line that focuses on the preschool children market. Management would like to develop a model to forecast sales, in millions of dollars, for the next four quarters. The Excel file **Toys Unlimited.xlsx** provides sales for each quarter for the previous five years.

a. Forecast Toys Unlimited sales for each quarter next year using a trend projection.
b. Forecast Toys Unlimited sales for each quarter next year using multiplicative decomposition.
c. Interpret the meaning of the seasonal components.
d. Which forecasting method would you choose for Toys Unlimited? Why?

16.50 Answer the following questions using the data from the Excel file **Toys Unlimited.xlsx** from Problem 16.49.

a. Forecast Toys Unlimited sales for each quarter next year using a multiple regression with seasonal dummy variables.
b. Interpret the meaning of the coefficients for the seasonal dummy variables.
c. Calculate the *MAD* for this forecast.

16.51 The U.S. stock market experienced an economic recovery during 2011 and 2012 after a major recession. The data in the Excel file **S&P 500.xlsx** show the end-of-month values for the S&P 500 Index during these two years.

a. Construct a graph showing the S&P Index over time.
b. Forecast the S&P Index for the end of January 2013 using exponential smoothing with $\alpha = 0.2$.
c. Calculate the *MAD* for the forecast in part b.
d. Forecast the S&P Index for the end of January 2013 using exponential smoothing with trend adjustment and setting $\alpha = 0.2$ and $\beta = 0.5$.
e. Calculate the *MAD* for the forecast in part d.
f. In which forecast do you have the most confidence?

16.52 Answer the following questions using the data from the Excel file **S&P 500.xlsx** described in Problem 16.51:

a. Forecast the S&P Index for the end of January 2013 using a trend projection.
b. Check the forecasting model in part a for the presence of autocorrelation using $\alpha = 0.05$.
c. Comment on the appropriateness of using trend projection for these data.

16.53 During the fiscal year 2012, the U.S. Postal Service experienced a record $15.9 billion in losses. In an effort to respond to this financial crisis, the postal service is considering closing many post office facilities that are operating at a loss. To help with this decision, suppose post office authorities would like to forecast the number of pieces of mail to be handled during 2013. Data in the Excel file **postal service.xlsx** show the number of pieces of mail, in billions, delivered by the U.S. Postal Service between 1983 and 2012.

Based on: U.S. Postal Service data.

a. Construct a graph showing the number of pieces of mail delivered over time.

b. Forecast the number of pieces of mail to be delivered during 2013 using a trend projection.

c. Check the forecasting model in part b for the presence of autocorrelation using $\alpha = 0.05$.

d. Comment on the appropriateness of using trend projection for these data.

16.54 There is recent speculation that the Super Bowl games, which determine the NFL champion, are becoming more competitive over time. The competitiveness of the game draws much attention from the gambling industry, which is affected by the winning margin, or point spread, of the outcome. To investigate this theory, I've constructed the Excel file **Super Bowl scores.xlsx**, which provides the winning and losing scores for each Super Bowl from 1986 to 2013.

a. Using these data and a significance level equal to 0.05, determine if the point spread of the game has changed significantly.

b. Provide a forecast for the point spread for the 2014 Super Bowl.

c. What are the limitations of your forecasting model?

CHAPTER 16 Solutions to Your Turn

YOUR TURN #1

a) $SMA(p = 2, \text{Fall, Senior}) = \dfrac{2.7 + 3.3}{2} = \dfrac{6.0}{2} = 3.0$

b)

Semester	Actual GPA, A_t	Forecast GPA, F_t	Forecasting Error, $A_t - F_t$	Absolute Forecasting Error, $\lvert A_t - F_t \rvert$
1	2.5			
2	2.2			
3	2.7	2.35	0.35	0.35
4	3.0	2.45	0.55	0.55
5	2.6	2.85	−0.25	0.25
6	3.0	2.80	0.20	0.20
7	3.2	2.80	0.40	0.40
8	2.7	3.10	−0.40	0.40
9	3.3	2.95	0.35	0.35
				$\sum \lvert A_t - F_t \rvert = 2.5$

$$MAD = \frac{\sum \lvert A_t - F_t \rvert}{n} = \frac{2.5}{7} = 0.357$$

YOUR TURN #2

a. $WMA(p = 2, \text{Fall, Senior}) = \dfrac{(1)(2.7) + (2)(3.3)}{1 + 2}$

$$= \frac{9.3}{3} = 3.1$$

b.

Semester	Actual GPA, A_t	Forecast GPA, F_t	Forecasting Error, $A_t - F_t$	Absolute Forecasting Error, $\lvert A_t - F_t \rvert$
1	2.5			
2	2.2			
3	2.7	2.30	0.40	0.40
4	3.0	2.53	0.47	0.47
5	2.6	2.90	−0.30	0.30
6	3.0	2.73	0.27	0.27
7	3.2	2.87	0.33	0.33
8	2.7	3.13	−0.43	0.43
9	3.3	2.87	0.43	0.43
				$\sum \lvert A_t - F_t \rvert = 2.63$

$$MAD = \frac{\sum \lvert A_t - F_t \rvert}{n} = \frac{2.63}{7} = 0.376.$$

c. The *MAD* for the *WMA* forecast is slightly higher than the *SMA* forecast. Therefore, the *SMA* forecast would be preferable.

YOUR TURN #3

Semester	Actual GPA, A_t	Forecast GPA, F_t	Forecasting Error, $A_t - F_t$	Absolute Forecasting Error, $\|A_t - F_t\|$
1	2.5			
2	2.2	2.50	−0.30	0.30
3	2.7	2.38	0.32	0.32
4	3.0	2.51	0.49	0.49
5	2.6	2.71	−0.11	0.11
6	3.0	2.67	0.33	0.33
7	3.2	2.80	0.40	0.40
8	2.7	2.96	−0.26	0.26
9	3.3	2.86	0.44	0.44
			$\sum \|A_t - F_t\| = 2.65$	

a. $F_{10} = F_9 + \alpha(A_9 - F_9)$

$F_{10} = 2.86 + (0.4)(3.3 - 2.86) = 3.04$

b. $MAD = \dfrac{\sum |A_t - F_t|}{n} = \dfrac{2.65}{8} = 0.331$

YOUR TURN #4

a.

Semester, t	Actual GPA, A_t	Smoothed Forecast, F_t	Trend, T_t	Forecast w/Trend, FIT_t	Absolute Error, $\|A_t - FIT_t\|$
1	2.5	2.50	0	2.5	—
2	2.2	2.50	0	2.5	0.30
3	2.7	2.35	−0.11	2.24	0.46
4	3.0	2.47	0.05	2.52	0.48
5	2.6	2.76	0.22	2.98	0.38
6	3.0	2.79	0.09	2.88	0.12
7	3.2	2.94	0.13	3.07	0.13
8	2.7	3.14	0.18	3.32	0.62
9	3.3	3.01	−0.04	2.97	0.33
				$\sum \|A_t - FIT_t\| = 2.82$	

$F_{10} = FIT_9 + \alpha(A_9 - FIT_9)$

$F_{10} = 2.97 + (0.5)(3.3 - 2.97) = 3.14$

$T_{10} = \beta(F_{10} - F_9) + (1 - \beta)T_9$

$T_{10} = (0.7)(3.14 - 3.01) + (1 - 0.7)(-0.04)$

$T_{10} = 0.09 - 0.01 = 0.08$

$FIT_{10} = F_{10} + T_{10}$

$FIT_{10} = 3.14 + 0.08 = 3.22$

b. $MAD = \dfrac{\sum |A_t - FIT_t|}{n} = \dfrac{2.82}{8} = 0.35$

YOUR TURN #5

a.

Semester, t	GPA, y	ty	t^2
1	2.5	2.5	1
2	2.2	4.4	4
3	2.7	8.1	9
4	3.0	12.0	16
5	2.6	13.0	25
6	3.0	18.0	36
7	3.2	22.4	49
8	2.7	21.6	64
9	3.3	29.7	81
$\sum t = 45$	$\sum y = 25.2$	$\sum ty = 131.7$	$\sum t^2 = 285$

$$b_1 = \frac{n\sum ty - (\sum t)(\sum y)}{n\sum t^2 - (\sum t)^2}$$

$$b_1 = \frac{(9)(131.7) - (45)(25.2)}{(9)(285) - (45)^2}$$

$$b_1 = \frac{1{,}185.3 - 1{,}134}{2{,}565 - 2{,}025} = \frac{51.3}{540} = 0.095$$

$$b_0 = \frac{\sum y}{n} - b_1\left(\frac{\sum t}{n}\right)$$

$$b_0 = \frac{25.2}{9} - (0.095)\left(\frac{45}{9}\right)$$

$$b_0 = 2.8 - (0.095)(5) = 2.325$$

$$\hat{y}_t = 2.325 + 0.095t$$

$$\hat{y}_{10} = 2.325 + 0.095(10) = 3.28$$

b.

Semester, t	Actual GPA, y_t	Forecast GPA, $\hat{y}_t$	Forecasting Error, $y_t - \hat{y}_t$	Absolute Forecasting Error, $\lvert y_t - \hat{y}_t \rvert$
1	2.5	2.42	0.08	0.08
2	2.2	2.52	−0.32	0.32
3	2.7	2.61	0.09	0.09
4	3.0	2.71	0.30	0.30
5	2.6	2.80	−0.20	0.20
6	3.0	2.90	0.11	0.11
7	3.2	2.99	0.21	0.21
8	2.7	3.09	−0.39	0.39
9	3.3	3.18	0.12	0.12
				$\sum \lvert y_t - \hat{y}_t \rvert = 1.82$

$$MAD = \frac{\sum \lvert y_t - \hat{y}_t \rvert}{n} = \frac{1.82}{9} = 0.20$$

	A	B	C	D	E	F	G	H
4	ANOVA							
5		df	SS	MS	F	Significance F		
6	Regression	1	0.5415	0.5415	8.2672	0.0238		
7	Residual	7	0.4585	0.0655				
8	Total	8	1.0000					
9								
10		Coefficients	Standard Error	t Stat	P-value	Lower 95%	Upper 95%	
11	Intercept	2.3250	0.1859	12.5048	0.0000	1.8853	2.7647	
12	Period	0.0950	0.0330	2.8753	0.0207	0.0169	0.1731	
13								
14	Observation	Period	Predicted Y	GPA	Residuals			
15	1	1	2.42	2.5	0.08			
16	2	2	2.52	2.2	-0.32			
17	3	3	2.61	2.7	0.09			
18	4	4	2.71	3.0	0.30			
19	5	5	2.80	2.6	-0.20			
20	6	6	2.90	3.0	0.11			
21	7	7	2.99	3.2	0.21			
22	8	8	3.09	2.7	-0.39			
23	9	9	3.18	3.3	0.12			

YOUR TURN #6

a.

	A	B
1	Durbin-Watson Calculations	
2		
3	Sum of Squared Difference of Residuals	268.6423
4	Sum of Squared Residuals	1086.0972
5		
6	Durbin-Watson Statistic	0.2473

$d = 0.247$

$d_L = 1.16$

$d_U = 1.39$

Because $d < d_L$, we reject the null hypothesis and conclude that positive autocorrelation exists in the permit time series.

b. The regression coefficients for the time series are shown here.

16		Coefficients
17	Intercept	48.9621
18	Period	-1.4299

$$\hat{y}_t = 48.9621 - 1.4299t$$
$$\hat{y}_1 = 48.9621 - 1.4299(1) = 47.53$$
$$e_1 = y_1 - \hat{y}_1 = 36.3 - 47.53 = -11.23$$
$$\hat{y}_2 = 48.9621 - 1.4299(2) = 46.10$$
$$e_2 = y_2 - \hat{y}_2 = 37.9 - 46.10 = -8.20$$
$$(e_2 - e_1)^2 = (-8.20 - (-11.23))^2 = (3.03)^2 = 9.181$$

The following spreadsheet shows the remaining values. Slight differences are due to rounding.

	A	B	C	D	E	F	G
1	Period	Percent	Predicted	Residual			
2	t	y_t	$\hat{y}_t$	e_t	e_{t-1}	$(e_t - e_{t-1})^2$	$(e_t)^2$
3	1	36.3	47.53	-11.23			126.162
4	2	37.9	46.10	-8.20	-11.23	9.180	67.278
5	3	39.9	44.67	-4.77	-8.20	11.764	22.776
6	4	41.6	43.24	-1.64	-4.77	9.796	2.698
7	5	42.7	41.81	0.89	-1.64	6.400	0.787
8	6	41.1	40.38	0.72	0.89	0.029	0.515
9	7	41.4	38.95	2.45	0.72	2.993	5.989
10	8	45.1	37.52	7.58	2.45	26.316	57.412
11	9	47.4	36.09	11.31	7.58	13.912	127.848
12	10	49.7	34.66	15.04	11.31	13.912	226.108
13	11	44.5	33.23	11.27	15.04	14.214	126.941
14	12	39.1	31.80	7.30	11.27	15.762	53.242
15	13	33.7	30.37	3.33	7.30	15.762	11.066
16	14	24.6	28.94	-4.34	3.33	58.830	18.866
17	15	18.3	27.51	-9.21	-4.34	23.718	84.890
18	16	19.7	26.08	-6.38	-9.21	8.008	40.752
19	17	15.0	24.65	-9.65	-6.38	10.694	93.196
20	18	18.8	23.22	-4.42	-9.65	27.352	19.571
21							
22					Total	268.642	1086.097

$$d = \frac{\sum_{t=2}^{n}(e_t - e_{t-1})^2}{\sum_{t=1}^{n} e_t^2} = \frac{268.642}{1{,}086.097} = 0.247$$

YOUR TURN #7

Because we have an odd number of seasons in a year (three), we can calculate the three-period centered moving average and the ratio-to-moving-average for Period 2 as follows:

$$CMA_2 = \frac{2.5 + 2.2 + 2.7}{3} = 2.47$$

$$RMA_2 = \frac{y_2}{CMA_2} = \frac{2.2}{2.47} = 0.8907$$

Continuing with these calculations for the remainder of the time series, we have the following:

Semester	Season	y_t	Three-Period Centered Moving Average	Ratio-to-Moving-Average
1	Fall	2.5		
2	Spring	2.2	2.47	0.8907
3	Summer	2.7	2.63	1.0266
4	Fall	3.0	2.77	1.0830
5	Spring	2.6	2.87	0.9059
6	Summer	3.0	2.93	1.0239
7	Fall	3.2	2.97	1.0774
8	Spring	2.7	3.07	0.8795
9	Summer	3.3		

Next, we calculate the seasonal factors for each semester:

	Fall	Spring	Summer
	1.0830	0.8907	1.0266
	1.0774	0.9059	1.0239
		0.8795	
Average	**1.0802**	**0.8920**	**1.0253**
Total = 2.9975			

Because this total does not equal 3, we need to normalize the seasonal factors, as follows:

$$NSF_{Fall} = \frac{3}{2.9975}(SF_{Fall}) = (1.0008)(1.0802) = 1.0811$$

$$NSF_{Spring} = \frac{3}{2.9975}(SF_{Spring}) = (1.0008)(0.8920) = 0.8927$$

$$NSF_{Summer} = \frac{3}{2.9975}(SF_{Summer}) = (1.0008)(1.0253) = 1.0261$$

$$\text{Total} = 2.999$$

Semester	Season	Seasonal Component
1	Fall	1.0811
2	Spring	0.8927
3	Summer	1.0261
4	Fall	1.0811
5	Spring	0.8927
6	Summer	1.0261
7	Fall	1.0811
8	Spring	0.8927
9	Summer	1.0261

YOUR TURN #8

The deseasonalized GPA for Period 1 would be as follows:

$$\frac{y_1}{S_1} = \frac{2.5}{1.0811} = 2.31$$

Applying this calculation to the remaining semesters results in the following:

Semester	Season	GPA, y_t	Seasonal Component, S_t	Deseasonalized GPA
1	Fall	2.5	1.0811	2.31
2	Spring	2.2	0.8927	2.46
3	Summer	2.7	1.0261	2.63
4	Fall	3.0	1.0811	2.77
5	Spring	2.6	0.8927	2.91
6	Summer	3.0	1.0261	2.92
7	Fall	3.2	1.0811	2.96
8	Spring	2.7	0.8927	3.02
9	Summer	3.3	1.0261	3.22

Using Excel to identify the regression coefficients with the deseasonalized GPA as the dependent variable and the semester as the independent variable provides the following results:

	A	B	C	D	E	F	G
1	Regression Analysis						
2							
3	ANOVA						
4		*df*	*SS*	*MS*	*F*	*Significance F*	
5	Regression	1	0.6263	0.6263	121.3780	0.0000	
6	Residual	7	0.0361	0.0052			
7	Total	8	0.6624				
8							
9		*Coefficients*	*Standard Error*	*t Stat*	*P-value*	*Lower 95%*	*Upper 95%*
10	Intercept	2.2892	0.0522	43.8669	0.0000	2.1658	2.4126
11	Period	0.1022	0.0093	11.0172	0.0000	0.0802	0.1241

The trend component is found with the following regression equation:

$T_t = 2.2892 + 0.1022t$

The forecast for the fall semester in the student's senior year (Period 10) is calculated as follows:

$$F_{10} = T_{10} \times S_{10}$$
$$T_{10} = 2.2892 + (0.1022)(10) = 3.31$$
$$S_{10} = S_{Fall} = 1.0811$$
$$F_{10} = (3.31)(1.0811) = 3.58$$

Performing these calculations with the remaining semesters results in the following:

Semester	Season	Trend Component, T_t	Seasonal Component, S_t	GPA Forecast, F_t
11	Spring	3.41	0.8927	3.04
12	Summer	3.52	1.0261	3.61

YOUR TURN #9

The trend component, T_t, for Period 1 $(t = 1)$ is calculated as follows:

$$T_t = 2.2892 + 0.1022t$$
$$T_1 = 2.2892 + 0.1022(1) = 2.39$$

The seasonal component for the fall semester is $S_1 = 1.0811$. Our GPA forecast for Period 1 is therefore as follows:

$$F_1 = T_1 \times S_1 = (2.39)(1.0811) = 2.58$$

For Period 1, our absolute forecasting error is the following:

$$|y_1 - F_1| = |2.5 - 2.58| = |-0.08| = 0.08$$

The absolute errors for the remaining semesters are as follows:

Semester, t	GPA, y_t	Trend Component, T_t	Seasonal Component, S_t	GPA Forecast, F_t	Absolute Forecasting Error, $\|y_t - F_t\|$
1	2.5	2.39	1.0811	2.58	0.08
2	2.2	2.49	0.8927	2.22	0.02
3	2.7	2.60	1.0261	2.67	0.03
4	3.0	2.70	1.0811	2.92	0.08
5	2.6	2.80	0.8927	2.50	0.10
6	3.0	2.90	1.0261	2.98	0.02
7	3.2	3.01	1.0811	3.25	0.05
8	2.7	3.11	0.8927	2.78	0.08
9	3.3	3.21	1.0261	3.29	0.01
					$\sum \|y_t - F_t\| = 0.47$

$$MAD = \frac{\sum |y_t - F_t|}{n} = \frac{0.47}{9} = 0.052$$

YOUR TURN #10

Because we have three seasons each year (Fall, Spring, Summer), we need two dummy variables, which are defined as follows:

Semester	Season	GPA, y_t	Dummy Variables SD_1	SD_2
1	Fall	2.5	0	0
2	Spring	2.2	1	0
3	Summer	2.7	0	1
4	Fall	3.0	0	0
5	Spring	2.6	1	0
6	Summer	3.0	0	1
7	Fall	3.2	0	0
8	Spring	2.7	1	0
9	Summer	3.3	0	1

The figure below shows the best subsets regression results using PHStat. The two models with the highest adjusted R^2 values have been highlighted.

10	Model	Cp	k+1	R Square	Adj. R Square	Std. Error
11	X1	52.3125	2	0.5415	0.4760	0.2559
12	X2	69.3750	2	0.4050	0.3200	0.2915
13	X3	97.5000	2	0.1800	0.0629	0.3423
14	X1X2	3.6875	3	0.9465	0.9287	0.0944
15	X1X3	47.6081	3	0.5951	0.4602	0.2598
16	X2X3	69.5000	3	0.4200	0.2267	0.3109
17	X1X2X3	4.0000	4	0.9600	0.9360	0.0894

Both highlighted models in the figure above have similar adjusted R^2 values (0.93). The model highlighted in yellow, however, would be preferable because it uses fewer independent variables.

	A	B	C	D	E	F	G
1	Best Subsets Analysis						
2	X1 X2						
3	*Regression Statistics*						
4	Multiple R	0.9729					
5	R Square	0.9465					
6	Adjusted R Square	0.9287					
7	Standard Error	0.0944					
8	Observations	9					
9							
10	ANOVA						
11		*df*	*SS*	*MS*	*F*	*Significance F*	
12	Regression	2	0.9465	0.4733	53.0748	0.0002	
13	Residual	6	0.0535	0.0089			
14	Total	8	1.0000				
15							
16		*Coefficients*	*Standard Error*	*t Stat*	*P-value*	*Lower 95%*	*Upper 95%*
17	Intercept	2.4750	0.0721	34.3175	0.0000	2.2985	2.6515
18	Sem	0.0950	0.0122	7.7929	0.0002	0.0652	0.1248
19	SD1	-0.4500	0.0668	-6.7395	0.0005	-0.6134	-0.2866

The final forecasting equation is as follows:

$$F_t = 2.475 + 0.095t - 0.45SD_1$$

The forecasts for the three semesters during the student's senior year are as follows:

$$\text{Fall semester } (t = 10): F_{10} = 2.475 + 0.095(10) - 0.45(0) = 3.43$$
$$\text{Spring semester } (t = 11): F_{11} = 2.475 + 0.095(11) - 0.45(1) = 3.07$$
$$\text{Summer semester } (t = 12): F_{12} = 2.475 + 0.095(12) - 0.45(0) = 3.62$$

To calculate *MAD*, we need to generate forecasts for the first nine semesters ($t = 1$ through 9). The forecast for the first semester is as follows:

$$\text{Fall semester } (t = 1): F_1 = 2.475 + 0.095(1) - 0.45(0) = 2.57$$

The forecasts for the remaining semesters, along with the forecasting errors, are shown in the following table.

Semester, t	GPA, y_t	GPA Forecast, F_y	Forecasting Error, $y_t - F_t$	Absolute Forecasting Error, $\lvert y_t - F_t \rvert$
1	2.5	2.57	−0.07	0.07
2	2.2	2.22	−0.02	0.02
3	2.7	2.76	−0.06	0.06
4	3.0	2.86	0.14	0.14
5	2.6	2.50	0.10	0.10
6	3.0	3.05	−0.05	0.05
7	3.0	3.14	0.06	0.06
8	2.7	2.79	−0.09	0.09
9	3.3	3.33	−0.03	0.03
				$\sum \lvert y_t - F_t \rvert = 0.62$

$$MAD = \frac{\sum \lvert y_t - F_t \rvert}{n} = \frac{0.62}{9} = 0.069$$

APPENDIX A: Tables

TABLE 1 | Binomial Probabilities

n	x	0.01	0.02	0.03	0.04	0.05	0.06	0.07	0.08	0.09
2	0	0.9801	0.9604	0.9409	0.9216	0.9025	0.8836	0.8649	0.8464	0.8281
	1	0.0198	0.0392	0.0582	0.0768	0.0950	0.1128	0.1302	0.1472	0.1638
	2	0.0001	0.0004	0.0009	0.0016	0.0025	0.0036	0.0049	0.0064	0.0081
3	0	0.9703	0.9412	0.9127	0.8847	0.8574	0.8306	0.8044	0.7787	0.7536
	1	0.0294	0.0576	0.0847	0.1106	0.1354	0.1590	0.1816	0.2031	0.2236
	2	0.0003	0.0012	0.0026	0.0046	0.0071	0.0102	0.0137	0.0177	0.0221
	3	0.0000	0.0000	0.0000	0.0001	0.0001	0.0002	0.0003	0.0005	0.0007
4	0	0.9606	0.9224	0.8853	0.8493	0.8145	0.7807	0.7481	0.7164	0.6857
	1	0.0388	0.0753	0.1095	0.1416	0.1715	0.1993	0.2252	0.2492	0.2713
	2	0.0006	0.0023	0.0051	0.0088	0.0135	0.0191	0.0254	0.0325	0.0402
	3	0.0000	0.0000	0.0001	0.0002	0.0005	0.0008	0.0013	0.0019	0.0027
	4	0.0000	0.0000	0.0000	0.0000	0.0000	0.0000	0.0000	0.0000	0.0001
5	0	0.9510	0.9039	0.8587	0.8154	0.7738	0.7339	0.6957	0.6591	0.6240
	1	0.0480	0.0922	0.1328	0.1699	0.2036	0.2342	0.2618	0.2866	0.3086
	2	0.0010	0.0038	0.0082	0.0142	0.0214	0.0299	0.0394	0.0498	0.0610
	3	0.0000	0.0001	0.0003	0.0006	0.0011	0.0019	0.0030	0.0043	0.0060
	4	0.0000	0.0000	0.0000	0.0000	0.0000	0.0001	0.0001	0.0002	0.0003
	5	0.0000	0.0000	0.0000	0.0000	0.0000	0.0000	0.0000	0.0000	0.0000
6	0	0.9415	0.8858	0.8330	0.7828	0.7351	0.6899	0.6470	0.6064	0.5679
	1	0.0571	0.1085	0.1540	0.1957	0.2321	0.2642	0.2922	0.3164	0.3370
	2	0.0014	0.0055	0.0120	0.0204	0.0305	0.0422	0.0550	0.0688	0.0833
	3	0.0000	0.0002	0.0005	0.0011	0.0021	0.0036	0.0055	0.0080	0.0110
	4	0.0000	0.0000	0.0000	0.0000	0.0001	0.0002	0.0003	0.0005	0.0008
	5	0.0000	0.0000	0.0000	0.0000	0.0000	0.0000	0.0000	0.0000	0.0000
	6	0.0000	0.0000	0.0000	0.0000	0.0000	0.0000	0.0000	0.0000	0.0000
7	0	0.9321	0.8681	0.8080	0.7514	0.6983	0.6485	0.6017	0.5578	0.5168
	1	0.0659	0.1240	0.1749	0.2192	0.2573	0.2897	0.3170	0.3396	0.3578
	2	0.0020	0.0076	0.0162	0.0274	0.0406	0.0555	0.0716	0.0886	0.1061
	3	0.0000	0.0003	0.0008	0.0019	0.0036	0.0059	0.0090	0.0128	0.0175
	4	0.0000	0.0000	0.0000	0.0001	0.0002	0.0004	0.0007	0.0011	0.0017
	5	0.0000	0.0000	0.0000	0.0000	0.0000	0.0000	0.0000	0.0001	0.0001
	6	0.0000	0.0000	0.0000	0.0000	0.0000	0.0000	0.0000	0.0000	0.0000
	7	0.0000	0.0000	0.0000	0.0000	0.0000	0.0000	0.0000	0.0000	0.0000
8	0	0.9227	0.8508	0.7837	0.7214	0.6634	0.6096	0.5596	0.5132	0.4703
	1	0.0746	0.1389	0.1939	0.2405	0.2793	0.3113	0.3370	0.3570	0.3721
	2	0.0026	0.0099	0.0210	0.0351	0.0515	0.0695	0.0888	0.1087	0.1288
	3	0.0001	0.0004	0.0013	0.0029	0.0054	0.0089	0.0134	0.0189	0.0255
	4	0.0000	0.0000	0.0001	0.0002	0.0004	0.0007	0.0013	0.0021	0.0031
	5	0.0000	0.0000	0.0000	0.0000	0.0000	0.0000	0.0001	0.0001	0.0002
	6	0.0000	0.0000	0.0000	0.0000	0.0000	0.0000	0.0000	0.0000	0.0000
	7	0.0000	0.0000	0.0000	0.0000	0.0000	0.0000	0.0000	0.0000	0.0000
	8	0.0000	0.0000	0.0000	0.0000	0.0000	0.0000	0.0000	0.0000	0.0000

(continued)

TABLE 1 | Binomial Probabilities (*Continued*)

n	x	0.01	0.02	0.03	0.04	0.05	0.06	0.07	0.08	0.09
9	0	0.9135	0.8337	0.7602	0.6925	0.6302	0.5730	0.5204	0.4722	0.4279
	1	0.0830	0.1531	0.2116	0.2597	0.2985	0.3292	0.3525	0.3695	0.3809
	2	0.0034	0.0125	0.0262	0.0433	0.0629	0.0840	0.1061	0.1285	0.1507
	3	0.0001	0.0006	0.0019	0.0042	0.0077	0.0125	0.0186	0.0261	0.0348
	4	0.0000	0.0000	0.0001	0.0003	0.0006	0.0012	0.0021	0.0034	0.0052
	5	0.0000	0.0000	0.0000	0.0000	0.0000	0.0001	0.0002	0.0003	0.0005
	6	0.0000	0.0000	0.0000	0.0000	0.0000	0.0000	0.0000	0.0000	0.0000
	7	0.0000	0.0000	0.0000	0.0000	0.0000	0.0000	0.0000	0.0000	0.0000
	8	0.0000	0.0000	0.0000	0.0000	0.0000	0.0000	0.0000	0.0000	0.0000
	9	0.0000	0.0000	0.0000	0.0000	0.0000	0.0000	0.0000	0.0000	0.0000
10	0	0.9044	0.8171	0.7374	0.6648	0.5987	0.5386	0.4840	0.4344	0.3894
	1	0.0914	0.1667	0.2281	0.2770	0.3151	0.3438	0.3643	0.3777	0.3851
	2	0.0042	0.0153	0.0317	0.0519	0.0746	0.0988	0.1234	0.1478	0.1714
	3	0.0001	0.0008	0.0026	0.0058	0.0105	0.0168	0.0248	0.0343	0.0452
	4	0.0000	0.0000	0.0001	0.0004	0.0010	0.0019	0.0033	0.0052	0.0078
	5	0.0000	0.0000	0.0000	0.0000	0.0001	0.0001	0.0003	0.0005	0.0009
	6	0.0000	0.0000	0.0000	0.0000	0.0000	0.0000	0.0000	0.0000	0.0001
	7	0.0000	0.0000	0.0000	0.0000	0.0000	0.0000	0.0000	0.0000	0.0000
	8	0.0000	0.0000	0.0000	0.0000	0.0000	0.0000	0.0000	0.0000	0.0000
	9	0.0000	0.0000	0.0000	0.0000	0.0000	0.0000	0.0000	0.0000	0.0000
	10	0.0000	0.0000	0.0000	0.0000	0.0000	0.0000	0.0000	0.0000	0.0000
11	0	0.8953	0.8007	0.7153	0.6382	0.5688	0.5063	0.4501	0.3996	0.3544
	1	0.0995	0.1798	0.2433	0.2925	0.3293	0.3555	0.3727	0.3823	0.3855
	2	0.0050	0.0183	0.0376	0.0609	0.0867	0.1135	0.1403	0.1662	0.1906
	3	0.0002	0.0011	0.0035	0.0076	0.0137	0.0217	0.0317	0.0434	0.0566
	4	0.0000	0.0000	0.0002	0.0006	0.0014	0.0028	0.0048	0.0075	0.0112
	5	0.0000	0.0000	0.0000	0.0000	0.0001	0.0002	0.0005	0.0009	0.0015
	6	0.0000	0.0000	0.0000	0.0000	0.0000	0.0000	0.0000	0.0001	0.0002
	7	0.0000	0.0000	0.0000	0.0000	0.0000	0.0000	0.0000	0.0000	0.0000
	8	0.0000	0.0000	0.0000	0.0000	0.0000	0.0000	0.0000	0.0000	0.0000
	9	0.0000	0.0000	0.0000	0.0000	0.0000	0.0000	0.0000	0.0000	0.0000
	10	0.0000	0.0000	0.0000	0.0000	0.0000	0.0000	0.0000	0.0000	0.0000
	11	0.0000	0.0000	0.0000	0.0000	0.0000	0.0000	0.0000	0.0000	0.0000
12	0	0.8864	0.7847	0.6938	0.6127	0.5404	0.4759	0.4186	0.3677	0.3225
	1	0.1074	0.1922	0.2575	0.3064	0.3413	0.3645	0.3781	0.3837	0.3827
	2	0.0060	0.0216	0.0438	0.0702	0.0988	0.1280	0.1565	0.1835	0.2082
	3	0.0002	0.0015	0.0045	0.0098	0.0173	0.0272	0.0393	0.0532	0.0686
	4	0.0000	0.0001	0.0003	0.0009	0.0021	0.0039	0.0067	0.0104	0.0153
	5	0.0000	0.0000	0.0000	0.0001	0.0002	0.0004	0.0008	0.0014	0.0024
	6	0.0000	0.0000	0.0000	0.0000	0.0000	0.0000	0.0001	0.0001	0.0003
	7	0.0000	0.0000	0.0000	0.0000	0.0000	0.0000	0.0000	0.0000	0.0000
	8	0.0000	0.0000	0.0000	0.0000	0.0000	0.0000	0.0000	0.0000	0.0000
	9	0.0000	0.0000	0.0000	0.0000	0.0000	0.0000	0.0000	0.0000	0.0000
	10	0.0000	0.0000	0.0000	0.0000	0.0000	0.0000	0.0000	0.0000	0.0000
	11	0.0000	0.0000	0.0000	0.0000	0.0000	0.0000	0.0000	0.0000	0.0000
	12	0.0000	0.0000	0.0000	0.0000	0.0000	0.0000	0.0000	0.0000	0.0000

TABLE 1 | Binomial Probabilities *(Continued)*

n	*x*	0.01	0.02	0.03	0.04	0.05	0.06	0.07	0.08	0.09
13	0	0.8775	0.7690	0.6730	0.5882	0.5133	0.4474	0.3893	0.3383	0.2935
	1	0.1152	0.2040	0.2706	0.3186	0.3512	0.3712	0.3809	0.3824	0.3773
	2	0.0070	0.0250	0.0502	0.0797	0.1109	0.1422	0.1720	0.1995	0.2239
	3	0.0003	0.0019	0.0057	0.0122	0.0214	0.0333	0.0475	0.0636	0.0812
	4	0.0000	0.0001	0.0004	0.0013	0.0028	0.0053	0.0089	0.0138	0.0201
	5	0.0000	0.0000	0.0000	0.0001	0.0003	0.0006	0.0012	0.0022	0.0036
	6	0.0000	0.0000	0.0000	0.0000	0.0000	0.0001	0.0001	0.0003	0.0005
	7	0.0000	0.0000	0.0000	0.0000	0.0000	0.0000	0.0000	0.0000	0.0000
	8	0.0000	0.0000	0.0000	0.0000	0.0000	0.0000	0.0000	0.0000	0.0000
	9	0.0000	0.0000	0.0000	0.0000	0.0000	0.0000	0.0000	0.0000	0.0000
	10	0.0000	0.0000	0.0000	0.0000	0.0000	0.0000	0.0000	0.0000	0.0000
	11	0.0000	0.0000	0.0000	0.0000	0.0000	0.0000	0.0000	0.0000	0.0000
	12	0.0000	0.0000	0.0000	0.0000	0.0000	0.0000	0.0000	0.0000	0.0000
	13	0.0000	0.0000	0.0000	0.0000	0.0000	0.0000	0.0000	0.0000	0.0000
14	0	0.8687	0.7536	0.6528	0.5647	0.4877	0.4205	0.3620	0.3112	0.2670
	1	0.1229	0.2153	0.2827	0.3294	0.3593	0.3758	0.3815	0.3788	0.3698
	2	0.0081	0.0286	0.0568	0.0892	0.1229	0.1559	0.1867	0.2141	0.2377
	3	0.0003	0.0023	0.0070	0.0149	0.0259	0.0398	0.0562	0.0745	0.0940
	4	0.0000	0.0001	0.0006	0.0017	0.0037	0.0070	0.0116	0.0178	0.0256
	5	0.0000	0.0000	0.0000	0.0001	0.0004	0.0009	0.0018	0.0031	0.0051
	6	0.0000	0.0000	0.0000	0.0000	0.0000	0.0001	0.0002	0.0004	0.0008
	7	0.0000	0.0000	0.0000	0.0000	0.0000	0.0000	0.0000	0.0000	0.0001
	8	0.0000	0.0000	0.0000	0.0000	0.0000	0.0000	0.0000	0.0000	0.0000
	9	0.0000	0.0000	0.0000	0.0000	0.0000	0.0000	0.0000	0.0000	0.0000
	10	0.0000	0.0000	0.0000	0.0000	0.0000	0.0000	0.0000	0.0000	0.0000
	11	0.0000	0.0000	0.0000	0.0000	0.0000	0.0000	0.0000	0.0000	0.0000
	12	0.0000	0.0000	0.0000	0.0000	0.0000	0.0000	0.0000	0.0000	0.0000
	13	0.0000	0.0000	0.0000	0.0000	0.0000	0.0000	0.0000	0.0000	0.0000
	14	0.0000	0.0000	0.0000	0.0000	0.0000	0.0000	0.0000	0.0000	0.0000
15	0	0.8601	0.7386	0.6333	0.5421	0.4633	0.3953	0.3367	0.2863	0.2430
	1	0.1303	0.2261	0.2938	0.3388	0.3658	0.3785	0.3801	0.3734	0.3605
	2	0.0092	0.0323	0.0636	0.0988	0.1348	0.1691	0.2003	0.2273	0.2496
	3	0.0004	0.0029	0.0085	0.0178	0.0307	0.0468	0.0653	0.0857	0.1070
	4	0.0000	0.0002	0.0008	0.0022	0.0049	0.0090	0.0148	0.0223	0.0317
	5	0.0000	0.0000	0.0001	0.0002	0.0006	0.0013	0.0024	0.0043	0.0069
	6	0.0000	0.0000	0.0000	0.0000	0.0000	0.0001	0.0003	0.0006	0.0011
	7	0.0000	0.0000	0.0000	0.0000	0.0000	0.0000	0.0000	0.0001	0.0001
	8	0.0000	0.0000	0.0000	0.0000	0.0000	0.0000	0.0000	0.0000	0.0000
	9	0.0000	0.0000	0.0000	0.0000	0.0000	0.0000	0.0000	0.0000	0.0000
	10	0.0000	0.0000	0.0000	0.0000	0.0000	0.0000	0.0000	0.0000	0.0000
	11	0.0000	0.0000	0.0000	0.0000	0.0000	0.0000	0.0000	0.0000	0.0000
	12	0.0000	0.0000	0.0000	0.0000	0.0000	0.0000	0.0000	0.0000	0.0000
	13	0.0000	0.0000	0.0000	0.0000	0.0000	0.0000	0.0000	0.0000	0.0000
	14	0.0000	0.0000	0.0000	0.0000	0.0000	0.0000	0.0000	0.0000	0.0000
	15	0.0000	0.0000	0.0000	0.0000	0.0000	0.0000	0.0000	0.0000	0.0000

(continued)

TABLE 1 | Binomial Probabilities *(Continued)*

n	x	0.01	0.02	0.03	0.04	0.05	0.06	0.07	0.08	0.09
20	0	0.8179	0.6676	0.5438	0.4420	0.3585	0.2901	0.2342	0.1887	0.1516
	1	0.1652	0.2725	0.3364	0.3683	0.3774	0.3703	0.3526	0.3282	0.3000
	2	0.0159	0.0528	0.0988	0.1458	0.1887	0.2246	0.2521	0.2711	0.2818
	3	0.0010	0.0065	0.0183	0.0364	0.0596	0.0860	0.1139	0.1414	0.1672
	4	0.0000	0.0006	0.0024	0.0065	0.0133	0.0233	0.0364	0.0523	0.0703
	5	0.0000	0.0000	0.0002	0.0009	0.0022	0.0048	0.0088	0.0145	0.0222
	6	0.0000	0.0000	0.0000	0.0001	0.0003	0.0008	0.0017	0.0032	0.0055
	7	0.0000	0.0000	0.0000	0.0000	0.0000	0.0001	0.0002	0.0005	0.0011
	8	0.0000	0.0000	0.0000	0.0000	0.0000	0.0000	0.0000	0.0001	0.0002
	9	0.0000	0.0000	0.0000	0.0000	0.0000	0.0000	0.0000	0.0000	0.0000
	10	0.0000	0.0000	0.0000	0.0000	0.0000	0.0000	0.0000	0.0000	0.0000
	11	0.0000	0.0000	0.0000	0.0000	0.0000	0.0000	0.0000	0.0000	0.0000
	12	0.0000	0.0000	0.0000	0.0000	0.0000	0.0000	0.0000	0.0000	0.0000
	13	0.0000	0.0000	0.0000	0.0000	0.0000	0.0000	0.0000	0.0000	0.0000
	14	0.0000	0.0000	0.0000	0.0000	0.0000	0.0000	0.0000	0.0000	0.0000
	15	0.0000	0.0000	0.0000	0.0000	0.0000	0.0000	0.0000	0.0000	0.0000
	16	0.0000	0.0000	0.0000	0.0000	0.0000	0.0000	0.0000	0.0000	0.0000
	17	0.0000	0.0000	0.0000	0.0000	0.0000	0.0000	0.0000	0.0000	0.0000
	18	0.0000	0.0000	0.0000	0.0000	0.0000	0.0000	0.0000	0.0000	0.0000
	19	0.0000	0.0000	0.0000	0.0000	0.0000	0.0000	0.0000	0.0000	0.0000
	20	0.0000	0.0000	0.0000	0.0000	0.0000	0.0000	0.0000	0.0000	0.0000

n	x	0.1	0.15	0.2	0.25	0.3	0.35	0.4	0.45	0.5
2	0	0.8100	0.7225	0.6400	0.5625	0.4900	0.4225	0.3600	0.3025	0.2500
	1	0.1800	0.2550	0.3200	0.3750	0.4200	0.4550	0.4800	0.4950	0.5000
	2	0.0100	0.0225	0.0400	0.0625	0.0900	0.1225	0.1600	0.2025	0.2500
3	0	0.7290	0.6141	0.5120	0.4219	0.3430	0.2746	0.2160	0.1664	0.1250
	1	0.2430	0.3251	0.3840	0.4219	0.4410	0.4436	0.4320	0.4084	0.3750
	2	0.0270	0.0574	0.0960	0.1406	0.1890	0.2389	0.2880	0.3341	0.3750
	3	0.0010	0.0034	0.0080	0.0156	0.0270	0.0429	0.0640	0.0911	0.1250
4	0	0.6561	0.5220	0.4096	0.3164	0.2401	0.1785	0.1296	0.0915	0.0625
	1	0.2916	0.3685	0.4096	0.4219	0.4116	0.3845	0.3456	0.2995	0.2500
	2	0.0486	0.0975	0.1536	0.2109	0.2646	0.3105	0.3456	0.3675	0.3750
	3	0.0036	0.0115	0.0256	0.0469	0.0756	0.1115	0.1536	0.2005	0.2500
	4	0.0001	0.0005	0.0016	0.0039	0.0081	0.0150	0.0256	0.0410	0.0625
5	0	0.5905	0.4437	0.3277	0.2373	0.1681	0.1160	0.0778	0.0503	0.0313
	1	0.3281	0.3915	0.4096	0.3955	0.3602	0.3124	0.2592	0.2059	0.1563
	2	0.0729	0.1382	0.2048	0.2637	0.3087	0.3364	0.3456	0.3369	0.3125
	3	0.0081	0.0244	0.0512	0.0879	0.1323	0.1811	0.2304	0.2757	0.3125
	4	0.0005	0.0022	0.0064	0.0146	0.0284	0.0488	0.0768	0.1128	0.1563
	5	0.0000	0.0001	0.0003	0.0010	0.0024	0.0053	0.0102	0.0185	0.0313
6	0	0.5314	0.3771	0.2621	0.1780	0.1176	0.0754	0.0467	0.0277	0.0156
	1	0.3543	0.3993	0.3932	0.3560	0.3025	0.2437	0.1866	0.1359	0.0938
	2	0.0984	0.1762	0.2458	0.2966	0.3241	0.3280	0.3110	0.2780	0.2344
	3	0.0146	0.0415	0.0819	0.1318	0.1852	0.2355	0.2765	0.3032	0.3125

TABLE 1 | Binomial Probabilities *(Continued)*

n	x	0.1	0.15	0.2	0.25	0.3	0.35	0.4	0.45	0.5
	4	0.0012	0.0055	0.0154	0.0330	0.0595	0.0951	0.1382	0.1861	0.2344
	5	0.0001	0.0004	0.0015	0.0044	0.0102	0.0205	0.0369	0.0609	0.0938
	6	0.0000	0.0000	0.0001	0.0002	0.0007	0.0018	0.0041	0.0083	0.0156
7	0	0.4783	0.3206	0.2097	0.1335	0.0824	0.0490	0.0280	0.0152	0.0078
	1	0.3720	0.3960	0.3670	0.3115	0.2471	0.1848	0.1306	0.0872	0.0547
	2	0.1240	0.2097	0.2753	0.3115	0.3177	0.2985	0.2613	0.2140	0.1641
	3	0.0230	0.0617	0.1147	0.1730	0.2269	0.2679	0.2903	0.2918	0.2734
	4	0.0026	0.0109	0.0287	0.0577	0.0972	0.1442	0.1935	0.2388	0.2734
	5	0.0002	0.0012	0.0043	0.0115	0.0250	0.0466	0.0774	0.1172	0.1641
	6	0.0000	0.0001	0.0004	0.0013	0.0036	0.0084	0.0172	0.0320	0.0547
	7	0.0000	0.0000	0.0000	0.0001	0.0002	0.0006	0.0016	0.0037	0.0078
8	0	0.4305	0.2725	0.1678	0.1001	0.0576	0.0319	0.0168	0.0084	0.0039
	1	0.3826	0.3847	0.3355	0.2670	0.1977	0.1373	0.0896	0.0548	0.0313
	2	0.1488	0.2376	0.2936	0.3115	0.2965	0.2587	0.2090	0.1569	0.1094
	3	0.0331	0.0839	0.1468	0.2076	0.2541	0.2786	0.2787	0.2568	0.2188
	4	0.0046	0.0185	0.0459	0.0865	0.1361	0.1875	0.2322	0.2627	0.2734
	5	0.0004	0.0026	0.0092	0.0231	0.0467	0.0808	0.1239	0.1719	0.2188
	6	0.0000	0.0002	0.0011	0.0038	0.0100	0.0217	0.0413	0.0703	0.1094
	7	0.0000	0.0000	0.0001	0.0004	0.0012	0.0033	0.0079	0.0164	0.0313
	8	0.0000	0.0000	0.0000	0.0000	0.0001	0.0002	0.0007	0.0017	0.0039
9	0	0.3874	0.2316	0.1342	0.0751	0.0404	0.0207	0.0101	0.0046	0.0020
	1	0.3874	0.3679	0.3020	0.2253	0.1556	0.1004	0.0605	0.0339	0.0176
	2	0.1722	0.2597	0.3020	0.3003	0.2668	0.2162	0.1612	0.1110	0.0703
	3	0.0446	0.1069	0.1762	0.2336	0.2668	0.2716	0.2508	0.2119	0.1641
	4	0.0074	0.0283	0.0661	0.1168	0.1715	0.2194	0.2508	0.2600	0.2461
	5	0.0008	0.0050	0.0165	0.0389	0.0735	0.1181	0.1672	0.2128	0.2461
	6	0.0001	0.0006	0.0028	0.0087	0.0210	0.0424	0.0743	0.1160	0.1641
	7	0.0000	0.0000	0.0003	0.0012	0.0039	0.0098	0.0212	0.0407	0.0703
	8	0.0000	0.0000	0.0000	0.0001	0.0004	0.0013	0.0035	0.0083	0.0176
	9	0.0000	0.0000	0.0000	0.0000	0.0000	0.0001	0.0003	0.0008	0.0020
10	0	0.3487	0.1969	0.1074	0.0563	0.0282	0.0135	0.0060	0.0025	0.0010
	1	0.3874	0.3474	0.2684	0.1877	0.1211	0.0725	0.0403	0.0207	0.0098
	2	0.1937	0.2759	0.3020	0.2816	0.2335	0.1757	0.1209	0.0763	0.0439
	3	0.0574	0.1298	0.2013	0.2503	0.2668	0.2522	0.2150	0.1665	0.1172
	4	0.0112	0.0401	0.0881	0.1460	0.2001	0.2377	0.2508	0.2384	0.2051
	5	0.0015	0.0085	0.0264	0.0584	0.1029	0.1536	0.2007	0.2340	0.2461
	6	0.0001	0.0012	0.0055	0.0162	0.0368	0.0689	0.1115	0.1596	0.2051
	7	0.0000	0.0001	0.0008	0.0031	0.0090	0.0212	0.0425	0.0746	0.1172
	8	0.0000	0.0000	0.0001	0.0004	0.0014	0.0043	0.0106	0.0229	0.0439
	9	0.0000	0.0000	0.0000	0.0000	0.0001	0.0005	0.0016	0.0042	0.0098
	10	0.0000	0.0000	0.0000	0.0000	0.0000	0.0000	0.0001	0.0003	0.0010
11	0	0.3138	0.1673	0.0859	0.0422	0.0198	0.0088	0.0036	0.0014	0.0005
	1	0.3835	0.3248	0.2362	0.1549	0.0932	0.0518	0.0266	0.0125	0.0054
	2	0.2131	0.2866	0.2953	0.2581	0.1998	0.1395	0.0887	0.0513	0.0269

(continued)

TABLE 1 | Binomial Probabilities (Continued)

n	x	0.1	0.15	0.2	0.25	0.3	0.35	0.4	0.45	0.5
	3	0.0710	0.1517	0.2215	0.2581	0.2568	0.2254	0.1774	0.1259	0.0806
	4	0.0158	0.0536	0.1107	0.1721	0.2201	0.2428	0.2365	0.2060	0.1611
	5	0.0025	0.0132	0.0388	0.0803	0.1321	0.1830	0.2207	0.2360	0.2256
	6	0.0003	0.0023	0.0097	0.0268	0.0566	0.0985	0.1471	0.1931	0.2256
	7	0.0000	0.0003	0.0017	0.0064	0.0173	0.0379	0.0701	0.1128	0.1611
	8	0.0000	0.0000	0.0002	0.0011	0.0037	0.0102	0.0234	0.0462	0.0806
	9	0.0000	0.0000	0.0000	0.0001	0.0005	0.0018	0.0052	0.0126	0.0269
	10	0.0000	0.0000	0.0000	0.0000	0.0000	0.0002	0.0007	0.0021	0.0054
	11	0.0000	0.0000	0.0000	0.0000	0.0000	0.0000	0.0000	0.0002	0.0005
12	0	0.2824	0.1422	0.0687	0.0317	0.0138	0.0057	0.0022	0.0008	0.0002
	1	0.3766	0.3012	0.2062	0.1267	0.0712	0.0368	0.0174	0.0075	0.0029
	2	0.2301	0.2924	0.2835	0.2323	0.1678	0.1088	0.0639	0.0339	0.0161
	3	0.0852	0.1720	0.2362	0.2581	0.2397	0.1954	0.1419	0.0923	0.0537
	4	0.0213	0.0683	0.1329	0.1936	0.2311	0.2367	0.2128	0.1700	0.1208
	5	0.0038	0.0193	0.0532	0.1032	0.1585	0.2039	0.2270	0.2225	0.1934
	6	0.0005	0.0040	0.0155	0.0401	0.0792	0.1281	0.1766	0.2124	0.2256
	7	0.0000	0.0006	0.0033	0.0115	0.0291	0.0591	0.1009	0.1489	0.1934
	8	0.0000	0.0001	0.0005	0.0024	0.0078	0.0199	0.0420	0.0762	0.1208
	9	0.0000	0.0000	0.0001	0.0004	0.0015	0.0048	0.0125	0.0277	0.0537
	10	0.0000	0.0000	0.0000	0.0000	0.0002	0.0008	0.0025	0.0068	0.0161
	11	0.0000	0.0000	0.0000	0.0000	0.0000	0.0001	0.0003	0.0010	0.0029
	12	0.0000	0.0000	0.0000	0.0000	0.0000	0.0000	0.0000	0.0001	0.0002
13	0	0.2542	0.1209	0.0550	0.0238	0.0097	0.0037	0.0013	0.0004	0.0001
	1	0.3672	0.2774	0.1787	0.1029	0.0540	0.0259	0.0113	0.0045	0.0016
	2	0.2448	0.2937	0.2680	0.2059	0.1388	0.0836	0.0453	0.0220	0.0095
	3	0.0997	0.1900	0.2457	0.2517	0.2181	0.1651	0.1107	0.0660	0.0349
	4	0.0277	0.0838	0.1535	0.2097	0.2337	0.2222	0.1845	0.1350	0.0873
	5	0.0055	0.0266	0.0691	0.1258	0.1803	0.2154	0.2214	0.1989	0.1571
	6	0.0008	0.0063	0.0230	0.0559	0.1030	0.1546	0.1968	0.2169	0.2095
	7	0.0001	0.0011	0.0058	0.0186	0.0442	0.0833	0.1312	0.1775	0.2095
	8	0.0000	0.0001	0.0011	0.0047	0.0142	0.0336	0.0656	0.1089	0.1571
	9	0.0000	0.0000	0.0001	0.0009	0.0034	0.0101	0.0243	0.0495	0.0873
	10	0.0000	0.0000	0.0000	0.0001	0.0006	0.0022	0.0065	0.0162	0.0349
	11	0.0000	0.0000	0.0000	0.0000	0.0001	0.0003	0.0012	0.0036	0.0095
	12	0.0000	0.0000	0.0000	0.0000	0.0000	0.0000	0.0001	0.0005	0.0016
	13	0.0000	0.0000	0.0000	0.0000	0.0000	0.0000	0.0000	0.0000	0.0001
14	0	0.2288	0.1028	0.0440	0.0178	0.0068	0.0024	0.0008	0.0002	0.0001
	1	0.3559	0.2539	0.1539	0.0832	0.0407	0.0181	0.0073	0.0027	0.0009
	2	0.2570	0.2912	0.2501	0.1802	0.1134	0.0634	0.0317	0.0141	0.0056
	3	0.1142	0.2056	0.2501	0.2402	0.1943	0.1366	0.0845	0.0462	0.0222
	4	0.0349	0.0998	0.1720	0.2202	0.2290	0.2022	0.1549	0.1040	0.0611
	5	0.0078	0.0352	0.0860	0.1468	0.1963	0.2178	0.2066	0.1701	0.1222
	6	0.0013	0.0093	0.0322	0.0734	0.1262	0.1759	0.2066	0.2088	0.1833
	7	0.0002	0.0019	0.0092	0.0280	0.0618	0.1082	0.1574	0.1952	0.2095
	8	0.0000	0.0003	0.0020	0.0082	0.0232	0.0510	0.0918	0.1398	0.1833
	9	0.0000	0.0000	0.0003	0.0018	0.0066	0.0183	0.0408	0.0762	0.1222

TABLE 1 | Binomial Probabilities (*Continued*)

n	*x*	0.1	0.15	0.2	0.25	0.3	0.35	0.4	0.45	0.5
	10	0.0000	0.0000	0.0000	0.0003	0.0014	0.0049	0.0136	0.0312	0.0611
	11	0.0000	0.0000	0.0000	0.0000	0.0002	0.0010	0.0033	0.0093	0.0222
	12	0.0000	0.0000	0.0000	0.0000	0.0000	0.0001	0.0005	0.0019	0.0056
	13	0.0000	0.0000	0.0000	0.0000	0.0000	0.0000	0.0001	0.0002	0.0009
	14	0.0000	0.0000	0.0000	0.0000	0.0000	0.0000	0.0000	0.0000	0.0001
15	0	0.2059	0.0874	0.0352	0.0134	0.0047	0.0016	0.0005	0.0001	0.0000
	1	0.3432	0.2312	0.1319	0.0668	0.0305	0.0126	0.0047	0.0016	0.0005
	2	0.2669	0.2856	0.2309	0.1559	0.0916	0.0476	0.0219	0.0090	0.0032
	3	0.1285	0.2184	0.2501	0.2252	0.1700	0.1110	0.0634	0.0318	0.0139
	4	0.0428	0.1156	0.1876	0.2252	0.2186	0.1792	0.1268	0.0780	0.0417
	5	0.0105	0.0449	0.1032	0.1651	0.2061	0.2123	0.1859	0.1404	0.0916
	6	0.0019	0.0132	0.0430	0.0917	0.1472	0.1906	0.2066	0.1914	0.1527
	7	0.0003	0.0030	0.0138	0.0393	0.0811	0.1319	0.1771	0.2013	0.1964
	8	0.0000	0.0005	0.0035	0.0131	0.0348	0.0710	0.1181	0.1647	0.1964
	9	0.0000	0.0001	0.0007	0.0034	0.0116	0.0298	0.0612	0.1048	0.1527
	10	0.0000	0.0000	0.0001	0.0007	0.0030	0.0096	0.0245	0.0515	0.0916
	11	0.0000	0.0000	0.0000	0.0001	0.0006	0.0024	0.0074	0.0191	0.0417
	12	0.0000	0.0000	0.0000	0.0000	0.0001	0.0004	0.0016	0.0052	0.0139
	13	0.0000	0.0000	0.0000	0.0000	0.0000	0.0001	0.0003	0.0010	0.0032
	14	0.0000	0.0000	0.0000	0.0000	0.0000	0.0000	0.0000	0.0001	0.0005
	15	0.0000	0.0000	0.0000	0.0000	0.0000	0.0000	0.0000	0.0000	0.0000
20	0	0.1216	0.0388	0.0115	0.0032	0.0008	0.0002	0.0000	0.0000	0.0000
	1	0.2702	0.1368	0.0576	0.0211	0.0068	0.0020	0.0005	0.0001	0.0000
	2	0.2852	0.2293	0.1369	0.0669	0.0278	0.0100	0.0031	0.0008	0.0002
	3	0.1901	0.2428	0.2054	0.1339	0.0716	0.0323	0.0123	0.0040	0.0011
	4	0.0898	0.1821	0.2182	0.1897	0.1304	0.0738	0.0350	0.0139	0.0046
	5	0.0319	0.1028	0.1746	0.2023	0.1789	0.1272	0.0746	0.0365	0.0148
	6	0.0089	0.0454	0.1091	0.1686	0.1916	0.1712	0.1244	0.0746	0.0370
	7	0.0020	0.0160	0.0545	0.1124	0.1643	0.1844	0.1659	0.1221	0.0739
	8	0.0004	0.0046	0.0222	0.0609	0.1144	0.1614	0.1797	0.1623	0.1201
	9	0.0001	0.0011	0.0074	0.0271	0.0654	0.1158	0.1597	0.1771	0.1602
	10	0.0000	0.0002	0.0020	0.0099	0.0308	0.0686	0.1171	0.1593	0.1762
	11	0.0000	0.0000	0.0005	0.0030	0.0120	0.0336	0.0710	0.1185	0.1602
	12	0.0000	0.0000	0.0001	0.0008	0.0039	0.0136	0.0355	0.0727	0.1201
	13	0.0000	0.0000	0.0000	0.0002	0.0010	0.0045	0.0146	0.0366	0.0739
	14	0.0000	0.0000	0.0000	0.0000	0.0002	0.0012	0.0049	0.0150	0.0370
	15	0.0000	0.0000	0.0000	0.0000	0.0000	0.0003	0.0013	0.0049	0.0148
	16	0.0000	0.0000	0.0000	0.0000	0.0000	0.0000	0.0003	0.0013	0.0046
	17	0.0000	0.0000	0.0000	0.0000	0.0000	0.0000	0.0000	0.0002	0.0011
	18	0.0000	0.0000	0.0000	0.0000	0.0000	0.0000	0.0000	0.0000	0.0002
	19	0.0000	0.0000	0.0000	0.0000	0.0000	0.0000	0.0000	0.0000	0.0000
	20	0.0000	0.0000	0.0000	0.0000	0.0000	0.0000	0.0000	0.0000	0.0000

n	*x*	0.55	0.6	0.65	0.7	0.75	0.8	0.85	0.9	0.95
2	0	0.2025	0.1600	0.1225	0.0900	0.0625	0.0400	0.0225	0.0100	0.0025
	1	0.4950	0.4800	0.4550	0.4200	0.3750	0.3200	0.2550	0.1800	0.0950
	2	0.3025	0.3600	0.4225	0.4900	0.5625	0.6400	0.7225	0.8100	0.9025

(*continued*)

TABLE 1 | Binomial Probabilities *(Continued)*

n	*x*	0.55	0.6	0.65	0.7	0.75	0.8	0.85	0.9	0.95
3	0	0.0911	0.0640	0.0429	0.0270	0.0156	0.0080	0.0034	0.0010	0.0001
	1	0.3341	0.2880	0.2389	0.1890	0.1406	0.0960	0.0574	0.0270	0.0071
	2	0.4084	0.4320	0.4436	0.4410	0.4219	0.3840	0.3251	0.2430	0.1354
	3	0.1664	0.2160	0.2746	0.3430	0.4219	0.5120	0.6141	0.7290	0.8574
4	0	0.0410	0.0256	0.0150	0.0081	0.0039	0.0016	0.0005	0.0001	0.0000
	1	0.2005	0.1536	0.1115	0.0756	0.0469	0.0256	0.0115	0.0036	0.0005
	2	0.3675	0.3456	0.3105	0.2646	0.2109	0.1536	0.0975	0.0486	0.0135
	3	0.2995	0.3456	0.3845	0.4116	0.4219	0.4096	0.3685	0.2916	0.1715
	4	0.0915	0.1296	0.1785	0.2401	0.3164	0.4096	0.5220	0.6561	0.8145
5	0	0.0185	0.0102	0.0053	0.0024	0.0010	0.0003	0.0001	0.0000	0.0000
	1	0.1128	0.0768	0.0488	0.0284	0.0146	0.0064	0.0022	0.0005	0.0000
	2	0.2757	0.2304	0.1811	0.1323	0.0879	0.0512	0.0244	0.0081	0.0011
	3	0.3369	0.3456	0.3364	0.3087	0.2637	0.2048	0.1382	0.0729	0.0214
	4	0.2059	0.2592	0.3124	0.3602	0.3955	0.4096	0.3915	0.3281	0.2036
	5	0.0503	0.0778	0.1160	0.1681	0.2373	0.3277	0.4437	0.5905	0.7738
6	0	0.0083	0.0041	0.0018	0.0007	0.0002	0.0001	0.0000	0.0000	0.0000
	1	0.0609	0.0369	0.0205	0.0102	0.0044	0.0015	0.0004	0.0001	0.0000
	2	0.1861	0.1382	0.0951	0.0595	0.0330	0.0154	0.0055	0.0012	0.0001
	3	0.3032	0.2765	0.2355	0.1852	0.1318	0.0819	0.0415	0.0146	0.0021
	4	0.2780	0.3110	0.3280	0.3241	0.2966	0.2458	0.1762	0.0984	0.0305
	5	0.1359	0.1866	0.2437	0.3025	0.3560	0.3932	0.3993	0.3543	0.2321
	6	0.0277	0.0467	0.0754	0.1176	0.1780	0.2621	0.3771	0.5314	0.7351
7	0	0.0037	0.0016	0.0006	0.0002	0.0001	0.0000	0.0000	0.0000	0.0000
	1	0.0320	0.0172	0.0084	0.0036	0.0013	0.0004	0.0001	0.0000	0.0000
	2	0.1172	0.0774	0.0466	0.0250	0.0115	0.0043	0.0012	0.0002	0.0000
	3	0.2388	0.1935	0.1442	0.0972	0.0577	0.0287	0.0109	0.0026	0.0002
	4	0.2918	0.2903	0.2679	0.2269	0.1730	0.1147	0.0617	0.0230	0.0036
	5	0.2140	0.2613	0.2985	0.3177	0.3115	0.2753	0.2097	0.1240	0.0406
	6	0.0872	0.1306	0.1848	0.2471	0.3115	0.3670	0.3960	0.3720	0.2573
	7	0.0152	0.0280	0.0490	0.0824	0.1335	0.2097	0.3206	0.4783	0.6983
8	0	0.0017	0.0007	0.0002	0.0001	0.0000	0.0000	0.0000	0.0000	0.0000
	1	0.0164	0.0079	0.0033	0.0012	0.0004	0.0001	0.0000	0.0000	0.0000
	2	0.0703	0.0413	0.0217	0.0100	0.0038	0.0011	0.0002	0.0000	0.0000
	3	0.1719	0.1239	0.0808	0.0467	0.0231	0.0092	0.0026	0.0004	0.0000
	4	0.2627	0.2322	0.1875	0.1361	0.0865	0.0459	0.0185	0.0046	0.0004
	5	0.2568	0.2787	0.2786	0.2541	0.2076	0.1468	0.0839	0.0331	0.0054
	6	0.1569	0.2090	0.2587	0.2965	0.3115	0.2936	0.2376	0.1488	0.0515
	7	0.0548	0.0896	0.1373	0.1977	0.2670	0.3355	0.3847	0.3826	0.2793
	8	0.0084	0.0168	0.0319	0.0576	0.1001	0.1678	0.2725	0.4305	0.6634
9	0	0.0008	0.0003	0.0001	0.0000	0.0000	0.0000	0.0000	0.0000	0.0000
	1	0.0083	0.0035	0.0013	0.0004	0.0001	0.0000	0.0000	0.0000	0.0000
	2	0.0407	0.0212	0.0098	0.0039	0.0012	0.0003	0.0000	0.0000	0.0000
	3	0.1160	0.0743	0.0424	0.0210	0.0087	0.0028	0.0006	0.0001	0.0000
	4	0.2128	0.1672	0.1181	0.0735	0.0389	0.0165	0.0050	0.0008	0.0000

TABLE 1 | Binomial Probabilities *(Continued)*

n	*x*	0.55	0.6	0.65	0.7	0.75	0.8	0.85	0.9	0.95
	5	0.2600	0.2508	0.2194	0.1715	0.1168	0.0661	0.0283	0.0074	0.0006
	6	0.2119	0.2508	0.2716	0.2668	0.2336	0.1762	0.1069	0.0446	0.0077
	7	0.1110	0.1612	0.2162	0.2668	0.3003	0.3020	0.2597	0.1722	0.0629
	8	0.0339	0.0605	0.1004	0.1556	0.2253	0.3020	0.3679	0.3874	0.2985
	9	0.0046	0.0101	0.0207	0.0404	0.0751	0.1342	0.2316	0.3874	0.6302
10	0	0.0003	0.0001	0.0000	0.0000	0.0000	0.0000	0.0000	0.0000	0.0000
	1	0.0042	0.0016	0.0005	0.0001	0.0000	0.0000	0.0000	0.0000	0.0000
	2	0.0229	0.0106	0.0043	0.0014	0.0004	0.0001	0.0000	0.0000	0.0000
	3	0.0746	0.0425	0.0212	0.0090	0.0031	0.0008	0.0001	0.0000	0.0000
	4	0.1596	0.1115	0.0689	0.0368	0.0162	0.0055	0.0012	0.0001	0.0000
	5	0.2340	0.2007	0.1536	0.1029	0.0584	0.0264	0.0085	0.0015	0.0001
	6	0.2384	0.2508	0.2377	0.2001	0.1460	0.0881	0.0401	0.0112	0.0010
	7	0.1665	0.2150	0.2522	0.2668	0.2503	0.2013	0.1298	0.0574	0.0105
	8	0.0763	0.1209	0.1757	0.2335	0.2816	0.3020	0.2759	0.1937	0.0746
	9	0.0207	0.0403	0.0725	0.1211	0.1877	0.2684	0.3474	0.3874	0.3151
	10	0.0025	0.0060	0.0135	0.0282	0.0563	0.1074	0.1969	0.3487	0.5987
11	0	0.0002	0.0000	0.0000	0.0000	0.0000	0.0000	0.0000	0.0000	0.0000
	1	0.0021	0.0007	0.0002	0.0000	0.0000	0.0000	0.0000	0.0000	0.0000
	2	0.0126	0.0052	0.0018	0.0005	0.0001	0.0000	0.0000	0.0000	0.0000
	3	0.0462	0.0234	0.0102	0.0037	0.0011	0.0002	0.0000	0.0000	0.0000
	4	0.1128	0.0701	0.0379	0.0173	0.0064	0.0017	0.0003	0.0000	0.0000
	5	0.1931	0.1471	0.0985	0.0566	0.0268	0.0097	0.0023	0.0003	0.0000
	6	0.2360	0.2207	0.1830	0.1321	0.0803	0.0388	0.0132	0.0025	0.0001
	7	0.2060	0.2365	0.2428	0.2201	0.1721	0.1107	0.0536	0.0158	0.0014
	8	0.1259	0.1774	0.2254	0.2568	0.2581	0.2215	0.1517	0.0710	0.0137
	9	0.0513	0.0887	0.1395	0.1998	0.2581	0.2953	0.2866	0.2131	0.0867
	10	0.0125	0.0266	0.0518	0.0932	0.1549	0.2362	0.3248	0.3835	0.3293
	11	0.0014	0.0036	0.0088	0.0198	0.0422	0.0859	0.1673	0.3138	0.5688
12	0	0.0001	0.0000	0.0000	0.0000	0.0000	0.0000	0.0000	0.0000	0.0000
	1	0.0010	0.0003	0.0001	0.0000	0.0000	0.0000	0.0000	0.0000	0.0000
	2	0.0068	0.0025	0.0008	0.0002	0.0000	0.0000	0.0000	0.0000	0.0000
	3	0.0277	0.0125	0.0048	0.0015	0.0004	0.0001	0.0000	0.0000	0.0000
	4	0.0762	0.0420	0.0199	0.0078	0.0024	0.0005	0.0001	0.0000	0.0000
	5	0.1489	0.1009	0.0591	0.0291	0.0115	0.0033	0.0006	0.0000	0.0000
	6	0.2124	0.1766	0.1281	0.0792	0.0401	0.0155	0.0040	0.0005	0.0000
	7	0.2225	0.2270	0.2039	0.1585	0.1032	0.0532	0.0193	0.0038	0.0002
	8	0.1700	0.2128	0.2367	0.2311	0.1936	0.1329	0.0683	0.0213	0.0021
	9	0.0923	0.1419	0.1954	0.2397	0.2581	0.2362	0.1720	0.0852	0.0173
	10	0.0339	0.0639	0.1088	0.1678	0.2323	0.2835	0.2924	0.2301	0.0988
	11	0.0075	0.0174	0.0368	0.0712	0.1267	0.2062	0.3012	0.3766	0.3413
	12	0.0008	0.0022	0.0057	0.0138	0.0317	0.0687	0.1422	0.2824	0.5404
13	0	0.0000	0.0000	0.0000	0.0000	0.0000	0.0000	0.0000	0.0000	0.0000
	1	0.0005	0.0001	0.0000	0.0000	0.0000	0.0000	0.0000	0.0000	0.0000
	2	0.0036	0.0012	0.0003	0.0001	0.0000	0.0000	0.0000	0.0000	0.0000
	3	0.0162	0.0065	0.0022	0.0006	0.0001	0.0000	0.0000	0.0000	0.0000

(continued)

TABLE 1 | Binomial Probabilities *(Continued)*

n	x	0.55	0.6	0.65	0.7	0.75	0.8	0.85	0.9	0.95
	4	0.0495	0.0243	0.0101	0.0034	0.0009	0.0001	0.0000	0.0000	0.0000
	5	0.1089	0.0656	0.0336	0.0142	0.0047	0.0011	0.0001	0.0000	0.0000
	6	0.1775	0.1312	0.0833	0.0442	0.0186	0.0058	0.0011	0.0001	0.0000
	7	0.2169	0.1968	0.1546	0.1030	0.0559	0.0230	0.0063	0.0008	0.0000
	8	0.1989	0.2214	0.2154	0.1803	0.1258	0.0691	0.0266	0.0055	0.0003
	9	0.1350	0.1845	0.2222	0.2337	0.2097	0.1535	0.0838	0.0277	0.0028
	10	0.0660	0.1107	0.1651	0.2181	0.2517	0.2457	0.1900	0.0997	0.0214
	11	0.0220	0.0453	0.0836	0.1388	0.2059	0.2680	0.2937	0.2448	0.1109
	12	0.0045	0.0113	0.0259	0.0540	0.1029	0.1787	0.2774	0.3672	0.3512
	13	0.0004	0.0013	0.0037	0.0097	0.0238	0.0550	0.1209	0.2542	0.5133
14	0	0.0000	0.0000	0.0000	0.0000	0.0000	0.0000	0.0000	0.0000	0.0000
	1	0.0002	0.0001	0.0000	0.0000	0.0000	0.0000	0.0000	0.0000	0.0000
	2	0.0019	0.0005	0.0001	0.0000	0.0000	0.0000	0.0000	0.0000	0.0000
	3	0.0093	0.0033	0.0010	0.0002	0.0000	0.0000	0.0000	0.0000	0.0000
	4	0.0312	0.0136	0.0049	0.0014	0.0003	0.0000	0.0000	0.0000	0.0000
	5	0.0762	0.0408	0.0183	0.0066	0.0018	0.0003	0.0000	0.0000	0.0000
	6	0.1398	0.0918	0.0510	0.0232	0.0082	0.0020	0.0003	0.0000	0.0000
	7	0.1952	0.1574	0.1082	0.0618	0.0280	0.0092	0.0019	0.0002	0.0000
	8	0.2088	0.2066	0.1759	0.1262	0.0734	0.0322	0.0093	0.0013	0.0000
	9	0.1701	0.2066	0.2178	0.1963	0.1468	0.0860	0.0352	0.0078	0.0004
	10	0.1040	0.1549	0.2022	0.2290	0.2202	0.1720	0.0998	0.0349	0.0037
	11	0.0462	0.0845	0.1366	0.1943	0.2402	0.2501	0.2056	0.1142	0.0259
	12	0.0141	0.0317	0.0634	0.1134	0.1802	0.2501	0.2912	0.2570	0.1229
	13	0.0027	0.0073	0.0181	0.0407	0.0832	0.1539	0.2539	0.3559	0.3593
	14	0.0002	0.0008	0.0024	0.0068	0.0178	0.0440	0.1028	0.2288	0.4877
15	0	0.0000	0.0000	0.0000	0.0000	0.0000	0.0000	0.0000	0.0000	0.0000
	1	0.0001	0.0000	0.0000	0.0000	0.0000	0.0000	0.0000	0.0000	0.0000
	2	0.0010	0.0003	0.0001	0.0000	0.0000	0.0000	0.0000	0.0000	0.0000
	3	0.0052	0.0016	0.0004	0.0001	0.0000	0.0000	0.0000	0.0000	0.0000
	4	0.0191	0.0074	0.0024	0.0006	0.0001	0.0000	0.0000	0.0000	0.0000
	5	0.0515	0.0245	0.0096	0.0030	0.0007	0.0001	0.0000	0.0000	0.0000
	6	0.1048	0.0612	0.0298	0.0116	0.0034	0.0007	0.0001	0.0000	0.0000
	7	0.1647	0.1181	0.0710	0.0348	0.0131	0.0035	0.0005	0.0000	0.0000
	8	0.2013	0.1771	0.1319	0.0811	0.0393	0.0138	0.0030	0.0003	0.0000
	9	0.1914	0.2066	0.1906	0.1472	0.0917	0.0430	0.0132	0.0019	0.0000
	10	0.1404	0.1859	0.2123	0.2061	0.1651	0.1032	0.0449	0.0105	0.0006
	11	0.0780	0.1268	0.1792	0.2186	0.2252	0.1876	0.1156	0.0428	0.0049
	12	0.0318	0.0634	0.1110	0.1700	0.2252	0.2501	0.2184	0.1285	0.0307
	13	0.0090	0.0219	0.0476	0.0916	0.1559	0.2309	0.2856	0.2669	0.1348
	14	0.0016	0.0047	0.0126	0.0305	0.0668	0.1319	0.2312	0.3432	0.3658
	15	0.0001	0.0005	0.0016	0.0047	0.0134	0.0352	0.0874	0.2059	0.4633
20	0	0.0000	0.0000	0.0000	0.0000	0.0000	0.0000	0.0000	0.0000	0.0000
	1	0.0000	0.0000	0.0000	0.0000	0.0000	0.0000	0.0000	0.0000	0.0000
	2	0.0000	0.0000	0.0000	0.0000	0.0000	0.0000	0.0000	0.0000	0.0000
	3	0.0002	0.0000	0.0000	0.0000	0.0000	0.0000	0.0000	0.0000	0.0000
	4	0.0013	0.0003	0.0000	0.0000	0.0000	0.0000	0.0000	0.0000	0.0000

TABLE 1 | Binomial Probabilities *(Continued)*

n	x	0.55	0.6	0.65	0.7	0.75	0.8	0.85	0.9	0.95
	5	0.0049	0.0013	0.0003	0.0000	0.0000	0.0000	0.0000	0.0000	0.0000
	6	0.0150	0.0049	0.0012	0.0002	0.0000	0.0000	0.0000	0.0000	0.0000
	7	0.0366	0.0146	0.0045	0.0010	0.0002	0.0000	0.0000	0.0000	0.0000
	8	0.0727	0.0355	0.0136	0.0039	0.0008	0.0001	0.0000	0.0000	0.0000
	9	0.1185	0.0710	0.0336	0.0120	0.0030	0.0005	0.0000	0.0000	0.0000
	10	0.1593	0.1171	0.0686	0.0308	0.0099	0.0020	0.0002	0.0000	0.0000
	11	0.1771	0.1597	0.1158	0.0654	0.0271	0.0074	0.0011	0.0001	0.0000
	12	0.1623	0.1797	0.1614	0.1144	0.0609	0.0222	0.0046	0.0004	0.0000
	13	0.1221	0.1659	0.1844	0.1643	0.1124	0.0545	0.0160	0.0020	0.0000
	14	0.0746	0.1244	0.1712	0.1916	0.1686	0.1091	0.0454	0.0089	0.0003
	15	0.0365	0.0746	0.1272	0.1789	0.2023	0.1746	0.1028	0.0319	0.0022
	16	0.0139	0.0350	0.0738	0.1304	0.1897	0.2182	0.1821	0.0898	0.0133
	17	0.0040	0.0123	0.0323	0.0716	0.1339	0.2054	0.2428	0.1901	0.0596
	18	0.0008	0.0031	0.0100	0.0278	0.0669	0.1369	0.2293	0.2852	0.1887
	19	0.0001	0.0005	0.0020	0.0068	0.0211	0.0576	0.1368	0.2702	0.3774
	20	0.0000	0.0000	0.0002	0.0008	0.0032	0.0115	0.0388	0.1216	0.3585

TABLE 2 | Poisson Probabilities

x	0.005	0.01	0.02	0.03	0.04	0.05	0.06	0.07	0.08	0.09
0	0.9950	0.9900	0.9802	0.9704	0.9608	0.9512	0.9418	0.9324	0.9231	0.9139
1	0.0050	0.0099	0.0196	0.0291	0.0384	0.0476	0.0565	0.0653	0.0738	0.0823
2	0.0000	0.0000	0.0002	0.0004	0.0008	0.0012	0.0017	0.0023	0.0030	0.0037
3	0.0000	0.0000	0.0000	0.0000	0.0000	0.0000	0.0000	0.0001	0.0001	0.0001

x	0.10	0.20	0.30	0.40	0.50	0.60	0.70	0.80	0.90	1.00
0	0.9048	0.8187	0.7408	0.6703	0.6065	0.5488	0.4966	0.4493	0.4066	0.3679
1	0.0905	0.1637	0.2222	0.2681	0.3033	0.3293	0.3476	0.3595	0.3659	0.3679
2	0.0045	0.0164	0.0333	0.0536	0.0758	0.0988	0.1217	0.1438	0.1647	0.1839
3	0.0002	0.0011	0.0033	0.0072	0.0126	0.0198	0.0284	0.0383	0.0494	0.0613
4	0.0000	0.0001	0.0003	0.0007	0.0016	0.0030	0.0050	0.0077	0.0111	0.0153
5	0.0000	0.0000	0.0000	0.0001	0.0002	0.0004	0.0007	0.0012	0.0020	0.0031
6	0.0000	0.0000	0.0000	0.0000	0.0000	0.0000	0.0001	0.0002	0.0003	0.0005
7	0.0000	0.0000	0.0000	0.0000	0.0000	0.0000	0.0000	0.0000	0.0000	0.0001

x	1.10	1.20	1.30	1.40	1.50	1.60	1.70	1.80	1.90	2.00
0	0.3329	0.3012	0.2725	0.2466	0.2231	0.2019	0.1827	0.1653	0.1496	0.1353
1	0.3662	0.3614	0.3543	0.3452	0.3347	0.3230	0.3106	0.2975	0.2842	0.2707
2	0.2014	0.2169	0.2303	0.2417	0.2510	0.2584	0.2640	0.2678	0.2700	0.2707
3	0.0738	0.0867	0.0998	0.1128	0.1255	0.1378	0.1496	0.1607	0.1710	0.1804
4	0.0203	0.0260	0.0324	0.0395	0.0471	0.0551	0.0636	0.0723	0.0812	0.0902
5	0.0045	0.0062	0.0084	0.0111	0.0141	0.0176	0.0216	0.0260	0.0309	0.0361
6	0.0008	0.0012	0.0018	0.0026	0.0035	0.0047	0.0061	0.0078	0.0098	0.0120
7	0.0001	0.0002	0.0003	0.0005	0.0008	0.0011	0.0015	0.0020	0.0027	0.0034
8	0.0000	0.0000	0.0001	0.0001	0.0001	0.0002	0.0003	0.0005	0.0006	0.0009
9	0.0000	0.0000	0.0000	0.0000	0.0000	0.0000	0.0001	0.0001	0.0001	0.0002

x	2.10	2.20	2.30	2.40	2.50	2.60	2.70	2.80	2.90	3.00
0	0.1225	0.1108	0.1003	0.0907	0.0821	0.0743	0.0672	0.0608	0.0550	0.0498
1	0.2572	0.2438	0.2306	0.2177	0.2052	0.1931	0.1815	0.1703	0.1596	0.1494
2	0.2700	0.2681	0.2652	0.2613	0.2565	0.2510	0.2450	0.2384	0.2314	0.2240
3	0.1890	0.1966	0.2033	0.2090	0.2138	0.2176	0.2205	0.2225	0.2237	0.2240
4	0.0992	0.1082	0.1169	0.1254	0.1336	0.1414	0.1488	0.1557	0.1622	0.1680
5	0.0417	0.0476	0.0538	0.0602	0.0668	0.0735	0.0804	0.0872	0.0940	0.1008
6	0.0146	0.0174	0.0206	0.0241	0.0278	0.0319	0.0362	0.0407	0.0455	0.0504
7	0.0044	0.0055	0.0068	0.0083	0.0099	0.0118	0.0139	0.0163	0.0188	0.0216
8	0.0011	0.0015	0.0019	0.0025	0.0031	0.0038	0.0047	0.0057	0.0068	0.0081
9	0.0003	0.0004	0.0005	0.0007	0.0009	0.0011	0.0014	0.0018	0.0022	0.0027
10	0.0001	0.0001	0.0001	0.0002	0.0002	0.0003	0.0004	0.0005	0.0006	0.0008
11	0.0000	0.0000	0.0000	0.0000	0.0000	0.0001	0.0001	0.0001	0.0002	0.0002
12	0.0000	0.0000	0.0000	0.0000	0.0000	0.0000	0.0000	0.0000	0.0000	0.0001

x	3.10	3.20	3.30	3.40	3.50	3.60	3.70	3.80	3.90	4.00
0	0.0450	0.0408	0.0369	0.0334	0.0302	0.0273	0.0247	0.0224	0.0202	0.0183
1	0.1397	0.1304	0.1217	0.1135	0.1057	0.0984	0.0915	0.0850	0.0789	0.0733
2	0.2165	0.2087	0.2008	0.1929	0.1850	0.1771	0.1692	0.1615	0.1539	0.1465
3	0.2237	0.2226	0.2209	0.2186	0.2158	0.2125	0.2087	0.2046	0.2001	0.1954
4	0.1733	0.1781	0.1823	0.1858	0.1888	0.1912	0.1931	0.1944	0.1951	0.1954
5	0.1075	0.1140	0.1203	0.1264	0.1322	0.1377	0.1429	0.1477	0.1522	0.1563
6	0.0555	0.0608	0.0662	0.0716	0.0771	0.0826	0.0881	0.0936	0.0989	0.1042

TABLE 2 | **Poisson Probabilities** *(Continued)*

x	3.10	3.20	3.30	3.40	3.50	3.60	3.70	3.80	3.90	4.00
7	0.0246	0.0278	0.0312	0.0348	0.0385	0.0425	0.0466	0.0508	0.0551	0.0595
8	0.0095	0.0111	0.0129	0.0148	0.0169	0.0191	0.0215	0.0241	0.0269	0.0298
9	0.0033	0.0040	0.0047	0.0056	0.0066	0.0076	0.0089	0.0102	0.0116	0.0132
10	0.0010	0.0013	0.0016	0.0019	0.0023	0.0028	0.0033	0.0039	0.0045	0.0053
11	0.0003	0.0004	0.0005	0.0006	0.0007	0.0009	0.0011	0.0013	0.0016	0.0019
12	0.0001	0.0001	0.0001	0.0002	0.0002	0.0003	0.0003	0.0004	0.0005	0.0006
13	0.0000	0.0000	0.0000	0.0000	0.0001	0.0001	0.0001	0.0001	0.0002	0.0002
14	0.0000	0.0000	0.0000	0.0000	0.0000	0.0000	0.0000	0.0000	0.0000	0.0001

x	4.10	4.20	4.30	4.40	4.50	4.60	4.70	4.80	4.90	5.00
0	0.0166	0.0150	0.0136	0.0123	0.0111	0.0101	0.0091	0.0082	0.0074	0.0067
1	0.0679	0.0630	0.0583	0.0540	0.0500	0.0462	0.0427	0.0395	0.0365	0.0337
2	0.1393	0.1323	0.1254	0.1188	0.1125	0.1063	0.1005	0.0948	0.0894	0.0842
3	0.1904	0.1852	0.1798	0.1743	0.1687	0.1631	0.1574	0.1517	0.1460	0.1404
4	0.1951	0.1944	0.1933	0.1917	0.1898	0.1875	0.1849	0.1820	0.1789	0.1755
5	0.1600	0.1633	0.1662	0.1687	0.1708	0.1725	0.1738	0.1747	0.1753	0.1755
6	0.1093	0.1143	0.1191	0.1237	0.1281	0.1323	0.1362	0.1398	0.1432	0.1462
7	0.0640	0.0686	0.0732	0.0778	0.0824	0.0869	0.0914	0.0959	0.1002	0.1044
8	0.0328	0.0360	0.0393	0.0428	0.0463	0.0500	0.0537	0.0575	0.0614	0.0653
9	0.0150	0.0168	0.0188	0.0209	0.0232	0.0255	0.0281	0.0307	0.0334	0.0363
10	0.0061	0.0071	0.0081	0.0092	0.0104	0.0118	0.0132	0.0147	0.0164	0.0181
11	0.0023	0.0027	0.0032	0.0037	0.0043	0.0049	0.0056	0.0064	0.0073	0.0082
12	0.0008	0.0009	0.0011	0.0013	0.0016	0.0019	0.0022	0.0026	0.0030	0.0034
13	0.0002	0.0003	0.0004	0.0005	0.0006	0.0007	0.0008	0.0009	0.0011	0.0013
14	0.0001	0.0001	0.0001	0.0001	0.0002	0.0002	0.0003	0.0003	0.0004	0.0005
15	0.0000	0.0000	0.0000	0.0000	0.0001	0.0001	0.0001	0.0001	0.0001	0.0002

x	5.10	5.20	5.30	5.40	5.50	5.60	5.70	5.80	5.90	6.00
0	0.0061	0.0055	0.0050	0.0045	0.0041	0.0037	0.0033	0.0030	0.0027	0.0025
1	0.0311	0.0287	0.0265	0.0244	0.0225	0.0207	0.0191	0.0176	0.0162	0.0149
2	0.0793	0.0746	0.0701	0.0659	0.0618	0.0580	0.0544	0.0509	0.0477	0.0446
3	0.1348	0.1293	0.1239	0.1185	0.1133	0.1082	0.1033	0.0985	0.0938	0.0892
4	0.1719	0.1681	0.1641	0.1600	0.1558	0.1515	0.1472	0.1428	0.1383	0.1339
5	0.1753	0.1748	0.1740	0.1728	0.1714	0.1697	0.1678	0.1656	0.1632	0.1606
6	0.1490	0.1515	0.1537	0.1555	0.1571	0.1584	0.1594	0.1601	0.1605	0.1606
7	0.1086	0.1125	0.1163	0.1200	0.1234	0.1267	0.1298	0.1326	0.1353	0.1377
8	0.0692	0.0731	0.0771	0.0810	0.0849	0.0887	0.0925	0.0962	0.0998	0.1033
9	0.0392	0.0423	0.0454	0.0486	0.0519	0.0552	0.0586	0.0620	0.0654	0.0688
10	0.0200	0.0220	0.0241	0.0262	0.0285	0.0309	0.0334	0.0359	0.0386	0.0413
11	0.0093	0.0104	0.0116	0.0129	0.0143	0.0157	0.0173	0.0190	0.0207	0.0225
12	0.0039	0.0045	0.0051	0.0058	0.0065	0.0073	0.0082	0.0092	0.0102	0.0113
13	0.0015	0.0018	0.0021	0.0024	0.0028	0.0032	0.0036	0.0041	0.0046	0.0052
14	0.0006	0.0007	0.0008	0.0009	0.0011	0.0013	0.0015	0.0017	0.0019	0.0022
15	0.0002	0.0002	0.0003	0.0003	0.0004	0.0005	0.0006	0.0007	0.0008	0.0009
16	0.0001	0.0001	0.0001	0.0001	0.0001	0.0002	0.0002	0.0002	0.0003	0.0003
17	0.0000	0.0000	0.0000	0.0000	0.0000	0.0001	0.0001	0.0001	0.0001	0.0001

(continued)

TABLE 2 | Poisson Probabilities *(Continued)*

x	6.10	6.20	6.30	6.40	6.50	6.60	6.70	6.80	6.90	7.00
0	0.0022	0.0020	0.0018	0.0017	0.0015	0.0014	0.0012	0.0011	0.0010	0.0009
1	0.0137	0.0126	0.0116	0.0106	0.0098	0.0090	0.0082	0.0076	0.0070	0.0064
2	0.0417	0.0390	0.0364	0.0340	0.0318	0.0296	0.0276	0.0258	0.0240	0.0223
3	0.0848	0.0806	0.0765	0.0726	0.0688	0.0652	0.0617	0.0584	0.0552	0.0521
4	0.1294	0.1249	0.1205	0.1162	0.1118	0.1076	0.1034	0.0992	0.0952	0.0912
5	0.1579	0.1549	0.1519	0.1487	0.1454	0.1420	0.1385	0.1349	0.1314	0.1277
6	0.1605	0.1601	0.1595	0.1586	0.1575	0.1562	0.1546	0.1529	0.1511	0.1490
7	0.1399	0.1418	0.1435	0.1450	0.1462	0.1472	0.1480	0.1486	0.1489	0.1490
8	0.1066	0.1099	0.1130	0.1160	0.1188	0.1215	0.1240	0.1263	0.1284	0.1304
9	0.0723	0.0757	0.0791	0.0825	0.0858	0.0891	0.0923	0.0954	0.0985	0.1014
10	0.0441	0.0469	0.0498	0.0528	0.0558	0.0588	0.0618	0.0649	0.0679	0.0710
11	0.0244	0.0265	0.0285	0.0307	0.0330	0.0353	0.0377	0.0401	0.0426	0.0452
12	0.0124	0.0137	0.0150	0.0164	0.0179	0.0194	0.0210	0.0227	0.0245	0.0263
13	0.0058	0.0065	0.0073	0.0081	0.0089	0.0099	0.0108	0.0119	0.0130	0.0142
14	0.0025	0.0029	0.0033	0.0037	0.0041	0.0046	0.0052	0.0058	0.0064	0.0071
15	0.0010	0.0012	0.0014	0.0016	0.0018	0.0020	0.0023	0.0026	0.0029	0.0033
16	0.0004	0.0005	0.0005	0.0006	0.0007	0.0008	0.0010	0.0011	0.0013	0.0014
17	0.0001	0.0002	0.0002	0.0002	0.0003	0.0003	0.0004	0.0004	0.0005	0.0006
18	0.0000	0.0001	0.0001	0.0001	0.0001	0.0001	0.0001	0.0002	0.0002	0.0002
19	0.0000	0.0000	0.0000	0.0000	0.0000	0.0000	0.0001	0.0001	0.0001	0.0001

x	7.10	7.20	7.30	7.40	7.50	7.60	7.70	7.80	7.90	8.00
0	0.0008	0.0007	0.0007	0.0006	0.0006	0.0005	0.0005	0.0004	0.0004	0.0003
1	0.0059	0.0054	0.0049	0.0045	0.0041	0.0038	0.0035	0.0032	0.0029	0.0027
2	0.0208	0.0194	0.0180	0.0167	0.0156	0.0145	0.0134	0.0125	0.0116	0.0107
3	0.0492	0.0464	0.0438	0.0413	0.0389	0.0366	0.0345	0.0324	0.0305	0.0286
4	0.0874	0.0836	0.0799	0.0764	0.0729	0.0696	0.0663	0.0632	0.0602	0.0573
5	0.1241	0.1204	0.1167	0.1130	0.1094	0.1057	0.1021	0.0986	0.0951	0.0916
6	0.1468	0.1445	0.1420	0.1394	0.1367	0.1339	0.1311	0.1282	0.1252	0.1221
7	0.1489	0.1486	0.1481	0.1474	0.1465	0.1454	0.1442	0.1428	0.1413	0.1396
8	0.1321	0.1337	0.1351	0.1363	0.1373	0.1381	0.1388	0.1392	0.1395	0.1396
9	0.1042	0.1070	0.1096	0.1121	0.1144	0.1167	0.1187	0.1207	0.1224	0.1241
10	0.0740	0.0770	0.0800	0.0829	0.0858	0.0887	0.0914	0.0941	0.0967	0.0993
11	0.0478	0.0504	0.0531	0.0558	0.0585	0.0613	0.0640	0.0667	0.0695	0.0722
12	0.0283	0.0303	0.0323	0.0344	0.0366	0.0388	0.0411	0.0434	0.0457	0.0481
13	0.0154	0.0168	0.0181	0.0196	0.0211	0.0227	0.0243	0.0260	0.0278	0.0296
14	0.0078	0.0086	0.0095	0.0104	0.0113	0.0123	0.0134	0.0145	0.0157	0.0169
15	0.0037	0.0041	0.0046	0.0051	0.0057	0.0062	0.0069	0.0075	0.0083	0.0090
16	0.0016	0.0019	0.0021	0.0024	0.0026	0.0030	0.0033	0.0037	0.0041	0.0045
17	0.0007	0.0008	0.0009	0.0010	0.0012	0.0013	0.0015	0.0017	0.0019	0.0021
18	0.0003	0.0003	0.0004	0.0004	0.0005	0.0006	0.0006	0.0007	0.0008	0.0009
19	0.0001	0.0001	0.0001	0.0002	0.0002	0.0002	0.0003	0.0003	0.0003	0.0004
20	0.0000	0.0000	0.0001	0.0001	0.0001	0.0001	0.0001	0.0001	0.0001	0.0002
21	0.0000	0.0000	0.0000	0.0000	0.0000	0.0000	0.0000	0.0000	0.0001	0.0001

x	8.10	8.20	8.30	8.40	8.50	8.60	8.70	8.80	8.90	9.00
0	0.0003	0.0003	0.0002	0.0002	0.0002	0.0002	0.0002	0.0002	0.0001	0.0001
1	0.0025	0.0023	0.0021	0.0019	0.0017	0.0016	0.0014	0.0013	0.0012	0.0011
2	0.0100	0.0092	0.0086	0.0079	0.0074	0.0068	0.0063	0.0058	0.0054	0.0050

TABLE 2 | Poisson Probabilities *(Continued)*

x	8.10	8.20	8.30	8.40	8.50	8.60	8.70	8.80	8.90	9.00
3	0.0269	0.0252	0.0237	0.0222	0.0208	0.0195	0.0183	0.0171	0.0160	0.0150
4	0.0544	0.0517	0.0491	0.0466	0.0443	0.0420	0.0398	0.0377	0.0357	0.0337
5	0.0882	0.0849	0.0816	0.0784	0.0752	0.0722	0.0692	0.0663	0.0635	0.0607
6	0.1191	0.1160	0.1128	0.1097	0.1066	0.1034	0.1003	0.0972	0.0941	0.0911
7	0.1378	0.1358	0.1338	0.1317	0.1294	0.1271	0.1247	0.1222	0.1197	0.1171
8	0.1395	0.1392	0.1388	0.1382	0.1375	0.1366	0.1356	0.1344	0.1332	0.1318
9	0.1256	0.1269	0.1280	0.1290	0.1299	0.1306	0.1311	0.1315	0.1317	0.1318
10	0.1017	0.1040	0.1063	0.1084	0.1104	0.1123	0.1140	0.1157	0.1172	0.1186
11	0.0749	0.0776	0.0802	0.0828	0.0853	0.0878	0.0902	0.0925	0.0948	0.0970
12	0.0505	0.0530	0.0555	0.0579	0.0604	0.0629	0.0654	0.0679	0.0703	0.0728
13	0.0315	0.0334	0.0354	0.0374	0.0395	0.0416	0.0438	0.0459	0.0481	0.0504
14	0.0182	0.0196	0.0210	0.0225	0.0240	0.0256	0.0272	0.0289	0.0306	0.0324
15	0.0098	0.0107	0.0116	0.0126	0.0136	0.0147	0.0158	0.0169	0.0182	0.0194
16	0.0050	0.0055	0.0060	0.0066	0.0072	0.0079	0.0086	0.0093	0.0101	0.0109
17	0.0024	0.0026	0.0029	0.0033	0.0036	0.0040	0.0044	0.0048	0.0053	0.0058
18	0.0011	0.0012	0.0014	0.0015	0.0017	0.0019	0.0021	0.0024	0.0026	0.0029
19	0.0005	0.0005	0.0006	0.0007	0.0008	0.0009	0.0010	0.0011	0.0012	0.0014
20	0.0002	0.0002	0.0002	0.0003	0.0003	0.0004	0.0004	0.0005	0.0005	0.0006
21	0.0001	0.0001	0.0001	0.0001	0.0001	0.0002	0.0002	0.0002	0.0002	0.0003
22	0.0000	0.0000	0.0000	0.0000	0.0001	0.0001	0.0001	0.0001	0.0001	0.0001

x	9.10	9.20	9.30	9.40	9.50	9.60	9.70	9.80	9.90	10.00
0	0.0001	0.0001	0.0001	0.0001	0.0001	0.0001	0.0001	0.0001	0.0001	0.0000
1	0.0010	0.0009	0.0009	0.0008	0.0007	0.0007	0.0006	0.0005	0.0005	0.0005
2	0.0046	0.0043	0.0040	0.0037	0.0034	0.0031	0.0029	0.0027	0.0025	0.0023
3	0.0140	0.0131	0.0123	0.0115	0.0107	0.0100	0.0093	0.0087	0.0081	0.0076
4	0.0319	0.0302	0.0285	0.0269	0.0254	0.0240	0.0226	0.0213	0.0201	0.0189
5	0.0581	0.0555	0.0530	0.0506	0.0483	0.0460	0.0439	0.0418	0.0398	0.0378
6	0.0881	0.0851	0.0822	0.0793	0.0764	0.0736	0.0709	0.0682	0.0656	0.0631
7	0.1145	0.1118	0.1091	0.1064	0.1037	0.1010	0.0982	0.0955	0.0928	0.0901
8	0.1302	0.1286	0.1269	0.1251	0.1232	0.1212	0.1191	0.1170	0.1148	0.1126
9	0.1317	0.1315	0.1311	0.1306	0.1300	0.1293	0.1284	0.1274	0.1263	0.1251
10	0.1198	0.1210	0.1219	0.1228	0.1235	0.1241	0.1245	0.1249	0.1250	0.1251
11	0.0991	0.1012	0.1031	0.1049	0.1067	0.1083	0.1098	0.1112	0.1125	0.1137
12	0.0752	0.0776	0.0799	0.0822	0.0844	0.0866	0.0888	0.0908	0.0928	0.0948
13	0.0526	0.0549	0.0572	0.0594	0.0617	0.0640	0.0662	0.0685	0.0707	0.0729
14	0.0342	0.0361	0.0380	0.0399	0.0419	0.0439	0.0459	0.0479	0.0500	0.0521
15	0.0208	0.0221	0.0235	0.0250	0.0265	0.0281	0.0297	0.0313	0.0330	0.0347
16	0.0118	0.0127	0.0137	0.0147	0.0157	0.0168	0.0180	0.0192	0.0204	0.0217
17	0.0063	0.0069	0.0075	0.0081	0.0088	0.0095	0.0103	0.0111	0.0119	0.0128
18	0.0032	0.0035	0.0039	0.0042	0.0046	0.0051	0.0055	0.0060	0.0065	0.0071
19	0.0015	0.0017	0.0019	0.0021	0.0023	0.0026	0.0028	0.0031	0.0034	0.0037
20	0.0007	0.0008	0.0009	0.0010	0.0011	0.0012	0.0014	0.0015	0.0017	0.0019
21	0.0003	0.0003	0.0004	0.0004	0.0005	0.0006	0.0006	0.0007	0.0008	0.0009
22	0.0001	0.0001	0.0002	0.0002	0.0002	0.0002	0.0003	0.0003	0.0004	0.0004
23	0.0000	0.0001	0.0001	0.0001	0.0001	0.0001	0.0001	0.0001	0.0002	0.0002
24	0.0000	0.0000	0.0000	0.0000	0.0000	0.0000	0.0000	0.0001	0.0001	0.0001

(continued)

TABLE 2 | Poisson Probabilities *(Continued)*

x	11.00	12.00	13.00	14.00	15.00	16.00	17.00	18.00	19.00	20.00
0	0.0000	0.0000	0.0000	0.0000	0.0000	0.0000	0.0000	0.0000	0.0000	0.0000
1	0.0002	0.0001	0.0000	0.0000	0.0000	0.0000	0.0000	0.0000	0.0000	0.0000
2	0.0010	0.0004	0.0002	0.0001	0.0000	0.0000	0.0000	0.0000	0.0000	0.0000
3	0.0037	0.0018	0.0008	0.0004	0.0002	0.0001	0.0000	0.0000	0.0000	0.0000
4	0.0102	0.0053	0.0027	0.0013	0.0006	0.0003	0.0001	0.0001	0.0000	0.0000
5	0.0224	0.0127	0.0070	0.0037	0.0019	0.0010	0.0005	0.0002	0.0001	0.0001
6	0.0411	0.0255	0.0152	0.0087	0.0048	0.0026	0.0014	0.0007	0.0004	0.0002
7	0.0646	0.0437	0.0281	0.0174	0.0104	0.0060	0.0034	0.0019	0.0010	0.0005
8	0.0888	0.0655	0.0457	0.0304	0.0194	0.0120	0.0072	0.0042	0.0024	0.0013
9	0.1085	0.0874	0.0661	0.0473	0.0324	0.0213	0.0135	0.0083	0.0050	0.0029
10	0.1194	0.1048	0.0859	0.0663	0.0486	0.0341	0.0230	0.0150	0.0095	0.0058
11	0.1194	0.1144	0.1015	0.0844	0.0663	0.0496	0.0355	0.0245	0.0164	0.0106
12	0.1094	0.1144	0.1099	0.0984	0.0829	0.0661	0.0504	0.0368	0.0259	0.0176
13	0.0926	0.1056	0.1099	0.1060	0.0956	0.0814	0.0658	0.0509	0.0378	0.0271
14	0.0728	0.0905	0.1021	0.1060	0.1024	0.0930	0.0800	0.0655	0.0514	0.0387
15	0.0534	0.0724	0.0885	0.0989	0.1024	0.0992	0.0906	0.0786	0.0650	0.0516
16	0.0367	0.0543	0.0719	0.0866	0.0960	0.0992	0.0963	0.0884	0.0772	0.0646
17	0.0237	0.0383	0.0550	0.0713	0.0847	0.0934	0.0963	0.0936	0.0863	0.0760
18	0.0145	0.0255	0.0397	0.0554	0.0706	0.0830	0.0909	0.0936	0.0911	0.0844
19	0.0084	0.0161	0.0272	0.0409	0.0557	0.0699	0.0814	0.0887	0.0911	0.0888
20	0.0046	0.0097	0.0177	0.0286	0.0418	0.0559	0.0692	0.0798	0.0866	0.0888
21	0.0024	0.0055	0.0109	0.0191	0.0299	0.0426	0.0560	0.0684	0.0783	0.0846
22	0.0012	0.0030	0.0065	0.0121	0.0204	0.0310	0.0433	0.0560	0.0676	0.0769
23	0.0006	0.0016	0.0037	0.0074	0.0133	0.0216	0.0320	0.0438	0.0559	0.0669
24	0.0003	0.0008	0.0020	0.0043	0.0083	0.0144	0.0226	0.0328	0.0442	0.0557
25	0.0001	0.0004	0.0010	0.0024	0.0050	0.0092	0.0154	0.0237	0.0336	0.0446
26	0.0000	0.0002	0.0005	0.0013	0.0029	0.0057	0.0101	0.0164	0.0246	0.0343
27	0.0000	0.0001	0.0002	0.0007	0.0016	0.0034	0.0063	0.0109	0.0173	0.0254
28	0.0000	0.0000	0.0001	0.0003	0.0009	0.0019	0.0038	0.0070	0.0117	0.0181
29	0.0000	0.0000	0.0001	0.0002	0.0004	0.0011	0.0023	0.0044	0.0077	0.0125
30	0.0000	0.0000	0.0000	0.0001	0.0002	0.0006	0.0013	0.0026	0.0049	0.0083
31	0.0000	0.0000	0.0000	0.0000	0.0001	0.0003	0.0007	0.0015	0.0030	0.0054
32	0.0000	0.0000	0.0000	0.0000	0.0001	0.0001	0.0004	0.0009	0.0018	0.0034
33	0.0000	0.0000	0.0000	0.0000	0.0000	0.0001	0.0002	0.0005	0.0010	0.0020
34	0.0000	0.0000	0.0000	0.0000	0.0000	0.0000	0.0001	0.0002	0.0006	0.0012
35	0.0000	0.0000	0.0000	0.0000	0.0000	0.0000	0.0000	0.0001	0.0003	0.0007
36	0.0000	0.0000	0.0000	0.0000	0.0000	0.0000	0.0000	0.0001	0.0002	0.0004
37	0.0000	0.0000	0.0000	0.0000	0.0000	0.0000	0.0000	0.0000	0.0001	0.0002
38	0.0000	0.0000	0.0000	0.0000	0.0000	0.0000	0.0000	0.0000	0.0000	0.0001
39	0.0000	0.0000	0.0000	0.0000	0.0000	0.0000	0.0000	0.0000	0.0000	0.0001

TABLE 3 | Cumulative Probabilities for the Standard Normal Distribution

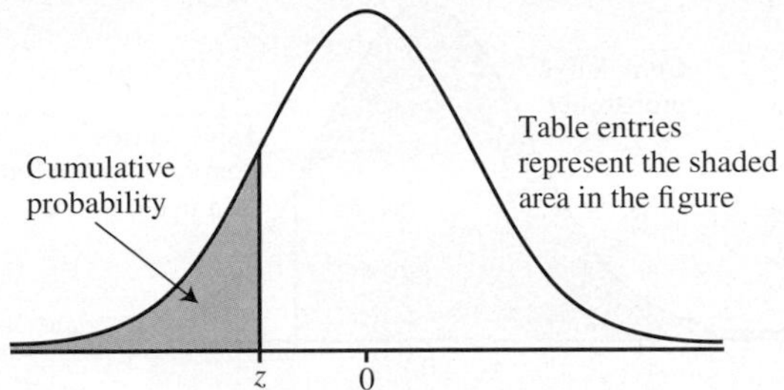

FIRST DIGIT OF Z	SECOND DIGIT OF Z									
z	0.00	0.01	0.02	0.03	0.04	0.05	0.06	0.07	0.08	0.09
−3.7 and lower	0.0001									
−3.6	0.0002	0.0002	0.0001	0.0001	0.0001	0.0001	0.0001	0.0001	0.0001	0.0001
−3.5	0.0002	0.0002	0.0002	0.0002	0.0002	0.0002	0.0002	0.0002	0.0002	0.0002
−3.4	0.0003	0.0003	0.0003	0.0003	0.0003	0.0003	0.0003	0.0003	0.0003	0.0002
−3.3	0.0005	0.0005	0.0005	0.0004	0.0004	0.0004	0.0004	0.0004	0.0004	0.0003
−3.2	0.0007	0.0007	0.0006	0.0006	0.0006	0.0006	0.0006	0.0005	0.0005	0.0005
−3.1	0.0010	0.0009	0.0009	0.0009	0.0008	0.0008	0.0008	0.0008	0.0007	0.0007
−3.0	0.0013	0.0013	0.0013	0.0012	0.0012	0.0011	0.0011	0.0011	0.0010	0.0010
−2.9	0.0019	0.0018	0.0018	0.0017	0.0016	0.0016	0.0015	0.0015	0.0014	0.0014
−2.8	0.0026	0.0025	0.0024	0.0023	0.0023	0.0022	0.0021	0.0021	0.0020	0.0019
−2.7	0.0035	0.0034	0.0033	0.0032	0.0031	0.0030	0.0029	0.0028	0.0027	0.0026
−2.6	0.0047	0.0045	0.0044	0.0043	0.0041	0.0040	0.0039	0.0038	0.0037	0.0036
−2.5	0.0062	0.0060	0.0059	0.0057	0.0055	0.0054	0.0052	0.0051	0.0049	0.0048
−2.4	0.0082	0.0080	0.0078	0.0075	0.0073	0.0071	0.0069	0.0068	0.0066	0.0064
−2.3	0.0107	0.0104	0.0102	0.0099	0.0096	0.0094	0.0091	0.0089	0.0087	0.0084
−2.2	0.0139	0.0136	0.0132	0.0129	0.0125	0.0122	0.0119	0.0116	0.0113	0.0110
−2.1	0.0179	0.0174	0.0170	0.0166	0.0162	0.0158	0.0154	0.0150	0.0146	0.0143
−2.0	0.0228	0.0222	0.0217	0.0212	0.0207	0.0202	0.0197	0.0192	0.0188	0.0183
−1.9	0.0287	0.0281	0.0274	0.0268	0.0262	0.0256	0.0250	0.0244	0.0239	0.0233
−1.8	0.0359	0.0351	0.0344	0.0336	0.0329	0.0322	0.0314	0.0307	0.0301	0.0294
−1.7	0.0446	0.0436	0.0427	0.0418	0.0409	0.0401	0.0392	0.0384	0.0375	0.0367
−1.6	0.0548	0.0537	0.0526	0.0516	0.0505	0.0495	0.0485	0.0475	0.0465	0.0455
−1.5	0.0668	0.0655	0.0643	0.0630	0.0618	0.0606	0.0594	0.0582	0.0571	0.0559
−1.4	0.0808	0.0793	0.0778	0.0764	0.0749	0.0735	0.0721	0.0708	0.0694	0.0681
−1.3	0.0968	0.0951	0.0934	0.0918	0.0901	0.0885	0.0869	0.0853	0.0838	0.0823
−1.2	0.1151	0.1131	0.1112	0.1093	0.1075	0.1056	0.1038	0.1020	0.1003	0.0985
−1.1	0.1357	0.1335	0.1314	0.1292	0.1271	0.1251	0.1230	0.1210	0.1190	0.1170
−1.0	0.1587	0.1562	0.1539	0.1515	0.1492	0.1469	0.1446	0.1423	0.1401	0.1379
−0.9	0.1841	0.1814	0.1788	0.1762	0.1736	0.1711	0.1685	0.1660	0.1635	0.1611
−0.8	0.2119	0.2090	0.2061	0.2033	0.2005	0.1977	0.1949	0.1922	0.1894	0.1867
−0.7	0.2420	0.2389	0.2358	0.2327	0.2296	0.2266	0.2236	0.2206	0.2177	0.2148
−0.6	0.2743	0.2709	0.2676	0.2643	0.2611	0.2578	0.2546	0.2514	0.2483	0.2451
−0.5	0.3085	0.3050	0.3015	0.2981	0.2946	0.2912	0.2877	0.2843	0.2810	0.2776
−0.4	0.3446	0.3409	0.3372	0.3336	0.3300	0.3264	0.3228	0.3192	0.3156	0.3121
−0.3	0.3821	0.3783	0.3745	0.3707	0.3669	0.3632	0.3594	0.3557	0.3520	0.3483
−0.2	0.4207	0.4168	0.4129	0.4090	0.4052	0.4013	0.3974	0.3936	0.3897	0.3859
−0.1	0.4602	0.4562	0.4522	0.4483	0.4443	0.4404	0.4364	0.4325	0.4286	0.4247
−0.0	0.5000	0.4960	0.4920	0.4880	0.4840	0.4801	0.4761	0.4721	0.4681	0.4641

Table 4 | Cumulative Probabilities for the Standard Normal Distribution

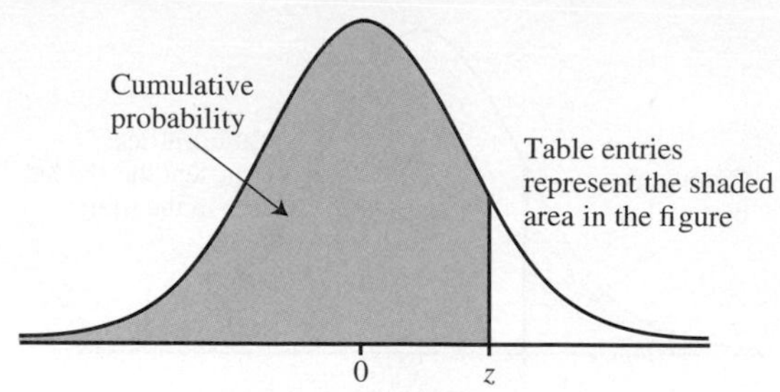

FIRST DIGIT OF Z	SECOND DIGIT OF Z									
z	0.00	0.01	0.02	0.03	0.04	0.05	0.06	0.07	0.08	0.09
0.0	0.5000	0.5040	0.5080	0.5120	0.5160	0.5199	0.5239	0.5279	0.5319	0.5359
0.1	0.5398	0.5438	0.5478	0.5517	0.5557	0.5596	0.5636	0.5675	0.5714	0.5753
0.2	0.5793	0.5832	0.5871	0.5910	0.5948	0.5987	0.6026	0.6064	0.6103	0.6141
0.3	0.6179	0.6217	0.6255	0.6293	0.6331	0.6368	0.6406	0.6443	0.6480	0.6517
0.4	0.6554	0.6591	0.6628	0.6664	0.6700	0.6736	0.6772	0.6808	0.6844	0.6879
0.5	0.6915	0.6950	0.6985	0.7019	0.7054	0.7088	0.7123	0.7157	0.7190	0.7224
0.6	0.7257	0.7291	0.7324	0.7357	0.7389	0.7422	0.7454	0.7486	0.7517	0.7549
0.7	0.7580	0.7611	0.7642	0.7673	0.7704	0.7734	0.7764	0.7794	0.7823	0.7852
0.8	0.7881	0.7910	0.7939	0.7967	0.7995	0.8023	0.8051	0.8078	0.8106	0.8133
0.9	0.8159	0.8186	0.8212	0.8238	0.8264	0.8289	0.8315	0.8340	0.8365	0.8389
1.0	0.8413	0.8438	0.8461	0.8485	0.8508	0.8531	0.8554	0.8577	0.8599	0.8621
1.1	0.8643	0.8665	0.8686	0.8708	0.8729	0.8749	0.8770	0.8790	0.8810	0.8830
1.2	0.8849	0.8869	0.8888	0.8907	0.8925	0.8944	0.8962	0.8980	0.8997	0.9015
1.3	0.9032	0.9049	0.9066	0.9082	0.9099	0.9115	0.9131	0.9147	0.9162	0.9177
1.4	0.9192	0.9207	0.9222	0.9236	0.9251	0.9265	0.9279	0.9292	0.9306	0.9319
1.5	0.9332	0.9345	0.9357	0.9370	0.9382	0.9394	0.9406	0.9418	0.9429	0.9441
1.6	0.9452	0.9463	0.9474	0.9484	0.9495	0.9505	0.9515	0.9525	0.9535	0.9545
1.7	0.9554	0.9564	0.9573	0.9582	0.9591	0.9599	0.9608	0.9616	0.9625	0.9633
1.8	0.9641	0.9649	0.9656	0.9664	0.9671	0.9678	0.9686	0.9693	0.9699	0.9706
1.9	0.9713	0.9719	0.9726	0.9732	0.9738	0.9744	0.9750	0.9756	0.9761	0.9767
2.0	0.9772	0.9778	0.9783	0.9788	0.9793	0.9798	0.9803	0.9808	0.9812	0.9817
2.1	0.9821	0.9826	0.9830	0.9834	0.9838	0.9842	0.9846	0.9850	0.9854	0.9857
2.2	0.9861	0.9864	0.9868	0.9871	0.9875	0.9878	0.9881	0.9884	0.9887	0.9890
2.3	0.9893	0.9896	0.9898	0.9901	0.9904	0.9906	0.9909	0.9911	0.9913	0.9916
2.4	0.9918	0.9920	0.9922	0.9925	0.9927	0.9929	0.9931	0.9932	0.9934	0.9936
2.5	0.9938	0.9940	0.9941	0.9943	0.9945	0.9946	0.9948	0.9949	0.9951	0.9952
2.6	0.9953	0.9955	0.9956	0.9957	0.9959	0.9960	0.9961	0.9962	0.9963	0.9964
2.7	0.9965	0.9966	0.9967	0.9968	0.9969	0.9970	0.9971	0.9972	0.9973	0.9974
2.8	0.9974	0.9975	0.9976	0.9977	0.9977	0.9978	0.9979	0.9979	0.9980	0.9981
2.9	0.9981	0.9982	0.9982	0.9983	0.9984	0.9984	0.9985	0.9985	0.9986	0.9986
3.0	0.9987	0.9987	0.9987	0.9988	0.9988	0.9989	0.9989	0.9989	0.9990	0.9990
3.1	0.9990	0.9991	0.9991	0.9991	0.9992	0.9992	0.9992	0.9992	0.9993	0.9993
3.2	0.9993	0.9993	0.9994	0.9994	0.9994	0.9994	0.9994	0.9995	0.9995	0.9995
3.3	0.9995	0.9995	0.9995	0.9996	0.9996	0.9996	0.9996	0.9996	0.9996	0.9997
3.4	0.9997	0.9997	0.9997	0.9997	0.9997	0.9997	0.9997	0.9997	0.9997	0.9998
3.5	0.9998	0.9998	0.9998	0.9998	0.9998	0.9998	0.9998	0.9998	0.9998	0.9998
3.6	0.9998	0.9998	0.9999	0.9999	0.9999	0.9999	0.9999	0.9999	0.9999	0.9999
3.7 and higher	0.9999									

TABLE 5 | Student's t-distribution

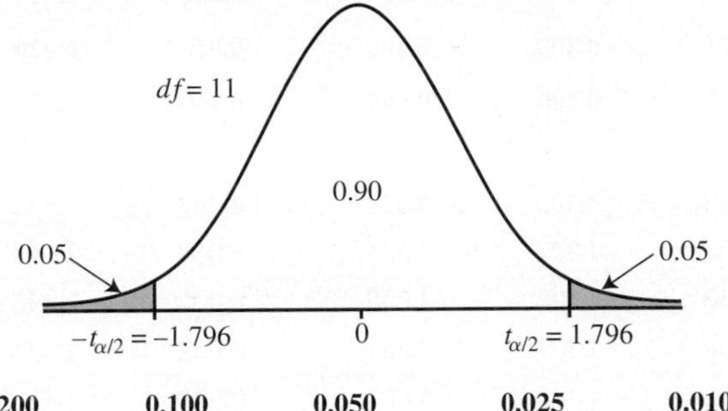

This table provides values for t_α (one-tail test) and $t_{\alpha/2}$ (two-tail test) that correspond to a given value of α and *df*. For example, for a two-tail test with $\alpha = 0.10$ and $df = 11$, $t_{\alpha/2} = 1.796$.

1 Tail	0.200	0.100	0.050	0.025	0.010	0.005
2 Tail	0.400	0.200	0.100	0.050	0.020	0.010
Conf Lev	0.600	0.800	0.900	0.950	0.980	0.990
df						
1	1.376	3.078	6.314	12.706	31.821	63.657
2	1.061	1.886	2.920	4.303	6.965	9.925
3	0.978	1.638	2.353	3.182	4.541	5.841
4	0.941	1.533	2.132	2.776	3.747	4.604
5	0.920	1.476	2.015	2.571	3.365	4.032
6	0.906	1.440	1.943	2.447	3.143	3.707
7	0.896	1.415	1.895	2.365	2.998	3.499
8	0.889	1.397	1.860	2.306	2.896	3.355
9	0.883	1.383	1.833	2.262	2.821	3.250
10	0.879	1.372	1.812	2.228	2.764	3.169
11	0.876	1.363	1.796	2.201	2.718	3.106
12	0.873	1.356	1.782	2.179	2.681	3.055
13	0.870	1.350	1.771	2.160	2.650	3.012
14	0.868	1.345	1.761	2.145	2.624	2.977
15	0.866	1.341	1.753	2.131	2.602	2.947
16	0.865	1.337	1.746	2.120	2.583	2.921
17	0.863	1.333	1.740	2.110	2.567	2.898
18	0.862	1.330	1.734	2.101	2.552	2.878
19	0.861	1.328	1.729	2.093	2.539	2.861
20	0.860	1.325	1.725	2.086	2.528	2.845
21	0.859	1.323	1.721	2.080	2.518	2.831
22	0.858	1.321	1.717	2.074	2.508	2.819
23	0.858	1.319	1.714	2.069	2.500	2.807
24	0.857	1.318	1.711	2.064	2.492	2.797
25	0.856	1.316	1.708	2.060	2.485	2.787
26	0.856	1.315	1.706	2.056	2.479	2.779
27	0.855	1.314	1.703	2.052	2.473	2.771
28	0.855	1.313	1.701	2.048	2.467	2.763
29	0.854	1.311	1.699	2.045	2.462	2.756
30	0.854	1.310	1.697	2.042	2.457	2.750

(continued)

TABLE 5 | Student's *t*-distribution (*Continued*)

1 Tail	0.200	0.100	0.050	0.025	0.010	0.005
2 Tail	0.400	0.200	0.100	0.050	0.020	0.010
Conf Lev	0.600	0.800	0.900	0.950	0.980	0.990
df						
31	0.853	1.309	1.696	2.040	2.453	2.744
32	0.853	1.309	1.694	2.037	2.449	2.738
33	0.853	1.308	1.692	2.035	2.445	2.733
34	0.852	1.307	1.691	2.032	2.441	2.728
35	0.852	1.306	1.690	2.030	2.438	2.724
36	0.852	1.306	1.688	2.028	2.434	2.719
37	0.851	1.305	1.687	2.026	2.431	2.715
38	0.851	1.304	1.686	2.024	2.429	2.712
39	0.851	1.304	1.685	2.023	2.426	2.708
40	0.851	1.303	1.684	2.021	2.423	2.704
41	0.850	1.303	1.683	2.020	2.421	2.701
42	0.850	1.302	1.682	2.018	2.418	2.698
43	0.850	1.302	1.681	2.017	2.416	2.695
44	0.850	1.301	1.680	2.015	2.414	2.692
45	0.850	1.301	1.679	2.014	2.412	2.690
46	0.850	1.300	1.679	2.013	2.410	2.687
47	0.849	1.300	1.678	2.012	2.408	2.685
48	0.849	1.299	1.677	2.011	2.407	2.682
49	0.849	1.299	1.677	2.010	2.405	2.680
50	0.849	1.299	1.676	2.009	2.403	2.678
51	0.849	1.298	1.675	2.008	2.402	2.676
52	0.849	1.298	1.675	2.007	2.400	2.674
53	0.848	1.298	1.674	2.006	2.399	2.672
54	0.848	1.297	1.674	2.005	2.397	2.670
55	0.848	1.297	1.673	2.004	2.396	2.668
56	0.848	1.297	1.673	2.003	2.395	2.667
57	0.848	1.297	1.672	2.002	2.394	2.665
58	0.848	1.296	1.672	2.002	2.392	2.663
59	0.848	1.296	1.671	2.001	2.391	2.662
60	0.848	1.296	1.671	2.000	2.390	2.660
61	0.848	1.296	1.670	2.000	2.389	2.659
62	0.847	1.295	1.670	1.999	2.388	2.657
63	0.847	1.295	1.669	1.998	2.387	2.656
64	0.847	1.295	1.669	1.998	2.386	2.655
65	0.847	1.295	1.669	1.997	2.385	2.654
66	0.847	1.295	1.668	1.997	2.384	2.652
67	0.847	1.294	1.668	1.996	2.383	2.651
68	0.847	1.294	1.668	1.995	2.382	2.650
69	0.847	1.294	1.667	1.995	2.382	2.649
70	0.847	1.294	1.667	1.994	2.381	2.648

TABLE 5 | Student's *t*-distribution (*Continued*)

1 Tail	0.200	0.100	0.050	0.025	0.010	0.005
2 Tail	0.400	0.200	0.100	0.050	0.020	0.010
Conf Lev	0.600	0.800	0.900	0.950	0.980	0.990
df						
71	0.847	1.294	1.667	1.994	2.380	2.647
72	0.847	1.293	1.666	1.993	2.379	2.646
73	0.847	1.293	1.666	1.993	2.379	2.645
74	0.847	1.293	1.666	1.993	2.378	2.644
75	0.846	1.293	1.665	1.992	2.377	2.643
76	0.846	1.293	1.665	1.992	2.376	2.642
77	0.846	1.293	1.665	1.991	2.376	2.641
78	0.846	1.292	1.665	1.991	2.375	2.640
79	0.846	1.292	1.664	1.990	2.374	2.640
80	0.846	1.292	1.664	1.990	2.374	2.639
81	0.846	1.292	1.664	1.990	2.373	2.638
82	0.846	1.292	1.664	1.989	2.373	2.637
83	0.846	1.292	1.663	1.989	2.372	2.636
84	0.846	1.292	1.663	1.989	2.372	2.636
85	0.846	1.292	1.663	1.988	2.371	2.635
86	0.846	1.291	1.663	1.988	2.370	2.634
87	0.846	1.291	1.663	1.988	2.370	2.634
88	0.846	1.291	1.662	1.987	2.369	2.633
89	0.846	1.291	1.662	1.987	2.369	2.632
90	0.846	1.291	1.662	1.987	2.368	2.632
91	0.846	1.291	1.662	1.986	2.368	2.631
92	0.846	1.291	1.662	1.986	2.368	2.630
93	0.846	1.291	1.661	1.986	2.367	2.630
94	0.845	1.291	1.661	1.986	2.367	2.629
95	0.845	1.291	1.661	1.985	2.366	2.629
96	0.845	1.290	1.661	1.985	2.366	2.628
97	0.845	1.290	1.661	1.985	2.365	2.627
98	0.845	1.290	1.661	1.984	2.365	2.627
99	0.845	1.290	1.660	1.984	2.365	2.626
100	0.845	1.290	1.660	1.984	2.364	2.626
∞	0.842	1.282	1.645	1.960	2.236	2.576

TABLE 6 | *F*-distribution

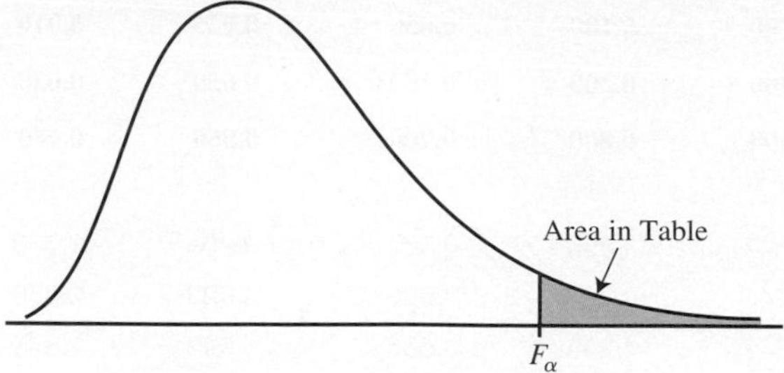

AREA IN THE RIGHT TAIL OF DISTRIBUTION = 0.10

	D_1									
D_2	1	2	3	4	5	6	7	8	9	10
1	39.863	49.500	53.593	55.833	57.240	58.204	58.906	59.439	59.858	60.195
2	8.526	9.000	9.162	9.243	9.293	9.326	9.349	9.367	9.381	9.392
3	5.538	5.462	5.391	5.343	5.309	5.285	5.266	5.252	5.240	5.230
4	4.545	4.325	4.191	4.107	4.051	4.010	3.979	3.955	3.936	3.920
5	4.060	3.780	3.619	3.520	3.453	3.405	3.368	3.339	3.316	3.297
6	3.776	3.463	3.289	3.181	3.108	3.055	3.014	2.983	2.958	2.937
7	3.589	3.257	3.074	2.961	2.883	2.827	2.785	2.752	2.725	2.703
8	3.458	3.113	2.924	2.806	2.726	2.668	2.624	2.589	2.561	2.538
9	3.360	3.006	2.813	2.693	2.611	2.551	2.505	2.469	2.440	2.416
10	3.285	2.924	2.728	2.605	2.522	2.461	2.414	2.377	2.347	2.323
11	3.225	2.860	2.660	2.536	2.451	2.389	2.342	2.304	2.274	2.248
12	3.177	2.807	2.606	2.480	2.394	2.331	2.283	2.245	2.214	2.188
13	3.136	2.763	2.560	2.434	2.347	2.283	2.234	2.195	2.164	2.138
14	3.102	2.726	2.522	2.395	2.307	2.243	2.193	2.154	2.122	2.095
15	3.073	2.695	2.490	2.361	2.273	2.208	2.158	2.119	2.086	2.059
16	3.048	2.668	2.462	2.333	2.244	2.178	2.128	2.088	2.055	2.028
17	3.026	2.645	2.437	2.308	2.218	2.152	2.102	2.061	2.028	2.001
18	3.007	2.624	2.416	2.286	2.196	2.130	2.079	2.038	2.005	1.977
19	2.990	2.606	2.397	2.266	2.176	2.109	2.058	2.017	1.984	1.956
20	2.975	2.589	2.380	2.249	2.158	2.091	2.040	1.999	1.965	1.937
21	2.961	2.575	2.365	2.233	2.142	2.075	2.023	1.982	1.948	1.920
22	2.949	2.561	2.351	2.219	2.128	2.060	2.008	1.967	1.933	1.904
23	2.937	2.549	2.339	2.207	2.115	2.047	1.995	1.953	1.919	1.890
24	2.927	2.538	2.327	2.195	2.103	2.035	1.983	1.941	1.906	1.877
25	2.918	2.528	2.317	2.184	2.092	2.024	1.971	1.929	1.895	1.866
26	2.909	2.519	2.307	2.174	2.082	2.014	1.961	1.919	1.884	1.855
27	2.901	2.511	2.299	2.165	2.073	2.005	1.952	1.909	1.874	1.845
28	2.894	2.503	2.291	2.157	2.064	1.996	1.943	1.900	1.865	1.836
29	2.887	2.495	2.283	2.149	2.057	1.988	1.935	1.892	1.857	1.827
30	2.881	2.489	2.276	2.142	2.049	1.980	1.927	1.884	1.849	1.819

TABLE 6 | F-distribution *(Continued)*

AREA IN THE RIGHT TAIL OF DISTRIBUTION = 0.10

D_2 \ D_1	11	12	13	14	15	16	17	18	19	20
1	60.473	60.705	60.903	61.073	61.220	61.350	61.464	61.566	61.658	61.740
2	9.401	9.408	9.415	9.420	9.425	9.429	9.433	9.436	9.439	9.441
3	5.222	5.216	5.210	5.205	5.200	5.196	5.193	5.190	5.187	5.184
4	3.907	3.896	3.886	3.878	3.870	3.864	3.858	3.853	3.849	3.844
5	3.282	3.268	3.257	3.247	3.238	3.230	3.223	3.217	3.212	3.207
6	2.920	2.905	2.892	2.881	2.871	2.863	2.855	2.848	2.842	2.836
7	2.684	2.668	2.654	2.643	2.632	2.623	2.615	2.607	2.601	2.595
8	2.519	2.502	2.488	2.475	2.464	2.455	2.446	2.438	2.431	2.425
9	2.396	2.379	2.364	2.351	2.340	2.329	2.320	2.312	2.305	2.298
10	2.302	2.284	2.269	2.255	2.244	2.233	2.224	2.215	2.208	2.201
11	2.227	2.209	2.193	2.179	2.167	2.156	2.147	2.138	2.130	2.123
12	2.166	2.147	2.131	2.117	2.105	2.094	2.084	2.075	2.067	2.060
13	2.116	2.097	2.080	2.066	2.053	2.042	2.032	2.023	2.014	2.007
14	2.073	2.054	2.037	2.022	2.010	1.998	1.988	1.978	1.970	1.962
15	2.037	2.017	2.000	1.985	1.972	1.961	1.950	1.941	1.932	1.924
16	2.005	1.985	1.968	1.953	1.940	1.928	1.917	1.908	1.899	1.891
17	1.978	1.958	1.940	1.925	1.912	1.900	1.889	1.879	1.870	1.862
18	1.954	1.933	1.916	1.900	1.887	1.875	1.864	1.854	1.845	1.837
19	1.932	1.912	1.894	1.878	1.865	1.852	1.841	1.831	1.822	1.814
20	1.913	1.892	1.875	1.859	1.845	1.833	1.821	1.811	1.802	1.794
21	1.896	1.875	1.857	1.841	1.827	1.815	1.803	1.793	1.784	1.776
22	1.880	1.859	1.841	1.825	1.811	1.798	1.787	1.777	1.768	1.759
23	1.866	1.845	1.827	1.811	1.796	1.784	1.772	1.762	1.753	1.744
24	1.853	1.832	1.814	1.797	1.783	1.770	1.759	1.748	1.739	1.730
25	1.841	1.820	1.002	1.785	1.771	1.758	1.746	1.736	1.726	1.718
26	1.830	1.809	1.790	1.774	1.760	1.747	1.735	1.724	1.715	1.706
27	1.820	1.799	1.780	1.764	1.749	1.736	1.724	1.714	1.704	1.695
28	1.811	1.790	1.771	1.754	1.740	1.726	1.715	1.704	1.694	1.685
29	1.802	1.781	1.762	1.745	1.731	1.717	1.705	1.695	1.685	1.676
30	1.794	1.773	1.754	1.737	1.722	1.709	1.697	1.686	1.676	1.667

AREA IN THE RIGHT TAIL OF DISTRIBUTION = 0.10

D_2 \ D_1	21	22	23	24	25	26	27	28	29	30
1	61.815	61.883	61.945	62.002	62.055	62.103	62.148	62.190	62.229	62.265
2	9.444	9.446	9.448	9.450	9.451	9.453	9.454	9.456	9.457	9.458
3	5.182	5.180	5.178	5.176	5.175	5.173	5.172	5.170	5.169	5.168
4	3.841	3.837	3.834	3.831	3.828	3.826	3.823	3.821	3.819	3.817
5	3.202	3.198	3.194	3.191	3.187	3.184	3.181	3.179	3.176	3.174
6	2.831	2.827	2.822	2.818	2.815	2.811	2.808	2.805	2.803	2.800
7	2.589	2.584	2.580	2.575	2.571	2.568	2.564	2.561	2.558	2.555
8	2.419	2.413	2.409	2.404	2.400	2.396	2.392	2.389	2.386	2.383
9	2.292	2.287	2.282	2.277	2.272	2.268	2.265	2.261	2.258	2.255
10	2.194	2.189	2.183	2.178	2.174	2.170	2.166	2.162	2.159	2.155
11	2.117	2.111	2.105	2.100	2.095	2.091	2.087	2.083	2.080	2.076

(continued)

TABLE 6 | *F*-distribution (*Continued*)

AREA IN THE RIGHT TAIL OF DISTRIBUTION = 0.10

D_2	D_1 = 21	22	23	24	25	26	27	28	29	30
12	2.053	2.047	2.041	2.036	2.031	2.027	2.022	2.019	2.015	2.011
13	2.000	1.994	1.988	1.983	1.978	1.973	1.969	1.965	1.961	1.958
14	1.955	1.949	1.943	1.938	1.933	1.928	1.923	1.919	1.916	1.912
15	1.917	1.911	1.905	1.899	1.894	1.889	1.885	1.880	1.876	1.873
16	1.884	1.877	1.871	1.866	1.860	1.855	1.851	1.847	1.843	1.839
17	1.855	1.848	1.842	1.836	1.831	1.826	1.821	1.817	1.813	1.809
18	1.829	1.823	1.816	1.810	1.805	1.800	1.795	1.791	1.787	1.783
19	1.807	1.800	1.793	1.787	1.782	1.777	1.772	1.767	1.763	1.759
20	1.786	1.779	1.773	1.767	1.761	1.756	1.751	1.746	1.742	1.738
21	1.768	1.761	1.754	1.748	1.742	1.737	1.732	1.728	1.723	1.719
22	1.751	1.744	1.737	1.731	1.726	1.720	1.715	1.711	1.706	1.702
23	1.736	1.729	1.722	1.716	1.710	1.705	1.700	1.695	1.691	1.686
24	1.722	1.715	1.708	1.702	1.696	1.691	1.686	1.681	1.676	1.672
25	1.710	1.702	1.695	1.689	1.683	1.678	1.672	1.668	1.663	1.659
26	1.698	1.690	1.683	1.677	1.671	1.666	1.660	1.656	1.651	1.647
27	1.687	1.680	1.673	1.666	1.660	1.655	1.649	1.645	1.640	1.636
28	1.677	1.669	1.662	1.656	1.650	1.644	1.639	1.634	1.630	1.625
29	1.668	1.660	1.653	1.647	1.640	1.635	1.630	1.625	1.620	1.616
30	1.659	1.651	1.644	1.638	1.632	1.626	1.621	1.616	1.611	1.606

AREA IN THE RIGHT TAIL OF DISTRIBUTION = 0.05

D_2	D_1 = 1	2	3	4	5	6	7	8	9	10
1	161.448	199.500	215.707	224.583	230.162	233.986	236.768	238.883	240.543	241.882
2	18.513	19.000	19.164	19.247	19.296	19.330	19.353	19.371	19.385	19.396
3	10.128	9.552	9.277	9.117	9.013	8.941	8.887	8.845	8.812	8.786
4	7.709	6.944	6.591	6.388	6.256	6.163	6.094	6.041	5.999	5.964
5	6.608	5.786	5.409	5.192	5.050	4.950	4.876	4.818	4.772	4.735
6	5.987	5.143	4.757	4.534	4.387	4.284	4.207	4.147	4.099	4.060
7	5.591	4.737	4.347	4.120	3.972	3.866	3.787	3.726	3.677	3.637
8	5.318	4.459	4.066	3.838	3.687	3.581	3.500	3.438	3.388	3.347
9	5.117	4.256	3.863	3.633	3.482	3.374	3.293	3.230	3.179	3.137
10	4.965	4.103	3.708	3.478	3.326	3.217	3.135	3.072	3.020	2.978
11	4.844	3.982	3.587	3.357	3.204	3.095	3.012	2.948	2.896	2.854
12	4.747	3.885	3.490	3.259	3.106	2.996	2.913	2.849	2.796	2.753
13	4.667	3.806	3.411	3.179	3.025	2.915	2.832	2.767	2.714	2.671
14	4.600	3.739	3.344	3.112	2.958	2.848	2.764	2.699	2.646	2.602
15	4.543	3.682	3.287	3.056	2.901	2.790	2.707	2.641	2.588	2.544
16	4.494	3.634	3.239	3.007	2.852	2.741	2.657	2.591	2.538	2.494
17	4.451	3.592	3.197	2.965	2.810	2.699	2.614	2.548	2.494	2.450
18	4.414	3.555	3.160	2.928	2.773	2.661	2.577	2.510	2.456	2.412
19	4.381	3.522	3.127	2.895	2.740	2.628	2.544	2.477	2.423	2.378
20	4.351	3.493	3.098	2.866	2.711	2.599	2.514	2.447	2.393	2.348
21	4.325	3.467	3.072	2.840	2.685	2.573	2.488	2.420	2.366	2.321

TABLE 6 | *F*-distribution (*Continued*)

AREA IN THE RIGHT TAIL OF DISTRIBUTION = 0.05

D_2 \ D_1	1	2	3	4	5	6	7	8	9	10
22	4.301	3.443	3.049	2.817	2.661	2.549	2.464	2.397	2.342	2.297
23	4.279	3.422	3.028	2.796	2.640	2.528	2.442	2.375	2.320	2.275
24	4.260	3.403	3.009	2.776	2.621	2.508	2.423	2.355	2.300	2.255
25	4.242	3.385	2.991	2.759	2.603	2.490	2.405	2.337	2.282	2.236
26	4.225	3.369	2.975	2.743	2.587	2.474	2.388	2.321	2.265	2.220
27	4.210	3.354	2.960	2.728	2.572	2.459	2.373	2.305	2.250	2.204
28	4.196	3.340	2.947	2.714	2.558	2.445	2.359	2.291	2.236	2.190
29	4.183	3.328	2.934	2.701	2.545	2.432	2.346	2.278	2.223	2.177
30	4.171	3.316	2.922	2.690	2.534	2.421	2.334	2.266	2.211	2.165

AREA IN THE RIGHT TAIL OF DISTRIBUTION = 0.05

D_2 \ D_1	11	12	13	14	15	16	17	18	19	20
1	242.983	243.906	244.690	245.364	245.950	246.464	246.918	247.323	247.686	248.013
2	19.405	19.413	19.419	19.424	19.429	19.433	19.437	19.440	19.443	19.446
3	8.763	8.745	8.729	8.715	8.703	8.692	8.683	8.675	8.667	8.660
4	5.936	5.912	5.891	5.873	5.858	5.844	5.832	5.821	5.811	5.803
5	4.704	4.678	4.655	4.636	4.619	4.604	4.590	4.579	4.568	4.558
6	4.027	4.000	3.976	3.956	3.938	3.922	3.908	3.896	3.884	3.874
7	3.603	3.575	3.550	3.529	3.511	3.494	3.480	3.467	3.455	3.445
8	3.313	3.284	3.259	3.237	3.218	3.202	3.187	3.173	3.161	3.150
9	3.102	3.073	3.048	3.025	3.006	2.989	2.974	2.960	2.948	2.936
10	2.943	2.913	2.887	2.865	2.845	2.828	2.812	2.798	2.785	2.774
11	2.818	2.788	2.761	2.739	2.719	2.701	2.685	2.071	2.658	2.646
12	2.717	2.687	2.660	2.637	2.617	2.599	2.583	2.568	2.555	2.544
13	2.635	2.604	2.577	2.554	2.533	2.515	2.499	2.484	2.471	2.459
14	2.565	2.534	2.507	2.484	2.463	2.445	2.428	2.413	2.400	2.388
15	2.507	2.475	2.448	2.424	2.403	2.385	2.368	2.353	2.340	2.328
16	2.456	2.425	2.397	2.373	2.352	2.333	2.317	2.302	2.288	2.276
17	2.413	2.381	2.353	2.329	2.308	2.289	2.272	2.257	2.243	2.230
18	2.374	2.342	2.314	2.290	2.269	2.250	2.233	2.217	2.203	2.191
19	2.340	2.308	2.280	2.256	2.234	2.215	2.198	2.182	2.168	2.155
20	2.310	2.278	2.250	2.225	2.203	2.184	2.167	2.151	2.137	2.124
21	2.283	2.250	2.222	2.197	2.176	2.156	2.139	2.123	2.109	2.096
22	2.259	2.226	2.198	2.173	2.151	2.131	2.114	2.098	2.084	2.071
23	2.236	2.204	2.175	2.150	2.128	2.109	2.091	2.075	2.061	2.048
24	2.216	2.183	2.155	2.130	2.108	2.088	2.070	2.054	2.040	2.027
25	2.198	2.165	2.136	2.111	2.089	2.069	2.051	2.035	2.021	2.007
26	2.181	2.148	2.119	2.094	2.072	2.052	2.034	2.018	2.003	1.990
27	2.166	2.132	2.103	2.078	2.056	2.036	2.018	2.002	1.987	1.974
28	2.151	2.118	2.089	2.064	2.041	2.021	2.003	1.987	1.972	1.959
29	2.138	2.104	2.075	2.050	2.027	2.007	1.989	1.973	1.958	1.945
30	2.126	2.092	2.063	2.037	2.015	1.995	1.976	1.960	1.945	1.932

(*continued*)

TABLE 6 | *F*-distribution *(Continued)*

AREA IN THE RIGHT TAIL OF DISTRIBUTION = 0.05

D_2 \ D_1	21	22	23	24	25	26	27	28	29	30
1	248.309	248.579	248.826	249.052	249.260	249.453	249.631	249.797	249.951	250.095
2	19.448	19.450	19.452	19.454	19.456	19.457	19.459	19.460	19.461	19.462
3	8.654	8.648	8.643	8.639	8.634	8.630	8.626	8.623	8.620	8.617
4	5.795	5.787	5.781	5.774	5.769	5.763	5.759	5.754	5.750	5.746
5	4.549	4.541	4.534	4.527	4.521	4.515	4.510	4.505	4.500	4.496
6	3.865	3.856	3.849	3.841	3.835	3.829	3.823	3.818	3.813	3.808
7	3.435	3.426	3.418	3.410	3.404	3.397	3.391	3.386	3.381	3.376
8	3.140	3.131	3.123	3.115	3.108	3.102	3.095	3.090	3.084	3.079
9	2.926	2.917	2.908	2.900	2.893	2.886	2.880	2.874	2.869	2.864
10	2.764	2.754	2.745	2.737	2.730	2.723	2.716	2.710	2.705	2.700
11	2.636	2.626	2.617	2.609	2.601	2.594	2.588	2.582	2.576	2.570
12	2.533	2.523	2.514	2.505	2.498	2.491	2.484	2.478	2.472	2.466
13	2.448	2.438	2.429	2.420	2.412	2.405	2.398	2.392	2.386	2.380
14	2.377	2.367	2.357	2.349	2.341	2.333	2.326	2.320	2.314	2.308
15	2.316	2.306	2.297	2.288	2.280	2.272	2.265	2.259	2.253	2.247
16	2.264	2.254	2.244	2.235	2.227	2.220	2.212	2.206	2.200	2.194
17	2.219	2.208	2.199	2.190	2.181	2.174	2.167	2.160	2.154	2.148
18	2.179	2.168	2.159	2.150	2.141	2.134	2.126	2.119	2.113	2.107
19	2.144	2.133	2.123	2.114	2.106	2.098	2.090	2.084	2.077	2.071
20	2.112	2.102	2.092	2.082	2.074	2.066	2.059	2.052	2.045	2.039
21	2.084	2.073	2.063	2.054	2.045	2.037	2.030	2.023	2.016	2.010
22	2.059	2.048	2.038	2.028	2.020	2.012	2.004	1.997	1.990	1.984
23	2.036	2.025	2.014	2.005	1.996	1.988	1.981	1.973	1.967	1.961
24	2.015	2.003	1.993	1.984	1.975	1.967	1.959	1.952	1.945	1.939
25	1.995	1.984	1.974	1.964	1.955	1.947	1.939	1.932	1.926	1.919
26	1.978	1.966	1.956	1.946	1.938	1.929	1.921	1.914	1.907	1.901
27	1.961	1.950	1.940	1.930	1.921	1.913	1.905	1.898	1.891	1.884
28	1.946	1.935	1.924	1.915	1.906	1.897	1.889	1.882	1.875	1.869
29	1.932	1.921	1.910	1.901	1.891	1.883	1.875	1.868	1.861	1.854
30	1.919	1.908	1.897	1.887	1.878	1.870	1.862	1.854	1.847	1.841

AREA IN THE RIGHT TAIL OF DISTRIBUTION = 0.025

D_2 \ D_1	1	2	3	4	5	6	7	8	9	10
1	647.789	799.500	864.163	899.583	921.848	937.111	948.217	956.656	963.285	968.627
2	38.506	39.000	39.165	39.248	39.298	39.331	39.355	39.373	39.387	39.398
3	17.443	16.044	15.439	15.101	14.885	14.735	14.624	14.540	14.473	14.419
4	12.218	10.649	9.979	9.605	9.364	9.197	9.074	8.980	8.905	8.844
5	10.007	8.434	7.764	7.388	7.146	6.978	6.853	6.757	6.681	6.619
6	8.813	7.260	6.599	6.227	5.988	5.820	5.695	5.600	5.523	5.461
7	8.073	6.542	5.890	5.523	5.285	5.119	4.995	4.899	4.823	4.761
8	7.571	6.059	5.416	5.053	4.817	4.652	4.529	4.433	4.357	4.295
9	7.209	5.715	5.078	4.718	4.484	4.320	4.197	4.102	4.026	3.964
10	6.937	5.456	4.826	4.468	4.236	4.072	3.950	3.855	3.779	3.717
11	6.724	5.256	4.630	4.275	4.044	3.881	3.759	3.664	3.588	3.526

TABLE 6 | *F*-distribution (*Continued*)

AREA IN THE RIGHT TAIL OF DISTRIBUTION = 0.025

D_2 \ D_1	1	2	3	4	5	6	7	8	9	10
12	6.554	5.096	4.474	4.121	3.891	3.728	3.607	3.512	3.436	3.374
13	6.414	4.965	4.347	3.996	3.767	3.604	3.483	3.388	3.312	3.250
14	6.298	4.857	4.242	3.892	3.663	3.501	3.380	3.285	3.209	3.147
15	6.200	4.765	4.153	3.804	3.576	3.415	3.293	3.199	3.123	3.060
16	6.115	4.687	4.077	3.729	3.502	3.341	3.219	3.125	3.049	2.986
17	6.042	4.619	4.011	3.665	3.438	3.277	3.156	3.061	2.985	2.922
18	5.978	4.560	3.954	3.608	3.382	3.221	3.100	3.005	2.929	2.866
19	5.922	4.508	3.903	3.559	3.333	3.172	3.051	2.956	2.880	2.817
20	5.871	4.461	3.859	3.515	3.289	3.128	3.007	2.913	2.837	2.774
21	5.827	4.420	3.819	3.475	3.250	3.090	2.969	2.874	2.798	2.735
22	5.786	4.383	3.783	3.440	3.215	3.055	2.934	2.839	2.763	2.700
23	5.750	4.349	3.750	3.408	3.183	3.023	2.902	2.808	2.731	2.668
24	5.717	4.319	3.721	3.379	3.155	2.995	2.874	2.779	2.703	2.640
25	5.686	4.291	3.694	3.353	3.129	2.969	2.848	2.753	2.677	2.613
26	5.659	4.265	3.670	3.329	3.105	2.945	2.824	2.729	2.653	2.590
27	5.633	4.242	3.647	3.307	3.083	2.923	2.802	2.707	2.631	2.568
28	5.610	4.221	3.626	3.286	3.063	2.903	2.782	2.687	2.611	2.547
29	5.588	4.201	3.607	3.267	3.044	2.884	2.763	2.669	2.592	2.529
30	5.568	4.182	3.589	3.250	3.026	2.867	2.746	2.651	2.575	2.511

AREA IN THE RIGHT TAIL OF DISTRIBUTION = 0.025

D_2 \ D_1	11	12	13	14	15	16	17	18	19	20
1	973.025	976.708	979.837	982.528	984.867	986.919	988.733	990.349	991.797	993.103
2	39.407	39.415	39.421	39.427	39.431	39.435	39.439	39.442	39.445	39.448
3	14.374	14.337	14.304	14.277	14.253	14.232	14.213	14.196	14.181	14.167
4	8.794	8.751	8.715	8.684	8.657	8.633	8.611	8.592	8.575	8.560
5	6.568	6.525	6.488	6.456	6.428	6.403	6.381	6.362	6.344	6.329
6	5.410	5.366	5.329	5.297	5.269	5.244	5.222	5.202	5.184	5.168
7	4.709	4.666	4.628	4.596	4.568	4.543	4.521	4.501	4.483	4.467
8	4.243	4.200	4.162	4.130	4.101	4.076	4.054	4.034	4.016	3.999
9	3.912	3.868	3.831	3.798	3.769	3.744	3.722	3.701	3.683	3.667
10	3.665	3.621	3.583	3.550	3.522	3.496	3.474	3.453	3.435	3.419
11	3.474	3.430	3.392	3.359	3.330	3.304	3.282	3.261	3.243	3.226
12	3.321	3.277	3.239	3.206	3.177	3.152	3.129	3.108	3.090	3.073
13	3.197	3.153	3.115	3.082	3.053	3.027	3.004	2.983	2.965	2.948
14	3.095	3.050	3.012	2.979	2.949	2.923	2.900	2.879	2.861	2.844
15	3.008	2.963	2.925	2.891	2.862	2.836	2.813	2.792	2.773	2.756
16	2.934	2.889	2.851	2.817	2.788	2.761	2.738	2.717	2.698	2.681
17	2.870	2.825	2.786	2.753	2.723	2.697	2.673	2.652	2.633	2.616
18	2.814	2.769	2.730	2.696	2.667	2.640	2.617	2.596	2.576	2.559
19	2.765	2.720	2.681	2.647	2.617	2.591	2.567	2.546	2.526	2.509
20	2.721	2.676	2.637	2.603	2.573	2.547	2.523	2.501	2.482	2.464
21	2.682	2.637	2.598	2.564	2.534	2.507	2.483	2.462	2.442	2.425
22	2.647	2.602	2.563	2.528	2.498	2.472	2.448	2.426	2.407	2.389

(*continued*)

TABLE 6 | *F*-distribution (*Continued*)

AREA IN THE RIGHT TAIL OF DISTRIBUTION = 0.025

D_2 \ D_1	11	12	13	14	15	16	17	18	19	20
23	2.615	2.570	2.531	2.497	2.466	2.440	2.416	2.394	2.374	2.357
24	2.586	2.541	2.502	2.468	2.437	2.411	2.386	2.365	2.345	2.327
25	2.560	2.515	2.476	2.441	2.411	2.384	2.360	2.338	2.318	2.300
26	2.536	2.491	2.451	2.417	2.387	2.360	2.335	2.314	2.294	2.276
27	2.514	2.469	2.429	2.395	2.364	2.337	2.313	2.291	2.271	2.253
28	2.494	2.448	2.409	2.374	2.344	2.317	2.292	2.270	2.251	2.232
29	2.475	2.430	2.390	2.355	2.325	2.298	2.273	2.251	2.231	2.213
30	2.458	2.412	2.372	2.338	2.307	2.280	2.255	2.233	2.213	2.195

AREA IN THE RIGHT TAIL OF DISTRIBUTION = 0.025

D_2 \ D_1	21	22	23	24	25	26	27	28	29	30
1	994.286	995.362	996.346	997.249	998.081	998.849	999.561	1000.22	1000.84	1001.41
2	39.450	39.452	39.454	39.456	39.458	39.459	39.461	39.462	39.463	39.465
3	14.155	14.144	14.134	14.124	14.115	14.107	14.100	14.093	14.087	14.081
4	8.546	8.533	8.522	8.511	8.501	8.492	8.483	8.476	8.468	8.461
5	6.314	6.301	6.289	6.278	6.268	6.258	6.250	6.242	6.234	6.227
6	5.154	5.141	5.128	5.117	5.107	5.097	5.088	5.080	5.072	5.065
7	4.452	4.439	4.426	4.415	4.405	4.395	4.386	4.378	4.370	4.362
8	3.985	3.971	3.959	3.947	3.937	3.927	3.918	3.909	3.901	3.894
9	3.652	3.638	3.626	3.614	3.604	3.594	3.584	3.576	3.568	3.560
10	3.403	3.390	3.377	3.365	3.355	3.345	3.335	3.327	3.319	3.311
11	3.211	3.197	3.184	3.173	3.162	3.152	3.142	3.133	3.125	3.118
12	3.057	3.043	3.031	3.019	3.008	2.998	2.988	2.979	2.971	2.963
13	2.932	2.918	2.905	2.893	2.882	2.872	2.862	2.853	2.845	2.837
14	2.828	2.814	2.801	2.789	2.778	2.767	2.758	2.749	2.740	2.732
15	2.740	2.726	2.713	2.701	2.689	2.679	2.669	2.660	2.652	2.644
16	2.665	2.651	2.637	2.625	2.614	2.603	2.594	2.584	2.576	2.568
17	2.600	2.585	2.572	2.560	2.548	2.538	2.528	2.519	2.510	2.502
18	2.543	2.529	2.515	2.503	2.491	2.481	2.471	2.461	2.453	2.445
19	2.493	2.478	2.465	2.452	2.441	2.430	2.420	2.411	2.402	2.394
20	2.448	2.434	2.420	2.408	2.396	2.385	2.375	2.366	2.357	2.349
21	2.409	2.394	2.380	2.368	2.356	2.345	2.335	2.325	2.317	2.308
22	2.373	2.358	2.344	2.331	2.320	2.309	2.299	2.289	2.280	2.272
23	2.340	2.325	2.312	2.299	2.287	2.276	2.266	2.256	2.247	2.239
24	2.311	2.296	2.282	2.269	2.257	2.246	2.236	2.226	2.217	2.209
25	2.284	2.269	2.255	2.242	2.230	2.219	2.209	2.199	2.190	2.182
26	2.259	2.244	2.230	2.217	2.205	2.194	2.184	2.174	2.165	2.157
27	2.237	2.222	2.208	2.195	2.183	2.171	2.161	2.151	2.142	2.133
28	2.216	2.201	2.187	2.174	2.161	2.150	2.140	2.130	2.121	2.112
29	2.196	2.181	2.167	2.154	2.142	2.131	2.120	2.110	2.101	2.092
30	2.178	2.163	2.149	2.136	2.124	2.112	2.102	2.092	2.083	2.074

TABLE 6 | *F*-distribution (*Continued*)

AREA IN THE RIGHT TAIL OF DISTRIBUTION = 0.01

D_2 \ D_1	1	2	3	4	5	6	7	8	9	10
1	4052.2	4999.5	5403.4	5624.6	5763.6	5859.0	5928.4	5981.1	6022.5	6055.8
2	98.503	99.000	99.166	99.249	99.299	99.333	99.356	99.374	99.388	99.399
3	34.116	30.817	29.457	28.710	28.237	27.911	27.672	27.489	27.345	27.229
4	21.198	18.000	16.694	15.977	15.522	15.207	14.976	14.799	14.659	14.546
5	16.258	13.274	12.060	11.392	10.967	10.672	10.456	10.289	10.158	10.051
6	13.745	10.925	9.780	9.148	8.746	8.466	8.260	8.102	7.976	7.874
7	12.246	9.547	8.451	7.847	7.460	7.191	6.993	6.840	6.719	6.620
8	11.259	8.649	7.591	7.006	6.632	6.371	6.178	6.029	5.911	5.814
9	10.561	8.022	6.992	6.422	6.057	5.802	5.613	5.467	5.351	5.257
10	10.044	7.559	6.552	5.994	5.636	5.386	5.200	5.057	4.942	4.849
11	9.646	7.206	6.217	5.668	5.316	5.069	4.886	4.744	4.632	4.539
12	9.330	6.927	5.953	5.412	5.064	4.821	4.640	4.499	4.388	4.296
13	9.074	6.701	5.739	5.205	4.862	4.620	4.441	4.302	4.191	4.100
14	8.862	6.515	5.564	5.035	4.695	4.456	4.278	4.140	4.030	3.939
15	8.683	6.359	5.417	4.893	4.556	4.318	4.142	4.004	3.895	3.805
16	8.531	6.226	5.292	4.773	4.437	4.202	4.026	3.890	3.780	3.691
17	8.400	6.112	5.185	4.669	4.336	4.102	3.927	3.791	3.682	3.593
18	8.285	6.013	5.092	4.579	4.248	4.015	3.841	3.705	3.597	3.508
19	8.185	5.926	5.010	4.500	4.171	3.939	3.765	3.631	3.523	3.434
20	8.096	5.849	4.938	4.431	4.103	3.871	3.699	3.564	3.457	3.368
21	8.017	5.780	4.874	4.369	4.042	3.812	3.640	3.506	3.398	3.310
22	7.945	5.719	4.817	4.310	3.988	3.758	3.587	3.453	3.346	3.258
23	7.881	5.664	4.765	4.264	3.939	3.710	3.539	3.406	3.299	3.211
24	7.823	5.614	4.718	4.218	3.895	3.667	3.496	3.363	3.256	3.168
25	7.770	5.568	4.675	4.177	3.855	3.627	3.457	3.324	3.217	3.129
26	7.721	5.526	4.637	4.140	3.818	3.591	3.421	3.288	3.182	3.094
27	7.677	5.488	4.601	4.106	3.785	3.558	3.388	3.256	3.149	3.062
28	7.636	5.453	4.568	4.074	3.754	3.528	3.358	3.226	3.120	3.032
29	7.598	5.420	4.538	4.045	3.725	3.499	3.330	3.198	3.092	3.005
30	7.562	5.390	4.510	4.018	3.699	3.473	3.304	3.173	3.067	2.979

AREA IN THE RIGHT TAIL OF DISTRIBUTION = 0.01

D_2 \ D_1	11	12	13	14	15	16	17	18	19	20
1	6083.3	6106.3	6125.9	6142.7	6157.3	6170.1	6181.4	6191.5	6200.6	6208.7
2	99.408	99.416	99.422	99.428	99.433	99.437	99.440	99.444	99.447	99.449
3	27.133	27.052	26.983	26.924	26.872	26.827	26.787	26.751	26.719	26.690
4	14.452	14.374	14.307	14.249	14.198	14.154	14.115	14.080	14.048	14.020
5	9.963	9.888	9.825	9.770	9.722	9.680	9.643	9.610	9.580	9.553
6	7.790	7.718	7.657	7.605	7.559	7.519	7.483	7.451	7.422	7.396
7	6.538	6.469	6.410	6.359	6.314	6.275	6.240	6.209	6.181	6.155
8	5.734	5.667	5.609	5.559	5.515	5.477	5.442	5.412	5.384	5.359
9	5.178	5.111	5.055	5.005	4.962	4.924	4.890	4.860	4.833	4.808
10	4.772	4.706	4.650	4.601	4.558	4.520	4.487	4.457	4.430	4.405
11	4.462	4.397	4.342	4.293	4.251	4.213	4.180	4.150	4.123	4.099

(*continued*)

TABLE 6 | F-distribution (Continued)

AREA IN THE RIGHT TAIL OF DISTRIBUTION = 0.01

D_2 \ D_1	11	12	13	14	15	16	17	18	19	20
12	4.220	4.155	4.100	4.052	4.010	3.972	3.939	3.909	3.883	3.858
13	4.025	3.960	3.905	3.857	3.815	3.778	3.745	3.716	3.689	3.665
14	3.864	3.800	3.745	3.698	3.656	3.619	3.586	3.556	3.529	3.505
15	3.730	3.666	3.612	3.564	3.522	3.485	3.452	3.423	3.396	3.372
16	3.616	3.553	3.498	3.451	3.409	3.372	3.339	3.310	3.283	3.259
17	3.519	3.455	3.401	3.353	3.312	3.275	3.242	3.212	3.186	3.162
18	3.434	3.371	3.316	3.269	3.227	3.190	3.158	3.128	3.101	3.077
19	3.360	3.297	3.242	3.195	3.153	3.116	3.084	3.054	3.027	3.003
20	3.294	3.231	3.177	3.130	3.088	3.051	3.018	2.989	2.962	2.938
21	3.236	3.173	3.119	3.072	3.030	2.993	2.960	2.931	2.904	2.880
22	3.184	3.121	3.067	3.019	2.978	2.941	2.908	2.879	2.852	2.827
23	3.137	3.074	3.020	2.973	2.931	2.894	2.861	2.832	2.805	2.781
24	3.094	3.032	2.977	2.930	2.889	2.852	2.819	2.789	2.762	2.738
25	3.056	2.993	2.939	2.892	2.850	2.813	2.780	2.751	2.724	2.699
26	3.021	2.958	2.904	2.857	2.815	2.778	2.745	2.715	2.688	2.664
27	2.988	2.926	2.871	2.824	2.783	2.746	2.713	2.683	2.656	2.632
28	2.959	2.896	2.842	2.795	2.753	2.716	2.683	2.653	2.626	2.602
29	2.931	2.868	2.814	2.767	2.726	2.689	2.656	2.626	2.599	2.574
30	2.906	2.843	2.789	2.742	2.700	2.663	2.630	2.600	2.573	2.549

AREA IN THE RIGHT TAIL OF DISTRIBUTION = 0.01

D_2 \ D_1	21	22	23	24	25	26	27	28	29	30
1	6216.1	6222.8	6229.0	6234.6	6239.8	6244.6	6249.1	6253.2	6257.1	6260.6
2	99.452	99.454	99.456	99.458	99.459	99.461	99.462	99.463	99.465	99.466
3	26.664	26.640	26.618	26.598	26.579	26.562	26.546	26.531	26.517	26.505
4	13.994	13.970	13.949	13.929	13.911	13.894	13.878	13.864	13.850	13.838
5	9.528	9.506	9.485	9.466	9.449	9.433	9.418	9.404	9.391	9.379
6	7.372	7.351	7.331	7.313	7.296	7.280	7.266	7.253	7.240	7.229
7	6.132	6.111	6.092	6.074	6.058	6.043	6.029	6.016	6.003	5.992
8	5.336	5.316	5.297	5.279	5.263	5.248	5.234	5.221	5.209	5.198
9	4.786	4.765	4.746	4.729	4.713	4.698	4.685	4.672	4.660	4.649
10	4.383	4.363	4.344	4.327	4.311	4.296	4.283	4.270	4.258	4.247
11	4.077	4.057	4.038	4.021	4.005	3.990	3.977	3.964	3.952	3.941
12	3.836	3.816	3.798	3.780	3.765	3.750	3.736	3.724	3.712	3.701
13	3.643	3.622	3.604	3.587	3.571	3.556	3.543	3.530	3.518	3.507
14	3.483	3.463	3.444	3.427	3.412	3.397	3.383	3.371	3.359	3.348
15	3.350	3.330	3.311	3.294	3.278	3.264	3.250	3.237	3.225	3.214
16	3.237	3.216	3.198	3.181	3.165	3.150	3.137	3.124	3.112	3.101
17	3.139	3.119	3.101	3.084	3.068	3.053	3.039	3.026	3.014	3.003
18	3.055	3.035	3.016	2.999	2.983	2.968	2.955	2.942	2.930	2.919
19	2.981	2.961	2.942	2.925	2.909	2.894	2.880	2.868	2.855	2.844
20	2.916	2.895	2.877	2.859	2.843	2.829	2.815	2.802	2.790	2.778
21	2.857	2.837	2.818	2.801	2.785	2.770	2.756	2.743	2.731	2.720
22	2.805	2.785	2.766	2.749	2.733	2.718	2.704	2.691	2.679	2.667

TABLE 6 | ***F*-distribution** *(Continued)*

AREA IN THE RIGHT TAIL OF DISTRIBUTION = 0.01

D_2	D_1 21	22	23	24	25	26	27	28	29	30
23	2.758	2.738	2.719	2.702	2.686	2.671	2.657	2.644	2.632	2.620
24	2.716	2.695	2.676	2.659	2.643	2.628	2.614	2.601	2.589	2.577
25	2.677	2.657	2.638	2.620	2.604	2.589	2.575	2.562	2.550	2.538
26	2.642	2.621	2.602	2.585	2.569	2.554	2.540	2.526	2.514	2.503
27	2.609	2.589	2.570	2.552	2.536	2.521	2.507	2.494	2.481	2.470
28	2.579	2.559	2.540	2.522	2.506	2.491	2.477	2.464	2.451	2.440
29	2.552	2.531	2.512	2.495	2.478	2.463	2.449	2.436	2.423	2.412
30	2.526	2.506	2.487	2.469	2.453	2.437	2.423	2.410	2.398	2.386

TABLE 7 | Critical Values of the Studentized Range, *Q*

0.05 LEVEL

D_2	D_1 = 2	3	4	5	6	7	8	9	10
1	17.97	26.98	38.32	37.08	40.41	43.12	45.40	47.36	49.07
2	6.09	8.33	9.80	10.88	11.74	12.44	13.03	13.54	13.99
3	4.50	5.91	6.82	7.50	8.04	8.48	8.85	9.18	9.46
4	3.93	5.04	5.76	6.29	6.71	7.05	7.35	7.60	7.83
5	3.64	4.60	5.22	5.67	6.03	6.33	6.58	6.80	6.99
6	3.46	4.34	4.90	5.30	5.63	5.90	6.12	6.32	6.49
7	3.34	4.16	4.68	5.06	5.36	5.61	5.82	6.00	6.16
8	3.26	4.04	4.53	4.89	5.17	5.40	5.60	5.77	5.92
9	3.20	3.95	4.41	4.76	5.02	5.24	5.43	5.59	5.74
10	3.15	3.88	4.33	4.65	4.91	5.12	5.30	5.46	5.60
11	3.11	3.82	4.26	4.57	4.82	5.03	5.20	5.35	5.49
12	3.08	3.77	4.20	4.51	4.75	4.95	5.12	5.27	5.39
13	3.06	3.73	4.15	4.45	4.69	4.88	5.05	5.19	5.32
14	3.03	3.70	4.11	4.41	4.64	4.83	4.99	5.13	5.25
15	3.01	3.67	4.08	4.37	4.59	4.78	4.94	5.08	5.20
16	3.00	3.65	4.05	4.33	4.56	4.74	4.90	5.03	5.15
17	2.98	3.63	4.02	4.30	4.52	4.70	4.86	4.99	5.11
18	2.97	3.61	4.00	4.28	4.49	4.67	4.82	4.96	5.07
19	2.96	3.59	3.98	4.25	4.47	4.65	4.79	4.92	5.04
20	2.95	3.58	3.96	4.23	4.44	4.62	4.77	4.90	5.01
24	2.92	3.53	3.90	4.17	4.37	4.54	4.68	4.81	4.92
30	2.89	3.49	3.85	4.10	4.30	4.46	4.60	4.72	4.82
40	2.86	3.44	3.79	4.04	4.23	4.36	4.52	4.63	4.73
60	2.83	3.40	3.74	3.98	4.16	4.31	4.44	4.55	4.65
120	2.80	3.36	3.68	3.92	4.10	4.24	4.36	4.47	4.56
∞	2.77	3.31	3.63	3.86	4.03	4.17	4.29	4.39	4.47

0.05 LEVEL

D_2	D_1 = 11	12	13	14	15	16	17	18	19	20
1	50.59	51.96	53.20	54.33	55.36	56.32	57.22	58.04	58.83	59.56
2	14.39	14.75	15.08	15.38	15.65	15.91	16.14	16.37	16.57	16.77
3	9.72	9.95	10.15	10.35	10.52	10.69	10.84	10.98	11.11	11.24
4	8.03	8.21	8.37	8.52	8.66	8.79	8.91	9.03	9.13	9.23
5	7.17	7.32	7.47	7.60	7.72	7.83	7.93	8.03	8.12	8.21
6	6.65	6.79	6.92	7.03	7.14	7.24	7.34	7.43	7.51	7.59
7	6.30	6.43	6.55	6.66	6.76	6.85	6.94	7.02	7.10	7.17
8	6.05	6.18	6.29	6.39	6.48	6.57	6.65	6.73	6.80	6.87
9	5.87	5.98	6.09	6.19	6.28	6.36	6.44	6.51	6.58	6.64
10	5.72	5.83	5.93	6.03	6.11	6.19	6.27	6.34	6.40	6.47
11	5.61	5.71	5.81	5.90	5.98	6.06	6.13	6.20	6.27	6.33
12	5.51	5.61	5.71	5.80	5.88	5.95	6.02	6.09	6.15	6.21
13	5.43	5.53	5.63	5.71	5.79	5.86	5.93	5.99	6.05	6.11
14	5.36	5.46	5.55	5.64	5.71	5.79	5.85	5.91	5.97	6.03
15	5.31	5.40	5.49	5.57	5.65	5.72	5.78	5.85	5.90	5.96

TABLE 7 | Critical Values of the Studentized Range, Q (*Continued*)

0.05 LEVEL

D_2	D_1 11	12	13	14	15	16	17	18	19	20
16	5.26	5.35	5.44	5.52	5.59	5.66	5.73	5.79	5.84	5.90
17	5.21	5.31	5.39	5.47	5.54	5.61	5.67	5.73	5.79	5.84
18	5.17	5.27	5.35	5.43	5.50	5.57	5.63	5.69	5.74	5.79
19	5.14	5.23	5.31	5.39	5.46	5.53	5.59	5.65	5.70	5.75
20	5.11	5.20	5.28	5.36	5.43	5.49	5.55	5.61	5.66	5.71
24	5.01	5.10	5.18	5.25	5.32	5.38	5.44	5.49	5.55	5.59
30	4.92	5.00	5.08	5.15	5.21	5.27	5.33	5.38	5.43	5.47
40	4.82	4.90	4.98	5.04	5.11	5.16	5.22	5.27	5.31	5.36
60	4.73	4.81	4.88	4.94	5.00	5.06	5.11	5.15	5.20	5.24
120	4.64	4.71	4.78	4.84	4.90	4.95	5.00	5.04	5.09	5.13
∞	4.55	4.62	4.68	4.74	4.80	4.85	4.89	4.93	4.97	5.01

0.01 LEVEL

D_2	D_1 2	3	4	5	6	7	8	9	10
1	90.03	135.0	164.3	185.6	202.2	215.8	227.2	237.0	245.6
2	14.04	19.02	22.29	24.72	26.63	28.20	29.53	30.68	31.69
3	8.26	10.62	12.17	13.33	14.24	15.00	15.64	16.20	16.69
4	6.51	8.12	9.17	9.96	10.58	11.10	11.55	11.93	12.27
5	5.70	6.98	7.80	8.42	8.91	9.32	9.67	9.97	10.24
6	5.24	6.33	7.03	7.56	7.97	8.32	8.61	8.87	9.10
7	4.95	5.92	6.54	7.01	7.37	7.68	7.94	8.17	8.37
8	4.75	5.64	6.20	6.62	6.96	7.24	7.47	7.68	7.86
9	4.60	5.43	5.96	6.35	6.66	6.91	7.13	7.33	7.49
10	4.48	5.27	5.77	6.14	6.43	6.67	6.87	7.05	7.21
11	4.39	5.15	5.62	5.97	6.25	6.48	6.67	6.84	6.99
12	4.32	5.05	5.50	5.84	6.10	6.32	6.51	6.67	6.81
13	4.26	4.96	5.40	5.73	5.98	6.19	6.37	6.53	6.67
14	4.21	4.89	5.32	5.63	5.88	6.08	6.26	6.41	6.54
15	4.17	4.84	5.25	5.56	5.80	5.99	6.16	6.31	6.44
16	4.13	4.79	5.19	5.49	5.72	5.92	6.08	6.22	6.35
17	4.10	4.74	5.14	5.43	5.66	5.85	6.01	6.15	6.27
18	4.07	4.70	5.09	5.38	5.60	5.79	5.94	6.08	6.20
19	4.05	4.67	5.05	5.33	5.55	5.73	5.89	6.02	6.14
20	4.02	4.64	5.02	5.29	5.51	5.69	5.84	5.97	6.09
24	3.96	4.55	4.91	5.17	5.37	5.54	5.69	5.81	5.92
30	3.89	4.45	4.80	5.05	5.24	5.40	5.54	5.65	5.76
40	3.82	4.37	4.70	4.93	5.11	5.26	5.39	5.50	5.60
60	3.76	4.28	4.59	4.82	4.99	5.13	5.25	5.36	5.45
120	3.70	4.20	4.50	4.71	4.87	5.01	5.12	5.21	5.30
∞	3.64	4.12	4.40	4.60	4.76	4.88	4.99	5.08	5.16

(*continued*)

TABLE 7 | Critical Values of the Studentized Range, Q *(Continued)*

0.01 LEVEL

	D_1									
D_2	11	12	13	14	15	16	17	18	19	20
1	253.2	260.0	266.2	271.8	277.0	281.8	286.3	290.4	294.3	298.0
2	32.59	33.40	34.13	34.81	35.43	36.00	36.53	37.03	37.50	37.95
3	17.13	17.53	17.89	18.22	18.52	18.81	19.07	19.32	19.55	19.77
4	12.57	12.84	13.09	13.32	13.53	13.73	13.91	14.08	14.24	14.40
5	10.48	10.70	10.89	11.08	11.24	11.40	11.55	11.68	11.81	11.93
6	9.30	9.48	9.65	9.81	9.95	10.08	10.21	10.32	10.43	10.54
7	8.55	8.71	8.86	9.00	9.12	9.24	9.35	9.46	9.55	9.65
8	8.03	8.18	8.31	8.44	8.55	8.66	8.76	8.85	8.94	9.03
9	7.65	7.78	7.91	8.03	8.13	8.23	8.33	8.41	8.49	8.57
10	7.36	7.49	7.60	7.71	7.81	7.91	7.99	8.08	8.15	8.23
11	7.13	7.25	7.36	7.46	7.56	7.65	7.73	7.81	7.88	7.95
12	6.94	7.06	7.17	7.26	7.36	7.44	7.52	7.59	7.66	7.73
13	6.79	6.90	7.01	7.10	7.19	7.27	7.35	7.42	7.48	7.55
14	6.66	6.77	6.87	6.96	7.05	7.13	7.20	7.27	7.33	7.39
15	6.55	6.66	6.76	6.84	6.93	7.00	7.07	7.14	7.20	7.26
16	6.46	6.56	6.66	6.74	6.82	6.90	6.97	7.03	7.09	7.15
17	6.38	6.48	6.57	6.66	6.73	6.81	6.87	6.94	7.00	7.05
18	6.31	6.41	6.50	6.58	6.65	6.73	6.79	6.85	6.91	6.97
19	6.25	6.34	6.43	6.51	6.58	6.65	6.72	6.78	6.84	6.89
20	6.19	6.28	6.37	6.45	6.52	6.59	6.65	6.71	6.77	6.82
24	6.02	6.11	6.19	6.26	6.33	6.39	6.45	6.51	6.56	6.61
30	5.85	5.93	6.01	6.08	6.14	6.20	6.26	6.31	6.36	6.41
40	5.69	5.76	5.83	5.90	5.96	6.02	6.07	6.12	6.16	6.21
60	5.53	5.60	5.67	5.73	5.78	5.84	5.89	5.93	5.97	6.01
120	5.37	5.44	5.50	5.56	5.61	5.66	5.71	5.75	5.79	5.83
∞	5.23	5.28	5.35	5.40	5.45	5.49	5.54	5.57	5.61	5.65

Source: H. L. Harter and D. S. Clemm, "The Probability Integrals of the Range and of the Studentized Range—Probability Integral, Percentage Points, and Moments of the Range," *Wright Air Development Technical Report* 58-484, Vol. I, 1959.

TABLE 8 | Chi-Square Distribution

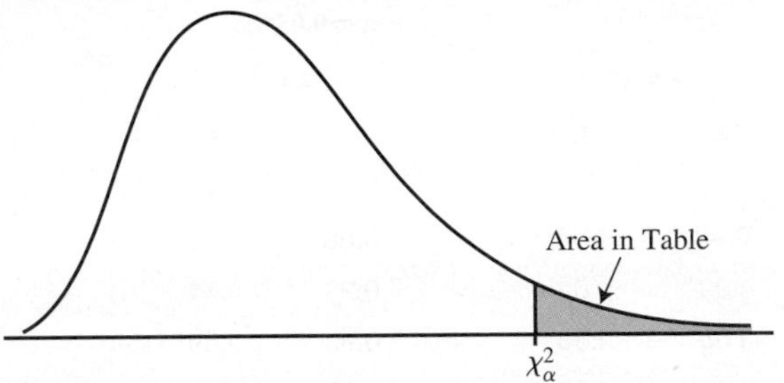

AREA IN RIGHT TAIL OF DISTRIBUTION

df	0.995	0.99	0.975	0.95	0.90	0.10	0.05	0.025	0.01	0.005
1	—	—	0.001	0.004	0.016	2.706	3.841	5.024	6.635	7.879
2	0.010	0.020	0.051	0.103	0.211	4.605	5.991	7.378	9.210	10.597
3	0.072	0.115	0.216	0.352	0.584	6.251	7.815	9.348	11.345	12.838
4	0.207	0.297	0.484	0.711	1.064	7.779	9.488	11.143	13.277	14.860
5	0.412	0.554	0.831	1.145	1.610	9.236	11.070	12.833	15.086	16.750
6	0.676	0.872	1.237	1.635	2.204	10.645	12.592	14.449	16.812	18.548
7	0.989	1.239	1.690	2.167	2.833	12.017	14.067	16.013	18.475	20.278
8	1.344	1.646	2.180	2.733	3.490	13.362	15.507	17.535	20.090	21.955
9	1.735	2.088	2.700	3.325	4.168	14.684	16.919	19.023	21.666	23.589
10	2.156	2.558	3.247	3.940	4.865	15.987	18.307	20.483	23.209	25.188
11	2.603	3.053	3.816	4.575	5.578	17.275	19.675	21.920	24.725	26.757
12	3.074	3.571	4.404	5.226	6.304	18.549	21.026	23.337	26.217	28.300
13	3.565	4.107	5.009	5.892	7.042	19.812	22.362	24.736	27.688	29.819
14	4.075	4.660	5.629	6.571	7.790	21.064	23.685	26.119	29.141	31.319
15	4.601	5.229	6.262	7.261	8.547	22.307	24.996	27.488	30.578	32.801
16	5.142	5.812	6.908	7.962	9.312	23.542	26.296	28.845	32.000	34.267
17	5.697	6.408	7.564	8.672	10.085	24.769	27.587	30.191	33.400	35.718
18	6.265	7.015	8.231	9.390	10.865	25.989	28.869	31.526	34.805	37.156
19	6.844	7.633	8.907	10.117	11.651	27.204	30.144	32.852	36.191	38.582
20	7.434	8.260	9.591	10.851	12.443	28.412	31.410	34.170	37.566	39.997
21	8.034	8.897	10.283	11.591	13.240	29.615	32.671	35.479	38.932	41.401
22	8.643	9.542	10.982	12.338	14.041	30.813	33.924	36.781	40.289	42.796
23	9.260	10.196	11.689	13.091	14.848	32.007	35.172	38.076	41.638	44.181
24	9.886	10.856	12.401	13.848	15.659	33.196	36.415	39.364	42.980	45.559
25	10.520	11.524	13.120	14.611	16.473	34.382	37.652	40.646	44.314	46.928
26	11.160	12.198	13.844	15.379	17.292	35.563	38.885	41.923	45.642	48.290
27	11.808	12.879	14.573	16.151	18.114	36.741	40.113	43.195	46.963	49.645
28	12.461	13.565	15.308	16.928	18.939	37.916	41.337	44.461	48.278	50.993
29	13.121	14.256	16.047	17.708	19.768	39.087	42.557	45.722	49.588	52.336
30	13.787	14.953	16.791	18.493	20.599	40.256	43.773	46.979	50.892	53.672

TABLE 9 | Critical Values for the Durbin-Watson Statistic

$\alpha = 0.05$

	$k=1$		$k=2$		$k=3$		$k=4$		$k=5$	
n	d_L	d_U	d_L	d_U	d_L	d_U	d_L	d_U	d_L	d_U
15	1.08	1.36	0.95	1.54	0.82	1.75	.69	1.97	.56	2.21
16	1.10	1.37	0.98	1.54	0.86	1.73	.74	1.93	.62	2.15
17	1.13	1.38	1.02	1.54	0.90	1.71	.78	1.90	.67	2.10
18	1.16	1.39	1.05	1.53	0.93	1.69	.82	1.87	.71	2.06
19	1.18	1.40	1.08	1.53	0.97	1.68	.86	1.85	.75	2.02
20	1.20	1.41	1.10	1.54	1.00	1.68	.90	1.83	.79	1.99
21	1.22	1.42	1.13	1.54	1.03	1.67	.93	1.81	.83	1.96
22	1.24	1.43	1.15	1.54	1.05	1.66	.96	1.80	.86	1.94
23	1.26	1.44	1.17	1.54	1.08	1.66	.99	1.79	.90	1.92
24	1.27	1.45	1.19	1.55	1.10	1.66	1.01	1.78	.93	1.90
25	1.29	1.45	1.21	1.55	1.12	1.66	1.04	1.77	.95	1.89
26	1.30	1.46	1.22	1.55	1.14	1.65	1.06	1.76	.98	1.88
27	1.32	1.47	1.24	1.56	1.16	1.65	1.08	1.76	1.01	1.86
28	1.33	1.48	1.26	1.56	1.18	1.65	1.10	1.75	1.03	1.85
29	1.34	1.48	1.27	1.56	1.20	1.65	1.12	1.74	1.05	1.84
30	1.35	1.49	1.28	1.57	1.21	1.65	1.14	1.74	1.07	1.83
31	1.36	1.50	1.30	1.57	1.23	1.65	1.16	1.74	1.09	1.83
32	1.37	1.50	1.31	1.57	1.24	1.65	1.18	1.73	1.11	1.82
33	1.38	1.51	1.32	1.58	1.26	1.65	1.19	1.73	1.13	1.81
34	1.39	1.51	1.33	1.58	1.27	1.65	1.21	1.73	1.15	1.81
35	1.40	1.52	1.34	1.58	1.28	1.65	1.22	1.73	1.16	1.80
36	1.41	1.52	1.35	1.59	1.29	1.65	1.24	1.73	1.18	1.80
37	1.42	1.53	1.36	1.59	1.31	1.66	1.25	1.72	1.19	1.80
38	1.43	1.54	1.37	1.59	1.32	1.66	1.26	1.72	1.21	1.79
39	1.43	1.54	1.38	1.60	1.33	1.66	1.27	1.72	1.22	1.79
40	1.44	1.54	1.39	1.60	1.34	1.66	1.29	1.72	1.23	1.79
45	1.48	1.57	1.43	1.62	1.38	1.67	1.34	1.72	1.29	1.78
50	1.50	1.59	1.46	1.63	1.42	1.67	1.38	1.72	1.34	1.77
55	1.53	1.60	1.49	1.64	1.45	1.68	1.41	1.72	1.38	1.77
60	1.55	1.62	1.51	1.65	1.48	1.69	1.44	1.73	1.41	1.77
65	1.57	1.63	1.54	1.66	1.50	1.70	1.47	1.73	1.44	1.77
70	1.58	1.64	1.55	1.67	1.52	1.70	1.49	1.74	1.46	1.77
75	1.60	1.65	1.57	1.68	1.54	1.71	1.51	1.74	1.49	1.77
80	1.61	1.66	1.59	1.69	1.56	1.72	1.53	1.74	1.51	1.77
85	1.62	1.67	1.60	1.70	1.57	1.72	1.55	1.75	1.52	1.77
90	1.63	1.68	1.61	1.70	1.59	1.73	1.57	1.75	1.54	1.78
95	1.64	1.69	1.62	1.71	1.60	1.73	1.58	1.75	1.56	1.78
100	1.65	1.69	1.63	1.72	1.61	1.74	1.59	1.76	1.57	1.78

TABLE 9 | Critical Values for the Durbin-Watson Statistic *(Continued)*

$\alpha = 0.01$

	$k=1$		$k=2$		$k=3$		$k=4$		$k=5$	
n	d_L	d_U	d_L	d_U	d_L	d_U	d_L	d_U	d_L	d_U
15	.81	1.07	.70	1.25	.59	1.46	.49	1.70	.39	1.96
16	.84	1.09	.74	1.25	.63	1.44	.53	1.66	.44	1.90
17	.87	1.10	.77	1.25	.67	1.43	.57	1.63	.48	1.85
18	.90	1.12	.80	1.26	.71	1.42	.61	1.60	.52	1.80
19	.93	1.13	.83	1.26	.74	1.41	.65	1.58	.56	1.77
20	.95	1.15	.86	1.27	.77	1.41	.68	1.57	.60	1.74
21	.97	1.16	.89	1.27	.80	1.41	.72	1.55	.63	1.71
22	1.00	1.17	.91	1.28	.83	1.40	.75	1.54	.66	1.69
23	1.02	1.19	.94	1.29	.86	1.40	.77	1.53	.70	1.67
24	1.04	1.20	.96	1.30	.88	1.41	.80	1.53	.72	1.66
25	1.05	1.21	.98	1.30	.90	1.41	.83	1.52	.75	1.65
26	1.07	1.22	1.00	1.31	.93	1.41	.85	1.52	.78	1.64
27	1.09	1.23	1.02	1.32	.95	1.41	.88	1.51	.81	1.63
28	1.10	1.24	1.04	1.32	.97	1.41	.90	1.51	.83	1.62
29	1.12	1.25	1.05	1.33	.99	1.42	.92	1.51	.85	1.61
30	1.13	1.26	1.07	1.34	1.01	1.42	.94	1.51	.88	1.61
31	1.15	1.27	1.08	1.34	1.02	1.42	.96	1.51	.90	1.60
32	1.16	1.28	1.10	1.35	1.04	1.43	.98	1.51	.92	1.60
33	1.17	1.29	1.11	1.36	1.05	1.43	1.00	1.51	.94	1.59
34	1.18	1.30	1.13	1.36	1.07	1.43	1.01	1.51	.95	1.59
35	1.19	1.31	1.14	1.37	1.08	1.44	1.03	1.51	.97	1.59
36	1.21	1.32	1.15	1.38	1.10	1.44	1.04	1.51	.99	1.59
37	1.22	1.32	1.16	1.38	1.11	1.45	1.06	1.51	1.00	1.59
38	1.23	1.33	1.18	1.39	1.12	1.45	1.07	1.52	1.02	1.58
39	1.24	1.34	1.19	1.39	1.14	1.45	1.09	1.52	1.03	1.58
40	1.25	1.34	1.20	1.40	1.15	1.46	1.10	1.52	1.05	1.58
45	1.29	1.38	1.24	1.42	1.20	1.48	1.16	1.53	1.11	1.58
50	1.32	1.40	1.28	1.45	1.24	1.49	1.20	1.54	1.16	1.59
55	1.36	1.43	1.32	1.47	1.28	1.51	1.25	1.55	1.21	1.59
60	1.38	1.45	1.35	1.48	1.32	1.52	1.28	1.56	1.25	1.60
65	1.41	1.47	1.38	1.50	1.35	1.53	1.31	1.57	1.28	1.61
70	1.43	1.49	1.40	1.52	1.37	1.55	1.34	1.58	1.31	1.61
75	1.45	1.50	1.42	1.53	1.39	1.56	1.37	1.59	1.34	1.62
80	1.47	1.52	1.44	1.54	1.42	1.57	1.39	1.60	1.36	1.62
85	1.48	1.53	1.46	1.55	1.43	1.58	1.41	1.60	1.39	1.63
90	1.50	1.54	1.47	1.56	1.45	1.59	1.43	1.61	1.41	1.64
95	1.51	1.55	1.49	1.57	1.47	1.60	1.45	1.62	1.42	1.64
100	1.52	1.56	1.50	1.58	1.48	1.60	1.46	1.63	1.44	1.65

Source: Computed from TSP 4.5 based on R. W. Farebrother, "A Remark on Algorithms AS106, AS153, and AS155: The Distribution of a Linear Combination of Chi-Square Random Variables," *Journal of the Royal Statistical Society*, Series C (Applied Statistics), 1984, 29, pp. 323–333.

APPENDIX B

Answers to Selected Even-Numbered Problems

Chapter 1

1.2 Quantitative/ratio. The differences between average monthly rainfalls are meaningful, and there is a true zero point, because there may be a month without any rainfalls.

1.4 Qualitative/nominal. The marital status is just a label without a meaningful difference or ranking.

1.6 Qualitative/nominal. The genders are merely labels with no ranking or meaningful difference)

1.8 Qualitative/nominal. The political affiliations are merely labels with no ranking or meaningful difference)

1.10 Qualitative/ordinal. You can rank the performance rating, but the differences between different performance ratings cannot be measured.

1.12 Qualitative/ordinal. The differences in the data values between class ranks are not meaningful.

1.14 Qualitative/nominal. The state in which the respondents in a survey reside is a label, and it is meaningless to talk about the rating of this value)

1.16 Qualitative/ordinal. You can rank movie ratings, but the differences between the ratings cannot be measured.

1.18 Qualitative/ordinal. The differences in the data values between ratings are not meaningful.

1.20 Time series: closing prices at specific days of the year.

1.22 Cross-sectional data: men and women workers' weekly earnings.

1.24 Time series: the number of 8 × 10 prints sold over the four years.

Time series: the number of 11 × 14 prints sold over the four years.

Time series: the number of 13 × 19 prints sold over the four years.

1.26 Inferential statistics, because the statement comparing the average costs of a hotel room in two cities is based on results from samples taken from two populations.

1.28 Descriptive statistics, because the average rating is based on the sample of reviewers who completed the review of the book.

1.30 Descriptive statistics, because this percentage represents the proportion of a specific group of customers arriving before 6 PM and is not making an inference about the entire population of customers.

Chapter 2

2.2 $2^6 = 64 > 50$; therefore, use six classes.

$$\text{Estimated class width} = \frac{74 - 16}{6} = 9.7 \approx 10$$

a. 16–25, 26–35, 36–45, 46–55, 56–65, 66–75

b. 16 to under 26, 26 to under 36, 36 to under 46, 46 to under 56, 56 to under 66, 66 to under 76

2.4 $2^5 = 32 > 30$; therefore, use five classes.

$$\text{Estimated class width} = \frac{42.8 - 13.9}{5} = 5.8 \approx 6$$

CLASS	FREQUENCY	RELATIVE FREQUENCY	CUMULATIVE RELATIVE FREQUENCY
13 to less than 19	6	0.200	0.200
19 to less than 25	11	0.367	0.567
25 to less than 31	4	0.133	0.700
31 to less than 37	7	0.233	0.933
37 to less than 43	2	0.067	1.0
Total	**30**	**1.00**	

2.6 $2^5 = 32 > 25$; therefore, use five classes.

$$\text{Estimated class width} = \frac{46 - 18}{5} = 5.6 \approx 6$$

a., b., c.

CLASS	FREQUENCY	RELATIVE FREQUENCY	CUMULATIVE RELATIVE FREQUENCY
18–23	2	0.08	0.08
24–29	6	0.24	0.32
30–35	5	0.20	0.52
36–41	5	0.20	0.72
42–47	7	0.28	1.00
Total	**25**	**1.00**	

d. The following histogram was constructed using bins 23, 29, 35, 41, and 47.

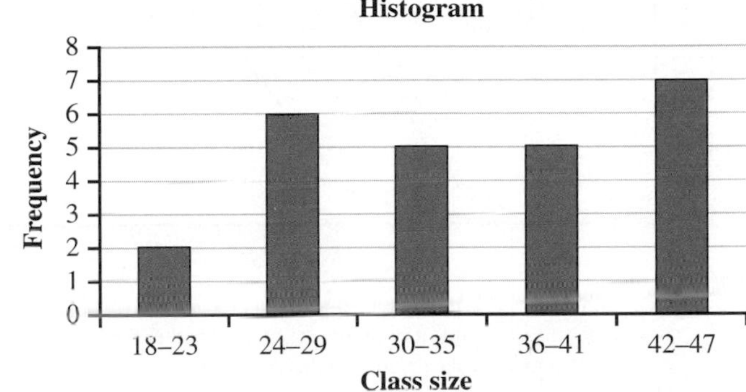

2.8 $2^6 = 64 > 40$; therefore, use six classes.

$$\text{Estimated class width (Current)} = \frac{76 - 19}{6} = 9.5 \approx 10$$

Results would be similar using the ages of laid-off employees.

CLASS	BINS	MIDPOINT
19 to less than 29	28.9	24
29 to less than 39	38.9	34
39 to less than 49	48.9	44
49 to less than 59	58.9	54
59 to less than 69	68.9	64
69 to less than 79	78.9	74

An extra bin (18.9) was added to Excel to provide the open-ended class required by PHStat.

a. **Percentage Polygon**

b. **Cumulative Percentage Polygon**

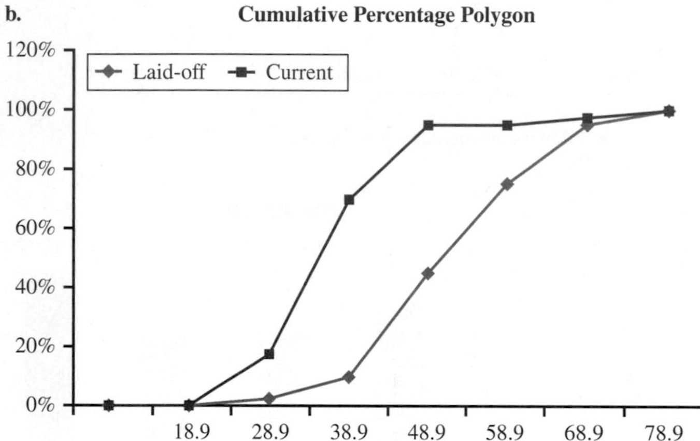

c. According to these polygons, it appears that the current workforce is younger than the laid-off employees. It appears that the laid-off employees may have a case for age discrimination.

2.10 $2^7 = 128 > 125$; therefore, use seven classes.

$$\text{Estimated class width} = \frac{83.2 - 71.0}{7} = 1.7 \approx 2$$

a., b., c.

CLASS	FREQUENCY	RELATIVE FREQUENCY	CUMULATIVE RELATIVE FREQUENCY
71 to less than 73	5	0.040	0.040
73 to less than 75	37	0.296	0.336
75 to less than 77	44	0.352	0.688
77 to less than 79	31	0.248	0.936
79 to less than 81	6	0.048	0.984
81 to less than 83	1	0.008	0.992
83 to less than 85	1	0.008	1.000
Total	**125**	**1.000**	

d. The following histogram was constructed using bins 72.99, 74.99, 76.99, 78.99, 80.99, 82.99, and 84.99.

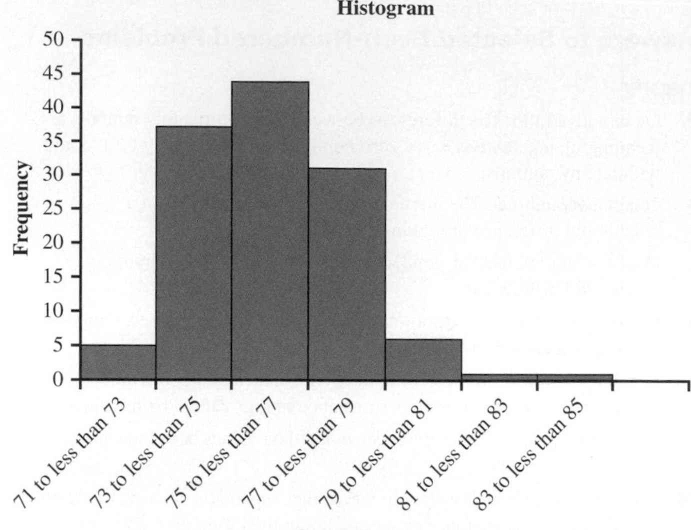

e. For 68.8% of the days, ocean temps were lower than 77 degrees.

2.12 a., b., c.

CATEGORY	FREQUENCY	RELATIVE FREQUENCY	CUMULATIVE RELATIVE FREQUENCY
Excellent	16	0.267	0.267
Good	31	0.517	0.783
Fair	8	0.133	0.917
Poor	5	0.083	1.000
Total	**60**	**1.000**	

d. **Dining Experience**

e. 78.3% rated their dining experience as either Excellent or Good.

2.14

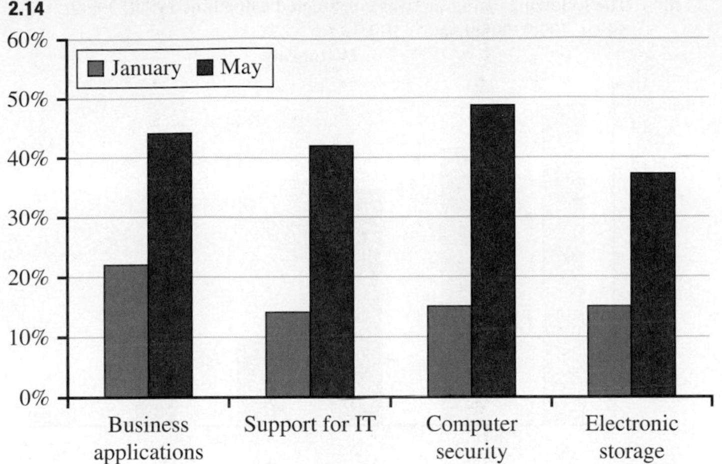

2.16

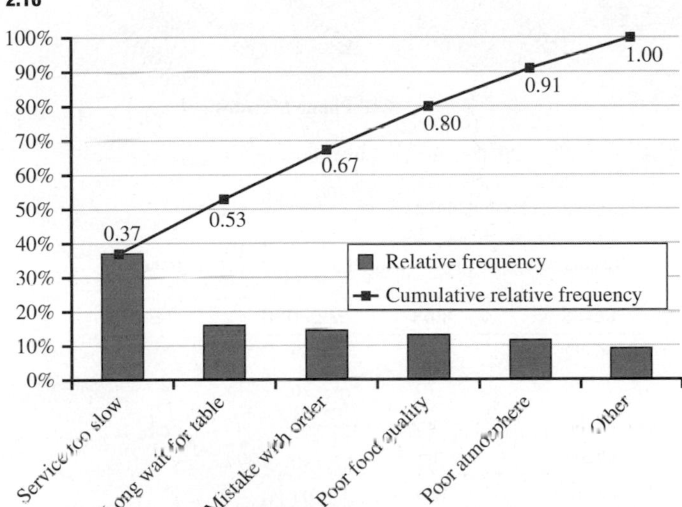

2.18 Gasoline Price Breakdown

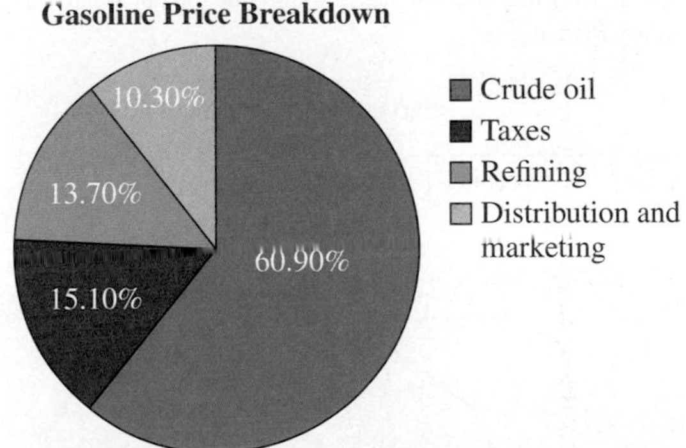

2.20 Because we are comparing data from a sample of countries over different time periods, a clustered bar chart would be a good choice to display these data. A stacked bar chart would not be the best choice because adding the GDPs for two time periods that are 10 years apart is not very meaningful.

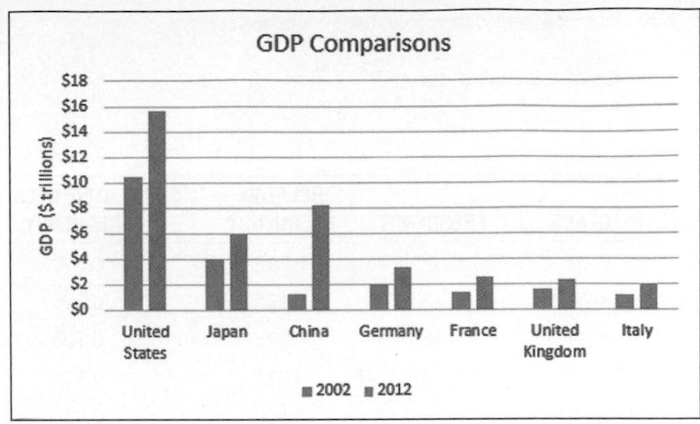

2.22

RATING	DARBY	EXTON	MEDIA	TOTAL
1	0	2	3	5
2	2	3	8	13
3	6	7	7	20
4	7	3	2	12
Total	**15**	**15**	**20**	**50**

Darby received 58% (7/12) of the four-star ratings even though they were only 30% (15/50) of the surveyed customers. Darby appears to have higher customer satisfaction when compared with the other two locations.

2.24
10 | 0 2 5 8 8 9
11 | 0 1 2 3 3 4 4 5
12 | 1 1 1 2 3 3 5 6 7 7 9
13 | 0 2 2 6 7 7 7 9
14 | 0 0 2 5 6
15 | 0

2.26 **a.**
2 | 3 4 6 7 8
3 | 0 0 1 2 2 2 4 4 5 5 5 5 6 7 7 9
4 | 2 2 3 5

b.
2 (0) | 3 4
2 (5) | 6 7 8
3 (0) | 0 0 1 2 2 2 4 4
3 (5) | 5 5 5 5 6 7 7 9
4 (0) | 2 2 3
4 (5) | 5

2.28 There does not appear to be a consistent relationship between order size and time on the Web site.

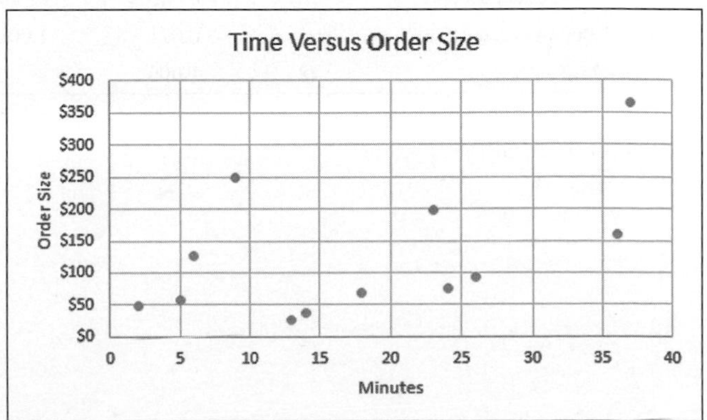

2.30 $2^6 = 64 > 40$; therefore, use six classes.

$$\text{Estimated class width} = \frac{23 - 0}{6} = 3.8 \approx 4$$

a., b., c.

CLASS	FREQUENCY	RELATIVE FREQUENCY	CUMULATIVE RELATIVE FREQUENCY
0–3	8	0.200	0.200
4–7	5	0.125	0.325
8–11	15	0.375	0.700
12–15	3	0.075	0.775
16–19	6	0.150	0.925
20–23	3	0.075	1.000
Total	**40**	**1.000**	

d. The following histogram was constructed using bins 3, 7, 11, 15, 19, and 23.

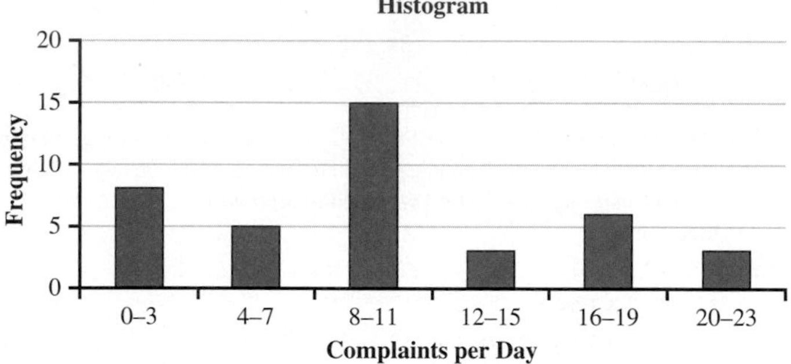

2.32 $2^6 = 64 > 48$; therefore, use six classes.

$$\text{Estimated class width} = \frac{1{,}187 - 43}{6} = 190.7 \approx 200$$

a., b., c.

CLASS	FREQUENCY	RELATIVE FREQUENCY	CUMULATIVE RELATIVE FREQUENCY
0 to under 200	15	0.313	0.313
200 to under 400	13	0.271	0.584
400 to under 600	11	0.229	0.813
600 to under 800	4	0.083	0.896
800 to under 1,000	4	0.083	0.979
1,000 to under 1,200	1	0.021	1.000
Total	**48**	**1.000**	

d. The following histogram was constructed using bins 199.9, 399.9, 599.9, 799.9, 999.9, and 1,199.9.

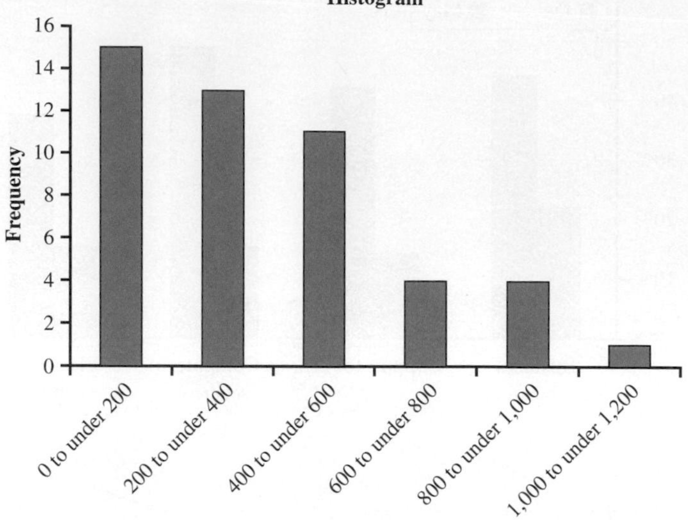

2.34 $2^5 = 32 > 30$; therefore, use five classes.

$$\text{Estimated class width (day)} = \frac{100 - 66}{5} = 6.8 \approx 7$$

Results would be similar using the evening-section grades.

CLASS	BINS	MIDPOINT
66–72	72	69
73–79	79	76
80–86	86	83
87–93	93	90
94–100	100	97

An extra bin (65) was added to Excel to provide the open-ended class required by PHStat.

a.

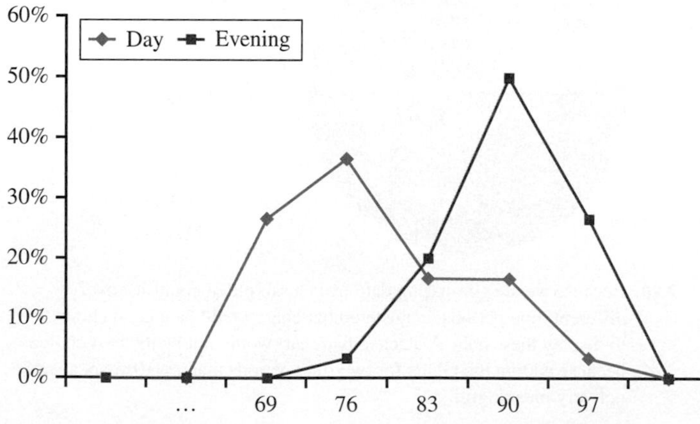

b.

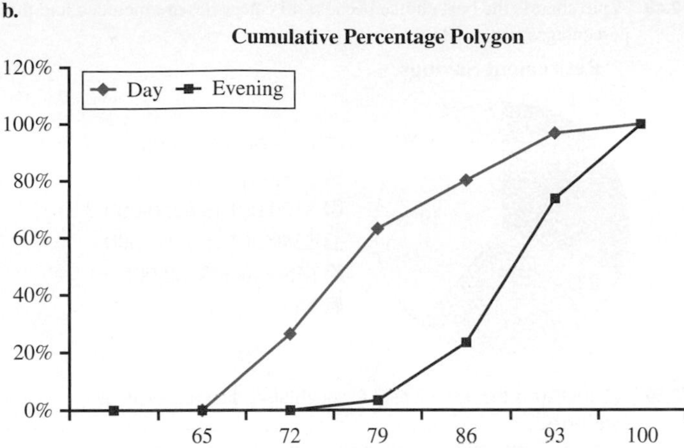

c. The evening-section grades appear to be noticeably higher than the day-section grades.

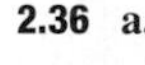

2.36 a.

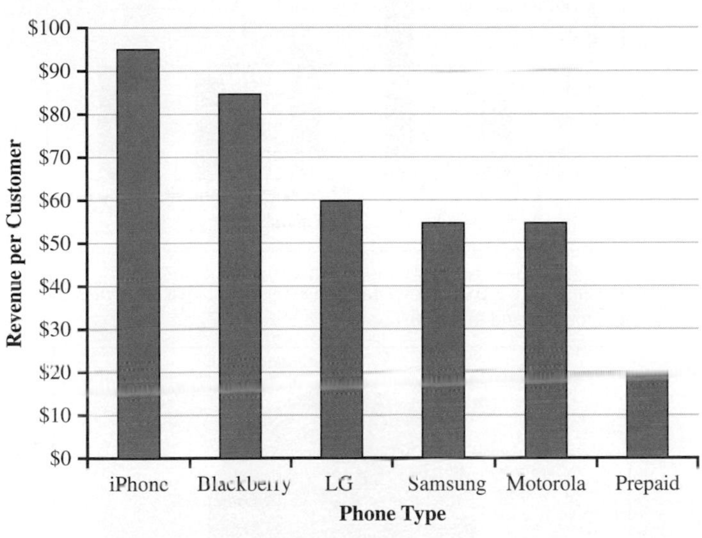

b.

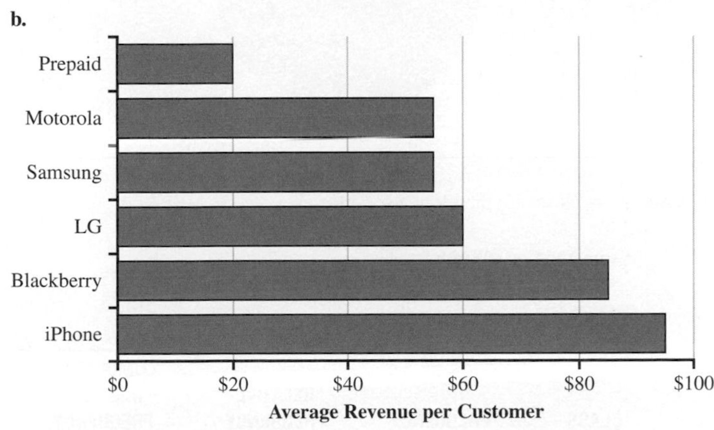

2.38 a.

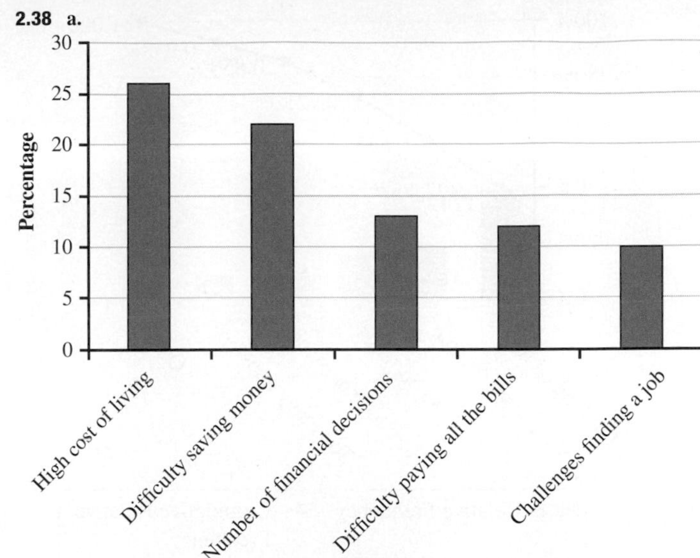

b.

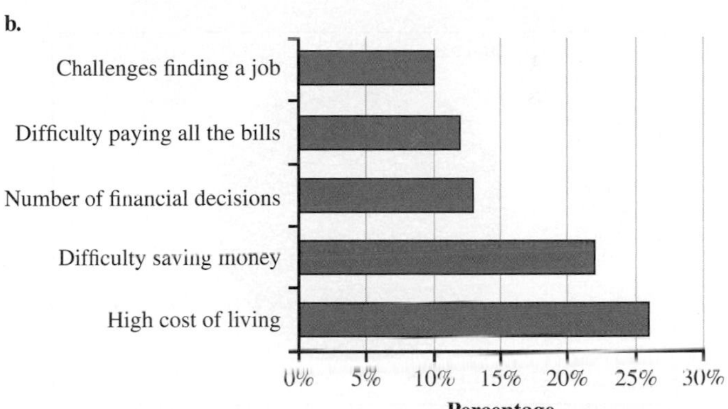

2.40

REASON	FREQUENCY	RELATIVE FREQUENCY	CUMULATIVE RELATIVE FREQUENCY
Too long on hold	47	0.392	0.392
Not knowledgeable	22	0.183	0.575
Not courteous	18	0.150	0.725
Hard to understand	15	0.125	0.850
Too many transfers	10	0.083	0.933
Other	8	0.067	1.000
Total	**120**		

100%
80%
60%
40%
20%
0%
0.392
0.575
0.725
0.850
0.933
1.000
Too long on hold
Not knowledgeable
Not courteous
Hard to understand
Too many transfers
Other
Relative Frequency
Cumulative Relative Frequency

2.42

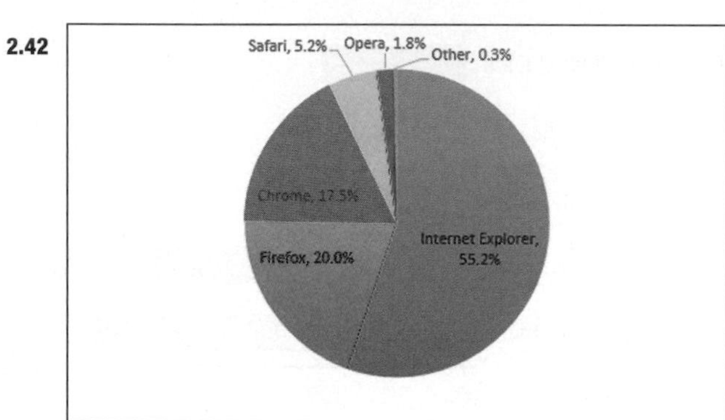

2.44

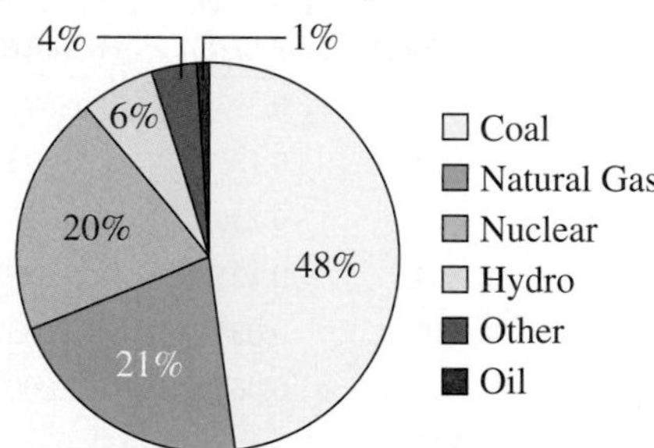

2.46 A clustered bar chart would be appropriate for these data. A stacked bar chart would also be an option.

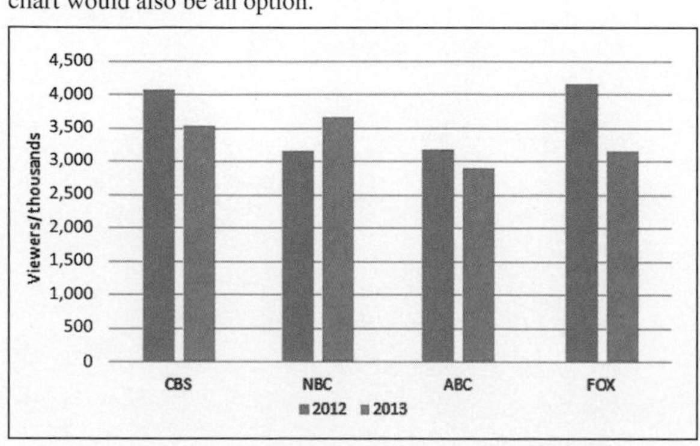

2.48 A pie chart is the best choice because all categories are included and the percentages sum to 100%.

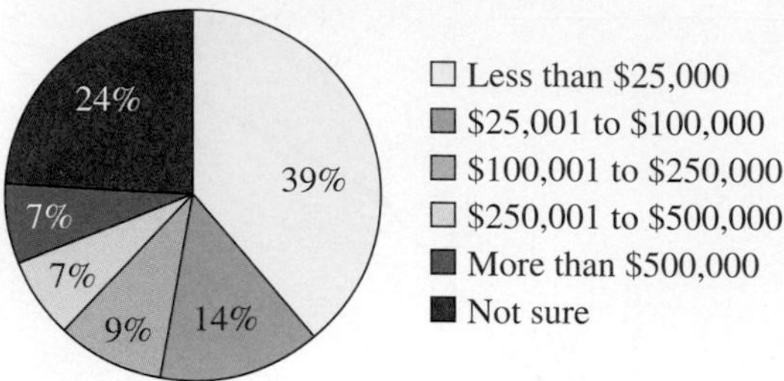

2.50 A bar chart is the best display for qualitative data organized in categories.

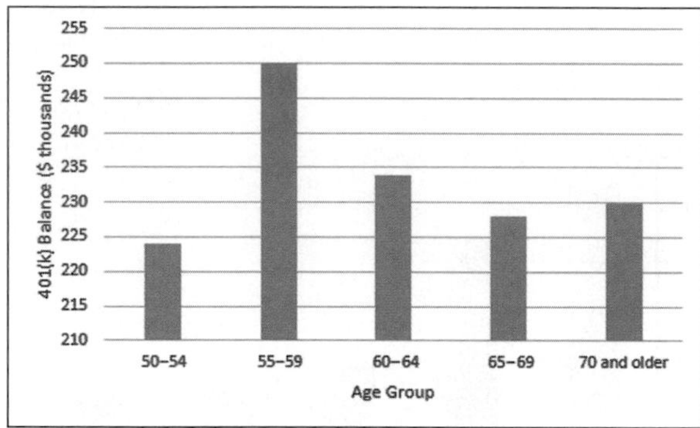

2.52 Pie charts are a good choice for displaying qualitative data when the proportions add to 100%.

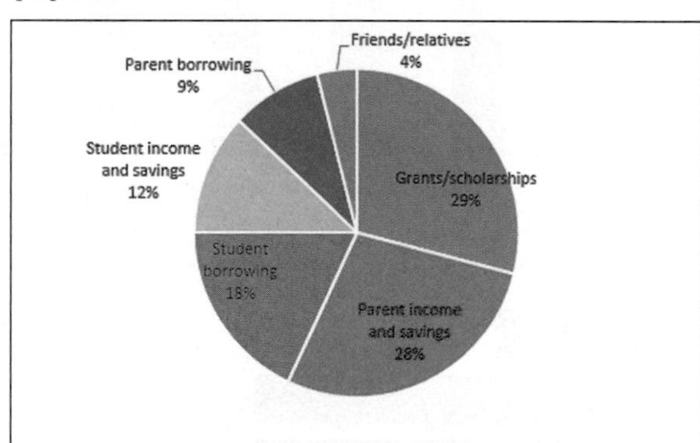

2.54 $2^6 = 64 \geq 55$; therefore, use 6 classes.

$$\text{Estimated Class Width} = \frac{66 - 26}{6} = 6.7 \approx 7$$

a., b., c.

CLASS	FREQUENCY	RELATIVE FREQUENCY	CUMULATIVE RELATIVE FREQUENCY
26–32	11	0.200	0.200
33–39	10	0.182	0.382
40–46	16	0.291	0.673
47–53	12	0.218	0.891
54–60	4	0.073	0.964
61–67	2	0.036	1.00
Total	**55**	**1.00**	

d. The following histogram was constructed using bins 32, 39, 46, 53, 60, and 67.

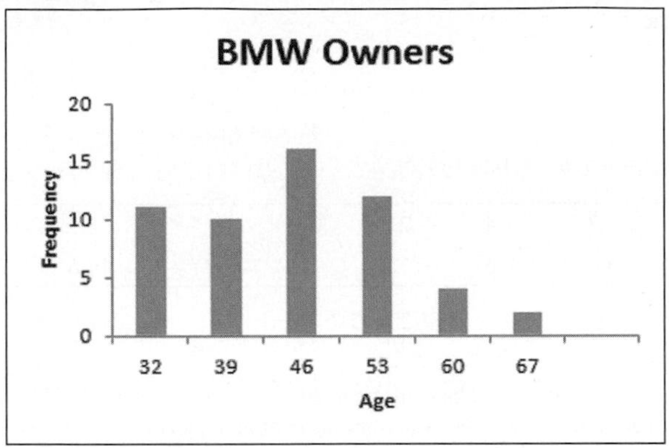

2.56 a., b., c.

CLASS	FREQUENCY	RELATIVE FREQUENCY	CUMULATIVE RELATIVE FREQUENCY
0	2	0.033	0.033
1	1	0.017	0.050
2	13	0.217	0.267
3	16	0.267	0.534
4	11	0.183	0.717
5	10	0.167	0.884
6	4	0.067	0.951
7	3	0.050	1.001
Total	**60**	**1.001**	

d. The following histogram was constructed using bins 0, 1, 2, 3, 4, 5, 6, and 7.

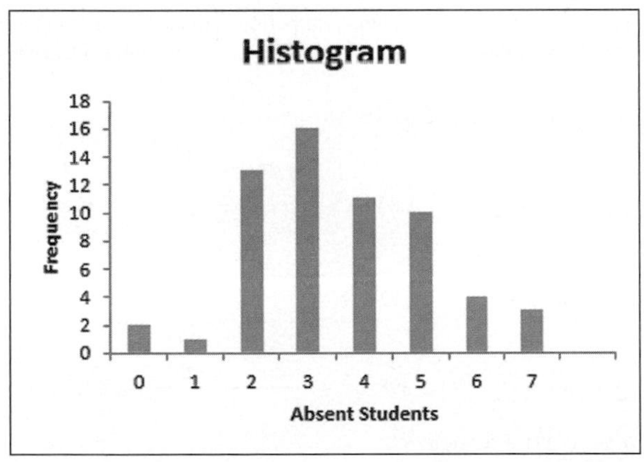

2.58 As the number of household members increases, the average monthly food costs also tend to increase

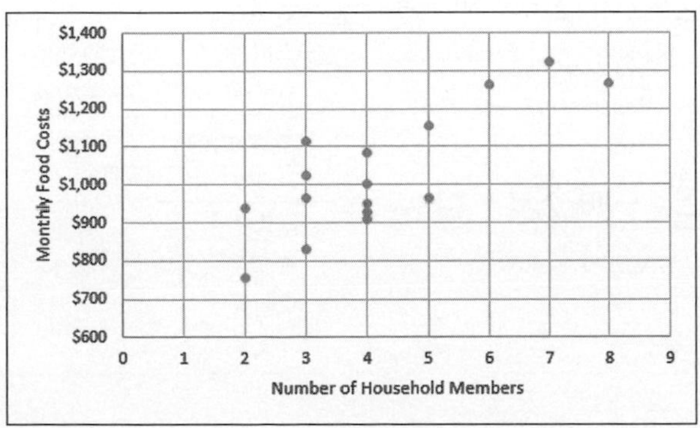

2.60

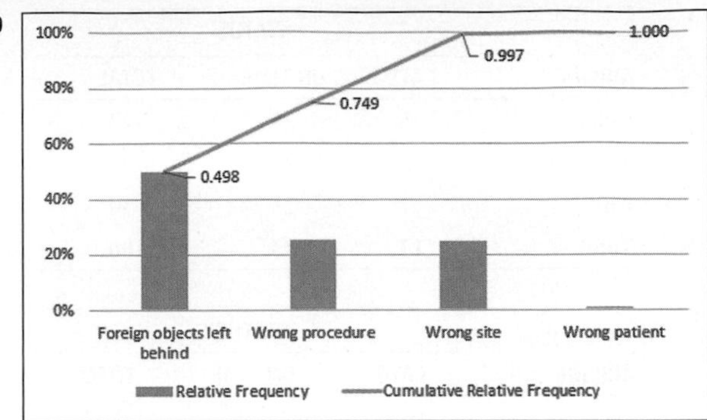

2.62
1 | 2 3 5 8
2 | 1 1 3 6 6 7 7 8
3 | 0 3 3 5 6 6 9
4 | 0 0 2 2 4 6 7 9
5 | 0 1 7

2.64

BRAND	DIET	REGULAR	TOTAL
Coke	6	6	12
Mt. Dew	2	8	10
Pepsi	4	7	11
Total	**12**	**21**	**33**

50% (6/12) of the Coke customers preferred Diet even though only 36% (12/33) of all the customers prefer Diet soda. Coke customers appear to have a higher percentage of customers who prefer diet soda than customers of other brands.

2.66 **a.**
1 | 8 9 9
2 | 0 0 0 2 2 3 3 5 5 5 6 8 8 8 8 9
3 | 0 1 1 1 1 2 2 3 5 5 5 6 6 9 9
4 | 1 3 3 5 6
5 | 1

b.
1 (5) | 8 9 9
2 (0) | 0 0 0 2 2 3 3
2 (5) | 5 5 5 6 8 8 8 8 9
3 (0) | 0 1 1 1 1 2 2 3
3 (5) | 5 5 5 6 6 9 9
4 (0) | 1 3 3
4 (5) | 5 6
5 (0) | 1

2.68

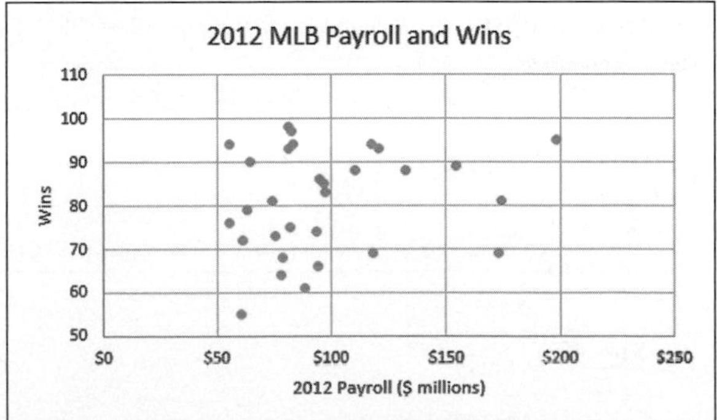

There does not appear to be a consistent relationship between payroll and wins during the 2010 season.

2.70 a.

	STATUS		
AIRLINE	LATE	ON TIME	TOTAL
Delta	5	38	43
Southwest	5	22	27
United	7	23	30
Total	**17**	**83**	**100**

b.

	STATUS		
AIRLINE	LATE	ON TIME	TOTAL
Delta	0.05	0.38	0.43
Southwest	0.05	0.22	0.27
United	0.07	0.23	0.30
Total	**0.17**	**0.83**	**1.00**

c. Delta has the highest on-time percentage $(38/43 = 0.88)$ while United has the lowest $(23/30 = 0.77)$

2.72 A line chart would be the best display for these data.

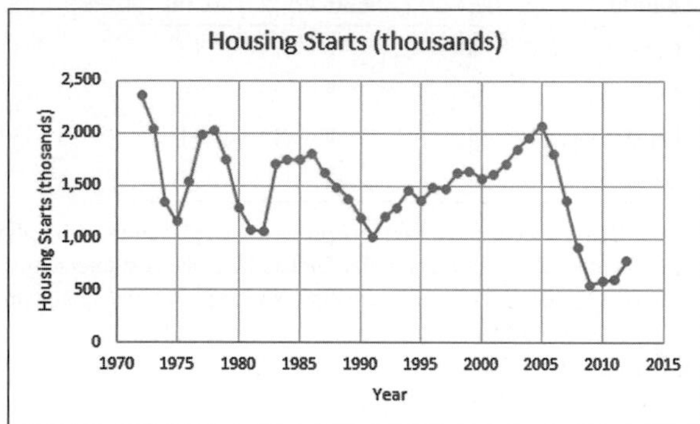

Chapter 3

3.2 a. $\bar{x} = \dfrac{\sum_{i=1}^{n} x_i}{n} = \dfrac{96}{8} = 12.0$

b. $i = 0.5(n) = 0.5(8) = 4$; median $= (14 + 16)/2 = 15$

c. Mode = 6, 17

d. Because the mean is less than the median, this distribution's shape would be described as left-skewed.

3.4 a. $\bar{x} = \dfrac{\sum_{i=1}^{n} x_i}{n} = \dfrac{68}{6} = 11.3$

b. $i = 0.5(n) = 0.5(6) = 3$; median $= (10 + 18)/2 = 14$

c. There is no mode.

d. Because the mean is lower than the median, this distribution's shape would be described as left-skewed.

3.6 a.

$$\bar{x} = \frac{\sum_{i=1}^{n} x_i}{n} = \frac{\$7.97 + \$9.57 + \$8.11 + \cdots + \$11.61 + \$11.32}{12}$$

$$= \frac{\$107.45}{12} = \$8.95$$

b. $i = 0.5(n) = 0.5(12) = 6$

\$7.34	\$7.35	\$7.97	\$7.99	\$8.11	\$8.18
\$8.83	\$9.32	\$9.57	\$9.86	\$11.32	\$11.61

Median = (\$8.18 + \$8.83)/2 = \$8.505

c. There is no mode.

d. Because the mean is higher than the median, this distribution's shape would be described as right-skewed.

3.8 a.

$$\bar{x} = \frac{\sum_{i=1}^{n} x_i}{n} = \frac{17.7 + 4.0 + 7.0 + \cdots + 1.3 + 8.6}{14} = \frac{189.4}{14} = 13.53$$

b. $i = 0.5(n) = 0.5(14) = 7$

1.3	1.4	2.1	4.0	5.8	6.3	7.0
8.4	8.6	11.2	16.2	17.7	19.6	79.8

Median $= (7.0 + 8.4)/2 = 7.7$

c. There is no mode.

d. Because 79.8 could be considered an outlier, the median would be the measurement that best describes the central tendency of these data.

e. Because the mean is higher than the median, this distribution's shape would be described as right-skewed.

3.10 a. 1986–1993: $\bar{x} = \dfrac{\sum_{i=1}^{n} x_i}{n} = \dfrac{229}{8} = 28.6;$

1994–2001: $\bar{x} = \dfrac{\sum_{i=1}^{n} x_i}{n} = \dfrac{354}{8} = 44.3$

b. $i = 0.5(n) = 0.5(8) = 4$

1986–1993: median $= (32 + 33)/2 = 32.5$

1994–2001: median $= (39 + 52)/2 = 45.5$

c. There is no mode in either data set.

d. Because the mean is lower than the median for the first eight years, this distribution's shape would be described as left-skewed. Because the mean is close to the median for the last eight years, this distribution's shape would be described as symmetrical.

e. The mean for the second eight-year period is much higher than the mean of the first eight-year period. There seems to be enough evidence to doubt his claim.

3.12 a. Range $= 23 - 5 = 18$

b. $\sum_{i=1}^{8} x_i = 114, \sum_{i=1}^{8} x_i^2 = 1{,}826, s^2 = \dfrac{1{,}826 - \dfrac{(114)^2}{8}}{8 - 1} = 28.8$

c. $s = \sqrt{28.8} = 5.37$

3.14 a. Range $= 34 - (-12) = 46$

b. $\sum_{i=1}^{6} x_i = 68, \sum_{i=1}^{6} x_i^2 = 2{,}398, \sigma^2 = \dfrac{2{,}398 - \dfrac{(68)^2}{6}}{6} = 271.2$

c. $\sigma = \sqrt{271.2} = 16.47$

3.16 a. Range $= 6 - 0 = 6$

b. $\sum_{i=1}^{9} x_i = 22, \sum_{i=1}^{9} x_i^2 = 80, s^2 = \dfrac{80 - \dfrac{(22)^2}{9}}{9 - 1} = 3.3$

c. $s = \sqrt{3.3} = 1.82$

3.18 a. Range $= 18 - 3 = 15$

b. $\sum_{i=1}^{10} x_i = 104, \sum_{i=1}^{10} x_i^2 = 1{,}280, s^2 = \dfrac{1{,}280 - \dfrac{(104)^2}{10}}{10 - 1} = 22.0$

c. $s = \sqrt{22.0} = 4.69$

3.20 **a.** Set 1: $\bar{x} = \frac{\sum_{i=1}^{n} x_i}{n} = \frac{31}{5} = 6.2$; Set 2: $\bar{x} = \frac{\sum_{i=1}^{n} x_i}{n} = \frac{34}{5} = 6.8$

Set 1: $s = \sqrt{\frac{207 - \frac{(31)^2}{5}}{5 - 1}} = 1.92;$

Set 2: $s = \sqrt{\frac{346 - \frac{(34)^2}{5}}{5 - 1}} = 5.36$

Set 1: $CV = 31.0\%$; Set 2: $CV = 78.8\%$

b. Set 2 has more variability because it has a higher coefficient of variation.

3.22 **a.** $z = 0.83$ **b.** $z = 2.08$

c. $z = -0.42$ **d.** $z = -2.50$

3.24 **a.** $z = -1.35$ **b.** $z = 1.99$

c. $z = -2.33$ **d.** $z = 0.65$

e. $z = 2.65$

3.26 **a.** $CV = 12.3\%$

b. $z = -0.38$

c. $x = \$325{,}000 + (2)(\$40{,}000) = \$405{,}000$
$x = \$325{,}000 \quad (2)(\$40{,}000) = \$245{,}000$

d. $x = \$325{,}000 + (4)(\$40{,}000) = \$485{,}000$
$x = \$325{,}000 - (4)(\$40{,}000) = \$165{,}000$

3.28 **a.** $CV = 8.9\%$

b. $z = -1.29$

c. $x = 31.6 + (3)(2.8) = 40.0$
$x = 31.6 - (3)(2.8) = 23.2$

d. $x = 31.6 + (4)(2.8) = 42.8$
$x = 31.6 - (4)(2.8) = 20.4$

e. $z = 2.24$
$x - 31.6 + (2.24)(2.8) - 37.9$
$x = 31.6 - (2.24)(2.8) = 25.3$

3.30 $\bar{x} \approx \frac{1{,}297.5}{75} = 17.3$

VALUE	m_i	f_i	$\bar{x}$	$(m_i - \bar{x})$	$(m_i - \bar{x})^2$	$(m_i - \bar{x})^2 f_i$
5 to under 10	7.5	15	17.3	−9.8	96.04	1,440.6
10 to under 15	12.5	9	17.3	−4.8	23.04	207.36
15 to under 20	17.5	21	17.3	0.2	0.04	0.84
20 to under 25	22.5	24	17.3	5.2	27.04	648.96
25 to under 30	27.5	6	17.3	10.2	104.04	624.24

$n = \sum f_i = 75$ $\qquad \sum (m_i - \bar{x})^2 f_i = 2{,}922$

$s \approx \sqrt{\frac{2{,}922}{75 - 1}} = 6.28$

3.32 $\bar{x} \approx \frac{14{,}810}{362} = \$40.9$

VALUE	m_i	f_i	$\bar{x}$	$(m_i - \bar{x})$	$(m_i - \bar{x})^2$	$(m_i - \bar{x})^2 f_i$
\$20 to under \$30	\$25	67	40.9	−15.9	252.81	16,938.27
\$30 to under \$40	\$35	111	40.9	−5.9	34.81	3,863.91
\$40 to under \$50	\$45	125	40.9	4.1	16.81	2,101.25
\$50 to under \$60	\$55	21	40.9	14.1	198.81	4,175.01
\$60 to under \$70	\$65	38	40.9	24.1	580.81	22,070.78

$n = \sum f_i = 362$ $\qquad \sum (m_i - \bar{x})^2 f_i = 49{,}149.22$

$s^2 \approx \frac{49{,}149.22}{362 - 1} = 136.15$

$s \approx \sqrt{136.15} = \$11.67$

3.34 $\bar{x} \approx \frac{3{,}380}{100} = 33.8$

VALUE	m_i	f_i	$\bar{x}$	$(m_i - \bar{x})$	$(m_i - \bar{x})^2$	$(m_i - \bar{x})^2 f_i$
0 to under 10	5	6	33.8	−28.8	829.44	4,976.64
10 to under 20	15	22	33.8	−18.8	353.44	7,775.68
20 to under 30	25	10	33.8	−8.8	77.44	774.40
30 to under 40	35	18	33.8	1.2	1.44	25.92
40 to under 50	45	28	33.8	11.2	125.44	3,512.32
50 to under 60	55	16	33.8	21.2	449.44	7,191.04

$n = \sum f_i = 100$ $\qquad \sum (m_i - \bar{x})^2 f_i = 24{,}256$

$s^2 \approx \frac{24{,}256}{100 - 1} = 245.01$

$s \approx \sqrt{245.01} = 15.65$

3.36 **a.** $i = \frac{P}{100}(n) = \frac{20}{100}(8) = 1.6$

20th percentile $= 20$

b. $i = \frac{P}{100}(n) = \frac{40}{100}(8) = 3.2$

40th percentile $= 38$

c. $i = \frac{P}{100}(n) = \frac{60}{100}(8) = 4.8$

60th percentile $= 54$

3.38 **a.** Percentile Rank $(50) = \frac{8 + 0.5}{10}(100) = 85$

b. Percentile Rank $(30) = \frac{4 + 0.5}{10}(100) = 45$

c. Percentile Rank $(15) = \frac{3 + 0.5}{10}(100) = 35$

3.40 **a.** $Q_1: i = \frac{P}{100}(n) = \frac{25}{100}(13) = 3.25$

$Q_1 = 15$

$Q_2: i = \frac{P}{100}(n) = \frac{50}{100}(13) = 6.5$

$Q_2 = 18$

$Q_3: i = \frac{P}{100}(n) = \frac{75}{100}(13) = 9.75$

$Q_3 = 22$

b. $IQR = Q_3 - Q_1 = 22 - 15 = 7$

3.42 **a.** $i = \frac{P}{100}(n) = \frac{60}{100}(12) = 7.2$

60th percentile $= 1.53$

b. $i = \frac{P}{100}(n) = \frac{20}{100}(12) = 2.4$

20th percentile $= 0.95$

c. $i = \frac{P}{100}(n) = \frac{85}{100}(12) = 10.2$

85th percentile $= 3.79$

3.44 **a.** $Q_1: i = \frac{P}{100}(n) = \frac{25}{100}(20) = 5$

$Q_1 = (58 + 59)/2 = 58.5$

$Q_2: i = \frac{P}{100}(n) = \frac{50}{100}(20) = 10$

$Q_2 = (71 + 75)/2 = 73$

$$Q_3: i = \frac{P}{100}(n) = \frac{75}{100}(20) = 15$$

$$Q_3 = (84 + 84)/2 = 84$$

b. $IQR = Q_3 - Q_1 = 84 - 58.5 = 25.5$

3.46 a. $\bar{x} = \frac{\sum_{i=1}^{n} x_i}{n} = \frac{25}{5} = 5.0 \quad \bar{y} = \frac{\sum_{i=1}^{n} y_i}{n} = \frac{30}{5} = 6.0$

$$\sum (x_i - \bar{x})(y_i - \bar{y}) = 11 \quad s_{xy} = \frac{\sum_{i=1}^{n} (x_i - \bar{x})(y_i - \bar{y})}{n - 1} = \frac{11}{5 - 1} = 2.75$$

b. $s_x = \sqrt{\frac{\sum_{i=1}^{n} (x_i - \bar{x})^2}{n - 1}} = \sqrt{\frac{16}{4}} = 2.0 \quad s_y = \sqrt{\frac{16}{4}} = 2.0$

$$r_{xy} = \frac{s_{xy}}{s_x s_y} = \frac{2.75}{(2.0)(2.0)} = 0.688$$

c. There is a positive linear relationship between these two variables.

3.48 a. x = minutes, y = rating

$$\bar{x} = \frac{\sum_{i=1}^{n} x_i}{n} = \frac{50}{10} = 5.0 \quad \bar{y} = \frac{\sum_{i=1}^{n} y_i}{n} = \frac{147}{10} = 14.7$$

$$\sum (x_i - \bar{x})(y_i - \bar{y}) = -41.0 \quad s_{xy} = \frac{\sum_{i=1}^{n} (x_i - \bar{x})(y_i - \bar{y})}{n - 1} = \frac{-41}{10 - 1} = -4.56$$

b. $s_x = \sqrt{\frac{\sum_{i=1}^{n} (x_i - \bar{x})^2}{n - 1}} = \sqrt{\frac{84}{9}} = 3.06 \quad s_y = \sqrt{\frac{70.1}{9}} = 2.79$

$$r_{xy} = \frac{s_{xy}}{s_x s_y} = \frac{-4.56}{(3.06)(2.79)} = -0.534$$

c. There is a negative linear relationship between these two variables.

3.50 a. x = shelf space, y = sales

$$\bar{x} = \frac{\sum_{i=1}^{n} x_i}{n} = \frac{36}{9} = 4.0 \quad \bar{y} = \frac{\sum_{i=1}^{n} y_i}{n} = \frac{63}{9} = 7.0$$

$$\sum (x_i - \bar{x})(y_i - \bar{y}) = 30.0 \; s_{xy} = \frac{\sum_{i=1}^{n} (x_i - \bar{x})(y_i - \bar{y})}{n - 1} = \frac{30.0}{9 - 1} = 3.75$$

b. $s_x = \sqrt{\frac{\sum_{i=1}^{n} (x_i - \bar{x})^2}{n - 1}} = \sqrt{\frac{16}{8}} = 1.41 \quad s_y = \sqrt{\frac{196}{8}} = 4.95$

$$r_{xy} = \frac{s_{xy}}{s_x s_y} = \frac{3.75}{(1.41)(4.95)} = 0.537$$

c. There is a positive linear relationship between these two variables.

3.52 Ford: $\bar{x} = \frac{104}{17} = 6.1$

Chevy: $\bar{x} = \frac{111}{17} = 6.5$

Honda: $\bar{x} = \frac{106}{17} = 6.2$

Choose Chevy because it has the highest weighted average.

3.54 a.

$$\bar{x} = \frac{\sum_{i=1}^{n} x_i}{n} = \frac{1.5 + 1.0 + 2.3 + \cdots + 1.5 + 12.4}{9} = \frac{93.0}{9} = 10.33$$

b. $i = 0.5(n) = 0.5(9) = 4.5$

1.0	1.5	1.5	2.3	8.8	12.1	12.4	13.2	40.2

Median = 8.8

c. Mode = 1.5

d. Because 40.2 could be considered an outlier, the median would be the measurement that best describes the central tendency of these data.

e. Because the mean is higher than the median, this distribution's shape would be described as right-skewed.

3.56 a. $\bar{x}$ = \$207.72

b. Median = \$196.87

c. There is no mode in this data set.

d. Because there do not appear to be any an outliers, the mean or the median would adequately describe the central tendency of these data.

e. Because the mean is more than the median, this distribution's shape would be described as right-skewed.

3.58 a. Range = 25.5 − 4.5 = 21.0

b. $s^2 = \frac{\sum_{i=1}^{n} x_i^2 - \frac{\left(\sum_{i=1}^{n} x_i\right)^2}{n}}{n - 1} = \frac{1{,}309.31 - \frac{(97.5)^2}{10}}{10 - 1} = 39.85$

c. $s = \sqrt{39.85} = 6.31$

3.60 a. Range = 5 − (−15) = 20

b. $\sum_{i=1}^{10} x_i = -69, \sum_{i=1}^{10} x_i^2 = 855, s^2 = \frac{855 - \frac{(-69)^2}{10}}{10 - 1} = 42.1$

c. $s = \sqrt{42.1} = 6.49$

3.62 a. Store 1:

$$\sum_{i=1}^{5} x_i = 29, \sum_{i=1}^{5} x_i^2 = 191, \bar{x} = 5.8, s = \sqrt{\frac{191 - \frac{(29)^2}{5}}{5 - 1}}$$

$$= 2.39, CV = 41.2\%$$

Store 2:

$$\sum_{i=1}^{5} x_i = 41, \sum_{i=1}^{5} x_i^2 = 341, \bar{x} = 8.2, s = \sqrt{\frac{341 - \frac{(41)^2}{5}}{5 - 1}}$$

$$= 1.10, CV = 13.4\%$$

b. Store 1 has more variability because it has a higher coefficient of variation.

3.64 $\bar{x} = \frac{\sum_{i=1}^{n} x_i}{n} = \frac{\$4{,}469}{20} = \$223.45$

$$s = \sqrt{\frac{\sum_{i=1}^{n} x_i^2 - \frac{\left(\sum_{i=1}^{n} x_i\right)^2}{n}}{n - 1}} = \sqrt{\frac{1{,}107{,}003 - \frac{(4{,}469)^2}{20}}{20 - 1}} = \$75.53$$

a. $CV = \frac{s}{\bar{x}}(100) = \frac{\$75.53}{\$223.45}(100) = 33.8\%$

b. $z = \frac{x - \bar{x}}{s} = \frac{\$200 - \$223.45}{\$75.53} = -0.31$

c. $x = \bar{x} + zs$

$x = \$223.45 + (1)(\$75.53) = \$298.98$

$x = \$223.45 - (1)(\$75.53) = \$147.92$

$16/20 = 80\%$ of the values are within this interval. This exceeds the 68% predicted by the Empirical Rule.

d. $x = \bar{x} + zs$

$x = \$223.45 + (2)(\$75.53) = \$374.51$

$x = \$223.45 - (2)(\$75.53) = \$72.39$

$18/20 = 90\%$ of the values are within this interval. This exceeds the 75% predicted by Chebyshev's Theorem.

3.66 a. $x =$ satisfaction, $y =$ activations

$$\bar{x} = \frac{\sum_{i=1}^{n} x_i}{n} = \frac{62.4}{8} = 7.8 \quad \bar{y} = \frac{\sum_{i=1}^{n} y_i}{n} = \frac{244}{8} = 30.5$$

$$\sum (x_i - \bar{x})(y_i - \bar{y}) = 39.3 \; s_{xy} = \frac{\sum_{i=1}^{n}(x_i - \bar{x})(y_i - \bar{y})}{n - 1} = \frac{39.3}{8 - 1} = 5.61$$

b. $$s_x = \sqrt{\frac{\sum_{i=1}^{n}(x_i - \bar{x})^2}{n - 1}} = \sqrt{\frac{5.68}{7}} = 0.90 \quad s_y = \sqrt{\frac{382.0}{7}} = 7.39$$

$$r_{xy} = \frac{s_{xy}}{s_x s_y} = \frac{5.61}{(0.90)(7.39)} = 0.843$$

c. There is a strong positive linear relationship between these two variables.

3.68 a. $$\mu \approx \frac{18{,}015}{62} = 290.6$$

VALUE	m_i	f_i	μ	$(m_i - \mu)$	$(m_i - \mu)^2$	$(m_i - \mu)^2 f_i$
278 to 282	280	6	290.6	−10.6	112.36	674.16
283 to 287	285	12	290.6	−5.6	31.36	376.32
288 to 292	290	21	290.6	−0.6	0.36	7.56
293 to 297	295	16	290.6	4.4	19.36	309.76
298 to 302	300	6	290.6	9.4	88.36	530.16
303 to 307	305	1	290.6	14.4	207.36	207.36

$N = \sum f_i = 62$ $\qquad \sum (m_i - \mu)^2 f_i = 2{,}105.32$

b. $$\sigma^2 \approx \frac{\sum_{i=1}^{k}(m_i - \mu)^2 f_i}{N} = \frac{2{,}105.32}{62} = 33.96$$

$\sigma \approx \sqrt{33.96} = 5.83$

3.70 a. $$i = \frac{P}{100}(n) = \frac{30}{100}(21) = 6.3$$

30th percentile $= \$10.75$

b. $$i = \frac{P}{100}(n) = \frac{45}{100}(21) = 9.45$$

45th percentile $= \$12.15$

c. $$i = \frac{P}{100}(n) = \frac{65}{100}(21) = 13.65$$

65th percentile $= \$14.00$

3.72 a. $$Q_1: i = \frac{P}{100}(n) = \frac{25}{100}(27) = 6.75$$

$Q_1 = 668$

$$Q_2: i = \frac{P}{100}(n) = \frac{50}{100}(27) = 13.5$$

$Q_2 = 919$

$$Q_3: i = \frac{P}{100}(n) = \frac{75}{100}(27) = 20.25$$

$Q_3 = 1{,}188$

$IQR = Q_3 - Q_1 = 1{,}188 - 668 = 520$

3.74 $$\text{Percentile rank (Freestyle 33 seconds)} = \frac{5 + 0.5}{8}(100) = 68.8$$

$$\text{Percentile rank (Backstroke 72 seconds)} = \frac{2 + 0.5}{10}(100) = 25.0$$

Because lower times are a measure of better performance, the swimmer performed better in the backstroke relative to the freestyle competition.

3.76 a. $$Q_1: i = \frac{P}{100}(n) = \frac{25}{100}(25) = 6.25$$

$Q_1 = 240$

$$Q_2: i = \frac{P}{100}(n) = \frac{50}{100}(25) = 12.5$$

$Q_2 = 271$

$$Q_3: i = \frac{P}{100}(n) = \frac{75}{100}(25) = 18.75$$

$Q_3 = 290$

$IQR = Q_3 - Q_1 = 290 - 240 = 50$

Upper Limit $= Q_3 + 1.5(IQR) = 290 + 1.5(50) = 365$

Lower Limit $= Q_1 - 1.5(IQR) = 240 - 1.5(50) = 165$

There are no outliers in this data set.

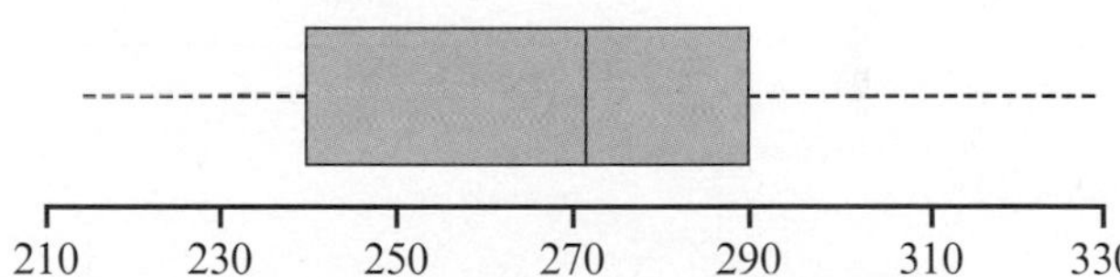

b. The five-number summary is 215, 240, 271, 290, 330.

3.78 a. $x =$ age, $y =$ credit score

$$\bar{x} = \frac{\sum_{i=1}^{n} x_i}{n} = \frac{400}{10} = 40.0 \quad \bar{y} = \frac{\sum_{i=1}^{n} y_i}{n} = \frac{693}{10} = 693.0$$

$$\sum (x_i - \bar{x})(y_i - \bar{y}) = 4{,}170.0 \; s_{xy} = \frac{\sum_{i=1}^{n}(x_i - \bar{x})(y_i - \bar{y})}{n - 1} = \frac{4{,}170.0}{10 - 1} = 463.3$$

b.

$$s_x = \sqrt{\frac{\sum_{i=1}^{n}(x_i - \bar{x})^2}{n - 1}} = \sqrt{\frac{1{,}164}{9}} = 11.37 \quad s_y = \sqrt{\frac{35{,}010}{9}} = 62.37$$

$$r_{xy} = \frac{s_{xy}}{s_x s_y} = \frac{463.33}{(11.37)(62.37)} = 0.653$$

c. There is a positive linear relationship between these two variables.

Chapter 4

4.2 $\frac{13}{52} = 0.25$

4.4
a. subjective
b. empirical
c. classical
d. empirical
e. classical

4.6
a. $\frac{32}{125} = 0.256$
b. $\frac{17}{125} = 0.136$
c. $\frac{49}{125} = 0.392$
d. empirical

4.8
a. 2
b. $\frac{2}{26} = 0.077$
c. $\frac{24}{26} = 0.923$
d. $\frac{11}{26} = 0.423$

4.10
a. $\frac{20}{50} = 0.40$
b. $\frac{30}{50} = 0.60$
c. $\frac{15}{50} = 0.30$
d. $\frac{25}{50} = 0.50$
e. $\frac{10}{50} = 0.20$

4.12
a. $\frac{39}{50} = 0.78$
b. $\frac{34}{50} = 0.68$
c. $\frac{23}{50} = 0.46$
d. 1

4.14 $\frac{0.42}{0.42 + 0.08} = \frac{0.42}{0.50} = 0.84$

4.16
a. Events are not mutually exclusive. They can occur at the same time.
b. Events are independent. The probability of the first event does not influence the occurrence of the second one.

4.18 75% + 80% − 70% = 85%

4.20
a. $\frac{205}{309} = 0.663$
b. $\frac{45}{107} = 0.421$
c. $\frac{\frac{2}{309}}{\frac{3}{309}} = \frac{2}{3} = 0.667$
d. $\frac{55}{136} = 0.404$
e. $\frac{\left(\frac{27}{309}\right)}{\left(\frac{79}{309}\right)} = \frac{27}{79} = 0.342$
f.

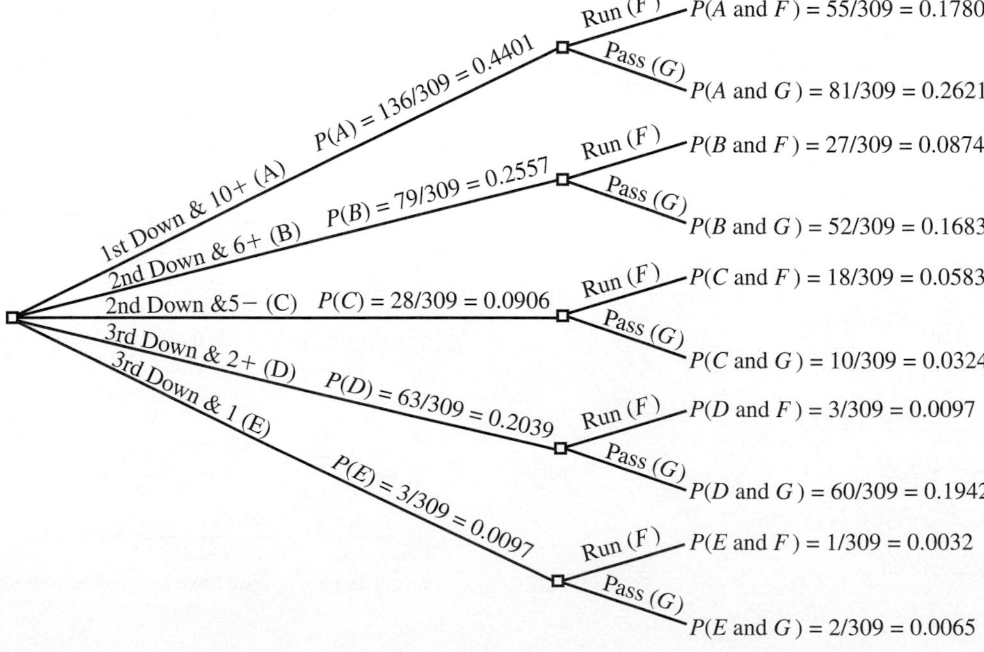

4.22 $(0.7)(0.7)(0.7)(0.7)(0.7)(0.7)(0.7) = 0.082$

4.24 $\frac{0.20}{0.35} = 0.571$

4.26 $(0.37)(0.37)(0.37) = 0.051$

4.28 **a.** $\frac{12}{75} = 0.16$

b. $\frac{32}{75} + \frac{23}{75} = 0.733$

c. $\frac{67}{75} = 0.893$

d. $\frac{20}{75} = 0.267$

e. $\frac{30}{75} + \frac{23}{75} - \frac{7}{75} = 0.613$

f. $\frac{\left(\frac{12}{75}\right)}{\left(\frac{30}{75}\right)} = \frac{12}{30} = 0.40$

g. $\frac{\left(\frac{2}{75}\right)}{\left(\frac{8}{75}\right)} = \frac{2}{8} = 0.25$

h.

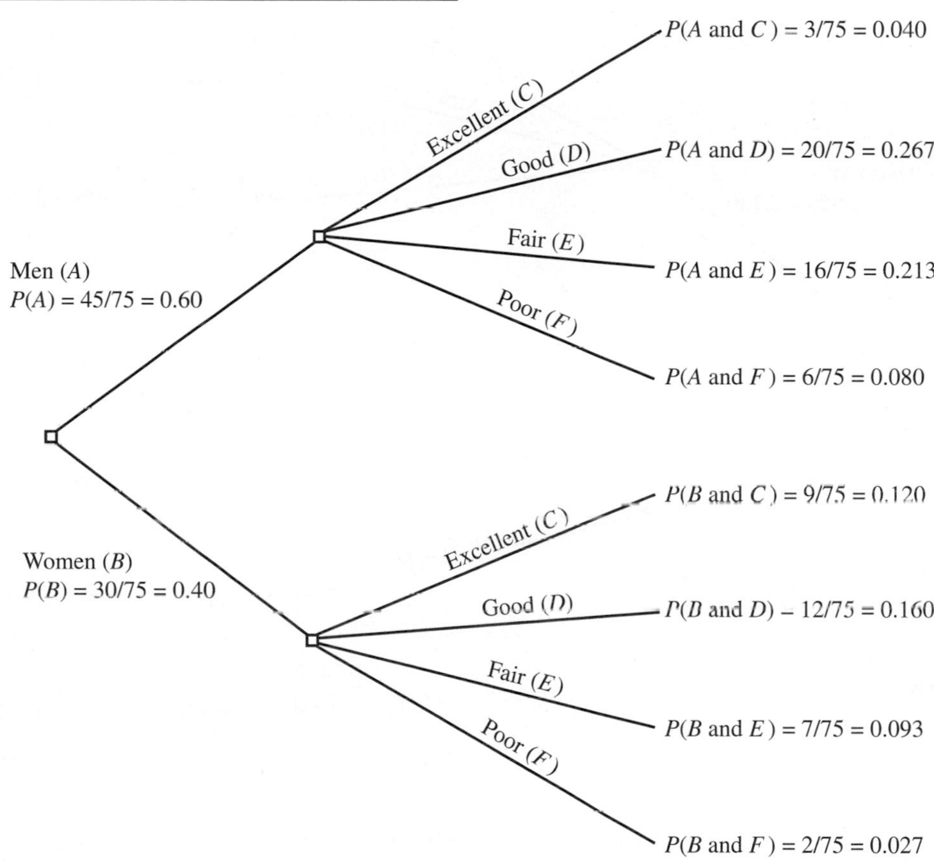

4.30 $\frac{(0.40)(0.30)}{(0.15)(0.67) + (0.45)(0.36) + (0.40)(0.30)} = \frac{0.12}{0.3825} = 0.314$

4.32 ${}_9P_2 = \frac{9!}{(9-2)!} = 72$

4.34 ${}_9C_2 = \frac{9!}{(9-2)!2!} = 36$

If order of objects is not of importance, combinations are used instead of permutations.

4.36 ${}_8P_3 = \frac{8!}{(8-3)!} = 336$

4.38 $\frac{(13)_4C_3(12)_4C_2}{_{52}C_5} = \frac{3{,}744}{2{,}598{,}960} = 0.00144$

4.40 ${}_4P_4 = 24$

4.42 ${}_9C_3 = 84$

4.44 $({}_{13}C_6)({}_{15}C_6) = 8{,}588{,}580$

4.46 $P(\text{Heart}) = \frac{13}{52} = 0.25$

4.48 **a.** empirical

b. classical

c. subjective

d. classical

4.50 **a.** 240

b. $\frac{240}{1{,}000} = 0.24$

c. $\frac{150}{1{,}000} = 0.15$

d. $\frac{610}{1{,}000} = 0.61$

4.52 **a.** Events are mutually exclusive

b. Events are dependent

4.54 a. Events are mutually exclusive

b. Events are dependent

4.56 a. $\frac{239}{968} = 0.247$

b. $\frac{243}{968} + \frac{707}{968} - \frac{180}{968} = 0.795$

c. $\frac{\left(\frac{130}{968}\right)}{\left(\frac{261}{968}\right)} = \frac{130}{261} = 0.498$

d. $\frac{\left(\frac{68}{968}\right)}{\left(\frac{307}{968}\right)} = \frac{68}{307} = 0.221$

e.

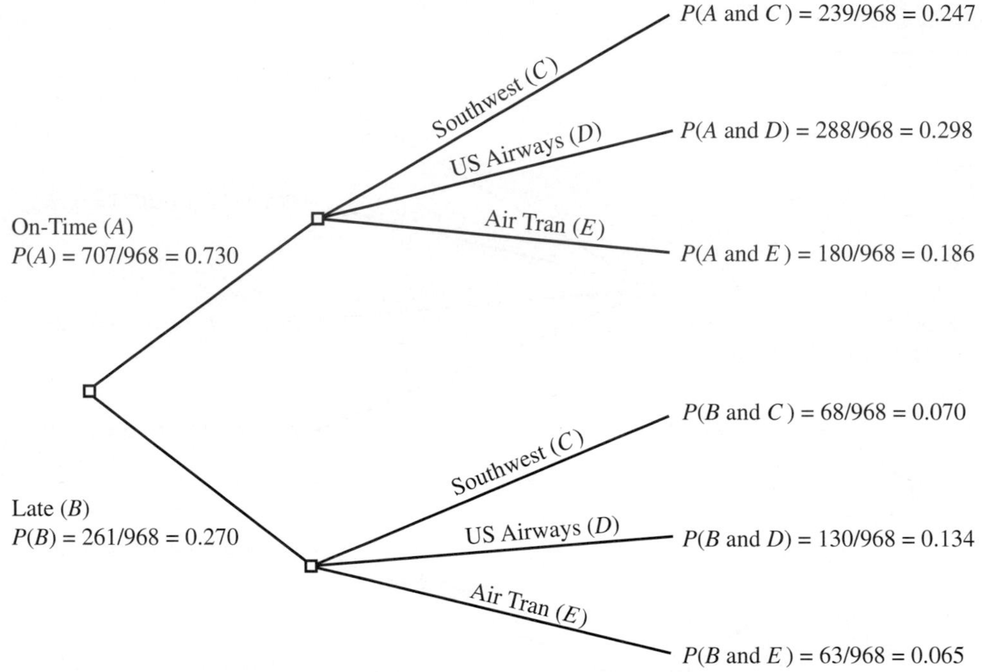

On-Time (A)
$P(A) = 707/968 = 0.730$

Southwest (C): $P(A \text{ and } C) = 239/968 = 0.247$

US Airways (D): $P(A \text{ and } D) = 288/968 = 0.298$

Air Tran (E): $P(A \text{ and } E) = 180/968 = 0.186$

Late (B)
$P(B) = 261/968 = 0.270$

Southwest (C): $P(B \text{ and } C) = 68/968 = 0.070$

US Airways (D): $P(B \text{ and } D) = 130/968 = 0.134$

Air Tran (E): $P(B \text{ and } E) = 63/968 = 0.065$

4.58 a. $\left(\frac{89}{165}\right)100 = 53.9\%$

b. $\left(\frac{69}{165}\right)100 = 41.8\%$

c. $\left(\frac{31}{165}\right)100 = 18.8\%$

d. $\left(\frac{89}{165} + \frac{44}{165} - \frac{30}{165}\right)100 = 62.4\%$

e. $\frac{\left(\frac{20}{165}\right)}{\left(\frac{76}{165}\right)}(100) = 26.3\%$

f. $\frac{\left(\frac{20}{165}\right)}{\left(\frac{36}{165}\right)}(100) = 55.6\%$

g. $P(A) = \frac{44}{165} = 0.267$

$P(A|B) = \frac{P(A \text{ and } B)}{P(B)}$

$P(A \text{ and } B) = \frac{14}{165} = 0.085 \quad P(B) = \frac{76}{165} = 0.461$

$P(A|B) = \frac{0.085}{0.461} = 0.184$

$P(A|B) \neq P(A)$

Events A and B are dependent.

4.60 $\frac{(0.50)(0.02)}{(0.20)(0.04) + (0.30)(0.03) + (0.5)(0.02)} = \frac{0.010}{0.027} = 0.370$

4.62 $(0.79)(0.79)(0.79)(0.79)(0.79) = 0.308$

4.64 Define A_1 = Order came from Mayfair store, A_2 = Order came from Claymont store, B = Delivery time exceeded 45 minutes.

$P(A_1) = 0.4$

$P(A_2) = 1 - 0.4 = 0.6$

$P(B|A_1) = 0.15$

$P(B|A_2) = 0.05$

$P(A_1|B) = \frac{(0.4)(0.15)}{(0.4)(0.15) + (0.6)(0.05)} = 0.667$

There is a 66.7% probability that the late order came from the Mayfair store.

4.66 $\frac{1}{{}_{30}C_5} = \frac{1}{142{,}506} = 0.000007$

4.68 ${}_{10}P_3 = \frac{10!}{(10-3)!} = 720$

4.70 $(5)(7) = 35$

4.72 $({}_{12}C_4)({}_{16}C_5) = (495)(4{,}368) = 2{,}162{,}160$

Chapter 5

5.2 **a.** $\mu = 2.61$

b. $\sigma = 1.019$

5.4 **a.** Not a discrete probability distribution because the sum of the probabilities of all outcomes is greater than 1

b. Discrete probability distribution

c. Discrete probability distribution

d. Not a discrete probability distribution because the probability of one outcome is greater than 1

e. Not a discrete probability distribution because the sum of the probabilities of all outcomes is less than 1

5.6 **a.** Stanton: $\mu = 3.7$, Newark: $\mu = 3.2$

b. Stanton: $\sigma = 1.14$, Newark: $\sigma = 1.39$

c. Stanton's fast-food restaurants have higher average customer satisfaction rating than ones in Newark. Customer satisfaction ratings for Stanton's fast-food restaurants are more consistent when compared with ones in Newark.

5.8 $EMV = \$19{,}200$

5.10 **a.** $P(2,7) = 0.0774$

b. $P(x) = P(0,7) + P(1,7) = 0.0016 + 0.0172 = 0.0188$

c. $P(6,7) + P(7,7) = 0.1306 + 0.0280 = 0.1586$

5.12 **a.** $P(4,5) = 0.0146$

b. $P(4,7) = 0.0577$

c. $P(4,10) = 0.1460$

5.14 $P(x \geq 14) = 0.1091 + 0.1746 + 0.2182 + 0.2054 + 0.1369 + 0.0576 + 0.0115 = 0.9133$

5.16 **a.** $P(7,8) = 0.3826$

b. $P(8,8) = 0.4305$

c. $1 - (P(6,8) + P(7,8) + P(8,8)) = 1 - (0.1488 + 0.3826 + 0.4305) = 0.0381$

d. $P(4,8) = 0.0046$

The probability of four out of eight customers being satisfied is very low, assuming that 90% of the customer base is satisfied. Based on this sample, it is not likely that 90% of the customers are satisfied.

5.18 **a.** $P(3,9) = 0.2716$

b. $P(x < 4) = P(0,9) + P(1,9) + P(2,9) + P(3,9) = 0.0207 + 0.1004 + 0.2162 + 0.2716 = 0.6089$

c. $P(x = 6 \text{ or } 7) = P(6,9) + P(7,9) = 0.0424 + 0.0098 = 0.0522$

d. $\mu = (9)(0.35) = 3.15; \sigma = \sqrt{(9)(0.35)(0.65)} = 1.43$

5.20 **a.** $P(0,15) = 0.3953$

b. $P(0,15) + P(1,15) + P(2,15) = 0.3953 + 0.3785 + 0.1691 = 0.9429$

c. $1 - (P(0,15) + P(1,15)) = 1 - (0.3953 + 0.3785) = 0.2262$

e. $P(4,15) = 0.0090$

The probability of 4 out of 15 customers making a purchase on the Web site is very low, assuming that 6% of the customers make a purchase. Based on this sample, it is not likely that 6% of the customers make purchases.

5.22 **a.** $P(3) = 0.2240$

b. $P(0) + P(1) + P(2) = 0.0498 + 0.1494 + 0.2240 = 0.4232$

c. $1 - (P(0) + P(1) + P(2) + P(3) + P(4)) = 1 - (0.0498 + 0.1494 + 0.2240 + 0.2240 + 0.1680) = 0.1848$

5.24 **a.** $P(4) = 0.0902$

b. $P(4) = 0.1680$

c. $P(4) = 0.1954$

d. As the value of λ approached 4.0, the probability that $x = 4$ increases.

5.26 **a.** $P(0) = 0.0743$

b. $P(0) + P(1) + P(2) + P(3) = 0.0743 + 0.1931 + 0.2510 + 0.2176 = 0.7360$

c. $1 - (P(0) + P(1)) = 1 - (0.0743 + 0.1931) = 0.7326$

5.28 **a.** $P(7) = 0.0824$

b. $P(0) + P(1) + P(2) = 0.0111 + 0.0500 + 0.1125 = 0.1736$

c. $1 - (P(0) + P(1) + P(2) + P(3) + P(4)) = 1 - (0.0111 + 0.0500 + 0.1125 + 0.1687 + 0.1898) = 0.4679$

5.30 **a.** $P(x) = P(2,22) = \dfrac{22!}{(22-2)!2!}(0.015)^2(0.985)^{20} = 0.0384$

b. $P(x) = P(2) = \dfrac{((22)(0.015))^2 2.71828^{-(22)(0.015)}}{2!} = 0.0391$

c. The probabilities are close enough, but fewer calculations were needed to obtain the result when using the Poisson distribution.

5.32 **a.** $P(3) = \dfrac{{}_{12-6}C_{5-3} \cdot {}_6C_3}{{}_{12}C_5} = 0.3788$

b. $P(2) = \dfrac{{}_{12-6}C_{5-2} \cdot {}_6C_2}{{}_{12}C_5} = 0.3788$

c. $P(0) + P(1) = \dfrac{{}_{12-6}C_{5-0} \cdot {}_6C_0}{{}_{12}C_5} + \dfrac{{}_{12-6}C_{5-1} \cdot {}_6C_1}{{}_{12}C_5} = 0.1212$

d. $\mu = 2.5; \sigma = 0.89$

5.34 $P(3) = \dfrac{{}_{14-6}C_{4-3} \cdot {}_6C_3}{{}_{14}C_4} = 0.1598$

5.36 **a.** $P(0) = \dfrac{{}_{9-2}C_{2-0} \cdot {}_2C_0}{{}_9C_2} = 0.5833$

b. $P(1) = \dfrac{{}_{9-2}C_{2-1} \cdot {}_2C_1}{{}_9C_2} = 0.3889$

c. $P(2) = \dfrac{{}_{9-2}C_{2-2} \cdot {}_2C_2}{{}_9C_2} = 0.0278$

d. $\mu = 0.444; \sigma = 0.55$

5.38 **a.** $P(3) = \dfrac{{}_{20-8}C_{3-3} \cdot {}_8C_3}{{}_{20}C_3} = 0.0491$

b. $P(1) = \dfrac{{}_{20-8}C_{3-1} \cdot {}_8C_1}{{}_{20}C_3} = 0.4632$

c. $P(2) = \dfrac{{}_{20-8}C_{3-2} \cdot {}_8C_2}{{}_{20}C_3} = 0.2947$

d. $P(0) = \dfrac{{}_{20-8}C_{3-0} \cdot {}_8C_0}{{}_{20}C_3} = 0.1930$

e. $\mu = 1.2; \sigma = 0.80$

5.40 **a.** $\mu = 1.53$

b. $\sigma = 1.22$

5.42 **a.** 8:00 A.M. class: $\mu = 2.58$; 10:00 A.M. class: $\mu = 1.79$

b. 8:00 A.M class: $\sigma = 1.39$; 10:00 A.M. class: $\sigma = 1.33$

c. More students miss the earlier class which is expected.

5.44 Portfolio A: $EMV = \$1,725$

Portfolio B: $EMV = \$1,700$

Investor should choose Portfolio A.

5.46 Profit = \$14 revenue + \$2 revenue − Cost to purchase calendars

The \$14 revenue is based on the number of calendars sold at \$14, which is the minimum of the supply of calendars and the eventual demand.

DEMAND	PROFIT (ORDER 100 CALENDARS)	PROBABILITY
100	$(100)(\$14) + (0)(\$2) - (100)(\$6) = \$800$	0.25
200	$(100)(\$14) + (0)(\$2) - (100)(\$6) = \$800$	0.40
300	$(100)(\$14) + (0)(\$2) - (100)(\$6) = \$800$	0.35

$EMV = (\$800)(0.25) + (\$800)(0.40) + (\$800)(0.35) = \$800$

DEMAND	PROFIT (ORDER 200 CALENDARS)	PROBABILITY
100	$(100)(\$14) + (100)(\$2) - (200)(\$6) = \$400$	0.25
200	$(200)(\$14) + (0)(\$2) - (200)(\$6) = \$1,600$	0.40
300	$(200)(\$14) + (0)(\$2) - (200)(\$6) = \$1,600$	0.35

$EMV = (\$400)(0.25) + (\$1,600)(0.40) + (\$1,600)(0.35) = \$1,300$

DEMAND	PROFIT (ORDER 300 CALENDARS)	PROBABILITY
100	$(100)(\$14) + (200)(\$2) - (300)(\$6) = \$0$	0.25
200	$(200)(\$14) + (100)(\$2) - (300)(\$6) = \$1,200$	0.40
300	$(300)(\$14) + (0)(\$2) - (300)(\$6) = \$2,400$	0.35

$EMV = (\$0)(0.25) + (\$1,200)(0.40) + (\$2,400)(0.35) = \$1,320$

Bob's Bookstore should order 300 calendars.

5.48 a. $P(6, 15) = 0.1914$

b. $P(9, 15) = 0.1048$

c. $P(4, 15) + P(5,15) = 0.0780 + 0.1404 = 0.2184$

d. $\mu = 6.75; \sigma = 1.926$

5.50 a. $P(4, 7) = 0.1640$

b. $P(x > 2) = 1.0 - P(0,7) - P(1,7) - P(2,7) = 1.0 - 0.0394 - 0.1619 - 0.2853 = 0.5134$

c. $\mu = (7)(0.37) = 2.59; \sigma = \sqrt{(7)(0.37)(0.63)} = 1.28$

5.52 a. $P(12, 12) = 0.0591$

b. $P(x > 9) = P(10, 12) + P(11, 12) + P(12, 12) = 0.2756 + 0.1885 + 0.0591 = 0.5232$

c. $P(x \leq 7) = 1.0 - P(8, 12) - P(9, 12) - P(10, 12) - P(11, 12) - P(12, 12) = 0.0866$

d. $\mu = (12)(0.79) = 9.48; \sigma = \sqrt{(12)(0.79)(0.21)} = 1.41$

5.54 a. $P(6, 6) = 0.4046$

b. $P(x \geq 4) = P(4, 6) + P(5, 6) + P(6, 6) = 0.1608 + 0.3952 + 0.4046 = 0.9606$

c. $P(x < 5) = 1.0 - P(5, 6) - P(6, 6) = 1.0 - 0.3952 - 0.4046 = 0.2002$

d. $\mu = (6)(0.86) = 5.16; \sigma = \sqrt{(6)(0.86)(0.14)} = 0.85$

5.56 a. $P(12, 20) = 0.0727$

b. $P(13, 20) + P(14, 20) + P(15, 20) + P(16, 20) + P(17, 20) + P(18, 20) + P(19, 20) + P(20, 20) = 0.0580$

c. $P(0, 20) + P(1, 20) + P(2, 20) + P(3, 20) + P(4, 20) + P(5, 20) + P(6, 20) + P(7, 20) + P(8, 20) + P(9, 20) = 0.5914$

d. $\mu = 9; \sigma = 2.2$

5.58 a. $P(2, 8) = 0.0324$

b. $P(x > 5) = P(6, 8) + P(7, 8) + P(8, 8) = 0.2297 + 0.1071 + 0.0218 = 0.3586$

c. $P(x \leq 3) = P(0, 8) + P(1, 8) + P(2, 8) + P(3, 8) = 0.0004 + 0.0057 + 0.0324 + 0.1058 = 0.1443$

d. $\mu = (8)(0.62) = 4.96; \sigma = \sqrt{(8)(0.62)(0.38)} = 1.37$

5.60 a. $P(6) = 0.0411$

b. $P(3) = 0.1133$

c. $P(x \geq 7) = 1.0 - P(x < 7) = 1.0 - 0.0786 = 0.9214$

d. $P(x < 10) = 0.3405$

5.62 a. $\lambda = (0.25)(16) = 4; P(2) = 0.1465$

b. $\lambda = (0.25)(16) = 4; P(4) = 0.1954$

c. $\lambda = (0.5)(16) = 8; P(6) = 0.1221$

d. $\lambda = (0.75)(16) = 12; P(6) = 0.0255$

5.64 a. $P(1) = 0.0098$

b. $P(x < 3) = 0.015 + 0.0098 + 0.0318 = 0.0431$

c. $P(x > 4) = 1.0 - P(x \leq 4) = 1.0 - 0.0015 - 0.0098 - 0.0318 - 0.0688 - 0.1118 = 0.7763$

d. $\sigma = \sqrt{6.5} = 2.55$

5.66 a. $P(1, 24) = \dfrac{24!}{(24-1)!1!}(0.025)^1(0.975)^{23} = 0.3352$

b. $P(4, 24) = \dfrac{24!}{(24-4)!4!}(0.025)^4(0.975)^{20} = 0.0025$

c. $P(1) = \dfrac{(0.60^1)(2.71828^{-0.60})}{1!} = 0.3293$

d. $P(4) = \dfrac{(0.60^4)(2.71828^{-0.60})}{4!} = 0.0030$

5.68 a. $P(3, 24) = \dfrac{24!}{(24-3)!3!}(0.035)^3(0.965)^{21} = 0.0411$

b. $P(x) = P(3) = \dfrac{((24)(0.035))^3 2.71828^{-(24)(0.035)}}{3!} = 0.0426$

c. The probabilities are very close.

5.70 a. $P(8) = \dfrac{{}_{19-14}C_{8-8} \cdot {}_{14}C_8}{{}_{19}C_8} = 0.0397$

b. $P(6) + P(7) + P(8) = \dfrac{{}_{19-14}C_{8-6} \cdot {}_{14}C_6}{{}_{19}C_8} + \dfrac{{}_{19-14}C_{8-7} \cdot {}_{14}C_7}{{}_{19}C_8} + \dfrac{{}_{19-14}C_{8-8} \cdot {}_{14}C_8}{{}_{19}C_8} = 0.6640$

c. There are only five returns that are not using the short form. If eight returns are selected, at least three returns must be short forms.

d. $\mu = 5.895; \sigma = 0.9737$

5.72 a. $P(4) = \dfrac{{}_{22-8}C_{10-4} \cdot {}_8C_4}{{}_{22}C_{10}} = 0.3251$

b. $P(6) = \dfrac{{}_{22-8}C_{10-6} \cdot {}_8C_6}{{}_{22}C_{10}} = 0.0433$

c. The proportion of cars (0.636) is much higher than the proportion of trucks (0.364) on the lot. Four trucks out of 10 vehicles have a higher probability than 4 cars out of 10 vehicles because the 0.40 proportion is very close to the proportion of trucks on the lot.

d. $\mu = 3.64; \sigma = 1.150$

5.74 a. $P(0) = \dfrac{{}_{52-12}C_{5-0} \cdot {}_{12}C_0}{{}_{52}C_5} = 0.2532$

b. $P(1) = \dfrac{{}_{52-12}C_{5-1} \cdot {}_{12}C_1}{{}_{52}C_5} = 0.4220$

c. $P(2) = \dfrac{{}_{52-12}C_{5-2} \cdot {}_{12}C_2}{{}_{52}C_5} = 0.2509$

d. $P(4) = \dfrac{{}_{52-12}C_{5-4} \cdot {}_{12}C_4}{{}_{52}C_5} = 0.0076$

e. $\mu = 1.154; \sigma = 0.9044$

Chapter 6

6.2 **a.** $P(z > 1.35) = 1.0 - 0.9115 = 0.0855$

b. $P(z > -0.42) = 1.0 - 0.3372 = 0.6628$

c. $P(-1.70 \le z \le -0.65) = 0.2578 - 0.0446 = 0.2132$

d. $P(-1.69 \le z \le 0.20) = 0.5793 - 0.0455 = 0.5338$

6.4 **a.** $z_{100} = \frac{100 - 124}{27} = -0.89$

$z_{140} = \frac{140 - 124}{27} = 0.59$

$P(100 \le x \le 140) = 0.7224 - 0.1867 = 0.5357$

b. $z_{130} = \frac{130 - 124}{27} = 0.22$

$z_{170} = \frac{170 - 124}{27} = 1.70$

$P(130 \le x \le 170) = 0.9554 - 0.5871 = 0.3683$

c. $z_{65} = \frac{65 - 124}{27} = -2.19$

$z_{90} = \frac{90 - 124}{27} = -1.26$

$P(65 \le x \le 90) = 0.1038 - 0.0143 = 0.0895$

d. $z_{120} = \frac{120 - 124}{27} = -0.15$

$z_{180} = \frac{180 - 124}{27} = 2.07$

$P(120 \le x \le 180) = 0.9808 - 0.4404 = 0.5404$

6.6 **a.** $\mu = (75)(0.22) = 16.5$

$\sigma = \sqrt{(75)(0.22)(1 - 0.22)} = 3.59$

b. $z_{10.5} = \frac{10.5 - 16.5}{3.59} = -1.67$

$z_{11.5} = \frac{11.5 - 16.5}{3.59} = -1.39$

$P(10.5 \le x \le 11.5) = 0.0823 - 0.0475 = 0.0348$

c. $z_{9.5} = \frac{9.5 - 16.5}{3.59} = -1.95;$

$z_{18.5} = \frac{18.5 - 16.5}{3.59} = 0.56$

$P(9.5 \le x \le 18.5) = 0.7123 - 0.0256 = 0.6867$

d. $z_{7.5} = \frac{7.5 - 16.5}{3.59} = -2.51$

$z_{15.5} = \frac{15.5 - 16.5}{3.59} = -0.28$

$P(7.5 \le x \le 15.5) = 0.3897 - 0.0060 = 0.3837$

6.8 **a.** **1.** $z_{250} = \frac{\$250 - \$237.22}{\$21.45} = 0.60$

$P(x < \$250) = 0.7257$

2. $z_{260} = \frac{\$260 - \$237.22}{\$21.45} = 1.06$

$P(x > \$260) = 1.0 - 0.8554 = 0.1446$

3. $z_{210} = \frac{\$210 - \$237.22}{\$21.45} = -1.27$

$z_{240} = \frac{\$240 - \$237.22}{\$21.45} = 0.13$

$P(210 \le x \le 240) = 0.5517 - 0.1020 = 0.4497$

b. Find the closest value to 0.80 in the body of Table 4 in Appendix A. This will be 0.7995 in row 0.8 and column 0.04. The z-score for the 80th percentile is therefore 0.84.
$x = \$237.22 + (0.84)(\$21.45) = \$255.24$

6.10 **a.** **1.** $z_7 = \frac{7 - 11.4}{3.6} = -1.22$

$P(x < 7) = 0.1112$

2. $z_9 = \frac{9 - 11.4}{3.6} = -0.67$

$P(x > 9) = 1.0 - 0.2514 = 0.7486$

3. $z_8 = \frac{8 - 11.4}{3.6} = -0.94$

$z_{12} = \frac{12 - 11.4}{3.6} = 0.17$

$P(8 \le x \le 12) = 0.5675 - 0.1736 = 0.3939$

4. $P(x = 10) = 0$

b. Find the closest value to 0.60 in the body of Table 4 in Appendix A. This will be 0.5987 in row 0.2 and column 0.05. The z-score for the 60th percentile is therefore 0.25.
$x = 11.4 + (0.25)(3.6) = 12.3$ lbs

6.12 **a.** **1.** $x = \$1{,}600 + (1)(\$75) = \$1{,}675$
$x = \$1{,}600 - (1)(\$75) = \$1{,}525$

2. $x = \$1{,}600 + (2)(\$75) = \$1{,}750$
$x = \$1{,}600 - (2)(\$75) = \$1{,}450$

3. $x = \$1{,}600 + (3)(\$75) = \$1{,}825$
$x = \$1{,}600 - (3)(\$75) = \$1{,}375$

b. The \$1,900 cost of this warranty is much higher than those of competing companies based on the fact that it is more than three standard deviations above the mean.

6.14 **a.** $x = \mu \pm z\sigma$
$x = 736 + (1)(40) = 776$
$x = 736 - (1)(40) = 696$

b. $x = 736 + (2)(40) = 816$
$x = 736 - (2)(40) = 656$

c. $x = 736 + (3)(40) = 856$
$x = 736 - (3)(40) = 616$

6.16 **a.** **1.** $z_{187} = \frac{187 - 185}{5} = 0.40$

$P(x > 187) = 1.0 - 0.6554 = 0.3446$

2. $z_{181} = \frac{181 - 185}{5} = -0.80$

$P(x < 181) = 0.2119$

3. $z_{180} = \frac{180 - 185}{5} = -1.00$

$z_{183} = \frac{183 - 185}{5} = -0.40$

$P(180 \le x \le 183) = 0.3446 - 0.1587 = 0.1859$

4. $z_{188} = \frac{188 - 185}{5} = 0.60$

$z_{193} = \frac{193 - 185}{5} = 1.60$

$P(188 \le x \le 193) = 0.9452 - 0.7257 = 0.2195$

6.18 **a.** $\mu = (24)(0.33) = 7.92$ adults

$\sigma = \sqrt{(24)(0.33)(1 - 0.33)} = 2.30$ adults

$z_{9.5} = \frac{9.5 - 7.92}{2.30} = 0.69$

$P(x \le 9.5) = P(z \le 0.69) = 0.7549$

b. $z_{5.5} = \frac{5.5 - 7.92}{2.30} = -1.05$

$z_{10.5} = \frac{10.5 - 7.92}{2.30} = 1.12$

$P(5.5 \le x \le 10.5) = 0.8686 - 0.1469 = 0.7217$

c. $z_{10.5} = \frac{10.5 - 7.92}{2.30} = 1.12$

$z_{14.5} = \frac{14.5 - 7.92}{2.30} = 2.86$

$P(10.5 \le x \le 14.5) = 0.9979 - 0.8686 = 0.1293$

d. $z_{6.5} = \frac{6.5 - 7.92}{2.30} = -0.62$

$z_{7.5} = \frac{7.5 - 7.92}{2.30} = -0.18$

$P(6.5 \le x \le 7.5) = 0.4286 - 0.2676 = 0.1610$

6.20 a. $\mu = (30)(0.392) = 11.76$

$\sigma = \sqrt{(30)(0.392)(1 - 0.392)} = 2.67$

b. $z_{12.5} = \dfrac{12.5 - 11.76}{2.67} = 0.28$

$P(x > 12.5) = 1.0 - 0.6103 = 0.3897$

c. $z_{13.5} = \dfrac{13.5 - 11.76}{2.67} = 0.65$

$z_{14.5} = \dfrac{14.5 - 11.76}{2.67} = 1.03$

$P(13.5 \le x \le 14.5) = 0.8485 - 0.7422 = 0.1063$

d. $z_{6.5} = \dfrac{6.5 - 11.76}{2.67} = -1.97$

$z_{9.5} = \dfrac{9.5 - 11.76}{2.67} = -0.85$

$P(6.5 \le x \le 9.5) = 0.1977 - 0.0244 = 0.1733$

e. $z_{13.5} = \dfrac{13.5 - 11.76}{2.67} = 0.65$

$z_{16.5} = \dfrac{16.5 - 11.76}{2.67} = 1.78$

$P(13.5 \le x \le 16.5) = 0.9625 - 0.7422 = 0.2203$

6.22 a. $\mu = 7$ minutes/customer

$\lambda = 1/7 = 0.1429$ customers/minute

$P(x > 12) = e^{-(12)(0.1429)} = 0.1800$

b. $P(x > 3) = e^{-(3)(0.1429)} = 0.6514$

c. $P(x \le 10) = 1 - e^{-(10)(0.1429)} = 0.7605$

$P(x \le 7) = 1 - e^{-(7)(0.1429)} = 0.6322$

$P(7 \le x \le 10) = 0.7605 - 0.6322 = 0.1283$

d. $P(x \le 5) = 1 - e^{-(5)(0.1429)} = 0.5106$

$P(x \le 1) = 1 - e^{-(1)(0.1429)} = 0.1332$

$P(1 \le x \le 5) = 0.5106 - 0.1332 = 0.3774$

6.24 a. $\lambda = \left(\dfrac{18 \text{ customers}}{1 \text{ hour}}\right)\left(\dfrac{1 \text{ hour}}{60 \text{ minutes}}\right) = 0.3$ customers/minute

$a = 45$ seconds $= 0.75$ minutes

$P(x \le 0.75) = 1 - e^{-(0.75)(0.3)} = 1 - 0.7985 = 0.2015$

b. $P(x \le 3) = 1 - e^{-(3)(0.3)} = 0.5934$

$P(x \le 1) = 1 - e^{-(1)(0.3)} = 0.2592$

$P(1 \le x \le 3) = 0.5934 - 0.2592 = 0.3342$

c. $P(x \le 5) = 1 - e^{-(5)(0.3)} = 0.7769$

$P(x \le 2) = 1 - e^{-(2)(0.3)} = 0.4512$

$P(2 \le x \le 5) = 0.7769 - 0.4512 = 0.3257$

d. $P(x \le 10) = 1 - e^{-(10)(0.3)} = 0.9502$

$P(x \le 4) = 1 - e^{-(4)(0.3)} = 0.6988$

$P(4 \le x \le 10) = 0.9502 - 0.6988 = 0.2514$

6.26 a. 1. $\mu = \dfrac{8 \text{ minutes}}{1 \text{ student}}$ $\quad \lambda = \dfrac{1 \text{ student}}{8 \text{ minutes}} = 0.125$ students/minute

$P(x \le 2) = 1 - e^{-(2)(0.125)} = 1 - 0.7788 = 0.2212$

2. $P(x \le 4) = 1 - e^{-(4)(0.125)} = 1 - 0.6065 = 0.3935$

3. $P(x \le 5) = 1 - e^{-(5)(0.125)} = 0.4647$

$P(x \le 3) = 1 - e^{-(3)(0.125)} = 0.3127$

$P(3 \le x \le 5) = 0.4647 - 0.3127 = 0.1520$

4. $P(x > 10) = e^{-(10)(0.125)} = 0.2865$

6.28 a. 1. $\mu = \dfrac{2.5 \text{ minutes}}{1 \text{ customer}}$

$\lambda = \dfrac{1 \text{ customer}}{2.5 \text{ minutes}} = 0.4$ customers/minute

$P(x \le 2) = 1 - e^{-(2)(0.4)} = 1 - 0.4493 = 0.5507$

2. $P(x > 5) = e^{-(5)(0.4)} = 0.1353$

3. $P(x \le 4) = 1 - e^{-(4)(0.4)} = 0.7981$

$P(x \le 1) = 1 - e^{-(1)(0.4)} = 0.3297$

$P(1 \le x \le 4) = 0.7981 - 0.3297 = 0.4684$

6.30 a. 1. $P(x > 63) = P(63 \le x \le 95) = \dfrac{95 - 63}{95 - 60} = 0.914$

2. $P(x > 70) = P(70 \le x \le 95) = \dfrac{95 - 70}{95 - 60} = 0.714$

3. $P(x > 88) = P(88 \le x \le 95) = \dfrac{95 - 88}{95 - 60} = 0.20$

4. $P(x = 75) = 0$

b. $\mu = \dfrac{60 + 95}{2} = 77.5$

$\sigma = \dfrac{95 - 60}{\sqrt{12}} = 10.12$

6.32 a. 1. $P(180 \le x \le 260) = \dfrac{260 - 180}{300 - 130} = 0.471$

2. $P(130 \le x \le 200) = \dfrac{200 - 130}{300 - 130} = 0.412$

3. $P(x > 150) = P(150 \le x \le 300) = \dfrac{300 - 150}{300 - 130} = 0.882$

b. $\mu = \dfrac{130 + 300}{2} = 215$

$\sigma = \dfrac{300 - 130}{\sqrt{12}} = 49.13$

6.34 a. $f(x) = \dfrac{1}{b - a} = \dfrac{1}{30 - 5} = \dfrac{1}{25} = 0.04$ if $5 \le x \le 30$

$f(x) = 0$ otherwise

b. $\mu = \dfrac{5 + 30}{2} = 17.5$ minutes

$\sigma = \dfrac{30 - 5}{\sqrt{12}} = 7.23$ minutes

c. $P(x \le 25) = P(5 \le x \le 25) = \dfrac{25 - 5}{30 - 5} = 0.80$

d. $P(x > 20) = P(20 \le x \le 30) = \dfrac{30 - 20}{30 - 5} = 0.40$

e. $P(8 \le x \le 15) = \dfrac{15 - 8}{30 - 5} = 0.28$

f. $P(x_1 \le x \le x_2) = \dfrac{x_2 - x_1}{b - a} = 0.75$

$\dfrac{x_2 - 5}{30 - 5} = 0.75$

$x_2 = 23.75$ minutes

6.36 a. $f(x) = \dfrac{1}{b - a} = \dfrac{1}{8.2 - 7.4} = \dfrac{1}{0.8} = 1.25$ ounces if $7.4 \le x \le 8.2$

$f(x) = 0$ otherwise

b. $\mu = \dfrac{7.4 + 8.2}{2} = 7.8$ ounces

$\sigma = \dfrac{8.2 - 7.4}{\sqrt{12}} = 0.231$ ounces

c. $P(x > 8.0) = P(8.0 \le x \le 8.2) = \dfrac{8.2 - 8.0}{8.2 - 7.4} = 0.25$

d. $P(x = 7.5) = 0$

e. $P(x < 8.1) = P(7.4 \le x \le 8.1) = \dfrac{8.1 - 7.4}{8.2 - 7.4} = 0.875$

f. $P(7.5 \le x \le 8.0) = \dfrac{8.0 - 7.5}{8.2 - 7.4} = 0.625$

g. $P(x_1 \le x \le x_2) = \dfrac{x_2 - x_1}{b - a} = 0.15$

$\dfrac{x_2 - 7.4}{8.2 - 7.4} = 0.15$

$x_2 = 7.52$ ounces

6.38 a. 1. $z_{80} = \dfrac{\$80 - \$86}{\$9.50} = -0.63$

$P(x < \$80) = 0.2643$

2. $z_{90} = \frac{\$90 - \$86}{\$9.50} = 0.42$

$P(x < \$90) = 0.6628$

3. $P(x = \$85) = 0$

4. $z_{75} = \frac{\$75 - \$86}{\$9.50} = -1.16$

$z_{95} = \frac{\$95 - \$86}{\$9.50} = 0.95$

$P(\$75 \le x \le \$95) = 0.8289 - 0.1230 = 0.7059$

c. Find the closest value to 0.75 in the body of Table 4 in Appendix A. This will be 0.7486 in row 0.6 and column 0.07. The z-score for the 75th percentile is therefore 0.67.

$x = \$86 + (0.67)(\$9.50) = \$92.37$

6.40 a. 1. $z_{195} = \frac{195 - 175}{16} = 1.25$

$P(x < 195) = 0.8944$

2. $z_{180} = \frac{180 - 175}{16} = 0.31$

$P(x > 180) = 1.0 - 0.6217 = 0.3783$

3. $P(x = 170) = 0$

4. $z_{150} = \frac{150 - 175}{16} = -1.56$

$z_{182} = \frac{182 - 175}{16} = 0.44$

$P(150 \le x \le 182) = 0.6700 - 0.0594 = 0.6106$

c. Find the closest value to 0.20 in the body of Table 3 in Appendix A. This will be 0.2005 in row -0.8 and column 0.04. The z-score for the 20th percentile is therefore -0.84.

$x = 175 + (-0.84)(16) = 161.6$ euros

6.42 a. $x = \$285{,}700 + (1)(\$46{,}100) = \$331{,}800$

$x = \$285{,}700 - (1)(\$46{,}100) = \$239{,}600$

b. $x = \$285{,}700 + (2)(\$46{,}100) = \$377{,}900$

$x = \$285{,}700 - (2)(\$46{,}100) = \$193{,}500$

c. $x = \$285{,}700 + (3)(\$46{,}100) = \$424{,}000$

$x = \$285{,}700 - (3)(\$46{,}100) = \$147{,}400$

6.44 a. 1. $z_{1,800} = \frac{1{,}800 - 2{,}090}{420} = -0.69$

$P(x < 1{,}800) = 0.2451$

2. $z_{2,000} = \frac{2{,}000 - 2{,}090}{420} = -0.21$

$z_{2,200} = \frac{2{,}200 - 2{,}090}{420} = 0.26$

$P(2{,}000 \le x \le 2{,}200) = 0.6026 - 0.4168 = 0.1858$

3. $z_{1,200} = \frac{1{,}200 - 2{,}090}{420} = -2.12$

$z_{1,600} = \frac{1{,}600 - 2{,}090}{420} = -1.17$

$P(1{,}200 \le x \le 1{,}600) = 0.1210 - 0.0170 = 0.1040$

4. $z_{2,300} = \frac{2{,}300 - 2{,}090}{420} = 0.50$

$z_{2,500} = \frac{2{,}500 - 2{,}090}{420} = 0.98$

$P(2{,}300 \le x \le 2{,}500) = 0.8365 - 0.6915 = 0.1450$

c. Find the closest value to 0.90 in the body of Table 4 in Appendix A. This will be 0.8997 in row 1.2 and column 0.08. The z-score for the 90th percentile is therefore 1.28.

$x = 2{,}090 + (1.28)(420) = 2{,}627.6$ hours

6.46 a. 1. $z_{900} = \frac{\$900 - \$822}{\$190} = 0.41$

$P(x < \$900) = 0.6591$

2. $z_{800} = \frac{\$800 - \$822}{\$190} = -0.12$

$z_{920} = \frac{\$920 - \$822}{\$190} = 0.52$

$P(\$800 \le x \le \$920) = 0.6985 - 0.4522 = 0.2463$

3. $z_{550} = \frac{\$550 - \$822}{\$190} = -1.43$

$z_{700} = \frac{\$700 - \$822}{\$190} = -0.64$

$P(\$550 \le x \le \$700) = 0.2611 - 0.0764 = 0.1847$

4. $z_{750} = \frac{\$750 - \$822}{\$190} = -0.38$

$z_{1,100} = \frac{\$1{,}100 - \$822}{\$190} = 1.46$

$P(\$750 \le x \le \$1{,}100) = 0.9279 - 0.3520 = 0.5759$

c. Find the closest value to 0.45 in the body of Table 3 in Appendix A. This will be 0.4483 in row -0.1 and column 0.03. The z-score for the 45th percentile is therefore -0.13.

$x = \$822 + (-0.13)(\$190) = \$797.30$

6.48 a. 1. $z_{11} = \frac{11 - 10}{3.2} = 0.31$

$P(x < 11) = 0.6217$

2. $z_{12} = \frac{12 - 10}{3.2} = 0.63$

$P(x > 12) = 1.0 - 0.7357 = 0.2643$

3. $z_7 = \frac{7 - 10}{3.2} = -0.94$

$z_9 = \frac{9 - 10}{3.2} = -0.31$

$P(7 \le x \le 9) = 0.3783 - 0.1736 = 0.2047$

4. $z_8 = \frac{8 - 10}{3.2} = -0.63$

$z_{15} = \frac{15 - 10}{3.2} = 1.56$

$P(8 \le x \le 15) = 0.9406 - 0.2643 = 0.6763$

c. Find the closest value to 0.70 in the body of Table 4 in Appendix A. This will be 0.6985 in row 0.5 and column 0.02. The z-score for the 70th percentile is therefore 0.52.

$x = 10 + (0.52)(3.2) = 11.7$

6.50 a. 1. $z_{18,500} = \frac{\$18{,}500 - \$16{,}230}{\$4{,}740} = 0.48$

$P(x < \$18{,}500) = 0.6844$

2. $z_{11,300} = \frac{\$11{,}300 - \$16{,}230}{\$4{,}740} = -1.04$

$P(x > \$11{,}300) = 1.0 - 0.1492 = 0.8508$

3. $z_{10,000} = \frac{\$10{,}000 - \$16{,}230}{\$4{,}740} = -1.31$

$z_{14,000} = \frac{\$14{,}000 - \$16{,}230}{\$4{,}740} = -0.47$

$P(\$10{,}000 < x < \$14{,}000) = 0.3192 - 0.0951 = 0.2241$

4. $z_{12,500} = \frac{\$12{,}500 - \$16{,}230}{\$4{,}740} = -0.79$

$z_{17,000} = \frac{\$17{,}000 - \$16{,}230}{\$4{,}740} = 0.16$

$P(\$12{,}500 < x < \$17{,}000) = 0.5636 - 0.2148 = 0.3488$

c. Find the closest value to 0.90 in the body of Table 4 in Appendix A. This will be 0.8997 in row 1.2 and column 0.08. The z-score for the 90th percentile is therefore 1.28.

$x = \$16{,}230 + (1.28)(\$4{,}740) = \$22{,}297.20$

6.52 a. 1. $z_{30} = \frac{30 - 60.3}{17.9} = -1.69$

$P(x < 30) = 0.0455$

2. $z_{45} = \frac{45 - 60.3}{17.9} = -0.85$

$P(x > 45) = 1.0 - 0.1977 = 0.8023$

3. $z_{50} = \dfrac{50 - 60.3}{17.9} = -0.58$

$z_{90} = \dfrac{90 - 60.3}{17.9} = 1.66$

$P(50 < x < 90) = 0.9515 - 0.2810 = 0.6705$

4. $z_{65} = \dfrac{65 - 60.3}{17.9} = 0.26$

$z_{85} = \dfrac{85 - 60.3}{17.9} = 1.38$

$P(65 < x < 85) = 0.9162 - 0.6026 = 0.3136$

c. Find the closest value to 0.35 in the body of Table 3 in Appendix A. This will be 0.3483 in row −0.3 and column 0.09. The z-score for the 35th percentile is therefore −0.39.
$x = 60.3 + (-0.39)(17.9) = 53.3$

6.54 **a.** $\mu = (20)(0.69) = 13.8$

$\sigma = \sqrt{(20)(0.69)(1 - 0.69)} = 2.07$

b. $z_{11.5} = \dfrac{11.5 - 13.8}{2.07} = -1.11$

$P(x > 11.5) = 1.0 - 0.1335 = 0.8665$

c. $z_{15.5} = \dfrac{15.5 - 13.8}{2.07} = 0.82$

$z_{16.5} = \dfrac{16.5 - 13.8}{2.07} = 1.30$

$P(15.5 \le x \le 16.5) = 0.9032 - 0.7939 = 0.1093$

d. $z_{10.5} = \dfrac{10.5 - 13.8}{2.07} = -1.59$

$z_{13.5} = \dfrac{13.5 - 13.8}{2.07} = -0.14$

$P(10.5 \le x \le 13.5) = 0.4443 - 0.0559 = 0.3884$

e. $z_{17.5} = \dfrac{17.5 - 13.8}{2.07} = 1.79$

$z_{19.5} = \dfrac{19.5 - 13.8}{2.07} = 2.75$

$P(17.5 \le x \le 19.5) = 0.9970 - 0.9633 = 0.0337$

6.56 **a.** $\mu = (40)(0.68) = 27.2$ teens

$\sigma = \sqrt{(40)(0.68)(1 - 0.68)} = 2.95$ teens

b. $z_{28.5} = \dfrac{28.5 - 27.2}{2.95} = 0.44$

$P(x \le 28.5) = 0.6700$

c. $z_{23.5} = \dfrac{23.5 - 27.2}{2.95} = -1.25$

$z_{24.5} = \dfrac{24.5 - 27.2}{2.95} = -0.92$

$P(23.5 \le x \le 24.5) = 0.1788 - 0.1056 = 0.0732$

d. $z_{32.5} = \dfrac{32.5 - 27.2}{2.95} = 1.80$

$P(x > 32.5) = 1.0 - 0.9641 = 0.0359$

e. $z_{25.5} = \dfrac{25.5 - 27.2}{2.95} = -0.58$

$z_{28.5} = \dfrac{28.5 - 27.2}{2.95} = 0.44$

$P(25.5 \le x \le 28.5) = 0.6700 - 0.2810 = 0.3890$

6.58 **a.** $\mu = (50)(0.475) = 23.75$ people

$\sigma = \sqrt{(50)(0.475)(1 - 0.475)} = 3.53$ people

b. $z_{19.5} = \dfrac{19.5 - 23.75}{3.53} = -1.20$

$P(x \le 19.5) = 0.1151$

c. $z_{26.5} = \dfrac{26.5 - 23.75}{3.53} = 0.78$

$z_{27.5} = \dfrac{27.5 - 23.75}{3.53} = 1.06$

$P(26.5 \le x \le 27.5) = 0.8554 - 0.7823 = 0.0731$

d. $z_{22.5} = \dfrac{22.5 - 23.75}{3.53} = -0.35$

$P(x > 22.5) = 1.0 - 0.3632 = 0.6368$

e. $z_{25.5} = \dfrac{25.5 - 23.75}{3.53} = 0.50$

$z_{28.5} = \dfrac{28.5 - 23.75}{3.53} = 1.35$

$P(25.5 \le x \le 28.5) = 0.9115 - 0.6915 = 0.2200$

6.60 **a.** $\lambda = \dfrac{22.1 \text{ fouls}}{40 \text{ minutes}} = 0.5525 \text{ fouls/minute}$

$P(x \le 1) = 1 - e^{-(1)(0.5525)} = 1 - 0.5755 = 0.4245$

b. $P(x \le 4) = 1 - e^{-(4)(0.5525)} = 0.8903$

$P(x \le 2) = 1 - e^{-(2)(0.5525)} = 0.6688$

$P(2 \le x \le 4) = 0.8903 - 0.6688 = 0.2215$

c. $P(x > 3) = e^{-(3)(0.5525)} = 0.1906$

e. $\sigma = \dfrac{1}{\lambda} = \dfrac{1}{0.5525} = 1.81$ minutes

6.62 **a.** $\mu = \dfrac{32 \text{ days}}{1 \text{ accident}} \quad \lambda = \dfrac{1 \text{ accident}}{32 \text{ days}} = 0.03125 \text{ accidents/day}$

$P(x \le 10) = 1 - e^{-(10)(0.03125)} = 1 - 0.7316 = 0.2684$

b. $P(x \le 25) = 1 - e^{-(25)(0.03125)} = 0.5422$

$P(x \le 15) = 1 - e^{-(15)(0.03125)} = 0.3742$

$P(15 \le x \le 25) = 0.5422 - 0.3742 = 0.1680$

c. $P(x > 40) = e^{-(40)(0.03125)} = 0.2865$

e. $\sigma = \mu = 32$ days

6.64 **a.** $\lambda = \left(\dfrac{10.8 \text{ customers}}{1 \text{ hour}}\right)\left(\dfrac{1 \text{ hour}}{60 \text{ minutes}}\right) = 0.18 \text{ customers/minute}$

$P(x \le 3) = 1 - e^{-(3)(0.18)} = 1 - 0.5827 = 0.4173$

b. $P(x \le 6) = 1 - e^{-(6)(0.18)} = 1 - 0.3396 = 0.6604$

$P(x \le 12) = 1 - e^{-(12)(0.18)} = 1 - 0.1153 = 0.8847$

$P(6 \le x \le 12) = 0.8847 - 0.6604 = 0.2243$

c. $P(x > 10) = e^{-(10)(0.18)} = 0.1653$

e. $\sigma = \dfrac{1}{\lambda} = \dfrac{1}{0.18} = 5.56$ minutes

6.66 **a.** $P(x > 3) = P(3 \le x \le 9) = \dfrac{9 - 3}{9 - 0.5} = 0.7059$

b. $P(x < 5.5) = P(0.5 \le x \le 5.5) = \dfrac{5.5 - 0.5}{9 - 0.5} = 0.5882$

c. $P(4 \le x \le 8) = \dfrac{8 - 4}{9 - 0.5} = 0.4706$

d. $\mu = \dfrac{0.5 + 9}{2} = 4.75$ minutes

$\sigma = \dfrac{9 - 0.5}{\sqrt{12}} = 2.45$ minutes

e. $x_2 = (0.80)(9 - 0.5) + 0.5 = 7.3$ minutes
Because 7.3 minutes exceeds the 6-minute target, this goal is not being met.

6.68 **a.** $P(x < 12) = P(4 \le x \le 12) = \dfrac{12 - 4}{18 - 4} = 0.5714$

b. $P(6 \le x \le 10) = \dfrac{10 - 6}{18 - 4} = 0.2857$

c. $P(x > 7) = P(7 \le x \le 18) = \dfrac{18 - 7}{18 - 4} = 0.7857$

d. $P(x = 15) = 0$

e. $\mu = \dfrac{4 + 18}{2} = 11$ minutes

$\sigma = \dfrac{18 - 4}{\sqrt{12}} = 4.05$ minutes

6.70 Find the closest value to 0.95 in the body of Table 4 in Appendix A. This will be in row 1.6, halfway between 0.9495 and 0.9505 in columns 0.04 and 0.05. The z-score for the 95th percentile is therefore 1.645.
$x = 60 + (1.645)(12) = 79.7 \approx 80$ boxes of golf balls

Chapter 7

7.2 **a.** $\mu = \dfrac{684}{20} = 34.2$

b. $\bar{x} = \dfrac{95}{5} = 19.0$

Sampling error $= -15.2$

c. $\bar{x} = \dfrac{286}{10} = 28.6$

Sampling error $= -5.6$

d. Sampling error decreases as the sample size increases.

e. Smallest $\bar{x} = \dfrac{60}{5} = 12.0$

Sampling error $= -22.2$

Largest $x = \dfrac{297}{5} = 59.4$

Sampling error $= 25.2$
Smallest sampling error $= -22.2$
Largest sampling error $= 25.2$

7.4 **a.** $\mu = \dfrac{181{,}200}{15} = 12{,}080.0$

b. $\bar{x} = \dfrac{69{,}175}{5} = 13{,}835.0$

Sampling error $= 1{,}755.0$

c. $\bar{x} = \dfrac{112{,}155}{10} = 11{,}215.5$

Sampling error $= -864.5$

d. Sampling error decreases as the sample size increases.

7.8 $\sigma_{\bar{x}} = \dfrac{15}{\sqrt{10}} = 4.75$

$z_{85} = \dfrac{85 - 80}{4.75} = 1.05$

$P(\bar{x} \leq 85) = 0.8531$

7.10 $\sigma_{\bar{x}} = \dfrac{9}{\sqrt{36}} = 1.50$

$\bar{x}_U = 45 + (1.96)(1.50) = 47.94$
$\bar{x}_L = 45 - (1.96)(1.50) = 42.06$

7.12 **a.** $\sigma_{\bar{x}} = \dfrac{\$0.50}{\sqrt{30}} = \$0.0912$

b. $z_{7.75} = \dfrac{\$7.75 - \$7.96}{\$0.0912} = -2.30$

$P(\bar{x} < \$7.75) = 0.0107$

c. $z_{8.10} = \dfrac{\$8.10 - \$7.96}{\$0.0912} = 1.54$

$P(\bar{x} < \$8.10) = 0.9382$

d. $z_{8.20} = \dfrac{\$8.20 - \$7.96}{\$0.0912} = 2.63$

$P(\bar{x} > \$8.20) = 1.0 - 0.9957 = 0.0043$

7.14 **a.** $\sigma_{\bar{x}} = \dfrac{\$26.00}{\sqrt{35}} = \$4.39$

b. $z_{160} = \dfrac{\$160 - \$156}{\$4.39} = 0.91$

$P(\bar{x} < \$160) = 0.8186$

c. $z_{163} = \dfrac{\$163 - \$156}{\$4.39} = 1.59$

$P(\bar{x} > \$163) = 1.0 - 0.9441 = 0.0559$

d. $z_{147} = \dfrac{\$147 - \$156}{\$4.39} = -2.05$

$z_{151} = \dfrac{\$151 - \$156}{\$4.39} = -1.14$

$P(\$147 \leq \bar{x} \leq \$151) = 0.1271 - 0.0202 = 0.1069$

7.16 **a.** $\sigma_{\bar{x}} = \dfrac{6.0}{\sqrt{30}} = 1.09$

$z_{51} = \dfrac{51 - 52.7}{1.09} = -1.56$

$P(\bar{x} < 51) = 0.0594$

b. $\sigma_{\bar{x}} = \dfrac{6.0}{\sqrt{45}} = 0.89$

$z_{51} = \dfrac{51 - 52.7}{0.89} = -1.91$

$P(\bar{x} < 51) = 0.0281$

c. $\sigma_{\bar{x}} = \dfrac{6.0}{\sqrt{60}} = 0.77$

$z_{51} = \dfrac{51 - 52.7}{0.77} = -2.21$

$P(\bar{x} < 51) = 0.0136$

d. With a larger sample size, standard error decreases and the sample means tend to move closer to the population mean of 52.7 MPH. Therefore, the probability of observing a sample mean less than 51.0 MPH decreases as the sample size increases.

7.18 **a.** $\sigma_{\bar{x}} = \dfrac{\$33}{\sqrt{31}} = \dfrac{\$33}{5.57} = \$5.92$

$z_{91} = \dfrac{\$91 - \$108}{\$5.92} = -2.87$

$P(\bar{x} < \$91) = 0.0021$

There's a 0.21% chance of observing a sample mean as low as \$91, if the population mean is \$108. This probability is low enough (less than 0.05) to contradict the findings of the Harris poll.

b. $\bar{x}_U = \mu_{\bar{x}} + z\sigma_{\bar{x}}$
$\bar{x}_U = \$108 + (1.96)(\$5.92) = \$119.60$
$\bar{x}_L = \mu_{\bar{x}} - z\sigma_{\bar{x}}$
$\bar{x}_L = \$108 - (1.96)(\$5.92) = \$96.40$

Note that the sample mean of \$91 is below the lower sample mean, confirming our answer to part a.

7.20 **a.** $\sigma_{\bar{x}} = \dfrac{6.5}{\sqrt{40}} = 1.03$

$z_{33} = \dfrac{33 - 30}{1.03} = 2.91$

$P(\bar{x} > 33) = 1.0 - 0.9982 = 0.0018$

Thus, there's less than a 1% chance of observing a sample mean as high as 33 minutes, if the population mean is 30 minutes. This probability is low enough (less than 0.05) to contradict the claim made by the pizza shop.

b. $\bar{x}_U = 30 + (1.96)(1.03) = 32.0$ minutes
$\bar{x}_L = 30 - (1.96)(1.03) = 28.0$ minutes

Note that the sample mean of 33 minutes is above the upper sample mean of 32 minutes, confirming our answer to part a.

7.22 **a.** $\sigma_{\bar{x}} = \dfrac{4.9}{\sqrt{32}}\sqrt{\dfrac{80 - 32}{80 - 1}} = 0.68$

b. $z_{87} = \dfrac{87 - 85.4}{0.68} = 2.35$

$P(\bar{x} < 87) = 0.9906$

c. $z_{86} = \dfrac{86 - 85.4}{0.68} = 0.88$

$P(\bar{x} > 86) = 1.0 - 0.8106 = 0.1894$

d. $z_{84.5} = \dfrac{84.5 - 85.4}{0.68} = -1.32$

$z_{86.5} = \dfrac{86.5 - 85.4}{0.68} = 1.62$

$P(84.5 \le \bar{x} \le 86.5) = 0.9474 - 0.0934 = 0.8540$

7.24 a. Using Excel, $\mu = 79.024$ in. and $\sigma = 3.608$ in. (Remember to use =STDEVP).

b. $\sigma_{\bar{x}} = \dfrac{3.608}{\sqrt{45}}\sqrt{\dfrac{335 - 45}{335 - 1}} = 0.501$

$z_{78} = \dfrac{78 - 79.024}{0.501} = -2.04$

$P(\bar{x} < 78) = 0.0207$

c. $z_{79.5} = \dfrac{79.5 - 79.024}{0.501} = 0.95$

$P(\bar{x} > 79.5) = 1.0 - 0.8289 = 0.1711$

d. $z_{78.5} = \dfrac{78.5 - 79.024}{0.501} = -1.05$

$z_{80} = \dfrac{80 - 79.024}{0.501} = 1.95$

$P(78.5 \le \bar{x} \le 80) = 0.9744 - 0.1469 = 0.8275$

7.26 a. $\sigma_p = \sqrt{\dfrac{(0.65)(1 - 0.65)}{125}} = 0.0427$

$\bar{p} = \dfrac{80}{125} = 0.64$

$z_{0.64} = \dfrac{0.64 - 0.65}{0.0427} = -0.23$

$P(\bar{p} \le 0.64) = 0.4090$

b. $\bar{p} = \dfrac{82}{125} = 0.656$

$z_{0.656} = \dfrac{0.656 - 0.65}{0.0427} = 0.14$

$P(\bar{p} \le 0.656) = 0.5557$

c. $\bar{p} = \dfrac{75}{125} = 0.60$

$z_{0.60} = \dfrac{0.60 - 0.65}{0.0427} = -1.17$

$P(\bar{p} \ge 0.60) = 1.0 - 0.1210 = 0.8790$

7.28 a. $\sigma_p = \sqrt{\dfrac{(0.4)(1 - 0.4)}{150}}\sqrt{\dfrac{400 - 150}{400 - 1}} = 0.0317$

$\bar{p} = \dfrac{50}{150} = 0.333$

$z_{0.333} = \dfrac{0.333 - 0.40}{0.0317} = -2.11$

$\bar{p} = \dfrac{54}{150} = 0.36$

$z_{0.36} = \dfrac{0.36 - 0.40}{0.0317} = -1.26$

$P(0.333 \le \bar{p} \le 0.36) = 0.1038 - 0.0174 = 0.0864$

b. $\bar{p} = \dfrac{55}{150} = 0.367$

$z_{0.367} = \dfrac{0.367 - 0.40}{0.0317} = -1.04$

$\bar{p} = \dfrac{62}{150} = 0.413$

$z_{0.413} = \dfrac{0.413 - 0.40}{0.0317} = 0.41$

$P(0.367 \le \bar{p} \le 0.413) = 0.6591 - 0.1492 = 0.5099$

c. $\bar{p} = \dfrac{53}{150} = 0.353$

$z_{0.353} = \dfrac{0.353 - 0.40}{0.0317} = -1.48$

$\bar{p} = \dfrac{70}{150} = 0.467$

$z_{0.467} = \dfrac{0.467 - 0.40}{0.0317} = 2.11$

$P(0.353 \le \bar{p} \le 0.467) = 0.9826 - 0.0694 = 0.9132$

7.30 a. $\sigma_p = \sqrt{\dfrac{(0.31)(1 - 0.31)}{175}} = 0.0350$

b. $\bar{p} = \dfrac{58}{175} = 0.331$

$z_{0.331} = \dfrac{0.331 - 0.31}{0.0350} = 0.60$

$P(\bar{p} < 0.331) = 0.7257$

c. $\bar{p} = \dfrac{62}{175} = 0.354$

$z_{0.354} = \dfrac{0.354 - 0.31}{0.0350} = 1.26$

$P(\bar{p} > 0.354) = 1.0 - 0.8962 = 0.1038$

d. $\bar{p} = \dfrac{52}{175} = 0.297$

$z_{0.297} = \dfrac{0.297 - 0.31}{0.0350} = -0.37$

$P(\bar{p} > 0.297) = 1.0 - 0.3557 = 0.6443$

e. $\bar{p} = \dfrac{44}{175} = 0.251$

$z_{0.251} = \dfrac{0.251 - 0.31}{0.0350} = -1.69$

$\bar{p} = \dfrac{50}{175} = 0.286$

$z_{0.286} = \dfrac{0.286 - 0.31}{0.0350} = -0.69$

$P(0.251 \le \bar{p} \le 0.286) = 0.2451 - 0.0455 = 0.1996$

7.32 a. $\sigma_p = \sqrt{\dfrac{(0.69)(1 - 0.69)}{140}} = 0.0391$

b. $\bar{p} = \dfrac{100}{140} = 0.714$

$z_{0.714} = \dfrac{0.714 - 0.69}{0.0391} = 0.61$

$P(\bar{p} \ge 0.714) = 1.0 - 0.7291 = 0.2709$

c. $\bar{p} = \dfrac{96}{140} = 0.686$

$z_{0.686} = \dfrac{0.686 - 0.69}{0.0391} = -0.10$

$\bar{p} = \dfrac{105}{140} = 0.75$

$z_{0.75} = \dfrac{0.75 - 0.69}{0.0391} = 1.53$

$P(0.686 \le \bar{p} \le 0.75) = 0.9370 - 0.4602 = 0.4768$

d. $\bar{p} = \dfrac{81}{140} = 0.579$

$z_{0.579} = \dfrac{0.579 - 0.69}{0.0391} = -2.84$

$P(\bar{p} \le 0.579) = 0.0023$

Thus, there's less than a 1% chance of observing a sample proportion as low as 0.579 if the population proportion is 0.69. This probability is low enough (less than 0.05) to contradict the claim made by the survey.

7.34 **a.** $\sigma_p = \sqrt{\frac{(0.36)(1-0.36)}{125}} = 0.0429$

b. $z_{0.30} = \frac{0.30 - 0.36}{0.0429} = -1.40$

$P(\bar{p} < 0.30) = 0.0808$

c. $z_{0.28} = \frac{0.28 - 0.36}{0.0429} = -1.86$

$z_{0.40} = \frac{0.40 - 0.36}{0.0429} = 0.93$

$P(0.28 \le \bar{p} \le 0.40) = 0.8238 - 0.0314 = 0.7924$

d. The standard error would be reduced as follows:

$\sigma_p = \sqrt{\frac{(0.36)(1-0.36)}{225}} = 0.0320$

This would, in turn, increase the probabilities that the sample proportions will be closer to the population proportion:

$z_{0.30} = \frac{\bar{p} - p}{\sigma_p} = \frac{0.30 - 0.36}{0.0320} = -1.88$

$P(\bar{p} < 0.30) = P(z < -1.88) = 0.0301$

$z_{0.28} = \frac{0.28 - 0.36}{0.0320} = -2.50$

$z_{0.40} = \frac{0.40 - 0.36}{0.0320} = 1.25$

$P(0.28 \le \bar{p} \le 0.40) = P(-2.50 \le z \le 1.25)$
$= 0.8944 - 0.0062 = 0.8882$

7.36 **a.** $\sigma_p = \sqrt{\frac{(0.56)(1-0.56)}{50}}\sqrt{\frac{200-50}{200-1}} = 0.0609$

$z_{0.60} = \frac{0.60 - 0.56}{0.0609} = 0.66$

$P(\bar{p} < 0.60) = 0.7454$

b. $\sigma_p = \sqrt{\frac{(0.56)(1-0.56)}{100}}\sqrt{\frac{200-100}{200-1}} = 0.0352$

$z_{0.60} = \frac{0.60 - 0.56}{0.0352} = 1.14$

$P(\bar{p} < 0.60) = 0.8729$

$\sigma_p = \sqrt{\frac{(0.56)(1-0.56)}{150}}\sqrt{\frac{200-150}{200-1}} = 0.0203$

$z_{0.60} = \frac{0.60 - 0.56}{0.0203} = 1.97$

$P(\bar{p} < 0.60) = 0.9756$

Increasing the sample size reduces the standard error. This, in turn, increases the probabilities that the sample proportions will be closer to the population proportion.

c. $\sigma_p = \sqrt{\frac{(0.56)(1-0.56)}{50}} = 0.0702$

$z_{0.60} = \frac{0.60 - 0.56}{0.0702} = 0.57$

$P(\bar{p} < 0.60) = 0.7157$

Without the finite correction factor the standard error is overestimated, causing the probability to be underestimated.

7.38 **a.** $\sigma_{\bar{x}} = \frac{\$15{,}300}{\sqrt{34}} = \frac{\$15{,}300}{5.83} = \$2{,}624.36$

$z_{70{,}000} = \frac{\$70{,}000 - \$74{,}804}{\$2{,}624.36} = -1.83$

$P(\bar{x} < \$70{,}000) = 0.0336$

b. $z_{74{,}000} = \frac{\$74{,}000 - \$74{,}804}{\$2{,}624.36} = -0.31$

$P(\bar{x} > \$74{,}000) = 1.0 - 0.3783 = 0.6217$

c. $z_{76{,}000} = \frac{\$76{,}000 - \$74{,}804}{\$2{,}624.36} = 0.46$

$z_{81{,}000} = \frac{\$81{,}000 - \$74{,}804}{\$2{,}624.36} = 2.36$

$P(\$76{,}000 < \bar{x} < \$81{,}000) = 0.9909 - 0.6772 = 0.3137$

7.40 **a.** $\sigma_{\bar{x}} = \frac{146}{\sqrt{4}} = 73.0$

$z_{1{,}200} = \frac{1{,}200 - 1{,}120}{73.0} = 1.10$

$P(\bar{x} > 1{,}200) = 1.0 - 0.8643 = 0.1357$

b. Because the sample size is less than 30, the weekly demand (population) must be normally distributed.

7.42 **a.** $\sigma_p = \sqrt{\frac{(0.10)(1-0.10)}{200}} = 0.0212$

$z_{0.12} = \frac{0.12 - 0.10}{0.0212} = 0.94$

$P(\bar{p} > 0.12) = 1.0 - 0.8264 = 0.1736$

b. $z_{0.14} = \frac{0.14 - 0.10}{0.0212} = 1.89$

$P(\bar{p} < 0.14) = 0.9706$

c. $z_{0.06} = \frac{0.06 - 0.10}{0.0212} = -1.89$

$z_{0.09} = \frac{0.09 - 0.10}{0.0212} = -0.47$

$P(0.06 \le \bar{p} \le 0.09) = 0.3192 - 0.0294 = 0.2898$

d. $\bar{p} = \frac{9}{200} = 0.045$

$z_{0.045} = \frac{0.045 - 0.10}{0.0212} = -2.59$

$P(\bar{p} \le 0.045) = 0.0048$

Thus, there's less than a 1% chance of observing a sample proportion as low as 0.045 if the population proportion is 0.1. This probability is low enough (less than 0.05) to conclude that the population proportion of left-handed golfers is less than 10%.

7.44 **a.** $\sigma_{\bar{x}} = \frac{\$7{,}500}{\sqrt{30}} = \$1{,}368.61$

$z_{24{,}000} = \frac{\$24{,}000 - \$23{,}200}{\$1{,}368.61} = 0.58$

$P(\bar{x} < \$24{,}000) = 0.7190$

b. $\bar{x}_U = \$23{,}200 + (1.96)(\$1{,}368.61) = \$25{,}882.48$

$\bar{x}_L = \$23{,}200 - (1.96)(\$1{,}368.61) = \$20{,}517.52$

c. $\sigma_{\bar{x}} = \frac{\$7{,}500}{\sqrt{60}} = \$967.74$

$z_{24{,}000} = \frac{\$24{,}000 - \$23{,}200}{\$967.74} = 0.83$

$P(\bar{x} < \$24{,}000) = 0.7967$

Increasing the sample size reduces the standard error. This, in turn, increases the probability that the sample mean will be closer to the population mean.

7.46 **a.** $\sigma_{\bar{x}} = \frac{3.0}{\sqrt{15}}\sqrt{\frac{90-15}{90-1}} = 0.71$

$z_{11} = \frac{11 - 12}{0.71} = -1.41$

$P(\bar{x} > 11) = 1.0 - 0.0793 = 0.9207$

b. $z_{12.5} = \frac{12.5 - 12}{0.71} = 0.70$

$P(\bar{x} > 12.5) = 1.0 - 0.7580 = 0.2420$

c. $z_{10} = \frac{10 - 12}{0.71} = -2.82$

$P(\bar{x} \le 10) = 0.0024$

Thus, there's less than a 1% chance of observing a sample mean as low as 10 minutes if the population mean is 12 minutes.

This probability is low enough (less than 0.05) to contradict the professor's claim that the average time to grade an exam is 12 minutes.

d. Because the sample size is less than 30, the time to correct exams must be normally distributed.

7.48 a. $\sigma_{\bar{x}} = \dfrac{\$95}{\sqrt{30}} = \$17.34$

$z_{475} = \dfrac{\$475 - \$460}{\$17.34} = 0.87$

$P(\bar{x} < \$475) = 0.8078$

b. $z_{450} = \dfrac{\$450 - \$460}{\$17.34} = -0.58$

$z_{465} = \dfrac{\$465 - \$460}{\$17.34} = 0.29$

$P(\$450 < \bar{x} < \$465) = 0.6141 - 0.2810 = 0.3331$

c. $\bar{x}_U = \mu_{\bar{x}} + z\sigma_{\bar{x}}$

$\bar{x}_U = \$460 + (1.96)(\$17.34) = \$493.99$

$\bar{x}_L = \mu_{\bar{x}} - z\sigma_{\bar{x}}$

$\bar{x}_L = \$460 - (1.96)(\$17.34) = \$426.01$

d. $z_{411} = \dfrac{\$411 - \$460}{\$17.34} = -2.83$

$P(\bar{x} \le \$411) = 0.0023$

There's a 0.23% chance of observing a sample mean as low as $411, if the population mean is $460. This probability is low enough (less than 0.05) to contradict the findings of the HomeAdvisor, Inc.

7.50 a. $\sigma_{\bar{x}} = \dfrac{5.0}{\sqrt{30}} = 0.912$

$z_{35.1} = \dfrac{35.1 - 34.5}{0.912} = 0.66$

$P(\bar{x} \ge 35.1) = 1.0 - 0.7454 = 0.2546$

There's a 25% chance of observing a sample mean as high as 35.1, if the population mean is 34.5. This probability is high enough (more than 0.05) to support the findings of the Pew Research Center.

b. $\bar{x}_U = \mu_{\bar{x}} + z\sigma_{\bar{x}}$

$\bar{x}_U = 34.5 + (1.96)(0.912) = 36.3$

$\bar{x}_L = \mu_{\bar{x}} - z\sigma_{\bar{x}}$

$\bar{x}_L = 34.5 - (1.96)(0.912) = 32.7$

7.52 a. $\sigma_{\bar{x}} = \dfrac{\$11,700}{\sqrt{40}} = \$1,851.27$

$z_{88,000} = \dfrac{\$88,000 - \$85,854}{\$1,851.27} = 1.16$

$P(\bar{x} < \$88,000) = 0.8770$

b. $z_{81,000} = \dfrac{\$81,000 - \$85,854}{\$1,851.27} = -2.62$

$P(\bar{x} > \$81,000) = 1.0 - 0.0044 = 0.9956$

c. $z_{83,000} = \dfrac{\$83,000 - \$85,854}{\$1,851.27} = -1.54$

$z_{85,000} = \dfrac{\$85,000 - \$85,854}{\$1,851.27} = -0.46$

$P(\$83,000 \le \bar{x} \le \$85,000) = 0.3228 - 0.0618 = 0.2610$

d. $z_{87,400} = \dfrac{\$87,400 - \$85,854}{\$1,851.27} = 0.84$

$P(\bar{x} \ge \$87,400) = 1.0 - 0.7995 = 0.2005$

There's a 20% chance of observing a sample mean as high as $87,400, if the population mean is $85,854. This probability is high enough (more than 0.05) to support the findings of the Graduate Management Admission Council.

7.54 a. $\dfrac{n}{N} = \dfrac{42}{286} = 0.147 > 0.05$

$\sigma_p = \sqrt{\dfrac{(0.39)(1 - 0.39)}{42}}\sqrt{\dfrac{286 - 42}{286 - 1}} = 0.0697$

$\bar{p} = \dfrac{15}{42} = 0.357$

$z_{0.357} = \dfrac{0.357 - 0.39}{0.0697} = -0.47$

$P(\bar{p} \le 0.357) = 0.3192$

b. $\bar{p} = \dfrac{18}{42} = 0.429$

$z_{0.429} = \dfrac{0.429 - 0.39}{0.0697} = 0.56$

$P(\bar{p} \ge 0.429) = 1.0 - 0.7123 = 0.2877$

c. $\bar{p} = \dfrac{17}{42} = 0.405$

$\bar{p} = \dfrac{22}{42} = 0.524$

$z_{0.405} = \dfrac{0.405 - 0.39}{0.0697} = 0.22$

$z_{0.524} = \dfrac{0.524 - 0.39}{0.0697} = 1.92$

$P(0.405 \le \bar{p} \le 0.524) = 0.9726 - 0.5871 = 0.3855$

7.56 a. $\sigma_p = \sqrt{\dfrac{(0.143)(1 - 0.143)}{180}} = 0.0261$

$z_{0.20} = \dfrac{0.20 - 0.143}{0.0261} = 2.18$

$P(\bar{p} \le 0.20) = 0.9854$

b. $z_{0.18} = \dfrac{0.18 - 0.143}{0.0261} = 1.42$

$P(\bar{p} \ge 0.18) = 1.0 - 0.9222 = 0.0778$

c. $z_{0.10} = \dfrac{0.10 - 0.143}{0.0261} = -1.65$

$z_{0.15} = \dfrac{0.15 - 0.143}{0.0261} = 0.27$

$P(0.10 \le \bar{p} \le 0.15) = 0.6064 - 0.0495 = 0.5569$

d. $\bar{p} = \dfrac{29}{180} = 0.161$

$z_{0.161} = \dfrac{0.161 - 0.143}{0.0261} = 0.69$

$P(\bar{p} \ge 0.161) = 1.0 - 0.7549 = 0.2451$

There's a 24% chance of observing a sample proportion as high as 0.161, if the population proportion is 0.143. This probability is high enough (more than 0.05) to support the findings of Catalyst.

7.58 a. $\sigma_p = \sqrt{\dfrac{(0.30)(1 - 0.30)}{140}} = 0.0387$

$\bar{p} = \dfrac{45}{140} = 0.321$

$z_{0.321} = \dfrac{0.321 - 0.30}{0.0387} = 0.54$

$P(\bar{p} \le 0.321) = 0.7054$

b. $\bar{p} = \dfrac{50}{140} = 0.357$

$z_{0.357} = \dfrac{0.357 - 0.30}{0.0387} = 1.47$

$P(\bar{p} \ge 0.357) = 1.0 - 0.9292 = 0.0708$

c. $\bar{p} = \dfrac{35}{140} = 0.250$

$\bar{p} = \dfrac{40}{140} = 0.286$

$$z_{0.250} = \frac{0.250 - 0.30}{0.0387} = -1.29$$

$$z_{0.286} = \frac{0.286 - 0.30}{0.0387} = -0.36$$

$P(0.250 \le \bar{p} \le 0.286) = 0.3594 - 0.0985 = 0.2609$

d. $\bar{p} = \frac{28}{140} = 0.20$

$$z_{0.20} = \frac{0.20 - 0.30}{0.0387} = -2.58$$

$P(\bar{p} \le 0.20) = 0.0049$

There's a 0.49% chance of observing a sample proportion as low as 0.20, if the population proportion is 0.30. This probability is low enough (less than 0.05) to contradict the findings of the University of Michigan Transportation Research Institute.

7.60 a. $\sigma_{\bar{x}} = \frac{0.5}{\sqrt{30}} = 0.09$

$\bar{x}_U = 16.0 + (3.0)(0.09) = 16.27$

$\bar{x}_L = 16.0 - (3.0)(0.09) = 15.73$

b. $P(-3.0 \le z \le 3.0) = 0.9987 - 0.0013 = 0.9974$

7.62 $\sigma_{\bar{x}} = \frac{\sigma}{\sqrt{n}}\sqrt{\frac{N-n}{N-1}} = \frac{0.9}{\sqrt{60}}\sqrt{\frac{570-60}{570-1}} = 0.11$

$$z_{7.75} = \frac{\bar{x} - \mu_{\bar{x}}}{\sigma_{\bar{x}}} = \frac{7.75 - 8.0}{0.11} = -2.27$$

$P(\bar{x} \le 7.75) = P(z \le -2.27) = 0.0116$

Thus, there's only a little over a 1% chance of observing a sample mean ranking as low as 7.75, if the population mean ranking is 8. This probability is low enough (less than 0.05) to conclude that the customer satisfaction goal of 8 is not being achieved.

Chapter 8

8.2 $\sigma_{\bar{x}} = \frac{30}{\sqrt{40}} = 4.74$

$UCL_{\bar{x}} = 45.00 + (2.575)(4.74) = 57.21$

$LCL_{\bar{x}} = 45.00 - (2.575)(4.74) = 32.79$

8.4 a. $\sigma_{\bar{x}} = \frac{12}{\sqrt{35}} = 2.03$

$UCL_{\bar{x}} = 60.00 + (2.330)(2.03) = 64.73$

$LCL_{\bar{x}} = 60.00 - (2.330)(2.03) = 55.27$

b. $\sigma_{\bar{x}} = \frac{12}{\sqrt{45}} = 1.79$

$UCL_{\bar{x}} = 60.00 + (2.330)(1.79) = 64.17$

$LCL_{\bar{x}} = 60.00 - (2.330)(1.79) = 55.83$

c. $\sigma_{\bar{x}} = \frac{12}{\sqrt{55}} = 1.62$

$UCL_{\bar{x}} = 60.00 + (2.330)(1.62) = 63.77$

$LCL_{\bar{x}} = 60.00 - (2.330)(1.62) = 56.23$

8.6 a. $\sigma_{\bar{x}} = \frac{50}{\sqrt{30}} = 9.13$

$ME_{\bar{x}} = (1.280)(9.13) = 11.69$

b. $\sigma_{\bar{x}} = \frac{50}{\sqrt{45}} = 7.45$

$ME_{\bar{x}} = (1.280)(7.45) = 9.54$

c. $\sigma_{\bar{x}} = \frac{50}{\sqrt{60}} = 6.45$

$ME_{\bar{x}} = (1.280)(6.45) = 8.26$

8.8 $\sigma_{\bar{x}} = \frac{17}{\sqrt{12}} = 4.91$

$UCL_{\bar{x}} = 60.00 + (2.575)(4.91) = 72.64$

$LCL_{\bar{x}} = 60.00 - (2.575)(4.91) = 47.36$

The population must be normally distributed.

8.10 a. $\sigma_{\bar{x}} = \frac{\$35}{\sqrt{35}} = \$5.92$

$UCL_{\bar{x}} = \$311.00 + (1.645)(\$5.92) = \$320.74$

$LCL_{\bar{x}} = \$311.00 - (1.645)(\$5.92) = \$301.26$

b. $ME_{\bar{x}} = (1.645)(\$5.92) = \$9.74$

8.12 a. $\sigma_{\bar{x}} = \frac{260}{\sqrt{32}} = 45.96$

$UCL_{\bar{x}} = 2{,}157.00 + (1.960)(45.96) = 2{,}247.08$

$LCL_{\bar{x}} = 2{,}157.00 - (1.960)(45.96) = 2{,}066.92$

b. $\sigma_{\bar{x}} = \frac{260}{\sqrt{32}} = 45.96$

$UCL_{\bar{x}} = 2{,}157.00 + (2.575)(45.96) = 2{,}275.35$

$LCL_{\bar{x}} = 2{,}157.00 - (2.575)(45.96) = 2{,}038.65$

c. $\sigma_{\bar{x}} = \frac{260}{\sqrt{32}} = 45.96$

$UCL_{\bar{x}} = 2{,}157.00 + (1.75)(45.96) = 2{,}237.43$

$LCL_{\bar{x}} = 2{,}157.00 - (1.75)(45.96) = 2{,}076.57$

8.14 a. $\sigma_{\bar{x}} = \frac{45}{\sqrt{45}} = 6.71$

$UCL_{\bar{x}} = 488.90 + (1.960)(6.71) = 502.05$

$LCL_{\bar{x}} = 488.90 - (1.960)(6.71) = 475.75$

Yes, this sample supports HP's claim that the cartridge will yield an average of 495 pages.

b. The margin of error:
CONFIDENCE.NORM (0.05, 45, 45) = 13.15

8.16 a. $\sigma_{\bar{x}} = \frac{2.3}{\sqrt{18}} = 0.542$

$UCL_{\bar{x}} = 27.5 + (1.96)(0.542) = 28.56$

$LCL_{\bar{x}} = 27.5 - (1.96)(0.542) = 26.44$

b. No, this sample does not support Toyota's claim that the average age of a Scion driver is 26 years.

c. The population must be normally distributed.

d. The margin of error: CONFIDENCE.NORM (0.05, 2.3, 18) = 1.06

8.18 $\hat{\sigma}_{\bar{x}} = \frac{8.5}{\sqrt{25}} = 1.70; df = 24$

$UCL_{\bar{x}} = 38.00 + (2.064)(1.70) = 41.51$

$LCL_{\bar{x}} = 38.00 - (2.064)(1.70) = 34.49$

The population's standard deviation is unknown, so we substitute the sample standard deviation and use the t-distribution. The population must be normally distributed.

8.20 a. $\hat{\sigma}_{\bar{x}} = \frac{32}{\sqrt{30}} = 5.84; df = 29$

$UCL_{\bar{x}} = 125.00 + (1.311)(5.84) = 132.66$

$LCL_{\bar{x}} = 125.00 - (1.311)(5.84) = 117.34$

b. $\hat{\sigma}_{\bar{x}} = \frac{32}{\sqrt{60}} = 4.13; df = 59$

$UCL_{\bar{x}} = 125.00 + (1.296)(4.13) = 130.35$

$LCL_{\bar{x}} = 125.00 - (1.296)(4.13) = 119.65$

c. $\hat{\sigma}_{\bar{x}} = \dfrac{32}{\sqrt{90}} = 3.37;\ df = 89$

$UCL_{\bar{x}} = 125.00 + (1.291)(3.37) = 129.35$

$LCL_{\bar{x}} = 125.00 - (1.291)(3.37) = 120.65$

8.22 a. $\hat{\sigma}_{\bar{x}} = \dfrac{40}{\sqrt{10}} = 12.65;\ df = 9$

$ME_{\bar{x}} = (2.262)(12.65) = 28.61$

b. $\hat{\sigma}_{\bar{x}} = \dfrac{40}{\sqrt{30}} = 7.30;\ df = 29$

$ME_{\bar{x}} = (2.045)(7.30) = 14.93$

c. $\hat{\sigma}_{\bar{x}} = \dfrac{40}{\sqrt{50}} = 5.66;\ df = 49$

$ME_{\bar{x}} = (2.009)(5.66) = 11.36$

8.24 a. $\hat{\sigma}_{\bar{x}} = \dfrac{1{,}755}{\sqrt{21}} = 382.97;\ df = 20$

$UCL_{\bar{x}} = 5{,}038 + (1.725)(382.97) = 5{,}698.62$

$LCL_{\bar{x}} = 5{,}038 - (1.725)(382.97) = 4{,}377.38$

b. =CONFIDENCE.T(0.10, 1755, 21) = 660.52

c. The population's standard deviation is unknown, so we substitute the sample standard deviation and use the *t*-distribution. The population must be normally distributed.

8.26 a. $\bar{x} = 4.59;\ s = 2.31$ (from Excel)

$\hat{\sigma}_{\bar{x}} = \dfrac{2.31}{\sqrt{12}} = 0.67;\ df = 11$

$UCL_{\bar{x}} = 4.59 + (2.201)(0.67) = 6.07$

$LCL_{\bar{x}} = 4.59 - (2.201)(0.67) = 3.11$

b. =CONFIDENCE.T(0.05, 2.31, 12) = 1.47

c. The population's standard deviation is unknown, so we substitute the sample standard deviation and use the *t*-distribution. The population must be normally distributed.

8.28 a. $\bar{x} = \$3.64;\ s = \$0.087;\ n = 15$

$\hat{\sigma}_{\bar{x}} = \dfrac{\$0.087}{\sqrt{15}} = \$0.0225;\ df = 14$

$UCL_{\bar{x}} = \$3.64 + (1.761)(\$0.0225) = \$3.68$

$LCL_{\bar{x}} = \$3.64 - (1.761)(\$0.0225) = \$3.60$

b. Because \$3.65 is within the confidence interval, the results from this sample validate AAA's findings.

c. CONFIDENCE.T(0.10, 0.087, 15) = 0.040

$UCL_{\bar{x}} = \$3.64 + \$0.040 = \$3.68$

$LCL_{\bar{x}} = \$3.64 - \$0.040 = \$3.60$

d. The population must be normally distributed.

8.30 $\bar{p} = 0.60;\ \sigma_p = \sqrt{\dfrac{(0.60)(1 - 0.60)}{150}} = 0.04$

$UCL_p = 0.60 + (1.960)(0.04) = 0.678$

$LCL_p = 0.60 - (1.960)(0.04) = 0.522$

8.32 a. $\bar{p} = 0.70;\ \sigma_p = \sqrt{\dfrac{(0.70)(1 - 0.70)}{125}} = 0.041$

$ME_p = (1.960)(0.041) = 0.080$

b. $\bar{p} = 0.70;\ \sigma_p = \sqrt{\dfrac{(0.70)(1 - 0.70)}{200}} = 0.032$

$ME_p = (1.960)(0.032) = 0.063$

c. $\bar{p} = 0.70;\ \sigma_p = \sqrt{\dfrac{(0.70)(1 - 0.70)}{250}} = 0.029$

$ME_p = (1.960)(0.029) = 0.057$

8.34 a. $\bar{p} = \dfrac{176}{225} = 0.7822;\ \sigma_p = \sqrt{\dfrac{(0.7822)(1 - 0.7822)}{225}} = 0.0275$

$UCL_p = 0.7822 + (1.960)(0.0275) = 0.8361$

$LCL_p = 0.7822 - (1.960)(0.0275) = 0.7283$

b. $ME_p = (1.960)(0.0275) = 0.0539$

c. There is no evidence that the proportion of individual tax returns that were filed electronically since 2012 has changed, since 81% is within the confidence interval.

8.36 a. $\bar{p} = \dfrac{127}{270} = 0.470;\ \sigma_p = \sqrt{\dfrac{(0.470)(1 - 0.470)}{270}} = 0.0304$

$UCL_p = 0.470 + (2.33)(0.0304) = 0.541$

$LCL_p = 0.470 - (2.33)(0.0304) = 0.399$

b. $ME_p = (2.33)(0.0304) = 0.0708$

c. There is no evidence to conclude that the homeownership rate in Germany has changed in 2014 since 44% is within the confidence interval.

8.38 $n = \dfrac{(1.645)^2(75)^2}{(12)^2} = 105.7$; use $n = 106$

8.40 a. $n = \dfrac{(1.960)^2(80)^2}{(10)^2} = 245.9$; use $n = 246$

b. $n = \dfrac{(1.960)^2(80)^2}{(15)^2} = 109.3$; use $n = 110$

c. $n = \dfrac{(1.960)^2(80)^2}{(20)^2} = 61.5$; use $n = 62$

8.42 $n = \dfrac{(1.645)^2(0.65)(1 - 0.65)}{(0.06)^2} = 171.0$; use $n = 171$

8.44 $n = \dfrac{(1.960)^2(1)^2}{(0.2)^2} = 96.04$; use $n = 97$

8.46 $n = \dfrac{(1.960)^2(0.02)^2}{(0.005)^2} = 61.5$; use $n = 62$

8.48 $n = \dfrac{(1.645)^2(0.50)(1 - 0.50)}{(0.04)^2} = 422.8$; use $n = 423$

8.50 $\dfrac{n}{N} = \dfrac{40}{400} = 0.10 > 0.05;\ \sqrt{\dfrac{(N - n)}{(N - 1)}} = \sqrt{\dfrac{360}{399}} = 0.9499$

$\sigma_{\bar{x}} = \dfrac{20}{\sqrt{40}} = 3.16$

$UCL_{\bar{x}} = 70.00 + (1.645)(3.16)(0.9499) = 74.94$

$LCL_{\bar{x}} = 70.00 - (1.645)(3.16)(0.9499) = 65.06$

8.52 $\dfrac{n}{N} = \dfrac{75}{500} = 0.15 > 0.05;\ \sqrt{\dfrac{(N - n)}{(N - 1)}} = \sqrt{\dfrac{425}{499}} = 0.9229;$

$\bar{p} = \dfrac{22}{75} = 0.2933;\ \hat{\sigma}_p = \sqrt{\dfrac{(0.2933)(1 - 0.2933)}{75}} = 0.0526$

$UCL_p = 0.2933 + (1.960)(0.0526)(0.9229) = 0.3884$

$LCL_p = 0.2933 - (1.960)(0.0526)(0.9229) = 0.1982$

8.54 a. $\dfrac{n}{N} = \dfrac{32}{105} = 0.30 > 0.05;\ \sqrt{\dfrac{(N - n)}{(N - 1)}} = \sqrt{\dfrac{73}{104}} = 0.8378$

$\sigma_{\bar{x}} = \dfrac{0.5}{\sqrt{32}} = 0.0884$

$UCL_{\bar{x}} = 1.4000 + (1.960)(0.0884)(0.8378) = 1.5452$

$LCL_{\bar{x}} = 1.4000 - (1.960)(0.0884)(0.8378) = 1.2548$

b. The average radon level is below the EPA's recommendation.

8.56 a. $\sigma_{\bar{x}} = \dfrac{\$4.30}{\sqrt{36}} = \$0.72$

$UCL_{\bar{x}} = \$21.32 + (2.030)(\$0.72) = \$22.77$

$LCL_{\bar{x}} = \$21.32 - (2.030)(\$0.72) = \$19.87$

The results of this sample are consistent with the claim made by the Bureau of Labor Statistics that the average hourly wage was $22.57.

b. $ME_{\bar{x}} = (2.030)(\$0.72) = \$1.46$

c. =CONFIDENCE.NORM(0.05, 4.3, 36) = 1.41

8.58 **a.** $\bar{p} = \frac{119}{210} = 0.567; \sigma_p = \sqrt{\frac{(0.567)(1 - 0.567)}{210}} = 0.0342$

$UCL_p = 0.567 + (1.96)(0.0342) = 0.634$

$LCL_p = 0.567 - (1.96)(0.0342) = 0.500$

b. $ME_p = (1.96)(0.0344) = 0.0674$

c. There is evidence to conclude that the proportion of women that breast-feed their six-month-old babies has increased since 2012.

8.60 **a.** $\bar{p} = \frac{5}{55} = 0.091$

$n = \frac{(2.330)^2(0.091)(1 - 0.091)}{(0.05)^2} = 179.6$

Use $n = 180$. Sample an additional 125.

8.62 **a.** $\hat{\sigma}_{\bar{x}} = \frac{76}{\sqrt{33}} = 13.23$

$UCL_{\bar{x}} = 222.00 + (1.694)(13.23) = 244.41$

$LCL_{\bar{x}} = 222.00 - (1.694)(13.23) = 199.59$

b. $\hat{\sigma}_{\bar{x}} = \frac{76}{\sqrt{33}} = 13.23$

$UCL_{\bar{x}} = 222.00 + (2.037)(13.23) = 248.95$

$LCL_{\bar{x}} = 222.00 - (2.037)(13.23) = 195.05$

c. $\hat{\sigma}_{\bar{x}} = \frac{76}{\sqrt{33}} = 13.23$

$UCL_{\bar{x}} = 222.00 + (2.738)(13.23) = 258.22$

$LCL_{\bar{x}} = 222.00 - (2.738)(13.23) = 185.78$

d. The higher the confidence level, the wider the confidence interval.

e. The population must be normally distributed.

8.64 **a.** $n = \frac{(1.645)^2(\$160)^2}{(\$20)^2} = 173.2$; use $n = 174$

b. $n = \frac{(1.960)^2(\$160)^2}{(\$20)^2} = 245.9$; use $n = 246$

c. $n = \frac{(2.330)^2(\$160)^2}{(\$20)^2} = 347.4$; use $n = 348$

d. To be more confident that the interval contains the true population parameter given a constant margin of error, a larger sample size is needed.

8.66 **a.** $\bar{x} = \$1{,}525; s = \$1{,}209.56; n = 20$

$\hat{\sigma} = \frac{\$1{,}209.56}{\sqrt{20}} = \$270.60; df = 19$

$UCL_{\bar{x}} = \$1{,}525 + (2.093)(\$270.60) = \$2{,}091.37$

$LCL_{\bar{x}} = \$1{,}525 - (2.093)(\$270.60) = \$958.63$

b. These results do validate the findings of Transparency International because $1,596 is within the confidence interval.

c. $ME_{\bar{x}} = (2.093)(\$270.60) = \$566.37$

d. The reason the margin of error is so large is that the sample standard deviation is large and the sample size is small.

e. CONFIDENCE.T(0.05, 1209.56, 20) = 566.09

$UCL_{\bar{x}} = \$1{,}525 + \$566.09 = \$2{,}091.09$

$LCL_{\bar{x}} = \$1{,}525 - \$566.09 = \$958.91$

8.68 $\bar{p} = \frac{274}{330} = 0.83; \sigma_p = \sqrt{\frac{(0.83)(1 - 0.83)}{330}} = 0.0207$

$UCL_p = 0.8300 + (1.645)(0.0207) = 0.8641$

$LCL_p = 0.8300 - (1.645)(0.0207) = 0.7959$

The results reported by GMAC are validated by this analysis, since 85% is included within the confidence interval.

8.70 **a.** $\bar{p} = \frac{47}{260} = 0.181; \hat{\sigma}_p = \sqrt{\frac{(0.181)(1 - 0.181)}{260}} = 0.0239$

$UCL_p = 0.181 + (1.645)(0.0239) = 0.220$

$LCL_p = 0.181 - (1.645)(0.0239) = 0.142$

b. $ME_p = (1.645)(0.0239) = 0.0393$

c. There is evidence to conclude that the proportion of new car loans between 73 and 84 months has increased since 2009 because 11% is below this interval.

8.72 **a.** $\bar{x} = \$321.83; s = \$90.66; n = 24$

$\sigma_{\bar{x}} = \frac{\$90.66}{\sqrt{24}} = \$18.51; df = 23$

$UCL_{\bar{x}} = \$321.83 + (2.807)(\$18.51) = \$373.79$

$LCL_{\bar{x}} = \$321.83 - (2.807)(\$18.51) = \$269.87$

b. $ME_{\bar{x}} = (2.807)(\$18.51) = \$51.96$

c. =CONFIDENCE.T(0.01, 90.66, 24) = 51.95

8.74 **a.** $\frac{n}{N} = \frac{27}{310} = 0.087 > 0.05; \sqrt{\frac{(N - n)}{(N - 1)}} = \sqrt{\frac{283}{309}} = 0.9570;$

$\bar{x} = 38.7; \hat{\sigma}_{\bar{x}} = \frac{6.8}{\sqrt{27}} = 1.3087; df = 26$

$UCL_{\bar{x}} = 38.70 + (2.056)(1.3087)(0.9570) = 41.27$

$LCL_{\bar{x}} = 38.70 - (2.056)(0.3087)(0.9570) = 36.13$

b. Because the population's standard deviation is unknown, the t-distribution needs to be used in calculations, and the finite population correction factor. The population also needs to be normally distributed.

8.76 **a.** $\frac{n}{N} = \frac{240}{872} = 0.275 > 0.05; \sqrt{\frac{(N - n)}{(N - 1)}} = \sqrt{\frac{632}{871}} = 0.8518$

$\bar{p} = \frac{77}{240} = 0.321; \hat{\sigma}_p = \sqrt{\frac{(0.321)(1 - 0.321)}{240}} = 0.0301$

$UCL_p = 0.321 + (1.960)(0.0301)(0.8518) = 0.371$

$LCL_p = 0.321 - (1.960)(0.0301)(0.8518) = 0.271$

b. $ME_p = (1.960)(0.0301)(0.8518) = 0.0503$

8.78 **a.** $\bar{x} = \$98.35; s = \$61.72; n = 350$

$\hat{\sigma}_{\bar{x}} = \frac{\$61.72}{\sqrt{350}} = \$3.30; df = 349$

$UCL_{\bar{x}} = \$98.35 + (1.960)(\$3.30) = \$104.82$

$LCL_{\bar{x}} = \$98.35 - (1.960)(\$3.30) = \$91.88$

b. $ME_{\bar{x}} = (1.960)(\$3.30) = \$6.47$

c. =CONFIDENCE.T(0.05, 61.72, 350) = 6.49

Chapter 9

9.2 **a.** $p\text{-value} = P(z_{\bar{x}} > 1.46) = 0.0721$

$p\text{-value} < 0.10 \rightarrow$ Reject H_0

b. $p\text{-value} = P(z_{\bar{x}} < -2.48) = 0.0066$

$p\text{-value} < 0.01 \rightarrow$ Reject H_0

c. $p\text{-value} = 2 \times P(z_{\bar{x}} < -1.92) = (2)(0.0274) = 0.0548$

$p\text{-value} > 0.01 \rightarrow$ Do not reject H_0

d. $p\text{-value} = 2 \times P(z_{\bar{x}} > 2.76) = (2)(1.0 - 0.9971) = 0.0058$

$p\text{-value} < 0.02 \rightarrow$ Reject H_0

9.4 **a.** $z_{\bar{x}} = \frac{111 - 120}{\frac{26}{\sqrt{40}}} = -2.19$

b. $p\text{-value} = 2 \times P(z_{\bar{x}} < -2.19) = (2)(0.0143) = 0.0286$

$p\text{-value} < 0.05 \rightarrow$ Reject H_0

9.6 **a.** $H_0: \mu = 1.7$ cups (status quo)
$H_1: \mu \neq 1.7$ cups

$$z_{\alpha/2} = 1.645; z_{\bar{x}} = \frac{1.95 - 1.70}{\frac{0.5}{\sqrt{34}}} = 2.92$$

$z_{\bar{x}} > z_{\alpha/2} \rightarrow$ Reject H_0
The coffee industry's claim is not supported.

b. p-value $= (2)(1.0 - 0.9982) = 0.0036$

9.8 **a.** $H_0: \mu \leq 40$ years (status quo)
$H_1: \mu > 40$ years

$$z_{\alpha} = 2.05; z_{\bar{x}} = \frac{42.7 - 40}{\frac{8.0}{\sqrt{60}}} = 2.614$$

$z_{\bar{x}} > z_{\alpha} \rightarrow$ Reject H_0
The sample provides enough evidence to refute the claim that the average age is less than or equal to 40 years.

b. p-value $= P(z_{\bar{x}} > 2.61) = 0.0045$

9.10 **a.** $H_0: \mu = 5$ minutes (status quo)
$H_1: \mu \neq 5$ minutes

$$z_{\alpha/2} = 2.33; z_{\bar{x}} = \frac{5.5 - 5.0}{\frac{1.7}{\sqrt{45}}} = 1.973$$

$|z_{\bar{x}}| \leq |z_{\alpha/2}| \rightarrow$ Do not reject H_0
This sample does not provide enough evidence to refute the claim that the average wait time equals 5 minutes.

b. p-value $= 2 \times P(z_{\bar{x}} > 1.97) = 0.0488$

9.12 **a.** $$-t_{\alpha} = -1.711; t_{\bar{x}} = \frac{58.8 - 65.0}{\frac{10.4}{\sqrt{25}}} = -2.981$$

$t_{\bar{x}} < -t_{\alpha} \rightarrow -2.981 < -1.711 \rightarrow$ Reject H_0

b. p-value $= 0.0032 < \alpha = 0.05 \rightarrow$ Reject H_0

9.14 **a.** $\bar{x} = 17.8; s = 3.29$ (from Excel)

$$t_{\alpha} = 1.833; t_{\bar{x}} = \frac{17.8 - 16.0}{\frac{3.29}{\sqrt{10}}} = 1.73$$

$t_{\bar{x}} \leq t_{\alpha} \rightarrow 1.73 < 1.833 \rightarrow$ Do not reject H_0

b. p-value $= 0.0590 > \alpha = 0.05 \rightarrow$ Do not reject H_0

9.16 **a.** $H_0: \mu \geq \$186$
$H_1: \mu < \$186$

$$-t_{\alpha} = -1.685; t_{\bar{x}} = \frac{\$178.10 - \$186.0}{\frac{\$22.4}{\sqrt{40}}} = -2.231$$

$t_{\bar{x}} < -t_{\alpha} \rightarrow -2.231 < -1.685 \rightarrow$ Reject H_0
This sample provides evidence that the average utility bill was smaller in the winter of 2013–2014 when compared to the winter of 2012–2013.

b. Yes, changing the value of α to 0.01 affects the conclusion.
$\alpha = 0.01; -t_{\alpha} = -2.426; t_{\bar{x}} = -2.231$
$t_{\bar{x}} \geq -t_{\alpha} \rightarrow -2.231 > -2.426 \rightarrow$ Do not reject H_0
A lower value of α makes it more challenging to reject the null hypothesis.

c. $\alpha = 0.05$: p-value $= 0.0158 < \alpha = 0.05 \rightarrow$ Reject H_0
$\alpha = 0.01$: p-value $= 0.0158 > \alpha = 0.01 \rightarrow$ Do not reject H_0

9.18 **a.** $H_0: \mu \geq \$373$ (status quo)
$H_1: \mu < \$373$
$\bar{x} = \$325.5; s = \$103.13$; (from Excel)

$$-t_{\alpha} = -1.753\ t_{\bar{x}} = \frac{\$325.5 - \$373.0}{\frac{\$103.13}{\sqrt{16}}} = -1.84$$

$t_{\bar{x}} < -t_{\alpha} \rightarrow -1.84 < -1.753 \rightarrow$ Reject H_0
This sample supports the retailers' concerns.

b. $|t_{\bar{x}}| = |-1.84| = 1.84$; $df = 15$; The p-value is between 0.025 and 0.05 which is less than α; therefore, we can reject the null hypothesis.

c. p-value = T.DIST(−1.84, 15, TRUE) = 0.0428

9.20 **a.** $H_0: \mu \leq 766$
$H_1: \mu > 766$
$\bar{x} = 771; \mu_{H_0} = 766; s = 21; n = 35; df = 34$

$$\alpha = 0.05; t_{\alpha} = 1.691; t_{\bar{x}} = \frac{771 - 766}{\frac{21}{\sqrt{35}}} = 1.41$$

$t_{\bar{x}} \leq t_{\alpha} \rightarrow 1.41 < 1.691 \rightarrow$ Do not reject H_0

b. $t_{\bar{x}} = 1.41$; $df = 34$; the p-value is between 0.05 and 0.10, which is greater than α; therefore we cannot reject the null hypothesis.

c. p-value = T.DIST.RT(1.41, 34) = 0.0838

e. Because the sample standard deviation was used to approximate the population standard deviation, the population needs to be normally distributed.

9.22 **a.** p-value $= P(z_p < -1.36) = 0.0869$
p-value $> 0.05 \rightarrow$ Do not reject H_0

b. p-value $= P(z_p > 1.28) = 0.1003$
p-value $> 0.10 \rightarrow$ Do not reject H_0

c. p-value $= 2 \times P(z_p > 2.29) = 0.0220$
p-value $< 0.05 \rightarrow$ Reject H_0

d. p-value $= 2 \times P(z_p < -0.90) = 0.3682$
p-value $> 0.01 \rightarrow$ Do not reject H_0

9.24 **a.** $$z_{\alpha} = 1.645; z_p = \frac{0.277 - 0.240}{\sqrt{\frac{(0.24)(1 - 0.24)}{130}}} = 0.99$$

$z_p \leq z_{\alpha} \rightarrow$ Do not reject H_0

b. p-value $= P(\bar{p} > 0.277) = P(z_p > 0.99) = 1.0 - 0.8389 = 0.1611$

9.26 **a.** $H_0: p \leq 0.26$ (status quo)
$H_1: p > 0.26$

$$\bar{p} = \frac{35}{100} = 0.35;\ p_{H_0} = 0.26;\ n = 100$$

$$\alpha = 0.05;\ z_{\alpha} = 1.645;\ z_p = \frac{0.35 - 0.26}{\sqrt{\frac{(0.26)(1 - 0.26)}{100}}} = 2.05$$

$z_p > z_{\alpha} \rightarrow 2.05 > 1.645 \rightarrow$ Reject H_0
This sample provides evidence that the proportion of admissions officers who visit an applying student's social network page has increased since 2012.

b. p-value $= P(\bar{p} > 0.35) = P(z_p > 2.05) = 1.0 - 0.9798 = 0.0202$

9.28 **a.** $H_0: p = 0.64$ (status quo)
$H_1: p \neq 0.64$

$$\bar{p} = \frac{103}{170} = 0.606; z_{\alpha/2} = 2.33$$

$$z_p = \frac{0.606 - 0.640}{\sqrt{\frac{(0.64)(1 - 0.64)}{170}}} = -0.924$$

$|z_p| \leq |z_{\alpha/2}| \rightarrow$ Do not reject H_0
We do not have enough evidence to conclude that the percentage of car owners who avoid repairs is different from 64%.

b. p-value $= 2 \times P(z_p < -0.924) = 0.3576$

9.30 **a.** $H_0: p \geq 0.26$ (status quo)
$H_1: p < 0.26$

$$\bar{p} = \frac{72}{360} = 0.20; p_{H_0} = 0.26; n = 360$$

$$\alpha = 0.01; -z_{\alpha} = -2.33; z_p = \frac{0.20 - 0.26}{\sqrt{\frac{(0.26)(1 - 0.26)}{360}}} = -2.60$$

$z_p < -z_{\alpha} \rightarrow -2.60 < -2.33 \rightarrow$ Reject H_0

This sample provides support that the proportion of Germans who feel leaving the Eurozone would be good for Germany has decreased since 2013.

b. p-value $= P(\bar{p} < 0.20) = P(z_p < -2.60) = 0.0047$

9.32 a. $z_\alpha = 1.645$

$$\text{Upper } \bar{x}_\alpha = 30.00 + (1.645)\left(\frac{6}{\sqrt{42}}\right) = 31.52$$

$$z = \frac{31.52 - 31.00}{\frac{6}{\sqrt{42}}} = 0.56$$

$$\beta = P(\bar{x}_\alpha \le 31.52) = P(z < 0.56) = 0.7123$$

b. $z_\alpha = 1.645$

$$\text{Upper } \bar{x}_\alpha = 30.00 + (1.645)\left(\frac{6}{\sqrt{42}}\right) = 31.52$$

$$z = \frac{31.52 - 32.00}{\frac{6}{\sqrt{42}}} = -0.52$$

$$\beta = P(\bar{x}_\alpha \le 31.52) = P(z < -0.52) = 0.3015$$

9.34 a. $z_\alpha = 1.645$

$$\text{Lower } p_\alpha = 0.720 - (1.645)\sqrt{\frac{(0.72)(1 - 0.72)}{100}} = 0.646$$

$$z = \frac{0.646 - 0.660}{\sqrt{\frac{(0.72)(1 - 0.72)}{100}}} = -0.31$$

$$\beta = P(p_\alpha > 0.646) = P(z > -0.31) = 0.6217$$

b. $z_\alpha = 1.645$

$$\text{Lower } p_\alpha = 0.72 - (1.645)\sqrt{\frac{(0.72)(1 - 0.72)}{100}} = 0.646$$

$$z = \frac{0.646 - 0.620}{\sqrt{\frac{(0.72)(1 - 0.72)}{100}}} = 0.5781$$

$$\beta = P(p_\alpha > 0.646) = P(z > 0.58) = 0.2810$$

9.36 a. $z_{\alpha/2} = 1.96$

$$\text{Upper } \bar{x}_{\alpha/2} = 120.00 + (1.96)\left(\frac{27}{\sqrt{60}}\right) = 126.83$$

$$\text{Lower } \bar{x}_{\alpha/2} = 120.00 - (1.96)\left(\frac{27}{\sqrt{60}}\right) = 113.17$$

$$\text{Upper } z = \frac{126.83 - 131.00}{\frac{27}{\sqrt{60}}} = -1.20$$

$$\text{Lower } z = \frac{113.17 - 131.00}{\frac{27}{\sqrt{60}}} = -5.12$$

$$\beta = P(-5.12 \le z \le -1.20) = 0.1151 - 0 = 0.1151$$

b. $z_{\alpha/2} = 1.96$

$$\text{Upper } \bar{x}_{\alpha/2} = 120.00 + (1.96)\left(\frac{27}{\sqrt{60}}\right) = 126.83$$

$$\text{Lower } \bar{x}_{\alpha/2} = 120.00 - (1.96)\left(\frac{27}{\sqrt{60}}\right) = 113.17$$

$$\text{Upper } z = \frac{126.83 - 115.00}{\frac{27}{\sqrt{60}}} = 3.39$$

$$\text{Lower } z = \frac{113.17 - 115.00}{\frac{27}{\sqrt{60}}} = -0.53$$

$$\beta = P(-0.53 \le z \le 3.39) = 0.9997 - 0.2981 = 0.7016$$

9.38 a. $H_0\colon \mu \ge \$243{,}000$
$H_1\colon \mu < \$243{,}000$
A Type I error can occur if the average listing price is above or equal to $243,000 and the null hypothesis is rejected. A Type II error can occur if the average listing price is below $243,000 and the null hypothesis is not rejected.

b. $H_0\colon \mu \ge \$243{,}000$ (status quo)
$H_1\colon \mu < \$243{,}000$
$-z_\alpha = -1.28$

$$\text{Lower } \bar{x}_\alpha = \$243{,}000 - (1.28)\left(\frac{\$45{,}000}{\sqrt{50}}\right) = \$234{,}854$$

$$z = \frac{\$234{,}854 - \$225{,}000}{\frac{\$45{,}000}{\sqrt{50}}} = 1.55$$

$$\beta = P(z > 1.55) = 0.0606$$

c. $H_0\colon \mu \ge \$243{,}000$ (status quo)
$H_1\colon \mu < \$243{,}000$
$-z_\alpha = -1.645$

$$\text{Lower } \bar{x}_\alpha = \$243{,}000 + (1.645)\left(\frac{\$45{,}000}{\sqrt{50}}\right) = \$232{,}531$$

$$z = \frac{\$232{,}531 - \$225{,}000}{\frac{\$45{,}000}{\sqrt{50}}} = 1.18$$

$$\beta = P(z > 1.18) = 0.1190$$

d. Reducing the value of α increases the value of β.

9.40 a. $H_0\colon p \ge 0.15$
$H_1\colon p < 0.15$
A Type I error can occur if the proportion of unsatisfied customers is above or equal to 0.15 and the null hypothesis is rejected. A Type II error can occur if the proportion of unsatisfied customers is below 0.15 and the null hypothesis is not rejected.

b. $H_0\colon p \ge 0.15$ (status quo)
$H_1\colon p < 0.15$
$-z_\alpha = 1.645$

$$\text{Lower } p_\alpha = 0.150 - (1.645)\sqrt{\frac{(0.15)(1 - 0.15)}{75}} = 0.082$$

$$z = \frac{0.082 - 0.110}{\sqrt{\frac{(0.15)(1 - 0.15)}{75}}} = -0.68$$

$$\beta = P(z > -0.68) = 1.0 - 0.2483 = 0.7517$$

c. $H_0\colon p \ge 0.15$ (status quo)
$H_1\colon p < 0.15$
$-z_\alpha = -1.645$

$$\text{Lower } p_\alpha = 0.150 - (1.645)\sqrt{\frac{(0.15)(1 - 0.15)}{75}} = 0.082$$

$$z = \frac{0.082 - 0.060}{\sqrt{\frac{(0.15)(1 - 0.15)}{75}}} = 0.53$$

$$\beta = P(z > 0.53) = 0.2981$$

9.42 a. $H_0\colon p = 0.80$
$H_1\colon p \ne 0.80$
A Type I error can occur if the proportion of plate appearances that result in the ball being put in play is equal to 0.80 and the null hypothesis is rejected. A Type II error can occur if the proportion of plate appearances that result in the ball being put in play is not equal to 0.80 and the null hypothesis is not rejected.

b. $H_0\colon p = 0.80$ (status quo)
$H_1\colon p \ne 0.80$
$z_{\alpha/2} = 1.96$

$$\text{Upper } p_{\alpha/2} = 0.80 + (1.96)\sqrt{\frac{(0.80)(1 - 0.80)}{250}} = 0.850$$

$$\text{Lower } p_{\alpha/2} = 0.80 - (1.96)\sqrt{\frac{(0.80)(1-0.80)}{250}} = 0.750$$

$$\text{Upper } z = \frac{0.850 - 0.77}{\sqrt{\frac{(0.80)(1-0.80)}{250}}} = 3.16$$

$$\text{Lower } z = \frac{0.750 - 0.77}{\sqrt{\frac{(0.80)(1-0.80)}{250}}} = -0.79$$

$\beta = P(-0.79 \le z \le 3.16) = 0.7844$

c. H_0: $p = 0.80$ (status quo)
H_1: $p \ne 0.80$
$z_{\alpha/2} = 1.96$

$$\text{Upper } p_{\alpha/2} = 0.80 + (1.96)\sqrt{\frac{(0.80)(1-0.80)}{250}} = 0.85$$

$$\text{Lower } p_{\alpha/2} = 0.80 - (1.96)\sqrt{\frac{(0.80)(1-0.80)}{250}} = 0.75$$

$$\text{Upper } z = \frac{0.85 - 0.88}{\sqrt{\frac{(0.80)(1-0.80)}{250}}} = -1.19$$

$$\text{Lower } z = \frac{0.75 - 0.88}{\sqrt{\frac{(0.80)(1-0.80)}{250}}} = -5.14$$

$\beta = P(-5.14 \le z \le -1.19) = 0.1170$

9.44 a. H_0: $p \le 0.39$ (status quo)
H_1: $p > 0.39$

b. $\bar{p} = \frac{126}{275} = 0.458; p_{H_0} = 0.39; n = 275$

$$\alpha = 0.05; z_\alpha = 1.645; z_p = \frac{0.458 - 0.39}{\sqrt{\frac{(0.39)(1-0.39)}{275}}} = 2.32$$

$z_p > z_\alpha \rightarrow 2.32 > 1.645 \rightarrow$ Reject H_0
This sample provides support that the proportion of smartphone using Apple's operating system has increased since 2013.

c. $p\text{-value} = P(\bar{p} > 0.458) = P(z_p > 2.32) = 1.0 - 0.9898 = 0.0102$
$p\text{-value} < 0.05 \rightarrow$ Reject H_0

9.46 a. H_0: $\mu \ge 30$ minutes (status quo)
H_1: $\mu < 30$ minutes

b. $\bar{x} = 27.8; s = 6.74$ (from Excel)

$$-t_\alpha = -1.363; t_{\bar{x}} = \frac{27.8 - 30.00}{\frac{6.74}{\sqrt{12}}} = -1.13$$

$t_{\bar{x}} \ge -t_\alpha \rightarrow -1.13 > -1.363 \rightarrow$ Do Not Reject H_0
This sample does not provide enough evidence to support Seasons Pizza's claim.

c. $|t_{\bar{x}}| = |-1.13| = 1.13; df = 11$; the p-value is between 0.10 and 0.20, which is greater than α; therefore we cannot reject the null hypothesis.

d. p-value = T.DIST(−1.13, 11, TRUE) = 0.1413

f. Season's Pizza increased its likelihood of rejecting the null hypothesis and finding support for its delivery claim by choosing a relatively high value of $\alpha = 0.10$.

g. Because the sample standard deviation was used to approximate the population standard deviation, the population needs to be normally distributed.

9.48 a. H_0: $p = 0.32$ (status quo)
H_1: $p \ne 0.32$

b. $\bar{p} = \frac{86}{225} = 0.382; z_{\alpha/2} = 1.645$

$$z_p = \frac{0.382 - 0.320}{\sqrt{\frac{(0.32)(1-0.32)}{225}}} = 1.994$$

$|z_p| > |z_{\alpha/2}| \rightarrow$ Reject H_0

This sample provides enough evidence that the proportion of Internet users who maintain the same passwords for all their social-networking sites has changed.

c. $p\text{-value} = 2 \times P(z_p > 1.994) = (2)0.0233 = 0.0466$
$p\text{-value} < 0.10 \rightarrow$ Reject H_0
Use of the p-value approach also proves that there is enough evidence to support H_1.

9.50 a. H_0: $\mu = \$77{,}300$ (status quo)
H_1: $\mu \ne \$77{,}300$

b. $\bar{x} = \$85{,}200; \mu_{H_0} = \$77{,}300; \sigma = \$21{,}000; n = 30$

$$\alpha = 0.02; z_{\alpha/2} = 2.33; z_{\bar{x}} = \frac{\$85{,}200 - \$77{,}300}{\frac{\$21{,}000}{\sqrt{30}}} = 2.06$$

$|z_{\bar{x}}| \le |z_{\alpha/2}| \rightarrow 2.06 < 2.33 \rightarrow$ Do not reject H_0
This sample does not provide enough evidence to prove that the average 401 (k) account balance has recently changed.

c. $p\text{-value} = 2 \times P(\bar{x} > \$85{,}200) = 2 \times P(z_{\bar{x}} > 2.06)$
$= (2)(1.0 - 0.9803) = 0.0394$
$p\text{-value} > 0.02 \rightarrow$ Do not reject H_0

e. $$\alpha = 0.05; z_{\alpha/2} = 1.96; z_{\bar{x}} = \frac{\$85{,}200 - \$77{,}300}{\frac{\$21{,}000}{\sqrt{30}}} = 2.06$$

$|z_{\bar{x}}| \ge |z_{\alpha/2}| \rightarrow 2.06 > 1.96 \rightarrow$ Reject H_0
Using $\alpha = 0.05$ rather than $\alpha = 0.02$ changes the conclusion. Increasing the value of α increases the likelihood of rejecting the null hypothesis.

9.52 a. H_0: $\mu = 6$ liters (status quo)
H_1: $\mu \ne 6$ liters

b. $\bar{x} = 7.48; \mu_{H_0} = 6; s = 3.66; n = 25; df = 24$

$$\alpha = 0.02; t_{\alpha/2} = 2.492; t_{\bar{x}} = \frac{7.48 - 6.000}{\frac{3.66}{\sqrt{25}}} = 2.02$$

$|t_{\bar{x}}| \le |t_{\alpha/2}| \rightarrow 2.02 < 2.492 \rightarrow$ Do not reject H_0
This sample does not provide enough evidence to conclude that the average gasoline consumption per car in the United States is different than 6 liters per day.

c. $t_{\bar{x}} = 2.02; df = 24$; the p-value is between 0.05 and 0.10, which is greater than α; therefore we cannot reject the null hypothesis.

d. p-value = T.DIST.2T(2.02, 24) = 0.0547

f. Because the sample standard deviation was used to approximate the population standard deviation, the population needs to be normally distributed.

9.54 a. H_0: $p = 0.12$ (status quo)
H_1: $p \ne 0.12$

b. $\bar{p} = \frac{29}{280} = 0.104; p_{H_0} = 0.12; n = 280$

$$\alpha = 0.10; z_{\alpha/2} = 1.645; z_p = \frac{0.104 - 0.12}{\sqrt{\frac{(0.12)(1-0.12)}{280}}} = -0.83$$

$|z_p| \le |z_{\alpha/2}| \rightarrow 0.83 < 1.645 \rightarrow$ Do not reject H_0
This sample does not provide enough evidence to conclude that the percentage of American adults who did not own a cell phone has changed since 2012.

c. $p\text{-value} = 2 \times P(\bar{p} < 0.104) = 2 \times P(z_p < -0.83)$
$= (2)(0.2033) = 0.4066$
$p\text{-value} > 0.10 \rightarrow$ Do not reject H_0

9.56 a. H_0: $\mu \ge 700$ (status quo)
H_1: $\mu < 700$

b. $\bar{x} = 620.15; \mu_{H_0} = 700; s = 325.97; n = 75; df = 74$

$$\alpha = 0.05; -t_\alpha = -1.666; t_{\bar{x}} = \frac{620.15 - 700}{\frac{325.97}{\sqrt{75}}} = -2.12$$

$t_{\bar{x}} < -t_\alpha \rightarrow -2.12 < -1.666 \rightarrow$ Reject H_0

This sample provides enough evidence to conclude that the average number of text messages per month has declined since 2012.

c. $|t_{\bar{x}}| = |-2.12| = 2.12$; $df = 74$; the p-value is between 0.01 and 0.025, which is less than α; therefore we can reject the null hypothesis.

d. p-value = T.DIST(−2.12, 74, TRUE) = 0.0187

9.58 a. $H_0: \mu \le \$86$
$H_1: \mu > \$86$
A Type I error can occur if the average monthly cable bill is below or equal to \$86 and the null hypothesis is rejected. A Type II error can occur if the average monthly cable bill is above \$86 and the null hypothesis is not rejected.

b. $H_0: \mu \le \$86$
$H_1: \mu > \$86$
$\mu = 92; \mu_{H_0} = 86; \sigma = 17; n = 52; \alpha = 0.01; z_\alpha = 2.33$

$$\text{Upper } \bar{x}_\alpha = 86 + (2.33)\left(\frac{17}{\sqrt{52}}\right) = 91.49$$

$$z = \frac{91.49 - 92}{\frac{17}{\sqrt{52}}} = -0.22$$

$$\beta = P(\bar{x}_\alpha \le 91.49) = P(z < -0.22) = 0.4129$$

c. $H_0: \mu \le \$86$
$H_1: \mu > \$86$
$\mu = 92; \mu_{H_0} = 86; \sigma = 17; n = 52; \alpha = 0.05; z_\alpha = 1.645$

$$\text{Upper } \bar{x}_\alpha = 86 + (1.645)\left(\frac{17}{\sqrt{52}}\right) = 89.88$$

$$z = \frac{89.88 - 92}{\frac{17}{\sqrt{52}}} = -0.90$$

$$\beta = P(\bar{x}_\alpha \le 89.88) = P(z < -0.90) = 0.1841$$

d. Increasing the probability of a Type I error, with all else constant, will decrease the probability of a Type II error.

9.60 a. $H_0: \mu \le 4.0$ hours
$H_1: \mu > 4.0$ hours
A Type I error can occur if the average operating time per charge is below or equal to 4.0 hours and the null hypothesis is rejected. A Type II error can occur if the average operating time per charge is above 4.0 hours and the null hypothesis is not rejected.

b. $H_0: \mu \le 4.0$ hours (status quo)
$H_1: \mu > 4.0$ hours
$z_\alpha = 1.645$

$$\text{Upper } \bar{x}_\alpha = 4.00 + (1.645)\left(\frac{0.7}{\sqrt{45}}\right) = 4.17$$

$$z = \frac{4.17 - 4.40}{\frac{0.7}{\sqrt{45}}} = -2.20$$

$$\beta = P(z < -2.20) = 0.0139$$

c. $H_0: \mu \le 4.0$ hours (status quo)
$H_1: \mu > 4.0$ hours
$z_\alpha = 2.33$

$$\text{Upper } \bar{x}_\alpha = 4.00 + (2.33)\left(\frac{0.7}{\sqrt{45}}\right) = 4.24$$

$$z = \frac{4.24 - 4.40}{\frac{0.7}{\sqrt{45}}} = -1.53$$

$$\beta = P(z < -1.53) = 0.0630$$

d. Reducing the value of α increases the value of β.

9.62 a. $H_0: \mu = 60$ days
$H_1: \mu \ne 60$ days
A Type I error can occur if the average number of days a home is on the market is equal to 60 and the null hypothesis is rejected. A Type II error can occur if the average number of days a home is on the market is not equal to 60 and the null hypothesis is not rejected.

b. $H_0: \mu = 60$ days (status quo)
$H_1: \mu \ne 60$ days
$z_{\alpha/2} = 1.96$

$$\text{Upper } \bar{x}_{\alpha/2} = 60.0 + (1.96)\left(\frac{25}{\sqrt{32}}\right) = 68.7$$

$$\text{Lower } \bar{x}_{\alpha/2} = 60.0 - (1.96)\left(\frac{25}{\sqrt{32}}\right) = 51.3$$

$$\text{Upper } z = \frac{68.7 - 54}{\frac{25}{\sqrt{32}}} = 3.33$$

$$\text{Lower } z = \frac{51.3 - 54}{\frac{25}{\sqrt{32}}} = -0.61$$

$$\beta = P(-0.61 \le z \le 3.33) = 0.7285$$

c. $H_0: \mu = 60$ days (status quo)
$H_1: \mu \ne 60$ days
$z_{\alpha/2} = 1.96$

$$\text{Upper } \bar{x}_{\alpha/2} = 60.0 + (1.96)\left(\frac{25}{\sqrt{32}}\right) = 68.7$$

$$\text{Lower } \bar{x}_{\alpha/2} = 60.0 - (1.96)\left(\frac{25}{\sqrt{32}}\right) = 51.3$$

$$\text{Upper } z = \frac{68.7 - 78}{\frac{25}{\sqrt{32}}} = -2.10$$

$$\text{Lower } z = \frac{51.3 - 78}{\frac{25}{\sqrt{32}}} = -6.04$$

$$\beta = P(-6.04 \le z \le -2.10) = 0.0179$$

d. As the true population mean moves away from the hypothesized mean, the probability of a Type II error decreases.

9.64 a. $H_0: p = 0.47$ (status quo)
$H_1: p \ne 0.47$

$$\bar{p} = \frac{55}{100} = 0.55; p_{H_0} = 0.47; n = 100$$

$$\alpha = 0.05; z_{\alpha/2} = 1.96; z_p = \frac{0.55 - 0.47}{\sqrt{\frac{(0.47)(1 - 0.47)}{100}}} = 1.60$$

$|z_p| \le |z_{\alpha/2}| \rightarrow 1.60 < 1.96 \rightarrow$ Do not reject H_0
This sample does not provide enough evidence to conclude that the percentage of small-business owners with more than a bachelor's degree is different than 47%.

b. $p\text{-value} = 2 \times P(\bar{p} > 0.55) = 2 \times P(z_p > 1.60)$
$= (2)(1.0 - 0.9452) = 0.1096$
p-value $> 0.05 \rightarrow$ Do not reject H_0

9.66 a. $H_0: \mu \ge \$11$ (status quo)
$H_1: \mu < \$11$

b. $\bar{x} = \$9.804; \mu_{H_0} = \$11; s = \$6.599; n = 65; df = 64$

$$\alpha = 0.05; -t_\alpha = -1.998; t_{\bar{x}} = \frac{\$9.804 - \$11.00}{\frac{\$6.599}{\sqrt{65}}} = -1.46$$

$t_{\bar{x}} \ge -t_\alpha \rightarrow -1.46 > -1.998 \rightarrow$ Do not reject H_0
This sample does not provide enough evidence to conclude that the average monthly revenue is less than \$11, and Vodafone should invest in the Nigerian market.

c. $|t_{\bar{x}}| = 1.46$; $df = 64$; the p-value is between 0.05 and 0.10, which is greater than α; therefore we cannot reject the null hypothesis.

d. p-value = T.DIST(−1.46, 64, TRUE) = 0.0746

Chapter 10

10.2 a. $H_0: \mu_1 - \mu_2 \le 0$
$H_1: \mu_1 - \mu_2 > 0$

$$\sigma_{\bar{x}_1-\bar{x}_2} = \sqrt{\frac{(24)^2}{50} + \frac{(18)^2}{55}} = 4.17$$

$$z_x = \frac{(86 - 78) - 0}{4.17} = 1.918$$

$\alpha = 0.10; z_\alpha = 1.280$

$z_{\bar{x}} > z_\alpha \rightarrow 1.918 > 1.280 \rightarrow$ Reject H_0

b. p-value $= P(z_{\bar{x}} > 1.92) = 1 - 0.9726 = 0.0274$
p-value $< \alpha \rightarrow 0.0274 < 0.10 \rightarrow$ Reject H_0

10.4 $\sigma_{\bar{x}_1-\bar{x}_2} = 1.315; z_{\alpha/2} = 1.96$
$UCL_{\bar{x}_1-\bar{x}_2} = 5.58$
$LCL_{\bar{x}_1-\bar{x}_2} = 0.42$

10.6 a. $H_0: \mu_1 - \mu_2 = 0$
$H_1: \mu_1 - \mu_2 \ne 0$

$$\sigma_{\bar{x}_1-\bar{x}_2} = \sqrt{\frac{(\$64)^2}{33} + \frac{(\$58)^2}{36}} = \$14.75$$

$$z_{\bar{x}} = \frac{(\$390.44 - \$359.52) - 0}{\$14.75} = 2.096$$

$z_{\alpha/2} = 1.960$
$|z_{\bar{x}}| > |z_{\alpha/2}| \rightarrow$ Reject H_0

b. p-value $= 2 \times P(z_{\bar{x}} > 2.10) = 0.036$
p-value $\le \alpha \rightarrow 0.036 < 0.05 \rightarrow$ Reject H_0
There is enough evidence to conclude that the average monthly utility bills of households in Baltimore and in Houston are different.

10.8 a. $H_0: \mu_1 - \mu_2 = 0$
$H_1: \mu_1 - \mu_2 \ne 0$

$$\sigma_{\bar{x}_1-\bar{x}_2} = \sqrt{\frac{(\$160)^2}{35} + \frac{(\$150)^2}{38}} = 36.38$$

$$z_{\bar{x}} = \frac{(\$606.40 - \$548.72) - 0}{36.38} = 1.585$$

$z_{\alpha/2} = 1.645$
$|z_{\bar{x}}| \le |z_{\alpha/2}| \rightarrow$ Do not reject H_0

b. p-value $= 2 \times P(z_{\bar{x}} > 1.59) = 0.112$
p-value $> \alpha \rightarrow 0.112 > 0.10 \rightarrow$ Do not reject H_0
There is not enough evidence to conclude that the average household back-to-school spending in 2013 was different than it was in 2014.

10.10 a. $$\sigma_{\bar{x}_1-\bar{x}_2} = \sqrt{\frac{(\$6{,}433)^2}{40} + \frac{(\$7{,}012)^2}{46}} = \$1{,}450; z_{\alpha/2} = 1.645$$

$UCL_{\bar{x}_1-\bar{x}_2} = \$5{,}729$
$LCL_{\bar{x}_1-\bar{x}_2} = \$959$

b. The confidence interval does not include zero, so there is enough evidence to conclude that the average salaries of the high school teachers in Pennsylvania and Ohio are different.

10.12 a. $H_0: \mu_1 - \mu_2 \le 10$
$H_1: \mu_1 - \mu_2 > 10$

$$s_p^2 = \frac{(16 - 1)(18.4)^2 + (20 - 1)(18.7)^2}{(16 - 1) + (20 - 1)} = 344.78$$

$$t_{\bar{x}} = \frac{(76.3 - 61.5) - 10}{\sqrt{(344.78)\left(\frac{1}{16} + \frac{1}{20}\right)}} = 0.7707$$

$df = 16 + 20 - 2 = 34; t_\alpha = 1.691$
$t_{\bar{x}} < t_\alpha \rightarrow$ Do not reject H_0

b. $|t_{\bar{x}}| = 0.7707; df = 34$
The p-value is greater than 0.20. Because this range is greater than $\alpha = 0.05$, we do not reject the null hypothesis.

c. p-value = T.DIST.RT(0.7707, 34) = 0.2231

10.14 a. $H_0: \mu_1 - \mu_2 \ge 0$
$H_1: \mu_1 - \mu_2 < 0$

$$t_{\bar{x}} = \frac{(144.0 - 156.3) - 0}{\sqrt{\frac{(16.8)^2}{27} + \frac{(27.0)^2}{21}}} = \frac{-12.3}{6.72} = -1.830$$

$$df = \frac{\left(\frac{(16.8)^2}{27} + \frac{(27.0)^2}{21}\right)^2}{\left(\frac{1}{27 - 1}\right)\left(\frac{(16.8)^2}{27}\right)^2 + \left(\frac{1}{21 - 1}\right)\left(\frac{(27.0)^2}{21}\right)^2}$$

$$= \frac{2{,}039.3}{64.5} = 31.62$$

$df = 31; -t_\alpha = -1.309$
$t_{\bar{x}} < -t_\alpha \rightarrow$ Reject H_0

b. $|t_{\bar{x}}| = 1.83; df = 31$
The p-value is between 0.025 and 0.05. Because this range is greater than $\alpha = 0.05$, we reject the null hypothesis.

c. p-value = T.DIST(−1.83, 31, TRUE) = 0.0384

10.16 $$s_p^2 = \frac{(10 - 1)(12.5)^2 + (14 - 1)(11.8)^2}{(10 - 1) + (14 - 1)} = 146.2$$

$df = 10 + 14 - 2 = 22; t_{\alpha/2} = 1.717$
$UCL_{\bar{x}_1-\bar{x}_2} = 2.20$
$LCL_{\bar{x}_1-\bar{x}_2} = -15.00$

10.18 a. $H_0: \mu_1 - \mu_2 \le 0.5$
$H_1: \mu_1 - \mu_2 > 0.5$

$$s_p^2 = \frac{(26 - 1)(\$1.25)^2 + (31 - 1)(\$1.2)^2}{(26 - 1) + (31 - 1)} = \$1.50$$

$$t_{\bar{x}} = \frac{(\$9.60 - \$8.60) - \$0.50}{\sqrt{(\$1.50)\left(\frac{1}{26} + \frac{1}{31}\right)}} = 1.534$$

$df = 26 + 31 - 2 = 55; t_\alpha = 1.673$
$t_{\bar{x}} \le t_\alpha \rightarrow$ Do not reject H_0
There is not enough evidence that the average hourly wage for day-care workers in the Northeast is $0.50 per hour higher than in the Midwest.

b. $|t_{\bar{x}}| = 1.534; df = 55$
The p-value is between 0.05 and 0.010. Because this range is greater than $\alpha = 0.05$, we do not reject the null hypothesis.

c. p-value = T.DIST.RT(1.534, 55) = 0.0654

d. Both populations need to be normally distributed.

10.20 a. $H_0: \mu_1 - \mu_2 = 0$
$H_1: \mu_1 - \mu_2 \ne 0$

$$t_{\bar{x}} = \frac{(38.1 - 32.6) - 0}{\sqrt{\frac{(10.6)^2}{11} + \frac{(13.2)^2}{12}}} = 1.107$$

$$df = \frac{\left(\frac{(10.6)^2}{11} + \frac{(13.2)^2}{12}\right)^2}{\left(\frac{1}{11 - 1}\right)\left(\frac{(10.6)^2}{11}\right)^2 + \left(\frac{1}{12 - 1}\right)\left(\frac{(13.2)^2}{12}\right)^2} = 20.67$$

$df = 20; t_{\alpha/2} = 2.086$
$|t_{\bar{x}}| \le |t_{\alpha/2}| \rightarrow$ Do not reject H_0
There is not enough evidence that the average class sizes from business and engineering departments are different.

b. $|t_{\bar{x}}| = 1.107; df = 20$
The p-value is between 0.20 and 0.40. Because this range is greater than $\alpha = 0.05$, we do not reject the null hypothesis.

c. p-value = T.DIST.2T(|1.107|, 20) = T.DIST.2T(1.107, 20) = 0.2814

d. Both populations need to be normally distributed.

10.22 a. $s_p^2 = \frac{(12-1)(130.8)^2 + (12-1)(133.7)^2}{(12-1)+(12-1)} = 17{,}492$

$df = 12 + 12 - 2 = 22;\ t_{\alpha/2} = 2.508$

$UL_{\bar{x}_1-\bar{x}_2} = 13.6$

$LCL_{\bar{x}_1-\bar{x}_2} = -257.2$

b. The confidence interval includes zero, so there is not enough evidence that the average number of words understood by first-born and later-born one-year-old children are different.

c. Both populations need to be normally distributed.

10.24 a. $H_0: \mu_d \le 0$

$H_1: \mu_d > 0$

b. $\bar{d} = 2.33;\ s_d = 2.338$

$t_{\bar{x}} = \frac{2.33 - 0}{\left(\frac{2.338}{\sqrt{6}}\right)} = 2.442$

$df = 5;\ t_\alpha = 2.015$

$t_{\bar{x}} > t_\alpha \rightarrow$ Reject H_0

c. The p-value is between 0.025 and 0.050. Because the p-value is less than $\alpha = 0.05$, we can reject H_0.

d. p-value $= 0.029$; p-value $< 0.05 \rightarrow$ Reject H_0

e. These samples should be treated as dependent.

10.26 a. $\bar{d} = 3.57;\ s_d = 3.55$

$df = 6;\ t_{\alpha/2} = 2.447$

$UCL_{\bar{d}} = 3.57 + (2.447)\left(\frac{3.55}{\sqrt{7}}\right) = 6.85$

$LCL_{\bar{d}} = 3.57 - (2.447)\left(\frac{3.55}{\sqrt{7}}\right) = 0.29$

b. The confidence interval does not include zero, so there is enough evidence to conclude that there is a difference in means between two populations.

10.28 a. $H_0: \mu_d = 0$

$H_1: \mu_d \ne 0$

$\bar{d} = 4.5;\ s_d = 5.911$

$t_{\bar{x}} = \frac{4.5 - 0}{\left(\frac{5.911}{\sqrt{10}}\right)} = 2.408$

$df = 9;\ t_{\alpha/2} = 2.262$

$|t_{\bar{x}}| > |t_{\alpha/2}| \rightarrow$ Reject H_0

b. The p-value is between 0.02 and 0.05. Because the p-value is less than $\alpha = 0.05$, we can reject H_0.

d. p-value $= 0.039$; p-value $< 0.05 \rightarrow$ Reject H_0

There is enough evidence to conclude that the average typing speed for the two input methods is different.

e. These samples are dependent and taken from normal populations.

10.30 a. $H_0: \mu_d \le 10$

$H_1: \mu_d > 10$

$\bar{d} = 13.5;\ s_d = 8.177$

$t_{\bar{x}} = \frac{13.5 - 10}{\left(\frac{8.177}{\sqrt{8}}\right)} = 1.211$

$df = 7;\ t_\alpha = 1.415$

$t_{\bar{x}} \le t_\alpha \rightarrow$ Do not reject H_0

b. The p-value is between 0.10 and 0.20. Because the p-value is greater than $\alpha = 0.10$, we cannot reject H_0.

c. $UCL_{\bar{d}} = 13.50 + (1.415)\left(\frac{8.177}{\sqrt{8}}\right) = 17.59$

$LCL_{\bar{d}} = 13.50 - (1.415)\left(\frac{8.177}{\sqrt{8}}\right) = 9.41$

Because 10 is within the interval, there is not enough evidence that the average weight loss is more than 10 pounds for participants in the weight-loss program.

e. p-value $= 0.133$; p-value $> 0.05 \rightarrow$ Do not reject H_0. There is not enough evidence to conclude that the average weight loss was more than 10 lbs for participants in the weight-loss program.

f. These samples should be treated as dependent.

10.32 a. $H_0: p_1 - p_2 \ge 0$

$H_1: p_1 - p_2 < 0$

$\hat{p} = \frac{60 + 72}{150 + 160} = 0.426$

$\bar{p}_1 = 0.40;\ \ \bar{p}_2 = 0.45$

$z_p = \frac{(0.40 - 0.45) - 0}{\sqrt{(0.426)(1 - 0.426)\left(\frac{1}{150} + \frac{1}{160}\right)}} = -0.893$

$-z_\alpha = -1.280$

$z_p \ge -z_\alpha \rightarrow$ Do not reject H_0

b. p-value $= P(z_p < -0.89) = 0.1867$

p-value $> \alpha \rightarrow 0.1867 > 0.10 \rightarrow$ Do not reject H_0

10.34 a. $H_0: p_1 - p_2 = 0$

$H_1: p_1 - p_2 \ne 0$

$\hat{p} = \frac{18 + 24}{85 + 105} = 0.221$

$\bar{p}_1 = 0.212;\ \ \bar{p}_2 = 0.229$

$z_p = \frac{(0.212 - 0.229) - 0}{\sqrt{(0.221)(1 - 0.221)\left(\frac{1}{85} + \frac{1}{105}\right)}} = -0.279$

$z_{\alpha/2} = 1.960$

$|z_p| \le |z_{\alpha/2}| \rightarrow$ Do not reject H_0

b. p-value $= 2 \times P(z_p < -0.28) = 0.779$

p-value $> \alpha \rightarrow 0.779 > 0.05 \rightarrow$ Do not reject H_0

10.36 $\bar{p}_1 = \frac{92}{130} = 0.708;\ \ \bar{p}_2 = \frac{76}{150} = 0.507$

$\hat{\sigma}_{p_1-p_2} = \sqrt{\frac{(0.708)(1 - 0.708)}{130} + \frac{(0.507)(1 - 0.507)}{150}}$

$= 0.057;\ z_{\alpha/2} = 1.645$

$UCL_{p_1-p_2} = 0.295$

$LCL_{p_1-p_2} = 0.107$

10.38 a. Define Population 1 as women and Population 2 as men.

$H_0: p_1 - p_2 \le 0$

$H_1: p_1 - p_2 > 0$

$\hat{p} = \frac{73 + 56}{170 + 150} = \frac{129}{320} = 0.403$

$\bar{p}_1 = \frac{73}{170} = 0.429;\ \ \bar{p}_2 = \frac{56}{150} = 0.373$

$z_p = \frac{(0.429 - 0.373) - 0}{\sqrt{(0.403)(1 - 0.403)\left(\frac{1}{170} + \frac{1}{150}\right)}} = \frac{0.056}{0.054945} = 1.02$

$\alpha = 0.10;\ z_\alpha = 1.28$

$z_p \le z_\alpha \rightarrow 1.02 < 1.28 \rightarrow$ Do not reject H_0

b. p-value $= P(z_p > 1.02) = 1 - 0.8461 = 0.1539$

p-value $> \alpha \rightarrow 0.1539 > 0.10 \rightarrow$ Do not reject H_0

There is not enough evidence to conclude that the proportions of women who leave the store with a purchase are higher than the percentage of men.

10.40 a. $\bar{p}_1 = \frac{24}{165} = 0.145;\ \ \bar{p}_2 = \frac{17}{145} = 0.117$

$\hat{\sigma}_{p_1-p_2} = \sqrt{\frac{(0.145)(1 - 0.145)}{165} + \frac{(0.117)(1 - 0.117)}{145}}$

$= 0.038;\ z_{\alpha/2} = 1.960$

$UCL_{p_1-p_2} = 0.102$

$LCL_{p_1-p_2} = -0.046$

The confidence interval includes zero, so there is not enough evidence to conclude that there is a difference in vacancy rates between Boston and Chicago.

10.42 a. $H_0: p_1 - p_2 \le 0$
$H_1: p_1 - p_2 > 0$
$$\hat{p} = \frac{23 + 7}{220 + 200} = 0.071$$
$\bar{p}_1 = 0.105; \;\; \bar{p}_2 = 0.035$
$$z_p = \frac{(0.105 - 0.035) - 0}{\sqrt{(0.071)(1 - 0.071)\left(\frac{1}{220} + \frac{1}{200}\right)}} = 2.800$$
$z_\alpha = 1.645$
$z_p > z_\alpha \rightarrow$ Reject H_0

b. p-value $= P(z_p > 2.80) = 0.026$
p-value $\le \alpha \rightarrow 0.026 < 0.05 \rightarrow$ Reject H_0
There is enough evidence to conclude that the proportion of loans from for-profit schools is larger than the proportion of loans from nonprofit schools.

c. $\bar{p}_1 = 0.105; \;\; \bar{p}_2 = 0.035$
$$\hat{\sigma}_{p_1 - p_2} = \sqrt{\frac{(0.105)(1 - 0.105)}{220} + \frac{(0.035)(1 - 0.035)}{200}}$$
$= 0.024; z_{\alpha/2} = 1.960$
$UCL_{p_1 - p_2} = 0.117$
$LCL_{p_1 - p_2} = 0.023$

10.44 a. $H_0: \mu_1 - \mu_2 \le 10$
$H_1: \mu_1 - \mu_2 > 10$
$$t_{\bar{x}} = \frac{(178.3 - 144.6) - 10}{\sqrt{\frac{(72.3)^2}{26} + \frac{(56.9)^2}{23}}} = 1.282$$
$$df = \frac{\left(\frac{(72.3)^2}{26} + \frac{(56.9)^2}{23}\right)^2}{\left(\frac{1}{26 - 1}\right)\left(\frac{(72.3)^2}{26}\right)^2 + \left(\frac{1}{23 - 1}\right)\left(\frac{(56.9)^2}{23}\right)^2} = 46.4$$
$df = 46; t_\alpha = 1.679$
$t_{\bar{x}} > t_\alpha \rightarrow$ Do not reject H_0

b. The p-value is between 0.100 and 0.200. Because the p-value is greater than $\alpha = 0.05$, we cannot reject H_0. There is not enough evidence to conclude that the men average 10 more online friends than the women.

c. p-value = T.DIST.RT(1.282, 46) = 0.1031

e. Both populations need to be normally distributed.

10.46 a. Define Population 1 as Greece and Population 2 as Spain.
$H_0: p_1 - p_2 = 0$
$H_1: p_1 - p_2 \ne 0$
$$\hat{p} = \frac{34 + 33}{120 + 135} = \frac{67}{255} = 0.263$$
$$\bar{p}_1 = \frac{34}{120} = 0.283; \bar{p}_2 = \frac{33}{135} = 0.244$$
$$z_p = \frac{(0.283 - 0.244) - 0}{\sqrt{(0.263)(1 - 0.263)\left(\frac{1}{120} + \frac{1}{135}\right)}} = \frac{0.039}{0.055236} = 0.71$$
$\alpha = 0.02; z_{\alpha/2} = 2.33$
$|z_p| \le |z_{\alpha/2}| \rightarrow 0.71 < 2.33 \rightarrow$ Do not reject H_0

b. p-value $= 2 \times P(z_p > 0.71) = 2 \times (1 - 0.7611) = 0.4778$
p-value $> \alpha \rightarrow 0.4778 > 0.02 \rightarrow$ Do not reject H_0
There is not enough evidence to conclude that the percentage of unemployed adults in Greece is different than the percentage of unemployed adults in Spain.

c. $\bar{p}_1 = 0.283; \bar{p}_2 = 0.263$
$$\hat{\sigma}_{p_1 - p_2} = \sqrt{\frac{(0.283)(1 - 0.283)}{120} + \frac{(0.244)(1 - 0.244)}{135}}$$
$= 0.0553; z_{\alpha/2} = 2.33$
$UCL_{p_1 - p_2} = (0.283 - 0.244) + (2.33)(0.0553)$
$= 0.039 + 0.129 = 0.168$
$LCL_{p_1 - p_2} = (0.283 - 0.244) - (2.33)(0.0553)$
$= 0.039 - 0.129 = -0.090$
Because zero is included in this interval, we have further evidence to conclude that the percentage of unemployed adults in Greece is not different than the percentage of unemployed adults in Spain.

10.48 a. $H_0: \mu_1 - \mu_2 = 0$
$H_1: \mu_1 - \mu_2 \ne 0$
$\bar{x}_1 = 3.43; s_1 = 1.636$
$\bar{x}_2 = 3.21; s_2 = 1.514$
$s_p^2 = 2.47$
$$t_{\bar{x}} = \frac{(3.43 - 3.21) - 0}{\sqrt{(2.47)\left(\frac{1}{18} + \frac{1}{20}\right)}} = 0.431$$
$df = 18 - 20 - 2 = 36; t_{\alpha/2} = 2.028$
$|t_{\bar{x}}| \le |t_{\alpha/2}| \rightarrow$ Do not reject H_0

b. The p-value is greater than 0.400. Because the p-value is greater than $\alpha = 0.05$, we cannot reject H_0.

c. $UCL_{\bar{x}_1 - \bar{x}_2} = 1.256$
$LCL_{\bar{x}_1 - \bar{x}_2} = -0.816$
The confidence interval includes zero, so there is not enough evidence to conclude that the average wait time experienced by drive-through customers is different from that experienced by customers using inside counters.

e. p-value $= 0.669$; p-value $> 0.05 \rightarrow$ Do not reject H_0. There is not enough evidence to conclude that the average wait time is different between these two locations of service.

f. Both populations need to be normally distributed.

10.50 a. $H_0: \mu_d \le 50$
$H_1: \mu_d > 50$
$\bar{d} = 69.92; s_d = 14.625$
$$t_{\bar{x}} = \frac{69.92 - 50}{\left(\frac{14.625}{\sqrt{12}}\right)} = 4.72$$
$df = 11; t_\alpha = 2.718$
$t_{\bar{x}} > t_\alpha \rightarrow$ Reject H_0

b. The p-value is less than 0.005. Because the p-value is less than $\alpha = 0.01$, we reject H_0. There is enough evidence to conclude that the average LDL level is more than 50 points lower for patients who have taken the new medication.

c. $$UCL_{\bar{d}} = 69.92 + (3.106)\left(\frac{14.625}{\sqrt{12}}\right) = 83.03$$
$$LCL_{\bar{d}} = 69.92 - (3.106)\left(\frac{14.625}{\sqrt{12}}\right) = 56.81$$
The confidence interval does not include 50, so there is enough evidence to conclude that there is a difference of more than 50 points in the LDL-level averages for patients before and after taking the new medication.

e. p-value $= 0.019$; p-value $< 0.05 \rightarrow$ Reject H_0

f. Both populations need to be normally distributed.

10.52 a. $H_0: \mu_1 - \mu_2 = 0$
$H_1: \mu_1 - \mu_2 \ne 0$
$\bar{x}_1 = 61.61; s_1 = 11.98$
$\bar{x}_2 = 69.66; s_2 = 7.85$
$$t_{\bar{x}} = \frac{(61.61 - 69.66) - 0}{\sqrt{\frac{(11.98)^2}{15} + \frac{(7.85)^2}{15}}} = -2.176$$
$$df = \frac{\left(\frac{(11.98)^2}{15} + \frac{(7.85)^2}{15}\right)^2}{\left(\frac{1}{15 - 1}\right)\left(\frac{(11.98)^2}{15}\right)^2 + \left(\frac{1}{15 - 1}\right)\left(\frac{(7.85)^2}{15}\right)^2} = 24.15$$

$df = 24; t_{\alpha/2} = 2.064$
$|t_{\bar{x}}| > |t_{\alpha/2}| \rightarrow$ Reject H_0

b. The p-value is between 0.02 and 0.05. Because the p-value is less than $\alpha = 0.05$, we can reject H_0. There is enough evidence to conclude that the fuel efficiency between Delta and US Airways is different.

d. p-value $= 0.0396$; p-value $< 0.05 \rightarrow$ Reject H_0. There is enough evidence to conclude that the fuel efficiency between Delta and US Airways is different.

e. Both populations need to be normally distributed.

10.54 a. $H_0: \mu_d \leq 0$
$H_1: \mu_d > 0$
$\bar{d} = 2.29; s_d = 2.66$

$$t_{\bar{x}} = \frac{2.29 - 0}{\left(\frac{2.66}{\sqrt{10}}\right)} = 2.73$$

$df = 9; t_\alpha = 1.833$
$t_{\bar{x}} > t_\alpha \rightarrow$ Reject H_0

b. The p-value is between 0.01 and 0.025. Because the p-value is less than $\alpha = 0.05$, we can reject H_0. There is evidence to conclude that a difference exists in the gas mileage between the two types of tires.

c. $UCL_{\bar{d}} = 3.83$
$LCL_{\bar{d}} = 0.75$
The confidence interval does not include zero, so there is evidence to conclude that a difference exists in the gas mileage between the two types of tires.

e. p-value $= 0.0117$; p-value $< 0.05 \rightarrow$ Reject H_0.

f. These samples are dependent and must be taken from populations that are normally distributed.

10.56 a. Define Population 1 as Chevrolet owners and Population 2 as Buick owners.
$H_0: p_1 - p_2 = 0$
$H_1: p_1 - p_2 \neq 0$

$$\hat{p} = \frac{68 + 76}{160 + 150} = \frac{144}{310} = 0.465$$

$$\bar{p}_1 = \frac{68}{160} = 0.425; \quad \bar{p}_2 = \frac{76}{150} = 0.507$$

$$z_p = \frac{(0.425 - 0.507) - 0}{\sqrt{(0.465)(1 - 0.465)\left(\frac{1}{160} + \frac{1}{150}\right)}} = \frac{-0.082}{0.056683} = -1.45$$

$\alpha = 0.05; z_{\alpha/2} = 1.96$
$|z_p| \leq |z_{\alpha/2}| \rightarrow 1.45 < 1.96 \rightarrow$ Do not reject H_0
There is not enough evidence to conclude that there is a difference in brand loyalty between Chevrolet and Buick owners.

b. $\bar{p}_1 = 0.425; \quad \bar{p}_2 = 0.507$

$$\hat{\sigma}_{p_1 - p_2} = \sqrt{\frac{(0.425)(1 - 0.425)}{160} + \frac{(0.507)(1 - 0.507)}{150}}$$
$$= 0.0565; z_{\alpha/2} = 1.96$$
$$UCL_{p_1 - p_2} = (0.425 - 0.507) + (1.96)(0.0565)$$
$$= -0.082 + 0.111 = 0.029$$
$$LCL_{p_1 - p_2} = (0.425 - 0.507) - (1.96)(0.0565)$$
$$= -0.082 - 0.111 = -0.193$$

Because zero is included in this interval, we have further evidence to conclude that there is no difference in brand loyalty between Chevrolet and Buick owners.

c. p-value $= 2 \times P(z_p < -1.45) = 2 \times (0.0735) = 0.1470$
p-value $> \alpha \rightarrow 0.1470 > 0.05 \rightarrow$ Do not reject H_0

10.58 a. Define Population 1 as Millennials and Population 2 as older than 34 years.
$H_0: p_1 - p_2 \leq 0$
$H_1: p_1 - p_2 > 0$

$$\hat{p} = \frac{112 + 84}{200 + 200} = \frac{196}{400} = 0.490$$

$$\bar{p}_1 = \frac{112}{200} = 0.560; \quad \bar{p}_2 = \frac{84}{200} = 0.420$$

$$z_p = \frac{(0.56 - 0.42) - 0}{\sqrt{(0.49)(1 - 0.49)\left(\frac{1}{200} + \frac{1}{200}\right)}} = \frac{0.14}{0.0500} = 2.80$$

$\alpha = 0.02; z_\alpha = 2.05$
$z_p > z_\alpha \rightarrow 2.80 > 2.05 \rightarrow$ Reject H_0
We have evidence to conclude that Millennials are more willing to share personal information online when compared to older individuals.

b. $\bar{p}_1 = 0.56; \quad \bar{p}_2 = 0.42$

$$\hat{\sigma}_{p_1 - p_2} = \sqrt{\frac{(0.56)(1 - 0.56)}{200} + \frac{(0.42)(1 - 0.42)}{200}}$$
$$= 0.0495; z_{\alpha/2} = 2.33$$
$$UCL_{p_1 - p_2} = (0.56 - 0.42) + (2.33)(0.0495)$$
$$= 0.14 + 0.115 = 0.255$$
$$LCL_{p_1 - p_2} = (0.56 - 0.42) - (2.33)(0.0495)$$
$$= 0.14 - 0.115 = 0.025$$

Because zero is not included in this interval, we have further evidence to conclude that Millennials are more willing to share personal information online when compared to older individuals.

c. p-value $= P(z_p > 2.80) = 1 - 0.9974 = 0.0026$
p-value $< \alpha \rightarrow 0.0026 < 0.02 \rightarrow$ Reject H_0

10.60 a. Define Population 1 as France and Population 2 as the Unites States.
$H_0: p_1 - p_2 \leq 0.05$
$H_1: p_1 - p_2 > 0.05$

$$\hat{p} = \frac{73 + 40}{240 + 225} = \frac{113}{465} = 0.243$$

$$\bar{p}_1 = \frac{73}{240} = 0.304; \quad \bar{p}_2 = \frac{40}{220} = 0.178$$

$$z_p = \frac{(0.304 - 0.178) - 0.05}{\sqrt{(0.243)(1 - 0.243)\left(\frac{1}{240} + \frac{1}{225}\right)}} = \frac{0.076}{0.03980} = 1.91$$

$\alpha = 0.10; z_\alpha = 1.28$
$z_p > z_\alpha \rightarrow 1.91 > 1.28 \rightarrow$ Reject H_0
We have evidence to conclude that the proportion of women on corporate boards of French companies is more than 5% higher than the proportion of women on boards of U.S. companies.

b. $\bar{p}_1 = 0.304; \quad \bar{p}_2 = 0.178$

$$\hat{\sigma}_{p_1 - p_2} = \sqrt{\frac{(0.304)(1 - 0.304)}{240} + \frac{(0.178)(1 - 0.178)}{225}}$$
$$= 0.0391; z_{\alpha/2} = 1.645$$
$$UCL_{p_1 - p_2} = (0.304 - 0.178) + (1.645)(0.0391)$$
$$= 0.126 + 0.0643 = 0.190$$
$$LCL_{p_1 - p_2} = (0.304 - 0.178) - (1.645)(0.0391)$$
$$= 0.126 - 0.0643 = 0.062$$

Because 0.05 is not included in this interval, we have further evidence to conclude that the proportion of women on corporate boards of French companies is more than 5% higher than the proportion of women on boards of U.S. companies.

c. p-value $= P(z_p > 1.91) = 1 - 0.9719 = 0.0281$
p-value $< \alpha \rightarrow 0.0281 < 0.10 \rightarrow$ Reject H_0

10.62 a. $H_0: \mu_1 - \mu_2 = 0$
$H_1: \mu_1 - \mu_2 \neq 0$
$\bar{x}_1 = \$365; s_1 = \$164.7$
$\bar{x}_2 = \$332; s_2 = \$172.5$
$s_p^2 = 28{,}362$

$$t_{\bar{x}} = \frac{(\$365 - \$332) - 0}{\sqrt{(28{,}362)\left(\frac{1}{45} + \frac{1}{40}\right)}} = 0.902$$

$df = 45 + 40 - 2 = 83; t_{\alpha/2} = 1.663$
$|t_{\bar{x}}| \leq |t_{\alpha/2}| \rightarrow$ Do not reject H_0

b. The p-value is between 0.200 and 0.400. Because the p-value is greater than $\alpha = 0.10$, we cannot reject H_0. There is not enough evidence to conclude that there is a difference in the average amounts spent by holiday shoppers in 2012 and 2013.

c. $UCL_{\bar{x}_1 - \bar{x}_2} = \$93.87$
$LCL_{\bar{x}_1 - \bar{x}_2} = -\$27.87$
The confidence interval includes zero, so there is not enough evidence to conclude that there is a difference in the average amounts spent by holiday shoppers in 2012 and 2013.

e. p-value $= 0.36$; p-value $> 0.10 \rightarrow$ Do not reject H_0.
There is not enough evidence to conclude that there is a difference in the average amounts spent by holiday shoppers in 2012 and 2013.

f. Both populations need to be normally distributed.

10.64 a. $H_0: \mu_1 - \mu_2 \geq 0$
$H_1: \mu_1 - \mu_2 < 0$
$\bar{x}_1 = \$1{,}008.84; s_1 = \$217.11$
$\bar{x}_2 = \$1{,}130.24; s_2 = \$337.79$
$s_p^2 = 80{,}619$

$$t_{\bar{x}} = \frac{(\$1{,}008.84 - \$1{,}130.24) - 0}{\sqrt{(80{,}619)\left(\frac{1}{25} + \frac{1}{25}\right)}} = -1.512$$

$df = 25 + 25 - 2 = 48; -t_\alpha = -1.677$
$t_{\bar{x}} \geq -t_\alpha \rightarrow$ Do not reject H_0

b. $UCL_{\bar{x}_1 - \bar{x}_2} = \$13.26$
$LCL_{\bar{x}_1 - \bar{x}_2} = -\$256.06$
The confidence interval includes zero, so there is not enough evidence to conclude that there is difference in average credit card balances for customers unaware and aware of the promotion.

d. p-value $= 0.0686$; p-value $> 0.05 \rightarrow$ Do not reject H_0.
There is not enough evidence to conclude that the average credit card balance after the promotion is higher than the average credit card balance before the promotion.

e. Both populations need to be normally distributed.

10.66 a. $H_0: \mu_d = 0$
$H_1: \mu_d \neq 0$
$\bar{d} = 0.83; s_d = 3.06$

$$t_{\bar{x}} = \frac{0.83 - 0}{\left(\frac{3.06}{\sqrt{24}}\right)} = 1.339$$

$df = 23; t_{\alpha/2} = 1.714$
$|t_{\bar{x}}| \leq |t_{\alpha/2}| \rightarrow$ Do not reject H_0

b. $$UCL_{\bar{d}} = 0.83 + (1.714)\left(\frac{3.06}{\sqrt{24}}\right) = 1.90$$

$$LCL_{\bar{d}} = 0.83 - (1.714)\left(\frac{3.06}{\sqrt{24}}\right) = -0.24$$

The confidence interval includes zero, so there is not enough evidence to conclude that a difference exists between the average taste-test scores of the two colas.

d. p-value $= 0.195$ p-value $> 0.10 \rightarrow$ Do not reject H_0.
There is not enough evidence to conclude that the average scores for Coke and Pepsi are different.

e. Both populations need to be normally distributed.

Chapter 11

11.2 a. $\sum_{j=1}^{3}\sum_{i=1}^{n_j} x_{ij} = 162; \sum_{j=1}^{3}\sum_{i=1}^{n_j} x_{ij}^2 = 2{,}436$

$$SST = 2{,}436 - \frac{(162)^2}{12} = 249$$

b. $\bar{x}_1 = 10.5; \bar{x}_2 = 18; \bar{x}_3 = 12; \bar{\bar{x}} = 13.5$
$SSB = 126$
$SSW = 123$

c. $MSB = 63; MSW = 13.67; F_{\bar{x}} = 4.609$
$D_1 = 2; D_2 = 9; F_\alpha = 4.256$
$F_{\bar{x}} > F_\alpha \rightarrow$ Reject H_0
There is enough evidence to conclude that not all three population means are equal.

11.4 a.

SOURCE	SUM OF SQUARES	DEGREES OF FREEDOM	MEAN SUM OF SQUARES	F
Between	50	2	25	5.000
Within	100	20	5	
Total	150	22		

b. 3

c. $D_1 = 2; D_2 = 20; F_\alpha = 5.849; F_{\bar{x}} = 5.000$
$F_{\bar{x}} \leq F_\alpha \rightarrow$ Do not reject H_0
There is not enough evidence to conclude that not all three population means are equal.

11.6 $MSW = 10.6; D_1 = 4; D_2 = 10; Q_\alpha = 5.77$
$|\bar{x}_1 - \bar{x}_2| = 6.5; CR_{1,2} = 10.15 \rightarrow$ Means are not different
$|\bar{x}_1 - \bar{x}_3| = 11.0; CR_{1,3} = 9.39 \rightarrow$ Means are different
$|\bar{x}_1 - \bar{x}_4| = 2.5; CR_{1,4} = 10.15 \rightarrow$ Means are not different
$|\bar{x}_2 - \bar{x}_3| = 4.5; CR_{2,3} = 10.15 \rightarrow$ Means are not different
$|\bar{x}_2 - \bar{x}_4| = 4.0; CR_{2,4} = 10.85 \rightarrow$ Means are not different
$|\bar{x}_3 - \bar{x}_4| = 8.5; CR_{3,4} = 10.15 \rightarrow$ Means are not different

11.8 a. $H_0: \mu_1 = \mu_2 = \mu_3$
H_1: Not all μs are equal
$\bar{x}_1 = 300; \bar{x}_2 = 296; \bar{x}_3 = 275; \bar{\bar{x}} = 289.2$

$$SST = 1{,}090{,}271 - \frac{(3{,}759)^2}{13} = 3{,}341.7$$

$SSB = 1{,}659.7$
$SSW = 1{,}682.0$
$MSB = 829.9; MSW = 168.2; \quad F_{\bar{x}} = 4.934$
$D_1 = 2; D_2 = 10; F_\alpha = 4.103$
$F_{\bar{x}} > F_\alpha \rightarrow 4.934 > 4.103 \rightarrow$ Reject H_0
There is enough evidence to conclude that there is a difference in the average driving distances of Mickelson, Woods, and Furyk.

b. $MSW = 168.2; D_1 = 3; D_2 = 10; Q_\alpha = 3.88$
$|\bar{x}_1 - \bar{x}_2| = 4; CR_{1,2} = 25.16 \rightarrow$ Means are not different
$|\bar{x}_1 - \bar{x}_3| = 25; CR_{1,3} = 23.87 \rightarrow$ Means are different
$|\bar{x}_2 - \bar{x}_3| = 21; CR_{2,3} = 23.87 \rightarrow$ Means are not different
There is enough evidence to conclude that the average driving distance by Mickelson is longer than the average driving distance by Furyk. There is not enough evidence to conclude that the average driving distance by Mickelson is different from the average driving distance by Woods and that the average driving distance between Woods is different than the average driving distance by Furyk.

11.10 a. $H_0: \mu_1 = \mu_2 = \mu_3 = \mu_4$
H_1: Not all μs are equal
$\bar{x}_1 = 10.9; \bar{x}_2 = 11.8; \bar{x}_3 = 17.7; \bar{x}_4 = 18.6;$

$$\bar{\bar{x}} = \frac{295.0}{20} = 14.75; \sum_{j=1}^{4}\sum_{i=1}^{n_j} x_{ij} = 295; \sum_{j=1}^{4}\sum_{i=1}^{n_j} x_{ij}^2 = 4{,}814.6$$

$SST = 463.35$
$SSB = 235.25$
$SSW = 228.10$
$MSB = 78.42; MSW = 14.26; F_{\bar{x}} = 5.499$
$D_1 = 3; D_2 = 16; F_\alpha = 3.239$
$F_{\bar{x}} > F_\alpha \rightarrow$ Reject H_0
There is enough evidence to conclude that there is a difference in the average mileage of the rental cars from Avis, Hertz, National, and Enterprise.

b. $MSW = 14.26; D_1 = 4; D_2 = 16; Q_\alpha = 4.05$

$CR_{1,2} = CR_{1,3} = CR_{1,4} = (4.05)\sqrt{\frac{14.26}{2}\left(\frac{1}{5}+\frac{1}{5}\right)} = 6.84$

$|\bar{x}_1 - \bar{x}_2| = 0.9; CR_{1,2} = 6.84 \rightarrow$ Means are not different
$|\bar{x}_1 - \bar{x}_3| = 6.8; CR_{1,3} = 6.84 \rightarrow$ Means are not different
$|\bar{x}_1 - \bar{x}_4| = 7.7; CR_{1,4} = 6.84 \rightarrow$ Means are different

There is enough evidence to conclude that the average mileage of the rental cars from Avis is lower than the average mileage of the rental cars Enterprise. There is not enough evidence to conclude that the average mileage of the rental cars from Avis is lower than the average mileage of the rental cars from Hertz or from National.

11.12 a. $H_0: \mu_1 = \mu_2 = \mu_3$
H_1: Not all μs are equal
$\bar{x}_1 = 8; \bar{x}_2 = 10; \bar{x}_3 = 7; \bar{\bar{x}} = 8.33$

$\sum_{j=1}^{3}\sum_{i=1}^{n_j} x_{ij} = 200; \sum_{j=1}^{3}\sum_{i=1}^{n_j} x_{ij}^2 = 2{,}472.54$

$SST = 2{,}472.54 - \frac{(200)^2}{24} = 805.9$

$SSB = 37.3$
$SSW = 768.6$
$MSB = 18.65; MSW = 36.6; F_{\bar{x}} = 0.510$
$D_1 = 2; D_2 = 21; F_\alpha = 3.467$
$F_{\bar{x}} \le F_\alpha \rightarrow$ Do not reject H_0

There is not enough evidence to conclude that there is a difference in the average package weights shipped by FedEx, UPS, and DHL.

b. There is no need to perform a multiple comparison test.

11.14 a. $H_0: \mu_1 = \mu_2 = \mu_3 = \mu_4$
H_1: Not all μs are equal
$\bar{x}_1 = 33.8; \bar{x}_2 = 15.0; \bar{x}_3 = 16.6; \bar{x}_4 = 19.0;$

$\bar{\bar{x}} = 21.56; \sum_{j=1}^{4}\sum_{i=1}^{n_j} x_{ij} = 388; \sum_{j=1}^{4}\sum_{i=1}^{n_j} x_{ij}^2 = 10{,}336$

$SST = 10{,}336 - \frac{(388)^2}{18} = 1{,}972.44$

$SSB = 1{,}070.44$
$SSW = 902.0$
$MSB = 356.81; MSW = 64.43; F_{\bar{x}} = 5.54$
$D_1 = 3; D_2 = 14; F_\alpha = 3.344$
$F_{\bar{x}} > F_\alpha \rightarrow$ Reject H_0

There is enough evidence to conclude that there is a difference in the average pizza-delivery times by the four drivers.

b. $MSW = 64.43; D_1 = 4; D_2 = 14; Q_\alpha = 4.11$
$|\bar{x}_1 - \bar{x}_2| = 18.8; CR_{1,2} = 15.65 \rightarrow$ Means are different
$|\bar{x}_1 - \bar{x}_3| = 17.2; CR_{1,3} = 14.75 \rightarrow$ Means are different
$|\bar{x}_1 - \bar{x}_4| = 14.8; CR_{1,4} = 15.65 \rightarrow$ Means are not different
$|\bar{x}_2 - \bar{x}_3| = 1.6; CR_{2,3} = 15.65 \rightarrow$ Means are not different
$|\bar{x}_2 - \bar{x}_4| = 4.0; CR_{2,4} = 16.50 \rightarrow$ Means are not different
$|\bar{x}_3 - \bar{x}_4| = 2.4; CR_{3,4} = 15.65 \rightarrow$ Means are not different

There is enough evidence to conclude that the average pizza-delivery time for Driver 2 and Driver 3 is less than the average pizza-delivery time for Driver 1. There is not enough evidence to conclude that the average pizza-delivery time for Driver 4 is different from other drivers, or that the delivery time for Driver 2 is different from that for Driver 3.

11.16 a. $\sum_{j=1}^{3}\sum_{i=1}^{n_j} x_{ij} = 63; \sum_{j=1}^{3}\sum_{i=1}^{n_j} x_{ij}^2 = 455$

$SST = 455 - \frac{(63)^2}{12} = 124.25$

b. Factor means
$\bar{x}_1 = 8; \bar{x}_2 = 4.75; \bar{x}_3 = 3$
Block means
$\bar{x}_1 = 5; \bar{x}_2 = 4; \bar{x}_3 = 3; \bar{x}_4 = 9$
$\bar{\bar{x}} = 5.25$
$SSB = 51.5$
$SSBL = 62.25$
$SSE = 10.50$

c. $MSB = 25.75; MSBL = 20.75; MSE = 1.75$
$F_{\bar{x}} = 14.714; D_1 = 2; D_2 = 6; F_\alpha = 5.143$
$F_{\bar{x}} > F_\alpha \rightarrow$ Reject H_0
$F_{BL} = 11.86; D_1 = 3; D_2 = 6; F_\alpha = 4.757$
$F_{BL} > F_\alpha \rightarrow$ Reject H_0

There is enough evidence to conclude that the three population means are different.

d. Because the blocking null hypothesis is rejected, there is evidence to conclude that the blocking factor is effective.

11.18 a.

SOURCE	SUM OF SQUARES	DEGREES OF FREEDOM	MEAN SUM OF SQUARES	F
Between	72	3	24.0	6.000
Block	168	6	28.0	7.000
Error	72	18	4.0	
Total	312	27		

b. 4

c. The main factor:
$D_1 = 3; D_2 = 18; F_\alpha = 3.160; F_{\bar{x}} = 6.000$
$F_{\bar{x}} > F_\alpha \rightarrow$ Reject H_0

There is enough evidence to conclude that not all four population means are equal.

The blocking factor:
$D_1 = 6; D_2 = 18; F_\alpha = 2.661; F_{BL} = 7.000$
$F_{BL} > F_\alpha \rightarrow$ Reject H_0

There is enough evidence to conclude that a difference between block means exists.

d. Because the blocking null hypothesis is rejected, there is evidence to conclude that the blocking factor is effective.

11.20 $MSE = 2.23; k = 4; b = 5; D_1 = 4; D_2 = 12; Q_\alpha = 4.20$
$CR_{1,2} = CR_{1,3} = CR_{1,4} = CR_{2,3} = CR_{2,4} = CR_{3,4}$
$= (4.20)\sqrt{\frac{2.23}{5}} = 2.8$

$|\bar{x}_1 - \bar{x}_2| = 0; CR_{1,2} = 2.8 \rightarrow$ Means are not different
$|\bar{x}_1 - \bar{x}_3| = 3.4; CR_{1,3} = 2.8 \rightarrow$ Means are different
$|\bar{x}_1 - \bar{x}_4| = 0.2; CR_{1,4} = 2.8 \rightarrow$ Means are not different
$|\bar{x}_2 - \bar{x}_3| = 3.4; CR_{2,3} = 2.8 \rightarrow$ Means are different
$|\bar{x}_2 - \bar{x}_4| = 0.2; CR_{2,4} = 2.8 \rightarrow$ Means are not different
$|\bar{x}_3 - \bar{x}_4| = 3.6; CR_{3,4} = 2.8 \rightarrow$ Means are different

11.22 a. $H_0: \mu_1 = \mu_2 = \mu_3$
H_1: Not all μs are equal
Factor means
$\bar{x}_1 = 25.98; \bar{x}_2 = 26.87; \bar{x}_3 = 27.08$
Block means
$\bar{x}_1 = 22.97; \bar{x}_2 = 29.23; \bar{x}_3 = 22.67; \bar{x}_4 = 29.03;$
$\bar{x}_5 = 25.93; \bar{x}_6 = 30.03$

$\bar{\bar{x}} = 26.64; \sum_{j=1}^{3}\sum_{i=1}^{n_j} x_{ij} = 479.6; \sum_{j=1}^{3}\sum_{i=1}^{n_j} x_{ij}^2 = 12{,}950.96$

$SST = 12{,}950.96 - \frac{(479.6)^2}{18} = 172.28$

$SSB = 4.07$
$SSBL = 161.24$
$SSE = 6.97$
$MSB = 2.03; MSBL = 32.25; MSE = 0.70$
$F_{\bar{x}} = 2.900; D_1 = 2; D_2 = 10; F_\alpha = 4.103$
$F_{\bar{x}} \le F_\alpha \rightarrow$ Do not reject H_0
$F_{BL} = 46.071; D_1 = 5; D_2 = 10; F_\alpha = 3.326$
$F_{BL} > F_\alpha \rightarrow$ Reject H_0

b. By rejecting the blocking null hypothesis, it seems there is evidence that the blocking factor is effective. But the main factor with the randomized block design is not significant, and we have to proceed to test the main factor with one-way ANOVA.

$SST = 172.28$

$SSB = 4.07$

$SSW = 168.21$

$MSB = 2.035; MSW = 11.214; F_{\bar{x}} = 0.181$

$D_1 = 2; D_2 = 15; F_\alpha = 3.682$

$F_{\bar{x}} \leq F_\alpha \rightarrow$ Do not reject H_0

There is not enough evidence to conclude that there is a difference in the averages in gas mileage using different grades of gasoline.

c. There is no need to perform a multiple comparison test, because the null hypothesis is not rejected.

11.24 a. $H_0: \mu_1 = \mu_2 = \mu_3$

H_1: Not all μs are equal

Factor means

$\bar{x}_1 = 228; \bar{x}_2 = 247; \bar{x}_3 = 233.75$

Block means

$\bar{x}_1 = 208; \bar{x}_2 = 242; \bar{x}_3 = 229; \bar{x}_4 = 240;$

$\bar{x}_5 = 259; \bar{x}_6 = 237; \bar{x}_7 = 240; \bar{x}_8 = 235$

$\bar{\bar{x}} = 236.25; \sum_{j=1}^{3}\sum_{i=1}^{n_j} x_{ij} = 5{,}670; \sum_{j=1}^{3}\sum_{i=1}^{n_j} x_{ij}^2 = 1{,}347{,}526$

$SST = 1{,}347{,}526 - \frac{(5{,}670)^2}{24} = 7{,}988.5$

$SSB = 1{,}519$

$SSBL = 4{,}294.5$

$SSE = 2{,}175$

$MSB = 759.5; MSBL = 613.5; MSE = 155.36$

$F_{\bar{x}} = 4.889; D_1 = 2; D_2 = 14; F_\alpha = 3.739$

$F_{\bar{x}} > F_\alpha \rightarrow$ Reject H_0

$F_{BL} = 3.949; D_1 = 7; D_2 = 14; F_\alpha = 2.764$

$F_{BL} > F_\alpha \rightarrow$ Reject H_0

There is enough evidence to conclude that there is a difference in the average driving yardage of the Top Flite, Pinnacle, and Titleist golf balls.

b. Because the blocking null hypothesis is rejected, there is evidence to conclude that the blocking factor is effective.

c. $MSE = 155.36; k = 3; b = 8; D_1 = 3; D_2 = 14; Q_\alpha = 3.70$

$CR_{1,2} = CR_{1,3} = CR_{2,3} = (3.70)\sqrt{\frac{155.36}{8}} = 16.3$

$|\bar{x}_1 - \bar{x}_2| = 19.00; CR_{1,2} = 16.3 \rightarrow$ Means are different

$|\bar{x}_1 - \bar{x}_3| = 5.75; CR_{1,3} = 16.3 \rightarrow$ Means are not different

$|\bar{x}_2 - \bar{x}_3| = 13.25; CR_{2,3} = 16.3 \rightarrow$ Means are not different

There is enough evidence to conclude that the average driving yardage of Pinnacle golf balls is greater than the average driving yardage of Top Flite golf balls. There is not enough evidence to conclude that there are differences in the average driving yardages of golf balls for all other possible pairs of the three companies.

11.26 a. $H_0: \mu_1 = \mu_2 = \mu_3$

H_1: Not all μs are equal

Factor means

$\bar{x}_1 = 160; \bar{x}_2 = 170; \bar{x}_3 = 142$

Block means

$\bar{x}_1 = 142; \bar{x}_2 = 160.7; \bar{x}_3 = 157.7; \bar{x}_4 = 139.3;$

$\bar{x}_5 = 147.7; \bar{x}_6 = 176; \bar{x}_7 = 178$

$\bar{\bar{x}} = 157.3; \sum_{j=1}^{3}\sum_{i=1}^{n_j} x_{ij} = 3{,}304; \sum_{j=1}^{3}\sum_{i=1}^{n_j} x_{ij}^2 = 529{,}536$

$SST = 529{,}536 - \frac{(3{,}304)^2}{21} = 9{,}706.7$

$SSB = 2{,}818.7$

$SSBL = 4{,}318$

$SSE = 2{,}570$

$MSB = 1{,}409.3; MSBL = 719.7; MSE = 214.2$

$F_{\bar{x}} = 6.579; D_1 = 2; D_2 = 12; F_\alpha = 3.885$

$F_{\bar{x}} > F_\alpha \rightarrow$ Reject H_0

$F_{BL} = 3.360; D_1 = 6; D_2 = 12; F_\alpha = 2.996$

$F_{BL} > F_\alpha \rightarrow$ Reject H_0

There is enough evidence to conclude that there is a difference in the average number of bagels sold per day by three stores of Bagel Boys.

b. Because the blocking null hypothesis was rejected, there is evidence to conclude that the blocking factor is effective.

c. $MSE = 214.2; k = 3; b = 7; D_1 = 3; D_2 = 12; \alpha = 0.05;$

$Q_\alpha = 3.77$

$CR_{1,2} = CR_{1,3} = CR_{2,3} = (3.77)\sqrt{\frac{214.2}{7}} = 20.85$

$|\bar{x}_1 - \bar{x}_2| = 10; CR_{1,2} = 20.85 \rightarrow$ Means are not different

$|\bar{x}_1 - \bar{x}_3| = 18; CR_{1,3} = 20.85 \rightarrow$ Means are not different

$|\bar{x}_2 - \bar{x}_3| = 28; CR_{2,3} = 20.85 \rightarrow$ Means are different

There is enough evidence to conclude that the average number of bagels sold per day in Store 2 is greater than the average number of bagels sold per day in Store 3. There is not enough evidence to conclude that there are differences in the average number of bagels sold per day when comparing Store 1 with Store 2 and Store 1 with Store 3.

11.28 a.

SOURCE	SUM OF SQUARES	DEGREES OF FREEDOM	MEAN SUM OF SQUARES	F
Factor A	100	2	50	5.000
Factor B	120	2	60	6.000
Interaction	60	4	15	1.500
Error	450	45	10	
Total	730	53		

b. 6

c. Interaction:

$D_1 = 4; D_2 = 45; F_\alpha = 2.579; F_{AB} = 1.500$

$F_{AB} \leq F_\alpha \rightarrow$ Do not reject H_0

d. Factor A:

$D_1 = 2; D_2 = 45; F_\alpha = 3.204; F_A = 5.000$

$F_A > F_\alpha \rightarrow$ Reject H_0

e. Factor B:

$D_1 = 2; D_2 = 45; F_\alpha = 3.204; F_B = 6.000$

$F_B > F_\alpha \rightarrow$ Reject H_0

11.30 Factor A:

$MSE = 40.2; a = 3; b = 2; r = 3$

$D_1 = 3; D_2 = 12; Q_A = 3.77$

$CR_A = (3.77)\sqrt{\frac{40.2}{(2)(3)}} = 9.76$

$|\bar{x}_1 - \bar{x}_2| = 4.6; CR_A = 9.76 \rightarrow$ Means are not different

$|\bar{x}_1 - \bar{x}_3| = 11.6; CR_A = 9.76 \rightarrow$ Means are different

$|\bar{x}_2 - \bar{x}_3| = 7.0; CR_A = 9.76 \rightarrow$ Means are not different

There is enough evidence to conclude that there is difference between Factor A the Level 1 and Level 3 means. There is not enough evidence to conclude that there are differences between the Level 1 and Level 2 means or between the Level 2 and Level 3 means.

Determining differences between level means of Factor B is not warranted because no difference in means between Factor B levels was found.

11.32

SOURCE	SUM OF SQUARES	DEGREES OF FREEDOM	MEAN SUM OF SQUARES	F	p-VALUE	F_a
Factor A	401.4	2	200.7	4.318	0.029	3.555
Factor B	1,780.1	2	890.0	19.148	0.00003	3.555
Interaction	98.1	4	24.5	0.528	0.716	2.928
Error	836.7	18	46.5			
Total	3,116.3	26				

Source of Variation	SS	df	MS	F	P-value	F crit
Sample	1780.074	2	890.037	19.14821	3.49E-05	3.554557
Columns	401.4074	2	200.7037	4.317928	0.029394	3.554557
Interaction	98.14815	4	24.53704	0.527888	0.716714	2.927744
Within	836.6667	18	46.48148			
Total	3116.296	26				

a. Interaction hypothesis: p-value $= 0.716 \rightarrow 0.716 > 0.05 \rightarrow$
Do not reject H_0
There is no interaction between Factors A and B, and we can test them individually.

b. Factor A hypothesis: p-value $= 0.029 \rightarrow 0.029 < 0.05 \rightarrow$ Reject H_0
There is enough evidence to conclude that the Factor A means are different.

c. Factor B hypothesis: p-value $= 0.00003 \rightarrow 0.00003 < 0.05 \rightarrow$
Reject H_0
There is enough evidence to conclude that the Factor B means are different.

11.34

SOURCE	SUM OF SQUARES	DEGREES OF FREEDOM	MEAN SUM OF SQUARES	F	p-VALUE	F_a
Factor A	123,215,833	2	61,607,917	5.174	0.017	3.555
Factor B	106,667	1	106,667	0.009	0.926	4.414
Interaction	21,225,833	2	10,612,917	0.891	0.427	3.555
Error	214,310,000	18	11,906,111			
Total	358,858,333	23				

a. Interaction hypothesis: p-value $= 0.427 \rightarrow 0.427 > 0.05 \rightarrow$
Do not reject H_0
There is no interaction between gender and major, and we can test them individually.

b. Factor A hypothesis: p-value $= 0.017 \rightarrow 0.017 < 0.05 \rightarrow$ Reject H_0
There is enough evidence to conclude that the person's starting salary is based on a person's major.

c. Factor B hypothesis: p-value $= 0.926 \rightarrow 0.926 > 0.05 \rightarrow$
Do not reject H_0
There is not enough evidence to conclude that the person's starting salary is based on a person's gender.

d. Factor A:
$MSE = 11{,}906{,}111;\ a = 3;\ b = 2;\ r = 4$
$D_1 = 3;\ D_2 = 18;\ Q_A = 3.61$

$$CR_A = (3.61)\sqrt{\frac{11{,}906{,}111}{(2)(4)}} = 4.404$$

$|\bar{x}_1 - \bar{x}_2| = 4{,}837.5;\ CR_A = 4.404 \rightarrow$ Means are different
$|\bar{x}_1 - \bar{x}_3| = 62.5;\ CR_A = 4.404 \rightarrow$ Means are not different
$|\bar{x}_2 - \bar{x}_3| = 4{,}775.0;\ CR_A = 4.404 \rightarrow$ Means are different
There is enough evidence to conclude that the starting salaries of finance majors and accounting majors are greater than the starting salary of marketing majors. There is not enough evidence to conclude that there are differences in finance and accounting majors' starting salaries.

e.

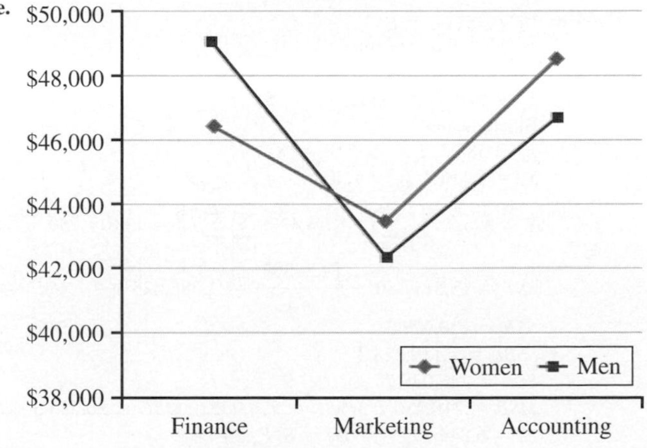

11.36

SOURCE	SUM OF SQUARES	DEGREES OF FREEDOM	MEAN SUM OF SQUARES	F	p-VALUE	F_α
Factor A	7,987.5	3	2,662.5	6.342	0.002	2.901
Factor B	2,205.2	1	2,205.2	5.253	0.029	4.149
Interaction	719.7	3	239.9	0.571	0.638	2.901
Error	13,434.0	32	419.8			
Total	24,346.4	39				

a. Interaction hypothesis: p-value
$= 0.638 \rightarrow 0.638 > 0.05 \rightarrow$ Do not reject H_0
There is no interaction between the city and time of the week, and we can test them individually.

b. Factor A hypothesis: p-value
$= 0.002 \rightarrow 0.002 < 0.05 \rightarrow$ Reject H_0
There is enough evidence to conclude that the city has an effect on the amount of time stuck in traffic.

c. Factor B hypothesis: p-value
$= 0.029 \rightarrow 0.029 < 0.05 \rightarrow$ Reject H_0
There is enough evidence to conclude that the time of the week has an effect on the amount of time stuck in traffic.

d. Factor A:
$MSE = 419.8;\ a = 4;\ b = 2;\ r = 5$
$D_1 = 4;\ D_2 = (4)(2)(5 - 1) = 32;\ \alpha = 0.05; Q_A = 3.84$

$$CR_A = (3.84)\sqrt{\frac{419.8}{(2)(5)}} = 24.9$$

$|\bar{x}_1 - \bar{x}_2| = |80.8 - 76.2| = 4.6;\ CR_A = 24.9 \rightarrow$ means are not different
$|\bar{x}_1 - \bar{x}_3| = |80.8 - 73.7| = 7.1;\ CR_A = 24.9 \rightarrow$ means are not different
$|\bar{x}_1 - \bar{x}_4| = |80.8 - 44.8| = 36.0;\ CR_A = 24.9 \rightarrow$ means are different
$|\bar{x}_2 - \bar{x}_3| = |76.2 - 73.7| = 2.5;\ CR_A = 24.9 \rightarrow$ means are not different
$|\bar{x}_2 - \bar{x}_4| = |76.2 - 44.8| = 31.4;\ CR_A = 24.9 \rightarrow$ means are different
$|\bar{x}_3 - \bar{x}_4| = |73.7 - 44.8| = 28.9;\ CR_A = 24.9 \rightarrow$ means are different
There is enough evidence to conclude that the amount of time stuck in traffic in New York is less than the amount of time stuck in traffic in Beijing, New Delhi, and Mexico City. There is not enough evidence to conclude that there are differences in the amount of time stuck in traffic between Beijing, New Delhi, and Mexico City.
Factor B:
No need for multiple comparisons as there are only two populations.

e.

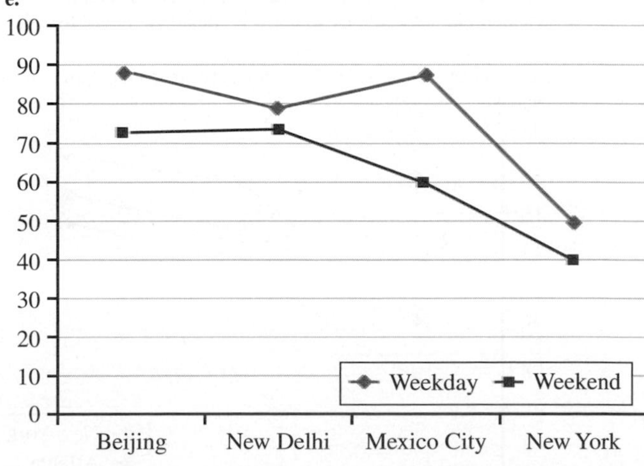

11.38

SOURCE	SUM OF SQUARES	DEGREES OF FREEDOM	MEAN SUM OF SQUARES	F	p-VALUE	F_α
Factor A	438.2	2	219.1	48.093	0.000	3.259
Factor B	96.8	2	48.4	10.629	0.0002	3.259
Interaction	16.9	4	4.2	0.927	0.459	2.634
Error	164	36	4.6			
Total	715.9	44				

a. Interaction hypothesis: p-value $= 0.459 \rightarrow 0.459 > 0.05 \rightarrow$ Do not reject H_0
There is no interaction between city and movie format, and we can test them individually.

b. Factor A hypothesis: p-value $= 0 \rightarrow 0 < 0.05 \rightarrow$ Reject H_0
There is enough evidence to conclude that the movie format has an effect on the cost of a movie.

c. Factor B hypothesis: p-value $= 0.0002 \rightarrow 0.0002 < 0.05 \rightarrow$ Reject H_0
There is enough evidence to conclude that the city has an effect on the cost of a movie.

d. Factor A:
$MSE = 4.6; a = 3; b = 3; r = 5$
$D_1 = 3; D_2 = 36;\ Q_A = 3.46$

$$CR_A = (3.46)\sqrt{\frac{4.6}{(3)(5)}} = 1.92$$

$|\bar{x}_1 - \bar{x}_2| = 5.53; CR_A = 1.92 \rightarrow$ Means are different
$|\bar{x}_1 - \bar{x}_3| = 7.33; CR_A = 1.92 \rightarrow$ Means are different
$|\bar{x}_2 - \bar{x}_3| = 1.80; CR_A = 1.92 \rightarrow$ Means are not different
There is enough evidence to conclude that there is a difference in average movie prices between 2D and 3D formats and between 2D and IMAX formats. There is no difference in average prices between 3D and IMAX formats.

Factor B:
$MSE = 4.6; a = 3; b = 3; r = 5$
$D_1 = 3; D_2 = 36;\ Q_B = 3.46$

$$CR_B = (3.46)\sqrt{\frac{4.6}{(3)(5)}} = 1.92$$

$|\bar{x}_1 - \bar{x}_2| = 1.20; CR_B = 1.92 \rightarrow$ Means are not different
$|\bar{x}_1 - \bar{x}_3| = 3.53; CR_B = 1.92 \rightarrow$ Means are different
$|\bar{x}_2 - \bar{x}_3| = 2.33; CR_B = 1.92 \rightarrow$ Means are different
There is enough evidence to conclude that there is a difference in average movie prices between New York and Dallas and between Atlanta and Dallas. There is no difference in average prices between New York and Atlanta.

e.

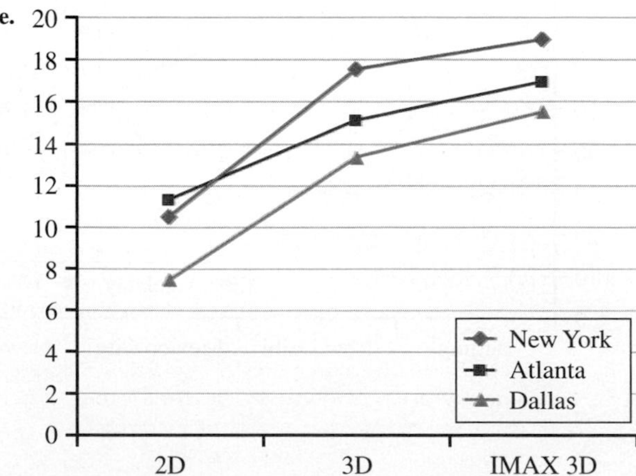

11.40 a. $H_0: \mu_1 = \mu_2 = \mu_3$
H_1: Not all μs are equal
$\bar{x}_1 = 33; \bar{x}_2 = 40; \bar{x}_3 = 17; \bar{\bar{x}} = 30$

$$\sum_{j=1}^{3}\sum_{i=1}^{n_j} x_{ij} = 450;\ \sum_{j=1}^{3}\sum_{i=1}^{n_j} x_{ij}^2 = 16{,}768$$

$$SST = 16{,}768 - \frac{(450)^2}{15} = 3{,}268$$

$SSB = 1{,}390$
$SSW = 1{,}878$
$MSB = 695; MSW = 156.5; F_{\bar{x}} = 4.441$
$D_1 = 2; D_2 = 12; F_\alpha = 3.885$
$F_{\bar{x}} > F_\alpha \rightarrow$ Reject H_0
There is enough evidence to conclude that there are differences in the average number of ER visits during three shifts.

b. $MSW = 156.5; D_1 = 3; D_2 = 12; Q_\alpha = 3.77$

$$CR_{1,2} = CR_{1,3} = CR_{2,3} = (3.77)\sqrt{\frac{156.5}{2}\left(\frac{1}{5} + \frac{1}{5}\right)} = 21.09$$

$|\bar{x}_1 - \bar{x}_2| = 7; CR_{1,2} = 21.09 \rightarrow$ Means are not different
$|\bar{x}_1 - \bar{x}_3| = 16; CR_{1,3} = 21.09 \rightarrow$ Means are not different
$|\bar{x}_2 - \bar{x}_3| = 23; CR_{2,3} = 21.09 \rightarrow$ Means are different
There is enough evidence to conclude that the average number of ER visits during the 3:00 P.M.–11:00 P.M. shift is greater than the average number of ER visits during the 11:00 P.M.–7:00 A.M. shift. There is not enough evidence to conclude that the average number of ER visits during the 7:00 A.M.–3:00 P.M. shift is different from that of the two other shifts.

c. You can add a blocking factor, such as day of the week.

11.42 a. $H_0: \mu_1 = \mu_2 = \mu_3 = \mu_4$
H_1: Not all μs are equal
$\bar{x}_1 = 198.0; \bar{x}_2 = 206.0; \bar{x}_3 = 163.6; \bar{x}_4 = 180.4;$

$$\bar{\bar{x}} = 187.0;\ \sum_{j=1}^{4}\sum_{i=1}^{n_j} x_{ij} = 3{,}740;\ \sum_{j=1}^{4}\sum_{i=1}^{n_j} x_{ij}^2 = 707{,}448$$

$$SST = 707{,}448 - \frac{(3{,}740)^2}{20} = 8{,}068$$

$SSB = 5{,}365.6$
$SSW = 2{,}702.4$
$MSB = 1{,}788.5; MSW = 168{,}9; F_{\bar{x}} = 10.6$
$D_1 = 3; D_2 = 16; F_\alpha = 3.239$
$F_{\bar{x}} > F_\alpha \rightarrow$ Reject H_0
There is enough evidence to conclude that there is a difference in the average ticket prices between these four teams.

b. $MSW = 168.9; D_1 = 4; D_2 = 16; Q_\alpha = 4.05.$
$|\bar{x}_1 - \bar{x}_2| = 8.0; CR_{1,2} = 23.54 \rightarrow$ Means are not different
$|\bar{x}_1 - \bar{x}_3| = 34.4; CR_{1,3} = 23.54 \rightarrow$ Means are different
$|\bar{x}_1 - \bar{x}_4| = 17.6; CR_{2,3} = 23.54 \rightarrow$ Means are not different
$|\bar{x}_2 - \bar{x}_3| = 42.4; CR_{2,3} = 23.54 \rightarrow$ Means are different
$|\bar{x}_2 - \bar{x}_4| = 25.6; CR_{2,3} = 23.54 \rightarrow$ Means are different
$|\bar{x}_3 - \bar{x}_4| = 16.8; CR_{2,3} = 23.54 \rightarrow$ Means are not different
There is enough evidence to conclude that the average ticket price for Green Bay is higher than the average price for Indianapolis. The average ticket price for New Orleans is higher than the average price of both Indianapolis and New York.

11.44 a. $H_0: \mu_1 = \mu_2 = \mu_3$
H_1: Not all μs are equal
Factor means
$\bar{x}_1 = 870; \bar{x}_2 = 1{,}112; \bar{x}_3 = 704$
Block means
$\bar{x}_1 = 585.3; \bar{x}_2 = 655; \bar{x}_3 = 821.7;$
$\bar{x}_4 = 1{,}116.7; \bar{x}_5 = 1{,}300$

$$\bar{\bar{x}} = 895.3;\ \sum_{j=1}^{3}\sum_{i=1}^{n_j} x_{ij} = 13{,}430;\ \sum_{j=1}^{3}\sum_{i=1}^{n_j} x_{ij}^2 = 13{,}811{,}150$$

$$SST = 13{,}811{,}150 - \frac{(13{,}430)^2}{15} = 1{,}786{,}823.3$$

$SSB = 420{,}973.3$
$SSBL = 1{,}119{,}823.3$
$SSE = 246{,}026.7$
$MSB = 210{,}486.7; MSBL = 279{,}955.8; MSE = 30{,}753.3$
$F_{\bar{x}} = 6.844; D_1 = 2; D_2 = 8; F_\alpha = 4.459$

$F_{\bar{x}} > F_\alpha \rightarrow$ Reject H_0
$F_{BL} = 9.103; D_1 = 4; D_2 = 8; F_\alpha = 3.838$
$F_{BL} > F_\alpha \rightarrow$ Reject H_0
There is enough evidence to conclude that there is a difference in the average prices of homes in Avalon, Stone Harbor, and Sea Isle City.

b. $MSE = 30{,}753; k = 3; b = 5; D_1 = 3; D_2 = 8; Q_\alpha = 4.04$

$$CR_{1,2} = CR_{1,3} = CR_{2,3} = (4.04)\sqrt{\frac{30{,}753.3}{5}} = 316.8$$

$|\bar{x}_1 - \bar{x}_2| = 242; CR_{1,2} = 316.8 \rightarrow$ Means are not different
$|\bar{x}_1 - \bar{x}_3| = 166; CR_{1,3} = 316.8 \rightarrow$ Means are not different
$|\bar{x}_2 - \bar{x}_3| = 408; CR_{2,3} = 316.8 \rightarrow$ Means are different
There is enough evidence to conclude that the average price of homes in Stone Harbor is higher than the average price of homes in Sea Isle City. There is not enough evidence to conclude that there are differences in the average price of homes when comparing Avalon with Stone Harbor or with Sea Isle City.

d. Because the blocking null hypothesis is rejected, there is evidence to conclude that the blocking factor is effective.

11.46 a. $H_0: \mu_1 = \mu_2 = \mu_3$
H_1: Not all μs are equal
$\bar{x}_1 = 97.4; \bar{x}_2 = 106.8; \bar{x}_3 = 100.4; \bar{\bar{x}} = 101.5$

$$\sum_{j=1}^{3}\sum_{i=1}^{n_j} x_{ij} = 1{,}523; \sum_{j=1}^{3}\sum_{i=1}^{n_j} x_{ij}^2 = 166{,}163$$

$$SST = 166{,}163 - \frac{(1{,}523)^2}{15} = 11{,}527.7$$

$SSB = 230.5$
$SSW = 11{,}297.2$
$MSB = 115.3; MSW = 941.4; F_{\bar{x}} = 0.122$
$D_1 = 2; D_2 = 12; F_\alpha = 3.885$
$F_{\bar{x}} < F_\alpha \rightarrow$ Do not reject H_0

b. Perform randomized block ANOVA with month as blocks:
Block means
$\bar{x}_1 = 66.7; \bar{x}_2 = 121; \bar{x}_3 = 106.3;$
$\bar{x}_4 = 75; \bar{x}_5 = 138.7$

$$\bar{\bar{x}} = 101.5; \sum_{j=1}^{3}\sum_{i=1}^{n_j} x_{ij} = 1{,}523; \sum_{j=1}^{3}\sum_{i=1}^{n_j} x_{ij}^2 = 166{,}163$$

$SST = 11{,}527.7$
$SSB = 230.5$
$SSBL = 11{,}107.7$
$SSE = 195.5$
$F_{\bar{x}} = 4.725; D_1 = 2; D_2 = 8; F_\alpha = 4.459$
$F_{\bar{x}} > F_\alpha \rightarrow$ Reject H_0
$F_{BL} = 113.746; D_1 = 4; D_2 = 8; F_\alpha = 3.838$
$F_{BL} > F_\alpha \rightarrow$ Reject H_0
There is enough evidence to conclude that the music has an effect on the average time spent using month as the blocking factor.

c. $MSE = 24.4; k = 3; b = 5; D_1 = 3; D_2 = 8; Q_\alpha = 4.04$

$$CR_{1,2} = CR_{1,3} = CR_{2,3} = (4.04)\sqrt{\frac{24.4}{5}} = 8.92$$

$|\bar{x}_1 - \bar{x}_2| = 9.4; CR_{1,2} = 8.92 \rightarrow$ Means are different
$|\bar{x}_1 - \bar{x}_3| = 3.0; CR_{1,3} = 8.92 \rightarrow$ Means are not different
$|\bar{x}_2 - \bar{x}_3| = 6.4; CR_{2,3} = 8.92 \rightarrow$ Means are not different
There is enough evidence to conclude that a difference exists in the amount of time spent at the table between no music and low music.

11.48 a. $H_0: \mu_1 = \mu_2 = \mu_3$
H_1: Not all μs are equal
$\bar{x}_1 = 36.0; \bar{x}_2 = 30.0; \bar{x}_3 = 42.0; \bar{\bar{x}} = 36.0$

$$SST = 16{,}102 - \frac{(432)^2}{12} = 550$$

$SSB = 288.0; MSB = 144.0$
$SSW = 262; MSW = 29.11; F_{\bar{x}} = 4.95$
$D_1 = 2; D_2 = 9; F_\alpha = 4.256$

Because $F_{\bar{x}} = 4.95$ is greater than $F_\alpha = 4.256$, we reject the null hypothesis. Therefore, we can conclude that a difference exists in the average number of hours that an employee works per week between these countries.

b. $D_1 = 3; D_2 = 9; MSW = 29.11$
$Q_\alpha = 3.95$

$$CR_{i,j} = (3.95)\sqrt{\frac{29.11}{2}\left(\frac{1}{4} + \frac{1}{4}\right)} = 10.7$$

$|\bar{x}_1 - \bar{x}_2| = 6; CR_{1,2} = 10.7 \rightarrow$ means are not different
$|\bar{x}_1 - \bar{x}_3| = 6; CR_{1,3} = 10.7 \rightarrow$ means are not different
$|\bar{x}_2 - \bar{x}_3| = 12; CR_{2,3} = 10.7 \rightarrow$ means are different
There is evidence that employees in China work more hours per week than employees in Sweden. There is no evidence of differences in worked hours per week between US and Sweden and between the US and China.

11.50 a. $H_0: \mu_1 = \mu_2 = \mu_3$
H_1: Not all μs are equal
$\bar{x}_1 = 15.2; \bar{x}_2 = 16.4; \bar{x}_3 = 13.4; \bar{\bar{x}} = 15.0$

$$SST = 3{,}461 - \frac{(225)^2}{15} = 86.0$$

$SSB = 22.8; MSB = 11.4$
$SSBL = 48.0; MSBL = 12.0$
$SSE = 15.2; MSE = 1.9; F_{\bar{x}} = 6.0$
$D_1 = 2; D_2 = 8; F_\alpha = 4.459$
Because $F_{\bar{x}} = 6.0$ is greater than $F_\alpha = 4.459$, we reject the null hypothesis. Therefore, we can conclude that a difference exists in the satisfaction scores between these three locations.

b. $H_0: \mu_{BL1} = \mu_{BL2} = \mu_{BL3} = \mu_{BL4} = \mu_{BL5}$
H_1: Not all μ_{BL}s are equal
$F_{BL} = 6.32$
$D_1 = 4; D_2 = 8; F_\alpha = 3.838$
Because $F_{BL} = 6.32$ is greater than $F_\alpha = 3.838$, we reject the null hypothesis. Therefore, we can conclude that the blocking factor was effective.

c. $D_1 = 3; D_2 = 8; MSE = 1.9$
$Q_\alpha = 4.04$

$$CR_{i,j} = (4.04)\sqrt{\frac{1.9}{5}} = (4.04)(0.616) = 2.49$$

$|\bar{x}_1 - \bar{x}_2| = 1.2; CR_{1,2} = 2.49 \rightarrow$ means are not different
$|\bar{x}_1 - \bar{x}_3| = 1.8; CR_{1,3} = 2.49 \rightarrow$ means are not different
$|\bar{x}_2 - \bar{x}_3| = 3.0; CR_{2,3} = 2.49 \rightarrow$ means are different
The average customer satisfaction score from Towson differs from the average customer satisfaction score from Dover.

11.52

ANOVA

SOURCE OF VARIATION	SS	df	MS	F	p-value	F crit
Sample	225	1	225	18.52699	0.000164	4.170877
Columns	96	2	48	3.952425	0.02995	3.31583
Interaction	12.66667	2	6.333333	0.5215	0.598912	3.31583
Within	364.3333	30	12.14444			
Total	698	35				

a. Interaction hypothesis: p-value $= 0.599 > 0.05 \rightarrow$ Do not reject H_0
There is no interaction between the type of diet and the reporting status of the individual.

b. Factor B hypothesis: p-value $= 0.00016 < 0.05 \rightarrow$ Reject H_0
There is enough evidence to conclude that the reporting status has an effect on the weight loss experienced by the individual.

c. Factor A hypothesis: p-value $= 0.02995 < 0.05 \rightarrow$ Reject H_0
There is enough evidence to conclude that the type of diet has an effect on the weight loss experienced by the individual.

d. $D_1 = 3; D_2 = 30; MSW = 12.144$
$Q_\alpha = 3.49$
$CR_{i,j} = (3.49)\sqrt{\frac{12.144}{(2)(6)}} = 3.49$
$|\bar{x}_1 - \bar{x}_2| = 2.0; CR_{1,2} = 3.49 \rightarrow$ means are not different
$|\bar{x}_1 - \bar{x}_3| = 2.0; CR_{1,3} = 3.49 \rightarrow$ means are not different
$|\bar{x}_2 - \bar{x}_3| = 4.0; CR_{2,3} = 3.49 \rightarrow$ means are different
The average weight loss from Diet 2 differs from the average weight loss from Diet 3.

11.54

SOURCE	SUM OF SQUARES	DEGREES OF FREEDOM	MEAN SUM OF SQUARES	F	p-VALUE	F_α
Factor A	90.94	3	30.31	1.658	0.182	2.708
Factor B	123.49	1	123.49	6.753	0.011	3.949
Interaction	2.33	3	0.78	0.042	0.988	2.708
Error	1,609.1	88	18.29			
Total	1,825.85	95				

a. Interaction hypothesis: p-value $= 0.988 \rightarrow 0.988 > 0.05 \rightarrow$
Do not reject H_0
There is no interaction between gender and state for the averages of BMI level, and we can test them individually.

b. Factor A hypothesis: p-value $= 0.182 \rightarrow 0.182 > 0.05 \rightarrow$
Do not reject H_0
There is not enough evidence to conclude that the state has an effect on BMI level.

c. Factor B hypothesis: p-value $= 0.011 \rightarrow 0.011 < 0.05 \rightarrow$ Reject H_0
There is enough evidence to conclude that gender has an effect on BMI level.

d. No need to perform a multiple comparison test because Factor B (gender) has only two populations.

e.

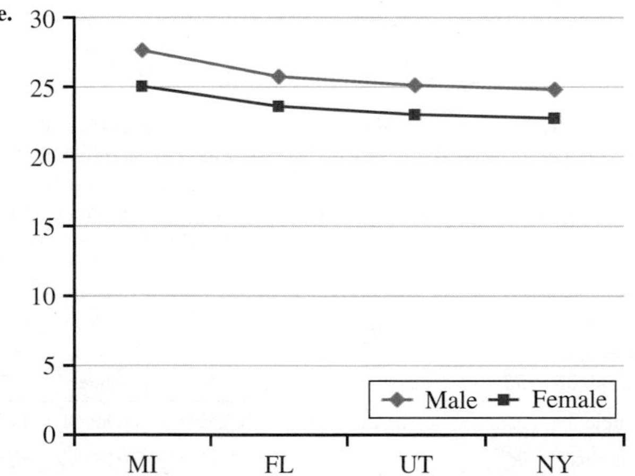

11.56 a. $H_0: \mu_1 = \mu_2 = \mu_3$
H_1: Not all μs are equal
$\bar{x}_1 = 3{,}617.2; \bar{x}_2 = 5{,}805.3; \bar{x}_3 = 4{,}462.4$
$\bar{\bar{x}} = 4{,}628.3; \sum_{j=1}^{3}\sum_{i=1}^{n_j} x_{ij} = 40{,}162; \sum_{j=1}^{3}\sum_{i=1}^{n_j} x_{ij}^2 = 673{,}594{,}727$
$SST = 673{,}594{,}727 - \frac{(40{,}162)^2}{27} = 95{,}215{,}052$
$SSB = 21{,}916{,}744$
$SSW = 73{,}298{,}308$
$MSB = 10{,}958{,}372; MSW = 3{,}054{,}096$
$F_{\bar{x}} = 3.588; D_1 = 2; D_2 = 24; F_\alpha = 3.403$
$F_{\bar{x}} > F_\alpha \rightarrow$ Reject H_0
There is enough evidence to conclude that there are differences in the credit card balances of the three groups.

b. $MSW = 3{,}054{,}096; D_1 = 3; D_2 = 24; Q_\alpha = 3.53$
$CR_{1,2} = CR_{1,3} = CR_{2,3} = (3.53)\sqrt{\frac{3{,}054{,}096}{2}\left(\frac{1}{9} + \frac{1}{9}\right)} = 2{,}056.3$
$|\bar{x}_1 - \bar{x}_2| = 2{,}188.1; CR_{1,2} = 2{,}056.3 \rightarrow$ Means are different
$|\bar{x}_1 - \bar{x}_3| = 845.2; CR_{1,3} = 2{,}056.3 \rightarrow$ Means are not different
$|\bar{x}_2 - \bar{x}_3| = 1{,}342.9; CR_{1,4} = 2{,}056.3 \rightarrow$ Means are not different
There is enough evidence to conclude that the average credit card balance for the "No promotion" group of customers is less than the average credit card balance for "E-mail promotion" group. There is not enough evidence to conclude that there are differences in the average credit card balance for the other two possible pairs of the three groups.

c. E-mail promotion appears to be an effective way to communicate with customers.

11.58 a. $H_0: \mu_1 = \mu_2 = \mu_3$
H_1: Not all μs are equal
$\bar{x}_1 = 278.0; \bar{x}_2 = 226.6; \bar{x}_3 = 205.2; \bar{x} = 236.6$
$SST = 339{,}748.9$
$SSB = 58{,}740.1; MSB = 29{,}370.1$
$SSW = 281{,}008.8; MSW = 4{,}683.5; F_{\bar{x}} = 6.27$
$D_1 = 2; D_2 = 60; F_\alpha = 3.150$
Because $F_{\bar{x}} = 6.27$ is greater than $F_\alpha = 3.150$, we reject the null hypothesis. Therefore, we can conclude that a difference exists in the average 401(k) balance between the three age groups.

b. $D_1 = 3; D_2 = 60; MSW = 4{,}683.5$
$Q_\alpha = 3.40$
$CR_{i,j} = (3.40)\sqrt{\frac{4{,}683.5}{2}\left(\frac{1}{21} + \frac{1}{21}\right)} = 50.8$
$|\bar{x}_1 - \bar{x}_2| = 51.4; CR_{1,2} = 50.8 \rightarrow$ means are different
$|\bar{x}_1 - \bar{x}_3| = 72.8; CR_{1,3} = 50.8 \rightarrow$ means are different
$|\bar{x}_2 - \bar{x}_3| = 21.4; CR_{2,3} = 50.8 \rightarrow$ means are not different
There is a difference in the average 401(k) balance between the 50- to 59-year age group and the 70 years or older age group. There is also a difference is the average 401(k) balance between the 50- to 59-year age group and the 60- to 69-year age group.

Chapter 12

12.2

POPULATION	f_o	f_e	$(f_o - f_e)$	$(f_o - f_e)^2$	$\frac{(f_o - f_e)^2}{f_e}$
A—yes	20	19	1	1	0.053
A—no	18	19	−1	1	0.053
B—yes	10	11	−1	1	0.091
B—no	12	11	1	1	0.091
Total					$\chi^2 = $ **0.288**

$k = 2; df = 1; \chi^2_{0.05} = 3.841$
$\chi^2 \leq \chi^2_{0.05} \rightarrow$ Do not reject H_0
The proportion of "Yes" observations does not differ between Populations A and B.

12.4

POPULATION	f_o	f_e	$(f_o - f_e)$	$(f_o - f_e)^2$	$\frac{(f_o - f_e)^2}{f_e}$
A—yes	10	13.76	−3.76	14.14	1.027
A—no	22	18.24	3.76	14.14	0.775
B—yes	16	18.06	−2.06	4.24	0.235
B—no	26	23.94	2.06	4.24	0.177
C—yes	17	11.18	5.82	33.87	3.030
C—no	9	14.82	−5.82	33.87	2.286
Total					$\chi^2 = $ **7.530**

$k = 3; df = 2; \chi^2_{0.05} = 5.991$

$\chi^2 > \chi^2_{0.05} \rightarrow$ Reject H_0

The proportion of "Yes" observations differs between Populations A, B, and C.

12.6 **a.** $\hat{p} = \dfrac{21 + 41 + 36 + 18}{700} = 0.166$

HOUSEHOLD INCOME	f_o	f_e	$(f_o - f_e)$	$(f_o - f_e)^2$	$\frac{(f_o - f_e)^2}{f_e}$
Less than $25,000 with health insurance	57	65.07	−8.07	65.12	1.002
Less than $25,000 without health insurance	21	12.93	8.07	65.12	5.044
$25,000–$49,999 with health insurance	142	152.67	−10.67	113.85	0.746
$25,000–$49,999 without health insurance	41	30.33	10.67	113.85	3.757
$50,000–$74,999 with health insurance	205	201.06	3.94	15.52	0.077
$50,000–$74,999 without health insurance	36	39.94	−3.94	15.52	0.388
$75,000 or more with health insurance	180	165.19	14.81	219.34	1.328
$75,000 or more without health insurance	18	32.81	−14.81	219.34	6.686
Total					$\chi^2 =$ **19.028**

$k = 4; df = 3; \chi^2_{0.01} = 11.345$

$\chi^2 > \chi^2_{0.01} \rightarrow$ Reject H_0

c. p-value $= 0.0003$. Because the p-value is smaller than $\alpha = 0.01$, there is enough evidence to reject the null hypothesis.

d. The proportion of households without health insurance differs by income bracket.

12.8 **a.** $H_0: p_1 = p_2$

$H_1: p_1 \neq p_2$

$\hat{p} = \dfrac{35 + 23}{75 + 80} = 0.374$

CATEGORY	f_o	f_e	$(f_o - f_e)$	$(f_o - f_e)^2$	$\frac{(f_o - f_e)^2}{f_e}$
Men—no sunscreen	35	28.05	6.95	48.303	1.722
Men—sunscreen	40	46.95	−6.95	48.303	1.029
Women—no sunscreen	23	29.92	−6.92	47.886	1.600
Women—sunscreen	57	50.08	6.92	47.886	0.956
Total					$\chi^2 =$ **5.307**

$k = 2; df = 1; \alpha = 0.01; \chi^2_{0.01} = 6.635$

$\chi^2 \leq \chi^2_{0.01} \rightarrow 5.307 < 6.635 \rightarrow$ Do not reject H_0

We have no evidence to conclude that the proportion of men who do not use sunscreen differs from the proportion of women.

b. p-value $=$ CHISQ.DIST.RT (5.307, 1) $= 0.0212$

Because the p-value $= 0.0212$ and is greater than $\alpha = 0.01$, we fail to reject the null hypothesis.

12.10 H_0: Random variable follows the Poisson distribution

H_1: Random variable does not follow the Poisson distribution $\lambda = 1.5$

RANDOM VARIABLE, x	f_o	$P(x)$	f_e	$(f_o - f_e)$	$(f_o - f_e)^2$	$\frac{(f_o - f_e)^2}{f_e}$
0	17	0.2231	22.31	−5.31	28.20	1.264
1	35	0.3347	33.47	1.53	2.341	0.070
2	30	0.2510	25.10	4.90	24.01	0.957
3 and more	18	0.1912	19.12	−1.12	1.25	0.065
Total	**100**					$\chi^2 =$ **2.356**

Note: Because the expected frequency for random variable "4 or more" is less than 5 it was combined with random variable "3" as "3 or more", and $P(3 \text{ or more}) = 1.0 - 0.2231 - 0.3347 - 0.2510 = 0.1912$

$k = 4; m = 0; df = 3; \chi^2_{0.05} = 7.815$

$\chi^2 \leq \chi^2_{0.05} \rightarrow$ Do not reject H_0

Conclusion: Random variable follows the Poisson distribution.

12.12 H_0: Random variable follows the normal probability distribution

H_1: Random variable does not follow the normal probability distribution $n < 75 \rightarrow$ number of intervals $= 4$

RANDOM VARIABLE, x	INTERVAL	f_o	$P(x)$	f_e	$(f_o - f_e)$	$(f_o - f_e)^2$	$\frac{(f_o - f_e)^2}{f_e}$
Less than 80	$z \leq -1$	10	0.1587	7.93	2.07	4.28	0.540
80 to under 100	$-1 < z \leq 0$	14	0.3413	17.07	−3.07	9.42	0.552
100 to under 120	$0 < z \leq 1$	19	0.3413	17.07	1.93	3.73	0.218
120 and more	$z > 1$	7	0.1587	7.93	−0.93	0.86	0.108
Total		50					$\chi^2 =$ **1.418**

$k = 4; m = 0; df = 3; \chi^2_{0.05} = 7.815$

$\chi^2 \leq \chi^2_{0.05} \rightarrow$ Do not reject H_0

Conclusion: Random variable follows the normal probability distribution.

12.14 **a.** H_0: U.S. market share for cars did not change between 2013 and 2014

H_1: U.S. market share for cars changed between 2013 and 2014

BRAND	f_o	$P(x)$	f_e	$(f_o - f_e)$	$(f_o - f_e)^2$	$\frac{(f_o - f_e)^2}{f_e}$
General Motors	35	0.185	40.70	−5.70	32.49	0.798
Ford Motors	37	0.165	36.30	0.70	0.49	0.013
Toyota	24	0.137	30.14	−6.14	37.70	1.251
Chrylser	20	0.122	26.84	−6.84	46.79	1.743
Honda	17	0.102	22.44	−5.44	29.59	1.319
Other	87	0.289	63.58	23.42	548.50	8.627
Total	**220**					$\chi^2 =$ **13.751**

$k = 6; df = 5; \alpha = 0.10; \chi^2_{0.10} = 9.236$

$\chi^2 > \chi^2_{0.10} \rightarrow 13.751 > 9.236 \rightarrow$ Reject H_0

We have evidence to conclude that the U.S. market share for cars has changed between 2013 and 2014.

b. p-value $=$ CHISQ.DIST.RT $(13.751, 5) = 0.0173$
Because the p-value $= 0.0173$ and is less than $\alpha = 0.10$, we reject the null hypothesis.

12.16 H_0: The number of touchdown passes thrown per game by Aaron Rodgers follows the Poisson probability distribution
H_1: The number of touchdown passes thrown per game by Aaron Rodgers does not follow the Poisson probability distribution
$\lambda = 1.7$

TOUCHDOWN PASSES	f_o	$P(x)$	f_e	$(f_o - f_e)$	$(f_o - f_e)^2$	$\frac{(f_o - f_e)^2}{f_e}$
0	4	0.1827	7.31	−3.31	10.96	1.499
1	12	0.3106	12.42	−0.42	0.18	0.014
2	14	0.2640	10.56	3.44	11.83	1.120
3 or more	10	0.2427	9.71	0.29	0.08	0.008
Total	**40**					$\chi^2 = $ **2.641**

$k = 4; m = 0; df = 3; \chi^2_{0.05} = 7.815$
$\chi^2 \leq \chi^2_{0.05} \rightarrow$ Do not reject H_0
Conclusion: The number of touchdown passes thrown per game by Aaron Rodgers follows the Poisson probability distribution.
The probability of 4 or more (0.0931) was combined with the probability of exactly 3 (0.1496) in the last category to ensure each cell has an expected frequency of at least five.

12.18 H_0: The number of correct answers per student follows the binomial probability distribution
H_1: The number of correct answers per student does not follow the binomial probability distribution
The probability of a success based on the sample with $n = 4$ is:

$$p = \frac{(4)(0.00) + (5)(0.25) + (12)(0.50) + (9)(0.75) + (10)(1.00)}{4 + 5 + 12 + 9 + 10} = 0.60$$

NUMBER OF CORRECT ANSWERS	f_o	$P(x)$	f_e	$(f_o - f_e)$	$(f_o - f_e)^2$	$\frac{(f_o - f_e)^2}{f_e}$
0 or 1	9	0.1792	7.17	1.83	3.35	0.467
2	12	0.3456	13.82	−1.82	3.31	0.240
3	9	0.3456	13.82	−4.82	23.23	1.681
4	10	0.1296	5.18	4.82	23.23	4.485
Total	**40**					$\chi^2 = $ **6.873**

Note: Because the expected frequency for the number of "yes" decisions "0" is less than 5 it was combined with the number of "yes" decisions "1" as "0 or 1," and $P(x) = 0.0256 + 0.1536 = 0.1792$
$k = 4; m = 1; df = 2; \chi^2_{0.05} = 5.991.$
$\chi^2 > \chi^2_{0.05} \rightarrow$ Reject H_0
Conclusion: The number of correct answers per student does not follow the binomial probability distribution.

12.20 H_0: The number of printers sold per week at the electronic store follows the normal probability distribution
H_1: The number of printers sold per week at the electronic store does not follow the normal probability distribution
$\bar{x} = 11.2; s = 4.3; n < 75 \rightarrow$ number of intervals $= 4$
$x = 11.2 + (1.0)(4.3) = 15.5$
$x = 11.2 - (1.0)(4.3) = 6.9$

x INTERVAL	z INTERVAL	f_o	$P(x)$	f_e	$(f_o - f_e)$	$(f_o - f_e)^2$	$\frac{(f_o - f_e)^2}{f_e}$
Less than 6.9	$z \leq -1$	7	0.1587	7.14	−0.14	0.02	0.003
6.9 to 11.2	$-1 < z \leq 0$	16	0.3413	15.36	0.64	0.41	0.027
11.2 to 15.5	$0 < z \leq 1$	14	0.3413	15.36	−1.36	1.85	0.120
More than 15	$z > 1$	8	0.1587	7.14	0.86	0.74	0.104
Total		**45**					$\chi^2 = $ **0.254**

$k = 4; m = 2; df = 1; \chi^2_{0.05} = 3.841$
$\chi^2 \leq \chi^2_{0.05} \rightarrow$ Do not reject H_0
Conclusion: There is enough evidence to conclude that the number of printers sold per week at the electronic store follows the normal probability distribution.

12.22 a. H_0: The row variable and column variable are independent of one another
H_1: The row variable and column variable are not independent of one another

b.

ROW VARIABLE	COLUMN VARIABLE C1	C2	C3
R1	$\frac{(26)(19)}{50} = 9.88$	$\frac{(26)(14)}{50} = 7.28$	$\frac{(26)(17)}{50} = 8.84$
R2	$\frac{(24)(19)}{50} = 9.12$	$\frac{(24)(14)}{50} = 6.72$	$\frac{(24)(17)}{50} = 8.16$

c.

CELL	f_o	f_e	$(f_o - f_e)$	$(f_o - f_e)^2$	$\frac{(f_o - f_e)^2}{f_e}$
R1–C1	9	9.88	−0.88	0.774	0.078
R1–C2	7	7.28	−0.28	0.078	0.011
R1–C3	10	8.84	1.16	1.346	0.152
R2–C1	10	9.12	0.88	0.774	0.085
R2–C2	7	6.72	0.28	0.078	0.012
R2–C3	7	8.16	−1.16	1.346	0.165
Total					$\chi^2 = $ **0.503**

d. $r = 2; c = 3; df = 2; \chi^2_{0.05} = 5.991$
$\chi^2 \leq \chi^2_{0.05} \rightarrow$ Do not reject H_0
Conclusion: The row and column variables are independent of one another.

12.24 a. H_0: Student's grade on the exam and hours spent studying are independent
H_1: Student's grade on the exam and hours spent studying are not independent

CELL	f_o	f_e	$(f_o - f_e)$	$(f_o - f_e)^2$	$\frac{(f_o - f_e)^2}{f_e}$
Less than 3 hours—A	4	11.1	−7.1	50.41	4.541
Less than 3 hours—B	18	13.2	4.8	23.04	1.745

CELL	f_o	f_e	$(f_o - f_e)$	$(f_o - f_e)^2$	$\frac{(f_o - f_e)^2}{f_e}$
Less than 3 hours—C	8	5.7	2.3	5.29	0.928
3–5 hours—A	15	12.95	2.05	4.20	0.324
3–5 hours—B	14	15.4	−1.4	1.96	0.127
3–5 hours—C	6	6.65	−0.65	0.42	0.063
More than 5 hours—A	18	12.95	5.05	25.50	1.969
More than 5 hours—B	12	15.4	−3.4	11.56	0.751
More than 5 hours—C	5	6.65	−1.65	2.72	0.409
Total					χ^2 = **10.860**

$r = 3; c = 3; df = 4; \chi^2_{0.05} = 9.488$

$\chi^2 > \chi^2_{0.05} \rightarrow$ Reject H_0

b. Conclusion: Student's grade on the exam and hours spent studying are not independent.

12.26 a. H_0: The type of the medal and country that earned it are independent
H_1: The type of the medal and country that earned it are not independent

CELL	f_o	f_e	$(f_o - f_e)$	$(f_o - f_e)^2$	$\frac{(f_o - f_e)^2}{f_e}$
United States—gold	46	41.99	4.01	16.08	0.383
United States—silver	29	31.74	−2.74	7.51	0.237
United States—bronze	29	30.27	−1.27	1.61	0.053
Germany—gold	11	17.77	−6.77	45.83	2.579
Germany—silver	19	13.43	5.57	31.02	2.310
Germany—bronze	14	12.81	1.19	1.42	0.111
Great Britain—gold	29	26.24	2.76	7.62	0.290
Great Britain—silver	17	19.84	−2.84	8.07	0.407
Great Britain—bronze	19	18.92	0.08	0.01	0.000
Total					χ^2 = **6.370**

$r = 3; c = 3; df = (3 - 1)(3 - 1) = 4; \alpha = 0.05; \chi^2_{0.05} = 9.488$
$\chi^2 \le \chi^2_{0.05} \rightarrow 6.370 < 9.488 \rightarrow$ Do not reject H_0

b. Conclusion: The type of the medal and country that earned it are independent.

c. p-value = CHISQ.DIST.RT (6.370, 4) = 0.1732
Because the p-value = 0.1732 and is greater than $\alpha = 0.05$, we fail to reject the null hypothesis.

12.28 a. $\hat{p} = \frac{9 + 7 + 13}{350} = 0.083$

INSTITUTION	f_o	f_e	$(f_o - f_e)$	$(f_o - f_e)^2$	$\frac{(f_o - f_e)^2}{f_e}$
Public and defaulted on loan	9	9.94	−0.94	0.88	0.089
Public and not defaulted on loan	111	110.06	0.94	0.88	0.008
Private and defaulted on loan	7	12.43	−5.43	29.48	2.372
Private and not defaulted on loan	143	137.57	5.43	29.48	0.214
For-profit and defaulted on loan	13	6.63	6.37	40.58	6.121
For-profit and not defaulted on loan	67	73.37	−6.37	40.58	0.553
Total					χ^2 = **9.360**

$k = 3; df = 2; \chi^2_{0.05} = 5.991$

$\chi^2 > \chi^2_{0.05} \rightarrow$ Reject H_0

c. p-value = 0.0093. Because the p-value is less than $\alpha = 0.05$, there is enough evidence to reject the null hypothesis.

d. The proportion of students who default on their student loans differs by the type of institution.

12.30 a. $\hat{p} = \frac{134 + 129 + 138}{580} = 0.691$

PITCHER	f_o	f_e	$(f_o - f_e)$	$(f_o - f_e)^2$	$\frac{(f_o - f_e)^2}{f_e}$
Stephen Strasburg—contacts made	134	145.11	−11.11	123.43	0.851
Stephen Strasburg—contacts missed	76	64.89	11.11	123.43	1.902
Clayton Kershaw—contacts made	129	124.38	4.62	21.34	0.172
Clayton Kershaw—contacts missed	51	55.62	−4.62	21.34	0.384
Tim Lincecum—contacts made	138	131.29	6.71	45.02	0.343
Tim Lincecum—contacts missed	52	58.71	−6.71	45.02	0.767
Total					χ^2 = **4.419**

$k = 3; df = 2; \chi^2_{0.05} = 5.991$

$\chi^2 \le \chi^2_{0.05} \rightarrow$ Do not reject H_0

The contact percentage does not differ among these three pitchers.

c. p-value = 0.11. Because the p-value is greater than $\alpha = 0.05$, there is not enough evidence to reject the null hypothesis.

12.32 **a.** $\hat{p} = \dfrac{10 + 10 + 13 + 8}{157} = 0.261$

STATE	f_o	f_e	$(f_o - f_e)$	$(f_o - f_e)^2$	$\frac{(f_o - f_e)^2}{f_e}$
Delaware—Follow the CDC	10	10.44	−0.44	0.19	0.018
Delaware— Do not follow	30	29.56	0.44	0.19	0.006
Maryland—Follow the CDC	10	8.35	1.65	2.72	0.326
Maryland— Do not follow	22	23.65	−1.65	2.72	0.115
New Jersey—Follow the CDC	13	13.05	0.05	0.002	0.000
New Jersey—Do not follow	37	36.95	−0.05	0.002	0.000
Pennsylvania—Follow the CDC	8	9.14	−1.14	1.30	0.142
Pennsylvania—Do not follow	27	25.86	1.14	1.30	0.050
Total					χ^2 = **0.657**

$k = 4; df = 3; \chi^2_{0.05} = 7.815$

$\chi^2 \le \chi^2_{0.05} \rightarrow$ Do not reject H_0

The proportion of adults who follow the CDC's guidelines does not differ among these four states.

c. p-value $= 0.88$. Because the p-value is greater than $\alpha = 0.05$, there is not enough evidence to reject the null hypothesis.

12.34 **a.** H_0: The proportions of Ohio voters by age group did not change from 2008 to 2014

H_1: The proportions of Ohio voters by age group changed from 2008 to 2014

AGE GROUP	f_o	$P(x)$	f_e	$(f_o - f_e)$	$(f_o - f_e)^2$	$\frac{(f_o - f_e)^2}{f_e}$
18–29	14	0.17	23.8	−9.8	96.04	4.035
30–44	18	0.27	37.8	−19.8	392.04	10.371
45–64	73	0.39	54.6	18.4	338.56	6.201
65 and older	35	0.17	23.8	11.2	125.44	5.271
Total	**140**					χ^2 = **25.887**

$k = 4; m = 0; df = 3; \chi^2_{0.05} = 7.815$

$\chi^2 > \chi^2_{0.05} \rightarrow$ Reject H_0

b. The proportions of Ohio voters by age group changed from 2008 to 2014.

12.36 **a.** H_0: The number of attempted shots does not differ across all six segments of the soccer goal

H_1: The number of attempted shots differs across all six segments of the soccer goal

SHOT LOCATION	f_o	f_e	$(f_o - f_e)$	$(f_o - f_e)^2$	$\frac{(f_o - f_e)^2}{f_e}$
Left	37	32.67	4.33	18.75	0.574
Middle	20	32.67	−12.67	160.53	4.914
Right	41	32.67	8.33	69.39	2.124
Total	**98**				χ^2 = **7.612**

$df = 2; \chi^2_{0.05} = 5.991$

$\chi^2 > \chi^2_{0.05} \rightarrow$ Reject H_0

Conclusion: The number of attempted shots differs across all six segments of the soccer goal, with a preference toward the right side of the goal.

b. H_0: The proportion of successful shots does not differ across all six segments of the soccer goal.

H_1: The proportion of successful shots differs across all six segments of the soccer goal.

$\hat{p} = \dfrac{25 + 12 + 30}{98} = 0.684$

SHOT LOCATION	f_o	f_e	$(f_o - f_e)$	$(f_o - f_e)^2$	$\frac{(f_o - f_e)^2}{f_e}$
Left—yes	25	25.3	−0.3	0.09	0.004
Left—no	12	11.7	0.3	0.09	0.008
Middle—yes	12	13.7	−1.7	2.89	0.211
Middle—no	8	6.3	1.7	2.89	0.459
Right—yes	30	28.0	2.0	4.00	0.143
Right–no	11	13.0	−2.0	4.00	0.308
Total					χ^2 = **1.133**

$df = 2; \chi^2_{0.05} = 5.99$

$\chi^2 \le \chi^2_{0.05} \rightarrow$ Do not reject H_0

Conclusion: The proportion of successful shots does not differ across all six segments of the goal.

c. Even though the preference is to attempt shots toward the right side of the goal, the proportion of successful shots does not differ across these segments.

12.38 H_0: The number of employees calling in sick per day follows the Poisson distribution

H_1: The number of employees calling in sick per day does not follow the Poisson distribution

$$\lambda = \frac{(0)(10) + (1)(7) + (2)(15) + (3)(12) + (4)(3) + (5)(3)}{50} = 2.0$$

NUMBER OF EMPLOYEES	f_o	$P(x)$	f_e	$(f_o - f_e)$	$(f_o - f_e)^2$	$\frac{(f_o - f_e)^2}{f_e}$
0	10	0.1353	6.77	3.23	10.432	1.541
1	7	0.2707	13.54	−6.54	42.772	3.159
2	15	0.2707	13.54	1.46	2.132	0.157
3 or more	18	0.3233	16.17	1.84	3.386	0.209
Total	**50**					χ^2 = **5.066**

Note: Because the expected frequencies for number of employees "4" and "5" are less than those when they were combined with number of employees "3" as "3 or more", and $P(x) = 1.0 - 0.1353 + 0.2707 + 0.2707 = 0.3233$

$k = 4; m = 1; df = 2; \chi^2_{0.01} = 9.210$

$\chi^2 \le \chi^2_{0.01} \rightarrow$ Do not reject H_0

Conclusion: The number of employees calling in sick per day follows the Poisson distribution.

12.40 H_0: The number of fairways hit per hole follows the binomial probability distribution

H_1: The number of fairways hit per hole does not follow the binomial probability distribution

$$p = \frac{(0)(32) + (1)(86) + (2)(88) + (3)(38) + (4)(6)}{(250)(4)} = 0.40$$

HIT PER HOLE	f_o	$P(x)$	f_e	$(f_o - f_e)$	$(f_o - f_e)^2$	$\frac{(f_o - f_e)^2}{f_e}$
0	32	0.130	32.5	−0.5	0.25	0.008
1	86	0.346	86.5	−0.5	0.25	0.003
2	88	0.346	86.5	1.5	2.25	0.026
3	38	0.154	38.5	−0.5	0.25	0.006
4	6	0.026	6.5	−0.5	0.25	0.038
Total	**250**					$\chi^2 = \mathbf{0.081}$

$k = 5; m = 1; df = 3; \chi^2_{0.05} = 7.815$

$\chi^2 \leq \chi^2_{0.05} \rightarrow$ Do not reject H_0

Conclusion: The number of the fairways the players hit per hole while teeing off follows the binomial probability distribution.

12.42 a. H_0: The number of annual snowfall amount in Minneapolis from 1884 until 2012 follows the normal probability distribution

H_1: The number of annual snowfall amount in Minneapolis from 1884 until 2012 does not follow the normal probability distribution

$\bar{x} = 46.3; s = 18.4; 75 < n < 220 \rightarrow$ number of intervals $= 5$

$x - 46.3 + (1.5)(18.4) = 73.9$

$x = 46.3 + (0.5)(18.4) = 55.5$

$x = 46.3 - (0.5)(18.4) = 37.1$

$x = 46.3 - (1.5)(18.4) = 18.7$

x INTERVAL	z INTERVAL	f_o	$P(x)$	f_e	$(f_o - f_e)$	$(f_o - f_e)^2$	$\frac{(f_o - f_e)^2}{f_e}$
Less than 18.7	$z \leq -1.5$	5	0.0668	8.55	−3.55	12.60	1.474
18.7 to 37.1	$-1.5 < z \leq -0.5$	40	0.2417	30.94	9.06	82.08	2.652
> 37.1 to 55.5	$-0.5 < z \leq 0.5$	47	0.3830	49.02	−2.02	4.08	0.083
> 55.5 to 73.9	$0.5 < z \leq 1.5$	25	0.2417	30.94	−5.94	35.28	1.140
More than 73.9	$z > 1.5$	11	0.0668	8.55	2.45	6.00	0.702
Total		**128**					$\chi^2 = \mathbf{6.051}$

$k = 5; m = 2; df = 5 - 2 - 1 = 2; \alpha = 0.01; \chi^2_{0.01} = 9.210$

$\chi^2 > \chi^2_{0.01} \rightarrow 6.051 > 9.210 \rightarrow$ Do not reject H_0

Conclusion: There is enough evidence to conclude that the annual snowfall amount in Minneapolis from 1884 until 2012 follows the normal probability distribution.

b. p-value $=$ CHISQ.DIST.RT (6.051, 2) $= 0.0485$

Because the p-value $= 0.0485$ and is greater than $\alpha = 0.01$, we fail to reject the null hypothesis.

12.44 a. H_0: Voters' responses about the economy and their party affiliations are independent

H_1: Voters' responses about the economy and their party affiliations are not independent

CELL	f_o	f_e	$(f_o - f_e)$	$(f_o - f_e)^2$	$\frac{(f_o - f_e)^2}{f_e}$
Get worse–Democrat	34	30.99	3.01	9.06	0.293
Get worse–Republican	30	32.65	−2.65	7.02	0.215
Get worse–Independent	19	19.37	−0.37	0.14	0.007
Stay the same–Democrat	17	17.17	−0.17	0.03	0.002
Stay the same–Republican	22	18.09	3.91	15.29	0.844
Stay the same–Independent	7	10.73	−3.73	13.91	1.299
Get better–Democrat	5	7.84	−2.84	8.07	1.029
Get better–Republican	7	8.26	−1.26	1.59	0.192
Get better–Independent	9	4.90	4.10	16.81	3.431
Total					$\chi^2 = \mathbf{7.312}$

$r = 3; c = 3; df = 4; \chi^2_{0.01} = 13.277$

$\chi^2 \leq \chi^2_{0.01} \rightarrow$ Do not reject H_0

b. Conclusion: Voters' responses about the economy and their party affiliations are independent.

12.46 a. $\hat{p} = \dfrac{7 + 11 + 7 + 8 + 5}{382} = 0.099$

DEALERSHIP	f_o	f_e	$(f_o - f_e)$	$(f_o - f_e)^2$	$\frac{(f_o - f_e)^2}{f_e}$
Aston—yes	7	5.64	1.36	1.85	0.328
Aston—no	50	51.36	−1.36	1.85	0.036
Dover—yes	11	9.01	1.99	3.96	0.440
Dover—no	80	81.99	−1.99	3.96	0.048
Springfield—yes	7	9.21	−2.21	4.88	0.530
Springfield—no	86	83.79	2.21	4.88	0.058
Media—yes	8	8.81	−0.81	0.66	0.075
Media—no	81	80.19	0.81	0.66	0.008
Newark—yes	5	5.15	−0.15	0.02	0.004
Newark—no	47	46.85	0.15	0.02	0.000
Total					$\chi^2 = \mathbf{1.527}$

$k = 5; m = 0; df = 4; \chi^2_{0.05} = 9.488$

$\chi^2 \leq \chi^2_{0.05} \rightarrow$ Do not reject H_0

The proportion of new cars requiring warranty work does not differ among these five dealerships.

c. p-value = 0.82. Because the p-value is greater than $\alpha = 0.05$, there is not enough evidence to reject the null hypothesis.

12.48 a. H_0: The number of cruises and a customer's satisfaction rating are independent

H_1: The number of cruises and a customer's satisfaction rating are not independent

CELL	f_o	f_e	$(f_o - f_e)$	$(f_o - f_e)^2$	$\frac{(f_o - f_e)^2}{f_e}$
Excellent/1–3	20	27.81	−7.81	61.00	2.193
Excellent/4–6	26	21.89	4.11	16.89	0.771
Excellent/7 or more	25	21.30	3.70	13.69	0.643
Good/1–3	42	32.12	9.88	97.61	3.041
Good/4–6	20	25.28	−5.28	27.88	1.104
Good/7 or more	20	24.60	−4.60	21.16	0.860
Average/1–3	18	17.62	0.38	0.14	0.008
Average/4–6	15	13.88	1.12	1.25	0.091
Average/7 or more	12	13.50	−1.5	2.25	0.167
Fair/1–3	10	9.40	0.60	0.36	0.038
Fair/4–6	6	7.40	−1.40	1.96	0.265
Fair/7 or more	8	7.20	0.80	0.64	0.089
Poor/1–3	4	7.05	−3.05	9.30	1.320
Poor/4–6	7	5.55	1.45	2.10	0.379
Poor/7 or more	7	5.40	1.60	2.56	0.474
Total					χ^2 = **11.443**

$r = 5; c = 3; df = 8; \chi^2_{0.05} = 15.507$

$\chi^2 \leq \chi^2_{0.05} \rightarrow$ Do not reject H_0

b. Conclusion: The number of cruises and a customer's satisfaction rating are independent.

12.50 a. H_0: The size of the employee's organization and his or her paid sick days category are independent

H_1: The size of the employee's organization and his or her paid sick days category are not independent

CELL	f_o	f_e	$(f_o - f_e)$	$(f_o - f_e)^2$	$\frac{(f_o - f_e)^2}{f_e}$
99 or less—yes	47	58.41	−11.41	130.19	2.229
99 or less—no	43	31.59	11.41	130.19	4.121
100 to 499—yes	53	51.92	1.08	1.17	0.023
100 to 499—no	27	28.08	−1.08	1.17	0.042
500 or more—yes	59	48.67	10.33	106.71	2.193
500 or more—yes	16	26.33	−10.33	106.71	4.053
Total					χ^2 = **12.661**

$r = 3; c = 2; df = (3 - 1)(2 - 1) = 2; \alpha = 0.05; \chi^2_{0.05} = 5.991$

$\chi^2 > \chi^2_{0.05} \rightarrow 12.661 > 5.991 \rightarrow$ Reject H_0

The size of the employee's organization and his or her paid sick days category are not independent.

b. p-value = CHISQ.DIST.RT (12.661, 2) = 0.0018

Because the p-value = 0.0018 and is less than $\alpha = 0.05$, we reject the null hypothesis.

12.52 a. H_0: The observed email frequency distribution is consistent with the Intermedia report

H_1: The observed email frequency distribution is not consistent with the Intermedia report

DAY	f_o	$P(x)$	f_e	$(f_o - f_e)$	$(f_o - f_e)^2$	$\frac{(f_o - f_e)^2}{f_e}$
Monday	33	0.15	30.0	3.0	9.0	0.300
Tuesday	51	0.23	46.0	5.0	25.0	0.543
Wednesday	48	0.22	44.0	4.0	16.0	0.364
Thursday	42	0.21	42.0	0.0	0.0	0.000
Friday	26	0.19	38.0	−12.0	144.0	3.789
Total	**200**					χ^2 = **4.996**

$k = 5; m = 0; df = 5 - 0 - 1 = 4; \alpha = 0.05; \chi^2_{0.05} = 9.488$

$\chi^2 \leq \chi^2_{0.05} \rightarrow 4.996 < 9.488 \rightarrow$ Do not reject H_0

The observed email frequency distribution is consistent with the Intermedia report.

b. p-value = CHISQ.DIST.RT (4.996, 4) = 0.2877

Because the p-value = 0.2877 and is greater than $\alpha = 0.05$, we fail to reject the null hypothesis.

12.54 a. H_0: The population bedroom distribution follows the stated distribution

H_1: The population bedroom distribution does not follows the stated distribution

BEDROOMS	f_o	f_e	$(f_o - f_e)$	$(f_o - f_e)^2$	$\frac{(f_o - f_e)^2}{f_e}$
2	4	6.0	−2.0	4.00	0.667
3	10	14.0	−4.0	16.00	1.143
4	27	17.5	9.5	90.25	5.157
5	8	7.5	0.5	0.25	0.033
6	1	5.0	−4.0	16.00	3.200
Total					$\chi^2 = \sum \frac{(f_o - f_e)^2}{f_e}$ = **10.200**

$df = k - m - 1 = 5 - 0 - 1 = 4; \alpha = 0.10; \chi^2_\alpha = 7.779.$

Because $\chi^2 = 10.2$ is more than $\chi^2_\alpha = 7.779$, we reject the null hypothesis and conclude that this sample does not support the stated probability distribution for number of bedrooms of rental properties.

b. p-value = CHISQ.DIST.RT (10.2, 4) = 0.0372

Because the p-value = 0.0372 and is less than $\alpha = 0.10$, we reject the null hypothesis.

12.56 H_0: The number of customers per day visiting Island Art follows the normal probability distribution

H_1: The number of customers per day visiting Island Art does not follow the normal probability distribution

$\bar{x} = 503; s = 198; n > 220 \rightarrow$ number of intervals = 6

$x = 503 + (2.0)(198) = 899$

$x = 503 + (1.0)(198) = 701$

$x = 503 - (1.0)(198) = 305$

$x = 503 - (2.0)(198) = 107$

x INTERVAL	z INTERVAL	f_o	P(x)	f_e	$(f_o - f_e)$	$(f_o - f_e)^2$	$\frac{(f_o - f_e)^2}{f_e}$
Less than 107	$z \le -2.0$	4	0.0228	5.5	−1.5	2.25	0.409
107 to 305	$-2.0 < z \le -1.0$	38	0.1359	32.6	5.4	29.16	0.894
305 to 503	$-1.0 < z \le 0.0$	80	0.3413	81.9	−1.9	3.61	0.044
503 to 701	$0.0 < z \le 1.0$	79	0.3413	81.9	−2.9	8.41	0.103
701 to 899	$1.0 < z \le 2.0$	31	0.1359	32.6	−1.6	2.56	0.079
More than 899	$z > 2.0$	8	0.0228	5.5	2.5	6.25	1.136
Total		**240**					$\chi^2 = 2.665$

$k = 6; m = 2; df = 3; \chi^2_{0.05} = 7.815$
$\chi^2 \le \chi^2_{0.05} \rightarrow$ Do not reject H_0
Conclusion: The number of customers per day visiting Island Art follows the normal probability distribution.

Chapter 13

13.2 $H_0: \sigma^2 \le 9.0$
$H_1: \sigma^2 > 9.0$
$$\chi^2 = \frac{(25 - 1)(3.4)^2}{9} = 30.827$$
$df = 24; \chi^2_{0.10} = 33.196$
$\chi^2 < \chi^2_{0.10} \rightarrow$ Do not reject H_0

13.4 $H_0: \sigma^2 = 39.0$
$H_1: \sigma^2 \ne 39.0$
$$\chi^2 = \frac{(40 - 1)(6.5)^2}{39} = 42.250$$
$df = 39; \chi^2_{0.975} = 23.654; \chi^2_{0.025} = 58.120$
$\chi^2_{0.975} \le \chi^2 \le \chi^2_{0.025} \rightarrow$ Do not reject H_0

13.6 **a.** $H_0: \sigma^2 \ge 144.0$
$H_1: \sigma^2 < 144.0$
$$s = 8.35; \chi^2 = \frac{(24 - 1)(8.35)^2}{144} = 11.14$$
$df = 23; \chi^2_{0.95} = 13.091$
$\chi^2 \le \chi^2_{0.95} \rightarrow$ Reject H_0

c. p-value $= 0.0182 < 0.05 \rightarrow$ Reject H_0
There is enough evidence to conclude that the standard deviation for the delivery times by Seasons Pizza is less than 12 minutes after improvements have been made.

13.8 **a.** $H_0: \sigma^2 = 16.0$
$H_1: \sigma^2 \ne 16.0$
$$s = 4.56; \chi^2 = \frac{(40 - 1)(4.56)^2}{16} = 50.68$$
$df = 39; \chi^2_{0.975} = 23.654; \chi^2_{0.025} = 58.120$
$\chi^2_{0.975} \le \chi^2 \le \chi^2_{0.025} \rightarrow$ Do not reject H_0

c. p-value $= 0.0996 > 0.05 \rightarrow$ Do not reject H_0
There is not enough evidence to conclude that the standard deviation of the temperature in the freezer of Amana's refrigerator is not equal to 4°F.

13.10 $H_0: \sigma_1^2 \le \sigma_2^2$
$H_1: \sigma_1^2 > \sigma_2^2$
$$F = \frac{(18)^2}{(15)^2} = 1.440; D_1 = 24; D_2 = 19; F_\alpha = 2.114$$
$F \le F_\alpha \rightarrow$ Do not reject H_0

13.12 $H_0: \sigma_1^2 = \sigma_2^2$
$H_1: \sigma_1^2 \ne \sigma_2^2$
$$F = \frac{(63)^2}{(41)^2} = 2.361; D_1 = 24; D_2 = 27; \alpha/2 = 0.025; F_{\alpha/2} = 2.195$$
$F > F_{\alpha/2} \rightarrow$ Reject H_0

13.14 **a.** $H_0: \sigma_1^2 \le \sigma_2^2$
$H_1: \sigma_1^2 > \sigma_2^2$
$$F = \frac{(10.4)^2}{(6.5)^2} = 2.560; D_1 = 23; D_2 = 20; F_\alpha = 2.092$$
$F > F_\alpha \rightarrow$ Reject H_0

c. p-value $= 0.0188 < 0.05 \rightarrow$ Reject H_0
There is enough evidence to conclude that Route 1 provides a more consistent commute time than Route 2.

13.16 **a.** $H_0: \sigma_1^2 = \sigma_2^2$
$H_1: \sigma_1^2 \ne \sigma_2^2$
$$F = \frac{(6300)^2}{(5200)^2} = 1.468; D_1 = 29; D_2 = 26; \alpha/2 = 0.025;$$
$F_{\alpha/2} = 2.165$
$F \le F_{\alpha/2} \rightarrow$ Do not reject H_0

c. p-value $= 0.326 > 0.05 \rightarrow$ Do not reject H_0
There is not enough evidence to conclude that there is a difference in the variability of the salaries for high school teachers in Cape May County compared with those for Camden County.

13.18 **a.** $H_0: \sigma^2 \ge 64.0$
$H_1: \sigma^2 < 64.0$
$$s = 6.13; \chi^2 = \frac{(20 - 1)(6.13)^2}{64} = 11.156$$
$df = 19; \chi^2_{0.95} = 10.117$
$\chi^2 > \chi^2_{0.95} \rightarrow$ Do not reject H_0

c. p-value $= 0.0815 > 0.05 \rightarrow$ Do not reject H_0
There is not enough evidence to conclude that the standard deviation of doctors' working hours per week is below 8 hours.

13.20 **a.** $H_0: \sigma_1^2 = \sigma_2^2$
$H_1: \sigma_1^2 \ne \sigma_2^2$
$s_1 = 2.48; n_1 = 10; s_2 = 2.21; n_2 = 10$
$$F = \frac{(2.48)^2}{(2.21)^2} = 1.259; D_1 = 9; D_2 = 9;$$
$\alpha/2 = 0.025; F_{\alpha/2} = 4.026$
$F \le F_{\alpha/2} \rightarrow 1.259 < 4.026 \rightarrow$ Do not reject H_0

c. p-value $= 0.743 > 0.05 \rightarrow$ Do not reject H_0
There is not enough evidence to conclude that there is a difference in the variability of the mileage obtained by the standard and low-profile types of tires.

13.22 a. $H_0: \sigma^2 \geq 0.0016$

$H_1: \sigma^2 < 0.0016$

$$s = 0.031;\ \chi^2 = \frac{(12-1)(0.031)^2}{0.0016} = 6.61$$

$df = 11;\ \chi^2_{0.95} = 4.575$

$\chi^2 > \chi^2_{0.95} \rightarrow$ Do not reject H_0

c. p-value $= 0.170 > 0.05 \rightarrow$ Do not reject H_0
There is not enough evidence to conclude that the standard deviation of the pretzel weights is less than 0.04 ounces.

13.24 a. $H_0: \sigma^2 \leq 9.0$

$H_1: \sigma^2 > 9.0$

$$s = 3.37;\ \chi^2 = \frac{(18-1)(3.37)^2}{9} = 21.45$$

$df = 17;\ \chi^2_{0.05} = 27.587$

$\chi^2 \leq \chi^2_{0.05} \rightarrow$ Do not reject H_0

c. p-value $= 0.207 > 0.05 \rightarrow$ Do not reject H_0
There is not enough evidence to conclude that the standard deviation of the tips at Tony's Bistro exceeds \$3.00, so there is no indication of inconsistent service.

13.26 a. $H_0: \sigma_1^2 = \sigma_2^2$

$H_1: \sigma_1^2 \neq \sigma_2^2$

$s_1 = 1.05;\ s_2 = 0.80;$

$$F = \frac{(1.05)^2}{(0.80)^2} = 1.72;\ D_1 = 10;\ D_2 = 11;$$

$\alpha/2 = 0.05;\ F_{\alpha/2} = 2.854$

$F \leq F_{\alpha/2} \rightarrow$ Do not reject H_0

b. p-value $= 0.393 > 0.10 \rightarrow$ Do not reject H_0
There is not enough evidence to conclude that there is a difference in the variability of the flight times for US Airways and Air France for nonstop flights from Paris to Philadelphia.

13.28 a. $H_0: \sigma^2 \geq 250{,}000$

$H_1: \sigma^2 < 250{,}000$

$$s = 378;\ n = 28;\ \chi^2 = \frac{(28-1)(378)^2}{250{,}000} = 15.43$$

$\alpha = 0.05;\ df = 27;\ \chi^2_{0.95} = 16.151$

$\chi^2 < \chi^2_{0.95} \rightarrow 15.43 < 16.151 \rightarrow$ Reject H_0

c. p-value $= 0.0371 < 0.05 \rightarrow$ Reject H_0
There is enough evidence to conclude that the population standard deviation for the life of Edalight's CFL bulbs is less than 500 hours. Therefore, their goal is being met.

13.30 a. $H_0: \sigma^2 = 0.09$

$H_1: \sigma^2 \neq 0.09$

$$s = 0.45;\ n = 15;\ \chi^2 = \frac{(15-1)(0.45)^2}{0.09} = 31.50$$

$\alpha = 0.05;\ df = 14;\ \chi^2_{0.975} = 5.629;\ \chi^2_{0.025} = 26.119$

$\chi^2 > \chi^2_{0.025} \rightarrow 31.50 > 26.119 \rightarrow$ Reject H_0

c. p-value $= 0.0047 < 0.05 \rightarrow$ Reject H_0
There is enough evidence to conclude that the standard deviation for the pH readings at 10:00 A.M. does not equal 0.30.

13.32 a. $H_0: \sigma_1^2 = \sigma_2^2$

$H_1: \sigma_1^2 \neq \sigma_2^2$

$s_1 = 147;\ n_1 = 23;\ s_2 = 102;\ n_2 = 27$

$$F = \frac{(147)^2}{(102)^2} = 2.08;\ D_1 = 22;\ D_2 = 26;\ \alpha/2 = 0.05;\ F_{\alpha/2} = 1.966$$

$F > F_{\alpha/2} \rightarrow 2.08 > 1.966 \rightarrow$ Reject H_0

c. p-value $= 0.0758 < 0.10 \rightarrow$ Reject H_0
There is enough evidence to conclude that there is a difference in the population variance for the miles driven per month for teenage males and teenage females.

13.34 a. $H_0: \sigma^2 \leq 0.0001$

$H_1: \sigma^2 > 0.0001$

$$s = 0.0110;\ \chi^2 = \frac{(25-1)(0.0110)^2}{0.0001} = 29.04$$

$df = 24;\ \chi^2_{0.05} = 36.415$

$\chi^2 \leq \chi^2_{0.05} \rightarrow$ Do not reject H_0

c. p-value $= 0.219 > 0.05 \rightarrow$ Do not reject H_0
There is not enough evidence to conclude that the standard deviation for the thickness of the glass exceeds 0.01 in.; the process does not need to be corrected.

13.36 a. $H_0: \sigma_1^2 \leq \sigma_2^2$

$H_1: \sigma_1^2 > \sigma_2^2$

$s_1 = 2.245;\ s_2 = 1.583;$

$$F = \frac{(2.245)^2}{(1.583)^2} = 2.011;\ D_1 = 23;\ D_2 = 23;\ F_\alpha = 2.014$$

$F \leq F_\alpha \rightarrow$ Do not reject H_0

c. p-value $= 0.0504 > 0.05 \rightarrow$ Do not reject H_0
There is not enough evidence to conclude that the variability in the ratings for the Pepsi product is greater than the variability in the ratings for the Coke product.

Chapter 14

14.2 $H_0: \rho = 0$

$H_1: \rho \neq 0$

$r = 0.672;\ df = 3;\ t_{\alpha/2} = 3.182$

$$t = \frac{0.672}{\sqrt{\dfrac{1-(0.672)^2}{5-2}}} = 1.570$$

$|t| \leq |t_{\alpha/2}| \rightarrow$ Do not reject H_0

14.4 $H_0: \rho \geq 0$

$H_1: \rho < 0$

$r = 0.420;\ df = 2;\ -t_\alpha = -2.920$

$$t = \frac{-0.420}{\sqrt{\dfrac{1-(-0.420)^2}{4-2}}} = -0.655$$

$t \geq -t_\alpha \rightarrow$ Do not reject H_0

14.6 $H_0: \rho = 0$

$H_1: \rho \neq 0$

$r = 0.716;\ n = 10;\ df = 8;\ t_{\alpha/2} = 2.896$

$$t = \frac{0.716}{\sqrt{\dfrac{1-(0.716)^2}{10-2}}} = 2.900$$

$|t| > |t_{\alpha/2}| \rightarrow$ Reject H_0

Conclusion: There is a significant correlation between a person's age and credit score.

14.8 $H_0: \rho \geq 0$

$H_1: \rho < 0$

$r = -0.892;\ n = 7;\ df = 5;\ -t_\alpha = -1.476$

$$t = \frac{-0.892}{\sqrt{\dfrac{1-(0.892)^2}{7-2}}} = -4.416$$

$t < -t_\alpha \rightarrow$ Reject H_0

Conclusion: There is enough evidence to conclude that the correlation between the selling price and the demand for the camera is less than zero.

14.10 $H_0: \rho \leq 0$

$H_1: \rho > 0$

$r = 0.802; n = 8; df = 6; t_\alpha = 1.943$

$$t = \frac{0.802}{\sqrt{\dfrac{1 - (0.802)^2}{8 - 2}}} = 3.287$$

$t > t_\alpha \rightarrow$ Reject H_0

Conclusion: There is enough evidence to conclude that the correlation between the starting salary and the GPA of a University of Delaware business graduate is greater than zero.

14.12 $H_0: \rho = 0$

$H_1: \rho \neq 0$

$r = 0.740; n = 7; df = 5; t_{\alpha/2} = 2.015$

$$t = \frac{0.740}{\sqrt{\dfrac{1 - (0.740)^2}{7 - 2}}} = 2.458$$

$|t| > |t_{\alpha/2}| \rightarrow$ Reject H_0

Conclusion: There is a significant correlation between a house's selling price and its square footage.

14.14 $R^2 = \dfrac{5.0625}{11.20} = 0.4518$

$H_0: \rho^2 \leq 0$

$H_1: \rho^2 > 0$

$D_1 = 1; D_2 = 3; F_\alpha = 10.128$

$$F = \frac{5.0625}{\left(\dfrac{6.1375}{(5 - 2)}\right)} = 2.475$$

$F \leq F_\alpha \rightarrow$ Do not reject H_0

14.16 $R^2 = \dfrac{10.3137}{13.00} = 0.793$

$H_0: \rho^2 \leq 0$

$H_1: \rho^2 > 0$

$D_1 = 1; D_2 = 2; F_\alpha = 18.513$

$$F = \frac{10.3137}{\left(\dfrac{2.6863}{(4 - 2)}\right)} = 7.679$$

$F \leq F_\alpha \rightarrow$ Do not reject H_0

14.18 **a.** $SST = 9{,}806 - \dfrac{(270)^2}{8} = 693.5$

b. $SSE = 279.3596$

$SSR = 414.1404$

c. $R^2 = \dfrac{414.1404}{693.5000} = 0.5972$

d. $H_0: \rho^2 \leq 0$

$H_1: \rho^2 > 0$

$D_1 = 1; D_2 = 6; F_\alpha = 5.987$

$$F = \frac{414.1404}{\left(\dfrac{279.3596}{(8 - 2)}\right)} = 8.895$$

$F > F_\alpha \rightarrow$ Reject H_0

14.20 **a.** $\sum x = 2{,}360; \sum y = 26.7; \sum xy = 7{,}939;$

$\sum x^2 = 701{,}600; \sum y^2 = 90.23$

$$b_1 = \frac{(8)(7{,}939) - (2{,}360)(26.7)}{(8)(701{,}600) - (2{,}360)^2} = 0.01157$$

$$b_0 = \frac{26.7}{8} - (0.01157)\left(\frac{2{,}360}{8}\right) = -0.07565$$

14.22 $s_e = \sqrt{\dfrac{9.727}{5 - 2}} = 1.801; x = 5$

$\hat{y} = 3.045 + (0.409)(5) = 5.09$

$\sum x = 19; \sum x^2 = 81$

$\bar{x} = \dfrac{19}{5} = 3.8; df = 3; t_{\alpha/2} = 3.182$

$$CI = 5.090 \pm (3.182)(1.801)\sqrt{\frac{1}{5} + \frac{(5 - 3.8)^2}{81 - \dfrac{(19)^2}{5}}}$$

$= 5.090 \pm 3.458$

$LCL = 1.632; UCL = 8.548$

14.24 $s_e = \sqrt{\dfrac{3.547}{6 - 2}} = 0.942; x = 3$

$\hat{y} = 1.679 + (0.584)(3) = 3.431$

$\sum x = 17; \sum x^2 = 71$

$\bar{x} = 2.833; df = 4; t_{\alpha/2} = 2.132$

$$CI = 2.833 \pm (2.132)(0.942)\sqrt{\frac{1}{6} + \frac{(3 - 2.833)^2}{71 - \dfrac{(17)^2}{6}}}$$

$= 2.833 \pm 0.823$

$LCL = 2.608; UCL = 4.254$

14.26 **a.** $\sum x = 232; \sum y = 1{,}181; \sum xy = 39{,}833;$

$\sum x^2 = 8{,}004; \sum y^2 = 203{,}415$

$$b_1 = \frac{(7)(39{,}833) - (232)(1{,}181)}{(7)(8{,}004) - (232)^2} = 2.196$$

$$b_0 = \frac{1{,}181}{7} - (2.1956)\left(\frac{232}{7}\right) = 95.946; SSE = 2{,}629.5$$

$s_e = \sqrt{\dfrac{2{,}629.5}{7 - 2}} = 22.933; x = 30$

$\hat{y} = 95.946 + (2.196)(30) = 161.826$

$\bar{x} = \dfrac{232}{7} = 33.14; df = 5; t_{\alpha/2} = 2.571$

$$CI = 161.83 \pm (2.571)(22.933)\sqrt{\frac{1}{7} + \frac{(30 - 33.14)^2}{8{,}004 - \dfrac{(232)^2}{7}}}$$

$= 161.83 \pm 24.65$

$LCL = 137.18; UCL = 186.48$

14.28 **a.** $\sum x = 168.8; \sum y = 62; \sum xy = 1{,}400.2;$

$\sum x^2 = 3{,}690.5; \sum y^2 = 582$

$$b_1 = \frac{(8)(1{,}400.2) - (168.8)(62)}{(8)(3{,}690.5) - (168.8)^2} = 0.714$$

$$b_0 = \frac{62}{8} - (0.714)\left(\frac{168.8}{8}\right) = -7.315$$

$SSE = 35.787$

$s_e = \sqrt{\dfrac{35.787}{8 - 2}} = 2.442; x = 21$

$\hat{y} = -7.315 + (0.714)(21) = 7.68$

$\bar{x} = 21.1; df = 6; t_{\alpha/2} = 1.943$

$$CI = 7.68 \pm (1.943)(2.442)\sqrt{\frac{1}{8} + \frac{(21 - 21.1)^2}{3{,}690.5 - \dfrac{(168.8)^2}{8}}}$$

$= 7.68 \pm 1.68$

$LCL = 6.00; UCL = 9.36$

14.30 a. $\sum x = 24{,}600;\ \sum y = 3{,}360;\ \sum xy = 8{,}376{,}000;$
$\sum x^2 = 61{,}520{,}000;\ \sum y^2 = 1{,}156{,}000$

$$b_1 = \frac{(10)(8{,}376{,}000) - (24{,}600)(3{,}360)}{(10)(61{,}520{,}000) - (24{,}600)^2} = 0.11$$

$$b_0 = \frac{3{,}360}{10} - (0.11)\left(\frac{24{,}600}{10}\right) = 65.4$$

$SSE = 14{,}896$

$$s_e = \sqrt{\frac{14{,}896}{10-2}} = 43.15;\ x = 2{,}400$$

$\hat{y} = 65.4 + (0.11)(2{,}400) = 329.40$

$\bar{x} = 2{,}460;\ df = 8;\ t_{\alpha/2} = 1.860$

$$CI = 329.4 \pm (1.860)(43.15)\sqrt{\frac{1}{10} + \frac{(2400 - 2{,}460)^2}{61{,}520{,}000 - \dfrac{(24{,}600)^2}{10}}}$$

$= 329.40 \pm 25.84$

$LCL = 303.56;\ UCL = 355.24$

14.32 $H_0\colon \beta_1 = 0$
$H_1\colon \beta_1 \neq 0$
$SSE = 0.7955;\ \sum x^2 = 81;\ n = 5;\ \bar{x} = 3.8$

$$s_e = \sqrt{\frac{0.7955}{3}} = 0.515;\ s_b = \frac{0.515}{\sqrt{81 - (5)(3.8)^2}} = 0.174$$

$b_1 = 0.977;\ df = 3;\ t_{\alpha/2} = 3.182$

$$t = \frac{0.977 - 0}{0.174} = 5.615$$

$|t| > |t_{\alpha/2}| \rightarrow$ Reject H_0

14.34 $H_0\colon \beta_1 = 0$
$H_1\colon \beta_1 \neq 0$
$SSE = 7.650;\ \sum x^2 = 71;\ \bar{x} = 2.83$

$$s_e = \sqrt{\frac{7.650}{4}} = 1.383;\ s_b = \frac{1.383}{\sqrt{71 - (6)(2.83)^2}} = 0.289$$

$b_1 = 0.285;\ df = 4;\ t_{\alpha/2} = 2.132$

$$t = \frac{0.285 - 0}{0.289} = 0.986$$

$|t| \leq |t_{\alpha/2}| \rightarrow$ Do not reject H_0

14.36 b. $\sum x = 122;\ \sum y = 16{,}900;\ \sum xy = 260{,}500;$
$\sum x^2 = 1{,}888;\ \sum y^2 = 36{,}510{,}000$

$$b_1 = \frac{(8)(260{,}500) - (122)(16{,}900)}{(8)(1{,}888) - (122)^2} = 100.91$$

$$b_0 = \frac{16{,}900}{8} - (100.91)\left(\frac{122}{8}\right) = 573.62$$

$H_0\colon \beta_1 = 0$
$H_1\colon \beta_1 \neq 0$
$SSE = 528{,}767$
$\bar{x} = 15.25$

$$s_e = \sqrt{\frac{528{,}767}{6}} = 296.9;\ s_b = \frac{296.9}{\sqrt{1{,}888 - (8)(15.25)^2}} = 56.62$$

$b_1 = 100.91;\ df = 6;\ t_{\alpha/2} = 2.447$

$$t = \frac{100.91 - 0}{56.62} = 1.782$$

$|t| \leq |t_{\alpha/2}| \rightarrow$ Do not reject H_0

14.38 b. $\sum x = 66;\ \sum y = 33.36;\ \sum xy = 202.71;\ \sum x^2 = 506;$
$\sum y^2 = 101.2966$

$$b_1 = \frac{(11)(202.71) - (66)(33.36)}{(11)(506) - (66)^2} = 0.023$$

$$b_0 = \frac{16{,}900}{11} - (0.023)\left(\frac{66}{11}\right) = 2.895$$

$H_0\colon \beta_1 = 0$
$H_1\colon \beta_1 \neq 0$
$SSE = 0.057$
$\bar{x} = 6$

$$s_e = \sqrt{\frac{0.057}{9}} = 0.08;\ s_b = \frac{0.08}{\sqrt{506 - (8)(6)^2}} = 0.0054$$

$b_1 = 0.023;\ df = 9;\ t_{\alpha/2} = 2.262$

$$t = \frac{0.023 - 0}{0.0054} = 4.259$$

$|t| > |t_{\alpha/2}| \rightarrow$ Reject H_0

c. There is a significant relationship between GPA and years, which supports the existence of grade inflation.

14.40 b. $\sum x = 213;\ \sum y = 1{,}510;\ \sum xy = 33{,}598;\ \sum x^2 = 5{,}281;$
$\sum y^2 = 304{,}162$

$$b_1 = \frac{(12)(33{,}598) - (213)(1{,}510)}{(12)(5{,}281) - (213)^2} = 4.53$$

$$b_0 = \frac{1{,}510}{12} - (4.53)\left(\frac{213}{12}\right) = 45.43$$

$H_0\colon \beta_1 = 0$
$H_1\colon \beta_1 \neq 0$
$SSE = 83{,}363.8$
$\bar{x} = 17.75$

$$s_e = \sqrt{\frac{83{,}363.8}{10}} = 91.3;\ s_b = \frac{91.3}{\sqrt{5{,}281 - (12)(17.75)^2}} = 2.36$$

$b_1 = 4.53;\ df = 10;\ t_{\alpha/2} = 2.228$

$$t = \frac{4.53 - 0}{2.36} = 1.919$$

$|t| \leq |t_{\alpha/2}| \rightarrow$ Do not reject H_0

c. There is no significant relationship between a purchaser's time on the Web site and his or her order size.

14.42 a. $\sum x = 25;\ \sum y = 30;\ \sum xy = 106;\ \sum x^2 = 121;$
$\sum y^2 = 178$

$$r = \frac{(6)(106) - (25)(30)}{\sqrt{[(6)(121) - (25)^2][(6)(178) - (30)^2]}} = -0.875$$

b. $H_0\colon \rho \geq 0$
$H_1\colon \rho < 0$
$r = -0.875;\ df = 4;\ -t_\alpha = -2.132$

$$t = \frac{-0.875}{\sqrt{\dfrac{1 - (0.875)^2}{6 - 2}}} = -3.616$$

$t < -t_\alpha \rightarrow$ Reject H_0

14.44 a. $R^2 = \dfrac{21.44}{48} = 0.447$

b. $H_0\colon \rho^2 \leq 0$
$H_1\colon \rho^2 > 0$
$D_1 = 1;\ D_2 = 4;\ F_\alpha = 7.709$

$$F = \frac{21.44}{\left(\dfrac{6.56}{(6-2)}\right)} = 13.07$$

$F > F_\alpha \rightarrow$ Reject H_0

14.46 a. $H_0\colon \beta_1 = 0$
$H_1\colon \beta_1 \neq 0$
$SSE = 6.56;\ \bar{x} = 4.17;\ s_e = 1.281$

$$s_b = \frac{1.281}{\sqrt{121 - (6)(4.17)^2}} = 0.3138$$

$b_1 = -1.1287; df = 4; t_{\alpha/2} = 2.776$

$$t = \frac{-1.1287 - 0}{0.3138} = -3.597$$

$|t| > |t_{\alpha/2}| \rightarrow$ Reject H_0

b. $b_1 = -1.1287; s_b = 0.3138; df = 4; t_{\alpha/2} = 2.776$

$CI = -1.1287 \pm (2.776)(0.3138) = -1.1287 \pm 0.8711$

$LCL = -1.9998; UCL = -0.2576$

14.48 a. $R^2 = \frac{76.97}{96.89} = 0.794$

b. $H_0: \rho^2 \le 0$

$H_1: \rho^2 > 0$

$D_1 = 1; D_2 = 7; F_\alpha = 5.591$

$$F = \frac{76.97}{\left(\frac{19.92}{(9-2)}\right)} = 27.048$$

$F > F_\alpha \rightarrow$ Reject H_0

c. $s_e = \sqrt{\frac{19.92}{9-2}} = 1.687; x = 2.5$

$\hat{y} = 37.722 - (4.729)(2.5) = 25.9$

$\bar{x} = 2.67; df = 7; t_{\alpha/2} = 2.365$

$$CI = 25.90 \pm (2.365)(1.687)\sqrt{\frac{1}{9} + \frac{(2.50 - 2.67)^2}{67.44 - \frac{(24)^2}{9}}}$$

$= 25.90 \pm 1.38$

$LCL = 24.52; UCL = 27.28$

d. $$PI = 25.90 \pm (2.365)(1.687)\sqrt{1 + \frac{1}{9} + \frac{(2.5 - 2.67)^2}{67.44 - \frac{(24)^2}{9}}}$$

$= 25.90 \pm 4.22$

$LPL = 21.68; UPL = 30.12$

14.50 b. $\sum x = 50; \sum y = 147; \sum xy = 694; \sum x^2 = 334;$
$\sum y^2 = 2{,}231$

$$b_1 = \frac{(10)(694) - (50)(147)}{(10)(334) - (50)^2} = -0.4881$$

$$b_0 = \frac{147}{10} - (-0.4881)\left(\frac{50}{10}\right) = 17.1405$$

c. Because the slope is negative, we can conclude that a 1-minute increase in the number of minutes the person waited on hold will decrease the company's customer rating by an average of 0.4881.

d. $SST = 2{,}231 - \frac{(147)^2}{10} = 70.1$

e. $SSE = 50.09$

$SSR = 20.01$

14.52 a. $H_0: \beta_1 = 0$

$H_1: \beta_1 \ne 0$

$SSE = 50.09; \bar{x} = 5.0; s_e = 2.502$

$$s_b = \frac{2.502}{\sqrt{334 - (10)(5.0)^2}} = 0.273$$

$b_1 = -0.4881; df = 8; t_{\alpha/2} = 2.306$

$$t = \frac{-0.4881 - 0}{0.273} = -1.788$$

$|t| \le |t_{\alpha/2}| \rightarrow$ Do not reject H_0

b. $b_1 = -0.4881; s_b = 0.273; df = 8; t_{\alpha/2} = 2.306$

$CI = -0.4881 \pm (2.306)(0.273) = -0.4881 \pm 0.6295$

$LCL = -1.1176; UCL = 0.1414$

c. We are 95% confident that the true regression slope is between −1.1176 and 0.1414. Because this interval does include zero, we do not have evidence to conclude that there is a linear relationship between number of minutes on hold and customer rating.

14.54 a. $R^2 = \frac{0.32}{1.27} = 0.252$

b. $H_0: \rho^2 \le 0$

$H_1: \rho^2 > 0$

$D_1 = 1; D_2 = 6; F_\alpha = 5.987$

$$F = \frac{0.32}{\left(\frac{0.95}{(8-2)}\right)} = 2.021$$

$F \le F_\alpha \rightarrow$ Do not reject H_0

c. $s_e = \sqrt{\frac{0.95}{8-2}} = 0.398; x = 14$

$\hat{y} = 5.4722 - (0.1137)(14) = 3.88$

$\bar{x} = 13.94; df = 6; t_{\alpha/2} = 2.447$

$$CI = 3.88 \pm (2.447)(0.398)\sqrt{\frac{1}{8} + \frac{(14.00 - 13.94)^2}{1{,}578.37 - \frac{(111.5)^2}{8}}}$$

$= 3.88 \pm 0.34$

$LCL = 3.54; UCL = 4.22$

d. $$PI = 3.88 \pm (2.447)(0.398)\sqrt{1 + \frac{1}{8} + \frac{(14.00 - 13.94)^2}{1{,}578.37 - \frac{(111.5)^2}{8}}}$$

$= 3.88 \pm 1.03$

$LPL = 2.85; UPL = 4.91$

14.56 b. $\sum x = 62.4; \sum y = 244; \sum xy = 1{,}942.5; \sum x^2 = 492.4;$
$\sum y^2 = 7{,}824$

$$b_1 = \frac{(8)(1{,}942.5) - (62.4)(244)}{(8)(492.4) - (62.4)^2} = 6.919$$

$$b_0 = \frac{244}{8} - (6.919)\left(\frac{62.4}{8}\right) = -23.4682$$

c. Because the slope is positive, we can conclude that a one-unit increase in the employees' satisfaction level will increase the number of weekly activations by an average of 6.919.

d. $\hat{y} = -23.4682 + 6.919(7.5) = 28.4$

e. $SST = 7{,}824 - \frac{(244)^2}{8} = 382$

f. $SSE = 110.08$

$SSR = 271.92$

14.58 a. $R^2 = \frac{271.92}{382} = 0.712$

b. $H_0: \rho^2 \le 0$

$H_1: \rho^2 > 0$

$D_1 = 1; D_2 = 6; F_\alpha = 13.745$

$$F = \frac{271.92}{\left(\frac{110.08}{(8-2)}\right)} = 14.821; F > F_\alpha \rightarrow \text{Reject } H_0$$

c. $s_e = \sqrt{\frac{110.08}{8-2}} = 4.283; x = 8.0$

$\hat{y} = -23.4682 + (6.919)(8.0) = 31.88$

$\bar{x} = 7.8; df = 6; t_{\alpha/2} = 3.707$

$$CI = 31.88 \pm (3.707)(4.283)\sqrt{\frac{1}{8} + \frac{(8.0 - 7.8)^2}{492.4 - \frac{(62.4)^2}{8}}}$$

$= 31.88 \pm 5.76$

$LCL = 26.12; UCL = 37.64$

d. $PI = 31.88 \pm (3.707)(4.283)\sqrt{1 + \frac{1}{8} + \frac{(8.0 - 7.8)^2}{492.4 - \frac{(62.4)^2}{8}}}$

$= 31.88 \pm 16.89$

$LPL = 14.99; UPL = 48.77$

14.60 b. $\sum x = 82.5; \sum y = 81.6; \sum xy = 676.9; \sum x^2 = 683.25;$
$\sum y^2 = 677.68$

$$b_1 = \frac{(10)(676.9) - (82.5)(81.6)}{(10)(683.25) - (82.5)^2} = 1.4095$$

$$b_0 = \frac{81.6}{10} - (1.4095)\left(\frac{82.5}{10}\right) = -3.4684$$

c. Because the slope is positive, we can conclude that a one-unit increase in a mother's shoe size will correspond with an increase in an infant's birth weight by an average of 1.4095 lbs.

d. $\hat{y} = -3.4684 + 1.4095(8.5) = 8.51$ ounces

e. $SST = 677.68 - \frac{(81.6)^2}{10} = 11.82$

f. $SSE = 6.61$

$SSR = 5.21$

14.62 a. $R^2 = \frac{5.21}{11.82} = 0.441$

b. $H_0: \rho^2 \leq 0$

$H_1: \rho^2 > 0$

$D_1 = 1; D_2 = 8; F_\alpha = 3.458$

$$F = \frac{5.21}{\left(\frac{6.61}{(10 - 2)}\right)} = 6.306$$

$F > F_\alpha \rightarrow$ Reject H_0

c. $s_e = \sqrt{\frac{6.61}{10 - 2}} = 0.909; x = 8.5$

$\hat{y} = -3.4684 + (1.4095)(8.5) = 8.51$

$\bar{x} = 8.25; df = 8; t_{\alpha/2} = 1.860$

$$CI = 8.51 \pm (1.860)(0.909)\sqrt{\frac{1}{10} + \frac{(8.5 - 8.25)^2}{683.25 - \frac{(82.5)^2}{10}}}$$

$= 8.51 \pm 0.60$

$LCL = 7.91; UCL = 9.11$

d. $PI = 8.51 \pm (1.860)(0.909)\sqrt{1 + \frac{1}{10} + \frac{(8.5 - 8.25)^2}{683.25 - \frac{(82.5)^2}{10}}}$

$= 8.51 \pm 1.79$

$LPL = 6.72; UPL = 10.30$

14.64 a. $\sum x = 91.3; \sum y = 98.3; \sum xy = 1{,}371.92; \sum x^2 = 1{,}299.17;$
$\sum y^2 = 1{,}456.51$

$$r = \frac{(7)(1{,}371.92) - (91.3)(98.3)}{\sqrt{[(7)(1{,}299.17) - (91.3)^2][(7)(1{,}456.51) - (98.3)^2]}}$$

$= 0.989$

b. $H_0: \rho \leq 0$

$H_1: \rho > 0$

$r = 0.989; df = 5; t_\alpha = 3.365$

$$t = \frac{0.989}{\sqrt{\frac{1 - (0.989)^2}{7 - 2}}} = 14.98$$

$t > t_\alpha \rightarrow$ Reject H_0

c. There is enough evidence to conclude that the correlation between domestic and international flights is greater than zero. Customers' satisfaction with international flights tends to increase with their satisfaction with domestic flights.

14.66 a. $r = \frac{(9)(296) - (36)(64)}{\sqrt{[(9)(160) - (36)^2][(9)(584) - (64)^2]}} = 0.881$

b. $H_0: \rho \leq 0$

$H_1: \rho > 0$

$r = 0.881; df = 7; t_\alpha = 1.895$

$$t = \frac{0.881}{\sqrt{\frac{1 - (0.881)^2}{9 - 2}}} = 4.922$$

$t > t_\alpha \rightarrow$ Reject H_0

c. According to this sample, there is enough evidence to conclude that the correlation coefficient between shelf space and weekly sales is greater than zero. In other words, there is a positive linear relationship between them.

14.68 a. $H_0: \beta_1 = 0$

$H_1: \beta_1 \neq 0$

$SSE = 28.89; \bar{x} = 4.0; s_e = 2.032$

$$s_b = \frac{2.032}{\sqrt{160 - (9)(4.0)^2}} = 0.508$$

$b_1 = 2.5; df = 7; t_{\alpha/2} = 2.365$

$$t = \frac{2.5 - 0}{0.508} = 4.921$$

$|t| > |t_{\alpha/2}| \rightarrow$ Reject H_0

b. $b_1 = 2.5; s_b = 0.508; df = 7; t_{\alpha/2} = 2.365$

$CI = 2.50 \pm (2.365)(0.508) = 2.5 \pm 1.2$

$LCL = 1.3; UCL = 3.7$

c. We are 95% confident that a one-foot increase in shelf space will increase weekly sales between an average of \$1.30 and \$3.70 per week.

14.70 a. $r = \frac{(9)(1{,}931) - (24)(767)}{\sqrt{[(9)(102) - (24)^2][(9)(66{,}059) - (767)^2]}}$

$= -0.704$

b. $H_0: \rho \geq 0$

$H_1: \rho < 0$

$r = -0.704; df = 7; -t_\alpha = -1.895$

$$t = \frac{-0.704}{\sqrt{\frac{1 - (0.704)^2}{9 - 2}}} = -2.627$$

$t < -t_\alpha \rightarrow$ Reject H_0

c. According to this sample, there is enough evidence to conclude that the correlation coefficient between the number of classes missed and the final grade is less than zero. In other words, there is a negative linear relationship between them.

14.72 a. $H_0: \beta_1 = 0$

$H_1: \beta_1 \neq 0$

$SSE = 349.54; \bar{x} = 2.67; s_e = 7.066$

$$s_b = \frac{7.066}{\sqrt{102 - (9)(2.67)^2}} = 1.149$$

$b_1 = -3.0088; df = 7; t_{\alpha/2} = 2.365$

$$t = \frac{-3.0088 - 0}{1.149} = -2.619$$

$|t| > |t_{\alpha/2}| \rightarrow$ Reject H_0

b. $b_1 = -3.0088; s_b = 1.149; df = 7; t_{\alpha/2} = 2.365$
$CI = -3.0088 \pm (2.365)(1.149) = -3.0088 \pm 2.7174$
$LCL = -5.7262; UCL = -0.2914$

c. We are 95% confident that the true regression slope is between −5.7262 and −0.2914. Because this interval does not include zero, we have evidence to conclude that there is a linear relationship between number of missed classes and the final grade.

14.74 a. $\sum x = 271 \; \sum y = 294 \; \sum xy = 12{,}034$

$\sum x^2 = 11{,}115 \; \sum y^2 = 16{,}344$

$$b_1 = \frac{(7)(12{,}034) - (271)(294)}{(7)(11{,}115) - (271)^2} = \frac{4{,}564}{4{,}364} = 1.0458$$

$$b_0 = \frac{294}{7} - (1.0458)\left(\frac{271}{7}\right) = 1.5126$$

b. $\hat{y} = 1.5126 + 1.0458(32) = \$34.98$

c. Because the slope is positive, we can conclude that the increase of one year in the customer's age will increase the order size by an average of $1.0458.

$$SST = 16{,}344 - \frac{(294)^2}{7} = 3{,}996$$

d. $SSE = (16{,}344) - (1.5126)(294) - (1.0458)(12{,}034) = 3{,}314.14$

e. $SSR = 3{,}996 - 3{,}314.14 = 681.86$

14.76 a. $H_0\colon \beta_1 = 0$
$H_1\colon \beta_1 \neq 0$
$SSE = 3{,}314.14; n = 7; \bar{x} = 38.71; s_e = 25.75$

$$s_b = \frac{25.75}{\sqrt{11{,}115 - (7)(38.71)^2}} = \frac{25.75}{25.015} = 1.03$$

$b_1 = 1.0458; \beta_1 = 0; df = 5; \alpha = 0.05; t_{\alpha/2} = 2.571$

$$t = \frac{1.0458 - 0}{1.03} = 1.015$$

$|t| < |t_{\alpha/2}| \rightarrow 1.03 < 2.571 \rightarrow$ Do Not Reject H_0

b. $b_1 = 1.0458; s_b = 1.03; df = 5; t_{\alpha/2} = 2.571$
$CI = 1.0458 \pm (2.571)(1.03) = 1.0458 \pm 2.648$
$LCL = -\$1.602; UCL = \$3.694$

c. We are 95% confident that the true regression slope is between −$1.602 and $3.694. Because this interval does include zero, we have evidence to conclude that there is not a linear relationship between the order size and age of a GNC customer.

14.78 a. $\hat{y} = 859.5991 - 10.2006(16) = \$696.390$
The expected selling price is $696,390.

$$R^2 = \frac{178{,}208.89}{1{,}975{,}324.17} = 0.090$$

b. 9.0% of the variation in selling price is explained by the age of the house.

c. $H_0\colon \rho^2 \leq 0$
$H_1\colon \rho^2 > 0$
$n = 30; \alpha = 0.01; D_1 = 1; D_2 = 30 - 2 = 28; F_\alpha = 7.636$

$$F = \frac{178{,}208.89}{\left(\frac{1{,}797{,}115.27}{30 - 2}\right)} = \frac{178{,}208.89}{64{,}182.69} = 2.78$$

$F < F_\alpha \rightarrow 2.78 < 7.636 \rightarrow$ Do Not Reject H_0

Based on this sample, we have enough evidence to conclude that the age of a house is not useful for predicting average selling price.

14.80 b. $b_1 = -0.0644; b_0 = 22{,}789.6$

c. An increase in one mile on the odometer will decrease the asking price by an average of $0.0644.

d. $H_0\colon \beta_1 = 0$
$H_1\colon \beta_1 \neq 0$
$s_e = 0.01985; df = 38; t_{\alpha/2} = 2.024$

$$t = \frac{-0.0644 - 0}{0.01985} = -3.244$$

$|t| > |t_{\alpha/2}| \rightarrow$ Reject H_0

Conclusion: The relationship between mileage and asking price is statistically significant.

e. $LCL = -0.1046; UCL = -0.0242$

We are 95% confident that the true regression slope is between −0.1046 and −0.0242. Because this interval does not include zero, we have evidence to conclude that there is a linear relationship between mileage and price.

f. $LCL = \$19{,}792; UCL = \$21{,}153$

g. $LPL = \$16{,}853; UPL = \$24{,}092$

Chapter 15

15.2 a. $\hat{y} = 3.7986 + 0.4428\,x_1 + 0.3618\,x_2$

b. Increasing x_1 by 1 unit increases y by an average of 0.4428.
Increasing x_2 by 1 unit increases y by an average of 0.3618.

c. $\hat{y} = 3.7986 + 0.4428\,(50) + 0.3618\,(15) = 31.37$

15.4 a. $LCL = 17.96; UCL = 30.67$

b. We are 90% confident that the average value of y using the given values of x_1 and x_2 is between 17.96 and 30.67.

c. $LPL = 13.07; UPL = 35.57$

d. We are 90% confident that a particular value of y using the given values of x_1 and x_2 is between 13.07 and 35.57.

15.6 a. Set x_1 = Age, x_2 = Days, x_3 = ICU
$\hat{y} = -462.495 + 113.556x_1 + 1{,}218.626x_2 + 2{,}213.213x_3$

b. Each additional year of the patient's age increases the hospital bill by an average of $114. Each additional day in the hospital increases the hospital bill by an average of $1,219. Each additional day in the ICU increases the hospital bill by an average of $2,213.

c. $\hat{y} = -462.495 + 113.556(53) + 1{,}218.626(3) + 2{,}213.213(0) = \$9{,}212$

d. $LCL = \$7{,}504; UCL = \$10{,}919$

We are 95% confident that the average hospital bill of patients described in part c is between $7,504 and $10,919.

e. $LPL = \$1{,}019; UPL = \$17{,}405$

We are 95% confident that the hospital bill for a particular patient described in part c is between $1,019 and $17,405.

15.8 a. Set x_1 = Total assets, x_2 = ROAA, x_3 = Previous EPS, x_4 = ROAE
$\hat{y} = 0.1941 - 0.1485x_1 + 1.0893x_2 + 0.1612x_3 - 0.0083x_4$

b. Each additional $1 billion in assets decreases the current earnings per share by an average of $0.1485. Each additional percent in the previous period's ROAA increases the current EPS by an average of $1.089. Each additional $1.00 for the previous period's EPS increases the current EPS by an average of $0.161. Each additional percent in the previous period's ROAE decreases the current EPS by an average of $0.008.

c. $\hat{y} = 0.1941 - 0.1485(2.6) + 1.0893(1.5) + 0.1612(1.80) - 0.0083(8.0) = \$1.666$ per share

d. $LCL = \$1.392; UCL = \$1.939$

We are 95% confident that the average EPS for banks described in part c is between $1.392 and $1.939.

e. $LPL = -\$0.528; UPL = \$3.860$

We are 95% confident that the EPS for a particular bank described in part c is between −$0.528 and $3.860.

15.10 a. Each additional square foot in the house will increase the average January heating bill by \$0.09. Each additional year in the age of the heating system will increase the average January heating bill by \$2.04. Each additional degree for the thermostat setting will increase the average January heating bill by \$10.83.

b. $\hat{y} = -652.2924 + 0.0904(2{,}850) + 2.0430(9) + 10.8250(72) = \$403.13$

15.12 a. $SSR = 401.0$; $SSE = 34.5$; $SST = 435.5$

b. $R^2 = \dfrac{401.0}{435.5} = 0.9208$

c. $F = \dfrac{200.5}{6.9} = 29.06$

H_0: $\beta_1 = \beta_2 = 0$
H_1: At least one $\beta_i \neq 0$
$D_1 = 2, D_2 = 5$
F.INV.RT(0.05, 2, 5) = 5.786

Because $F = 29.06$ is greater than $F_\alpha = 5.786$, we reject H_0 and conclude that at least one of the population coefficients for our independent variables is not equal to zero.

d. Because the p-value for the overall regression model is 0.0018, which is less than 0.05, the model is significant.

e. $R_A^2 = 1 - \left[(1 - 0.9208)\left(\dfrac{8-1}{8-2-1}\right)\right] = 0.8891$

15.14 a. 35

b. 4

c. $R^2 = \dfrac{1{,}600}{2{,}800} = 0.5714$

d. $F = \dfrac{400}{40} = 10.0$

H_0: $\beta_1 = \beta_2 = \beta_3 = \beta_4 = 0$
H_1: At least one $\beta_i \neq 0$
$D_1 = 4, D_2 = 30$
F.INV.RT(0.05, 4, 30) = 2.690

Because $F = 10.0$ is greater than $F_\alpha = 2.690$, we reject H_0 and conclude that at least one of the population coefficients for our independent variables is not equal to zero.

e. $R_A^2 = 1 - \left[(1 - 0.5714)\left(\dfrac{35-1}{35-4-1}\right)\right] = 0.5143$

15.16 a. Set x_1 = Square feet, x_2 = Number of rooms, x_3 = Number of bathrooms, x_4 = Size of crew
$\hat{y} = 159.6400 - 0.0016x_1 + 5.7563x_2 - 3.6582x_3 - 18.8169x_4$

b. $R^2 = 0.3935$

c. $F = 10.54$

H_0: $\beta_1 = \beta_2 = \beta_3 = \beta_4 = 0$
H_1: At least one $\beta_i \neq 0$; $D_1 = 4, D_2 = 65$
F.INV.RT(0.05, 4, 65) = 2.513

Because $F = 10.54$ is greater than $F_\alpha = 2.513$, we reject H_0 and conclude that at least one of the population coefficients for our independent variables is not equal to zero.

d. $R_A^2 = 1 - \left[(1 - 0.3935)\left(\dfrac{70-1}{70-4-1}\right)\right] = 0.3561$

15.18 a. Set x_1 = Bedrooms, x_2 = Age, x_3 = Blocks
$\hat{y} = 1{,}742.863 + 1{,}092.525x_1 + 63.456x_2 - 1{,}750.951x_3$

b. $R^2 = 0.5271$

c. $F = 31.21$

H_0: $\beta_1 = \beta_2 = \beta_3 = 0$
H_1: At least one $\beta_i \neq 0$
$D_1 = 3, D_2 = 84$
F.INV.RT(0.05, 3, 84) = 2.713

Because $F = 31.21$ is greater than $F_\alpha = 2.713$, we reject H_0 and conclude that at least one of the population coefficients for our independent variables is not equal to zero.

d. $R_A^2 = 1 - \left[(1 - 0.5271)\left(\dfrac{88-1}{88-3-1}\right)\right] = 0.5102$

15.20 a. Set x_1 = Age, x_2 = Days, x_3 = ICU
$\hat{y} = -462.495 + 113.556x_1 + 1{,}218.626x_2 + 2{,}213.213x_3$

b. $R^2 = 0.7517$

c. $F = 46.41$

H_0: $\beta_1 = \beta_2 = \beta_3 = 0$
H_1: At least one $\beta_i \neq 0$
$D_1 = 3, D_2 = 46$
F.INV.RT(0.05, 3, 46) = 2.807

Because $F = 46.41$ is greater than $F_\alpha = 2.807$, we reject H_0 and conclude that at least one of the population coefficients for our independent variables is not equal to zero.

d. $R_A^2 = 1 - \left[(1 - 0.7517)\left(\dfrac{50-1}{50-3-1}\right)\right] = 0.7355$

15.22 a. $R^2 = \dfrac{102{,}454.94}{163{,}613.50} = 0.6262$

b. $MSR = \dfrac{102{,}454.94}{3} = 34{,}151.65$

$MSE = \dfrac{61{,}158.56}{32-3-1} = 2{,}184.23$

$F = \dfrac{34{,}151.65}{2{,}184.23} = 15.64$

H_0: $\beta_1 = \beta_2 = \beta_3 = 0$
H_1: At least one $\beta_i \neq 0$
$D_1 = 3, D_2 = 28$
F.INV.RT(0.05, 3, 28) = 2.947

Because $F = 15.64$ is to the right of $F_\alpha = 2.947$, we reject H_0 and conclude that at least one of the population coefficients for our independent variables is not equal to zero.

c. $R_A^2 = 1 - \left[(1 - 0.6262)\left(\dfrac{32-1}{32-3-1}\right)\right] = 0.5862$

15.24 a. $\hat{y} = 3.7986 + 0.4428x_1 + 0.3618x_2$

b. H_0: $\beta_i = 0$
H_1: $\beta_i \neq 0$
$df = 6$; T.INV.2T(0.10, 6) = 1.943

x_1: $t = \dfrac{0.4428 - 0}{0.1076} = 4.12$; therefore, reject the null

x_2: $t = \dfrac{0.3618 - 0}{0.3782} = 0.96$; therefore, do not reject the null

c. The p-value for x_1 (0.0063) is less than 0.10 and is significant. The p-value for x_2 (0.3757) is greater than 0.10 and is not significant.

15.26 a. $CI = 0.4428 \pm (1.943)(0.1076)$
$LCL = 0.2337$, $UCL = 0.6519$

We are 90% confident that the true regression coefficient for x_1 is between 0.2337 and 0.6519. Because this interval does not include zero, the x_1 variable is significant.

b. $CI = 0.3618 \pm (1.943)(0.3782)$
$LCL = -0.3730$, $UCL = 1.0966$

We are 90% confident that the true regression coefficient for x_2 is between −0.3730 and 1.0966. Because this interval includes zero, the x_2 variable is not significant.

15.28 a. Set x_1 = Assists, x_2 = Rebounds, x_3 = Turnovers, x_4 = Personal fouls
$\hat{y} = -23.1391 + 1.1690x_1 + 0.8630x_2 - 0.4041x_3 - 0.4209x_4$

b. H_0: $\beta_i = 0$
H_1: $\beta_i \neq 0$
$df = 61$; T.INV.2T(0.10, 61) = 1.670

Assists: $t = \frac{1.1690 - 0}{0.3745} = 3.12$; therefore, reject the null

Rebounds: $t = \frac{0.8630 - 0}{0.2126} = 4.06$; therefore, reject the null

Turnovers: $t = \frac{-0.4041 - 0}{0.4315} = -0.94$; therefore, do not reject the null

Personal fouls: $t = \frac{-0.4209 - 0}{0.3022} = -1.39$; therefore, do not reject the null

c. The *p*-values for both Assists (0.0028) and Rebounds (0.0001) are both less than 0.10 and are significant. The *p*-values for Turnovers (0.3527) and Personal fouls (0.1687) are both greater than 0.10 and are not significant.

d. $CI = -0.4209 \pm (1.670)(0.3022)$
$LCL = -0.9256$, $UCL = 0.0838$
We are 90% confident that an extra personal foul committed by Villanova will change the average point differential per game between −0.9256 and 0.0838 points.

e. Because this interval does include zero, the personal foul variable is not significant.

15.30 a. Set x_1 = Total assets, x_2 = ROAA, x_3 = Previous EPS, x_4 = ROAE
$\hat{y} = 0.1941 - 0.1485x_1 + 1.0893x_2 + 0.1612x_3 - 0.0083x_4$

b. H_0: $\beta_i = 0$
H_1: $\beta_i \neq 0$
$df = 216$; T.INV.2T(0.05, 216) = 1.971

Total assets: $t = \frac{-0.1485 - 0}{0.0737} = -2.01$; therefore, reject the null

ROAA: $t = \frac{1.0893 - 0}{0.0743} = 14.66$; therefore, reject the null

Previous EPS: $t = \frac{0.1612 - 0}{0.0518} = 3.13$; therefore, reject the null

ROAE: $t = \frac{-0.0083 - 0}{0.0046} = -1.80$; therefore, do not reject the null

c. The *p*-values for Total assets (0.0450), ROAA (3.06E-34), and Previous EPS (0.0021) are less than 0.05 and are significant. The *p*-value for Previous ROAE (0.0752) is greater than 0.05 and is not significant.

d. $CI = 1.0893 \pm (1.971)(0.0743)$
$LCL = 0.94$, $UCL = 1.24$
We are 95% confident that an extra 1% to previous ROAA will increase the average EPS between \$0.94 and \$1.24.

e. Because this interval does not include zero, the Previous ROAA variable is significant.

15.32 a. H_0: $\beta_i = 0$
H_1: $\beta_i \neq 0$
$df = n - k - 1 = 28 - 3 - 1 = 24$, T.INV.2T(0.05, 24) = 2.064

TV: $t = \frac{11.9025 - 0}{3.2437} = 3.67$, therefore, reject the null

People: $t = \frac{7.3994 - 0}{2.7922} = 2.65$, therefore, reject the null

Years: $t = \frac{-0.8577 - 0}{1.2931} = -0.66$, therefore, do not reject the null

b. TV:
$CI = 11.9025 \pm (2.064)(3.2437)$
$LCL = 5.21$, $UCL = 18.60$
We are 95% confident that an extra television in the household will increase the average monthly cable bill between \$5.21 and \$18.60. Because this interval does not include zero, the TV variable is significant.

People:
$CI = 7.3994 \pm (2.064)(2.7922)$
$LCL = 1.64$, $UCL = 13.16$
We are 95% confident that an extra person in the household will increase the average monthly cable bill between \$1.64 and \$13.16. Because this interval does not include zero, the People variable is significant.

Years:
$CI = -0.8577 \pm (2.064)(1.2931)$
$LCL = -3.53$, $UCL = 1.81$
We are 95% confident that an additional year that a household is a customer will result in a change in the average monthly cable bill between a decrease of \$3.53 and an increase of \$1.81. Because this interval does include zero, the Years variable is not significant.

15.34 a. Create the dummy variable x_3, which equals 1 for male and 0 for female student.
$\hat{y} = 13.2377 + 1.0002x_1 - 0.3389x_2 + 0.2684x_3$

b. Increasing x_1 by 1 unit increases y by 1.002. Increasing x_2 by 1 unit decreases y by 0.3389. Males increase the average value of y by 0.2684 when compared with females.

15.36 Create the dummy variable Gender, which equals 1 for male and 0 for female student.

a. Set x_1 = GPA, x_2 = Hours, x_3 = Absences, x_4 = Gender
$\hat{y} = 55.559 + 7.197x_1 + 1.882x_2 - 1.141x_3 - 0.585x_4$

b. $F = \frac{313.8}{40.5} = 7.75$
H_0: $\beta_1 = \beta_2 = \beta_3 = \beta_4 = 0$
H_1: At least one $\beta_i \neq 0$
$D_1 = 4$, $D_2 = 35$
F.INV.RT(0.10, 4, 35) = 2.113
Because $F = 7.75$ is greater than $F_\alpha = 2.113$, we reject H_0 and conclude that at least one of the population coefficients for our independent variables is not equal to zero.

c. The female students are the base gender. The male students average 0.6 points lower on the exam when compared with female students.

d. The *p*-values for both GPA (0.0136) and Hours (0.0046) are less than 0.10 and are significant. The *p*-values for both Absences (0.1123) and Gender (0.7747) are greater than 0.10 and are not significant.

e. Set x_1 = GPA, x_2 = Hours
$\hat{y} = 51.3632 + 8.0357(3.45) + 1.8083(4.0) = 86.3$

15.38 Set dummy variable Loc = 1 for a home game and 0 for an away game (this choice is arbitrary).

a. Set x_1 = Assists, x_2 = Rebounds, x_3 = Turnovers, x_4 = Personal fouls, x_5 = Location
$\hat{y} = -24.5780 + 0.9294x_1 + 0.8448x_2 - 0.3340x_3 - 0.3556x_4 + 6.5060x_5$

b. $F = \frac{1,306.3}{140.3} = 9.31$
H_0: $\beta_1 = \beta_2 = \beta_3 = \beta_4 = 0$
H_1: At least one $\beta_i \neq 0$
$D_1 = 5$, $D_2 = 60$
F.INV.RT(0.10, 5, 60) = 1.946

Because $F = 9.31$ is greater than $F_\alpha = 1.946$, we reject H_0 and conclude that at least one of the population coefficients for our independent variables is not equal to zero.

c. The home game point differential averages 6.5 more points per game than away games.

d. The variables x_1 (Assists), x_2 (Rebounds), and x_5 (Location) all have p-values less than 0.10 and are significant.

e. Set x_1 = Assists, x_2 = Rebounds, x_3 = Location

$$\hat{y} = -37.0615 + 1.0348(8) + 0.8279(37) + 7.2878(1)$$
$$= 9.1 \text{ points}$$

15.40

MONTH	DUMMY VARIABLES MON1	MON2
June	0	0
July	1	0
August	0	1

a. Set x_1 = Bedrooms, x_2 = Age, x_3 = Blocks, x_4 = Mon1, x_5 = Mon2

$$\hat{y} = 1{,}119.036 + 984.403x_1 + 51.628x_2 - 1{,}655.564x_3 + 1{,}462.510x_4 + 1{,}479.476x_5$$

b. $F = \dfrac{67{,}615{,}406.5}{2{,}828{,}625.8} = 23.90$

H_0: $\beta_1 = \beta_2 = \beta_3 = \beta_4 = \beta_5 = 0$

H_1: At least one $\beta_i \neq 0$

$D_1 = 5, D_2 = 82$

F.INV.RT(0.05, 5, 82) = 2.326

Because $F = 23.90$ is greater than $F_\alpha = 2.326$, we reject H_0 and conclude that at least one of the population coefficients for our independent variables is not equal to zero.

c. June is the base month. July rentals average $1,463 more per week than June rentals. August rentals average $1,479 more per week than June rentals.

d. The variables x_1 (bedrooms), x_3 (blocks), x_4 (Mon1), and x_5 (Mon2) all have p-values less than 0.05 and are significant.

e. Set x_1 = Bedrooms, x_3 = Blocks, x_4 = Mon1, x_5 = Mon2

$$\hat{y} = 1{,}632.018 + 992.244(3) - 1{,}683.708(2) + 1{,}519.933(0) + 1{,}508.962(1) = \$2{,}750 \text{ per week}$$

15.42

INDEPENDENT VARIABLES	*VIF* WITH ALL VARIABLES	*VIF* WITHOUT x_1
x_1	5.93	—
x_2	2.85	2.61
x_3	5.91	2.61

Removing the variable x_1 eliminates the presence of multicollinearity.

15.44 a.

10	Model	Cp	k+1	R Square	Adj. R Square	Std. Error
11	X1	14.0275	2	0.7064	0.6738	7.5339
12	X2	21.1704	2	0.6067	0.5630	8.7201
13	X3	64.3002	2	0.0046	-0.1060	13.8730
14	X4	9.7890	2	0.7656	0.7396	6.7319
15	X1X2	13.4130	3	0.7429	0.6787	7.4776
16	X1X3	4.0738	3	0.8733	0.8417	5.2492
17	X1X4	10.8511	3	0.7787	0.7234	6.9380
18	X2X3	22.5473	3	0.6154	0.5193	9.1462
19	X2X4	8.6641	3	0.8092	0.7616	6.4416
20	X3X4	5.4932	3	0.8535	0.8169	5.6449
21	X1X2X3	5.9001	4	0.8758	0.8225	5.5577
22	X1X2X4	10.6204	4	0.8099	0.7284	6.8753
23	X1X3X4	3.1838	4	0.9137	0.8767	4.6326
24	X2X3X4	5.3380	4	0.8836	0.8337	5.3793
25	X1X2X3X4	5.0000	5	0.9162	0.8604	4.9289

$$\hat{y} = 35.8512 + 0.3536x_1 + 0.4943x_3 - 0.6887x_4$$

b.

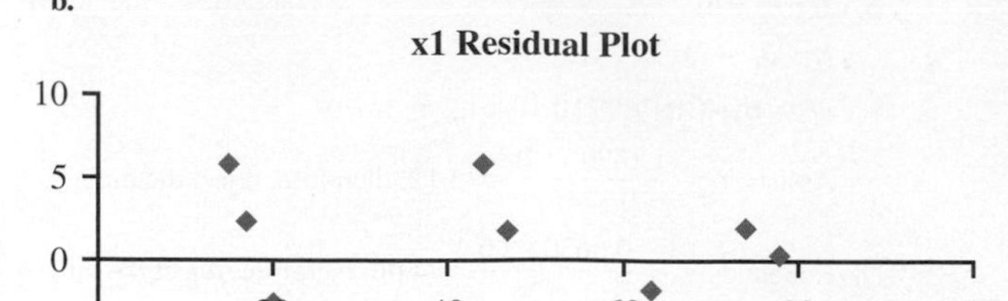

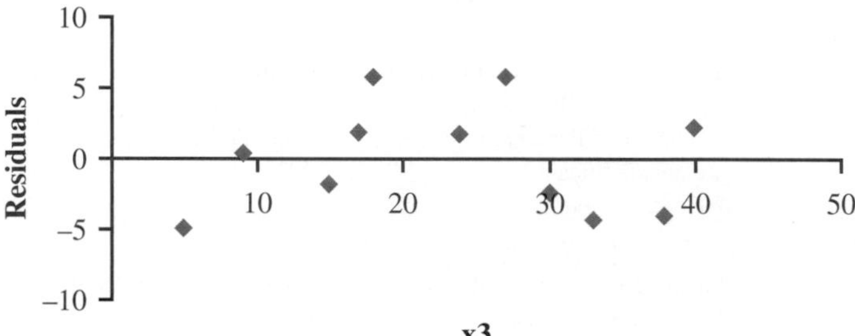

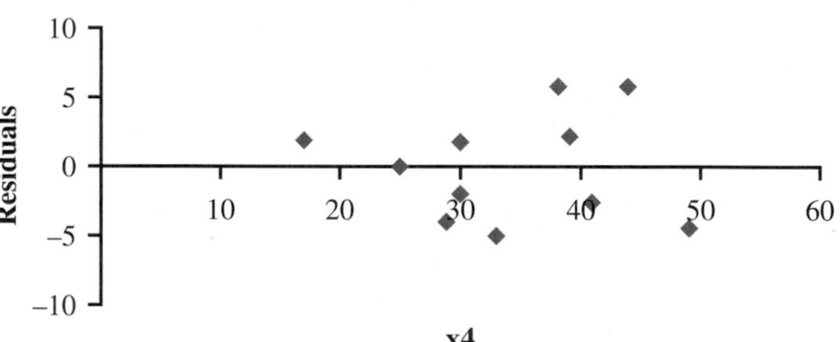

The residual plots do not show any significant violation of the constant variance assumption.

15.46 a.

INDEPENDENT VARIABLES	*VIF* WITH ALL VARIABLES
GPA	1.22
Hours	1.19
Absences	1.04
Gender	1.00

b. There is no evidence that multicollinearity is present with these three independent variables.

c.

4	GPA entered.						
5		*df*	*SS*	*MS*	*F*	*Significance F*	
6	Regression	1	801.4950278	801.4950278	16.27918655	0.000254691	
7	Residual	38	1870.904972	49.23434137			
8	Total	39	2672.4				
9							
10		*Coefficients*	*Standard Error*	*t Stat*	*P-value*	*Lower 95%*	*Upper 95%*
11	Intercept	49.50650966	8.915820117	5.552659094	2.33847E-06	31.45737544	67.55564387
12	GPA	11.14115969	2.7613029	4.034747396	0.000254691	5.55119421	16.73112516
13							
14	Hours entered.						
15		*df*	*SS*	*MS*	*F*	*Significance F*	
16	Regression	2	1146.271718	573.1358591	13.89531079	3.15324E-05	
17	Residual	37	1526.128282	41.24671032			
18	Total	39	2672.4				
19							
20		*Coefficients*	*Standard Error*	*t Stat*	*P-value*	*Lower 95%*	*Upper 95%*
21	Intercept	51.36323752	8.18582668	6.274654904	2.66918E-07	34.7771772	67.94929784
22	GPA	8.035710976	2.746177239	2.926144337	0.005835303	2.471427351	13.5999946
23	Hours	1.808347137	0.625471482	2.891174401	0.006389469	0.541021535	3.07567274
24							
25	No other variables could be entered into the model. Stepwise ends.						
26							

d. Set x_1 = GPA, x_2 = Hours

$\hat{y} = 51.3632 + 8.0357x_1 + 1.8083x_2$

e.

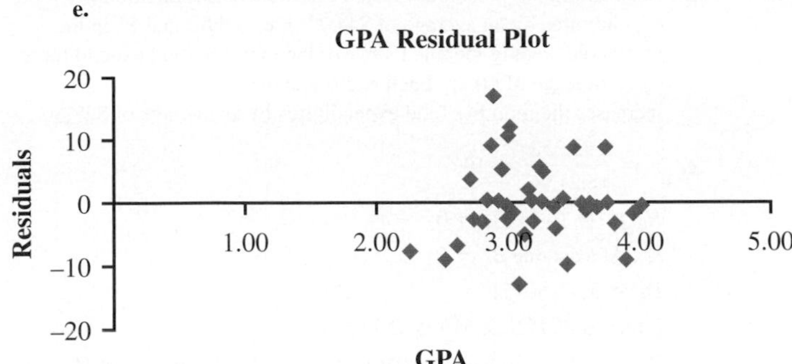

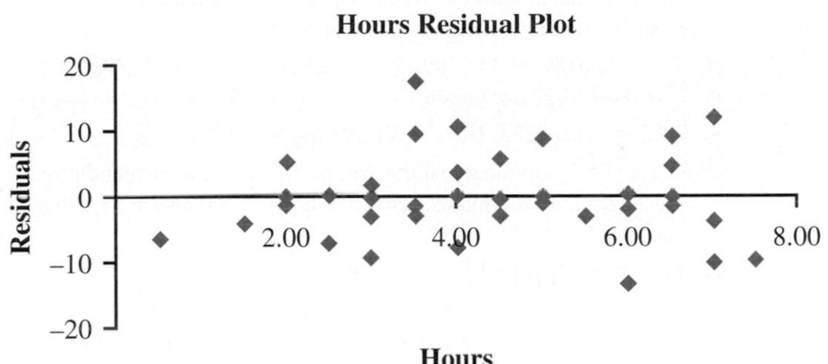

The residual plots do not show any significant violation of the constant variance assumption.

15.48 a.

INDEPENDENT VARIABLES	*VIF* WITH ALL VARIABLES	*VIF* WITHOUT BATHROOM
Square feet	4.88	3.80
Rooms	5.10	3.79
Bathroom	5.34	—
Crew	1.12	1.08
Children	1.08	1.07

b. Removing the Bathroom variable eliminates the presence of multicollinearity.

c. Set x_1 = Square feet, x_2 = Rooms, x_3 = Crew, x_4 = Child

10	Model	Cp	k+1	R Square	Adj. R Square	Std. Error
11	X1	74.7162	2	0.1324	0.1196	24.1946
12	X2	66.0829	2	0.1856	0.1737	23.4407
13	X3	53.3730	2	0.2640	0.2532	22.2844
14	X4	50.1825	2	0.2837	0.2731	21.9845
15	X1X2	68.0708	3	0.1857	0.1614	23.6139
16	X1X3	42.8284	3	0.3413	0.3217	21.2377
17	X1X4	34.5733	3	0.3922	0.3741	20.4006
18	X2X3	35.1399	3	0.3887	0.3705	20.4592
19	X2X4	21.3249	3	0.4739	0.4582	18.9802
20	X3X4	25.3363	3	0.4492	0.4327	19.4213
21	X1X2X3	36.8451	4	0.3906	0.3629	20.5829
22	X1X2X4	22.1112	4	0.4814	0.4578	18.9870
23	X1X3X4	15.8654	4	0.5199	0.4981	18.2685
24	X2X3X4	4.6795	4	0.5889	0.5702	16.9054
25	X1X2X3X4	5.0000	5	0.5992	0.5746	16.8191
26						

The models highlighted in yellow and orange are both candidates.

Orange: $\hat{y} = 142.6829 - 0.0121x_1 + 6.4635x_2 - 14.9177x_3 + 24.2465x_4$

The yellow model would be preferable for two reasons. The adjusted R^2 values are very similar, but the yellow model contains one less variable (square feet). In addition, the regression coefficient for square feet for the orange model is negative, which is counterintuitive. According to this model, a house with more square feet will require less time to clean.

d.

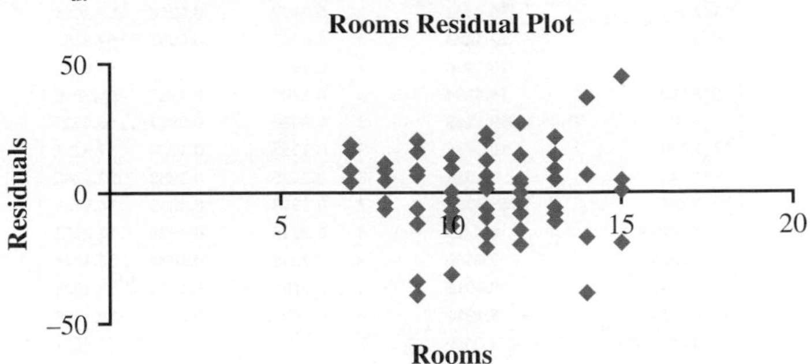

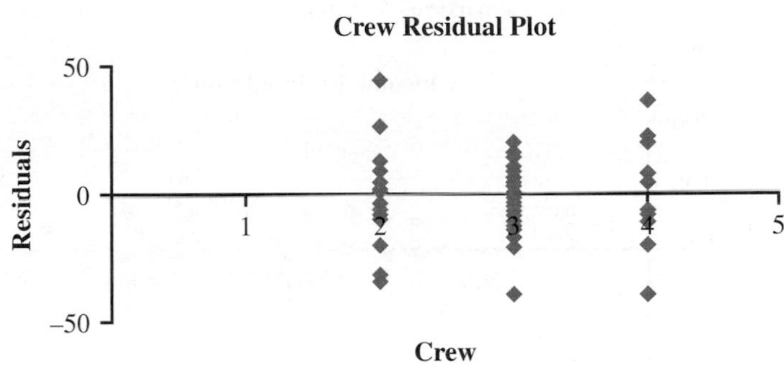

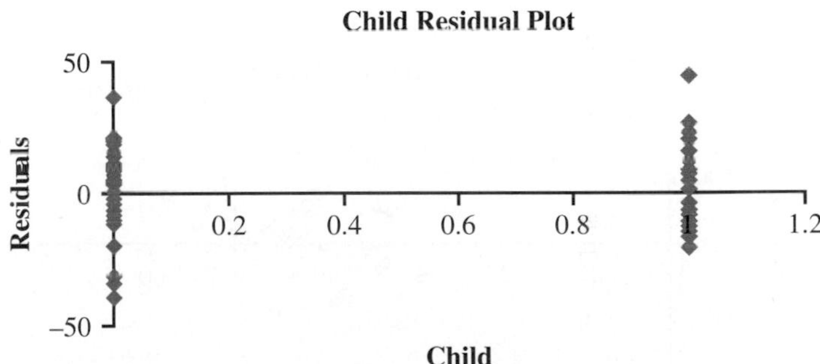

The residual plots do not show any significant violation of the constant variance assumption.

15.50 a.

MONTH	DUMMY VARIABLES EDUC1	EDUC2
High school	0	0
Bachelor	1	0
Graduate	0	1

INDEPENDENT VARIABLES	*VIF* WITH ALL VARIABLES
Income	1.16
Age	1.15
Educ1	1.33
Educ2	1.28

b. There is no evidence that multicollinearity is present with these four independent variables.

c. Set x_1 = Income, x_2 = Age, x_3 = Educ1, x_4 = Educ2

	Model	Cp	k+1	R Square	Adj. R Square	Std. Error
11	X1	18.4024	2	0.0726	0.0567	56.4325
12	X2	10.1714	2	0.1752	0.1610	53.2195
13	X3	20.4441	2	0.0472	0.0308	57.2015
14	X4	22.1023	2	0.0265	0.0097	57.8185
15	X1X2	10.3350	3	0.1981	0.1700	52.9341
16	X1X3	14.9294	3	0.1409	0.1107	54.7916
17	X1X4	19.1198	3	0.0886	0.0567	56.4325
18	X2X3	10.3035	3	0.1985	0.1704	52.9211
19	X2X4	9.1025	3	0.2135	0.1859	52.4246
20	X3X4	15.3338	3	0.1358	0.1055	54.9521
21	X1X2X3	9.4729	4	0.2338	0.1928	52.2032
22	X1X2X4	9.9548	4	0.2278	0.1864	52.4074
23	X1X3X4	10.8918	4	0.2161	0.1741	52.8023
24	X2X3X4	5.1312	4	0.2879	0.2498	50.3259
25	X1X2X3X4	5.0000	5	0.3145	0.2646	49.8252
26						

d. $\hat{y} = 481.0039 + 0.03179x_1 + 2.3984x_2 + 39.6920x_3 + 54.5480x_4$

e.

Income Residual Plot

Residuals

Income

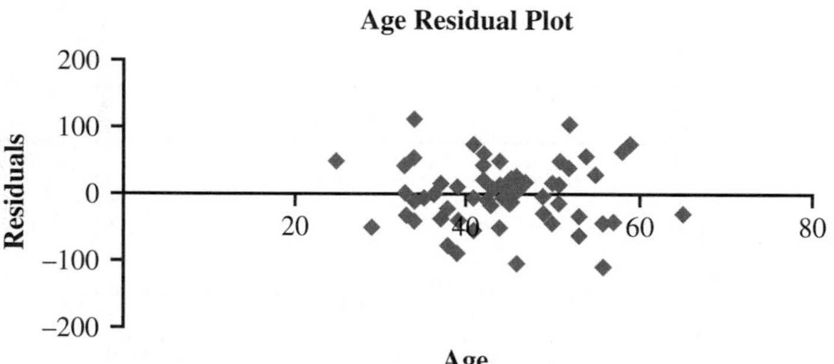

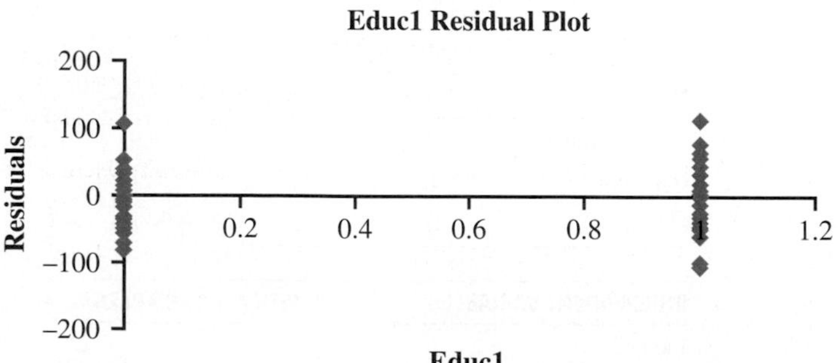

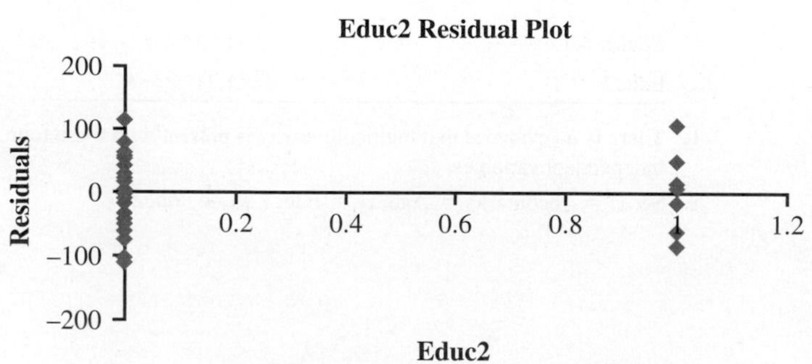

The residual plots do not show any significant violation of the constant variance assumption.

15.52 a. Set x_1 = People, x_2 = Income, x_3 = Teenagers

$\hat{y} = 592.6149 + 44.2289x_1 + 0.2522x_2 + 27.8032x_3$

b. Each additional person in the household increases the monthly food expenditures by an average of \$44.23. Each additional \$1 in the household weekly income increases the monthly food expenditures by an average of \$0.25. Each additional teenager in the household increases the monthly food expenditures by an average of \$27.80.

c. $F = \dfrac{193{,}252}{18{,}213.5} = 10.61$

$H_0: \beta_1 = \beta_2 = \beta_3 = 0$

H_1: At least one $\beta_i \neq 0$

$D_1 = 3, D_2 = 51$

F.INV.RT$(0.05, 3, 51) = 2.7862$

Because $F = 10.61$ is greater than $F_\alpha = 2.7862$, we reject H_0 and conclude that at least one of the population coefficients for our independent variables is not equal to zero.

d. $\hat{y} = 592.6149 + 44.2289(5) + 0.2522(1{,}200) + 27.8032(1)$
$= \$1{,}144.20$ per month

e. $LCL = \$1{,}096.83$, $UCL = \$1{,}191.64$

We are 95% confident that the average monthly food expenditure for the sample of families described in part d is between \$1,096.83 and \$1,191.64.

f. $LPL = \$869.18$; $UPL = \$1{,}419.29$

We are 95% confident that the monthly food expenditure for the particular family described in part d is between \$869.18 and \$1,419.29.

g. $H_0: \beta_i = 0$

$H_1: \beta_i \neq 0$

$df = 51$, T.INV.2T$(0.05, 51) = 2.008$

People: $t = \dfrac{44.2289 - 0}{12.2088} = 3.62$; therefore, reject the null

Income: $t = \dfrac{0.2522 - 0}{0.0698} = 3.61$; therefore, reject the null

Teenagers: $t = \dfrac{27.8032 - 0}{24.5021} = 1.13$; therefore, do not reject the null

h. $CI = 27.8032 \pm (2.008)(24.5021)$

$LCL = -21.40$, $UCL = 77.00$

We are 95% confident that an extra teenager in the household will increase the average monthly food expenditures between \$21.40 less and \$77 more per week. Because this interval does include zero, the teenager variable is not significant.

i.

	Model	Cp	k+1	R Square	Adj. R Square	Std. Error
11	X1	16.8511	2	0.1808	0.1654	152.7004
12	X2	14.9346	2	0.2040	0.1890	150.5284
13	X3	26.9853	2	0.0585	0.0407	163.7074
14	X1X2	3.2876	3	0.3687	0.3445	135.3310
15	X1X3	15.0429	3	0.2268	0.1971	149.7730
16	X2X3	15.1240	3	0.2258	0.1961	149.8678
17	X1X2X3	4.0000	4	0.3843	0.3481	134.9583
18						

The models highlighted in yellow and orange are both candidates with adjusted R^2 values around 35%.

Yellow: $\hat{y} = 591.5999 + 45.0267x_1 + 0.2692x_2$

The yellow model would be preferable because it contains one less variable (teenager).

15.54 a.

INDEPENDENT VARIABLES	*VIF* WITH ALL VARIABLES
Bill	1.40
Diners	1.22
Table minutes	1.21
Day	1.24

There is no evidence that multicollinearity is present with these four independent variables.

b. Create the dummy variable Day, which equals 1 for a weekend and 0 for a weekday.

Set x_1 = Bill, x_2 = Diners, x_3 = Table minutes, x_4 = Day
$\hat{y} = 1.1826 + 0.0854x_1 + 0.6563x_2 + 0.0490x_3 + 0.7076x_4$

c. Each additional $1 on the total bill increases the tip by an average of $0.085. Each additional diner at the table increases the tip by an average of $0.656. Each additional minute that the diners are at their table increases the tip by an average of $0.049. Weekend tips average $0.708 more than weekday tips.

d. $F = \frac{322.02}{5.71} = 56.44$

H_0: $\beta_1 = \beta_2 = \beta_3 = \beta_4 = 0$
H_1: At least one $\beta_i \neq 0$
$D_1 = 4, D_2 = 75$
F.INV.RT(0.02, 4, 75) = 3.112

Because $F = 56.44$ is greater than $F_\alpha = 3.112$, we reject H_0 and conclude that at least one of the population coefficients for our independent variables is not equal to zero.

e. The p-values for Bill (2.04E-15), Diners (0.0113), and Table minutes (0.0112) are all less than 0.02 and are significant. The p-value for Day (0.2638) is greater than 0.02 and is not significant.

f. $df = 75$, T.INV.2T(0.02, 75) = 2.377
$CI = 0.0854 \pm (2.377)(0.008557)$
$LCL = 0.0651, UCL = 0.1057$

We are 98% confident that an additional $1 in the total bill increases the average tip between $0.065 and $0.106.

g.

10	Model	Cp	k+1	R Square	Adj. R Square	Std. Error
11	X1	18.66256	2	0.685254	0.681218701	2.631419
12	X2	153.3466	2	0.237439	0.22766205	4.095070
13	X3	160.9416	2	0.212187	0.202086379	4.163144
14	X4	169.6977	2	0.183073	0.172599602	4.239371
15	X1X2	10.36263	3	0.7195	0.712214713	2.500218
16	X1X3	9.04438	3	0.723884	0.716711643	2.480606
17	X1X4	17.64033	3	0.606273	0.687367688	2.606068
18	X2X3	122.2194	3	0.347585	0.330638811	3.813061
19	X2X4	120.1395	3	0.3545	0.337734103	3.792798
20	X3X4	134.5665	3	0.306532	0.288519436	3.931199
21	X1X2X3	4.267691	4	0.746415	0.736405581	2.392829
22	X1X2X4	9.768301	4	0.728126	0.717394515	2.477615
23	X1X3X4	9.748135	4	0.728193	0.717464214	2.477309
24	X2X3X4	102.7058	4	0.419116	0.396186209	3.621555
25	X1X2X3X4	5	5	0.75063	0.737330768	2.388626
26						

The models highlighted in yellow and orange are both candidates with adjusted R^2 values around 74%. The yellow model would be preferable because it contains one less variable (teenager).

Yellow: $\hat{y} = 0.9664 + 0.0886x_1 + 0.6576x_2 + 0.0527x_3$

h. $\hat{y} = 0.9664 + 0.0886(125) + 0.6576(4) + 0.0527(95) = \$19.68$

15.56 a.

INDEPENDENT VARIABLES	*VIF* WITH ALL VARIABLES	*VIF* WITHOUT EXPERIENCE
Performance (x_1)	1.08	1.08
College (x_2)	1.07	1.07
Age (x_3)	10.30	1.12
Student Eval (x_4)	1.07	1.04
Experience (x_5)	10.44	—
Gender (x_6)	1.04	1.04

College is a dummy variable which equals 1 for business and 0 for arts and science. Gender is a dummy variable which equals 1 for male and 0 for female. Removing the variable Experience eliminates the presence of multicollinearity.

b. $\hat{y} = -13{,}092.751 + 1{,}867.843x_1 + 20{,}237.204x_2 + 641.323x_3 + 321.285x_4 + 3{,}159.078x_6$

c. Increasing the performance score by one point corresponds to an average salary increase of $1,868. Associate professors in the business college average $20,237 more in annual salary than associate professors in the arts and science college. Increasing the faculty's age by one year corresponds to an average salary increase of $641. Increasing the average student evaluation score by one percentage point corresponds to an average salary increase of $321. Male associate professors earn an average of $3,159 more in salary than female associate professors.

d. $F = \frac{2{,}793{,}294{,}896.3}{140{,}880{,}400.1} = 19.83$

H_0: $\beta_1 = \beta_2 = \beta_3 = \beta_4 = \beta_5 = 0$
H_1: At least one $\beta_i \neq 0$
$D_1 = 5, D_2 = 79$
F.INV.RT(0.01, 5, 79) = 3.258

Because $F = 19.83$ is greater than $F_\alpha = 3.258$, we reject H_0 and conclude that at least one of the population coefficients for our independent variables is not equal to zero.

e. The p-values for Performance (0.0034), College (5.36E-11), and Age (0.0005) are all less than 0.01 and are significant. The p-value for Student (0.0931) and Gender (0.2327) is greater than 0.01 and is not significant.

f.

4	College entered.						
5		*df*	*SS*	*MS*	*F*	*Significance F*	
6	Regression	1	9218424576.7780	9218424576.7780	48.1892	0.0000	
7	Residual	83	15877601515.5750	191296403.8021			
8	Total	84	25096026092.3529				
9							
10		*Coefficients*	*Standard Error*	*t Stat*	*P-value*	*Lower 95%*	*Upper 95%*
11	Intercept	71928.0750	2186.8722	32.8908	0.0000	67578.4741	76277.6759
12	College	20864.1917	3005.5684	6.9418	0.0000	14886.2370	26842.1463
13							
14	Age entered.						
15		*df*	*SS*	*MS*	*F*	*Significance F*	
16	Regression	2	12116918476.7543	6058459238.3772	38.2764	0.0000	
17	Residual	82	12979107615.5986	158281800.1902			
18	Total	84	25096026092.3529				
19							
20		*Coefficients*	*Standard Error*	*t Stat*	*P-value*	*Lower 95%*	*Upper 95%*
21	Intercept	38067.9332	8158.7961	4.6659	0.0000	21837.4886	54298.3777
22	College	22299.4472	2754.4345	8.0958	0.0000	16819.9997	27778.8948
23	Age	764.3373	178.6135	4.2793	0.0001	409.0181	1119.6565
24							
25	Performance entered.						
26		*df*	*SS*	*MS*	*F*	*Significance F*	
27	Regression	3	13370678687.7025	4456892895.9008	30.7887	0.0000	
28	Residual	81	11725347404.6504	144757375.3661			
29	Total	84	25096026092.3529				
30							
31		*Coefficients*	*Standard Error*	*t Stat*	*P-value*	*Lower 95%*	*Upper 95%*
32	Intercept	15411.1853	10961.1295	1.4060	0.1636	-6398.0241	37220.3947
33	College	20910.3292	2676.0864	7.8138	0.0000	15585.7566	26234.9017
34	Age	646.8709	175.4138	3.6877	0.0004	297.8525	995.8893
35	Performance	1845.0668	626.9389	2.9430	0.0042	597.6551	3092.4785
36							
37	No other variables could be entered into the model. Stepwise ends.						

$\hat{y} = 15{,}411.185 + 1{,}845.067x_1 + 20{,}910.329x_2 + 646.871x_3$

g. $\hat{y} = 15{,}411.185 + 1{,}845.067(17) + 20{,}910.329(1) + 646.871(41) = \$94{,}209$

h. $LCL = \$88{,}934$
$UCL = \$99{,}485$

We are 99% confident that the average salary for faculty members that fit this description will be between these limits.

i. $LPL = \$62{,}036$
$UPL = \$126{,}383$

We are 99% confident that the salary from a particular faculty member that fits this description will be between these limits.

j.

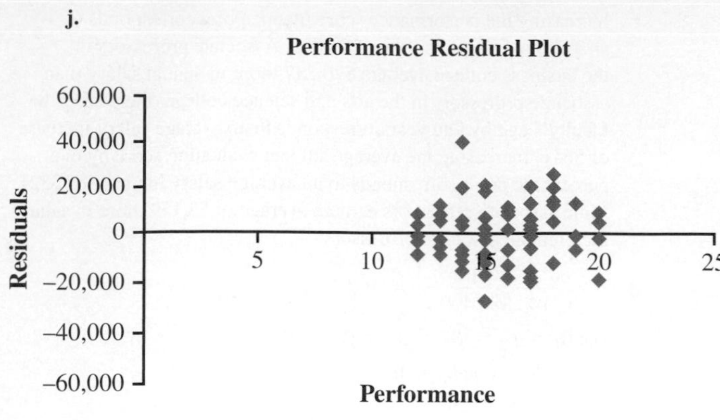

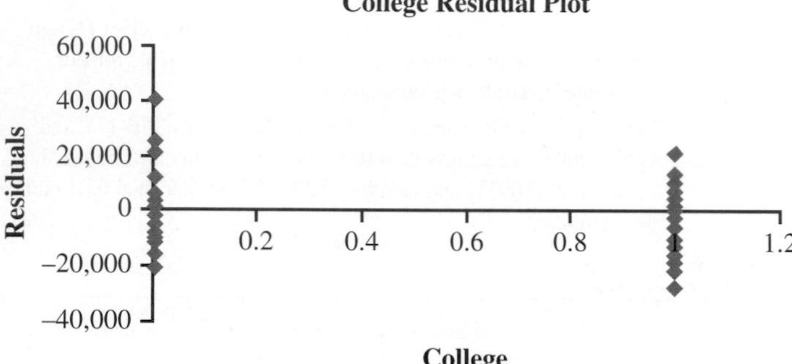

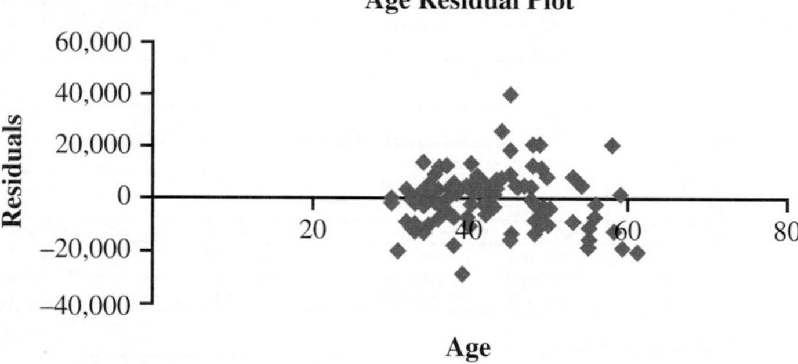

The residual plots do not show any significant violation of the constant variance assumption.

15.58 Create the dummy variable Location, which equals 0 for a wooded lot and 1 for a lot on the golf course.

INDEPENDENT VARIABLES	*VIF* WITH ALL VARIABLES	*VIF* WITHOUT ASKING PRICE
Bedrooms (x_1)	4.84	4.45
Bathrooms (x_2)	2.42	2.41
Days on market (x_3)	1.21	1.20
Age (x_4)	2.77	2.41
Square feet (x_5)	4.94	3.11
Location (x_6)	1.34	1.34
Asking price (x_7)	6.60	—

Removing the Asking price variable eliminates the presence of multicollinearity.

Performing best subsets regression on the remaining six independent variables produces the following results. The following figure shows only the models with adjusted R^2 values exceeding 83%.

10	Model	Cp	k+1	R Square	Adj. R Square	Std. Error
11	X1X4X5	4.284284	4	0.851754	0.847121702	95.56325
12	X1X2X4X5	6.187536	5	0.851903	0.845667688	96.01662
13	X1X3X4X5	4.800333	5	0.854039	0.847893446	95.32174
14	X1X4X5X6	5.080922	5	0.853607	0.847443243	95.4627
15	X2X3X4X5	15.36594	5	0.837772	0.83094099	100.4933
16	X3X4X5X6	14.854	5	0.83856	0.831762401	100.2489
17	X1X2X3X4X5	6.773306	6	0.854081	0.846319118	95.81377
18	X1X2X4X5X6	6.758972	6	0.854103	0.846342361	95.80652
19	X1X3X4X5X6	5.191991	6	0.856515	0.84888332	95.01107
20	X2X3X4X5X6	15.57666	6	0.840527	0.832043921	100.165
21	X1X2X3X4X5X6	7	7	0.856811	0.847573082	95.42207
22						

The models with the five highest adjusted R^2 values are highlighted in the previous figure. The yellow model would be the best choice because it has the fewest independent variables with essentially the same adjusted R^2 values as the other four models.

$\hat{y} = 168.2365 + 74.2955x_1 - 6.1373x_4 + 0.1529x_5$

Test the significance of the overall model using $\alpha = 0.01$:

$$F = \frac{1{,}679{,}052.7}{9{,}132.3} = 183.86$$

H_0: $\beta_1 = \beta_4 = \beta_5 = 0$

H_1: At least one $\beta_i \neq 0$

$D_1 = k = 3, D_2 = n - k - 1 = 100 - 3 - 1 = 96$

$\text{F.INV.RT}(0.01, 3, 96) = 3.992$

Because $F = 183.86$ is greater than $F_\alpha = 3.992$, we reject H_0 and conclude that at least one of the population coefficients for our independent variables is not equal to zero.

The *p*-values for Bedrooms (0.0002), Age (0.0005), and Square feet (4.04E-12) are all less than 0.01 and are significant.

Each additional bedroom increases the selling price by an average of \$74,296. Each additional year in age of the house decreases the selling price by an average of \$6,137. Each additional square foot of space in the house increases the selling price by an average of \$152.90.

The predicted selling price of the home described in the problem is as follows:

$$\hat{y} = 168.2365 + 74.2955(4) - 6.1373(18) + 0.1529(2{,}800) = \$783{,}067$$

$LCL = \$752{,}816$

$UCL = \$813{,}575$

We are 99% confident that the average selling price for homes that fit this description will be between these limits.

$LPL = \$530{,}223$

$UPL = \$1{,}036{,}168$

We are 99% confident that the selling price for a specific home that fits this description will be between these limits.

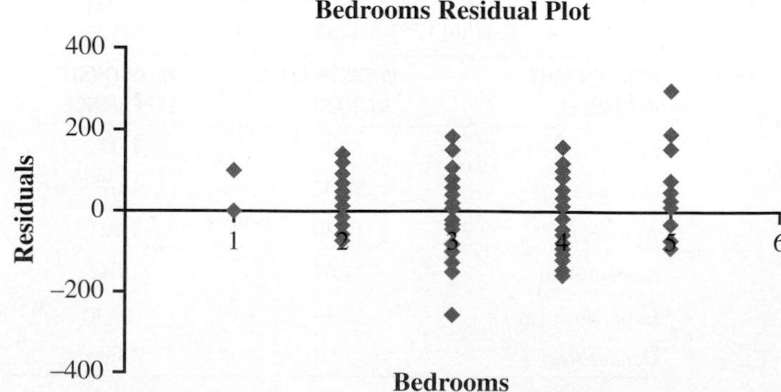

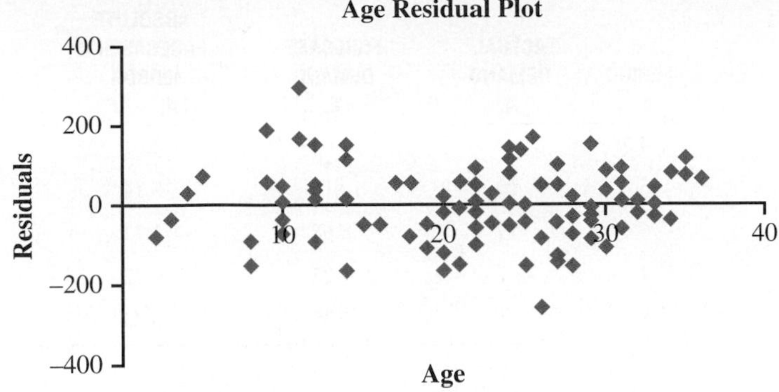

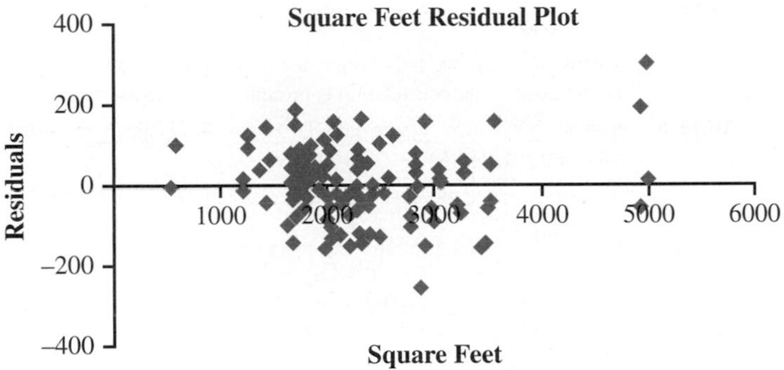

The residual plots do not show any significant violation of the constant variance assumption.

Chapter 16

16.2 a. $WMA(p = 3, \text{Period } 8, \text{Demand}) = \dfrac{(1)(19) + (3)(16) + (4)(10)}{1 + 3 + 4} = 13.38$

b. $MAD = \dfrac{18.25}{4} = 4.56$

16.4 a.

PERIOD t	ACTUAL DEMAND A_t	SMOOTHED FORECAST DEMAND F_t	TREND T_t	FORECAST W/TREND FIT_t	ABSOLUTE FORECASTING ERROR $\|A_t - FIT_t\|$
1	15	15	0	15	
2	24	15	0	15	9
3	26	18.6	2.5	21.1	4.9
4	33	23.1	3.9	27.0	6.0
5	20	29.4	5.6	35.0	15.0
6	22	29.0	1.4	30.5	8.4
7	27	27.0	−1.0	26.1	0.9
8	20	26.4	−0.7	25.8	5.8

$F_9 = 25.8 + (0.4)(20 - 25.8) = 23.2;$
$T_9 = 0.7(23.5 - 26.4) + 0.3(-0.7) = -2.2$
$FIT_9 = 23.5 - 2.2 = 21.3$

b. $MAD = \dfrac{50.0}{7} = 7.14$

16.6 a.

ACTUAL CPI A_t	SMOOTHED FORECAST CPI F_t	TREND T_t	FORECAST W/TREND FIT_t	ABSOLUTE FORECASTING ERROR $\|A_t - FIT_t\|$
184.0	184.0	0	184.0	
188.9	184.0	0	184.0	4.9
195.3	185.5	0.8	186.3	9.0
201.6	189.0	2.1	191.1	10.5
207.3	194.3	3.7	198.0	9.3
215.3	200.8	5.1	205.9	9.4
214.5	208.7	6.5	215.2	0.7
218.1	215.0	6.4	221.4	3.3
224.9	220.4	5.9	226.3	1.4
229.6	225.9	5.7	231.6	2.0

$F_{2013} = 231.6 + (0.3)(229.6 - 231.6) = 231.0$
$T_{2013} = 0.5(231.0 - 225.9) + 0.5(5.7) = 5.4$
$FIT_{2013} = 231.0 + 5.4 = 236.4$

b. $MAD = \dfrac{50.5}{9} = 5.61$

16.8 a. $WMA(p = 3, 2014) = \dfrac{(1)(20.6) + (2)(14.9) + (3)(12.1)}{1 + 2 + 3}$
$= 14.45$

b.

YEAR t	VIEWERS A_t	FORECAST VIEWERS F_t	ABSOLUTE FORECASTING ERROR $\|A_t - F_t\|$
2005	30.3		
2006	31.8		
2007	25.3		
2008	27.1	28.30	1.20
2009	23.8	27.28	3.48
2010	20.1	25.15	5.05
2011	20.6	22.50	1.90
2012	14.9	20.97	6.07
2013	12.1	17.67	5.57

$MAD = \dfrac{23.27}{6} = 3.88$

c. $F_{2014} = 16.4 + (0.4)(12.1 - 16.4) = 14.7$
$T_{2014} = 0.2(14.7 - 18.1) + 0.8(-1.7) = -2.0$
$FIT_{2014} = 14.7 - 2.0 = 12.7$

d. $MAD = \dfrac{28.5}{8} = 3.56$

e. The forecast using exponential smoothing with trend adjustment would be preferable to the three-period weighted moving average because its *MAD* is lower.

16.10 a. $SMA(p = 4, \text{Year } 2011, \text{Enrollment})$

$$= \frac{630 + 625 + 641 + 656}{4} = 638$$

b. $MAD = \frac{55.0}{4} = 13.75$

c.

YEAR t	ACTUAL ENROLLMENT A_t	SMOOTHED FORECAST ENROLLMENT F_t	ABSOLUTE FORECASTING ERROR $\lvert A_t - F_t \rvert$
2006	624	624	
2007	645	624	21
2008	659	632.4	26.6
2009	643	643	0
2010	630	643	13
2011	625	637.8	12.8
2012	641	632.7	8.3
2013	656	636	20

$$F_{2014} = 636 + (0.4)(656 - 636) = 644$$

d. $MAD = \frac{101.7}{7} = 14.52$

e. The forecast using four-period simple moving average would be preferable because its MAD is lower than the forecast that uses exponential smoothing.

16.12 a. $SMA(p = 3, \text{Month } 11, \text{Expenses})$

$$= \frac{\$312 + \$364 + \$345}{3} = \$340.3$$

$$MAD = \frac{153.0}{7} = 21.86$$

b. $WMA(p = 3, \text{Month } 11, \text{Expenses})$

$$= \frac{(0.1)(\$312) + (0.2)(\$364) + (0.7)(\$345)}{0.1 + 0.2 + 0.7} = 345.5$$

$$MAD = \frac{159.2}{7} = 22.74$$

c. $F_{11} = 340.0 + (0.1)(345 - 340) = 340.5$

$$MAD = \frac{174.3}{9} = 19.36$$

d. The forecast using exponential smoothing would be preferable because its MAD is lower than the forecast that uses either three-period simple moving average or three-period weighted moving average.

16.14 a. $n = 8; \sum t = 36; \sum y = 87; \sum ty = 330; \sum t^2 = 204$

$$b_1 = \frac{(8)(330) - (36)(87)}{(8)(204) - (36)^2} = -1.464$$

$$b_0 = \frac{87}{8} - (-1.464)\left(\frac{36}{8}\right) = 17.463$$

$$\hat{y}_9 = 17.463 + (-1.464)(9) = 4.29$$

c.

PERIOD t	ACTUAL DEMAND A_t	FORECAST DEMAND F_t	ABSOLUTE FORECASTING ERROR $\lvert A_t - F_t \rvert$
1	15	16.00	1.00
2	17	14.54	2.46
3	14	13.07	0.93
4	7	11.61	4.61
5	10	10.14	0.14
6	12	8.68	3.32
7	7	7.22	0.22
8	5	5.75	0.75

$$MAD = \frac{13.43}{8} = 1.68$$

16.16 a. $d = \frac{330.09}{166.84} = 1.978; d_L = 1.08; d_U = 1.36$

Because $d > d_U$, we fail to reject the null hypothesis and conclude that no positive autocorrelation is present in this time series.

16.18 b. $n = 9; \sum t = 45; \sum y = 903.3; \sum ty = 4,712.5; \sum t^2 = 285$

$$b_1 = \frac{(9)(4,712.5) - (45)(903.3)}{(9)(285) - (45)^2} = 3.2667$$

$$b_0 = \frac{903.3}{9} - (3.2667)\left(\frac{45}{9}\right) = 84.0332$$

$$\hat{y}_{2014} = 84.0332 + (2.865)(10) = 112.68$$

c. $MAD = \frac{17.26}{9} = 1.92$

16.20 b. $n = 8; \sum t = 36; \sum y = 3,130; \sum ty = 14,828; \sum t^2 = 204$

$$b_1 = \frac{(8)(14,828) - (36)(3,130)}{(8)(204) - (36)^2} = 17.690$$

$$b_0 = \frac{3,130}{8} - (17.690)\left(\frac{36}{8}\right) = 311.645$$

$$\hat{y}_9 = 311.645 + (17.69)(9) = 470.9$$

c. $MAD = \frac{140.19}{8} = 17.524$

d. $t = \frac{500 - 311.645}{17.69} = 10.6 \approx 11$

The number of minutes will exceed the plan's limit in the 11th's month.

16.22 b. $n = 21; \sum t = 231; \sum y = 12,449; \sum ty = 178,744;$ $\sum t^2 = 3,311$

$$b_1 = \frac{(21)(178,744) - (231)(12,449)}{(21)(3,311) - (231)^2} = 54.2922$$

$$b_0 = \frac{12,449}{21} - (54.2922)\left(\frac{231}{21}\right) = -4.4047$$

$$\hat{y}_{2013} = -4.4047 + (54.2922)(22) = \$1,190.02$$

c. $MAD = \frac{4,596}{21} = \$218.86$

d. $d = \frac{196,683.5}{1,368,963.5} = 0.144; n = 21; \alpha = 0.05; d_L = 1.22;$

$d_U = 1.42$

Because $d < d_L$, we reject the null hypothesis and conclude that a positive autocorrelation is present in this time series.

e. The graph of the data from part a does not appear to follow a linear pattern and positive autocorrelation is present. This forecasting method does not appear to be appropriate for this data.

16.24 a.

PERIOD	SEASON	DEMAND Y_t	SEASONAL COMPONENT S_t	DESEASONALIZED DEMAND
1	Y1-Q1	6	0.7929	7.6
2	Y1-Q2	11	1.4425	7.6
3	Y1-Q3	9	1.1001	8.2
4	Y1-Q4	5	0.6645	7.5
5	Y2-Q1	8	0.7929	10.1
6	Y2-Q2	14	1.4425	9.7
7	Y2-Q3	10	1.1001	9.1
8	Y2-Q4	7	0.6645	10.5
9	Y3-Q1	7	0.7929	8.8
10	Y3-Q2	15	1.4425	10.4
11	Y3-Q3	14	1.1001	12.7
12	Y3-Q4	9	0.6645	13.5

$$T_t = 6.5964 + 0.47t$$
$$F_{Y4\text{-}Q1} = T_{13} \times S_{13} = [6.5964 + 0.47(13)](0.7929) = 10.1$$
$$F_{Y4\text{-}Q2} = T_{14} \times S_{14} = [6.5964 + 0.47(14)](1.4425) = 19.0$$
$$F_{Y4\text{-}Q3} = T_{15} \times S_{15} = [6.5964 + 0.47(15)](1.1001) = 15.0$$
$$F_{Y4\text{-}Q4} = T_{16} \times S_{16} = [6.5964 + 0.47(16)](0.6645) = 9.4$$

b. Quarter 2 has the highest demand, followed by Quarters 3, 1, and 4, in that order.

c. $MAD = \dfrac{8.49}{12} = 0.71$

16.26 a.

	DUMMY VARIABLES		
	SD1	SD2	SD3
Quarter 1	0	0	0
Quarter 2	1	0	0
Quarter 3	0	1	0
Quarter 4	0	0	1

Set x_1 = Period, x_2 = SD1, x_3 = SD2, x_4 = SD3

Model	Cp	k+1	R Square	Adj. R Square	Std. Error
X1	79.1219	2	0.1594	0.0753	3.1881
X2	47.4286	2	0.4652	0.4117	2.5430
X3	88.7619	2	0.0664	-0.0270	3.3599
X4	72.7619	2	0.2208	0.1428	3.0696
X1X2	27.6982	3	0.6749	0.6026	2.0900
X1X3	75.8719	3	0.2101	0.0345	3.2578
X1X4	45.1841	3	0.5061	0.3964	2.5758
X2X3	22.0000	3	0.7298	0.6698	1.9052
X2X4	42.5714	3	0.5314	0.4272	2.5092
X3X4	73.5714	3	0.2323	0.0616	3.2117
X1X2X3	5.0035	4	0.9131	0.8806	1.1459
X1X2X4	14.9936	4	0.8167	0.7480	1.6643
X1X3X4	47.1748	4	0.5062	0.3211	2.7318
X2X3X4	24.0000	4	0.7298	0.6285	2.0207
X1X2X3X4	5.0000	5	0.9325	0.8939	1.0801

$$F_t = 4.812 + 0.438t + 5.896SD_1 + 3.125SD_2 - 1.312SD_3$$
$$F_{Y4\text{-}Q1} = 4.812 + 0.438(13) + 5.896(0) + 3.125(0) - 1.312(0) = 10.5$$
$$F_{Y4\text{-}Q2} = 4.812 + 0.438(14) + 5.896(1) + 3.125(0) - 1.312(0) = 16.8$$
$$F_{Y4\text{-}Q3} = 4.812 + 0.438(15) + 5.896(0) + 3.125(1) - 1.312(0) = 14.5$$
$$F_{Y4\text{-}Q4} = 4.812 + 0.438(16) + 5.896(0) + 3.125(0) - 1.312(1) = 10.5$$

b. Quarter 2 has an average demand that is 5.9 units above that for Quarter 1. Quarter 3 has an average demand that is 3.1 units above that for Quarter 1. Quarter 4 has an average demand that is 1.3 units below that for Quarter 1.

c. $MAD = \dfrac{7.81}{12} = 0.651$

16.28 a.

	DUMMY VARIABLES	
	SD1	SD2
Fall	0	0
Spring	1	0
Summer	0	1

Set x_1 = Period, x_2 = SD1, x_3 = SD2

b.

Model	Cp	k+1	R Square	Adj. R Square	Std. Error
X1	1806.0797	2	0.0272	-0.0701	110.0305
X2	1626.0438	2	0.1238	0.0361	104.4280
X3	1113.7026	2	0.3985	0.3383	86.5215
X1X2	1577.2849	3	0.1510	-0.0377	108.3536
X1X3	1113.2252	3	0.3998	0.2665	91.1009
X2X3	8.0775	3	0.9925	0.9908	10.2171
X1X2X3	4.0000	4	0.9957	0.9941	8.1693

$$F_t = 262.717 + 1.733t - 193.983SD_1 - 235.967SD_2$$
$$F_{Y5\text{-Fall}} = 262.717 + 1.733(13) - 193.983(0) - 235.967(0) = 285.25 \approx 285$$
$$F_{Y5\text{-Spring}} = 262.717 + 1.733(14) - 193.983(1) - 235.967(0) - 93$$
$$F_{Y5\text{-Summer}} = 262.717 + 1.733(15) - 193.983(0) - 235.967(1) = 52.75 \approx 53$$

c. The spring semester has an average enrollment that is 194.0 students below that of the fall semester. The summer semester has an average enrollment that is 236.0 students below that of the fall semester.

d. $MAD = \dfrac{68.4}{12} = 5.7$

16.30 b.

PERIOD	SEASON	REVENUE y_t	SEASONAL COMPONENT S_t	DESEASONALIZED REVENUE
1	10-Q1	346	0.9799	353.1
2	10-Q2	297	0.9778	303.7
3	10-Q3	293	0.9644	303.8
4	10-Q4	332	1.0779	308.0
5	11-Q1	313	0.9799	319.4
6	11-Q2	319	0.9778	326.2
7	11-Q3	318	0.9644	329.7
8	11-Q4	364	1.0779	337.7
9	12-Q1	330	0.9799	336.8
10	12-Q2	338	0.9778	345.7
11	12-Q3	340	0.9644	352.6
12	12-Q4	411	1.0779	381.3

$$T_t = 304.8485 + 4.3566t$$
$$F_{2013\text{-}Q1} = T_{13} \times S_{13} = [304.8485 + 4.3566(13)](0.9799) = \$354.21$$
$$F_{2013\text{-}Q2} = T_{14} \times S_{14} = [304.8485 + 4.3566(14)](0.9778) = \$357.72$$
$$F_{2013\text{-}Q3} = T_{15} \times S_{15} = [304.8485 + 4.3566(15)](0.9644) = \$357.02$$
$$F_{2013\text{-}Q4} = T_{16} \times S_{16} = [304.8485 + 4.3566(16)](1.0779) = \$403.73$$

c. AOL's advertising revenue is highest during Quarter 4.

d. $MAD = \dfrac{136.92}{12} = 11.41$

e. AOL's advertising revenue is increasing by an average of $4.36 million per quarter.

16.32 b.

	DUMMY VARIABLES			
	SD1	**SD2**	**SD3**	**SD4**
Monday	0	0	0	0
Tuesday	1	0	0	0
Wednesday	0	1	0	0
Thursday	0	0	1	0
Friday	0	0	0	1

Set x_1 = Period, x_2 = SD1, x_3 = SD2, x_4 = SD3, x_5 = SD4

Model	Cp	k+1	R Square	Adj. R Square	Std. Error
X1X2X3	24.5488	4	0.6541	0.5598	14.4971
X1X2X4	52.9025	4	0.3433	0.1641	19.9762
X1X2X5	30.9257	4	0.5842	0.4708	15.8949
X1X3X4	46.6620	4	0.4117	0.2512	18.9070
X1X3X5	28.1270	4	0.6149	0.5098	15.2971
X1X4X5	38.0944	4	0.5056	0.3708	17.3321
X2X3X4	14.3730	4	0.7657	0.7018	11.9323
X2X3X5	31.1380	4	0.5819	0.4678	15.9393
X2X4X5	49.8544	4	0.3767	0.2067	19.4613
X3X4X5	42.8469	4	0.4535	0.3045	18.2225
X1X2X3X4	5.6038	5	0.8837	0.8372	8.8149
X1X2X3X5	14.2441	5	0.7890	0.7046	11.8750
X1X2X4X5	32.6638	5	0.5871	0.4219	16.6130
X1X3X4X5	29.5473	5	0.6212	0.4697	15.9108
X2X3X4X5	16.3161	5	0.7663	0.6728	12.4980
X1X2X3X4X5	6.0000	6	0.9013	0.8465	8.5602

$F_t = 177.733 - 1.9t - 35.433SD_1 - 37.867SD_2 - 22.967SD_3 + 9.267SD_4$

$F_{\text{Monday-Week4}} = 177.733 - 1.9(16) - 35.433(0) - 37.867(0) - 22.967(0) + 9.267(0) = 147.33$

$F_{\text{Tuesday-Week4}} = 177.733 - 1.9(17) - 35.433(1) - 37.867(0) - 22.967(0) + 9.267(0) = 110.00$

$F_{\text{Wednesday-Week4}} = 177.733 - 1.9(18) - 35.433(0) - 37.867(1) - 22.967(0) + 9.267(0) = 105.67$

$F_{\text{Thursday-Week4}} = 177.733 - 1.9(19) - 35.433(0) - 37.867(0) - 22.967(1) + 9.267(0) = 118.67$

$F_{\text{Friday-Week4}} = 177.733 - 1.9(20) - 35.433(0) - 37.867(0) - 22.967(0) + 9.267(1) = 149.00$

c. Tuesday has an average chlorine demand that is 35.4 tons below that for Monday. Wednesday has an average chlorine demand that is 37.9 tons below that for Monday. Thursday has an average chlorine demand that is 23.0 tons below that for Monday. Friday has an average chlorine demand that is 9.3 tons above that for Monday.

d. $MAD = \dfrac{76.67}{15} = 5.111$

16.34 b. $T_t = 589.2219 + 4.5064t$

$F_{\text{Monday-Week4}} = T_{16} \times S_{16} = [589.2219 + 4.5064(16)](1.1538) = \$763.04$

$F_{\text{Tuesday-Week4}} = T_{17} \times S_{17} = [589.2219 + 4.5064(17)](0.8894) = \$592.19$

$F_{\text{Wednesday-Week4}} = T_{18} \times S_{18} = [589.2219 + 4.5064(18)](1.2134) = \$813.39$

$F_{\text{Thursday-Week4}} = T_{19} \times S_{19} = [589.2219 + 4.5064(19)](0.8403) = \$567.07$

$F_{\text{Friday-Week4}} = T_{20} \times S_{20} = [589.2219 + 4.5064(20)](0.9029) = \$613.39$

c. The highest sales occur on Wednesday, followed by Monday, Friday, Tuesday, and Thursday, in that order.

d. $MAD = \dfrac{\$310.68}{15} = \$20.71$

16.36 a.

YEAR t	ACTUAL PERCENT A_t	FORECAST PERCENT F_t	ABSOLUTE FORECASTING ERROR $\lvert A_t - F_t \rvert$
2005	32		
2006	29		
2007	41		
2008	59	34.0	25.0
2009	51	43.0	8.0
2010	38	50.3	12.3
2011	42	49.3	7.3
2012	37	43.7	6.7

$SMA(p = 3, \text{Year 2013, Percent}) = \dfrac{37 + 42 + 38}{3} = 39.0$

b. $MAD = \dfrac{59.3}{5} = 11.9$

c.

YEAR t	ACTUAL PERCENT A_t	FORECAST PERCENT F_t	ABSOLUTE FORECASTING ERROR $\lvert A_t - F_t \rvert$
2005	32		
2006	29		
2007	41		
2008	59	36.0	23.0
2009	51	49.7	1.3
2010	38	52.6	14.6
2011	42	44.7	2.7
2012	37	41.7	4.7

$WMA(p = 3, \text{Year 2013, Percent}) = \dfrac{(5)(37) + (3)(42) + (1)(38)}{5 + 3 + 1} = 38.8$

d. $MAD = \dfrac{46.3}{5} = 9.3$

e. The forecast using three-period weighted moving average would be preferable because its *MAD* is lower than the forecast that uses three-period simple moving average.

16.38 a.

DAY t	CUSTOMERS A_t	FORECAST CUSTOMERS F_t	ABSOLUTE FORECASTING ERROR $\lvert A_t - F_t \rvert$
1	260		
2	243		
3	232		
4	277	245.0	32.0
5	270	250.7	19.3
6	285	259.7	25.3
7	248	277.3	29.3
8	254	267.7	13.7

$$SMA(p = 3, \text{Day 9, Customers}) = \frac{285 + 248 + 254}{3} = 262.3$$

b. $MAD = \dfrac{119.6}{5} = 23.92$

c.

DAY t	CUSTOMERS A_t	SMOOTHED FORECAST CUSTOMERS F_t	FORECASTING ERROR $A_t - F_t$	ABSOLUTE FORECASTING ERROR $\|A_t - F_t\|$
1	260	260		
2	243	260	−17	17
3	232	258.3	−26.3	26.3
4	277	255.7	21.3	21.3
5	270	257.8	12.2	12.2
6	285	259.0	26.0	26.0
7	248	261.6	−13.6	13.6
8	254	260.2	−6.2	6.2

$$F_9 = 260.2 + (0.1)(254 - 260.2) = 259.6$$

d. $MAD = \dfrac{122.6}{7} = 17.51$

e. The forecast using exponential smoothing would be preferable because its MAD is lower than the forecast that uses three-period simple moving average.

16.40 b. $n = 8; \sum t = 36; \sum y = 23.8; \sum ty = 108.7; \sum t^2 = 204$

$$b_1 = \frac{(8)(108.7) - (36)(23.8)}{(8)(204) - (36)^2} = 0.038$$

$$b_0 = \frac{23.8}{8} - (0.038)\left(\frac{36}{8}\right) = 2.804$$

$$\hat{y}_{2014} = 2.804 + (0.038)(9) = 3.15$$

c.

YEAR	PERIOD t	ACTUAL GPA A_t	FORECAST GPA F_t	ABSOLUTE FORECASTING ERROR $\|A_t - F_t\|$
2006	1	2.94	2.84	0.10
2007	2	2.82	2.88	0.06
2008	3	2.90	2.92	0.02
2009	4	2.96	2.96	0.00
2010	5	2.85	2.99	0.14
2011	6	3.08	3.03	0.05
2012	7	3.15	3.07	0.08
2013	8	3.10	3.11	0.01

There is an indication that grade inflation is present at Newark College because the actual GPA and forecasted GPA are constantly growing over time.

16.42 a.

	DUMMY VARIABLES	
	SD1	SD2
Fall	0	0
Spring	1	0
Summer	0	1

Set x_1 = Period, x_2 = SD1, x_3 = SD2

Model	Cp	k+1	R Square	Adj. R Square	Std. Error
X1	48.8818	2	0.1373	0.0980	0.2095
X2	59.1736	2	0.0084	-0.0367	0.2246
X3	14.7090	2	0.5653	0.5455	0.1487
X1X2	50.2145	3	0.1456	0.0642	0.2134
X1X3	9.7500	3	0.6524	0.6193	0.1361
X2X3	8.0925	3	0.6732	0.6421	0.1320
X1X2X3	4.0000	4	0.7495	0.7119	0.1184

$$F_t = 2.65 + 0.0087t + 0.1651SD_1 + 0.4139SD_2$$
$$F_{\text{Fall-2014}} = 2.65 + 0.0087(25) + 0.1651(0) + 0.4139(0) = 2.87$$
$$F_{\text{Spring-2014}} = 2.65 + 0.0087(26) + 0.1651(1) + 0.4139(0) = 3.04$$
$$F_{\text{Summer-2014}} = 2.65 + 0.0087(27) + 0.1651(0) + 0.4139(1) = 3.30$$

b. The spring semester has an average GPA that is 0.17 points higher than the fall semester.

c. The summer semester has an average GPA that is 0.41 points higher than the fall semester.

d. $MAD = \dfrac{2.357}{24} = 0.098$

16.44 a.

YEAR	PERIOD t	ACTUAL BONUS A_t	SMOOTHED FORECAST BONUS F_t	ABSOLUTE FORECASTING ERROR $\|A_t - F_t\|$
2005	1	149.8	149.80	
2006	2	191.4	149.80	41.60
2007	3	177.8	170.60	7.20
2008	4	100.9	174.20	73.30
2009	5	140.6	137.55	3.05
2010	6	139.0	139.08	0.08
2011	7	111.3	139.04	27.74
2012	8	121.9	125.17	3.27

$$F_{2013} = 125.17 + (0.5)(121.9 - 125.17) = 123.54$$

b. $MAD = \dfrac{156.24}{7} = 22.32$

c.

PERIOD t	ACTUAL BONUS A_t	SMOOTHED FORECAST BONUS F_t	TREND T_t	FORECAST W/TREND FIT_t	ABSOLUTE FORECASTING ERROR $\|A_t - FIT_t\|$
1	149.8	149.80	0.00	149.80	
2	191.4	149.80	0.00	149.80	41.60
3	177.8	170.60	10.40	181.00	3.20
4	100.9	179.40	9.60	189.00	88.10
5	140.6	144.95	−12.43	132.52	8.08
6	139.0	136.56	−10.41	126.15	12.85
7	111.3	132.58	−7.19	125.39	14.09
8	121.9	118.35	−10.71	107.64	14.26

$$F_{2013} = 107.64 + (0.5)(121.9 - 107.64) = 114.77$$
$$T_{2013} = 0.5(114.77 - 118.35) + 0.5(-10.71) = -7.15$$
$$FIT_{2013} = 114.77 - 7.15 = 107.62$$

d. $MAD = \dfrac{182.18}{7} = 26.03$

e. The forecast using exponential smoothing would be preferable because its *MAD* is lower than the forecast using exponential smoothing with trend adjustment.

16.46 b. $n = 9; \sum t = 45; \sum y = 132.1; \sum ty = 790.1; \sum t^2 = 285$

$$b_1 = \frac{(9)(790.1) - (45)(132.1)}{(9)(285) - (45)^2} = 2.1600$$

$$b_0 = \frac{132.1}{9} - (2.1600)\left(\frac{45}{9}\right) = 3.8778$$

$$\hat{y}_{10} = 3.8778 + (2.1600)(10) = 25.48$$

c.

YEAR	PERIOD t	ACTUAL RATE A_t	FORECAST RATE F_t	ABSOLUTE FORECASTING ERROR $\lvert A_t - F_t \rvert$
2004	1	10.4	6.04	4.36
2005	2	9.2	8.20	1.00
2006	3	8.1	10.36	2.26
2007	4	8.3	12.52	4.22
2008	5	11.3	14.68	3.38
2009	6	18.0	16.84	1.16
2010	7	20.1	19.00	1.10
2011	8	21.7	21.16	0.54
2012	9	25.0	23.32	1.68

$$MAD = \frac{19.7}{9} = 2.19$$

16.48 a. $SMA(p = 4, 2013) = \frac{9.69 + 9.01 + 9.46 + 9.49}{4} = 9.413$

b. $MAD = \frac{3.852}{12} = 0.321$

c. $F_{2013} = 9.138 + (0.7)(9.69 - 9.138) = 9.524$

d. $MAD = \frac{3.639}{16} = 0.243$

e. The forecast using exponential smoothing would be preferable because its *MAD* is lower than the forecast using a four-period simple moving average.

16.50 a.

10	Model	Cp	k+1	R Square	Adj. R Square	Std. Error
11	X1	276.6899	2	0.0764	0.0251	1.9556
12	X2	181.2109	2	0.3777	0.3431	1.6053
13	X3	300.9048	2	0.0000	-0.0555	2.0349
14	X4	48.3537	2	0.7969	0.7857	0.9170
15	X1X2	164.0328	3	0.4382	0.3721	1.5694
16	X1X3	278.5832	3	0.0768	-0.0318	2.0120
17	X1X4	43.7807	3	0.8177	0.7962	0.8941
18	X2X3	167.5859	3	0.4270	0.3596	1.5850
19	X2X4	14.5247	3	0.9100	0.8994	0.6282
20	X3X4	19.7287	3	0.8936	0.8810	0.6831
21	X1X2X3	149.1353	4	0.4915	0.3962	1.5391
22	X1X2X4	9.9516	4	0.9307	0.9177	0.5681
23	X1X3X4	17.8051	4	0.9060	0.8883	0.6619
24	X2X3X4	7.9150	4	0.9372	0.9254	0.5411
25	X1X2X3X4	5.0000	5	0.9527	0.9400	0.4850

$$F_t = 5.1775 + 0.0425t - 1.1825SD_1 + 0.8150SD_2 + 3.7725SD_3$$

$$F_{6-Q1} = 5.1775 + 0.0425(21) - 1.1825(0) + 0.8150(0) + 3.7725(0) = 6.07$$

$$F_{6-Q2} = 5.1775 + 0.0425(22) - 1.1825(1) + 0.8150(0) + 3.7725(0) = 4.93$$

$$F_{6-Q3} = 5.1775 + 0.0425(23) - 1.1825(0) + 0.8150(1) + 3.7725(0) = 6.97$$

$$F_{6-Q4} = 5.1775 + 0.0425(24) - 1.1825(0) + 0.8150(0) + 3.7725(1) = 9.97$$

b. Quarter 2 has average sales that are \$1.18 million below Quarter 1. Quarter 3 has average sales that are \$0.815 million above Quarter 1. Quarter 4 has average sales that are \$3.77 million above Quarter 1.

c. $MAD = \frac{6.20}{20} = 0.31$

16.52 a. $n = 24; \sum t = 300; \sum y = 32{,}006; \sum ty = 407{,}255; \sum t^2 = 4{,}900$

$$b_1 = \frac{(24)(407{,}255) - (300)(32{,}006)}{(24)(4{,}900) - (300)^2} = 6.2435$$

$$b_0 = \frac{32{,}006}{24} - (6.2435)\left(\frac{300}{24}\right) = 1{,}255.5396$$

$$\hat{y}_{\text{Jan-2013}} = 1{,}255.5396 + (6.2435)(25) = 1{,}411.6$$

b. $d = \frac{53{,}496.4}{87{,}393.7} = 0.612; n = 24; \alpha = 0.05; d_L = 1.27; d_U = 1.45$

Because $d < d_L$, we should reject the null hypothesis and conclude that there is a positive autocorrelation in this time series.

c. The trend projection method is not appropriate for the forecast of the S&P 500 Index because of the presence of autocorrelation that can lead to unreliable forecasts.

16.54 b. $n = 28; \sum t = 406; \sum y = 398; \sum ty = 4{,}299; \sum t^2 = 7{,}714$

$$b_1 = \frac{(28)(4{,}299) - (406)(398)}{(28)(7{,}714) - (406)^2} = -0.8057$$

$$b_0 = \frac{398}{28} - (-0.8057)\left(\frac{406}{28}\right) = 25.8969$$

$$\hat{y}_{2014} = 25.8969 - (0.8057)(29) = 2.53 \approx 3$$

$$MAD = \frac{216.7}{28} = 7.7$$

c. $d = \frac{8,617.4}{2,742.7} = 3.142; n = 28; \alpha = 0.05; d_L = 1.33; d_U = 1.48$

Because $d > d_U$, we fail to reject the null hypothesis and conclude that no positive autocorrelation is present in this time series, so the trend projection method is appropriate.

d. The limitation is that the downward trend can't continue because the point spread cannot be negative. The winning team must have more winning points than the losing team.

Photo Credits

CHAPTER 1

Pages 1 and **16**, Fotolia; **Page 2**, Ruslan Ivantsov/Shutterstock; **Page 3**, Shutterstock; **Page 7**, Robert Donnelly; **Page 12**, Oliver Hoffmann/Shutterstock; **Page 13**, Picture-Factory/Fotolia; **Page 15**, Fotolia.

CHAPTER 2

Pages 21 and **66**, Shutterstock; **Page 23**, Laborant/Shutterstock; **Page 26**, Fotolia; **Page 42**, Alexander Raths/Shutterstock; **Page 50**, Shutterstock; **Page 61**, Fotolia.

CHAPTER 3

Pages 77 and **132**, Shutterstock; **Page 81**, Michael Jung/Fotolia; **Page 84**, Shutterstick; **Page 100**, Robert Donnelly; **Page 105**, Shutterstock; **Page 117**, Dan Race/Fotolia; **Page 122**, Robert Donnelly; **Page 126**, Andres Rodriguez/Fotolia.

CHAPTER 4

Pages 147 and **183**, Volodymyr Krasyuk/Shutterstock; **Page 151**, Monkey Business Images/Shutterstock; **Page 161**, Valerie Potapova/Fotolia; **Page 170**, Fotolia.

CHAPTER 5

Page 193 and **235**, Shutterstock; **Page 194**, Danny E. Hooks/Shutterstock; **Page 196**, Shutterstock; **Page 205**, VikOl/Shutterstock; **Page 214**, C. A. Carrigan/Shutterstock; **Page 226**, Ersler Dmitry/Shutterstock.

CHAPTER 6

Pages 247 and **279**, Pitrs/Fotolia; **Page 248**, Robert Donnelly; **Page 257**, Fotolia; **Page 263**, Fotolia; **Page 272**, Tyler Olson/Fotolia.

CHAPTER 7

Pages 289 and **323**, Tom Hauck/AP Images; **Page 291**, Alysta/Shutterstock; **Page 296**, Monkey Business/Fotolia; **Page 308**, Dmitry Kalinovsky/Shutterstock; **Page 313**, Fotolia.

CHAPTER 8

Pages 333 and **371**, Shutterstock; **Page 338**, R. Gino Santa Maria/Shutterstock; **Page 342**, Andy Dean/Fotolia; **Page 346**, Teekaygee/Shutterstock; **Page 362**, Robert Donnelly; **Page 367**, Tyler Olson/Fotolia.

CHAPTER 9

Pages 383 and **425**, Harry Hu/Shutterstock; **Page 385**, R. Mackay Photography/Shutterstock; **Page 389**, Ever/Fotolia; **Page 401**, Xy/Fotolia; **Page 412**, Pressmaster/Shutterstock; **Page 417**, Boykov/Shutterstock.

CHAPTER 10

Pages 437 and **484**, Moodboard/Getty Images; **Page 438**, Robert Donnelly; **Page 462**, Jose Gil/Shutterstock; **Page 471**, Lichtmeister/Fotolia; **Page 475**, Amy Walters/Shutterstock; **Page 481**, Iofoto/Shutterstock.

CHAPTER 11

Pages 501 and **557**, iStockphoto/Thinkstock; **Page 507**, Carmen Steiner/Shutterstock; **Page 526**, Minerva Studio/Fotolia; **Page 541**, Pink Badger/Fotolia; **Page 548**, Floydine/Fotolia.

CHAPTER 12

Pages 575 and **612**, Marcio Jose Bastos Silva/Shutterstock; **Page 577**, Sedin/Shutterstock; **Page 585**, Beth Ponticello/Shutterstock; **Page 597**, R Mackay/Fotolia; **Page 609**, Monkey Business/Fotolia.

CHAPTER 13

Pages 625 and **644**, Arsel/Fotolia; **Page 626**, Tyler Olson/Fotolia; **Page 631**, Sixninepixels/Shutterstock; **Page 634**, Ministr-84/Shutterstock; **Page 639**, Shutterstock.

CHAPTER 14

Pages 651 and **697**, Scanrail/Fotolia; **Page 657**, Robert Donnelly; **Page 667**, Jack Hollingsworth/Photodisc/Thinkstock; **Page 689**, Danny Hooks/Fotolia.

CHAPTER 15

Pages 709 and **756**, Egd/Shutterstock; **Page 714**, Waynerd/Fotolia; **Page 732**, Pangfolio.com/Shutterstock; **Page 739**, Kadmy/Fotolia.

CHAPTER 16

Pages 767 and **814**, Diego Cervo/Fotolia; **Page 774**, Lightpoet/Fotolia; **Page 795**, Trekandshoot/Fotolia.

COVER PHOTOS

Trading screen financial data, Simon Smith/Getty Images; *Red empty stadium seats,* Ollo/Getty Images; *Apples and red peppers ready to be bought,* Antonio Rosario/Getty Images; *Jet plane in a sunset sky. Panoramic composition in high resolution,* Mo Ses/Shutterstock; *Row of different cars parked in a crowded city,* Radu Razvan/Shutterstock; *Touching stock market graph on a touch screen device,* Bloomua/Shutterstock; *FitBit image,* Courtesy of FitBit, Inc.

Index

D

G

H

Q

R

S

V

W

Y

Z

TABLE 3 | Cumulative Probabilities for the Standard Normal Distribution

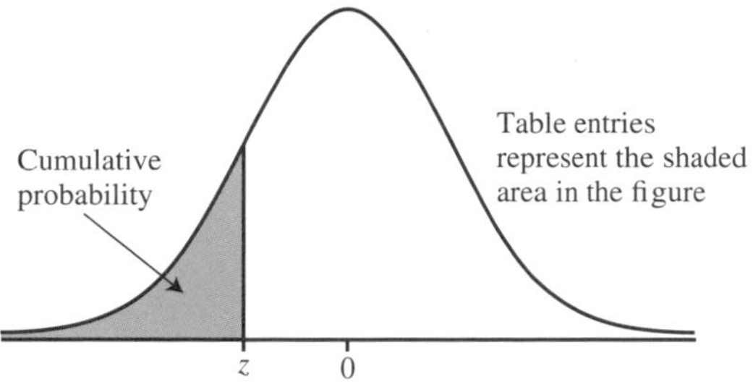

FIRST DIGIT OF *Z* / SECOND DIGIT OF *Z*

z	0.00	0.01	0.02	0.03	0.04	0.05	0.06	0.07	0.08	0.09
−3.7 and lower	0.0001									
−3.6	0.0002	0.0002	0.0001	0.0001	0.0001	0.0001	0.0001	0.0001	0.0001	0.0001
−3.5	0.0002	0.0002	0.0002	0.0002	0.0002	0.0002	0.0002	0.0002	0.0002	0.0002
−3.4	0.0003	0.0003	0.0003	0.0003	0.0003	0.0003	0.0003	0.0003	0.0003	0.0002
−3.3	0.0005	0.0005	0.0005	0.0004	0.0004	0.0004	0.0004	0.0004	0.0004	0.0003
−3.2	0.0007	0.0007	0.0006	0.0006	0.0006	0.0006	0.0006	0.0005	0.0005	0.0005
−3.1	0.0010	0.0009	0.0009	0.0009	0.0008	0.0008	0.0008	0.0008	0.0007	0.0007
−3.0	0.0013	0.0013	0.0013	0.0012	0.0012	0.0011	0.0011	0.0011	0.0010	0.0010
−2.9	0.0019	0.0018	0.0018	0.0017	0.0016	0.0016	0.0015	0.0015	0.0014	0.0014
−2.8	0.0026	0.0025	0.0024	0.0023	0.0023	0.0022	0.0021	0.0021	0.0020	0.0019
−2.7	0.0035	0.0034	0.0033	0.0032	0.0031	0.0030	0.0029	0.0028	0.0027	0.0026
−2.6	0.0047	0.0045	0.0044	0.0043	0.0041	0.0040	0.0039	0.0038	0.0037	0.0036
−2.5	0.0062	0.0060	0.0059	0.0057	0.0055	0.0054	0.0052	0.0051	0.0049	0.0048
−2.4	0.0082	0.0080	0.0078	0.0075	0.0073	0.0071	0.0069	0.0068	0.0066	0.0064
−2.3	0.0107	0.0104	0.0102	0.0099	0.0096	0.0094	0.0091	0.0089	0.0007	0.0004
−2.2	0.0139	0.0136	0.0132	0.0129	0.0125	0.0122	0.0119	0.0116	0.0113	0.0110
−2.1	0.0179	0.0174	0.0170	0.0166	0.0162	0.0158	0.0154	0.0150	0.0146	0.0143
−2.0	0.0228	0.0222	0.0217	0.0212	0.0207	0.0202	0.0197	0.0192	0.0188	0.0183
−1.9	0.0287	0.0281	0.0274	0.0268	0.0262	0.0256	0.0250	0.0244	0.0239	0.0233
−1.8	0.0359	0.0351	0.0344	0.0336	0.0329	0.0322	0.0314	0.0307	0.0301	0.0294
−1.7	0.0446	0.0436	0.0427	0.0418	0.0409	0.0401	0.0392	0.0384	0.0375	0.0367
−1.6	0.0548	0.0537	0.0526	0.0516	0.0505	0.0495	0.0485	0.0475	0.0465	0.0455
−1.5	0.0668	0.0655	0.0643	0.0630	0.0618	0.0606	0.0594	0.0582	0.0571	0.0559
−1.4	0.0808	0.0793	0.0778	0.0764	0.0749	0.0735	0.0721	0.0708	0.0694	0.0681
−1.3	0.0968	0.0951	0.0934	0.0918	0.0901	0.0885	0.0869	0.0853	0.0838	0.0823
−1.2	0.1151	0.1131	0.1112	0.1093	0.1075	0.1056	0.1038	0.1020	0.1003	0.0985
−1.1	0.1357	0.1335	0.1314	0.1292	0.1271	0.1251	0.1230	0.1210	0.1190	0.1170
−1.0	0.1587	0.1562	0.1539	0.1515	0.1492	0.1469	0.1446	0.1423	0.1401	0.1379
−0.9	0.1841	0.1814	0.1788	0.1762	0.1736	0.1711	0.1685	0.1660	0.1635	0.1611
−0.8	0.2119	0.2090	0.2061	0.2033	0.2005	0.1977	0.1949	0.1922	0.1894	0.1867
−0.7	0.2420	0.2389	0.2358	0.2327	0.2296	0.2266	0.2236	0.2206	0.2177	0.2148
−0.6	0.2743	0.2709	0.2676	0.2643	0.2611	0.2578	0.2546	0.2514	0.2483	0.2451
−0.5	0.3085	0.3050	0.3015	0.2981	0.2946	0.2912	0.2877	0.2843	0.2810	0.2776
−0.4	0.3446	0.3409	0.3372	0.3336	0.3300	0.3264	0.3228	0.3192	0.3156	0.3121
−0.3	0.3821	0.3783	0.3745	0.3707	0.3669	0.3632	0.3594	0.3557	0.3520	0.3483
−0.2	0.4207	0.4168	0.4129	0.4090	0.4052	0.4013	0.3974	0.3936	0.3897	0.3859
−0.1	0.4602	0.4562	0.4522	0.4483	0.4443	0.4404	0.4364	0.4325	0.4286	0.4247
−0.0	0.5000	0.4960	0.4920	0.4880	0.4840	0.4801	0.4761	0.4721	0.4681	0.4641

TABLE 4 | Cumulative Probabilities for the Standard Normal Distribution

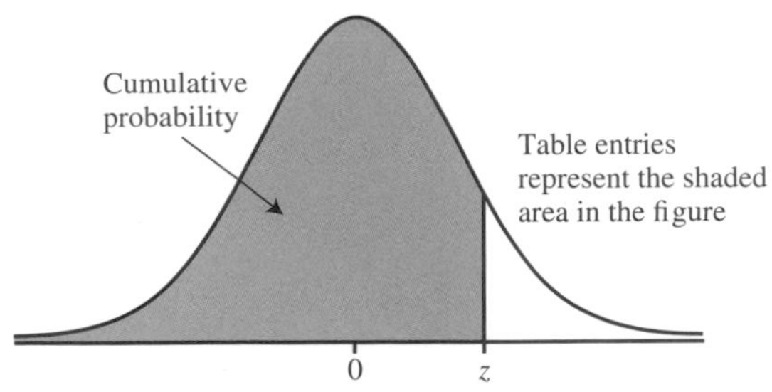

FIRST DIGIT OF Z					SECOND DIGIT OF Z					
z	0.00	0.01	0.02	0.03	0.04	0.05	0.06	0.07	0.08	0.09
0.0	0.5000	0.5040	0.5080	0.5120	0.5160	0.5199	0.5239	0.5279	0.5319	0.5359
0.1	0.5398	0.5438	0.5478	0.5517	0.5557	0.5596	0.5636	0.5675	0.5714	0.5753
0.2	0.5793	0.5832	0.5871	0.5910	0.5948	0.5987	0.6026	0.6064	0.6103	0.6141
0.3	0.6179	0.6217	0.6255	0.6293	0.6331	0.6368	0.6406	0.6443	0.6480	0.6517
0.4	0.6554	0.6591	0.6628	0.6664	0.6700	0.6736	0.6772	0.6808	0.6844	0.6879
0.5	0.6915	0.6950	0.6985	0.7019	0.7054	0.7088	0.7123	0.7157	0.7190	0.7224
0.6	0.7257	0.7291	0.7324	0.7357	0.7389	0.7422	0.7454	0.7486	0.7517	0.7549
0.7	0.7580	0.7611	0.7642	0.7673	0.7704	0.7734	0.7764	0.7794	0.7823	0.7852
0.8	0.7881	0.7910	0.7939	0.7967	0.7995	0.8023	0.8051	0.8078	0.8106	0.8133
0.9	0.8159	0.8186	0.8212	0.8238	0.8264	0.8289	0.8315	0.8340	0.8365	0.8389
1.0	0.8413	0.8438	0.8461	0.8485	0.8508	0.8531	0.8554	0.8577	0.8599	0.8621
1.1	0.8643	0.8665	0.8686	0.8708	0.8729	0.8749	0.8770	0.8790	0.8810	0.8830
1.2	0.8849	0.8869	0.8888	0.8907	0.8925	0.8944	0.8962	0.8980	0.8997	0.9015
1.3	0.9032	0.9049	0.9066	0.9082	0.9099	0.9115	0.9131	0.9147	0.9162	0.9177
1.4	0.9192	0.9207	0.9222	0.9236	0.9251	0.9265	0.9279	0.9292	0.9306	0.9319
1.5	0.9332	0.9345	0.9357	0.9370	0.9382	0.9394	0.9406	0.9418	0.9429	0.9441
1.6	0.9452	0.9463	0.9474	0.9484	0.9495	0.9505	0.9515	0.9525	0.9535	0.9545
1.7	0.9554	0.9564	0.9573	0.9582	0.9591	0.9599	0.9608	0.9616	0.9625	0.9633
1.8	0.9641	0.9649	0.9656	0.9664	0.9671	0.9678	0.9686	0.9693	0.9699	0.9706
1.9	0.9713	0.9719	0.9726	0.9732	0.9738	0.9744	0.9750	0.9756	0.9761	0.9767
2.0	0.9772	0.9778	0.9783	0.9788	0.9793	0.9798	0.9803	0.9808	0.9812	0.9817
2.1	0.9821	0.9826	0.9830	0.9834	0.9838	0.9842	0.9846	0.9850	0.9854	0.9857
2.2	0.9861	0.9864	0.9868	0.9871	0.9875	0.9878	0.9881	0.9884	0.9887	0.9890
2.3	0.9893	0.9896	0.9898	0.9901	0.9904	0.9906	0.9909	0.9911	0.9913	0.9916
2.4	0.9918	0.9920	0.9922	0.9925	0.9927	0.9929	0.9931	0.9932	0.9934	0.9936
2.5	0.9938	0.9940	0.9941	0.9943	0.9945	0.9946	0.9948	0.9949	0.9951	0.9952
2.6	0.9953	0.9955	0.9956	0.9957	0.9959	0.9960	0.9961	0.9962	0.9963	0.9964
2.7	0.9965	0.9966	0.9967	0.9968	0.9969	0.9970	0.9971	0.9972	0.9973	0.9974
2.8	0.9974	0.9975	0.9976	0.9977	0.9977	0.9978	0.9979	0.9979	0.9980	0.9981
2.9	0.9981	0.9982	0.9982	0.9983	0.9984	0.9984	0.9985	0.9985	0.9986	0.9986
3.0	0.9987	0.9987	0.9987	0.9988	0.9988	0.9989	0.9989	0.9989	0.9990	0.9990
3.1	0.9990	0.9991	0.9991	0.9991	0.9992	0.9992	0.9992	0.9992	0.9993	0.9993
3.2	0.9993	0.9993	0.9994	0.9994	0.9994	0.9994	0.9994	0.9995	0.9995	0.9995
3.3	0.9995	0.9995	0.9995	0.9996	0.9996	0.9996	0.9996	0.9996	0.9996	0.9997
3.4	0.9997	0.9997	0.9997	0.9997	0.9997	0.9997	0.9997	0.9997	0.9997	0.9998
3.5	0.9998	0.9998	0.9998	0.9998	0.9998	0.9998	0.9998	0.9998	0.9998	0.9998
3.6	0.9998	0.9998	0.9999	0.9999	0.9999	0.9999	0.9999	0.9999	0.9999	0.9999
3.7 and higher	0.9999									